Foldout Documenting Sources: APA Style

19 Documenting Sources: APA Style 347
a. APA In-Text Citations 347
b. APA Reference List 358
c. APA Style Notes 376
d. APA Format 377

Student Model Research Project: APA Style 381

20 Documenting Sources: *Chicago* Style 389
a. *Chicago*-Style Notes and Bibliography 390
b. *Chicago* Style Tables and Figures 407
c. *Chicago*-Style Research Project 407

Student Model Research Project: *Chicago* Style 408

21 Documenting Sources: CSE Style 416
a. CSE In-Text Citations 416
b. CSE Reference List 418
c. CSE Format 428

Student Model Research Project: CSE-Style Reference List 429

Part Six   Genre Matters   431

22 Writing in Literature and the Other Humanities 432
a. Approach 432
b. Resources 435
c. Citing, Documenting Sources 437
d. Language 437
e. Writing about Fiction 440
f. Writing about Poetry 446
g. Writing about Drama 451

Student Models Textual Analysis 434; Writing about Fiction: Interpretive Analysis 442; Writing about Poetry: Explication 446
Professional Model Writing about Drama: Review of a Play 451

23 Writing in the Sciences and Social Sciences 455
a. Approach 455
b. Research Methods 456
c. Citing, Documenting Sources 457
d. Language 457
e. Writing Assignments 459

Student Model Research Report 461

24 Preparing for and Taking an Essay Exam 469
a. Preparing for an Exam 469
b. Previewing the Exam 471
c. Writing an Effective Answer 472

Student Model Effective Essay Exam: Response 474

25 Writing in Business and as a Citizen 476
a. Business Letter Formats 476
b. Business Letters 479
c. Business Memos 481
d. Job Application Letters 482
e. Résumés 486
f. Reports and Proposals 490
g. Press Releases 492

Student Models Job Application 485; Traditional Résumé 487; Scannable Résumé 489
Professional Models Business Letter: Apology 480; Business Memo 482; Press Release 493

Part Seven   Style Matters   495

26 Writing Concisely 496
a. Wordy Expressions 497
b. Unnecessary Repetition 499
c. Indirect Constructions 500
d. Consolidation 502

27 Using Coordination and Subordination 505
a. Coordinating Terms, Phrases, Clauses 506
b. Effective Coordination 507
c. Main Ideas, Supporting Information 510
d. Coordination and Subordination 515

28 Using Parallelism 518
a. Pairs and Series 520
b. Comparisons 522
c. Function 522
d. Lists and Outlines 523
e. Emphasis 525

29 Variety and Emphasis 527
a. Varying Sentence Length 528
b. Varying Sentence Openings 529
c. Emphasis with Rhythm 531
d. Emphasis with Punctuation 533
e. Questions, Commands, Exclamations 534
f. Strategic Repetition 534
g. Emphatic Verbs 535
h. Active or Passive Voice 535
i. **Writing Responsibly** Blending Voices in Your Text 538

30 Appropriate Language 540
a. Language in Context 540
b. Biased or Hurtful Language 544

31 Effective Word Choice 548
a. Diction 548
b. Compelling Words and Figures 550
c. Idioms 554
d. Clichés 555

c. Common Spelling Problems 562
d. Spelling Rules 564
e. Plurals 569
f. Improving Your Spelling 571

Part Eight   Grammar Matters   573

Foldout Common Sentence Problems

33 Grammar 574
THE PARTS OF SPEECH
a. Nouns 575
b. Pronouns 577
c. Verbs 577
d. Adjectives 580
e. Adverbs 581
f. Prepositions 582
g. Conjunctions 583
h. Interjections 584
SENTENCE STRUCTURE
i. Subjects 585
j. Predicates 587
k. Verb Types, Sentence Patterns 588
l. Phrases 591
m. Clauses 594
n. Sentence Types 597

34 Sentence Fragments 600
a. Recognizing Fragments 600
b. Correcting Fragments 604
c. Intentional Fragments 609

35 Comma Splices and Fused Sentences 611
a. Joining Independent Clauses 611
b. Identifying Comma Splices, Fused Sentences 612
c. Avoiding Spliced, Fused Sentences 613
d. Correcting Spliced, Fused Sentences 615

36 Agreement 620
SUBJECT-VERB AGREEMENT
a. Subjects and Verbs Agree 620
b. Intervening Words 622
c. Compound Subjects 623
d. Indefinite Pronouns 625
e. Collective Noun 625
f. Measurements, Numbers 626
g. Singular Nouns with *–s* 627
h. Titles, Words as Words, Gerund 627
i. *Who*, *Which*, or *That* 628
j. Subject after Verb 629
k. Linking Verbs 629
PRONOUN ANTECEDENT AGREEMENT
l. Indefinite and Generic Words 631
m. Collective Nouns 634
n. Compound Antecedents 634

37 Verbs 636

VERB FORMS
a. Basic Forms 636
b. Regular and Irregular Verbs 638
c. Complete Verbs 639
d. *-s* or *-es*, *-d* or *-ed* Endings 642
e. *Rise/Raise*, *Sit/Set*, *Lie/Lay* 643

TENSE
f. Verb Tenses 644
g. Uses of the Present Tense 647
h. Tense Sequence 648

MOOD
i. Verb Mood 650
j. Subjunctive Mood 650

VOICE
k. Verb Voice 652
l. Active vs. Passive 653

38 Pronoun Case, Reference 656

PRONOUN CASE
a. Subject Complements 658
b. Case in Compounds: *She and I* vs. *Her and Me* 658
c. Appositives 660
d. *We* and *Us* before Nouns 660
e. Infinitives 661
f. Case with *-ing* Words 661
g. Comparisons with *Than* or *As* 662
h. *Who/Whom, Whoever/Whomever* 663

PRONOUN REFERENCE
i. Ambiguous Reference 665
j. Broad Reference 665
k. Implied Reference 666
l. *You* for Direct Address 666
m. Indefinite *They, It* 666
n. *Who, Whom* vs. *That, Which* 667

39 Adjectives and Adverbs 669

a. Adjectives vs. Adverbs 669
b. Subject Complements 670
c. *Bad* vs. *Badly*, *Good* vs. *Well* 671
d. Double Negatives 673
e. Nouns as Adjectives 673
f. Comparatives and Superlatives 674

40 Confusing Shifts 678

a. Tense 678
b. Mood and Voice 679
c. Person and Number 681
d. Direct and Indirect Quotations 683

41 Misplaced and Dangling Modifiers 686

MISPLACED MODIFIERS
a. Confusing Placement 687
b. Disruptive Placement 689

DANGLING MODIFIERS
c. Identifying 692
d. Correcting 693

42 Mixed and Incomplete Constructions 695

MIXED CONSTRUCTIONS
a. Mixed Constructions 695

b. Subjects and Predicates 697

INCOMPLETE CONSTRUCTIONS
c. Essential Words 700
d. Comparisons 701

Part Nine Language Matters 703

43 English Sentence Structure 704

a. Normal Word Order 704
b. Stated Subject 704
c. *There* and *It* Sentences 705
d. Redundant Pronouns 706
e. Objects 707
f. Questions 709
g. Inversions 710

44 Nouns 713

a. Noun Types 713
b. Articles, Other Determiners 714

45 Verb Issues 722

a. Phrasal Verbs 722
b. Gerunds and Infinitives 725
c. Participles as Adjectives 727
d. Helping Verbs 728

46 Adjectives and Adverbs 732

a. Adjective Order 732
b. Prepositions with Adjectives 733
c. Adverb Placement 734
d. Confusing Adverbs 736

47 Prepositions 739

a. Recognizing Prepositions 739
b. Functions of Prepositions 740
c. Using Prepositions 744
d. Necessary, Unnecessary Prepositions 745

Part Ten Detail Matters 747

48 Commas 748

a. Compound Sentences 750
b. Introductory Elements 751
c. Conjunctive Adverbs, Transitional Phrases 753
d. Interjections, Contrasting Information, 753
e. Items in a Series 754
f. Coordinate Adjectives 755
g. Nonessential Elements 757
h. Quotations 759
i. Numbers, Names, Titles, Dates, etc. 760
j. Avoiding Ambiguity 762
k. Avoiding use Between Subjects/Verbs, Verbs/Objects 763

49 Semicolons 766

a. Linking Independent Clauses 767
b. Conjunctive Adverbs, Transitional Phrases 768
c. Series with Commas 769
d. Comma Splices, Fused Sentences 769
e. Misuse 770

50 Apostrophes 773

a. Possession 773
b. Contractions, Abbreviated Years 777
c. Avoiding Use with Plurals of Dates, Abbreviations, Numbers, etc. 777

51 Quotation Marks 780

a. Direct Quotations 780
b. Titles of Short Works 783
c. Words Used in a Special Sense 784
d. Misuse 784
e. Punctuating Quotations 785
f. Altering Quotations: Ellipses, Square Brackets 786
g. Introducing, Identifying Quotations 787
h. **Writing Responsibly** Acknowledging Indirect Sources 790

52 End Punctuation 792

a. Periods 792
b. Question Marks 793
c. Exclamation Points 794

53 Dashes, Parentheses, Colons, Ellipses, and Other Marks 796

a. Dashes 796
b. Parentheses 798
c. Brackets 800
d. Colons 800
e. Ellipses 803
f. Slashes 805

54 Capitalizing 807

a. First Word of a Sentence 807
b. Proper Nouns, Proper Adjectives 809
c. Titles and Subtitles 810
d. Pronoun *I* and Interjection *O* 811
e. Abbreviations and Acronyms 812

55 Italics and Underlining 814

a. Titles of Longer Works 814
b. Emphasis 816
c. Names of Vehicles 816
d. Words, Letters, Numbers as Words 816
e. Non-English Words; Latin Genus, Species 817
f. Hyperlinks 817

56 Abbreviations 820

a. Titles 822
b. Acronyms and Initialisms 822
c. Years, Hours, Numbers, Dollars 823
d. Misuse with Names, Words, States, etc. 823
e. Latin Abbreviations 824

57 Numbers 826

a. When to Spell Out 827
b. With Dates, Times, Addresses, Money, etc. 827

58 Using Hyphens 830

a. Compounds 830
b. Breaking Words 833

REBECCA MOORE HOWARD
Syracuse University

SECOND EDITION

WRITING MATTERS

A **HANDBOOK** FOR WRITING AND RESEARCH

McGraw Hill
Connect
Learn
Succeed

WRITING MATTERS: A HANDBOOK FOR WRITING AND RESEARCH, SECOND EDITION

Published by McGraw-Hill, a business unit of The McGraw-Hill Companies, Inc., 1221 Avenue of the Americas, New York, NY 10020. Copyright © 2014 by The McGraw-Hill Companies, Inc. All rights reserved. Printed in the United States of America. Previous edition © 2010. No part of this publication may be reproduced or distributed in any form or by any means, or stored in a database or retrieval system, without the prior written consent of The McGraw-Hill Companies, Inc., including, but not limited to, in any network or other electronic storage or transmission, or broadcast for distance learning.

Some ancillaries, including electronic and print components, may not be available to customers outside the United States.

This book is printed on acid-free paper.

3 4 5 6 7 8 9 0 QTN/QTN 1 0 9 8 7 6 5 4

ISBN: 978-0-07-340595-7
MHID: 0-07-340595-7

Senior Vice President, Products & Markets: *Kurt L. Strand*
Vice President, General Manager, Products & Markets: *Michael Ryan*
Vice President, Content Production & Technology Services: *Kimberly Meriwether David*
Managing Director: *David S. Patterson*
Director: *Susan Gouijnstook*
Senior Brand Manager: *Nancy Huebner*
Senior Director of Development: *Dawn Groundwater*
Senior Development Editor: *Michael O'Loughlin*
Executive Market Development Manager: *Nanette Giles*
Senior Marketing Manager: *Kevin Colleary*
Digital Product Analyst: *Janet Byrne Smith*
Content Project Manager: *Sandy Wille*
Buyer: *Nicole Baumgartner*
Cover/Interior Design: *Preston Thomas, Cadence Design Studio*
Cover Illustration: *Lachina Publishing Services*
Content Licensing Specialist: *Shawntel Schmitt*
Photo Researcher: *Deborah Anderson*
Compositor: *Thompson Type*
Typeface: *10.5/12 Garamond Premier Pro*
Printer: *Quad/Graphics*

All credits appearing on page or at the end of the book are considered to be an extension of the copyright page.

Library of Congress Cataloging-in-Publication Data

Howard, Rebecca Moore.
　Writing matters : a handbook for writing and research / Rebecca Moore Howard, Syracuse University.—Second edition.
　　pages cm
　Includes index.
　ISBN-13: 978-0-07-340595-7—ISBN-10: 0-07-340595-7 (Hard Copy)
　1. English language-Rhetoric.　2. Report writing.　I. Title.
PE1408.H685247 2013
808'.042-dc23
　　　　　　　　　　　　　　　　　　　　　　　　　　　　　2012038887

The Internet addresses listed in the text were accurate at the time of publication. The inclusion of a website does not indicate an endorsement by the authors or McGraw-Hill, and McGraw-Hill does not guarantee the accuracy of the information presented at these sites.

www.mhhe.com

Writing Matters is dedicated
to the memory of my sister, Sandy

Dear Colleagues:

Thank you for taking the time to consider *Writing Matters!*
I started this project as a way of giving back to the composition community and helping students with their development as writers. Working on this handbook has also been a source of my own development: My life and teaching have been immeasurably enriched by the students and instructors I have met during my travels to discuss *Writing Matters* and my responsibilities-focused approach to writing.

While developing on the second edition of *Writing Matters*, I have also been working on the Citation Project, a nationwide study of the researched writing of 174 students for their composition classes. Some of the results of that research are available on the Citation Project website: citationproject.net. There you will see a variety of signs that students may not be reading their sources carefully and completely and that their research projects suffer accordingly. This edition includes newly developed materials that teach concrete skills, such as marking where the source material ends and the writer's own voice begins. On a larger scale, these materials encourage students to invest themselves in their writing.

Rebecca Moore Howard is Professor of Writing and Rhetoric at Syracuse University. Her recent work on the Citation Project is part of a collaborative endeavor to study how students really use resources.

In *Writing Matters*, I draw on three decades' worth of teaching, writing, and research—as well as on my recent travels—to focus sustained attention on **writers' responsibilities to other writers, to their readers, to their topics,** and most especially, **to themselves.** The result is a teaching and learning framework that unites research, rhetoric, documentation, grammar, and style into a cohesive whole, helping students to find consistency in rules that might otherwise confound them. Students experience responsible writing not only by citing the work of other writers accurately but also by treating those writers' ideas fairly. They practice responsible writing by providing reliable information about a topic at a depth that does the topic justice. Most importantly, they embrace responsible writing by taking their writing seriously and approaching writing assignments as opportunities to learn about new topics and to expand their scope as writers.

Students are more likely to write well when they think of themselves as writers rather than as error-makers. By explaining rules in the context of responsibility, I address composition students respectfully as mature and capable fellow participants in the research and writing process.

Sincerely,

Rebecca Moore Howard

Change the Conversation . . .

Writing Matters offers instructors and students a four-part framework that focuses the rules and conventions of writing through a lens of responsibility, ultimately empowering students to own their ideas and to view their writing as consequential.

Writing Matters helps students see the conventions of writing as a network of **responsibilities . . .**

> **to other writers** by treating information fairly and accurately, and crafting writing that is fresh and original
>
> **to the audience** by writing clearly, and providing readers with the information and interpretation they need to make sense of a topic
>
> **to the topic** by exploring a topic thoroughly and creatively, assessing sources carefully, and providing reliable information at a depth that does the topic justice
>
> **to themselves** by taking writing seriously, and approaching the process as an opportunity to learn about a topic and to expand research and writing skills

Make It Your Own! **McGraw Hill connect plus+ | COMPOSITION**

WRITING MATTERS eBook

The **CONNECT COMPOSITION PLUS 2.0 eBook** provides *Writing Matters* content in a digital format that is accessible from within Connect and Blackboard. In support of the engaged learning experience, students can link directly to activities and assignments within **CONNECT** from the eBook. Students can have all the resources from *Writing Matters* right on their desktops!

Personal Learning Plan (PLP)

Through an intuitive, adaptive diagnostic that assesses proficiencies in five core areas of grammar and mechanics, students generate a personalized learning plan tailored to address their needs within the timeframe students determine they want to study. The personalized program includes contextualized grammar and writing lessons, videos, animations, and interactive exercises and provides immediate feedback on students' work and progress. Based on metacognitive learning theories, the **PERSONAL LEARNING PLAN** continually adapts with each interaction, while built-in time management tools keep students on track to ensure they achieve their course goals. The Personal Learning Plan is designed to improve student writing, allow classroom instruction to focus on critical writing processes, and support the goals of writing programs and individual instructors with reports that present data related to progress, achievement, and students who may be at risk.

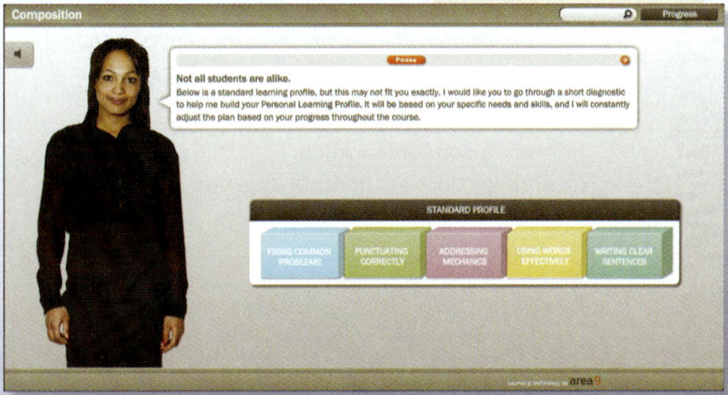

Writing Matters Instructors Matter

Change, Rearrange, Exchange . . .   McGraw-Hill create

Your courses evolve over time—shouldn't your course material? With **McGraw-Hill Create™**, you can easily arrange and rearrange material from a variety of sources, including your own. You can select content by discipline or collection, including 4,000 textbooks, 5,500 articles, 25,000 cases, and 11,000 readings. When you build a **CREATE** book, you will receive a complimentary print review copy in 3 to 5 business days or a complimentary electronic review copy (eComp) via e-mail in about one hour. Go to **mcgrawhillcreate.com** and register today.

With Create you can:

choose which chapters in the handbook you want from

- *Writing Matters* Comprehensive with exercises
- *Writing Matters* Tabbed with or without exercises
- *Writing Matters* Pocket
- McGraw-Hill texts

choose which resources you want from

- other McGraw-Hill collections, such as *The Ideal Reader* (800 readings by genre, mode, theme, discipline, and author), *Annual Editions* (5,500 articles from journals and periodicals), *Traditions* (readings in the humanities), *Sustainability* (readings with an environment focus), and *American History and World Civilization Documents* (primary sources including maps, charters, letters, memoirs, and essays)

- your own works, such as syllabi, institutional information, study guides, assignments, diagrams, and artwork; and student writing, art, and photos

choose which format you want

- print
- electronic

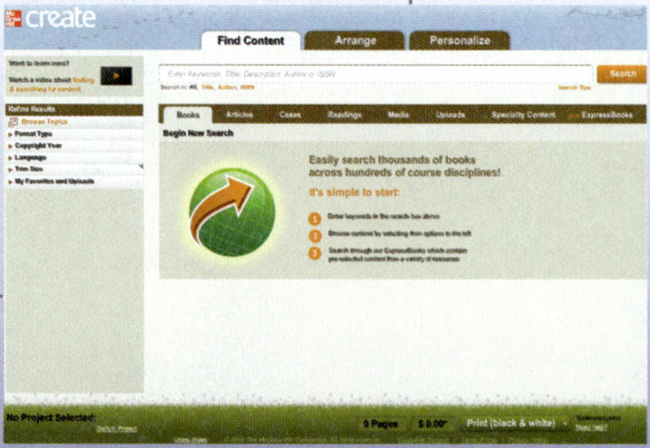

Make It Your Own!

Connect Composition Plus 2.0

When you draw upon **CONNECT COMPOSITION PLUS 2.0** with *WRITING MATTERS* to implement your curriculum, you use digital tools developed by composition experts to create a state-of-the-art teaching and learning environment that engages your students with their course assignments, including:

- group assignments
- blog assignments
- discussion board assignments
- writing assignments with accurate formatting

The flexible content and powerful tools found in **CONNECT COMPOSITION PLUS 2.0 with *WRITING MATTERS*** work well in traditional course settings as well as in online or hybrid courses.

Peer Review

CONNECT COMPOSITION PLUS 2.0 offers writing assignments with superior peer reviewing capability that helps instructors easily assign and manage groups and peer review exercises. This program gives students an engaging space in which to collaborate online, benefit from their classmates' comments, and participate in a crucial step in the writing process. Managed through an efficient and fun-to-use online system, this collaborative experience prepares students for the group writing projects they will encounter throughout their college careers and in the workplace.

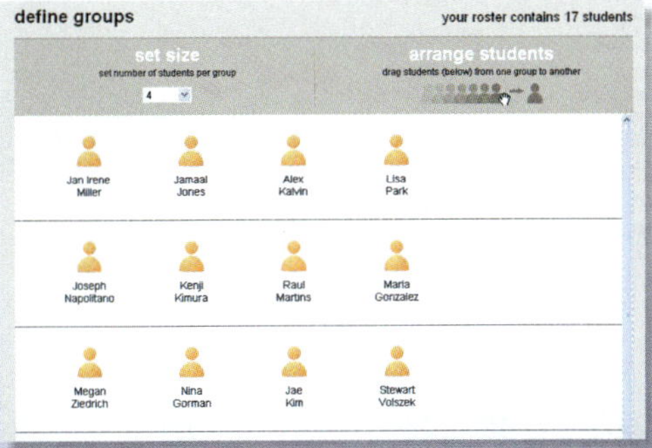

Outcomes-Based Assessment of Writing

CONNECT's powerful **OUTCOMES-BASED ASSESSMENT** tool generates clear, simple reports—suitable for program evaluation or accrediting bodies—allowing a variety of stakeholders a view of student progress toward program goals. Prebuilt, customizable grading rubrics, written specifically for composition programs, can be adapted to your unique assignments and objectives to make the set-up, management, and reporting of outcomes-based writing assessment efficient, professional, and useful.

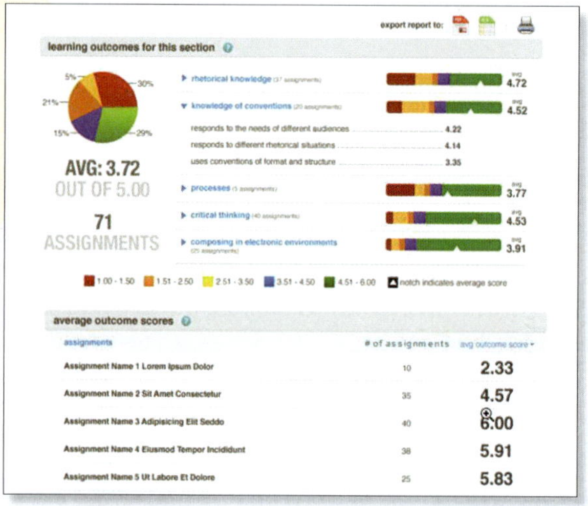

Make It Your Own!

Blackboard® and MH Campus®

All the content of *Writing Matters*—writing instruction, readings, assignments, documentation flowcharts—is integrated with your program's course management system to offer single sign-on, seamless use of all **CONNECT COMPOSITION PLUS 2.0** assets and synchronization for all assignment and grade book utilities.

Tegrity

TEGRITY CAMPUS is a service that makes class time available all the time. It automatically captures every lecture in a searchable format, allowing students to review course material when they study and complete assignments. With a simple one-click start-and-stop process, you capture all computer screens and corresponding audio. Students replay any part of any class with easy-to-use, browser-based viewing on a PC or Mac.

McGraw-Hill Makes Change Easier

McGraw-Hill is firmly committed to the success and professional growth of our customers as they use our digital course solutions. We understand that incorporating new systems and technologies into your programs can feel daunting. But we know it also can be transformative. The following programs support instructors of all proficiencies in a variety of formats, with the goal of helping every one of our customers exceed their expectations.

- **Digital Success Academy**—The Digital Success Academy offers a wealth of training resources and course creation tips for instructors. Presented in easy-to-navigate, easy-to-complete sections, the Digital Success Academy includes the popular *Connect 100* and *Connect 200* video shorts, step-by-step *Clickthrough Guides*, and *First Day of Class* materials that explain how to use both the Connect platform and its course-specific tools and features.

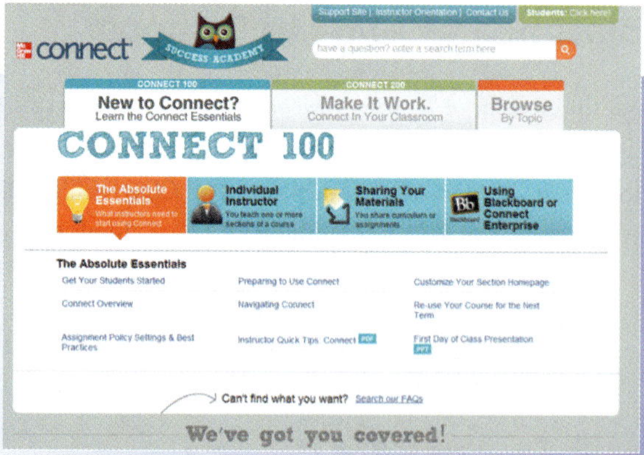

  http://create.mcgraw-hill.com/wordpress-mu/success-academy

- **Digital Success Team**—The Digital Success Team is a group of McGraw-Hill professionals dedicated to working online with instructors—one-on-one—to demonstrate how the Connect platform works and to help incorporate Connect into a customer's specific course design and syllabus. You can request a Digital Success Team personal consultation through your McGraw-Hill sales representative or by visiting our Digital Products Support Center. **http://mpss.mhhe.com/orientation.php**

- **Digital Learning Consultants**—Digital Learning Consultants are local resources who work closely with your McGraw-Hill sales representative. They can provide face-to-face faculty support and training. You can request a Digital Learning Consultation through your McGraw-Hill sales representative. http://catalogs.mhhe.com/mhhe/findRep.do

- **Digital Faculty Consultants**—Digital Faculty Consultants are experienced instructors who have utilized Connect in their classroom. These instructors are available to offer suggestions, advice, and training about how best to use Connect in a real classroom. To request a Digital Faculty Consultant to speak with, please e-mail your McGraw-Hill sales representative.

- **National Training Webinars**—McGraw-Hill offers an ongoing series of webinars for instructors to learn and master the Connect platform as well as its course-specific tools and features. We hope you will refer to our online schedule of national training webinars and sign up to learn more about Connect! https://mhhe.webex.com/mhhe/onstage/g.php?p=280&t=m

- **Customer Experience Group (CXG)**—McGraw-Hill is dedicated to making sure instructors and students can reach out and receive help with any of our digital products. To contact our customer support team, please call us at 800-331-5094 or visit us online at http://mpss.mhhe.com/contact.php. Hours of operation are Sunday 6 p.m.–11 p.m., Monday–Thursday 8 a.m.–11 p.m., and Friday 8 a.m.–6 p.m. Please note that all times are Central.

  > McGraw-Hill is focused on delivering a memorable and rewarding service experience to instructors and students using our digital products. Our Customer Experience Group is a dedicated support team available to assist all faculty and students with support questions and inquiries as they relate to McGraw-Hill digital products.

- **The Connect Community**—The Connect Community brings together faculty from across the country to discuss critical issues, answer questions, and share best practices. As a member, you can participate in lively conversations, lead new groups and forums based on the issues you would like to explore, and get up-to-date news and information about Connect. Join the Community today and engage. http://theconnectcommunity.com

Components of *Writing Matters*

Writing Matters includes an array of resources for instructors and students. Under the leadership of Rebecca Moore Howard, experienced instructors created supplements that help instructors and students fulfill their course responsibilities.

Instruction Matters

Instruction Matters includes teaching tips and learning outcomes. It connects each instructor and student resource to the core material and makes the exercises relevant to instructors and students.

Assessment Matters

Assessment Matters offers more than a thousand test items.

Practice Matters offers three sets of grammar and ESL activities and exercises to practice writing well.

Exercises for ESL Students

Exercises for Students

Grammar Exercises for Students

Presentation Matters

This PowerPoint deck is designed to give new teachers confidence in the classroom and can be used as a teaching tool by all instructors. The PowerPoint slides emphasize key ideas from *Writing Matters* and help students take useful notes. Instructors can alter the slides to meet their own needs.

Acknowledgments

The creation and evolution of *Writing Matters* has been an exciting and humbling experience. I began in the belief that I knew what I was doing, but I quickly realized that I had embarked upon a path not only of sharing what I know but also of learning what I should know. *Writing Matters* lists a single author, Rebecca Moore Howard, but that author is actually the central figure in a collaboration of hundreds of students, teachers, and editors.

I thank the instructors who have provided invaluable insights and suggestions as reviewers and members of the board of advisors. Talking with instructors at all sorts of institutions and learning from them about the teaching of writing has been an unparalleled experience. As a result of this project, I have many new colleagues, people who care deeply about teaching writing and who are experts at doing so. I also thank the many students who have shared their thoughts with us through class tests and design reviews. I particularly thank the students who have shared their writing with me and allowed me to publish some of it in this book. *Writing Matters* has been improved greatly by their contributions.

Acknowledgments

Manuscript Reviewers

Abraham Baldwin Agricultural College: Jeff Newberry
Allen County Community College: Tracy R. Lee (*Board of Advisors*), Bruce Symes,
Baton Rouge Community College: Rosemary Mack, Jaimie Stallone (*Board of Advisors*)
Boise State University: Gail Shuck
Bowie State University: Stephanie Johnson, Sidney Walker
Brigham Young University: Brian Jackson, Brett McInelly
Butler Community College: John Buaas, Sheryl LeSage, Troy Nordman (*Board of Advisors*)
Butte College: Molly Emmons, John Osbourne
Caldwell Community College: Paula Rush
Cameron University: William Carney, John Hodgson, Carolyn Lindsey Kinslow
Catawba Valley Community College: Polly Watson
Central Piedmont Community College: Amy Bagwell, Brad Bostian, Patricia Bostian (*Board of Advisors*), Jack Summers, Barbara Urban
Clark State Community College: Laurie Buchanan, Cecilia Kennedy, Kathryn Ward
Clayton State University: Mary Lamb, Dan Mills
Community College of Allegheny County: Pamela Jean Turley
Delaware Technical and Community College Dover: Bonnie Ceban, Nicholas David, Theodore A. Legates
Eastern Arizona College: Ida Nunley, Margaret Simonton
Florence-Darlington Technical College: Marjory Hall, Mark Rooze, Alan M. Trusky
Florida International University: Andrew Golden, Kimberly Harrison, Ben Lauren, Robert Saba, Andrew Strycharski
Frederick Community College: Kenneth P. Kerr, Kelly Trigger
Georgia College and State University: Craig Callender, Robert Viau
Georgia Gwinnett College: A. Keith Kelly, Scott Reed
Georgia State University: Lynee Lewis Gaillet, Marti Singer
Greenville Technical College: Julie Gibson
Harding University: Nicholas Boone, Terry Engel (*Board of Advisors*)
Hutchinson Community College: Bonnie Feeser, Trudy Zimmerman
Indian River State College: Camila Alvarez, Ray Considine, Roderick Hofer, Tammy Powley (*Board of Advisors*), Donald Skinner, April Van Camp
Indiana University-Northwest-Gary: Pat Buckler, William K. Buckley, Lou Ann Karabel, Doug Swartz
Indiana University-Purdue University Indianapolis: Steve Fox
John Jay College: Tim McCormack
Jones County Junior College: David Lowery, Patti Smith, Tammy Townsend, Cheryl Windham
KCTCS Western Kentucky Community and Technical College: Kimberly Russell
Kent State University: Andrea Adolph, Charles Douglas Baker, Robert Miltner, Stephen E. Neaderhiser, Beverly Neiderman, Lindsay Steiner
Kent State University-Stark: Brooke Horvath
Lamar State College: Andrew Preslar, Arlene Turkel, Gwen Whitehead
Loyola University of Chicago: Victoria Anderson, Margaret Loweth, Sherrie Weller
Luzerne County Community College: Stephen Housenick, Mary Stchur
Marist College: Joseph Zeppetello
Marquette University: Virginia Chappell
Marshalltown Community College: Connie Adair, Carolyn Briggs
Metropolitan State College of Denver: Jane Chapman Vigil, Elizabeth Kleinfeld, Mikkilynn Olmstead, Jessica Parker, Jim Sundeen
Miami University of Ohio: Heidi McKee, Jason Palmeri, James E. Porter (*Board of Advisors*)
Morehouse College: Consuella Bennett, Albert Turner, Corey Stayton
Mount Hood Community College: Jonathan Morrow
New England College: Susan Nagelsen
New Jersey Institute of Technology: Mark Arnowitz, Norbert Elliot
Northern Virginia Community College-Alexandria: Shonette H. Grant (*Board of Advisors*)
Northwest Florida State College: Vickie Hunt, Julie Nichols
Norwalk Community College: Cindy Casper (*Board of Advisors*), Lisa Dresdner
Olympic College: Sonia Begert, Ian Sherman
Palo Alto College: Ruth Ann Gambino, Caroline Mains, Diana Nystedt
Purdue University-Calumet-Hammond: Karen Bishop-Morris, Susan Roach
Robert Morris University: Diane Todd Bucci, Tracy Gorrell, Edward Karshner, Sylvia Pamboukian, Connie Ruzich, Scott Wyatt
Rutgers University-Camden: William FitzGerald
Saint Johns River State College: Paul Robert Andrews, Melody Hargraves, Jeannine Morgan, Roger Vaccaro

Salisbury University: Elizabeth Curtin, Loren Loving Marquez (*Board of Advisors*), Nicole Munday
San Diego State University: Candace Boeck (*Board of Advisors*), Chris Werry
Seton Hall University: Gita Dasbender, Edmund H. Jones, Judith Pike
Shawnee Community College: Susan Woolridge
Snow College: Melanie Jenkins
Southwestern Oklahoma State College: Jill T. Jones, Kelly S. Moor, Valerie A. Reimers
Syracuse University: Patrick Williams
University of Cincinnati-Blue Ash College: Sonja Andrus
University of Illinois-Urbana-Champaign: Courtney Caudle, Cara Finnegan, Grace Giorgio, Greg Webb, Jessica Wong
University of Miami: Andrew Green, Gina Maranto
University of Utah: Jay Jordan
University of Wisconsin-River Falls: Kathleen Hunzer
US Air Force Academy: Andrea Van Nort
Waynesburg University: Jill Moyer Sunday
Wayne State University: Jeff Pruchnic
Weatherford College: Sarah Lock
Weber State University: Sylvia Newman, Scott Rogers
Wichita State University: Darren DeFrain
York College of Pennsylvania: Julie S. Amberg

Personal Acknowledgments

Writing Matters is the result of rich collaboration with a creative, supportive, knowledgeable team who have a deep understanding of both teaching and publishing: Tom Howard, senior lecturer in University Studies at Colgate University, has worked with me from the beginning to the end, and his intelligence and ingenuity are evident everywhere in this project. Colleagues have also drafted sections of *Writing Matters:* Amy Rupiper Taggart from North Dakota State University drafted "Designing in Context: Academic and Business Documents"; Ted Johnston, formerly of El Paso Community College, and Maggie Sokolik, University of California, Berkeley, drafted "Language Matters: Issues for Multilingual Writers" and the ESL Notes that appear throughout *Writing Matters;* and Sandra Jamieson, Drew University, and Bruce R. Thaler, drafted many of the exercises.

McGraw-Hill has supported the project from beginning to end. My thanks go out to David Patterson, Managing Director; Susan Gouijnstook, Director; Dawn Groundwater, Director of Development; Nanette Giles, Executive Market Development Manager; Nancy Huebner, Brand Manager; and Kevin Colleary, Marketing Manager. My special thanks go to Michael O'Loughlin, my brilliant Senior Development Editor, whose energy, patience, and intelligence have made a second edition that shines.

In addition, *Writing Matters* has benefited greatly from the efforts of an extended editorial team: Christopher Bennem, David Chodoff, Paul Banks, Janet Byrne Smith, Elizabeth Murphy, Dana Wan, and Stephanie Lippitt. It has been a pleasure to work with an outstanding production team: Terri Schiesl, Debra Hash, Preston Thomas, Shawntel Schmitt, Nicole Baumgartner, Lenny Behnke, Deborah Anderson, Kay J. Brimeyer, Debra DeBord, and Nancy Ball. In particular, I would like to thank Jennifer Gordon, the copyeditor, whose careful eye saved me from many embarrassing errors, and Sandy Wille, our fabulous production editor, who juggled schedules and personalities with aplomb.

Contents

Part One: Writing Matters Planning, Drafting, Revising, Editing, Proofreading, and Formatting 1

1 Writing Responsibly in the Information Age 2
a. Writing Today 2
b. The Writer's Responsibilities 3
Writing Responsibly Your Responsibilities as a Writer 5
Writing Responsibly Taking Yourself Seriously as a Writer 7
Student Model Newspaper Article 8

2 Planning Your Project 9
a. Analyzing Your Writing Situation 9
Writing Responsibly Seeing and Showing the Whole Picture 13
b. Analyzing an Assignment 17
c. Generating Ideas 20
Writing Responsibly Note Taking and Plagiarism 21
d. Narrowing or Broadening a Topic 25
e. Working with Others: Planning a Collaborative Project 26
Student Model Freewrite 21; Brainstorm 22; Journalists' Questions 24

3 Organizing and Drafting Your Project 29
a. Crafting an Effective Thesis 29
b. Organizing Your Ideas 33
c. Preparing to Draft 38
d. Drafting: Explaining and Supporting Your Ideas 40
Writing Responsibly Made-up Evidence 41
e. Writing with Others: Collaborative Projects 45
Student Model Informal (or Scratch) Outline 36; Topic Outline and Sentence Outline 36; First Draft 42

4 Crafting and Connecting Paragraphs 46
a. Writing Relevant Paragraphs 47
b. Writing Unified Paragraphs 47
c. Writing Coherent Paragraphs 52
Writing Responsibly Guiding the Reader 56
d. Developing Paragraphs Using Patterns 59
e. Writing Introductory Paragraphs 63
f. Writing Concluding Paragraphs 65
g. Connecting Paragraphs 69
Professional Model Editorial 69

5 Drafting and Revising Visuals 73
a. Deciding Whether to Illustrate College Writing Projects 73
b. Using Visuals as Evidence 74
Writing Responsibly Exploitative Images 78

xvii

c. Deciding Whether to Copy Visuals or to Create Them 78
d. Revising Visuals 78

6 Revising, Editing, Proofreading, and Formatting 82

Revising Globally: Analyzing Your Own Work
a. Gaining Perspective 82
b. Revising Your Draft 83
Writing Responsibly The Big Picture 85
c. Reconsidering Your Title 86
Revising Locally: Editing Words and Sentences
d. Choosing Your Words with Care 87
e. Editing Your Sentences 88
Writing Responsibly Making an Essay Long Enough without Wordiness 89
Revising with Others
f. Revising with Peers 90
g. Revising with a Tutor or an Instructor 92
Proofreading and Formatting
h. Proofreading 93
Writing Responsibly Beware the Spelling Checker! 93
i. Formatting an Academic Text 95
j. Creating and Submitting a Portfolio 99
k. **Writing Responsibly** Explaining Your Choice of Sources 104
Student Model Final Draft 95;
Personal Statement 101

Part Two Reasoning Matters Reading, Thinking, and Arguing 107

7 Thinking and Reading Critically 108

a. Comprehending 108
Writing Responsibly Engaging with What You Read 108
b. Reflecting 114
c. Preparing to Write 119
Writing Responsibly Drawing Inferences 124
Writing Responsibly Understanding *Criticism* 125
d. **Writing Responsibly** Understanding and Representing the Entire Source 132
Professional Model Essay 112; **Editorial** 115
Student Model Summary 111; **Double-Entry Reading Journal** 118; **Claims and Evidence Analysis** 121; **Advertisement Critique** 121; **Prewrite** 123; **Critical Response Essay** 127

8 Analyzing and Crafting Arguments 134

a. Persuading and Exploring 134
Writing Responsibly The Well-Tempered Tone 136
b. Making Claims 138
Writing Responsibly Choosing an Engaging Topic 140
c. Choosing Evidence Rhetorically 142
Writing Responsibly Establishing Yourself as a Responsible Writer 144
Writing Responsibly Preparing Oral Arguments 144
d. Considering Alternative Viewpoints 145
e. Discovering Assumptions and Common Ground 147
f. Organizing Arguments: Classical, Rogerian, and Toulmin Models 154
g. Avoiding Logical Fallacies 156
Writing Responsibly Visual Claims and Visual Fallacies 156
Student Model Exploratory Argument 147

Contents **xix**

Part Three — Media Matters: Designing, Writing, and Presenting 161

9 Designing Printed and Electronic Documents 162

a. Understanding the Four Principles of Design 162
b. Planning Your Design Project 163
c. Applying the Principles of Design 164

Writing Responsibly Selecting Fonts with Readers in Mind 165

Writing Responsibly Establishing a Consistent Font 166

Writing Responsibly Designing for Those with Impaired Color Vision 168

10 Writing for Multiple Media 171

a. Writing and Answering E-mail 172

Writing Responsibly Maintaining Confidentiality in E-mail 173

Writing Responsibly Making Considerate Attachments 174

Writing Responsibly Understanding E-mail and Privacy 175

b. Creating Websites and Web Pages 176

Writing Responsibly Checking Accessibility 181

c. Writing in Interactive Media 181

Writing Responsibly Flaming 182

11 Presenting with Multiple Media 183

a. Identifying Your Purpose, Audience, Context, and Genre 183
b. Devising a Topic and Thesis 184
c. Organizing the Presentation 185
d. Preparing and Rehearsing the Presentation 186
e. Delivering the Presentation 189
f. Speaking Responsibly 189

Writing Responsibly Listening Actively 190

Part Four — Research Matters: Finding, Evaluating, and Citing Sources 191

12 Planning a Research Project 192

a. Analyzing the Assignment's Purpose, Audience, and Method of Development 192
b. Setting a Schedule 194
c. Choosing and Narrowing a Research Topic 195
d. Drafting Research Questions and Hypotheses 195

Writing Responsibly Using Printed Sources 197

e. Choosing Research Sources Strategically 197

f. Establishing a Research Log 198

Writing Responsibly Avoiding Accidental Plagiarism 199

g. Building and Annotating a Working Bibliography 200

13 Finding Information 206

a. Finding Reference Works 206

Writing Responsibly Using Wikipedia Responsibly 208

Writing Responsibly Going Beyond Reference Sources 210

b. Finding Information on the Web 210
   c. Finding Reliable Interactive Media 214
   d. Finding Articles in Journals and Other Periodicals Using Databases and Indexes 215
   Writing Responsibly *Really* Reading *Real* Sources 216
   e. Finding Books Using Library Catalogs 220
   f. Finding Government Information 224
   g. Finding Multimedia Sources 225
   h. Conducting and Reporting Field Research 226
   Writing Responsibly Conducting Interviews Fairly 227
   Writing Responsibly Avoiding Manipulation and Bias in Observations 228
   Writing Responsibly Reporting Results Fairly 229

14 Evaluating Information 230
   a. Evaluating for Relevance and Reliability 230
   Writing Responsibly Keeping an Open, Inquiring Mind 234
   Writing Responsibly Online Plagiarism 236
   b. Evaluating Online Texts: Websites, Blogs, Wikis, and Discussion Forums 236
   c. Evaluating Visual Sources 239
   d. **Writing Responsibly** Choosing and Unpacking Complex Sources 244

15 Using Information Responsibly: Taking Notes and Avoiding Plagiarism 246
   a. Valuing Research 248
   b. Using Information Ethically: What You Do and Do Not Have to Acknowledge 248

   Writing Responsibly Using Illustrations and Avoiding Plagiarism 249
   c. Making Notes That Help You Avoid Plagiarizing 250
   d. Making Notes That Help You Research 251
   Writing Responsibly Highlighting versus Making Notes 251
   e. Paraphrasing without Patchwriting 252
   f. Summarizing 256
   g. Quoting 259
   Writing Responsibly Using Quotations Fairly 260
   h. Using Analysis, Interpretation, Synthesis, and Critique in Your Notes 262
   <mark>Student Model</mark> Summary 257;
   Reading Note 261; Summary Note with Writer's Assessment 263

16 Writing the Research Project 264
   a. Drafting a Thesis Statement 264
   b. Organizing Your Ideas 266
   Writing Responsibly Acknowledging Counterevidence 267
   c. Drafting Your Research Project 270
   d. Revising, Proofreading, Formatting, and Publishing Your Project 273
   <mark>Student Model</mark> Thesis Statement 265;
   Outline 268

17 Citing Expertly 274
   a. Integrating Source Material Responsibly 275
   b. Showing Source Boundaries 276
   c. Emphasizing Your Voice 278
   d. Providing Context 280
   e. Integrating Altered Quotations 284

Part Five — Documentation Matters: Creating Citations and Informational Notes 287

Foldout Documentation Matters:
MLA Style and APA Style

18 Documenting Sources: MLA Style 288

a. Creating MLA-Style In-Text Citations 288
Writing Responsibly Citing and Documenting Sources 288
Writing Responsibly Using Signal Phrases to Demonstrate Your Relationship with Sources 293
b. Preparing an MLA-Style List of Works Cited 305
Books—Printed and Electronic 305
Periodicals—Printed and Electronic 315
Other Electronic Sources 319
Audio and Visual Sources 322
Miscellaneous Sources—Printed and Electronic 328
c. Using MLA Style for Informational Notes 331
d. Formatting a Paper in MLA Style 332
Writing Responsibly Of Deadlines and Paperclips 334
Student Model Research Project: MLA Style 336

19 Documenting Sources: APA Style 347

a. Creating APA-Style In-Text Citations 347
Writing Responsibly Citing and Documenting Sources 347
b. Preparing an APA-Style Reference List 358
Books—Printed and Electronic 358
Periodicals—Printed and Electronic 366
Other Electronic Sources 370
Audio and Visual Sources 372
Miscellaneous Sources—Printed and Electronic 374
c. Using APA Style for Informational Notes 376
d. Formatting a Paper in APA Style 377
Writing Responsibly Of Deadlines and Paperclips 380
Student Model Research Project: APA Style 381

20 Documenting Sources: *Chicago* Style 389

Writing Responsibly Citing and Documenting Sources 389
a. Creating *Chicago*-Style Notes and Bibliography Entries 390
Books—Printed and Electronic 390
Periodicals—Printed and Electronic 397
Other Electronic Sources 402
Audio and Visual Sources 404
Miscellaneous Sources—Printed and Electronic 406
b. Using *Chicago* Style for Tables and Figures 407
c. Formatting a *Chicago*-Style Research Project 407
Student Model Research Project: *Chicago* Style 408
Writing Responsibly Of Deadlines and Paperclips 408

21 Documenting Sources: CSE Style 416

a. Creating CSE-Style In-Text Citations 416
Writing Responsibly Citing and Documenting Sources 416
b. Preparing a CSE-Style Reference List 418
Books—Printed and Electronic 418
Periodicals—Printed and Electronic 422

Miscellaneous Sources—Printed and Electronic 426
c. Formatting a CSE-Style Research Project 428

Student Model Research Project: CSE-Style Reference List 429
Writing Responsibly Of Deadlines and Paperclips 429

Part Six Genre Matters Writing in and beyond College 431

22 Writing in Literature and the Other Humanities 432

a. Adopting the Approach of Literature and the Other Humanities 432
Writing Responsibly Reading with Study Guides 433
b. Using the Resources of Literature and the Other Humanities 435
c. Citing and Documenting Sources—MLA and *Chicago* Style 437
d. Using the Language of Literature and the Other Humanities 437
e. Writing about Fiction 440
f. Writing about Poetry 446
g. Writing about Drama 451
Student Model Textual Analysis 434; Writing about Fiction: Interpretive Analysis 442; Writing about Poetry: Explication 446
Professional Model Writing about Drama: Review of a Play 451

23 Writing in the Sciences and Social Sciences 455

a. Adopting the Approach of the Sciences and Social Sciences 455
b. Using the Research Methods of the Sciences and Social Sciences 456
Writing Responsibly Presenting Data Accurately 456
c. Citing and Documenting Sources—APA and CSE Style 457
d. Using the Language of the Sciences and Social Sciences 457

e. Writing Assignments in the Sciences and Social Sciences 459
Student Model Research Report 461

24 Preparing for and Taking an Essay Exam 469

a. Preparing for an Essay Exam 469
b. Previewing the Exam 471
c. Writing an Effective Answer 472
Writing Responsibly Using Your Computer during an Essay Exam 473
Student Model Effective Essay Exam: Response 474

25 Writing in Business and as a Citizen 476

a. Using Business Letter Formats 476
b. Writing Business Letters 479
Writing Responsibly Letters to the Editor 479
c. Writing Business Memos 481
d. Writing Job Application Letters 482
Writing Responsibly Personal E-mails and IM at Work 484
e. Writing Résumés 486
f. Writing Reports and Proposals 490
g. Writing Press Releases 492
Student Model Job Application 485; Traditional Résumé 487; Business Letter: Scannable Résumé 489
Professional Model Business Letter: Apology 480; Business Memo 482; Press Release 493

Contents **xxiii**

Part Seven Style Matters 495

26 Writing Concisely 496

Writing Responsibly Conciseness versus the Too-Short Paper 496
a. Eliminating Wordy Expressions 497
b. Eliminating Ineffective or Unnecessary Repetition 499
c. Avoiding Indirect Constructions 500
d. Consolidating Phrases, Clauses, and Sentences 502

27 Using Coordination and Subordination 505

a. Coordinating Terms, Phrases, and Clauses 506
b. Coordinating Effectively 507
c. Identifying Important Ideas and Supporting Information with Subordination 510
d. Using Coordination and Subordination Together 515

28 Using Parallelism 518

a. Using Parallelism for Paired Items and Items in a Series 520
b. Maintaining Parallelism in Comparisons 522
c. Including Function Words to Maintain Parallelism 522
Writing Responsibly Using Parallelism to Clarify Relationships among Ideas 523
d. Maintaining Parallelism for Items in Lists and Outlines 523
e. Using Parallelism to Create Emphasis 525

29 Engaging Readers with Variety and Emphasis 527

a. Varying Sentence Length and Structure 528
b. Varying Sentence Openings 529
c. Creating Emphasis with Rhythm 531
d. Creating Emphasis with Punctuation 533
e. Using Questions, Commands, and Exclamations 534
f. Using Strategic Repetition 534
g. Creating Emphasis with Emphatic Verbs 535
h. Choosing the Active or Passive Voice 535
Writing Responsibly Voice and Responsibility 536
i. **Writing Responsibly** Blending Voices in Your Text 538

30 Choosing Appropriate Language 540

a. Using Language in Context 540
Writing Responsibly Avoiding Online Shortcuts 542
Writing Responsibly Euphemisms and Doublespeak 544
b. Avoiding Biased or Hurtful Language 544

31 Choosing Effective Words 548

a. Diction: Finding the Right Word 548
b. Choosing Compelling Words and Figures 550
Writing Responsibly Word Choice and Credibility 551
c. Mastering Idioms 554
d. Avoiding Clichés 555

32 Using the Dictionary and Spelling Correctly 558

a. Choosing a Dictionary 558
Writing Responsibly Choose Accurate Synonyms 560

b. Using a Dictionary 560
c. Avoiding Common Spelling Problems 562
d. Remembering Spelling Rules 564

Writing Responsibly Spelling Errors 564
e. Forming Plurals 569
f. Improving Your Day-to-Day Spelling 571

Part Eight Grammar Matters Writing with Clarity 573

33 Understanding Grammar 574

Writing Responsibly Why Grammar Matters 574

Parts of Speech
a. Nouns 575
b. Pronouns 577
c. Verbs 577
d. Adjectives 580
e. Adverbs 581
f. Prepositions 582
g. Conjunctions 583
h. Interjections 584

Sentence Structure
i. Subjects 585
j. Predicates 587
k. Verb Types and Sentence Patterns 588
l. Phrases 591
m. Independent and Subordinate Clauses 594
n. Sentence Types 597

34 Avoiding Sentence Fragments 600

a. Recognizing Fragments 600
b. Correcting Fragments 604

Writing Responsibly Sentence Fragments and Context 604

c. Using Intentional Fragments Effectively and Judiciously 609

35 Avoiding Comma Splices and Fused Sentences 611

a. Correctly Joining Independent Clauses 611
b. Identifying Incorrectly Joined Independent Clauses: Comma Splices and Fused Sentences 612

Writing Responsibly Clarifying Boundaries 612

c. Recognizing When Comma Splices and Fused Sentences Tend to Occur 613

Writing Responsibly Is a Comma Splice Ever Acceptable? 614

d. Correcting Comma Splices and Fused Sentences 615

36 Maintaining Agreement 620

Subject-Verb Agreement
a. Understanding How Subjects and Verbs Agree 620

Writing Responsibly Dialect Variation in Subject-Verb Agreement 622

b. Ignoring Words That Intervene between the Subject and the Verb 622
c. Distinguishing Plural from Singular Compound Subjects 623
d. Distinguishing Singular and Plural Indefinite Pronouns 625
e. Understanding Collective Noun Subjects 625
f. Finding Agreement When the Subject Is a Measurement, a Number, or the Word *Number* 626
g. Recognizing Nouns That Are Singular Even Though They End in *–s* 627

Contents **xxv**

    h. Treating Titles, Words as Words, and Gerund Phrases as Singular 627
    i. Matching a Relative Pronoun (*Who, Which,* or *That*) to Its Antecedent When the Pronoun Is the Subject of a Subordinate Clause 628
    j. Finding Agreement When the Subject Follows the Verb 629
    k. Matching a Linking Verb with Its Subject, Not Its Subject Complement 629

Pronoun-Antecedent Agreement
    l. Matching Pronouns with Indefinite Pronoun and Generic Noun Antecedents 631
    Writing Responsibly Using a Plural Pronoun with a Singular Antecedent 633
    m. Matching Pronouns with Collective Noun Antecedents 634
    n. Matching Pronouns with Compound Antecedents 634

37 Using Verbs 636

Verb Forms
    a. Understanding the Basic Forms of Verbs 636
    b. Using Regular and Irregular Verb Forms Correctly 638
    c. Combining Main Verbs with Helping Verbs to Form Complete Verbs 639
    d. Including *-s* or *-es*, *-d* or *-ed* Endings When Required 642
    e. Distinguishing *Rise* from *Raise*, *Sit* from *Set*, *Lie* from *Lay* 643

Tense
    f. Understanding Which Verb Tense to Use 644
    g. Following Conventions for the Use of the Present Tense 647
    h. Using Tense Sequence to Clarify Time Relationships 648

Mood
    i. Understanding Verb Mood 650
    j. Using the Subjunctive Mood Correctly 650
    Writing Responsibly Using the Subjunctive in Formal Writing 651

Voice
    k. Understanding Voice 652
    l. Choosing between the Active and Passive Voice 653

38 Understanding Pronoun Case and Reference 656

Pronoun Case
    a. Using the Subjective Case for Subject Complements 658
    b. *She and I* or *Her and Me*? Keeping Track of Case in Compounds 658
    c. Keeping Track of Pronoun Case in Appositives 660
    d. Deciding between *We* and *Us* before Nouns 660
    e. Using the Objective Case Both before and after an Infinitive 661
    f. Deciding on Pronoun Case with the *-ing* Form of a Verb 661
    g. Clarifying Pronoun Case in Comparisons with *Than* or *As* 662
    h. Using *Who, Whom, Whoever,* and *Whomever* 663
    Writing Responsibly Case and Tone 663

Clear Pronoun Reference
    i. Avoiding Ambiguous Reference 665
    j. Avoiding Confusingly Broad Reference with *It, This, That,* and *Which* 665
    k. Avoiding Implied Reference 666
    l. Reserving *You* for Directly Addressing the Reader 666
    m. Avoiding the Indefinite Use of *They* and *It* 666
    n. Designating People with *Who, Whom,* and *Whose,* not *That* and *Which* 667

39 Using Adjectives and Adverbs 669
a. Differentiating Adjectives and Adverbs 669
b. Using Adjectives, Not Adverbs, as Subject Complements after Linking Verbs 670
c. Choosing *Bad* or *Badly, Good* or *Well* 671
d. Using Negatives Correctly 673
e. Avoiding Long Strings of Nouns Used as Adjectives 673
f. Using Comparative and Superlative Adjectives and Adverbs 674

40 Avoiding Confusing Shifts 678
a. Avoiding Awkward Shifts in Tense 678
b. Avoiding Awkward Shifts in Mood and Voice 679
c. Avoiding Awkward Shifts in Person and Number 681
d. Avoiding Awkward Shifts in Direct and Indirect Quotations and Questions 683

41 Avoiding Misplaced and Dangling Modifiers 686
Misplaced Modifiers
a. Avoiding Confusing or Ambiguous Placement 687
b. Avoiding Disruptive Placement 689
Writing Responsibly Misplaced Modifiers in the Real World 690
Dangling Modifiers
c. Identifying Dangling Modifiers 692
d. Correcting Dangling Modifiers 693

42 Avoiding Mixed and Incomplete Constructions 695
Mixed Constructions
a. Recognizing and Correcting Grammatically Mixed Constructions 695
b. Recognizing and Correcting Mismatched Subjects and Predicates 697
Incomplete Constructions
c. Adding Essential Words to Compound and Other Constructions 700
d. Avoiding Incomplete or Ambiguous Comparisons 701

Part Nine Language Matters Issues for Multilingual Writers
(by Ted E. Johnston and M. E. Sokolik) 703

43 Understanding English Word Order and Sentence Structure 704
a. Observing Normal Word Order 704
b. Including a Stated Subject 704
c. Managing *There* and *It* Constructions 705
d. Eliminating Redundant Subject and Object Pronouns 706
e. Structuring Sentences with Direct Objects, Indirect Objects, and Object Complements 707
f. Observing Word-Order Patterns in Questions 709
g. Observing Inverted Word Order When Certain Conjunctions or Adverbs Begin a Clause 710

44 Using Nouns and Noun Determiners 713
a. Understanding Different Types of Nouns 713
b. Using Nouns with Articles (*a, an, the*) and Other Determiners 714

Contents **xxvii**

45 Managing English Verbs 722
    a. Using Phrasal Verbs 722
    b. Using Gerunds and Infinitives after Verbs and Prepositions 725
    c. Using Participles as Adjectives 727
    d. Using Helping Verbs for Verb Formation 728

46 Managing Adjectives and Adverbs 732
    a. Placing Adjectives in the Proper Order 732
    b. Choosing the Correct Prepositions with Adjectives 733
    c. Placing Adverbs Correctly 734
    d. Dealing with Confusing Adverbs 736

47 Using Prepositions 739
    a. Recognizing Prepositions 739
    b. The Functions of Prepositions 740
    c. Using Prepositions Correctly 744
    d. Necessary and Unnecessary Prepositions 745

Part Ten Detail Matters Punctuation and Mechanics 747

48 Using Commas 748
    Writing Responsibly Commas and Clarity 748
    a. Using Commas in Compound Sentences 750
    b. Using a Comma after Introductory Elements 751
    c. Using Commas to Set Off Conjunctive Adverbs and Most Transitional Phrases 753
    d. Inserting Commas to Set Off Interjections, Contrasting Information, Expressions of Direct Address, Parenthetical and Conversational Expressions, and Tag Questions 753
    e. Using Commas to Separate Items in a Series 754
    f. Using Commas to Separate Coordinate, Not Cumulative, Adjectives 755
    g. Using Commas to Set Off Nonessential Appositives, Phrases, and Clauses 757
    h. Using Commas with Quotations 759
    i. Using Commas with Numbers, Names and Titles, Place Names and Addresses, and Dates 760
    j. Using Commas to Avoid Ambiguity 762
    k. Avoiding Commas between Subjects and Verbs, Verbs and Objects 763

49 Using Semicolons 766
    Writing Responsibly Sending a Signal with Semicolons 766
    a. Using a Semicolon to Link Independent Clauses 767
    b. Using a Semicolon before a Conjunctive Adverb or Transitional Phrase Linking Two Independent Clauses 768
    c. Using a Semicolon to Mark a Series with Internal Commas 769
    d. Repairing a Comma Splice 769
    e. Avoiding Overuse 770

50 Using Apostrophes 773
    a. Using an Apostrophe to Indicate Possession 773
    Writing Responsibly Contractions in Formal Writing 773

b. Using Apostrophes in Contractions and Abbreviated Years 777
   c. Moving Away from Using Apostrophes to Form Plurals of Abbreviations, Dates, Numbers, and Words or Letters Used as Words 777

51 Using Quotation Marks 780

   a. Setting Off Direct Quotations 780
   Writing Responsibly Using Quotations Fairly 781
   b. Indicating Titles of Short Works 783
   c. Indicating Words Used in a Special Sense 784
   d. Misusing Quotation Marks 784
   e. Punctuating Quotations 785
   f. Altering Quotations with Ellipses and Square Brackets 786
   g. Introducing and Identifying Quotations 787
   h. **Writing Responsibly** Acknowledging Indirect Sources 790

52 Using End Punctuation: Periods, Question Marks, and Exclamation Points 792

   a. Using Periods to End Statements and Mild Commands 792
   b. Using Question Marks to End Direct (Not Indirect) Questions 793
   Writing Responsibly Quotation Marks and Exclamation Points 793
   c. Using Exclamation Points with Strong Commands or to Express Excitement or Surprise 794

53 Using Other Punctuation: Dashes, Parentheses, Brackets, Colons, Ellipses, and Slashes 796

   a. Using Dashes 796
   b. Using Parentheses 798
   Writing Responsibly Dashes, Parentheses, or Commas? 798
   c. Using Brackets 800
   d. Using Colons 800
   Writing Responsibly Using *[sic]* 800
   e. Using Ellipses 803
   Writing Responsibly Altering Quotations 803
   f. Using Slashes 804

54 Capitalizing 807

   a. Capitalizing the First Word of a Sentence 807
   b. Capitalizing Proper Nouns and Proper Adjectives 809
   c. Capitalizing Titles and Subtitles 810
   d. Capitalizing the First-Person Pronoun *I* and the Interjection *O* 811
   Writing Responsibly Capitalizing in E-mail and IM 811
   e. Capitalizing Abbreviations and Acronyms 812

55 Italics and Underlining 814

   a. Italicizing Titles of Longer Works 814
   Writing Responsibly Using Italics for Emphasis 816
   b. Italicizing for Emphasis 816
   c. Italicizing Names of Vehicles 816
   d. Italicizing Words, Letters, or Numbers Used as Words 816
   e. Italicizing Unfamiliar Non-English Words and Latin Genus and Species 817
   f. Underlining Hyperlinks 817

56 Using Abbreviations 820

   a. Abbreviating Titles before and after Names 822
   b. Using Familiar Abbreviations: Acronyms and Initialisms 822
   Writing Responsibly Using Online Abbreviations Appropriately 823

c. Using Abbreviations with Specific Years (BC, BCE, AD, CE), Hours (a.m., p.m.), Numbers (no.), and Dollars ($) 823
d. Avoiding Abbreviations of Names, Words, Courses, Parts of Books, States and Countries, Days and Months, Holidays, and Units of Measurement in Prose 823
e. Replacing Latin Abbreviations with English Equivalents in Formal Prose 824

57 Using Numbers 826

Writing Responsibly Ethos and Convention 826

a. Spelling Out Numbers When They Can Be Expressed in One or Two Words 827
b. Following Conventions for Dates, Times, Addresses, Specific Amounts of Money and Other Quantitative Information, and Divisions of Literary Works 827

58 Using Hyphens 830

a. Using Hyphens to Form Compounds 830
Writing Responsibly Hyphenating with Readers in Mind 831
b. Using Hyphens to Break Words at the Ends of Lines 833

Glossary of Key Terms G1
Glossary of Usage G14
Credits C1
Index I1
ESl Index ESL1

Part One

Writing Matters

Planning, Drafting, Revising, Editing, Proofreading, and Formatting

1. Writing Responsibly in the Information Age   2
2. Planning Your Project   9
3. Organizing and Drafting Your Project   29
4. Crafting and Connecting Paragraphs   46
5. Drafting and Revising Visuals   73
6. Revising, Editing, Proofreading, and Formatting   82

1 Writing Responsibly in the Information Age

IN THIS CHAPTER

a. Writing today, 2

b. Writer's responsibilities: to audience, topic, other writers, self, 3

Student Model
Newspaper Article, 8

In 2004, the National Commission on Writing published a report called "Writing: A Ticket to Work . . . Or a Ticket Out," surveying 120 of the largest corporations in America. Among the results: American corporations expect their salaried employees to be able to write clearly, correctly, and logically. Eighty percent of finance, insurance, and real estate employers take writing skills into consideration when hiring salaried employees. For these employers, good writing is a "threshold skill." To get a good job, to keep that job, or to get promoted, you must write clearly, logically, and accurately; for the appropriate audience; and with the necessary level of support and documentation. As you write projects for your college courses, you are, in effect, standing before the elevator to your own future. You decide whether the elevator will take you up.

But writing well is more than a ticket to a good job. Whether drafting business e-mails or making PowerPoint presentations, texting friends or commenting on a Facebook page, posting a tweet or even composing a paper for a college course, we write to develop and evaluate beliefs and ideas, to move others, to express ourselves, and to explore possibilities. For all these reasons and more, writing matters!

1a Writing Today

Long before Johannes Gutenberg introduced the printing press, in the fifteenth century, a *page* was seen as a sheet of paper covered with text, and *literacy* meant the ability to read and write a text, whether written on the page or carved in stone. But as the Internet revolution changes our understanding of what a page is, it also expands our concept of literacy (Figure 1.1). Today, a page can be a sheet of paper, but it can also be a screen in a website or an e-mail message on a

FIGURE 1.1 The media revolution In the fifteenth century, few could read (or had access to) the Gutenberg Bible. Today, readers can view its pages on their phones, but to do so they must be multiliterate: Not only must they be able to read and write, but they must also know how to access multiple media online.

Droid; it can include not only words, but also images and sound files, links to other web pages, and Flash animations. The ability to understand, interpret, and use these new kinds of pages—by contributing to a class wiki or making an online presentation, for example—requires not just print literacy but multiple literacies (visual literacy, digital literacy, information literacy).

Like most people reading this book, you are probably already multiliterate: You "code shift," switching from medium to medium easily because the "literacies" required for each medium are not entirely separate. Whether penning a thank-you note, searching a library database, reading an advertisement, composing a college paper, or texting your best friend, you analyze and interpret, adjusting your message in response to your purpose, audience, context, and medium: When texting a friend you may ignore the conventions of punctuation and capitalization, for example, but you would not do so when writing a résumé.

This handbook focuses on print literacy because it remains central to communication; yet *Writing Matters* also addresses digital, visual, oral, and information literacies because they have become impossible to separate from one another and from traditional print literacy. As a reader, you must be able not only to decipher written language but also to interpret visuals—drawing meaning from advertisements, for example, and subjecting them to the scrutiny of a careful shopper. As a writer, you may incorporate graphics into papers in economics and psychology; contribute to class blogs or Twitter discussions; search online databases and electronic library catalogs; or create presentations using Prezi and Jing. As both a reader and a writer, you will be expected to manage all the information you receive and transmit. Being multiliterate *means* being information literate.

› **More about**
Writing business memos, 481–82
Creating PowerPoints, 187
Creating websites, 176–81
Writing in literature and other humanities, 432–54 (ch. 22)
Writing in the sciences and social sciences, 455–68 (ch. 23)
Reading critically, 108–33 (ch. 7)
Interpreting visuals, 119, 122, 126
Incorporating visuals, 95, 306–07, 327–28, 334–36, 379–80

1b The Writer's Responsibilities

With opportunities to express and even create yourself in words come responsibilities to your readers, to the topics you address, to the other writers from whom you borrow and to whom you respond, and perhaps especially to yourself as a writer with ideas and ideals to express.

1. Your responsibilities to your audience

Audience members make a commitment to you by spending their time reading your work. To make your readers feel that this commitment was worthwhile, you can do the following:

- Choose a topic that your audience will find interesting and about which you have something you want to say.
- Make a claim that will help your audience follow your thoughts.
- Support your claim with thoughtful, logical, even creative evidence drawn from sources that you have evaluated carefully for relevance and reliability.
- Write clearly so that your audience (even if that audience is your composition teacher) does not have to struggle to understand. To write clearly, build a logical structure, use transitional techniques to guide readers, and correct errors of grammar, punctuation, and spelling.
- Write appropriately by using a tone and vocabulary that are right for your topic, audience, context, and genre.
- Write engagingly by varying sentence structures and word choices, avoiding wordiness, and using repetition only for special effect.

2. Your responsibilities to your topic

Examples of writers who did not take seriously their responsibility to their topic are everywhere. Here are three:

- A six-year-old child who won tickets to a Hannah Montana concert with an essay about her father's Iraq War death; her father had *not* been killed in Iraq. She lost those tickets.
- Jayson Blair, a *New York Times* reporter who concocted stories without leaving his apartment; he was forced to resign.
- The president of Raytheon Company, who plagiarized large sections of his book *Swanson's Unwritten Rules of Management* from a book published in 1944; he was fined a million dollars by the company's shareholders.

You treat your topic responsibly when you explore it thoroughly and creatively, rely on trustworthy sources, and offer supporting evidence that is accurate, relevant, and reliable. You show respect for your topic when you provide

---

> **More about**
> Writing Responsibly, foldout preceding ch. 1
> List of Writing Responsibly boxes, pages facing inside back cover
> Devising a topic, 20–25
> Finding information, 206–29 (ch. 13)
> Using supporting evidence, 40–42
> Evaluating sources, 230–45 (ch. 14)
> Organizing, 33–37
> Providing transitions, 54–55
> Correcting grammar, 574–702 (part 8, Grammar Matters)
> Correcting punctuation, 748–835 (part 10, Detail Matters)
> Writing with flair, 496–572 (part 7, Style Matters)

enough evidence to persuade readers of your claims and when you acknowledge viewpoints that do not support your position. In a college writing project, not fulfilling your responsibilities to your topic might lead to a bad grade. In the workplace, it could have great financial, even life-and-death, consequences: The Merck pharmaceutical company, for example, was accused of suppressing evidence that its drug Vioxx could cause heart attacks and strokes. As a result, Merck faced a host of lawsuits, trials, and out-of-court settlements.

> **Writing Responsibly** | **Your Responsibilities as a Writer**
>
> When you write, you have four areas of responsibility:
>
> 1. To your audience
> 2. To your topic
> 3. To other writers
> 4. To yourself

3. Your responsibilities to other writers

You have important responsibilities to other writers whose work you may be using.

Acknowledge your sources Writing circulates easily today, and vast quantities of it are available online, readily accessible through search engines such as Bing and Google and databases such as JSTOR. It may seem natural, then, simply to copy the information you need from a source and paste it into your own text, as you might if you were collecting information about a disease you were facing or a concert you hoped to attend. But when you provide readers with information, ideas, language, or images that others have collected or created, you also have a responsibility to *acknowledge* those sources. Such acknowledgment gives credit to those who contributed to your thinking, and it allows your readers to read your sources for themselves. Acknowledging your sources also protects you from charges of plagiarism, and it builds your authority and credibility as a writer by establishing that you have reviewed key sources on a topic and taken other writers' views into consideration.

To acknowledge sources in academic writing, you must do *all three* of the following:

1. When quoting, copy accurately and use quotation marks or block indention to signal the beginning and end of the copied passage; when paraphrasing or summarizing, put the ideas fully into your own words and sentences.
2. Include an in-text citation to the source, whether you are quoting, paraphrasing, or summarizing.

> **More about**
> Avoiding hypothetical evidence, 41
> Avoiding altering images inappropriately, 78–81

> **More about**
> Using a search engine, 210–13
> Using an online database, 215–20
> Using an electronic library catalog, 220–26

> **More about**
> When to quote, paraphrase, or summarize, 252–63
> Using quotation marks, 780–91 (ch. 51)
> Formatting block quotations, 334, 377, 782–83
> Adjusting quotations using brackets and ellipses, 786, 800, 803–04

More about
Citing and documenting sources, 288–430 (part 5, Documentation Matters)
Avoiding plagiarism and "patchwriting," 250–56, 274–76

3. **Document the source**, providing enough information for your readers to locate the source and to identify the type of source you used. This documentation usually appears in a bibliography (often called a list of works cited or a reference list) at the end of college research projects.

Writing Responsibly around the World Concepts of plagiarism vary from one culture or context to another. Where one may see cooperation, another may see plagiarism. Even if borrowing ideas and language without acknowledgment is a familiar custom for you, writers in the United States (especially in academic contexts) must explicitly acknowledge all ideas and information borrowed from another source.

Obtain copyright clearance While plagiarism is concerned with acknowledging sources of ideas or language, copyright focuses on the right to compensation for the use of writers' words and ideas in a public context. When writers use a substantial portion of another writer's text, they must not only acknowledge the source but may also need to obtain the original author's permission, often in exchange for a fee.

As a student, your use of sources is covered under the *fair use* provision of copyright law, which allows you to include copyrighted material without permission when you are doing your college assignments. What counts as fair use cannot be expressed in percentages or checklists. The Center for Social Media at American University offers a "Code of Best Practices in Fair Use for Media Literacy Education" that you can find online. It explains that if you copy someone else's text or music files and avoid paying for it, you are violating copyright. But if you are using parts of a text or a song for educational purposes, and if you are not interfering with the copyright owner's ability to profit from the material, you are making fair use of it and do not need the copyright owner's

---

Quick Reference **Your College's Plagiarism Policy**

Most colleges publish their plagiarism policies in their student handbook, which is often available online. **Find your plagiarism policy** by searching the student handbook's table of contents or index. Or search your college's website, using key terms such as *plagiarism, cheating policy, academic honesty,* or *academic integrity*. Before writing a research project, **read your school's plagiarism policy** carefully. If you are unsure what the policy means, talk with your adviser or instructor. In addition to the general policy for your college, **read your course syllabi** carefully to see what specific guidelines your instructors may provide there.

permission. Because plagiarism and copyright are separate issues, though, you must always acknowledge your source, even when no permission is needed.

Copyright protections also apply to you as a writer: Anything you write is protected by US copyright law—even your college assignments.

Treat other writers fairly Your responsibility to other writers does not end with the need to acknowledge your use of their ideas or language. You must also represent *accurately* and *fairly* what your sources say: Quoting selectively to distort meaning or taking a comment out of context is irresponsible. So is treating other writers with scorn.

> **More about**
> Bias, 544–47
> Ad hominem, 159

It is perfectly acceptable to criticize the ideas of others. In fact, examining ideas under the bright light of careful scrutiny is central to higher education. But treating the people who developed the ideas with derision is not. Avoid *ad hominem* (or personal) attacks, and focus your attention on other writers' ideas and their expression of them.

4. Your responsibilities to yourself

You have a responsibility to yourself as a writer. Writers represent themselves on paper and screen through the words and images (and even sounds) they create and borrow, so submitting a project as your own that someone else has written is a form of impersonation—it does not represent you. Make sure that the writing "avatar," or **persona,** you create is the best representation of yourself it can be. Encourage readers to view you with respect by treating others—not only other writers but also other people and groups—respectfully and without bias. Earn your audience's respect by synthesizing information from sources to produce new and compelling ideas and by using language clearly, correctly, logically, and with flair.

> **More about**
> Synthesis, 123–25
> Common sentence problems, fold-out preceding part 8, Grammar Matters
> Style, 496–572 (part 7, Style Matters)
> Grammar, 574–702 (part 8, Grammar Matters)
> Punctuation and mechanics, 748–835 (part 10, Detail Matters)

If you graduate from college having learned to be an effective writer, you will have learned something employers value highly. More importantly, though, you will have fulfilled a key responsibility to yourself.

Writing Responsibly | **Taking Yourself Seriously as a Writer**

Many students enter writing classes thinking of themselves as "bad writers." This belief can be a self-fulfilling prophecy—students fail to engage because they already believe they are doomed to fail. Remember that writing is not an inborn talent but a skill to be learned. Instead of thinking of yourself as a bad writer, think of yourself as a writer-in-progress, someone who has something to say and who is learning how to say it effectively. If you speak or have studied another language, think of yourself as someone who is learning to draw on that experience.

to SELF

> **EXERCISE 1.1** **Assessing the writer's responsibilities**
>
> Read "Plagiarism Cheats Students," written by Salt Lake Community College student Jeff Gurney for his college newspaper, *The Globe*. To what extent do you agree with Gurney's argument? What reservations do you have about it? What other writers' responsibilities might a revision of the article take into account?

Student Model Newspaper Article

Plagiarism Cheats Students

By JEFF GURNEY

In the world of higher education, your growth as a student comes with a heavy price. Many hours are spent reading, researching and writing for required reports in most of your classes. This means staying up many nights until almost dawn and drinking a lot of coffee.

Or at least this is how it should be. Unfortunately, an amazing number of students are getting into buying ready-made reports. There are many places that you can go online and pick the type of paper you want. For a fee they will send you the paper and all you have to do is change a few sentences. Once that part is done all you need to do is turn it in.

This is the way some students have made it through college. Then the professors got smart and noticed that there were a lot of papers that sounded pretty much the same or had just about the same content.

Along come services like Turnitin.com where the professor tells you to first send the report online, and for a fee, usually paid for by the school, your paper is compared to many different papers and texts that are in a massive database. The service can tell in percentages how much content in your paper was gleaned from other sources.

This service also provides [instructors] with the results of the scan and tells them what your scores are in each of several categories.

Over the past few years there have been several writers working for very prominent media services that have been caught plagiarizing, and surprisingly they were using quite a bit of other people's stuff. The most amazing thing about this misuse is that they worked for trusted publications and broke that trust for money.

In a recent study reported by Mark Edmundson in the *New York Times* (September 9, 2003, p. A29), 38 percent of American college students admitted to committing "cut and paste" plagiarism. This percentage is up 10 percent from 2000.

These numbers pose a question. What is the reason we go to college? Are you attending SLCC merely to get a better job, or to learn something in the process for that job? An unknown author once said, "If it were easy then everybody would have done it." This is the ideal that those that started higher education probably had in mind. It is much more valuable, that diploma in hand, when you earn it yourself.

2 Planning Your Project

IN THIS CHAPTER

a. Writing situation, 9

b. Analyzing an assignment, 17

c. Generating ideas, topics, 20

d. Narrowing, broadening a topic, 25

e. Collaboration, 26

Student Models
Freewrite, 21; **Brainstorm,** 22, 26; **Journalists' Questions,** 24

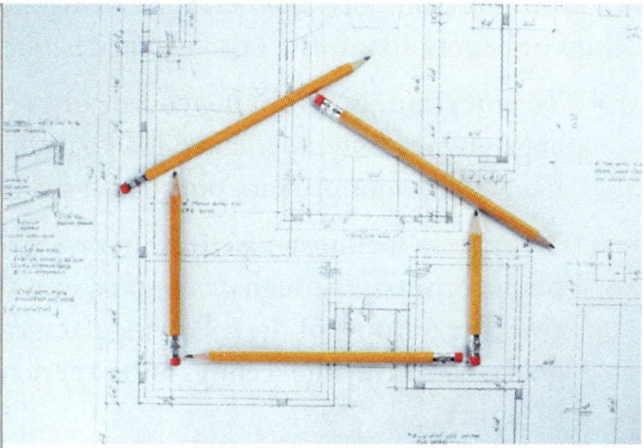

Just as an architect creates a blueprint to show how to fit together the concrete footings, steel beams, and electrical wiring of a building, so, too, does a writer create a plan that takes into account the project's purpose, audience, context, and genre. Just as an architect must choose the right materials and devise plans to complete the project on budget and on schedule, a writer must select an engaging topic, devise ideas that will resonate with the reader, fulfill the terms of the assignment, and do it all on time.

2a Analyzing Your Writing Situation

The first step in planning a writing project is analyzing the ***writing situation:***

- What is your **purpose**? What do you hope to accomplish with the text?
- Who is your **audience**? Who will be reading the text you produce and why?
- What **topics** will interest them?
- What **tone** is appropriate to your purpose and audience?
- What are the **context** (academic, business, personal) and **genre** (or type) of writing you will produce (research report, résumé, Facebook status update)? How will your context and genre affect the way you write this project?

Throughout the writing process—planning, drafting, revising, and editing—you can refine or reconsider your initial decisions.

1. Establish a purpose.

The classical reasons, or *purposes,* for writing are to entertain, to express your feelings or beliefs, to inform, or to persuade your audience.

- **To entertain.** Entertaining your readers (by providing them with an engaging reading experience) is a goal all writers share, but it is unlikely to be your primary purpose in academic or business writing.

- **To express feelings or beliefs.** In *expressive* writing, an experience is often conveyed through *description,* and the language is richly evocative. The purpose of the following paragraph is expressive; the writer's goal is to convey the feelings and experiences of a small would-be ballerina.

> *More about*
> Description, 59

> She stood in the doorframe shivering. She was a tiny girl, about four years old, and her wispy blonde hair was tied back with a pink satin ribbon. Leaning against her mother's leg, she gazed into the unfamiliar room. Other girls her age were twirling and jumping with confidence, laughing at their reflections in the mirrors, spinning on the slippery wooden floors. The girl's mother handed her the ballet shoes, gave her a quick peck on the cheek, and stepped back into the snowstorm. Alone now, the girl retreated to the wall and slid into a dark corner. She bent her knees against her chest and wrapped her arms around her legs. There she sat.
> —Amanda Godfrey, McHenry County College, "Ballet Blues"

In most college courses, an expressive purpose is unlikely to be primary, but it may well play a secondary role, as you draw on your own experiences to illustrate a point.

Writing about Personal Experiences Depending on your cultural background or educational experiences, writing about personal issues and experiences may seem odd in an academic writing course. Instructors at US colleges and universities, however, sometimes assign expressive essays as a way to get their students to write about something they already know. If you are uncomfortable writing on a personal topic, discuss the issue with your instructor.

- **To inform.** An *informative* (or *expository*) text may explain a concept, describe a sequence of events or a process, or analyze a relationship. Scientific, technical, journalistic, and business writing are typically informative. The abstract below, which comes from a psychology research paper, is expository because it informs the reader of the results of a psychological study:

> This study explores the potential influence of stereotypical appearances on male subjects' stated opinions regarding entertainment perceived as "feminine." The findings show that participants were more likely to give a favorable ranking of a "chick flick" in the presence of a counter-stereotypical male than in the presence of a stereotypical male. The discussion focuses on possible explanations for participant behavior, with a theoretical basis in gender role conflict.
> —Heather DeGroot, James Madison University, "The Power of Wardrobe: Male Stereotype Influences"

- **To persuade or argue.** Texts that try to convince readers to adopt beliefs or opinions or to take action have a ***persuasive*** (or ***argumentative***) purpose. Editorials, book and movie reviews, grant proposals, and much academic writing all have a persuasive purpose. The paragraph below comes from an editorial. It draws on evidence from studies to support its claim that Head Start is a worthwhile program:

> Head Start, the federally funded pre-kindergarten program, has been under attack recently as a waste of money, because some say the effects don't last long enough to make a difference later in life. I beg to differ. Studies show that eighth graders who were in Head Start do as well as kids who received education from a private pre-school. Poor children who do not attend Head Start do no better than their parents. To raise our population out of poverty, children must learn at an early age to have confidence, have goals and strive for them, and receive the best education they can. Head Start provides a good start.
> —Lynn Holmlund, Bentley College, "Going Public: Head Start"

Student Models
Informative projects
"Alternative Energy: Does It Really Offer an Alternative?" Betsy Smith, 95–99
"The Power of Wardrobe," Heather DeGroot, 381–88
"Nature vs. Nurture," Robyn Worthington, 461–68

> **More about**
> Analyzing and crafting arguments, 134–60 (ch. 8)

EXERCISE 2.1 Analyzing purpose

Read the following passages and determine whether the primary purpose of each passage is expressive, informative, or persuasive:

> Camels do not store water in their humps. They drink furiously, up to twenty-eight gallons in a ten-minute session, then distribute the water evenly throughout their bodies. Afterward, they use the water stingily. They have viscous urine and dry feces. They breathe through their noses, and keep their mouths shut. They do sweat, but only as a last resort, after first allowing their body temperatures to rise 10 degrees Fahrenheit. As they begin to dehydrate, the volume of

their blood plasma does not at first diminish. They can survive a water loss of up to one-third of their body weight, then drink up and feel fine. Left alone, unhurried and unburdened, they can live two weeks between drinks.

—William Langewiesche, *Sahara Unveiled*

Gentlemen, I want you to suppose a case for a moment. Suppose that all the property you were worth was in gold, and you had to put it in the hands of Blondin, the famous rope-walker, to carry across the Niagara Falls on a tight rope. Would you shake the rope while he was passing over it, or keep shouting to him, "Blondin, stop a little more! Go a little faster!"? No. I am sure you would not. You would hold your breath as well as your tongue and keep your hand off until he was safely over. Now the Government is in the same situation. It is carrying an immense weight across a stormy ocean. Untold treasures are in its hands. It is doing the best it can. Don't badger it! Just keep still, and it will get you safely over.

—Abraham Lincoln, "Reply to Critics of His Administration"

Have you ever had to ask for help, knowing your children will suffer unless you get it? Think about asking for a loan from a relative, if this is the only way you can imagine asking for help. I will tell you how it feels. You find out where the office is that you are supposed to visit. You circle that block four or five times. Thinking of your children, you go in. Everybody is very busy. Finally, someone comes out and you tell her that you need help. That never is the person you need to see. You go see another person, and after spilling the whole shame of your poverty all over the desk between you, you find that this isn't the right office after all—you might repeat the whole process, and it never is any easier at the next place.

—Jo Goodwin Parker, "What Is Poverty?"

2. Identify and address your audience.

A text is seldom written for the writer alone. Rather, it is intended for an ***audience,*** and this fact shapes the text in large and small ways. That is why, for a piece of writing to be effective, the writer must make a careful analysis of the intended reader (or readers).

Before putting fingers to keyboard, consider the characteristics of your audience, such as age and gender, occupation and interests, educational background, political or cultural affiliations, and ethnic or religious background. Then, consider the audience's expectations:

Writing Responsibly
Seeing and Showing the Whole Picture

As a writer, you have a responsibility to look beyond your own experiences and beliefs, beyond your own self-interest. As you explore an issue, give thorough, respectful attention to interpretations that contradict or conflict with yours. Figure out what motivates the supporters of opposing positions. Consider whether your own opinion should be revised. Then, as you write, no matter which position you support in your text, let your audience see all the viewpoints and the reasons for them.

to AUDIENCE

- Are your readers already well informed about the topic, or are they reading your text to learn about something new to them?
- Are your readers eager to learn about your topic, or do they have only a passing interest?
- Do readers hold strong opinions about your topic, or are they likely to be open-minded?

Next, consider what will make your writing most effective for this audience:

- **What information will your audience need in order to understand and appreciate what you are saying?** A general audience will need you to define all specialized terms as you use them, as well as to provide any background information necessary for them to understand the topic. A specialist audience, on the other hand, may be bored by too much explanation, but these readers will still need you to define any terms you are using in an unusual sense and to provide background information about aspects of the topic likely to fall outside of their area of expertise. An instructor, while an expert, may expect you to write for a nonspecialist reader.

- **What kinds of language, examples, evidence, or reasons will be most effective?** Someone arguing for the legalization of marijuana in front of a group of college students will make very different choices than will someone arguing the same position in front of an audience filled with their parents or with police officers.

One way to write for an audience is, first, to picture a few specific people (representative of your audience) and then to think about what each of them will need in order to understand and appreciate what you are saying.

Getting Help in Understanding Your Audience If you have a different cultural or linguistic background than your prospective readers—whether you are a native English speaker or not—try to find classmates, peers, instructors, tutors, or advisers who may share experiences with the readers you have in mind. They might be able to help you determine how much background information your readers will need and what kinds of evidence they will find most effective.

The excerpt below shows a writer crafting a text with her audience in mind:

> *More about*
> Writing letters,
> 476–94 (ch. 25)

Dear Governor:

Your effort to improve education has been quite extensive. Throughout these past few years the creation of after-school programs that have offered tutoring for students has been possible because of your involvement. You have also formed the National Teachers Academy in Illinois, which works to improve the quality of teaching in schools. In addition, you secured several hundred million dollars that gave libraries the ability to replace many outdated books. Although you have made some great accomplishments for education, the conditions of our schools still call for much improvement. By striving to implement a voucher system, you could cause a nationwide education reform, and give every child a chance at a quality education. . . .

—Amanda Godfrey, McHenry County College

By imagining the governor's reactions, what he might appreciate and what he might resist, Godfrey knows to start her letter by listing the actions he has already taken to improve the state's schools. *Then* Godfrey argues for a new school voucher program.

> *More about*
> Reading to comprehend, 108–14
> Reading to reflect, 114–19
> Reading to write, 119–27
> Analysis, 120–22
> Synthesis, 123–25

In much of your college writing, you will have an audience of one—your instructor. To satisfy that audience, begin with a careful analysis of what the instructor hopes you will learn from the assignment. These objectives may be specified in the assignment or in the course syllabus, but sometimes you will simply need to ask. Generally, your instructor will be a specialist reader who wants to be reassured that you have done the reading, understood the issues, and synthesized the information from classroom lectures, discussions, and assigned reading. In addition, most instructors want to see that you can express yourself clearly and correctly in writing. To accomplish these goals, provide the following:

- Important background information
- Definitions of key terms
- Explanations of key concepts

- Analysis of the issues
- Synthesis of evidence from assigned reading and classroom discussion to support claims
- Citations and a list of works cited or references for source-based writing

3. Match your tone to your purpose and your audience.

When you speak, your ***tone*** of voice, gestures, facial expressions, and body language all convey your attitude. Are you patient, annoyed, angry, pleasantly surprised? All of these attitudes are conveyed in a moment by the pitch of your voice or the look on your face. Writers also convey their attitude toward their readers and their subject through their tone. In writing, tone is conveyed primarily through ***level of diction*** (formal or informal) and the ***connotation*** (emotional resonance) of the words you choose. To write at a formal level of diction, use standard American English; avoid regionalisms (such as *y'all*), colloquial language (such as *what up*), and slang (such as *hot* rather than *good* or *exciting*); and write in complete sentences (*Are you coming?* rather than just *Coming?*).

Although most college instructors will expect you to adopt a formal level of diction, the individual decisions you make will vary from course to course and discipline to discipline. In some courses, using the first-person pronoun *I* might be perfectly acceptable or even required, but for others (such as economics and sociology) it might be considered too informal.

Recognizing Differences in Connotation A word in your first language may share a literal meaning with a word in another language but have a very different connotation. The word *ambitious* ("eager for success"), for example, can be positive or negative in English; in Spanish, *ambición* is generally negative. If you are not sure how key words are used by your prospective readers, consult a cross-language or bilingual dictionary or check with classmates, a writing tutor, or your instructor.

Whatever the particular demands of your course, all disciplines expect you to adopt a measured tone. In general, opt for connotatively neutral language: Shrill or sarcastic prose will suggest to your audience that your opinions spring from your heart and not your head. This does not mean that emotional topics are off limits or that you may not express your beliefs, but temperance (moderation, self-restraint) is highly valued in academic discourse. Your instructor

> **More about**
> Citing and documenting sources, 288–346 (MLA style, ch. 18), 347–88 (APA style, ch. 19), 389–415 (*Chicago* style, ch. 20), 416–30 (CSE style, ch. 21)

> **More about**
> Developing a thesis, 29–33
> Level of diction, 543
> Connotation and denotation, 548–50

> **More about**
> Dictionaries for second-language learners, 559

> **More about**
> Writing in literature and the other humanities, 432–54 (ch. 22)
> Writing in the sciences and social sciences, 455–68 (ch. 23)
> Exploratory arguments, 134–35
> Considering alternative viewpoints, 145–47

will expect you to have looked at all sides of an issue carefully before drawing a conclusion and to exhibit respect for those with whom you disagree.

Make It **Your Own**

Draft a paragraph on one of the topics below as if you were writing to knowledgeable adults (perhaps even college professors). Carefully consider your purpose and your audience as you do so. Next, revise the paragraph to address an audience of high school students. Finally, revise it to appeal to a general audience.

1. The importance of participating in local government
2. Restrictions on language, dress, and behavior in public schools
3. Cell phone etiquette
4. Individual participation in recycling projects

Work **Together**

Working in pairs or small groups, compare your paragraphs with those of your classmate(s). Are the purpose and audience clear for each? Discuss the connotations of specific words, assess the level of formality of each sample paragraph, and point to words or sentences that make the diction more formal or less formal.

Next, write a paragraph reflecting on this process. Consider the similarities and differences you observed among the paragraphs and the things that surprised you. Make a note of the challenges you faced as you drafted your paragraphs and how you responded to those challenges. List the strategies you plan to use next time you write for a specific audience.

> **More about**
> Business writing, 476–94
> Public writing, 478–81

4. Consider context and genre.

As earlier sections on addressing an academic audience have implied, the *context* (or setting) in which your text is to be read will affect all your writing decisions. So, too, will the *genre* (or type) of writing you produce.

The contexts in which you are likely to write, now and in the future, are *academic, business, public,* and *personal*. Like academic writing, business writing generally adopts a formal level of diction and uses words with neutral connotations. Public writing, which ranges from letters to the editor to press releases and reports, generally maintains a formal level of diction (it is directed to a wide-ranging audience), but its tone may be more impassioned than would be appropriate in an academic or business context. An informal tone is most appropriate in a personal context, but even then, the audience makes a difference: A casual, bantering tone and highly informal level of diction might be appropriate in a text message to a friend, while a warm but slightly more formal tone might be appropriate for an e-mail to a grandparent. Whenever you write in an unfamiliar context, consulting examples can help you hit the right note.

In literature classes, you may have learned that poetry, drama, fiction, and nonfiction were the four major literary genres, but genre extends beyond literature. If you are unfamiliar with the genre in which you will be writing, read several examples to determine what they have in common. This handbook contains sample documents in a variety of genres. Your instructor may also be able to provide examples, or you could locate examples in your library or on the Internet. Whether you are writing a business e-mail, a scientific report, a grant proposal, or a letter to the editor, the expectations readers have for this type of writing will affect every choice you make.

> **Student Models**
> Editorial (public), 8
> Essay (academic), 42–44, 95–99, 127–30, 442–46, 446–51
> Research project (academic), 147–53, 336–46, 381–88, 408–15
> Essay exam (academic), 474–75
> Memo (business), 482
> Résumés (business), 487, 489
>
> **Professional Models**
> Editorials (public), 69–71, 115–17
> Article (public), 112–14
> Review (public), 443–46
> Letter (business), 480
> Press release (public), 493

2b Analyzing an Assignment

Recognizing the purpose of an assignment is crucial to success. If you are asked to *argue* for or against the goals of the plain speech movement of the 1920s, for example, and, instead, you *describe* those goals, you will probably not get an *A*. When analyzing an assignment, look for words that indicate purpose.

The audience for an assignment is, of course, your instructor, and the instructor's goal in assigning the project is to assess your knowledge of the facts, to gauge how well you have synthesized this information with other knowledge, and to assess your ability to express your understanding in writing. Occasionally, your instructor may ask you to imagine another audience—the readership of a particular magazine, for example.

Frequently, an assignment will specify the approach you should take. If you are asked to analyze, for example, your instructor will expect you to break a topic, issue, or text into its component parts and, perhaps, evaluate each one. If your instructor asks you to summarize a reading assignment, you will be expected to write the main idea and key supporting points briefly, in your own words and using your own sentence structures.

Sometimes, an assignment will specify the genre, although the genre may be taken for granted. A biology instructor teaching a laboratory class may

> **More about**
> Analyzing, 120–22, 270–72
> Summarizing, 110–11

> **Quick Reference** — **Analyzing the Purpose of an Assignment**
>
> | If the assignment asks you to... | The purpose is... | The approach is... |
> |---|---|---|
> | describe, explain | informative (expository) | to put into words what something looks, sounds, feels, smells, or tastes like; to discuss *how* something functions |
> | assess, evaluate, argue | persuasive | to make a judgment based on evidence or offer an interpretation based on close reading, and to explain *why* |
> | analyze, consider, discuss | informative or persuasive | to break a topic, reading assignment, or issue into its component parts and explain how it works; to reflect critically on the pros and cons of an issue, offer an interpretation based on a close reading, and sometimes explain why you have reached this conclusion |

assume that you understand that a laboratory report is required. If you are not sure what the genre of the assignment is, or what it requires, ask your instructor.

Finally, an assignment will generally include a due date. In order to meet that date, you will have to create a realistic schedule. Start by listing the steps in the writing process in reverse order on a sheet of paper or in a new computer file so that you can work back from the due date. Next, list all your other obligations: other assignments, studying for exams, work, rehearsals or team practices, family and social obligations. Then work backward to figure out how much time you can allot to each task. The more obligations you have, the more time you will need to leave between steps. Finally, write the intermediate due dates on a calendar—a date book, the calendar on your computer, or your phone. For each of these due dates, write down not just the name of the project ("English paper") but also the specific action that you need to have taken by that date ("outline English paper"). A schedule for a five-page paper that does not require research might look like that shown in Figure 2.1.

> **More about**
> Time management, 194
> Online assignment calendar, 194

EXERCISE 2.2 Analyzing an assignment

Read the following assignments; indicate whether their purpose is informative, persuasive, or both; and underline the words that indicate purpose.

1. Describe two or three medical services available to families in your community, and explain how a family nurse-practitioner could use these services.

Writing Matters • Analyzing an Assignment **2b** 19

SEPTEMBER						
Sunday	Monday	Tuesday	Wednesday	Thursday	Friday	Saturday
		19 Track meet	20	21 Comp. assignment distributed	22 Analyze Comp. assignment and writing situation	23 Work Date with the "girls"
24 Generate ideas, develop topic, draft thesis for comp. paper	25 Review notes, draft outline for comp. paper	26 Study for Econ quiz	27 Write first draft, make appt. at Writing Center	28 Econ quiz	29 Bring draft to class for peer review	30 Work

OCTOBER						
Sunday	Monday	Tuesday	Wednesday	Thursday	Friday	Saturday
1 Lunch with Mom & Dad	2 Bring essay to Writing Center	3 Revise comp. essay ————	4	5	6 ——→ Revise comp. essay	7 Work Proofread & edit comp. paper
8 Format & print comp. paper	9 Comp. paper due	10 Study for psych midterm ————	11	12	13 ——→ Psych midterm!	14 Work

FIGURE 2.1 A sample calendar Your calendar will differ depending on the complexity of the assignment, the time you have to complete it, and your other obligations.

2. Evaluate the constitutionality of judicial review, explaining its origins and offering several examples from US Supreme Court decisions.

3. Analyze the impact an increase in the price of higher education in the United States would have on the market for higher education in India.

4. Assess the main arguments of Handlin's *Boston's Immigrants* (1941) in light of the other assigned course reading. Are they still persuasive? Why or why not?

Make It **Your Own**

For an upcoming writing assignment or one already under way, analyze the assignment and set up a schedule that takes into account all your other obligations.

2c Generating Ideas

For some writing projects, especially in college or business, your *topic* will often be assigned. When you are required to come up with a topic on your own, ask yourself these questions:

- What topics are appropriate to the assignment?
- What topics will interest, exasperate, or intrigue me *and* my reader?
- What topics do I have special access to or knowledge about?

> **More about**
> Finding information, 206–29 (ch. 13)
> Reading and thinking critically, 108–33 (ch. 7)

You will be most engaged when you choose a topic that interests you, but your reader will be most engaged when you offer some special knowledge or insight into what you are writing about. You can create that special knowledge by doing research, but you can also create special knowledge by thinking critically about your topic.

Invention techniques, like those outlined below, can help you devise and develop a topic. No single strategy works for everyone, and most writers use several methods. If you have tried some of these before, experiment with the others. Drawing on new techniques may increase your creativity.

Generating Ideas in English or Your First Language If English is not your first language, you might find it helpful to keep a journal, freewrite, or brainstorm in English. If you get stuck, try using words and phrases from your first language. But be careful when returning to your notes to translate not merely your *words* but also your *ideas* into English appropriate for your readers.

1. Keep an idea journal or commonplace book.

In the nineteenth century, the philosopher Ralph Waldo Emerson wrote his essays from ideas he had jotted down in a notebook. In the twenty-first century, writers often use tablets, smartphones, or online tools like Google Docs to store ideas. Whatever medium you use, you may find that keeping an *idea journal* or a *commonplace book* (or both) is an effective part of the creative process.

> **More about**
> Keeping a reading journal, 117–18
> Keeping a research log, 198–99
>
> **More about**
> Avoiding accidental plagiarism, 250–51, 252–56

Like a diary, an idea journal is something to write in every day. Unlike a diary, it is not a record of your life but rather of your thoughts. A commonplace book records the ideas (quotations, summaries, paraphrases) of others that you might find useful in the future. You can also use your commonplace book to record your reactions to those ideas. As you jot notes in your commonplace book, record your sources and use quotation marks to separate carefully the words of others from your own.

Writing Responsibly — Note Taking and Plagiarism

Many people have unintentionally plagiarized sources because of a faulty note-taking system, saying that they did not record the source when taking notes or that they failed to put quotation marks around passages they copied. To avoid finding yourself in such a situation, consider putting all quotations, summaries, and paraphrases in one column of your journal or commonplace book and your own comments and reactions in another. That way, even if you forget to put quotation marks around a quotation or to record a page number, you will not be lulled into believing the words or ideas were your own—and your sources will get proper credit.

to OTHER WRITERS

Make It Your Own

Keep an idea journal for one week. Write in it daily about the topics discussed in your classes, and at the end of the week read through your notes. What topics have arisen repeatedly? Which are most engaging? What ideas could be developed into a paper?

2. Freewrite.

Have you ever found yourself sitting in front of a blank screen, knowing you had to begin writing but just not being able to get started? Try *freewriting:* writing the first thing that enters your head and then continuing to write non-stop for ten to fifteen minutes (or for a set number of pages). What you write about does not matter; if you draw a blank, just write (or type) the same word over and over again until something comes to you.

To be useful, freewriting must be fast and spontaneous. If you find that you cannot resist correcting and revising, turn the brightness down until your screen is very dim or even black. Here is a sample of freewriting for Betsy Smith's essay:

Student Models
Draft thesis, 30
Revised thesis, 31–33
Outlines, 35–38
First draft, "Is Alternate Energy Really Good for the Environment?" 42–44
Final draft, "Alternative Energy: Does It Really Offer an Alternative?" 95–99

Student Model — Freewrite

Drawing a blank about what to write about. Maybe should go to the park for a run. Need to figure out schedule for next sem. Can't decide b/w bio and environ science. Oooh, that reminds me I need to find out if I can recycle my old notebooks somewhere.

Once the time has elapsed, read through what you wrote. Even among random thoughts you might find a usable idea. Betsy Smith's essay topic—the environmental movement—appears in this freewriting snippet, for example. But the exercise is also beneficial for freeing the mind and exorcising writer's block.

A variation of freewriting is *focused freewriting.* Instead of starting from the first idea to pop into your head, start from something specific: your topic, a quotation, a memory, an image. If you stray from the topic, just keep writing, trying to circle back to it.

3. Brainstorm.

Brainstorming (or *listing*) is writing down everything you can think of on a topic. Brainstorming helps get ideas percolating and provides a record of that percolation. Here is a snippet of Betsy Smith's brainstorm on the environmental movement:

Student Model Brainstorm

- Types of alternative energy: solar, wind, hydro.
- Advantages/disadvantages of each.
- Alt energy may benefit consumers; might harm wildlife.
- Who is for it, against it. Their different arguments.
- Where is alt energy movement strongest, weakest? Why?
- Why alternatives to fossil fuels needed.
- History of oil exploration and development of alternatives.

After you have amassed a useful number of items, sort through the material to make connections: Move items around or draw lines to connect related items. Then brainstorm about the idea groups that seem most important, interesting, or challenging.

4. Cluster.

Clustering (or *mapping*) is a visual method for identifying and developing ideas. To create a cluster or idea map, follow these steps:

1. Write your topic in the middle of the page, and draw a circle around it.
2. Write other ideas related to your topic around the central idea bubble, and draw a circle around each of those.

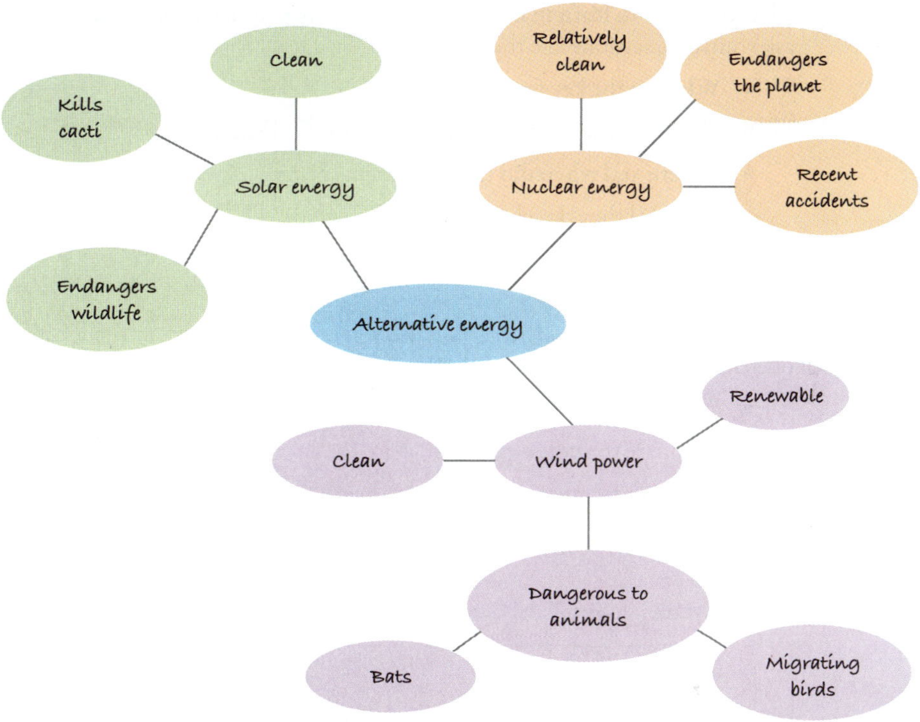

FIGURE 2.2 A sample cluster diagram

3. Draw connecting lines from the word bubbles to the central topic or to the other word bubbles to show the relationships among the ideas.

When creating a cluster, keep two things in mind:

1. Keep your topic and idea notes brief—if you write more than a word or two, the diagram will quickly become difficult to read.
2. Use a pencil—you will probably make many changes as you work.

The cluster diagram above (Figure 2.2) shows some of Betsy Smith's ideas for her paper on alternative energy.

5. Answer the journalists' questions.

The *journalists' questions*—*who, what, where, when, why,* and *how*—not only can help you generate ideas about your topic but also can help you figure out what you need to learn in order to write the paper. When considering a topic, ask yourself questions like these:

- **Who** are the key figures?
- **What** did they accomplish, or what are the issues?
- **Where** and **when** did the main events occur?
- **Why** did they do what they did, or why did these events transpire as they did?
- **How** did it happen?

As a college student, you will also benefit from adding two additional questions to the journalists' list:

- What is the **significance**?
- What are the **consequences**?

The journalists' questions tailored to Betsy Smith's topic are shown in Figure 2.3.

Student Model Journalists' Questions

- Who is affected by the building of wind farms? Who will benefit from their being built?
- What other sources of energy do we have? What impact do they have on the environment? What impact will the wind farms have?
- Where are wind farms being built?
- When will the wind farms go online? When will the courts rule on the challenges to these wind farms?
- Why is there disagreement within the environmental community about whether wind farms should be built?
- How will the issues be resolved? How can animals be protected?

FIGURE 2.3 The journalists' questions

6. Discuss your topics with friends and classmates.

Sometimes just batting ideas around with friends or classmates can help you generate ideas. This can be as casual as a late-night chat with your roommate or texting with a friend ("What do you think about . . . ?"), or it can be as formal as a scheduled brainstorming session with a collaborative writing group. Whatever approach you take, keep the discussion open enough that people feel free to speak their minds but focused enough that your discussion does not drift too far from your topic, and always be ready to record ideas.

7. Use the Internet, the library, and classroom tools.

Surfing the Internet can provide direction and stimulate ideas when you are faced with a new topic. Start by searching a ***subject directory,*** a collection of websites organized into groups by topic and arranged hierarchically from most general to most specific to get a sense of the range of related subtopics. Subject directories are useful for narrowing or expanding your topic. For very current topics, searching a news site or locating a specialized blog can also be useful.

> **More about**
> Subject directories, 212–13
> Blogs, 214–15
> Evaluating online sources, 236–39

The reference sources provided by your college library are another resource for generating ideas. Browse through general encyclopedias and dictionaries to get a sense of how your topic is usually discussed, or turn to specialized dictionaries or encyclopedias to get a more detailed introduction. Some reference sources may be available online through your college library's website.

Finally, because you will often be writing about topics that were introduced in class, you can get ideas by reading (or rereading) course materials, such as your textbook, class notes, and any handouts your instructor has distributed. All can provide context or help you identify a topic that interests you.

> **More about**
> Reference sources, 206–10

Make It **Your Own**

Use focused freewriting, brainstorming, or clustering to develop one of the ideas that came out of your weeklong experiment with keeping an idea journal (p. 20) or an idea from the reading in one of your classes.

> **More about**
> Note taking, 119–27, 250–51
> Annotating, 114–17

2d Narrowing or Broadening a Topic

Once you have devised a topic, consider whether you can do justice to it in the assigned length. In most cases, you will need to narrow your topic further; occasionally, you may have to broaden it.

1. Narrow your topic.

To narrow an overly general topic, use brainstorming or one of the other idea-generating techniques to develop a list of subtopics. Betsy Smith wanted to write about alternative energy, but the topic was so big, she could not cover it in a three- to five-page paper; she had to narrow it. Some of her possible subtopics are listed in the brainstorming example below.

Student Model Brainstorm

> The green movement has been around for a while but has been gaining in recognition in recent years.
> Many aspects of the green/environmentalist movement: climate change, preservation, endangered species, alternatives to fossil fuels, etc.
> People can feel very strongly about these issues. Some modify how they eat and what they buy; some join groups like Greenpeace and are willing to be arrested and/or put themselves in danger to fight for change.
> Are there conflicts within the green movement? What might they entail?

2. Broaden your topic.

While you are much more likely to have to narrow your topic, you may occasionally find yourself struggling to come up with something to say about the topic you have selected, in which case your topic may be too narrow. If, for example, you were thinking about exploring whether social workers in your town are pressured to overreport their contact hours with Medicare patients, but you were finding too little research on this topic, you could broaden your topic by expanding the region (from social workers in your town to social workers throughout the country), or you could broaden the type of caregivers you studied by including medical personnel (doctors, nurses, and technicians) and social workers. The idea-generating techniques discussed above can help you broaden, as well as narrow, your topic.

2e Working with Others: Planning a Collaborative Project

In academic and professional contexts, collaborative work is common. Working in a group can be challenging, but there are several steps you can take to make collaborative work more satisfying and less frustrating.

1. Form a cohesive group.

Start group projects by establishing rapport. A few small steps taken at the outset can help:

- Meet face-to-face, at least at the start.
- Start your first meeting by having group members introduce themselves and mention some detail—hometown, favorite book, a special interest or talent—to help everyone get to know one another.
- Make an effort to learn everyone's name.
- Distribute the contact information, such as e-mail addresses and phone numbers (with best times to call), for every group member at the end of the first session.

2. Anticipate pitfalls.

Anyone who has participated in a collaborative project knows that pitfalls abound: One person is consistently late, another lets other team members do all the work, a third dominates the proceedings, and a fourth is resentful but never says a word. Before starting a project, work together to figure out the likely pitfalls and to decide in advance how the group will respond:

- What will you do if someone does not complete assigned work?
- What will you do if someone does assigned work badly?
- How will you want the instructor to grade the completed project, if it is a class assignment?

Once you have developed a list of potential problems and how the group will resolve them, put it in writing, have everybody sign the document, and

Self Assessment

To ensure your group is effective, pause regularly to reflect on every member's contribution. Be sure every member participates in the following tasks:
- ☐ Deciding on a topic
- ☐ Drafting a thesis statement
- ☐ Brainstorming ideas
- ☐ Organizing the project
- ☐ Assigning tasks

distribute copies to all members. This written agreement not only will provide a record but also will remind all members of their responsibilities to the group. If something does go wrong, address the problem immediately; do not let it fester.

3. Devise a schedule and assign tasks.

The writing process for individual projects applies to collaborative projects as well. Some additional steps include the following:

> **More about**
> Analyzing the writing situation, 9–17
> Devising a topic, 20–25
> Drafting, 38–42
> Revising globally and locally, 82–89
> Drafting and revising visuals, 73–81 (ch. 5)
> Proofreading and formatting, 93–95

- Select a secretary. That role can be performed by one person or can rotate among group members.
- Brainstorm project ideas, making sure everyone participates.
- List component tasks (such as coordinating the group; researching the topic; drafting, revising, and editing the text; identifying or creating appropriate visuals).
- Establish dates by which each task needs to be completed, and construct a timetable.
- Divide the work among group members, taking into account people's talents, interests, and schedules and the difficulty of each task. Keep in mind that some phases of the project should be done by the entire group. (See the Self-Assessment checklist on p. 27.)
- Plan periodic meetings to discuss progress and problems.
- Distribute a schedule of meetings and due dates.

3 Organizing and Drafting Your Project

IN THIS CHAPTER

a. Thesis, 29
b. Organization, 33
c. Preparing to draft, 38
d. Drafting, 40
e. Collaboration, 45

Student Models
Informal (Scratch) Outline, 36; Topic and Sentence Outlines, 37; First Draft, 42

Before producing a new line of clothing or an automobile, designers sketch the product, planning and arranging the shapes before dressing them in colors and textures. Writers, too, begin with a plan. They take into account the writing situation (purpose, audience, topic, context, and genre), then sketch their ideas in words and arrange them in sentences and paragraphs. Both designers and writers sometimes erase initial ideas and revise early efforts. For both, until that first sketch is penned, the finished work is merely an idea.

3a Crafting an Effective Thesis

A ***thesis*** is a brief statement (one or two sentences) of the central claim you will make. It gives your audience an indication of the focus and direction of your project. Drafting a preliminary thesis statement as early as possible and then revising it as you develop your project will help you focus and clarify your ideas.

Stating the Main Idea In some contexts and cultures, it is appropriate to imply the main idea rather than state it explicitly. However, readers in the United States, especially in academic and business contexts, will usually expect you to express your main idea clearly and directly, usually at the beginning of your written document or project.

29

> **More about**
> Generating ideas,
> 20–25

1. Devise a thesis statement.

Before you begin to draft a thesis, review your notes. Do any ideas jump out? If not, return to the idea-generating stage. If so, focus on an aspect of your topic that will engage you and your reader and that is appropriate to your purpose, context, and genre. Next, ask yourself probing questions about your topic and then answer them. Review your answers, looking for ones that identify your topic and make a claim about it. Choose one that will allow you to bring your own insights to the topic, and use that as your preliminary thesis. Here are some sample questions and answers, with the claim highlighted in yellow and the topic underlined:

Questions	Answers
Should members of political parties be barred from overseeing presidential elections?	Members of political parties should be barred from overseeing presidential elections to avoid even the suspicion of electoral manipulation such as occurred in Florida in 2000 and Ohio in 2004.
What drove the ivory-billed woodpecker to near-extinction in the United States?	The direct effects of the two world wars led to the near-extinction of the ivory-billed woodpecker.
What kinds of privacy violations or other social mischief occur with social networking sites like Google+ and Facebook?	Social networking sites open new avenues for privacy violations and other social dangers, such as publication of incriminating photographs, stalking, and contact with inappropriate new "friends."
What motivates students to plagiarize, and what can we do to reduce the number of incidents?	Reducing the incidents of plagiarism among college students requires understanding its causes, which include late-night desperation, fear of a bad grade, lack of interest in a course, ignorance of citation requirements, and societal norms.

> **Student Model**
> Exploratory argument:
> "Why Students Cheat,"
> Tom Hackman,
> 147–53

If you are not sure how to answer your question, use idea-generating techniques to develop possibilities.

> **EXERCISE 3.1** Selecting a topic and developing a preliminary thesis
> Make a list of at least five topics that interest you. Select two of the topics (or two from the following list) and write one or more questions for each. Then answer those questions to create a preliminary thesis.

Optional Topics
1. Violence in college sports
2. Compulsory military service
3. Standardized testing
4. Passenger screening in airports

Underline each of your two topics, and circle your claims.

2. Revise a thesis statement.

A well-crafted thesis statement should indicate your topic and make a claim that is appropriate to your purpose, and it should do so in language that will engage the reader. Only rarely does a writer accomplish all of these objectives in the first draft of the thesis. Most writers need to revise the thesis statement repeatedly as they draft.

Purpose: Informative The thesis of an *informative* essay makes a *claim of fact*, a claim that can be verified. To be engaging, an informative thesis must make a claim of fact that is not yet widely known to or accepted by the audience, and it must be specific enough that the writer can explore it in depth.

> **More about**
> Claims of fact, 138–42
> Common knowledge, 249–50

DRAFT THESIS
This paper is about conflicts within the environmental movement. [Topic]

This draft thesis establishes a topic but does not make a claim of fact, and it is far too general to explore in depth.

REVISION 1—FOR AN INFORMATIVE PROJECT
There are many conflicts within the environmental movement. [Topic]

Self Assessment

When revising a thesis, ask yourself the following questions. If the answer to any question is no, make the revisions necessary to strengthen your thesis.
- ☐ Does your thesis identify your **topic**?
- ☐ Does it indicate your **purpose** (informative or persuasive)?
- ☐ Does it make a **claim** (or assertion) that you can support—a *claim of fact* (a verifiable issue) for an informative project, or a *claim of judgment* or *value* (a belief or opinion that can be supported by evidence) for a persuasive project?
- ☐ Will it **interest** your readers?

This thesis statement establishes the topic and makes a claim of fact, but the claim is too broad. Because the writer has not specified which conflicts she has in mind, she would potentially have to explain all possible conflicts within the environmental movement to satisfy the promise of the thesis.

REVISION 2—FOR AN INFORMATIVE PROJECT

[Topic] Among the conflicts within the environmental movement is that between those who want to reduce global warming by replacing fossil fuels with alternatives, like wind energy and solar energy, and those who fear that new energy generating plants will harm local wildlife.

The thesis statement now narrows the claim—makes it specific—so that it focuses solely on one area of conflict within the environmental movement. It will intrigue readers interested in environmental issues and inform those who know little about the conflicts.

> **More about**
> Claims of value, 139
> Claims of judgment, 139–40

Purpose: Persuasive The thesis of a *persuasive* writing project must make a *claim of value* (a belief about the way the world should be) or *judgment* (an opinion or a provisional decision that is not widely shared). The claim must be one that can be supported with reasons and evidence. The revised informative thesis above clearly specifies a topic and will probably intrigue readers, but it is not appropriate for a persuasive project because it makes a claim of fact, not a claim of value or judgment.

REVISION 3—FOR AN ARGUMENTATIVE PROJECT

[Topic] As serious and time-sensitive as the issue of climate change is, alternative energy is not a solution if it will be just as harmful to wildlife as conventional energy.

This thesis still specifies the topic, but it now also makes a *claim of judgment* ("alternative energy is not a solution"). Because it is narrow, focusing on just one issue ("alternative energy [that] is . . . harmful to wildlife"), it can be explained in a brief essay. And because it demonstrates the importance of the topic ("As serious and time-sensitive as the issue of climate change is"), it is likely to interest readers.

When drafting your thesis statement, make sure it focuses on a claim you can support and that will interest your reader. When revising your thesis statement, focus on making sure your reasons and evidence actually support your claim. If not, either replace the irrelevant reasons and evidence or revise your thesis so that the support you offer is pertinent.

> **EXERCISE 3.2 Revising a thesis statement**
> Revise the thesis statements you drafted in Exercise 3.1, and explain why you made your revisions.

> **Make It Your Own**
>
> For an essay that you are currently working on in this or another class, draft and revise your thesis statement so that it makes a claim you can support convincingly.

3b Organizing Your Ideas

Most essays benefit from attention to organization both *before* and *after* the essay is drafted. Organizing beforehand makes the essay easier to write; reviewing the structure after you have written a draft can show you where you need more support, whether the essay is logically organized, and whether any of the evidence is irrelevant.

> **More about**
> Reorganizing a draft, 83–86

1. Review your prewriting and make a list of ideas.

Start organizing by reviewing all the preparatory writing you have done. Then write your preliminary thesis statement at the top of a clean sheet of paper or in a new electronic document. Below the thesis statement, list all the ideas that might be relevant to it.

> **More about**
> Keeping a journal, 20–21
> Freewriting, 21–22
> Brainstorming, 22
> Clustering, 23–24
> Journalists' questions, 23–24

2. Arrange your ideas into logical groupings.

Read through your list of ideas. How are they related? Create a cluster diagram or table to group ideas by topic. Or create a ***tree diagram*** to arrange ideas from most general to most specific: Write your main idea at the top of the page and let subsequent ideas branch off below it (Figure 3.1).

> **More about**
> Cluster diagrams, 23

3. Consider your essay's overall shape.

The typical essay has three basic parts:

- Introduction
- Body
- Conclusion

> **More about**
> Organizing paragraphs, 49–51, 60–61

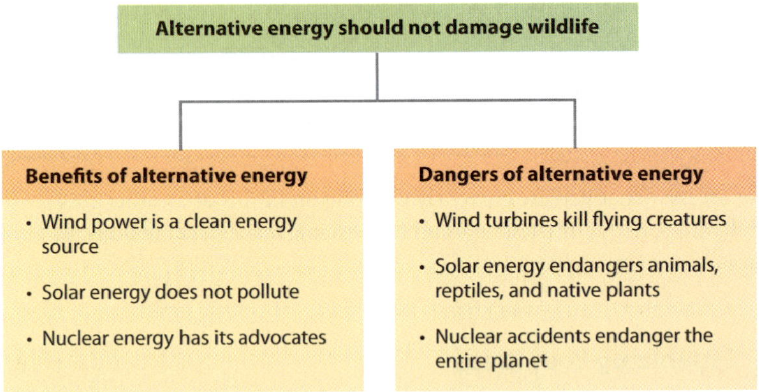

```
                    ┌─────────────────────────────────────────────┐
                    │  Alternative energy should not damage wildlife │
                    └─────────────────────────────────────────────┘
                                         │
                    ┌────────────────────┴────────────────────┐
```

Benefits of alternative energy	**Dangers of alternative energy**
• Wind power is a clean energy source	• Wind turbines kill flying creatures
• Solar energy does not pollute	• Solar energy endangers animals, reptiles, and native plants
• Nuclear energy has its advocates	• Nuclear accidents endanger the entire planet

FIGURE 3.1 A tree diagram A tree diagram can help you organize your thoughts before you begin writing.

In its simplest form, the typical essay becomes a "five-paragraph theme": one paragraph for the introduction, three for the body, and one for the conclusion. Of course, college writing seldom takes such a tidy form. Instead, it is more likely to unfold in this manner:

> **More about**
> Writing the introduction, 63–65

Introduction The introduction is typically brief (one to three paragraphs, depending on the length of the essay). Often the thesis statement appears in the introduction, where it can shape the reader's expectations of the essay. What goes into the introduction depends on the essay's purpose, audience, context, and genre, but it should entice readers to carry on and should prepare them for what follows.

> **More about**
> Relevance, 47, 230–31
> Unity, 47–48
> Coherence, 52–58
> Development, 59–63
> Reasons and evidence, 40–42
> Conclusion, 65–68

Body The body is the longest portion of the essay, with length depending on the complexity of ideas being conveyed and the quantity of support needed to convince the audience. Each paragraph in the body should make one main point, expressed in a topic sentence; the body paragraphs should supply reasons and evidence that support the topic sentence; and each topic sentence should support the thesis.

Conclusion Like the introduction, the conclusion is usually rather brief (one to three paragraphs, depending on the length of the essay). Just as the introduction should entice readers, so the conclusion should convince them that they have spent their time well.

4. Choose an organizational strategy.

Once you have collected and organized your notes, choose the order in which to present your ideas that best fits your thesis and supporting materials. Some organizational patterns include the following:

Chronological organization Use *chronological* (or *time*) order to tell a story (narrative) or explain a process (process analysis).

Spatial organization Organize your essay spatially—from left to right, inside to outside, top to bottom—when describing a scene or structure.

Logical organization This is probably the most common organizational scheme for academic essays: Begin with an introduction that includes a general statement—the thesis—and then proceed to the body of the essay, where specific reasons and evidence are provided. With indifferent or even hostile readers, consider reversing this order: Begin with something specific—an interesting anecdote, some dramatic statistics, a provocative illustration—that will gain your audience's interest, attention, or sympathy, and then move on to the general conclusion.

If you are writing for an audience likely to balk when faced with new ideas or ideas that challenge their beliefs, organize your essay from *familiar to unfamiliar*. To startle your readers into seeing a familiar issue in a new light, use *unfamiliar-to-familiar order*.

You may choose to organize your body paragraphs in *climactic order*, from least to most exciting. You might even save your thesis until the end of the essay.

> **More about**
> Description, 59
> Narration, 59–60
> Exemplification, 60
> Comparison-
>   contrast, 60–61
> Cause-effect, 62
> Analysis, 62
> Definition, 62–63

> **EXERCISE 3.3 Reviewing organizational strategies**
> Read the student models beginning on pages 337 and 409. What organizational strategies does each use? What organizational changes would you recommend?

5. Choose an outlining technique that is appropriate for you.

Outlines, whether formal or informal, not only guide you as you draft, but also allow you to experiment with ways of sequencing your supporting paragraphs.

An informal outline An *informal* (or *scratch*) *outline* is simply a list of the ideas in your essay in the order you want to present them. You can jot down your ideas in words, phrases, complete sentences, even pictures—whatever you need to jog your memory about what to put next. Here is a sample scratch outline for Betsy Smith's draft essay on conflicts within the environmental movement.

Student Model Informal (or Scratch) Outline

```
Intro
Green/environmental movement: brief explanation
Growing importance and awareness in recent years → conflict
within the movement about how to handle these issues
Thesis: A major goal of the green movement is to find fossil fuel
alternatives, but some members are concerned that wind, solar, and
nuclear power sites will also harm the environment.

Body
Benefits/importance of alternative energy; types of alternative fuel
being proposed: wind, solar, nuclear
Problems with alternative energy sources: harmful to animals, scenic
views, safety for humans

Conclusion
Conflicts might be inevitable, but we have to move forward, find
creative compromises, use less energy
```

Student Models
Essays by Betsy Smith: First draft, "Is Alternative Energy Really Good for the Environment?" 42–44
Final draft, "Alternative Energy: Does It Really Offer an Alternative?" 95–99

A formal outline (topic or sentence) A formal outline uses roman numerals (I, II, III), capital letters (A, B, C), arabic numerals (1, 2, 3), lowercase letters (a, b, c), and indentions of five spaces (or half an inch) to indicate level of generality, with roman numeral headings being most general and lowercase letters most specific. Each level of your outline should include at least two entries.

A *topic outline* uses words and phrases to indicate the ideas to be discussed. A *sentence outline* uses complete sentences. Some writers prefer a topic outline because it is easier to construct. Others prefer a sentence outline because it provides a starting point for drafting. Which type of outline you choose depends entirely on your own preferences, the complexity of your essay, and your instructor's expectations.

Student Models Topic Outline and Sentence Outline

Compare a section of a topic outline with a section of a sentence outline for a later draft of Betsy Smith's essay:

Thesis: A major goal of the green movement is to find fossil fuel alternatives, but some members are concerned that wind, solar, and nuclear power sites will also harm the environment.

Topic Outline

I. Divisions within environmental movement over alternative energy
   A. Benefits of alternative fuel
      1. Fewer greenhouse gas emissions/less warming
      2. Sustainable renewable energy sources: the sun, wind, and water
   B. Drawbacks
      1. Bad for environment: scenery, humans
      2. Destruction of animal habitats, extinction
      3. Future problems unknown without tests

Sentence Outline

I. When it comes to alternative energy sources, environmentalists are divided.
   A. There are numerous potential benefits of using alternative fuel sources.
      1. Alternative energy produces fewer carbon dioxide and other greenhouse gas emissions, improving air quality and slowing the rate of global warming.
      2. Renewable energy sources, including the sun, wind, and water, are sustainable; they cannot be depleted and therefore can be used for the foreseeable future.
   B. Although there are many advantages to alternative fuel sources, there are drawbacks as well.
      1. New structures can have negative consequences on their surroundings, ranging from ruining picturesque views to endangering human health.
      2. Animal habitats may be destroyed, leading to extinction of species.
      3. The long-term effects of building new facilities is still largely unknown and could present even greater problems in the future.

6. Check your outline for unity and coherence.

Once you have completed your outline, review it critically for *unity* and *coherence.* Unity is achieved when all the supporting paragraphs are relevant to the thesis and when all the examples, reasons, and evidence are relevant to the main idea of the supporting paragraph. Coherence is achieved when the supporting paragraphs, with all their reasons, evidence, and examples, are organized logically so that readers can move from idea to idea without having to pause to consider the relationships among the parts.

> **More about**
> Coherence, 52–59
> Unity, 47–52

EXERCISE 3.4 Creating an informal outline

Using the thesis statement below, arrange the ideas in the list that follows into an informal (or scratch) outline for an essay.

> **Thesis:** Effectively combating plagiarism, in all its forms, requires a fuller understanding of how and why students break the rules

List of Ideas

- Many honest students plagiarize accidentally because they don't know the rules.
- One commonly held myth is that plagiarism is the result of slothfulness.
- The Internet makes it harder for students to separate their words from those of others and to keep track of where ideas come from.
- Some students plagiarize because they lack interest in the course or paper topic.
- What is considered acceptable source use in some cultures is called plagiarism in others.
- Plagiarism is often treated as a crime committed through laziness.
- High-achieving students sometimes plagiarize to maintain high grades.

EXERCISE 3.5 Creating a topic outline

Use the ideas in Exercise 3.4 to create a formal topic outline. Then compare the two outlines you created for this list of ideas and note how they differ. Review them for unity and coherence; then write a paragraph describing other possible organizations you could have used and explaining why you selected these.

3c Preparing to Draft

When the moment comes to combine words and sentences into paragraphs and paragraphs into an essay, set aside some time and find a place where you can concentrate. Begin drafting by reviewing the writing you have done while generating ideas, drafting your thesis, and creating an outline. Even in the best circumstances, you may encounter writer's block, but by using the appropriate techniques, you should be able to get past it. If you get stuck, try the strategies outlined in the Quick Reference box on page 40.

1. Get ready: Allocate enough time and find a good place to write.

Ideally, set aside a substantial block of time for writing your first draft. How you define *substantial* depends on how long or complex your project will be: An hour or two might be enough for a three- to five-page essay; a longer paper will require more. If you are unable to find a block of time, work in smaller chunks over several days. Do not delay starting just because you can cobble together only a half hour at a time.

Next, consider what place is best for you: a study carrel in the library or a table at a sidewalk café? Whatever your preference, focus on the task at hand by turning off your phone and closing your Internet browser.

2. Start writing.

The writing you have done while analyzing your writing situation and devising your topic, drafting your thesis, and organizing your ideas will provide you with a starting point. Begin by reviewing this material, and then try one of the following methods (or a combination of them):

- **Method 1: Fill in your outline.** Use your outline as scaffolding, filling it in and fleshing it out until it becomes a first draft.

- **Method 2: Start with what you have.** Instead of beginning at the beginning, start writing whatever parts of the essay you feel confident about—an interesting example, a descriptive passage in support of one of your ideas, or even just a sentence or a phrase that captures a relevant thought. Continue writing out-of-order thoughts until you can stitch them together and fill in the gaps.

- **Method 3: Write straight from your brain.** Type your thesis statement at the top of a computer file, and then just start writing. This may produce a very brief, general first draft, but it will be one that actually speaks from what you have to say. You can supplement it later.

Whatever method you choose, do not worry about the language you use to present your ideas. Just get words on paper. You can smooth out the kinks later, when you revise and edit.

3. Overcome writer's block.

Gene Fowler—a newspaper columnist, novelist, and screenwriter—once said, "Writing is easy: All you do is sit staring at a blank sheet of paper until drops of blood form on your forehead." Fortunately, there are techniques to help you avoid writing trauma.

Writing Matters • Organizing and Drafting Your Project

> **More about**
> Finding information, 206–29 (ch. 13)

Quick Reference: Overcoming Writer's Block

- **Take a break.** Doing something else, like taking a walk or doing your laundry, can help.
- **Write something else.** Just the act of writing can help unblock you.
- **Write what you can.** You do not have to start at the beginning and keep writing until you get to the conclusion. Instead, write the parts you *can* write, even if you cannot yet string them together.
- **Start from what you already have.** Use your outline, brainstorming, and other notes to jump-start your writing.
- **Write a message to yourself.** Write a note to yourself: "What I want to say is . . . ," and then finish the sentence.
- **Talk, text, or e-mail.** Tell a tutor, instructor, classmate, or friend what your paper will be about. Then use your own words as a starting point for writing.
- **Change your situation.** Switch media—from pencil and paper to word processor, or vice versa—or change the setting in which you are writing.
- **Avoid perfection.** It is the rare writer who produces a masterpiece on the first try. If you cannot avoid focusing on problems, turn off your computer screen so that you cannot see what you have written until it is time to start revising.

3d Drafting: Explaining and Supporting Your Ideas

To draft a thesis statement for your paper, you asked yourself a question and wrote a tentative answer. The body of your essay will explain *why* you believe that your answer is true and why your readers should agree with you. The topic sentence (or main idea) in each supporting paragraph will form the backbone of your essay, and the reasons and evidence you supply will be the flesh that covers the skeleton.

Specific evidence is needed to make your writing convincing and interesting. Some kinds of evidence you can draw on include the following:

- Facts and statistics
- Expert opinion
- Examples
- Observations
- Case studies
- Anecdotes
- Passages from the text you are studying

Writing Responsibly — Made-up Evidence

In May 2005, a stem cell expert resigned his position at Seoul National University following revelations by the journal *Nature* that his lab had falsified data. Woo Suk Hwang's case is not an isolated one: In 2009, for example, noted anesthesiologist Scott S. Rubin was fired by Massachusetts' Baystate Medical Center, then sent to prison and ordered to pay $420,000 in restitution, for falsifying data. Commentators have noted that competition was a factor in these cases: The desire for acclaim had become more important than the desire for truth.

The highly competitive academic environment may tempt you, too, to make up "facts" to support a thesis in a paper. It is easy to alter data, invent statistics or quotations, or manipulate an image so that it "shows" what you want it to. Resist the temptation: The short-term benefits are not worth it. Not only are you likely to get caught—fabricated evidence often *sounds* fake—but you are also sacrificing the opportunity to learn something about your topic and about the writing process.

to TOPIC

The paragraph below uses facts and examples:

> The physical demands on competitive cyclists are immense. [Topic sentence] One day, they will have to ride two hundred kilometres through the mountains; the next day there might be a long, flat sprint lasting seven hours. Because cyclists have such a low percentage of body fat, they are more susceptible to infections than other people. (At the beginning of the Tour, Armstrong's body fat is around four or five percent; this season Shaquille O'Neal, the most powerful player in the N.B.A., boasted that his body-fat level was sixteen percent.) [Support: Facts/Examples]
> —Michael Specter, "The Long Ride," *New Yorker*

This paragraph uses facts and statistics:

> One of the most important, if often unnoticed, features of American life in the late twentieth century was the aging of the American population. [Topic sentence] After decades of steady growth, the nation's birth rate began to decline in the 1970s and remained low through the 1980s and 1990s. In 1970, there were 18.4 births for every 1,000 people in the population. By 1996, the rate had dropped to 14.8 births. The declining birth rate and a significant rise in life expectancy produced a substantial increase in the proportion of elderly citizens. Almost 13 percent of the population was more than sixty-five years old in 2000, as compared with 8 percent in 1970. The median age in 2000 was 35.3, the highest in the nation's history. In 1970, it was 28.0. [Support: Facts and statistics]
> —Alan Brinkley, *American History: A Survey*

As you draft, ask yourself: Have I supplied *enough* reasons and evidence to persuade my reader? Is the evidence I have supplied relevant?

> **More about**
> Relevance, 47, 230–31

> **Tech** **Protecting Your Work**
>
> Because terrible things happen to computer files all the time, it is important to **save early and often,** and to **save your file in multiple locations:** Burn it to a disc, save it on a flash drive, or e-mail a copy to yourself. Remember to date each version of a file so you know which is the most recent and have a backup of your research.

> **EXERCISE 3.6 Analyzing evidence**
>
> Analyze the sample paragraphs on page 41 and list the types of evidence provided. Note whether there is sufficient evidence to support the topic sentence and explain your response.

> **Make It Your Own**
>
> For a paper that you are working on, produce a first draft using one of the drafting methods described in this section.

Student Model First Draft

The first draft of Betsy Smith's essay on conflict within the environmental movement appears on the pages that follow. Note that in this draft she does not worry about polished writing or even perfect grammar and spelling. She knows she can make changes as she revises. For now, her focus is on getting her ideas down in a logical order and on supporting her thesis. Consider what she will need to do as she revises to fulfill her responsibilities to her reader, her topic, other writers, and herself.

Student Models
Draft thesis, 30
Revised thesis, 31–32
Outlines, 36–37
Final draft, 95–99

Smith 1

Betsy Smith

Professor Locke

Composition 102

4 Oct. 2012

Is Alternative Energy Really Good for the Environment?

The Environmental, or Green, Movement has been around for many years. Although the movement includes many areas (politics, economics, agricultureetc.), most environmentalists want to create and maintain a healthy planet. But the green movement is made up of many different individuals with different opinions about how to best preserve nature. The result is conflict. Recently, with the growing attenention to global warming in recent years, these agreuments have tended to involve alternitive fuel sources. A major goal of the green movement is to find fossil fuel alternitives, but some environmentalists are concerned that wind, solar, and nuclear power sites will also harm the environment.

One example of this green vs. green debate was recently featured in *The Washington Post*. In this case, the company Invenergy is trying to build a wind power facility on Beech Ridge in West Virginia, but it is being fought by David Cowan, a nearby resident who is a bat enthusiast. He argues that the wind turbines that spin as part of the process are harmful to the surrounding wildlife, namely the endangered Indiana Bat. Even though "Cowan and other plaintiffs, including the D.C.-based Animal Welfare Institute, support wind power as one way to mitigate climate change." These members of the environmental movement are also worried about the dangers of the new technology alternitive energy requires (Glod).

The Beech Ridge case is not the only example of this debate. In Imperial County, CA, near San Diego, environmentalists are fighting the construction of a solar energy project. They claim that the project's location would hurt the bighorn sheep there and also be harmful to the flat-tailed horned lizard. Another solar project in the Mojave Desert is being opposed because it will threaten California desert tortoises and endangered cacti (Breen).

When it comes to using alternitive energy, greenies disagree. There are numerous environmental benefits of using alternitive fuel sources. Alternitive energy produces fewer carbon dioxide and other greenhouse gas emissions, which improve air quality and reduce pollution. Renewable energy sources, including the sun, wind, and water, are sustainable; they can't be depleted and therefore can continue to be used ("Environmental Benefits . . .").

Smith 2

> [Topic sentence introduces discussion of drawbacks to alternative fuel sources]

While there are many advantages to alternitive fuel sources, there are drawbacks as well. New structures can hurt their surroundings ranging from ruining picturesque views to endangering some species of animal to, in the case of nuclear, poisoning human beings (Breen, Glod, Mark).

> [Sentence fragment]

Due to the fact that the long term effects of new facility production are still largely unknown and could present even greater problems that we do not yet comprehend.

> [Topic sentence introduces discussion of nuclear fuel, with its advantages, disadvantage]

Another source of alternitive energy now being reexamined is nuclear. Now that climate change has become such a dominant factor, some environmentalists feel that increasing nuclear power production is better than burning fossil fuels. Nuclear power has divided the movement more than wind and solar power, largely because

> [Quotation not cited]

"more than 50 years after the establishment of the civilian atomic energy program, the country still lacks a way to safely handle the radioactive waste formed during the fission process." But even some of the most invested environmentalists believe that in the face of climate change, we may have to turn to nuclear power (Mark).

> [Conclusion]

Even though these issues are complex, there are efforts being made to find solutions. In West Virginia, there is research being done to reduce the number of bats the wind turbines will harm,

> [Quotation does not offer an example of "research" as claimed in first half of sentence]

"including stopping the turbines at certain times or using sound to deter the bats" (Glod). New locations for construction are being explored, and all over the world, new theories about how to safely handle nuclear waste are being proposed and tested. Our planet is in it's current bad situation because of our recklessness with natural resources, and as serious and time-sensitive as the issue of climate change is, alternitive energy is not a solution if it will be just as harmful to wildlife as conventional energy. Until we make wind, solar and nuclear power sites that are safe for the living things surrounding them, there will continue to be conflict within the green movement.

--------------------- [new page] ---------------------

Works Cited

> [Cites sources even in first draft]

> [Citations need revision to follow MLA style]

Breen, Steve. "Green vs. green," *The San Diego Union Tribune.* Oct. 21, 2009.

"Environmental Benefits of Renewable Energy," *Clean Energy.* Union of Concerned Scientists, 2009.

Glod, Maria. "Tiny Bat Pits Green against Green," *The Washington Post.* Oct. 22, 2009.

Mark, Jason. The Fission Division: "Will nuclear power split the green movement?" *Earth Island Journal* 22.3 (2007).

> **EXERCISE 3.7 Analyzing a draft**
> Create a topic outline for Betsy Smith's draft above. (Tip: Outlines of the first part of her draft appear on pages 36 and 37.) Based on your outline, how unified is her draft? How cohesive is it? Now consider the evidence she provides: Is there enough? Is it specific enough?

3e Writing with Others: Collaborative Projects

The work of many academic courses is conducted collaboratively, as are many workplace writing projects. Collaboration may mean that each team member is responsible for a separate part of the project, but often projects are *coauthored:* Group members work together to draft a thesis, devise an outline, and even write the text.

Drafting collaboratively can be a difficult process to manage, but it can also be rewarding and creative. The following principles will help keep the experience a happy one:

- If possible, keep groups small; smaller groups can reach the "critical mass" needed for creativity without the many management difficulties (such as finding a time to meet) that larger groups face.

- As with planning, it is important to the drafting process that each member has an opportunity to contribute. Make an effort to restrain overbearing members and to encourage reluctant participants.

- Treat everyone's writing respectfully. Some group members may be more skilled than others, but insightful ideas can be coaxed from initially unimpressive material.

- Whether your group is collaborating over e-mail or courseware such as Blackboard, in a Facebook group, or face-to-face, make sure everyone has a copy of the latest draft and schedule following each session.

> **More about**
> Planning a collaborative project, 26–28
> Peer response, 90–92

Make It Your Own

Use the material in this chapter to analyze an essay you are writing or have recently written. Identify the essay's thesis statement or main idea, then analyze how well each paragraph supports it. Does the evidence support each paragraph's main point? If so, write a note in the margin explaining how; if not, revise the paragraph. Finally, make a topic outline from the essay and use it to check for unity and cohesion.

4 Crafting and Connecting Paragraphs

IN THIS CHAPTER

a. Relevant paragraphs, 47
b. Unified paragraphs, 47
c. Coherent paragraphs, 52
d. Developed paragraphs, 59
e. Introductory paragraphs, 63
f. Concluding paragraphs, 65
g. Connecting paragraphs, 69

Professional Model
Editorial, 69

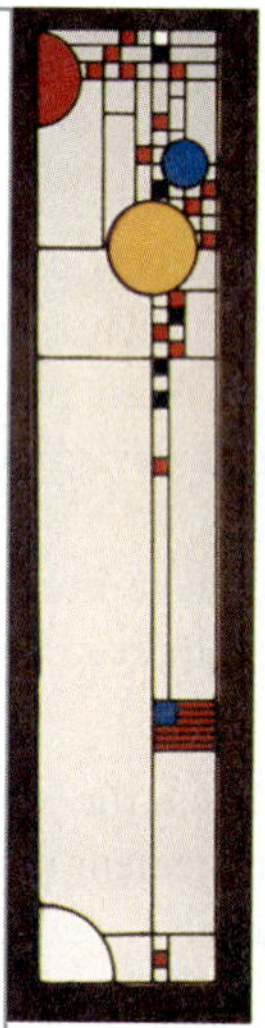

Frank Lloyd Wright, stained glass window, 1912

American architect Frank Lloyd Wright claimed that "[t]rue ornament is not a matter of prettifying externals. It is organic with the structure it adorns...." He designed furniture and stained glass windows (like the one here) that were as much a part of the structure as the walls that surrounded them.

Similarly, a writing project will be most effective when each paragraph is essential to the whole. When is a paragraph essential? It is essential when it is relevant, unified, coherent, well developed, interesting, and carefully connected to the paragraphs that come before and after it. A paragraph will be an essential part of the whole when it is all of the following:

- **Relevant.** It must support the main idea of the paper (your *thesis*) and, when possible, remind readers of what that thesis is.
- **Unified.** It should have a clear point (*topic*) and include only the material that explains that point.
- **Coherent.** It should include connections that make relationships among sentences clear to readers.
- **Well developed.** It should supply the information your readers need to be persuaded of your point.
- **Connected.** It should begin and end so that your readers can see how it relates to the paragraphs that precede and follow it.
- **Interesting.** It should make your readers want to move on to the next paragraph.

4a Writing Relevant Paragraphs

A *relevant* paragraph not only addresses the general topic of your paper but also contributes to the reader's understanding of or belief in the main idea of the paper (the *thesis*). Compare this paragraph to the essay's thesis:

Thesis:
... [Staples's] argument fails to be persuasive for several reasons: He doesn't account for the influence positive role models have, he ignores the fact that art frequently depicts violence without dire consequences to its consumers, and he overlooks the broad spectrum of hip-hop to focus on only a single strand.

Second, by calling hip-hop a "lethal genre," Staples places it into a category separate from other works of art that are not as "virulent." Yes, many hip-hop lyrics are violent, but that does not distinguish the songs from many other artistic works. Edgar Allan Poe, considered one of America's greatest writers, wrote numerous stories about murder and death, including "The Tell-Tale Heart," whose narrator is a confessed killer. *The Talented Mr. Ripley,* a novel by Patricia Highsmith, and the movie based on this novel, make Tom Ripley, an unrepentant murderer, a sympathetic character. Sculptor Kiki Smith depicts mutilated or deformed bodies in her art (see fig. 1) and, instead of being criticized, she is considered one of today's most important sculptors. No one would claim, I think, that Kiki Smith influences her viewers to commit mayhem. Clearly, hip-hop artists are not alone in depicting horrible people and events; they should not be singled out for doing so, and it should not be assumed that their audience will blindly follow suit.

- Topic Sentence
- Concession/rebuttal
- Example 1
- Example 2
- Example 3
- Concluding Sentence (also recalls thesis)

Fig. 1 Kiki Smith, *Untitled* (1993).

—Alea Wratten, SUNY–Geneseo, "Reflecting on Brant Staples's Editorial 'How Hip-Hop Music Lost Its Way and Betrayed Its Fans'"

Student Model
Alea Wratten's complete essay, 127–30

4b Writing Unified Paragraphs

Paragraphs are ***unified*** when they focus on a single main idea. Unifying a paragraph is easiest when it includes a ***topic sentence,*** a single sentence (sometimes two) that clearly states the main idea of the paragraph. That way, you can check each supporting sentence against this main idea and eliminate all those that are not relevant.

1. Focus the paragraph on a central idea and delete irrelevant details.

All the sentences in a supporting paragraph should support or explain the paragraph's main idea or topic, and each supporting paragraph should provide evidence for or develop further the text's main idea.

> **Topic Sentence**
>
> **Irrelevant:** Focus of ¶ is on how writer came to inherit, not writer's or city attorney's reaction or library's location—cut
>
> **Relevant:** Explains why writer inherited library

Last year I inherited a library—not just the books, but the whole building. I didn't see it as a boon at first; I saw it only as a legal nuisance. In the 1950s, my grandfather, I discovered, had donated the library to the town. Fifty years later, when the townspeople built a new library and decided to sell the old building, they discovered that they couldn't: The deed specified that if they ceased to use the building as a library, it would revert to the owner or his heirs. When the city attorney found the deed, he called every member of the town council. I was that heir. So now I owned the library in which I had spent so many hours as a girl. The building stands on a shady corner in what was once a quiet town.

When revising, hone your paragraphs until they focus on a single supporting idea: No matter how much you may like a certain sentence, if it does not support the main idea of the paragraph, it must be cut.

→ EXERCISE 4.1 Unifying a paragraph

Underline the topic sentence or main idea of the sample paragraph below. Then cross through any sentences that do not support that main idea.

> As we consider American dietary habits we also need to think about how people learn about nutrition. How do we know if our favorite foods are good for us? The national shift to convenience food is a problem too, because we don't know what is in it. Few people know that since 1909 Americans doubled the amount of sugar we eat (Amrock 8). Schools teach about the Federal Dietary Recommendations, but they change. First we had a Food Pyramid, and now we have a plate with different sized portions of food types. Davis and Saltos explain that it changes as understanding of nutrition grows (34). How can we trust something that keeps changing? The Food Pyramid said 6-11 servings of grains and only 3-5 of vegetables (www.nal.usda.gov/fnic/Fpyr/pmap.htm), but now portions of grains and vegetables are the same size (choosemyplate.gov). Having fewer vegetables was easier and popular with kids. Some people cut fat or carbohydrates to lose weight. My friends just exercise a lot or count calories. People can also get nutritional information from websites, but not all of them are healthy. The Harvard School of Public Health has an interactive website that clarifies nutritional information ("Knowledge for Healthy Eating").

EXERCISE 4.2 Writing unified paragraphs

Using the topic sentence and some of the supporting details given below, write a unified paragraph. Be selective: Not all the supporting details provided may be relevant.

> **Topic sentence:** Over the last three and a half decades, the average American has increased the amount of food eaten from 16.4 pounds to 18.2 pounds per week and Americans' obesity rate has doubled.

Possible Supporting Details

1. The government recommends that fruits and vegetables should make up half of what we eat (choosemyplate.gov).
2. The US Department of Agriculture (USDA) compiles food consumption figures.
3. Corn syrup consumption in the US increased by 387% from 1970 to 2005 (Wells & Buzby 17).
4. What we eat is as important as how much we eat.
5. In 2005, 86 pounds of added fats and oils were consumed per person in the United States; we consumed 53 pounds in 1970 (Wells & Buzby 12).
6. In 1970, US consumption of added sugars and sweeteners was 119 pounds per person and by 2005 that number was 142 pounds (Wells & Buzby 17-18).
7. According to Schlosser, half of the US food budget is spent on fast food.
8. The National Health Nutrition Examination Survey (NHANES) tracks obesity.
9. In 2008, NHANES found that 72 million adult Americans (34.2%) were obese.

2. Place the topic sentence appropriately.

Topic sentences can appear at the beginning, middle, or end of a paragraph, but most commonly they appear at the beginning or end of the paragraph.

Topic sentence at beginning of paragraph The most common placement for a topic sentence is at the beginning of the paragraph:

> Environmentalists paint a bleak picture of aquaculture. The David Suzuki Foundation, for example, maintains that fish waste contained in the fishery pens kills organisms living in the seabed. Yvon Gesinghaus, a manager of a

Topic sentence

> tribal council in British Columbia, Canada, also notes that the scummy foam from the farms collects on the beaches, smothering the clams that provide the natives with food and money. George K. Iwama, Biksham Gujja, and Andrea Finger-Stich point to the destruction of coastal habitats in Africa and Southeast Asia to make room for shrimp ponds.
>
> —Adrianne Anderson, Texas Christian University

In the paragraph above, the main idea is spelled out in the first sentence, so readers can easily see the relationship between the main idea and the supporting reasons and evidence that follow.

Topic sentence at end of paragraph Writers may place the topic sentence at the end of a paragraph to draw a conclusion based on the evidence presented and to enhance dramatic effect.

> When I was a little girl, Walt Disney's *The Little Mermaid* was my favorite movie, and Ariel (the title character) was my favorite character. I watched this movie three times a day, repeating Ariel's lines word for word. I wanted to be like her—cute and little and sweet and lovable, with big eyes and a tiny waist. But when I watched *The Little Mermaid* for the first time in more than seven years, I noticed things I had overlooked as a child. Was Ariel unhealthily thin? Was she more childlike than a full-grown woman should be? Was Ariel too willing to make sacrifices for Prince Charming? **Maybe *The Little Mermaid* wasn't the innocent entertainment I had once thought.**
>
> —Heidi Johnson, North Dakota State University

Holding the topic sentence until the end of the paragraph and starting with dramatic statistics or (as in the example above) a provocative anecdote may stimulate interest before you draw your conclusion. Remember, though: The relationship between evidence and main point must be clear, or you might leave your readers puzzled.

Topic sentence in middle of paragraph Occasionally writers will place the topic sentence somewhere in the middle of the paragraph:

> Biology is destiny—or at least more and more people seem ready to believe that it is. Perhaps this is because recent scientific advances—gene splicing, in vitro fertilization, DNA identification of criminals, mapping the human genome—have been repeatedly echoed and amplified by popular culture. **From science fact to science fiction (and back again), the gene has become a pervasive cultural symbol.** It crops up not just in staid scientific journals and

PBS documentaries, but also with increasing regularity in political discourse, popular entertainment, and advertising.

—Jeff Reid, "The DNA-ing of America," *Utne Reader*

In cases where the main idea appears in the middle of the paragraph, it acts as a linchpin: In this example, the paragraph begins with examples of genetic advances, and it ends with a sentence supporting the widespread cultural importance of these genetic tests. The topic sentence links these two different kinds of support.

3. Decide whether to leave the main idea unstated.

Some paragraphs (especially descriptive and narrative ones) may leave the main idea unstated. The main idea of the paragraph below, for example, is implied by the details and the word choices. The words and phrases that suggest the main idea are highlighted.

> The sound of discreet footsteps echoed in my ears as our choir followed a monk through one of the dark, damp archways into a grand hall furnished with ancient tables and chairs; it had been immaculately preserved by the family that had inhabited the old palace, which now served as a monastery, school, and museum. From the hall we passed into a room filled with religious relics that had belonged to the old prince. In another room, brown music manuscripts in Beethoven's and Haydn's own handwriting lay in crystal cases. In a third, bright tapestries woven from gold thread hung from the shiny stone walls, and sparkling crown jewels bedecked glass cabinets. We passed quickly through room after room filled with rusty (or bloodstained?) torture devices. Just before we reached an open-air walkway, we passed doors that seemed to belong to dwarves: They were entrances to the rooms of children who attended school here.
>
> —Christina Huey, Georgia Southern University

In this paragraph, the implied main idea—something like "Everything in the monastery seemed strange and remarkable"—comes through without Huey's having to state it explicitly. But be careful: Including just one irrelevant idea in a paragraph without an explicit topic sentence can confuse your readers.

EXERCISE 4.3 Identifying the topic sentence

Identify the topic sentence (main idea) in the following paragraphs:

1. Rock music had always been a vehicle to express frustration, rebellion, and obloquy, but as the 1970s proceeded, these themes were often softened to achieve mass acceptance. The notion of rock as mainstream

entertainment was gaining ground steadily. David Bowie, for example, who in an earlier era might have been considered too inaccessible a figure for television audiences, turned up as a smiling guest on Cher's variety show in 1975. Rock was becoming a common language, the reference point for a splintered culture. In March 1976, presidential candidate Jimmy Carter told a lecture audience that Bob Dylan, Led Zeppelin, and the Grateful Dead were among the artists who had inspired him to work hard as governor of Georgia, and once he won the election, Carter continued to court rock by inviting numerous musicians to the White House. —Ken Tucker, "The Seventies and Beyond," in *Rock of Ages: The Rolling Stone History of Rock & Roll*, p. 520

2. Straddling the top of the world, one foot in China and the other in Nepal, I cleared the ice from my oxygen mask, hunched a shoulder against the wind, and stared absently down at the vastness of Tibet. I understood on some dim, detached level that the sweep of earth beneath my feet was a spectacular sight. I'd been fantasizing about this moment, and the release of emotion that would accompany it, for many months. But now that I was finally here, actually standing on the summit of Mount Everest, I just couldn't summon the energy to care.
—Jon Krakauer, *Into Thin Air*, p. 5

> **Make It Your Own**
>
> Select a paragraph from a recent or current writing project. Underline the topic sentence or main idea; then cross through any sentences that do not support it.

4c Writing Coherent Paragraphs

A paragraph is *coherent* when readers can understand the relationships among the sentences without having to pause or ponder. Readers are most likely to find a paragraph coherent when all the sentences in the paragraph are relevant, when the paragraph is clearly organized, and when transitional strategies link sentences.

1. Organize your paragraphs logically.

There are many ways to organize a paragraph logically. Most paragraphs follow deductive order: They begin with a topic sentence (the most general statement in the paragraph) and the supporting evidence follows:

> The handbags in the museum exhibition were hardly Murakami's only contribution to the Roppongi Hills complex of glass-and-steel towers. Cute cartoonlike characters that he had created as branding elements for the center—Barney-like brontosaurs, droopy-eared rabbits, and smiling aliens—grinned down on me from pennants and from express buses to Roppongi Hills. In the same development, at a large Vuitton store, new handbags in a cherry design by Murakami would soon be introduced, along with a couple of the artist's sculptures of a red, smiling cherry. Last year at another Vuitton shop in Tokyo, Murakami displayed a large fiberglass sculpture and a four-panel screen painted in his LV monogram design.
> —Arthur Lubow, "The Murakami Method," *New York Times*

A less common option is to organize the paragraph inductively, so that it begins with the supporting details and concludes with the topic sentence:

> His trademark character Mr. DOB (who appears in the sculpture *DOB in the Strange Forest*) is reminiscent of both Mickey Mouse and Sonic the Hedgehog. But there's something heavier going on here. It's hinted at in the manic eyes of Murakami's characters. It's unleashed fully in the show's centerpiece painting *Tan Tan Bo Puking*, aka *Gero Tan*, where the cartoon character subject is bearing fearsome jagged teeth, and the whole lot is melting. It's like cartoon Dali, sure, but it's also another reminder that Japan experienced the flesh-melting horror of atomic attack.
> —Daniel Etherington, "Nasty Cartoons from Japan," bbc.co.uk

The painting referred to in the paragraph above is shown in the background of Figure 4.1.

A third option is to organize the paragraph by increasing order of emphasis or interest:

> Monotonously the trucks sway, monotonously come the calls, monotonously falls the rain. It falls on our heads and on the heads of the dead up the line, on the body of the little recruit with the wound that is so much too big for his hip; it falls on Kemmerich's grave; it falls in our hearts.
> —Erich Maria Remarque, *All Quiet on the Western Front*

FIGURE 4.1 The painting *Tan Tan Bo Puking*—a.k.a. *Gero Tan*—and sculptures by artist Takashi Murakami

A fourth option is to organize the paragraph by posing a problem or question and then resolving it:

Question
Answer

So why exactly is the protagonist drawn to the dreams of the past? It may be because those dreams are not the trivialities of modern times. They are not about realizing suddenly that you are standing at your locker naked or unable to get to the airport in time for your flight. Instead, the dreams of the past are dreams of death, of unknown gods, of devouring monsters.

—Michael Parr, McHenry Community College, "The Importance of Dreaming in Sylvia Plath's 'Johnny Panic and the Bible of Dreams'"

2. Use transitions within (and between) paragraphs.

In addition to omitting irrelevancies and being well organized, a coherent paragraph provides guideposts that point readers from one sentence to the next. These are ***transitional words and phrases.*** They alert readers to the significance of what you are saying and point up the relationships among your ideas. The following paragraph uses transitional words and phrases to guide readers through a comparison of two books:

Contrast

Baron's book, which is written in the relentlessly melodramatic style of *Jaws*, describes cougars spreading inexorably eastward. By contrast, Elizabeth Marshall Thomas, in *The Tribe of Tiger: Cats and Their Culture*, argues that cougars were never fully exterminated in the East and instead survived in remote areas by being especially stealthy around humans. The difference is significant.

If you accept Marshall Thomas's argument, **then** the eastern seaboard sounds a great deal like pre–cougar-resurgence Colorado. **Indeed**, the herds of deer plaguing the unbroken strip of Eastern suburbs makes a replay of the Boulder situation likely—but on a far larger scale. **Already**, bears and coyotes are invading the Eastern suburbs. Can cougars and wolves be far behind?
—Peter Canby, "The Cat Came Back," *Harper's*

> Cause-effect
> Emphasis
> Time

Make sure you choose the appropriate transition for the situation, and vary your selection to avoid ineffective repetition. (For some example transitions, see the Quick Reference box below.)

> **More about**
> Avoiding repetition, 499

3. Repeat words, phrases, and sentence structures.

Repetition—especially repetition used for padding—can annoy readers, but repetition used consciously, to knit sentences into a cohesive paragraph or to call attention to an idea, can be an asset. The following paragraph repeats words and phrases (*deer hunting, hunting, deer season*) to emphasize the point made in the final sentence, where the writer uses the word *deer* on its own.

> **More about**
> Developing without padding, 89
> Effective repetition, 534–35

I don't object to deer hunting: let everyone have his sport, I say. I don't for a moment doubt the value, importance, and dignity of hunting for those who

> Repeated structure
> Repeated words

Quick Reference — **Sample Transitional Expressions**

To add to an idea: *again, also, and, and then, besides, further, furthermore, in addition, incidentally, likewise, moreover, next, still, too*
To indicate cause or effect: *accordingly, as a result, because, consequently, hence, since, then, therefore, thus*
To indicate chronology (time sequence): *after, afterward, as long as, as soon as, at last, before, earlier, finally, first, formerly, immediately, in the first place, in the interval, in the meantime, in the next place, in the last place, later, latter, meanwhile, next, now, often, once, previously, second, shortly, simultaneously, since, sometime later, subsequently, suddenly, then, third, today, tomorrow, until, until now, when, years ago, yesterday*
To conclude: *all in all, finally, in brief, in conclusion, in other words, in short, in sum, in summary, that is, to summarize*
To concede: *certainly, granted, of course*
To compare: *alike, also, in the same way, like, likewise, resembling, similarly*

To contrast: *after all, and yet, although, but, conversely, despite, difference, dissimilar, even so, even though, granted, however, in contrast, in spite of, instead, nevertheless, nonetheless, notwithstanding, on the contrary, on the other hand, otherwise, regardless, still, though, unlike, while this may be true, yet*
To emphasize: *after all, certainly, clearly, even, indeed, in fact, in other words, in truth, it is true, moreover, of course, undoubtedly*
To offer an example: *as an example, for example, for instance, in other words, namely, specifically, that is, thus, to exemplify, to illustrate*
To indicate spatial relationships: *above, adjacent to, against, alongside, around, at a distance from, behind, below, beside, beyond, encircling, far off, farther along, forward, here, in front of, inside, near the back, near the end, nearly, next to, on, over, surrounding, there, through, to the left, to the right, to the north, to the south, up front*

do it. Deer hunting teaches skill, discipline, and patience. More than that, it teaches the moral lesson of seriousness—that certain things must be entered into advisedly, done with care, and done right. That hunting provides an education I am very willing to believe. And yet deer season is for me a sad couple of weeks. Because with all its profound advantages for the hunter, the fact remains that deer season is a little tough on the deer.

—Castle Freeman, "Surviving Deer Season: A Lesson in Ambiguity," *Atlantic*

The paragraph above repeats sentence structures ("I don't object," "I don't . . . doubt"; "Deer hunting teaches," "It teaches") but largely relies on the repetition of words (*deer, hunting, season*) for emphasis. The paragraph below uses related concepts (the word *gangster,* the names of gangsters and others from the FBI's Most Wanted list), but it mainly relies on repetition of phrase and sentence structures to lend emphasis.

When he said he'd been a gangster, they smiled. Sure you were, pops. When he said he'd been Public Enemy Number One—right after John Dillinger, Pretty Boy Floyd, and his old protégé Baby Face Nelson—people turned away and rolled their eyes. When he said he and his confederates had single-handedly "created" J. Edgar Hoover and the modern FBI, well, then he would get bitter and people would get up and move to another table. He was obviously unstable. How could you believe anyone who claimed he was the only man in history to have met Charles Manson, Al Capone, and Bonnie and Clyde?

—Bryan Burrough, *Public Enemies*

4. Use pronouns, synonyms, and equivalent expressions.

Pronouns (I, you, he, she, it, we, they), synonyms (words that mean the same thing), and equivalent expressions not only help writers avoid having to repeat the same word over and over (unintentional repetition) but also create coherence by establishing links to words and phrases that appeared earlier. The

> **Writing Responsibly** — Guiding the Reader
>
> As a writer, you have a responsibility to guide your reader from point to point, highlighting the relationships among your words, sentences, and paragraphs. Do not leave readers to puzzle out the relationships among your ideas for themselves. Few academic readers in the United States will think that explicit claims and transitions insult their intelligence.
>
> to AUDIENCE

following paragraph, for example, uses several equivalent expressions for the word *gossip* as well as the pronoun *it* to refer to this concept:

> The first law of gossip is that you never know how many people are talking about you behind your back. The second law is thank God. The third—and most important—law is that as gossip spreads from friends to acquaintances to people you've never met, it grows more garbled, vivid, and definitive. Out of stray factoids and hesitant impressions emerges a hard mass of what everyone knows to be true. Imagination supplies the missing pieces, and repetition turns these pieces into facts; gossip achieves its shape and amplitude only in the continual retelling. The best stories about us are told by perfect strangers.
> —Tad Friend, "The Harriet-the-Spy Club," *New Yorker*

Key concept
Repeated structure
Pronouns
Equivalent expressions

5. Combine techniques.

The example paragraphs in *section c* used more than one technique to achieve coherence. When revising your own paragraphs, draw on a variety of techniques to make your paragraphs cohere.

EXERCISE 4.4 Analyzing coherence

For each of the following paragraphs, identify how the paragraph is organized, underline the transitional words and phrases, and circle the words that are repeated or the pronouns or synonyms that replace them.

1. Readers of this novel can attribute multiple meanings to the word *paradise* depending on whose point of view they are looking from. The founders of Ruby consider *paradise* to consist of preserving the history of the Old Fathers and remaining isolated from outsiders, but this view proves faulty and falls apart. On their journey toward seeking comfort, the women of the convent realize that *paradise* means coming to terms with one's past instead of running from it or letting it determine who they are, and this understanding leads them to show compassion and mercy toward those who have harmed them. —Sonu Ray, Drew University, "Journey to *Paradise*: Discovering Its Gateway"

2. The group worshipped unharassed until 1667. At that time, the Court acted on the complaints of the orthodox churches of the area against Myles and his followers. In an order from the Plymouth Court dated July 2, 1667, the members were fined five pounds each for "setting up of a public meeting without the knowledge and approbation of the Court to the disturbance of the peace of the place" (King 30–31). The

Court offered them three alternatives: They could discontinue their worship services, leave the town, or petition the Court for an alternate site of worship. Mr. Myles moved his church to New Meadow Neck, just south of Rehoboth, which is today in Barrington, Rhode Island.
—Robyn Worthington, Bristol Community College, "The Covenant between Church and Town in Swansea, Massachusetts"

3. First, use the cork borer to cut 2 cylinders out of the potato and then slice the cores into pieces 2 cm long. It is a good idea to place the slices in a beaker to prevent them from drying out. There should be two potato cylinders for each treatment. Weigh the two cylinders for each treatment and record the weight in grams: that is your initial weight. Next, blot the cylinders with a paper towel and put each of the sets of cylinders into 100 ml beakers (there should be five) and place 50 ml of each solution in the beakers. —Stephanie Warnekros, Johnson County Community College, "Osmosis in Potato Cubes"

EXERCISE 4.5 Unscrambling the "Gettysburg Address"

The sentences below make up the final paragraph of Abraham Lincoln's "Gettysburg Address," but they have been scrambled. Without checking the original, use the clues within the paragraph to restore Lincoln's sentences to their proper order. Then list the coherence techniques that helped you put the paragraph back together again.

1. It is rather for us to be here dedicated to the great task remaining before us—that from these honored dead we take increased devotion to that cause for which they gave the last full measure of devotion—that we here highly resolve that these dead shall not have died in vain—that this nation, under God, shall have a new birth of freedom—and that government of the people, by the people, for the people, shall not perish from the earth.
2. The world will little note, nor long remember, what we say here, but it can never forget what they did here.
3. But, in a larger sense, we cannot dedicate—we cannot consecrate—we cannot hallow—this ground.
4. The brave men, living and dead, who struggled here, have consecrated it, far above our poor power to add or detract.
5. It is for us the living, rather, to be dedicated here to the unfinished work which they who fought here have thus far so nobly advanced.

Writing Matters • Developing Paragraphs Using Patterns   **4d**   59

> **Make It Your Own**
>
> Select a paragraph from a current or recent writing project and assess its coherence. List the techniques you used to weave the sentences together into a paragraph and note what you could do to make it even more coherent.

4d Developing Paragraphs Using Patterns

Using *patterns*—description, narration or process analysis, exemplification, comparison and contrast, cause and effect, analysis, and definition—can help you develop your paragraphs (and your essay) into a cohesive and unified whole.

Description When describing, include details that appeal to the senses (sight, sound, taste, smell, touch) and organize them spatially (from left to right, top to bottom, near to middle to far) to mimic how we normally take in a scene. Spatially organized paragraphs rely on indications of place or location to guide the reader by the mind's eye (or ear or nose).

> A few moments later French announces, "Bottom contact on sonar." The seafloor rolls out like a soft, beige carpet. Robison points to tiny purple jellies floating just above the floor. Beyond them, lying on the floor itself, are several bumpy sea cucumbers, sea stars with skinny legs, pink anemones, and tube worms, which quickly retract their feathery feeding arms at *Tiburon*'s approach. A single rattail fish hangs inches above the bottom, shoving its snout into the sediments in search of a meal.
> —Virginia Morell, "OK, There It Is—Our Mystery Mollusk,"
> *National Geographic*

[Sensory description]

[Indications of place or location]

Narration and process analysis A paragraph that tells a story or describes a process unrolls over time. Include each step or key moment, and describe it in enough detail that readers can envision it.

> The very first trick ever performed by Houdini on the professional stage was a simple but effective illusion known generally as the "Substitution Trunk," though he preferred to call it "Metamorphosis." Houdini and his partner would bring a large trunk onto the stage. It was opened and a sack or bag produced from inside it. Houdini, bound and handcuffed, would get into the sack, which was then sealed or tied around the neck. The trunk was closed

[Step 1]

[Step 2]

[Step 3]

over the bag and its occupant. It was locked, strapped, and chained. Then a screen was drawn around it. The partner (after they married, this was always Mrs. Houdini) stepped behind the screen which, next moment, was thrown aside—by Houdini himself. The partner had meanwhile disappeared. A committee of the audience was called onstage to verify that the ties, straps, etc. around the trunk had not been tampered with. These were then laboriously loosened; the trunk was opened and there, inside the securely fastened bag, was—Mrs. Houdini!

—Ruth Brandon, *The Life and Many Deaths of Harry Houdini*

The sequence of events in the Substitution, or Metamorphosis, trick is depicted in Figure 4.2.

Exemplification: Explaining through example Exemplification works by providing examples to make a general point specific:

For many years I believed that women had only one thing to learn from men: how to get the attention of a waiter by some means short of kicking over the table and shrieking. Never in my life have I gotten the attention of a waiter, unless it was an off-duty waiter whose car I'd accidentally scraped in a parking lot somewhere. Men, however, can summon a maître d' just by thinking the word "coffee," and this is a power women would be well-advised to study. What else would we possibly want to learn from them? How to interrupt someone in midsentence as if you were performing an act of conversational euthanasia? How to drop a pair of socks three feet from an open hamper and keep right on walking? How to make those weird guttural gargling sounds in the bathroom?

—Barbara Ehrenreich, "What I've Learned from Men: Lessons for a Full-Grown Feminist," *Ms.*

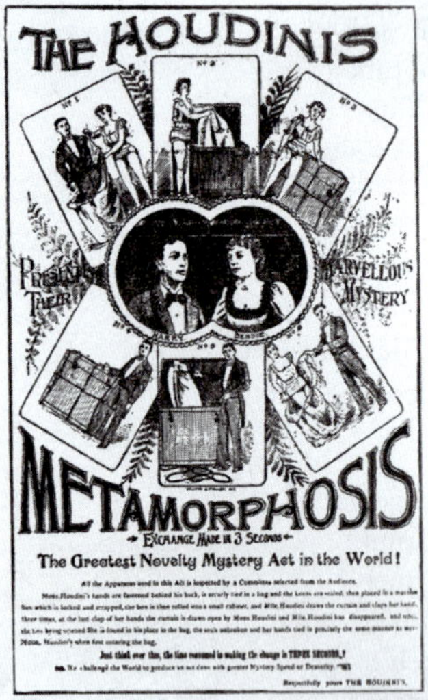

Comparison-contrast: Showing similarities and differences A paragraph that is developed using comparison-contrast points out similarities or differences (sometimes both). A comparison-contrast paragraph can proceed by either the ***block method*** or the ***alternating method.*** In the block method, the writer groups all the traits of the first item together before discussing the second item. In the alternating method, the writer proceeds point by point, discussing each common or divergent trait of both items before moving to the next trait. In the block method, readers must remember everything you have said about item A while they read about

FIGURE 4.2 **A visual process analysis**

item B, so the more complex your material, the more your readers are likely to need the alternating method.

Block Method	**Alternating Method**
A	A
A	B
A	
	A
B	B
B	
B	A
	B

The first paragraph below uses the alternating method; the second uses the block method.

> At first glance, it would appear that surgery and writing have little in common, but I think that is not so. For one thing, they are both sub-celestial arts; as far as I know, the angels disdain to perform either one. In each of them you hold a slender instrument that leaves a trail wherever it is applied. In one, there is the shedding of blood; in the other it is ink that is spilled upon a page. In one, the scalpel is restrained; in the other, the pen is given rein. The surgeon sutures together the tissues of the body to make whole what is sick or injured; the writer sews words into sentences to fashion a new version of human experience. A surgical operation is rather like a short story. You make the incision, rummage around inside for a bit, then stitch up. It has a beginning, a middle and an end. If I were to choose a medical specialist to write a novel, it would be a psychiatrist. They tend to go on and on. And on.
> —Richard Selzer, "The Pen and the Scalpel," *New York Times*

Surgery

Writing

> Europeans interpreted the simplicity of Indian dress in two different ways. Some saw the lack of clothing as evidence of "barbarism." André Thevet, a shocked French visitor to Brazil in 1557, voiced this point of view when he attributed nakedness to simple lust. If the Indians could weave hammocks, he sniffed, why not shirts? But other Europeans viewed unashamed nakedness as the Indians' badge of innocence. As remnants of a bygone "golden age," they believed, Indians needed clothing no more than government, laws, regular employment, or other corruptions of civilization.
> —James West Davidson et al., *Nation of Nations,* 5th ed.

"Barbarism"

"Innocence"

Cause-and-effect: Reasons and consequences A cause-and-effect paragraph explains why something happened or what its consequences are:

> When we exhibit these [positive] emotions, society showers us with positive reinforcement; we learn this even before we get out of diapers. When, as children, we hug our rotten little puke of a sister and give her a kiss, all the aunts and uncles smile and twit and cry, "Isn't he the sweetest little thing?" Such coveted treats as chocolate-covered graham crackers often follow. But if we deliberately slam the rotten little puke of a sister's fingers in the door, sanctions follow—angry remonstrance from parents, aunts, and uncles; instead of a chocolate-covered graham cracker, a spanking.
> —Stephen King, "Why We Crave Horror Movies," *Playboy*

Analysis: Dividing a whole into its parts Analysis divides a single entity into its component parts:

> The central United States is divided into two geographical zones: the Great Plains in the west and the prairie in the east. Though both are more or less flat, the Great Plains—extending south from eastern Montana and western North Dakota to eastern New Mexico and western Texas—are the drier of the two regions and are distinguished by short grasses, while the more populous prairie to the east (surrounding Omaha, St. Louis, and Fort Leavenworth) is tall-grass country. The Great Plains are the "West"; the prairie, the "Midwest."
> —Robert D. Kaplan, *An Empire of Wilderness*

Definition: Explaining the meaning of a word or concept Like those in a dictionary, a definition explains the meaning of a word or concept by grouping it into a class and then providing the distinguishing characteristics that set it apart from other members of that class:

Term to Be Defined	Class	Distinguishing Characteristics
Argument is	a way to discover truth	by examining all sides of the issue.

Extended definitions (definitions that run to a paragraph or more) analyze in detail what a term does or does not mean. They go beyond a desktop dictionary, often using anecdotes, examples, or reasons for using the word in this particular way:

> The international movement known as *theater of the absurd* so vividly captured the anguish of modern society that late twentieth-century critics called it "the true theater of our time." Abandoning classical theater from Sophocles

and Shakespeare through Ibsen and Miller, absurdist playwrights rejected traditional dramatic structure (in which action moves from conflict to resolution), along with traditional modes of character development. The absurdist play, which drew stylistic inspiration from dada performance art and surrealist film, usually lacks dramatic progression, direction, and resolution. Its characters undergo little or no change, dialogue contradicts actions, and events follow no logical order. Dramatic action, leavened with gallows humor, may consist of irrational and grotesque situations that remain unresolved at the end of the performance—as is often the case in real life.

—Gloria Fiero, *The Humanistic Tradition,* 5th ed.

> Distinguishing characteristics

Make It **Your Own**

Write two paragraphs. For each, choose one of the patterns of development discussed on pp. 59–63. Check to make sure that they are unified and that they use appropriate transitions to guide the reader.

Work **Together**

Exchange paragraphs with a classmate and make a note of which patterns you see. Mark any places where the paragraph lacks coherence or needs additional transitions.

4e Writing Introductory Paragraphs

Introductory paragraphs shape readers' attitudes toward the rest of the text. Yet writers often have a hard time producing these paragraphs. Many writers find it helpful to draft the body of the essay before tackling the introduction.

Avoid Praising the Reader in Your Introduction In some contexts and cultures, writers win the approval of readers by overtly praising their taste, character, or intelligence, whether the writing is intended to be wholly personal or not. Generally, however, this is considered inappropriate for a college paper, and academic and professional writers in the United States avoid referring directly to the reader and occasionally will actually challenge the reader's beliefs.

Whether you write the introduction first or last, it should prepare the reader for what follows. In many cases, this means including the thesis in the introduction. A common placement for the thesis statement is at the end of the introduction—this is the *funnel introduction.*

Regardless of whether you include your thesis in your introduction, hold it until your conclusion, or merely imply your main idea, your introduction should identify and convey your stance toward your topic, establish your purpose, and engage readers to make them want to read on. One or more of the following strategies can help you write an effective introduction:

- Begin with a vivid quotation, a compelling question, or some interesting data.
- Start with an engaging—and relevant—anecdote.
- Offer a surprising but apt definition of a key term.
- Provide background information.
- State a commonly held belief and then challenge it.
- Explain what interesting, conflicting, difficult, or misunderstood territory the essay will explore.

(For some opening gambits to avoid, see the Quick Reference box on page 65.)

In the introductory paragraph that follows, the writer uses several effective strategies: She begins with a question that challenges the audience to examine some common assumptions about the topic, she provides background information that her readers may lack, and she concludes with a thesis statement that explains why reading her text should be important to the audience.

Opening question — Many people enjoy sitting down to a nice seafood dinner, but how many of those people actually stop to think about where the fish on their plate came from? *Answer that provides background information* — With many species of wild fish disappearing because of overfishing, increasingly the answer will be a fish farm. But while fish farming can help to supply the demand, it can threaten the environment and cause problems with wild fish. It can also threaten the health of consumers by increasing the risk of disease and increasing the quantity of antibiotics consumed. *Thesis* — In fact, as a careful and conscientious consumer, you would do well to learn the risks involved in buying and eating farm-raised fish before one winds up on your dinner plate.

—Adrianne Anderson, Texas Christian University

Brief essays may require only a one-paragraph introduction, but longer texts often need more. A text of twenty pages may have an introduction that runs several paragraphs, and introductions to books are generally the length of a short chapter. While there are no firm rules about the length of the introduction, they should be in proportion to the essay's length.

> **Quick Reference — Seven Don'ts for Introductions**
>
> Avoid common problems that can undermine your introduction's success:
>
> 1. **"In my paper I will do..."** While announcing your topic is acceptable in some academic disciplines (in the sciences, for example), announcing what your paper is or will do is usually unnecessary and boring. Also avoid referring to your own text by its title.
>
> 2. **"In this paper I hope to..." or "In this paper I will try to..."** These openers share the shortcomings of *"In my paper I will do..."*; they also state something your instructor already assumes, and they undermine your credibility by emphasizing your lack of confidence.
>
> 3. **"I don't know much about this topic, but..."** Introductions that apologize for your amateur status undermine your credibility as a writer and give readers an excuse to stop reading.
>
> 4. **"I have a lot of expertise in this topic."** Refrain from claiming more prestige or credit than is your due.
>
> 5. **"According to *Merriam-Webster's Third Unabridged Dictionary*,..."** While starting with a definition can be an effective opening strategy, merely providing readers with a definition they could easily find for themselves is tedious.
>
> 6. **"Ever since the beginning of time,..."** Start your paper at the beginning of your material, not before recorded history.
>
> 7. **"The greatest problem facing our society today..."** Do not make claims that your project cannot support with concrete evidence.

4f Writing Concluding Paragraphs

As with the introduction, the conclusion is a part of the essay that readers are likely to remember. In fact, because it is the last thing the audience will read, it is what they will probably remember best. Thus, it demands a writer's best work.

The shape of the conclusion is often what might be called an ***inverted funnel:*** While the introduction often starts at a general level and then narrows down to the thesis, a common strategy for the conclusion is to start out specific—with a restatement and development of the thesis (in different words)—and then to broaden out. The restatement of your thesis should add perspectives that you have developed in the body of your project and not be a simple paraphrase of what appeared in your introduction. The final draft of Betsy Smith's project (pp. 95–99) demonstrates the technique:

Thesis in the introduction

As serious and time-sensitive as the issue of climate change is, alternative energy is not a solution if it will be just as harmful to wildlife as conventional energy.

Restated thesis in the conclusion

Clearly, it is important that we reduce our carbon footprint, but it is also important that we protect the living things with which we share the planet.

In Smith's introduction, the thesis raises a problem and indicates the possible conflicts. In Smith's conclusion, the *if* is gone, replaced by *clearly*. The body of Smith's project has described the conflicts as being very real, so in her conclusion she can state her thesis in much more definite terms.

The purpose of the conclusion is to provide readers with a sense of closure and to make them feel that reading the text was worthwhile. To achieve closure and convey the importance of the essay, try one or more of the following strategies:

- Return to the anecdote, question, or quotation with which you began.
- Summarize your findings (especially in long or technical projects).
- Discuss how what you have learned has changed your thinking.
- Suggest a possible solution (or solutions) to the problems raised in the text.
- Indicate additional research that needs to be conducted or what the reader can do to help solve the problem.
- Leave readers with a vivid and pertinent image, quotation, or anecdote.

(For some strategies to avoid when writing your conclusion, see the Quick Reference box on the next page.)

The concluding paragraph below provides an example of an effective conclusion.

> The farmers of nineteenth-century America could afford to do here what they had not dared to do in the Old World: hope. This hope—for greater economic security, for more opportunity for themselves, their children, and their grandchildren—is the optimism and idealism that has carried our country forward and that, indeed, still carries us forward. Although the American dream has evolved across the centuries, it survives today and is a cornerstone

Makes reader feel time reading was well spent by showing importance of American dream

Restates thesis (American dream = hope for greater security, opportunity)

Achieves closure by recurring to introduction with mention of American dream

> **Quick Reference** — **Five Don'ts for Conclusions**
>
> Avoid common problems that can undermine your conclusion's success:
>
> 1. **Don't offer additional support for your thesis in your conclusion.** Such conclusions undermine the feeling of closure and leave readers wanting and expecting more.
> 2. **Don't end with a generality or a cliché.** Almost nothing will undermine the readers' sense that they have spent their time well than ending with something trite.
> 3. **Don't apologize for the shortcomings of your paper.** Such an ending will leave readers feeling they have wasted their time. If your paper is truly bad, you should have revised your draft, not passed it on to readers; if it is not, you have nothing to apologize for.
> 4. **Don't repeat your introduction.** It may be useful to return to the anecdote or statistics with which you began, but merely repeating your introduction or thesis will insult your audience. They do not want to read the same text a second time.
> 5. **Don't announce what your essay has done or shown** ("In my paper, I have shown . . ."). In a long or complicated text, a summary can be useful to readers, but your readers will be reminded of what your text has done when they read your summary; there is no need to announce it.

of American philosophy. It is what underlies our Constitution and our laws, and it is a testimony to the vision of the farmers who founded this nation.
—Leonard Lin, University of Southern California, "The Middle Class Farmers and the American Philosophy"

EXERCISE 4.6 Writing introductory paragraphs

Revise the following introductory paragraph to make it more effective:

> People aged 50 and older cannot see as well at night as younger people. The small muscles that control the size of the pupil get weaker with age, and with age there may be a loss of rods, which are crucial for night vision. This affects older people's ability to adapt to the dark. This can cause problems when driving at night after the bright headlights of a car pass or just walking from well-lit to dark parts of a home. Older people need to recognize their decreased ability to see at night and to take measures that will help them be safe in the dark, whether driving, walking outdoors, or getting around the home. This paper presents the reasons why night vision is weaker in older people and some methods of compensating for this problem.

EXERCISE 4.7 Writing concluding paragraphs

Revise the following concluding paragraph to make it more effective:

> To summarize the point of this essay, the majority of experts acknowledge that every one of the world's seven species of marine turtles is threatened by extinction. At present humans are causing more turtle deaths than natural forces. A key cause is habitat destruction and alteration. Coastal development is rapidly eliminating access to beaches for female turtles to nest and lay eggs. Another important cause is predation for turtle meat, eggs, hides, and shells. Incidental capture in fisheries increases the loss of turtles. Masking the threat is the slow maturation of turtles, which can hide the effect of overexploitation for many years. We need to greatly expand our knowledge of marine turtle life history patterns and the true conservation status of turtle populations, as well as the level and types of exploitation. With this knowledge we need to formulate and implement effective management and conservation strategies to preserve viable marine turtle populations. If we do not, time will run out for one of the most intriguing creatures on the face of the earth.

Make It **Your Own**

Review the introduction and conclusion of a current or recent writing project. What strategies did you use? Referring to the Quick Reference boxes and the strategies discussed in this chapter, revise your introduction and conclusion.

Work **Together**

Exchange your revised introductions and conclusions and note what strategies your classmate used in the revision. Did they work? What strategies might make these paragraphs more powerful?

Before reviewing your classmate's comments, write a paragraph reflecting on this process. What did you learn about effective introductions and conclusions by reading and evaluating someone else's? Did your classmate use any strategies you might try? Now review the comments you received and make a note of any revisions that you plan to make.

4g Connecting Paragraphs

Readers need to know not only how sentences connect to one another but also how paragraphs are connected. One way to connect paragraphs is by using one of the patterns of development (pp. 59–63) for the essay, just as you would do with individual paragraphs; you can also link paragraphs using these transitional devices:

- Providing transitional expressions (and sentences)
- Repeating words and phrases strategically
- Using pronouns and synonyms to refer back to words and ideas
- Creating parallel sentence structures

A final way to create coherence among paragraphs is by referring back to the essay's main idea.

The essay excerpted below, by former vice president and 2007 Nobel Peace Prize recipient Al Gore, uses all of these strategies to create a unified and cohesive text:

Professional Model Editorial

An Inconvenient Truth

By AL GORE

Some experiences are so **intense** while they are happening that **time seems to stop** altogether. When it begins again and our lives resume their normal course, those intense experiences remain vivid, refusing to stay in the past, remaining always and forever with us.

Seventeen years ago my youngest child was badly—almost fatally—injured. This is a story I have told before, but its meaning for me continues to change and to deepen.

That is **also** true of the story I have tried to tell for many years about the global environment. It was during **that** interlude 17 years ago when I started writing my first book, *Earth in the Balance*. It was because of my son's accident and the way it abruptly interrupted the flow of my days and hours that I began to rethink everything, especially what my priorities had been. Thankfully, my son has long since recovered completely. **But** it was during that traumatic period that I made at least two enduring changes: I vowed always to put my family first, and I also vowed to make the climate crisis the top priority of my professional life.

Unfortunately, in the intervening years, **time has not stood still** for the global environment. The pace of destruction has worsened and the urgent need

Keywords, phrases (highlighted on first use)

¶ 2 provides an example of the intense experiences mentioned in ¶ 1.

Transitional words, expressions

Adjective *that* in "that interlude 17 years ago," "that traumatic period" refers back to period of child's injury, introduced in ¶ 2.

"abruptly . . . hours" refers back to "time seems to stand still" (¶ 1).

"Time has not stood still" refers back to "time seems to stop" (¶ 1).

> ¶ 5 sets up logical (problem-solution) structure of essay: Global warming is a crisis that is dangerous but also presents opportunities. The words *danger* and *opportunity* and synonyms for these words appear throughout.

> This section elaborates on the idea that global warming puts the earth in *danger*.

for a response has grown more acute.

. . . I also want to convey my strong feeling that what we are facing is not just a cause for alarm, it is paradoxically also a cause for hope. The Chinese expression for "crisis" consists of two characters side by side. The first is the symbol for "danger," the second the symbol for "opportunity."

The climate crisis is, indeed, extremely dangerous. In fact it is a true planetary emergency. Two thousand scientists, in a hundred countries, working for more than twenty years in the most elaborate and well-organized scientific collaboration in the history of humankind, have forged an exceptionally strong consensus that all the nations on Earth must work together to solve the crisis of global warming. . . .

So the message is unmistakably clear. This crisis means "danger!"

Why do our leaders seem not to hear such a clear warning? Is it simply that it is inconvenient for them to hear the truth?

> "Unwelcome" is a synonym for "inconvenient" in previous ¶.

If the truth is unwelcome, it may seem easier just to ignore it. But we know from bitter experience that the consequences of doing so can be dire. For example, when we were first warned that the levees were about to break in New Orleans because of Hurricane Katrina, those warnings were ignored. Later, a bipartisan group of members of Congress chaired by Rep. Tom Davis (R-Va.) said in an official report, "The White House failed to act on the massive amounts of information at its disposal," and that a "blinding lack of situational awareness and disjointed decision-making needlessly compounded and prolonged Katrina's horror."

Today, we are hearing and seeing dire warnings of the worst potential catastrophe in the history of human civilization: a global climate crisis that is deepening and rapidly becoming more dangerous than anything we have ever faced. And yet these dire warnings are also being met with a "blinding lack of situational awareness"—in this case, by the Congress, as well as the president.

As Martin Luther King Jr. said in a speech not long before his assassination: "We are now faced with the fact, my friends, that tomorrow is today. We are confronted with the fierce urgency of now. In this unfolding conundrum of life and history, there is such a thing as being too late."

But along with the danger we face from global warming, this crisis also brings unprecedented opportunities. There will be plenty of new jobs and new profits—we can build clean engines; we can harness the sun and the wind; we can stop wasting energy; we can use our planet's plentiful coal resources without heating the planet. . . .

But there's something even more precious to be gained if we do the right thing. The climate

> "Today" contrasts with "when we were first warned . . ." in previous ¶.

> Repetition of "blinding lack of situational awareness" connects this ¶ to the previous one.

> This section elaborates on the *opportunities* global warming presents.

> Transitional sentence refers to list of opportunities in previous ¶.

Writing Matters • Connecting Paragraphs   4g   71

Uses *chance* as synonym for *opportunity*.	
	Reference to Dr. King and repetition of "Tomorrow is today" connect this ¶ to earlier ¶ above.
Repetition of *rise* and sentence structure ("When we...") ties these 3 ¶s together.	
	Emphasis on pronouns, contrast, connects final ¶ with previous ¶s.
"This too is a moral moment" and "This is a moral, ethical, and spiritual challenge" hearken back to "moral and spiritual challenge" in previous ¶.	

crisis also offers us the chance to experience what very few generations in history have had the privilege of knowing: a generational mission; the exhilaration of a compelling moral purpose, a shared and unifying cause; the thrill of being forced by circumstances to put aside the pettiness and conflict that so often stifle the restless human need for transcendence; the opportunity to rise.

When we do rise, it will fill our spirits and bind us together. Those who are now suffocating in cynicism and despair will be able to breathe freely. Those who are now suffering from a loss of meaning in their lives will find hope.

When we rise, we will experience an epiphany as we discover that this crisis is not really about politics at all. It is a moral and spiritual challenge. At stake is the survival of our civilization and the habitability of the Earth. . . .

This too is a moral moment, a crossroads. This is not ultimately about any scientific discussion or political dialogue. It is about who we are as human beings. It is about our capacity to transcend our own limitations, to rise to this new occasion. To see with our hearts, as well as our heads, the response that is now called for. This is a moral, ethical and spiritual challenge.

We should not fear this challenge. We should welcome it. We must not wait. In the words of Dr. King, "Tomorrow is today."

I began with a description of an experience 17 years ago that, for me, stopped time. During that painful period I gained an ability I hadn't had before to feel the preciousness of our connection in our children and the solemnity of our obligation to safeguard their future and protect the Earth we are bequeathing to them.

Imagine with me now that once again, time has stopped—for all of us—and before it starts again, we have the chance to use our moral imaginations and to project ourselves across the expanse of time, 17 years into the future, and share a brief conversation with our children and grandchildren as they are living in the year 2023.

Will they feel bitterness toward us because we failed in our obligation to care for the Earth that is their home and ours? Will the Earth have been irreversibly scarred by us? Imagine now that they are asking us: "What were you thinking? Didn't you care about our future? Were you really so self-absorbed that you couldn't—or wouldn't—stop the destruction of Earth's environment?" What would our answer be?

We can answer their questions now by our actions, not merely with our promises. In the process, we can choose a future for which our children will thank us.

EXERCISE 4.8 Identifying paragraph-building techniques

Review the excerpt from Al Gore's "An Inconvenient Truth" as follows:

1. Check each paragraph for relevance, unity, and coherence. Highlight topic sentences and identify the patterns used to develop paragraphs. (Patterns may be mixed.) Note examples of strategies described in this chapter.
2. Identify and review the introductory and concluding paragraphs. Note the techniques used to begin and end the essay.
3. Identify the methods Gore used to weave the paragraphs into a unified and cohesive whole: Circle the repeated words, underline the transitional expressions, and draw a box around the pronouns and synonyms that refer back to earlier passages.

Make It **Your Own**

Select a current or recent writing project and review it using the three steps described in Exercise 4.8. Write your observations in the margin and note any revisions you might make to develop your ideas more fully. If this is a paper you are currently drafting, use this review to help you revise it.

5 Drafting and Revising Visuals

IN THIS CHAPTER

a. Illustrating a college project, 73
b. Visuals as evidence, 74
c. Copying and creating visuals, 78
d. Revising visuals, 78

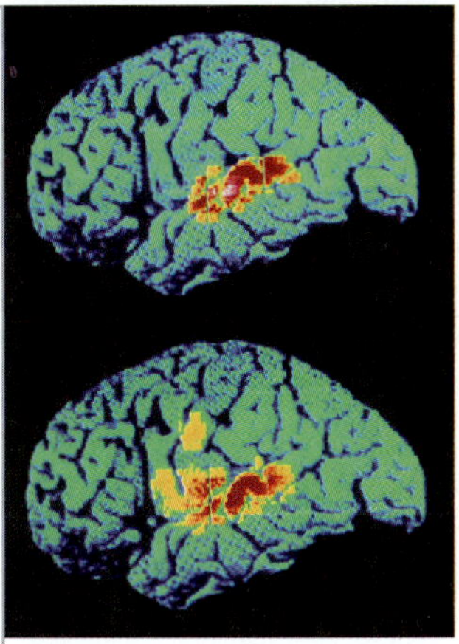

Visuals can bring life to a written text: A Facebook page, a political ad, a website—all would be boring without images. Visuals play a much more important role than mere decoration, however; they help us understand the world. The colors in these PET scans, for example, inform researchers about the portions of the brain that are activated while a subject is listening to words (top) or repeating them (bottom). Images from the Hubble Space Telescope make the theoretical real: They inform viewers about the universe that surrounds our home planet.

5a Deciding Whether to Illustrate College Writing Projects

In personal writing, visuals are often used to entertain or express the writer's thoughts or feelings. In business and public writing, visuals can make an arguable claim and provide evidence for it. In academic writing, visuals may help to engage or persuade readers, but their primary role is to aid understanding. A photograph of a painting you are analyzing for an art history course, a graph comparing voter turnout among age groups for a political science project, a video or animation that describes the course of a disease for a biology assignment—all these would be appropriate illustrations in an academic text.

To determine whether a visual is appropriate in a college project, ask yourself these questions:

> **More about**
> Purpose, 10–12
> Audience, 12–15
> Context and genre, 16–17

- **Does this visual reinforce my purpose?** The primary purpose of visuals in academic writing is to inform. They may

73

Student Models
Visual support, 129, 149, 340, 341, 343, 388, 410, 468

have a secondary persuasive purpose—evidence should be chosen that the reader will find convincing—but the primary purpose will be informative.

- **Is this visual appropriate to my audience, context, and genre?** To determine whether illustrations are appropriate, look at articles from journals in your field or ask your instructor.

Photographs in Job Applications In Europe and Asia it is common to include a personal photograph with a job application. In the United States, however, it is generally considered inappropriate for a résumé to include a photograph (or a description of the job candidate). In fact, employers are barred by law from asking applicants personal questions, such as their age, marital status, race, religion, or sexual orientation.

- **Does the "tone" of the visual match that of the text?** While a caricature might be appropriate in a political magazine like the *Nation*, it would not be appropriate in most college projects (Figure 5.1).

FIGURE 5.1 Caricature versus photograph Unless you were analyzing the political content of such an image, a caricature like this one of former president George W. Bush would not be appropriate in a college project.

5b Using Visuals as Evidence

In academic writing, visuals are used primarily as evidence. Choose the right type of illustration for the information you wish to convey.

1. Information graphics

Information graphics—such as tables, bar graphs, line graphs, and pie charts—convey and depict relationships among data.

Tables Tables, such as Table 5.1, organize large amounts of information in rows and columns for easy viewing. The information in a table can be textual, graphic, or numeric, but it is usually numeric. Tables are frequently the best choice for presenting data on more than four variables or data that include decimals.

Bar graphs and pie charts Bar graphs and pie charts allow comparison of data in two or more categories. A bar graph (Figure 5.2) uses bars of different colors and heights (or lengths). A

Quick Reference: Matching Visual Evidence to Claims

- **Tables.** Use to display large amounts of information, data that include decimals, or information on multiple variables that are difficult to convey in a graph.
- **Pie charts.** Use to convey significant divisions in a single entity that add up to 100 percent.
- **Bar graphs.** Use to compare two or more variables.
- **Line graphs.** Use to show changes among variables over time.
- **Diagrams.** Use to model processes or locations.
- **Maps.** Use to represent geographic locations; may also include data.
- **Photographs.** Provide readers with a reference point or example, or depict a process (two or more photographs needed).
- **Movie stills.** Provide a reference point, offer an example, show a process (two or more stills needed).
- **Screenshots.** Provide a reference point or example from an electronic resource, such as a website.

TABLE 5.1 | CHILDREN 3 TO 21 YEARS OLD SERVED IN FEDERALLY SUPPORTED PROGRAMS FOR THE DISABLED, BY TYPE OF DISABILITY (2006–09)

Type of Disability	2005–06	2006–07	2007–08	2008–09
Autism	3.3	3.9	4.5	5.2
Developmental delay	5.1	5.0	5.4	5.5
Emotional disturbance	7.1	6.9	6.7	6.5
Hearing impairments	1.2	1.2	1.2	1.2
Intellectual disability	8.3	8.0	7.6	7.4
Multiple disabilities	2.1	2.1	2.1	2.0
Orthopedic impairments	1.1	1.0	1.0	1.1
Other health impairments	8.5	9.1	9.7	10.2
Specific learning disabilities	40.7	39.9	39.0	38.2
Speech or language impairments	21.9	22.1	22.0	22.0
Visual impairments	0.4	0.4	0.4	0.4
Traumatic brain injury	0.4	0.4	0.4	0.4

Source: US Dept. of Educ., Inst. of Educ. Sciences, Natl. Center for Educ. Statistics, *Digest of Education Statistics,* US Dept. of Educ., 2010; Print; table 45.

pie chart (Figure 5.3) uses segments of a circle to depict portions of a whole. Choose a pie chart when comparing percentages that add up to 100. Both bar graphs and pie charts work best with a small number of categories where the differences among them are clear. Tom Hackman, Robyn Worthington, and Heather DeGroot use bar graphs to supply evidence succinctly.

Student Models
"Why Students Cheat," Tom Hackman, 147–53
"Nature versus Nurture," Robyn Worthington, 461–68
"The Power of Wardrobe: Male Stereotype Influences," Heather DeGroot, 381–88

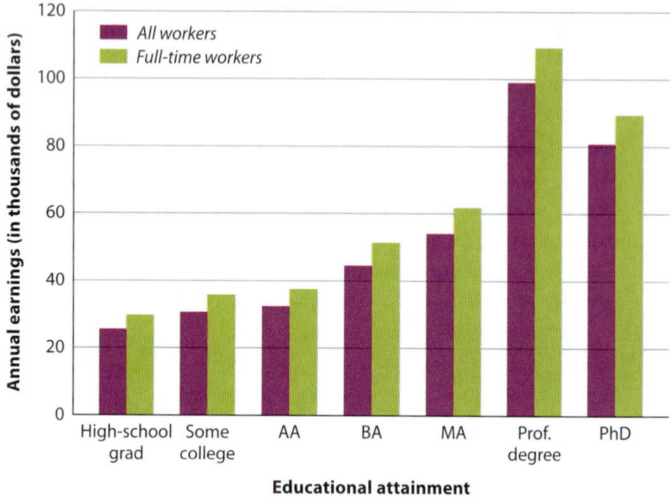

FIGURE 5.2 Work experience and average annual earnings of workers 25–62 by educational attainment The bar graph shown here uses bars of different colors to compare earnings of full-time workers against all workers (both full-time and part-time) by education level. (US Census Bureau, *Current Population Surveys*, Mar. 1998, 1999, 2000. Print.)

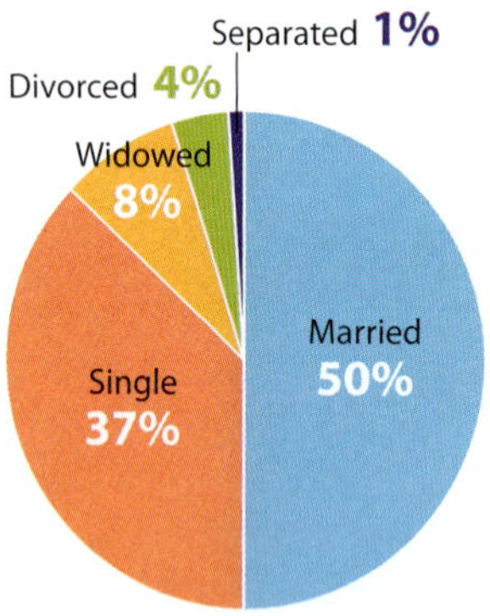

FIGURE 5.3 Who reads romance? This pie chart breaks down the total number of romance readers (100 percent) into groups. Because the information to be conveyed is relatively simple and all of one type (marital status of romance readers), it can readily be conveyed by a pie chart. (Data from "About the Romance Genre," *The Voice of Romance*, Romance Writers of America. 2008. Web.)

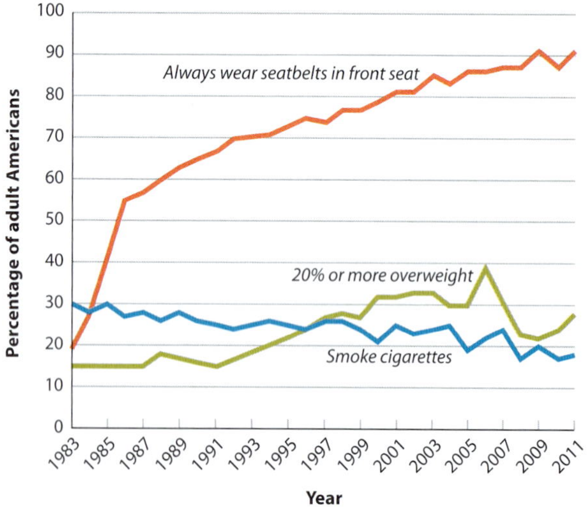

FIGURE 5.4 Smoking, overweight, and seatbelt use, trends 1983–2011 This line graph allows readers to see at a glance the trend in these behaviors and to compare the trends for the three variables: The graph shows that, while the number of smokers has declined slightly over the period, the number of overweight Americans has increased, and the number of Americans wearing seatbelts has skyrocketed. (Data from the Harris Poll, 1983–2011. www.harrisinteractive.com.)

Line graphs Line graphs (such as Figure 5.4) are especially useful in illustrating change over time. The more lines, the more types of data can be compared (but the more complex the graphic). As with bar graphs and pie charts, line graphs work best when you are comparing only a few variables—the more variables, the more difficult it will be to convey the information clearly.

2. Images

Academic writers use images (photographs, screenshots, film stills, architectural renderings, and the like) as references, as when writing about a work of art or a scene from a movie, and they use them as examples. The photograph in Figure 5.5 would provide an effective example in a project discussing the connections between the women's movement of the 1970s and Vietnam War protests.

Abrams Conrad includes an image of a 1794 map to show readers the area studied by the first European explorers of the Pacific Northwest. Alea Wratten uses a photograph of a sculpture as a visual example. Lydia Nichols uses illustrations from superhero and underground comics to demonstrate the differences between these two types of comic books. Heather DeGroot shows photographs of a proctor in stereotypical, counterstereotypical, and "control" outfits.

Student Models
"Exploration and Empire: James Cook and the Pacific Northwest," Abrams Conrad, 408–15
"Reflecting on Brent Staples's Editorial, . . ." Alea Wratten, 127–30
"Holy Underground Comics, Batman!" Lydia Nichols, 336–46
"The Power of Wardrobe: Male Stereotype Influences," Heather DeGroot, 381–88

FIGURE 5.5 Photographs in history Photographs are frequently used in history to supply visual evidence.

EXERCISE 5.1 Using visuals as evidence

For one of the thesis statements you revised in Exercise 3.2, describe the type of visuals you might use as support.

> **Writing Responsibly**
>
> **Exploitative Images**
>
> When using images in your academic work, keep in mind that scholarly essays refrain from including images that may be seen as emotionally manipulative of the reader, as well as those that might be emotionally exploitative of those whom they depict. As you review your selection of images, think about what is right for your topic and how much respect you are extending to the people depicted and how they might feel about the use of the image.
>
> to TOPIC

> **More about**
> Placing visuals on the page, 334–36 (MLA), 379–80 (APA)

5c Deciding Whether to Copy Visuals or to Create Them

Original artwork, like original thoughts, can often be more effective than material "quoted" from others. Some illustrations, however, must come from an outside source, either because the subject is inaccessible (as with a historical photograph) or because the software needed to create the visual is beyond the writer's ability.

Whenever you borrow images from an outside source, be sure to indicate your source, either in the figure caption (for most illustrations) or in a source note (for tables). While you are not required to obtain permission to use a visual in an unpublished academic work, you will need permission if you plan to publish your project, even on the web.

5d Revising Visuals

As with the words you have written, reconsider your supporting visuals while revising to make sure they are clear, they are accurate, and they avoid distortion.

1. Avoid visual clutter.

Your readers will understand your information graphics best when they are clean and simple. Omit lines around cells in a table; use them only to set off headings or to indicate major divisions (Table 5.2). Leave space between columns, and align numbers to make graphics easier to read. Avoid using special views or shading that could make your visual more difficult to interpret (Figure 5.6).

2. Keep visuals clear and accurate.

Double-check the numbers in tables and figures to make sure totals are accurate and that percentages in a pie chart total 100. (If rounding the numbers up

> **Tech** **Consider the Size of Your Document**
>
> Submitting an illustrated document brings with it certain concerns:
>
> - If you will be submitting your project on paper, make sure you have access to a printer of sufficient quality that it can handle your graphics.
> - If you will be submitting your project electronically, think about how large a file your e-mail program—and that of your recipient—can handle. Image files dramatically increase the size of a document file.
> - If you will be delivering your project online, make sure to optimize your graphics for the web so that they load quickly into the reader's browser.

or down has caused inaccuracy, indicate this in a note.) Label all parts of your tables and figures (columns, rows, vertical and horizontal axes, "slices" of a pie chart) so that readers can understand them without having to read the text. Avoid abbreviations that might be unfamiliar or confusing (Figure 5.6).

Johnsville Boxers, Batting Statistics

NAME	AB	R	H	SO	BA
Tammy	12	2	5	7	.416
Alyssa	14	0	1	13	.071
Travis	12	5	7	5	.583
Jose	15	3	5	10	.333
Akira	13	6	8	5	.615
Walt	14	7	7	7	.500
Taylor	5	4	1	4	.200
Leslie	11	2	4	7	.363
Chloe	9	3	5	4	.555
Derek	8	7	6	2	.250
Maria	14	4	6	8	.571
Lance	12	5	3	9	.250
Carlos	12	4	4	8	.333
Antoine	14	6	5	9	.357
B.J.	5	2	2	3	.400
Sasha	15	7	6	9	.400

NAME	AT BATS	RUNS	HITS	STRIKE OUTS	BATTING AVERAGE
Tammy	12	2	5	7	.416
Alyssa	14	0	1	13	.071
Travis	12	5	7	5	.583
Jose	15	3	5	10	.333
Akira	13	6	8	5	.615
Walt	14	7	7	7	.500
Taylor	5	4	1	4	.200
Leslie	11	2	4	7	.363
Chloe	9	3	5	4	.555
Derek	8	7	6	2	.250
Maria	14	4	6	8	.571
Lance	12	5	3	9	.250
Carlos	12	4	4	8	.333
Antoine	14	6	5	9	.357
B.J.	5	2	2	3	.400
Sasha	15	7	6	9	.400

TABLE 5.2 Less is more Instead of enhancing clarity, lines around cells and abbreviations in headings in the table on the left make the visual more difficult to read.

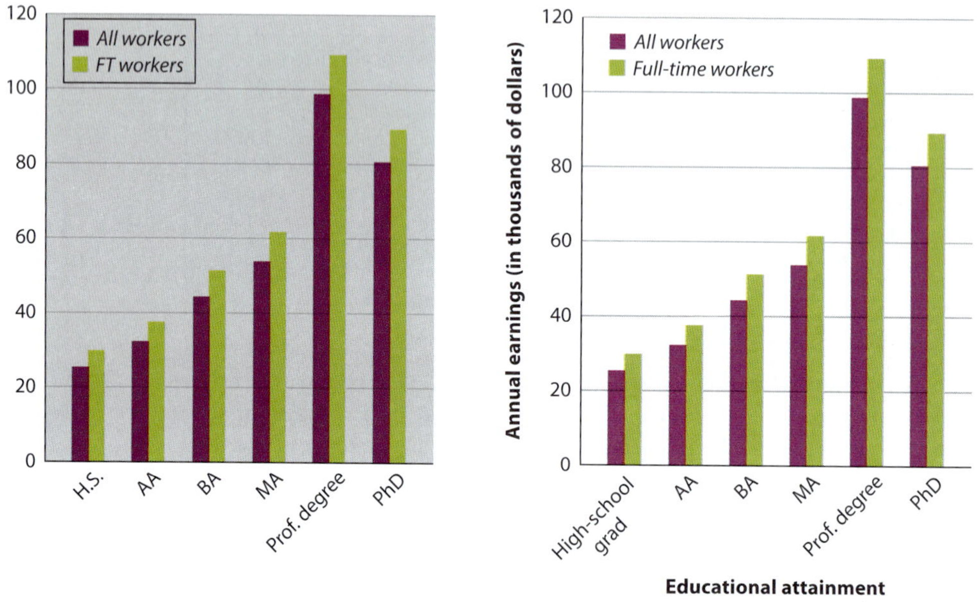

FIGURE 5.6 Clarity and precision The bar graph at left will be more difficult for readers to interpret than the graph at right: "Full-time" is abbreviated to FT and "high-school" to H.S., which could be confusing; no indication is given that the dollar amounts are in thousands; and the shading and the box around the legend make the figure unnecessarily busy.

3. Avoid distortion.

Make sure the information supplied in visuals is complete. The graph on the left in Figure 5.7 distorts the disparity in number of Democratic and Republican voters by starting the scale at 104. Changing the vertical axis in the revised graph on the right more accurately reflects the difference. Cropping photographs to eliminate background or to focus on the main action is acceptable, but cropping to distort information is unethical, as is using image-processing programs to change or distort an image.

> *More about*
> Logical appeals
>   (logos), 142–43
> Emotional appeals
>   (pathos), 144–45

4. Do not manipulate.

Advertisements may use photographs that tug on readers' heartstrings (Figure 5.8). An academic audience, however, will expect images that stir the emotions to be supported by arguments grounded in logic.

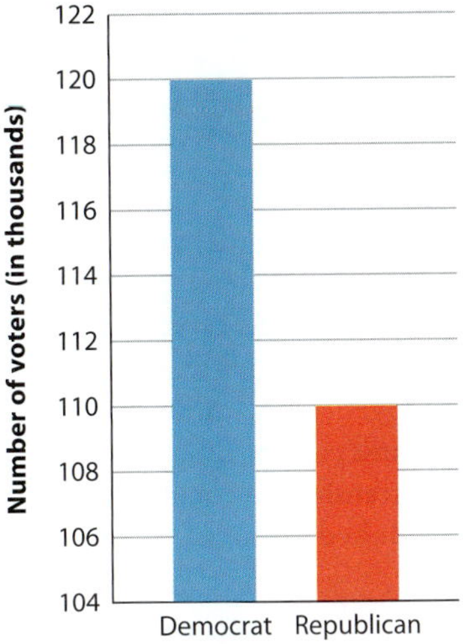

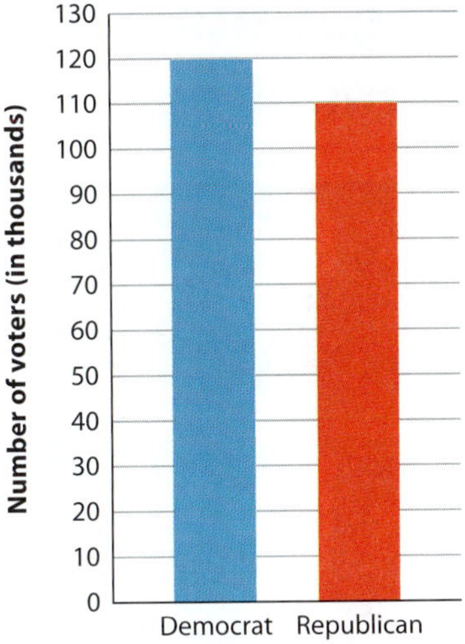

FIGURE 5.7 Distortion in scale By starting the vertical scale at 104, the graph at left distorts the difference in the number of voters. The graph at the right more accurately depicts the differences.

FIGURE 5.8 Manipulative images in advertising This famous advertisement, showing a tearful Iron Eyes Cody, makes a powerful emotional argument in favor of protecting the environment, but it does not offer a reasoned position that would be expected in an academic or business context.
www.adcouncil.org/files/pollution_historic_cody.gif

6 Revising, Editing, Proofreading, and Formatting

IN THIS CHAPTER

REVISING GLOBALLY

a. Gaining perspective, 82

b. Revising your draft, 83

c. Reconsidering your title, 86

REVISING LOCALLY

d. Choosing words carefully, 87

e. Editing sentences, 88

REVISING WITH OTHERS

f. Peer revising, 90

g. Working with a tutor or instructor, 92

PROOFREADING AND FORMATTING

h. Proofreading, 93

i. Formatting, 95

j. Creating and submitting a portfolio, 99

k. Writing Responsibly
Explaining Your Choice of Sources, 104

Student Models
Final Draft, 95–99; Personal Statement, 101–103

As writers revise, they chisel meaning from their first words and sentences, they erase and redraw parts of the broad outline, they carve out details from generalities, and they sand down rough edges. Only through revising, editing, and proofreading carefully can a writer transform a rough-hewn draft into a polished work.

REVISING GLOBALLY: ANALYZING YOUR OWN WORK

Revising globally means learning to re-see—looking at the big picture to address elements like thesis, evidence, audience, context, genre, and ethical responsibilities. The first step toward assessing these aspects of your writing is to take a step backward to gain the distance needed for being objective about your own work. The second is to dive in, adjusting focus and organization, making changes to address your audience more effectively, and developing your ideas more fully.

6a Gaining Perspective

Writers generally feel a sense of "ownership" toward the texts they compose. This helps them produce an authentic voice and a commitment toward the ideas they express. But that sense of ownership can hold a writer back from making needed changes. To gain the objectivity they need, writers can draw on a wide range of techniques, such as those described in the Quick Reference box on the next page.

Quick Reference — Seven Ways to Gain Objectivity about Your Work

1. **Allow time between drafts.** A few days or even a few hours between drafts can provide the distance you need.
2. **Clear your mind.** Do something to get your mind off your paper, such as going for a run or playing a quick game of Guitar Hero.
3. **Learn from other readers.** Having others read and react to your draft will give you a sense of what your text is (and is not) communicating.
4. **Analyze the work of a fellow writer.** Most tutors and teachers will tell you that they learn as much from the coaching experience as do the people whom they coach.
5. **Listen to your draft being read aloud.** Every time your reader stumbles, pauses, or has to reread a passage, mark the spot. Then figure out what caused the interruption and revise accordingly.
6. **Outline your draft.** Once your outline is complete, read it through carefully. If any sections seem unconnected to the thesis or to the sections before or after, reorganize.
7. **Compare your text to others in the target context and genre.** When writing in an unfamiliar context or genre, consider reading professional texts to help you see what does and does not work in your own writing.

> *More about*
> Peer revising,
> 90–92

6b Revising Your Draft

Begin revising by rereading the text. Read your project through to the end before making any changes. Then reread and take notes. Work through each paragraph, focusing on the global issues of thesis, evidence, organization, and development. Most writers focus on just one issue at a time, rereading for each issue. At this stage you should skip over local issues such as spelling and punctuation; do not let them distract you.

1. Thesis and introduction

Because writers often discover and develop their ideas as they compose, the draft thesis may not capture the evolving project's main idea. (Often, the true thesis appears in the conclusion of the first draft.) This might mean you should adjust your evidence to your thesis. More frequently it means you should revise your thesis to match the evidence offered in your draft. Check your draft, too, to be sure that the introduction indicates your purpose—your reasons for writing—and your attitude toward your material. Are you skeptical? Enthusiastic? Still figuring it out?

> *More about*
> Drafting a thesis,
> 30–31
> Revising a thesis,
> 31–33
> Drafting an introduction, 63–65

In addition to revising your thesis, consider your introduction. Is the length proportionate to the whole project? A three-paragraph introduction is fine for a seven-page paper, but if the whole project is only four paragraphs long, the introduction should be very short. Does the introduction provide necessary background, a relevant anecdote, or compelling statistics that will give the audience a context for the thesis?

2. Evidence and counterevidence

> **More about**
> Organizing arguments, 154–55

In rereading your text, you may have had concerns about the evidence you offered in support of your thesis. Perhaps you noticed something weak, irrelevant, or overly general, or that you just did not supply enough evidence. If you need more or better evidence, go back to the idea-generating stage or do additional research. Perhaps your draft talked only about the evidence for your thesis, while ignoring conflicting information and alternative interpretations. An effective argument shows both evidence and counterevidence and explains why the writer believes the evidence is more valid or useful than the counterevidence.

3. Audience

> **More about**
> Audience, 12–15
> Introduction, 63–65
> Development, 40–41, 59–63
> Connotation, 15, 550
> Level of formality, 15, 543
> Conclusions, 65–67

After rereading your text, consider how your readers will react. Have you won them over? Think about your introduction. Does it make your audience want to keep reading? Next, consider the evidence in your body paragraphs. Will it persuade the people who will be reading your project? Now consider your word choice. Is the language appropriate to those people? An academic or business audience will expect a more formal tone but will not need you to define specialized terms; a general audience may be more engaged by an informal tone and may need specialized terms clearly defined. Finally, review your conclusion. Does it provide readers with a feeling of closure? There are many ways to create this sense of closure. Tailor the conclusion to your readers. For a long or complex text, readers may need a summary; for a persuasive essay, readers may want to take action, so offer them a plan.

4. Organization

> **More about**
> Unity, 47–51
> Coherence, 52–57
> Transitions, 276–78, 753

Rereading your text may have alerted you to problems with organization. When revising, make sure that your essay is both unified and coherent. In a unified essay, all the paragraphs support the thesis, and all the details in each paragraph support the paragraph's main idea. When revising, be prepared to

Writing Responsibly — The Big Picture

Another way to think about revising is to focus on your responsibilities to your audience, your topic, other writers, and yourself:

- Have you provided your audience with a worthwhile reading experience?
- Have you covered your topic fully and creatively?

- Have you represented borrowed ideas accurately and acknowledged all your sources, whether you have quoted, summarized, or paraphrased?
- Have you developed a stance that readers will find credible, represented your ideas clearly and powerfully, and written in a voice that is a reflection of your best self?

to SELF

Self Assessment

As you revise, check your draft for the following elements. If the answer to any question is no, make the revisions necessary.

Introduction

- ☐ **Thesis** Does my thesis state my main claim? Does my thesis match the evidence in my draft? Does the introduction indicate my purpose and attitude toward my topic?
- ☐ **Evidence and counterevidence** Does my introduction indicate the complexity of my topic and how I will support my thesis?
- ☐ **Audience** Does my introduction provide needed background information? Will the introduction be engaging or compelling for the people reading my project?
- ☐ **Organization** Does my introduction give readers a sense of how the body of my essay will develop my ideas?

Body Paragraphs

- ☐ **Thesis** Does my whole draft explain why I believe the thesis? Is each body paragraph relevant to my thesis? Is the evidence in each paragraph relevant to the paragraph's topic?
- ☐ **Evidence and counterevidence** Is the evidence I supply relevant? Do I supply enough evidence? Is the evidence compelling? Do I show counterevidence to my thesis? Do I credit my sources?
- ☐ **Audience** Will my readers need more (or less) information? Are my tone and word choices appropriate for this audience?
- ☐ **Organization** Does my organizational pattern suit my evidence? Does each paragraph lead logically to the next?

Conclusion

- ☐ **Thesis** Is my conclusion focused on a relevant issue that shows the importance of my topic? Does it reinforce my purpose?
- ☐ **Evidence and counterevidence** Does my conclusion avoid introducing new supporting evidence?
- ☐ **Audience** Does my conclusion provide an action plan, reflection, or necessary summary?
- ☐ **Organization** Does my conclusion follow logically from my body paragraphs?

delete ideas, facts, and even whole paragraphs—no matter how much you like them—if you notice that they do not support your thesis.

In a coherent essay, the relationship among the paragraphs is clear and logical. Sometimes a text lacks coherence because the writer has not included transitional words and phrases that signal the relationships among ideas. Sometimes a text lacks coherence because a step in the argument has been omitted or the ideas are not fully supported. Also, be sure to clarify the relationships among your paragraphs, by adding or changing transitions or by tightening the logic of your argument or both.

> **More about**
> Relevance, 47, 230–36
> Generating ideas, 20–25
> Developing paragraphs, 59–63
> Finding information, 206–29 (ch. 13)

6c Reconsidering Your Title

Once you have revised your draft globally, revisit your title. It should prepare the audience for what it will read in your essay. In most college projects, your title should accurately reflect not only the topic but also your approach to the topic:

- The Power of Wardrobe: <u>An Analysis</u> of Male Stereotype Influences
- Transcending Stereotypes in Hurston's *Their Eyes Were Watching God*

> Note how these writers use a descriptive phrase (underlined) to make their titles more specific.

You might also use a clever turn of phrase, a quotation, or a question to intrigue your readers and draw them into your project (Figure 6.1):

- Holy Underground Comics, Batman! <u>Moving Away from the Mainstream</u>
- My View from the Sidelines: <u>A Close Reading</u> of Gary Snyder's "Front Lines"

> Note how these writers indicate their approach in their titles (highlighted).

FIGURE 6.1 The importance of a title The title plays an important role in guiding your audience. Consider this painting. Without knowing the title, a viewer might have seen this as a painting of trees. By calling it *Farmhouse in Normandy,* the artist, Paul Cézanne (1839–1906), shifts the viewer's focus from the dense foliage in the foreground to the small building in the background.

A question in your title can also suggest your approach (analysis, comparison-contrast, cause-effect).

- Differing Intentions? Comparing Raphael's Painting with a Print of Raphael's *Saint Cecilia*

> ### Make It **Your Own**
>
> Take a writing project you have gotten back from an instructor, and write a paragraph explaining how you fulfilled your responsibilities as a writer. (See "The Big Picture," p. 85.) Are there any global issues you would revise now if you had the opportunity? Explain.

REVISING LOCALLY: EDITING WORDS AND SENTENCES

Your writing is a reflection of you—your ideas and your attitude toward your topic and audience. Revise locally to make sure that your words and sentences reflect your meaning and that together they create a ***persona*** that is appropriate for your purpose, audience, context, and genre.

persona The apparent personality of the writer as conveyed through tone and style

6d Choosing Your Words with Care

When revising, reconsider your word choices. Each word should reflect your intended meaning; it should have the right ***denotation***. Be very careful to use the word that expresses your exact meaning: Readers may sometimes guess your intent, but you cannot count on this, and you should not expect readers to be charitable.

In addition to denotations, words carry ***connotations***—emotional associations that affect readers' interpretations. Compare *freedom fighter* with *terrorist*. Both words have roughly the same denotation; both refer to people who use violence to achieve political ends, but the connotative difference is enormous.

Next, consider the level of formality that is appropriate to your audience, context, and genre: A text message to a friend may be filled with slang and acronyms, but this informality is rarely appropriate in business or academic writing. Writers who intend to sound sophisticated by trotting out a word like *progenitor* to mean *parent* or even *mom* or *dad* may instead make themselves sound pompous. All writing, though, benefits from avoiding biased language—language that unfairly or offensively characterizes groups or individuals.

> **More about**
> Denotation, 15, 548–49, 551
> Connotation, 15, 550, 551
> Levels of formality, 15, 543
> Biased language, 544–47
> General and specific language, 542–51

> **More about**
> Common sentence problems, fold-out preceding part 8, Grammar Matters
> Sentence types, 597–99
> Sentence variety, 528
> Writing concisely, 496–504 (ch. 26)
> Style, 495–572 (part 7)
> Grammar, 573–702 (part 8)
> Punctuation and mechanics, 747–843 (part 10)

Finally, consider whether you have combined general, abstract language with specific, concrete words; explaining broad issues requires abstract language, but specific words will make your writing more compelling.

6e Editing Your Sentences

When revising, reconsider the structure of your sentences:

1. Are they grammatically correct?
2. Are they varied, and do they emphasize the most important information?
3. Are they as concise as they can be without losing meaning or affecting style?

In most contexts (academic and business, in particular), readers expect sentences to be formed according to the conventions of English grammar. Nongrammatical sentences may confuse, distract, or even annoy readers. Edit your prose to conform to standard written English.

Once you are sure that your sentences are clear and correct, shape them to reflect your emphases. A good way to begin editing for style is to read your draft out loud—or better still, get a friend to read it to you. Listen to the rhythm of your sentences. Do they all sound alike? If so, your sentences probably use the same sentence structure or they all begin the same way.

> **More about**
> Writing concisely, 496–504 (ch. 26)
> Coordination and subordination, 505–17 (ch. 27)
> Parallelism, 518–27 (ch. 28)
> Variety and emphasis, 528–39 (ch. 29)

To correct this problem, consider the information in your sentences. Combine related information in a single sentence by putting the most important information in the independent clause and additional information in the subordinate, or dependent, clause. If the information is of equal weight, use compound sentences and parallel structures to emphasize this balance. Where appropriate, use questions, commands, and exclamations for variety or emphasis.

In addition to writing varied sentences, hone them to eliminate clutter and polish them to add luster to your ideas. Try these strategies to revise for wordiness:

- Eliminate empty expressions, intensifiers, roundabout expressions, and redundancies.
- Eliminate ineffective repetition.
- Favor the active voice.

Writing Responsibly: Making an Essay Long Enough without Wordiness

When your paper is not long enough, you may be tempted to pad, but that might make it hard (and boring) to read. Instead, try these tips:

- Revisit your thesis: Is it too narrow? If so, explore strategies for broadening it.
- Check your evidence: Have you offered facts, statistics, expert testimony, and examples to support your thesis? If not, return to the library or its website to search for more information. Have you explained your evidence so that your audience will understand it? Have you specified exactly how your evidence supports your thesis?
- Analyze your counterevidence: Are you showing your audience the whole range of perspectives or only the data that support your thesis? Most audiences will appreciate knowing not just why you believe your thesis but also why you believe it even though there are other possible interpretations of the issue.

to TOPIC

Writing concisely for the web is particularly important, as most users prefer pages that are easy to scan.

Because not every writer makes the same kinds of mistakes, a personalized editing checklist can come in handy. To create one, try the following:

1. Review the last five texts that you have produced, looking for the kinds of common sentence errors noted in the Grammar Matters foldout preceding part 8.
2. Make a list of the issues you find (or that your instructor marked).
3. Reorganize the list so that the type of mistake you make most frequently is at the top.

Each time you write, use the top five items on your editing checklist to guide your local revisions. Over time, you are likely to find that you make fewer of these errors and can add some of your less common mistakes.

> **More about**
> Empty phrases, 497
> Roundabout and redundant expressions, 498–99
> Ineffective repetition, 499
> Using the active voice, 535–36

NOTE Instructors often use symbols to indicate the most common mistakes. Learn these symbols so that you can correct errors your instructor identifies and improve your draft.

> **More about**
> List of editing symbols, inside back cover

REVISING WITH OTHERS

As writers we can be touchy. We pour ourselves into our texts and feel hurt that others might not understand or appreciate what we have written. Little wonder, then, that we often feel defensive when others read our work before it is finished. Yet paradoxically, getting feedback from a real, live audience is one of the best ways to make sure readers—who do not have you standing by to explain—will understand your writing, will be convinced by your evidence, will be persuaded by your conclusion, and will form a high opinion of you as a responsible, authoritative writer.

6f Revising with Peers

One common way to get feedback from readers is to solicit comments from your peers. In business, this might mean sharing your text with coworkers online or via e-mail. In school, this usually means sharing your draft with your classmates face-to-face, through a class blog or wiki, or in an online writing environment like Connect Composition 2.0, which accompanies this book (mcgrawhillconnect.com). Whether in a business or academic context, the role of writer and peer editor carries its own responsibilities.

1. The writer's role

When readers respond to your text, adopt a stance that is both engaged and receptive:

- **Talk.** Before readers begin to comment, explain what you are trying to accomplish and what you would like help with.
- **Listen.** As others respond to your draft, listen instead of arguing or defending. If readers seem uninformed or inattentive, figure out how you can revise the text so that even an uninformed or inattentive reader can understand what you are trying to say.

Peer Review with Multilingual Students Many students are nervous about working in peer groups. But participation can reduce people's fears by showing that everyone makes mistakes and benefits from their experience with diversity. Group work helps non-native speakers of English become more familiar with the rules and idiosyncrasies of English—resolving difficult issues of idiom and word choice, for example—and more trustful of native speakers' natural abilities with their language.

Native English-speaking students may also be hesitant to work in groups with peers from different language backgrounds. However, workplaces, like college, are increasingly diverse, and just as it is excellent practice for any students to hear responses to their writing, it can be especially valuable coming from classmates who have diverse experiences with language. Your multilingual peers may have perspectives on your topic, organization, word choice, and style that you have not considered.

- **Question.** If your readers are not addressing your concerns or are speaking in generalities, ask them to point to specific passages. Ask yourself what underlying issue they are trying to get at. Do not settle for a disappointing response.

- **Write.** Take notes as your readers talk. What they say may be vivid at the time, but you will be surprised by how quickly you forget the details.

- **Evaluate.** You are the person who must make the final decision. Be open to advice, and consider whether there may be a better way of solving the problem.

2. The peer editor's role

As a reader of a classmate's paper, keep the following guidelines in mind:

- **Stay positive.** Tell the writer what is working well, along with what could be improved (Figure 6.2).

- **Talk to the writer.** Listen and respond to the writer's concerns, whether conducting the session face-to-face or electronically.

- **Look at the big picture, but be specific.** Focus on what the writer is trying to achieve, but back up general comments by pointing to

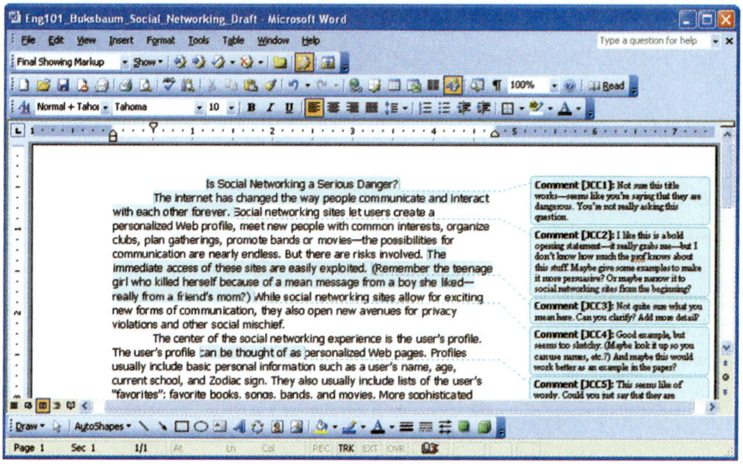

FIGURE 6.2 Electronic peer review If conducting peer review electronically, remember that there is a person on the receiving end of your comments. Stay positive, helpful, and friendly, and link each comment to something specific in the text.

specific passages in the text and explaining as best you can why they do not work for you.

- **Be a reader and a fellow writer—not a teacher, editor, or critic.** Your job is not to judge the text or to rewrite it, but to participate in its composition by helping the writer recognize and resolve issues.

6g Revising with a Tutor or an Instructor

Many colleges sponsor a writing center that offers free tutoring or online services such as NetTutor or Smarthinking. Many instructors also allow students to submit a rough draft of their papers for comment. Take full advantage of these opportunities, and when you do, follow these guidelines:

> **More about**
> Time management, 18–19, 194

- **Be prepared.** Bring a copy of your assignment, your textbook or handbook, any sources you are using, and whatever writing you have already done on the assignment, even if that writing is very informal or a work in progress.

- **Be open to advice.** Bring your own list of issues or concerns about the text or project, but also be receptive to broader issues or suggestions. Your tutor or instructor may have concerns that go beyond your list and that require you to rethink your assumptions, revise your thesis, or revisit the library for additional research.

- **Be an active participant.** If the tutor or instructor makes a suggestion that you do not understand, ask for an explanation (and take notes). If you do not agree with a suggestion, consider the underlying issue and offer an alternative resolution. Then revise thoughtfully and fully.

Work **Together**

Exchange with a classmate a paper you are working on or recently completed. Explain what you are trying to accomplish, and listen to your classmate's comments, asking for clarification and taking notes. Now respond to your classmate's draft. Remember to point to specific words, sentences, and paragraphs.

Make It **Your Own**

> Using comments you received from your classmate, revise your draft. After completing the process, write a paragraph discussing which of your peer's suggestions made the biggest difference in your revision, and why. If you did not find the process helpful, discuss what you or your classmate might have done to make it more productive.

PROOFREADING AND FORMATTING

6h Proofreading

> *More about*
> Using a dictionary, 560–62
> Usage glossary, G14–G19
> Homonyms and near homonyms, 563–65

When revising, your focus is on your ideas and how you express them; when you proofread, you pull back from the content of the essay to concentrate on correcting errors.

To proofread effectively, divorce yourself from the content you know so well, so that you can see the text as it appears on the page. An effective way to achieve this distance is to print out your draft and read the hard copy line by line from the bottom up. Mark each correction on the printout as you read; enter them one by one, and then check to make sure that you have made each correction without introducing additional errors. Another option for proofreading is to work in teams: One person reads the text (including punctuation marks) out loud, while the other person marks errors on the printout.

Writing **Responsibly** — Beware the Spelling Checker!

While spell-check software can be very helpful in catching typos, it cannot distinguish between homonyms (*they're, their*) or other frequently confused words (*lay, lie; affect, effect*). Spelling checkers may even lead you astray, suggesting words that are close to the word you mistyped (*defiant* for the misspelled *definate*) but worlds away from the word you intended (*definite*). As a writer, you have a responsibility to use words that communicate what you want to say and to not leave your reader guessing. Do not merely run your computer's spell-check software; also use a dictionary to double-check the spelling checker's suggestions, check usage in the usage glossary, and proofread your text carefully yourself. Only you can know what you *meant* to say!

to SELF

Self Assessment — A Checklist for Proofreading

Before you submit your text to your instructor, check the following elements. If you answer no to any of the questions, make the revisions necessary.

Spelling
- ☐ Did you spell-check your project using your word processing software?
- ☐ Did you read through the text carefully, looking for misused words?
- ☐ Did you check specifically for words you frequently confuse or misspell?

Punctuation
- ☐ Did you check sentence punctuation, especially use of the comma and the apostrophe?
- ☐ Did you double check that, in a text with dialog or in a research project, all quotations have quotation marks and that end punctuation and in-text citations are correctly placed?
- ☐ Did you check specifically for errors you regularly make (for example, comma splices or fused sentences)?

Other Errors
- ☐ Did you check to make sure that remnants of previous corrections—an extra word, letter, or punctuation mark—do not remain?
- ☐ Did you check that you have included all in-text citations where needed (for summaries, paraphrases, quotations, or ideas you have borrowed for a research project)?
- ☐ Did you check that all in-text citations are included in the reference list or list of works cited, and make sure that all formats are correct and consistent?

Proofreading When English Is Not Your First Language If you have difficulty proofreading a project, try reading it aloud; this may help you recognize errors. Also, ask your instructor if you can have a friend, classmate, or tutor help you proofread. A visit to the writing center may result in some helpful tips or practice, as well.

Make It Your Own

Customize the proofreading checklist in the Self-Assessment on this page to reflect your own needs by adding the errors you have made on your last two or three writing projects.

Work Together

Working in pairs, trade printed copies of a writing project. Have the other student read the text out loud while you mark corrections. When the process is complete for one text, trade roles with your partner and repeat the process.

> **More about**
> Visual design, 162–70 (ch. 9)
> MLA format, 332–36
> APA format, 377–81

6i Formatting an Academic Text

The Quick Reference box on this page provides guidelines for formatting an academic text. More coverage of formatting and incorporating visuals appears elsewhere in this book.

> **More about**
> Prewriting and earlier drafts of "Alternative Energy: Does It Really Offer an Alternative?":
> Freewriting, 21–22
> Brainstorming, 22, 26
> Cluster diagramming, 23
> Journalists' questions, 24
> Thesis, 30–32
> Tree diagram, 34
> Outline, 36–37
> First draft, 42–44

Quick Reference — Formatting Academic Texts

- Leave 1- to 1.5-inch margins.
- Indent the first line of each paragraph by half an inch.
- Use a standard font, such as Times New Roman or Cambria, in 12-point size.
- Use headings, headers, page numbers, and paragraph indents to help readers navigate the text easily.
- Format headings of the same level the same way throughout the project.
- Use figure and table numbers to guide the reader from text to visual.
- Use a style guide that is appropriate to your discipline.
- Keep your design simple; focus on content.

Student Model Final Draft

You have seen Betsy Smith's essay as it developed, from freewriting and brainstorm, to draft thesis statement and outline, to initial draft. Now consider her final draft. If you compare this to Smith's earlier draft, you will see how she has revised globally and locally to tighten her thesis, develop her evidence, and make her introduction and conclusion more compelling.

Smith 1

Betsy Smith

Professor Locke

Composition 102

18 Oct. 2012

Alternative Energy: Does It Really Offer an Alternative?

In general, members of the environmental, or green, movement work toward a common goal: to establish and maintain a healthy planet. Although environmentalists might agree on this overarching objective, groups within the movement have different opinions about how best to preserve nature. Some focus on the big picture—stopping climate change—and so they work to reduce our carbon emissions by providing alternatives to fossil fuels; others focus on local issues, and so they work to preserve habitats for local plants and animals. Often, the result is conflict.

When it comes to alternative energy, environmentalists are divided. There are those who see the numerous environmental benefits of using alternative fuel sources. Alternative energy reduces greenhouse gas emissions, which improves air quality and slows the rate of global warming. Renewable energy sources—namely, the sun, wind, and water—are sustainable; they cannot be depleted and therefore can be used for the foreseeable future ("Environmental Benefits"). Even when they acknowledge these advantages, however, opposing environmentalists point out that there are drawbacks as well. New structures needed to generate this energy can have negative consequences on their surroundings, causing problems that range from ruining picturesque views to endangering some species of animals to, in the case of nuclear energy, poisoning human beings (Breen, Glod, Mark). As serious and time-sensitive as the issue of climate change is, alternative energy is not a solution if it will be just as harmful to wildlife as conventional energy.

One type of alternative energy that seems safe on the surface is wind energy: It relies on a clean, renewable resource that will have little effect on the local environment. Or will it? Wind turbines reach hundreds of feet into the air (Glod), endangering any bird or bat that flies through this air space. Eric Glitzenstein, an attorney with a public-interest law firm and president of the Wildlife Advocacy Project, testified before Congress that a 44-turbine wind farm in West Virginia killed dozens of migrating birds in a single night (6). The *New York Times* reported that both parties to a lawsuit over construction of a wind farm in Greenbrier County, West Virginia, acknowledge that more than 100,000 bats will be killed over twenty years by the 122 proposed turbines. Some of those killed might be the endangered Indiana bat, whose population has already fallen by half since 1967 (Glod). Opponents of this wind farm recognize that alternative energy sources, like wind power, are necessary if we are to slow global warming, but they are also concerned about the hazards the new technology creates.

Topic sentence introduces example 1

Transition

Body

Solar energy plants, too, are an alternative to more polluting fossil fuels, but they may also threaten local wildlife. The *San Diego Union Tribune* reports that some environmentalists in Imperial County, California, are fighting the construction of solar energy facilities. They argue that the facility will endanger both flat-tailed horned lizards and peninsular bighorn sheep (Breen). Another solar project in the Mojave Desert is being opposed on the grounds that it will threaten California desert tortoises and endangered cacti (Breen).

Topic sentence introduces example 2

Transition

Smith 3

Nuclear energy is also being touted as a clean alternative to fossil fuels. With the looming threat of global warming, some environmentalists now feel that increasing nuclear power production is preferable to burning fossil fuels. According to Stewart Brand, the founder and editor of the *Whole Earth Catalog,* "Climate change . . . changes priorities. Suddenly, worrying about radiation 6,000 years from now kind of goes down the list" (qtd. in Mark). Antinuclear activists, however, remind us of the accidents that occurred at nuclear power plants in Three Mile Island, Pennsylvania, and Chernobyl, Ukraine, in the 1970s and 1980s; they also warn that there is still no safe way to dispose of radioactive fuel rods and that, since we have not yet found a way to store nuclear waste safely, using even more nuclear energy will increase the environmental damage (Mark).

Clearly, it is important that we reduce our carbon footprint, but it is also important that we protect the living things with which we share the planet. In the face of green versus green conflicts, we must look for realistic solutions. In some cases, that is already being done. Wind-power company Invenergy, for example, has proposed several compromises with Greenbrier County residents to reduce the number of bats killed, including using sound to keep bats away from the turbines (Glod). In the Imperial County and Mojave Desert cases, new locations for construction are being considered (Breen). In terms of nuclear power, new theories about how to store nuclear waste safely are being proposed and tested (Mark). More importantly, however, we must change the way we approach the problem. Yes, we will continue to need energy, but shouldn't we also consider how we can reduce our energy demands as well? We are faced with the prospect of climate change today because of our recklessness with natural resources. It is time to consider how we can do more with less.

Smith 4

Works Cited

Breen, Steve. "Green vs. Green." *SignonSanDiego.com*. San Diego Union Tribune, 21 Oct. 2009. Web. 6 Oct. 2010.

Glitzenstein, Eric. "Testimony of Eric R. Glitzenstein before the House Subcommittee on Fisheries, Wildlife, and Oceans, House Committee on Resources, May 1, 2007." *Wildlife Advocacy Project.* Meyer, Glitzenstein, & Crystal, n.d. Web. 6 Oct. 2010.

Glod, Maria. "Tiny Bat Pits Green against Green." *Washington Post.* Washington Post, 22 Oct. 2009. Web. 6 Oct. 2010.

Mark, Jason. "The Fission Division: Will Nuclear Power Split the Green Movement?" *Earth Island Journal* 22.3 (2007): n. pag. Web. 6 Oct. 2010.

List of works cited follows MLA style

EXERCISE 6.1 Assessing a revision

Compare the final version of Betsy Smith's essay (above) with the earlier version (pp. 42–44). Which of her changes are global and which are local? Is there anything more that you would suggest she do with this essay before submitting it? Explain.

6j Creating and Submitting a Portfolio

Some instructors (and prospective employers) may ask you to submit a writing portfolio. A portfolio may contain any of the following:

- A collection of texts that show your best work

- A collection of texts (such as a proposal, a formal report, a set of instructions, a website) that demonstrate the range of work you have produced
- A collection of texts from a single project (such as journal entries, freewriting and brainstorming, outline, first draft, revised draft) that show your writing process

What you include depends on the portfolio's purpose, audience, and context: You may create a portfolio of your best work to demonstrate your writing skills for admission to a course (a creative writing course, for example); you may create a portfolio showing the range of writing you have done to apply for a job; or you may create a portfolio to demonstrate the process you followed for a composition class.

As you select the contents, consider your audience:

- What kinds of writing projects will interest your readers?
- How many examples will your readers expect you to include? Will they want to see multiple examples of the same type of work, or is one example sufficient? Will they be interested in work you have created in electronic media, or will they focus exclusively on your writing?
- How will they want you to submit the portfolio—electronically or in print?

Once you have selected the items to be included, think about how you want to arrange the contents. A portfolio that shows your writing process should be arranged chronologically; a portfolio that includes a range of your work might be arranged from strongest to weakest; and a portfolio that includes your best work might be arranged in order of interest to your audience. While the contents of a portfolio will vary, in general, include the following:

Title page or home page For a printed portfolio, include a title page with the following information:

- Title (for example, "One Writer's Journey through Sophomore Composition" or "Portfolio for Application to Stockbridge Writers' Group")
- Identifying information (name, course, contact information)
- Date of submission

For an electronic portfolio, include this information in a separate document or on the home page.

Table of contents or menu with hyperlinks For a printed portfolio, include a table of contents listing the items in the order in which they are arranged, number the pages sequentially, and provide page references in your table of contents. An electronic portfolio should include a menu with hyperlinks to the contents.

Personal statement Whether submitted electronically or in print, a portfolio should include a personal statement that describes the contents of the portfolio and explains your choice and arrangement of selections and what the selections demonstrate about you as a writer. For portfolios submitted electronically, consider embedding links to your writing selections from your personal statement as well as from the menu.

> ### Make It **Your Own**
>
> Review three recent writing projects and consider what they reveal about you as a writer. Think about the process you used to write them, the choices you made as you worked on them, and your level of satisfaction with the finished pieces. Then write a two-page reflective essay that could be used as the basis for a personal statement to introduce them in a portfolio. Use specific examples from these texts to support your claims.

Submission Submitting a printed portfolio is straightforward: You assemble the contents, make sure each page is clearly labeled with your name and a brief title, place the contents in a folder or three-ring binder with your identifying information on the front, double-check the contents against the table of contents, and hand it in.

Submitting an electronic portfolio offers more options: You might create an electronic folder that contains your documents and either save the documents to a disc and mail it or attach the folder to an e-mail. Alternatively, you might create a website, post the contents to a server, and send the URL to recipients. Consult your recipient in advance to determine the best method of electronic submission.

> **More about**
> Creating a website, 176–81

Student Model Personal Statement

Consider the following personal statement. Notice how Rachana Ky lists the items he included in his writing portfolio, briefly describes his reasons for selecting them, and points out what he believes are the strengths of each.

Dear Professor Howard:

Here is my writing portfolio, the culmination of the semester's work. The selections I have included are the literacy development essay and ethnography from Writing 205 (Sophomore Composition) and a paper on the Parthenon from Architecture 133 (History of Architecture). The purpose of including these papers is to show how I write on a range of assignments, from the personal to the purely academic. The literacy development essay was based on my own life experience. The ethnography describes my observations in the weight room but is more objective than the literacy development essay. The Parthenon essay is the most objective of the three, focusing on a topic about which I have no personal knowledge.

Each of these three pieces of work reflects different qualities or characteristics that reveal me as a writer. The literacy development essay describes my intellectual growth. This piece was written for a broad audience. To show my own growth, I used simple, direct language in the early parts of the essay and more sophisticated language later. My development is best reflected through the verb choices: From simple forms of "to be" and "learned," I moved on to "flogged," "balked," and "superseded."

My ethnography strives to capture the mood of the weight room, and I used descriptive language to convey the smell of body odor, the feel of extreme exertion, and the look of the sweaty, muscular bodies. I also tried to capture the different mind-sets of those using the weight room, from steroidal bodybuilders to svelte women striving for better abs.

The paper on the Parthenon shows my writing when it is limited to the language of architecture. It describes the Parthenon, what it meant to the people who built it, and the history of the building (what remains and how pieces of it were dispersed across the Western world). I notice that in this essay, my word choices were fairly simple, but I was still able to get my point across without using all the fancy words used by architecture critics.

I believe the introduction to each paper is strong. In general, when I cannot come up with a good start to a paper, I notice that I have problems developing the rest of the essay, so I work hard to develop an introduction that creates a sense of what my paper will discuss and how. The first two samples in particular, where I was not limited to following a certain style, have particularly engaging introductions that, I hope, have captured the reader's imagination.

I look forward to hearing your thoughts about the enclosed.

Rachana

Rachana Ky

6k Writing Matters · Revising, Editing, Proofreading, and Formatting

Writing Responsibly
Explaining Your Choice of Sources

> **Make It Your Own!** When college writers share their opinion of their sources, their text is more interesting and convincing. Rather than just quoting from your sources, tell *why* you are quoting them, and your writing will be more persuasive.

In much of your college writing, you select and work with sources: You decide how to use sources to help convey your thesis. Your basic responsibility is to acknowledge those sources, cite them correctly, and provide full publication information about them at the end of your paper. When you talk *about* your sources—tell what you think of your source and its information—you invite your audience into your thinking processes and portray yourself as an experienced academic writer.

When college writing instructors involved in the Citation Project studied research papers from US colleges, they noticed how few students talked about their sources. Most of the papers just pulled out information—usually a brief quotation—from sources, as if all the sources were alike. The nature of the sources and the student's thoughts about them remained invisible to the audience. The following example, from a paper on sexism and sexual violence, shows the drab result:

First draft

[Student's voice] Hostility toward women can be seen even in the ancient West. [Citation] Stevenson observes, [Quotation] "Livy's underlying message, it would seem, is that Roman men have to regulate public contributions by prominent women, and not accept female advice too easily, without prolonged consideration" (189).

The material from the Stevenson source is accurately quoted and cited, and the sentences flow. But the passage provokes questions rather than insights. Who are Stevenson and Livy? Where did this source come from? Why did the writer choose it? Why should the writer's audience respect Stevenson's opinions? What else did the source say? What was the context in which the quotation appeared? These are the kinds of questions readers ask, and answering them will bring your text to life:

Revised draft

[Student's voice] Hostility toward women can be seen even in the ancient West. [Credentials of author and publisher] Tom Stevenson, a classics scholar at the University of Queensland, writes in the scholarly journal *Classical World* [Citation] that the Roman historian Livy described women who supported their menfolks' success, which might seem to be a compliment to the women. But notice that the women aren't having their own successes. Furthermore, all of Livy's women are either described too briefly, or they are flawed. [Summary of the remainder of the source] Even as Stevenson provides this analysis, he also cautions against

Revised draft continued

> being too simplistic about Livy's portrayal of women; some of their faults were because their men were flawed. Still, Stevenson concludes, "Livy's underlying message, it would seem, is that Roman men have to regulate public contributions by prominent women, and not accept female advice too easily, without prolonged consideration" (189).

- Counter-evidence
- Quotation
- Citation

Source: Stevenson, Tom. "Women of Early Rome as *Exempla* in Livy, *AB Urbe Condita*, Book 1." *Classical World* 104.2 (Winter 2011): 175–189. Print.

Now, not only is the material from the source accurately quoted and cited, but Levy has been identified, and Stevenson's credentials and the authority of the publication have been established, along with a description of his argument.

Sometimes you choose to use a source because you like its argument or presentation of information, even if it may not be particularly scholarly. In these cases, too, you should let your audience know why you have chosen the source:

> One good way to understand the treatment of women in contemporary society is to consult newsmedia. They are not reports of research written by experts, but rather are sources that reflect and shape popular opinion. *Time* magazine publishes an article on date rape because it believes this is an issue that readers will or should care about. It also reports on current events. So it is *Time* that reports on a congressional bill intended to reduce sexual violence in colleges. Why is the bill needed? The answer is in the shocking numbers the magazine cites: "One in five college women will be the victim of a sexual assault (and 6% of men)" (Webley).

- Information about why the writer chose this source
- Summary of some information in the source
- Student's voice
- Quotation
- Citation

Source: Webley, Kayla. "It's Not Just Yale: Are Colleges Doing Enough to Combat Sexual Violence?" *Time.com* 18 Apr. 2011: n. pag. Web. 20 Apr. 2011.

Self Assessment

Review your work with each source. Have you done the following?

- ☐ Identify the author of the source and his or her credentials. Did you show what makes you trust this person? ▶ *Analyzing and crafting arguments, 134–60*
- ☐ Identify the publisher of the source and its credentials. Did you show what makes you trust this organization? ▶ *Finding information, 206–29*
- ☐ Consider the date of publication. Did you provide and comment on the publication date, if it affects your trust in the source?
- ☐ Summarize the source. Did you indicate how the selection you have drawn from contributed to the argument the source was making? ▶ *Evaluating information, 230–45*
- ☐ Provide additional discussion. Did you help your audience understand the reasons you chose this source and your selections from it?

Part Two

Reasoning Matters

Reading, Thinking, and Arguing

7 Thinking and Reading Critically 108
8 Analyzing and Crafting Arguments 134

7 Thinking and Reading Critically

IN THIS CHAPTER

a. Comprehending, 108

b. Reflecting, 114

c. Preparing to write, 119

d. Writing Responsibly
   Understanding, representing the entire source, 132

Student Models
Summary, 111; Double-Entry Reading Journal, 118; Claims and Evidence Analysis, 121; Advertisement Critique, 121; Prewrite, 123; Critical Response Essay, 127

Professional Models
Essay, 112; Editorial, 115

When you read critically, you peel back a text to uncover its meaning. You begin with comprehension, just getting the gist of the text. Next comes reflection, when you annotate and analyze the text. As you prepare to write, you explore not only what is written but also what is left unstated, and you draw on your own experience and other texts to hone your evaluation. The process of peeling a text, as you would the layers of an onion, is what drives and deepens the intellectual process.

7a Comprehending

In our day-to-day lives, we read constantly, and the texts range from instant messages to thousand-page books. Some texts, like street signs (Figure 7.1), are simple messages of just a few words or images; they are designed to communicate information quickly, simply, and clearly.

Most of the texts you read in college were written to inform or educate you about an issue or topic. They may also have a secondary

---

Writing Responsibly / Engaging with What You Read

When conducting research, you have a responsibility to engage with the texts you read. If you are struggling, begin by determining what barrier is keeping you from making a connection with the text: Is the language too challenging? Is the topic unfamiliar or too familiar? Is your concentration poor because you did not eat lunch? Then try to overcome the barrier: Use a dictionary to acquaint yourself with the unfamiliar vocabulary; consider the material as a primer or a recapitulation of an important topic; eat a sandwich.

to TOPIC

purpose: to persuade you to accept a position on that issue or topic. Because most college-level reading assignments attempt to engage you in the complexities of an issue, you should read the text several times. You will get the most out of complex texts if you preview the text, read through it quickly to get the gist, write a brief summary, and, most importantly, enjoy what you read!

Reading for Comprehension Many people think the key to better reading is to read slower. Native and non-native English speakers may slow their *speech* to help their listeners comprehend, but the same idea may not work for *reading*. In fact, research shows that reading faster can help increase your comprehension, because you associate ideas more easily.

1. Preview the text.

The more you know about a text before you begin reading, the more efficiently you will be able to read. Unless you are reading a work of literature—a novel, a poem, or a play—resist the urge to dive in and read the text from beginning to end. Instead, start by ***previewing:***

- **Note the title and subtitle.** The title sets the stage for the work and may reveal its topic, its approach, and even its tone.
- **Read the abstract, introduction, conclusion, and sidebars.** Many scholarly journals place an ***abstract,*** or summary, at the beginning of each article; abstracts also appear in article database entries. Other texts may offer overviews of main ideas and important questions in introductions, prologues, conclusions, boxes, or sidebars. Textbook chapters often conclude with study questions that provide a framework for thinking about key topics.
- **Read first sentences and paragraphs.** In short texts, read the first sentence of each paragraph; in longer texts, read the first paragraph of each section. From this you will gain a preliminary sense of the topic and argument of the text.
- **Note the key terms.** In textbooks, important terms are often indicated in italic or boldfaced type and may also be listed at the end of the chapter or in a glossary. Terms are generally defined in the body or margins of a text; the text may also have a glossary.
- **Read the headings and subheadings.** If the text is organized into sections with headings, skim them for an outline.

FIGURE 7.1 Everyday texts Street signs convey information through words, shapes, and images. They are simple, so we can act on them immediately, almost without thinking.

- **Scan figures and illustrations.** Figures may signal important ideas. Visuals convey complex processes quickly and are often accompanied by a succinct explanation (Figure 7.2).

2. Get the gist.

> **More about**
> Paraphrasing and patchwriting, 252–56

After surveying the text, you are ready to read it once through from beginning to end to get the *gist*, or basic idea. As you read, circle words or phrases you have questions about, but press on without looking them up—yet. When you have finished, close the book and write down what you remember. Try to *paraphrase*, to state the ideas in your own words, rather than reproducing the language of the text. If you can accurately paraphrase the text's major points without *patchwriting*, you have grasped its literal meaning. If you cannot, read the text again, close the book, and try to paraphrase once more.

> **patchwriting** Using the language or sentence structure of the source; not putting the content into fresh words

3. Summarize the text.

When you feel you have a good (though not necessarily perfect) grasp of the text, *summarize* it. A paraphrase may be as long as (or longer than) the passage it restates, but a summary shortens it by restating only the main idea and major supporting points of a text. To qualify as a summary, what you write should be at least 50 percent shorter than the text it restates; many summaries are only 10 percent (or less) as long as the original. The summary on the next page captures

Ancestor to whales. *Ambulocetus*, an ancestor to modern whales, dated to 50 MYA. The presence of limbs is evidence that land-based mammals gave rise to whales.

FIGURE 7.2 Preview figures Previewing the figures can also provide insight. This figure, for example, emphasizes the descent of whales, pointing to an emphasis on evolution.
(From Mader, *Biology*, 9th ed., New York, McGraw-Hill, 2007, p. 297)

the main idea and major supporting points of the Brent Staples editorial that Alea Wratten writes about later in this chapter. The original editorial, which starts on page 116, is about 730 words; this summary is about 140, a bit less than a quarter of the original.

Student Model — "Reflecting on Brent Staples's Editorial 'How Hip-Hop Music Lost Its Way and Betrayed Its Fans,'" Alea Wratten, 128–30

Student Model Summary

> Summary of "How Hip-Hop Music Lost Its Way and Betrayed Its Fans"
>
> In this editorial, *New York Times* writer Brent Staples claims that both rap music and the way it is marketed perpetuate racial stereotypes and glorify violence, materialism, and sexism. Citing the example of an actual gang war in the 1990s, Staples argues that rival rappers use their music to insult each other and initiate violence. 50 Cent, for instance, timed a post–radio-interview gun battle to coincide with the release of his album *Massacre*. Staples worries that rap will influence inner-city kids, who already face poverty and violence, to adopt the glamorous "gangsta" lifestyle and maybe even wind up in prison. He also blames producers like Jimmy Iovine and Dr. Dre for the direction hip-hop has taken. Staples ends by saying that he feels the public will not stand for much more of this; if hip-hop continues in this vein, he thinks, it won't last.

For any complex reading assignment, writing a summary will help you to remember the main points of the text, and the summary you create will also provide a useful reference. As with paraphrasing, avoid patchwriting: The more you can write about a reading in your own words, the better you will understand it.

4. Enjoy the text.

You are most likely to comprehend a text when you enjoy it, and you are far more likely to do so if you *think* about the text as you read. Engage with it as you would with a message from a friend or with a new movie you have been anticipating. Pleasure often lies in the details: a nice turn of phrase, a subtle joke, or a clever comparison. Enjoyment does not require total agreement with—or

> **More about**
> Synthesis, 123–25, 262–63

even a complete understanding of—every word on the page. It requires only active engagement and an open mind. This approach can also improve your academic performance and your ability to connect (or *synthesize*) what you read with material from other classes and your own life.

EXERCISE 7.1 Comprehending the text

Look at the title of the article below, and then write a sentence indicating what you think the essay will be about, based on the title alone. Next, read the essay and summarize the text. Finally, write one or two sentences explaining what you found surprising, interesting, or challenging about this essay, and why.

Professional Model Essay

Why Uncertainty May Be Bad for Your Health
By Wray Herbert

   I recall sitting once before an open window, listening to the radio. Outside it was pouring rain. I mean horizontal monsoon, umbrellas buckling in people's hands. But on the radio, the DJ was calmly announcing "a chance of showers today." He's right, I remember thinking, an excellent chance.

   The English language is not very helpful when it comes to talking about uncertainty. What does it really mean when a report forecasts "a possibility" of rain or snow today or a friend assures you that there's "not much chance" of dying in a plane crash? And when it comes to personal health, the vocabulary of likelihood is often even foggier because it's so laden with emotion. How do you respond if you're told that it's "possible" your breast cancer will recur, or that a serious side effect of treatment is "unlikely"?

   According to a new study, there's a good chance you end up misinformed and make unwise health decisions as a result. That's not only because language is inexact, but also because quirks of our psychology make it very difficult to convey probabilities as simply that: probabilities. Instead, because of a deep-seated motivation to be polite and tactful, we clumsily try to make things seem better than they are and often end up making them worse.

   Much of this miscommunication has to do with what social scientists call "face work." . . . When we are forced by circumstance to do things that threaten someone—disagreeing with a colleague, for example—we resort to strategies that we hope will dampen the threat and help them save face. One strategy is to fall back on words like "possibly."

   Doctor-patient conversation is an example of such a face-threatening situation, because doctors often have to tell people unwanted news. They often resort to qualifiers when speaking with patients about the risks of developing certain medical conditions or about potential side effects to a drug or a procedure. Psychologist Jean-François Bonnefon of the University of Toulouse in France wanted to explore whether misuse of probability language might have untoward health consequences. Specifically, he wanted to know: when delivering bad news to a patient, do physicians help unfortunate patients save face by using words like "possibly" just to be polite? And if they do, are they more apt to use face-saving language if the health threat is more severe? How do patients interpret such polite euphemisms? Do they work, or backfire?

To explore this idea in the laboratory, Bonnefon had several hundred people imagine that they were patients and that their family doctor had given them some bad news: for some the news was that they would "possibly" develop insomnia within the year. Others were told that they would "possibly" go deaf inside a year. The psychologist then asked the participants if the doctor meant "possibly" to mean 10 percent, 20 percent and so on up to 100 percent. They were also asked whether they thought the doctor was actually making a medical risk assessment, or just being nice.

The results, as reported in the September issue of the journal *Psychological Science,* were unambiguous. When the "doctor" talked about the possibility of deafness, patients believed he was describing a much greater likelihood than when he discussed the possibility of insomnia. Bonnefon labels this phenomenon the "severity bias," meaning that "possibly" is taken as an actual prediction of modest risk when the subject is something like insomnia—a condition that is unpleasant, certainly, but not devastating. But with deafness, the same probability word is taken as diplomatic finessing of dire news. In other words, the "patients" didn't believe the doctor when the threat was serious. They knew intuitively that he was not being forthcoming, and they gave the news the worst possible spin. . . .

These findings have some serious implications for personal health choices and for health policy. Doctors are encouraged to be direct about potential side effects of treatments. They use qualifiers like "possibly" and "likely" all the time, as do package inserts that accompany prescription drugs. Such terms are nebulous enough. If a side effect or medical condition is "possible," should a patient take precautions—or seek potential treatment to lower their perceived risk? But the confusion only grows if patients don't know a phrase's true intended purpose—if they're unsure whether the doctor is being kind to save face or is serious about the risk assessment. That patient could easily end up reading the remark as tactfulness and so assume that the news is far worse than it is. Treatment choices made as a result of such misunderstandings would be at best uninformed, and at worst life-threatening.

Though it may go against all of our natural impulses, physicians need to forget about tact and social niceties when talking to patients about risk, Bonnefon concludes. This means avoiding vague words like "possibly" and stating explicitly the known risk (whether it's one in 100 or one in 10) whenever possible. It may not seem nice. But it's better than taking the risk of killing a patient with kindness.

—*Newsweek*, 19 Sept. 2006. Web. 15 Mar. 2007.

Make It **Your Own**

Find a photograph in a printed or online newspaper or use one from this book, and write a one- or two-paragraph description of it. Be sure to indicate your first impression and what the photo depicts. Then photocopy the image, but place it behind your description so that readers will see the description *before* they see the image.

Work **Together**

Trade descriptions with a classmate and without looking at the photograph, try to form a mental picture of the image. Now look at the photograph. Discuss how well the description captured the image and what you would change. Did the description change what you noticed or the impact the image had on you?

7b Reflecting

Reflecting refers to the important transition between getting the general idea (the gist) and fully comprehending a text. Steps in reflecting on a text may include annotating it or writing about it in your reading journal.

1. Annotate the text.

A first step in reflecting upon a text is to reread it with a pencil or pen in hand (or a computer at the ready). Careful annotations can be useful when it comes

> **Tech** Annotating Online Texts
>
> When you read from a screen instead of a page, consider saving the text to your hard drive, flash drive, or network drive and using Track Changes or footnoting options to comment on a text or the highlighting function to mark key ideas.

Reasoning Matters • Reflecting   **7b**   115

> ## Self Assessment
>
> When annotating an image, analyze the following elements. Be sure to answer each of these questions and take the suggested steps to offer a thorough critique.
> - ☐ **Tone.** Does it strike you as warm, amused, angry, dispassionate? Point to specific parts of the image that convey the tone.
> - ☐ **Responses.** What responses does the image elicit from you, and why? Again, tie your responses directly to elements of the image.
> - ☐ **Biases.** Do you detect any assumptions or biases? If so, tell what they are and how the visual indicates them.
> - ☐ **Connections.** Does this image remind you of another visual or printed text? If so, in what ways? (Be specific.) Make any connections between the visual and your own experience change question mark to a period.

time to study for a test or to respond to a text in writing. As you annotate, focus on some or all of the following:

- **Definitions.** Look up and write down definitions of unfamiliar words.
- **Concepts.** Underline the most important, interesting, or difficult concepts.
- **Tone.** Note the writer's tone—sarcastic, sincere, witty, shrill.
- **Biases.** Look out for the writer's biases and unstated assumptions (and your own).
- **Fallacies.** Is the text illogical or misleading?
- **Responses.** Ask questions and note your own reactions and insights.
- **Connections.** Make connections with other texts you have read or your own experiences.

Read footnotes and any text in parentheses: They seldom contain the main claims or supporting evidence, but they can provide key background information, references to additional scholarship on a topic, and juicy tidbits the writer felt compelled to share.

> **More about**
> Tone, 15–16, 136, 543, 548–50
> Bias, 544–47
> Avoiding logical fallacies, 156–60
> Note taking, 250–63
> Working bibliography, 200–05

Professional Model Editorial

Read the following newspaper editorial by Brent Staples. The annotations to this editorial, which appeared in the *New York Times,* reflect Alea Wratten's thoughts, insights, and struggles with a text she would later write about. The comments define unfamiliar vocabulary, note reflections, and make connections.

How Hip-Hop Music Lost Its Way and Betrayed Its Fans

By BRENT STAPLES

(12 May 2005)

I loved "Just Walk on By" (same author)

There are certainly negative images out there, but there are many positive African American role models, too (including Staples).

virulent—extremely infectious or damaging. Why is rap the most "virulent" music?

Central argument—raises an important issue but over-generalizes.

"palette" compares music to painting

misogyny—hatred of women

Have things changed since then?

Is this logic backwards? Sometimes gangsta rappers are violent, but does their music describe the violence or cause it?

The "rap community" isn't entirely gangsta rap; there are other kinds of rap/hip-hop out there.

African-American teenagers are beset on all sides by dangerous myths about race. The most poisonous one defines middle-class normalcy and achievement as "white," while embracing violence, illiteracy and drug dealing as "authentically" black. This fiction rears its head from time to time in films and literature. But it finds its most virulent expression in rap music, which started out with a broad palette of themes but has increasingly evolved into a medium for worshiping misogyny, materialism and murder.

This dangerous narrowing of hip-hop music would be reason for concern in any case. But it is especially troubling against the backdrop of the 1990's, when rappers provoked a real-world gang war by using recordings and music videos to insult and threaten rivals. Two of the music's biggest stars—Tupac Shakur and the Notorious B.I.G.—were eventually shot to death.

People who pay only minimal attention to the rap world may have thought the killings would sober up the rap community. Not quite. The May cover of the hip-hop magazine *Vibe* was on the mark when it depicted fallen rappers standing among tombstones under the headline: "Hip-Hop Murders: Why Haven't We Learned Anything?"

The cover may have been prompted in part by a rivalry between two rappers that culminated in a shootout at a New York radio station, Hot 97, earlier this spring. The events that led up to the shooting show how recording labels now exploit violence to make and sell recordings.

At the center of that Hot 97 shootout was none other than 50 Cent, whose given name is Curtis Jackson III. Mr. Jackson is a confessed former drug dealer who seems to revel in the fact that he was shot several times while dealing in Queens. He has also made a career of "beef" recordings, in which he whips up controversy and heightens tension by insulting rival artists.

He was following this pattern in a radio interview in March when a rival showed up at the station. The story's murky, but it appears that the rival's entourage met Mr. Jackson's on the street, resulting in gunfire.

Mr. Jackson's on-air agitation was clearly timed to coincide with the release of "The Massacre," his grotesquely violent and misogynist compact disc. The CD cover depicts the artist standing before a wall adorned with weapons, pointing what appears to be a shotgun at the

Too strong? Rap sometimes glamorizes, but it can raise awareness, too.

Many people "learned" or were not involved in the violence: Kanye West, Chuck D., Public Enemy, etc.

True—recording labels are marketing an image.

Example: 50 Cent and the release/marketing of "The Massacre"

No concrete proof that 50 Cent planned a gunfight to promote his album. Is the inference fair? I think so.

camera. The photographs in the liner notes depict every ghetto stereotype—the artist selling drugs, the artist in a gunfight—and includes a mock autopsy report that has been seen as a covert threat aimed at some of his critics.

The "Massacre" promotion raises the ante in a most destructive way. New artists, desperate for stardom, will say or do anything to win notice—and buzz—for their next projects. As the trend escalates, inner-city listeners who are already at risk of dying prematurely are being fed a toxic diet of rap cuts that glorify murder and make it seem perfectly normal to spend your life in prison.

Critics who have been angered by this trend have pointed at Jimmy Iovine, the music impresario whose Interscope Records reaped millions on gangster rap in the 90's. Mr. Iovine makes a convenient target as a white man who is lording over an essentially black art form. But also listed on "The Massacre" as an executive pro-

ducer is the legendary rapper Dr. Dre, a black man who happens to be one of the most powerful people in the business. Dr. Dre has a unique vantage point on rap-related violence. He was co-founder of Death Row Records, an infamous California company that marketed West Coast rap in the 1990's and had a front-row seat for the feud that led to so much bloodshed back then.

The music business hopes to make a financial killing on a recently announced summer concert tour that is set to feature 50 Cent and the mega-selling rap star Eminem. But promoters will need to make heavy use of metal detectors to suppress the kind of gun-related violence that gangster artists celebrate. That this lethal genre of art has grown speaks volumes about the industry's greed and lack of self-control.

But trends like this reach a tipping point, when business as usual becomes unacceptable to the public as a whole. Judging from the rising hue and cry, hip-hop is just about there.

> *Is it the marketing or the art itself that is "misogynistic" and "supremely violent"? Note: Listen to this song.*

> *In many neighborhoods, kids grow up seeing people going to prison all the time, so for them it is normal.*

> *I wonder who these other critics are?*

> *impresario—entertainment manager or promoter*

> *Good example of author's point—even in the name of the record company.*

> *A pun?*

> *Can art be "lethal"?*

> *tipping point—the moment when something rare becomes much more common*

> *Hip-hop is still popular. Does he just mean against gangsta rap?*

EXERCISE 7.2 Annotating a text

Using the annotations to the Staples essay above as a model, annotate the essay by Wray Herbert (pp. 112–114).

2. Keep a journal.

Articulating your responses in a ***journal*** is a good way to build a deeper understanding and a sense of taking part in—not just taking in—what you read. A journal entry can do any of the following:

- Analyze the writer's purpose: Is it to entertain, inform, persuade?
- Develop insights through freewriting.

> **More about**
> Purpose, 10–11
> Generating ideas, 20–25
> Outlining, 35–38
> Synthesizing, 123–25, 262–63

- Brainstorm reasons to support or oppose the writer's claims.
- Organize your ideas through clustering or outlining.
- Synthesize ideas from the text with ideas of your own or ideas from other sources.

A double-entry reading journal provides a column for quotations, summaries, or paraphrases and a column for your responses. This technique can help you avoid plagiarism by keeping your own ideas separate from the ideas you have found in the text.

The entries from the reading journal below reflect one student's thoughts about the Wray Herbert article that appears in Exercise 7.1.

Student Model Double-Entry Reading Journal

Quotation/Summary/Paraphrase	Response
"I recall sitting once before an open window, listening to the radio. Outside it was pouring rain. I mean horizontal monsoon, umbrellas buckling in people's hands. But on the radio, the DJ was calmly announcing 'a chance of showers today.' He's right, I remember thinking, an excellent chance." (par 1)	This opening story made me laugh. It was a great way to introduce a key point: language can often confuse what we mean instead of making it clearer.
Doctors try to avoid hurting patients' feelings in what Herbert calls "face-threatening situations" (par 5), which means they often use "euphemisms" (par 5) when they have to deliver bad news.	"Saving face" applies to the classroom, too. When we peer edit papers, we don't want to hurt anyone's feelings; I definitely hold back and say "you might need a better example" because the word "might" makes it sound nicer.
What Dr. Bonnefon calls a "severity bias" made more (fake) patients overestimate the likelihood they'd go deaf (a worse outcome) than that they'd develop insomnia (a less bad result). (par 6–7)	I learned about confirmation bias (the tendency to look for supporting evidence) and the representativeness bias (the tendency to overestimate the likelihood of things that seem common) in my psychology class; this severity bias must be a tendency to overestimate the likelihood that something bad will happen.

EXERCISE 7.3 Writing a journal entry

Using the journal entry above as a model, write a journal entry on either the Herbert essay (pp. 112–14) or the Staples editorial (pp. 116–17). If you quote any material, note where it comes from, in case you have to cite it later.

EXERCISE 7.4 Writing about an image

Find a striking photograph online or in a magazine, newspaper, or textbook. Using the sample below as a model, write a journal entry about the image, relating your thoughts, feelings, and reactions to the photograph as a whole or to specific parts of it.

The colors in this photo are vibrant; robe concealing the woman in the foreground is almost the same shade of blue as the blue blouse that Preety Zinta is wearing.

Is the subject the woman in the foreground, covered head to toe, or the glamour shots of models and actresses (especially Preety Zinta) in the background? Preety Zinta almost looks like the woman's reflection. Her set expression reveals very little, almost as little as the covered woman's.

It's interesting to wonder what the woman in the foreground is thinking. Does she want to uncover her head (like Preety Zinta) or is she shocked by Zinta's flowing hair and red lipstick?

The contrast here makes me think about what these photos say about the way women are perceived and treated by their society (and ours).

7c Preparing to Write

Often, critical readers are readying themselves for the next step: writing. Having something interesting to say about a reading selection will come from *analyzing* the text carefully; *interpreting* the text to find or create a new, deeper meaning; *synthesizing* what you have learned from the text with what you have learned elsewhere; and *critiquing,* or evaluating, the text.

1. Analyze.

> **More about**
> Analysis, 59–60, 62
> Evaluating claims, 134–41
> Evidence, 40–41
> Analyzing works of literature, 432–54 (ch. 22)

To comprehend a text fully, you must ***analyze*** it: Take it apart, consider its components, figure out how the parts fit together, and assess how the text as a whole convinces its audience of its claims. When analyzing a text, consider the following:

- The major claims a text makes. Are all the claims backed by evidence (such as examples, facts, and expert testimony)?
- The type and quality of the evidence offered to support the claims. How appropriate and satisfying is the evidence? Is it sufficient to support the claims?
- The presence or absence of counterevidence. Does the text inform its audience of weaknesses in its claims or evidence, or offer alternative perspectives?
- The sources the author draws on (if any). How reliable are they, and what is the author's attitude toward them?
- The organization of the argument (classical, Rogerian, Toulmin). What does the organization suggest about the writer's purpose?
- The rhetorical appeals used in the text. Where can you see the author using logos (rational, logical claims or evidence), ethos (where the texts shows the expertise or credibility of the author or the sources), or pathos (drawing on the audience's emotions or sympathy)? How approropriate are the rhetorical appeals for the audience, context, and purpose?

> **More about**
> Purpose, 10–11
> Audience, 12–16
> Organization: classical, Rogerian, Toulmin, 154–55
> Rhetorical appeals (logos, ethos, pathos), 142–45
> Tone, 15–16, 136, 543, 548–50
> Style, 496–572 (part 7, Style Matters)

- The tone and style. What do these reflect about the author's purpose in writing this piece or attitudes toward the topic or audience?
- The logical pattern used in the text, which provides information about the author's purpose. Exploratory arguments are likely to use ***inductive logic,*** citing particular examples and then drawing a general conclusion. Persuasive arguments are likely to use ***deductive logic,*** offering generally accepted truths from which conclusions can be drawn about specific instances. How appropriate are the logical patterns for the audience, context, and purpose?

Quick Reference: Steps in Developing Critical Understanding

- **Analyze.** Divide a text into its component parts to understand *how* it reaches its audience.
- **Interpret.** Dig below the surface to draw conclusions based on the author's assumptions and motives, omissions, and the circumstances in which the text was written.
- **Synthesize.** Connect ideas in a text to relevant ideas in other texts or experiences; analyze the relationships among ideas or draw comparisons and contrasts.
- **Critique.** Evaluate based on evidence gathered through careful reading, analysis, interpretation, and synthesis.

Student Model: Claims and Evidence Analysis

In analyzing the Staples editorial (p. 115), Alea Wratten identified its main claim and the reasons and evidence provided to support that claim:

> Major claims:
> 1. Today's hip-hop music spreads a dangerous myth that an authentic black experience is violent.
> 2. This has serious consequences for listeners.
>
> Evidence:
> - Lyrics promote racism, sexism, violence
> - Behavior of hip-hop artists promotes violence: Deaths of Tupac Shakur, Notorious B.I.G.
> - 50 Cent's insulting rivals and shootout at Hot 97 to promote record
> - Violent imagery on cover of The Massacre and in liner notes
> - Dr Dre—cofounder of Death Row Records, executive producer of 50 Cent's record
> - Need for metal detectors at concerts

Student Model: Advertisement Critique

An analysis of an advertisement—focusing on the claims it makes, the relation between image and text, and the reaction the advertisement is trying to elicit from the reader—appears on the next page.

This advertisement for Adopt Us Kids, sponsored by the Ad Council, appeared in a variety of magazines. It makes two explicit claims: "You don't have to be perfect to be a perfect parent" and "There are thousands of teens in foster care who would love to put up with you." These two claims suggest a third: *Readers should consider adopting a child in foster care.* The ad relies on the assumption that people don't adopt because they worry they won't be good parents.

The image of a flawed but still inviting birthday cake illustrates the first claim. This cake may sag a bit, but it's been placed in an elegant serving dish and lit up with polka-dotted candles. Atop the cake is the number 16—a milestone age that people associate with sweet sixteen parties and driver's licenses.

The specificity of this age implies a particular person, and an engaged reader can't help but wonder about all the kids in foster care who turn sixteen without this rite of passage, the luxury of a birthday cake, or the love of a parent who'd buy or make one. The image elicits our emotional response, but the written text articulates and clarifies its message: What matters in parenthood is effort and love, not perfection. Omission is also used powerfully here; what is *missing* from the photograph—a child—might be missing from a reader's life, too.

2. Interpret.

After analyzing the text to determine how it works, consider the significance or meaning of the elements you have identified, and draw inferences about what may be below the surface of the text. Use the following questions to help guide your *interpretation* of a text:

> **More about**
> Identifying assumptions, 147
> Identifying stakeholders, 233
> Interpreting, 262–63, 270–72

- What assumptions does the writer make about the subject or audience? Why are such assumptions significant?

- What does the text omit (evidence, opposing views), and what might these omissions indicate?

- What conclusions can you draw about the author's attitude from the tone? What motives can you infer from the author's background or previous publications?
- Who published this text or sponsored the research, and what influence might these sponsors have upon the way the information, arguments, or evidence is presented?
- In what context was the text written—place, time, cultural environment—and how might this context have influenced the writer?

Student Model Prewrite

In prewriting for her critical response essay, Alea Wratten considered Staples's assumptions, omissions, and possible motivations:

> Staples treats hip-hop and rap as synonyms. He refers to the "dangerous narrowing" of this kind of music, but there is no discussion of what this narrowed from. He gives examples of rappers whose albums glorify violence, but not of hip-hop artists with other themes. Also, while Staples states twice that rap is misogynistic, he doesn't provide any lyrics or examples to prove it. Is he relying on his readers to know enough about rap to know this is true? I don't think so—people who read the *New York Times* editorial page are probably mostly white, middle-aged, and well off, not the kind of folks who are usually into hip-hop. And he mustn't think his readers really know about hip-hop because he has to tell them what *Vibe* is ("the hip-hop magazine"). So are these gaps typical of editorials? They do have to be short, so not a lot of room for examples. And since they're directed toward a general audience, they're more likely to use this kind of dramatic language. Or is this an indication of a blind spot about hip-hop? This is something I think a lot of people from the Beatles or Motown generation—like my mom!—share.

3. Synthesize.

College assignments often ask you to *synthesize*—to connect what you have read to ideas in other texts or to the world around you. You may begin to synthesize early on, as you read and annotate the text. You will probably develop these connections in your reading journal and as you draft and revise your essay.

More about
Synthesizing, 262–63
Comparing and contrasting, 60–61

To synthesize, ask yourself the following questions:

- What else have you read or experienced that this text may explain, illustrate, clarify, complicate, or contradict?
- How do the author's other writings amplify, clarify, complicate, or contradict the selection you are writing about?
- What outside forces (historical events, socioeconomic forces, cultural shifts) might influence or underlie the text?
- What claims or points in each text do you find especially compelling? How do compelling points in one text connect to ideas in the other(s)?
- What claims could these texts, taken together, provide evidence for?
- How is your understanding of a topic enhanced or your thinking changed by putting these texts together? What might others gain by seeing these texts together?

Writing Responsibly — Drawing Inferences

An inference is only as good as what it is based on. Inferences based on facts are fair; those based on personal values and beliefs or on a faulty understanding of the text are apt to be one-sided and unfair. Aim for the former and avoid the latter.

to TOPIC

An excerpt from prewriting for Alea Wratten's essay draws connections between Brent Staples's editorial "How Hip-Hop Music Lost Its Way and Betrayed Its Fans" and the hip-hop music she listens to.

Staples uses examples of gangsta rappers like 50 Cent and Eminem to support his claim that hip-hop promotes negative stereotypes and violence. Sure, 50 Cent's music may try to make violence look cool, but not all hip-hop is ultra-violent. Kanye West is a big star, and he has gone platinum with positive, even spiritual messages. Lauren Hill, Kam, KRS One, Arrested Development, Chuck D, and Public Enemy are just a few of the artists on my iPod who set positive examples for listeners.

Wratten's inferences are fair: They are based on facts (other hip-hop stars who are successful without violence) and on her analysis of Staples's omissions.

Make It Your Own

College assignments often ask you to synthesize ideas found in two or more texts. Using the questions on page 124 as a guide, write a 350- to 500-word essay that synthesizes "Why Uncertainty May Be Bad for Your Health" (Exercise 7.1, p. 112) with the information below and any other texts or experiences that are relevant.

> How we state propositions can influence how we try to solve a problem, reason through a decision, or make a judgment (Anderson, 1991). For example, in one study college students who were told that a cancer treatment had a 50 percent success rate judged the treatment to be significantly more effective and expressed a greater willingness to have it administered to a family member than did participants who were told it had a 50 percent failure rate (Kahneman & Tversky, 1979). Representing outcomes in terms of positives or negatives has this effect because people tend to assign greater costs to negative outcomes (such as losing $100) than they assign value to an equivalent positive outcome (finding $100). The proposition that "there is a 50 percent chance of failure" evokes thoughts about the patient's dying and causes the "50-50" treatment to appear more risky (Slovic et al., 1988). Thus differences in how we verbally represent choices and goals can make a difference in our perceptions and decisions.
>
> —Michael W. Passer and Ronald E. Smith, *Psychology: The Science of Mind and Behavior,* 2nd ed.

4. Critique.

A *critique* is a well-informed evaluation. It may be positive, negative, or a bit of both. A movie review, for example, is a critique; it provides readers with an evaluation to help them decide whether or not to see the film. A reviewer's opinion alone is usually not enough to sway a would-be audience member. The reviewer must also provide evidence for the judgment by describing the performances, the screenplay, or the director's vision. Similarly, critiques

---

Writing Responsibly — **Understanding *Criticism***

In everyday speech, *criticism* is often used simply to mean "finding fault." But in academic disciplines, *criticizing* means "evaluating a work's merits based on a careful and fair analysis." The ideal critic approaches a text skeptically yet with an open mind and provides evidence for the judgments she makes. If you are used to thinking about published texts as absolutely authoritative sources of information, it is important for you to realize that *all* texts present only partial views that can always be challenged.

to OTHER WRITERS

Professional Model
Review, 451–54

written for college courses offer judgments based on careful analysis of the text's component parts. They may also be informed by other texts, your own knowledge and experience, or both.

As you prepare to write a critique, consider the following issues:

- **The writer's aims.** What are the author's goals? Does she or he achieve them? Are they worth achieving?
- **The writer's claims.** What are the writer's claims? How much are you persuaded by them? Why?
- **The writer's evidence.** How credible is the evidence? How verifiable and relevant is the evidence? How sound is the reasoning?
- **The writer's authority.** What expertise or life experience does the writer bring to the topic, and is it relevant?

Self Assessment: Preparing to Write about a Visual

When exploring a visual, especially if writing about it, ask yourself the following questions. Does evidence support your answers?

Analysis

- ☐ **Parts and patterns.** What are the relationships among the parts? Does the image include or imply a comparison or contrast, a cause or effect?
- ☐ **Purpose.** Is the visual's purpose to inform, persuade, entertain, or express emotion? If the visual is persuasive, what does it claim and how does it support this claim?
- ☐ **Attitude.** What is the artist's attitude toward the subject or audience? On what basis can you make this inference?
- ☐ **Context.** Where is the image set? When was it created? Who produced or sponsored it, and why? How do accompanying words inform your reading?

Interpretation

- ☐ **Assumptions.** What values does the image assume or promote? How do those values match, contrast with, or challenge those of its audience?

- ☐ **Omissions.** Is something missing? Has the visual been cropped to eliminate background? If so, how does this affect your understanding?
- ☐ **Audience.** Who is the intended audience? Where was the visual originally published, or where did you find it? How was the image received by its original audience?

Synthesis

- ☐ **Other sources.** How is this image similar to or different from others that you know? Have you read or studied anything that could help you understand this visual?
- ☐ **Background.** What knowledge or personal experiences do you have that might deepen your understanding?

Critique

- ☐ **Aims.** Based on your analysis, what were the artist's aims, and were they achieved?
- ☐ **Claims.** What claims is the artist making, and are you persuaded?
- ☐ **Authority.** What expertise or experience does the artist bring?

Also consider your own goals and position:

- **Your aims, claims, and evidence.** Why are you writing the critique? What claims are you making? What evidence will you use to support those claims?
- **Your authority.** What authority do you have, and why might readers value your judgment and evaluation? You may not be an expert, but your opinion can be valid and interesting if it is based on thoughtful analysis.
- **Your audience.** What are your readers' interests and knowledge about the subject? What background information will you need to provide? Will they be sympathetic to your claims, or will you have to work hard to persuade them?

> **More about**
> Claims, 138–41
> Evidence, 40–41
> Authority, 143, 233
> Relevance, 230–31
> Reliability, 232–39
> Audience, 12–15

EXERCISE 7.5 Analyzing an article

Analyze the Al Gore essay on pages 69–71. In two or three paragraphs, describe the author's assumptions and attitude. Also consider how circumstances (Hurricane Katrina, the 2000 presidential election) might have affected its reception.

Work Together

In groups of three or more, compare your syntheses. How effectively do your classmates' syntheses draw connections between the two texts? In what ways are they similar to and different from your own? Discuss the strategies you used to complete this synthesis and any revisions that could make them more effective. Make a note of strategies you might use in the future.

Student Model Critical Response Essay

In the essay that follows, Alea Wratten (SUNY–Geneseo) analyzes Brent Staples's essay "How Hip-Hop Music Lost Its Way and Betrayed Its Fans" and draws on her knowledge of hip-hop to create this critical response.

Wratten 1

Reflecting on Brent Staples's Editorial "How Hip-Hop
Music Lost Its Way and Betrayed Its Fans"

Hip-hop is among today's most popular forms of American music. You can hear it walking through the mall, during TV commercials, and on nearly anyone's iPod (including mine). Despite, or perhaps because of, this popularity, Brent Staples, in his *New York Times* editorial, "How Hip-Hop Music Lost Its Way and Betrayed Its Fans," calls hip-hop a "lethal genre of art" (26), claiming the music brainwashes and endangers black kids, who will identify blackness with the criminal underworld depicted in these songs. He claims that hip-hop "has evolved into a medium for worshiping misogyny, materialism, and murder" (26) and that it is only getting worse. Staples raises some excellent concerns about the dangers of marketing violence to young people, but ultimately his argument fails to be persuasive for several reasons: He does not account for the influence positive role models have, he ignores the fact that art frequently depicts violence without dire consequences to its consumers, and he overlooks the broad spectrum of hip-hop to focus on only a single strand.

First, it is distressing that Staples, who himself presents a positive role model for black teens, would assume that black teens would be likely to identify with violent, misogynistic lyrics, associating success and respect for the law with whiteness and poverty, crime, and sexism with blackness. Staples, who grew up poor and black, was likely smarter than this, and so are today's black teens. They see successful black men and women all around them—our president, the nation's wealthiest and most popular talk show host, an influential editorial writer for the New York Times, not to mention scores of business men and women, actors, comedians, and sports

---

Introduction: Brief summary of editorial to which it is responding

Thesis: Acknowledges strengths of Staples's editorial but also lists three problems

Topic sentence: Analyzes assumption that black teens use rap stars as models

Counterevidence

figures—all of whom are role models that black teens might identify with and aspire to become. With this range of possible models before them, it is unlikely that many black teens would be deluded about the world because they had listened to offensive hip-hop lyrics.

Topic sentence: Analyzes assumption that hip-hop is different from other art forms

Second, by calling hip-hop a "lethal genre," Staples places it into a category separate from other works of art that are not as "virulent." Yes, many hip-hop lyrics are violent, but that does not distinguish them from many other artistic works. Edgar Allan Poe, considered one of America's greatest writers, wrote numerous stories about murder and death, including "The Tell-Tale Heart," whose narrator is a confessed killer. *The Talented Mr. Ripley,* a novel by Patricia Highsmith, and the movie based on this novel, make Tom Ripley, an unrepentant murderer, a sympathetic character. Sculptor Kiki Smith depicts mutilated bodies in her art (see fig. 1), and, instead of being criticized, she is considered one of today's most important sculptors. No one would claim, I think, that Kiki Smith influences her viewers to commit mayhem. Clearly, hip-hop artists are not alone in depicting horrible people and events; they should not be singled out for doing so, and it should not be assumed that their audience will blindly follow suit.

Counterexamples

Body: Analyzes author's assumptions, claims, and evidence, and provides counterexamples based on knowledge of hip-hop and other information

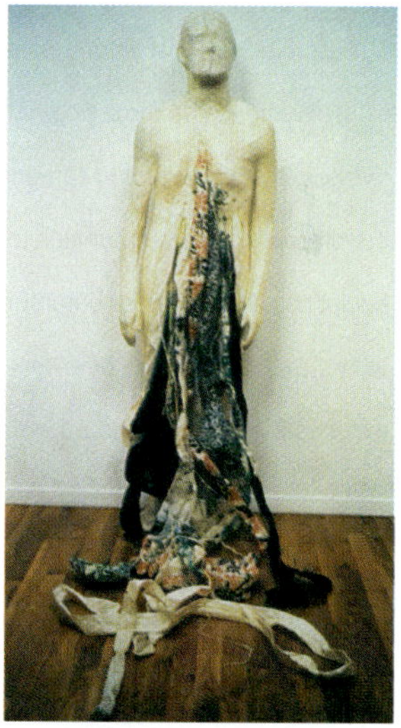

Fig. 1. Kiki Smith, *Untitled,* 1993. Paper and papier-mâché. Pace Wildenstein Gallery, New York.

Visual counterexample

> **Topic sentence: Challenges assumption that all hip-hop is *gangsta***

Finally, tarring all of hip-hop with one brush is a mistake. While gangsta rap continues to be very popular, hip-hop includes many bands and artists who write uplifting and socially aware lyrics. Kanye West, for instance, currently among hip-hop's biggest stars, offers a positive, spiritual message in his music, a message of which Staples would likely approve. In his song "Family Business," West explains,

> **Counterexamples**

"I woke up early this mornin' with a new state of mind / A creative way to rhyme without usin' nines and guns / keep your nose out the sky, keep your heart to God / and keep your face to the risin' sun" (West). And West is not alone: Lauren Hill, Kam, KRS One, Arrested Development, Chuck D, and Public Enemy are just a few of the musicians and bands on my iPod that explore hip-hop's more socially responsible side. These artists show that the strand of hip-hop that Staples accuses of providing a "toxic diet" (25) for listeners is just one of many.

> **Conclusion: Acknowledges violent and misogynistic lyrics in hip-hop but offers different interpretation**

Some of the most popular hip-hop songs do revolve around violent or sexist themes. It is important to remember, though, that these themes draw attention to conditions in the communities out of which hip-hop developed. They bring important social problems of poor communities to the attention of a wide audience—black and white. So hip-hop may offer more than just a catchy beat; it is also a way for artists to express themselves and a form of art that tells their stories.

Works Cited

Staples, Brent. "How Hip-Hop Music Lost Its Way and Betrayed Its Fans." Editorial. *New York Times* 12 May 2005: A25. Print.

West, Kanye. "Family Business." *The College Dropout*. Roc-a-Fella, 2004. CD.

EXERCISE 7.6 Writing a critique

Find an editorial in a printed or online newspaper. First, read the editorial using the techniques discussed in this chapter and write a summary noting the editorial's main idea and major supporting points. Then, write a paragraph-long critical response to it using analysis, interpretation, synthesis, and critique.

EXERCISE 7.7 Interpreting a graphic

The bar graph below appeared on the front page of the newspaper *USA Today* with no accompanying story. Based on the graphic alone, write a one- to two-paragraph story to accompany it. What is the main claim of the graphic? What evidence does it use to support its main claim?

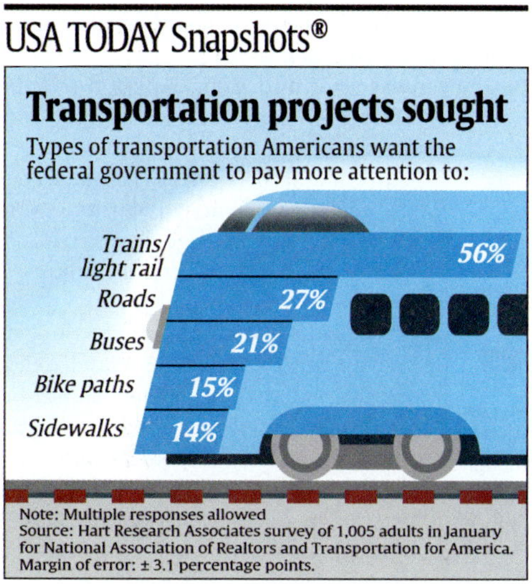

USA TODAY Snapshots®

Transportation projects sought
Types of transportation Americans want the federal government to pay more attention to:

- Trains/light rail: 56%
- Roads: 27%
- Buses: 21%
- Bike paths: 15%
- Sidewalks: 14%

Note: Multiple responses allowed
Source: Hart Research Associates survey of 1,005 adults in January for National Association of Realtors and Transportation for America. Margin of error: ± 3.1 percentage points.

By Anne R. Carey and Sam Ward, USA TODAY

7d Reasoning Matters • Thinking and Reading Critically

Writing Responsibly
Understanding and Representing the Entire Source

> **Make It Your Own!** For a research project to be worthwhile, it should represent the overall arguments of its sources—more than just a few sentences—so that readers can understand what the sources were saying and how they fit together.

Each time you write from sources, push yourself to work with them in more substantial ways. Take the time to read each source—the entire source—carefully. Next, **summarize** it, as a way of processing the information: Restate, concisely and in fresh language, the main claims (and the most important supporting evidence) of an entire source. Then when you draft your research project, blend in summaries of your important sources, so that your readers understand how they, too, contribute to your discussion.

You can also draw from sources by quoting or paraphrasing brief passages. But if you simply paste a quotation into your draft, how much do you or your audience actually understand the source or even the passage you are quoting? **Paraphrasing** is a better alternative, because it pushes you to think about the passage: to know the material well enough to restate it in your own words. Changing just a few words in the passage, however, is not paraphrasing; it is **patchwriting**: a mixture of your words and the source's. This is an error interpreted by most readers as plagiarism.

Because quoting and patchwriting do not require much comprehension and are easy to do, inexperienced college writers rely on them too heavily. Frequently, too, the quotations come from the first few pages of the source—which some students feel is all they have to read. Researchers with the Citation Project found that the majority of college writers' citations came from the first two pages of the source (see chart) and felt the quality of these papers suffered. That is because, in most sources, the first few pages discuss only general findings, while the insightful, detailed examples and evidence that are important to a good analysis or argument are deeper in the text.

When a writer provides only isolated quotations from sources ("dropped quotations"), the result may be uninformative, like this passage from a paper about social media and individual identity:

Page Cited
DATA FROM **The Citation Project**

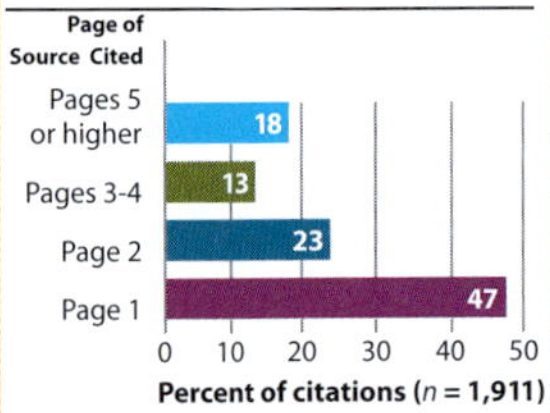

Page of Source Cited	Percent of citations (n = 1,911)
Pages 5 or higher	18
Pages 3–4	13
Page 2	23
Page 1	47

Researchers found that although most college writers quote from the first pages of a source, the best research projects drew from the entire source.

First draft

Student's voice: People value their personal lives and try to separate their private and public selves. Many are aware of being different people in the workplace, in school, on a date.

All this may be changing, though. **Quotation:** "The fact that the Internet never seems to forget is threatening, at an almost existential level, our ability to control our identities; to preserve the option of reinventing ourselves and starting anew; to overcome our checkered pasts" (Rosen). **Parenthetical citation**

Reasoning Matters • Understanding and Representing the Entire Source **7d** 133

Notice how, in this draft, readers are given no information about the source; they are presented only with one sentence from it. This causes the reader to wonder: Does the writer understand the source, or has she simply found a "killer quote" that supports her argument? Because the writer provides only the isolated quotation, it is not even clear what her purpose is in including it.

Now consider how this passage is transformed by adding a summary and contextualized quotations:

Revised draft

> [Student's voice] People value their personal lives, and many deliberately work to keep their private and public selves separate. Many of us are aware, too, of being different people in the workplace, in school, on the athletic field, on a date. Some value these differences, happy to switch from dedicated intellectual in the classroom to enthusiastic player on the soccer field.
>
> All this may be changing, though. [Signal phrase providing information about the author] Writing in the *New York Times*, journalist Jeffrey Rosen points out that [Summary of the parts of the source relevant to the student's argument] we may no longer be in control of the multiple identities that were previously taken for granted. In our online lives, what we post on Facebook and Twitter can easily merge with what we post on a school blog, in our comments on a news story, or in our pictures on Flickr. Rosen explains that even in untagged pictures, our faces can be identified through facial-recognition technology. [Summary of the remainder of the source] He also describes the privacy-protecting laws that are in development and the companies that offer services to clean up our online reputations. [Student's voice] Most central to my research, though, is his explanation for this claim: [Quotation (no page reference because source is unpaginated)] "The fact that the Internet never seems to forget is threatening, at an almost existential level, our ability to control our identities; to preserve the option of reinventing ourselves and starting anew; to overcome our checkered pasts."

Source: Rosen, Jeffrey. "The Web Means the End of Forgetting." *New York Times* 21 July 2010: n. pag. Web. 1 Feb. 2011.

The writer has shown responsibility to her source, her topic, and her audience. Because she has taken the time to read and understand the source, she is able to summarize it to show what its main claims are. Her audience now knows how the quotation was used in the source and how it supports her argument. With this brief summary, the writer has also explained her ideas clearly and established a "conversation" between herself, her source, and her audience—that is, rather than just "using" sources, she is thinking about them, interacting with them, and giving her audience enough information that they can do the same.

Self Assessment

Review and revise your work with each source. Have you done the following?

- ☐ Read, understand, and accurately represent the whole source. Did you look for the details deeper in the source?
- ☐ Summarize the main ideas of the source. Did you put the source's ideas in your own words, fairly and accurately? ▶ *Paraphrasing, 252–56*
- ☐ Incorporate your summary into your source analysis. Did you use the best examples and evidence?
- ☐ Locate the most relevant passages. Did you cite from *throughout* the source? ▶ *Critical reading, 108–33*

8 Analyzing and Crafting Arguments

IN THIS CHAPTER

a. Persuading and exploring, 134

b. Making claims, 138

c. Choosing evidence rhetorically, 142

d. Considering alternative viewpoints, 145

e. Discovering assumptions and common ground, 147

f. Organizing arguments: Classical, Rogerian, Toulmin, 154

g. Avoiding logical fallacies, 156

Student Model
Exploratory Argument, 147

> **More about**
> Crafting a thesis, 29–32, 139, 264–66
> Claims of judgment, 139–40
> Tone, 15–16, 136, 543, 548–50
> Diction, 15–16, 538–39

This advertisement uses text and a visual to argue that drinking and driving is wrong because of the harm drunk drivers can cause to others. Visually, the ad is powerful because the symbol, a broken heart, shows a human profile in red, suggesting the absence of a loved one. The white type on a stark black background adds drama and highlights the message. The placement of the advertisement is also persuasive: That it is on the back of a bus stop bench suggests an alternative to driving under the influence.

Arguments like this one are all around us—from television and Facebook, to editorials and blogs. As readers, we have a responsibility to think critically about whether such arguments are logical, provide evidence to support their claims, and are underlain by assumptions we share. As writers, we have a responsibility to explore issues with an open mind and to support our positions with sound reasoning and compelling evidence.

8a Persuading and Exploring

Arguments may be ***persuasive*** (thesis driven, claim based) or ***exploratory*** (thesis seeking, inquiry based). In a persuasive argument, the writer's purpose is to convince readers to agree with or at least to respect a position on a debatable issue. A persuasive argument articulates and advocates for a *claim of judgment*. It will be most effective when it provides compelling reasons and evidence in support of the claim and when the writer's tone is reasonable. The advertisement in Figure 8.1 makes a persuasive argument.

In an exploratory argument, the writer's purpose is to consider a wide range of evidence and eventually to arrive at the most plausible position. An exploratory argument begins by examining the evidence, which it then uses to arrive at a conclusion—its thesis. Exploratory arguments are useful for assessing complex issues and developing well-informed opinions about them, even if such opinions are provisional, subject to change when new information or a better interpretation becomes available. They can also be a useful way to convince those who disagree to reconsider the evidence.

1. Reason with inductive logic.

Exploratory arguments are likely to use *inductive logic:* They cite particular examples or specific instances and then draw a conclusion or claim. For instance, imagine that, over a period of months or years, you take exams, sometimes after a good night's sleep and sometimes after staying up late cramming. Reflecting back on your experience, you draw the conclusion that you get better grades on tests after getting a good night's sleep before an exam. This is inductive reasoning. Notice that *counterevidence,* evidence that undermines your claim, can weaken a conclusion reached inductively. Acing an exam after getting only three hours' sleep means that, in at least this one instance, your conclusion is false.

When supporting your claim with inductive logic or analyzing an argument based on inductive logic, consider not only evidence that supports the claim but also evidence that undermines it. Have you explained why the claim is still persuasive despite the counterevidence? If not, revise your claim. Also avoid blanket statements that include words like *always* and *never.* Absolute claims like "I always do better on exams after a good night's sleep" are almost always false.

FIGURE 8.1 Arguing to persuade This advertisement argues that taking your lunch to work saves money over time; it first asserts this claim, then backs it up with evidence.

2. Reason with deductive logic.

Persuasive arguments are likely to use *deductive logic.* They start from a general premise to draw conclusions about specific instances. Continuing with the example from the section above, consider this general premise: "Test-takers do their best work after a good night's sleep." From this premise, you might draw the conclusion that, before your next psychology exam, you should get a good night's sleep. If the general premise is true, then the conclusion is inescapable, but is the general premise true?

Imagine that you have not read the assigned chapters and that you have put off studying for the exam. In that case, all the sleep in the world is unlikely to improve your performance, and studying for the exam late into the night might be your best option. When writing or assessing arguments based on deductive logic, be sure to consider alternative explanations for the conclusion and to examine carefully the assumptions underlying the premises.

In this excerpt from his journal, student William Archer explores two possible ways to understand the Vietnam War in the context of a class discussion of tragedy; he begins with a question, considers the evidence, and weighs his findings to arrive at a tentative position:

> Should the Vietnam War be viewed more as a Greek or Christian tragedy? Viewing the war as a Christian tragedy would suggest that if certain things had been done differently, a more positive outcome might have resulted; officials made mistakes (moral and strategic) that led to their downfall (and the deaths of soldiers), and those mistakes could have been avoided. Viewing the war as a Greek tragedy would imply that nothing those involved did could have made any difference; officials had character flaws and destinies that ultimately led to their downfall.
>
> There is valid evidence to support either claim. Someone could take the Christian tragedy outlook and argue that had the United States chosen to maintain democratic principles instead of overthrowing President Diem, then we might have avoided the war altogether. Others could take the Greek tragedy outlook and claim that under our government's built-in fear of the spread of communism, war in Southeast Asia was inevitable.
>
> For now, I view the war more as a Greek tragedy; given the historical context following World War II, a proxy war between key powers was bound to happen somewhere in the region. I wonder what would have happened if the United States had chosen a different Southeast Asian nation to "draw the line" with?
>
> —William Archer, Colgate University

Writing Responsibly: The Well-Tempered Tone

In public discourse, especially in public blogs, the "zinger," or clever put-down, is often used to trump an opponent. Sarcasm also thrives: Some bloggers take a sarcastic tone toward whatever they oppose. But if you want your argument (and yourself) to be taken seriously—especially in academic and business circles—and if you want to persuade people who do not already agree with you, establishing a fair, even-tempered tone and avoiding sarcasm are crucial. Use logic and sound evidence, not snide comments, to make your point.

to SELF

Academic writing like Archer's is frequently exploratory in its early stages and becomes persuasive as the essay develops. Working this way often yields a more thoughtful, considered position than does beginning from a predetermined position.

Exploratory versus Persuasive Approaches to Argument For personal or cultural reasons, you may be more comfortable seeking consensus than stating an opinion. Seek help in formulating a Rogerian or Toulmin argument, or if you want to write an exploratory argument, check with your instructor to be sure this approach is acceptable.

EXERCISE 8.1 Choosing an approach to argument

Consider the assignments below and decide whether each calls for a persuasive or exploratory argument; be prepared to explain your answer.

1. Drawing on ideas and issues raised in lecture, discussion, and readings throughout the term, find, read, and critically analyze one or two newspaper articles on a controversial topic, focusing on the different points of view and assumptions underlying the press coverage. . . .
   (Anthropology 300, Portland State University)

2. Present a health promotion or nursing intervention that can be applied to a specific risk behavior or health problem. Include material from professional journals and clinical experiences about the risk behavior or health problem and information about the group of people at risk. Then identify and analyze a nursing intervention that can lead to risk reduction or that promotes improved health.
   (Nursing 224, University of Rhode Island)

3. Darwin, Marx, Nietzsche: Which one of the three was the most important "challenge" to the orthodoxy of his day? Why? Do you feel that the impact of the three was largely the same or significantly different? Why? (CORE 152, Colgate University)

> **More about**
> Analyzing an assignment, 17–18, 192–93

Work **Together**

In small groups, discuss your analysis of the assignments in Exercise 8.1. Come to a consensus about each assignment and present your conclusions to the class. Finally, consider the process by which your group reached consensus: Was the debate more persuasive or exploratory?

8b Making Claims

> **More about**
> Prejudice, 139–40

Just about every text—speeches, advertisements, websites, journal or magazine articles—has a main point or thesis that makes a claim (Figure 8.2). When faced with any kind of text, begin your critical evaluation by determining whether the thesis makes a claim of *fact, opinion,* or *belief,* or whether it simply expresses a *superstition* or *prejudice.*

1. A claim of fact can be verified.

A text whose main claim is a statement of fact is *informative* (or *expository*):

> **More about**
> Informative purpose, 10–11, 31–32

> Susan B. Anthony and Martha Carey Thomas worked for women's voting rights in the United States.
>
> Denmark became a constitutional monarchy in 1849.
>
> The square root of 4 is 2.

A *claim of fact* is not debatable and *cannot* be the central claim in an argument. For this reason, claims of fact are sometimes called *weak claims.*

Superstitions are claims with no basis in fact:

> **More about**
> Warrants, 155

> A wish made on a falling star will come true.
>
> The Chicago Cubs will never win a World Series because of the curse of the Billy Goat.
>
> If you don't forward this e-mail to five friends, you'll suffer ten years of bad luck.

FIGURE 8.2 *Adoriction Lifevest* **by Erik Adigaard** Claims can be advanced visually as well as in writing. This visual makes a claim about the relationship between junk food and obesity. Bring the same critical acumen to assessing the claims made through visuals that you bring to assessing print texts.

> **Quick Reference** — **Devising an Arguable Thesis**
>
> In an argumentative essay, make sure your thesis makes a claim of judgment or value:
>
> **Claim of Judgment (Opinion)**
> The use of e-mail in the workplace reduces personal interactions among colleagues.
>
> **Claim of Value (Personal Belief)**
> Electronic communications ruin interpersonal relationships.
>
> **Claim of Fact**
> E-mail has surpassed the telephone as the most popular way to communicate in the workplace.
>
> Also, consider qualifying your position with words like *often, sometimes, some,* and *most* to avoid committing yourself to a stronger position than you can effectively defend. Do not, however, use these qualifiers as a way of making claims that cannot be supported.

2. A claim of value is based on moral or religious beliefs.

Values are fundamental principles that an individual or a group holds to be inarguably true; they are based on a moral or religious belief system:

> Humans should not eat animals.
>
> All people should be treated fairly under the law.
>
> Stealing is unjustifiable.

People tend to defend their beliefs with great passion, and ***claims of value,*** like the three statements above, are frequently at the heart of argumentative (or persuasive) texts. As you craft your own argument or read the arguments of others, carefully assess the relationship between a claim of value and the assumptions (or warrants) underlying it, whether you are assessing an argument or crafting one.

3. A claim of judgment reflects a reasoned opinion.

The holder of an opinion regards it as the most plausible answer *for now,* based on an evaluation of the available information:

> Graduates with engineering degrees are likely to find high-paying jobs.
>
> The healthiest diet is low in carbohydrates.
>
> The Adam Ezra Group is destined to have a number-one hit song.

Supplied with identical facts, not everyone will hold the same opinion. For this reason, the main claim of an argumentative text is often based on an opinion, or ***claim of judgment.*** Sometimes it makes a ***claim of policy*** (a claim about what we should do or how we should solve a problem). Sometimes it makes a *claim of causation* (a claim about the causes or effects of a problem).

When opinions are not provisional or temporary, they become **prejudices,** usually expressed in stereotypes:

> Athletes are poor students.
>
> Women are too emotional to be president.
>
> Blondes are dumb.

> **More about**
> Counterevidence, 135
> Sweeping generalizations, 156

Prejudice is by its very nature unfair because it ascribes qualities to an individual based on generalities about a group, generalities that are themselves often inaccurate. Whenever you suspect that a prejudice is operating as a claim, examine the evidence—and more importantly, the counterevidence—for the claim. Often a prejudice is based on an overgeneralization, and counterexamples are easy to come by. A claim based on prejudice never makes an effective thesis in an argumentative essay.

When writing an argumentative essay, ask yourself the following question: Do I take an arguable position on which reasonable people could disagree? A claim of fact (or a widely held opinion) is not debatable; reasonable people would not disagree about the number of Electoral College votes needed to win a US presidential election (270) or about the temperature at which water boils at sea level (212 degrees Fahrenheit).

A claim of value (personal conviction or belief) is often difficult to support with objective evidence, as such claims rest on shared assumptions. Writers often find it difficult, if not impossible, to conduct an open-minded exploration of such issues. Writing about claims of value is an important way of exploring and sharing your beliefs, but if your assignment is to craft a persuasive argument, focusing on a claim of value can make your task extremely difficult.

Writing Responsibly — Choosing an Engaging Topic

In addition to making sure your topic is arguable, you should also ask yourself the following questions:

1. Is my topic fresh?
2. Do I have something to add?
3. Is it worth reading (and writing) about?

Thinking critically about saturated topics (such as abortion and gun control) is difficult. Instead of articulating your own reasons, you can easily wind up offering a rehash of other people's.

The topics about which you can write most interestingly are those on which you have a distinctive perspective. Almost any eighteen-year-old can write passionately about the drinking age, for example, but to justify resuscitating tired topics, you must have something original to add. Whatever topic you choose, you will have your best shot at engaging your readers and doing justice to your topic when you write about something you and your readers find compelling.

to TOPIC

EXERCISE 8.2 Assessing claims

Determine whether each of the following topics makes a claim of judgment, a claim of fact, or a claim of value. Explain each of your answers in a sentence or two.

EXAMPLE

It is illegal in this town for grocery stores to use plastic bags.

This is a claim of fact because it can be verified.

1. Grocery stores should charge customers for plastic bags to encourage people to recycle their old bags or to use canvas sacks instead.
2. Expecting customers to provide their own bags is ridiculous.
3. In some areas of the country, subsidizing solar energy is a waste of government money.
4. Solar panels have become much less expensive over the last ten years.
5. It is too difficult to be a vegetarian.

EXERCISE 8.3 Assessing thesis statements

Determine whether the following thesis statements are arguable or not, and explain why.

EXAMPLE

Theodore Roosevelt's sickly and weak physical condition as a child had a critical influence on many of his later personal and political decisions.

This is arguable because we have extensive factual information about Roosevelt's childhood physical condition as well as his later personal and political decisions, and a writer can form a knowledgeable and defensible opinion about the importance of the connection between them.

1. Using animals for drug experimentation is barbaric, cruel, and immoral.
2. Exposure to secondhand smoke significantly increases the risk of lung cancer and heart disease in nonsmokers, as well as several respiratory illnesses in young children.
3. Bilingual education is not effective in areas with large non-English-speaking populations of the United States.
4. Advertisements cause significant harm to people and our society as a whole.
5. Many invasive plants now threatening native species in the United States were deliberately planted by home gardeners.

> **Make It Your Own**
>
> Draft an arguable thesis for one of the topics in Exercise 3.1 or 3.2. If you completed Exercise 3.3, select a different topic.

8c Choosing Evidence Rhetorically

An argument will be only as persuasive as the reasons and evidence, or *grounds,* that support the claim. Support can appeal to your readers' intellect, it can draw on the authority of a figure they respect, or it can appeal to their emotions. Each of these is a *rhetorical appeal.* The ancient Greeks called these appeals logos, ethos, and pathos. Each has a place in responsible writing. As you develop your evidence, you have a responsibility, to your audience and to yourself, to make rhetorical appeals that your audience will find appropriate and persuasive.

1. Appeal to your readers' intellect (logos).

Logos refers to evidence that is rational and consistent; it appeals to readers by engaging their logical powers. Academic writing, such as the excerpt from Rachel Bateman's essay below, relies heavily on reasoned support and concrete evidence:

> Research suggests that violence in the media adversely affects a particularly vulnerable subset of children (usually males): those with Attention Deficit Disorder or information-processing disorders. These children have a hard time understanding the moral context of violence when it is used as entertainment; they may not differentiate enough between an action sequence in a movie and a face-to-face interaction in their daily lives (Gerteis 1993). Television viewing of children with these disorders should be carefully monitored, and role-models—parents, doctors, and teachers—should work with these kids to help them better understand the meaning and consequences of real-life violence.
>
> —Rachel Bateman, University of Kansas,
> "A Closer Look at the Causes of Violence"

A logical appeal can effectively reach a wide range of readers—from sympathetic to hostile—by reinforcing or challenging opinions with reasoned support.

Visuals that provide strong, quantifiable evidence—facts, data, statistics—appeal to the reader's intellect. This evidence may be displayed in a graph, chart, or map or in a before-after photo pair (Figure 8.3). They are effective for convincing a skeptical audience and are appropriate in all types of texts, especially academic texts, where logical reasoning is highly valued.

Logos and Ethos in the United States In academic and business writing in the United States, argument relies primarily on rational appeals. Mentioning highly revered traditional authorities or sources (such as important political figures or religious works) is not considered a sufficient form of support. Instead, evaluate the arguments and supporting evidence of these authorities, and include their work as support only if it directly contributes to your argument.

2. Appeal to your readers by establishing your credibility (ethos).

Establishing a credible *ethos*—good character, sound knowledge, or good reputation—encourages readers to have confidence in what you say. Maxine Paetro, for example, establishes her credentials before she expresses her judgments:

> As the executive recruiter for several major ad agencies, I've eyeballed more than 40,000 cover letters. Some were winners. Some should have been deleted before ever seeing the light of print.
> —Maxine Paetro, "Mission: Employable," *Mademoiselle*

Ethical appeals can be very effective with wavering readers. When people are undecided about an issue, they often want to learn more about it from a person of good character who has considered both sides and provides sound judgments.

FIGURE 8.3 Shrinking area of Arctic permafrost, 1979–2003 These photographs make a logical appeal: They provide factual (verifiable) evidence for global warming.

Writing Responsibly — Establishing Yourself as a Responsible Writer

As a writer, you can establish your ethos not only by offering your credentials, but also by providing readers with sound and sufficient evidence drawn from recognized authorities on the topic, thereby demonstrating your grasp of the material. By adopting a reasonable tone and treating alternative views fairly, you demonstrate that you are a sensible person. By editing your prose carefully, you establish your respect for your readers.

to SELF

3. Appeal to your readers' emotions (pathos).

> **More about**
> Making a presentation, 183–90 (ch. 11)
> Tone, 15–16, 136, 543, 548–50

Using *pathos* to support a claim means stirring the audience's emotions in an effort to elicit sympathy and, thus, agreement. Pathos often relies on examples, stories, or anecdotes to persuade readers. It also uses a tone that stimulates readers' feelings. Visuals that appeal to the readers' emotions or beliefs (Figures 8.4 and 8.5) make an emotional (or *pathetic*) appeal. Use pathos cautiously: Arguments that appeal solely to readers' emotions can be manipulative, even unethical, unless they are backed by strong logical evidence. In addition, many academic disciplines respect only logos and ethos as rhetorical appeals.

Many emotional appeals make use of visuals, especially photographs, because of the immediate impact they can have on the hearts of audience members. Photographs that tug on the readers' emotions are common in advertising but rare in academic or business writing, where judgments are more likely to be made on a logical basis.

EXERCISE 8.4 Assessing logos, ethos, and pathos

Examine the evidence Brent Staples offers in his editorial (pp. 116–17). Classify it as logical, ethical, or emotional. Now classify the evidence in Alea Wratten's critique of the Staples editorial (pp. 128–30) in the same way. Finally, write a paragraph explaining which of these two texts you find more persuasive and why.

Writing Responsibly — Preparing Oral Arguments

When you write formal arguments for college courses, rational and ethical appeals are often more appropriate to your context and genre. But when you deliver a speech, presentation, or other form of oral argument, supplement logical and ethical appeals with vivid emotional appeals that your audience will remember. Be sure to support emotional appeals with logical and ethical appeals: After telling a moving story about an individual, use statistics or an expert's opinion to show how the issue affects others. Without logical evidence and ethical appeals, an emotional appeal is merely manipulative.

to AUDIENCE

Reasoning Matters • Considering Alternative Viewpoints   **8d**   **145**

FIGURE 8.4 Loss of sea ice poses a threat to the polar bear This photograph makes a strong emotional appeal—we fear for the safety and well-being of the polar bear—but it would be out of place in an academic text without statistics that show a clear relationship between dropping polar bear populations and reduced ice coverage caused by global warming.

FIGURE 8.5 Visual pathos Charitable organizations like Save the Children often use pathos to elicit donations.

EXERCISE 8.5 Assessing visual appeals
Write a paragraph in which you argue that illustrations in one of the student projects in this book make a logical, ethical, or emotional appeal.

Student Models
Illustrated projects: 128, 148, 337, 382, 409, 462

8d Considering Alternative Viewpoints

To consider an issue in all its complexity, you must consider alternative viewpoints. When reading or writing an argument, consider ***counterevidence:*** the doubts you or other reasonable people might have or the objections that opponents might raise. Ask friends or colleagues to help you brainstorm alternative positions or search for alternative voices in print and online sources. When assessing an argument, consider whether the writer has taken these alternative viewpoints into consideration and how well the writer responds to critics' concerns.

Responses to alternative viewpoints can take several approaches:

- You can provide counterevidence that refutes the opposition. Consider a supporting paragraph from Alea Wratten's response to the Bret Staples editorial on the ill effects of hip-hop music:

    Refutation
    Counterevidence

    ... While gangsta rap continues to be very popular, hip-hop includes many bands and artists who pen uplifting and socially aware lyrics. Kanye West, for instance, currently among hip-hop's biggest stars, offers a positive, spiritual message in his music, a message of which Staples would likely approve.... And West is not alone: Lauren Hill, Kam, KRS One, Arrested Development, Chuck D, and Public Enemy are just a few of the musicians and bands on my iPod that explore hip-hop's more socially responsible side. These artists show that the strand of hip-hop that Staples accuses of providing a "toxic diet" for listeners is just one of many.
    —Alea Wratten, SUNY–Geneseo, "Reflecting on Brent Staples's Editorial"

    Student Model
    Critique: 127–30

- You can acknowledge alternative views and explain why your position is still the most reasonable *despite* this counterevidence. In the introduction to her essay, Shona Sequiera creates an appealing tension by indicating what both her counterevidence and her evidence will be:

    Concession
    Explanation of why opposing position is less important than the writer's

    Although *Their Eyes Were Watching God* has been widely criticized for painting too romantic a picture of African American life, Hurston's heroine Janie is ultimately able to transcend oppressive stereotypes and successfully come into her own. Her journey towards self-identity and self-knowledge harbors the celebratory ethnic notion that black is not just a color but a culture as well.
    —Shona Sequiera, Connecticut College, "Transcending Stereotypes in Hurston's *Their Eyes Were Watching God*"

- You can revise your thesis to include concessions, exceptions, or qualifiers such as *some* or *usually*:

    Concession

    Qualifier

    While the media may have an effect on some young adults, bursts of violence, like those at Columbine High School, Virginia Tech, and Northern Illinois University, are far more complex and have many more underlying causes than anti–media violence activists usually acknowledge: Mental illness, alienation, availability of weapons, and defects in school security are also components of the motivation to become violent.
    —Rachel Bateman, University of Kansas, "A Closer Look at the Causes of Violence"

EXERCISE 8.6 Assessing the strength of a conclusion

Reread the student essay by Alea Wratten that appears at the end of chapter 7 (pp. 128–30). Does the writer include enough evidence to persuade you of her claim? Does she consider evidence that undermines her claim? How reasonable is her tone? Write a paragraph discussing these issues. Draw specific evidence from the essay to support your claims.

8e Discovering Assumptions and Common Ground

In order to persuade an audience of the truth of a claim, the writer must persuade readers to accept certain common assumptions. For Tom Hackman to convince us that colleges and universities should take the motivations for plagiarism into consideration when devising academic integrity policies, we must first assume that plagiarism is a widespread problem and that it is wrong. If you do not share these basic assumptions (and most of us do), then you would not be convinced that rethinking plagiarism policies is worth the time and trouble. When Martin Luther King, Jr., said, "The nations of Asia and Africa are moving with jet-like speed toward gaining political independence, but we still creep at horse-and-buggy pace toward gaining a cup of coffee at a lunch counter," he assumed that American progress should not lag behind that of Africa and Asia. Is this assumption correct? That depends upon whether you share it. Dr. King knew that most people in his audience—US citizens—would. An African or Asian audience, on the other hand, might be less likely to share this assumption about American progress.

As you read and write arguments, consider carefully the assumptions, or *warrants,* that underlie the claims being made: On what common ground must both reader and writer stand before they can discuss a topic productively? What must both writer and audience agree is true without argument or evidence?

EXERCISE 8.7 Identifying main claim and evidence

Read (or reread) the essay "An Inconvenient Truth" (pp. 69–71), identify the main claim, and assess the evidence provided in support of this claim.

Student Model Exploratory Argument

In the following exploratory argument, Tom Hackman, a student at Syracuse University, first analyzes plagiarism and then uses his analysis as the basis of a claim that universities should take these differences into consideration when devising their plagiarism policies.

Student Models
Persuasive arguments, 127, 337, 443, 462

Hackman 1

Tom Hackman

Professor Howard

Writing 109

28 September 2012

Why Students Cheat: The Complexities and Oversimplifications of Plagiarism

> Introduction: Explains why topic matters

The system of American higher education is founded on principles of honesty and academic integrity. For this reason, nearly all those invested in this system—students, instructors, and administrators—recognize that plagiarism cannot be tolerated. They also agree that a lot of plagiarism is occurring. A survey published

> Background: Describes extent and severity of plagiarism

in *Who's Who among American High School Students* (reported by Newberger) indicated that 15% of top-ranked high schoolers plagiarize. Practices among higher education students are not much better. According to research by Donald L. McCabe, a professor at Rutgers University who has done extensive work on cheating, 38% of college students admitted to committing forms of plagiarism in the previous year (Rimer 7). A recent study by Hard, Conway, and Moran showed that plagiarism was common among the 421 students who participated in their research. Fig. 1 illustrates the various forms this plagiarism took.

There is a commonly held myth about how most plagiarism occurs. Late at night, a student sits staring at a computer screen. A paper is due the following morning, and research needs to be done, notes need to be taken, and, in the end, an essay needs to be written and edited. Instead of completing this immense task, though, the student succumbs to the temptations of plagiarism—"cutting and pasting" from sources, downloading an essay from the Internet, or simply buying a paper from

> Counter-evidence: Describes alternative perspectives

148

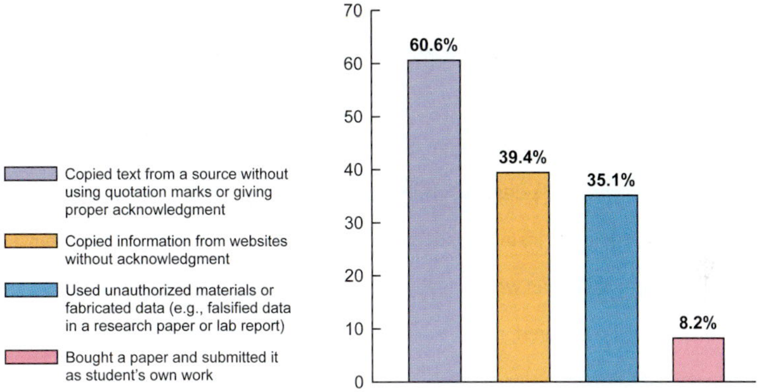

Hackman 2

Fig. 1. Common types of plagiarism and the percentage of students who commit them. (Data and categories from Hard, Conway, and Moran 1069)

another student. In this myth, students are too apathetic and slothful to complete their assignments on their own; instead, they cheat.

<mark>Undeniably, some plagiarism occurs because students find it easier than simply doing the work required.</mark> The mind of a plagiarist, however, cannot be fit so easily into a single stereotype. The argument that laziness is the main cause of plagiarism is at best incomplete, and moreover it seems fed by unfair stereotypes of modern students as bored by academic rigor, more interested in video games or their Facebook page than the hard work of learning.

    In fact, some plagiarism grows from the opposite of these characteristics. High-achieving students, for example, fear what a bad grade will do to their

> Concession

> Evidence: Expert opinions, examples

Hackman 3

otherwise stellar GPA. Such students treat the attainment of impressive marks as a necessity and will betray the very academic system they revere in order to sustain their average.

Other students plagiarize more from lack of interest in a particular course than general idleness. Students who view writing papers as hoops they must jump through to graduate, for instance, are more likely simply to download a paper from an online "paper mill" than write one themselves. For them, a college writing class is something to be endured, rather than an opportunity for learning. Russell Hunt, a professor at St. Thomas University in Canada, explains this attitude in point 2 of his article:

> If I wanted to learn how to play the guitar, or improve my golf swing, or write HTML, "cheating" would be the last thing that would ever occur to me. It would be utterly irrelevant to the situation. On the other hand, if I wanted a certificate saying that I could pick a jig, play a round in under 80, or produce a slick webpage (and never actually expected to perform the activity in question), I might well consider cheating. . . .

Students draw a distinction between their interests and their academic assignments. They rationalize their plagiarism as a way to escape an "unfair" academic obligation. Websites such as essaytown.com, which will write a paper to order, cater to students like these, who consider at least some aspects of academia essentially useless.

Many other instances of plagiarism are committed by students with honest intentions but who are ignorant of citation methods. Michael Gunn, a British student,

[Margin note: Quotes authority to support claim; notes qualifications of authority]

[Margin note: Provides example that illustrates claim]

copied quotations from Internet sources in numerous papers over several years and was shocked to learn that this qualified as plagiarism (Baty). Even students who recognize the importance of citation may not know how to cite their sources correctly. A student who omits the source of a paraphrase in a paper would probably be surprised to learn that he or she is often considered as guilty of plagiarism as the student who downloads an essay.

The Internet has compounded confusion with regard to citation. The Internet is a place of free exchange where information moves from computer to computer with the click of a mouse. In this environment, ownership and citation become hazy. As John Leland, a reporter for the New York Times, writes, "Culture's heat now lies with the ability to cut, paste, clip, sample, quote, recycle, customize, and re-circulate." Many students find it is easy and "natural" to take text from an online source—for instance, by highlighting the text, copying it, and pasting it into a word processing document. Because it can be difficult to keep track of everything they have read, the chances of accidental plagiarism (forgetting to cite the copied text) increase. So, too, does the likelihood of "patchwriting," substituting synonyms or moving sentences around, but not fully putting the borrowed text into the writer's own words (Howard 233). Finally, some students will also be tempted to commit intentional plagiarism, choosing to leave a block of copied text uncited.

Quotes authority to corroborate claim; notes qualifications of authority

Paraphrases authority to corroborate claim

To add to the complexity of the plagiarism issue, societal norms play a significant role in students' and even scholars' views about fair use of another's work. Unlike in the West, Chinese culture largely accepts appropriating others' ideas and holds that private property is less important than the needs of the people. Professors

Quotes and summarizes source to support claim

copy from other professors, and students follow their lead. The "culture of copying" is prevalent throughout Chinese academia (Jiang A45).

Yet despite the many varieties and causes of plagiarism, college instructors and administrators too often treat the issue simply as a crime committed by the laziest of pupils. Birchard quotes a dean of Canada's Simon Fraser University, who voices a typical view: "We have a zero tolerance policy for cheating. . . . And we hope the severity of the penalties sends a strong message to other students who might be tempted to cheat or cut academic corners." Granted, there is ultimately no excuse for plagiarism, and any honest student should share the goal of eliminating it from academic life. Yet a less simplistic response to plagiarism would ultimately be more productive than the widespread law-and-order mentality that now exists.

Counterevidence

Concession and rebuttal

Conclusion: Restates counterevidence and rebuttal, states thesis

The motivations behind plagiarism, and the situations that give rise to it, are varied. Importantly, much plagiarism occurs without the guilty student understanding that what he or she is doing represents academic dishonesty. Effectively combating plagiarism, in all its forms, requires a fuller understanding of how and why students break the rules. Academic policy writers must realize that plagiarism is not a single offense but a general term for a lack of citation, and plagiarism must be recognized as dynamic behavior, with many motivations, including social expectations, desires for high GPAs, disregard for the value of learning or intellectual property, and unawareness of citation standards. A regular user of a paper mill website has far different attitudes than a nonciting Chinese exchange student (or professor). The various categories of plagiarism threaten academia to varying extents and therefore demand a flexible response based upon the specifics of each incident. Only through this approach will plagiarism, in all its forms, be reduced.

Returns to thesis

Works Cited

Baty, Phil. "Plagiarist Student to Sue University." *Times Education Supplement* [London] 28 May 2004: n. pag. *TimesOnline.* Web. 15 Sept. 2009.

Birchard, Karen. "Canada's Simon Fraser U. Suspends 44 Students in Plagiarism Scandal." *Chronicle of Higher Education* 53.8 (2004): 46. *EbscoHost.* Web. 21 Sept. 2009.

Hard, Stephen F., James M. Conway, and Antonia C. Moran. "Faculty and College Student Beliefs about the Frequency of Student Academic Misconduct." *Journal of Higher Education* 77.6 (2006): 1058–80. Print.

Howard, Rebecca Moore. "A Plagiarism *Pentimento.*" *Journal of Teaching Writing* 11.3 (1993): 233–46. Print.

Hunt, Russell. "Four Reasons to Be Happy about Internet Plagiarism." *Teaching Perspectives.* Dec. 2002. St. Thomas University, Canada. Web. 15 Sept. 2005.

Jiang, Xueqin. "Chinese Academics Consider a 'Culture of Copying.'" *Chronicle of Higher Education* 48.36 (2002): A45–46. *EbscoHost.* Web. 21 Sept. 2009.

Leland, John. "Beyond File Sharing: A Nation of Copiers." *New York Times* 14 Sept. 2003, sec. 9:1. *LexisNexis.* Web. 15 Sept. 2009.

Newberger, Eli H. "Why Do Students Cheat?" *School for Champions.* School for Champions, 6 Dec. 2003. Web. 16 Sept. 2009.

Rimer, Sara. "A Campus Fad That's Being Copied: Internet Plagiarism Seems on the Rise." *New York Times* 3 Sept. 2003: 7. *LexisNexis.* Web. 15 Sept. 2009.

8f Organizing Arguments: Classical, Rogerian, and Toulmin Models

>*More about*
Organizing, 33–35
Explaining and supporting your ideas, 40–41
Purpose, 10–11
Audience, 12–15

As with any writing, an argument is most effective when it is carefully organized. The following are three widely used models for organizing arguments. Each one serves certain purposes of argument.

Before choosing a structure, consider which of these models is best suited to your purpose and audience.

1. The classical model

The *classical model* of argumentation derives from the work of ancient Greek and Roman orators. It is well suited to persuasive arguments and is composed of five parts, usually presented in this order:

1. **Introduction.** Acquaint readers with your topic, give them a sense of why it is important and why you are qualified to address it, suggest your paper's purpose, and state the essay's main claim (or thesis) in one or two sentences.
2. **Background.** Provide basic information to help your audience understand and appreciate your position. You might include a brief review of major sources on the subject or offer a chronology of relevant events.
3. **Reasons and evidence.** Explain to readers why you believe what you do, and offer logical, well-chosen examples and data as support. Appeal to readers through their intellect, their respect for you and for your sources, and their emotions (if emotional appeals can be supported logically). This is the heart of your essay, and it should be the longest section, constituting at least 50 percent of the whole.
4. **Counterevidence.** Describe and explain alternative viewpoints, treating opponents fairly.
5. **Conclusion.** Leave readers with a strong sense of why they should agree with you by suggesting solutions, calling for action, or re-emphasizing the value of your position. If your essay's argument is complex, it may also be helpful to summarize it briefly here.

>*More about*
Deduction, 135–37

The classical argument uses deductive reasoning and is well suited to persuasive arguments.

2. The Rogerian model

The purpose of *Rogerian* argument is to build common ground on complex issues, not to "win" an argument. It was developed by Carl Rogers, a twentieth-century psychologist, who hoped this method would make discussion more productive. The Rogerian model is composed of the same five parts as the classical model, but in a different order:

1. **Introduction**
2. **Background**
3. **Counterevidence**
4. **Reasons and evidence**
5. **Conclusion**

In a Rogerian argument, the counterevidence appears before the evidence because the presentation of counterevidence helps establish the complexity of the issue. Instead of refuting the counterevidence, the writer explores its legitimacy first and then explains why he or she nevertheless believes the thesis. Tom Hackman's essay earlier in this chapter follows the Rogerian model.

3. The Toulmin model

The model for arguments developed by philosopher Stephen *Toulmin* includes five parts, but the parts are somewhat different from those of classical and Rogerian argument:

1. **Claim:** your thesis, the central argument
2. **Grounds:** the reasons you believe the claim and evidence supporting your claim
3. **Warrants:** any assumptions that explain how the grounds support the claim
4. **Backing:** supporting evidence for the warrants; they require their own supporting evidence because they are themselves claims
5. **Rebuttal:** counterevidence and your response

Like classical argument, the Toulmin model is persuasive. Like classical argument, Toulmin presents the main claim and evidence before counterevidence. One distinctive feature of Toulmin argument is that it places counterevidence last, and it also refutes the counterevidence, leaving less doubt that the main claim is the best perspective. It also recognizes that assumptions underlie all claims and brings those assumptions to the surface, making the search for common ground easier (or at least clarifying the terms of the discussion).

> **More about**
> Revising, 82–92
> Claims of value, judgment, 139–40
> Reasons and evidence, 40–41
> Appeals, 142–45
> Counterevidence, 135, 145–46
> Persuading and exploring, 134–37

8g Avoiding Logical Fallacies

When assessing an argument that seems persuasive, keep an eye out for logical *fallacies.* Because inductive arguments depend on examples and the conclusions you draw from them, fallacies like the following can creep in:

- **Hasty generalization (jumping to conclusions).** *Look at her, running that stop sign! She's a terrible driver!*

    A hasty generalization occurs when a general conclusion is based on insufficient evidence: Since even the best drivers occasionally make mistakes, this one piece of evidence is not enough to incriminate this driver.

- **Sweeping generalization.** *Women are terrible drivers! My girlfriend ran a stop sign the other day and almost got us both killed!*

    Sweeping generalizations apply a claim to *all* cases when it actually applies to only a few or maybe to none. Stereotypes are often based on a sweeping generalization. (Whenever words like *all, every,* and *none* are used in an argument, take a closer look; these often signal that a sweeping generalization is coming.)

- **False analogy.** *Our candidate's victories over his enemies during the war will ensure his victory over his political opponents in the election.*

    A false analogy draws a connection between two items or events that have few or no relevant common characteristics. This false analogy

Writing Responsibly — Visual Claims and Visual Fallacies

In academic writing, you might use a visual to *support* a claim, but you should be cautious about using a visual to *make* a claim. Visual claims are effective sales tools (they are common in advertisements), but they are likely to commit a visual fallacy, such as *overgeneralization*—drawing a conclusion based on too little evidence. (Is it reasonable to assume that *all* women using a certain brand of soap will look like a movie star simply because one celebrity claims to use the product?) This ad may also commit the fallacy of false authority. (Is the actress an authority on whose expertise we can rely when buying soap?)

to TOPIC

does not explain how the two things resemble each other: Why would a military victory guarantee a political victory? Is the political process really like a military campaign? Are opposition candidates really like enemy soldiers?

- **Stacking the deck (special pleading).** *Got dandruff? Our shampoo contains MarvEll, guaranteed to end your dandruff problems!*

  An argument that stacks the deck focuses only on supporting evidence and ignores counterevidence that casts reasonable doubt upon it. In this case, the dandruff-killing properties of the shampoo may also make your hair brittle, but the ad would not mention that fact.

- **False authority.** *My mother says that ice cream is more nourishing than a bowl of oatmeal.*

  Unless your mother is a nutritionist, her word alone is insufficient. An argument that appeals to a false authority draws evidence from someone who is *not* an expert on the topic.

- **Bandwagon appeal.** *Mom and Dad, you have to buy me an SUV; all my friends have one!*

  The bandwagon appeal implies that the majority opinion is the right opinion and invites you to climb aboard. Some bandwagon appeals may be based on poll results, lending them the impression of reliability. But poll results merely report what the majority of respondents *believe* to be true. Many Americans in 1860 might have believed that holding other people in slavery was perfectly acceptable, which goes to show that the majority can be wrong.

The power of deductive arguments depends on the validity of the conclusion or the appeal of the premises, so watch out for arguments based on dubious logic or hidden or missing premises:

- **Begging the question (circular reasoning).** *You must believe me because I never lie.*

  An argument that begs the question uses the conclusion (in a disguised form) as one of the premises in the argument. In this example, the second half of the sentence repeats the conclusion rather than offering a premise from which it can be derived.

- **Non sequitur (irrelevant argument).** *You can solve a lot of problems with money, so the rich must be much happier than we are.*

A non sequitur (which means "it does not follow" in Latin) draws a conclusion from a premise that does not follow logically. The conclusion in the statement above equates money with happiness, but anyone with money will tell you that the two do not go hand in hand.

- ***Post hoc, ergo propter hoc* (false cause).** *This ring must be lucky: I wore it for the first time today, and I pitched a perfect game.*

  Post hoc, ergo propter hoc means "after this, therefore, because of this" in Latin. In a *post hoc* fallacy, the speaker wrongly assumes that the first event caused the second: Just because the player wore a ring while pitching a perfect game does not mean that the ring is "lucky"; maybe he was just having a good day or the other team's hitters were weak.

- **Either-or fallacy (false dilemma).** *You're either for us or against us!*

  The either-or fallacy allows, misleadingly, for only two choices or sides in an argument, never allowing for other options, never acknowledging compromise or complexity. (A visual false dilemma occurs in the image shown in Figure 8.6.)

- **Red herring.** *Reporter: "Mayor, what do you have to say about the dangerous decay of the city's flood walls?" Mayor: "I'm proud of the accomplishments in my administration: We have a much larger, better-equipped police force than when I took office."*

  According to the *Oxford English Dictionary*, a red herring is a smoked fish with a distinctive odor used to train dogs to follow a scent. As early as 1884, it was used to mean an irrelevance used to distract attention from the real issue. In the example above, the mayor is trying to dodge a difficult question by changing the subject.

FIGURE 8.6 Either-or fallacy on a website This image from an anti–gun control website suggests that there are only two ways to protect yourself. A third option might be to call the police. (Source: http://bbvm.wordpress.com/2009/03/12/two-ways-to-shield-yourself-from-a-violent-attack-see-women-of-caliber/)

Reasoning Matters • Avoiding Logical Fallacies   **8g**   159

> ## Self Assessment
>
> As you revise your argument, consider the following features. If your answer to any of these questions is no, make the necessary revisions.
>
> ☐ **Claim.** Do you take an arguable position based on an opinion or belief on which reasonable people could disagree? Have you modified it to avoid making a stronger claim than you can effectively support? Does your introduction show why your topic is important?
>
> ☐ **Evidence.** Do you supply evidence in support of your claim? Do you use rational, ethical, or emotional appeals that are appropriate to your topic, purpose, and audience? Do you use visuals, where appropriate, to make or support claims?
>
> ☐ **Counterevidence.** Have you acknowledged alternative interpretations of your evidence, as well as evidence that undermines your claims? Have you explained why your position is the most reasonable despite these objections?
>
> ☐ **Organization.** Have you followed an appropriate model of argument, such as a classical, Rogerian, or Toulmin model? Is the organizational structure appropriate to your overall aim—persuasion or exploration?

- **Ad hominem (personal attack).** *His views on how to resolve the parking problem on campus are ridiculous! What would you expect from a member of a frat that has its own parking lot?*

  An ad hominem (personal) attack attempts to undermine an opposing viewpoint by criticizing the motives or character of the individual offering the alternative view. When writers use ad hominem attacks, they focus their critiques on aspects of a person's character without connecting character flaws to the issues in question.

- **Guilt by association.** *Tiffany is the most treacherous person I ever met. If Makoto is Tiffany's friend, he can't be trusted.*

  Guilt by association dismisses or condemns people because of the relationships they have. Just because Tiffany is untrustworthy (if indeed she is) does not mean that everyone who befriends her is also untrustworthy.

- **Slippery slope.** *If we exempt one person from the physical education requirement, everybody will want an exemption.*

  The slippery slope fallacy implies that one event will initiate an unstoppable sequence of events. But as any skier can tell you, a slippery slope does not always mean that you will slide uncontrollably to the bottom of the hill. It is not impossible to exempt some students (those with a good excuse) while requiring the rest to take gym.

Reasoning Matters • Analyzing and Crafting Arguments

> **EXERCISE 8.8 Locating logical fallacies in political websites**
>
> Locate three logical fallacies in the websites of political figures—the president, your city's mayor, a senator from your home state, a candidate running for an upcoming election. (Go beyond the home page, deeper into the site, at least twice.) In a paragraph, name the fallacy and explain how the text (or visual) commits it.

Work Together

Exchange your revised project with a fellow student. Read each other's work carefully. Does it commit any of the fallacies listed on pages 156–59? If so, mark them and explain what makes them fallacies. If the project is fallacy-free, explain why its claims are logical.

Make It Your Own

Write a paragraph reflecting on the material in this chapter and your responses. What did you learn about effective argumentation and logic by reading and evaluating other people's writing? What surprised you? Have you noticed the use of ethos, logos, or pathos in your daily life, or caught any logical fallacies? If so, what effect did these things have on the argument being made? Has your opinion of argument changed as a result of your increased understanding of it? End with a checklist of five specific issues to check as you revise future papers.

Part Three

Media Matters

Designing, Writing, and Presenting

9 Designing Printed and Electronic Documents   162
10 Writing for Multiple Media   171
11 Presenting with Multiple Media   183

9 Designing Printed and Electronic Documents

IN THIS CHAPTER

a. Understanding design principles, 162

b. Planning your design project, 163

c. Applying design principles, 164

The early Peruvians wove this design to represent and honor their sun god. They used proximity to connect the head and tail to the figure's torso. They used the alignment of short yellow and red lines and the repetition of shapes (straight lines at right and left, red and yellow emblems above and below) to create the background against which the figure stands out. They used contrast of white outline against brown background to define the figure, and they inserted a rectangle in the center of the figure, which contrasts with the rest because it is filled in by color. This contrasting element attracts the eye and draws attention to the figure's core. According to renowned designer Robin Williams, these four principles—proximity, alignment, repetition, and contrast—are the pillars on which effective design rests.

9a Understanding the Four Principles of Design

Designer Robin Williams explains how the four principles work:

- **Proximity** (or nearness) suggests that content is related.
- **Alignment,** arrangement in a straight line (vertical, horizontal, or diagonal), creates connections among parts and ideas.
- **Repetition** of a design element lends unity (oneness).
- **Contrast** among design elements calls attention through difference.

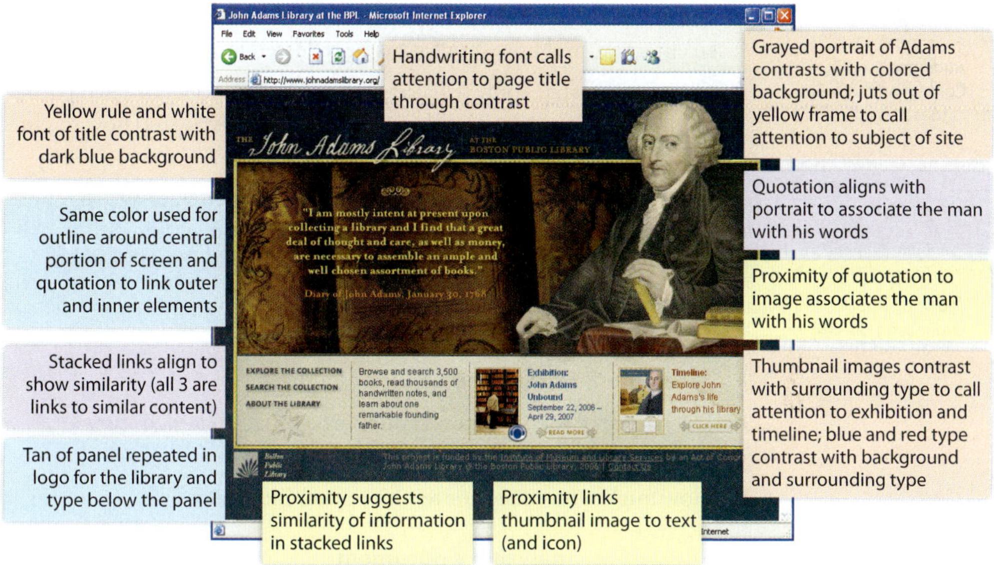

Media Matters • Planning Your Design Project   **9b**   163

[Annotated screenshot of a web page from the Boston Public Library's John Adams Library website, with the following callouts:]

- Yellow rule and white font of title contrast with dark blue background
- Same color used for outline around central portion of screen and quotation to link outer and inner elements
- Tan of panel repeated in logo for the library and type below the panel
- Handwriting font calls attention to page title through contrast
- Proximity suggests similarity of information in stacked links
- Proximity links thumbnail image to text (and icon)
- Grayed portrait of Adams contrasts with colored background; juts out of yellow frame to call attention to subject of site
- Quotation aligns with portrait to associate the man with his words
- Proximity of quotation to image associates the man with his words
- Stacked links align to show similarity (all 3 are links to similar content)
- Thumbnail images contrast with surrounding type to call attention to exhibition and timeline; blue and red type contrast with background and surrounding type

FIGURE 9.1 A web page from the Boston Public Library's website

In an effective design, such as that in the web page in Figure 9.1, these four principles work together to direct readers to the most important information and to highlight relationships among the elements on the page or screen.

> **EXERCISE 9.1 Analyzing a design**
> Find a web page, brochure, or advertisement (in print or online) that you think makes good use of words and graphics, and in two or three paragraphs explain how it uses the four principles of design.

9b Planning Your Design Project

To figure out how best to apply the four principles of design to your project, begin with a careful consideration of your writing situation:

- **Topic.** What is your topic, and how can you reflect that topic through your design?
- **Audience.** Who will your audience be, what kind of expectations do they bring with them, and what kind of relationship do you have (or want to have) with them?

> **More about**
> Purpose, 9–11
> Audience, 12–15
> Context and genre, 16–17

- **Purpose.** Is your purpose to inform, to persuade, to express yourself, or to entertain, and how should this be reflected in your design?
- **Context.** In what context (academic, business, public) or setting (over the Internet, in person) will your project be received, and how might this affect its design?
- **Genre.** What type of project (résumé, business letter, essay, lab report) will best fulfill your purpose, and what design conventions are associated with this genre?

> **More about**
> Organizing, 33–38

Next determine how the pieces of information you want to convey relate to one another:

- What information is most and least important?
- Does some of the information support a broader claim or provide evidence for this claim?
- How might you convey or reinforce your ideas visually?

EXERCISE 9.2 Analyzing a document

Return to the web page, brochure, or advertisement that you used in Exercise 9.1. Analyze its purpose, audience, context, and genre. What pieces of information (if any) did the designer use to organize the document?

Make It **Your Own**

For an organization you are involved with or endorse, plan a promotional web page, brochure, or advertisement to solicit members or advertise an event. How will the purpose of your document affect its design? What audience will you appeal to? What information will they need, or what information will persuade them to join or attend an event?

9c Applying the Principles of Design

Once you have organized your project, you are ready to begin designing it.

1. Create an overall impression.

Start by considering the overall impression you want to give the reader: Should the design be conservative or trendy, serious or playful? Let your decision about the style of your project guide you in your choice of colors, fonts, and visuals.

> **More about**
> Colors, 167–68
> Fonts, 165–66
> Visuals, 74–81, 169–70
> White space, 166

2. Plan the layout.

Next consider the overall *layout,* the visual arrangement of text and images. An effective layout should use proximity, alignment, repetition, and contrast to make the relationships among the elements clear. Keep your layout simple, and use it to direct the reader's eye to the most important pieces of information.

3. Format the document.

Once you have sketched your layout, you are ready to create a cohesive and attractive design by using the following elements:

Fonts Word processors give writers a wide range of fonts (or typefaces) to choose from. Serif fonts (fonts with a little tail on the ends of letters, like Cambria and Times New Roman) are easier to read when printed on paper, while sans serif fonts (such as Arial and Calibri) are easier to read on screen and are preferred for web publishing.

In addition to selecting the font family, you can set your font in a variety of styles, including **boldface,** *italics,* underlining, or color. Use color or **boldface** for emphasis and contrast, but do so consistently and sparingly: The more they are used, the less attention they will call to themselves. Since *italics* and underlining often have a specific meaning, avoid using them except when required.

> **More about**
> Using italics and underlining, 814–19

When choosing a font size, make sure it will be easy to read (especially if you are using it for the body of your project). Generally, a 10- or 12-point type will be legible to most readers, but print out a page of text to check the font size: 10-point type in one font may look larger than 12-point in another.

The font you choose can also add contrast, or it can group items through repetition: If most of your text is in a serif font, a sans serif font (or the same font in bold or a different color) can call attention to a heading. Use the same style, size, color, and type of font for all the headings at the same level and for all text of the same type.

Keep in mind, too, that the fonts you use (especially in headings) can reinforce the overall impression you are trying to create. A typeface such as 𝔒𝔩𝔡 𝔈𝔫𝔤𝔩𝔦𝔰𝔥, for

Writing Responsibly

Selecting Fonts with Readers in Mind

Not all readers have perfect vision. If your audience includes members over forty (or under twelve), use a font size of at least 12 points to make the reading experience easier and more pleasant. If your audience includes visually impaired people, increase your font size even more.

to AUDIENCE

> **More about**
> Using information responsibly, 246–63 (ch. 15)

Writing Responsibly: Establishing a Consistent Font

When you copy material from a source, you have the responsibility of citing the source, indicating that it is a direct quotation, and providing full information about the source in a bibliography. When you cut and paste your direct copy from an electronic source, you also have the responsibility of converting its font to the one you are using for your main text. Otherwise, when the font suddenly shifts from black to blue, or from Times to Arial, the audience may be distracted from your message.

to OTHER WRITERS

> **More about**
> Page layout:
> MLA style, 332–36 (ch. 18)
> APA style, 277–81 (ch. 19)
> *Chicago* style, 407–08 (ch. 20)
> CSE style, 428–29 (ch. 21)

example, might be appropriate in a poster announcing the first meeting of the Shakespeare Society. Be careful: For a text-heavy document, legibility is more important than drama. More than a few words in an ornate font like *Edwardian Script* or **Haettenschweiler** will be hard to read. Setting lengthy passages on a website in a serif font may also make the text difficult to read on screen, though such fonts can be used effectively for headings online.

NOTE For college writing, check the style guide for your discipline to make sure these design decisions will be acceptable.

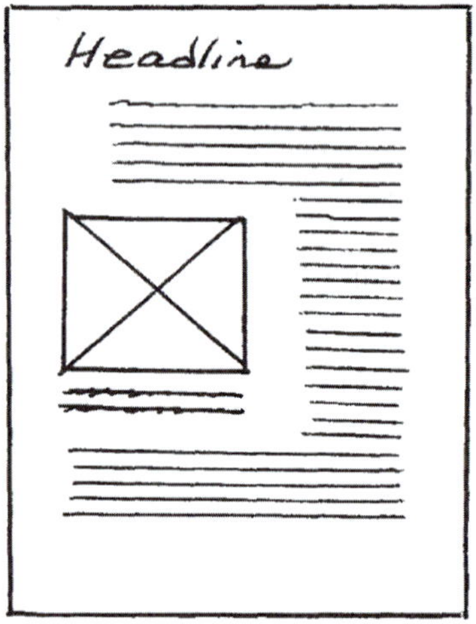

White space The portion of a page or screen with no text or images, the *white space,* does not literally have to be white (Figure 9.2). The margins at top, bottom, left, and right of a page provide white space, as does the extra space before a paragraph or around a heading. Extra white space above or around text or a visual groups elements into a section. Using the same amount of white space around headings at the same level or visuals of the same type lends consistency to your layout. Adding extra white space lends emphasis through contrast. Ample white space makes a page inviting and easy to read; without it, a page looks crowded, and the eye has difficulty knowing where to focus (Figure 9.3).

FIGURE 9.2 Using white space to group elements Adding white space above a heading or around a figure and its caption groups the information into a unit for readers.

Lists Another strategy for grouping related items (and for adding white space) is to use lists (see Figure 9.3). Keep lists succinct to allow readers to skim them for information. They can be particularly effective in web pages to summarize and

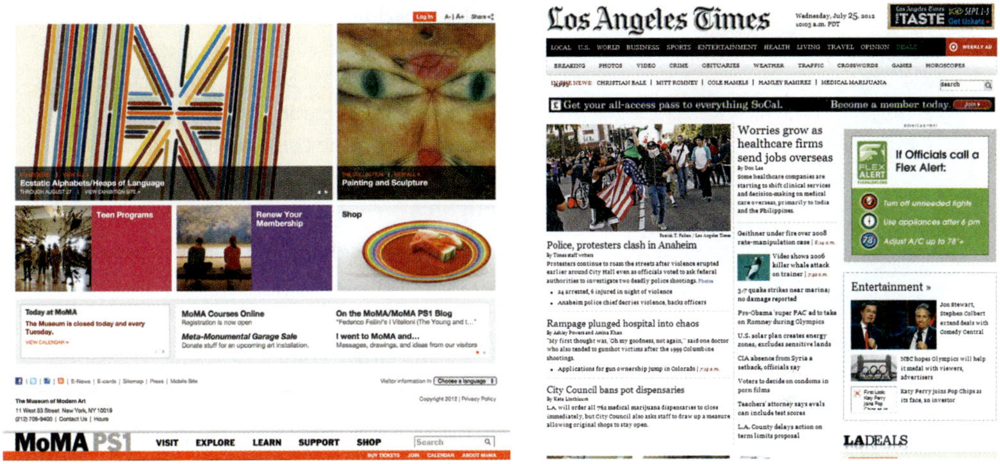

FIGURE 9.3 Formatting a web page The web pages from the Museum of Modern Art in New York (*left*) and the *Los Angeles Times* (*right*) use font size, style, color, and white space to highlight information and make the page attractive. A news page is by necessity crowded with information, so it also uses lists, boxes, and bullets to make the page easier to navigate.

break up blocks of text on the screen. When creating lists, regardless of your medium, remember to do the following:

- Keep list items parallel (use all phrases or all sentences, for example).
- Keep the number of items in a list small (four to six).
- Begin list items with a dot, diamond, or square, and align all items at left.
- Use numbered lists to indicate steps in a process and bulleted lists to group related information.

While lists are common in business writing (as in résumés and PowerPoint presentations), they are used sparingly in most academic writing.

Color Color, through contrast, calls the reader's attention to what is important in the text: Headings; bullets or numbers in lists; boxes, charts and graphs; or illustrations often appear in color so that readers will notice them. Use color judiciously:

- Use a limited color palette. Too many colors in close proximity will create a hodgepodge effect.

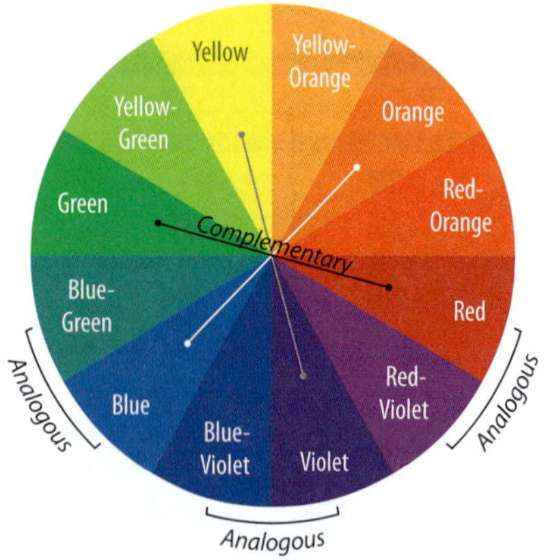

FIGURE 9.4 **The color wheel** Colors opposite each other on the color wheel are complementary; colors adjacent to each other are analogous.

- Use a pleasing color palette. Analogous colors, those adjacent to each other on a color wheel (Figure 9.4), create a softer, more harmonious look. Complementary colors, those opposite each other on the color wheel, contrast with each other, each making the other color look brighter.

- Use readable color combinations. Make sure colors contrast enough with their background that they are legible.

- Use appropriate colors. Consider the associations colors and combinations of colors carry: pastel pinks and blues for new babies, bright yellow and black for warnings, green for nature.

- Use colors consistently. The repetition of colors will group items of the same type.

Headings Writers often use headings and subheadings to group text and guide readers. They can help readers comprehend a text's structure at a glance. The principles of repetition and contrast are crucial with headings:

> **More about**
> Parallelism, 518–26 (ch. 28)

- Set all headings of the same level in the same font, style, and color, and align them in the same way on the page or screen:

   First-level heading

   Second-level heading

   Third-level heading

- Use the same grammatical structure for all headings of the same level. For example, use all *-ing* phrases (*Containing the Economic Downturn,*

Writing Responsibly — Designing for Those with Impaired Color Vision

Most people with a color-vision impairment are unable to distinguish between red and green: Both colors appear gray. A smaller number are unable to distinguish between blue and yellow. To be sure that those with a color-vision impairment can obtain important information, avoid the red/green or blue/yellow color combination, or use labels or underlining in addition to color.

to AUDIENCE

Bailing Out Wall Street) or all *noun phrases* (*Economic Downturn Ahead, Wall Street Bailout*).

- Distinguish among heading levels by setting all headings of the same level in a specific font, style, or color or by placing them differently on the page (flush left, centered).

> **More about**
> Visual arguments, 134–60 (ch. 8)
> Visuals in college writing assignments, 73–74

4. Add visuals.

Visuals are the first thing readers notice when they look at your text. For this reason, they are integral to documents geared toward the general public and must thus catch the eye of potential readers. Visuals are appropriate in some academic genres—in economics, for example, graphs are used frequently—but they are not customary in all academic disciplines. Ideally, any visuals you include in a document should be visually compelling. This does not mean that you should choose images just because they will capture the reader's attention. To be effective, images must be compelling *and* must expand your readers' understanding of your text. They must also be appropriate to your writing situation.

Place visuals on a page as soon as possible after the text discussion that refers to them. In academic and business writing, include a reference to the figure or table in your text, numbered in order of appearance (such as *figure 1* or *table 2*). Provide a caption that includes this number and, wherever possible,

> **More about**
> Incorporating visuals, 306–07, 334–36 (MLA), 379–90 (APA)
> Choosing the right type of visual, 74–77
> Revising visuals, 78–81
> Academic writing, 432–75
> Business writing, 476–94

Quick Reference: Including Visuals (Images and Graphics)

	Images	**Graphics**
Type	Photographs, drawings and sketches, screenshots, film stills.	Tables, flowcharts, pie charts, line and bar graphs, diagrams, timelines, maps.
Purpose	Depict or explain an event, object, or process, or illustrate a concept.	Convey complex information in an easily readable form.
Audience	Use images to draw readers in.	Use graphics to help readers understand complex data, trends, processes.
Context and Genre	In academic and business contexts and genres, use images to provide evidence, to help readers grasp a point, or to provide an example. In personal and public writing, use images for these purposes, as well as to capture interest, make an argument, or reinforce a point.	In every context and genre, use graphics to help readers understand complex data quickly.

adds information that is not included in the text. The overall effect is usually best if images are placed at the top or bottom of the page and are either centered or placed flush with the left or right margin.

> **EXERCISE 9.3 Analyzing layout**
> Return once again to the design you analyzed in Exercises 9.1 and 9.2. In one or two paragraphs, analyze its layout. Consider its overall impression (trendy or conservative, playful or serious); its use of white space, lists, color, and headings to create proximity, alignment, repetition, and contrast; its use of fonts and visuals, and how the visuals function (do they reinforce product identity, provide an example, offer additional information, further the argument, demonstrate a process?). Has your assessment of the document's purpose, audience, context, and genre changed as you studied it more closely?

Make It **Your Own**

Using the plan you developed for the Make It Your Own exercise on page 164, sketch the web page, brochure, or advertisement you planned. Consider the overall impression that would be most appropriate given your writing situation.

Work **Together**

In groups of three or four, critique the documents you produced in the Make It Your Own exercise above. How well has each designer used proximity, alignment, repetition, and contrast? How well does each design express the purpose of the group or event? How well does it appeal to the target audience?

10 Writing for Multiple Media

IN THIS CHAPTER

a. Writing and answering e-mail, 172

b. Creating websites and web pages, 176

c. Writing in interactive media, 181

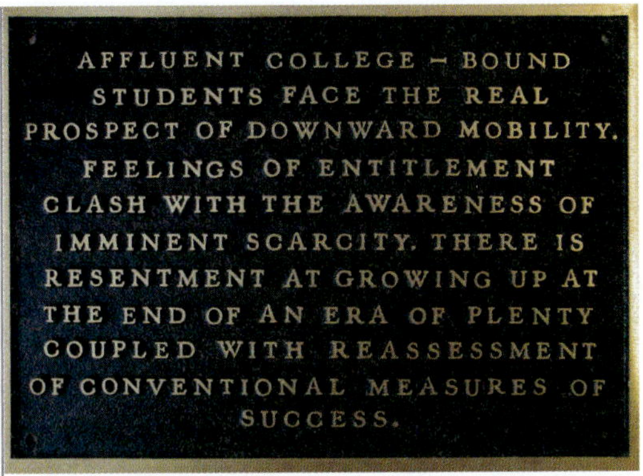

> AFFLUENT COLLEGE – BOUND STUDENTS FACE THE REAL PROSPECT OF DOWNWARD MOBILITY. FEELINGS OF ENTITLEMENT CLASH WITH THE AWARENESS OF IMMINENT SCARCITY. THERE IS RESENTMENT AT GROWING UP AT THE END OF AN ERA OF PLENTY COUPLED WITH REASSESSMENT OF CONVENTIONAL MEASURES OF SUCCESS.

Jenny Holzer, *Affluent College Bound Students*, 1981

Contemporary artists struggle to choose a medium—paint on canvas; charcoal and ink on paper; neon tubing; or, as in this work by artist Jenny Holzer above, raised lettering on a bronze plaque. They choose the medium that will best express their idea to their audience. Here, Holzer uses the contrast between her words (describing the situation of many college-bound adolescents today) and a medium closely associated with commemorating historical figures. These choices enable her to challenge both her viewers (including students and faculty at the University of Chicago, where this work was shown at a gallery on campus) and the very concept of art.

Like contemporary artists, writers today have an array of media to choose from: pen and paper, e-mail, instant message, website, blog, wiki. From these many choices, they must select the medium that will be most appropriate to their message, their purpose, and their audience. They must also choose a medium that will help them meet their responsibilities as writers. This chapter offers guidelines for matching medium to message, for deciding on the most appropriate style and tone, and for meeting your responsibilities to yourself and your readers.

10a Writing and Answering E-mail

Writers in many contexts have embraced e-mail because it offers a convenient and speedy way to communicate in writing, but its very speed creates the need for special care. Before you press the Send button, consider whether you have selected and arranged your words to create the appropriate *tone*. If you have doubts, revisit your message or consider picking up the phone or paying a visit instead.

1. Write e-mail.

> **More about**
> Tone, 15–16, 115, 136, 548–49
> Business e-mails, memos, 481–82
> Acronyms, 542, 822

To deal efficiently with the volume of e-mail most of us get, even personal e-mail should take on the characteristics of the traditional business memo: limiting the number of recipients, providing an appropriate Subject line, getting right to the point, and sticking to a single topic.

Recipients Include in the To line only those recipients who need to take action on the message; include in the Cc line anyone who must be kept informed but from whom you do not need a reply.

Subject line Provide a short, descriptive title in the Subject line of your e-mail: "A question about tomorrow's assignment." The Subject line should reflect the content of the message; alter it, in a reply or when forwarding a message, only when doing so is necessary or useful.

Salutation Many business communities use formal salutations ("Dear Dr. Mansfield") in their e-mails; others do not. Pay attention to e-mails you have

---

Quick Reference — Consider Your Writing Situation When Composing E-mail

Purpose and Focus
The primary purpose of most e-mail messages is to inform, so focus on a single issue, state it briefly in the Subject line, repeat it in the first paragraph, and keep the e-mail brief.

Audience and Context
While e-mail is generally somewhat informal, adjust your tone and level of formality to the context in which you are writing and in which your words will be read. Unless you are writing to a close friend, avoid *emoticons*—representations of emotions on faces, such as :) (happy) and ;) (wink). Also avoid IM acronyms—IMO for "in my opinion" or FWIW for "for what it's worth"—and nonstandard capitalization, grammar, punctuation, and spelling. If you are replying to an earlier message, select Reply rather than starting a new e-mail, to avoid creating filing problems for your audience.

Writing Responsibly

Maintaining Confidentiality in E-mail

You may have noticed the Bcc ("blind carbon copy") option in the header of your e-mail messages. Any recipient you list in this line will receive a copy of your message but will not be identified to other recipients. Sending blind copies can be ethical or unethical: Use the Bcc option to keep the e-mail addresses of recipients private, as when sending a message to a group of people who do not know one another. Do not blind-copy a recipient to deceive your correspondent into believing a message is confidential. So your readers will not mistakenly believe they are the only recipient of a message, mention in the body of the message that it is being shared with others. If you wish to forward another's e-mail, first obtain permission.

to OTHER WRITERS

previously received from the people to whom you are writing, and follow their lead. When in doubt, include the formal salutation.

Task-Oriented E-mails Get Right to the Point The tone of an e-mail should be appropriate to the task. An e-mail to a professor or business associate should not be as informal as a note to a friend. Indeed, in formal settings in the United States, e-mails that are task oriented frequently dispense with formalities and personal touches and get right to the point following the greeting. In some cultures, such messages would be considered rude. US readers view them as efficient and timesaving.

Organization and length State your purpose in the first paragraph, and keep the paragraphs short. If an e-mail must be long, use numbered lists, headings, and transitions to make the organization clear and to help the recipient understand the content quickly.

Style To avoid embarrassing gaffes, treat the writing context as being slightly more formal than you think it is.

Design Some e-mail programs allow for text styling such as boldface and italics; others allow only plain text. When you are not sure whether your recipient will see formatting, use the following conventions:

1. For book titles and other text you would normally italicize, place an underline before and after the title: _Lone Survivor_ by Marcus Luttrell.

Media Matters • Writing for Multiple Media

> **More about**
> URLs, 236–39
> Block style letters, 477
> Font types and styles, 165–66
> Discussion groups, 181–82, 215

2. For emphasis, place an asterisk before and after the word to be highlighted: *Recommendations*.
3. Place URLs on a separate line to make it easy for your readers to copy and paste them into the address bar of their web browser.
4. Avoid special characters, like dashes, that may disappear or become garbled in transmission.

Some discussion groups require that messages be sent in plain text. In general, format paragraphs in block style, with no indention of the first line, and separate paragraphs with a blank space. Choose a standard sans serif font such as Arial or Verdana in a 10- or 12-point font size. Keep the font black.

Closing If your e-mail begins with a formal salutation, provide a pleasant or complimentary closing ("Yours truly," "Best wishes," "Sincerely"), as well.

Contact information After your name, list contact information such as your mailing address, telephone number, or website address.

> **More about**
> Spelling, 558–72 (ch. 32)
> Punctuation, 748–806 (ch. 47–53)
> Capitalization, 807–813 (ch. 54)

Revision Edit for grammatical and typographical errors and be sure you included your attachments. If your emotions are involved, delay sending for an hour or even a day, until you are calm and reasonable. Hostile e-mail can establish you as an unreasonable person; it may also circulate beyond your intended recipients, doing even more harm.

Archiving Consider whether sent messages need to be preserved. You may find it helpful to "tag" e-mails—establish topical archive folders for your correspondence (Figure 10.1). Merely saving e-mail messages in your inbox will make them difficult to find later and may use up limited storage space.

Writing Responsibly / **Making Considerate Attachments**

When your recipients receive your e-mail with attachments, they may download it to their computers. Before you attach your file, give it a name that will make sense when it appears on the recipients' hard drive. Often this will mean including your name in the file name, along with a label identifying the text, such as "Rivera Graphs.doc." In the body of your e-mail, name and describe your attachments; otherwise your recipients may be afraid to open them. While you may be able to e-mail large files as attachments, your recipients' servers may not accommodate them. Consider sending big files through a free third-party program such as Dropbox, Google Docs, Windows SkyDrive, or YouSendIt.

to OTHER WRITERS

Writing Responsibly | Understanding E-mail and Privacy

E-mail is not a private medium: A confidential message to a friend may get forwarded to others (intentionally or accidentally as part of an e-mail thread), and work sent from a company computer—even when using a web-based e-mail program—may be read by security or by your boss, even after it has been deleted. For your own peace of mind, do not write messages that might harm your reputation or those of others.

to SELF

2. Answer e-mail.

Answering e-mail messages involves not only the issues related to writing e-mail but also the following:

Timing Read and reply to your e-mail every day. If replying to a particular e-mail will take more time than you have, send an immediate reply so that the sender knows you received the message, and indicate when you will respond. If you are going to be away from e-mail for a day or more, add an auto-reply message to alert correspondents.

Context Before answering, read all the messages that have been sent to you on that topic. If your e-mail program allows, sort your messages by subject to be sure that you have read everything in the thread you are responding to. So that your recipient has a context for what you are saying, quote pertinent passages from the e-mail to which you are responding, or refer your reader to an earlier message in the thread.

FIGURE 10.1 Folders for archived e-mail

Recipients Most people get more e-mail than they can handle, so always consider carefully before selecting Reply All. Does everybody on the list really need to be included?

➤ EXERCISE 10.1 Analyzing an e-mail message

Analyze an e-mail message you wrote to a boss, an instructor, or an older family member (parent or grandparent, aunt or uncle): Is it focused on a single topic? Does it include an appropriate Subject line? Is the message logically organized? Is it of an appropriate length? Is the tone appropriate given the recipient of the message? Does the message avoid errors of grammar, spelling, punctuation, and mechanics? In one or two paragraphs, explain how you might revise the message. Next, rewrite the e-mail for a different audience and, asking the same questions, describe the differences.

10b Creating Websites and Web Pages

Writing for the web generally means creating a ***website,*** a collection of files located at a single address, or URL, on the World Wide Web.

1. Plan your site.

Every website begins with a ***home page,*** the page designed to introduce visitors to the site. The home page should include the website's title, the date the site was created or last updated, and links to a site map (or table of contents), contact information, and a copyright or Creative Commons notice. Most sites also have additional ***web pages***—documents that, like the home page itself, may include text, audio and video, still images, and database files.

To make your website useful to others, plan the overall structure of the site carefully. Then create each page as a separate document (or file) on your computer, and save all the pages—with any video, image, or sound files you plan to include—in a common folder. This will save you time and trouble when you upload your files to a server.

Quick Reference — Creating a Website? Consider Your Writing Situation

Purpose and Focus
Readers scan websites quickly, so keep your sentences brief and clear and your focus tight. Images, sound files, and design should reflect your purpose and capture readers' attention.

Context and Audience
Consider any restrictions of your host or site sponsor as you plan your site. Consider, too, the needs and expectations of your readers, but remember that unintended readers may also see what you post on the open Web, so avoid language or content that you or others might find embarrassing or offensive.

Genre
If you will be providing information that will remain current for a long time, create a website that you update once or twice a year; if your site requires daily or weekly updates, create a blog; if you want readers to participate in the creation of the site's content, create a wiki.

Unlike print documents in which reading proceeds *linearly* (the document is arranged so that all readers begin at page 1 and read through to the end), most websites are *hypertextual* (users may enter the site at any page and follow their own path through the website). Just how easy it is for users to find their way around your site depends on its structure and on the navigation tools you provide.

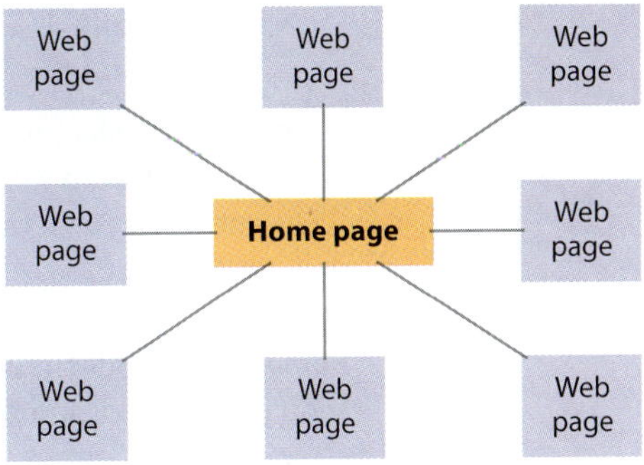

Site structure When creating a website, consider how the various pages will relate to one another and how users will move among them. A site that includes a home page and a handful of web pages with loosely related content may work best with a hub-and-spoke structure (Figure 10.2). If your website will offer a series of pages with related content, a hierarchical arrangement, with links from home page to lower-level pages and from page to page, may be more useful (Figure 10.3).

FIGURE 10.2 **A hub-and-spoke structure**

Navigation tools Navigation tools include the following:

- **Menus.** Placed at the top, bottom, left, or right side of the web page, menus list main sections of your website and are consistent from page to page.

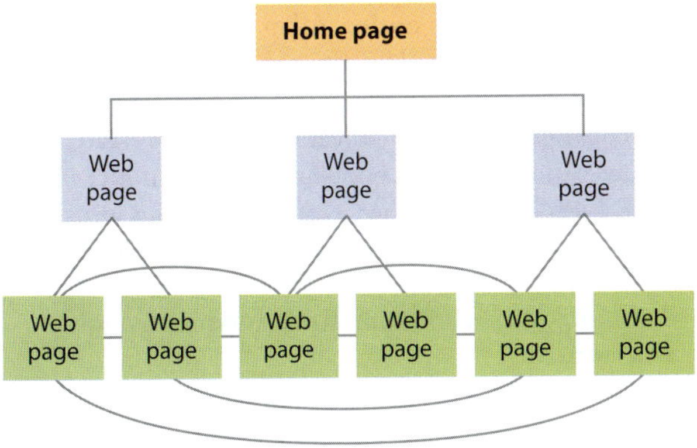

FIGURE 10.3 **A hierarchical, treelike structure, with additional links**

- **Click trails.** Used to show the path you took to the page you are on, click trails offer users an easy way to jump back to higher-level pages.
- **Hyperlinks (or links).** Used to jump from place to place on a web page or from web page to web page, links appear as highlighted words or images on a web page.

The website shown in Figure 10.4 offers these navigation tools.

Home page While the contents of your home page will depend on the purpose, audience, context, and genre of your site, users will benefit from the following:

- **Title.** The home page (and each additional web page) should include a title that clearly and succinctly indicates the type of information your site will include.
- **Date created, last updated.** Providing a copyright date or indicating when you last updated the site lets readers know how current your site is and enables users to create a complete bibliographic citation.
- **Link to a site map.** A site map is a table of contents for the site; it helps users find the information they are looking for quickly and easily.
- **Link to contact information.** Provide a link to your basic contact information, including an e-mail address, your name, and your role. To avoid possible cyberstalking, reveal only as much information as you are willing for the entire world to know, and establish a separate e-mail address exclusively for correspondence from your website.
- **Copyright or Creative Commons notice.** All material published on the web is automatically protected by copyright. Remind readers of this fact by including a copyright notice: "Copyright © 2010 Paul Jefferson." For the copyright date, use the year in which you created or last updated the page. An increasingly popular alternative notice is a Creative Commons License. Browse the Creative Commons website (http://creativecommons.org/) to learn more about this project.

> **EXERCISE 10.2 Examining the navigation tools and home page of a website**
>
> Analyze your school's website or another website you visit regularly. In a paragraph or two, discuss the strengths and weaknesses of the site's structure and navigation tools. What tools do you use regularly and why? Now study the website's home page. Which elements discussed in this chapter are included? Which would you like to see added, and why?

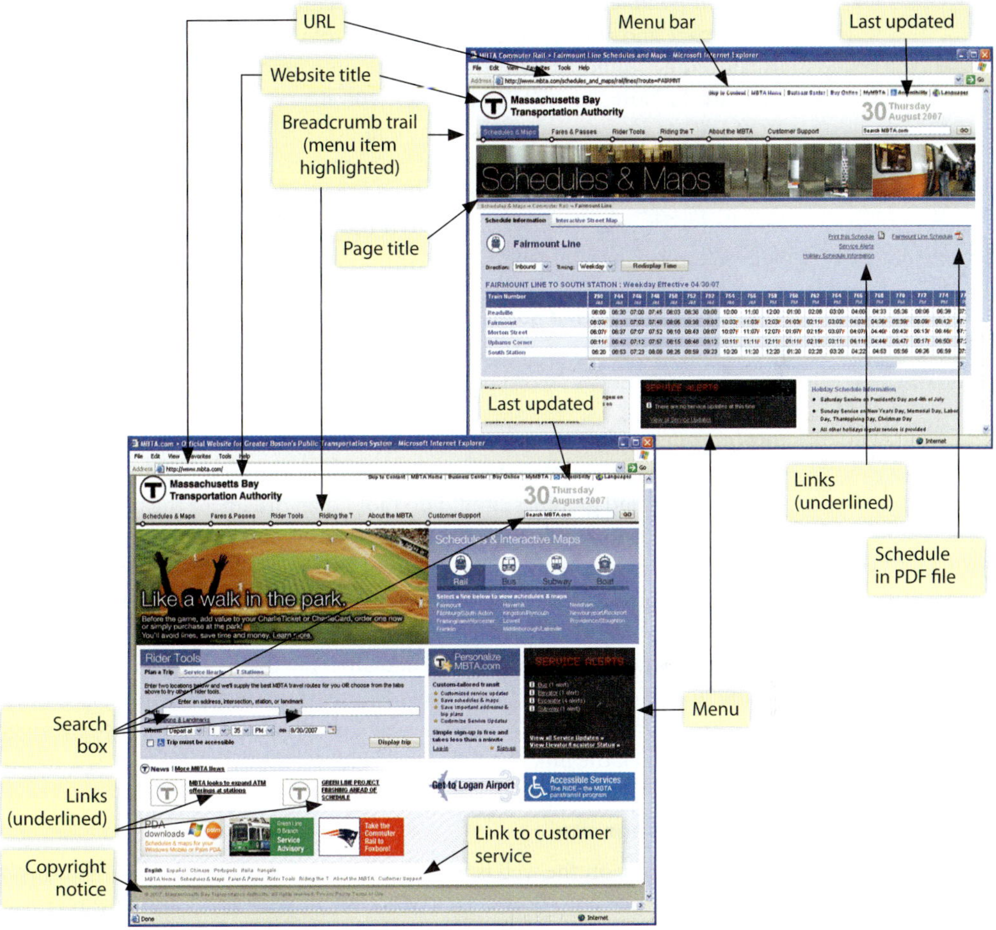

FIGURE 10.4 The Massachusetts Bay Transportation Authority's website This Webby–award-winning site includes menus, search boxes, and a click trail that reinforces the sponsoring organization's identity by resembling a subway map. It appeals to its target audience by placing convenient links to schedules and maps, rider tools, and subway advisories on its home page (*left*) and featuring a photograph of Boston's beloved Fenway Park.

2. Create your website's content.

To populate your own web pages, you can either create the content from scratch using an HTML editor or convert print-based documents.

Using an HTML editor Choose an **HTML** editor that automatically sets up a basic page and allows you to select styles from a menu. A free HTML editor usually comes bundled with the software on a new computer—TextEdit on a Macintosh, Notepad on Windows. Or you may want a simpler-to-use visual, WYSIWYG ("what you see is what you get") editor that allows you to create a web page as easily as creating a word processing document. You may not need to buy a visual editor; many are available for free (one may even come bundled with your browser), and often they are loaded onto the machines in your school's computer labs.

> **PDF** Portable Document Format; created by Adobe, PDF format allows a document to be opened in different systems without losing its formatting

Converting print-based documents Texts originally prepared on a word processor can be converted into web pages or **PDFs** for posting online. Check the Help function in your word processing program for instructions.

Incorporating image, sound, and video files Web pages more easily attract an audience when they include multimedia files—images, graphics, sound, or video. Images and graphics should do more than ornament the page, however; they should also provide useful information, set an appropriate tone, or suggest useful perspectives on the content of the page. When adding images and graphics to your site, consider how much is enough. Just as a visually bland web page can fail to stir readers' interest, a visually cluttered page can distract them.

Since not every site visitor will actually play the files (and some may not be able to see or hear the files), provide a written description of any that are crucial to your point. A description may also pique visitors' curiosity enough for them to click the link or file you provide.

3. Design your site.

Communicating on the web is inescapably visual, and the design of your website will influence both how clear and accessible your site is and how receptive users are to your message. To make your site visually effective, plan it carefully and apply the principles of design.

Tech   Use a Lower Resolution to Avoid Memory-Hogging Image Files

Including high-resolution image files or a large quantity of lower-resolution image files can make loading a web page so time-consuming that visitors become exasperated and give up. Avoid this problem by reducing the size of your images. Most image files will look fine online at 72 dots per inch.

4. Revise and edit your website.

A website full of errors will undermine your credibility with readers long before they ever assess the content on your site, so check your website carefully before bringing it "live":

- Since most readers scan websites for information, make sure your prose is clear and concise.
- Check that visual, audio, and multimedia files add value and are not merely ornamental.
- Check that your design is attractive and consistent.
- Check that image, audio, and other media files open properly.
- Check all links to make sure they work.
- Ask friends to read your pages: Users with different hardware and software will run into different problems.
- Edit and proofread your site carefully for errors in spelling, grammar, punctuation, and mechanics.

> **More about**
> Writing concisely, 496–504 (ch. 26)
> Deciding to illustrate, 73–74
> Designing printed and electronic documents, 162–70 (ch. 9)
> Evaluating websites, 136–39
> Editing and proofreading, 87–89, 93–94

> **Writing Responsibly** — **Checking Accessibility**
>
> Make sure your site is accessible to visually impaired users by running your pages through an accessibility checker. The Assistive Technology Resource Center (atrc.colostate.edu) provides a list of programs, some of which are free.
>
> *to AUDIENCE*

5. Maintain your website.

Once your website is up and running, check it every month or so:

- Make sure the site continues to run on different browsers.
- Delete, replace, or repair broken links.
- Make sure image files appear; if a small icon appears instead, check to make sure the image file is in your server folder and that its URL is typed correctly (including the file extension, such as .jpg or .gif).

10c Writing in Interactive Media

With the rapid spread of broadband access, online communication has become an increasingly familiar part of our lives: Instant messaging and chat rooms, bulletin boards and discussion groups, and wikis and blogs are now common additions to the classroom, newsroom, and living room. The very familiarity of these media can lull writers into making errors that they later regret. Many of the principles described in *sections a* and *b* for e-mail and website writing

> ## Writing Responsibly
> ### Flaming
>
> The quick interactivity and the anonymity of online media present a special challenge: keeping your temper. ***Flaming***—writing a scathing response to someone with whom you disagree—is a great temptation, but it shuts down reasoned discourse, instead encouraging ad hominem attack. Flaming may convey a sense of power for your having found a biting way to put down an opponent, but it also minimizes the likelihood of anyone's listening to or being influenced by you.
>
> to OTHER WRITERS

> **More about**
> Ad hominem and other logical fallacies, 156–59

> **More about**
> Discussion lists, 215
> Blogs, 215
> Documenting posts to discussion lists, 321 (MLA), 371 (APA), 404 (*Chicago*), 427 (CSE)
> Citing blogs and blog posts, 321 (MLA), 371 (APA), 404 (*Chicago*), 427 (CSE)

also apply to these other forms of online writing. In particular, be sure to think about your purpose and to tailor your writing style and tone to your intended audience, considering carefully how your readers might interpret your message *before* sending or posting it.

The goal of online discussions, as with live discussions, is to learn collaboratively through give and take; however, because participants are not physically present, the temptation to go off on a tangent may be great. To avoid this, focus on responding directly to the comments of other participants and summarizing the discussion before moving on. Your online voice can be casual, but strive to keep your comments clear and to maintain a voice that is friendly and polite, even when you disagree.

When participating in a discussion in ***asynchronous media*** (media that do not require participants to sign on at a specific date and time), take advantage of the opportunity to reflect on and proofread your comments before posting them. Asynchronous discussions usually require participants to make a commitment to sign on regularly and to make comments at least once a week.

> **More about**
> Collaborative writing projects, 26–28, 45

In ***synchronous media*** such as instant messaging and chat, where communication occurs in real time, participants must make a commitment to sign on at a specific time and to focus attention on the discussion while it is occurring. Reflection and careful proofreading are not possible, but synchronous discussions are useful for brainstorming and for developing a sense of community.

11 Presenting with Multiple Media

IN THIS CHAPTER

a. Identifying purpose, audience, context, genre, 183

b. Devising a topic and thesis, 184

c. Organizing the presentation, 185

d. Preparing and rehearsing the presentation, 186

e. Delivering the presentation, 189

f. Speaking responsibly, 189

"Future generations may well have occasion to ask themselves, 'What were our parents thinking? Why didn't they wake up when they had a chance?'" So speaks Al Gore in this presentation on global warming. He gave his presentation to groups large and small across the country and around the world. It was captured in the documentary *An Inconvenient Truth,* which has been seen by thousands and thousands of viewers, both in theaters and on DVD. Very few of us ever have an opportunity to reach out to such a large audience on a topic of global importance. Still, we are often called upon to present our ideas at school, at work, and in our communities. If we can present them clearly and compellingly, using multiple media when they will help us reach listeners, we, too, can effect change.

11a Identifying Your Purpose, Audience, Context, and Genre

> **More about**
> Purpose, 10–11
> Audience, 12–15
> Context and genre, 16–17

As with any writing project, begin planning a presentation by considering your *purpose, audience, context,* and *genre*. In an academic or business context, your primary *purpose* is likely to be the same as for a

183

written text: to present information or to persuade others to accept your position or to take action. Even more so than a written text, an oral presentation is likely also to have a secondary purpose: to engage the imagination or emotions of the audience so that members can more readily identify with and remember the key points.

When addressing classmates or colleagues, you will probably have a sense of the needs and expectations of your *audience*. When addressing an unfamiliar group, ask yourself why the group has assembled and what they hope to get out of your presentation. It may be useful to ask the event organizers what kind of audience to expect.

The *context,* or setting, in which you deliver your presentation will affect the kinds of equipment you will need, the types of multimedia aids you create, and the relationship you can establish with your audience. When addressing a small group in a college classroom, for example, you will probably not need any special equipment, whereas in larger settings you may need a projector, a sound system, and special lighting.

Finally, consider the *genre* of your presentation. As a college student, you are most likely to be asked to contribute to or lead a class discussion, or to give a presentation online or in person to a class, student group, or social service organization. In business, you may be asked to train colleagues or make a sales pitch to potential customers.

Contributing to Class Discussion In US schools, active participation in class is an important part of the learning experience, and it may even play a role in instructors' grades. If you are uncomfortable with the idea of speaking in class, let your instructor know. If students in your class seem uncomfortable when they speak, remember that you are responsible for being an effective listener as well as a speaker. That means listening patiently and respectfully at all times.

11b Devising a Topic and Thesis

> *More about*
> Devising a topic, 20
> Narrowing, expanding a topic, 25–26
> Devising a thesis, 30–31

A presentation, like a written text, begins with an appropriate topic and a well-focused thesis. Your topic and approach should engage you and your audience and offer special insight. Craft a thesis that conveys your purpose and that will engage and guide your audience.

11c Organizing the Presentation

It is more difficult for people to understand and remember ideas they have heard than those they have read. Organize your talk to help your audience hold your main points in memory while the presentation unfolds.

1. Introduction

Use your introduction (10–15 percent of your presentation) to develop a rapport with your audience and to establish the key points of your presentation. Your introduction should accomplish the following:

- Specify your topic and approach, and convey the topic's importance.
- Engage your audience: A compelling anecdote, startling statistics, or an apt quotation are all good opening gambits.
- Establish your credentials: Knowledge, experience, or the research you have conducted all give you special expertise.
- Provide a brief overview of your main points so that the audience will know in advance what they should be listening for.

> **More about**
> Introductions, 63–65

2. Body

The body (75–85 percent of your presentation) should explain the points that you previewed in your introduction. It should be clearly and logically organized, so listeners know where you are going and where you have been. Use transitions such as "first," "second," and "third" to guide your audience, and provide a brief summary of the main points you made earlier ("As I explained a few minutes ago . . .") and a preview of the points you are about to discuss ("Next I will show how . . .").

For each claim you make, supply appropriate, relevant evidence, such as specific examples drawn from your reading or your experience. Facts and statistics can be very effective as long as you do not burden your audience with more numbers than it can process. (Presenting statistics in information graphics can help.) Engaging anecdotes or stories that use concrete, descriptive language, on the other hand, are more easily remembered.

> **More about**
> Organizing, 33–37, 47–51, 266–69
> Transitions, 54–55
> Explaining and supporting ideas, 40–44, 59–63, 270–72
> Using visuals as evidence, 74–77
> Finding information, 206–29 (ch. 13)

3. Conclusion

Keep your conclusion brief (5–10 percent of your presentation). Use it to reinforce the main point of the presentation: Repeat the main idea and key points, end with a brief but powerful statement, or return to the opening anecdote, example, or statistic.

> **More about**
> Conclusions, 65–67

11d Preparing and Rehearsing the Presentation

For an oral presentation, the following methods of delivery are common:

- **Speaking off-the-cuff.** If you are an expert on a topic about which your audience knows little, you may be able to speak engagingly and informatively with little special preparation.
- **Reading a written presentation aloud.** If your material is highly technical or if you are anxious about speaking, reading your presentation may work. Since you will lose eye contact with the audience and risk losing their attention, build in opportunities to speak without a script to engage your listeners.
- **Speaking from your notes.** Speaking from notes will keep you organized and prevent you from forgetting important points while allowing you to make eye contact with the audience.

1. Prepare a speaking outline.

> **More about**
> Topic outlines, 36–37, 268–69

When speaking from notes, create a speaking outline by jotting notes on a topic outline about where to pause, when to increase the urgency in your voice, and when to advance to the next slide or visual aid. Add content notes, too, but keep them brief, including only as much information as you need to remind yourself of the point you want to make.

2. Use language effectively.

Well-chosen language can help listeners understand and remember your main points. As you draft and rehearse your presentation, do the following:

> **More about**
> Abstract versus concrete language, 550–52
> Eliminating wordiness, 497–99
> Figures of speech, 553
> Parallelism, 518–26 (ch. 28)
> Repetition (intentional), 534–35

- Use clear, familiar language.
- Choose concrete words. When abstract words are needed, support them with concrete examples.
- Eliminate wordiness.
- Keep sentences relatively short.
- Include vivid figures of speech, such as metaphors and similes, that link an unfamiliar notion to a familiar or striking one.
- Use parallelism and repetition to emphasize your main points.

3. Create visual, audio, and multimedia aids.

Visual, audio, and multimedia aids can enhance your presentation by clarifying or providing additional information, by showing what you are describing, and by countering stage fright (directing attention away from you). When using visual or multimedia aids during a presentation, make sure the aids are relevant, that you explain them clearly and succinctly, that you do not provide so many that the audience pays attention to them rather than to you, and that you speak to your audience, not to your visual aids.

> **More about**
> Using visuals as support, 74–77

Presentation software such as Microsoft PowerPoint or Apple Keynote usefully projects visual, audio, and multimedia aids. However, overuse of presentation software or poor preparation of slides can overwhelm or distract the audience. (For advice on effective use of presentation software, see the Self Assessment box on the next page.)

4. Rehearse your presentation.

Practice your presentation out loud in front of a mirror, a group of friends or family, or a video camera. Reading the slides word-for-word can bore your audience, so learn your material well. Use at least two or three practice sessions to make sure of the following:

- You are comfortable with the content of your presentation.
- Your presentation is the right length (long enough but not too long).
- Your delivery is polished: You are familiar with the pronunciation of all words and names, you know when to pause or gesture, and you are comfortable making eye contact with the audience (or with yourself in the mirror).

> **More about**
> Visual design, 162–70 (ch. 9)
> Matching visual to information, 74–77

Quick Reference — Overcoming Presentation Anxiety

The following tips may help you get through your presentation with a minimum of nerves.

- Envision your success: Picture yourself calm and relaxed at the podium; imagine your sense of accomplishment at the end of the presentation.
- Take several slow, deep breaths, or tighten and relax your muscles just before you take the podium.
- Ignore your racing heart or clammy hands. Instead, use the adrenaline surge to add energy to your presentation.
- Focus on your message: Get excited about what you have to say, and you will bring the audience with you.
- Accept the fact that you may stumble, and be prepared to go on.

Self Assessment: Ten Steps to Using Presentation Software Effectively

When preparing a presentation, reflect on your work. Ask yourself the following questions, revising and practicing as necessary.

- ☐ **Did you review your outline to determine where slides would enhance your presentation?** Do not overwhelm your presentation by creating a slide for every moment.
- ☐ **Did you begin with a title slide?** This slide should include the title of your presentation, your name, and any other useful identifying information.

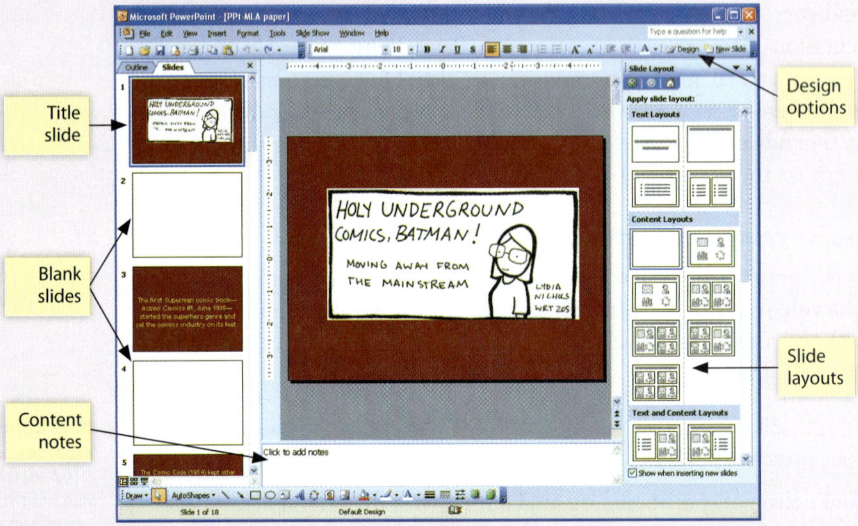

[Screenshot of Microsoft PowerPoint interface with labels: Title slide, Blank slides, Content notes, Design options, Slide layouts]

- ☐ **Did you keep text brief, design uniform, and contents varied?** The audience should be listening to you, not reading your slides. To make slides easy to absorb, maintain a consistent design. To enhance interest, vary the other components (images, information graphics, video clips).
- ☐ **Did you add blank slides?** Go to a blank slide when no illustration is relevant.
- ☐ **Did you check that slides are visually pleasing?** Keep slides uncluttered and balanced; limit your use of animations (the way text or images enter a slide).
- ☐ **Did you proofread your slides?** Make sure all text is clear, and correct all misspellings and all mistakes of grammar, punctuation, and mechanics.
- ☐ **Did you learn your software's commands?** Keystroke commands allow you to advance or return to slides, use the animation effects, and end the slide show.
- ☐ **Did you practice your presentation with your slides in advance?** Use animations to bring information forward, and do not leave slides up after you have moved on to the next topic.
- ☐ **Did you check your equipment in advance?** Make sure that cords are long enough, that you can lower the lights and cover windows, and so forth.
- ☐ **Did you practice giving your presentation without your slides?** Murphy's Law—whenever something *can* go wrong, it *will* go wrong—applies to presentation software. If the power fails or your computer dies, you should still be able to go on with the show.

- You deploy and discuss visual aids with grace.
- You have good posture and avoid nervous fidgeting and irritating mannerisms (such as the repetition of "um" or "like").

If possible, rehearse in the space where you will be making your presentation to determine how loudly you will have to speak, to test placement of visual aids or screens, and to check your equipment.

Adjusting Your Gestures to Appeal to a Multicultural Audience Gestures vary from culture to culture. As you prepare to give formal presentations, pay attention to the gestures commonly made by classmates or other peers who represent your prospective audience. How do they differ from gestures you are accustomed to? Are you aware of any gestures you should not use while speaking to a multicultural audience?

11e Delivering the Presentation

When the time comes to make your presentation, approach the podium, wait for your audience to settle down, and then begin:

- **Connect with the audience.** Introduce yourself, thank the audience for attending, and smile.
- **Maintain eye contact with the audience.** As you speak, look out at the audience, turning to the left, the right, and center, so all members of the audience feel included.
- **Control your pacing, volume, and tempo.** Speak slowly and clearly. Pause between sections of your presentation. Vary the tone of your voice. If you sense that you are losing your audience, slow your pace, increase your volume, or step closer to the audience.

11f Speaking Responsibly

As you prepare your presentation, keep your responsibilities as a speaker in mind:

- **Know your material and your purpose.** For an informative speech, be sure your information is current and your examples pertinent. For a

Writing Responsibly — Listening Actively

When attending a presentation, be fair to the speaker by listening actively:

- Give the speaker your undivided attention.
- Make an effort to understand the speaker's point of view.
- Set aside prejudices based on the speaker's appearance, accent, rate of speech, or apparent level of comfort.
- Listen for the speaker's main points.
- Identify and assess the evidence presented.

to OTHER WRITERS

> **More about**
> Biased language, 544–47
> Logical fallacies, 156–59
> Patchwriting, 247, 252–56
> Signal phrases, 276–78, 288–89 (MLA), 348–49 (APA)
> Revising visuals, 78–81
> Contextualizing sources, 276–78

persuasive speech, adopt a position that you believe in, one for which you can offer compelling, concrete evidence.

- **Acknowledge counterevidence and alternative interpretations.** Do not alter quotations unfairly or misuse statistics. Avoid words and images that manipulate your audience or that rely on logical fallacies.

- **Use signal phrases.** Since readers will not have access to your written text, acknowledge sources with signal phrases such as "Alison Ling's research shows . . ." and be prepared to provide a list of works cited if requested.

- **Practice before presenting.** Respect the time and attention of your audience by practicing your presentation until you can deliver it with confidence and grace.

Work Together

With two to four classmates, listen to a complete speech posted on YouTube or a website such as American Rhetoric (http://americanrhetoric.com/). As you listen, take notes on the main point of the speech, the organization of the speech, the transitions or other signposts the speaker used, and the speaker's language and delivery. Compare your notes. What did you notice that other group members did not (and vice versa)?

Part Four

Research Matters

Finding, Evaluating, and Citing Sources

12 Planning a Research Project   192
13 Finding Information   206
14 Evaluating Information   230
15 Using Information Responsibly: Taking Notes and Avoiding Plagiarism   246
16 Writing the Research Project   264
17 Citing Expertly   274

12 Planning a Research Project

IN THIS CHAPTER

a. Analyzing purpose, audience, and method of development, 192

b. Setting a schedule, 194

c. Choosing and narrowing a research topic, 195

d. Drafting research questions and hypotheses, 195

e. Choosing sources strategically, 197

f. Establishing a research log, 198

g. Building and annotating a working bibliography, 200

> *More about*
> Purpose, 10–12
> Audience, 12–15

Jan Cartwright, collage, Self-Portrait, 2001

To create this collage, the artist had to devise a plan, gather the right materials, and assemble them to create a unified whole. Yet it took more than just the right materials; it took an idea that would unify them and engage the viewer. Similarly, when you write a research project, you not only must devise a plan and gather supporting information, but you must also have a vision. Your goal should be to present the research in your text in a way that engages and even enlightens the reader. The first stage of the research process—planning—is crucial to the success of this endeavor.

12a Analyzing the Assignment's Purpose, Audience, and Method of Development

Most research projects will have one of two purposes:

- **To inform:** to explain an issue, compare proposed solutions, or review the research on a specific topic
- **To persuade:** to argue for a claim

Figure out the purpose of the assignment by looking closely at the words it uses:

If the assignment asks you to . . .	your purpose is likely to be . . .
describe, compare, discuss, review, analyze	informative (expository)
assess, evaluate, argue	persuasive

192

Sometimes, college research assignments specify the method of development to use: comparison-contrast, cause-effect, and so on. One of the most frequently used methods of development is *analysis*—the writer divides the issue, proposal, or event into its component parts; explains how the parts work together; and discusses the implications.

As a writer, you have a responsibility to shape your project with the needs and expectations of your audience in mind, so consider who that audience will be. For most college assignments, your audience will include your instructor and perhaps your fellow students. Your instructor will want to see not only that you understand the material covered in class, but also that you can interpret it, analyze it, and think creatively and critically about it. Fellow students may need you to define terms or provide background.

> **More about**
> Arguing for a claim, 138–42
> Methods of development, 59–63
> Interpretation, analysis, synthesis, and critique, 62, 119–31, 262–63, 270–72
> Generating ideas, 20–25

EXERCISE 12.1 Writing with your audience in mind

For each of the assignments listed below, determine whether the purpose is informative or persuasive. Then choose one assignment and write a paragraph about how you would approach it if you were writing for an academic audience, for the readers of your college newspaper, and for a website appealing to readers already interested in the topic.

1. Analyze the effect that monitoring Internet searches at the library would have on patrons.
2. Argue for or against the monitoring of Internet searches at libraries.
3. Evaluate the treatment options for gambling addictions—which option is most effective, and why?
4. Describe the symptoms of a gambling addiction.
5. Explain how genetic engineering is currently used to diagnose and control disease in humans.
6. Argue for or against the use of genetic engineering to control disease in humans.
7. Compare the results of homeschooling and traditional classroom education on academic success in college.
8. Evaluate the effects of homeschooling on children.
9. Define "reality television."
10. Argue for or against this statement: The nightly news is reality television.

> **Quick Reference — Factors in Planning a Research Project**
>
> - When is the project due?
> - How long is the project to be?
> - What type of research is required?
> - What types of sources are more useful—scholarly books and articles only, or a mix of scholarly and popular sources?
> - How many sources will you need to answer your research questions fully and accurately?
> - On what criteria will the project be evaluated?
> - What other work and activities will compete for your time and attention?

12b Setting a Schedule

> **More about**
> Setting a realistic schedule, 18–21

Set a schedule for your research project that allows time for each of the following steps:

- Analyzing the assignment, taking its scope and purpose into consideration
- Analyzing your audience to determine what your reader will expect from you
- Choosing a topic that is appropriate to your assignment and your audience
- Narrowing your topic to one that can be fully explored within the time you have available to devote to it
- Framing research questions and developing a hypothesis that will structure and focus your research project
- Creating a working bibliography to keep track of the information you will need for documenting your sources later
- Annotating your working bibliography so that you can remember what these sources cover and how you expect to use them

Check with your instructor if you do not know the answer to these questions.

> **Tech — Using an Assignment Calculator**
>
> To set a realistic schedule, try using an online assignment calculator like the one offered by the University of Minnesota Libraries (www.lib.umn.edu/help/calculator). Such tools divide the writing process into steps and suggest a date by which each step should be completed. Check your own library's website to see whether a time management calculator is provided, or search for one by typing "assignment calculator" into the search box of a search engine such as Yahoo! or Google.

> **Make It Your Own**
>
> For a research project you have been assigned, answer the questions in the Quick Reference box on the previous page, and then set up a schedule for each stage of your research project. Be sure to leave time for other assignments and for unexpected delays.

12c Choosing and Narrowing a Research Topic

When the choice is up to you, select a topic that will interest your readers and you, ideally one about which you already have some knowledge and insight. Idea-generating techniques such as freewriting and brainstorming can help you devise a topic that will be of interest to your readers, and they can help you narrow your topic so that you can write about it specifically and insightfully. For college research projects, conducting preliminary research or reviewing assigned reading or class notes may be the most helpful in choosing and narrowing your topic. You might try putting your general topic into the search box of a library catalog or database to see what topics arise in the results that are returned. A search in the database PsycINFO on "peer influence" generated topics from smoking and group initiation to copycat crime among juvenile offenders.

More about
Generating ideas, 20–25
Narrowing a topic, 25–26

> **Make It Your Own**
>
> Use two or more of the idea-generating techniques in chapter 2, *section 2c*, to devise and narrow a research topic for this or another class.

12d Drafting Research Questions and Hypotheses

After you have tentatively chosen a topic but before you begin searching for sources, list a number of questions about your topic that research might answer. These are your ***research questions.*** Next, write the answers you expect to find. These answers are the ***hypotheses*** that your research will test. The following examples show research questions and hypotheses for Lydia Nichols's paper on underground comics and for Heather DeGroot's paper on the effects of wardrobe on social influence.

Student Models
Research projects: "Holy Underground Comics, Batman!" Lydia Nichols, 336–46
"The Power of Wardrobe," Heather DeGroot, 381–88

> **Research question:** What are the characteristics that distinguish underground comics from mainstream comics?
>
> **Hypothesis:** Unlike mainstream comics, underground comics focus on topics that challenge social mores, have an author or author team that has creative control, and appeal to an adult readership.

> **Research question:** Does the clothing a man wears influence the behavior of other men?
>
> **Hypothesis:** The clothing a man wears will influence the behavior of other men when he is in a position of authority relative to the rest of the group.

As you conduct your research, you will continually revise your research questions and hypotheses; the more you learn, the more you know about what questions can be answered and what hypotheses are most plausible. You will also reduce the number of questions you are asking. Your finished project will probably answer only one of the questions you generated at the beginning of the process, and your *thesis* will probably come directly from the hypothesis that you generated to answer that question.

> *More about*
> Devising a thesis, 29–31
> Revising a thesis, 31–33

EXERCISE 12.2 Devising research questions and hypotheses

Devise a research question for one of the assignments you analyzed in Exercise 12.1. Then answer it to create a research hypothesis. (You may need to use the idea-generating techniques discussed in chapter 2.) If your research question cannot be readily answered through research, divide it into several more specific questions that can be.

Make It Your Own

Create three to five questions that could guide your research on the topic you devised and narrowed in the second Make It Your Own activity on page 195. Remember that your questions must be answerable through research. If they are too broad, divide them into more specific questions. Then turn one of your questions into a hypothesis.

Writing Responsibly — Using Printed Sources

With so much information available online, you might think that you no longer need to consult printed materials. However, many classic and scholarly books are not (yet) available digitally, and your library may not subscribe to the electronic versions of important newspapers, magazines, and scholarly journals. Dedicate yourself to finding the best information available, whether you access it through a search engine, through an online database like Academic Search Premier or Web of Science, or through trips to your library's stacks.

to TOPIC

12e Choosing Research Sources Strategically

Your research project must reflect real research, instead of just creating the appearance of it. The sources you choose are key to fulfilling your responsibilities to your reader, your topic, and yourself. When choosing sources, ask yourself these questions:

- Have you visited your library and its academic databases (not just Google) to see what kinds of resources are available?
- Have you consulted, for background, general reference sources that provide basic facts about your topic?
- Have you consulted, for an authoritative overview, specialized reference sources that discuss the debates and issues about your topic?
- Have you found in-depth analyses and arguments written by experts on your topic?
- Have you located—after finding a journalist, blogger, or website discussing research results—the research report itself, instead of settling for secondhand information?
- Are your sources either up-to-date or classics that established the principles for studying the topic you are researching?
- Have you consulted enough sources to develop a broad understanding of your topic?
- Have you consulted sources that offer a variety of perspectives on your topic, rather than just searching for sources that agree with your hypothesis?
- Have you consulted the best sources, even if they are not available online?

> *More about*
> Reliability, 232–43
> Scholarly versus popular sources, 232–34
> Counterevidence, 145–47
> Finding online sources, 210–15
> Finding articles in journals, magazines, and newspapers, 215–20
> Finding specialized reference sources, 212–13
> Finding books, 220–24
> Finding government documents, 224
> Finding multimedia sources, 225
> Field research: interviews, observational studies, surveys, 226–30

- Have you conducted experiments, observations, surveys, or interviews, when relevant, to develop information of your own?

You may need help to determine whether a source is up-to-date or reliable or to locate sources online or in your library's print collection. When you do, consult a research expert—a reference librarian.

> ### Work **Together**
>
> Skim Lydia Nichols's "Holy Underground Comics, Batman!" (pp. 336–46) or Heather DeGroot's "The Power of Wardrobe: Male Stereotype Influences" (pp. 381–88). Then, with a classmate, evaluate the writer's choice of sources. What types of sources were consulted? How authoritative are they? Would you suggest any strategic changes in source choices? Why or why not?

> ### Make It **Your Own**
>
> For the research hypothesis you devised in the Make It Your Own activity on page 196, make a list of sources that would allow you to uncover useful information. Write a paragraph about these sources, answering the questions following the bullets in *section 12e*.

> **More about**
> Keeping an idea journal or commonplace book, 20
> Keeping a reading journal, 117–18
> Annotating, 114–17
> Making notes, 250–56
> Avoiding patchwriting, 250–51, 274–86
> Research questions and hypotheses, 195–96
> Search terms (keywords), 210–11
> Interpretation, analysis, synthesis, and critique, 120–22, 262–63, 270–72

12f Establishing a Research Log

A *research log* is a journal in which you record research questions and hypotheses; your working thesis; your search terms; information from sources; your interpretation, analysis, synthesis, and critique of sources; and your ideas for where to go next.

1. Set up the research log.

A research log can be compiled in any of the following media: index cards, a notebook, or a file in a computer, tablet, or smartphone.

Before you set up your research log, consider the advantages and disadvantages of each medium: Index cards may seem old-fashioned in the digital age, yet they are easy to arrange in outline order or to "storyboard" when it comes time to write your paper. Notebooks are easy to carry around and more

> **Tech** **Back Up Your Electronic Research Log**
>
> Do not be a victim of a computer crash: If you keep your research log in electronic form, be sure to back up your files after every session, and store the backup files in a separate place—on a flash drive, for example. If you cannot save your files to a second device, e-mail the files to yourself or print out the new material after each session.

difficult to lose than note cards. Keeping notes on index cards or in a notebook forces you to interact with your sources, rather than just cutting and pasting information into a word processing file. Keeping a research log on a computer (especially a laptop or tablet) or smartphone makes it possible to search your notes electronically, to rearrange them into outline order, and to copy material from your notes directly into your paper. A phone is likely to be with you at all times, and you can sync it with your computer.

2. Define the components of a research log.

Divide your research log into sections for different categories of notes:

- The research assignment
- Purpose statement and audience profile
- Your research schedule
- A list of possible research questions
- Your working hypothesis
- Notes taken while reading sources
- Your own ideas
- Your working bibliography

Writing Responsibly — Avoiding Accidental Plagiarism

The facility with which you can cut and paste material from sources into a digital file makes it easy to fall into unintentional plagiarism. If you are maintaining an electronic research log, it is especially important to mark clearly what you have copied directly from a source and what you have paraphrased, summarized, or commented upon. Consider supplementing your electronic research log with a folder for printouts and photocopies, and check your text against it.

to SELF

> **More about**
> Taking notes to avoid plagiarism, 250–51
> Patchwriting, 252–55

Make It Your Own

Using the information you have generated in the other Make It Your Own activities in this chapter (pp. 195, 196, 198), establish a research log.

12g Building and Annotating a Working Bibliography

Start your research by gathering potential sources and reviewing them to discover whether they are relevant and reliable. Then set up a ***working bibliography*** to record those that might be useful. Annotate each entry so that you can remember why you thought the source was worth examining.

1. Identify the components of a working bibliography.

A working bibliography should include the information you will need for locating and documenting your sources:

To locate and document...	include in the working bibliography...
a printed book or an article or chapter in a printed book	the call number, the name of the author or editor, the title of the book, the title of the article or chapter (if relevant), the publisher, the place of publication, the date of publication, and the medium of publication (for example, Print).
an e-book or an article or chapter in an e-book	all of the above minus the call number, plus the DOI or URL; include the e-book format (for example, Kindle e-book, Nook e-book) as the medium.
a printed article	the name of the author, the title of the article, the title of the journal, the volume and issue number of the journal, the year of publication, the page numbers of the article, and the medium of publication (in this case, Print).
an article accessed through a database	all of the above, plus the name of the database, the DOI or, if there is no DOI, the URL for the journal's home page, and the date you last accessed the file. If no page numbers are provided, include paragraph numbers or section name. (The medium will be Web.)
an article in an online journal	all of the above. (The medium will be Web.)
a web page, wiki entry, or entry in a blog or discussion list	the name of the author, the title of the web page or entry title, the title of the website or blog, the sponsor, and the publication date or the date you last accessed the file. (The medium will be Web.)

DOI (digital object identifier) A permanent tag that does not change over time or from database to database

> **More about**
> Publication information, foldouts accompanying ch. 18, 19
> Digital object identifiers (DOI), 200, 358–59, 370, 399

As you construct the entries in your working bibliography, follow the documentation style that you will use in your project. Writers in literature typically use MLA style (ch. 18), writers in psychology and other social sciences

> **Tech** **Citation Management Software**
>
> Citation management software—such as the proprietary EndNote and RefWorks and the open source Zotero—can format the entries in your bibliography no matter what documentation style you choose. Your library may make such software available to you for free. Use the documentation chapters in this handbook to test your program for accuracy; not every program performs to perfection, and you are the writer and the person responsible for providing your audience with error-free documentation that does not cause confusion.

typically use APA style (ch. 19), writers in the humanities (except for literature) typically use *Chicago* style (ch. 20), and writers in the sciences typically use CSE style (ch. 21). (If you are not sure which documentation style to use, consult your instructor.) Using the appropriate style in the planning stage will save you time later, when you are formatting your finished project.

Saving a copy of an e-file or photocopying a printed document is prudent in case the source becomes unavailable later. Some instructors may also require you to submit copies of your sources with your final project. A PDF generally captures an article as it looked (or would have looked) in print, while an HTML copy provides the text, but not the formatting or illustrations. If both a PDF and an HTML file are available, select the PDF, which will enable you to cite the page numbers of the article and see any illustrations.

2. Recognize the title of the source and name of the publisher.

For many projects, you will be using sources found through library databases or on the web. As you construct your working bibliography, you may be challenged to figure out the title of your source or the name of the publication. Often it is difficult to identify which is the name of the publication and which is the sponsor of the publication. This is even more confusing when the sponsor is identified as "Publisher" (as in Figure 12.3, p. 204). Another problem arises when the name of a subsection of the publication looks like the name of the publication or the title of the source.

The following strategies should be helpful in your search for accurate information to include in your working bibliography:

- **Explore links.** Links labeled "about" or "contact us" often contain revealing information. You can also try clicking on the website logo.
- **Look for a bibliographic entry.** Many library databases not only provide you with the source itself but also with a model bibliographic entry for it. You may have to convert the model from one style (APA,

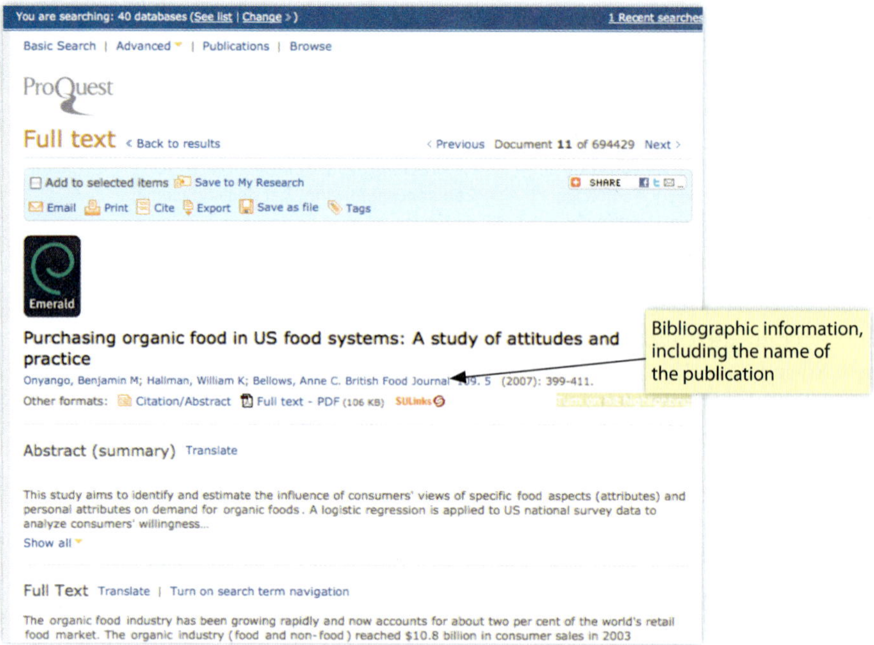

FIGURE 12.1 Locating the title in the model bibliographic information In this source retrieved from a database, it is only in the bibliographic information that the name of the publication, *British Food Journal,* appears.

for example) to another (perhaps MLA), but from the model you will at least know the correct name of the publication. Figure 12.1 shows a search result from a library database. It seems clear that the source title is "Purchasing Organic Food in U.S. Food Systems: A Study of Attitudes and Practices." The name of the publication, however, is not as clear. Is it *ProQuest* or *Emerald*? Fortunately, a bibliographic citation immediately follows the title, and that identifies the publication as the *British Food Journal.*

- **Look for an organizational path.** Many online publications have a small bar that shows where the current page appears in the site's organization. The current page usually will be on the right-hand side of the organizational path, with increasingly larger categories to the left.
- **Look for a volume and issue number.** The name of the publication usually accompanies this information (Figures 12.3 and 12.4).

FIGURE 12.2 Locating the publisher by following the organizational path The name of the publication *WebMD* is the first item on the left of the organizational path, followed by the name of the site subsection, "Healthy Eating & Diet," in which the current page is filed. The title of this source, "Organic Foods—Overview," appears below the organizational path.

- **Look for the name of an organization or university.** These are usually the sponsor of the publication, rather than the name of the publication itself. Once you have eliminated the sponsor, keep looking around the page for the name of the publication. Figure 12.3 shows the process.
- **Look at the top of the page.** Websites often place the sponsor's or database's name at the top, followed by the name of the publication, and then the title and author of the source (Figure 12.4).

3. Annotate the working bibliography.

An annotated entry in a working bibliography includes not only the information you will need to document and locate the source, but also a brief note that will remind you what the source is about and how you might use it in your project. Annotating sources will save you time later when you return to sources that looked promising or when you decide to do more research on the topic.

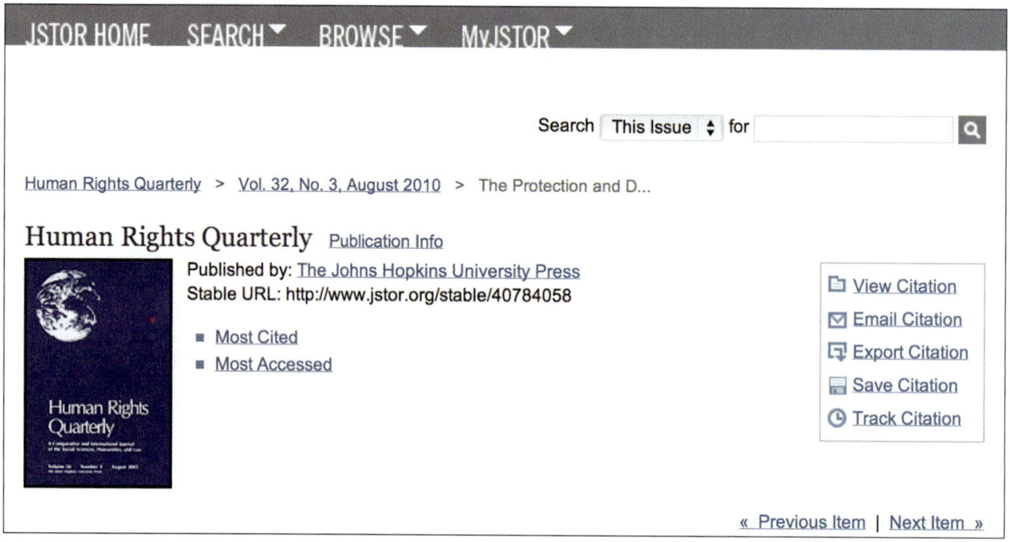

Research Matters • Planning a Research Project

FIGURE 12.3 Sorting organizational and institutional sponsors from the name of the publication The page identifies "Johns Hopkins University Press" as the publisher, but clicking on that name brings up a list of all the journals Johns Hopkins University Press publishes. Above the publisher information is the name of the publication, *Human Rights Quarterly*, followed by a link to "publication info." Note that above that is an organizational path showing the name of the publication and volume and issue number. At the very top is the name of the database, *JSTOR*.

Student Model
Research project:
"Holy Underground Comics, Batman!"
Lydia Nichols, 336–46

Below is a sample entry from a working bibliography for Lydia Nichols's research paper:

Fenty, Sean, Trena Houp, and Laurie Taylor. "Webcomics: The Influence and Continuation of the Comix Revolution." *ImageTexT* 1.2 (2004): 22 pars. Web. 18 March 2007.

An article in a peer-reviewed online journal. Good history of Underground Comics movement; definitions. Covers importance of comics on the Internet. Compares & contrasts Underground Comics and webcomics. Mentions *The Comics Journal*—check that out.

- Author names
- Publication info:
  – Title of journal
  – Volume, number, year of publication
  – Number of paragraphs (no page numbers)
- Article title
- Medium
- Date accessed

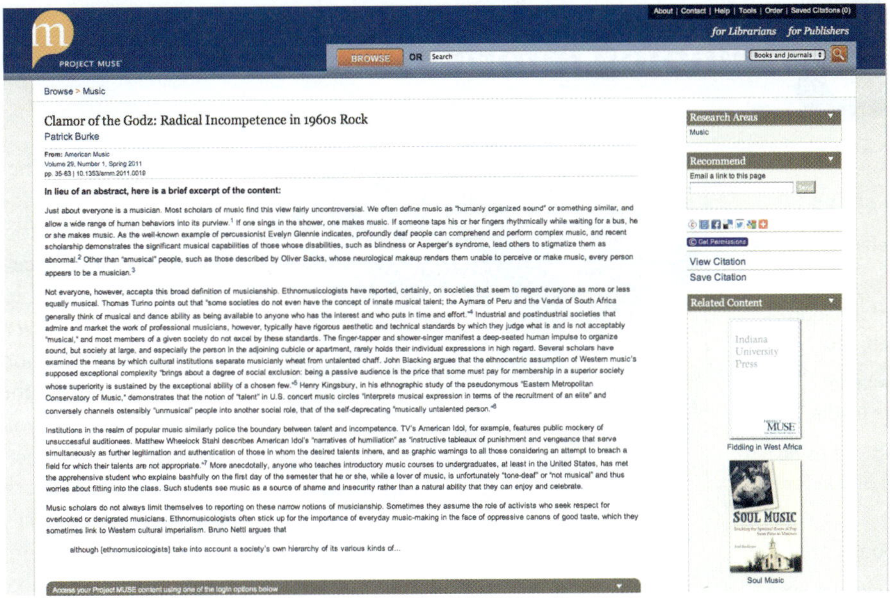

FIGURE 12.4 Locating the title by finding volume and issue numbers and by the organizational path At the top is the database name, Project Muse. Below that is the organizational path, which often identifies the database, publication, and volume and issue number. Some databases and publications put the name of the publication, volume, and issue number in the banner, as in this case. Further down is the title of the source, "Clamor of the Godz: Radical Incompetence in 1960s Rock," and under that, the author's name.

Make It Your Own

For the research project that you have been working on through the Make It Your Own assignments in this chapter, create a working bibliography of at least ten sources. Choose a mix of source types, including at least three books, three scholarly articles, and one or more newspaper or magazine articles, reference works, websites, pamphlets, government publications, or visual, multimedia, or audio sources. Then locate and annotate the five most promising sources, recording complete publication information and taking preliminary notes on what the source covers and how it might be useful to your research project.

> **More about**
> Finding information, 206–29 (ch. 13)
> Scholarly versus popular sources, 232–34

13 Finding Information

IN THIS CHAPTER

a. Finding reference works, 206
b. Finding information on the web, 210
c. Finding reliable interactive media, 214
d. Finding articles using databases and indexes, 215
e. Finding books, 220
f. Finding government information, 224
g. Finding multimedia sources, 225
h. Conducting field research, 226

> **More about**
> Reliability, 232–43
> Scholarly versus popular sources, 232–34

A simple Internet search can provide ready access to information—some excellent, much unreliable. It will not, however, help you strike a good balance among the types of sources you consult in your research. A web search for sources too easily becomes an issue of quantity, collecting "enough sources." The inexperienced researcher may tend to choose brief, quickly available online resources that are easy to read but that lead to a shallow paper relying on general facts or pieces that do not fit. Experienced researchers use advanced techniques that yield a good balance between general reference sources, specialized reference sources, popular opinion, and expert insight. They also go beyond the web to find scholarly resources—the print, electronic, and multimedia gems.

13a Finding Reference Works

Unless you are already an expert on your research topic, your search for sources should include both general and specialized reference works such as dictionaries, encyclopedias, biographical sources, bibliographies, almanacs, yearbooks, and atlases. General reference sources, written for newcomers to the topic, can do the following:

- Introduce you to your topic and help you determine whether it will sustain your interest
- Provide an overview and basic facts

Your search should also include specialized, subject-specific reference works written for researchers wanting in-depth understanding of the topic; these can:

- Introduce you to the issues and debates on your topic
- Help you get a sense of subtopics you might want to explore
- Provide lists of reliable sources on the topic
- Introduce and define special terminology, which will help you develop a list of keywords that you can use in further searching for sources

You will find reference works listed in your library's catalog. You may also be able to link to electronic reference sources through your library's home page or databases. As you search reference works, you may have to generate keywords for increasingly general search terms: If you cannot find good overview sources on "bats AND wind turbines," for example, you may have to search separately for "dangers of alternative energy sources" or "wildlife AND alternative energy." If you cannot find good overview sources on "ghostwriting," you might try the larger category of "plagiarism" or the even larger category of "ethics." Reference sources on related issues that include your topic may help you understand and explain the context for your research or its importance.

> **More about**
> Searching a library catalog, 220–24

1. Use dictionaries and encyclopedias.

In addition to whatever online tools they may use, most writers keep a collegiate dictionary at hand to verify spellings, look up definitions, and gather additional brief information about words. An *unabridged* dictionary provides more—more words, more examples of usage, more complete descriptions of the word's roots in other languages. The most extensive unabridged dictionary is the *Oxford English Dictionary* (or *OED*), a multivolume work providing the entire history of English words and showing the ways in which their meanings have changed over time. Unabridged dictionaries, including the *OED,* may be available in print or online.

Specialized dictionaries are written for students and scholars in specific academic fields. In addition to defining terms, subject-specific dictionaries may also provide a comprehensive introduction to the topic, as well as a list of further resources. If, for example, you want a deeper understanding of what *absolutism* means to a political scientist, you can turn to a source like the *Blackwell Dictionary of Political Science,* which offers a long paragraph explaining the term, followed by three recommended sources on the topic.

> **More about**
> Selecting a dictionary, 558–60
> Using a dictionary, 560–62

Writing Responsibly: Using Wikipedia Responsibly

Wikipedia (www.wikipedia.org) is an online encyclopedia created and revised by users. Its ongoing updates make its entries more up-to-date than those in most other encyclopedias. Most Wikipedia updates, however, are done by a relatively small number of people whose average age is 27, which means most entries are not validated by experts—unlike a source such as the *Encyclopedia Brittanica*. Approach Wikipedia with care, and verify the information you find there. Wikipedia is not an authoritative source for most college-level research projects, and its use in your project could subject you to the sort of ridicule that a US presidential candidate encountered when she cited Wikipedia in a campaign ad.

to TOPIC

Encyclopedias such as the *Concise Columbia Electronic Encyclopedia* and Wikipedia are available for free online. Others, such as *The New Encyclopedia Britannica,* are available in print but may also be accessible through your library's website.

> **More about**
> Reliability, 232–43

General encyclopedias provide a useful introduction to your topic, and some may offer a list of further resources. Specialized encyclopedias, on the other hand, provide not only an introduction to the topic, but also a sense of how scholars in the field approach the topic. They are also likely to provide a brief list of authoritative sources. If your library makes Reference Universe or Credo available, you can search across all the library's reference works, both online and in print.

Quick Reference: Dictionaries and Encyclopedias

Specialized Dictionaries
- *The Bedford Glossary of Critical and Literary Terms*
- *Dictionary of American History*
- *Dictionary of American Literary Characters*
- *Grove Dictionary of Art*
- *Dictionary of 20th-Century World Politics*
- *Public Policy Dictionary*

Specialized Encyclopedias
- *The Advertising Age Encyclopedia of Advertising*
- *Cambridge Encyclopedia of the English Language*
- *Encyclopedia of African-American Culture and History*
- *Encyclopedia of American Cultural and Intellectual History*
- *Encyclopedia of Bioethics*
- *Encyclopedia of Government and Politics*
- *Encyclopedia of Latin American History and Culture*
- *Encyclopedia of Religion*
- *Garland Encyclopedia of World Music*
- *McGraw-Hill Encyclopedia of Engineering*
- *McGraw-Hill Encyclopedia of Science and Technology*
- *Routledge Encyclopedia of Philosophy*
- *Women's Studies Encyclopedia*

2. Refer to almanacs and yearbooks.

Almanacs and yearbooks are annual publications offering facts and statistics, such as when each phase of the moon will occur and annual per capita income of nations. The best-known general-purpose almanac is the *World Almanac and Book of Facts,* which has been published annually since 1923. Subject-specific almanacs and yearbooks, such as the *Almanac of American Politics* and the *Yearbook of Immigration Statistics,* provide a wide body of statistical and tabular data on specific topics. Today, much of the information once most readily found in an almanac or yearbook is now available online at sites such as the *CIA Factbook* and the Research Tools page at the *Economist* magazine's website.

> **Quick Reference**
>
> **Almanacs and Yearbooks**
> *Almanac of American Politics*
> *Americana Annual*
> *Britannica Book of the Year*
> *Congressional Quarterly Almanac Plus*
> *Facts on File Yearbook*
> *Information Please Almanac*
> *Statistical Abstract of the United States*
> *UNESCO Statistical Yearbook*

3. Check out biographical reference works.

Biographical reference sources can provide you with the facts and events of people's lives (both the famous and the fairly obscure), such as their education, their accomplishments, and their current position. They can also help you understand the historical context in which the person lived or in which his or her works were produced. Numerous biographical resources are available to researchers; two of the most commonly consulted are the *American National Biography* and the *Dictionary of National Biography* (British).

> **Quick Reference**
>
> **Biographical Reference Sources**
> *Baker's Biographical Dictionary of Musicians*
> *Biographical Dictionary of American Indian History to 1900*
> *Cambridge Biographical Encyclopedia*
> *Cambridge Dictionary of American Biography*
> *Fifty Major Thinkers on Education*
> *McGraw-Hill Encyclopedia of World Biography*
> *Mexican American Biographies: A Historical Dictionary, 1836–1987*
> *Notable American Women: A Biographical Dictionary*
> *Notable Black American Women*
> *Webster's New Biographical Dictionary*
>
> **Bibliographical Resources**
> *Bibliographic Guide to Education*
> *Bibliographic Guide to Psychology*
> *Bibliographic Guide to the History of Computing, Computers, and the Information Processing Industry*
> *Film Research: A Critical Bibliography*
> *Information Sources in the Life Sciences*
> *Information Sources of Political Science*
> *International Bibliography of the Social Sciences*
> *MLA International Bibliography of Books and Articles on the Modern Languages and Literatures*
> *Sociology: A Guide to Reference and Information Sources*

> **Writing Responsibly** — **Going beyond Reference Sources**
>
> Because both general and specialized reference works provide background information to orient you to your topic, they are an essential starting point in your research. For a college-level research project, however, reference works are only the beginning; to fulfill your responsibilities to your topic and audience, you must go beyond these sources to find books, articles, and websites that treat your topic in depth.
>
> to TOPIC

4. Use bibliographies.

Bibliographies list sources on a particular topic, providing the information needed to locate the source. They often provide an abstract or brief summary of each source, so you can tell whether it is likely to be relevant to your research.

13b Finding Information on the Web

Engines like Google and Yahoo! search billions of web pages for whatever words the user enters and then return links in order of relevance, as determined by the search engine's criteria. (Google, for example, ranks its results based on the number of other pages that link to a site, as well as advertising.) The results retrieved can differ based on the criteria the search engine uses to rank relevance, as well as on the web pages it indexes. For that reason, running a search on multiple engines is a good idea. A list of alternative search engines appears in the Quick Reference box on page 213.

Before using a search engine for the first time, read about how it works. Look for links (often at the bottom of the page) called "About" or "Help" to find answers to frequently asked questions (FAQs) or for advice about how best to conduct a search on that site. Look, too, for advanced search options; these will help you focus your search.

1. Use keywords.

The most common way to begin a web search is with a simple keyword search. A search on Google using the term "underground comics"—the topic of Lydia Nichols's paper at the end of chapter 18—yielded more than 2 million hits (Figure 13.1).

This kind of searching is very easy, and it yields plenty of results—too many. No one could look at all 2 million results, and most are not even relevant. To

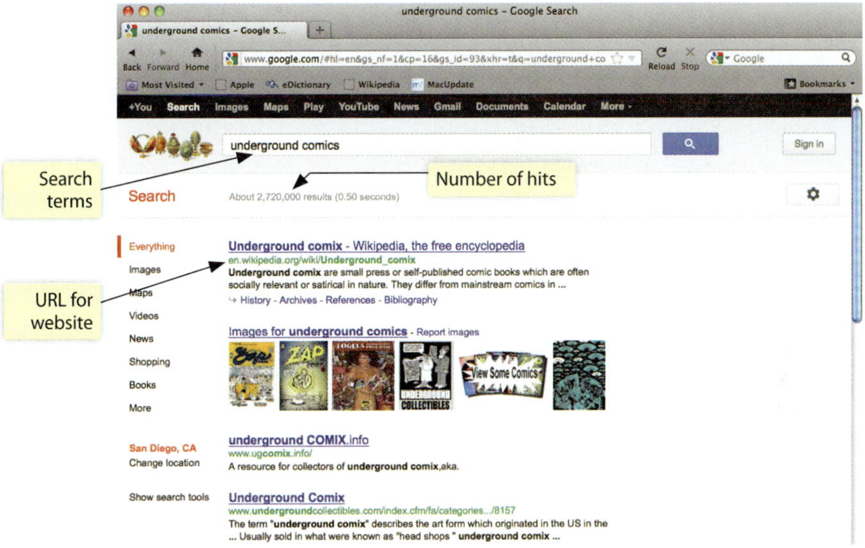

FIGURE 13.1
A simple keyword search on Google

narrow the results to a more manageable number, and to focus more closely on sites that will be relevant to your research, you can group terms using quotation marks or use a combination of terms. A search on "underground comics" and "history," for example, reduced the number of hits from 2 million to 34,300—still too many but a definite improvement.

> **More about**
> Relevance, 230–31

2. Use advanced search options.

You can narrow search results further with advanced search options (Figure 13.2), which can limit results by language, file type (Word, rich text, PDF, or Excel), domain (.org, .gov, .edu, or .com), and other options. Limiting the search on "'underground comics' history" to sites with the domain .edu, for example, reduced the number of hits to 1,420.

3. Use metasearch engines.

Because search engines index different web pages and use different methods to rank sites, using more than one engine increases your odds of finding useful resources. To search multiple sites simultaneously, use *metasearch engines,* which

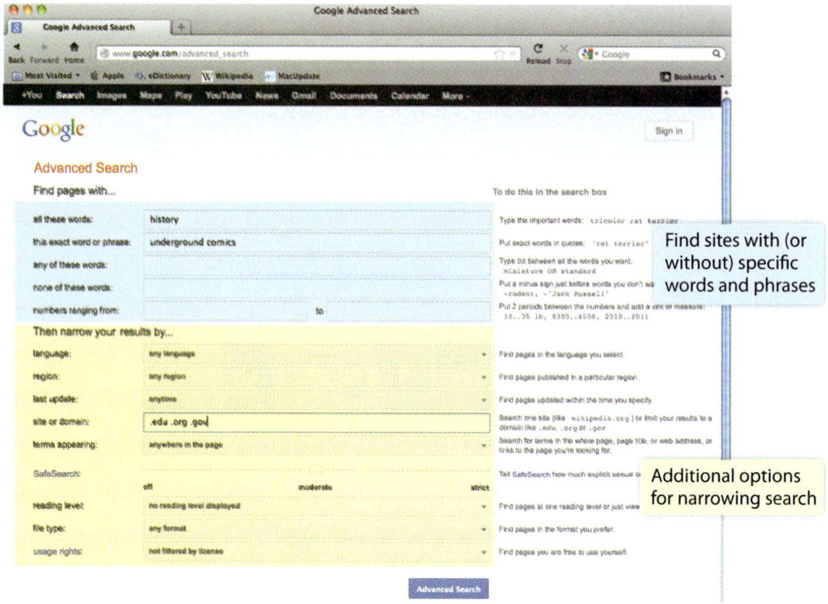

FIGURE 13.2 An advanced search on Google

return the top search results from several search engines at once, with duplicate entries deleted. (A list of metasearch engines appears in the Quick Reference on the next page.) Searching on the terms "underground comics" and "history" on InfoSpace, for example, produced three pages of hits (not 3 million).

4. Use subject directories.

> **More about**
> Devising a topic, 20–25, 195
> Narrowing or broadening a topic, 25–26

Subject directories list websites by topic. Their organization—from general to specific—can provide an effective overview of a topic and can help you discover, narrow, or expand your topic. The Quick Reference box on the next page lists some useful subject directories; your library may also make subject guides available. Check your library's website or consult a reference librarian.

NOTE Most subject directories today emphasize keyword searching but still list websites by category.

> **EXERCISE 13.1** Conducting a simple keyword search
>
> Using the topic you selected for Exercise 12.1 (p. 193), generate three or more keywords and use them to conduct keyword searches on two of

> **Quick Reference** — **Search Engines and Subject Directories**
>
> **Search Engines**
> Ask: www.ask.com
> Bing: www.bing.com
> Gigablast: gigablast.com
> Google: www.google.com
> Lycos: www.lycos.com
> Yahoo!: www.yahoo.com
>
> **Metasearch Engines**
> Info.com: www.info.com
> Infospace: infospace.com
> Search.com: www.search.com
> Yippy: Yippy.com
>
> **Subject Directories**
> Academic Info: www.academicinfo.net/subject-guides
> Bubl Link: bubl.ac.uk
> Infomine: infomine.ucr.edu
> IPL2: www.ipl.org
> Open Directory Project: www.dmoz.org

the search engines listed in the Quick Reference box above. Write a paragraph comparing your results: Did each search engine generate the same number of results? How do the top ten results differ? What about the next ten?

EXERCISE 13.2 Conducting an advanced keyword search

Return to the same search engines you used in Exercise 13.1 and use the same keywords, but this time select the advanced search feature to narrow your search to sites within the domains .edu, .gov, and .org. Write a paragraph comparing the results from the advanced search with those from the simple search you conducted in Exercise 13.1.

EXERCISE 13.3 Conducting a search with a subject directory

Using the keywords you generated for Exercise 13.1, conduct a search using one of the subject directories listed in the Quick Reference box above. Write a paragraph comparing the results from the subject directory with those you generated in Exercise 13.1 and Exercise 13.2.

Make It Your Own

Review the sources generated in Exercises 13.1, 13.2, and 13.3 and create a working list of sources you might use for a paper on the topic. Write a paragraph explaining why this combination of sources seems appropriate.

> **Make It Your Own**
>
> For a research project you are developing, create a list of keywords. Use the advanced search option of one of the search engines listed in the Quick Reference Box on the previous page to help you find .edu, .gov, or .org sources for these keywords. Now use the same keywords to search in one of the subject directories listed in the same Quick Reference box. Bookmark any sources that seem as if they will be useful, and make a note of the search term and the title in your research notebook. Write one sentence about why that source might be useful for your paper.

13c Finding Reliable Interactive Media

> **More about**
> Documenting a blog, 321 (MLA), 371 (APA), 404 (*Chicago*), 427 (CSE)
> Documenting a discussion list, 321 (MLA), 371 (APA), 404 (*Chicago*), 427 (CSE)
> Reliability, 232–43
> Netiquette, 483

In addition to conventional websites, a variety of other electronic sources—including blogs, discussion lists, and groups on social networking sites like Facebook—can offer you insight into your topic. Such sources are often contributed to by experts, so they have become an important source for up-to-the-minute news.

Of course, not all blogs, discussion lists, and groups are equally authoritative. Evaluate the reliability of such sites by finding out the qualifications of the writers, and verify the information you glean from such sources by consulting additional sources.

To find a blog or discussion list on your topic, use a specialized search engine. (Some are listed in the Quick Reference box on the next page.) You can also enter your keyword with "blog," "listserv," "newsgroup," or "chat room" in a search engine.

News alerts and RSS feeds collect news stories on topics you specify. Registering for alerts at sites such as Google (www.google.com/alerts) will bring daily updates on your chosen topics to your e-mail box. As of this writing, to read RSS feeds you must first download a news reader to your computer or create a personal web page at a site like Yahoo! or AOL; then you can register at sites to have stories "clipped" and saved for you.

Sites for sharing information, whether in print or other media, are being born and expiring (or at least fading in popularity) almost every day; as this book goes to press, YouTube, Twitter, Pinterest, and Flickr are widely used for sharing information and media files on topics of common interest, but new possibilities constantly arise.

Research Matters • Finding Articles in Journals and Other Periodicals Using Databases and Indexes

Quick Reference: Blog and Discussion List Search Engines

Blog Search Engines
Blogarama: ww1.blogarama.com
Blogdigger: http://blogdigger.com/index.html
Google Blog Search: www.google.com/blogsearch
Technorati: technorati.com

Discussion List Search Engines
CataList: www.lsoft.com/catalist.html
Google Groups: https://groups.google.com/?pli=1
Yahoo! Groups: groups.yahoo.com

> **EXERCISE 13.4** Researching electronic sources
> Find a blog or discussion group on the topic you explored in Exercises 13.1 and 13.2. Who are the contributors to this site? Conduct a web search to learn about contributors.

13d Finding Articles in Journals and Other Periodicals Using Databases and Indexes

A *periodical* is a publication, like a magazine, newspaper, or scholarly journal, that is issued at regular intervals—daily, weekly, monthly, quarterly. A search engine such as Google or Ask can point you to articles published online in magazines, newspapers, and some journals, but many articles in academic journals are not available for free on the web, and many magazines and newspapers require subscriptions before you can access their content. For a comprehensive listing of articles published in periodicals, turn to the databases available through your college library's website. (You may be prompted to sign in.)

Library databases are organized so that you can search for articles by author, title, subject, date, and other fields. Some databases provide only an *abstract,* or summary, but many provide the complete text, either in a **PDF** (sometimes called "full text PDF") file, which shows the article more or less as it would have appeared in print, or in an **HTML** (sometimes called "full text") file, which provides the text but not the formatting or illustrations that would have appeared in the printed text.

1. Choose an appropriate database.

Most college libraries provide a wide variety of databases. Most will offer an all-purpose database like ProQuest Central, Academic Search Premier, or Academic OneFile that indexes both popular magazines and scholarly journals, as

Writing Responsibly — *Really* Reading *Real* Sources

As you choose your sources, it may seem efficient to select only those that are short and easy to read. Resist this temptation; fulfill your responsibility to your topic by pushing beyond easy, basic information. If you controlled for page length in your source selection, you would be writing your research project from uninsightful sources that would produce a shallow, uninteresting paper. Instead, when your source selection is finished, include substantial sources that treat complex questions in complex ways. Reading these sources will be a greater challenge, but you will be able to produce richer, more successful writing from them.

to TOPIC

> **More about**
> Writing situation, 9–17

well as discipline-specific databases, such as Education FullText, PsycINFO, and Science Direct. They may also offer LexisNexis Academic, which indexes news reports from around the world. A reference librarian can help you learn which databases available at your library will best suit your research needs.

When searching for articles, be sure to consider the types of sources that are most appropriate to your topic and writing situation. In particular,

Tech — Using Google Scholar

> **More about**
> Evaluating sources, 230–45 (ch. 14)

Google Scholar (scholar.google.com) allows users to search the web for scholarly materials—articles in academic journals, theses, books, and abstracts.

Pros

- Google Scholar can help you locate material that you would otherwise need both your library's catalog and subscription databases to find.
- It may even link to your own library's digital holdings (see the preferences settings in Google Scholar).
- It links to many citation management software types.
- It indicates how many online sites have cited the source and provides links to those citations.

Cons

- Google has its own definition of *scholarly*, so some hits may be to works your instructor may not consider authoritative.
- You may be shifted to sites where you will be asked to pay for full-text versions of the source. (Always check your library's holdings or try interlibrary loan—a system for borrowing from another library—before paying for access.)
- Because of Google's search and ranking methods, the most recent sources may not be included, or they may appear at the end of the list. (You can include a date range in Advanced Scholar Search.)

Research Matters • Finding Articles in Journals and Other Periodicals Using Databases and Indexes **13d** 217

consider whether you should use popular sources, scholarly sources, or a combination of the two.

For Heather DeGroot, writing for her psychology class, PsycINFO (a database that indexes articles from psychology journals) was a good starting place for her periodicals search. For Lydia Nichols, researching the characteristics of underground comics, a general database (such as ProQuest Central or Academic Search Premier), which indexes both popular and scholarly sources, was a good place to start.

> **Student Models**
> Research projects:
> "The Power of Wardrobe," Heather DeGroot, 381–88
> "Holy Underground Comics, Batman!" Lydia Nichols, 336–46

2. Search the database.

Searching a database is much like using a search engine such as Google or Yahoo! You type in a search term and hit Return to generate a list of articles that include your keywords. Unlike a search engine, however, the database limits its search to selected publications, so the items returned are more likely to be reliable.

To make sure the results of a database search are relevant, narrow your search by combining search terms and using the advanced search options the database makes available. Typing "comic books" in the search box of a database like Academic Search Premier generates a list of over 17,000 items—fewer than with a Google search but still far too many to be helpful. As with a web search engine, combining terms ("comic books AND underground") narrows the search. The search could be narrowed further by using the database's search options. The menu bars on the left and right in Figure 13.3 show some of the options for narrowing a search.

NOTE Databases differ from vendor to vendor and are updated frequently, so check the Help screens or ask a librarian for advice.

If narrowing your search by combining terms and using the database's narrowing options is not getting you the results you need, try the following:

- Conduct your search again with alternative or refined search terms. Check your database's subject or topics list (sometimes called

---

Tech Hidden Benefits of Library Databases

In addition to their superiority in finding sources, a library database may be linked to RefWorks or another citation management software to which your library subscribes. When you choose a source in the database, the software makes a bibliographic entry in whatever style—MLA, APA, and so forth—you select.

> **More about**
> Relevance, 230–31
> Citation management programs, 201

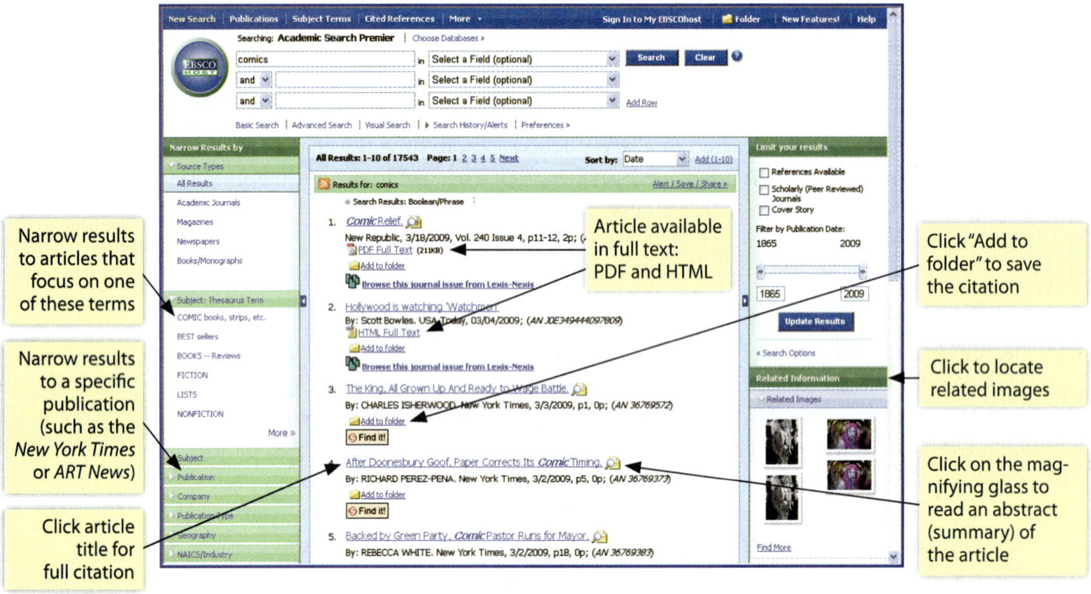

FIGURE 13.3 Search results for "underground comics AND genre"

Callouts on figure:
- Narrow results to articles that focus on one of these terms
- Narrow results to a specific publication (such as the *New York Times* or *ART News*)
- Click article title for full citation
- Article available in full text: PDF and HTML
- Click "Add to folder" to save the citation
- Click to locate related images
- Click on the magnifying glass to read an abstract (summary) of the article

Thesaurus) for the terms with which your topic was indexed and use those terms in your search.

- Narrow (or expand) your search using Boolean logic. (See the Quick Reference box on the next page.)
- Return to the library's database menu to run your search on other databases.

As you find promising sources, create entries for them in your working bibliography, or follow directions on the database for e-mailing entries to yourself.

Just as metasearch engines allow you to send your keyword search out to several search engines simultaneously, some database vendors allow you to search simultaneously through all their databases. Increasingly, libraries

> **More about**
> Creating a working bibliography, 200–05

Tech — **HTML versus PDF**

Articles accessed through a database are often available in both HTML and PDF versions. The HTML (often called *full text*) version will download much more quickly, but the PDF (often called *full text PDF*) version may be a duplicate of the article as it appears in the publication, including illustrations and page numbers, which you can then include in your reference list or list of works cited.

Research Matters • Finding Articles in Journals and Other Periodicals Using Databases and Indexes **13d** **219**

Quick Reference: Conducting a Boolean Search

Most databases (and search engines like Yahoo!) narrow a search with Boolean logic, which relies on the words *and, not,* and *or* to expand or narrow a search and parentheses or quotation marks to group words. Most databases also use wildcard characters (* or ?) to stand in place of letters, allowing you to search for different forms of a word at the same time. Check Help screens or consult a reference librarian to learn how to use Boolean logic in searching your library's databases.

AND	Comics AND history 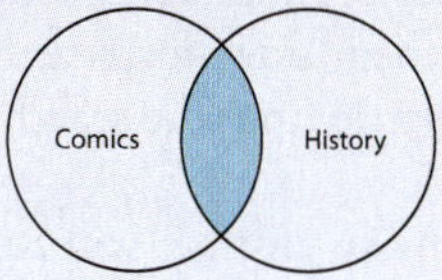	Narrows a search by retrieving items that include *both* terms.
OR	Comics OR history 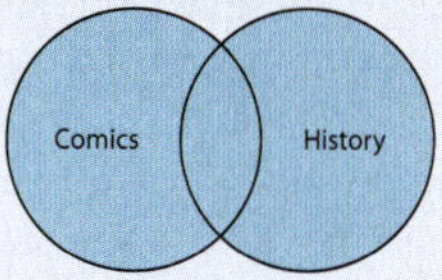	Expands a search by retrieving items that include *either* term.
NOT	Comics NOT history 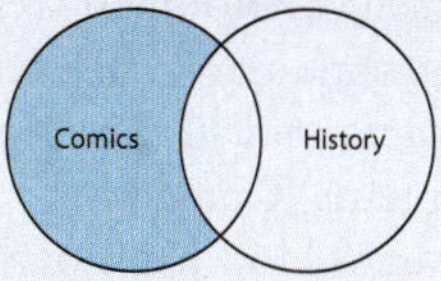	Narrows a search by retrieving items that include one term but not the other.
" "	"graphic novel"	Quotation marks group terms to retrieve pages with these words in this order.
( )	(comics OR comix) AND (underground)	Parentheses group terms so complex alternatives can be retrieved.
* / ?	comi* (or comi?) to search for comic, comics, and comix simultaneously	Wildcard characters allow you to search for more than one version of a word at the same time by replacing the letters that are different in each word with an asterisk (*) or question mark (?).

are also offering *federated searching,* which allows you to search across many databases simultaneously. Check your library's website to see what multiple-database searching options are available to you.

3. Find copies of articles.

Once you have generated a list of articles from your database search, you are ready to retrieve copies of the articles. Some articles you can access directly from the database search page (look for links saying something like "Find It in Full Text") and you can then print them, download them to your hard drive, or e-mail them to yourself. The first article from the search screen in Figure 13.3, for example, is available online.

For some articles, however, only an abstract will be available through the database; in a few cases, only a bibliographic citation may be available. While it may be tempting to skip articles that you cannot have delivered instantly to your desktop, you may miss out on important sources of information, especially classics published before the Internet revolution. To find articles you cannot link to from the database, consult your library's website (or a librarian) for a list of journals available through your library or through interlibrary loan.

> **EXERCISE 13.5 Conducting a database search**
>
> Using one or more keywords that you generated in Exercise 13.1, conduct a search using a general database such as ProQuest Central or Academic Search Premier. Now conduct the same search using an appropriate subject-specific database. (Ask your instructor or a librarian for help in determining which databases might be appropriate.) Compare the results: How many articles were returned on each search? How many of the same articles were listed on the first two pages of results?

> **EXERCISE 13.6 Locating an article**
>
> For one of the searches you performed in Exercise 13.5, find an article that is not available as a link from the database results page. Then write a paragraph describing the steps you took to find it.

13e Finding Books Using Library Catalogs

While reference works can give you an overview or direct you to other sources, it is in books that you are most likely to find extensive, in-depth treatments of your topic—especially in the humanities and some social sciences. One or two well-chosen books, supplemented by a selection of journal articles and other sources, can round out your research and deepen your understanding of your topic.

1. Search the catalog.

Libraries index all their holdings in catalogs, which in most cases you can access through your library's website. Most library catalogs allow users to search for resources by author, title, and subject heading. Some include additional search options such as call number or keyword (Figure 13.4). Because catalogs differ from library to library, check the Help or Search Tips screen before beginning a search. If your library's catalog allows keyword searching, you may find it

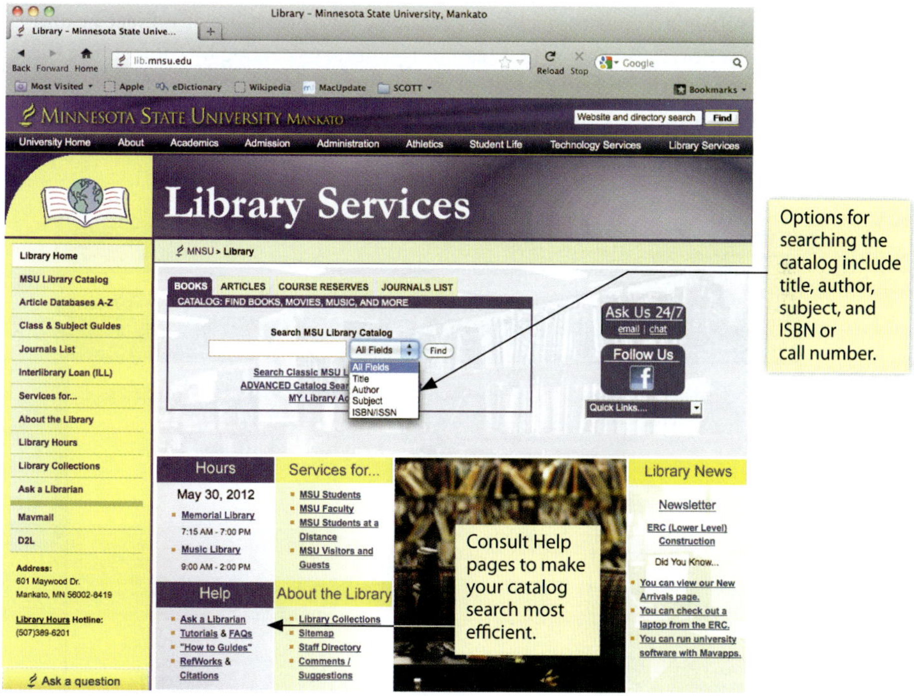

FIGURE 13.4 A library website Students at Minnesota State University, Mankato, and other colleges and universities around the country now search their library's catalog directly from their library's home page.

useful to conduct a "keyword anywhere" search, using your search terms. Most library catalogs include tables of contents for anthologies and edited books, so a keyword search may yield useful results.

NOTE Some catalogs may require you to specify the category (such as author or title) in which you wish to search. If you do not, the program may default to a category you are not expecting. For example, if you are looking for books *about* Herman Melville and do not specify that you are searching by subject, your library's program may default to searching for books *by* Melville and provide you with a list of books by him as well as about him.

>**More about**
Keyword searching, 210–11

Search a library's catalog much as you do a search engine or a periodical database: Type a keyword or a combination of words in the search box and hit Enter. Whereas Google and other web search engines allow you to use any keyword related to your topic, library catalogs use a preset list of subject headings to index library books. When searching a library's catalog by subject, use these preset headings. To find the subject headings the library has used, go to a catalog entry for a book on your topic that you have already identified as relevant. The book's record will list the subject headings used (Figure 13.5). Clicking

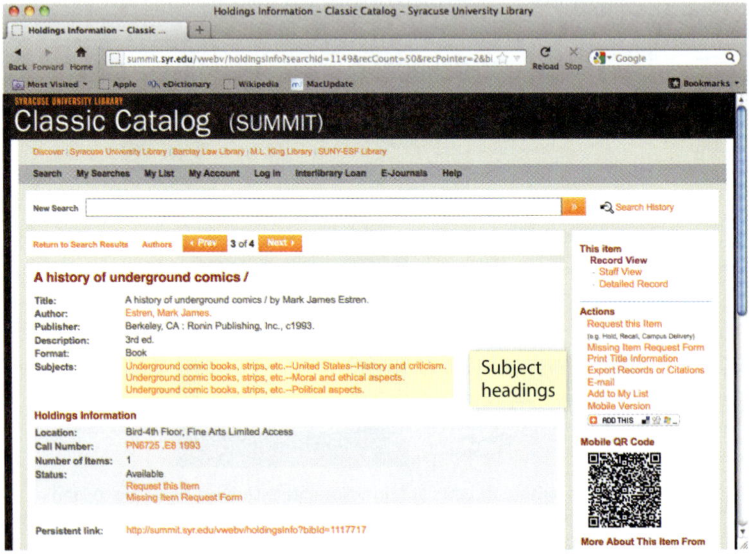

FIGURE 13.5 Finding subject headings in a library record

on them will bring you to a list of related subject headings and to other books cataloged using the same terms. Repeat the process with other useful books to add subject terms.

2. Browse the stacks or the catalog.

Many researchers enjoy browsing library stacks to find books on their topic: Since books on a topic all share the first part of a call number, they are shelved close together. If you are free to wander in your library's stacks, check for other books on your topic shelved close to those you have identified as relevant. If your library catalog allows it, search for other books on your subject by inserting the first part of a relevant book's call number in the catalog's search box. (The screenshot in Figure 13.6 shows a search for items whose call number begins with PN 6725.) Or the results page in an online catalog search on your library's website might show you sources on related topics.

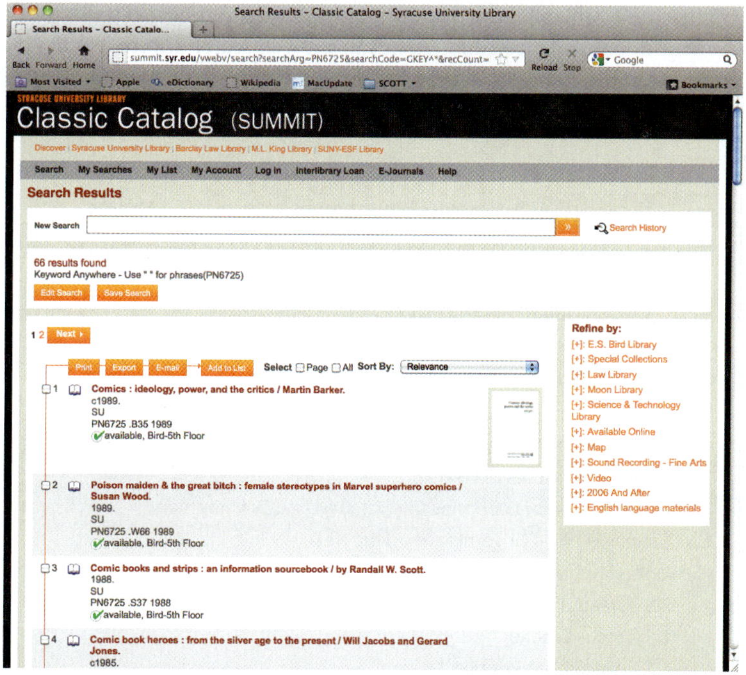

**FIGURE 13.6
Browsing by call number**

> **EXERCISE 13.7 Using the library catalog**
>
> Using the keywords you generated in Exercise 13.1, find a book using your library's catalog. Then refine your search using the subject headings and call number. Write a paragraph describing the process and analyzing your results.

13f Finding Government Information

Although you will usually rely on books and articles in your college research, government publications can provide you with rich resources, including congressional records, government reports, and legal documents. The federal government makes more than 300,000 documents available online, free of charge, from all three branches of the government—executive, legislative, and judicial. Most state and local governments also post their documents on the web, as do many governments around the world. If you are researching a social, legal, or political issue or if you need up-to-date statistics about almost any group, you may find valuable information in government publications. To locate government documents, conduct an advanced web search limited to the domain .gov or search databases such as CQ Press Electronic Library and LexisNexis Congressional.

Quick Reference Accessing Government Information Online

The websites for the following all provide access to government documents and datasets online:

- European Union
- FedStats
- FedWorld Information Network
- FirstGov
- Library of Congress
- National Institutes of Health
- Organization for Economic Cooperation and Development
- State and Local Government on the Net
- United Nations
- US Bureau of Labor Statistics
- US Census Bureau
- US Government Printing Office

> **Quick Reference** — **Multimedia Resources**
>
> Academy of American Poets
> American Rhetoric: The Power of Oratory in the United States
> Archive.org
> Library of Congress
> MIT Open Courseware
> National Aeronautics and Space Administration (NASA)
> National Park Service
> New York Public Library
> Perry Castañeda Library Map Collection, University of Texas
> Smithsonian Institution

13g Finding Multimedia Sources

Photographs, graphs, charts, and drawings have long been a staple of research papers in disciplines such as art history, film studies, history, geography, geology, political science, sociology, and psychology. With research in all disciplines now being shared through multimedia presentations and websites, the use of multimedia resources has also expanded. To find multimedia resources, start with your library's catalog. Besides the video clips you can find on YouTube and Hulu, you may also find appropriate multimedia resources online at the sites hosted by the organizations listed in the Quick Reference box on this page.

NOTE Because you need to cite your media sources, remember to add them to your working bibliography.

> **More about**
> Working bibliography, 200–01

Make It Your Own

For a research assignment for this or another class, create a working bibliography of at least ten items. Include at least one of the following:

- Website
- Article in a scholarly journal
- Article in a newspaper
- Article in a magazine
- Subject-specific reference book
- Book
- Government publication
- Media resource

Which are available online? Which can you locate in your library?

Work Together

In small groups or as a class, take a tour of the library. (You will need to arrange this in advance.) Come prepared with a topic, and ask a librarian for advice on how best to conduct a database search or find resources on your topic in the library's catalog. Explore the library's multimedia offerings, and check out at least one book on your topic. Finally, prepare a brief report listing at least three things you learned about the library that you did not know before your visit.

13h Conducting and Reporting Field Research

Field research is often part of a research project in which the writer begins by reviewing information from secondary sources (reports of others' research) and then adds to the body of information by conducting a fresh inquiry. The most common types of field research are interviews, observational studies, and surveys.

1. Interviews

Expertise and the knowledge that comes with experience can often be gained only through an interview. Media such as e-mail, text messaging, and even the telephone extend your range of possible interviewees, but face-to-face interviews give you an opportunity to read the other person's body language—facial expressions and bodily gestures—which can provide insight and direction for follow-up questions.

Instructors with special expertise in your subject make good subjects for an interview; government agencies, businesses, and public service organizations can also connect you with experts. When researching cultural or historical events, consider interviewing participants—the attorneys in a legal case, your soldier-cousin for her experience in Iraq, organizers of a demonstration for immigrants' rights.

Consider these tips for making the best use of your time:

Before the Interview

- Consider your purpose, and shape your questions accordingly.
- Select your interviewee with care, and contact that person for an appointment.

Writing Responsibly

Conducting Interviews Fairly

- To project professionalism, show up for the interview on time and prepared.
- Ask only for information that your expert alone could provide, not information you could easily gather on your own.
- Tell the interviewee up front how you will use the information you gather, and get her or his written consent.
- Ask for permission to record the interview, and confirm any quotations you may want to use.
- Offer the interviewee an opportunity to review your notes or your draft document. (You need not change your notes or document in response, but you should acknowledge any difference of opinion.)

to SELF

- Conduct background research on the topic and on the person whom you are interviewing, and develop ten to fifteen open-ended questions. (Ask "How would you rate the job the president of the Student Senate is doing, and why?" *not* "Is the president of the Student Senate doing a good job?") Avoid questions that prompt an interviewee to provide a particular answer. (Ask "How do you think the stock market will react in the coming year, and why?" *not* "How far will the stock market fall in the coming year?")

During the Interview

- Set your interviewee at ease, but remain politely neutral.
- Use your prepared questions and listen carefully to the answers; also listen for surprises and ask follow-up questions.
- Take extensive notes or, if permitted, record the interview.
- Avoid interrupting or talking about yourself.

After the Interview

- Reflect on your notes while the interview is still fresh, recording your thoughts and any additional questions you would like to ask; then phone or e-mail the interviewee *once* for follow-up. (Multiple follow-up calls are likely to annoy.)
- Make a transcript of the interview, and send a copy to your interviewee for comment or confirmation.
- Send a thank-you note within twenty-four hours of your interview, and send the interviewee a copy of your finished project with a note of appreciation.

Writing Responsibly: Avoiding Manipulation and Bias in Observations

- Ask permission to observe organized groups. Let the group's leader decide whether all should be informed, but reveal your purpose if asked.
- Resist manipulating the site or the community to get the results you want.
- Move around the scene to change your perspective.
- Provide groups the opportunity to read and respond to your study before you submit it. (You need not change your report, but you should acknowledge differences of opinion.)
- Alert readers to the limitations of your study or to ways your own experiences and perspectives may have influenced your observations.

to TOPIC

2. Observational studies

Observational studies are common in the social sciences, particularly in psychology, sociology, and anthropology. Consider the following before beginning an observational study:

> **More about**
> Devising a hypothesis, 195–96

- **Your hypothesis.** What do you expect to learn? You can refine your hypothesis as your observations continue, but starting out with a hypothesis will help guide your observations and note taking.

- **Your role.** Will you participate in the group, or observe the group from outside? The role you play will influence your perspective and affect your observations. Consider the steps you can take to minimize bias.

- **Your methods.** Establish categories for the observations you expect, and adjust them in response to your observations. Make notes immediately after a research session rather than during it, so your presence will be less obtrusive.

3. Surveys

Surveys are used frequently in politics and marketing but are useful in many types of research to assess beliefs, opinions, and behavior. When developing a survey, consider these issues:

- **Your hypothesis.** What do you expect to learn from your survey?
- **Your target population.** What group will you reach and how will you contact them? Strive to include a broad and representative range of respondents.

> **Tech** **Online Surveys**
>
> A variety of web-based survey tools allows you to conduct surveys online. The following are among the most popular:
>
> - Google Docs
> - SurveyMonkey
> - SurveyGizmo
> - Zoomerang
>
> Each allows users to create and send out a basic survey to a limited number of respondents for free.
>
> You might also consider conducting your survey with the help of social media such as Facebook or Twitter.

- **Your survey.** What type of questions will you ask, how many questions will you include, and how will you administer the survey?

Most surveys offer true-false, yes-no, and multiple-choice questions because these are easier to tabulate, but a few open-ended questions may deepen your sense of the respondents' feelings, and quotations can be used in your project. Whatever type of questions you ask, be sure your answer options are fair and that they offer an adequate range of choices. Because respondents are not likely to spend more than a few minutes answering questions, surveys should be brief—one to two pages is a reasonable limit.

> **Writing Responsibly** **Reporting Results Fairly**
>
> As you integrate the results of your field research into your larger project, explain how you chose your research participants, how many you invited, and how many agreed to participate. Do not, however, name or indirectly identify your participants unless they have agreed to their identity being made public. When you quote from an interview or survey, indicate how typical the quotation is. Did you choose it just because it supports your thesis, or is it typical of the majority of responses?
>
> to AUDIENCE

14 Evaluating Information

IN THIS CHAPTER

a. Evaluating for relevance and reliability, 230

b. Evaluating online texts, 236

c. Evaluating visual sources, 239

d. Writing Responsibly Choosing, unpacking complex sources, 244

CLOTHING

"Do you have this in sheep?"

In Aesop's fable "The Wolf in Sheep's Clothing," the wolf uses a sheep's skin to lull his intended dinner into a false sense of security. Texts, too, can be a kind of wolf in sheep's clothing. They can appear to be wonderful resources, full of interesting facts and persuasive arguments, while hiding misinformation and faulty reasoning. For this reason, it is crucial that researchers dig below the surface to evaluate their sources carefully for relevance and reliability. Just as a wolf can hide under a sheep's clothing, a book should not be judged by its cover!

14a Evaluating for Relevance and Reliability

Evaluating sources means assessing how ***relevant,*** or useful, a source is to your research and determining the source's ***reliability***—how much you can count on it.

1. Relevance

When considering a potential source, first consider its relevance: Does the source offer information that could enrich your understanding of your topic, provide background information or evidence to support your claims, or suggest alternative perspectives? Before taking the time to read the text, determine its likely relevance by *previewing* it:

- **Check the publication date.** Recently published works are most likely to be of the greatest relevance, as they will probably provide the most up-to-date information. Be alert, though, to classics; they contain information or ideas on which researchers still rely. Classics will be cited frequently by other reliable sources; your instructor can also help you identify them.

- **Read the abstract, foreword, introduction, or lead** (first paragraph in a newspaper article). These usually provide a summary, overview, or key facts discussed in detail in the source.

- **Read the headings and subheadings.** These will provide an outline of the work.

- **Scan figures and illustrations.** These might signal important ideas and explain complex processes.

- **Read the conclusion.** The conclusion—the last few paragraphs in a journal or magazine article or the final chapter of a book—often reiterates the central idea and argument, important questions, and major findings.

- **Consult the index.** Check it for key terms in your research.

> **abstract** A summary of the text's main claims and most important supporting evidence

> **More about**
> Previewing a text, 109–10
> Finding the copyright date, foldout accompanying ch. 18, 19
> Primary versus secondary sources, 435–37

Quick Reference: Judging Reliability

Scholarly work. Was the source published in a scholarly journal or book, or in a popular magazine, newspaper, or book?

Expertise. Is the author an authority on the subject?

Objectivity. Do tone, logic, quality of the evidence, and coverage of the opposition suggest that the source is unbiased?

Scope. Does the author attempt to test his or her own assumptions and explore alternatives?

Citations. Does the text cite sources, and is it cited in other texts?

Scrutiny. Was the text subjected to scrutiny by someone else before you saw it? For example, was it selected by the library, reviewed by another scholar, or fact-checked for accuracy?

Presentation. Is the text clearly written, well organized, and carefully edited and proofread?

Domain. Does the main portion of the URL end in .edu or .org, suggesting a noncommercial purpose, or does it end with .com, suggesting a commercial purpose?

Site sponsor or host. Is the site's host identified? Does the host promote a viewpoint or position that might bias the content?

FIGURE 14.1 Popular versus scholarly books *The South Beach Diet* (Rodale) is a popular-press book aimed at a general audience: people wanting to lose weight. *Unbearable Weight: Feminism, Western Culture, and the Body* (University of California Press), on the other hand, is a scholarly book about our culture's obsession with women's weight; its target audience is scholars in fields such as women's studies and cultural studies.

2. Reliability

Judging reliability is not a simple, yes-or-no litmus test. Instead, it is a balancing act: You rate a source on a variety of criteria; the more criteria on which you can rate the source highly, the more reliable it is likely to be. Here are several criteria to consider:

- **Is the source scholarly or popular?** Scholarly sources (Figure 14.1) include articles published in academic journals and books published by scholarly presses. They typically include citations of their own sources and full bibliographic information for them, either in notes or in a bibliography. They are written by subject-matter experts, not for profit but as a contribution to knowledge, and they are reviewed by other subject-matter experts (*peer review*) before being accepted for publication.

    In contrast, articles in magazines and books published by the popular press are commercial; they were selected by an editor who believes that an audience will be interested enough in the material to buy it. Often these articles include advertisements that sometimes accompany an "objective" story. Popular sources may be fact-checked, but they are not reviewed by experts.

    Sources published in popular publications with a sophisticated or expert audience are likely to be more reliable than sources in general-audience publications, but those in scholarly publications are likely to be the most reliable of all. If you find in a popular publication a story describing research that someone has conducted, find the original report of the research rather than relying solely on a journalist's description of it.

> **More about**
> Biographical reference works, 209–10

- **Is the author an expert on the topic?** Does the author have advanced training in the subject? You can determine this by reading about the author in a biographical reference work, by finding other works the author has published, by considering the author's academic background, and by determining whether the author has been cited in the footnotes or bibliographies of other reliable sources.

- **Does the source seem objective?** Does the source have an objective tone, make reasonable claims supported by logical reasons and solid evidence, recognize alternative perspectives, and treat opponents with respect? Or does it contain emotionally loaded language, make exaggerated claims, or support those claims with faulty logic and questionable or scanty evidence? An author may care deeply and write passionately about a subject, but if he or she characterizes groups unfairly or offensively or treats the individuals making up the group as if they are all the same, then you should suspect bias.

> **More about**
> Tone, 15–16, 136, 543, 548–50
> Opinion versus belief, 138–40
> Types of evidence, 40–44
> Bias, 544–47

- **Is the type of source appropriate to your purpose?** Or are you choosing it just because it was easy to find, is short, or is easy to read? Most college projects are designed to explore complex issues. Does your source offer a detailed exploration of the debates about your issue, or does it offer just basic facts or a condensed overview? You cannot write an insightful argument based only on a shallow understanding of your issue.

- **Does the author or publisher have a vested interest?** Consider author, audience, and purpose: Who is writing, to whom, and why? How does the author stand to benefit from the work? Most authors will benefit in some way: through sales of the book or through the prestige of publishing. But consider whether the author or publisher will benefit in some other way: Is the author promoting a product or process from which she will benefit financially? Will the author or publisher gain adherents to a political position? Check the author's or publisher's website for advertisements and to see whether a mission statement reveals an agenda.

Quick Reference: Scholarly versus Popular Periodicals

Scholarly

- Articles are written by scholars, specialists, researchers
- Use technical terminology
- Tend to be long—typically, ten pages or more
- Include citations in the text and a list of references
- Are reviewed by other scholars before publication
- Acknowledge any conflicts of interest (such as research support from a pharmaceutical company)
- Generally look serious; unlikely to include color photographs, but may include charts, graphs, and tables
- Published by professional organizations

Popular

- Articles are written by journalists or professional writers
- Avoid technical terminology
- Tend to be brief—as little as one or two pages
- Do not include citations or a list of references
- May be fact-checked but not reviewed by experts
- Unlikely to acknowledge conflicts of interest
- Often published on glossy paper with eye-catching color images
- Published by commercial companies

Writing Responsibly: Keeping an Open, Inquiring Mind

As a researcher, you have a responsibility to avoid bias: Read sources with an open mind, use reliable sources, avoid exaggerated claims and logical fallacies, and criticize unreasonable or poorly supported conclusions but not the people who hold them. Make sure to consider all sides of an argument, especially those that challenge the positions you hold. Use difficult sources, too: Do not reject a source because it is written to a more expert audience than you. Find the time to study it carefully and gain at least a preliminary understanding of it.

to TOPIC

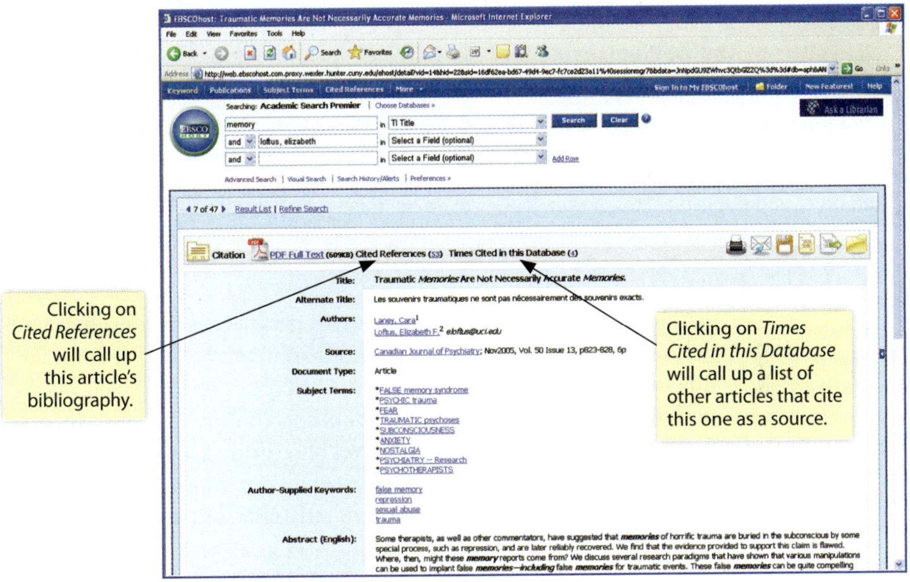

Research Matters • Evaluating for Relevance and Reliability

FIGURE 14.2 Determining reliability by assessing citations Both the number of times an article has been cited and the citations in the article itself are useful ways of determining an article's reliability.

- **Does the text cite its sources?** Most scholarly articles and books and some popular books will include a bibliography, and some journal databases will list the article's sources in the citation. Reputable newspapers and magazines will check a writer's sources, though they often go unnamed, identified only as a "White House source" or a "source close to the investigation."

- **Do other scholars cite the text?** Also important is the number of times a source has been cited by other scholarly works. Some journal databases indicate the number of times an article has been cited by other articles indexed by that database (Figure 14.2). Citation indexes such as Web of Knowledge, Scopus, Microsoft Academic Search, and Google Scholar also provide this information. If you find very few citations to your source, check the publication date: Sources published within the previous three years may not yet have any citations at all. Citation frequency does not itself determine reliability; it is just one test.

- **How did you find the source?** Sources located through your college library are more likely to be reliable than are sources located through

> **More about**
> Exploratory arguments, 134–37
> Reasoning logically, 138–40
> Using evidence as support, 40–41, 59–63
> Citing sources, 288–346 (MLA style, ch. 18), 347–88 (APA style, ch. 19), 389–415 (*Chicago* style, ch. 20), 416–30 (CSE style, ch. 21)
> Choosing a citation style, 437, 457

Writing Responsibly

Online Plagiarism

The ease with which users can cut and paste information from one site into another means you must be wary of online sites, especially if they are self-sponsored. Unreliable sites frequently copy directly from other, more reliable sites. If you suspect plagiarism, copy a passage and paste it into a search engine's search box. Do any of your hits use the same (or very similar) language? The best way to avoid using material plagiarized from another site is to evaluate sites carefully for reliability.

to SELF

---

a Google search because library sources are selected in consultation with subject-matter experts, in response to reviews, or after considering where the source was published. A source published solely on the web (unless in a scholarly journal published online) is not likely to have been subjected to the same level of scrutiny. Google searches will return such sites, but library databases will not. Finding a source on a library database is not a guarantee of reliability, but it is one indicator.

- **Is the source well written and edited?** Has the writer approached the task with a sense of responsibility—by writing, organizing, editing, and proofreading the material carefully? Is the page design easy to follow? Are the visuals appropriate to the audience and purpose and free from manipulation or distortion?

14b Evaluating Online Texts: Websites, Blogs, Wikis, and Discussion Forums

> **More about**
> Websites, 176–81, 214–20
> Interactive media, 181–82, 214

Anyone can create a website, post a blog, or contribute to an open wiki or discussion forum. This freedom makes the web exciting, but it also means researchers should evaluate online sources with special care. In addition to the general criteria listed above, consider these factors when evaluating websites:

URL A site's ***URL*** (short for *universal resource locator*, its web address) appears at the top of the browser window (Figure 14.3). Every item on the web has a URL, and all URLs end with an extension, or *domain*, that indicates the type of site it is. The most common domains are these:

- **.com** (commercial): sites hosted by businesses
- **.edu** (educational): sites sponsored by colleges and universities

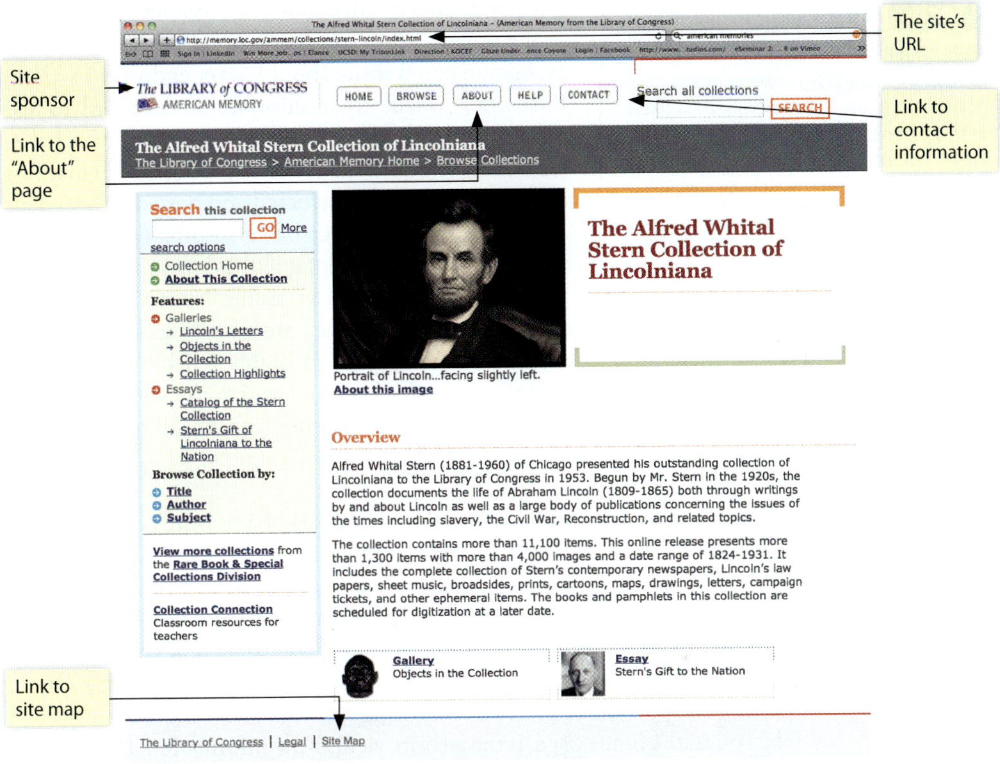

Research Matters • Evaluating Online Texts: Websites, Blogs, Wikis, and Discussion Forums

FIGURE 14.3 A web page The URL appears at the top of the browser window. Note that the Library of Congress's website indicates the sponsoring organization prominently and provides links to pages providing information about the organization and site.

- **.gov** (governmental): sites sponsored by some branch of federal, state, or local government
- **.net** (network): typically, sites sponsored by businesses selling Internet infrastructure services (such as Internet providers) but also sometimes chosen by businesses that want to appear technologically sophisticated or organizations that want to indicate that they are part of a network
- **.org** (organization): usually sites sponsored by nonprofit groups (though sometimes the nonprofit status of these groups may be questionable)

> **Tech — Identifying Personal Websites**
>
> A URL that includes a personal name (jsmith) plus a tilde (~) or percent sign (%) or words like "users" or "members" is likely to be personal (not sponsored by a larger organization). Before using information from a personal site, investigate the author's credentials carefully.

Sites sponsored by educational, governmental, and nonprofit organizations are likely to be reliable, but your evaluation of a website should never end with its URL. Businesses usually offer information intended to sell products or services, yet commercial sites can nevertheless be highly informative. A site ending in .edu may just as easily have been constructed and posted by a student as by an expert, and much of the information posted on university websites is designed to entice new students and is thus a type of advertising. Nonprofit organizations are not trying to sell a product, but they are usually seeking support. Government sites, too, while often a source of highly reliable information, are unlikely to publish information that will undermine the administration's agenda. The reliability of information from all sites (indeed, all texts) must be evaluated with care.

> **lurk** Read online discussions without contributing

Sponsor As with any publication, the credentials of a website's creator are an important factor in assessing reliability, but websites frequently lack an identified author. Instead, they have ***sponsors***—corporations, agencies, and organizations that are responsible for creating content and making it available. To determine who sponsors a site, jump to the home page, link to pages called "About" or "Contact us," or click on the website's logo (see Figure 14.3). Often, deleting the portion of the URL following the domain (.com, .edu, .org) will take you to the home page. If the website yields little information, try conducting a web search on the site's name; you might even try including the word "scam" or "fraud" in that search. You can also go to the Whois site (whois.net) to search for information about your website.

Open or moderated? The reliability of online discussion forums depends in large part on their contributors. Sources to which anyone can contribute should be screened carefully; nonexpert enthusiasts can post inaccurate information, and people can deliberately insert distorted "truths." For example, Wikipedia once had to block certain web addresses on Capitol Hill to keep congressional staffers from altering—and falsifying—the biographies of their bosses or their bosses' political opponents.

Wikis and web forums in which prospective contributors are screened by the site's owner, or *moderator*, are more likely to be reliable. The wiki Encyclopedia of Life, for example, promises to provide reliable information because it will be created and moderated by a consortium of highly regarded scientific

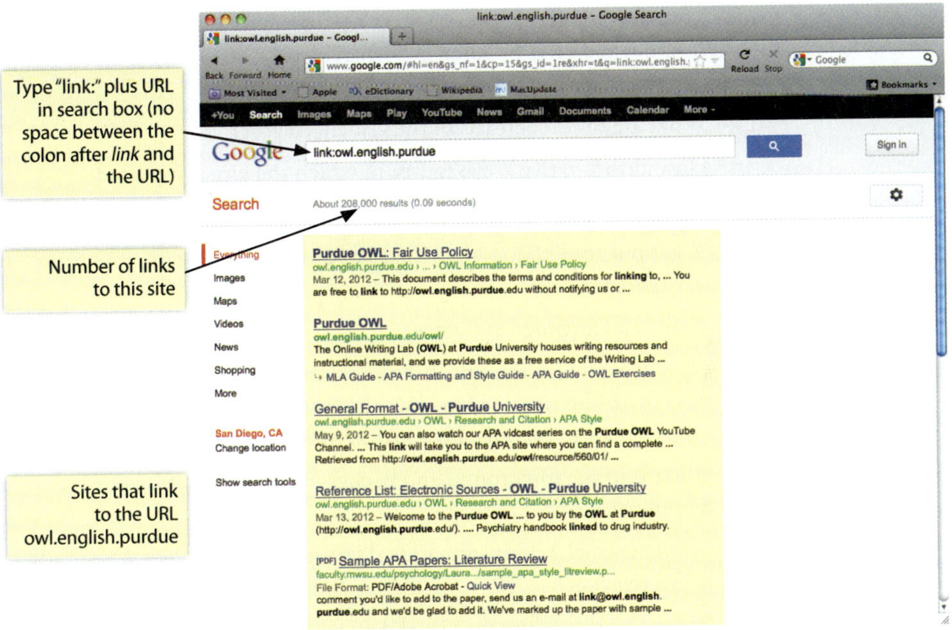

FIGURE 14.4 Using the links to a page to assess reliability

institutions. Some scholars are even writing wiki textbooks to which they invite other experts to contribute.

Links An additional step in assessing the reliability of a website is to determine the number and type of sites that link to it. From the Google search page, you can determine the number of times a site has been linked to and review the linked sites (Figure 14.4): Type "link:" plus the URL in the search box and click Search or hit Return. Popularity alone does not guarantee reliability—the site may just be fun to read or authored by a celebrity—but when coupled with other criteria, it can be one indication of reliability.

14c Evaluating Visual Sources

Visual texts such as information graphics (tables, graphs, flowcharts) and photographs convey their messages powerfully yet sometimes so subtly that uncritical viewers may accept their claims without even realizing that a claim is being

> **More about**
> Visual arguments,
> 134–35, 138,
> 142–45, 156, 158,
> 169–70

Research Matters • Evaluating Information

made. As with printed texts, researchers need to evaluate visual texts carefully to determine whether the source is both relevant and reliable. To determine relevance and reliability, consider the following:

- What are the credentials of the visual's creator?
- How authoritative is the source in which the visual appeared?
- On what date was the image created or the photograph taken?
- What purpose(s) does the visual serve? Is it to entertain, to inform, or to persuade?
- Who is its intended audience?
- How accurate are the title, headings, labels, and any other text that appears with the visual? How does the text influence how you "read" the visual? How relevant is the visual to the accompanying text?
- What is in the foreground and background, and what is your eye drawn to?
- To what social, ethnic, or national groups do the subjects belong, and is this relevant?
- What emotions does the visual depict? What emotions does it elicit from you or other viewers?
- Has the visual been manipulated or cropped to omit or distort information? (See Figure 14.5.)

> **More about**
> Purpose, 10–12
> Avoiding distortion, manipulation, 80, 81, 144–45

FIGURE 14.5 FDR in a wheelchair Although many Americans knew that President Roosevelt had been partially paralyzed by polio, only two photographs were taken of the president in a wheelchair. Were photographers protecting FDR's privacy or suppressing important information?

Research Matters • Evaluating Visual Sources 14c 241

For graphics, also consider the following:
- What do the data represent?
- What relationships does the graphic show?
- How up-to-date is the information in the graphic?
- Are the data complete? Are there any gaps in years covered or groups represented?
- Are the data presented fairly?
- Is the source of the data unbiased?

➔ EXERCISE 14.1 Evaluating reliability

Using the criteria discussed in *section a* in this chapter, write a paragraph in which you rate the reliability of the article excerpted below. Be sure to explain why you rated the article as you did.

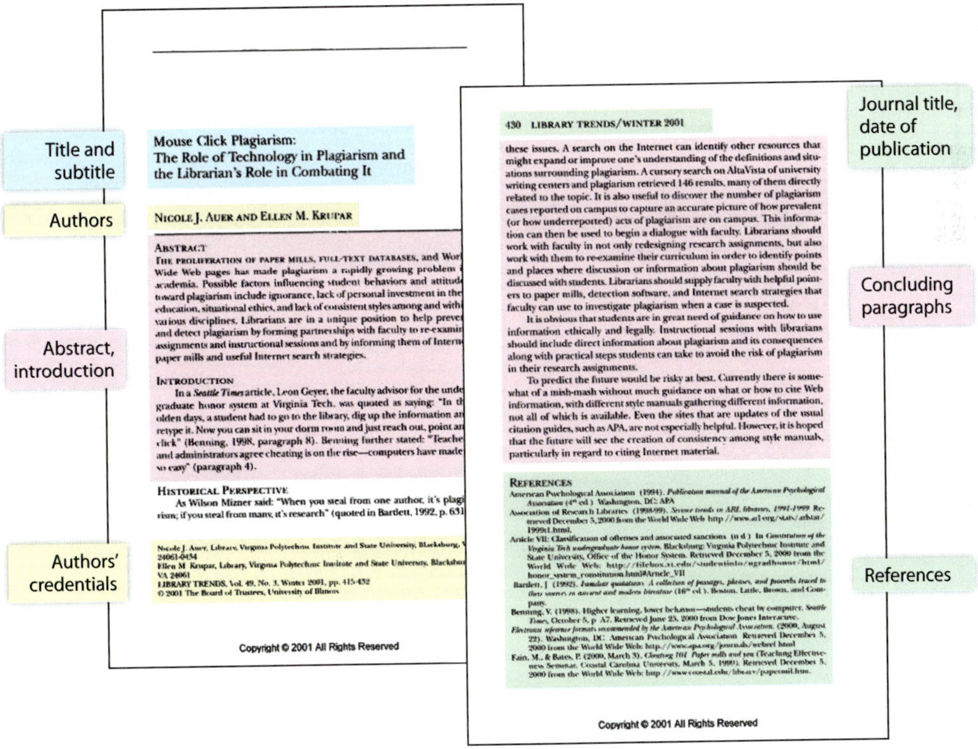

[Annotated article excerpt with labels:]

- Title and subtitle: **Mouse Click Plagiarism: The Role of Technology in Plagiarism and the Librarian's Role in Combating It**
- Authors: Nicole J. Auer and Ellen M. Krupar
- Abstract, introduction
- Authors' credentials
- Journal title, date of publication: LIBRARY TRENDS/WINTER 2001
- Concluding paragraphs
- References

Copyright © 2001 All Rights Reserved

EXERCISE 14.2 Evaluating web pages

Using the criteria discussed in *sections a* and *b*, evaluate the two web pages shown on this page. Which would you consider the more reliable source on plagiarism, and why?

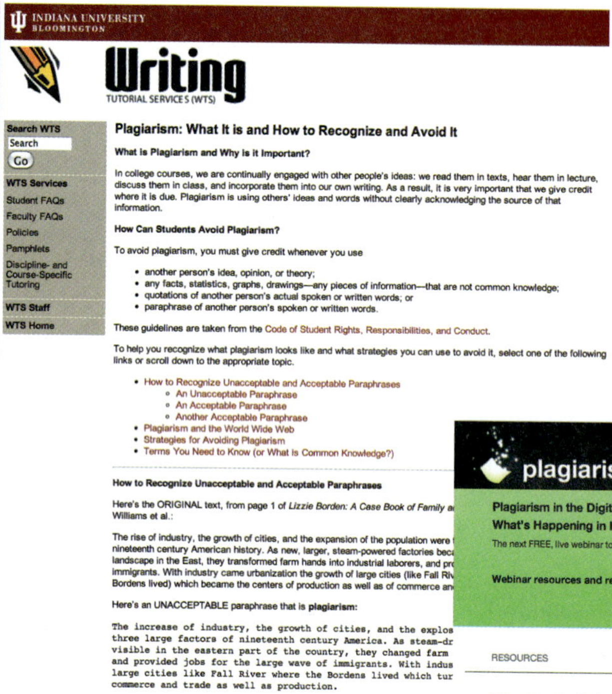

EXERCISE 14.3 Evaluating a graph

Using the criteria discussed in *section c*, write a paragraph evaluating the graph below. Be sure to support your assessment with specific reasons.

PINCHED FOR TIME: MORE WOMEN THAN MEN
Percentage of Americans Who Always Feel Rushed

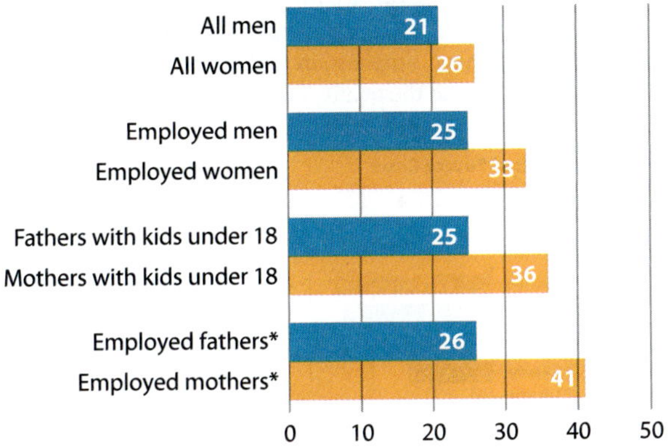

All men	21
All women	26
Employed men	25
Employed women	33
Fathers with kids under 18	25
Mothers with kids under 18	36
Employed fathers*	26
Employed mothers*	41

*Employed fathers, employed mothers refers to employed parents with children under age 18. Employed does not include people who identify as retired but also work for pay.
Source: Pew Research Center

Make It Your Own

Using the criteria in this chapter, write a paragraph evaluating three sources in the working bibliography that you began in the Make It Your Own exercise in chapter 12, page 205, or that you found for a research project in this or another class.

Work Together

In small groups, discuss your evaluations from Exercises 14.1, 14.2, and 14.3. Where do you agree or disagree in your evaluations, and why?

Writing Responsibly

Choosing and Unpacking Complex Sources

Make It Your Own! Research projects that rely heavily on short, simple sources tend to be simplistic and awkward. If you find, read, and write about lengthy, complex sources, you will produce superior scholarship.

Everyone wants to be efficient, yet college writers trying to save time may inadvertently do themselves and their audience a disservice when they write. While incorporating research into their papers, too many writers choose only short, simple sources that can be read quickly (see chart), and the quality of their papers suffers.

Researchers with the Citation Project were struck by the extent to which the quality of students' research projects was reduced by the shallowness of their sources. More than half of the papers' citations were to a source no longer than five pages, resulting in projects that were simplistic and unimpressive. They lacked the complex information and in-depth opinions that are essential to good research and interesting writing.

Length of Source Cited
DATA FROM **The Citation Project**

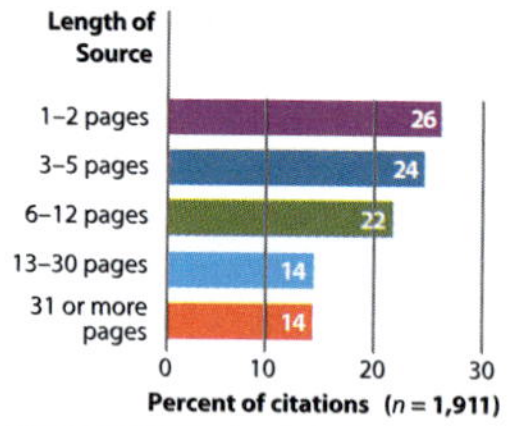

Length of Source	Percent of citations (n = 1,911)
1–2 pages	26
3–5 pages	24
6–12 pages	22
13–30 pages	14
31 or more pages	14

Researchers found that while most college research writers choose short, simple sources, the best writers work from lengthy, complex sources that bring details and insight—and not just basic facts—to the topic.

Writers relying on short sources work with too small a toolbox. Their papers will have very little to say if there is very little to draw on. Sources that are more extensive, in contrast, explore the interesting complexities and important debates about their topic. Such sources give writers—and the writers' audience—things to think about and talk about. They provide essential research material that leads to rich analysis and well-grounded argument.

Simply choosing lengthy sources is not enough, however. You should also "unpack" your sources—share with your audience the complexities and insights of your sources. Note how, in the following example, from an article on unnecessary medical procedures, complexity is lacking when the writer simply drops a quotation into his text and lets it speak for him:

First draft

> [Student's voice] Every time a person goes to the doctor, he or she should be aware of the risks of unnecessary medical testing. [Signal phrase] A doctor from San Francisco says, [Quotation] "[M]ost experts agree that overuse needs to be curbed. If it isn't, we could face a future public health problem of rising cancer rates, thanks to our medical overzealousness" [Parenthetical citation] (Parikh).

Research Matters • Choosing and Unpacking Complex Sources

The writer offers a quotation that supports his argument, and he has cited the quotation correctly. He has also provided some information about the writer of the source. However, because this quotation stands alone, readers of this student's paper may think that the source made this statement as a simple directive: *Overuse of medical tests should stop.* In fact, the source offered a detailed review of the reasons for the overuse of CT scans, as well as a thoughtful set of recommendations.

Such information deserves to be represented. It is part of your responsibility to your audience and topic to show the whole picture that the source offers. Consider how much more interesting, informative, and persuasive the passage becomes when it provides more information and context:

Revised draft

> [Student's voice] Every time a person goes to the doctor, he or she should be aware of the risks of unnecessary medical testing. [Signal phrase] San Francisco Bay Area pediatrician Rahul Parikh says that CT scans are a dangerously overused test, putting children in particular risk for cancer due to the radiation levels in the procedure. [Quotation] "[M]ost experts agree that overuse needs to be curbed. If it isn't, we could face a future public health problem of rising cancer rates, thanks to our medical overzealousness," says Parikh. [Signal phrase] He notes, though, that the test is quick and easy. Moreover, television medical shows give people a general awareness of tests like the CT scan, and thus patients may demand it even when it is not medically necessary. Doctors, too, have a reason for overusing the test: It is financially profitable. In addition to recommending that the test be administered less often, [Signal phrase] Parikh advocates adjusting the radiation dose when the CT scan is administered to children.

[Summary that clarifies the argument of the source]
[Summary of the source's complex treatment of the topic]

Source: Parikh, Rahul. "How TV Illustrates a Disturbing Medical Trend." *Salon* 18 Apr. 2011: n. pag. Web. 18 Apr. 2011.

Notice that in the first draft, it sounds as if the doctor quoted is talking about all medical testing; the second draft shows that in fact Parikh was talking about a specific test, the CT scan. Choosing extensive sources, paying attention to the complexity of the material, and incorporating that complexity into your paper not only increases the sophistication of your own writing; it can also save you from misrepresenting the source.

Self Assessment

Review your work with each source, revising as necessary, to be sure you:

- ☐ Choose lengthy, detailed sources. Did you find material that provides insights and debates on the topic? ▶ *Finding information, 206–29*
- ☐ Discuss the complexities of your sources' treatment of their topic. Did you go beyond simple, basic facts? ▶ *Analyzing, interpreting, synthesizing, and critiquing, 262–63*; "Understanding and Representing the Entire Source," 132–33
- ☐ Explain any material you quote. Did you give background on every source? ▶ *Relevance and reliability, 230–36*

15 Using Information Responsibly: Taking Notes and Avoiding Plagiarism

IN THIS CHAPTER

a. Valuing research, 248

b. Using information ethically, 248

c. Making notes that help you avoid plagiarizing, 250

d. Making notes that help you research, 251

e. Paraphrasing without patchwriting, 252

f. Summarizing, 256

g. Quoting, 259

h. Using analysis, interpretation, synthesis, and critique in your notes, 262

Student Models
Summary, 257; Reading Note, 261; Summary Note with Writer's Assessment, 263

Doris Kearns Goodwin

Harold Garner

Ibrahim al-Marashi

Plagiarism makes news. In 2002, historian Doris Kearns Goodwin was accused of plagiarizing portions of her book *The Fitzgeralds and the Kennedys.* She admitted that she had carelessly included some sentences word for word from her sources without putting those sentences in quotation marks. Her publisher was forced to make a financial settlement with the writer whose sentences she lifted, and Goodwin's credibility was severely undermined.[1]

The next year, the British government "borrowed" information from Ibrahim al-Marashi's doctoral thesis to make its case for war against Iraq—without citing the author of the thesis. Exposure of the appropriation undermined the British government's credibility.[2]

Then in 2007, Mounir Errami and Harold Garner (University of Texas Southwestern Medical Center) used text-matching software to test a portion of the abstracts in *Medline,* a database listing reports of medical research. They came up with some 420 potential duplicates, of which 73 were written by different authors, leading them to suspect widespread plagiarism. Errami and Garner conducted their research because they

---

[1] Mark Lewis, "Doris Kearns Goodwin and the Credibility Gap," *Forbes* 27 Feb. 2002. Web. 30 Dec. 2012.

[2] Gaby Hinsliff, Martin Bright, Peter Beaumont, and Ed Vulliamy, "First Casualties in the Propaganda Firefight," *Guardian.co.uk* [Manchester, Eng.] 9 Feb. 2003. Web. 14 Dec. 2012; "The Plagiarism Plague," *BBC News Online.* BBC, 7 Feb. 2003. Web. 17 Dec. 2012.

were concerned that the publication of plagiarized drug-safety studies gives practitioners a false assessment of the risk associated with the drugs tested.[3]

Plagiarism involves the presentation of another person's work—a paper or story, a photograph or graphic, a speech or song, a web page or e-mail message—without indicating that it came from a source. Buying a paper or "borrowing" a sentence (without citation and quotation marks) are both classified as plagiarism.

Sometimes plagiarism may be inadvertent—Kearns Goodwin, for example, claimed that she had copied passages word for word into her notes and then forgot that these passages were not her own.[4] Whether intentional or not, such borrowings are still considered unacceptable.

Student plagiarism may not be reported in the *New York Times,* but to many instructors, it is even more objectionable than the cases discussed here, because when students are given a writing assignment, they are expected to learn something about the topic and about writing itself, and plagiarism prevents this learning.

Also be alert to the possibility of ***patchwriting,*** copying and only partially changing the language of a source. The National Council of Writing Program Administrators defines *patchwriting* as a misuse of sources. Sometimes, though, instructors and college policies categorize it as plagiarism. In either case, patchwriting is not good writing. It often results not from an intention to present another's words and ideas as one's own but, rather, from inaccurate note taking, misunderstanding the source, incorrect use of or omitting quotation marks, or incomplete paraphrasing.

Plagiarism and Culture Attitudes toward and definitions of plagiarism vary from one culture to another. Some individualist cultures, like that of the United States, see words and ideas as personal property that can be "stolen" by plagiarists. Some collectivist cultures view information as a shared good. Whether your home culture tends to be more individualist or collectivist, when writing for a US academic audience, be especially careful to mark borrowed language as quotation, to provide a citation whenever you borrow language or ideas, and to document sources fully.

> **citation** The acknowledgment of sources in the body of a research project

> **documentation** Information in a footnote, bibliography, reference list, or list of works cited that allows readers to locate the source cited in the text

---

[3] Mounir Errami and Harold Garner, "Commentary: A Tale of Two Citations," *Nature* 451.7177 (2008): 397–99. *Academic Search Premier*. Web. 17 Dec. 2012.
[4] Kirkpatrick, David. "Historian Says Borrowing Was Wider Than Known," *New York Times* 23 Feb. 2002. Web. 30 Dec. 2012.

Inform yourself in detail about what your instructor and your college (or your employer) define as ethical writing; although everyone rejects plagiarism, the definition of what constitutes plagiarism can vary subtly from one discipline or profession to another. Still, as you follow the guidelines for writing described in this chapter (and throughout this book), you can be confident that the work you produce represents its sources responsibly.

15a Valuing Research

One of the keys to avoiding plagiarism is understanding why instructors value source acknowledgment: Seeking the truth is the heart of all academic work. To achieve this goal, academic researchers—from architects to anthropologists, psychologists to physicists—build on the work of others. They must be able to trace ideas to their source because one faulty piece of information can invalidate the whole research project. That is why failing to credit previous researchers is considered such a serious breach of academic discipline, and cheating in all its forms—from distorting an opponent's position to doctoring a quotation, manipulating an image, falsifying data, or taking credit for someone else's work—is punished so severely.

For students, conducting research and learning to write clearly and accurately has another value: It develops the intellectual, rhetorical, and ethical skills and practices needed in college, at work, and in one's community. Plagiarism averts that learning.

> **More about**
> Using quotation marks, 780–89 (ch. 51)
> Block indention for long quotations, 292, 334 (MLA), 377 (APA)
> Citing sources, 288–305 (MLA), 347–57 (APA), 389–407 (*Chicago*), 416–18 (CSE)
> Documenting sources, 305–31 (MLA), 358–76 (APA), 390–407 (*Chicago*), 416–28 (CSE)
> Using signal phrases, 274–86, 291, 348–49

15b Using Information Ethically: What You Do and Do Not Have to Acknowledge

The first step toward avoiding plagiarism is approaching your writing tasks with a clear sense of what you are and are not expected to cite and document.

1. What you *do* have to cite: Quotations, paraphrases, summaries, and *un*common knowledge

You must document quotations, paraphrases, summaries, and information that is unlikely to be known by nonexperts:

- **Quotations.** Enclose short quotations in quotation marks, and indent long quotations as a block. Name the author either in a signal phrase ("Professor Jones argues") or in a parenthetical citation, and include

- **Paraphrases and summaries.** Provide a citation each time you use a source, even when you are not quoting. As with quotations, cite the author and page number in the text, and include full source information in your bibliography, references list, or list of works cited.

- **Ideas and information.** Acknowledge the source of any information or ideas that are *not* common knowledge. As with quotations, paraphrases, and summaries, cite the author and page number in your text and provide full source information in your bibliography, references list, or list of works cited. A piece of information from the Internet needs to be cited every bit as much as does a piece of information gleaned from a journal article or book.

2. What you do *not* have to cite: Common knowledge (facts, dates, events, cultural knowledge)

You do *not* have to document ***common knowledge*** (unless it is included in a quotation)—even if you learned the information from a source. Common knowledge is general information that is available in a number of different sources and that is considered factual and incontestable. Here are some examples:

Facts
- On average, the Earth is about 93 million miles from the sun.
- Labor organizer "Mother" Jones worked on behalf of the United Mine Workers of America.

Dates
- The spring equinox occurred on March 20 in 2012.
- US women won the right to vote on August 26, 1920, when the Nineteenth Amendment was passed.

Writing Responsibly — Using Illustrations and Avoiding Plagiarism

The web contains a variety of images, videos, and sound files that you can download to your word processor: A click of the mouse, and they are yours. Or are they? Keep full records of who created them, where you found them, and on what date you downloaded them so that you can cite them fully.

to OTHER WRITERS

> **More about**
> Citing media illustrations, 327–28 (MLA), 374 (APA), 405 (*Chicago*)

Events
- James Earl Ray was convicted of the assassination of civil rights leader Martin Luther King, Jr.
- Francis Crick, James Watson, and Maurice Wilkins are credited with discovering the structure of DNA.

Cultural Knowledge
- The composer Wolfgang Amadeus Mozart was a child prodigy.
- Elvis Presley made the song "Hound Dog" a smash hit, although he did not write it.

Everything outside of these categories should be cited in the text of your project and documented in a footnote or in your bibliography, references list, or list of works cited.

15c Making Notes That Help You Avoid Plagiarizing

Inadvertent plagiarism is a growing problem for researchers today because cutting and pasting material from online sources into notes is so easy. It is easy to lose track of which material has been borrowed, and it is easy to lose track of which material came from which source. The following strategies for maintaining good research notes can help you avoid problems:

> **More about**
> Research log, 198–99
> Working bibliography, 200–05

- **Keep two sets of notes—bibliography and content.** For every source you consult, create a bibliographic note in your working bibliography and create content notes in a separate section of your research log.

- **Indicate the source and page number for all content notes.** Keying your notes to a source page will help you find the source passage when you return to the notes later and will also allow you to cite the source fully.

- **Make a fresh computer file, card, or notebook section for notes on each source, and include the author and page number in each note.** Separating notes helps you avoid confusing one source with another.

- **Use columns or different colored fonts or cards to mark different types of notes.** If done consistently, using one column or color for your own comments, another for quotations, and a third for summaries and paraphrases can provide a useful visual cue for identifying source material and avoiding unintentional plagiarism.

- **Create a Favorites list or bookmark useful web pages.** If taking notes on a computer, bookmark or create a Favorites list for sites you have visited, so you can track your sources.

> **Tech** — **Bookmarking and Listing Favorites**
>
> If you will not always be working from a single computer, set up bookmarks on a social bookmarking site like Pinterest or Twitter, which allow you to store, tag, and share bookmarks.

15d Making Notes That Help You Research

Research note making involves the following activities:

- Annotating sources
- Summarizing sources accurately and without patchwriting
- Paraphrasing sources accurately and without patchwriting
- Recording quotations that you may want to use later
- Analyzing sources by dividing them into their component parts
- Interpreting the meaning of sources
- Synthesizing information from one source with information from other sources
- Critiquing, or evaluating, sources
- Recording source information, including the page number on which the material appears

> **More about**
> Annotation, 114–17
> Summarizing, 110–11, 256–59
> Patchwriting, 252–55
> Quoting, 259–62, 272
> Analyzing, 120–22, 262–63, 270–72
> Interpreting, 122–23, 262–63, 270–72
> Synthesizing, 123–25, 262–63, 270–72
> Critiquing, 125–27, 260–63, 270–72

Writing Responsibly — Highlighting versus Making Notes

While highlighting is a useful way to signal important information in a source, it is not a substitute for writing your own notes about a text. Highlighting can help you mark what is important, but annotating will push you to engage with the text and save you from leafing through page after highlighted page, looking for a passage that you faintly recall having read. So even though it may seem more time-consuming than highlighting, making notes will actually serve you better in the long run.

to SELF

15e Paraphrasing without Patchwriting

A *paraphrase* restates someone else's ideas in fresh words and sentences. Paraphrase a source when you want to do the following:

- Understand the logic of complex passages
- Convey ideas from a source in your own words
- Mention examples and details from the source

After summarizing, paraphrasing is the technique you should use most often when making notes from sources.

Making Notes in English If you are a non-native writer of English, you may want to save time by copying passages in English into your notes word for word or by copying your own translation of the material into your notes. However, your English language skills will improve more quickly if you make an effort to paraphrase, and you will also be less likely to commit unintentional plagiarism. Remember that writing with sources in US academic and professional settings often means using your sources critically—another reason to avoid simply copying them.

Because you are including all of the writer's main ideas, a paraphrase is often as long as, and sometimes even longer than, the original. Like a summary, a paraphrase must not use the same language as the original (except for keywords), and the order of ideas and the sentence structures must be fresh as well. Just as you would cite the source of a quotation, you must also cite the source when you paraphrase.

Writers who are inexperienced with paraphrasing often *patchwrite:* They replace some terms with synonyms, delete a few words, or alter the grammar slightly, but they do not put the passage fully into fresh words and sentences. Patchwriting commonly happens as writers work with sources on complex, unfamiliar topics. Good writers rewrite their patchwriting, turning it into effective paraphrase; in doing this, they push themselves toward a better understanding of the source.

To paraphrase *without* patchwriting, follow these steps:

1. Read the source until you feel you understand it. Think about the overall meaning of the passage you are borrowing. Figure out whether there are any key terms that must be retained in your paraphrase.
2. Close the text and walk away. Do something else for a few minutes or a few hours.

3. Come back to your desk and write what you remember. If you cannot remember anything, repeat steps 1 and 2.
4. Check your paraphrase against the source to make sure you have correctly represented what it said. If you have closely followed any of the source language (other than key terms), either copy exactly and supply quotation marks or revise your note.

When your paraphrase is complete, check to be sure that you have done *all* of the following:

- Used synonyms rather than the words of the source where possible; used key terms and technical language from the source when no synonym is reasonable.
- Quoted specialized terms the first time used but not thereafter.
- Used different sentence structures from those in the original passage. If you find yourself borrowing the sentence structures of your source, try dividing or combining sentences or varying their length and structure to alter their rhythm and blend them into your own text.

> **More about**
> Varying sentence length and structure, 528

- Cited the source of the paraphrase in your text, usually by bookending the paraphrase with a signal phrase and a page reference in parentheses.
- Documented the source in your bibliography, reference list, or list of works cited.

The following examples illustrate techniques for revising passages to avoid patchwriting:

Passage from Source

With these caveats, we argue more limitedly that digital technology offers new avenues of aesthetic experimentation for comic artists and that the internet has given some comic artists a modest prosperity that they would not have without the internet as a means of distribution. (Sean Fenty, Trena Houp, and Laurie Taylor, "Webcomics: The Influence and Continuation of the Comix Revolution," *ImageTexT* 1.2 [2004]: par. 2. Web. 18 Mar. 2007.)

Note with Patchwriting

Fenty, Houp, and Taylor argue that digital technology provides comic artists with an opportunity for artistic experimentation and that some have more success than they would have without the Internet (par. 2).

> Authors
>
> Picks up language from source
>
> Uses synonym or word in another form
>
> Paragraph reference (use only when source numbers its paragraphs)

Note without Patchwriting

> According to Fenty, Houp, and Taylor, comic artists use the computer to experiment and the internet to publish their works, allowing them more creative options and earning them more money than they made in the pre-Internet era (par. 2).

Notice that the patchwritten note relies heavily not only on the language but also on the sentence structure of the source. The note without patchwriting captures the main ideas of the passage without borrowing sentence structures or more than a few key words from the original.

Here is another example:

Passage from Source

Until recently, the Church was one of the least studied aspects of the Cuban revolution, almost as if it were a voiceless part of Cuban society, an institution and faith that had little impact on the course of events. (Super, John C. "Interpretations of Church and State in Cuba, 1959–1961." *The Catholic Historical Review* 89.3 [2003]: 511–529. Print.)

Note with Patchwriting

> Super 511
>
> According to Super, the Catholic Church until recently was not much studied as an aspect of the Cuban revolution. It was as if the Church was voiceless in Cuban culture, as if it had little influence on events (511).

- Authors
- Picks up language from source
- Uses synonym or word in another form
- Page reference

Note without Patchwriting

> Super argues that scholarship on the Cuban revolution is only beginning to recognize the influential role of the Church (511).

The revised note still retains key terms from the source: "Cuban revolution" and "Church" appear in both the original passage and the revised note because there can be no synonyms for proper nouns (names). But the passage no longer draws heavily on the source's sentence structure, organization, or word choices.

Writing from sources without patchwriting is an advanced skill; learning how to avoid patchwriting requires conscious, ongoing effort. You will find it hard at first, but it gets easier with practice. Remember, if you find yourself leaning heavily on the wording of the source in your first-draft paraphrases, revise them. Work for greater comprehension of the text by looking up unfamiliar words or thinking about concepts you do not understand. Then turn away from the source and write from your head rather than from the source. As long as you are looking at the source and asking yourself, "How else can I say this?" you are playing with words rather than comprehending the source.

EXERCISE 15.1 Correcting a paraphrase to avoid patchwriting

Study the following source and the first draft of a paraphrase that follows. Circle words in the note that appear in the source, and underline synonyms or words in another form. Then revise the note to avoid the patchwriting.

Passage from Source

Washington has posed a special problem for *Wikipedia,* which is monitored by 800 to 1,000 active editor-volunteers. In the recent flare-up, a community of *Wikipedia* editors read a story in the *Lowell Sun* newspaper in which staffers for [Representative Marty] Meehan acknowledged replacing an entry on him [in *Wikipedia*] with more flattering verbiage. That prompted last week's Capitol Hill *Wikipedia* blackout; all computers connected to servers at the House of Representatives, identified by a numerical Web address, were denied access.

—Yuki Noguchi, "On Capitol Hill, Playing WikiPolitics," *Washington Post*

Draft Note

Noguchi A1

Wikipedia and its active editor-volunteers have a special problem with Washington. Recently the editors read a *Lowell Sun* newspaper story about Meehan's staffers having acknowledged that they had replaced an entry on him with more flattering words. That resulted in last week's Wikipedia blackout on Capitol Hill computers, which were denied access.

EXERCISE 15.2 Paraphrasing without patchwriting

Using the guidelines for paraphrasing without patchwriting in *section d* in this chapter, choose a key sentence from the passage in Exercise 15.1 and paraphrase it. Then compare your paraphrase with the original. Is your paraphrase accurate? Does it avoid patchwriting? Revise your paraphrase until it is accurate and written completely in fresh words and sentence structures.

Make It **Your Own**

From a source for a research project (or from another college-level text), choose three sentences you consider important. Then paraphrase them following the guidelines in *section d*. Attach a copy of the source to your paraphrase.

Work **Together**

In groups of two or three, compare the original source with the paraphrases that each group member wrote for the Make It Your Own exercise above. Did group members paraphrase accurately? Did they avoid patchwriting? Discuss any sentences that may lean too heavily on the language or sentence structure of the original source. What might the writer do to avoid patchwriting? If the paraphrase avoids patchwriting, identify the paraphrasing strategies each writer used.

15f Summarizing

An effective *summary* briefly restates the main claims and supporting evidence of a source. By forcing you to identify the main claims and understand them well enough to state them accurately in fresh words, writing an accurate summary helps you understand a difficult text. Most of your content notes should summarize your sources.

In general, a summary should be at least 50 percent shorter than the material you are summarizing, but most summaries go far beyond that: A single paragraph, for example, might summarize a 25-page essay. Your summary should be only as long as needed to capture the main claim and major supporting evidence accurately. To summarize a source, follow these steps:

1. Read the source, underlining key terms and looking up words that you do not know. For short sources, one or two careful readings may be enough; for longer or more complex sources, you may need to reread the source several times.
2. Annotate the source. Underline or highlight the thesis or main idea of the source, and identify the main supporting ideas. For a longer source, creating an outline may be helpful.
3. Write down, without looking at the source, the thesis or main claim in a sentence or two. For each group of supporting paragraphs, write a one- or two-sentence summary in your own words.

4. Combine your sentences into a paragraph, editing to omit repetition and using transitions to make logical connections between sentences clear.
5. Check your summary against the source. Have you used fresh words and sentence structures? If not, this may be a sign that you do not yet understand the source. Go back and read the material again, and revise your summary to avoid patchwriting.
6. Credit the original source when you incorporate your summary into your paper. Use a signal phrase to indicate where the summary begins and a page reference (in parentheses) to indicate where it ends.

> **More about**
> Transitions, 54–55
> Placing signal phrases and page references, 276–77, 288–90, 348–50

Student Model Summary

Below is an example of an effective summary of an original source:

Passage from Source

Before exploring these connections, however, webcomics must be more clearly defined. Many people are only familar with webcomics through Scott McCloud's explanation of them in *Reinventing Comics,* where he took on the role of a spokesperson for webcomics. While McCloud offered an initial study on webcomics, this paper does not operate within a McCloudian definition of comics, where he expounds upon their potential to revolutionize all comics production. In this paper, the term webcomics must be distinguished from hyperbolic proclamations about the internet as an inevitable site of radical aesthetic evolution and economic revolution for comics. The problems

Self Assessment

When you summarize, check for these elements. Have you done *all* of the following?

- ☐ Made clear that you are writing a summary of a source, not your own ideas.
- ☐ Cited the source you are summarizing.
- ☐ Rearranged the ideas of the source so that they make sense in your own text. For example, if the source presents a cause and its effects, you can present the effects first and the causes second, if that will work better in your paper.
- ☐ Provided transitions to clarify relationships among ideas.
- ☐ Kept your own ideas, examples, and interpretations out (unless you were asked to analyze, respond, or interpret in addition to summarizing).
- ☐ Included page citations wherever you are summarizing an identifiable part of the source.
- ☐ Maintained the balance of the ideas in the source, without emphasizing one more than it was emphasized in the source.
- ☐ Made sure that your omissions and deletions do not alter or distort the meaning of the source.
- ☐ Documented the source in your bibliography, reference list, or list of works cited.

with McCloud's claims about the liberatory and radical properties of the internet have been addressed by others, like Gary Groth in his article for *The Comics Journal*, "McCloud Cuckoo Land." Our argument does not claim that the internet is a superior comic medium, free of those "tiny boxes" and "finite canvases" that seem to trouble McCloud (online). Further, we recognize that the internet has not offered a level playing field, free of corporate domination, "a world," to quote McCloud's *Reinventing Comics*, "in which the path from selling ten comics to selling ten thousand comics to selling ten million comics is as smooth as ice" (188, Panel 1). With these caveats, we argue more limitedly that digital technology offers new avenues of aesthetic experimentation for comic artists and that the Internet has given some comic artists a modest prosperity that they would not have without the internet as a means of distribution. (Sean Fenty, Trena Houp, and Laurie Taylor, "Webcomics: The Influence and Continuation of the Comix Revolution," *ImageTexT* 1.2 [2004]: par. 2. Web. 18 Mar. 2007.)

Summary

Scott McCloud claims that the Internet will free underground comic artists from the restrictions of print distribution and make it possible for underground comic artists to reach huge audiences. Fenty, Houp, and Taylor, on the other hand, focus on the possibilities for experimentation on the web and argue that the web provides better opportunities to make money publishing underground comics than does print. (Fenty, Houp, and Taylor par. 2)

Notice that the writer of the summary captures the main idea of the source in her own words and sentence structures. Her summary is about one quarter the length of the original material.

EXERCISE 15.3 Summarizing accurately

Write one or two sentences summarizing the following passages:

1. HAZARD, Ky.— On a rainy day in mid-January, Alan Maimon, a reporter here for the Louisville *Courier-Journal,* packed up his desktop computer, fax machine and printer in his company-owned Ford Explorer. He then drove three hours to Louisville, turned in the equipment to the newspaper and, with that, officially brought to a close *The Courier-Journal*'s storied Hazard bureau in Eastern Kentucky. . . . From the heart of coal country, the reporters used the megaphone of *The Courier-Journal*'s front page to tell the world about mining disasters and the strip mining that cut across the roller-coaster terrain here. The strip mining articles won the paper a Pulitzer Prize for public service in

1967. In 1998, its reporters wrote about the widespread doctoring of air quality tests in the mines, which left hundreds of miners breathing dangerous levels of coal dust, leading to black lung disease. And always, the paper served as a roll call for the region's dead—38 miners killed near Hyden in 1970; 15 in the Scotia mines in Whitesburg in 1976; and then, two days later, 11 more; seven in Floyd County in 1982; and so on. —Katharine Q. Seelye, "A Fabled Bureau Exits Eastern Kentucky's Coal Country"

2. Though the studies are few in number, there is some convincing evidence that children may indeed experience musical performance anxiety at least as early as sixth grade. Additionally, there is some evidence that gender may also play a role in a musician's experience of musical performance anxiety. Several studies have noted differences in the level of anxiety reported by men and women (Abel and Larkin, 1990; LeBlanc et al., 1997; Nagel, 1988; Widmer et al., 1997). In each case, females reported more performance anxiety than males. Other studies have noted physiological differences, with females experiencing higher heart rates (LeBlanc et al., 1997) and greater levels of hyperventilation (Widmer et al., 1997). In addition, men and women have shown different means of coping with musical performance anxiety. Wolfe (1990) found that women tended to use emotion-focused strategies, whereas men tended towards problem-focused strategies. The emotion-focused strategies were related to greater confidence and competence and less self-consciousness, distractibility and disruptive cognitive activity than the problem-focused strategies. The evidence seems to suggest the possibility of systematic differences between the genders on the experience of musical performance anxiety. —Charlene Ryan, "Gender Differences in Children's Experience of Musical Performance Anxiety"

15g Quoting

A *quotation* is someone else's words transcribed exactly, with quotation marks or block indention to signal that it is from a source. Quote from a source under the following circumstances:

- When your source uses particularly vivid or engaging language
- When you want to reproduce a subtle idea that might be difficult to paraphrase or summarize without distortion
- When your source conveys technical information that is difficult to paraphrase

> **More about**
> Using quotation marks, 780–91 (ch. 51)
> Indention for longer quotations, 292, 334 (MLA), 377 (APA)
> Deciding when to create or borrow visuals, 78
> Obtaining permission, 6–7, 227
> Ellipses in quotations, 786, 803–04
> Brackets in quotations, 786, 800
> Interviews, 226–27
> Surveys, 228–29
> Writing about literature, 432–54 (ch. 22)

- When you want to convey ideas in an expert's own words
- When you want to analyze or highlight the specific language used in your source (as when studying a work of literature or a historical document)
- When you want to emphasize an important point

When making notes, copy quotations word for word, and double-check them against the source. Whether you transcribe a quotation or cut and paste it into your notes, put quotation marks around it to avoid any confusion later. In your writing project, adjust quotations to integrate them into your own sentences, using ellipses to signal cuts and brackets to indicate any words you have added or changed. In your notes, the quotation should appear exactly as it did in the source.

When working with primary sources such as interviews and surveys that you have conducted or works of literature you are studying, you are likely to use quotations extensively. In contrast, secondary sources such as newspaper articles, scholarly articles, and books are already quoting, summarizing, and paraphrasing their sources, so you should limit the number of direct quotations you copy from them. Use summary and paraphrase instead.

If you find that you are copying a lot of quotations but are paraphrasing little and summarizing even less, you may not be fully comprehending what you are reading. In these situations, try the following:

> **More about**
> Evaluating sources, 230–45 (ch. 14)

- Read the source again.
- Look up words you do not understand.
- Consult reference sources that can provide background knowledge.
- Discuss the source with your instructor, classmates, or friends.

Writing Responsibly | Using Quotations Fairly

We have all seen ellipsis-laden quotations praising a new movie, and we have all wondered whether a crucial word or words might have been omitted: "This is the . . . movie of the year!" could well have been "This is the *worst* movie of the year!" in the original review. That is one reason to be skeptical when reading such advertisements. (Another is the advertiser's desire for the movie to succeed at the box office.)

In academic writing, you can adjust a quotation to bring the punctuation or grammar into line with your own text, or to remove extraneous information, as long as your changes are indicated with ellipses or brackets and you do not distort the author's point. Protect your credibility and be fair to your source by altering quotations accurately.

to OTHER WRITERS

Good scholarship requires that you work to understand the whole source rather than just quoting from the sections that you believe you understand or that you think sound authoritative. Understanding the difficult parts is important, for they may well change the meaning of what you thought at first you understood.

Student Model Reading Note

The following reading note correctly uses quotation marks to signal material taken word for word from the source, yet it indicates that the writer does not fully understand what she is writing about.

Draft Note

> Milne 140
>
> The "free-black community . . . of Five Points" is not reflected in "the areas of Block 160 that were excavated." "All that survived . . . were the remains of their ancestors interred in the mostly forgotten burying ground, a few intriguing and unusual items discarded in the defunct privies and cisterns, and a handful of church addresses." But "it is probable that many members of this community remained in the neighborhood, living 'off-the-grid.'. . ."

This note is merely a string of quotations, sewn together with a few of the note-taker's own words. Using these notes as is would produce a research paper that would similarly be a mosaic of quotation, difficult to read and lacking the researcher's insight and critical judgment. Rereading the source in order to gain a better understanding of it enabled the writer to summarize with much less quotation. The following revision is much easier to read as well:

Revised Note

> Milne 140
>
> Very few items belonging to members of the African American population in Five Points have been excavated, most likely because members of this community were not part of mainstream society—they were "living 'off the grid'" (140)—not because they had all moved away.

Other chapters in this text discuss the mechanics of using quotation marks and integrating quotations into your text. Consult these sections before you begin your research, as you make notes on sources, and as you draft and revise your text. Applying these principles will enable you to be responsible to the writers from whom you borrow, to your readers, and to yourself.

> **More about**
> Integrating borrowed ideas and words, 272, 275–78

Self Assessment

When analyzing, interpreting, synthesizing, and critiquing a source, ask yourself the following questions. If the answer is not clear, reread and reevaluate the source, as necessary.

Analysis
- What is the purpose of the source?
- Who is the intended audience?
- What major claims does the source make?
- What evidence (reasons, facts, statistics, examples, expert testimony) does the source use to support these claims?

Interpretation
- What assumptions does the author make about the subject or audience, and why are such assumptions significant?
- What does the source omit (evidence, opposing views), and what might these omissions indicate?
- What conclusions can you draw about the author's attitude from the text's tone? What motives can you infer from the author's background?
- Who published this text or sponsored the research, and what influence might these sponsors have upon the way the information, arguments, or evidence is presented?
- In what context was the text written— place, time, cultural environment—and how might this context have influenced the author?
- What expertise or life experience does the author bring to the subject, and is it relevant to the topic?

Synthesis
- Do any other sources make a similar (or opposing) claim, reach a similar (or opposing) conclusion, or offer similar (or opposing) evidence?
- Do any other sources identify similar causes or effects?
- What else do you know about this topic?

Critique
- What are the aims of the source, how worthwhile are they, and how well are they achieved?
- What claims does the source make? Are you persuaded by them? Why or why not?
- How credible is the evidence? Is evidence based on verifiable facts? How relevant is the evidence?
- How logical is the source? Does the author commit any fallacies?
- How fairly does the source treat alternative viewpoints?

> **More about**
> Analysis, interpretation, synthesis, and critique, 119–33, 270–71
>
> **Student Models**
> Research projects:
> "Holy Underground Comics, Batman!" Lydia Nichols, 336–46
> "The Power of Wardrobe," Heather DeGroot, 381–88

15h Using Analysis, Interpretation, Synthesis, and Critique in Your Notes

In addition to recording information from sources, the note-taking stage is also the time to start analyzing, interpreting, synthesizing, and critiquing what you read. The Self-Assessment box above lists questions to ask yourself as you read and take notes on your sources.

The following note for Lydia Nichols's research project provides a summary of the source while also including her own assessment of it:

Research Matters • Using Analysis, Interpretation, Synthesis, and Critique in Your Notes   15h   263

Student Model Summary Note with Writer's Assessment

> Heller
>
> Provides a history of *Zap* comics from the first issue by Robert Crumb in 1968 to the most recent issue in 1994. Describes *Zap* as founding the underground "comix" movement in reaction to the superhero comics that adhered to the 1950s Comics Code and spurred on by late 1960s cultural challenges to the status quo, but doesn't go into detail or identify any comics it inspired. Identifies artists who joined forces with Crumb, and highlights their contributions. Discusses censorship battle over *Zap* #4, which was accused of violating community standards of decency. But not sure what happened: Bookstore owner was fined, but article doesn't indicate what other legal troubles it caused. Later issues continued to be sexually explicit, but they also satirized contemporary mores and included "comic documentary" similar to comic books published during World War II. Article provides a good overview of the history of *Zap* comics (including showing all 14 covers); it assumes that readers will already know a good deal about the history of comics. "Good Shall Triumph" and "Comic Book Code" provide more info. about the Comics Code Authority, but I would like to know more about early examples of documentary comics. Heller is obviously a fan of *Zap* comics (I read online that he was an art director at the *NY Times*) but I would like to know more about what motivated Crumb and the others to rebel.

Margin notes: Summary that includes analysis and interpretation; Critique; Synthesis

Work **Together**

Read the research project in chapter 18 (pp. 337–46) or 19 (pp. 382–88). In small groups of two or three, use the criteria in the bulleted list in *section g* to categorize the writer's use of quotations. Has she used quotations effectively? Why or why not?

Make It **Your Own**

Create a content note on a source for an upcoming research project. First, paraphrase or summarize the source, following the instructions in *sections e* and *f.* Then ask yourself three or more of the questions in the Self-Assessment box on p. 262 and create a note on the source. Bring it to class.

16 Writing the Research Project

IN THIS CHAPTER

a. Drafting a thesis statement, 264

b. Organizing your ideas, 266

c. Drafting your research project, 270

d. Revising, proofreading, formatting, and publishing your project, 273

Student Models
Thesis Statement, 265;
Outline, 268

The Hubble Space Telescope, taking pictures of the cosmos since 1990, has provided enough data to keep scientists busy for years, long after the telescope stops functioning. So far, scientists have published over six thousand articles based on what they have learned from Hubble. These articles have given us a clearer idea of the age of our universe, a better understanding of how galaxies evolve, and information about what happens when stars collapse. Until these papers were published, the Hubble merely provided pretty pictures to the rest of us.

Like the scientific articles published from the Hubble data, your college research projects are an opportunity to share what you have read and studied; they are an opportunity to provide readers with a synthesis of the information you have gleaned from a variety of sources and to present what you have learned, filtered through the lens of your understanding. They are the culmination of your research and an expression of yourself.

16a Drafting a Thesis Statement

As you began your research, you chose and defined a *topic* that would be appropriate to your purpose and of interest to your reader. You

> **Quick Reference** — **Drafting the Research Paper**
>
> - **Thesis.** Draft a one- or two-sentence thesis statement that grows out of your research questions and hypothesis. Revise your thesis as you draft your project.
> - **Organization.** List and explain the reasons you believe your thesis statement or why you think it is the most reasonable way to address a difficult issue. Sort research notes into separate piles for each of your reasons. Draft an outline that organizes your material so that readers can follow your logic and maintain interest to the end.
> - **Analysis, interpretation, synthesis, critique.** Divide ideas into their component parts and think about what they mean. Then combine ideas from sources with your own ideas to come up with something fresh. Decide whether sources have achieved their goals and whether their goals were worthwhile.
> - **Evidence and counterevidence.** Incorporate evidence, making sure it is relevant. Use summaries, paraphrases, and a few quotations as support. Acknowledge opposing evidence and explain why your position is reasonable despite this. (If your position does *not* seem reasonable in light of counterevidence, revise your thesis.) Make sure you provide enough evidence—and the appropriate types of evidence—to persuade your readers.
> - **Citation and documentation.** Cite sources in the text. Double-check that you have used quotation marks where needed and that paraphrases do not slip into patchwriting. Document sources in a list of works cited (MLA), reference list (APA, CSE), or bibliography (*Chicago*).

> **More about**
> Assessing the writing situation, 9–17, 192–93
> Devising a thesis, 29–32, 195–96
> Choosing a topic, 20–25, 195
> Using evidence, 40–41
> Finding information, 206–29 (ch. 13)
> Acknowledging alternative views, 145–47
> Organizing, 33–37, 52–57, 154–55, 266–69
> Drafting, 40–44, 270–72
> Summary, paraphrase, and quotation, 256–58, 272
> Avoiding patchwriting, 252–55, 274–78
> Relevance, 230–31

then framed *research questions* and turned them into a *hypothesis* that you tried to confirm (and undermine) through your research. Now, with research data in hand, you are ready to draft a *thesis statement* that will serve as the focus of your project.

This thesis should be a one- or two-sentence statement that grows out of your research hypothesis (or hypotheses), revised in light of what you learned through the research process. It should be a statement that you are prepared to defend, using the information you gleaned from sources and your own ideas, and it should convey your *purpose*.

Student Model Thesis Statement

Read the research question, hypothesis, and thesis statement for the student research essay by Lydia Nichols:

> **Research question:** What are the characteristics of underground comics?
>
> **Hypothesis:** The characteristics of underground comics are a focus on topics that ❶challenge social mores, ❷an author or author team that has creative control, and ❸an adult readership.
>
> **Thesis statement:** While far less well-known than their superhero counterparts, underground comics offer an innovative and sophisticated alternative to mainstream titles.

Hypothesis answers research question by listing three distinguishing traits.

Thesis statement makes purpose clear: uses comparison of comic types to persuade readers that underground comics are more innovative and sophisticated. It transforms specifics of hypothesis into a broader, more engaging claim.

As you draft your research project, you may discover that the counterevidence is overwhelming or that the body of your draft offers a different answer to your research question than the one in your thesis. (Frequently, the true thesis takes shape in the conclusion of the first draft.) So be prepared to revisit your thesis as you draft, revising or even replacing it as necessary.

Make It **Your Own**

For a research paper that you are working on, draft (or revise) a thesis statement. Does the thesis statement concisely assert your central idea? Will it appeal to your readers? Does it convey your purpose?

16b Organizing Your Ideas

The process of organizing your ideas begins with assembling the materials you will need. These include the following:

- Your research log and any other notes you have taken
- Any photocopies or printouts of sources
- A copy of your thesis statement
- Any office supplies you may need (pens, pencils, highlighters, stick-on notes, index cards, a notebook)

> **More about**
> Research log, 198–99
> Annotating, 114–17
> Generating ideas, 20–25
> Making notes, 117–18, 250–51, 259-63

1. Organize your ideas and notes.

With your preliminary thesis statement drafted and necessary materials at hand, you are ready to begin organizing your ideas and notes.

1. Start by listing the reasons you believe your thesis is true. While these reasons may be derived from your research sources, they should be *your* reasons, stated in your own words. (The strategies for generating ideas can help.)
2. Review the notes you took while reading sources: Do they provide evidence that supports your reasons for believing your thesis? Organize your notes according to which of your reasons they support: Separate index cards into piles, or cut and paste notes into separate computer files for each supporting point.
3. Assess your stock of evidence: The size of a computer file or stack of index cards will indicate how much information you have collected in support of each of your reasons for believing the thesis. If a set of notes looks skimpy, find more supporting evidence, revise your thesis, or delve deeper into your reasons for believing your thesis.

2. Outline your project.

After you have organized your ideas and notes, outline your essay to determine the most effective order for presenting your ideas. Some writers prefer a sentence outline because it aids drafting. (Each sentence in the outline becomes the topic sentence of a paragraph.) Others, eager to start writing, prefer a scratch (informal) outline that simply lists their reasons and the major supporting points in order of presentation. Still others prefer a topic outline: It is quicker to write than a sentence outline, but its formal structure of roman numerals and letters makes the structure of the draft clearer.

> **More about**
> Scratch outlines, 35–36
> Sentence outlines, 36–37
> Topic outlines, 36–37

Writing Responsibly — Acknowledging Counterevidence

While sorting your notes, be sure to retain *counterevidence*—evidence that *undermines* your claims. If some of your research contradicts or complicates your thesis or supporting reasons, do not suppress it. Instead, revise your thesis or supporting reasons on the basis of this counterevidence, or acknowledge the counterevidence and explain why the reasons for believing your thesis are more convincing than those that challenge it. Your readers will appreciate your presentation of multiple perspectives.

to AUDIENCE

Student Model Outline

The topic outline below shows the structure of the first part of Lydia Nichols's research paper. Note that the roman numeral sections list Nichols's reasons; the capital letter and arabic numeral sections list the evidence in support of her reasons.

> Thesis: While far less well-known than their superhero counterparts, underground comics offer an innovative and sophisticated alternative to mainstream titles.
>
> I. Success of superhero comics in the late 1930s led to homogenization
>   A. Superhero defined
>   B. Superman debuted June 1938
>   C. Copycat superheroes ride Superman's success
> II. Further homogenization in the 1950s, with creation of Comics Code Authority (1954)
>   A. Specific rules of CCA code—example: letters of the word "crime" cannot be bigger than other letters on the cover
>   B. General rules of CCA code
>   1. Show respect for parents, morality (good triumphs over evil)
>   2. Portray criminals, crimes negatively
>   3. Religion treated respectfully
>   4. No profanity
>   C. Violators not distributed (EC Comics and others); conformers gained market share
> III. Homogenization, superhero domination undermined by appearance of underground "comix" in late 1960s
>   A. Underground comix defined
>   1. Not submitted to CCA for approval
>   2. Satirized conservative beliefs

Overall organization: Chronological (1930s, 1950s, 1960s)

Uses example to support claim

Uses definition to support claim

Research Matters • Organizing Your Ideas — 16b

3. Included political and sexual content (fetishism)
4. Challenged social norms
5. Offered insightful commentary on society
6. Example: Robert Crumb's *Zap,* first issue released in 1968

B. Underground comix contrasted with CCA-approved comics
   1. *Amazing Fantasy* (1962) (Visual: Cover of *Amazing Fantasy* #15)
      a. Comics Code Authority approval stamp in upper-right corner of *Amazing Fantasy*
      b. Traditional superhero
      c. Traditional drawing
   2. *Snarf* (1976) (Visual: *Snarf* #6)
      a. Not CCA-approved (no stamp)
      b. Depicts regular guy fighting real problems (big oil—an important issue in the mid-1970s)
      c. Takes on political issues
      d. Drawing crude

Supports claim by showing and analyzing contrasting visuals

Make It **Your Own**

For a research paper that you are working on, do the following:

- List reasons for believing your thesis. Include supporting evidence and illustrations.
- Decide on the best order in which to present your material, and make an outline (sentence, scratch, or topic) from which to work.

16c Drafting Your Research Project

When drafting your research project, your goal is to draw on information in sources to support your own ideas, weaving that information into your sentences and paragraphs so that it supports your ideas without overwhelming them. Draw on your analysis of sources, your own interpretations of what you have read, and your synthesis of ideas from sources. To support your claims, incorporate summaries, paraphrases, and quotations from your notes, using signal phrases to identify the source of borrowed ideas and to provide context for your sources.

> **Make It Your Own**
>
> For a research paper that you are working on, compose a first draft. As you write, reread the tips in the Quick Reference box below as necessary. You will revise this draft later, so for now you can just relax.

1. Use analysis, interpretation, and synthesis to support your claims.

When you read sources and took notes, you analyzed your material to break it down into its component parts, and you interpreted what you read to

>**More about**
>Drafting, 40–44

Quick Reference — **Writing the First Draft**

As you begin writing, keep in mind that you are composing a draft—what you write will be revised—so do not worry about whether you are saying it "right." A few writers' tricks will help you produce that first draft:

- Keep your thesis statement in front of you to help you stay focused as you write.
- Start with the sections that are easiest to write, and then organize and fill in the gaps later.
- Begin writing *without* consulting your sources. Then draw on sources for evidence to support what you have drafted on your own.
- When incorporating quotations, paraphrases, or summaries, note which source the material comes from (including the page number) to avoid having to track down this information later and, perhaps, plagiarizing inadvertently.
- Draft with a notepad next to you or another file open on your computer, so you can jot down ideas that come to you while writing another section.
- Include visuals that support your points and that help your reader understand what you are writing about.

Research Matters • Drafting Your Research Project   16c   271

determine its meaning. You also synthesized sources: You may have identified ideas in one source that were supported by information in others, described areas of agreement (or disagreement) among sources, or explained which sources were most persuasive and why. The work you have already done to analyze, interpret, and synthesize sources is what you will draw on as you draft your research project. Use it to show readers how borrowed material is relevant; do not expect readers to figure this out without your help.

Examine the paragraph below from Lydia Nichols's essay on underground comics to see how she uses analysis, interpretation, and synthesis to support her own claims.

Student Model
Research project: "Holy Underground Comics, Batman," Lydia Nichols, 336–46

Underground artists not only push the envelope in terms of content, but they also incorporate experimental visual devices, earning critical praise for breaking away from traditional comic layouts in favor of more artistic perspectives. Artists such as Daniel Clowes argue that comic art can be more evocative than film, especially in the use of nonlinear storytelling techniques (Hignite 18). *New York Times* columnist John Hodgman agrees: Discussing a moment of existential crisis in Kevin Huizenga's *Ganges* #1, he writes, "I have never seen any film . . . that gets at that frozen moment when we suddenly feel our mortality, when God is seen or denied, as effectively as a comic panel." Artist Chris Ware manipulates the borders and frames in his comics so extensively that even reading his works can feel like an art to be mastered (see fig. 3). The demands his comics place on the reader create an interaction between viewer and artist that is unheard of in the pages of superhero titles.

Sentence 1: Nichols's claim (topic sentence) offers her interpretation.

Sentences 2 and 3 synthesize information from sources to support her claim.

Sentences 4 and 5 provide her own analysis to support her claim.

Fig. 3. Cover from Chris Ware's *Jimmy Corrigan: The Smartest Kid on Earth* (New York: Pantheon, 2000). Critically acclaimed *Jimmy Corrigan* comics use visual storytelling techniques, pushing the limitations of comics and forcing the reader to work to achieve understanding.

Illustration provides an example that supports Nichols's claim, and caption offers interpretation of what the reader is seeing there.

Instead of merely stringing together material from sources, Nichols integrates her own ideas with information from sources to craft a paragraph that readers will find persuasive. She analyzes primary sources (examples of underground comics) to determine what makes them visually exciting, she interprets her sources to determine which support her claim, and she synthesizes evidence to make her case.

2. Use summary, paraphrase, and some quotations to support your claims.

> **More about**
> Quoting, paraphrasing, or summarizing, 250–62
> Signal phrases, 276–77, 290–92, 348–50
> Avoiding patchwriting, 252–56
> Quotation marks, 780–91 (ch. 51)

So that your paper will not seem like a series of quotations strung together with a few words of your own, use quotations sparingly. Instead, put borrowed ideas into your own words, by either paraphrasing or summarizing. Use quotations only when the language is particularly vivid or technical, when you want to borrow the authority of the speaker, or when you are analyzing the language of the source. In the sample paragraph on the previous page, Lydia Nichols uses a combination of quotation and summary to support her claims. She quotes Hodgman because the quotation is especially vivid, but she summarizes Clowes's ideas to convey his argument concisely.

NOTE When summarizing or paraphrasing, work to avoid patchwriting, and, when quoting, use quotation marks or indent longer quoted passages as a block.

---

3. Acknowledge your sources.

> **More about**
> Citing sources, 288–305 (MLA), 347–57 (APA), 389–406 (*Chicago*), 416–28 (CSE)
> Documenting sources, 305–30 (MLA), 358–76 (APA), 389–407 (*Chicago*), 416–28 (CSE)

Even while working on your first draft, you should acknowledge information you have borrowed from sources—quotations, paraphrases, summaries, illustrations, data, or other information—by citing them in the text and providing full documentation in a list of works cited, a reference list, or a bibliography. Both citation and documentation are necessary to support your credibility as a writer and to avoid plagiarism. No matter which citation and documentation style you use, your entries should be complete and consistent so that readers can locate your sources and enter into the conversation you have contributed to in your research project.

16d Revising, Proofreading, Formatting, and Publishing Your Project

Once you have composed a first draft, however rough it may be, you can begin the process of shaping and polishing it—the process of *revision*. First, attend to big picture, or global, issues, such as clarifying your purpose, making sure your essay is cohesive and unified, and making sure your ideas are fully developed. Next, attend to local issues, such as making sure your word choices reflect your meaning and are at the appropriate level, that you have varied your sentences, and that your prose is concise.

Once revision is complete, edit your text to correct errors of grammar, punctuation, and mechanics. Then proofread carefully—remember that spell-check software can help, but it cannot replace a careful human proofreader. Finally, format your project following the requirements of your discipline.

> **More about**
> Global revision, 82–87
> Local revision (editing), 87–89
> Peer editing, 89–92
> Proofreading, 93–94
> Formatting, 95, 332–36 (MLA), 377–81 (APA), 407–08 (*Chicago*), 428–29 (CSE)

17 Citing Expertly

IN THIS CHAPTER

a. Integrating source material responsibly, 275

b. Showing source boundaries, 276

c. Emphasizing your voice, 278

d. Providing context, 280

e. Integrating altered quotations, 284

When you research a topic, you work with sources with multiple viewpoints, settling on those that further the conversation on your topic, and then present your sources' ideas in ways that allow readers to see your text clearly.

Source citations are necessary in a researched paper, yet simple citations do not help readers see the clarity of your thinking. For your readers, the clarity of your project comes when you go beyond simply naming the source. When you cite expertly, you use accurate signal verbs, show source boundaries, emphasize your own voice, provide context for the source, and accurately integrate altered quotations. Expert citation makes your conversation with sources, like the image or message in a glass paperweight, "transparent": Others can see how your ideas developed and how you are relating to your sources and the information in them.

Citations are an essential part of academic writing. They name the sources you are using—the other writers with whom you are talking. At more expert levels of researched writing, *rhetorical citations* accomplish this task and more: They provide helpful information about your sources; they reveal your attitude toward, and judgment of, your sources; and they highlight your own contributions to the "conversation" that takes place between you and your sources.

17a Integrating Source Material Responsibly

> **More about**
> Using information responsibly, 246–63
> In-text citation, 288–305 (MLA style, ch. 18)
> Ethos, 143–44

When writing from sources, your most basic responsibility is to let your audience know whenever your text is drawing on a source. This protects you from charges of plagiarism. It also fulfills a responsibility to your audience, by letting readers know who is speaking in your text. It fulfills a responsibility to yourself, as well: Careful citation increases your writerly ethos; it makes you a more credible, respected writer. In MLA style, *in-text citation*—whether through parenthetical references, signal phrases, or a combination of the two—accomplishes all of this.

Having a Conversation with Sources You may consider published sources to be authorities, but an important aspect of academic writing is learning how to be critical even of authoritative material. You are free to agree or disagree with any source, but it is important that you use sources to support your claims, rather than simply repeating a source's language and ideas.

1. Parenthetical citations

You can cite your sources by using the author's last name and relevant page number(s) in a ***parenthetical citation.***[1] Place that citation at the end of the material from your source:

> *Quotation marks indicate the beginning and end of the source's exact words*
>
> "His name was Mark Zuckerberg, he was a sophomore, and although Eduardo had spent a fair amount of time at various Epsilon Pi events with him, along with at least one prepunch Phoenix event that Eduardo could remember, he still barely knew the kid"
>
> *Source author (last name only)* (Mezrich 15). *Page in source*

When you are paraphrasing or summarizing material, you should also use parenthetical citation to acknowledge that your material comes from a source:

---

[1] The terms *parenthetical citation, parenthetical note,* and *parenthetical reference* are often interchangeable.

> Who wouldn't envy the genius and wealth of the person who invented Facebook? But who wouldn't pity a person who has no close friends? Mark Zuckerberg may have great wealth, but he has few confidantes (Denby 98).

Source author (last name only): Denby
Page in source: 98

2. Signal phrases

To incorporate borrowed material smoothly into your prose, introduce it with a ***signal phrase.*** One part of the signal phrase is an identification (usually the name) of the writer from whom you are borrowing. The other part is a verb; choose one that conveys your sense of the writer's intention.

In choosing your signal verb, consider the attitude or position of the writer you are quoting. Is the writer making a claim? Is she or he agreeing or disagreeing or even conceding a point? Or is the writer's position neutral? It is easy to choose a neutral verb, such as *writes, says,* or *comments.* Whenever possible, though, go beyond these neutral verbs to indicate the writer's attitude:

> Oscar Wilde quipped, "A poet can survive everything but a misprint."

For the quotation above, *quipped* (which means "uttered a witty remark") is clearly appropriate, given the cleverness of the sentence quoted. *Snarled,* on the other hand, would not be appropriate: Although Wilde's quip may have an edge to it, few would agree that the comment conveys the anger or viciousness associated with the verb *snarl*.

To maintain your audience's interest, vary the signal words you use, while avoiding verbs that might misrepresent the writer's intentions. (A list of signal verbs appears in the Quick Reference box on p. 277.) You can also vary your placement of the signal phrase:

> E. M. Forster asked, "How do I know what I think until I see what I say?"

> "How do I know what I think," E. M. Forster asked, "until I see what I say?"

> "How do I know what I think until I see what I say?" E. M. Forster asked.

> **More about**
> Verb tense, 644–49

> **More about**
> Paraphrasing, 250–56
> Summarizing, 256–59
> Using quotation marks, 259–60, 780–91

17b Showing Source Boundaries

When the material from your source is a quotation, it is easy for the audience to see the source boundaries: The quotation marks indicate where your use of

Quick Reference: Signal Verbs

Neutral Signal Verbs

analyzes	introduces
comments	notes
compares	observes
concludes	records
contrasts	remarks
describes	reports
discusses	says
explains	shows
focuses on	states
illustrates	thinks
indicates	writes

Writers in literature and the other humanities typically use present tense verbs in signal phrases; writers in the sciences use the present or past tense, depending on the context.

Signal Verbs That Indicate:

Claim/Argument

argues	finds
asserts	holds
believes	maintains
charges	points out
claims	proposes
confirms	recommends
contends	suggests
demonstrates	

Disagreement

complains	questions
contradicts	refutes
criticizes	rejects
denies	warns
disagrees	

Concession

- acknowledges
- admits
- concedes
- grants

Agreement

- agrees
- concurs
- confirms
- supports

---

source material begins and ends. When you are paraphrasing or summarizing the source, the place where you begin to use source material may not be clear. Signal phrases help solve the problem; you can place a signal phrase at the beginning of the source material and a parenthetical reference at the end.

Consider this example:

> Who wouldn't envy the genius and wealth of the person who invented Facebook? But who wouldn't pity a person who has no close friends? David Denby describes Mark Zuckerberg as having great wealth, but he has few confidantes. "*The Social Network* is shrewdly perceptive about such things as class, manners, ethics, and the emptying out of self that accompanies a genius's absorption in his work" (98).

Signal phrase includes source author (full name on first reference)

Quotation marks indicate the beginning and end of the source's exact words

Page in source

In the example above, it is clear that the first two sentences are the writer's statement of her own ideas, the third sentence is a paraphrase from the Denby source, and the fourth a quotation from Denby. Notice that when the author's name is included in the signal phrase, it does not need to be included in the parenthetical reference.

1. Unpaginated source material

Many sources are accessed electronically and have no page numbers. For an unpaginated source, include only the author's last name in the parenthetical reference:

> "Facebook, which surpassed MySpace in 2008 as the largest social-networking site, now has nearly 500 million members, or 22 percent of all Internet users, who spend more than 500 billion minutes a month on the site" (**Rosen**).

Source author (last name only)

When you are quoting from the source, the quotation marks show where the source use begins and ends.

When you are paraphrasing or summarizing from an electronic source with no page numbers, however, you must work subtly with the material to show your audience where the source use begins and ends. Usually you can do this by using the author's name in the parenthetical reference, and describing the author in a signal phrase:

Signal phrase describes source author

> A writer for the *New York Times* explains how damaging Facebook material can be when one searches for a job (**Rosen**).

Parenthetical reference identifies source author (last name only)

17c Emphasizing Your Voice

Just as important as signaling source boundaries is the need to signal your own voice. Your readers want to know clearly when it is *you* talking. In the following example it is not clear where the student writer stops drawing from the Rosen source and begins to state his own ideas:

> *Signal phrase* — Rosen explains, "Seventy percent of U.S. recruiters report that they have rejected candidates because of information found online, like photos and discussion-board conversations and membership in controversial groups." With 500 million people on Facebook, the dangers are widespread. It is ironic that this phenomenon of personal data revealed to the world was begun by a person who himself had poor social skills.

The use of a signal phrase with a parenthetical reference shows the boundaries of the information from Rosen:

> *Signal phrase describes source author* — A writer for the *New York Times* explains, "Seventy percent of U.S. recruiters report that they have rejected candidates because of information found online, like photos and discussion-board conversations and membership in controversial groups." With 500 million people on Facebook, the dangers are widespread *Parenthetical reference identifies source author (last name only)* — (Rosen). It is ironic that this phenomenon of personal data revealed to the world was begun by a person who himself had poor social skills.

The final sentence in this passage is an interesting one, and the student writer wants to emphasize that it is his own insight. That could be done with first-person singular phrases such as "I believe" or "in my opinion."

Yet in some genres and writing situations (including many college assignments), first-person singular is inappropriate. Fortunately, there are more sophisticated ways to handle the task. One option is to speak in the first-person plural, subtly drawing the audience into the conversation:

> **More about**
> First-person pronouns, 438–39, 681–82

> A writer for the *New York Times* explains, "Seventy percent of U.S. recruiters report that they have rejected candidates because of information found online, like photos and discussion-board conversations and membership in controversial groups." With 500 million people on Facebook, the dangers are widespread (Rosen). We cannot escape the irony that this phenomenon of personal data revealed to the world was begun by a person who himself had poor social skills.

Parenthetical reference shows end of source material

First-person plural suggests shift to student writer's voice

It is even better to comment upon the source or its information:

> A writer for the *New York Times* explains, "Seventy percent of U.S. recruiters report that they have rejected candidates because of information found online, like photos and discussion-board conversations and membership in controversial groups." With 500 million people on Facebook, the dangers are widespread (Rosen). Such information suggests an irony: This phenomenon of personal data revealed to the world was begun by a person who himself had poor social skills.

Parenthetical reference shows end of source material

Transition to student writer's interpretation of source material

In this version, the writer's voice is implicitly clear. He uses the adjective *such* to point to the previous material and then provides his interpretation. Demonstrative pronouns (*this, that, these, those*) can also be used as a transition to the student writer talking about source material.

17d Providing Context

Readers appreciate knowing not only when you are speaking and when your sources are, but also *who* your sources are and why you chose them. **Rhetorical citations** provide this information smoothly: Your citations can explain why you chose the source, what kind of source it is, when the source was published, and what its argument is.

1. Explain your choice of sources.

Unless your readers are familiar with your sources, they may have no reason to respect them and thus no reason to believe your claims. You can avoid this problem with rhetorical citations that not only name your source but also indicate why you respect the source, as this writer does:

> **More about**
> Evaluating sources, 230–45 (ch. 14)

Signal phrase includes student writer's opinion of the source

> Gary Wolf provides a helpful, wide-ranging overview of our motivations for gathering and sharing data about ourselves, offering examples like this: "*Foursquare*, a geo-tracking application with about one million users, keeps a running tally of how many times players 'check in' at every locale, automatically building a detailed diary of movements and habits; many users publish these data widely."

In the example above, the writer establishes that the source can be respected for its thorough treatment of the topic.

The selection below acknowledges the shortcomings of the source while also asserting its usefulness:

Signal phrase becomes extended explanation of student writer's opinion of the source

> Mezrich has made up parts of his story about Zuckerberg's rise, while claiming he is sticking as closely as possible to reality. Yet his fiction is worth reading; it shows how people perceive Harvard and its geniuses: "There was something playful about those eyes—but that was where any sense of natural emotion or readability ended. His narrow face was otherwise devoid of any expression at all. And his posture, his general aura—the way he seemed closed in on himself, even while engaged in a group dynamic, even here, in the safety of his own fraternity—was almost painfully awkward" (15).

Page in source

2. Identify the type of source.

Is your source a newspaper column? A blog? A scholarly article? The differences among types of sources are important. If you want up-to-the-minute information, a newspaper or blog is likely to have it. If you want carefully researched, accurate information, a scholarly journal article is a good choice. Your readers want to know that you have made appropriate source choices, and you can provide such information in rhetorical citations:

> *[Signal phrase describes and identifies source author and his credentials]* Writing in the *New York Times*, journalist Gary Wolf provides a wide-ranging overview of our motivations for gathering and sharing data about ourselves, offering examples like this: "*Foursquare,* a geo-tracking application with about one million users, keeps a running tally of how many times players 'check in' at every locale, automatically building a detailed diary of movements and habits; many users publish these data widely."

3. Identify the date of publication.

For many topics, the date of publication is important. The number of people who use the Foursquare application, for example, changes constantly. Providing the date on which such information was published helps readers know how fresh the numbers are and how accurate they might still be:

> *[Signal phrase includes publication date of time-sensitive information]* In a 2010 article in the *New York Times*, journalist Gary Wolf says, "*Foursquare,* a geo-tracking application with about one million users, keeps a running tally of how many times players 'check in' at every locale, automatically building a detailed diary of movements and habits; many users publish these data widely."

4. Identify the larger discussion in the source.

For the most successful, persuasive writing from sources, you need to *read* the sources, rather than just pulling sentences from them. That allows you not only to position the quotation, paraphrase, or summary in your text, but also to indicate how it contributed to the source text's discussion. Build a brief source summary into rhetorical citation:

> **More about**
> Critical reading, 108–33
> Avoiding plagiarism, 246–63 (ch. 15)

Extended signal phrase includes summary of the source

In a 2010 article in the *New York Times,* journalist Gary Wolf provides a wide-ranging overview of our motivations for gathering and sharing data about ourselves, offering examples like this: "*Foursquare,* a geo-tracking application with about one million users, keeps a running tally of how many times players 'check in' at every locale, automatically building a detailed diary of movements and habits; many users publish these data widely."

The phrase "overview of our motivations for gathering and sharing data about ourselves" summarizes the source.

Citation is not only ethical but rhetorical; in addition to protecting you against charges of plagiarism, it also creates a sophisticated, readable document that audiences are likely to trust.

▶ EXERCISE 17.1 Integrating and identifying source material

Read Lydia Nichols's essay "Holy Underground Comics, Batman! Moving Away from the Mainstream" (pp. 337–44) and note how she integrates her source material. Use one of four different colored highlighting markers to identify each of the different rhetorical moves she uses:

- Parenthetical references that are the *only* acknowledgment of the source in the sentence (that is, any sentences that have no signal phrases or other cues; just the parenthetical reference)
- Signal phrases
- Phrases that clearly signal her own voice speaking
- References to context: explaining her choice of source, the type of source, or the date of publication

When you have finished highlighting, use what you have learned in this chapter to evaluate how Nichols integrates her sources. What changes would you recommend if she were to revise this essay? Include the page reference in this book where she can read an explanation of each.

Research Matters • Citing Expertly

> ### Make It **Your Own**
>
> Choose a source-based paper you have already written or a draft in progress, and working on a printout of your paper, use one of four different colored highlighting markers to identify each of the four different rhetorical moves described in Exercise 17.1.
>
> ### Work **Together**
>
> When you have completed the highlighting, exchange papers with another student and use his or her highlighting and what you have learned so far in this chapter to evaluate the ways he or she integrates sources. For any revisions you recommend, be sure to include the page reference in this book where an explanation can be found.
>
> Now review your own paper and the comments and suggestions made by your reader and look for patterns. Which types of signals do you use most? Which do you use least? Make a checklist of issues and use it to help you revise papers in the future.
>
> If this is a paper you are currently drafting, revise to include some of these rhetorical cues in the sections where you seem to have the least transparency regarding sources. Before you look at your paper again, write a brief reflection on this process. What did you learn about how sources can be used effectively by reading and evaluating someone else's paper? Did your fellow student use any strategies that you think you might try? Did he or she use sources in a way that you would prefer to avoid?

17e Integrating Altered Quotations

Sometimes you may need to alter a quotation so that it fits into your sentence. In her draft on page 271, Nichols deletes words from the Hodgman quotation because those words do not help her make her point. As long as the meaning is not significantly changed, writers may do any of the following to fit quoted material more fluidly into their own sentences:

> **More about**
> Using ellipses in quotations, 786, 803–04
> Using square brackets in quotations, 786, 800

- Quote short phrases rather than full sentences
- Add or change words for clarity
- Change capitalization
- Change grammar

All added or changed words should be placed in square brackets; deleted words should be marked with ellipses. The example below shows a responsible alteration of a quotation:

Quotation Integrated into Student Text

Certain portions of the Comic Book Code were incredibly specific and controlling, such as the rule that forbade "[t]he letters of the word 'crime' on a comics magazine . . . [to] be appreciably greater in dimension than the other words contained in the title" (qtd. in "Good Shall Triumph over Evil").

Original Quotation

The letters of the word "crime" on a comics magazine shall never be appreciably greater in dimension than the other words contained in the title.

A capital letter was changed to a lowercase letter, double quotation marks were changed to single, one word was added and a couple of others were omitted, but the overall meaning of the passage remains the same.

Imagine, however, that the writer had made these changes instead:

Quotation Unfairly Altered

Certain portions of the code allowed some flexibility. Consider, for example, the rule that allowed "[t]he letters of the word 'crime' on a comics magazine . . . [to] be appreciably greater in dimension than the other words contained in the title" (qtd. in "Good Shall Triumph over Evil").

Original Quotation

The letters of the word "crime" on a comics magazine shall never be appreciably greater in dimension than the other words contained in the title.

Clearly this alteration of the quotation is not acceptable, as it changes the meaning of the passage completely.

EXERCISE 17.2 Integrating quotations

Read the passage below. Then, in the following quotations, circle the numbers for those that alter the quotation fairly, and cross through the numbers of those that change the meaning of the quotation.

> The meeting of Normans and Anglo-Saxons at Hastings was the most decisive battle of the Middle Ages and one of the determining days in the making of the West. Hastings changed Britain, which had been dominated since the end of Roman rule by invading tribes from the Continent and the North—Angles, Saxons, and Vikings. This day more than any other turned Britain away from

its Scandinavian past and toward Europe. Hastings inaugurated the era of the knight, the social dominance of those who fought with lance on horseback.

—Howard R. Bloch, *A Needle in the Right Hand of God.* New York: Random House, 2006, p. 7.

1. Bloch maintains that the Battle of Hastings "turned Britain away from its Scandinavian past" and from Europe as well (7).

2. The Battle of Hastings, notes Bloch, gave the "invading tribes from the Continent and the North" new power over Britain (7).

3. "[T]hose who fought with lance on horseback" became dominant after the Battle of Hastings, observes Bloch (7).

4. Bloch concludes that the fight between the Romans and the invading tribes from the Continent and the North was "the most decisive battle of the Middle Ages" (7).

Self Assessment

As you revise projects that use sources, review your draft, revising as necessary, to be sure you:

- ☐ Cite your sources. Did you name any from which you are paraphrasing, summarizing, or quoting?
- ☐ Use signal verbs. Did you convey the attitude of your source?
- ☐ Use signal phrases and parenthetical references. Did you show where each source use begins and ends, even when it is unpaginated?
- ☐ Emphasize your own insights. Did you comment on or analyze the source, rather than just repeat it?
- ☐ Provide relevant contextual information. Did you identify the type of source, its date of publication, and its publisher?
- ☐ Reveal your reasoning. Did you explain why you chose and trusted your sources?

Make It Your Own

Choose a source-based paper you have already written or a draft in progress, and use the material in this chapter and the tips in the Self-Assessment box above to help you review the ways you use and incorporate source material. Make a note of changes that would strengthen your use of source material, and add any new items you identify to the checklist in the Self-Assessment.

MLA

Journal Article from an Online Database

Decker, Alicia, and Mauricio, Castro. "Teaching History with Comic Books: A Case Study of Violence, War, and the Graphic Novel." *History Teacher:* 45.2 (2012): 169-188. *Academic Search Elite.* Web. 17 Dec. 2012.

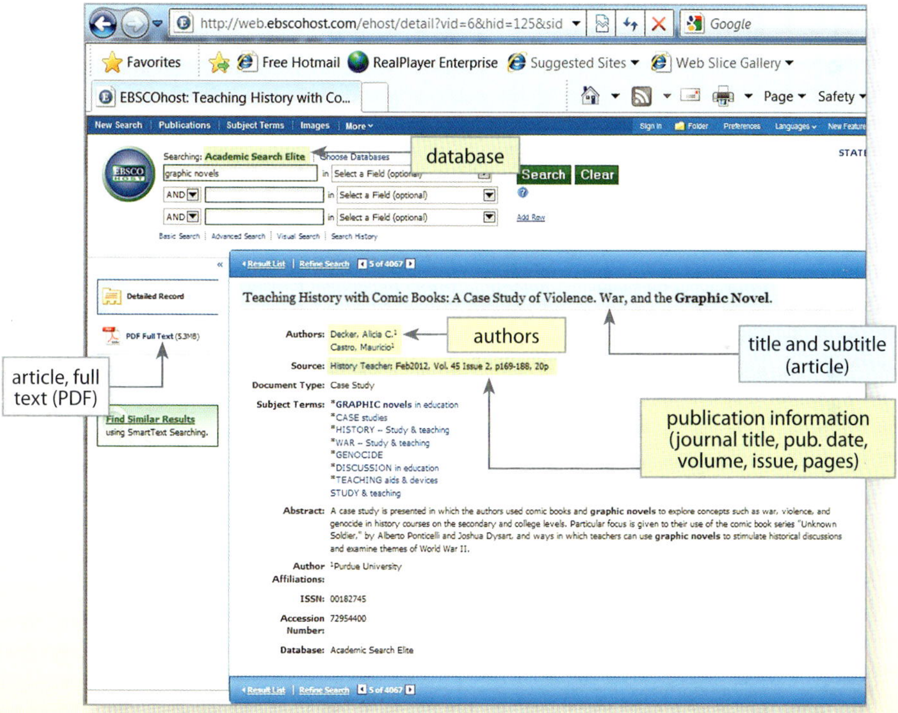

Database screen: full record of article

Look for the information you need to document an article you accessed through an online database on the search results screen, the full record of the article, or the first and last pages of the article itself. The access date is the date you last consulted the source; record this date in your notes. (For more about documenting an article accessed through an online database, see pp. 316–18.)

MLA

Journal Article (Printed)

author — title and subtitle (article)
Stewart, Mary Amanda. "Juxtaposing Immigrant and Adolescent Girl Experiences: Literature for All Readers."
title (journal)   issue   medium
English Journal 101.5 (2012): 17–22. Print.
           vol.   year   pages

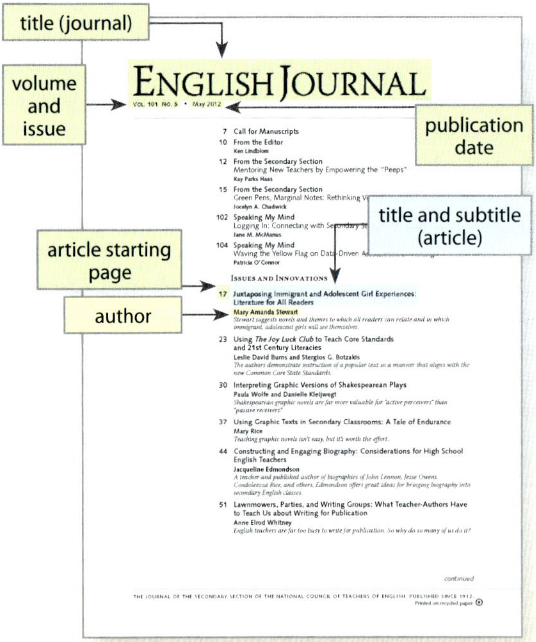

Journal table of contents

First page of article

- title (journal)
- volume and issue
- publication date
- article starting page
- author
- title and subtitle (article)
- author
- title and subtitle (article)
- article starting page
- title (journal), volume, number, publication date

Look for the information you need to document a journal article on the cover or table of contents of the journal and on the first and last pages of the article. (For more about documenting an article from a printed or online periodical, see pp. 315–19.)

Documentation Matters | Documenting a Source: MLA Style

Book (Printed)

author   *title*   *publication information*   *medium*
Woolf, Virginia. *Three Guineas*. San Diego: Harvest-Harcourt, Inc., 1966. Print.
                                            place of publication   *imprint-publisher*   *publication date*

Title page

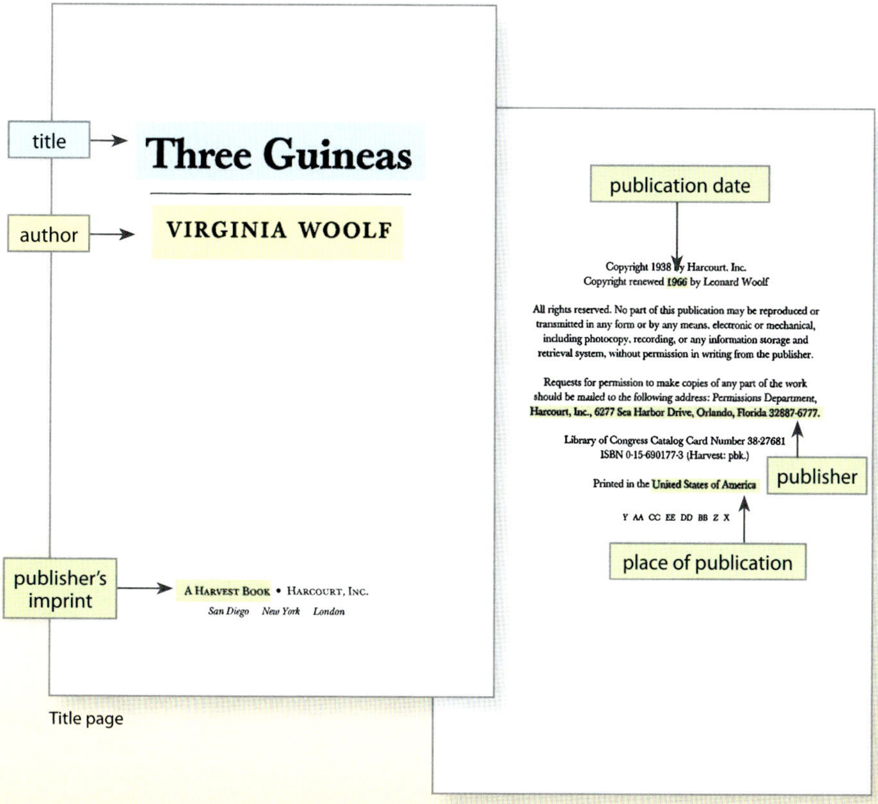

- title → **Three Guineas**
- author → VIRGINIA WOOLF
- publisher's imprint → A HARVEST BOOK · HARCOURT, INC. San Diego New York London

Copyright page

- publication date → Copyright 1938 by Harcourt, Inc. Copyright renewed 1966 by Leonard Woolf
- All rights reserved. No part of this publication may be reproduced or transmitted in any form or by any means, electronic or mechanical, including photocopy, recording, or any information storage and retrieval system, without permission in writing from the publisher.
- Requests for permission to make copies of any part of the work should be mailed to the following address: Permissions Department, Harcourt, Inc., 6277 Sea Harbor Drive, Orlando, Florida 32887-6777.
- Library of Congress Catalog Card Number 38-27681
- ISBN 0-15-690177-3 (Harvest: pbk.)
- publisher → Printed in the United States of America ← place of publication
- Y AA CC EE DD BB Z X

Look for the information you need to document a printed book on the book's title page and copyright page. If more than one location for the publisher is listed on the title page, use the first. (For more about documenting a book, see pp. 305–15.)

MLA

Short Work on a Website

Esposito, Joseph. "E-books and the Personal Library." *The Scholarly Kitchen.* Society for Scholarly Publishing, Aug. 20, 2012. Web. 17 Dec. 2012.

(Labels: author, web page title, website title, sponsor/publisher, medium, access date, ©date/last update)

Web page

Frequently, the information you need to create a complete entry in the list of works cited is missing or difficult to find on web pages. Look at the top or bottom of the web page or home page or for a link to an "About" or "Contact Us" page. If no sponsor or publisher is listed, use *n.p.*; if no publication date is available, use *n.d.* (For more about documenting online sources, see pp. 319–22.)

Part Five

Documentation Matters

18   Documenting Sources: MLA Style   288
19   Documenting Sources: APA Style   347
20   Documenting Sources: *Chicago* Style   389
21   Documenting Sources: CSE Style   416

18 Documenting Sources: MLA Style

IN THIS CHAPTER

a. In-text citations, 288
b. Works-cited list, 305
c. Informational notes, 331
d. Formatting, 332

Student Model
Research Project:
MLA Style, 336

Developed by the Modern Language Association (MLA), MLA style guidelines are used by many researchers in the humanities—especially in languages and literature—to cite and document sources and to format papers in a uniform way. The *MLA Handbook for Writers of Research Papers* (7th ed.) requires that sources be acknowledged in two ways:

- **Citation:** In the body of your project, provide an in-text citation for each source used.
- **Documentation:** At the project's end, provide a list of all the works you cited in the project.

In-text citations appear in the body of your paper. They mark each use you make of a source, regardless of whether you are quoting, paraphrasing, summarizing, or drawing ideas from it. They also alert readers to a shift between *your* ideas and those you have borrowed.

> **More about**
> Popular academic styles per discipline, 437, 457
> APA style, 347–88 (ch. 19)
> *Chicago* style, 389–415 (ch. 20)
> CSE style, 416–30 (ch. 21)

18a Creating MLA-Style In-Text Citations

You can cite a source in your text by using a signal phrase and page reference (in parentheses) or a parenthetical citation:

Writing Responsibly — Citing and Documenting Sources

When you cite and document sources, you demonstrate how thoroughly you have researched your topic and how carefully you have thought about your sources, which encourages your audience to believe you are a credible researcher. In your citations and documentation you acknowledge any material that you have borrowed from a source and you join the conversation on your topic by adding your own interpretation. Accurate entries in the body of your project and list of works cited allow your audience to find and read your sources so that they can evaluate your interpretation and learn more about the subject themselves. Accurate entries also demonstrate the care with which you have written your research project, which further reinforces your credibility, or ethos.

to AUDIENCE

- **Signal phrase.** Include the author's name and an appropriate verb in your sentence before the borrowed material, and put the page number(s) in parentheses after the borrowed material. Often you will use just the author's surname, and you should never use the author's first name alone.

> While encouraging writers to use figurative language, <u>journalist</u> <u>Constance Hale cautions</u> [signal phrase] that "a metaphor has the shelf life of a fresh vegetable" <u>(224)</u> [page no.], illustrating the warning with her own lively metaphor.

Qualifications of source author

Using a signal phrase allows you to integrate the borrowed material into your sentence, to put the source in context by adding your own interpretation, and to describe the qualifications of the source author. For these reasons, most summaries, paraphrases, and quotations should be introduced by a signal phrase.

- **Parenthetical citation.** Include in parentheses the author's surname plus the page number(s) from which the borrowed material comes:

> While figurative language can make a passage come alive, be aware that metaphors have "the shelf life of a fresh vegetable" <u>(Hale 224)</u> [parenthetical note].

Parenthetical citations are useful when you are citing more than one source, when you are establishing facts, or when the author's identity is not relevant to the point you are making.

NOTE The works-cited entry is the same whether you use a signal phrase or a parenthetical citation:

> <u>Hale, Constance.</u> [author] *<u>Sin and Syntax.</u>* [title] <u>New York: Broadway, 2001.</u> [publication info.] <u>Print.</u> [medium]

1. Include enough information to lead readers to the source in your list of works cited.

Whether you are using a signal phrase or a parenthetical citation, in-text citations should provide enough information for readers to locate the source in the

18a Documentation Matters • Documenting Sources: MLA Style

> **More about**
> What you do and do not need to cite, 348–50
> Signal phrases, 274–86
> Signal verbs (list), 277
> Integrating borrowed material into your text, 274–76

> **Quick Reference** — **General Principles of In-Text Citation**
>
> - Cite not only direct quotations but also paraphrases, summaries, and information gathered from a source, whether printed or online.
> - In most cases, include the author's surname and a page reference. For one-page and unpaginated sources (such as websites), provide only the author's name.
> - Place the name(s) either in a signal phrase or in a parenthetical citation. A signal phrase makes it easier to integrate borrowed information or the author's credentials into your own prose. A parenthetical citation is appropriate when establishing facts or citing more than one source for a piece of information.
> - For two or more sources by the same author, include the title—either a complete title in the text or an abbreviated title in the parenthetical citation.
> - Whenever you add a title or abbreviated title, insert a comma between the surname and the title, but not between the title and the page number. In parenthetical citations, do not insert punctuation between the author's surname and the page number.

List of works cited. In most cases, providing the author's surname and a page reference is enough. Occasionally, however, you may need to provide more information:

> Example 6, 296

- If you cite more than one source by the same author, mention the title of the work in the text or include a shortened form of the title in the in-text citation. (You may also want to mention the title of the work, if it is relevant to the point you are making.)

> Example 7, 296

- If you refer to sources by two different authors who have the same surname, mention the authors' first names in the text, or include the authors' first initials in the in-text citation.

> Example 8, 296
> Example 16a, 302

Occasionally, you may need to include less information. For example, you would omit a page number when you are summarizing an entire source, when your source is just one page long, or when your source, such as a web page, is not paginated.

2. Place in-text citations to avoid distracting readers and show them where borrowed material starts and stops.

When you incorporate a quotation, paraphrase, summary, or idea from a source into your own text, carefully consider the placement of the in-text citation, keeping the following goals in mind:

> **Tech** **Page References and Web Pages**
>
> Despite the term *web page,* most websites do not have page numbers in the sense that printed books do. Your browser may number the pages when you print a web page from a website, but this numbering appears only on your printed copy. Different computers and printers break pages differently, so your printed page 5 might be someone else's page 4 or 6. For this reason, in-text citations of most web pages include only the author's name. If a website numbers its paragraphs, provide that information in place of a page reference.

- To make clear exactly which material is drawn from the source
- To avoid distracting your reader

Signal phrase When using a signal phrase, bookend the borrowed information: Insert the author's name *before,* and the page number *after,* the cited material.

> **Daniels,** who has written several books about DC Comics' creations, **notes** that underground comics artists are not controlled by corporate interests that discourage daring material **(165)**.

Signal phrase

Page number

Parenthetical citation When using a parenthetical citation, place the note at a natural pause—at the end of a phrase, clause, or sentence—right after the borrowed material and before any punctuation.

> **More about**
> Phrases, 591–94
> Clauses, 594–97
> Sentences, 597–99

Following a sentence

> Common themes of underground comics include sex and sexual identity, politics, and social issues (**Daniels 165**).

Following a clause

> Other common themes of underground comics include sex and sexual identity, politics, and social issues (**Daniels 165**), as shown in Robert Crumb's *Snarf* comics.

Following a phrase

> The themes of underground comics, such as sex and sexual identity, politics, and social issues (Daniels 165), are all demonstrated in Robert Crumb's *Snarf* comics.

> **More about**
> Block quotations, 299, 334

Block quotations When the text you are quoting takes up more than four lines of your project, indent the borrowed material as a block by one inch from the left margin, and place the parenthetical citation one space *after* the closing punctuation mark. No quotation marks should be used when indenting quoted material as a block.

Example

> *signal phrase*
> Howard and Kennedy assert that parents and school officials tend to ignore hazing until an incident becomes public knowledge. They describe a concrete incident that demonstrates their claims:
>
> > In general, the Bredvik school community (parents, teachers, coaches, and students) condoned or ignored behaviors that could be called "hazing" or "sexual harassment." However, when the incident was formally brought to the attention of the larger, public audience, a conflict erupted in the community over how to frame, understand, and react to the event. (347-48)

3. Adjust in-text citations to match your source.

The exact form of an in-text citation depends on the source. Does it have one author, several authors, or no authors? Is the source paginated? Is the source a novel, a story in an anthology, or a PowerPoint presentation? The examples below cover the most common source types. (A list of in-text citation examples in MLA style appears on page 294.) For more unusual sources, study the general principles as outlined here and in the *MLA Handbook for Writers of*

Writing Responsibly
Using Signal Phrases to Demonstrate Your Relationship with Sources

As you consider using a source, think about *why* you want to use it. Does it provide a supporting reason or illustration? Does it provide an authoritative voice? Does it make a point that contrasts with your own? Then include a signal phrase that reflects your answer to that question.

> Tom Bergin, who covers the oil and gas industry for Reuters, provides one example of the consequences of offshore drilling.
>
> Neurobiologist Catherine Levine agrees with this point of view.
>
> The views of meteorologist John Coleman contrast dramatically with those of the majority of climate scientists.

to TOPIC

> **More about**
> Integrating supporting material, 275–76
> When to use signal phrases, 276, 759

Research Papers, 7th ed. (available in any library), and adapt them to your special circumstances.

1. One author

a. Signal phrase

> Cahill cautions responsible historians against disparaging the Middle Ages. Medieval Europe's reputation as a time of darkness, ignorance, and blind faith is "largely (if not wholly) undeserved" (310).
>
> *page no.*

b. Parenthetical citation

> The Middle Ages are often unjustly characterized as a time of darkness, ignorance, and blind faith (Cahill 310).

2. Two or three authors
Include the surnames of all the authors in your signal phrase or parenthetical citation; use *and,* not an ampersand (&), in the parenthetical citation.

> To write successfully about their families, authors must have motives beyond merely exposing secret histories (Miller and Paola 72).

> **MLA In-Text Citations Index**
> 1. One author
> 2. Two or three authors
> 3. More than three authors
> 4. Group, government, or corporate author

MLA In-Text Citations Index

1. One author
2. Two or three authors
3. **More than three authors**
4. Group, government, or corporate author
5. Unnamed author

Quick Reference — Examples of MLA-Style In-Text Citations

1. One author 293
   a. Signal phrase 293
   b. Parenthetical note 293
2. Two or three authors 293
3. More than three authors 294
4. Group, government, or corporate author 295
5. Unnamed author 295
6. Two or more sources by the same author 296
7. Two or more authors with the same surname 296
8. Entire source (including a one-page source) 296
9. Selection from an anthology 297
10. Multivolume source 297
11. Literary source 297
    a. Novel 298
    b. Play 298
    c. Poem 298
12. Sacred text 299
13. Motion picture, television or radio broadcast 300
14. Indirect source 300
15. Dictionary or encyclopedia entry 301
16. Website or other online source 302
    a. Without page, paragraph, screen, or slide numbers 302
    b. With paragraph, screen, or slide numbers 302
    c. In a PDF file 303
17. Personal communication (e-mail, letter, interview) 303
18. Table, chart, or figure 303
19. Government document 304
20. Legal source 304
21. Multiple sources in one sentence 304
22. Multiple sources in one citation 305

3. More than three authors For sources with more than three authors, you may either list each author by surname (following the order in the text) or insert the Latin phrase *et al.* following the first author's surname.

et al. Abbreviation of the Latin phrase *et alii*, "and others"

NOTE *al.* is an abbreviation, so it requires a period; *et* is a complete word, so it does not. There should be no punctuation between the author's name and *et al.*

---

all authors in signal phrase
Visonà, Poynor, Cole, Harris, Abiodun, and Blier stress that symbols used in African art are not intended to be iconic but instead to suggest a wide variety of meanings. The authors liken this complexity to "a telephone line that carries multiple messages simultaneously" (19).

> Symbols used in African art are not intended to be iconic but rather to suggest a complex range of meanings (**Visonà et al.** 19).
>
> *1st author + et al.*

Whichever you choose, do the same in your list of works cited.

> Example 3, 308

4. Group, government, or corporate author When a government agency, corporation, or other organization is listed as the author, use that organization's name in your in-text citation. The MLA suggests incorporating names into your sentence in a signal phrase to avoid long parenthetical citations.

> *government agency as author*
> **The Federal Emergency Management Agency** indicates that Kansas City is located in a region of frequent and intense tornado activity (4).

If a parenthetical citation makes more sense in the context, use common abbreviations ("US" for *United States*, "Corp." for *Corporation*) to shorten the name where you can.

5. Unnamed author If the author is unnamed and the work is alphabetized by title in the list of works cited, use the title in your in-text citation. Abbreviate long titles in parenthetical citations.

> One nineteenth-century children's book vows that "when examined by the microscope, the flea is a pleasant object," and the author's vivid description of this sight—a body "curiously adorned with a suit of polished armor, neatly jointed, and beset with a great number of sharp pins almost like the quills of a porcupine"—may win readers' curiosity, if not their sympathy (*Insects* 8).
>
> *title*

If you do abbreviate the title, start your abbreviation with the word by which the title will be alphabetized in your list of works cited. Also, only if the author is listed specifically as "Anonymous" should you use that designation.

> Example 4, 308

MLA In-Text Citations Index

2. Two or three authors
3. More than three authors
4. **Group, government, or corporate author**
5. **Unnamed author**
6. Two or more sources by the same author
7. Two or more authors with the same surname

6. Two or more sources by the same author When you draw on two or more sources by the same author, differentiate between those sources by including titles.

> In her book *Nickel and Dimed*, [book title] social critic Barbara Ehrenreich demonstrates that people cannot live on the then-current minimum wage (60). Perhaps, as she notes in her blog entry "'Values' Voters Raise Minimum Wages," [blog entry title] they will be a little better able to hold their own in the six states (Arizona, Colorado, Montana, Missouri, Nevada, Ohio) that have recently raised their minimum wage.

7. Two or more authors with the same surname When you cite sources by two different authors with the same surname, differentiate them by including their first names (the first time you mention them in a signal phrase) or by including their first initials (in a parenthetical reference or subsequent in-text citations).

> Including citations is important not only because they give credit but also because they "organize a field of inquiry, create order, and allow for accountability" (S. Rose 243). This concern for acknowledging original sources dates back to the early eighteenth century: Joseph Addison was one of the first to argue for "the superiority of original to imitative composition" (M. Rose 114).

8. Entire source (including a one-page source) Mention an entire source—whether it is a film or a website, a book or an article, a painting or a graphic novel—in your text using the information that begins the entry in your list of works cited.

MLA In-Text Citations Index

4. Group, government, or corporate author
5. Unnamed author
6. Two or more sources by the same author
7. Two or more authors with the same surname
8. Entire source
9. Selection from an anthology
10. Multivolume source

> The film *The Lady Eve* asks whether love is possible without trust.

> Example 41b, 323

9. Selection from an anthology If your source is a selection from an anthology, reader, or other collection, your citation should name the author of the selection—not the editor of the anthology. In the example below, Faulkner is the author of the selection "A Rose for Emily," a story that appears in a literature anthology edited by Robert DiYanni.

> Example 10, 310

MLA In-Text Citations Index

8. Entire source
9. Selection from an anthology
10. Multivolume source
11. Literary source
12. Sacred text

> Southern fiction often explores the marked curiosity that women of stature and mystery inspire in their communities. [author of selection] Faulkner's "A Rose for Emily," for example, describes the title character as "a tradition, a duty, and a care; a sort of hereditary obligation upon the town . . ." (79).

10. Multivolume source If you use information from more than one volume of a multivolume work, your in-text citation must indicate both the volume and the page from which you are borrowing. (This information can be omitted if you use only one volume of the work, since your works-cited entry will indicate which volume you used.)

> Example 15b, 312

> [author] Tarbell writes that in 1847 Abraham Lincoln was a popular man of "simple, sincere friendliness" who was an enthusiastic—though awkward—bowler [vol. no. pg. no.] (1: 210).

The words *volume* and *page* (or their abbreviations) are not used.

11. Literary source Because many classics of literature—novels, poems, plays—are published in a number of editions (printed and digital) with pagination that varies widely, your citation should provide your readers with the information they will need to find the passage, regardless of which edition they are reading.

a. Novel Include the chapter number (with the abbreviation *ch.*) after the page number (or location reference for digital books) from your edition.

> Joyce shows his protagonist's dissatisfaction with family, faith, and country through the adolescent Stephen Daedalus's first dinner at the adult table, an evening filled with political and religious discord (274; ch. 1).
>
>   pg. no. ch. no.

Use arabic (2, 9, 103), not roman (ii, ix, ciii), numerals, regardless of what your source uses.

If the novel has chapters grouped into parts or books, include both the part or book number and the chapter number, using the appropriate abbreviation (*pt.* for *part* or *bk.* for *book*).

> Even though New York society declares the Countess Olenska beyond her prime, Newland Archer sees in her the "mysterious authority of beauty" (Wharton 58; bk. 1, ch. 8).

MLA In-Text Citations Index

9. Selection from an anthology
10. Multivolume source
11. **Literary source**
12. Sacred text
13. Motion picture, television or radio broadcast

b. Play When citing plays, use act, scene, and line numbers (in that order), not page numbers or location numbers (used in digital editions). Do not label the parts. Instead, separate them with periods.

> When the ghost of Hamlet's father cries, "Adieu, adieu, adieu! remember me," Hamlet wonders if he must "remember" his father through vengeance (1.5.91).

Use arabic (1, 5, 91), not roman (i, v, xci), numerals for act, scene, and line numbers, and omit spaces after periods between numbers.

c. Poem For poetry, use line numbers, rather than page or location numbers. With the first reference to line numbers, use the word *line* or *lines;* omit it thereafter.

> In Audre Lorde's poem "Hanging Fire," her fourteen-year-old frets, "What if I die / before morning" (lines 7-8) [1st ref.], making me remember my own teenage worries of just a few years ago. Each of the three stanzas ends with "and momma's in the bedroom / with the door closed" (9-10, 20-21, 32-33) [later refs.], bringing me back to my "now": I am that mother who does not understand.

Audre Lorde, "Hanging Fire," *The Collected Poems of Audre Lorde*. Copyright © 1978 by Audre Lorde. Used by permission of W. W. Norton & Company, Inc. This selection may not be reproduced, stored in a retrieval system, or transmitted in any form or by any means without the prior written permission of the publisher.

MLA In-Text Citations Index

10. Multivolume source
11. Literary source
12. Sacred text
13. Motion picture, television or radio broadcast
14. Indirect source

For long poems that are divided into sections (books, parts, numbered stanzas), provide section information as well, omitting the section type (such as *book* or *part*) and separating the section number from the line number(s) with a period.

> David Mason's *Ludlow* (2007) begins with a description that captures Luisa's life:
>
>   Down below
> the mesa, smells of cooking rose from shacks
> in rows, and there Luisa scrubbed the pot
> as if she were some miner's wife and not
> a sapper's daughter, scrawny, barely twelve. (1.5-8)
>
> [sec.] [lines.]

Use arabic (*1, 5, 8*), not roman (*i, v, viii*), numerals, and omit spaces.

12. Sacred text Cite sacred texts (such as the Bhagavad-Gita, the Talmud, the Qur'an, and the Bible) not by page number but by book title (abbreviated in parenthetical citations), chapter number, and verse number(s), and separate each section with a period. Do not italicize book titles or put them in quotation marks, and do not italicize the name of the sacred text, unless you are referring to a specific edition.

MLA In-Text Citations Index

11. Literary source
12. Sacred text
13. **Motion picture, television or radio broadcast**
14. Indirect source
15. Dictionary or encyclopedia entry
16. Website or other online source

> Example 41b, 323

> **sacred text**
> In the **Bible's** timeless love poetry, the female speaker concludes her description of her lover with this proclamation: "This is my beloved and this is my friend, / O daughters of Jerusalem" (Song of Sol. 5.16).
>
> *book* — *ch.verse*
> *No space*

> **specific edition**
> The *New Oxford Annotated Bible* offers a moving translation of the timeless love poetry in the **Song of Solomon**. The female speaker concludes her description of her lover with this proclamation: "This is my beloved and this is my friend, / O daughters of Jerusalem" (5.16).
>
> *book* — *ch.verse*

13. Motion picture, television or radio broadcast The information you include in an in-text citation for a motion picture or for a television or radio broadcast depends on what you are emphasizing in your project. When you are emphasizing the work itself, use the title; when you are emphasizing the director's work, use the director's name; when you are emphasizing an actor's work, use the actor's name. Start your works-cited entry with whatever you have used in your in-text citation.

> **title**
> While *The Lady Eve* is full of slapstick humor, it is mainly remembered for its snappy dialogue, at once witty and suggestive.

> **actor's name**
> Barbara Stanwyck's portrayal of Jean Harrington is at once sexy and wholesome.

14. Indirect source When you can, avoid quoting from a secondhand source. When you cannot use the original source, mention the name of the person you are quoting in your sentence. In your parenthetical citation, include *qtd. in* (for *quoted in*) plus the name of the author of the source in which you found the quotation.

> Handel's stock among opera-goers rose considerably over the course of the twentieth century. In 1912, an English music critic, **H. C. Colles,** [author quoted] maintained that "it would be difficult, if not impossible, to make any one of Handel's operas tolerable to a modern audience" (**qtd. in Orrey** [source of quotation] 62). Today, however, Handel's operas are performed around the world.

In your list of works cited, include the *indirect* source (*Orrey*), not the source being quoted (*H. C. Colles*).

15. Dictionary or encyclopedia entry In the citation of a dictionary or encyclopedia entry, omit the page number on which you found the item. For a dictionary entry, place the defined word in quotation marks, followed by the abbreviation *def.* Follow this with the letter or number of the definition you wish to reference.

> Another definition of *honest* is "respectable" (**"Honest," def. 6**), but what, if anything, does truth have to do with respectability?

In the parenthetical citation for an encyclopedia entry, include the entry's full title in quotation marks.

> The study of ethics is not limited to philosophers, as its "all-embracing practical nature" makes it an applicable or even necessary course of study in a wide variety of disciplines, from biology to business (**"Ethics"**).

If you are citing two entries with the same title from different reference sources, add an abbreviated form of the reference work's title to each entry.

MLA In-Text Citations Index

13. Motion picture, television or radio broadcast
14. Indirect source
15. **Dictionary or encyclopedia entry**
16. Website or other online source
17. Personal communication

> **More about**
> Parts of a dictionary entry, 560–62

> While the word *ethics* is commonly understood to mean "moral principles" ("Ethics," def. 4, *Random House Webster's*), to philosophers it is "the evaluation of human conduct" ("Ethics," *Philosophical Dict.*).

16. Website or other online source Cite electronic sources such as websites, online articles, e-books, and e-mails as you would print sources, even though many of these sources do not use page numbers.

a. Without page, paragraph, screen, or slide numbers Unless there is another numbering system at work (such as numbered paragraphs, screens, or slides), cite the author without a page reference.

> When first published in 1986, Alan Moore's *Watchmen* revolutionized the comic book. Today, even its harshest critics acknowledge the book's landmark status (Shone). *[author only]*

You may credit your source more elegantly by mentioning the author in a signal phrase and omitting the parenthetical citation altogether.

> Reading Alan Moore's *Watchmen* in 2005, critic Tom Shone found it *[signal phrase]* "underwhelming," but he admitted that in 1986 the comic book was "unquestionably a landmark work."

b. With paragraph, screen, or slide numbers If an electronic source numbers its paragraphs, screens, or slides, you can reference these numbers as you would pages (with an appropriate identifying abbreviation—*par.* or *pars., screen* or *screens*).

MLA In-Text Citations Index

14. Indirect source
15. Dictionary or encyclopedia entry
16. **Website or other online source**
17. Personal communication
18. Table, chart, or figure

> The Internet has also become an outlet for direct distribution through artist websites, making independent titles not only more accessible to consumers but also more affordable for individual artists to produce and market (Fenty, Houp, and Taylor par. 1).

c. In a PDF file Online documents offered as a PDF (portable document format) file include all the elements of the printed document, including the page number. Since pages are fixed, you can and should cite page numbers.

17. Personal communication (e-mail, letter, interview) As with other unpaginated sources, when citing information from a letter, e-mail message, interview, or other personal communication, you should include the author's name in a signal phrase or parenthetical citation. Also indicate the type of source you are citing.

> Many people have asked why teachers cannot do more to prevent school shootings; in an e-mail to this author, one instructor responds: "As creative writing teachers untrained in psychology, can we really determine from a student's poetry whether he or she is emotionally disturbed—even a threat to others?" (Fox).

18. Table, chart, or figure If a copy of the visual you are discussing is *not* included in your project, include relevant information in the text (artist's name or table title, for example), and include an entry in your list of works cited.

> There is no experience quite like standing in front of a full-size painting by Jackson Pollock. His paintings have an irresistible sense of movement to them, the particular quality of which is unique to his work. This is especially evident in *One (Number 31, 1950),* which currently hangs on the fourth floor of New York's Museum of Modern Art.

> **More about**
> PDF files, 180, 215, 218

MLA In-Text Citations Index

14. Indirect source
15. Dictionary or encyclopedia entry
16. Website or other online source
17. Personal communication
18. Table, chart, or figure
19. Government document
20. Legal source

> Examples 47–51, 327–28

TABLE 1 | THE DEMISE OF THE THREE-DECKER NOVEL

Year	No. of 3-deckers published
1894	184
1895	52
1896	—
1897	4
1898	0

Source: Information from John Feather, *A History of British Publishing* (Clarendon: Crown Helm, 1988; print; 125).

FIGURE 18.1 Table in MLA style

If a copy of the visual *is* included in your project, reference it in your text and include the source information in a table's source note (Figure 18.1) or in a figure's caption (see the figure caption on p. 339 in the student model project at the end of this chapter).

19. Government document Because government documents are alphabetized in the list of works cited by the name of the nation that produced them, mention the country as well as the agency in your text.

> Example 52, 328

Just as the nation was entering World War II, the United States War Department published a book outlining what it had learned about reading aerial photographs.

> Example 53, 329

20. Legal source Laws, acts, and legal cases are typically referred to by name either in your sentence or in a parenthetical citation. Laws and acts are neither italicized nor enclosed in quotation marks.

In 2008 the U.S. Congress passed the Combat Bonus Act.

Legal cases are italicized in your text, but not in the list of works cited.

In 1963 the Supreme Court ruled that poor defendants should receive legal representation, even if they could not pay for it themselves (*Gideon v. Wainright*).

21. Multiple sources in one sentence When you use different information from multiple sources within a single sentence, give separate citations in the appropriate place.

MLA In-Text Citations Index

17. Personal communication
18. Table, chart, or figure
19. Government document
20. Legal source
21. Multiple sources in one sentence
22. Multiple sources in one citation

> Other common themes of underground comics include sex and sexual identity, politics, and social issues (Daniels 165), as shown in Crumb's work, which is well known for its satirical approach to countercultural topics (Heller 101-02).

MLA In-Text Citations Index

20. Legal source
21. Multiple sources in one sentence
22. **Multiple sources in one citation**

22. Multiple sources in one citation When you draw information from more than one source, follow the borrowed material with a list of all relevant sources, separated by semicolons.

> Jamestown was once described as a failed colony populated by failed colonists, but new findings suggest that the colonists were resourceful survivors (Howard; Lepore 43).

Entire source—no page reference

18b Preparing an MLA-Style List of Works Cited

The list of works cited, which comes at the end of your research project, includes information about the sources you have cited in your text. (A bibliography that includes sources you read but did not cite in your research project is called a *list of works consulted*.) Your list of works cited provides readers with the information they need to locate the material you used in your project. The format of each entry depends in part on the type of source it is. (See the Quick Reference box on pp. 306–07 for a list of MLA-style examples included in this chapter.)

MLA Works-Cited Entries

1. **One author**
2. Two or three authors
3. More than three authors

Books—Printed and Electronic

In a printed book, most or all of the information you need to create an entry in the list of works cited appears on the title and copyright pages, which are located at the beginning of the book. In an online or e-book, print and electronic publication information often appears at the top or bottom of the first page or screen or is available through a link.

> Annotated visual of where to find author, title, and publication information, on foldout accompanying this chapter

1. One author
a. Printed The basic entry for a printed book looks like this:

> Author's surname, First name. *Title: Subtitle.* Place of publication: Publisher (shortened), date of publication. Medium of publication.

Reference: Examples of MLA-Style Works-Cited Entries

Books—Printed and Electronic

1. One author 305
   a. Printed 305
   b. Database 306
   c. E-book 307
2. Two or three authors 308
3. More than three authors 308
4. Unnamed (anonymous) author 308
5. Author using a pen name (pseudonym) 309
6. Two or more works by the same author 309
7. Group or corporate author 309
8. Edited book or anthology (printed or online) 309
9. Author and editor or translator 309
10. One or more selections from an edited book or anthology (printed or online) 310
11. Edition other than the first 311
12. Imprint (division) of a larger publishing company 311
13. Introduction, preface, foreword, or afterword 311
14. Entry in a reference work 311
    a. Printed 312
    b. Online 312
    c. CD-ROM or DVD-ROM 312
15. Multivolume work 312
    a. Multiple volumes 312
    b. One volume 312
16. Book in a series 313
17. Republished book 313
18. Title within a title 313
19. Sacred text 313
20. Missing publication information 314
21. Pamphlet, brochure, or press release 314
22. Conference proceedings 314
23. Dissertation 314

Periodicals—Printed and Electronic

24. Article in a scholarly journal 315
    a. Printed 315
    b. Accessed through a database 316
    c. Online 316
25. Article in a magazine (weekly, monthly) 316
    a. Printed 316
    b. Accessed through a database 317
    c. Online 317
26. Article in a newspaper 317
    a. Printed 317
    b. Accessed through a database 318
    c. Online 318
27. Article on microform 318
28. Review (printed or online) 319
29. Editorial (printed or online) 319
30. Letter to the editor (printed or online) 319

Other Electronic Sources

31. Website 320
32. Web page or short work on a website 320
33. Home page (academic) 320
    a. Course 320
    b. Department 321
34. Discussion list posting 321
35. Article on a wiki 321

MLA Works-Cited Entries

1. One author
2. Two or three authors
3. More than three authors

Here is an example of an actual entry in the list of works cited:

author — *title* — *publication information* — *medium*
Morrison, Toni. *Home.* New York: Knopf, 2012. Print.
                                       place   *pub.* *date*

b. Database Some books are available in online, full-text archives, or databases, such as Bartleby.com. When you are documenting a book you accessed through a database, add the name of the database and change the medium of

36. Blog 321
    a. Blog 321
    b. Blog posting 321
    c. Comment on a blog posting 321
37. Avatar 322
38. Source published in more than one medium 322
39. Computer software 322
40. Video game 322

Audio and Visual Sources

41. Motion picture 323
    a. Film 323
    b. Video or DVD 323
    c. Internet download 324
    d. Online video clip 324
    e. DVD extras 324
42. Television or radio broadcast 324
    a. Series 324
    b. Episode 325
    c. Single program 325
    d. Podcast 325
43. Musical or other audio recording 325
    a. CD, LP, audiobook 325
    b. Song or selection from a CD or LP or a chapter from an audiobook 325
    c. Compressed music file (MP3, MP4) 326
    d. Online sound file or clip 326
44. Live performance 326
    a. Ensemble 326
    b. Individual 326

45. Musical composition 326
46. Lecture, speech, or debate 327
47. Table 327
48. Work of art 327
    a. Original work 327
    b. Reproduction of a work of art 327
49. Comic or cartoon 327
    a. Cartoon or comic strip 328
    b. Comic book or graphic novel 328
50. Map or chart 328
51. Advertisement 328

Miscellaneous Sources—Printed and Electronic

52. Government document 328
    a. Printed 329
    b. Online 329
53. Legal source 329
54. Letter (published) 329
    a. Single letter 329
    b. Collection of letters 330
55. Interview 330
56. Personal correspondence 330
    a. Letter 330
    b. E-mail 330
    c. Memorandum 330
    d. Instant message (IM) 330
57. Diary or journal 330
    a. Single entry, published 330
    b. Single entry, unpublished 331
    c. Diary or journal, published 331

publication from *Print* to *Web*. Also, add the date (day, month, and year) on which you accessed the work.

Wharton, Edith. *The Age of Innocence*. New York: D. Appleton, 1920.
Bartleby.com. Web. 5 July 2007.
  [database]   [date accessed]
        [medium]

c. E-book The citation for an electronic version of a book is the same as for a printed book except that the medium of publication changes from *Print* to the

MLA Works-Cited Entries

1. One author
2. Two or three authors
3. More than three authors

specific type of e-book file you read: Nook file, Microsoft Reader file, Kindle file, and so on.

> Morrison, Toni. *Home*. New York: Knopf, 2012. Kindle file.
> [medium: Kindle file]

2. Two or three authors List authors in the order in which they appear on the title page. Only the first author should be listed with surname first.

> Miller, Brenda, and Suzanne Paola. *Tell It Slant*. New York: McGraw-Hill, 2004. Print.
> [author 1: Miller, Brenda; author 2: Suzanne Paola]

> Fullagar, Simone, Kevin W. Markwell, and Erica Wilson. *Slow Tourism: Experiences and Mobilities*. Bristol: Multilingual Matters, 2012. Print.
> [author 1: Fullagar, Simone; author 2: Kevin W. Markwell; author 3: Erica Wilson]

> **More about**
> *et al.*, 153
>
> Example 3, 294

3. More than three authors Either list all the authors, or just list the first and add *et al*. Whichever you choose, do the same in your in-text citation.

> Visonà, Monica Blackmun, Robin Poynor, Herbert M. Cole, Michael D. Harris, Rowland Abiodun, and Suzanne Preston Blier. *A History of Art in Africa*. New York: Abrams, 2001. Print.

> Visonà, Monica Blackmun, et al. *A History of Art in Africa*. New York: Abrams, 2001. Print.

> **MLA Works-Cited Entries**
>
> 1. One author
> 2. Two or three authors
> 3. More than three authors
> 4. Unnamed (anonymous) authors
> 5. Author using a pen name
> 6. Two or more works by the same author

4. Unnamed (anonymous) author Start the entry with the title.

> *Terrorist Hunter: The Extraordinary Story of a Woman Who Went Undercover to Infiltrate the Radical Islamic Groups Operating in America*. New York: Ecco-HarperCollins, 2003. Print.
> [title]

Alphabetize the entry in your list of works cited using the first significant word of the title (not an article like *a*, *an*, or *the*). Only if the author is listed specifically as "Anonymous" should you use that designation in the works-cited entry (and in your text).

> Anonymous. *Go Ask Alice*. Englewood Cliffs: Prentice, 1971. Print.

5. **Author using a pen name (pseudonym)** If the author is using a pen name (or *pseudonym*), document the source using the author's pen name and insert the author's actual name in brackets following the pseudonym.

> Keene, Carolyn [Edward Stratemeyer]. *The Secret of the Old Clock.* New York:
>
> Grosset, 1930. Print.

6. **Two or more works by the same author** Alphabetize the entries by the first important word in each title. Supply the author's name only with the first entry. For subsequent works, replace the author's name with three hyphens.

> Lethem, Jonathan. *The Ecstasy of Influence: Nonfictions, Etc.* New York:
>
> Doubleday, 2011. Print.
>
> ---. *Gun, with Occasional Music.* Philadelphia: Harvest, 2003. Print.

7. **Group or corporate author** Treat the sponsoring organization as the author.

> corporate author
> Blackfoot Gallery Committee. *The Story of the Blackfoot People:*
>
> *Nitsitapiisinni.* Richmond Hill: Firefly, 2002. Print.

8. **Edited book or anthology (printed or online)** When citing the book as a whole, treat the editor as the author and insert the abbreviation *ed.* (or *eds.* if there is more than one editor) after the name.

> Furman, Laura, ed. *The O. Henry Prize Stories: The Best Stories of the Year.*
>
> New York: Anchor, 2011. Print.
>
> Delbanco, Nicholas, and Alan Cheuse, eds. *Literature: Craft and Voice.* New
>
> York: McGraw-Hill, 2009. Print.

9. **Author and editor or translator** List the author first. After the title, include the abbreviation *Ed.* or *Trans.* (as appropriate) before the editor's or translator's name. If the book was accessed online, add the information shown in item 1b–c.

> Larsson, Asa. *Sun Storm.* Trans. Marlaine Delargy. New York: Delacorte, 2006.
>
> Print.

MLA Works-Cited Entries

3. More than three authors
4. Unnamed (anonymous) authors
5. Author using a pen name
6. Two or more works by the same author
7. Group or corporate author
8. Edited book or anthology
9. Author and editor or translator
10. One or more selections from an edited book or anthology
11. Edition other than the first

MLA Works-Cited Entries

8. Edited book or anthology
9. Author and editor or translator
10. **One or more selections from an edited book or anthology**
11. Edition other than the first
12. Imprint (division) of a larger publishing company

> Example 8, 309

> Example 24 a–c, 315–16

NOTE When the abbreviation appears before the editor's or translator's name, it means *edited by* or *translated by,* so use the same abbreviation regardless of whether there is one editor or translator or many. When the abbreviation *ed.* appears after the name, it means *editor,* so add an *-s* (*eds.*) if more than one editor is listed. The abbreviation *trans.* does not change.

---

10. One or more selections from an edited book or anthology (printed or online) If you are citing a selection from an edited book or anthology, start the entry with the selection's author and title. Include the page numbers for the entire selection (even if you used only part).

author   title (selection)
Faulkner, William. "A Rose for Emily." Literature: Reading Fiction, Poetry, and Drama. Ed. Robert DiYanni. 6th ed. New York: McGraw-Hill, 2009.
pages (selection)
79-84. Print.

When documenting a longer work, such as a novel or a play, that is included in the anthology or collection, italicize the work's title.

title (selection)
Ives, David. *Sure Thing.* Literature: Reading Fiction, Poetry, and Drama. . . .

If you are citing more than one selection in the anthology or collection, include an entry for the collection as a whole.

DiYanni, Robert D., ed. *Literature: Reading Fiction, Poetry, and Drama.* 6th ed. New York: McGraw-Hill, 2009. Print.

Then, for each selection you use from the anthology, include only the author and title of the selection, the surname of the anthology's editor, and the page numbers of the selection.

Faulkner, William. "A Rose for Emily." DiYanni 79-84.

For a scholarly article included in an edited book, include the article's original publication information first, the abbreviation *Rpt. in* for *reprinted in,* and then the publication information for the anthology.

original publication info.
Stock, A. G. "Yeats and Achebe." *Journal of Commonwealth Literature*
reprint publication info.
5.3 (1970): 105-11. Rpt. in *Things Fall Apart.* By Chinua Achebe.
Ed. Francis Abiola Irele. New York: Norton, 2008. 271-77. Print.

If the book was accessed online, add the information shown in item 1b–c.

11. Edition other than the first Insert the edition number (*2nd ed., 3rd ed.*) or edition name (*Rev. ed.* for "revised edition") before the publication information. The edition number or name should appear on the title page.

> Feather, John. *The Information Society: A Study of Continuity and Change.* 5th ed. London: Facet, 2008. Print.

12. Imprint (division) of a larger publishing company Name both the imprint and the publisher, separating them with a hyphen.

> Betcherman, Lita-Rose. *Court Lady and Country Wife: Two Noble Sisters in Seventeenth-Century England.* New York: William Morrow-HarperCollins, 2005. Print.

(imprint: William Morrow; publisher: HarperCollins)

13. Introduction, preface, foreword, or afterword Begin with the name of the person who wrote this section of the text. Then provide a descriptive label (such as *Introduction* or *Preface*), the title of the book, and the name of the book's author. (If the author of the section and the book are the same, use only the author's surname after the title.) Include the page numbers for the section.

> Camuto, Christopher. Introduction. *The Shenandoah.* By Julia Davis. Morgantown: West Virginia UP, 2011. 7-30. Print.

(author of intro. | label | title of book | author of book | pages (intro.))

If this section has a title, include it before the descriptive label.

> Burton, Larry W. "Countering the Naysayers: Independent Writing Programs as Successful Experiments in American Education." Afterword. *A Field of Dreams: Independent Writing Programs and the Future of Composition Studies.* Ed. Peggy O'Neill, Angela Crow, and Larry W. Burton. Logan: Utah State UP, 2002. 295-300. Print.

14. Entry in a reference work Format an entry in a dictionary or encyclopedia as you would a selection from an edited book or anthology. For signed articles, include the author's name. (Articles in reference works often carry the author's

---

MLA Works-Cited Entries

9. Author and editor or translator
10. One or more selections from an edited book or anthology
11. Edition other than the first
12. Imprint (division) of a larger publishing company
13. Introduction, preface, foreword, or afterword
14. Entry in a reference work
15. Multivolume work
16. Book in a series

MLA Works-Cited Entries

12. Imprint (division) of a larger publishing company
13. Introduction, preface, foreword, or afterword
14. **Entry in a reference work**
15. **Multivolume work**
16. Book in a series
17. Republished book

initials only, so you may need to cross-reference the initials with a list of contributors in the front or back of the book.) If an article is unsigned, begin with its title.

a. Printed For familiar reference works, omit publication information other than the edition, year of publication, and medium. If the entries are arranged alphabetically, omit a page reference.

"Culture." *Oxford English Dictionary.* Compact 2nd ed. 1991. Print.

Green, Michael. "Cultural Studies." *A Dictionary of Cultural and Critical Theory.* Cambridge: Blackwell, 1996. Print.

b. Online For online reference works, add the site's sponsor, change the medium of publication to *Web,* and add the date you accessed the site.

"Culture." *Merriam-Webster Online Dictionary.* Merriam-Webster Online [sponsor], 2008. Web [medium]. 3 Mar. 2012 [access date].

c. CD-ROM or DVD-ROM Although CD-ROMs have largely been replaced by the Internet, you may still need to use them. If the CD-ROM or DVD-ROM is published in versions rather than editions, use the abbreviation *Vers.* and include the version number before the publication information. Change the medium of publication to *CD-ROM* or *DVD-ROM.*

Cooley, Marianne. "Alphabet." *World Book Multimedia Encyclopedia.* Vers. 6.0.2 [version]. Chicago: World Book, 2002. CD-ROM [medium].

15. Multivolume work

> Example 10, 297

a. Multiple volumes Indicate the total number of volumes, followed by the abbreviation *vols.,* and indicate the span of years in which the volumes were published. Specify the volume from which you borrowed a particular passage or idea in your in-text citation.

Tarbell, Ida M. *The Life of Abraham Lincoln.* 2 vols [no. of vols]. New York: Lincoln Memorial Assn., 1895-1900 [pub. dates]. Print.

b. One volume If you used only one volume, include the number of the volume you used before the publication information, and give only the publication date of that volume.

                                                        vol. used

Tarbell, Ida M. *The Life of Abraham Lincoln.* Vol. 1. New York: Lincoln
                            pub. date
    Memorial Assn., 1895. Print.

16. Book in a series If the book you are citing is part of a series, the series title will usually be noted on the book's title page or on the page before the title page. Insert the series title (with no quotation marks or italics) after the medium of publication. If books in the series are numbered, include the number following the series title.

Todorov, Tzvetan. *Mikhail Bakhtin: The Dialogical Principle.* Trans. Wlad
                                                                   series title
    Godzich. Minneapolis: U of Minnesota P, 1995. Print. Theory and
                    no.
    Hist. of Lit. 13.

17. Republished book If a book has been republished, its original date of publication will appear on the book's copyright page. If the original publication date may be of interest to your readers, include it before publication information for the version you consulted. If the book was edited or an introduction was added, include that information before the republication information.

                                orig.
                            pub. date   *editors*
Burroughs, William S. *Naked Lunch.* 1959. Ed. James Grauerholz and
                repub. info.
    Barry Miles. New York: Grove, 2001. Print.

18. Title within a title Omit italics from any title that would normally be italicized when it falls within the main title of a book.

                        book title   *title within title*
Blamires, Harry. *The New Bloomsbury Book: A Guide Through* Ulysses.
    3rd ed. London: Routledge, 2006. Print.

If the title within the title would normally appear in quotation marks, retain the quotation marks and italicize both titles.

19. Sacred text Italicize the title of the edition you are using. Editors' and translators' names follow the title.

MLA Works-Cited Entries

14. Entry in a reference work
15. Multivolume work
16. Book in a series
17. Republished book
18. Title within a title
19. Sacred text
20. Missing publication information
21. Pamphlet, brochure, or press release

MLA Works-Cited Entries

18. Title within a title
19. Sacred text
20. Missing publication information
21. Pamphlet, brochure, or press release
22. Conference proceedings
23. Dissertation
24. Article in a scholarly journal
25. Article in a magazine

> Example 1, 305

> Example 46, 327

The New Oxford Annotated Bible. Ed. Michael D. Coogan, Marc Z. Brettler, Carol A. Newsom, and Pheme Perkins. Augmented 3rd ed. New York: Oxford UP, 2007. Print. Rev. Standard Vers. with Apocrypha.

The Holy Qur'an. Ed. and trans. Abdullah Yusuf Ali. 10th ed. Beltsville: Amana, 1997. Print.

20. Missing publication information Replace missing information with an appropriate abbreviation, such as *n.d.* for *no date* or *n.p.* for *no publisher* or *no place of publication*. (The letter *n* is capitalized following a period and lowercased after a comma.)

Barrett, Edgar, ed. *Football West Virginia 1960.* N.p.: West Virginia University, n.d. Print.

21. Pamphlet, brochure, or press release Follow the format for book entries. For a press release, include day, month, and year of publication, if available.

"Family Teams Key to March for Babies." Fargo: March of Dimes, 17 Jan. 2008. Print.

If the item was e-mailed or published online, document it as you would a book published online.

22. Conference proceedings Include the title of the conference, the sponsoring organization (if its name is not cited in the conference title), and the date and location of the conference, if that information is not already included in the publication's title.

Bizzell, Patricia, ed. *Proceedings of the Rhetoric Society of America:* [sponsor] *Rhetorical Agendas: Political, Ethical, Spiritual.* 28–31 May 2004, [title (conference)] [date] U of Texas—Austin. Mahwah, NJ: Erlbaum, 2005. Print. [location]

For a paper delivered at a conference, follow the format for a lecture.

23. Dissertation Include the abbreviation *Diss.*, the school to which the dissertation was submitted (abbreviate *University* to *U*), and the year it was submitted. For published dissertations, italicize the title.

Agopsowicz, William Joseph. *In Praise of Fantasy: A Study of the Nineteenth Century American Short Story (Poe, Hawthorne, Irving, Melville, Bierce, James)*. Diss. Arizona State U, 1992. Ann Arbor: UMI, 1992. Print.

For unpublished dissertations, put the title in quotation marks.

Brommer, Stephanie. "We Walk with Them: South Asian Women's Organizations in Northern California Confront Domestic Abuse." Diss. U of California—Santa Barbara, 2004. Print.

> **MLA Works-Cited Entries**
>
> 22. Conference proceedings
> 23. Dissertation
> **24. Article in a scholarly journal**
> 25. Article in a magazine
> 26. Article in a newspaper

Periodicals—Printed and Electronic

A periodical is a publication issued at regular intervals—newspapers are typically published every day, magazines every week or month, and scholarly journals four times a year. Most researchers today find articles in periodicals by searching their library's **databases,** online indexes that provide citation information as well as an abstract (or summary) and sometimes an electronic copy of the article itself, in either PDF or HTML format. (A PDF file shows the article more or less as it would have appeared in print; an HTML file includes the text of the article but not the illustrations or formatting of the print version.) For all periodicals, include not only the title of the article (in quotation marks) but also the title of the periodical (in italics). The other publication information you include depends on the type of periodical you are documenting.

24. Article in a scholarly journal The information you need to create an entry for a printed journal article is on the cover or in the table of contents of the journal and on the first and last page of the article. For articles downloaded from a database, the information you need appears on the screen listing the articles that fit your search terms, on the first and last page of the file you download, or in the full record for the article you select. For articles that appear in journals published solely online, you may find the information you need on the website's home page, in the journal's table of contents, or on the first screen of the article. Access dates for database and online articles should come from your notes.

> Annotated visual of where to find author, title, publication, and other information, on foldout accompanying this chapter

a. Printed The basic entry for an article in a printed journal looks like this:

Surname, First name. "Article Title." *Journal Title* volume.issue (year): pages. Medium of publication.

MLA Works-Cited Entries

22. Conference proceedings
23. Dissertation
24. **Article in a scholarly journal**
25. **Article in a magazine**
26. Article in a newspaper
27. Article on microform

Here is an example of an actual entry:

author — Weaver, Karen. *article title* — "A Game Change: Paying for Big-Time College Sports."
journal title — *Change* *issue* 43.1 *year* (2011): *pages* 14-21. *medium* Print.
vol.

b. Accessed through a database When you document an article from a scholarly journal that you accessed through an online database, add the name of the database (in italics), change the medium of publication to *Web*, and add the date (day, month, year) on which you accessed the work at the end of the entry.

Weaver, Karen. "A Game Change: Paying for Big-TIme College Sports." *Change* 43.1 (2011): 14-21. *database* — *EBSCOhost Education Research Complete*. *medium* Web. *access date* 3 Mar. 2010.

c. Online To document an online journal article, follow the model for a printed journal article, change the medium to *Web*, and add the date on which you accessed the article at the end of the entry. Although many journals that are published only online do not provide all the information that is available for printed journals, your entry should include as much of that information as possible. If the article you are documenting omits page numbers, use *n. pag.* in their place. Include the article's URL only if readers will not be able to find the article by searching for the author or title. (The parts that are different from a printed journal article are highlighted.)

Woolums, Viola. "Gendered Avatar Identity." *Kairos* 16.1 (2011): n. pag. *medium* Web. *access date* 3 Jan. 2012.

25. **Article in a magazine (weekly, monthly)**

a. Printed Provide the issue's publication date (month and year or day, month, and year) and the page range for the article, but not the magazine's volume or issue number, even when they are available.

Fuller, Alexandra. "Her Heart Inform Her Tongue: Language Lost and Found." *Harper's* *pub. date* Jan. 2012: *pgs.* 60-64. Print.

Collins, Lauren. "The King's Meal." *New Yorker* 21 Nov. 2011: 66–71. Print.

If the article appears on nonconsecutive pages (the first part appears on p. 2 but the rest of the article is continued on p. 10), include a plus sign after the first page number (*2+*).

b. Accessed through a database

> Fuller, Alexandra. "Her Heart Inform Her Tongue: Language Lost and Found." *Harper's* Jan. 2012: 60-64. [database] WilsonWeb. [medium] Web. [access date] 13 Apr. 2012.

c. Online If you are documenting the online edition of a magazine that also appears in print, use the site name (usually a variation on the print title, such as *Progressive.org* or *Vanity Fair Online*).

> Carr, Nicholas. "Is Google Making Us Stupid?" *The Atlantic.com*. [website] Atlantic Monthly Group, [site sponsor] July/Aug. 2008. Web. 2 Dec. 2008.

> Stevenson, Seth. "Ads We Hate." *Slate.com*. [website] WashingtonPost.Newsweek [site sponsor] Interactive, 28 Dec. 2009. Web. 3 Mar. 2010.

26. Article in a newspaper The information you need to create an entry for a printed newspaper article is on the masthead of the newspaper (at the top of the first page) and on the first and last page of the article. For newspaper articles downloaded from a database, the information you need appears on the screen listing the articles that fit your search terms or on the first and last page of the article itself. Articles that appear in online versions of the newspaper usually contain all the information you need at the top of the first screen. Use conventional capitalization of titles even when your original source does not.

a. Printed For an article in a daily newspaper, include the date (day, month, year). If the paper paginates sections separately, include the section number, letter, or name immediately before the page number.

> Richtel, Matt, and Julie Bosman. "To Serve the Young, E-Book Fans Prefer Print." *New York Times* [date] 21 Nov. 2011: [sec. & pg.] B1. Print.

If the section number or letter is not part of the page number, add the abbreviation *sec.* and the section name, number, or letter. If the section is named, add the section name before the abbreviation *sec.* If no author is listed, begin

---

Documentation Matters • Preparing an MLA-Style List of Works Cited **18b**

MLA Works-Cited Entries

23. Dissertation
24. Article in a scholarly journal
25. **Article in a magazine**
26. **Article in a newspaper**
27. Article on microform
28. Review (printed or online)

> Annotated visual of where to find author, title, publication, and other information, on foldout accompanying this chapter

> **More about**
> Title capitalization, 810–11

MLA Works-Cited Entries

24. Article in a scholarly journal
25. Article in a magazine
26. **Article in a newspaper**
27. **Article on microform**
28. Review
29. Editorial

> Example 24a, 315
> Example 25a, 316
> Example 26a, 317

the entry with the title of the article. If the article continues on a nonconsecutive page, add a plus sign after the first page number (*A20+*). If the newspaper's masthead specifies an edition (such as late edition or national edition), include that information after the date.

> Keller, Julia. "Viral Villainy." *Chicago Tribune* 22 Mar. 2009, final ed., sec. 6: [section / edition]
> 1+. Print. [nonconsecutive pg.]

If the name of the city in which the newspaper is published does not appear in the newspaper's title, include it in brackets after the title.

> Willman, David. "NIH Calls Actions of Senior Researcher 'Serious
> Misconduct.'" *Plain Dealer* [Cleveland] 10 Sept. 2006: A15. Print. [newspaper / city]

For well-known national newspapers (such as the *Christian Science Monitor,* *USA Today,* and the *Wall Street Journal*), no city or state is needed. If you are unsure whether the newspaper is well known, consult your instructor or a reference librarian.

b. Accessed through a database For a newspaper article accessed through a database, add the database name, change the medium to *Web,* and add the access date.

> Richtel, Matt, and Julie Bosman. "To Serve the Young, E-Book Fans
> Prefer Print." *New York Times* 21 Nov. 2011: B1. Factiva. Web. [database / medium]
> 2 Feb. 2012. [access date]

c. Online For an online newspaper article, provide the site name and sponsor, and include your date of access.

> Do not italicize a sponsor's name unless the sponsor is itself a publication.

> Netburn, Deborah. "Theaters Set Aside Tweet Seats for Twitter Users."
> LATimes.com. *Los Angeles Times,* 6 Dec. 2011. Web. 23 Jan. 2012. [website / sponsor / access date]

27. Article on microform Many libraries still store some back issues of periodicals on microform, a photograph of a periodical printed on plastic and viewed through a special microform reader. Your entry for an article on microform is the same as for a printed article.

If your source is preserved on microform in a reference source such as NewsBank, change the medium of publication to *Microform* and add the title of the reference source and any access numbers (such as fiche and grid numbers) following the medium of publication.

28. Review (printed or online) Begin with the reviewer's name (if provided), followed by the title of the review (if any) and the label *Rev. of* (for *Review of*). Then include the title and author of the work being reviewed. Finally, include the title of the periodical and its publication information. If the review was accessed online, add information as shown in item 24b–c, 25b–c, or 26b–c.

> Example 24a–c, 315–16
> Example 25a–c, 316–17
> Example 26a–c, 317–18

<pre>
   reviewer   title (review)   title (book)
Grover, Jan. "Unreliable Narrator." Rev. of Love Works Like This: Opening
                                    author
     One's Life to a Child, by Lauren Slater. Women's Review of Books
     19.10-11 (2002): 40. Print.
</pre>

29. Editorial (printed or online) Often editorials are unsigned. When that is the case, begin with the title of the editorial (if any). Then insert the label *Editorial* and follow with the periodical's publication information.

<pre>
                       editorial title
"Expanding the Horizon: OSU President Seeks to Give Students a New
                                     label
     View of Their Place in the World." Editorial. Columbus [OH] Dispatch
     12 Mar. 2009: 8A. Print.
</pre>

If the editorial was accessed online, add information as shown in item 24b–c, 25b–c, or 26b–c.

30. Letter to the editor (printed or online) Begin with the author's name, followed by the label *Letter* and the periodical's publication information.

<pre>
 letter author   label
Park, John. Letter. Time 5 Dec. 2011: 9. Print.
</pre>

If the letter to the editor has a title, add it (in quotation marks) after the author's name. If the letter to the editor was accessed online, add information as shown in item 24b–c, 25b–c, or 26b–c.

Other Electronic Sources

While it is usually easy to find the information you need to create a complete entry for a book or an article in a periodical, websites can be a bit trickier. Most of the information you need will appear on the site's home page, usually

> **MLA Works-Cited Entries**
>
> 26. Article in a newspaper
> 27. Article on microform
> **28. Review**
> **29. Editorial**
> **30. Letter to the editor**
> 31. Website
> 32. Web page or short work on a website

> Example 24a–c, 315–16
> Example 25a–c, 316–17
> Example 26a–c, 317–18

> Annotated visual of where to find author, title, and publication information, on foldout accompanying this chapter

MLA Works-Cited Entries

29. Editorial
30. Letter to the editor
31. **Website**
32. **Web page or short work on a website**
33. **Home page (academic)**
34. Discussion list posting
35. Article on a wiki

at the bottom or top of the page, or on the web page you are documenting. Sometimes you may need to look further: Click on links such as "About us" or "More information." Frequently, websites do not provide complete information, so include as much as you can.

31. Website The basic entry for a website looks like this:

> Author's surname, First name. *Website title.* Site sponsor, Publication date or date last updated. Medium. Access date.

Here is an example of an actual entry:

> McGann, Jerome J., ed. [editor] *The Complete Writings and Pictures of Dante Gabriel Rossetti: A Hypermedia Archive.* [title (website)] Institute for Advanced Technology in the Humanities, U of Virginia, and Networked Infrastructure for [site sponsors] Nineteenth-Century Electronic Scholarship, 2008. [update] Web. [medium] 15 Feb. 2012. [access date]

If no author or editor is listed, begin with the website's title.

32. Web page or short work on a website Add the title of the web page to the entry for a website.

> Bahri, Deepika. "Yehuda Amichai." [page title] *Postcolonial Studies.* Dept. of English, Emory U, 13 Nov. 2002. Web. 17 Feb. 2012.

Personal websites often do not provide all the information needed to create a complete entry. If the site does not have a title, include the identifier "home page" or "website" in its place; if the title includes the author's name, do not restate it.

33. Home page (academic)

a. Course

> Gray, David. [instructor] "Introduction to Ethics." [title (course)] *Dept. of Philosophy.* [title (website)] Carnegie [site sponsor] Mellon U, Spring 2006. Web. [medium] 17 Apr. 2007. [access date]

b. Department

English Dept. Home page. *U of California—Santa Barbara.* UCSB, 2010.

Web. 20 July 2010.

34. Discussion list posting Treat the subject line (or *thread*) as the title, and include the name of the list, the sponsoring group, and the date of the posting.

Rendleman, Eliot. "Binge Writing and Moderation Writing." *Writing Program Administration Discussion List.* WPA, 21 Aug. 2011. Web. 27 Sept. 2012.

35. Article on a wiki Since wikis are written and edited collaboratively, there is no author to cite. Instead, begin the entry with the article title.

"Harry Potter—Is It Worth the Hype?" *ChildLitWiki.* 21 July 2007. Web. 12 Dec. 2011.

36. Blog

a. Blog

Ebert, Roger. *Roger Ebert's Journal. Chicago Sun-Times,* 2012. Web. 12 June 2011.

b. Blog posting

Luther, Jason. "Our Failed Writing Center: A Response." *Taxomania!,* 11 Nov. 2011. Web. 30 Nov. 2011.

c. Comment on a blog posting

Danderson, Mark. "Some Tough Love for Authors." *The Scholarly Kitchen.* Society for Scholarly Publishing, 25 Oct. 2011. Web. 19 Mar. 2012.

If the comment's author uses a screen name, use that; if the actual name is available and of interest to readers, provide that as well, following the screen name, in square brackets.

MLA Works-Cited Entries

31. Website
32. Web page or short work on a website
33. Home page (academic)
34. Discussion list posting
35. Article on a wiki
36. Blog
37. Avatar
38. Source published in more than one medium

Do not italicize a sponsor's name unless the sponsor is itself a publication.

MLA Works-Cited Entries

35. Article on a wiki
36. Blog
37. Avatar
38. Source published in more than one medium
39. Computer software
40. Video game
41. Motion picture
42. Television or radio broadcast

37. Avatar If the author/speaker uses an avatar with a different name than the writer's actual name, use the avatar's name, but if the writer's actual name is available and of interest to readers (it may lend credibility, for example), provide it in square brackets following the avatar name.

<u>avatar</u> <u>actual name</u>
Reuters, Eric [Eric Krangel]. "*Second Life* on *The Daily Show*." *Second Life News Center/Reuters*. Second Life, 8 Apr. 2007. Web. 10 Feb. 2008.

38. Source published in more than one medium Some sources may include multiple media. For example, a printed book may come with a supplementary website or CD-ROM. In the entry in your list of works cited, follow the entry format for the part of the source that you mainly used, but list all the media you consulted in alphabetical order.

Davis, Robert L., H. Jay Siskin, and Alicia Ramos. *Entrevistas: An Introduction to Language and Culture*. 2nd ed. New York: McGraw-Hill, 2005.
<u>list of media</u>
Print, website.

39. Computer software

<u>title</u> <u>vendor</u> <u>release date</u> <u>download date</u>
PowerResearcher. Atlanta: Uniting Networks, 2004. 8 June 2004.

40. Video game

<u>game</u> <u>publisher</u>
Rock Band 2. Wii. Nintendo, 2008.
<u>platform</u> <u>release date</u>

Audio and Visual Sources

The information you need to create an entry for most audio and visual sources will appear on the cover, label, or program of the work or in the credits at the end of a film. The person you list in the "author" position—the director, performer, artist, or composer—will vary depending on what you have emphasized in your research project. If you are writing about a director's body of work, put the director's name first; if you are writing about a performance, put the performer's name first. If it is the work itself that you are writing about, put the title of the work first. (This decision should be mirrored in your in-text citation.) However you choose to organize the entry, indicate the role of those whom you list, using abbreviations such as *perf.* (*performer*), *dir.* (*director*), and *cond.* (*conductor*).

As with any other entry, italicize the titles of complete or longer works (such as albums, films, operas, and original works of art) and place quotation marks around the titles of shorter works or works published as part of a larger whole (such as songs on a CD or a single episode of a television show). Publication information includes the name of the distributor, production company, or network, as well as the date on which the audio or visual was created, recorded, or broadcast. The medium will be *Film, DVD, Television, Radio, Podcast*—however you accessed the work. If you found the audio or visual source online, also include the date on which you last accessed it.

> **MLA Works-Cited Entries**
>
> 39. Computer software
> 40. Video game
> **41. Motion picture**
> 42. Television or radio broadcast
> 43. Musical or other audio recording

41. Motion picture
a. Film

    title   *director*   *release distributor date medium*
Good Deeds. Dir. Tyler Perry. Lionsgate, 2012. Film.

If other artists besides the director are relevant to your project, list them between the director and the distributor.

                                performers
Good Deeds. Dir. Tyler Perry. Perf. Tyler Perry and Thandie Newton.

    Lionsgate, 2012. Film.

If your project stresses the director, performer, or other contributor, place that information at the beginning of the citation.

Perry, Tyler, dir. *Good Deeds.* Perf. Tyler Perry and Thandie Newton. Lionsgate,

    2012. Film.

b. Video or DVD Include the original release date, when relevant, before the distributor, and include the medium you viewed.

The Lady Eve. Dir. Preston Sturges. Perf. Barbara Stanwyck and Henry

           orig. release   *distributor*   *medium*
    Fonda. 1941. Universal Home Entertainment, 2006. DVD.

MLA Works-Cited Entries

39. Computer software
40. Video game
41. **Motion picture**
42. **Television or radio broadcast**
43. Musical or other audio recording
44. Live performance

c. Internet download Include the date on which you accessed the film.

> *Juno.* Screenplay by Diablo Cody. Dir. Jason Reitman. Perf. Ellen Page, Michael Cera, Jennifer Garner, Jason Bateman. Fox Searchlight, 2007. iTunes, 2008. Internet download. 19 Jan. 2012. *(access date)*

d. Online video clip Cite a video clip on YouTube or a similar site as you would a web page.

> Ok Go. "This Too Shall Pass—Rube Goldberg Machine Version." *YouTube.* YouTube, 2 Mar. 2010. Web. 4 Mar. 2012.
> *(performer) (video clip title) (website) (site sponsor) (medium) (date posted) (date accessed)*

e. DVD extras Add the title of the extra (in quotation marks).

> "The Making of *Winter's Bone*." *(DVD extra)* *Winter's Bone.* Dir. Debra Granik. Perf. Jennifer Lawrence and John Hawkes. 2010. Lionsgate, 2010. DVD.

42. Television or radio broadcast In most cases, begin with the title of the series or episode. Follow that with a list of the relevant contributors and information about the local station that broadcast the program (omit for cable). Because the director may change from episode to episode, other contributors, such as the creator or producer, may be more relevant. Include the date of the program and the medium in which you accessed it. If your project emphasizes an individual, begin with that person's name. Add any supplementary information at the end of the entry.

a. Series

> *The Office.* *(series title)* Creat. and exec. prod. Greg Daniels, Ricky Gervais, and Stephen Merchant. Perf. Steve Carell, Rainn Wilson, John Krasinski, and Jenna Fischer. NBC. *(network)* WNBC, New York, *(city of local station)* 24 Mar. 2005–20 May 2010. *(broadcast dates)* Television. *(call letters) (medium)*

> *Bridging the Morphine Gap.* Host Mukti Jain Campion. BBC. Radio 4, London, 3 Mar. 2008. Radio.

b. Episode

"In Buddy's Eyes." Internet download, television. *Desperate Housewives*.

    Perf. Teri Hatcher, Felicity Huffman, Marcia Cross, Eva Longoria,

    and Nicollette Sheridan. ABC. KNXV, Phoenix, 20 Apr. 2008.
supplementary info.
    iTunes, 2008. 5 Jan. 2013.

c. Single program

Persuasion. By Jane Austen. Adapt. Simon Burke. Perf. Julia Davis and Rupert

    Penry-Jones. PBS. WGBH, Boston, 13 Jan. 2008. Television.

d. Podcast For a podcast, replace the original medium of publication with the word *Podcast,* and add the date on which you accessed the file.

"The Giant Pool of Money." Narr. Ira Glass. *This American Life*. Natl. Public

    medium   *access date*
    Radio. WBEZ, Chicago, 27 Sept. 2008. Podcast. 3 Oct. 2008.

43. Musical or other audio recording

Begin with whichever part of the entry is more relevant to your project—the name of the composer or performer, or the title of the CD or song. Place the title of shorter works, such as a song, in quotation marks. Italicize the titles of longer works, such as the title of an opera, but not the titles of symphonies identified only by form, number, and key, such as Brahms's Symphony no. 1.

a. CD, LP, audiobook

Adamo, Mark. *Little Women*. Perf. Stephanie Novacek, Chad Shelton,

    Margaret Lloyd, and Stacey Tappan. Houston Grand Opera. Cond.
    prod. co. & release date
    Patrick Summers. Ondine, 2001. CD.
                  medium

Brahms, Johannes. Symphony no. 1. Chicago Symphony Orchestra. Cond.

    Georg Solti. Decca, 1992. CD.

b. Song or selection from a CD or LP or a chapter from an audiobook

Los Campesinos. "My Year in Lists." *Hold on Now, Youngster. . . .* Arts & Crafts,

    2008. CD.

MLA Works-Cited Entries

40. Video game
41. Motion picture
42. **Television or radio broadcast**
43. **Musical or other audio recording**
44. Live performance
45. Musical composition

c. Compressed music file (MP3, MP4)

Los Campesinos. "My Year in Lists." *Hold on Now, Youngster.* . . . Arts & Crafts, 2008. Download. iTunes, 2008. MP3. 16 Dec. 2008.
— supplementary info: iTunes, 2008; download date: 16 Dec. 2008

d. Online sound file or clip

For a sound recording accessed online, combine the format for a web page with the format for a sound recording.

Chaucer, Geoffrey. "'The Miller's Tale': Nicholas Seduces Alisoun." Perf. Alfred David. *The Canterbury Tales.* "The Criyng and the Soun": The Chaucer Metapage Audio Files. VA Military Inst. Dept. of Eng. and Fine Arts, 2009. Web. 20 June 2012.

— author: Chaucer, Geoffrey; selection title: "'The Miller's Tale': Nicholas Seduces Alisoun."; title of work: *The Canterbury Tales*; website: "The Criyng and the Soun"; sponsor: The Chaucer Metapage Audio Files; date posted: 2009; date accessed: 20 June 2012; medium: Web

44. Live performance The entry for a performance is similar to that for a film. Instead of the distributor, year of release, and medium of publication, include the group (if any), the venue and city of the performance, the date of the performance you attended, and the label *Performance*. If your project emphasizes the composer, writer, or performer, begin the entry with that information. If the performance is untitled, include a descriptive label.

a. Ensemble

The Importance of Being Earnest. By Oscar Wilde. Dir. Jerry Chipman. Perf. Brian Everson, Stephen Garrett, and Bennett Wood. Theatre Memphis. Lohrey Stage, Memphis, TN. 27 Jan. 2012. Performance.

— group: Theatre Memphis; venue: Lohrey Stage; city: Memphis, TN; perf. date: 27 Jan. 2012

b. Individual

Hartig, Caroline. Clarinet recital. Brigham Young University. 18 Nov. 2011. Performance.

— performer: Hartig, Caroline; label: Clarinet recital

45. Musical composition To document a musical composition itself rather than a specific performance, recording, or published version of it, include only the composer and the title of the work (in italics unless the composition is identified only by form, number, and key).

Schumann, Robert. Symphony no. 1 in B-flat major, op. 38.

— composer: Schumann, Robert; untitled symphony: Symphony no. 1 in B-flat major, op. 38

MLA Works-Cited Entries

41. Motion picture
42. Television or radio broadcast
43. Musical or other audio recording
44. Live performance
45. Musical composition
46. Lecture, speech, or debate
47. Table

46. Lecture, speech, or debate Treat the speaker as the author; place the title in quotation marks (if there is one); and indicate the occasion and sponsoring organization (if relevant), location, date, and mode of delivery. If the lecture, speech, or debate is untitled, replace the title with a brief descriptive label.

> *speaker*   *title*   *sponsor*
> Capri, Frank. "The Peace Movement of the 1960s." 92nd Street Y,
>   *location*   *date*   *medium*
> New York. 14 Mar. 2010. Lecture.

47. Table For a table included in your project, place source information in a note below the table. For a table that you are discussing but that does not appear in your paper, include an entry in your list of works cited following the model below.

> *Example 18, 303*

> *author*   *title*   *label*   *website*
> United States. Senate. "Senate Salaries since 1789." Table. *US Senate.*
>   *sponsor*   *medium*
> US Senate, 7 June 2012. Web.

48. Work of art For a work of art included in your project, place source information in the figure caption. For a work that you discuss but that does not appear in your project, include an entry in your list of works cited following the models below.

> *Example 18, 303*

a. Original work

>   *date of*
> *artist*   *title*   *production*   *medium*
> Pollack, Jackson. *One (Number 31).* 1950. Acrylic on canvas.
>   *location*
> Museum of Mod. Art, New York.

b. Reproduction of a work of art

> Lichtenstein, Roy. *Whaam!* 1963. Tate Gallery, London. *Responding to Art:*
> *Form, Content, and Context.* By Robert Bersson. New York: McGraw-Hill,
> 2004. Print.

49. Comic or cartoon For a cartoon reproduced in your project, provide source information in the caption. For cartoons that you discuss without providing a copy of the image in your project, include an entry in your list of works cited following these models:

MLA Works-Cited Entries

44. Live performance
45. Musical composition
46. Lecture, speech, or debate
47. Table
48. Work of art
49. Comic or cartoon
50. Map or chart
51. Advertisement

a. Cartoon or comic strip

artist — *title* — *label* — *publication information*
Thaves, Bob. "Frank and Ernest." Comic strip. *Evening Sun* [Norwich, NY]
medium
9 Dec. 2011: 16. Print.

b. Comic book or graphic novel

authors — *title*
Pekar, Harvey, and Joyce Brabner, writers. *Our Cancer Year.* Illus. Frank
pub. info. — *medium*
Stack. Philadelphia: Running Press, 1994. Print.

> Example 18, 303

50. Map or chart For a map or chart reproduced in your project, provide source information in the caption. For a map or chart discussed but not included in your project, include an entry in your list of works cited following the model below.

"The Invasion of Sicily: Allied Advance to Messina (23 July-17 August
label
1943)." Map. *The West Point Atlas of American Wars.* Ed.

Vincent J. Esposito. Vol. 2. New York: Praeger, 1959. 247. Print.

MLA Works-Cited Entries

47. Table
48. Work of art
49. Comic or cartoon
50. Map or chart
51. Advertisement
52. Government document
53. Legal source
54. Letter (published)

51. Advertisement For an advertisement reproduced in your project, provide source information in the caption. For an advertisement discussed but not included in your project, include an entry in your list of works cited following the models below.

label
Earthlink Cable Internet. Advertisement. *Metro* 17 Apr. 2007: 11. Print.

date accessed
Infiniti. Advertisement. *Yahoo.com.* Web. 20 Apr. 2007.

Domino's Pizza. Advertisement. Comedy Central. Television.
date broadcast
2 Aug. 2006.

Miscellaneous Sources—Printed and Electronic

> Example 7, 309
> Example 19, 304

52. Government document If no author is listed, use the name of the governing nation and the government department and agency (if any) that produced the document, as you would for a work with a corporate author. Abbreviate Government Printing Office as *GPO*.

United States. War Department. *Advanced Map and Aerial Photograph*
    Reading. Washington, DC: GPO, 1941. Print.

[nation: United States.] [department: War Department.]

For congressional documents, include the number and session of Congress and the number and type of document. Common abbreviations in US government documents include the following:

Doc.	Document	**Rept.**	Report
GPO	Government Printing Office	**Res**	Resolution
HR	House of Representatives	**S**	Senate
		Sess.	Session

a. Printed

United States. Cong. House. *Combat Bonus Act.* 110th Cong., 2nd sess. HR
    6760. Washington, DC: GPO, 2008. Print.

b. Online

United States. Cong. House. *Combat Bonus Act.* 110th Cong., 2nd sess.
    HR 6760. *Thomas.gov.* Lib. of Cong., 31 July 2008. Web.
    16 May 2012.

[website: Thomas.gov.] [sponsor: Lib. of Cong.] [access date: 16 May 2012.]

53. Legal source

Gideon v. Wainwright. 372 US 335. Supreme Court of the US. 1963.
    FindLaw. Thomas Reuters, 2010. Web. 16 Dec. 2008.

[legal case: Gideon v. Wainwright.] [case number: 372 US 335.] [court: Supreme Court of the US.] [decision yr: 1963.]
[website: FindLaw.] [sponsor: Thomas Reuters,] [update: 2010.] [medium: Web.] [access date: 16 Dec. 2008.]

54. Letter (published)

a. Single letter Cite a single letter as you would a selection from an edited book or anthology but add the recipient's name, the date the letter was written, and the letter number (if there is one).

Brooks, Phillips. "To Agnes." 24 Sept. 1882. *Children's Letters: A Collection*
    of Letters Written to Children by Famous Men and Women. Ed. Elizabeth
    Colson and Anna Gansevoort Chittenden. New York: Hinds, 1905. 3-4.
    Print.

[author: Brooks, Phillips.] [recipient: "To Agnes."] [date written: 24 Sept. 1882.]

MLA Works-Cited Entries

50. Map or chart
51. Advertisement
52. **Government document**
53. **Legal source**
54. **Letter (published)**
55. Interview
56. Personal correspondence

> Example 10, 310

> Example 8, 309

b. Collection of letters Cite as you would an edited book or anthology.

> Examples 24–25, 315–17
> Example 42, 324

55. Interview Treat a published interview as you would an article in a periodical. Treat an interview broadcast on radio or television or podcasted as you would a broadcast. For an unpublished interview you conducted, include the name of the person interviewed, the label *Personal interview, Telephone interview,* or *E-mail interview,* and the date on which the interview took place.

person interviewed *label* *date*
Harberg, Amanda. Personal interview. 11 Feb. 2012.

56. Personal correspondence To document personal correspondence, such as a letter or e-mail message you received, include a descriptive label such as *Letter to the author* or *Message to the author,* as well as the medium (*MS* for "manuscript," *E-mail*).

a. Letter

letter writer *label* *date written*
Gould, Stephen Jay. Letter to the author. 13 Nov. 1986. MS.
medium

MLA Works-Cited Entries

52. Government document
53. Legal source
54. Letter (published)
55. Interview
56. Personal correspondence
57. Diary or journal

b. E-mail

e-mail author *subject line* *label*
Elbow, Peter. "Re: bibliography about resistance." Message to the author.
date sent *medium*
12 Apr. 2004. E-mail.

A mass e-mail or electronic memo should include a label describing recipients, such as *E-mail to ENG 204 students*.

c. Memorandum Very few institutions send out printed memos anymore, but if you need to document one, treat it as you would an e-mail message, replacing the word *e-mail* with the word *memo* at the end of your entry.

d. Instant message (IM)

Grimm, Laura. Message to the author. 14 June 2012. Instant message.

57. Diary or journal

> Example 10, 310

a. Single entry, published Treat an entry in a published diary or journal like an article in an edited book or anthology, but include a descriptive label (*Diary entry*) and the date of composition after the entry title.

b. Single entry, unpublished

author — Zook, Aaron. *title* — "Sketches for *Aesop's Foibles* (new musical)." *label* — Journal entry. *entry date* — 1 May 2007. *medium* — MS.

c. Diary or journal, published Treat a complete diary or journal as you would an edited book or anthology. ▸ Example 8, 309

18c Using MLA Style for Informational Notes

In addition to in-text citations, MLA style allows researchers to include informational notes to provide relevant, but potentially distracting, content or to provide bibliographic information about one or more sources. MLA style recommends using a list of endnotes at the end of the project. To identify informational notes in the text, include a superscript (above-the-line) arabic number that corresponds to the note number in the list of endnotes. Include an entry for each source in your list of works cited.

Beneath the crude humor of *Zap* and similar comics lay insightful commentary on society and its principles, which many readers found to be a refreshing change from mainstream superhero titles.[1] . . . Comics like Tomine's provide a subject or situation that readers can identify with more easily than, say, Superman's battles with Brainiac.[2]

Notes *Heading (centered), new page*

⟵½"⟶ 1. According to Schnakenberg, more than two million copies of *Zap* comics were in print by 1999.

2. For an intriguing argument that the world of classic comic book superheroes is not so different from our own—including a discussion of how comics before World War II commented on then current events—see Wright 1-28.

Use **content notes** to provide information that clarifies or justifies a point in your text, but avoid notes that include interesting digressions that could distract your readers. Lydia Nichols's essay at the end of this chapter includes a content note. You can also use content notes to acknowledge the contributions of others (tutors, classmates, and so on) to the preparation of your paper.

Bibliographic notes can add information about a source or point readers to other sources on the topic. If several sources provide the same information, cite the most valuable source in your text, and list the others in a bibliographic note. Then include the full citation of all these sources in your list of works cited.

18d Formatting a Paper in MLA Style

The care with which you cite and document your sources reflects the care you have taken in writing your research project. Continue that care by formatting your project in the way your readers expect. For most writing projects in literature and composition, follow the MLA's formatting guidelines.

1. Margins and spacing

> **Student Model**
> Research project, MLA style, 336–46

Set one-inch margins at the top, bottom, and sides of your paper. Double-space the entire paper, including long quotations, the list of works cited, and any endnotes. Indent the first line of each paragraph by half an inch, and do not add an extra space between paragraphs. Use a hanging indent for each entry in the list of works cited: The first line should be flush with the left margin with subsequent lines indented half an inch. (For more on creating a hanging indent in a word processing program, see the Tech box on the next page.)

> **More about**
> Choosing a typeface and type size, 165–66

2. Typeface

Choose a standard typeface, such as Times New Roman or Arial, in an easily readable size (usually 12 points).

Tech Creating a Header

Most word processing programs allow you to insert a header. In Microsoft Word, select "Header" from the Insert tab. Any information you type into the header space will then appear at the top of every page of your manuscript. You can also choose to insert page numbers to paginate your project automatically.

3. Header

MLA style requires that each page of your project include a header, consisting of your surname and the page number. Place the header in the upper right-hand corner, a half inch from the upper edge and one inch from the right edge of the page.

4. Identifying information

No title page is required in MLA style. Instead, include the following identifying information in the upper left-hand corner of the first page of your research project, one inch from the top and left edges of the paper:

- Your name
- Your instructor's name
- The number of the course in which you are submitting the paper
- The date

Tech • Indention

The major style guides (MLA, APA, *Chicago*, CSE) were initially written before the widespread use of personal computers, when most writers still worked on typewriters. To create a paragraph or hanging indention on a typewriter, the typist would hit the space bar five times or set a tab. Now, just about everyone creates writing projects on a computer, where paragraph and hanging indentions are created using the Ruler or Paragraph Dialog box.

Ruler

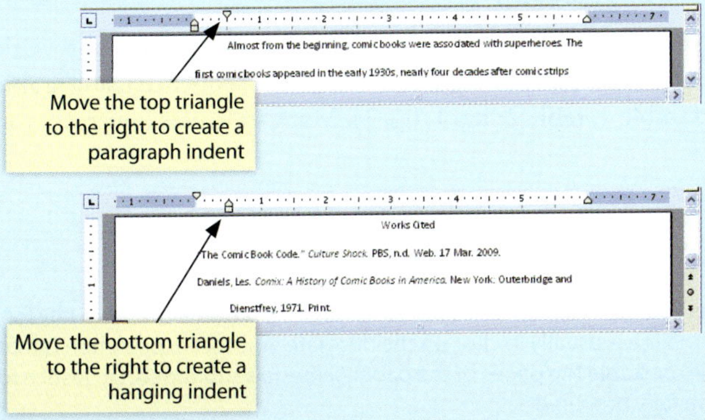

Move the top triangle to the right to create a paragraph indent

Move the bottom triangle to the right to create a hanging indent

Paragraph Dialog Box

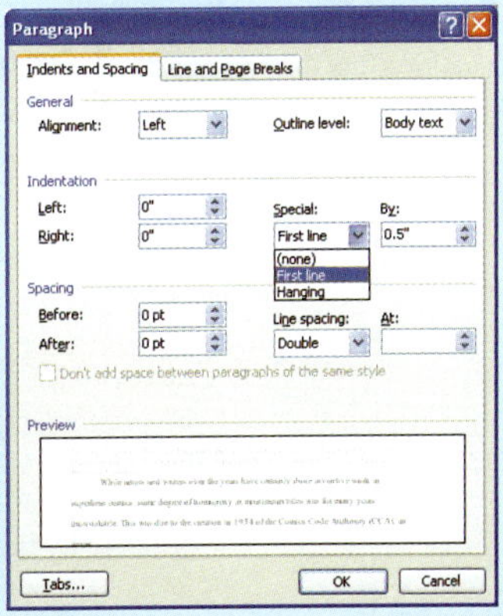

If your instructor requires a title page, ask for formatting instructions or follow the model on page 382.

5. Title

> **More about**
> Crafting a title, 86–87

Center the title of your project and insert it two lines below the date. Do not put quotation marks around your title or italicize it. Drop down two more lines before beginning to type the first paragraph of your research project.

6. Long quotations

> **More about**
> Block quotations, 292, 299, 338, 782–83
> Sample block quotations, 292 (prose), 299 (poetry)

Set quotations of prose longer than four lines of your text as a block: Omit the quotation marks, and indent the entire quotation one inch from the left margin of your text. When quoting four or more lines of poetry, indent all the lines one inch from the left margin; keep the same indention and line breaks that were in the original poem, and include the line numbers of the passage quoted. If a line of the poem is too long to fit on a single line of your page, indent the continuation by an extra quarter of an inch.

7. Tables and figures

> Sample tables and figures, 74–81, 303–04, 340, 341, 343

Tables and figures (photographs, cartoons, graphs, and charts) are most effective when they appear as close as possible after the text in which they are first discussed. (If placing figures and tables appropriately is awkward, consider including them in an appendix at the end of your project.) Labeling your tables and figures, both in the text and in your caption, will help readers connect your discussion with the illustration:

- Refer to the visual in your text using the word *table* or the abbreviation *fig.*, and number tables and figures in a separate sequence using arabic numerals (table 1, table 2; fig. 1, fig. 2). MLA style uses lowercase for

---

Writing Responsibly — **Of Deadlines and Paperclips**

Instructors expect students to turn in thoughtful, carefully proofread, and neatly formatted papers on time—usually in class on the due date. Another expectation is that the writer will clip or staple the pages of the paper *before* it is submitted. Do justice to yourself by being fully prepared.

to SELF

in-text references to tables and figures unless they begin a sentence: "Table 1 presents 2010 data, and table 2 presents 2012 data."

- Accompany each illustration with the word *Table* or the abbreviation *Fig.*, the appropriate number, and a brief, explanatory title. Customarily, table numbers and titles appear above the table, and figure numbers and titles appear below the figure. Generally, they use the same margins as the rest of the paper.
- If additional information is needed, provide an explanatory caption after the number and title. (Remember that your text should explain what the figure or table demonstrates. That information should not be repeated in the caption.)
- If you borrow the illustration or borrow information needed to create the illustration, cite your source. Any photographs or drawings you create yourself should identify the subject but do not need a citation. Citations usually appear below the table in a source note or in the figure caption. If you document the illustration in a figure caption or source note, you do not need to include an entry in your list of works cited.

8. Printing and binding

If you are submitting a hard copy of your project, print it using a high-quality printer (make sure it has plenty of ink), on opaque 8½ × 11–inch white paper. Most instructors do not want you to enclose your project in a binder. Unless your instructor tells you otherwise, staple or paperclip the pages together in the upper left-hand corner.

9. Portfolios

Many instructors ask students to submit the final draft of the research project in a portfolio, which may include an outline, preliminary notes and drafts, a working or annotated bibliography, and a personal statement describing their writing process and what they have learned from the experience (Figure 18.2).

> **More about**
> Outlining, 35–37, 267–69
> Note taking, 714–17, 250–51
> Writing a first draft, 38–44
> Working or annotated bibliography, 200–05

FIGURE 18.2 Page 1 of Lydia Nichols's personal statement Nichols created a visual personal statement to explain how her interest in underground comics developed.

Student Model Research Project: MLA Style

In the student model research project that follows, Lydia Nichols fulfills her responsibilities to topic and audience. She uses comparison-contrast to support her claim that underground comics are more innovative than their mainstream cousins, and she provides a historical overview to fill in the background her readers lack. Her research draws on a variety of print and online sources, and she uses visuals to support some of her points.

Lydia Nichols

Prof. Concannon

Writing 205

6 April 2012

Holy Underground Comics, Batman! Moving Away from the Mainstream

When most people think of comic books, predictable images usually come to mind: caped heroes, maniacal villains, deeds of incredible strength, and other typical elements of super-powered adventures. Undeniably, characters like Batman, Superman, and Spider-Man are the most prominent features of the comic book landscape, in terms of both popularity and revenue (Wright xiv). However, there is more to comic books than superpowers and secret identities. Underground comics (also known as *comix*), printed by small publishers or by individual artists, are very different from what is usually expected in the genre. While far less well-known than their superhero counterparts, underground comics often offer an innovative and more sophisticated alternative to mainstream titles.

Almost from the beginning, comic books were associated with superheroes. The first comic books appeared in the early 1930s, nearly four decades after comic strips such as *Yellow Boy* began appearing in the major newspapers. However, Les Daniels, who has written extensively on conventional and underground comics, points out that comic books did not gain widespread popularity until June of 1938, when writer Jerry Siegel and artist Joe Shuster debuted their character Superman in *Action Comics* #1 (9). Daniels reports that Superman was an immediate success, and the character quickly inspired the creation of copycat superheroes in other comic books. The protagonists of these comics each had their own strengths and vulnerabilities, but the stories all shared a basic formula: individuals with extraordinary abilities battling against evil and struggling to maintain a secret identity. These superhero comics, though similar to each other, set the comic book industry on its

Nichols 2

feet, paving the way to profits and sustained success. Over the decades and even today, superhero comics are what are typically seen on store shelves.

While artists and writers over the years have certainly done inventive work in superhero comics, some similarity in mainstream titles was for many years unavoidable due to the creation in 1954 of the Comics Code Authority (CCA), an organization formed by a number of the leading comic publishers to regulate the content of comics ("Good Shall Triumph"). It set very explicit standards, dictating what content was allowed in comic books and what content was expected. Some parts of the code were incredibly specific and controlling:

> The letters of the word "crime" on a comics magazine shall never be appreciably greater in dimension than the other words contained in the title. The word "crime" shall never appear alone on a cover. . . . Restraint in the use of the word "crime" in titles or subtitles shall be exercised. (qtd. in "Good Shall Triumph")

Other rules were more general—vague enough to allow the CCA a free hand in shaping content. One read, "Respect for parents, the moral code, and for honorable behavior shall be fostered" (qtd. in "Good Shall Triumph"). The CCA also regulated the presentation of criminals and criminal acts, themes of religion and race, and dialogue, especially profanity. While the CCA had no legal authority, major magazine distributors refused comics that did not have CCA approval. Many comic publishers, such as EC Comics (*Vault of Horror, Tales from the Crypt*), were virtually forced out of business as a result of the CCA, though the banned titles would eventually gain the appreciation of collectors and aspiring comic artists such as Art Spiegelman, author of the graphic novel *Maus* (1986) ("Comic Book Code"). Other publishers, including DC Comics, made their artists abide by CCA rules in order to continue selling to a wide audience ("Good Shall Triumph"). The result was that the comics with the largest distribution were those that conformed to the CCA's strict rules about appropriate language, subjects, and tone.

In the 1960s, in contrast to mainstream CCA-approved superhero comics, alternatives began to appear. According to Steven Heller, an art director at the *New York Times* and a

338

founder of the Masters in Graphic Arts Program at the School for Visual Arts in New York, Robert Crumb's *Zap* (1968) initiated the "underground comix revolution" (101). Crumb and other like-minded artists did not submit their comics for CCA approval. Though this limited the distribution of their work, it allowed them artistic freedom. From its first issue, *Zap* satirized mainstream, conservative beliefs and did not shy away from sexual or political content (Heller 101-02). Beneath the crude humor of *Zap* and similar comics lay insightful commentary on society and its principles, which many readers found to be a refreshing change from mainstream superhero titles.[1]

    To see the contrast between these mainstream and underground comics, compare the two covers in fig. 1 (on the next page). The *Amazing Fantasy* cover (left) includes the Comics Code Authority approval stamp in its upper right corner, while the *Snarf* cover (right) does not. The *Snarf* cover actually pokes fun at covers like the one at left; on the *Amazing Fantasy* cover, superhero Spider-Man dangles from a high building by a thread, proclaiming his "awesome might" to the world, while on the *Snarf* cover, a geeky guy in an unwieldy homemade contraption wants to save the world by fighting "the big companies," which include oil companies (the "Gas" industry this inventor is trying to boycott) and probably DC Comics, too.

    Underground comics continue to be less well-known than superhero comics, but they are better-respected among mature readers for their bold and inventive content. Graphic novels, such as Spiegelman's *Maus* and Harvey Pekar and Joyce Brabner's *Our Cancer Year* (1994), have successfully addressed some of the most highly charged and sensitive subjects in modern society. Both of these show the subtlety and wide range of topics that underground comics explore. Daniels notes that underground comics frequently explore themes of sex and sexual identity, politics, and social issues (165), as shown in Crumb's work, which Heller describes as taking a satirical approach to countercultural topics (101-02).

    Mainstream superhero comics are set on an epic scale—depicting amazing feats, heroic battles between good and evil, and the like—while underground comics tend to

Nichols 4

Fig. 1. Mainstream versus Underground Comics. Spider-Man (left) extols (and exhibits) his prowess as superhero, while (right) a less conventional comic book "hero" struts his stuff. (Left: Cover from Jack Kirby and Steve Ditko, *Amazing Fantasy* #15. [New York: Marvel Comics, 1962; print]; right: Cover from Robert Crumb, *Snarf* #6 [Amherst: Kitchen Sink Enterprises, 1976; print])

focus on everyday life. Steven Weiner, who reviews graphic novels for *Library Journal,* called Adrian Tomine, for example, "a master of pseudorealistic stories" due to his ability to present an ordinary situation as profoundly interesting and complex (58; see fig. 2, next page). Comics like Tomine's provide a subject or situation that readers can identify with more easily than, say, Superman's battles with Brainiac.[2]

The quirky perspectives of underground artists would be impossible in mainstream comics because the structure for producing and publishing mainstream comics limits the input of the artists working on them. The modern comic book industry is a huge business,

340

Nichols 5

Fig. 2. Comic whose characters face realistic challenges—the loss of a loved one, parental guilt—that readers can easily relate to. From Adrian Tomine, *Optic Nerve* #6 (Montreal: Drawn and Quarterly, Feb. 1999; print; 22).

selling not only comics but also related merchandise such as T-shirts, toys, and video games, not to mention tickets to comic book–inspired movies. Story decisions involving major characters such as Batman and the Hulk have to be made with profits in mind. Because mainstream comic publishers often change the creative teams working on their titles (Herndon 23) and because teams can include dozens of members (McCloud 180),

Citation: Placement clarifies which information comes from which source

341

individual artists can have only so much impact on a particular character or story. Most mainstream comics are the result of work done by many different people.

In contrast, the individual artist in the underground realm has almost total control in creating his or her comic book. The creative teams working on underground titles are usually very small, and they rarely change (Herndon 23). Daniels notes that underground comic artists are not controlled by corporate interests that discourage daring material that might not sell (165, 180). This freedom allows for the uninhibited creativity that distinguishes underground comics from their more commercially oriented counterparts.

Underground artists not only push the envelope in terms of content but they also incorporate experimental visual devices, earning critical praise for breaking away from traditional comic layouts in favor of more artistic perspectives. Artists such as Daniel Clowes argue that comic art can be more evocative than film, especially in the use of nonlinear storytelling techniques (Hignite 18). *New York Times* columnist John Hodgman agrees: Discussing a moment of existential crisis in Kevin Huizenga's *Ganges* #1, he writes, "I have never seen any film or read any prose that gets at that frozen moment when we suddenly feel our mortality, when God is seen or denied, as effectively as a comic panel" (18). Artist Chris Ware manipulates the borders and frames in his comics so extensively that even reading his works can feel like an art to be mastered (see fig. 3, page 7). The demands his comics place on the reader create an interaction between viewer and artist that is unheard of in the pages of superhero titles.

While Ware and Clowes demonstrate how the page can be used to create innovative and complicated layouts, other underground artists excel at creating simple, striking visuals. Unlike mainstream comics, which depict dynamic scenes through loud, flamboyant colors, underground comics often achieve their effects through simplicity. Frequently, they are printed in black and white or with limited colors, with characters rendered in clean, bold lines. The clarity and lack of clutter in such art allows for immediate, striking storytelling (see fig. 2, page 5).

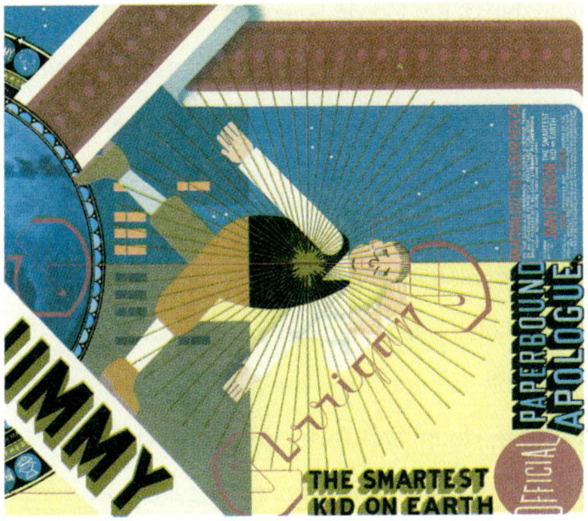

Fig. 3. Cover from Chris Ware's *Jimmy Corrigan: The Smartest Kid on Earth* (New York: Pantheon, 2000; print). Critically acclaimed *Jimmy Corrigan* comics use visual storytelling techniques, pushing the limitations of comics and forcing the reader to work to achieve understanding.

Caption explains how visual supports claim

Obviously, most underground comics are not intended for young children. Yet because of the childish connotations of the term "comic," most adults overlook the fascinating work that underground comic artists do. The association of comics with superheroes and children has made reading comics a source of shame or embarrassment for many adults. As Clowes comments, "I think that the average reader is far more open to a well-designed book than a standard comic book. . . . Very few would feel comfortable reading a standard comic book pamphlet" (qtd. in Hignite 17). Artists such as Scott McCloud have changed this perception of comic books by offering a broader definition of what a comic is. According to McCloud, comics are "juxtaposed pictorial and other images in a deliberate sequence" (12). This definition includes not only what one might find in the latest Spider-Man comic, but also all the experimental work that McCloud and his underground colleagues are creating.

Establishes credibility

Signal phrase and parenthetical page reference bookend apt quotation

McCloud and others have succeeded in bringing underground comics to a wider audience. Since the 1980s, underground comics have been finding their way into gallery

Conclusion: Provides closure

and museum exhibitions, where the craftsmanship of the individual comic book artist can be better appreciated (Hignite 18). Major newspapers like the *New York Times* have begun featuring underground comics in their pages, including serialized graphic novels such as *George Sprott (1894-1975)* and *Watergate Sue*. The market for underground comics has also expanded through Internet venues such as *eBay,* where interested readers can find not only new titles but also classic comix otherwise available only in specialty shops. The Internet has also become an outlet for direct distribution through artists' websites, making independent titles not only more accessible to consumers but also more affordable for individual artists to produce and market (Fenty, Houp, and Taylor, par. 1). While underground comics may never sell as well or be as large a part of popular culture as Superman and his ilk, their creators will likely continue to be heroes to anyone seeking courage, creativity, and artistic quality in their comics.

> Revisits thesis, states why underground comics provide more sophisticated alternative

Notes Heading (centered), new page

½" 1. According to Schnakenberg, more than two million copies of *Zap* comics were in print by 1999.

2. For an intriguing argument that the world of classic comic book superheroes is not so different from our own—including a discussion of how comics before World War II commented on then current events—see Wright 1-28.

Works Cited

"The Comic Book Code." *Culture Shock.* PBS, n.d. Web. 17 Mar. 2009.

Daniels, Les. *Comix: A History of Comic Books in America.* New York: Outerbridge, 1971. Print.

Fenty, Sean, Trena Houp, and Laurie Taylor. "Webcomics: The Influence and Continuation of the Comix Revolution." *ImageTexT* 1.2 (2004): 22 pars. Web. 18 Mar. 2009.

"'Good Shall Triumph over Evil': The Comic Book Code of 1954." *History Matters: The U.S. History Survey Course on the Web.* American Social History Project/Center for Media and Learning, CUNY, and the Center for History and New Media, George Mason University, 2006. Web. 22 Mar. 2009.

Heller, Steven. "Zap Comics." *Print* May/June 2000: 100-05. *Academic Search Complete.* Web. 26 Mar. 2009.

Herndon, L. Kristen. "Mainstream Culture Is in Trouble, and Superman's Not Gonna Save It. But the Simpsons Might." *Art Papers* 21.1 (1997): 22-25. *Art Index.* Web. 10 Mar. 2009.

Hignite, M. Todd. "Avant-Garde and Comics: Serious Cartooning." *Art Papers* 26.1 (2002): 17-19. *Art Index.* Web. 10 Mar. 2009.

Hodgman, John. "Comics Chronicle." *New York Times* 4 June 2006, late ed., sec. 7: 18. *LexisNexis.* Web. 19 Mar. 2009.

McCloud, Scott. *Understanding Comics, the Invisible Art.* New York: Harper Perennial, 1994. Print.

Schnakenberg, Robert E. "Zap Comix." *St. James Encyclopedia of Popular Culture.* Detroit: St. James Press, 2002. *Find Articles.* Web. 17 Mar. 2009.

Weiner, Stephen. "Beyond Superheroes: Comics Get Serious." *Library Journal* 7.2 (2002): 55-58. *Academic Search Complete.* Web. 10 Mar. 2009.

Wright, Bradford W. *Comic Book Nation: The Transformation of Youth Culture in America.* Baltimore: Johns Hopkins UP, 2001. Print.

APA

Journal Article from an Online Database

<u>author</u> <u>year</u> <u>article title and subtitle</u>
Fancher, R. E. (2009). Scientific Cousins: The relationship between Charles Darwin and Francis Galton.
  <u>publication information</u> <u>digital object identifier</u>
American Psychologist 64, 84–92. doi:10.1037/a0013339
  <u>journal title</u> <u>volume pages</u>

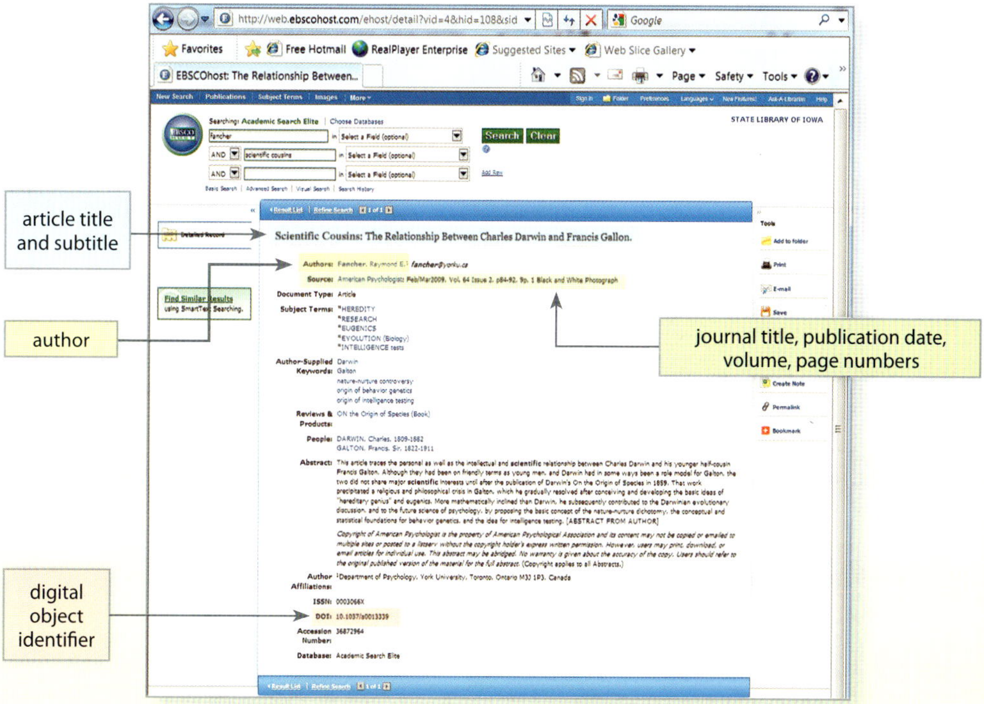

Database screen

Look for the information you need to document an article you accessed through an online database on the search results screen, the full record of the article, or the first and last pages of the article itself. When there is a subtitle, include this information. Include a digital object identifier (DOI) if one is provided. No access date is needed. (For more about documenting an article accessed through an online database, see pp. 366–68.)

APA

Journal Article (Printed)

author — year — article title and subtitle
Willingham, D. T., (2012). Ask the cognitive scientist: Why does family wealth affect learning?
publication information
American Educator, 36(1), 33–39.
journal title — volume — pages

- journal title
- volume, number, and publication date
- article title and subtitle
- author
- article title and subtitle
- author
- journal title, publication date
- article starting page

Journal table of contents

First page of article

Look for the information you need to document a journal article on the cover or table of contents of the journal and on the first and last pages of the article. (Turn to the last page of the article for the last page number.) If each issue of the journal begins with page 1, include the issue number, in parentheses, after the volume number. (For more about documenting an article from a printed or online periodical, see pp. 366–70.)

Documentation Matters | Documenting a Source: APA Style

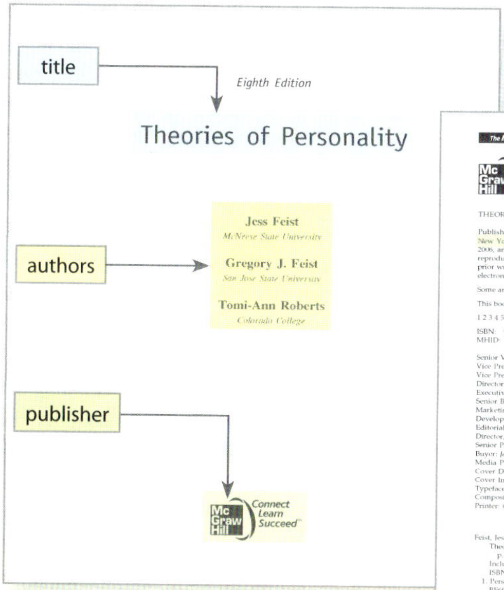

Book (Printed)

authors   *publication date*   *title*
Feist, J., Feist, G.J., & Roberts, T. (2013). *Theories of personality.*
  publication information
  New York: McGraw-Hill.
   place of   *publisher*
   publication

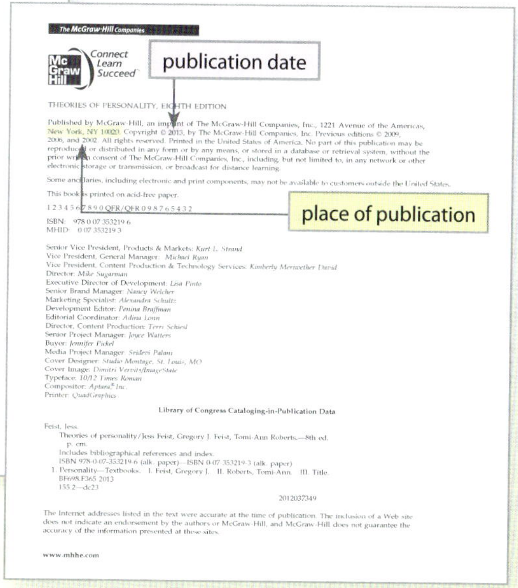

Title page

Copyright page

Look for the information you need to document a printed book on the book's title page and copyright page. If more than one location for the publisher is listed on the title page, use the first or the publisher's home office location (if indicated). (For more about documenting a book, see pp. 358–65.)

APA

Short Work on a Website

corporate author/publisher: **PsyBlog**
©date/last update: **(2012, August 28).**
web page title (and subtitle when available): **Memory enhanced by a simple break after reading.**
retrieval statement: **Retrieved from**
URL for web page: **http://www.spring.org.uk/2012/08/memory-enhanced-by-a-simple-break-after-reading.php**

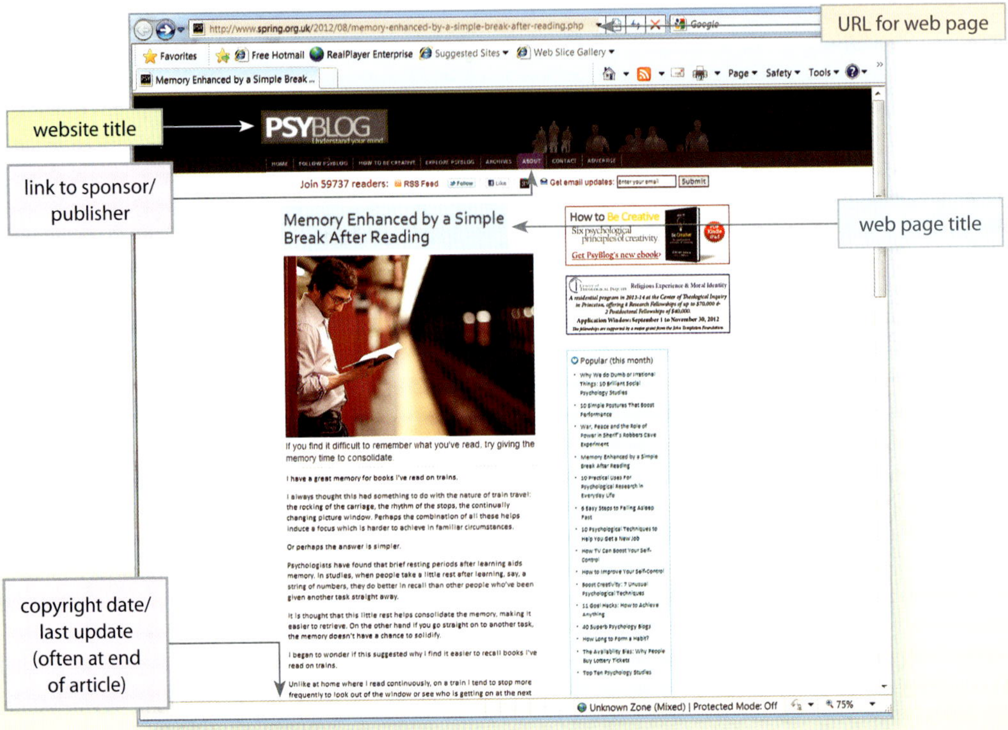

Callouts on screenshot:
- URL for web page
- website title
- link to sponsor/publisher
- web page title
- copyright date/last update (often at end of article)

Frequently, the information you need to create a complete entry in the reference list is missing or difficult to find on web pages. Look at the top or bottom of the web page or home page or find the link to an "About" or "Contact Us" page. If no author is cited, move the title to the author position. If the web page is untitled, add a description (in brackets) in place of the title. If the page was created and published by the same group, omit the publisher name from the retrieval statement; if not, add the publisher's name before the URL (*Retrieved from APA website:*). (For more about documenting online sources, see pp. 370–72.)

19 Documenting Sources: APA Style

IN THIS CHAPTER

a. In-text citations, 347
b. Reference list, 358
c. Informational notes, 376
d. Formatting, 377

Student Model
Research Project:
APA Style, 381

> **More about**
> MLA style, 288–346 (ch. 18)
> *Chicago* style, 389–415 (ch. 20)
> CSE style, 416–30 (ch. 21)

Developed by the American Psychological Association, APA style is used by researchers in psychology and many other social science disciplines, such as education, social work, and sociology. The *Publication Manual of the American Psychological Association* (6th ed.) requires that sources be cited in two ways:

- **Citation:** In the body of your project, provide an in-text citation for each source used.
- **Documentation:** At the project's end, provide a reference list.

19a Creating APA-Style In-Text Citations

In-text citations appear in the body of your project. They mark each use you make of a source, regardless of whether you are quoting, paraphrasing, or drawing on an idea. In-text citations should include just enough information for readers to locate the source in your reference list, which appears at the end of the project. They should also alert readers to shifts between *your* ideas and those you have borrowed from a source.

Writing Responsibly | Citing and Documenting Sources

When you cite and document sources, you demonstrate how thoroughly you have researched your topic and how carefully you have thought about your sources, which encourages your audience to believe you are a credible researcher. In your citations and documentation, you acknowledge any material that you have borrowed from a source, and you join the conversation on your topic by adding your own interpretation. Accurate entries in the body of your project and list of references allow your audience to find and read your sources so that they can evaluate your interpretation and learn more about the subject themselves. Accurate entries also demonstrate the care with which you have written your research project, which further reinforces your credibility, or ethos.

to AUDIENCE

> **Quick Reference — General Principles of In-Text Citation**
>
> - Cite not only direct quotations but also paraphrases, summaries, and information gathered from a source, whether printed or online.
> - Include the author's surname and the year of publication. You may place the name(s) in a signal phrase or in a parenthetical citation.
> - Place parenthetical citations after the borrowed material; if the author is named in a signal phrase, insert the year of publication, in parentheses, immediately following the author's name and the page reference at the end of the borrowed passage.
> - For works with no author, use the first few words of the title in the author position.
> - For works with multiple authors, use the word *and* before the last author in a signal phrase; replace the word *and* with an ampersand (&) in a parenthetical citation.
> - Include a page or paragraph number when borrowing specific information but not when summarizing an entire source.

1. Place in-text citations so that readers know where borrowed material starts and stops.

> **More about**
> What you do and do not need to cite, 348–50
> Signal phrases, 274–86 (ch. 17)
> Integrating borrowed material into your text, 274–76

When you incorporate a quotation, paraphrase, summary, or idea from a source into your own prose, carefully consider the placement of the in-text citation, keeping the following goals in mind:

- To make clear exactly which material is drawn from the source
- To avoid distracting your reader

You can cite a source in your text in two ways:

- ***Signal phrase.*** Include the author's name (often just the surname) and an appropriate verb in your sentence, and place the date of publication, in parentheses, immediately following the author's name.

> Psychologist G. H. Edwards (1992) found that subtypes or subcategories of beliefs emerge from within gender categories.

A signal phrase often makes it easier for readers to determine where your ideas end and borrowed material begins. It also allows you to integrate the borrowed material into your sentence and to put the source in context by adding your own interpretation and the qualifications of the source author. For these reasons, most of your summaries, paraphrases, and quotations should be introduced by a signal phrase.

- **Parenthetical citation.** In parentheses, provide the author's surname, followed by a comma and the year in which the source was published. Place the note immediately after the borrowed material.

> Subtypes or subcategories of beliefs emerge from within gender categories (Edwards, 1992).

Parenthetical citations are most appropriate when citing more than one source or establishing facts.

NOTE The reference list entry is the same, regardless of whether you use a signal phrase or a parenthetical citation:

> *author* *pub. year* *title*
> Edwards, G. H. (1992). The structure and content of the male gender role
> *publication info.*
> stereotype: An exploration of subtypes. *Sex Roles, 27,* 553–561.

> **More about**
> Creating reference list entries, 358–76

Provide enough information in your in-text citation for readers to locate the source in the reference list. In most cases, the author's surname and the date of publication are sufficient. Occasionally, you may need to provide more information. When citing works by authors with the same surname, also include the authors' initials.

> Examples 1–2, 350–53

> Example 11, 355
> Example 7, 362

> While subtypes or subcategories of beliefs may emerge from within gender categories (Edwards, G. H., 1992), broader categories of beliefs emerge from within cultural groups (Edwards, C. P., 1988).

Quick Reference — Examples of APA-Style In-Text Citations

1. One author, paraphrase or summary 350
   a. Signal phrase 351
   b. Parenthetical citation 351
2. One author, quotation 351
   a. Signal phrase 351
   b. Parenthetical citation 352
3. Two authors 352
4. Three to five authors 352
5. Six or more authors 353
6. Group or corporate author 353
7. Unnamed (anonymous) author 354
8. Two or more sources in one citation 354
9. Two or more sources by the same author in one citation 354
10. Two or more sources by the same author in the same year 355
11. Two or more authors with the same surname 355
12. Reprinted or republished work 355
13. Sacred or classical source 356
14. Indirect source 356
15. Website or other online source 357
16. Personal communication (e-mail, letter, interview) 357

> Example 2, 351

When quoting from a source, include page numbers.

> The stereotype effect occurs when "individual members . . . are judged in a direction consistent with group-level expectations . . ." (Biernat, 2003, p. 1019).

APA In-Text Citations

1. **One author, paraphraase or summary**
2. One author, quotation
3. Two authors

2. Adjust in-text citations to match your source.

The exact form of an in-text citation depends on the type of source you are citing. The examples that follow cover the most common types. For more unusual sources, study the general principles outlined here and adapt them to your special circumstances or consult the *Publication Manual of the American Psychological Association*, 6th ed. (available in any library).

1. One author, paraphrase or summary The APA does not require that writers include a page reference for summaries and paraphrases, but your instructor may. If your instructor does want you to include a page reference, follow the model for a quotation on the next page.

a. Signal phrase

> signal phrase
> **Plummer** (2001) **indicates** that boys begin pressuring one another to conform in childhood, telling each other to toughen up or to stop acting like a baby.

b. Parenthetical citation

> This pressure to conform to recognized masculine norms typically begins at a very young age, and boys may tell each other to toughen up or to stop acting like a baby (**Plummer,** 2001).

2. One author, quotation If you are borrowing specific language from your source, include the author's name, the year of publication, and a page reference.

NOTE The APA suggests, but does not require, that writers include a page reference for summaries and paraphrases when readers may need help finding the cited passage. Your instructor may require that you always include one, so be sure to ask. If your instructor *does* want you to include a page reference, follow examples 2a–b.

APA In-Text Citations

1. **One author, paraphraase or summary**
2. **One author, quotation**
3. Two authors
4. Three to five authors

a. Signal phrase In a signal phrase, insert the year of publication immediately after the author's name and a page reference at the end of the cited passage. This not only provides source information but also makes clear what part of your text comes from the source.

> **Plummer** (2001) argues that an overt pressure to conform to recognized norms of masculinity typically begins at a very young age, with boys discouraging one another from being "soft" or "artistic" (p. 18).

b. Parenthetical citation In a parenthetical citation, include all three pieces of information at the end of the passage cited.

> This overt pressure to conform to recognized norms of masculinity typically begins at a very young age, with boys discouraging each other from being "soft" or "artistic" (Plummer, 2001, p. 18).

3. Two authors List two authors by surnames in the order listed by the source; be sure to use this same order in your reference list entry. In a signal phrase, spell out the word *and* between the two surnames; in a parenthetical citation, replace the word *and* with an ampersand (&).

> signal phrase (*and* spelled out)
> Iezzoni and Long-Bellil (2012) observe that "with limited exceptions, physicians have little training in addressing the wide-ranging needs of persons with disabilities" (p. 136).

> Most physicians, the authors observe, "have little training in addressing the
> parenthetical citation (ampersand)
> wide-ranging needs of persons with disabilities" (Iezzoni & Long-Bellil, 2012, p. 136).

4. Three to five authors When a source has three, four, or five authors, list them all in your first in-text citation.

> The research of Oller, Pearson, and Cobo-Lewis (2007) suggests that bilingual children may have a smaller vocabulary in each of their languages than monolingual children have in their sole language.

APA In-Text Citations

1. One author, paraphrase or summary
2. **One author, quotation**
3. **Two authors**
4. **Three to five authors**
5. Six or more authors
6. Group or corporate author

In subsequent citations, list only the first author, representing the others with the abbreviation *et al.* In APA style, this abbreviation should not be underlined or italicized.

> The bilingual children in the study were all Spanish-English speakers (Oller et al., 2007).

NOTE *al.* is an abbreviation, so it requires a period; *et* is a complete word, so it does not. There should be no punctuation between the author's name and *et al.*

et al. Abbreviation of the Latin phrase *et alii*, "and others"

5. Six or more authors If the source has six or more authors, use only the surname of the first author plus *et al.* unless confusion will result.

> The researchers note that "there is less direct experimental evidence for the effect of grazing animal species on biodiversity" (Rook et al., 2003, p. 141).

acronym A word formed from the first letters of words in a name or phrase, such as NASA from National Aeronautics and Space Administration

6. Group or corporate author Provide the full name of the group in your signal phrase or parenthetical citation. If you are going to cite this source again in your project, use the group's name in a signal phrase and insert an abbreviation of the name in parentheses. In subsequent in-text references, use only the abbreviation.

> *full name*
> In 2003 the National Commission on Writing in America's Schools and
> *acronym*
> Colleges (NCWASC) demanded that "the nation's leaders . . . place writing squarely in the center of the school agenda, and [that] policymakers at the state and local levels . . . provide the resources required to improve writing" (p. 3). The NCWASC also noted that . . .

APA In-Text Citations

3. Two authors
4. Three to five authors
5. **Six or more authors**
6. **Group or corporate author**
7. Unnamed (anonymous) author
8. Two or more sources in one citation

Alternatively, include the full name in a parenthetical citation, and insert the abbreviation in square brackets afterward.

> If writing is to improve, our society "must place writing squarely in the center of the school agenda, and policymakers at the state and local levels must provide the resources required to improve writing" (National Commission on Writing in America's Schools and Colleges [NCWASC], 2003, p. 3).
>
> full name — abbreviation

More about
Quotation marks with titles, 783–84
Italics with titles, 814–15

7. Unnamed (anonymous) author When no author is listed for a source, use the first few words of the reference list entry (usually the title) instead.

> On average, smokers shave about 12 minutes off their life for every cigarette smoked ("A Fistful of Risks," 1996, pp. 82–83).
>
> title

Set titles of articles or parts of books in quotation marks and titles of books and other longer works in italics.

8. Two or more sources in one citation When the information you are drawing on comes from more than one source, follow the borrowed material with a list of all relevant sources, separated by semicolons. List the sources in alphabetical order, the same order in which they appear in the reference list.

> When placed in well-structured rehabilitative programs, juvenile offenders—even those who commit serious crimes such as murder—can become more mature thinkers, more involved and loving members of their families, and more successful workers and learners (Beyer, 2006; Burns & Hoagwood, 2002).

9. Two or more sources by the same author in one citation When citing two or more sources by the same author in a single citation, name the author once but include all publication years, separating them with commas.

> Wynn's work explores the ability of human infants to perform mathematical functions, such as addition and subtraction (1992, 2000).
> *(Wynn = author; 1992 = pub. year 1; 2000 = pub. year 2)*

> Human infants have shown surprising abilities to perform mathematical functions, such as addition and subtraction (Wynn, 1992, 2000).
> *(1992 = pub. year 1; 2000 = pub. year 2)*

10. Two or more sources by the same author in the same year When your reference list includes two or more publications by the same author in the same year, add a letter following the year (*2006a, 2006b*). Use these year-and-letter designations in your in-text citations and in your reference list.

> Example 6, 360

> The brain not only controls the senses of sight and sound, but it also plays an important role in associating emotions such as fear with particular situations (Barinaga, 1992b).
> *(1992b = letter assigned)*

11. Two or more authors with the same surname If your reference list includes works by different authors with the same surname, include the authors' initials to differentiate them.

> Rehabilitation is a viable option for many juvenile offenders, whose immaturities and disabilities can, with institutional support and guidance, be overcome as the child matures (M. Beyer, 2006).
> *(M. Beyer = first initial + surname)*

If a source has more than one author, include initials for the first author only.

12. Reprinted or republished work Include both dates in your in-text citation, with the original date of publication first.

APA In-Text Citations

8. Two or more sources in one citation
9. Two or more sources by the same author in one citation
10. Two or more sources by the same author in the same year
11. Two or more authors with the same surname
12. Reprinted or republished work
13. Sacred or classical source
14. Indirect source

APA In-Text Citations

11. Two or more authors with the same surname
12. Reprinted or republished work
13. **Sacred or classical source**
14. **Indirect source**
15. Website or other online source
16. Personal communication (e-mail, letter, interview)

> Danon-Boileau (2005/2006) takes a cross-disciplinary approach to the study of language disorders in children.
>
> *[orig. year / reprint year]*

13. Sacred or classical source Cite sacred texts, such as the Bible, the Talmud, or the Qur'an, in the body of your research project using standard book titles, chapter numbers, and verse numbers, and indicate the version you used.

> In the Song of Solomon, the female speaker concludes her description of her lover with this proclamation: "His mouth is sweetness itself, he is all delight. / Such is my lover, and such my friend, O daughters of Jerusalem" (5:16, Revised Standard Version).
>
> *[ch.:verse, version]*

For classical works, cite the year of the translation or version you used: (Plato, trans. 1968).

14. Indirect source When you can, avoid quoting from a secondhand source (source material you have learned about through its mention in another source). When you cannot locate or translate the original source, mention the original author's name in a signal phrase. In your parenthetical citation, include *as cited in* followed by the name of the author of the source in which you found the information, and conclude with the year of that source's publication.

> Choy, Fyer, and Lipsitz (as cited in King, 2008) make the distinction that people with phobias, unlike those with general anxiety, can identify specific causes for their feelings of nervousness and dread.

In the reference list, provide only the source you used: For the example above, include a reference list entry for King, not Choy, Fyer, and Lipsitz.

15. Website or other online source Frequently, the information you need to create a complete in-text citation is missing. Electronic sources may lack fixed page numbers: Page 5 in one printout may be page 4 or 6 in another. Use page numbers only when they are fixed, as in a PDF file. When paragraph numbers are provided, include those (with the abbreviation *para.*) instead of a page number.

> **More about**
> PDF files, 180, 215, 218

> The Internet has also become an outlet for direct distribution of underground comics through artist websites, making independent titles more affordable to market (Fenty, Houp, & Taylor para. 1).

When paragraphs are not numbered, include the title of the section and number of the paragraph in which the material you are citing appears. If the author is unnamed, use the first few words of the title.

> Examples 27–28, 370–71

> Cell-phone use while driving can impair performance as badly as drinking alcohol does ("Driven to Distraction," 2006, para. 1).

If no date is provided, use *n.d.* for *no date*.

> Barrett (n.d.) unwittingly reveals the sexism prevalent on college campuses in the early 1960s through his account of a football game.

16. Personal communication (e-mail, letter, interview) For sources such as personal e-mail messages, interviews, and phone calls that your readers cannot retrieve and read, mention the communication in your text or provide a parenthetical citation, but do not include an entry in the reference list.

> The scientist himself was much more modest about the development (S. J. Gould, personal communication, November 13, 1986).

APA In-Text Citations

13. Sacred or classical source
14. Indirect source
15. **Website or other online source**
16. **Personal communication (e-mail, letter, interview)**

APA Reference List Entries

1. One author
2. Two authors
3. Three to seven authors

19b Preparing an APA-Style Reference List

The reference list, which comes after the body of your research project, lists the sources you have cited in your text. The format of each entry in the list depends in part on the type of source you are citing, such as a printed book, an article in an electronic journal or accessed through a database, or an audio recording. (See the Quick Reference box on pp. 360–61 for a list of APA-style reference list examples.)

Books—Printed and Electronic

> Annotated visual of where to find author, title, and publication information, on foldout accompanying this chapter

In a printed book, the information you need to create a reference list entry appears on the title and copyright pages at the beginning of the book. In an online book or e-book, print and electronic publication information appears at the top or bottom of the first page or is available through a link.

1. One author

a. Printed The basic entry for a printed book looks like this:

Author's surname, Initial(s). (Year of publication). *Title: Subtitle.* Place of publication (city, state [abbreviated]): Publisher.

Here is an example of an actual citation:

> For books, only first word of title and subtitle (plus names) are capitalized.

Pollock, J. (2012). *Crime and justice in America: An introduction to criminal justice.* Maryland Heights, MO: Anderson Publishing.

b. E-book Works published electronically or made accessible online are now frequently tagged with a digital object identifier (DOI). Unlike a URL that may change or stop working, a DOI is a permanent identifier that will not change over time or from database to database. If the e-book you are documenting is tagged with a DOI, use that identifier instead of publication information or URL, and add a description of the source type in brackets after the title. If no DOI has been assigned, replace publication information with the URL from which the electronic file can be obtained. If you accessed the source on a device such as a Kindle or Nook, no URL should be included.

> **More about**
> Digital object identifiers, 366–67, 370
> URLs, 236–38

Carter, J. (2003). *Nasty people: How to stop being hurt by them without stooping to their level* [Adobe Digital Editions version]. doi:10.1036/0071410228

Documentation Matters • Preparing an APA-Style Reference List   **19b**   359

> **Tech**   **Citing Electronic Sources: Digital Object Identifiers (DOIs) and URLs**
>
> Because URLs change and links break, the APA now recommends using a digital object identifier (DOI), a permanent identifying code, whenever available; use a URL, or web address, only when no DOI is available. Most electronic books and articles in academic journals now include a DOI. When your citation ends with a DOI or URL, do *not* add a period after it. Break a DOI or URL (if necessary) only after a slash or before a dot or other punctuation mark; do not add a hyphen.

> von Hippel, E. (n.d.). *Democratizing Innovation.* Retrieved from http://web.mit
>
>   .edu/evhippel/www/democ.htm

If no publication date available, use n.d.

2. Two authors   When there are two authors, list them in the order in which they appear on the title page.

> author 1   author 2
> Raskin, H., & Rabiner, D. (2012). *College drinking and drug use*.
>
>   New York, NY: Guilford.

Use an ampersand (&) between names.

3. Three to seven authors   When the book has three to seven authors, list all their names.

> James, J., Burks, W., & Eigenmann, P. (2011). *Food allergy*. Philadelphia, PA:
>
>   Saunders.

Use an ampersand (&) between the last two names.

4. Eight or more authors   When the book has eight or more authors, list the first six authors followed by three ellipsis points and the last author's name.

> Masters, R., Skrapec, C., Muscat, B., Dussich, J. P., Pincu, L., Way,
>
>   L. B., . . . Gerstenfeld, P. (2010). *Criminal justice: Realities and challenges*.
>
>   New York, NY: McGraw-Hill.

5. Unnamed (anonymous) author   Start the entry with the title followed by the publication date. Alphabetize the entry in the reference list using the first significant word in the title (not an article such as *a, an,* or *the*).

> *And still we conquer! The diary of a Nazi Unteroffizier in the German Africa*
>
>   *Corps.* (1968). University, AL: Confederate Publishing.

APA Reference List Entries

1. One author
2. **Two authors**
3. **Three to seven authors**
4. **Eight or more authors**
5. **Unnamed (anonymous) author**
6. Two or more books by the same author
7. Two or more authors with the same surname and first initial

Reference — Examples of APA-Style Reference List Entries

Books—Printed and Electronic
1. One author 358
   a. Printed 358
   b. E-book 358
2. Two authors 359
3. Three to seven authors 359
4. Eight or more authors 359
5. Unnamed (anonymous) author 359
6. Two or more books by the same author 360
7. Two or more authors with the same surname and first initial 362
8. Group or corporate author 362
9. Author and editor or translator 362
10. Edited book or anthology 363
11. Selection from an edited book or anthology 363
12. Edition other than the first 363
13. Introduction, preface, foreword, or afterword 363
14. Entry in an encyclopedia or other reference work 364
    a. Printed 364
    b. Online 364
15. Multivolume work 364
16. Republished book 364
17. Title within a title 364
18. Sacred or classical source 365
19. Dissertation or thesis 365
    a. Published 365
    b. Unpublished 365
    c. Abstracted in DAI 365

Periodicals—Printed and Electronic
20. Article in a scholarly journal 366
    a. Printed 366
    b. Online or accessed through a database 366
21. Special issue of a journal 367
22. Article in a magazine 367
    a. Printed or accessed through a database 367
    b. Online 367
23. Article in a newspaper 368
    a. Printed or accessed through a database 368
    b. Online 368

APA Reference List Entries

- 5. Unnamed (anonymous) author
- **6. Two or more books by the same author**
- 7. Two or more authors with the same surname and first initial

Example 10, 355

6. Two or more books by the same author For multiple books by the same author (or authors), arrange the entries in order of publication (from least to most recent).

Rose, G. (1993). *Feminism and geography: The limits of geographical knowledge.* Minneapolis: University of Minnesota Press.

Rose G. (2011). *Visual methodologies: An introduction to researching with visual materials.* Thousand Oaks, CA: Sage.

When books were written by the same author(s) in the same year, alphabetize the entries by title and add the letter *a* following the publication date of the first entry, *b* following the publication date of the second entry, and so on.

Dobrin, S. I. (2011a). *Ecology, Writing Theory, and New Media: Writing Ecology.* New York, NY: Routledge.

Documentation Matters • Preparing an APA-Style Reference List

24. Review (printed or online) 369
25. Letter to the editor (printed or online) 369
26. Abstract (printed or online) 369

Other Electronic Sources
27. Website 370
28. Web page 371
29. Discussion list posting 371
30. Article on a wiki 371
31. Blog 371
    a. Blog posting 371
    b. Comment on a blog posting 372
32. Computer software 372
33. Presentation slides 372

Audio and Visual Sources
34. Motion picture 372
35. Online video or video blog (vlog) 372
36. Television or radio broadcast 373
    a. Series 373
    b. Episode 373
    c. Podcast 373
37. Musical or other audio recording 373
    a. CD, LP, or audiobook 373
    b. Selection or song on a CD, LP, or audiobook 373
38. Lecture, speech, conference presentation, or poster session 373
39. Work of art 374
40. Advertisement 374
41. Map 374

Miscellaneous Sources—Printed and Electronic
42. Government publication 374
    a. Printed 374
    b. Online 375
43. Report (nongovernmental) 375
44. Data set 375
45. Fact sheet, brochure, pamphlet 375
46. Conference proceedings 376
47. Legal source (printed or online) 376
48. Interview (published or broadcast) 376
49. Personal communication (e-mail, letter, interview) 376

Dobrin, S. I. (2011b). *Postcomposition.* Carbondale: Southern Illinois

University Press.

Works written by a single author should be listed *before* sources written by that same author plus a coauthor, regardless of publication dates.

Morrison, J. R. (2007). *Diagnosis made easier: Principles and techniques for*

mental health clinicians. New York, NY: Guilford.

Morrison, J. R., & Anders, T. F. (1999). *Interviewing children and adolescents:*

Skills and strategies for effective DSM-IV *diagnosis.* New York, NY:

Guilford.

APA Reference List Entries

5. Unnamed (anonymous) author
6. **Two or more books by the same author**
7. Two or more authors with the same surname and first initial

APA Reference List Entries

6. Two or more books by the same author
7. **Two or more authors with the same surname and first initial**
8. Group or corporate author
9. Author and editor or translator
10. Edited book or anthology

No state abbreviation if state included in name of university press

When citing multiple sources by an author and various coauthors, alphabetize entries by the surname of the second author.

>Clarke-Stewart, A., & Allhusen, V. D. (2005). *What we know about childcare.*
>
>>Cambridge, MA: Harvard University Press.
>
>Clarke-Stewart, A., & Brentano, C. (2006). *Divorce: Causes and consequences.*
>
>>New Haven, CT: Yale University Press.

7. Two or more authors with the same surname and first initial When your reference list includes sources by two different authors with the same surname and first initial, differentiate them by including their first names in brackets.

>Cohen, A. [Andrew]. (1994). *Assessing language ability in the classroom.*
>
>>Boston, MA: Heinle.
>
>Cohen, A. [Anne]. (1973). *Poor Pearl, poor girl! The murdered girl stereotype in*
>
>>*ballad and newspaper.* Austin: University of Texas Press.

8. Group or corporate author List the sponsoring organization as the author. Use the full name, and alphabetize it in the reference list according to the name's first significant word (ignoring articles such as *a, an,* or *the*). If the same group or corporation is also listed as the publisher, replace the name of the publisher with the word *Author*.

>Fabian Society, Commission on Life Chances and Child Poverty. (2006).
>
>>*Narrowing the gap: The final report of the Fabian Commission on Life*
>>
>>*Chances and Child Poverty.* London, UK: Author.

9. Author and editor or translator If the source originally appeared earlier than the edited or translated version, add the date of original publication at the end of the entry. If the work has an editor, use the abbreviation *Ed.* For a translator, use the abbreviation *Trans.*

Alvtegen, K. (2010). *Shame* (S. Murray, Trans.). New York, NY: Felony and

Mayhem. (Original work published 2006)

10. Edited book or anthology Put the editor's name in the author position.

Ghosh, R. A. (Ed.). (2005). *CODE: Collaborative ownership and the digital*

economy. Boston, MA: MIT Press.

For a book with multiple editors, change the abbreviation to *Eds.*

11. Selection from an edited book or anthology Begin with the selection's author, followed by the publication date of the book and the selection's title (with no quotation marks or other formatting). Then insert the word *In*, the editors' names, and the title of the book or anthology (italicized). Next include page numbers for the entire selection (even if you used only part of it). Conclude the entry with the publication information for the book in which the selection appeared.

selection author   selection title   editors
Smither, N. (2000). Crime scene cleaner. In J. Bowe, M. Bowe, & S.

                                                        selection pg. nos.
Streeter (Eds.), *Gig: Americans talk about their jobs* (pp. 96–103).

New York, NY: Crown.

12. Edition other than the first Insert the edition number (*2nd ed., 3rd ed.*) or edition name (*Rev. ed.* for "revised edition") after the book's title. (The edition number or name usually appears on the title page.)

Nier, J. A. (2013). *Taking sides: Clashing Views in Social Psychology* (4th ed.).

New York, NY: McGraw-Hill.

13. Introduction, preface, foreword, or afterword The sixth edition of the *Publication Manual of the APA* does not provide an example of an entry for an introduction, preface, foreword, or afterword, but based on other examples, such an entry might look like the one below:

foreword's author   label   book's author   book's title
Andretti, M. (2008). Foreword. In D. Daly, *Race to win: How to become a*

                       pg. nos. (foreword)
complete champion (pp. 2–3). Minneapolis, MN: Quayside-Motorbooks.

APA Reference List Entries

8. Group or corporate author
9. Author and editor or translator
10. Edited book or anthology
11. Selection from an edited book or anthology
12. Edition other than the first
13. Introduction, preface, foreword, or afterword
14. Entry in an encyclopedia or other reference work
15. Multivolume work

14. Entry in an encyclopedia or other reference work Format an entry in a reference work as you would a selection from an edited book. For signed articles, include the author's name. (Articles in reference works often carry the author's initials only, so you may need to cross-reference the initials with a list of contributors in the front or back of the book.) If an article is unsigned, begin with its title.

a. Printed

entry author　　　　　　　　　　　entry title
Treffert, D. A. (2000). Savant syndrome. In A. E. Kazdin (Ed.), *Encyclopedia*
　　　　　　　　　　　　entry page nos.
　　of psychology (pp. 144–148). New York, NY: Oxford University Press.

b. Online

Depression, reactive. (2001). In E. Reber & A. Reber (Eds.), *Penguin*
　　　　　　　　　　　　　　　　　　　　　　　　　　URL
　　dictionary of psychology. Retrieved from http://www.credoreference.com

15. Multivolume work

Tomasello, M. (Ed.). (1998–2003). *The new psychology of language: Cognitive

　　and functional approaches to language structure* (Vols. 1–2). Mahwah, NJ:

　　Erlbaum.

16. Republished book

Huxley, E. (2006). *Red strangers.* New York, NY: Penguin Group. (Original work

　　published 1939)

17. Title within a title The sixth edition of the *Publication Manual of the APA* does not provide an example of an entry for a book with a title within the book's title, but based on other examples, such an entry might look like the one below:

　　　　　　　　　　　　　　　title within title
Porter, L. (1987). The interpretation of dreams: *Freud's theories revisited.*

　　Boston, MA: Twayne.

Omit italics from any title that would normally be italicized when it falls within the main title of a book. If the title within the title would normally appear in quotation marks, retain the quotation marks and italicize both titles.

18. Sacred or classical source No entry in the reference list is needed for a sacred source, such as the Bible, the Talmud, or the Qur'an, or a classical source, such as Plato's *Republic*.

> Example 13, 356

19. Dissertation or thesis Indicate whether the work is a doctoral dissertation or a master's thesis. If the dissertation or thesis was accessed through a database service, include the name of the database from which it was obtained and provide any identifying number. If it was obtained from a university or personal website, include the URL.

a. Published

>   Song, L. Z. (2003). *Relations between optimism, stress and health in Chinese and American students* (Doctoral dissertation). Available from ProQuest Dissertations and Theses database. (UMI No. AAI3107041)

>   Lillie, A. S. (2008). *MusicBox: Navigating the space of your music* (Master's thesis, Massachusetts Institute of Technology). Retrieved from http://thesis.flyingpudding.com/documents/Anita_FINAL_THESIS.pdf

b. Unpublished

>   Luster, L. (1992). *Schooling, survival and struggle: Black women and the GED* (Unpublished doctoral dissertation). Stanford University, Stanford, CA.

c. Abstracted in DAI If you used the abstract in the *Dissertation Abstracts International* database, include that information in the entry. Remember, though, that reading the abstract is no substitute for reading the actual source.

>   Kelley, E. (2008). Parental depression and negative attribution bias in parent reports of child symptoms. *Dissertation Abstracts International: Section B. Sciences and Engineering, 69*(7), 4427.

APA Reference List Entries

16. Republished book
17. Title within a title
18. **Sacred or classical source**
19. **Dissertation or thesis**
20. Article in a scholarly journal
21. Special issue of a journal

Periodicals—Printed and Electronic

A periodical is a publication issued at regular intervals—newspapers are generally published every day, magazines every week or month, and scholarly journals four times a year. For periodicals, include not only the title of the article (with no quotation marks or italics) but also the title of the periodical (in italics, all important words capitalized). Other publication information you include depends on the type of periodical you are citing.

> Annotated visual of where to find author, title, publication, and other information, on foldout accompanying this chapter

20. Article in a scholarly journal The information needed to create a reference list entry for a printed journal article appears on the cover or in the table of contents of the journal and on the first and last page of the article. For articles downloaded from a database, the information appears on the search results screen, in the full record of the article, or on the first and last page of the downloaded file. For articles that appear in journals that are published solely online, the needed information may be on the website's home page, in the journal's table of contents, or on the first page of the article.

> More about Formatting author information: Examples 1–11, 350–55

a. Printed The basic citation for an article in a printed journal looks like this:

Author's surname, Initial(s). (Year of publication). Article title. *Journal Title, vol no.,* pages.

APA Reference List Entries

Here is an example of an actual citation:

Wright, S. (2011). Invasive species and the loss of beta diversity. *Ethics and the Environment, 16,* 79–98.

18. Sacred or classical source
19. Dissertation or thesis
20. Article in a scholarly journal
21. Special issue of a journal
22. Article in a magazine

If the article is published in a journal that starts each issue with page 1, provide the issue number after the volume number (not italicized, in parentheses).

Sui, C. (2007). Giving indigenous people a voice. *Taiwan Review, 57*(8), 40.

> More about Digital object identifiers (DOIs), PDFs, 180, 215, 218, 358–59, 370

b. Online or accessed through a database More and more, researchers access journal articles electronically, either through online journals or through databases that provide access to articles in PDF or HTML format. Articles accessed electronically now frequently include a digital object identifier (DOI). The DOI is a permanent code that does not change from library to library or from

Documentation Matters • Preparing an APA-Style Reference List

database to database. The DOI makes URLs unnecessary. Whenever a DOI is provided, include it at the end of your reference list entry. The basic citation for an article in an online journal or accessed through an online database that has a DOI is the same as for a printed journal article except that the DOI appears at the end of the citation.

> Luo, Y. (2011). Do 10-month-old infants understand others' false beliefs? *Cognition, 121,* 289–298. doi:10.1016/j.cognition.2011.07.011 [DOI]

For an article in an online journal that does *not* provide a DOI, include the phrase *Retrieved from* followed by the URL for the journal's home page.

> Janyam, K. (2011). The influence of job satisfaction on mental health of factory workers. *The Internet Journal of Mental Health, 7*(1). Retrieved from http://www.ispub.com/journal/the_internet_journal_of_mental_health/

21. Special issue of a journal

> Leong, F. (Ed.). (2009). History of racial and ethnic minority psychology [special issue title] [Special issue] [label]. *Cultural Diversity and Ethnic Minority Psychology, 15.*

22. Article in a magazine

a. Printed or accessed through a database Provide the full publication date of the issue (year, month, and day or year and month). If the volume and issue number of the magazine are available, include that information as you would for a journal article.

> Greene, K. (2011, December). Our data, ourselves. *Discover,* 42–47.

> Pelusi, N. (2009, January/February). The appeal of the bad boy. *Psychology Today, 42*(1), 58–59.

b. Online Include the URL for the magazine's home page.

> Fairhall, D. (2011, December 10). Welcome to the new Arctic. *Salon.* Retrieved from http://www.salon.com

---

APA Reference List Entries

19. Dissertation or thesis
20. Article in a scholarly journal
21. Special issue of a journal
22. Article in a magazine
23. Article in a newspaper
24. Review (printed or online)

> Example 20, 366

APA Reference List Entries

21. Special issue of a journal
22. Article in a magazine
23. **Article in a newspaper**
24. Review (printed or online)
25. Letter to the editor (printed or online)

If the magazine is available in a printed edition but the article is only available online, include the phrase *Supplemental material* in brackets after the article's title.

> Daniller, A. (2007, December). Psychology research done right [Supplemental material]. *GradPSYCH.* Retrieved from http://gradpsych.apags.org

23. Article in a newspaper The information you need to create a reference list entry for a printed newspaper article is on the masthead of the newspaper (at the top of the first page) and on the first and last page of the article. For newspaper articles downloaded from a database, the information you need appears on the search results screen, the full record of the article, or the article itself. For articles that appear in online versions of the newspaper, the information you need is usually at the top of the first page of the article.

a. Printed or accessed through a database

> *author* — Ritter, M. *pub. date* — (2011, December 1). *title* — Mouse study offers hope for new HIV protection. *newspaper* — *Atlanta Journal-Constitution,* *sec./pg. no.* — p. A7.

If the title of a newspaper does not include its place of publication, supply the city and state, in square brackets, following the title.

> Esch, M. (2011, July 1). New York may ban gas drilling in watersheds, state land. *Evening Sun* [Norwich, NY], pp. 1, 3.

If the pages of the article are not continuous, provide all page numbers.

> Vergano, D. (2011, July 3). Shuttles proved humans could work together in space. *Press & Sun-Bulletin* [Binghamton, NY], pp. A1, A4.

To cite a newspaper article downloaded from a database, follow the model for a printed newspaper article, but omit the page numbers, and change the comma after the newspaper's title to a period.

b. Online Follow the format for a printed newspaper article, but omit the page reference and include the words *Retrieved from* and the URL for the newspaper's home page.

Smyth, J. C., & Thompson, D. (2011, December 10). Public retirement ages come under greater scrutiny. *Denver Post*. Retrieved from http://www.denverpost.com

24. Review (printed or online) Follow the model for the type of periodical in which the review appeared. In the author position, insert the name of the author of the review; if the review is titled, insert that title in the title position (no italics or quotation marks); and add in brackets the label *Review of the book* (or *Review of the film,* and so forth) followed by the title and author of the reviewed work. End with publication information for the periodical in which the review appeared.

> Examples 20 and 20–23, 367–69

review author   *review title*   *label*
Balk, D. E. (2007). Diamonds and mummies are forever [Review of the book *Remember me,* by L. T. Cullen]. *Death Studies, 31,* 941–947. doi:10.1080/07481180701603436

Comma between title, author

If the review is untitled, substitute the label *Review of the book,* the book's title, and the book's author in brackets.

Hurdley, R. (2011, September). [Review of the book *Gripes: The little quarrels of couples,* by J. Kaufmann]. *Cultural Sociology, 5,* 452–453.

Comma between title, author

25. Letter to the editor (printed or online) Follow the model for the type of periodical in which the letter appeared, and insert the label *Letter to the editor* in brackets following the letter's title.

> Examples 20 and 20–23, 367–69

APA Reference List Entries

letter author   *letter title*   *label*
Richmond, A. (2009, May). Miracle drug? [Letter to the editor]. *The Atlantic, 303*(4), 14.

If the letter is untitled, put the label *Letter to the editor,* in brackets, in the title position.

26. Abstract (printed or online) It is always better to read and cite the article itself. However, if you relied only on the abstract, or summary, cite only the abstract to avoid misrepresenting your source and your research.

Loverock, D. S. (2007). Object superiority as a function of object coherence and task difficulty [Abstract]. *American Journal of Psychology, 120,* 565–591.

23. Article in a newspaper
24. Review (printed or online)
25. Letter to the editor (printed or online)
26. Abstract (printed or online)
27. Website

Tebeaux, E. (2011). Technical writing and the development of the English paragraph 1473–1700. *Journal of Technical Writing and Communication, 41*, 219–253. Abstract retrieved from http://www.ebscohost.com

Other Electronic Sources

> Annotated visual of where to find author, title, and publication information, on foldout accompanying this chapter

While it is usually easy to find the information you need to create a complete citation for a book or an article in a periodical, websites can be a bit trickier. Most of the information you need will appear on the site's home page, usually at the bottom or top of that page, or on the web page you are citing. Sometimes, however, you may need to look further. Click on links with titles such as "About us" or "More information." Frequently, websites do not provide complete information, in which case include as much information in your entry as you can.

> Example 15, 357

27. Website In general, when mentioning an entire website in a research project, you do not have to include an entry in your reference list. However, if you quote or paraphrase content from the site or interact with it in a substantial way, include it, following this model:

APA Reference List Entries

25. Letter to the editor (printed or online)
26. Abstract (printed or online)
27. **Website**
28. Web page
29. Discussion list posting

Author's surname, Initial(s). (Copyright date or date last updated). *Website title.* Retrieved from + URL

Here is an example of an actual citation:

Gilbert, R. (2001). *Shake your shyness.* Retrieved from http://shakeyourshyness.com

---

Tech **Checking URLs and DOIs**

DOIs. If your entry includes a DOI, check it before submitting your project by visiting crossref.org and inserting the DOI into the search box.

URLs. Just before submitting your paper, test all the URLs. Sometimes web addresses change or content is taken down.

If the URL you provided no longer works, search for the work online by title or keyword; you may find it "cached" on the web even though the owner of the original site has taken the work down. Then use the URL for the cached version in your bibliographic entry.

If no author is cited, move the title to the author position. If the web page is untitled, add a description in brackets. If no date is provided, insert *(n.d.)* following the author's name.

> Example 5, 359

28. Web page Provide the title of the page (with no formatting) and the URL for the specific page you are citing.

American Psychological Association. (2011). [web page title] Treatment for binge eating. Retrieved from [URL for web page] http://www.apa.org/

29. Discussion list posting Treat the subject line (or *thread*) as the title, and include the label *Discussion list post* (in brackets).

Arendes, L. [date posted] (2008, July 9). [subj. line] Objectivity [label] [Discussion list post]. Retrieved from [URL] news://sci.psychology.research

If the name of the list is not included in the URL, add it to the retrieval statement: *Retrieved from Early Childhood Education Discussion List: http://www.dmoz.org/Reference/Education/Early_ Childhood*

30. Article on a wiki Cite a wiki article as you would a web page. Because wikis are written and edited collaboratively, there is no author to cite; begin with the article's title. If the date of the most recent update is not noted, include the abbreviation *n.d.* (*no date*) in its place. Always include a retrieval date and direct URL.

Battered person syndrome. (n.d.). Retrieved April 22, 2012, from http:// [URL] psychology.wikia.com

31. Blog Include a screen name if the author's name is not provided.
a. Blog posting

Dean, J. [post author] (2009, January 1). [post date] Gratitude enhanced by focusing on end [post title] of pleasurable experience [label] [Web log post]. Retrieved from [URL (post)] http://www.spring.org.uk/2009_01_01_blogarchive.php

APA Reference List Entries

26. Abstract (printed or online)
27. Website
28. Web page
29. Discussion list posting
30. Article on a wiki
31. Blog
32. Computer software
33. Presentation slides

b. Comment on a blog posting

Carosin, R. *[comment author]* (2011, December 11). *[date posted]* Re: An untranslatable mind *[subject line (thread title)]* [Web log comment]. Retrieved from http://mindhacks.com/ *[URL]*

32. Computer software Provide an entry for computer software only if it is unfamiliar to your readers and it is necessary to a computation you have made.

Power Researcher *[title]* [Computer software]. *[label]* Atlanta: Uniting Networks.

If the software you are citing is available in more than one version, add a version number in parentheses between the title of the software and the identifying label.

33. Presentation slides The sixth edition of the *Publication Manual of the APA* does not provide an example of an entry for presentation slides, but based on other examples such an entry might look like the one below:

Doyle, T. (2009). *Privacy, free expression, and compromising images* [PowerPoint slides]. *[label]* Retrieved from http://library.hunter.cuny.edu/pdf/Privacyfreeexpression.ppt

Audio and Visual Sources

The information you need to create an entry for most audio and visual sources appears on the cover, label, or program of the work or in the credits at the end of a film or television show. As with other citations, italicize the titles of longer works, such as CDs and films, and do not format or add quotation marks to the titles of shorter works, such as single songs or single episodes of television programs.

34. Motion picture

Grazer, B. (Producer), & Howard, R. (Director). (2001). *[release]* *A beautiful mind* *[title]* [Motion picture]. United States: Warner Bros. *[distributor]*

35. Online video or video blog (vlog)

ATTC Network. (2007, July 12). Michael–Clinical psychologist [Video file]. Retrieved from http://www.youtube.com/watch?v=4OAYT5P6xaQ

36. Television or radio broadcast

a. Series

Garcia, R. (Executive producer). (2008–2009). *In treatment* [Television series]. New York, NY: HBO.

b. Episode

Reingold, J. (Writer), & Barclay, P. (Director). (2009). Mia: Week three [Television series episode]. In R. Garcia (Executive producer), *In treatment*. New York, NY: HBO.

c. Podcast

Mitchell, N. (Producer). (2008, March 15). The psyche on death row. *All in the mind* [Audio podcast]. Retrieved from http://www.abc.net.au/rn/allinthemind/default.htm

37. Musical or other audio recording

a. CD, LP, or audiobook

Gore, A. (Writer), & Patton, W. (Narrator). (2007). *The assault on reason* [CD]. New York, NY: Penguin Audio.

b. Selection or song on a CD, LP, or audiobook

writers   *© date*   *performers*
Dilly, D., & Wilkin, M. (1959). The long black veil [Recorded by H. Dickens & A. Gerrard]. On *Pioneering women of bluegrass* [CD]. Washington, DC: Smithsonian/Folkways Records. (1996).
recording date

38. Lecture, speech, conference presentation, or poster session

Krauss, S. A., & Dahlsgaard, K. K. (2011, May 21). *Work after war: National Guard soldiers' experience of the postdeployment return to civilian employment.* Paper presented at the 2011 Conference on Work, Stress, and Health, Orlando, FL.

APA Reference List Entries

34. Motion picture
35. Online video or video blog (vlog)
36. Television or radio broadcast
37. Musical or other audio recording
38. Lecture, speech, conference presentation, or poster session
39. Work of art
40. Advertisement

Ferandi, A. B. (2009, April). *The effect of stable unions on child health, nutrition, and development.* Poster session presented at the annual meeting of the Population Association of America, Detroit, MI.

39. Work of art The sixth edition of the *Publication Manual of the APA* does not provide an example of an entry for a work of art such as a painting or a sculpture, but based on other examples, such an entry might look like the one below.

                     date   title of
     artist   completed   artwork   label   location
McElheny, J. (2008). *Island universe* [Sculpture]. White Cube, London, UK.

40. Advertisement The sixth edition of the *Publication Manual of the APA* does not provide an example of an entry for an advertisement, but based on other examples, such an entry might look like the one below:

company or product   label   source of advertisement
Regal Cinemas [Advertisement]. (2010, March 10). *Los Angeles Times.* Retrieved from http://www.latimes.com/

41. Map

U.S. Census Bureau, Geography Division (Cartographer). (2001). Mean center of population for the United States: 1790 to 2000 [Demographic map]. Retrieved from http://www.census.gov/geo/www/cenpop/meanctr.pdf

Miscellaneous Sources—Printed and Electronic

42. Government publication

a. Printed

U.S. Department of Health and Human Services, National Institutes of Health, National Institute of Mental Health. (2008). *Bipolar disorder* (NIH Publication No. 3679). Washington, DC: Government Printing Office.

APA Reference List Entries

37. Musical or other audio recording
38. Lecture, speech, conference presentation, or poster session
39. **Work of art**
40. **Advertisement**
41. **Map**
42. **Government publication**
43. Report (non-governmental)
44. Data set

U.S. Department of Health and Human Services. (2005). *Steps to a healthier US*. Washington, DC: Author.

> Example 8, 362

b. Online

U.S. General Accounting Office. (1993, September 21). *North American Free Trade Agreement: A focus on the substantive issues* (Publication No. GAO/T-GGD-93-44). Retrieved from http://www.gpoaccess.gov/gaoreports/search.html

43. Report (nongovernmental)

American Psychological Association, Task Force on Gender Identity and Gender Variance. (2008). *Report of the Task Force on Gender Identity and Gender Variance*. Retrieved from http://www.apa.org/pi/lgbc/transgender/2008TaskForceReport.pdf

44. Data set

U.S. Department of Justice, Federal Bureau of Investigation. (2007, September). *2006 Crime in the United States* [Data set]. Retrieved from http://www.data.gov/raw/310

45. Fact sheet, brochure, pamphlet

Department of Health and Human Services, Centers for Disease Control and Prevention. (2005, May 3). *Basic information about SARS* [Fact sheet]. Retrieved from http://www.cdc.gov/ncidod/SARS/factsheet.htm

If no author is listed, move the title to the author position. If no publication date is available, insert *n.d.* (for *no date*) in its place.

APA Reference List Entries

40. Advertisement
41. Map
42. Government publication
43. Report (nongovernmental)
44. Data set
45. Fact sheet, brochure, pamphlet
46. Conference proceedings
47. Legal source (printed or online)

Example 10, 355
Example 21, 367

APA Reference List Entries

44. Data set
45. Fact sheet, brochure, pamphlet
46. Conference proceedings
47. Legal source (printed or online)
48. Interview (published or broadcast)
49. Personal communication (e-mail, letter, interview)

Example 16, 357

46. Conference proceedings Cite conference proceedings either as an edited book or as the special issue of a journal, depending on how they were published.

47. Legal source (printed or online)

case title (abbreviated) *U.S. Reports vol.* *no.* *decision date*
Lynn v. Alabama, 493 U.S. 945 (1989). Retrieved from *Open Jurist* website:
URL
http://openjurist.org/493/us/945/lynn-v-alabama

48. Interview (published or broadcast)

interview subject   *broadcast date*
Cameron, J. (2009, December 18). James Cameron, a king with a soft

touch. Interview by M. Norris [Digital download]. National Public

Radio, Washington, DC. Retrieved from http://www.npr.org

49. Personal communication (e-mail, letter, interview) Cite personal communications that are not available to the public in the body of the research project, but do not include an entry in the reference list.

19c Using APA Style for Informational Notes

In addition to in-text citations, APA style allows researchers to include informational notes. These notes may provide supplementary information, acknowledge any help the writer received, or call attention to possible conflicts of interest.

To add supplementary information, include a superscript (above-the-line) arabic number in the text and at the beginning of the note (either at the bottom of the page for a footnote or in a list of notes at the end of the project).

The participants in each condition were told at the beginning of the experiment that they were participating in a memory-recall task. They were to identify what they could remember from a clip from the movie *Pretty Woman* (Milchan, Reuther, & Marshall, 1990),[1] a stereotypical "chick-flick."

> **Notes**
>
> ⸺½"→ ¹This romantic comedy starring Julia Roberts and Richard Gere (dir. Garry Marshall) was extremely popular, grossing nearly $464 million worldwide, according to the site Box Office Mojo (http://www.boxofficemojo.com/movies/?id=prettywoman.htm). Nevertheless, participants had not seen the film before participating in the experiment.

Add notes to acknowledge help or possible conflicts of interest to the title page, four lines below the date.

> Sample title page, 382

19d Formatting a Paper in APA Style

The care with which you cite and document your sources reflects the care you have taken in writing your research project. Continue that care by formatting your project in the way your readers expect. For most writing projects in the social sciences, follow the APA's formatting guidelines. The *Publication Manual of the APA* offers guidance for writers submitting projects for publication in scholarly journals, so not all its formatting requirements are appropriate for student projects. Ask your instructor about making reasonable modifications.

> **Student Model**
> Research project, APA style: "The Power of Wardrobe," Heather DeGroot, 381–88

1. Margins and spacing

- Set margins of at least one inch at the top, bottom, and left- and right-hand sides of your paper.
- Indent the first line of each paragraph half an inch.
- Indent quotations of forty or more words as a block, half an inch from the left margin.
- Double-space the entire paper, including the abstract, title page, block quotations, footnotes, figure captions, and the reference list. Set the text so that the right margin is uneven (ragged), and do not hyphenate words at the ends of lines.
- Insert two spaces after punctuation at the end of a sentence.

> **More about**
> Block quotations, 782–83

> Sample reference list, 387

- Use a hanging indent for each reference list entry: The first line should be flush with the left margin with subsequent lines indented half an inch.

2. Typeface, header, and page number

> More about
> Choosing a typeface and type size, 165–66

Use a standard typeface such as Times New Roman or Arial in a readable size (usually 12 points). Include a header, or *running head,* consisting of the first two or three words of the title (no more than fifty characters) in the upper left-hand corner of the page, half an inch from the upper edge. Include the page number half an inch from the top and one inch from the right edge of the page. Use your word processor's header feature to insert the running head and number the pages automatically.

> More about
> Crafting a title, 86–87
> Notes acknowledging help or conflicts, 376–77, 382

3. Title page

- Insert the title, typed in upper- and lowercase letters, centered on the top half of the page.
- Insert a blank line and then type your name.

Tech — **Indention**

The major style guides (MLA, APA, *Chicago*, CSE) were initially written before the widespread use of personal computers, when most writers still worked on typewriters. To create a paragraph or hanging indention on a typewriter, the typist would hit the space bar five times or set a tab. Now, just about everyone creates writing projects on a computer, where paragraph and hanging indentions are created using the Ruler or Paragraph Dialog box.

Ruler

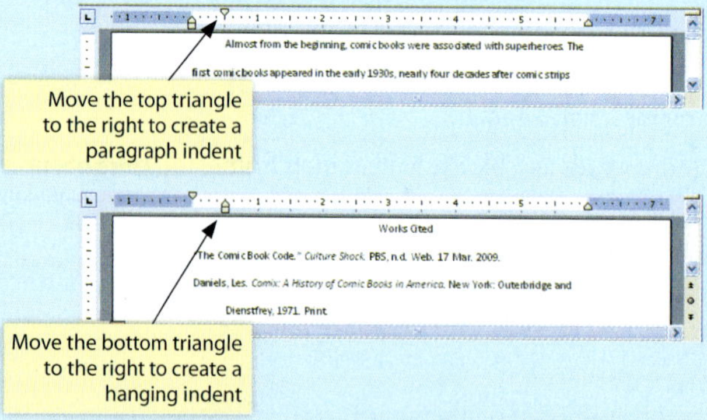

Move the top triangle to the right to create a paragraph indent

Move the bottom triangle to the right to create a hanging indent

Paragraph Dialog Box

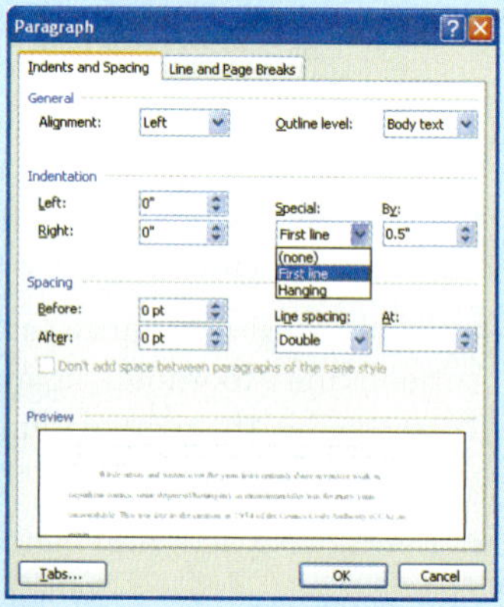

> **Tech** **Creating a Header**
> Word processing programs allow you to insert a header automatically. In Microsoft Word, select "Header and Footer" under the View menu. If you have any questions about creating a header, consult your program's Help directory.

- Papers for submission to a scholarly journal include the author's university or college affiliation; student writers usually include the course number, the name of the instructor to whom the project will be submitted, and the date of submission, each centered on separate lines.
- If you need to acknowledge help you received—for example, in conducting your research or interpreting your results—include a note on the title page, four lines below the identifying information.

> Sample title page, APA style, 382

4. Abstract

The abstract generally includes a one-sentence summary of the most important points in each section of the project:

> Sample abstract, APA style, 382

- Introduction—problem you are investigating
- Methods—number and characteristics of the participants and your research methods
- Results—your outcomes
- Discussion—implications of your results. This section concludes your text.

The abstract follows the title page and appears on its own page, headed with the word *Abstract* centered at the top of the page. The abstract should be no more than 150–250 words.

5. Tables and figures

- Refer to tables and figures in the text, using the word *Table* or *Figure* followed by the number of the table or figure in sequence. (The first figure is Figure 1; the first table is Table 1.) Discuss the significance of tables and figures in the text, but do not repeat the information that appears in the table or figure itself.
- Include a caption with each figure. The caption should begin with the word *Figure* and the number assigned in the text (both in italics). The

> Sample figure captions, APA style, 388

caption, which follows the figure, should describe the figure briefly but not repeat the information in your text. If you borrowed the figure or the data to create the figure, include the source information at the end of your caption.

- Include the word *Table* and the table number (no italics) on one line and, on the next line, the table title (in italics). The table itself should appear below the table number and title. If you borrowed the table or the data to create the table, include source information below the table, preceded by the word *Note* (in italics, followed by a period).

- In research projects submitted for publication, tables should appear, each on a new page, after the reference list or endnotes (if any). Figures (graphs, charts, photographs, maps, and so on) should appear, each on a new page, following the tables. In college research projects, however, your instructor may prefer to see tables and figures in the body of your research project, as close as possible following their first mention in the text. Check with your instructor before formatting your project.

> Sample figures, APA style, 388

6. Reference list

- Center the heading "References" at the top of the page.
- Use a hanging indent for each reference list entry: The first line should be flush with the left margin, with subsequent lines indented half an inch.
- Alphabetize the entries in the reference list by the surname of the author or, if no author is listed, by the first important word in the title (ignoring *A, An,* or *The*).
- Italicize all titles of books and websites, but do not enclose titles of articles or book chapters in quotation marks.

> **More about**
> Italics with titles, 814–15

Writing Responsibly — Of Deadlines and Paperclips

Instructors expect students to turn in thoughtful, carefully proofread, and neatly formatted papers on time—usually in class on the due date. Another expectation is that the writer will clip or staple the pages of the paper *before* the paper is submitted. Do justice to yourself by being fully prepared.

to SELF

- Capitalize the first word, the first word following a colon or a dash, and proper nouns in titles of books, articles in periodicals, websites and web pages, films, and so on. Capitalize all major words in journal titles: *Psychology, Public Policy, and Law; Monitor on Psychology.*

> **More about**
> Capitalization, 810–11
> Proper nouns, 809–10

7. Printing, paper, and binding

Print your project using a high-quality printer (make sure it has plenty of ink), on opaque, 8½ × 11–inch white paper. Most instructors do not want you to enclose your paper in a binder, but if you are in doubt, ask. If it is not submitted in a binder, paperclip or staple the pages together.

Student Model Research Project: APA Style

In the sample student research project that follows, Heather DeGroot examines the influence that gender stereotypes can have on behavior. She fulfills her responsibilities to topic and audience by drawing on a variety of relevant and reliable sources to provide the background that her readers will need, by including visuals that help her readers understand her project, and by following the format for an APA-style research project, the format her readers expect. By acknowledging her sources, she fulfills her responsibility to the other writers from whom she has borrowed information. By conducting her primary research with care, by thanking Patrick Brown for the assistance he provided, by acknowledging the limitations of her project, and by revising, editing, and proofreading her project carefully, she demonstrates her own credibility as a researcher and writer.

> **More about**
> Writing in the sciences and social sciences, 455–68 (ch. 23)
> Appendixes, 460–61

1″ 1″ 1″ 1″

Running head: POWER OF WARDROBE 1

Running head: Shortened title pg. no.

The words *Running head,* followed by a colon, may not be needed for college research projects in APA style.

The Power of Wardrobe: Male Stereotype Influences

Heather DeGroot

Psychology 220

Dr. Lawrence

May 2, 2012

Identifying information (double spaced)

Author Note

I would like to thank Patrick Brown for playing the proctor in each of the three conditions.

½″ 1″ ½″ 1″ 1″ 1″

POWER OF WARDROBE 2

Abstract

Heading (centered, 1″ from top), new page

This study explores the potential influence of stereotypical appearances on male subjects' stated opinions regarding entertainment perceived as "feminine." Results are based on responses from 26 undergraduate males. Data were analyzed using one-way variance tests and Tukey HSD post hoc tests. The findings show that participants were more likely to give a favorable rating to a "chick-flick" in the presence of a counterstereotypical male (M = 8.67, SD = 1.53) than in the presence of a stereotypical male (M = 5.31, SD = 1.97) or control proctor (M = 5.20, SD = 1.99). Results suggest that participants may have experienced gender role conflict.

Abstract: Summary of problem, methods, results, discussion

The Power of Wardrobe: Male Stereotype Influences

Stereotypes—expectations placed upon people because of their gender, race, or religion—may be discouraged in their most overt forms, but they continue to flourish in the media. In contemporary American culture, this sort of bias places an exaggerated emphasis on physical appearance. Such attitudes are not isolated features of media programming; rather, they influence many interactions in everyday life. Sontag, Peteu, and Lee (1999) indicate that this is especially true among adolescents and young adults, for whom clothing, personal image, and identity tend to be inextricably bound.

Impressions of other people can be classified into two categories: stereotypes and individuating information. Stereotypes focus on social categories, while individuating information is the focus of other factors, including personality, actions of the individual, and so forth (Kunda & Thagard, 1996). The stereotype effect, as defined by researcher Monica Biernat (2003), is "a finding that individual members (comparable in all ways except their category membership) are judged in a direction consistent with group-level expectations or stereotypes" (p. 1019). Under such circumstances, people are judged more by the category in which one can group them than by their qualities or skills as individuals. However, according to Kunda and Thagard (1996), the division of these types of judgment is not always clear. This was the influence for their impression-formation theory in which stereotypes, traits, and behaviors are all constrained by positive and negative associations. In their research, they found that appearance was crucial in this process.

The influential power of stereotypes is particularly interesting when gender boundaries are crossed. In a 2003 study, researchers Vescio, Snyder, and Butz found that while membership in a socioeconomic class or "power position" (p. 1062) tended to give participants a biased or predetermined opinion about the beliefs and behaviors (such as work ethic) by which a person in another category lived, gender exerted at least as great an influence on the manner in which people were categorized. Mansfield (2006) demonstrated that males in power positions were likely to be viewed differently than females in the same positions.

POWER OF WARDROBE 4

Would these findings remain consistent if only one gender were used in the study? That is, can we identify intra-gender roles or stereotypes that similarly affect perception and beliefs about individuals? A study by G. H. Edwards (1992) found that beliefs regarding men and women transcend gender, with subtypes or categories (such as for men, businessman, athlete, or loser) emerging within each sex. Typically, such seeming variations represent varying degrees of a supposed normative "masculinity," rather than truly distinct expressions of a male gender role. Rudman and Fairchild (2004) write that "for men, a lifetime of experience observing one's peers being teased or ostracized for 'effeminate' behavior may evoke strong normative pressures toward highly masculine self-presentations" (p. 160). Plummer (2001) indicates that boys begin pressuring one another to conform in childhood, telling each other to toughen up or to stop acting like a baby.

The purpose of this study is to observe whether male participants are likely to be influenced by a stereotypically "male" opinion. Are college-aged males more swayed by the "jock" or "cool guy on campus" than by those with an "average Joe" or a "metrosexual" appearance? Hypothetically, male participants should more likely be swayed by the opinions of the stereotypical male than by those of the control group ("average Joe") or the experimental group (counterstereotypical).

Methods

Participants

Twenty-six undergraduate males from a large southeastern university (mean age = 19) participated in this study in order to fill a course requirement in their general psychology classes.

Procedure

The participants were randomly assigned to one of three conditions in the study: the stereotypically "male" proctor group, the counterstereotypical proctor group, and the control group. The proctor was the same person in each condition, but his appearance was different in each (Figure 1). In the stereotypically male proctor condition, the proctor wore an outfit consisting of team sports apparel: a baseball cap, a basketball jersey, shorts, and sneakers. In the counterstereotypical condition, he wore a long-sleeved, light pink button-down shirt (tucked in), creased khaki pants, and dress shoes. In the control condition, the proctor wore a short-sleeved blue polo shirt (not tucked in), khaki shorts, and sneakers.

The participants in each condition were told at the beginning of the experiment that they were participating in a memory-recall task. They were to identify what they could remember from a clip from the movie *Pretty Woman* (Milchan, Reuther, & Marshall, 1990), a stereotypical "chick-flick." During the ten-minute film clip, which was constant for each of the three conditions, the proctor read scripted lines such as "Oh! I love this part!" and "I'm seriously such a sap, but this film is just so good!" The script was a constant in each of the three conditions.

> Ampersand used in parenthetical citation

After the clip was viewed by all, the proctor handed out a questionnaire to conduct the "memory-recall task." The questionnaire contained diversion questions such as "What color is the dress that Vivian (Julia Roberts's character) wears in the scene?" and "What game do Edward and Vivian play after the performance?" At the end of the questionnaire, the participants rated the movie on an opinion scale from 1 to 10, with 10 being the highest overall liking.

After the experiment was over, participants in each condition were debriefed as a group and were dismissed from the study.

Results

A one-way analysis of variance (ANOVA) was conducted on the data in order to determine whether males are more influenced by a stereotypically "male" proctor in comparison to the counterstereotypical and control-group proctors. The analysis demonstrated that at least one group was significantly different from the others, $F(2, 23) = 4.08$, $p < .05$. Tukey HSD post hoc tests were performed to measure the difference between the groups individually. The Tukey HSD revealed that the participants were more likely to give a favorable movie rating under the influence of the counterstereotypically masculine proctor ($M = 8.67$, $SD = 1.53$) than the stereotypically masculine proctor ($M = 5.31$, $SD = 1.97$) or the control proctor ($M = 5.20$, $SD = 1.99$) (see Figure 2).

> Results: DeGroot summarizes data and research findings; includes figures, pp. 241–42.

There were no significant differences in movie ratings between those in the stereotypically masculine proctor's group and those in the control proctor's. These results were contrary to the study's initial hypothesis, and they suggest that male participants are more likely to defy gender roles in the presence of a counterstereotypical proctor than in the presence of a stereotypically masculine proctor.

Discussion

The study elicited something beyond stereotypical responses from the participants. In fact, the participants may have experienced gender role conflict. Instead of scoring favorably when the masculine male proctor said he enjoyed the film, the participants scored the film lower than initially expected. The presence of a highly or moderately "masculine" male, though he made favorable comments in each condition, may have caused the participants to adhere more rigidly to socialized male gender roles and thus rate the movie lower than subjects in the atypically "masculine" proctor group, who did not feel the pressure to assert masculinity in their rating of *Pretty Woman*. (See McCreary et al., 1996.)

Certain irregularities in the study provoked questions that might be investigated in future research. Due to factors beyond the researcher's control, each condition had a different number of participants. The counterstereotypical condition, which had significant findings, had the smallest number of participants; as a result, those scores are subject to greater statistical variation due to strong individual opinion. However, one might also question whether the number of males present influences a subject's tendency to admit to a counterstereotypical opinion or value judgment. If the study were to be replicated to find for stereotype differences alone, it would be crucial for the number of participants in each condition to be the same. On the other hand, a separate study might use multiple viewing groups of varying individual sizes to determine the effect of group size in gender-stereotype-determined valuations.

Another issue to consider is the effect of the fictional nature of the film to which the male viewers were asked to react. A study reported in *Business Week* suggests that men are more willing to show empathy when they know the stories eliciting their emotional response are fictional. Jennifer Argo, one of the authors of the study, is quoted as saying that fictional works provide "an excuse to relax gender stereotypes" (as cited in Coplan, 2008, p. 17). This factor was not considered in the study reported here.

References

Biernat, M. (2003). Toward a broader view of social stereotyping. *American Psychologist, 58,* 1019–1027. doi:10.1037/0003-066X.58.12.1019

Coplan, J. H. (2008, January 28). When it's all right for guys to cry. *Business Week, 4068,* 17. Retrieved from http://www.businessweek.com

Edwards, G. H. (1992). The structure and content of the male gender role stereotype: An exploration of subtypes. *Sex Roles: A Journal of Research, 27,* 553–551.

Kunda, Z., & Thagard, P. (1996). Forming impressions from stereotypes, traits, and behaviors: A parallel-constraint-satisfaction theory. *Psychological Review, 103,* 284–308.

Mansfield, H. C. (2006). *Manliness.* New Haven, CT: Yale University Press.

McCreary, D. R., Wong, F. Y., Wiener, W., Carpenter, K. M., Engle, A., & Nelson, P. (1996). The relationship between masculine gender role stress and psychological adjustment: A question of construct validity? *Sex Roles: A Journal of Research, 34,* 507–516.

Milchan, A. (Producer), Reuther, S. (Producer), & Marshall, G. (Director). (1990). *Pretty woman* [DVD]. USA: Touchstone Home Video.

Plummer, D. C. (2001). The quest for modern manhood: Masculine stereotypes, peer culture and the social significance of homophobia. *Journal of Adolescence, 24,* 15–23.

Rudman, L. A., & Fairchild, K. (2004). Reactions to counterstereotypic behavior: The role of backlash in cultural stereotype maintenance. *Journal of Personality and Social Psychology, 87,* 157–176.

Sontag, M. S., Peteu, M., & Lee, J. (1999). *Clothing in the self-system of adolescents: Relationships among values, proximity of clothing to self, clothing interest, anticipated outcomes and perceived quality of life.* Retrieved from Michigan State University Extension website: http://web1.msue.msu.edu/msue/imp/modrr/rr556098.html

Vescio, T. K., Snyder, M., & Butz, D. A. (2003). Power in stereotypically masculine domains: A social influence strategy X stereotype match model. *Journal of Personality and Social Psychology, 85,* 1062. doi:10.1037/0022-3514.85.6.1062

Figure caption: Label *(Figure)* and number in italics; caption below illustration

POWER OF WARDROBE 8

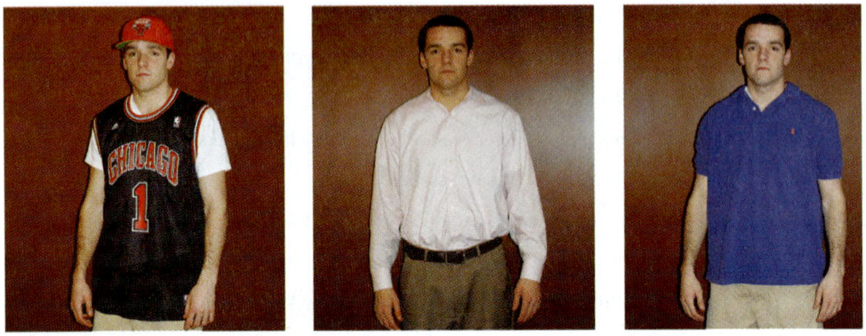

(a) (b) (c)

Figure 1. Male proctor in three conditions: (a) stereotypical, (b) counterstereotypical, and (c) control.

POWER OF WARDROBE 9

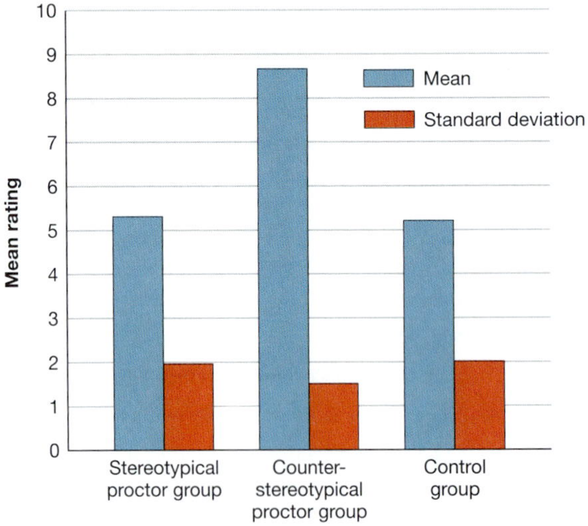

Figure 2. Tukey HSD post hoc test results for the three groups: Group with the stereotypical proctor, group with counterstereotypical proctor, and control group.

20 Documenting Sources: *Chicago* Style

IN THIS CHAPTER

a. Notes and bibliography entries, 390

b. Tables and figures, 407

c. Formatting, 407

Student Model
Research Project: *Chicago* Style, 408

More about
MLA style, 288–346 (ch. 18)
APA style, 347–88 (ch. 19)
CSE style, 416–30 (ch. 21)

Written by editors at the University of Chicago Press, the *Chicago Manual of Style* (16th ed.) provides advice to help writers and editors produce clear and consistent copy for their readers. Many writers in the humanities and social sciences (in history, economics, and philosophy, for example) follow the guidelines provided by the *Chicago Manual* for citing and documenting sources.

Editors at the University of Chicago Press recognize that readers from different disciplines may have different expectations about how in-text citations and bibliography entries should look, so the *Chicago Manual* provides an author-date system similar to that of the American Psychological Association (APA) and the Council of Science Editors (CSE) for writers in the sciences. It also provides a note and bibliography system for writers in the humanities and social sciences. If your readers (including your instructor) expect you to use the author-date system, consult the *Chicago Manual* itself or follow the style detailed in the APA and CSE chapters in this book.

This chapter includes examples of the most common types of *Chicago*-style notes and bibliography entries. For more information or for examples of less common types of sources, consult the *Chicago Manual* itself. You can also subscribe to the *Chicago Manual* online.

Writing Responsibly / Citing and Documenting Sources

When you cite and document sources, you demonstrate how thoroughly you have researched your topic and how carefully you have thought about your sources, which encourages your audience to believe you are a credible researcher. In your citations and documentation you acknowledge any material from which you have quoted, paraphrased, summarized, or drawn information, and you join the conversation on your topic by adding your own interpretation. Accurate entries in the body of your project and bibliography allow your audience to find and read your sources so that they can evaluate your interpretation and learn more about the subject themselves. Accurate entries also demonstrate the care with which you have written your research project, which further reinforces your credibility, or ethos.

to AUDIENCE

20a Creating *Chicago*-Style Notes and Bibliography Entries

> **footnote** Note that appears at the bottom of the page

> **endnote** Note that appears in a list of notes at the end of the project

The note system offered by the *Chicago Manual* allows you to include full bibliographic information in a footnote or endnote or to use an abbreviated footnote or endnote with a bibliography. The University of Chicago Press recommends using abbreviated notes with a bibliography.

Examples of the *complete* form of notes and bibliography entries for different types of sources appear in the next section. An *abbreviated* note typically includes enough information for readers to recognize the work and find it in the bibliography. It usually includes the author's surname, a shortened version of the title that includes the title's keywords in the same order as they appear on the title page, and the page number you are citing. Here is an example of an abbreviated note and a bibliography entry for the same book:

NOTE (ABBREVIATED) 1. Vancouver, *Voyage of Discovery*, 283.

BIBLIOGRAPHY Vancouver, George. *A Voyage of Discovery to the North Pacific Ocean and Round the World, 1791–1795.* Edited by W. Kaye Lamb. London: Hakluyt Society, 1984.

A complete bibliographic note or bibliography entry includes three parts: the author's name, the title of the work, and the publication information (print, electronic, or both). The information you include in each of these parts will differ depending on the type of source you are citing. There are many models, but every variation cannot be covered, so be prepared to adapt a model to your special circumstances.

> Annotated visual of where to find author and publication information, on foldouts accompanying ch. 18 and ch. 19

> **More about**
> Formatting notes (*Chicago* style), 407–08
> Formatting bibliographies (*Chicago* style), 408

Books—Printed and Electronic

In a printed book, the information you need to create a note and bibliography entry (with the exception of the page numbers) is on the title and copyright

Tech | Creating Footnotes and Endnotes

Most word processing programs, including Microsoft Word and Google Docs, allow you to insert footnotes and endnotes easily. This automated system for inserting footnotes will automatically renumber all the notes in your project if you add or delete one. However, the software for managing notes may not provide many formatting options, so check with your instructor in advance to make sure the software's default format is acceptable.

Reference Examples of *Chicago*-Style Note and Bibliography Entries

Books—Printed and Electronic
1. One author 391
    a. Printed 391
    b. Database 392
    c. E-book 392
2. Two or three authors 393
3. More than three authors 393
4. Unnamed (anonymous) author 393
5. Two or more works by the same author 394
6. Group or corporate author 394
7. Editor (no author) 394
8. Author and editor or translator 395
9. Selection from an edited book or anthology 395
10. Edition other than the first 395
11. Introduction, preface, foreword, or afterword by a different writer 396
12. Entry in an encyclopedia or dictionary 396
    a. Printed 396
    b. Online 396
13. Multivolume work 396
14. Book in a series 397
15. Sacred text 397
16. Dissertation or thesis 397

Periodicals—Printed and Electronic
17. Article in a scholarly journal 398
    a. Printed 398
    b. Accessed through a database 399
    c. Online 399
18. Article in a magazine 400
    a. Printed 400
    b. Accessed through a database 400
    c. Online 400
19. Article in a newspaper (signed) 400
    a. Printed 400
    b. Accessed through a database 401
    c. Online 401
20. Article or editorial in a newspaper (unsigned) 401
21. Review 402
22. Letter to the editor 402

Other Electronic Sources
23. Website 403
24. Web page or wiki article 403
25. Discussion list or blog posting 404
26. CD-ROM 404

Audio and Visual Sources
27. Motion picture (film, video, DVD) 404
28. Music or other audio recording 405
29. Podcast 405
30. Performance 405
31. Work of art 405

Miscellaneous Sources—Printed and Electronic
32. Government publication 406
33. Interview (published or broadcast) 406
    a. Printed or broadcast 406
    b. Online 406
34. Personal communication 406
    a. Letter 406
    b. E-mail 406
35. Indirect source 407

---

pages, at the beginning of the book. In an online or e-book, print and electronic publication information often appears at the top or bottom of the first screen or is available through a link.

1. One author

a. Printed The basic note for a printed book looks like this:

Ref. No. Author's first name Surname, *Title: Subtitle* (Place of Publication: Publisher, date of publication), page(s).

Chicago Note & Bibliography Entries

1. **One author**
2. Two or three authors
3. More than three authors

Chicago Note & Bibliography Entries

1. **One author**
2. Two or three authors
3. More than three authors

Here is an example of an actual note:

> 1. Richard Wrangham, *Catching Fire: How Cooking Made Us Human* (New York: Basic Books, 2011), 96–98.

The basic bibliography entry for a printed book looks like this:

> Author's surname, First Name. *Title: Subtitle.* Place of publication: Publisher, date of publication.

Here is an example of an actual bibliography entry:

> Wrangham, Richard. *Catching Fire: How Cooking Made Us Human.* New York: Basic Books, 2011.

The *Chicago Manual* allows for either full publishers' names (the name minus words like *Incorporated* or *Publishers*) or abbreviated versions (*Wiley* instead of *John Wiley & Sons,* for example). Be consistent within your research project. This chapter uses full names.

b. Database

> 2. W. E. B. Du Bois, *The Souls of Black Folk* (1903; Bartleby.com, 1999), chap. 1, www.bartleby.com/114/.

> Du Bois, W. E. B. *The Souls of Black Folk.* Reprint of the 1903 edition, Bartleby.com, 1999. www.bartleby.com/114/.

If the online book is *not* available in print or is not yet in final form and might change by the time your readers seek it out, provide your access date immediately before the DOI or URL. Separate the access date from the surrounding citation by commas in a note and by periods in a bibliography entry.

Tech — Guidelines for Formatting URLs

In *Chicago* style, if a URL will not fit on a single line, break it after a colon or a double slash (//), before or after an ampersand (&) or equals sign, and before a dot or other punctuation mark.

c. E-book

> 3. Charles C. Mann, *1491: New Revelations of the Americas before Columbus* (New York: Alfred A. Knopf, 2005), Adobe Reader e-book, chap. 3.

Mann, Charles C. *1491: New Revelations of the Americas before Columbus.* New York: Alfred A. Knopf, 2005. Adobe Reader e-book.

2. Two or three authors

4. Peter Bernstein and Annalyn Swan, *All the Money in the World* (New York: Random House, 2008), 122.

5. William Rick Crandall, John A. Parnell, and John E. Spillan, *Crisis Management: Leading in the New Strategy Landscape* (Thousand Oaks, CA: Sage, 2012), 119.

Bernstein, Peter, and Annalyn Swan. *All the Money in the World.* New York: Random House, 2008.

Crandall, William Rick, John A. Parnell, and John E. Spillan. *Crisis Management: Leading in the New Strategy Landscape.* Thousand Oaks, CA: Sage, 2012.

3. More than three authors

6. Lawrence Niles et al., *Life Along the Delaware Bay: Cape May Gateway to a Million Shorebirds* (Piscataway, NJ: Rutgers University Press, 2012), 87.

Niles, Lawrence, Joanna Burger, Amanda Dey, and Jan Van der Kam. *Life Along the Delaware Bay: Cape May Gateway to a Million Shorebirds.* Piscataway, NJ: Rutgers University Press, 2012.

4. Unnamed (anonymous) author If no author is listed, begin with the title.

7. *Terrorist Hunter: The Extraordinary Story of a Woman Who Went Undercover to Infiltrate the Radical Islamic Groups Operating in America* (New York: Ecco, 2003), 82.

Chicago Note & Bibliography Entries

1. One author
2. **Two or three authors**
3. **More than three authors**
4. **Unnamed (anonymous) author**
5. Two or more works by the same author
6. Group or corporate author

1st author only listed surname first

1st author plus *et al.* ("and others" in Latin) in note

All authors in bibliography entry

Terrorist Hunter: The Extraordinary Story of a Woman Who Went Undercover to Infiltrate the Radical Islamic Groups Operating in America. New York: Ecco, 2003.

5. Two or more works by the same author Your note will be the same as for any book by one or more authors. In your bibliography, alphabetize the entries by the first important word in the title, and replace the author's name with three dashes in entries after the first.

> Examples 1–3, 391–93

Howard, Philip K. *Life Without Lawyers: Restoring Responsibility in America.* New York: W. W. Norton, 2011.

———. *Sacred Cows: How Dead Laws Drag Down Democracy.* New York: W. W. Norton, 2012.

6. Group or corporate author

8. Blackfoot Gallery Committee, *The Story of the Blackfoot People: Nitsitapiisinni* (Richmond Hill, ON: Firefly Books, 2002), 15. [group as author]

Blackfoot Gallery Committee. *The Story of the Blackfoot People: Nitsitapiisinni.* Richmond Hill, ON: Firefly Books, 2002. [group as author]

7. Editor (no author)

9. Robbie B. H. Goh, ed., *Narrating Race: Asia, (Trans)Nationalism, Social Change.* (New York: Ridopi, 2011), 37.

Goh, Robbie B. H., ed. *Narrating Race: Asia, (Trans)Nationalism, Social Change.* New York: Ridopi, 2011.

NOTE When the abbreviation *ed.* appears after a name, it means *editor,* so for more than one editor, change the abbreviation from *ed.* to *eds.*

Chicago Note & Bibliography Entries

3. More than three authors
4. Unnamed (anonymous) author
5. **Two or more works by the same author**
6. **Group or corporate author**
7. **Editor (no author)**
8. Author and editor or translator
9. Selection from an edited book or anthology

8. Author and editor or translator

10. John Locke, *The Second Treatise of Government,* ed. Thomas P. Peardon (Indianapolis: Oxford University Press, 1990), 124.

11. Adania Shibli, *We Are All Equally Far from Love,* trans. Paul Starkey (Northhampton, MA: Interlink Books, 2012), 71.

Locke, John. *The Second Treatise of Government.* Edited by Thomas P. Peardon. Indianapolis: Oxford University Press, 1990.

Shibli, Adania. *We Are All Equally Far from Love.* Translated by Paul Starkey. Northhampton, MA: Interlink Books, 2012.

Edited by, Translated by, in bibliography

NOTE When the abbreviation *ed.* appears before a name, it means *edited by,* so do not add an *-s* when there is more than one editor.

---

9. Selection from an edited book or anthology

12. Rebecca Arnold, "Fashion," in *Feminist Visual Culture,* ed. Fiona Carson and Claire Pajaczkowska (New York: Routledge, 2001), 208.

[selection author] [selection title] [title of book in which selection appears]

Arnold, Rebecca. "Fashion." In *Feminist Visual Culture,* edited by Fiona Carson and Claire Pajaczkowska, 207–22. New York: Routledge, 2011.

[selection pgs.]

10. Edition other than the first

13. James A. Herrick, *The History and Theory of Rhetoric: An Introduction,* 3rd ed. (Boston: Allyn & Bacon, 2005), 50.

Herrick, James A. *The History and Theory of Rhetoric: An Introduction.* 3rd ed. Boston: Allyn & Bacon, 2005.

Chicago Note & Bibliography Entries

6. Group or corporate author
7. Editor (no author)
8. **Author and editor or translator**
9. **Selection from an edited book or anthology**
10. **Edition other than the first**
11. Introduction, preface, foreword, or afterword by a different writer
12. Entry in an encyclopedia or dictionary

Chicago Note & Bibliography Entries

- 10. Edition other than the first
- 11. Introduction, preface, foreword, or afterword by a different writer
- 12. Entry in an encyclopedia or dictionary
- 13. Multivolume work
- 14. Book in a series

s.v. Abbreviation of the Latin phrase *sub verbo,* "under the word"

11. Introduction, preface, foreword, or afterword by a different writer

14. Mario Andretti, foreword to *Race to Win: How to Become a Complete Champion,* by Derek Daly (Minneapolis: Motorbooks, 2008), 7.

[label: foreword to]

Andretti, Mario. Foreword to *Race to Win: How to Become a Complete Champion,* by Derek Daly, 7–8. Minneapolis: Quayside-Motorbooks, 2008.

12. Entry in an encyclopedia or dictionary

For a well-known reference work such as the *American Heritage Dictionary* or the *Encyclopedia Britannica,* a bibliography entry is not necessary.

a. Printed

15. *The American Heritage Dictionary,* 2nd college ed., s.v. "plagiarism."

b. Online Unless a "last updated" date appears on the site, include an access date before the URL.

16. *Dictionary.com,* s.v. "plagiarism," accessed July 14, 2010, http://dictionary.reference.com/browse/plagiarism.

13. Multivolume work

Vols. published in different years with different titles

17. Robert Caro, *The Years of Lyndon Johnson,* vol. 3, *Master of the Senate* (New York: Alfred A. Knopf, 2002), 4.

[labels: vol., vol. title]

Vols. published in same year with same title

18. George Brown Tindall and David E. Shi, *America: A Narrative History,* 8th ed. (New York: W. W. Norton, 2003), 2:123.

[labels: vol. pg.]

Caro, Robert. *The Years of Lyndon Johnson.* Vol. 3, *The Master of the Senate.* New York: Alfred A. Knopf, 2002.

Tindall, George Brown, and David E. Shi. *America: A Narrative History.* 8th ed. 2 vols. New York: W. W. Norton, 2003.

14. Book in a series

19. Oleg V. Khlevnyuk, ed., *The History of the Gulag: From Collectivization to the Great Terror,* Annals of Communism (New Haven, CT: Yale University Press, 2004), 186–87.

Khlevnyuk, Oleg V., ed. *The History of the Gulag: From Collectivization to the Great Terror.* Annals of Communism. New Haven, CT: Yale University Press, 2004.

15. Sacred text

20. 1 Kings 3:23–26 (King James Version).

21. Qur'an 17:1–2.

Generally, sacred texts are not included in the bibliography.

16. Dissertation or thesis For an unpublished dissertation or thesis, place the title in quotation marks; titles of published dissertations or theses are italicized. Include the type of document (*PhD diss., MA thesis*), the university where it was submitted, and the date of submission.

22. Jessica Davis Powers, "Patrons, Houses and Viewers in Pompeii: Reconsidering the House of the Gilded Cupids" (PhD diss., University of Michigan, 2006), 43–57, ProQuest (AAI 3208535).

Powers, Jessica Davis. "Patrons, Houses and Viewers in Pompeii: Reconsidering the House of the Gilded Cupids." PhD diss., University of Michigan, 2006. ProQuest (AAI 3208535).

Periodicals—Printed and Electronic

A periodical is a publication issued at regular intervals—newspapers are generally published every day, magazines every week or month, and scholarly journals four times a year. For periodicals, include not only the title of the article

---

***Chicago* Note & Bibliography Entries**

12. Entry in an encyclopedia or dictionary
13. Multivolume work
14. Book in a series
15. Sacred text
16. Dissertation or thesis
17. Article in a scholarly journal
18. Article in a magazine

> Annotated visual of where to find author, title, and publication information, on foldouts accompanying ch. 18 and ch. 19

(in quotation marks) but also the title of the periodical (in italics). The type of publication information you include depends on the type of periodical you are citing.

> **More about**
> Formatting author information: Examples 1–6, 391–94

17. Article in a scholarly journal The information you need to create a note and bibliography entry for a printed journal article appears on the cover or title page of the journal and on the first and last page of the article. For articles downloaded from a database, the information appears on the screen listing the articles that fit your search terms, on the full record of the article, or on the first and last page of the file you download. For articles that appear in journals published solely online, you will find the publication information on the website's home page, in the journal's table of contents, or on the first page of the article.

a. Printed The basic note for an article in a printed journal looks like this:

Ref. No. Author's first name and Surname, "Title of Article," *Title of Journal* Vol. no., issue no. (Year of publication): Pages.

Months (May) or seasons (Winter) may be included before the year of publication, but they are not required. If a journal is paginated by volume—for example, if issue 1 ends on page 175 and issue 2 begins on page 176—the issue number may be omitted. Here are examples of notes and bibliography entries of journals with and without issue numbers.

Chicago Note & Bibliography Entries

15. Sacred text
16. Dissertation or thesis
17. **Article in a scholarly journal**
18. Article in a magazine
19. Article in a newspaper (signed)

Paginated by Issue (Issue Number Included)

23. Bishupal Limbu, "Democracy, Perhaps: Collectivity, Kinship, and the Politics of Friendship," *Comparative Literature* 63, no. 1 (2011): 92.
                                                               vol. no.   issue no.

Limbu, Bishupal. "Democracy, Perhaps: Collectivity, Kinship, and the Politics of Friendship." *Comparative Literature* 63, no. 1 (2011): 92.

Paginated by Volume (No Issue Number)

24. Sarah Brown, "The Role of Elite Leadership in the Southern Defense of Segregation, 1954–1964," *Journal of Southern History* 77 (2011): 832.
                                                      vol. no.

Brown, Sarah. "The Role of Elite Leadership in the Southern Defense of Segregation, 1954–1964." *Journal of Southern History* 77 (2011): 827–64.

b. Accessed through a database Most researchers locate journal articles through subscription databases available through their college library. Frequently, articles indexed in such databases are also available in HTML or PDF format through the database. If the article you are citing is available in PDF format, include the page numbers you are citing in your note and the page range in your bibliography entry. If the article is available only in HTML format, add a subhead or paragraph number to your note if this will help readers locate the passage you are citing. To cite an article accessed through a subscription database, add the name of the database and reference number (if any) at the end of your entry, or include the URL if stable. More and more academic journals are also adding digital object identifiers (DOIs); if the article you are citing includes a DOI, add it in place of the database information.

> **HTML** Hypertext markup language, the coding system used to create websites and web pages

> **PDF** Portable document format, a method for sharing documents without losing formatting

> **DOI** Digital object identifier, a permanent identifier given to electronic sources

> 25. Jazmin A. Reyes and Maurice J. Elias, "Fostering Social-Emotional Resilience among Latino Youth," *Psychology in the Schools* 48, no. 7 (2011): 729, doi:10.1002/pits.20580. EBSCOHost (AN6242560).
> [DOI]

> Reyes, Jazmin A., and Maurice J. Elias. "Fostering Social-Emotional Resilience among Latino Youth." *Psychology in the Schools* 48, no. 7 (2011): 723–37. doi:10.1002/pits.20580.

c. Online Online journals may not provide page numbers. Provide a subheading or paragraph number (if the article provides them), and include the DOI (if there is one) or the URL for the article (if there is not).

> 26. Margaret F. Gibson, "Stressing Reproduction: Reading into Parents of Disabled Children." *Disability Studies Quarterly* 32, no. 1 (2012), http://www.dsq-sds.org/article/view/1654/3055.

> Gibson, Margaret F. "Stressing Reproduction: Reading into Parents of Disabled Children." *Disability Studies Quarterly* 32, no. 1 (2012), http://www.dsq-sds.org/article/view/1654/3055.

Chicago Note & Bibliography Entries

15. Sacred text
16. Dissertation or thesis
17. **Article in a scholarly journal**
18. Article in a magazine
19. Article in a newspaper (signed)

Chicago Note & Bibliography Entries

18. Article in a magazine Omit volume and issue numbers, and replace the parentheses around the publication date (month and year or month, day, and year) with commas. Page numbers may be omitted.

a. Printed

27. Marian Smith Holmes, "The Freedom Riders," *Smithsonian,* February 2009, 72.

Holmes, Marian Smith. "The Freedom Riders." *Smithsonian,* February 2009, 70–75.

b. Accessed through a database

28. Jesse Ellison, "The Refugees Who Saved Lewiston," *Newsweek,* January 17, 2009, 69, LexisNexis Academic.

Ellison, Jesse. "The Refugees Who Saved Lewiston." *Newsweek,* January 17, 2009, 69. LexisNexis Academic.

c. Online

29. Alice Karekezi, "The Science of Warp," *Salon,* December 11, 2011, www.salon.com/2011/12/11/the_science_of_warp/.

Karekezi, Alice. "The Science of Warp." *Salon,* December 11, 2011. www.salon.com/2011/12/11/the_science_of_warp/.

19. Article in a newspaper (signed) Because page numbers may differ from edition to edition, use the edition name and section letter or number (if available) instead. A bibliography entry may be omitted.

a. Printed

30. John M. Broder, "Geography Is Dividing Democrats over Energy," *New York Times,* January 26, 2009, national edition, sec. 1.

Broder, John M. "Geography Is Dividing Democrats over Energy." *New York Times,* January 26, 2009, national edition, sec. 1.

If the city in which the newspaper is published is not identified on the newspaper's masthead, add it in parentheses; if it might be unfamiliar to readers, add the state, also.

31. Jim Kenneally, "When Brockton Was Home to a Marathon," *Enterprise* (Brockton, MA), April 20, 2006, sec. 1.

Kenneally, Jim. "When Brockton Was Home to a Marathon." *Enterprise* (Brockton, MA), April 20, 2006, sec. 1.

For well-known national newspapers (such as the *Christian Science Monitor, USA Today,* and the *Wall Street Journal*), no city or state is needed. If you are unsure whether the newspaper is well known, consult your instructor or a reference librarian.

b. Accessed through a database

32. John M. Broder, "Geography Is Dividing Democrats over Energy," *New York Times,* January 26, 2009, late edition, sec. A, LexisNexis Academic. [database]

Broder, John M. "Geography Is Dividing Democrats over Energy." *New York Times,* January 26, 2009, late edition, sec. A. LexisNexis Academic.

c. Online

33. Victor Davis Hanson, "Oil-Rich America?" *Chicago Tribune,* December 8, 2011, www.chicagotribune.com/news/politics/sns-201112080900--tms--vdhansonctnvh-a20111208dec08,0,6557873.column [article URL]

Hanson, Victor Davis. "Oil-Rich America?" *Chicago Tribune,* December 8, 2011. www.chicagotribune.com/news/politics/sns-201112080900--tms--vdhansonctnvh-a20111208dec08,0,6557873.column

20. Article or editorial in a newspaper (unsigned) When no author is named, place the newspaper's title in the author position in your bibliography entry.

Chicago Note & Bibliography Entries

19. Article in a newspaper (signed)
20. Article or editorial in a newspaper (unsigned)
21. Review
22. Letter to the editor
23. Website
24. Web page or wiki article

(*Chicago* style does not require a bibliography entry for unsigned newspaper articles or editorials, but your instructor might.)

    34. "Health before Ideology," *Los Angeles Times,* January 27, 2009, sec. A.

Los Angeles Times. "Health before Ideology." January 27, 2009, sec. A.

21. Review

    35. Anthony Tommasini, review of *Siegfried,* by Richard Wagner, conducted by Fabio Luisi, Metropolitan Opera, New York, *New York Times,* October 29, 2011, sec. C.

Tommasini, Anthony. Review of *Siegfried,* by Richard Wagner, conducted by Fabio Luisi, Metropolitan Opera, New York. *New York Times,* October 29, 2011, sec. C.

22. Letter to the editor
Omit the letter's title, page numbers, and the edition name or number.

    36. John A. Beck, letter to the editor, *Los Angeles Times,* March 16, 2010.

Beck, John A. Letter to the editor. *Los Angeles Times,* March 16, 2010.

Other Electronic Sources

Although it is usually easy to find citation information for books and articles in periodicals, websites can be a bit trickier. Most of the information you need will appear at the bottom or top of the web page or on the site's home page. Sometimes, however, you may need to look further. Click on links such as "About us" or "More information." Frequently, websites do not provide complete information, so provide as much information as you can. If no author is listed, place the site's sponsor in the "author" position. If key information is missing, include a phrase describing the site, in case the URL changes.

> Annotated visual of where to find publication information, on foldouts accompanying ch. 18 and ch. 19

23. Website The basic note for a website looks like this:

> Ref. No. Website Title, Author, Sponsoring Organization, last update or access date if last update not provided, URL.

However, website titles that are the same as book titles or other types of publications should follow the styling for that publication. Here is an example of an actual note for a website that has the same title as a book:

> 37. *Victorian England: An Introduction,* Christine Roth, University of Wisconsin–Oshkosh, Department of English, accessed April 2, 2012, www.english.uwosh.edu/roth/VictorianEngland.htm.

The bibliography entry for the note above looks like this:

> Roth, Christine. *Victorian England: An Introduction.* University of Wisconsin–Oshkosh, Department of English. Accessed April 2, 2012. www.english.uwosh.edu/roth/VictorianEngland.htm.

Include an access date only when the publication date or last update is not indicated. *Chicago* style does not require an entry in the bibliography for web content, but if your instructor does, follow the example above.

24. Web page or wiki article When referring to a specific page or article on a website or wiki, place that page's title in quotation marks. For a wiki article, begin with the article's title.

> 38. "Centennial Farm and Ranch Program," Montana History Wiki, Montana Historical Society, last modified August 4, 2011, http://montanahistorywiki.pbworks.com/w/page/21639590/Centennial%20Farm%20and%20Ranch%20Program.

> Montana History Wiki, Montana Historical Society. "Centennial Farm and Ranch Program." Last modified August 4, 2011. http://montanahistorywiki.pbworks.com/w/page/21639590/Centennial%20Farm%20and%20Ranch%20Program.

Chicago Note & Bibliography Entries

21. Review
22. Letter to the editor
23. **Website**
24. **Web page or wiki article**
25. Discussion list or blog posting
26. CD-ROM

Chicago Note & Bibliography Entries

23. Website
24. Web page or wiki article
25. **Discussion list or blog posting**
26. **CD-ROM**
27. **Motion picture (film, video, DVD)**
28. Music or other audio recording
29. Podcast

25. Discussion list or blog posting A blog post need not be included in the bibliography.

39. Francis Heaney, "The Tie Project, Days 164–173," *Heaneyland* (blog), July 28, 2007, www.yarnivore.com/francis/archives/001900.html#more.

Heaney, Francis. *Heaneyland* (blog). www.yarnivore.com/francis/archives/001900.html#more.

26. CD-ROM If there is more than one version or edition of the CD-ROM add that information after the title.

40. *History through Art: The 20th Century* (San Jose, CA: Fogware Publishing, 2000), CD-ROM, chap. 1.

History through Art: The 20th Century. San Jose, CA: Fogware Publishing, 2000. CD-ROM.

Audio and Visual Sources

The information you need to create notes and bibliography entries for most audio and visual sources appears on the cover, label, or program or in the credits at the end of a film or a television show. Begin with the author, director, conductor, or performer, or begin your citation with the name of the work, depending on what your project emphasizes. The *Chicago Manual* provides few models of audiovisual sources. Those below are based on the principles explained in *Chicago*.

27. Motion picture (film, video, DVD)

41. *Juno*, directed by Jason Reitman, written by Diablo Cody (2007; Los Angeles: Fox Searchlight Home Entertainment, 2008), DVD.

Juno. Directed by Jason Reitman, written by Diablo Cody. 2007. Los Angeles: Fox Searchlight Home Entertainment, 2008. DVD.

28. Music or other audio recording

    42. Johannes Brahms, *Piano Concerto no. 1 in D minor, op. 15,* Berliner Philharmoniker, conducted by Claudio Abbado, Philips Classics Productions BMG D153907, 1986, compact disc.

Brahms, Johannes. *Piano Concerto no. 1 in D minor, op. 15.* Berliner
    Philharmoniker. Claudio Abbado (conductor). Philips Classics Productions
    BMG D153907, 1986, compact disc.

29. Podcast

    43. Melvyn Bragg, host, "The Indian Mutiny," *In Our Time,* BBC Radio 4, podcast audio, February 18, 2010, www.bbc.co.uk/programmes/b00qprnj.

Bragg, Melvyn, host. "The Indian Mutiny." *In Our Time,* BBC Radio 4, February
    18, 2010. Podcast audio. www.bbc.co.uk/programmes/b00qprnj.

30. Performance

    44. Jay O. Sanders, *Titus Andronicus,* dir. Michael Sexton, Anspacher Theater, New York, November 29, 2011.

Sanders, Jay O. *Titus Andronicus.* Directed by Michael Sexton. Anspacher
    Theater, New York, November 29, 2011.

31. Work of art

If a reproduction of the work appears in your project, identify the work in a figure caption. If you discuss the work but do not show it, cite it in your notes but do not provide an entry in your bibliography. If the reproduction is taken from a book, follow the model for a selection from an edited book or anthology.

    45. Alexander Calder, *Two Acrobats,* 1929, wire sculpture, Menil Collection, Houston.

Chicago Note & Bibliography Entries

- 26. CD-ROM
- 27. Motion picture (film, video, DVD)
- **28. Music or other audio recording**
- **29. Podcast**
- **30. Performance**
- **31. Work of art**
- 32. Government publication
- 33. Interview (published or broadcast)

> **More about**
> Figure captions (*Chicago* style), 407

> Example 9, 395

Miscellaneous Sources—Printed and Electronic

32. Government publication For documents published by the Government Printing Office (or GPO), including the publisher is optional. If you omit the publisher, change the colon after the location to a period.

> 46. US Department of Education, Office of Communications and Outreach, *Parent Power: Build the Bridge to Success* (Washington, DC: US Government Printing Office, 2010), 19.

> US Department of Education, Office of Communicaitons and Outreach. *Parent Power: Build the Bridge to Success*. Washington, DC: US Government Printing Office, 2010.

33. Interview (published or broadcast)

a. Printed or broadcast

> 47. Barack Obama, interview by Maria Bartiromo, *Closing Bell,* CNBC, March 27, 2008.

> Obama, Barack. Interview by Maria Bartiromo. *Closing Bell*, CNBC, March 27, 2008.

b. Online

> 48. Barack Obama, interview by Maria Bartiromo, *Closing Bell,* CNBC, March 27, 2008, www.cnbc.com/id/23832520.

> Obama, Barack. Interview by Maria Bartiromo. *Closing Bell*. CNBC, March 27, 2008. www.cnbc.com/id/23832520.

34. Personal communication Unless your instructor requires it, no bibliography entry is needed for a personal communication.

a. Letter

> 49. Evan Marks, letter to the author, August 13, 2005.

b. E-mail

> 50. Chris M. Anson, e-mail message to the author, November 11, 2011.

35. Indirect source If you do not have access to the original source, your note and bibliography entry should name both the original source and the source from which you borrowed the material.

> 51. Theophrastus, *The Characters of Theophrastus,* ed. J. M. Evans and G. E. V. Austen (London: Blackie and Sons, 1904), 48, quoted in Henry Gleitman, *Psychology,* 5th ed. (New York: W. W. Norton, 2000).

> Theophrastus. *The Characters of Theophrastus.* Edited by J. M. Edmonds and G. E. V. Austen. London: Blackie and Sons, 1904, 48. Quoted in Henry Gleitman. *Psychology.* 5th ed. New York: W. W. Norton, 2000.

> **Chicago** Note & Bibliography Entries
>
> 33. Interview (published or broadcast)
> 34. Personal communication
> **35. Indirect source**

20b Using *Chicago* Style for Tables and Figures

The *Chicago Manual* recommends that you number tables and figures in a separate sequence (*Table 1, Table 2, Figure 1, Figure 2*) both in the text and in the table title or figure caption. Tables and figures should be placed as close as possible after the text reference. For tables, provide a brief identifying title and place it above the table. For figures, provide a caption that includes any information about the figure that readers will need to identify it, such as the title of a work of art, the artist's name, the work's location, and a brief description. If the figure or table, or information used to create the figure or table, comes from another source, provide a source note. Source notes for tables generally appear below the table, while source information for figures appears at the end of the figure caption.

20c Formatting a *Chicago*-Style Research Project

The *Chicago Manual* provides detailed instructions about manuscript preparation for authors submitting their work for publication, but it does not offer formatting instructions for college projects. Follow the formatting instructions provided in chapter 9 or chapter 18, or consult your instructor.

> **More about**
> MLA-style formatting, 332–36
> Formatting college projects, 95

1. Format notes.

The *Chicago Manual* recommends numbering bibliographic notes consecutively throughout the project, using superscript (above-the-line) numbers.

> While acknowledging that not all scholars agree, Mann observes, "If Monte Verde is correct, as most believe, people were thriving from Alaska to Chile while much of northern Europe was still empty of mankind and its works."[8]

Type the heading "Notes" at the top of a new page following the end of the text, and type the notes below the heading. (You may need to insert a page break if your word processor has automatically created endnotes on the last page of your paper.)

2. Format the bibliography.

To begin your list of works cited, type the heading "Bibliography," "References," or "Works Cited" at the top of a new page. (Ask your instructor which heading is preferred.) Entries should be formatted with a hanging indent: Position the first line of each entry flush with the left margin, and indent subsequent lines by half an inch. Entries should be alphabetized by the author's surname.

> **More about**
> Hanging indent, 333, 378

Student Model Research Project: *Chicago* Style

The research project that follows was written by Abrams Conrad for a history course at American University. Conrad fulfills his responsibilities to topic and audience by drawing on a variety of relevant and reliable sources to make his case. He fulfills his responsibility to the writers from whom he borrows information and ideas by citing them in abbreviated notes in the text and by providing a complete entry for each work in the list of works cited at the end of the project. He demonstrates his credibility as a researcher and a writer by providing evidence to support his claims and by revising, editing, and proofreading his project carefully.

Writing Responsibly **Of Deadlines and Paperclips**

Instructors expect students to turn in thoughtful, carefully proofread, and neatly formatted papers on time—usually in class on the due date. They also expect writers to clip or staple the pages of the paper *before* submitting. Do justice to yourself by being fully prepared.

to SELF

Abrams Conrad

History 235

Professor Burke

December 15, 2012

Exploration and Empire: James Cook and the Pacific Northwest

Exploration of the Pacific Northwest begins and ends with Captain James Cook, the first British explorer to reach the area, map it, and study its peoples, and with those who had sailed and trained under his command. While others sailed to the Pacific Northwest, their motivation was largely for trade. Cook's voyage and those of his successors were motivated as much by a desire to understand the region and its peoples as by the desire for financial gain.

In the late 1770s, the Pacific Northwest was the globe's last temperate coast to be explored and mapped, primarily due to its remoteness from Europe. To get there, ships had to sail around Cape Horn at the tip of South America. Cook's third voyage, begun in 1778, was undertaken to discover a Northwest Passage, an inland waterway connecting the Pacific Ocean with the Atlantic that would shorten the sailing time from Europe to Asia. The Admiralty had instructed him "to search for, and to explore, such Rivers or Inlets as may appear to be of a considerable extent and pointing towards Hudsons or Baffins Bay."[1] While his findings were negative—he all but eliminated the possibility of an inland passage—he was the first Briton to make contact with the area and truly to study the geography and culture of the region.

Cook made anchor in Nootka Sound for most of April 1778 and then ventured north along the Canadian coast, searching for a waterway northeast, until he put in at Prince William Sound.[2] He made a detailed survey of the coast, a portion of which is shown in Figure 1.

Cook's third voyage was also politically strategic: to thwart Spanish and Russian claims to the Pacific Northwest.[3] With the Spanish in the south and moving north, and the Russians in the north and moving south, the northwest coast, or "New Albion," was a place where the British could establish a claim and perhaps eventually a colony.[4]

Another reason for Cook's exploration of the Northwest was the man himself. Cook was the quintessential explorer; he "never missed an opportunity to chart a reef or an island," wrote Ernest Dodge of the Peabody Museum in Salem, Massachusetts.[5] Cook stood out because he was so

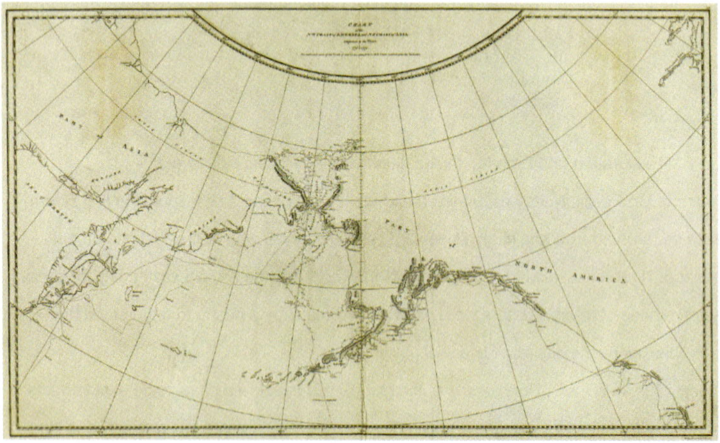

Figure identified in caption

Figure 1. A chart of the northwest coast of America and the northeast coast of Asia, explored in the years 1778 and 1779. Prepared by Lieut. Henry Roberts, under the immediate inspection of Capt. Cook. (1794), David Rumsey Map Coll.

methodical. He was exact in his measurements and never missed an opportunity to learn or write about indigenous peoples.

Claim in topic sentence; supporting facts in balance of ¶

Note numbers placed at natural pause

Cook's explorations of the Pacific Northwest ended with his death in the Hawaiian Islands in early 1779, but his explorations of the Pacific Northwest had direct consequences for traders. James King, who took over command of the expedition after Cook's death, received 800 Spanish dollars in return for twenty sea otter pelts he brought back from the Pacific Northwest—and those were the ragged ones; King received 120 dollars each for pelts in pristine condition, an immense amount of money at that time.[6] It is doubtful the price ever went that high again,[7] but this sum put the region on the map for traders and spawned a new series of voyages.

Claim in topic sentence; supported by comparison in next 4 ¶s

Example 1

What made Cook so important to the Pacific Northwest were the explorations of the area by those who had sailed with him. In this regard, it is interesting to compare the results of those who sailed under Cook with those who did not. Some of the first voyages to the area after Cook's death were the trading voyages of James Hanna, James Strange, and John Meares. Hanna sailed from Macao to Nootka

Sound (in what is now British Columbia) in 1784–86.[8] His voyage produced few results except those of trade, collecting more than 500 skins.[9] Strange sailed from India; his mission was to proceed to the Northwest, trade at Nootka Sound and Alaska, make discoveries, and sail through the Bering Strait and Arctic Ocean, as far north as the North Pole.[10] While his instructions stated discovery as the primary goal, his investors looked upon trade as the focus of the expedition, and Strange ended up doing neither very well. He brought back barely 600 skins, not enough to offset the costs of the voyage, and though he tried to put together another trip, he was unsuccessful.[11]

John Meares led a voyage in 1785 to the Gulf of Alaska, where he anticipated better trading and finer pelts; he proved ignorant both of Russian control over the area and of the harsh Alaskan climate.[12] Meares lost twenty-three men to disease.[13] He also got his ship stuck in the ice and was released only with warm weather and the help of George Dixon and Nathanial Portlock (both had sailed with Cook), who provided aid if he promised to leave at once.[14] While Meares showed some bad judgment, he was ultimately successful in trade in the Northwest, but he was not committed to exploration of the coast or the discovery and naming of locations.[15] Meares himself refers to his voyages as "commercial" and describes people and geography in terms of "extension of our particular commerce."[16] Compare Meares's voyages with those of Portlock, Dixon, and Vancouver, all students of Cook.

In May 1785, the King George's Sound Company sent Nathanial Portlock out on a mission to control the region where furs came from. Portlock, who had been to the Northwest with Cook, sailed from London in September 1785 with two ships, the *King George* and the *Queen Charlotte,* captained by George Dixon, another Cook disciple.[17] They became the first men to drop anchor in Hawaii, specifically Kealakekua Bay, since Cook's death. Their primary goal was to collect furs and trade them in Macao or Canton on the Chinese coast. While they did return with a surplus, they made no real killing.[18] Their journals, published in 1789, heavily advocated advancement of the fur trade, but their voyage became known for its geographical results.[19] They discovered the Queen Charlotte Islands off what is now British Columbia, and their accounts of the local people ultimately proved more important than whatever furs they sold.[20] In their accounts, Cook's influence is easily seen. Both made detailed observations, were meticulous in their calculations, and proved to be just as interested in who sold them goods as in the goods themselves.

Conrad 4

Example 6

It is in the voyage of George Vancouver where Cook's influence is clearest. Sailing from England in 1791, Vancouver's voyage was one part discovery, one part trade, and one part diplomacy. He was to chart the coast from Nootka Sound to Cook Sound for traders, investigate the possibility of an inland northwest passage,[21] retrieve the territory taken by the Spanish around Nootka Sound, and, in the winter months, survey all of the Hawaiian Islands.[22] Arriving in the Strait of Juan de Fuca in late April 1792, Vancouver immediately began his survey of the coast north of California, accomplishing much during the summer of 1792. He missed the Columbia River, much to his dismay, but he mapped and named Puget Sound.[23] His survey finally revealed most of the hazards of the Northwest coastline and negated the idea of an inland northwest passage and a large inland sea.[24] In late August, he met with the Spanish to negotiate the restitution of Nootka Sound. Reaching an impasse, he sent his executive officer back to England requesting instructions and sailed for Hawaii, where he surveyed the Islands.[25] There, in February 1794 (in contrast with Cook), he concluded a treaty with the Hawaiian king, actually gaining control of the islands for England, though the treaty was not ratified in London.[26]

Conclusion: Provides summary and explains significance of research

When comparing the voyages of Hanna, Strange, and Meares with those of Portlock, Dixon, and Vancouver, a glaring difference stands out: While all the voyages shared similar objectives, the *approach* to those objectives was vastly different. Hanna, Strange, and Meares were concerned with trade, pure and simple; Cook's men were also concerned with trade, but as Dodge writes, "[t]he drilling of the Master was notable."[27] The men who had served under Cook considered it their duty both to fulfill their trade objectives and to explore, chart, discover, and explain as much of the region as they could. The missions to the Pacific Northwest that were motivated by trade alone yielded only temporary results. The geographic information gained from the exploratory expeditions of Cook's men paid dividends for years to come. Not only did they provide information for those who followed, both traders and scholars, but they also contributed to the British goal of empire building. Empire is not just geography or territory. It is also about having gone somewhere, mapped it, and named the places. In the Pacific, where the British played a major role in discovery, there are British names in every corner of the sea.[28] Cook and his men were letting it be known worldwide that they had been there. Seeing all those vastly different places, all with British names, added to the inquisitive and the imperialistic mindset of the British. It is at least part of the reason they were so ready to go to war over places so distant.

Notes

1. Cook, *The Journals*, 220–24.
2. Ibid., 230.
3. Rose, "Captain Cook," 102–9.
4. Schwantes, *The Pacific Northwest*, 41.
5. Dodge, *Beyond the Capes*, 15.
6. Schwantes, *The Pacific Northwest*, 43.
7. Ibid.
8. Blumenthal, *The Early Exploration*, 3.
9. Dodge, *Beyond the Capes*, 43–44.
10. Gough, "India-Based Expeditions," 219.
11. Ibid., 217–19.
12. Ibid., 220.
13. Ibid.
14. Blumenthal, *The Early Exploration*, 4; *Oxford Dictionary of National Biography*, s.v. "Meares, John," accessed April 28, 2009, www.oxforddnb.com/subscribed.
15. Blumenthal, *The Early Exploration*, 3.
16. Ibid., 3, 10.
17. Dodge, *Beyond the Capes*, 44.
18. Ibid., 43–58.
19. *Oxford Dictionary of National Biography,* s.v. "Portlock, Nathanial," accessed April 28, 2009, www.oxforddnb.com/subscribed.
20. Dodge, *Beyond the Capes*, 53.
21. Ibid., 135–55.
22. Vancouver, *Voyage of Discovery*, 283–88.
23. Ibid.
24. Ibid., 288.

25. Dodge, *Beyond the Capes,* 135–55.

26. Ibid.

27. Ibid., 43.

28. Dobbie, "Pacific Place Names," 258–65.

Works Cited

Blumenthal, Richard W., ed. *The Early Exploration of Inland Washington Waters: Journals and Logs from Six Expeditions, 1786–1792*. Jefferson, NC: McFarland, 2004.

Cook, James. *The Journals of Captain James Cook on His Voyages of Discovery*. Edited by J. C. Beaglehole. Vol. 3. Cambridge: Cambridge University Press, 1967.

Dobbie, Elliot V. K. "Pacific Place Names and the History of Discovery." *American Speech* 36 (1961): 258–65.

Dodge, Ernest S. *Beyond the Capes: Pacific Exploration from Captain Cook to the Challenger, 1776–1877*. Boston: Little, Brown, 1971.

Gough, Barry M. "India-Based Expeditions of Trade and Discovery in the North Pacific in the Late Eighteenth Century." *Geographical Journal* 155, no. 2 (1989): 215–23. http://www.jstor.org/stable/635063.

Rose, J. Holland. "Captain Cook and the Founding of British Power in the Pacific." *Geographical Journal* 73, no. 2 (1929): 102–22. http://www.jstor.org/stable/1783522.

Schwantes, Carlos A. *The Pacific Northwest: An Interpretive History*. Lincoln: University of Nebraska Press, 1989.

Vancouver, George. *A Voyage of Discovery to the North Pacific Ocean and Round the World, 1791–1795: With an Introduction and Appendices*. Edited by W. Kaye Lamb. Vol. 1. London: Hakluyt Society, 1984.

21 Documenting Sources: CSE Style

IN THIS CHAPTER

a. In-text citations, 416
b. Reference list, 418
c. Formatting, 428

Student Model
Research Project: CSE-Style Reference List, 429

More about
MLA style, 288–346 (ch. 18)
APA style, 347–88 (ch. 19)
Chicago style, 389–415 (ch. 20)

Writers in the sciences customarily use formatting and documentation guidelines from *Scientific Style and Format: The CSE Manual for Authors, Editors, and Publishers* (7th ed.) published by the Council of Science Editors (CSE). CSE style requires that sources be cited briefly in the text and documented in a reference list at the end of the project. The goal of providing in-text citations and a list of references is to allow readers to locate and read the sources for themselves and to distinguish the writer's ideas from those borrowed from sources.

21a Creating CSE-Style In-Text Citations

In-text citations, which appear in the body of your paper, identify any material borrowed from a source, whether it is a quotation, paraphrase, summary, or idea. The CSE offers three formats for citing sources in the body of the project:

- Name-year
- Citation-sequence
- Citation-name

> **Writing Responsibly** — **Citing and Documenting Sources**
>
> When you cite and document sources, you acknowledge any material from which you have quoted, paraphrased, summarized, or drawn information, and you join the conversation on your topic by adding your own interpretation, data, methods, and results. Simultaneously, you give interested readers (including your instructor) a way to join the conversation. Accurate entries allow your audience to find and read your sources so that they can evaluate your research and learn more about the subject themselves. Accurate entries also demonstrate the care with which you have written your project, which reinforces your credibility, or ethos.
>
> to AUDIENCE

The ***name-year system*** requires you to include the last name of the author and the year of publication in parentheses whenever the source is cited:

> Advances have clarified the role of betalains and carotenoids in determining the color of flowers (Grotewold 2006).

author: Grotewold; date: 2006

If you use the author's name in your sentence, include just the year of publication in parentheses:

> Christoffel (2007) argues that public health officers adopted the strategies they did because they were facing a crisis.

author: Christoffel; date: 2007

The name-year system tells readers immediately who wrote the source and how current it is, which is particularly crucial in the sciences. This system involves many rules for creating in-text citations (for example, how to create in-text citations for several authors, with organizations as authors, and so on), which can make it difficult to apply the rules consistently.

The ***citation-sequence*** and ***citation-name systems*** use a superscript number (the same number for a source each time it is cited) to refer the reader to a list of references at the end of the project.

> Some testing of the River Invertebrate Prediction and Classification System (RIVPACS) had already been conducted[1]. Biologists in Great Britain then used environmental data to establish community type[2], and two studies developed predictive models for testing the effects of habitat-specific sampling[3,4]. These did not, however, account for the earlier RIVPACS research[1].

Place reference numbers before punctuation marks. When drawing information from multiple sources, include multiple citations, separated by commas (no space between commas and reference numbers).

Tech — Creating Superscript Numbers

The footnoting function in your word processing program will not work for inserting reference numbers for the citation-sequence or citation-name systems because it will only insert the reference marks in sequence (1, 2, 3, . . .), whereas the CSE system requires that you use the same superscript number for a source each time you cite it. Instead, insert superscript numbers manually, without using your word processing program's footnote function, and type your list of references separately. (Use the Help Directory function to learn about inserting superscript numbers.)

When using the citation-sequence system, arrange the sources in your reference list in order of first mention in your research report and then number them. (The first work cited is number 1, the second work cited is number 2, and so on.) When using the citation-name system, alphabetize sources and then number them. (The first work alphabetically is number 1, the second work alphabetically is number 2, and so on.)

The citation-sequence and citation-name systems need no rules about how to form in-text citations, but they do require readers to turn to the reference list to see the name of the author and the source's date of publication. Since the word processor's footnoting system cannot be used, numbering (and renumbering) of notes must be done by hand. To avoid the confusion that can arise during revision and editing, consider using a simplified author-date system while drafting the research project and inserting the numbers for the citation-sequence or citation-name system in the final draft.

Check with your instructor about which system to use, and use it consistently. If your instructor does not have a preference, consider the advantages and drawbacks of each system before making your choice.

CSE Reference List Entries

1. One author
2. Two or more authors
3. Group or corporate author

21b Preparing a CSE-Style Reference List

A research report or project in CSE style ends with a list of cited references. How you format those references depends on the type of source and the system you use.

Books—Printed and Electronic

> Annotated visual of where to find author and publication information, on foldouts accompanying ch. 18 and ch. 19

In a printed book, you can find most or all of the information you need to create a reference list entry on the copyright and title pages at the beginning of the book. In an online or e-book, print and electronic publication information often appears at the top or bottom of the first page or is available through a link.

1. One author

a. Printed The basic format for a printed book looks like this:

Name-year system

> No punctuation between surname and initials and no period or space between initials

Author's surname First and Middle Initials. Date of publication. Title: subtitle.

Place of publication: Publisher.

Reference: Examples of CSE-Style Reference List Entries

Books—Printed and Electronic
1. One author 418
   a. Printed 418
   b. Online 420
2. Two or more authors 420
3. Group or corporate author 420
4. Edited book 421
5. Selection from an edited book or conference proceedings 421
6. Dissertation 422

Periodicals—Printed and Electronic
7. Article in a scholarly journal 422
   a. Printed 422
   b. Accessed through a database 423
   c. Online 424
8. Article in a magazine 424
   a. Printed 424
   b. Accessed through a database 424
   c. Online 425
9. Article in a newspaper 425
   a. Printed 425
   b. Accessed through a database 425
   c. Online 426

Miscellaneous Sources—Printed and Electronic
10. Website 426
11. Web page 427
12. Discussion list or blog posting 427
13. E-mail message 428
14. Technical report or government document 428

Citation-sequence and citation-name systems

Ref. No. Author's surname First and Middle Initials. Title: subtitle. Place of publication: Publisher; date of publication.

> Lines after the first align with the author's name, not the reference number.

NOTE Book titles are neither italicized nor underlined in CSE style.

Here are examples of actual reference list entries:

Name-year system

Wedge, M. 2012. Pills are not for preschoolers: a drug-free approach for troubled kids. New York (NY): W. W. Norton.

Citation-sequence and citation-name systems

1. Wedge, M. Pills are not for preschoolers: a drug-free approach for troubled kids. New York (NY): W. W. Norton; 2012.

> Annotated visual of where to find author, title, and publication information, on foldouts accompanying ch. 18 and ch. 19

CSE Reference List Entries

1. One author
2. Two or more authors
3. Group or corporate author

CSE Reference List Entries

1. One author
2. **Two or more authors**
3. **Group or corporate author**
4. Edited book
5. Selection from an edited book or conference proceedings

Period after citation only if it concludes in a forward slash

b. Online

Name-year system

Stroup A. 1990. A company of scientists: botany, patronage, and community at the seventeenth-century Parisian Royal Academy of Sciences [Internet]. Berkeley (CA): University of California Press. [cited 2012 Mar 2]. Available from: http://ark.cdlib.org/ark:/13030/ft587006gh/.

print publication information — *access date* — *URL (permalink)*

Citation-sequence and citation-name systems

2. Stroup A. A company of scientists: botany, patronage, and community at the seventeenth-century Parisian Royal Academy of Sciences [Internet]. Berkeley (CA): University of California Press; 1990 [cited 2012 Mar 2]. Available from: http://ark.cdlib.org/ark:/13030/ft587006gh/.

2. Two or more authors

Name-year system

Follow the order of authors on the title page. No and *before last author.*

Jamieson BGM, Dallai R, Afzelius BA. 1999. Insects: their spermatozoa and phylogeny. Enfield (NH): Science Publishers.

Citation-sequence and citation-name systems

3. Jamieson BGM, Dallai R, Afzelius BA. Insects: their spermatozoa and phylogeny. Enfield (NH): Science Publishers; 1999.

If the source has more than ten authors, list the first ten; after the tenth author, insert the words *et al.*

3. Group or corporate author

Name-year system

Institute of Medicine Committee on the Use of Complementary and Alternative Medicine by the American Public. 2005. Complementary and alternative medicine in the United States. Washington (DC): National Academies Press.

Citation-sequence and citation-name systems

    4. Institute of Medicine Committee on the Use of Complementary and Alternative Medicine by the American Public. Complementary and alternative medicine in the United States. Washington (DC): National Academies Press; 2005.

4. Edited book
Name-year system

    Whelan CT, Mason NJ, editors. 2005. Electron scattering: from atoms, molecules, nuclei, and bulk matter. New York (NY): Kluwer Academic/Plenum.

Citation-sequence and citation-name systems

    5. Whelan CT, Mason NJ, editors. Electron scattering: from atoms, molecules, nuclei, and bulk matter. New York (NY): Kluwer Academic/Plenum; 2005.

5. Selection from an edited book or conference proceedings
Name-year system

    selection author   *selection title*
    Berkenkotter C. 2000. Scientific writing and scientific thinking: writing the
                                       book title
    scientific habit of mind. In: Goggin MD, editor. Inventing a discipline: rhetoric scholarship in honor of Richard E. Young. Urbana (IL): National
                          selection pages
    Council of Teachers of English. p. 270–284.

Citation-sequence and citation-name systems

    6. Berkenkotter C. Scientific writing and scientific thinking: writing the scientific habit of mind. In: Goggin MD, editor. Inventing a discipline: rhetoric scholarship in honor of Richard E. Young. Urbana (IL): National Council of Teachers of English; 2000. p. 270–284.

To cite a paper published in the proceedings of a conference, add the number and name of the conference, the date of the conference, and the location of the conference (separated by semicolons and ending with a period) after the title of the book and before the publication information.

CSE Reference List Entries

2. Two or more authors
3. Group or corporate author
4. **Edited book**
5. **Selection from an edited book or conference proceedings**
6. Dissertation
7. Article in a scholarly journal

CSE Reference List Entries

4. Edited book
5. Selection from an edited book or conference proceedings
6. **Dissertation**
7. **Article in a scholarly journal**
8. Article in a magazine
9. Article in a newspaper

> **More about**
> Formatting author information: Examples 1–5, 418–22

> Annotated visual of where to find author and publication information, on foldouts accompanying ch. 18 and ch. 19

48th Annual American Society for Cell Biology Conference; 2008

Dec 13–17; San Francisco.

6. Dissertation For dissertations published by University Microfilms International (UMI), include the access number.

Name-year system

Song LZ. 2003. Relations between optimism, stress and health in Chinese and American students [dissertation]. Tucson (AZ): University of Arizona.
Available from: UMI, Ann Arbor, MI; AAI3107041.
access information   location   access no.

Citation-sequence and citation-name systems

7. Song LZ. Relations between optimism, stress and health in Chinese and American students [dissertation]. Tucson (AZ): University of Arizona; 2003. Available from: UMI, Ann Arbor, MI; AAI3107041.

If the location of the college is not listed on the title page of the dissertation, place square brackets around this information: [Tucson (AZ)].

Periodicals—Printed and Electronic

The information needed to document a printed journal article is on the cover or table of contents of the journal and the first and last pages of the article. For articles downloaded from a database, the information you need appears on the screen listing the articles that fit your search terms, on the full record of the article, or on the first (and last) page of the file you download. For journal articles published online, the information you need appears on the website's home page, on that issue's web page, or on the first screen of the article.

7. Article in a scholarly journal

a. Printed The basic citation for an article in a scholarly journal looks like this:

Name-year system

Author's surname First and Middle Initials. Year of publication. Title: subtitle.
Abbreviated Journal Title. Vol. number(Issue number):page numbers.

Citation-sequence and citation-name systems

Ref. No. Author's surname First and Middle Initials. Title:subtitle. Abbreviated Journal Title. Year of publication;Vol. number(Issue number):page numbers.

Here is an actual citation of each type:

Name-year system

Cox L. 2007. The community health center perspective. Behav Healthc. 27(3):20–21.

> Journal titles: Omit punctuation, articles (*an, the*), and prepositions (*of, on, in*), and abbreviate most words longer than 5 letters (except 1-word titles like *Science* and *Nature*).

Citation-sequence and citation-name systems

8. Cox L. The community health center perspective. Behav Healthc. 2007;27(3):20–21.

b. Accessed through a database Most researchers locate journal articles through subscription databases available through their college library. Frequently, articles indexed in such databases are available in HTML or PDF format through a link from the database. As yet, the CSE does not provide a model for an article accessed through an online database, but since most library databases are by subscription, readers will probably find the URL of the database's home page more useful than a direct link to the article itself. If a DOI is available, include it.

> **DOI** Digital object identifier, a permanent identifier assigned to electronic articles

Name-year system

Yuan F, Mayer B. 2012. Chemical and isotopic evaluation of sulfur sources and cycling in the Pecos River, New Mexico, USA. Chem Geol [Internet]. [cited 2012 Aug 7];291(1–2):13–22. In: Science Direct. Available from: www.sciencedirect.com doi:10.1016/j.chemgeo.2011.11.014

> No period after URL or DOI

CSE Reference List Entries

6. Dissertation
7. **Article in a scholarly journal**
8. Article in a magazine

Citation-sequence and citation-name systems

9. Yuan F, Mayer B. Chemical and isotopic evaluation of sulfur sources and cycling in the Pecos River, New Mexico, USA. Chem Geol [Internet]. 2004 [cited 2012 Aug 7];291(1–2):13–22. Available from: www.sciencedirect.com doi:10.1016/j.chemgeo.2011.11.014

CSE Reference List Entries

6. Dissertation
7. Article in a scholarly journal
8. **Article in a magazine**
9. Article in a newspaper
10. Website

c. Online Omit page numbers for online articles. When a subscription is not required to access the article, provide a direct permalink URL to the article; otherwise, provide the URL to the journal's home page. If a DOI is provided, include it.

Name-year system

Patten SB, Williams HVA, Lavorato DH, Eliasziw M. 2009. Allergies and major depression: a longitudinal community study. Biopsychosoc Med [Internet]. [cited 2012 Feb 5];3(3). Available from: www.bpsmedicine.com/content/3/1/3 doi:10.1186/1751-0759-3-3

[Internet] — URL (permalink) — DOI annotations]

Citation-sequence and citation-name systems

10. Patten SB, Williams HVA, Lavorato DH, Eliasziw M. Allergies and major depression: a longitudinal community study. Biopsychosoc Med [Internet]. 2012 [cited 2009 Feb 5];3(3). Available from: www.bpsmedicine.com/content/3/1/3 doi:10.1186/1751-0759-3-3

8. Article in a magazine
a. Printed

Name-year system

Gladwell M. 2006 Oct 16. The formula. New Yorker. 138–149.

Citation-sequence and citation-name systems

11. Gladwell M. The formula. New Yorker. 2006 Oct 16;138–149.

b. Accessed through a database

Name-year system

No period after URL (unless it concludes with a forward slash) or DOI

Gladwell M. 2006 Oct 16 [cited 2012 Apr 23]. The formula. New Yorker [Internet]:138–149. Available from: www.ebscohost.com/.

Citation-sequence and citation-name systems

12. Gladwell M. The formula. New Yorker [Internet]. 2006 Oct 16 [cited 2012 Apr 23]:138–149. Available from: www.ebscohost.com/.

c. Online
Name-year system

Coghlan A. 2007 May 16 [cited 2012 May 19]. Bipolar children—is the US overdiagnosing? NewScientist.com [Internet]. Available from: www.newscientist.com/channel/health/mg19426043.900-bipolar-children--is-the-us-overdiagnosing.html/.

Citation-sequence and citation-name systems

13. Coghlan A. Bipolar children—is the US overdiagnosing? NewScientist.com [Internet]. 2007 May 16 [cited 2012 May 19]. Available from: www.newscientist.com/channel/health/mg19426043.900-bipolar-children--is-the-us-overdiagnosing.html/.

9. Article in a newspaper
a. Printed
Name-year system

LaFraniere S. 2009 Feb 6. Scientists point to possible link between dam and China quake. New York Times (Late Ed.). Sect. A:1 (col. 3).

Citation-sequence and citation-name systems

14. LaFraniere S. Scientists point to possible link between dam and China quake. New York Times (Late Ed.). 2009 Feb 6;Sect. A:1 (col. 3).

b. Accessed through a database
Name-year system

LaFraniere S. 2009 Feb 6 [cited 2009 Feb 28]. Scientists point to possible link between dam and China quake. New York Times [Internet]. Sect. A:1. Available from: www.lexisnexis.com/.

Citation-sequence and citation-name systems

15. LaFraniere S. Scientists point to possible link between dam and China quake. New York Times [Internet]. 2009 Feb 6 [cited 2011 Feb 28];Sect. A:1. Available from: www.lexisnexis.com/.

CSE Reference List Entries

6. Dissertation
7. Article in a scholarly journal
8. Article in a magazine
9. Article in a newspaper
10. Website
11. Web page

c. Online

Name-year system

> LaFee S. 2006 May 17. Light can hold fatal attraction for many nocturnal animals. San Diego Union-Tribune [Internet]. [cited 2011 May 20]. [about 11 paragraphs]. Available from: www.signonsandiego.com/news/science/.

length

Citation-sequence and citation-name systems

> 16. LaFee S. Light can hold fatal attraction for many nocturnal animals. San Diego Union-Tribune [Internet]. 2006 May 17 [cited 2011 May 20]. [about 11 paragraphs]. Available from: www.signonsandiego.com/news/science/.

Include permalink URL if available; if not, use URL of home page.

Miscellaneous Sources—Printed and Electronic

Annotated visual of where to find author, title, and publication information, on foldouts accompanying ch. 18 and ch. 19

The information needed to document a website or web page usually appears at the top or bottom of the home page or web page. You may also need to look for a link to a page labeled "About us" or "Contact us." Frequently, information needed for a complete reference list entry is missing, in which case provide as much information as you can.

10. Website

Name-year system

In the name-year system, a sample reference entry for a website looks like this:

> Author. Title of website [Medium (Internet)]. Publication date [Access date].
>
> Available from: URL (home page)

Here is an example of an actual entry:

> MIT news [Internet]. 2009 Feb 9 [cited 2012 Mar 10]. Available from: http://web.mit.edu/newsoffice/index.html/.

The site has no author, so the reference list entry begins with the name of the site's sponsor.

CSE Reference List Entries

7. Article in a scholarly journal
8. Article in a magazine
9. **Article in a newspaper**
10. **Website**
11. Web page
12. Discussion list or blog posting

Citation-sequence and citation-name systems

When referencing an entire website, the only difference between the name-year system and the citation-sequence and citation-name systems is that the citation-sequence and citation-name entries add a reference number at the beginning of the entry.

11. Web page When documenting a web page or a document on a website, provide the URL for the web page, not the site's home page.

Name-year system

    article author   *article title*
Schorow S. 2009 Feb 5. Aliens at sea: anthropologist Helmreich studies
                                     website
researchers studying ocean microbes. MIT News [Internet]. [cited 2012 Mar 10].
                            URL (web page)
Available from: http://web.mit.edu/newsoffice/2012/alien-ocean-0205.html

Citation-sequence and citation-name systems

17. Schorow S. Aliens at sea: anthropologist Helmreich studies researchers studying ocean microbes. MIT News [Internet]. 2009 Feb 5 [cited 2012 Mar 10]. Available from: http://web.mit.edu/newsoffice/2009/alien-ocean-0205.html

12. Discussion list or blog posting

Name-year system

             date/time posted
Hall A. 2004 Aug 5, 11:33 am [cited 2012 Jan 30]. Biology of deep Gulf of
                  disc. list   *medium*
Mexico shipwrecks. In: FISH-SCI [Internet discussion list]. [Lulea (Sweden): National Higher Research and Education Network]. [about 4 paragraphs]. Available from: http://segate.sunet.se/archives/fish-sci.html

Citation-sequence and citation-name systems

18. Hall A. Biology of deep Gulf of Mexico shipwrecks. In: FISH-SCI [Internet discussion list]. [Lulea (Sweden): National Higher Research and Education Network]; 2004 Aug 5, 11:33 am [cited 2012 Jan 30]. [about 4 paragraphs]. Available from: http://segate.sunet.se/archives/fish-sci.html

---

CSE Reference List Entries

9. Article in a newspaper
10. Website
11. **Web page**
12. **Discussion list or blog posting**
13. E-mail message
14. Technical report or government document

CSE Reference List Entries

11. Web page
12. Discussion list or blog posting
13. **E-mail message**
14. **Technical report or government document**

13. E-mail message

Name-year system

e-mail author — *date/time sent* — *subject line*
Martin SP. 2012 Nov 18, 3:31 pm. Revised results [E-mail]. Message to: Lydia Jimenez [cited 2012 Nov 20]. [about 2 screens].
e-mail recipient — *length*

Citation-sequence and citation-name systems

19. Martin SP. Revised results [E-mail]. Message to: Lydia Jimenez. 2012 Nov 18, 3:31 pm [cited 2012 Nov 20]. [about 2 screens].

14. Technical report or government document

If no author is listed, use the name of the governing nation and the government agency that produced the document, and include any identifying number.

Name-year system

Department of Health and Human Services (US). 1985 May. Women's health. Report of the Public Health Service Task Force on Women's Health Issues. [publisher unknown]. PHS:85-50206.

Citation-sequence and citation-name systems

20. Department of Health and Human Services (US). Women's health. Report of the Public Health Service Task Force on Women's Health Issues. [publisher unknown]; 1985 May. PHS:85-50206.

21c Formatting a CSE-Style Research Project

> **More about**
> Writing an abstract, 379
> Formatting college papers, 95
> Formatting a paper in APA style, 377–81

The CSE does not specify a format for the body of a college research report, but most scientific reports include the following sections:

- Abstract
- Introduction
- Methods
- Results

- Discussion
- References

Ask your instructor for formatting guidelines, refer to the general formatting guidelines provided in chapter 9, or follow the formatting guidelines for APA style in chapter 19.

Start a new page for your reference list, and title it "References."

Name-year system List entries in alphabetical order by author's surname. If no author is listed, alphabetize by the first main word of the title (omitting articles such as *the, a,* and *an*). Do not number the entries.

Citation-sequence system Number your entries in order of their appearance in your paper. Each work should appear in your reference list only once, even if it is cited more than once in your project. Double-check to make sure that the numbers in your reference list match the numbers in your text.

Citation-name system Alphabetize the entries in your reference list first (by the author's surname or the first main word of the title if no author is listed). Then number them. Each work should appear in your reference list only once, even if it is cited more than once in your project. Double-check to make sure that the numbers in your reference list match the numbers in your text.

Student Model Research Project: CSE-Style Reference List

The sample reference list on page 430 is taken from a laboratory report by Alicia Keefe, University of Maryland. Keefe fulfilled her responsibility to the writers from whom she borrowed information and ideas by supplying a complete citation for each source. She fulfilled her responsibility to her reader by formatting the entries using the name-year system in CSE style, in keeping with her reader's expectations.

Writing Responsibly: Of Deadlines and Paperclips

Instructors expect students to turn in thoughtful, carefully proofread, and neatly formatted papers on time—usually in class on the due date. They also expect writers to clip or staple the pages of the paper *before* the paper is submitted. Do justice to yourself by being fully prepared.

to SELF

References

Geiger P. 2002. Introduction to *Drosophila melanogaster.* Tucson (AZ): University of Arizona, General Biology Program for Teachers, Biology Department [Internet] [cited 2008 Apr 30]. Available from: http://biology.arizona.edu/sciconn/lessons2/geiger/intro.htm

Hoikkala A, Aspi J. 1993 [cited 2008 Apr 28]. Criteria of female mate choice in *Drosophila littoralis, D. montana,* and *D. ezoana.* Evolution [Internet]. 47(3):768–778. Available from: http://web.ebscohost.com

Ives JD. 1921. Cross-over values in the fruit fly, *Drosophila ampelophila,* when the linked factors enter in different ways. Am Naturalist. 6:571–573.

Mader S. 2005. Lab manual. 9th ed. New York (NY): McGraw-Hill.

Marcillac F, Bousquet F, Alabouvette J, Savarit F, Ferveur JF. 2005 [cited 2008 Apr 28]. A mutation with major effects on *Drosophila melanogaster* sex pheromones. Genetics [Internet]. 171(4):1617–1628. Available from: http://web.ebscohost.com doi:10.1534/genetics.104.033159

Service PM. 1991. Laboratory evolution of longevity and reproductive fitness components in male fruit flies: mating ability. Evolution. 47:387–399.

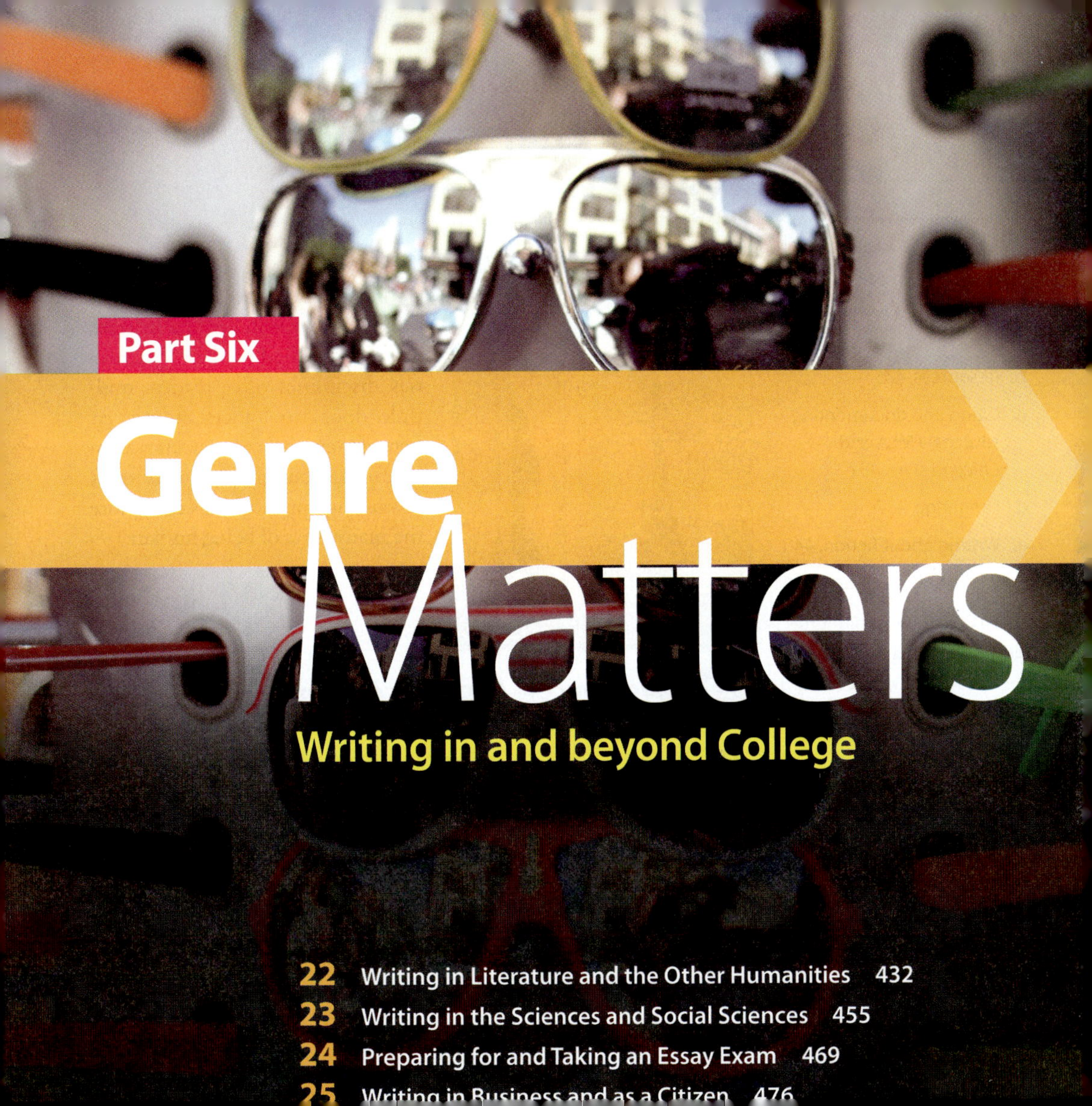

Part Six

Genre Matters

Writing in and beyond College

22 Writing in Literature and the Other Humanities 432
23 Writing in the Sciences and Social Sciences 455
24 Preparing for and Taking an Essay Exam 469
25 Writing in Business and as a Citizen 476

22 Writing in Literature and the Other Humanities

IN THIS CHAPTER

a. Approach, 432
b. Resources, 435
c. Citing and documenting sources—MLA and *Chicago* style, 437
d. Language, 437
e. Writing about fiction, 440
f. Writing about poetry, 446
g. Writing about drama, 451

Student Models
Textual Analysis, 434; Writing about Fiction: Interpretive Analysis, 442; Writing about Poetry: Explication, 446

Professional Model
Writing about Drama: Review of a Play, 451

> *More about*
> Summarizing, 110–11, 256–58
> Annotating, 114–17
> Reading journal, 117–18
> Enjoying what you read, 111–12

There is rarely one right way to interpret or appreciate literature, art, music, or events in history. Instead, the texts studied in these humanities disciplines offer readers multiple doors to understanding. At first glance, these doors may seem confusing, but they actually offer rewarding opportunities to explore the many ways of being human.

22a Adopting the Approach of Literature and the Other Humanities

Whether focused solely on the text and the reader's experience of it or on its social, historical, or cultural contexts, writing in the humanities is an act of interpretation. Yet while those who study the humanities produce multiple meanings, each interpretation must be based on evidence from the text that will persuade others to accept the writer's position.

1. Read actively and reflectively.

Understanding works of literature and other texts in the humanities is not merely a matter of extracting information, but it does begin with reading to gain a basic understanding of the text. Begin by summarizing: What is the main point of the work? In literature, this is the ***theme***. A summary will help you get to the heart of the matter, but keep in mind that literary analysis must do more than summarize what the text says.

Next, annotate or make notes about the work. Some of your notes may provide perspectives on the work that you can use later when writing. The notes in Figure 22.1 (p. 434), for example, show the beginnings of themes that Rita McMahan explores in her analysis of Gary Snyder's poem "Front Lines."

Finally, enjoy what you are reading. If you make an effort to appreciate the language, note insights, or make connections to something in your own experience, you will get more out of your reading.

> **Student Model**
> Explication: "My View from the Sidelines," Rita McMahan, 446

2. Analyze the text.

Understanding a historical event or work of literature, philosophy, or art involves analysis, dividing the work or event into its component parts to see how they work together.

Usually you will need to study the text again (and again) to identify the elements from which it is constructed and to determine how these parts work together. The Quick Reference box on page 435 lists some of the elements that a literary analysis should take into consideration.

> **More about**
> Analysis, 120–22, 262–63, 270–72

> **More about**
> Person, 438–39, 620–21
> Level of diction, 15–16, 543–44
> Style, 495–572 (part 7, Style Matters)
> Figures of speech, 552–53

3. Adopt a critical framework.

Coming to terms with a text requires even more than comprehension and analysis. It also requires *interpretation* (determining what the elements *mean*), *synthesis* (connecting the text to what you already know and to other works you have read), and sometimes *critique* (evaluating the methods and effects of a work). You may compare two or more texts as an aid to understanding, or you may adopt a critical, theoretical approach to the work.

In introductory classes in literature and the other humanities, students are often expected to take a ***formalist approach***, looking closely at the work itself (the primary source) to understand how it functions. Examples of other popular approaches are outlined in the Quick Reference box on page 436.

Before adopting a critical approach, consider the issues you have discussed in class or in other classes you are taking. A psychology class, for example, may

> **More about**
> Interpretation, 122–23, 262–63, 270–72
> Synthesis, 123–25, 262–63, 270–72
> Critique, 125–27, 262–63, 270–72

Writing Responsibly — **Reading with Study Guides**

SparkNotes and similar study guides, long a staple of college bookstores and now available online, may tempt struggling students to substitute the guide for the text itself. Do not succumb! You not only deprive yourself of a learning experience, but you may also find that the study guide leaves you unprepared for the sophisticated level of understanding your instructor expects. If you are having difficulty making sense of a text, discuss the work with classmates, read essays about or reviews of the work at your college library, watch a reading or a performance of the work, or seek advice from your instructor.

to SELF

Student Model: Textual Analysis

> Battlelines? Reminds me of a Buffalo Springfield song my parents used to play—"For What It's Worth?"—from sort of the same period, I think—"Battlelines being drawn..."

FRONT LINES
Gary Snyder

The edge of the (cancer) — *A tumor, sickness, death... scary*
[Yuck!] Swells against the hill—we feel
A foul breeze—
[Sounds like "stinks"] And it (sinks) back down.
The deer winter is here
A chainsaw (growls) in the gorge. — *Animal noise*

Ten wet days and the log trucks stop, — *Not real breather*
The trees breathe.
Sunday the 4 wheel jeep of the
Realty Company brings in
Landseekers, lookers, they say — *Pornography?*
To the land,
[Rape!? Prostitution?] (Spread your legs.)

(The jets crack sound overhead, it's OK here;) — *Hard to read this line out loud*
[Rhythm] Every pulse of the rot at the heart
[Heart disease?] In the (sick fat veins) of (Amerika) — *Why with a "k"?*
[Edge of what? The cancer? Amerika?] Pushes the edge up closer

A bulldozer (grinding) and (slobbering)
Sideslipping and (belching) on top of
[Makes the bushes seem human] The skinned-up bodies of still live bushes
In the pay of a man — *Bulldozer = mercenary*
From town.

[Same rhythm]
Behind is a forest that goes to the Arctic
And a desert that still belongs to the Piute
And here we must draw
Our line. — *Relates to title?*

FIGURE 22.1 Notes from a close reading of the poem "Front Lines," by Gary Snyder

Quick Reference: Elements of Literature

When writing about a work of literature, consider the following elements and ask yourself these questions:

Genre. Into what broad category, or *genre* (fiction, poetry, drama), does the work fit? Into what narrower category (mystery, sci-fi; sonnet, ode; comedy, tragedy) does the work belong? What expectations are set up by the genre, and how does the work adhere to or violate these expectations?

Plot. What happens? Does the plot unfold chronologically (from start to finish), or does the text use flashbacks or flash-forwards? Does the plot proceed as expected, or is there a surprise?

Setting. Where and when does the action occur? Is the setting identifiable? If not, what hints does the text give about the where and when? Are time and place consistent, or do elements from other times or places intrude?

Character. Who is the *protagonist*, or main character? Who are the supporting characters? How believable are the characters? Do they represent types or individuals?

Point of view. Who is telling the story—one of the characters or a separate narrator? What point of view does the narrator take—the first-person (*I*) or third-person (*she, he, it*)? Does the narrator have special insight into the characters or recount events as an outsider?

Language/style. What level of diction (formal, informal, colloquial, dialect) does the text use, and why? How are words put together? Does the text contain long, complex sentences or short, direct ones? Does the text contain figurative language (such as metaphor and simile), or is the writing more literal?

Theme. What is the main point of the story? If you were to tell the story as a fable, what would its moral be?

Symbol. Do any of the characters, events, or objects represent something more than their literal meaning?

Irony. Is there a contrast between what is said and what is meant, between what the characters know and what the reader knows?

Allusion. Does the work contain references to literary and cultural classics or sacred texts?

---

provide a theory that will help you explain the behavior of a character; an economics class may help you understand the market forces affecting the plot; a women's studies class may provide methods of interpretation that will give you new perspectives on historical events.

22b Using the Resources of Literature and the Other Humanities

As you prepare to write about a text, ask your instructor whether you should consult outside sources. ***Primary sources*** for studying a literary work include the work itself; they may include the author's letters or e-mail messages, diaries, interviews, annotated manuscripts, or performances (live or recorded). To write about Gary Snyder's poem "Front Lines," Rita McMahan not only analyzed the poem but also watched a video of Snyder reading and talking about

> **Quick Reference — Critical Approaches to Literature**
>
> **Biographical approach.** Focus on the author's life to understand the work. Does the work reflect the trajectory of the author's own life or perhaps depict a working out in literature of something the author was unable to work out in reality?
>
> **Deconstructionist approach.** Focus on gaps, discontinuities, or inconsistencies in the text that reveal or challenge the assumptions of the dominant culture. What do these inconsistencies communicate that the author may not have intended?
>
> **Feminist approach.** Focus on the power relations between men and women (or elements in the work that take on gender traits). Does the work reinforce traditional power relations or challenge them?
>
> **Marxist approach.** Focus on the power relations among social classes (or among elements that take on class characteristics). Does the work reinforce the status quo or challenge it?
>
> **New historicist approach.** Focus on the social-historical moment in which the work was created. How does the work reflect that historical moment?
>
> **Postcolonial approach.** Focus on the power relations between colonizing and colonized peoples (or on elements in the work that reflect traditional power dynamics). Does the work reinforce or challenge those power relations?
>
> **Queer approach.** Focus on the power relations between "normal" and "deviant." How differently can a text be read when the reader rejects this dichotomy?
>
> **Reader response approach.** Focus not on the author's intentions or the text's meaning but on the experience of the individual reader. How does the individual reader construct meaning in the act of reading?

his poetry and his life, and she arranged to interview the poet via e-mail. Primary sources in the other humanities might include any of the following:

- In film studies, a classic film like *Citizen Kane* (1941) or a popular movie like *Slumdog Millionaire* (2008); a director's annotated script; or a series of storyboards, comic-strip-like sketches showing the main characters, action, and shot sequences in a film

- In classics, a lyric poem by the ancient Greek poet Sappho; a history of ancient Rome by Livy (59 BCE–17 CE), or a vase depicting an important event in classical history

- In art history, a painting, sculpture, or other artistic production or a video of an artist at work

- In philosophy, a text like Plato's *Meno* or a lecture by a philosopher like Peter Singer

- In history, a historical document, such as the Mayflower Compact (1620), or court records detailing an event like the My Lai massacre during the Vietnam War

Secondary sources are works about the author, period, text, or critical framework you are using. They provide information about the primary source you are studying. Use secondary sources to develop and support, not to substitute for, your own interpretation. Shona Sequiera used the framework provided by the documentary *Ethnic Notions*, a secondary source, to assess the main character in Zora Neale Hurston's novel *Their Eyes Were Watching God* (1937), her primary source. You can find secondary sources by searching your library's catalog, specialized databases (such as the *MLA International Bibliography*, *Historical Abstracts*, the *Arts and Humanities Citation Index*, or the *Philosopher's Index*), the *Book Review Digest*, and the *Literary Criticism Index*.

> **Student Model**
> Interpretative analysis: "Transcending Stereotypes in Hurston's *Their Eyes Were Watching God*," Shona Sequiera, 442–46

> **More about**
> Finding information, 206–29 (ch. 13)

22c Citing and Documenting Sources—MLA and *Chicago* Style

Whenever you borrow ideas or information or quote from a work, you must cite the source in the text and document it in a bibliography or list of works cited. While there are other style guides, most writers in literature and the other humanities use either the style detailed in the *MLA Handbook for Writers of Research Papers*, 7th edition, or in the *Chicago Manual of Style*, 16th edition. Ask your instructor which you should use.

> **More about**
> In-text citation (MLA), 288–305
> Works-cited list (MLA), 305–31
> Notes and bibliography (*Chicago*), 390–405

22d Using the Language of Literature and the Other Humanities

Each discipline uses language distinctively, and your writing will be most effective when it follows conventions that are accepted in the discipline in which you are writing.

1. Use the specialized vocabulary of the discipline correctly.

Most academic disciplines in the humanities use specialized vocabulary. Learning that vocabulary will help you understand sources and communicate effectively with your audience. To master this new language, consult discipline-specific dictionaries and encyclopedias, such as the *Penguin Dictionary of Literary Terms and Literary Theory*, *The Columbia Dictionary of Modern Literary and Cultural Criticism*, or *The Oxford Encyclopedia of British Literature*. Consider the terms in context, and ask your instructor for help.

> **More about**
> Finding subject-specific reference works, 208

2. Use past and present tense correctly.

More about Tense, 644–650

Writers in the humanities, including literary studies, usually choose the present tense when writing about the work being studied (the events, characters, and setting) or the ideas of other scholars, and they use the present or past tense (as appropriate) when discussing actual events, such as the author's death or a historical or cultural event from the time that the work was published.

Present Tense

Uses present tense to discuss the work studied

These witches and ghosts are real, and often present, for Haun's characters, and "witch doctors" have busy practices fending them off. Dreams and visions are carefully noted and heeded, and the natural world is festooned with warning signs.
—Lisa Alther, "The Shadow Side of Appalachia: Mildred Haun's Haunting Fiction"

Past Tense

Uses past tense to discuss past events

Margaret Lindsey, defamed as a sorceress (incantatrix) by three men in 1435, successfully purged herself with the help of five women; her accusers were warned against making further slanders under pain of excommunication.
—Kathleen Kamerick, "Shaping Superstition in Late Medieval England"

3. Use first and third person correctly.

More about Person, 458, 620–21

The use of the first person (*I, we*) or third person (*he, she, it, they, Elena, the conflict*) pronoun varies from one humanities discipline to another. In part, this reflects a difference in emphasis: Are writers emphasizing their arguments or the evidence on which they are based? In philosophy, the goal is often to advance one's own perspective:

First person (I)

I begin, in Section 1, by clarifying the kind of groups and the type of collective rights that I shall be concerned with.
—Steven Wall, "Collective Rights and Individual Autonomy"

In literary studies, the emphasis is on the work of literature, so writers use the third person whenever reasonable. Compare these two versions of a sentence from Rita McMahan's essay on the poem "Front Lines":

First Person

When I first read the poem, I thought the conflict was over property on a hillside, . . . but a closer look revealed to me that the conflict was a war between the developers (and their technology) and the hillside, or Earth, itself.

Third Person

A first reading suggests a conflict over property on a hillside, . . . but a closer look reveals that the war is between the developers (and their technology) and the hillside, or Earth, itself.

The version in the third person shifts the emphasis from the writer to the poem and is thus less personal and more persuasive. (Notice also that it shifts to the present tense.)

4. Use the active voice.

In the humanities, writers typically use the active voice:

ACTIVE   Janie's relationship with her third husband, Tea Cake, plays a key role in transforming her concept of racial identity.

PASSIVE   A key role in transforming her concept of racial identity was played by Janie's relationship with her third husband, Tea Cake.

> **More about**
> Active versus passive voice, 535–37

Use of the active voice promotes a clear, concise style and specifies who did what to whom. Of course, some circumstances may require the passive voice, as when the "who" is unknown or when you want to emphasize the action rather than the actor.

5. Use the author's full name at first mention and surname only thereafter.

In writing about the works of others, provide the author's complete name ("Zora Neale Hurston") the first time it is mentioned; subsequently, use the author's surname ("Hurston") only, unless this will cause confusion. (When writing about the Brontë sisters, for example, you may need to specify whether you are discussing Charlotte or Emily Brontë.) You may use the first name when writing about a fictional character, but it is not customary to refer to an author by first name.

More about
Capitalizing titles, 810–11
Quotation marks versus italics for titles, 783–84, 810–11, 814–16

More about
Analyzing assignments, 17–18, 192–93, 471–72

Student Models
Interpretive analysis: "Transcending Stereotypes in Hurston's *Their Eyes Were Watching God*," Shona Sequiera, 442–46
Explication: "My View from the Sidelines," Rita McMahan, 446–51

Professional Model
Review: "Rash and Unadvis'd in Verona Seeks Same," Ben Brantley, 451–54

6. Include the work's title in your title.

When writing about a work of literature or another text (a painting or film, for example), provide the title of the work in the title or subtitle of your project and again in the first paragraph of your text. Capitalize the title correctly and use italics or quotation marks as needed.

22e Writing about Fiction

A common assignment in the humanities is the ***interpretive analysis,*** which calls on the writer to study one or more elements of a text; in literature, a writer might study a character or the setting; in philosophy, a writer might study the use of a particular word or concept (*freedom, free will*); in history, a writer might study the repercussions of a historical event. In some disciplines (such as literature, philosophy, or film), a writer might analyze a single primary source or compare one or more primary sources. Often (particularly in history and art history), students will be asked to draw on secondary as well as primary resources in addition to providing their own analysis.

Another writing assignment that is common in literature and the performing arts is the ***critique*** or review: an assessment of a work of literature or art or of a performance (a play, concert, or film). Some disciplines, such as literature or philosophy, may call on students to ***explicate*** a text, or provide a close reading (line by line or even word by word). Often, a close reading will focus on one or more of the elements of literature. (See the Quick Reference box on p. 435.)

Of course, many writing assignments in college will combine assignment types: To write an academic essay about a work of literature, follow the steps in the writing process discussed in part 1 (pp. 2–105) and the specific recommendations in the sections below.

1. Devise a literary thesis.

Narrow your focus to an idea you can develop fully in the assigned length. To devise a topic in literature, ask yourself questions about the elements of the work:

- What are the central conflicts among or within characters?
- What aspects of the plot puzzled or surprised you, and why?

- How might the setting (time and place) have influenced the behavior of the characters?
- Did the writer use language in a distinctive (or difficult or obscure) way, and why?
- What images recurred or were especially powerful, and why?
- What other works did you think about as you were reading this one, and why?

Then answer one of your questions. Your answer can be your **working thesis**.

As you draft your paper, you should analyze or interpret (not merely summarize) the text, as these contrasting examples demonstrate:

SUMMARY THESIS	In this poem, Snyder shows that development destroys nature.
INTERPRETIVE/ ANALYTICAL THESIS	In this poem, Snyder uses symbolism and rhythm to urge readers to see the conflict between "development" and ecological sustainability.

To support the first thesis, the writer could merely report the poem's main point. To support the second thesis, however, the writer must analyze the poem's symbolism and rhythm and then use that analysis to explain her interpretation of the poem's central conflict.

> **More about**
> Writing ethically, 2–8 (ch. 1), Writing Responsibly boxes (listed on the last pages facing inside back cover)
> Planning, 9–28 (ch. 2)
> Organizing and drafting, 29–45 (ch. 3)
> Crafting and connecting paragraphs, 46–72 (ch. 4)
> Drafting and revising visuals, 73–81 (ch. 5)
> Revising, editing, proofreading, and formatting, 82–105 (ch. 6)

> **More about**
> Devising a thesis, 30

2. Support your claims with reasons and evidence from the text.

As with any writing project, you can use idea-generating techniques like brainstorming, freewriting, and clustering to figure out what your thesis is and why you believe it. Then turn back to the text: What details from the work illustrate or support your reasons? These are the *evidence* your readers will need. Consider this passage from Rita McMahan's essay:

> **More about**
> Idea-generating techniques, 20–25

The title, "Front Lines," implies that a battle (or perhaps multiple battles) is occurring—wars are fought on the front lines; a first reading suggests a conflict over property on a hillside between two opponents, but a closer look reveals that the war is between the developers (and their technology) and the hillside, or Earth, itself. The juxtaposition of the deer and the chainsaw in the first stanza— "The deer winter here / A chainsaw growls in the gorge" (lines 5–6)—pits them on opposite sides of this battle, as does the placement of "log trucks" and "trees" (7–8) and "bulldozer" and "bushes" (18–20).

Topic sentence: States claim

Evidence: Uses quotations and summary from the poem and explains their relevance

> **More about**
> Incorporating evidence, 40–41, 270–72

McMahan argues that Snyder uses the symbolism of war between the developers and nature, and she offers concrete evidence from the text—some quoted, some summarized—to support the claim. Note that McMahan does not merely drop the evidence from the poem into her essay but instead explains its relevance.

3. Support your claims with evidence from outside the text.

Depending on your approach, you may also draw on evidence from outside the text. In the essay in the section that follows, Shona Sequiera draws her critical framework from a documentary film she watched in class. She also draws counterevidence from a secondary source, an essay in a scholarly collection.

Student Model Writing about Fiction: Interpretive Analysis

The essay that follows by Shona Sequiera, a student at Connecticut College, offers an interpretation of the main character in Zora Neale Hurston's novel *Their Eyes Were Watching God* (1937). In her essay, Sequiera rebuts a common criticism of Hurston's characters—that they are "folk," simple, colorful, but not fully human. Measuring the protagonist (or main character), Janie Crawford, against the analysis of caricatured black roles described in the documentary *Ethnic Notions*, Sequiera argues that Janie develops over the course of the novel into a fully developed character who escapes stereotype.

Shona Sequiera

Professor Flood

English 342

3 May 2012

Transcending Stereotypes in Hurston's

Their Eyes Were Watching God

Title: Includes author's surname and title of novel

Parodic images of African Americans permeated popular culture—art, film, and stage performance—from the 1820s through the 1960s, becoming deeply ingrained in the American psyche and shaping "the most gut level feelings about race" in the United States (*Ethnic Notions*). These images form a damaging visual tapestry of white-constructed black identity. As an African American writer, Zora Neale Hurston carried the burden of telling stories *of* her people and *for* her people in a manner that both protested and counteracted false representations of them in mainstream culture. Although *Their Eyes Were Watching God* (1937) has been widely criticized for painting a caricatured picture of African American life (Spencer 113–14), Hurston's heroine, Janie, is ultimately able to transcend oppressive stereotypes and come into her own.

Names author, includes title of work in first ¶

Thesis statement

As presented in the novel, Janie Crawford is not a stereotype but a sexual, romantic, feeling woman who immerses herself in the "great fish-net" (193) of life. After her second husband Jody's death, Janie scrutinizes "her skin and features" (83) to find that "the young girl was gone but a handsome woman had taken her place" (83), a textual moment in which the heroine looks past her skin color and into the life experiences that molded and situated her within the framework of her

Topic sentence

Page reference for quote from *Their Eyes*

Supporting evidence: Uses quotations from novel and explains relevance cultural community. Janie's setting free "the weight, the length, the glory" (83) of her "plentiful hair" (83) is a metaphorical rejection of the control Jody tried to impose upon her sexuality. While Janie may retain the self-assertiveness and independence with men of the mammy figure (*Ethnic Notions*), her physical beauty, lack of fulfillment in motherhood, and disdain for mundane domestic life separate her from that figure. Instead of a stereotypical character, Janie's taking "careful stock of herself" (83) allows her to move from under the control of men to a position of self-assertiveness and independence. By the novel's end, Janie comes to represent a positive image of black women who are not merely color-coded mammy figures (*Ethnic Notions*) but valuable contributors to and members of black culture.

Evidence and interpretation: Refers to stereotype in *Ethnic Notions* and explains why stereotype does not apply

Topic sentence

Like the stereotypical black comedian *Ethnic Notions* identifies as a common type, Janie acts for other people's pleasure. After Jody's death she "starched and ironed her face, forming it into just what people wanted to see" (83). Unlike those figures, however, she does not appear to be content and yet crumble with depression, humiliation, and self-hatred. She rejoices within—"She sent her face to Joe's funeral, and herself went rollicking with the springtime across the world" (88).

Supporting evidence: Uses quotation as support and explains relevance

Topic sentence

In particular, Janie's relationship with her third husband, Tea Cake, plays a key role in transforming her from a stereotype into a realistic black character. Over the course of the novel, Janie journeys from believing that she "wuz just like de rest" (9) of the white Washburn children to marrying the dark-complexioned Tea Cake, who teaches her to love the skin she lives in. Unlike Mrs. Turner, the mulatto who despises her own blackness, Janie learns both to value skin color as an important component of herself and her culture and to look beyond external appearance to

Supporting evidence: Uses quotation and summary, and explains relevance see that the life Tea Cake represents—a happy-go-lucky, romantic, and adventurous existence—is the one that most fulfills her.

Conclusion: Restates thesis (in different words)

Historically, African Americans have been called upon to be the vessels through which damaging white notions of blackness have been showcased (*Ethnic Notions*). Yet Janie Crawford transcends the stereotypical roles expected of her and proves that even though (or especially because) all three husbands are "gone from [her]" (83) upon her return to Eatonville, she values herself enough to move on with her life. Janie plays for neither a white nor a black audience but for herself. As a result, she defies white and black expectations of African American women and is able to experience the depths of love in a period when a black person must not love a thing too much (Morrison 45). In painting a romantic yet realistic portrait of Janie's joy *and* suffering, Hurston argues that the African American experience cannot be defined through distorted notions of color, but that it must be celebrated as a culture of living, fully human beings. Janie's journey toward constructing self-identity provided a model for the African American community, demonstrating how to change their notions of themselves and the ways in which they cater to the dictates of the dominant white culture. Unlike Ethel Waters, who laments in *Ethnic Notions* that "darkies never dream," Janie Crawford dares not only to dream, but to follow her dreams and defy societal guidelines that restrict people on the basis of race, class, and gender.

Shows importance of her analysis

Emphasizes contrast between analysis in *Ethnic Notions* and her own conclusions about Janie's character

Sequiera 4

Works Cited

Ethnic Notions. Dir. Marlon Riggs. KQED, San Francisco, 1986. Videocassette.

Hurston, Zora Neale. *Their Eyes Were Watching God.* 1937. New York:

   Perennial-HarperCollins, 2000. Print.

Morrison, Toni. *Beloved.* New York: Plume-Penguin. 1987. Print.

Spencer, Stephen. "Racial Politics and the Literary Reception of Zora Neale

   Hurston's *Their Eyes Were Watching God.*" *Multiethnic Literature and Canon*

   Debates. Ed. Mary Jo Bona and Irma Maini. Albany: State U of New York P,

   2006. 111–26. Print.

22f Writing about Poetry

While the shape of the poem on the page can be important, poetry is traditionally a spoken art form. When writing about poetry, start by reading the poem aloud or listening to the poet read the work. In addition to the issues that apply to writing about literature generally, pay special attention to the sound, structure, and language of the work. (For more information on writing about poetry, see the Quick Reference box on the next page.)

Student Model Writing about Poetry: Explication

The essay that begins on page 448 was written by Rita McMahan, a student at Eastern Oregon State University. McMahan draws evidence from a close reading of the poem "Front Lines" (see Figure 22.1) to support her claim that poet Gary Snyder uses symbolism and rhythm to persuade readers to accept his view of development. To build her case, McMahan also draws on other primary sources, including a video showing Snyder reading his poetry and information gleaned from an e-mail correspondence with the poet.

Quick Reference: Writing about Poetry

When writing about a poem, consider the following elements and ask yourself these questions:

Sound

Rhythm. Is the rhythm part of the traditional form of the poem? If not, which words are stressed, and how is this relevant to the poem's meaning?

Rhyme. Is the rhyme scheme part of the traditional form of the poem? If not, what is the purpose of the rhyme scheme? If the poem does not rhyme, are there any other sounds linking words or lines in the poem?

Alliteration/Assonance/Consonance. Does the poem use alliteration (the repetition of a consonant sound at the beginning of a stressed syllable) to link lines or words within a line? Does the poem use assonance or consonance, the repetition of a vowel or consonant sound, to link lines or words in a line? What effects do these choices have on the reader or listener?

Structure

Verse form. Is the poem written in a traditional verse form (such as the sonnet or the limerick), or is the form open, or free? Does the verse form relate to the meaning of the poem?

Line length. Are the poem's lines of regular length, or do lengths vary from line to line or from stanza to stanza? Do sentences carry over from line to line, or does each line express a complete thought? If line lengths are irregular, does length emphasize or de-emphasize a thought?

Stanzas. Are lines grouped into regular (or irregular) stanzas? If so, does the stanza convey a single unit of thought, or does an idea or sentence continue across stanzas?

Language

Imagery. What sensory "pictures" does the poem call to mind—the stultifying warmth of a July day in the Deep South? The luxuriant springtime riot of mountaintop flowers? What is the relationship between the images the poem calls forth and the ideas it conveys?

Figurative language. Simile (a comparison using *like* or *as*—"My love is like an ice pick"), metaphor (a comparison that does not use *like* or *as*—"My love is an ice pick"), and a host of other figures of speech create images in the reader's mind. Can you identify any figures of speech in the poem and, if so, how do they affect meaning?

Connotation. Poets choose words for their connotative (implicit) as well as for their denotative (literal) meanings. Consider the emotional difference between the verbs *gripe* and *lament*. Both mean "to complain," but, oh, the difference between the two. Note the connotations of the words in the poem you are studying and how they help create the overall effect of the poem.

Repetition. Poets may choose to repeat an important word or phrase. If a word or phrase is repeated (as is the word *and* in "The Raven"), consider its significance. How does this repetition affect your understanding and experience of the poem?

The last stanza from Edgar Allan Poe's "The Raven" (lines 103–8) demonstrates the issues of sound, structure, and language:

And the ráven, never flítting, **still is sítting,**
　　***still* is sítting**
On the pállid bust of Pállas just above my
　　chamber door´;
And his eyes´ have all the see´ming of a
　　démon's that is drea´ming,
And the lámp-light o'er him strea´ming
　　throws his **shádow on the floor´**;
And my soul´ from out that **shádow** that
　　lies floa´ting **on the floor´**
　　　Shall be lifted—nevermore´

McMahan 1

Rita McMahan

Professor Mencelly

English 110

5 May 2012

My View from the Sidelines: Gary Snyder's "Front Lines"

Gary Snyder might be classified as not only a poet and free thinker, but also as an agent for change—a visionary. One of the Beat generation writers of San Francisco, Snyder has worked as a logger, seaman, trail crew member, and firewatcher (Maxwell); his poetry can be seen as an intersection between his alternative cultural viewpoints and his experiences in nature. In fact, many of Snyder's works focus on maintaining Earth's ecological balance, and "Front Lines," in particular, expresses his passionate feelings on the subject. In this poem, Snyder uses symbolism and rhythm to urge readers to see development and ecological sustainability in a new light.

The title, "Front Lines," implies that a battle is occurring—wars are fought on the front lines; a first reading suggests a conflict over property on a hillside between two opponents, but a closer look reveals that the war is between the developers (and their technology) and the hillside, or Earth, itself. The juxtaposition of the deer and the chainsaw in the first stanza—"The deer winter here / A chainsaw growls in the gorge" (lines 6–7)—pits them on opposite sides of this battle, as does the placement of "log trucks" and "trees" (7–8) and "bulldozer" and "bushes" (18–20).

Snyder employs another symbol to represent the nature of this conflict: cancer. "The edge of the cancer" (1) creates fear in the reader, since cancer strikes without warning, spreading quickly and unpredictably. Likewise, Snyder implies that no one

McMahan 2

is safe from the ravages of unchecked, exploitive growth. Snyder's use of cancer to communicate the destruction of the environment raises what may be perceived as a benign issue—the protection of trees or deer habitat—to something more obviously dangerous, possibly fatal.

In addition to the cancer symbolism, Snyder conjures up the fearful image of rape: "To the land / Spread your legs" (12–13). This appears as a direct order, unlike any other line in the poem, and it is aggressive, not erotic. Because of its consequences to the victim, no restitution can ever be made; what is lost in the act is lost for all time. Similarly, the land can never be returned to its original state after its exploitation by developers. Like the battlefield and cancer, Snyder chooses rape as a symbol for the attack on the land, and as the images accumulate, a feeling of danger and damage overtakes the reader.

Explains significance of symbol

Connects symbolism in this paragraph with other symbols

In addition to symbolism, Snyder employs rhythm to convey this sense of danger. In a 1989 video of Snyder reading his poetry and discussing his techniques with students (*Writers Uncensored*), the way he enunciated each word and gave certain phrases special emphasis made it obvious that he wanted us to notice the sound of each syllable. Snyder explains in the video that "Sometimes driven behind the origin is the rhythm. . . . Rhythm is in a very real sense, primary" (*Writers Uncensored*). Reading "Front Lines," one can infer that Snyder tries to make the reader *feel* "the pulse of the rot at the heart" (15–16) through the way the words themselves are chosen and arranged, with the stress on *pulse, rot,* and *heart*.

Topic sentence (begins second half of essay body)

Integrates quotation as support

Links Snyder's commentary to poem under discussion

There is no single rhythmic pattern at work in the poem, but the second, fourth, and fifth stanzas all end in short, choppy lines, which themselves end in

449

one-syllable words that draw the reader's attention. Furthermore, lines 21–22 ("In the pay of a man / From town") and 25–26 ("And here we must draw / Our line") have a marching cadence, a rhythm that reinforces the battlefield symbolism. Snyder's words and lines are short and easy to read, but their rhythmic impact makes the reader sit up and take notice that something important is being communicated.

Topic sentence

Line 14 ("The jet crack sounds overhead, it's OK here") contains a similar choppy rhythm. In an e-mail, Snyder explained that he chose words to communicate exactness or precision. He said that the printed version of the poem is actually wrong—"jet" should be plural, and "sounds" should be singular, referring to the sound barrier. He explained that the line is meant to convey the sound of jets making sonic booms while going faster than the speed of sound. The rhythm of the line echoes the startling sounds of the sonic booms. As with Snyder's symbolism, his use of rhythm is not simply for decoration, but helps reinforce and make vivid his activist message.

Uses information from e-mail interview with poet as support

Topic sentence

Throughout the poem, Snyder uses symbolism and rhythm to compel the reader to defend the natural world, rather than to "develop" or destroy it, and his use of these techniques generates strong feelings and associations—especially if you have the chance to hear him read his own work, when his words seem even more particular and expressive. The fight to protect the environment continues, as does Snyder's advocacy. At 77, he serves as a professor emeritus at the University of California–Davis, where he continues to influence a new generation of writers and motivate readers to meet the challenges of the modern world (Maxwell).

Conclusion: Thesis restated, importance of poem's theme reiterated

Provides closure by circling back to poet

McMahan 4

Works Cited

Maxwell, Glyn. "About Gary Snyder." *Modern American Poetry: An Online Journal
 and Multimedia Companion to the Anthology of Modern American Poetry
 (OUP, 2000)*. Ed. Ian Hamilton. Dept. of English, University of Illinois at
 Urbana-Champaign, 2002. Web. 15 March 2009.

Snyder, Gary. "Front Lines." *No Nature: New and Selected Poems.* New York:
 Pantheon, 1992. 218. Print.

Snyder, Gary. E-mail interview. 8 Nov. 2008.

Writers Uncensored: Gary Snyder. Prod. Lewis MacAdams and John Dorr. Perf.
 Gary Snyder. Lannan Foundation, 1989. MPEG.

22g Writing about Drama

Like students of fiction, students of drama focus on character, plot, the language and symbols the playwright uses, and the theme (or main point) of the work. Unlike fiction, plays are written to be acted. When writing about drama, you may be asked to go beyond the words on the page, to watch a performance of a play and to critique it in a review. When writing about a performance, offer an assessment not only of the actors' performances and the director's staging, but also of the set, costumes, props, lighting, and sound design, analyzing whether they helped to create a distinctive overall effect. Some issues to consider when critiquing a play are listed in the Quick Reference box on the next page.

> **More about**
> Elements of literature, 435

Professional Model Writing about Drama: Review of a Play

In the review that follows, Ben Brantley of the *New York Times* says little about the play itself; the audience is expected to know the basic plot of Shakespeare's classic tragedy *Romeo and Juliet* and to accept the play as a powerful drama. Instead, he concentrates on assessing the performance—acting, direction, sets, costumes, and lighting—as a guide to potential audience members.

Quick Reference: Writing about Drama

When writing about drama, consider the following elements and ask yourself these questions:

Actors' performances. How well did the actors depict the characters? Did they bring something more to the character than you had recognized on the printed page? Did they build on an unspoken motive, a lie, or omission from the dialogue?

Direction. How effective was the director in shaping the overall production? Were the design elements consistent with the script and performances? Were the pacing and mood of the performance appropriate?

Stage set. Were the stage sets realistic or abstract? Did they reinforce the setting (the place and time) of the play, or were they in contrast to the conventional setting? How effective were the stage sets in reinforcing the themes of the play?

Costumes. Were the costumes appropriate to the characters? Were they appropriate to the period in which the play was set, or were they in contrast to that period? How effective were the costumes in advancing the themes?

Props. What stage properties (props) were used, and what symbolic value might they have?

Lighting and sound design. How effective was the lighting in contributing to the mood of the play? Did music underscore scene changes or contribute to the mood? Was sound used to create appropriate atmospheric effects? How effective were lighting and sound design in reinforcing the themes of the play?

Rash and Unadvis'd in Verona Seeks Same

Playful title to appeal to general audience

By BEN BRANTLEY

Lauren Ambrose plays Juliet on a watery stage Verona in Central Park.

A battle of the elements is being pitched at the Delacorte Theater in Central Park, where "Romeo and Juliet" opened last night in a terrifically exciting new production, starring Lauren Ambrose as a Juliet truly to die for.

Thesis: Indicates review is positive (Note: One-sentence paragraphs okay in newspapers)

On the one hand there's water, lots of it, in the form of a big, baffling pond that stretches across the stage, presumably for symbolic purposes, something to muse upon in perplexity as the actors slosh through it in rubber boots. On the other hand there's the fire that rages in the blood of every performance, a

Support: Examples from the production to support claim that "battle of the elements is being pitched"

Genre Matters • Writing about Drama   **22g**   453

> [Critique: Indicates early in review that performance is a success]

conflagration so consuming that it threatens to turn the show into a collective funeral pyre.

Great news: Fire wins.

Most of the advance word about this four-alarm retelling of the ultimate tragic love story, directed by Michael Greif, has centered on the body of water (70 feet round, one and a half inches deep) that has been made on the stage by the designer Mark Wendland. It looks great, reflecting twilight and moonlight as evening bleeds into night. But to be honest, [Critique: Choice does not support play's central image. (Note: Quotation marks for titles in newspapers)] it doesn't make much sense for either dramatic or poetic purposes.

For maritime Shakespearean endeavors like "The Tempest," "Twelfth Night" or even "The Comedy of Errors," turn on the taps all you want. But for "Romeo and Juliet," a play famous for its imagery of flame and lightning?

I'm not going to pretend that Mr. Greif justifies his watery conceit. [Critique: Shifts from criticism to praise] But he doesn't let it bog down the real, dangerous business of the title characters' love either. . . .

In "Romeo and Juliet" all the performances are so focused and purposeful that no oversize puddle is going to deter them in their zealous course.

For [Critique: Praise for director's vision] what Mr. Greif and his cast have achieved, and what most productions of "Romeo and Juliet" fatally lack, is a sense of infectious, instinctive urgency. Blood is boiling in everybody's veins, whether from love or hate or an addling cocktail of the two, and it breeds impulsive action.

Led by Ms. Ambrose and Oscar Isaac as a Juliet and Romeo whose theme song would never be [Allusion: Motown/Supremes song most readers will know] "You Can't Hurry Love," this production advances with hotheaded speed, even when it's standing still.

"Too rash, too unadvis'd, too sudden, too like the lightning," words with which the perceptive Juliet characterizes her newly discovered passion, apply throughout the show. [Critique: Praise for director's tempo] It's a tempo that inevitably makes for bad ends and wonderful drama.

Mr. Greif and his designers who include Emilio Sosa (costumes) and Donald Holder (lighting) have turned Verona into a cross-cultural watering hole that suggests Venice mixed with Marrakesh and Seville, a place of open-air produce markets (convenient for food fights) and flamenco dancing (good for checking out the erotic chops of potential partners). [Support: Description of set, costumes, lighting]

Quick-Temper Town would be a good nickname for this restless, bustling Verona. Mr. Greif plants storm signals even in the prologue, spoken not with the usual cosmic sadness but in high dudgeon by Mercutio (Christopher Evan Welch), Romeo's wild and crazy best friend. . . . [Support: Evidence for claim that director's vision is appropriate]

It is clear in this context that when Romeo and Juliet instantly fall for each other, and then hightail it to the wedding chapel, they're just doing what comes naturally in Verona. Haste—a word that crops up a lot in the text—is the watchword for everyone's behavior. . . .

Mr. Isaac, last seen in the park as Proteus in "Two Gentlemen of Verona" two years ago, is sweetly and convincingly in thrall to his Juliet, a clumsy, overgrown puppy with the loyalty of a one-owner dog. But it's Ms. Ambrose who gives the production its devastatingly torn heart.

Best known as the petulant Claire in "Six Feet Under," Ms. Ambrose, who recently appeared on Broadway in "Awake and Sing!," makes Juliet into a compelling bundle of mixed instincts. Even at 13, she's the smartest person in Verona, capable of analyzing exactly what's happening to her. Had she lived, she might have been a Viola or Rosalind, a Shakespeare heroine to tutor brash men in the finer arts of loving.

But because she is 13 (and you don't doubt it), Juliet leads not with her head but her hormones. Every line she utters is infused with equal amounts of intelligence and impetuosity. She has enough erotic life force for both herself and Romeo, but Mr. Isaac gallantly contributes his share. And without a hint of the now usually obligatory nudity, this couple can make a drawn-out kiss light up the night, as Michael Friedman's mood-enhancing (but never mood-pushing) music swells in the background.

Red-haired and luminously pale, this Juliet is such a brightly glowing candle that the water motif at last makes perfect sense in that final, fatal scene in the Capulet family tomb. It takes a whole lot of water to quench such a flame. But, ah my friends, before then, it gave a lovely light.

Annotations:
- Critique: Praise for actor's performance
- Background: Identification of actor, other roles readers may know
- Allusion: Other Shakespeare characters familiar to most readers
- Support: Evidence for praise of performance
- Conclusion: Returns to "two elements" theme of introduction
- Allusion: Popular poem, "First Fig," by Edna St. Vincent Millay

Work Together

In groups of three or four, discuss the differences between the review above (pp. 452–54) and one of the student papers in this chapter (pp. 443–46, 448–51). How does the difference in purpose, audience, context, and genre affect the tone, the type of evidence provided, and the focus of the writing project?

23 Writing in the Sciences and Social Sciences

IN THIS CHAPTER

a. Approach, 455
b. Research methods, 456
c. Citing and documenting sources—APA and CSE style, 457
d. Language, 457
e. Common writing assignments, 459

Student Model
Research Report, 461

A scientist—a biologist, nurse, or physicist, for example—looking at these women playing volleyball would focus on their heart or respiration rates, or on the velocity at which the ball is traveling, because scientists focus on the characteristics, systems, and processes of the natural world, whether of people, plants, or planets. A social scientist—an anthropologist, economist, or sociologist, for example—would focus on who they are and how they work together, because social scientists focus on the behavior of people, as individuals and in groups. What unites the sciences with the social sciences, though, is a reliance on *empirical* (experimental, observational) research.

23a Adopting the Approach of the Sciences and Social Sciences

The search for verifiable data anchors the writing produced by both scientists and social scientists. Writing is integral to the work of these disciplines because it is the basic tool for keeping records and sharing results. Researchers make their notebooks and reports useful to other researchers by doing the following:

- Explaining their methods clearly and carefully so that others can repeat the experiment
- Describing data accurately and thoroughly (including the data that *disprove* the hypothesis)

- Placing their findings in the context of research conducted by others
- Offering reasonable conclusions based on those data

23b Using the Research Methods of the Sciences and Social Sciences

> **More about**
> Observational studies, 228
> Surveys, 228–29
> Interviews, 226–28

The research on which scientists base their claims is ***primary:*** They collect data by conducting tests—experiments, observational studies, and surveys, questionnaires, and interviews—to challenge their hypotheses. Scientists usually collect *quantitative* (numerical) data, while social scientists may collect quantitative or *qualitative* (descriptive) data.

Quantitative data, which might include the temperature at which a liquid vaporizes or the number of subjects who answer a question in the same way, can be gathered through experiments, surveys, questionnaires, and interviews. For quantitative data to be meaningful, it must be based on careful measurements and observations, and it must be gathered from a sample that is both representative of the group and large enough that unusual responses will not skew the results. Any scientist who conducts the same experiment should achieve the same results.

Qualitative, or nonnumerical, data provide information about the experiences of individuals. This information may be drawn from interviews, observation, or both, and it often takes the form of a case study or ethnography. Qualitative data might include reports on the feeling a medication induces or descriptions of a subject's behavior. For qualitative research to be useful, the data must be based on a rich understanding of the phenomenon or issues being

---

Writing Responsibly — Presenting Data Accurately

Writing in the spring 2003 issue of the *Quarterly Journal of Medicine,* Christopher Martyn explains the importance of accurately representing research:

> Time, energy and public money are wasted when researchers follow false leads. . . . [E]very time a case of fraud hits the headlines, the reputation of scientists and scientific research takes a knock. In biomedical research, patients may even be harmed, if conclusions are drawn from fraudulent clinical studies (244).

When conducting an experiment, be especially careful to record data accurately. You are far more likely to receive a bad grade for falsifying data than for acknowledging that your experiment did not achieve the desired result.

to TOPIC

studied and must provide great detail. Qualitative data must be organized carefully for the researcher to make sense of the information.

23c Citing and Documenting Sources—APA and CSE Style

Whenever you borrow ideas or information or quote from a work, you must cite the source. While there are a variety of style guides, many scientists use the style developed by the Council of Science Editors to document their sources, while social scientists often use the style devised by the American Psychological Association. Ask your instructor which you should use. All academic documentation styles require you both to cite sources in your text and to provide full bibliographic information in a reference list at the end of your project.

> *More about*
> APA style, 347–88 (ch. 19)
> CSE style, 416–30 (ch. 21)

23d Using the Language of the Sciences and Social Sciences

Since the goal of scientists and social scientists is to convey information, writers in these disciplines concentrate on making their language as clear and precise as possible. Your writing will be most effective when it follows conventions for writing that are accepted in the discipline in which you are writing.

> *More about*
> Figures of speech, 552–53
> Writing concisely, 496–504 (ch. 26)

1. Learn the discipline's vocabulary.

Even at the introductory level, most writing in the sciences and social sciences requires that you learn some specialized terminology and use it with precision. You can learn vocabulary from the context or from the word parts (prefixes, roots, and suffixes) that form the term. The following resources can provide comprehensive explanations:

- Discipline-specific dictionaries and encyclopedias: Since each discipline will have its own terminology, search your library's catalog for appropriate reference sources using the words *dictionary* or *encyclopedia* and the name of the discipline (such as *sociology* or *biology*). Some discipline-specific reference works may be available via your library's website.

> *More about*
> Searching an online library catalog, 220–24

- Textbooks: Most textbooks in the sciences and social sciences set key terms in boldfaced or italic type and define them at first use. Check for an index or glossary at the back of the book or for a list of key terms in the margins or at the end of each chapter.

- Your instructors: Pay attention in lectures not just to what your instructors *say* but also to how they *use* words. Instructors may also define key terms or list them on slides, handouts, or the board.

The following excerpt from a student's report demonstrates both an understanding of and comfort with the specialized vocabulary of her discipline:

> The Mars Global Surveyor (MGS) magnetometer experiment was most useful due to its examination of magnetic properties present in Mars' crust. The most constructive portion was gained when the spacecraft altitude was below 200 km to as low as 101 km during the first ten minutes of periapsis (the period during which MGS was closest to the planet's surface).
>
> —Molly Patterson, Colgate University, Untitled report for Geology 105

2. Use the third person and passive voice to describe how research was conducted.

Scientists and social scientists write research reports so that other researchers can follow their procedures and produce an identical result. Since (in principle) the individual conducting the research is unimportant, researchers in the sciences typically use the third person and passive voice to describe how research was conducted:

> The materials consisted of two PsyScope computer programs run on Macintosh computers and a paper and pencil questionnaire. The participant was first assigned a room for experiment one (conditioning manipulation). The participant was then given the informed consent form, which was signed prior to the start of the experiment. The lights were turned off and the participant read the instruction. The experimenter asked if there were any questions.
>
> —Amy M. Ehret, Illinois State University, "Effects of Stigma on Approach and Avoidance Behaviors in Social Situations"

Some social scientists use the first person (*I, we*) when discussing observations they made as a participant or the conclusions they drew from their research. Social scientists typically avoid the passive voice when describing the actions of participants.

3. Use the past tense to discuss methods and present tense to discuss implications.

Scientists and social scientists use the past tense to discuss methods of data collection or the behavior of research participants, and they use the present tense to discuss the implications of their research. This is neatly demonstrated in the sentence below:

> Since this study **included** only middle-class Caucasians, it **is** not representative of the population as a whole.
>
> —Robyn Worthington, Bristol Community College,
> "Nature versus Nurture: Does Birth Order Shape Personality?"

Past tense
Present tense

23e Writing Assignments in the Sciences and Social Sciences

Common types of writing projects in the sciences and social sciences include the following:

- Literature review: In a literature review, writers summarize research on a specific topic, analyze and evaluate the sources and the research on which these studies were based, and synthesize sources to develop a thorough understanding of the topic.

- Research or laboratory notebook: In a research or laboratory notebook, writers record in precise detail (1) the materials (including sketches of setups if complex) in the order used; (2) a chronological list of the procedures followed; and (3) the results (raw data, clearly labeled and logically organized), including any graphs or calculations.

- Research or laboratory report: In a research or laboratory report, writers provide a detailed description of research, including methods, results, and discussion.

Unlike a humanities research paper, a research or laboratory report in the sciences and social sciences usually follows a standard format:

Title page The title page should include the following information:

- Title: Titles should accurately describe the project; titles should avoid playfulness or puns and should convey as briefly as possible the most important aspects of the report.
- Author's name
- Instructor's name and course number
- Date of submission
- Author notes

> **Student Model**
> Research report "Nature versus Nurture," Robyn Worthington, 461–68

> **More about**
> Summarizing, 110–11, 256–58
> Analyzing, 120–22, 262–63, 270–72
> Evaluating sources, 230–45 (ch. 14)
> Synthesizing, 123–25, 262–63, 270–72

> **More about**
> Author notes, 376–77

Abstract A brief summary of the report, the *abstract* usually includes a one-sentence summary of the most important points in each section of the report. The abstract should be no longer than 150–250 words.

Introduction The introduction provides necessary background, such as a brief review of other, closely related studies, indicates the purpose of conducting the research, and states the limits of what the research is intended to show.

Methods The methods section provides the following:

- Information about participants or subjects, including the number of participants and any relevant demographic information about them
- A description of the methods used to collect information (for example, face-to-face interview, online questionnaire, or telephone survey) or to conduct the experiment
- The equipment used (if any)
- The methods of recording data

The methods section must provide enough detail that others could repeat the study or experiment and achieve the same results.

> **More about**
> Matching graphic to information, 74–78
> Numbering figures and tables, 379–80 (APA)

Results The results section provides details of your outcomes. Information graphics are used to convey results succinctly.

Discussion The discussion section of the report offers readers an interpretation of the results, showing how the data collected support (or fail to support) the hypothesis. The discussion indicates the limitations of the data (what they do not indicate), and it relates the results to those of earlier researchers. (Do the data confirm, undermine, or extend earlier research?) The discussion concludes with an analysis of the implications of the research.

> **More about**
> Creating an APA-style reference list, 358–76
> Creating a CSE-style reference list, 418–28

References The reference list includes secondary sources and begins on a new page, with the heading (the word *References*) centered at the top of the page.

Tables and figures Tables follow the reference list; figures follow tables. Each table or figure appears on a separate page.

Appendixes Appendixes include any figures, tables, photographs, or other materials that amplify but are not central to the discussion. Appendixes should be mentioned in the main body of the text so that readers know to consult them. Each appendix should include only one figure, set of data, and so on, but a report can include several appendixes. If more than one appendix is included, each should be assigned a letter (Appendix A, Appendix B, and so on). Arrange the appendixes in the order in which they are mentioned in the text, and give each appendix a succinct, descriptive title, such as "Appendix A: Background Questions."

> ## Work Together
>
> Read the research report on pages 462–68. Then in groups of three or four, discuss the differences between the research report and one of the student projects in the previous chapter (pp. 443–46, 448–51). How do the approach, language, and structure of the two writing projects differ?

Student Model Research Report

The research report that follows describes a study on birth order and personality conducted by Robyn Worthington, a student at Bristol Community College. Worthington's study follows APA style.

Running head: NATURE VERSUS NURTURE 1

Nature versus Nurture: Does Birth Order Shape Personality?

Robyn Worthington

Dr. Mary Zahm

Psychology 52

December 17, 2012

Title page: Includes title that accurately reflects research topic

---

NATURE VERSUS NURTURE 2

Abstract

Psychological researchers agree that the personalities of siblings differ, but there is much disagreement about the reasons for the differences. Many variables have been studied, including age range, birth order, gender, and nonshared environmental factors. This study examines the extent to which birth order affects personality and attempts to show a correlation. A revised sample of 51 participants completed a Myers-Briggs Type Indicator Test. Results show a significant relationship between birth order and introversion/extraversion, but they do not support the hypothesis fully.

Abstract: Provides summary of most important points in each section.

Introduction

[Margin note: Uses first person to emphasize personal observation]

As the mother of three boys, I have been stunned by the differences in their personalities. Despite having the same parents and the same home environment, their personality differences are great. Researchers in psychology agree that

[Margin note: Shifts to third person]

siblings differ, but there is much disagreement about the reasons for the differences. Variables such as age range, birth order, gender, and nonshared environmental factors have been studied as possible causes. This study investigates a possible correlation between birth order and personality.

[Margin note: Introduction: Explains issues under consideration, offers brief review of related studies]

Darwin's theory of evolution, specifically his principle of divergence, has been used as a possible explanation for the differences in sibling personality (Sulloway, 1996). Darwin theorized that "given enough time, species tend to evolve multiple forms that diverge in character, a process called adaptive radiation" (p. 85). One factor in adaptive radiation is development in different environmental niches. According to Sulloway (1996), the family environment is not a single environment, but a collection of microenvironments. The oldest child comes into an (intact) family of two; the family environment the next child experiences includes two parents and a sibling with whom the second child must compete; the third child finds a family with two parents and two siblings with each of whom the third child must compete, and so on. In short, as each child is born, the family environment changes, including the way that the parents interact with each child and the way the children interact with each other, and this difference in family environment can affect personality (Leman, 1985). By developing diverging personalities, younger siblings avoid competing with older, bigger, more experienced siblings on the same grounds (Sulloway, 1996).

[Topic sentence] Certain characteristics of personality have been associated with birth order. Oldest, or first borns, have been characterized as ambitious high achievers who are usually confident, organized, and conservative (Leman, 1985; Sulloway, 1996). Both Sulloway and Leman suggest that children born second tend to diverge as much as possible from the first born, taking on a totally different set of characteristics. They are noted as being more sociable, more cooperative, and more open to experience than their conservative older siblings, who have a tendency to relate strongly with their parents. Youngest children tend to be charming, affectionate, outgoing, and used to being the center of attention; they may also be spoiled and impatient (Leman, 1985).

[Support: Uses evidence from sources (Sulloway, Leman)]

[Topic sentence] Gender, age range, and nonshared environment are also thought to be factors in personality differences in siblings. In a study of university psychology students, Tammy Mann (1993) predicted that nonshared environmental factors would account for personality differences more than other factors. However, the results showed that the family constellation variables of age, birth order, and gender may be more firmly associated with personality differences in siblings than the nonshared environment. In fact, 27% of the correlations between constellation variables and sibling personality differences were statistically significant (Mann, 1993).

[Support: Uses facts, statistics from source (Mann)]

Methods

This study used Darwin's theory of evolution as well as the theory proposed by Frank Sulloway concerning birth order and personality as models. [Hypothesis] The hypothesis to be tested is that birth order would account for the differences in personality among

Defines key term

siblings. Birth order was defined as either oldest, middle, youngest, or only child. Personality was assessed by the Myers-Briggs Type Indicator (Briggs & Myers, 1980), in the categories of extraversion/introversion, sensing/intuition, thinking/feeling, and judging/perceiving.

The initial sample consisted of 70 randomly selected adolescents and adults from whom 55 surveys were returned. For statistical calculations, only-children were eliminated from the sample, as their number was too few. The revised sample consisted of 51 people ranging in age from 14 to 90 years of age. All were European American and considered themselves of middle-class backgrounds. Of the 51 subjects, 16 reported being an oldest sibling, 17 reported being a middle sibling, and 18 reported being a youngest sibling.

Methods: Description of participants, materials; explanation of how data were collected and analyzed

The Myers-Briggs Type Indicator Test was distributed to the participants along with a background questionnaire (Appendix) on which subjects supplied personal data, including birth order. The surveys were collected, scored, and labeled with four letters which corresponded to the participants' personality type:

E (extraversion) or I (introversion)

N (intuitive) or S (sensing)

F (feeling) or T (thinking)

J (judging) or P (perceiving)

The information collected was statistically evaluated by establishing a null and an alternate hypothesis for each personality trait. The scores were placed in a contingency table, and the calculations were performed and evaluated using the chi-square test for goodness of fit.

Results: Explains outcomes (with visual representation of results) and discloses shortcomings

Results

A statistically significant relationship between birth order and personality traits was found in one of the four areas. Calculations revealed a significant relationship between extraversion/introversion at the .005 (0.5%) level of significance. Of the 16 oldest children, 14 preferred introversion, 10 out of 17 middle siblings showed a preference for extraversion, and 12 out of 18 youngest siblings showed a preference for extraversion. (See Figure 1.) In all other areas, the calculations fell short of a reliable level of significance. In the traits of sensing/intuition, thinking/feeling, and judging/perceiving, the test values were below 1, too low for even a .005 (0.5%) level of significance.

Discussion: Interprets results

Discussion

While this study was able to demonstrate a significant relationship between birth order and the traits of extraversion/introversion, the data collected do not support the hypothesis that birth order can account for the differences in other aspects of personality in siblings. The variables involved may be too difficult to assess using the statistical methods of this study. Other characteristics, such as gender and number or spacing of children, all influence the way that parents relate to their children and the way that siblings relate to each other, so these factors, too, are likely to affect personality. Other factors include genetics and nonshared environmental experiences such as playgroups and nursery school/day care, friends, teachers, and so forth—all of which may have an impact on personality.

With so many variables, assessing the causes of personality differences in siblings is extremely difficult. Based on the results of this study, I have concluded that personality development is not likely the result of any one factor but, instead, a combination of many. Further, since this study included only middle-class European Americans, it cannot be assumed to be representative of the population as a whole. Future research might include a cross-sectional study of various ethnic and socioeconomic groups as a better representation of the population.

An interesting result of the study was that, when the personality traits were divided by gender, 24 out of 31 females demonstrated a preference for the trait of feeling to that of thinking. Future research might include a study of the effect of gender on personality differences or personality differences among siblings based on gender.

> Conclusion: Summarizes findings, acknowledges shortcomings, suggests new avenues for research

References

Briggs, K. C., & Myers, I. B. (1980). *Myers-Briggs Type Indicator.* Palo Alto, CA: Consulting Psychologists Press.

Leman, K. (1985). *The birth order book.* Tappan, NJ: Revell.

Mann, T. L. (1993). A failure of nonshared environmental factors in predicting sibling personality differences. *Journal of Psychology, 127,* 79–86. Retrieved from http://www.heldref.org/pubs/jrl/about.html

Sulloway, F. J. (1996). *Born to rebel: Birth order, family dynamics, and creative lives.* New York, NY: Random House.

> References: Provides full bibliographic information in APA style for all sources cited in report

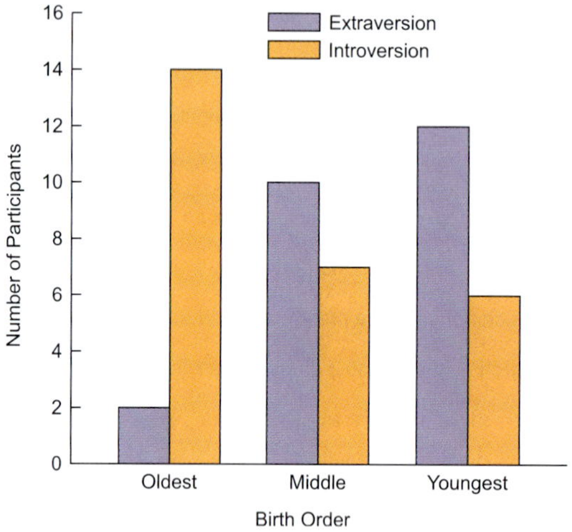

Figure 1. Preference for extraversion/introversion among siblings.

Appendix: Background Questions

Date of birth: _____

Sex: M _____   F _____

How many siblings do you have? _____ (Brothers _____ Sisters _____)

What is your birth order?   Oldest _____   Middle _____

Youngest _____   Only child _____

How many years separate you from the siblings who were born just before and/or just after you?   A brother _____ years older   A sister _____ years older

A brother _____ years younger   A sister _____ years younger

As a young child, did you attend day care or nursery school?   Yes _____   No _____

If yes, how old were you when you first attended? _____

How many years did you attend? _____

24 Preparing for and Taking an Essay Exam

IN THIS CHAPTER

a. Preparing, 469
b. Previewing, 471
c. Writing an effective answer, 472

Student Model
Effective Essay Exam Response, 474

Long before marathon runners cross the finish line, they get ready for the 26.2-mile race. They practice regularly, eat well, and learn the terrain ahead of time. They also use strategy, knowing how to pace themselves and when to turn up the heat. And they do not panic if someone else dashes ahead. Runners know that being prepared is crucial to running a good race.

Students who succeed on essay exams have many of these attributes. They prepare by reviewing their notes and answering practice questions, and they have a test-taking strategy that allows them to get to the finish line. All of this preparation—not cramming the night before—is what leads to a good grade.

24a Preparing for an Essay Exam

You begin to prepare for any college test by reading, taking notes, listening, and working on your assignments. An essay exam, however, requires some special preparation.

> *More about*
> Annotating, 114–17
> Taking notes, 250–63
> Keeping a reading journal, 117–19
> Summarizing, 110–11, 256–58
> Outlining, 35–37, 267–69

1. Take good notes and review them often.

Stay up-to-date on your reading assignments, and take good notes:

- Highlight and underline important terms and concepts, but do not overdo it—highlighting everything means you must reread everything.

- Write down your thoughts and questions, and connect what you are reading to other ideas or situations.
- Note any statements in the text that strike you as especially crucial or interesting—or that might show up on an essay exam.
- For complicated texts, write outlines or summaries that will help you figure out what is going on, keep track of the development of ideas, and recall the material later on.
- When taking notes in class, focus on the major points your instructor is making—do not try to write down every detail.

Keep all your notes in a reading journal. As you review them, focus on the most important ideas and information. Using a highlighter or a pen in a new color, take notes *on* your notes, marking the big topics or drawing connections among major ideas. Reviewing your notes regularly (not just the day before an exam) will help you learn important concepts and identify material you are likely to be asked about.

Study Groups An alternative to coming up with questions on your own is to work in small study groups. Each member could devise a question or an outline for the rest of the group, or members might work together to come up with questions and answers. Study groups work well when members share their ideas and learn from one another; they fail when some members rely too heavily on others to do their thinking for them. Group work can be a challenge when members do not share the same goals, experiences, or cultural or linguistic backgrounds. Before any project starts, be sure to discuss members' expectations.

2. Devise and answer practice questions.

After reviewing your notes, consider the terms and concepts that seem essential, and identify issues or patterns that have arisen repeatedly in readings and lectures. Then brainstorm questions based on these terms, concepts, issues, and patterns. As you brainstorm, be sure to include questions that you fear will be asked, as well as ones you hope will be on the exam. For each of the questions you develop, devise a brief outline and draft a practice answer.

3. Understand the rules for the exam.

Regardless of how you study, ask your instructor exactly what will be required and what will be allowed.

- Is use of a dictionary, thesaurus, or writer's handbook permitted during the exam? What about phones, tablets, or laptops?
- How many questions will there be? Will different questions be worth different numbers of points, or will all questions be equally weighted?
- Is partial credit available for partial answers or for an outline of an answer?
- Are sample questions and answers available?

24b Previewing the Exam

When you sit down to take an essay exam—or any test, for that matter—you may have the impulse to start writing immediately. It is a good idea, though, to take a few minutes to look over the exam, decide on a strategy, and make sure you understand the questions.

1. Read the exam, and develop a test-taking strategy.

The first step in writing a successful exam is to read the entire exam before writing anything. As you read, develop a strategy for taking the test:

- Determine how many points are assigned to each question, and set a time limit for answering each part. Give yourself more time for the questions that are worth more points: Finishing a 50-point question is more important than finishing a 10-pointer.
- Check off the questions that you find easy and can complete quickly. You may want to start with some of those.
- Leave yourself a little time to read through your answers to add or clarify information; to correct errors of spelling, usage, and grammar; and to rewrite illegible words.

2. Analyze the questions: What do they ask you to do?

When you read an exam question, it may be easier to identify the topic than to know what you are supposed to *do* with it. *Compare* is quite different from *define* or *summarize*, so pay close attention to the verbs and do what they tell you. (See the Quick Reference box on page 472 for sample question analyses.)

Also be on the lookout for two-part questions; make sure you answer both parts. Ask your instructor to clarify any question that is vague or confusing.

> **More about**
> Analyzing the assignment, 17–19, 192–93
> Writing about literature, 432–54 (ch. 22)
> Writing in the sciences and social sciences, 455–68 (ch. 23)
> Comparison-contrast, 60–61
> Definition, 62–63
> Summarizing, 110–11, 256–59

> **Quick Reference** — **Common Verbs on Essay Exams**
>
> **What Is the Question?**
>
> 1. **Analyze** the architectural style of Frank Lloyd Wright.
> 2. **Compare and contrast** the major economic problems of the North and South during the Civil War.
> 3. **Define** the terms *denotation* and *connotation,* and discuss these terms in regard to the word *brother.*
> 4. **Describe** how bees build a hive.
> 5. **Evaluate** John F. Kennedy's performance as commander in chief during the Cuban Missile Crisis.
> 6. **Illustrate** the effects of global warming on mammals of the Arctic, including the walrus and the polar bear.
> 7. **List** and **explain** the four main causes of an economic recession.
> 8. **Summarize** Carl Rogers's humanist approach to psychology.
>
> **What Am I Supposed to Do?**
>
> 1. **Name** the elements of his style, and then **critically examine** those elements and the style as a whole.
> 2. Name the economic problems, and explain how they were **similar and different** in the North and South.
> 3. Give the **main characteristics** of the terms. **Show that you understand** the definitions by applying them to *brother.*
> 4. Create, in words, a **step-by-step** picture of what bees do.
> 5. State what you think of Kennedy's performance, and give specific and concrete **evidence** for your opinion(s).
> 6. Give specific **examples** of the effects on the animals named and at least one additional animal.
> 7. **Jot down** the causes and **tell clearly** how each results in a recession.
> 8. Give the **main points** of his approach, and keep your answer **concise.**

Asking for the answer (or even a hint) is inappropriate (and probably will not work), but asking your instructor to define an unfamiliar word (as long as it is not a key term) is perfectly reasonable.

24c Writing an Effective Answer

To structure an essay exam answer, follow the same rules that guide you when you write any other essay.

1. Respond to the question, provide support, organize logically, and review your work.

Writing an effective answer means answering the question you are asked, providing sufficient supporting evidence, and organizing your response clearly and logically, then reviewing your work. Use these tips for showing off what you have learned.

> ### Writing Responsibly
> **Using Your Computer during an Essay Exam**
>
> Check with your instructor in advance of an essay exam to see whether you can write your exam on a laptop. The computer will allow you to present a readable copy: You can use cut-and-paste to revise and reorganize your answer and run a spell-check program to catch and correct the most obvious typos. It would be inappropriate—and unfair to your classmates—to do anything other than write, so avoid the temptation to consult online sources; only open your word processing program and leave your browser closed.
>
> to OTHER WRITERS

- Write a thesis statement, one or two sentences that express your main point and that respond directly to the question.
- Outline the points you want to make. Jot down the evidence you will use.
- Draft your answer. Start with your thesis and use your outline to fill in your explanation of the thesis.
- Leave ample margins on each side of the page and several blank lines below each answer, in case you decide to add information later on.
- When you have finished your draft, reread it, correcting any problems with coherence, correctness, and legibility.

> **More about**
> Informal (scratch) outlines, 35–36
> Thesis statements, 29–33
> Transitions, 54–55
> Supporting your ideas, 40–42

Quick Reference: What an Effective Answer Does—and Does Not Do

An effective answer . . .	An effective answer does not . . .
has a clear thesis that answers the question	answer the question you hoped would be asked
answers the question that was asked	stick in information on the topic that is unrelated to the question
provides ample and accurate supporting evidence	pad the answer by repeating what you have already said
answers the question parts in the order they were asked	make personal judgments that the question does not ask for
uses the method of development suggested by the question (such as analysis, comparison-contrast, definition)	

Student Model | Effective Essay Exam Response

The sample answer on page 475 responds directly to the exam question by comparing *The Big Lebowski* and *The Big Sleep* and by including the core concept "film noir" in the answer. Notice that this writer fulfills his responsibility to his reader (and to himself) by demonstrating that he understands the issues discussed in class and can synthesize information from films he has seen to support his claims.

Essay Exam Question

Identify and compare/contrast the films from which the stills below are taken. Be sure to include in your discussion at least one of the core concepts we have discussed in class, such as genre, dialogue, film noir, etc. (30 points)

Thesis: Big Lebowski is new kind of film noir, main difference is kind of hero

> **Thesis answers question**
>
> **Core concept discussed in class**

Though The Big Lebowski is generally considered a parody of film noir detective stories such as The Big Sleep, it might also be categorized as a contemporary variation on the style. As the still photos show, the differences are obvious: gonzo comedy aside, Lebowski chiefly differs in the nature and quality of its hero.

> **Emphasizes contrast between heroes**

Instead of the occasionally superhuman wit and capability of Philip Marlowe, we have The Dude, called by the film's narrator "one of the laziest people on the planet Earth." However, though The Dude's ineptitude is largely played for laughs, much of the humor derives from discomfort and even dread; his insufficiency as a hero only heightens the sense of alienation.

> **Supports claims with details about heroes from these films**

    At the beginning of The Big Sleep, Marlowe is made to sit in an orchid hothouse, where he proceeds to grow more physically uncomfortable with every passing moment, but he is able to speak his client's language, anticipate his interests and needs, and ultimately earn the general's quiet admiration. The Dude, in contrast, is so out of his depth that he seems incapable of scoring a single point against anyone he meets. When The Dude finds himself in a shadow-drenched room, the viewer may not feel an immediate sense of dread, but it does seem clear that the protagonist has little hope of prevailing. In a particularly revealing scene, The Dude's "client" taunts him with the failure of his generation's ideals, and our hero has no real answer.

> **Conclusion compares/contrasts heroes**

    These two scenes reveal the core of the typical noir hero: the individual who loses, over and over again, and who is compelled to absorb these defeats and continue on, often with a diminished sense of self. The hero responds by creating a persona to act as surrogate for this loss—one as the hard-boiled detective (Marlowe), and the other as the hyper-passive Dude.

> **Returns to key concept and how these heroes display it**

25 Writing in Business and as a Citizen
by Amy Rupiper Taggart

IN THIS CHAPTER

a. Business letter formats, 476
b. Business letters, 479
c. Business memos, 481
d. Job application letters, 482
e. Résumés, 486
f. Reports and proposals, 490
g. Press releases, 492

Student Models
Job Application, 485;
Traditional Résumé, 487;
Scannable Résumé, 489

Professional Models
Business Letter: Apology, 480; Business Memo, 482;
Press Release, 493

If you bought a bag of apples at the grocery store on Wednesday and discovered on Thursday that most of them were rotten, you would probably complain to the produce manager and ask for a refund. If this kind of thing happened often, you might write a letter to the store's owner. If you found something rotten in a government agency or corporation, you might write a letter to the editor to bring the problem to the attention of your community. If you found an issue that you could help resolve, you might offer a proposal for solving the problem and promote your program with a press release. Business writing, then, is more than memos or résumés and cover letters. It is something we all do, whether as employees or as citizens.

25a Using Business Letter Formats

Regardless of what you do after college, you will need to know how to write a good business letter. In company settings, letters are used to communicate with people outside the office—with customers, for example. While some business communications may be sent by e-mail (letters to the editor, for example, are frequently submitted electronically), more formal communications or communications that should remain private (such as notifying employees of a salary increase) are best communicated in printed form.

In your personal life, you may need to write a business letter to request information, thank someone, or comment on a product or service. The formality of the context can serve as a guide in determining whether e-mail or a printed letter is more appropriate.

Whether sending letters by conventional mail or e-mail, be considerate of your reader's time and present information courteously and concisely. These guidelines can help you write an effective business letter:

- **State your purpose in the first paragraph.** Businesspeople want to see at a glance what the letter is about.
- **Be clear and specific throughout the letter.** A vague, muddled, or repetitious letter may be ignored.
- **Keep your paragraphs short.** This will help your reader grasp your major points quickly.
- **Adopt a positive yet somewhat formal tone.** Make sure the tone fits the audience and purpose.
- **Reread and edit your letter.** Clarify your points, reduce wordiness, and correct all errors. Grammatical and typographical errors may severely diminish your credibility with your reader.

1. Use a standard letter format.

Whatever the purpose of your business letter, follow one of two standard formats:

1. **Full block style.** Align all text with the left-hand margin. This is the best choice when you are writing a letter on letterhead stationery.
2. **Modified block style.** Align the following elements just to the right of the center of the page: return address, date, closing, and signature. Align everything else with the left-hand margin.

> **Professional Models**
> Business Letters:
> Full block style, 480
> Modified block style, 485

In addition to using an appropriate letter style, follow these design guidelines:

- Use 8 ½ × 11–inch white or off-white paper. You may also use letterhead stationery, especially if you are communicating as a representative of a company or organization.
- Single-space your paragraphs and insert an extra line of space between them; do not indent paragraphs.
- Use a standard size (number 10) envelope, and fold the letter horizontally in thirds.
- Follow standard practice for addressing the envelope: addressee's full name, title, and address (with zip code) in the middle of the envelope;

and your name and address in the upper left-hand corner. Use your computer's software to generate a neatly typed envelope or address label.

2. Include standard elements.

As you type your letter, incorporate the typical elements of a business letter:

Return address and date If you are using letterhead stationery with a preprinted address, add just the date. Otherwise, include your full address. Spell out the names of months.

Inside address Give the name, title (if appropriate), and full address of the person to whom you are writing. Spell out words like *Street* or *Road,* but use the two-letter postal abbreviations for states.

Salutation In some instances, you may address a letter to a company or organization (*Dear Habitat for Humanity*) or to a job title (*Dear Shipping Department Manager*), but it is preferable to address your letter to an actual person, even if you have to contact the company to determine who that person is. Also, use appropriate titles (abbreviated before the name), such as *Mr., Ms., Dr., Gen., Prof.,* or *Rev.* Professional titles supersede gender-specific titles. For example, if you were writing to a female minister, you would address the letter to *Rev. Aldrich,* not *Ms. Aldrich.* If you have the person's name but do not know the gender, use the whole name: *Dear Pat Gonzalez.*

> **More about**
> Titles before and after names, 822
> Abbreviating titles, 821–22

Body Type each paragraph flush with the left margin and put a line of space between paragraphs. Do not use paragraph indention.

Closing and signature Using the formality of the letter as a guide, choose an appropriate closing phrase, such as *Sincerely, Yours truly,* or *Best regards.* Four lines (two double spaces) below the closing, type your full name, and sign in the space above.

Additional information Below your name, include other kinds of information, such as *Cc.* (*enclosure*) if you are enclosing items with the letter.

Sample business letter, block style The letter in full-block style on page 480 (Figure 25.1) is on letterhead stationery that includes the company's address and other contact information. If this letter had been written on plain paper, a return address would be needed directly above the date. Most items and all paragraphs are separated by two lines (one double space), but below the date and below the closing, four lines of space are required.

25b Writing Business Letters

The letters you write as an employee or in your personal life will have a variety of purposes. On Monday you may be a businessperson writing a letter of apology to a customer, and on Tuesday you might be a private citizen writing a letter of complaint. It is helpful, then, to look at some guidelines for writing different kinds of business letters.

1. Letters of complaint

When writing a letter of complaint, your challenge is to exercise restraint. Be reasonable and informed, and get to the point. Effective complaint letters do not cast the recipient of the letter in a negative light. When writing a letter of complaint, follow these four steps:

1. Describe the problem at the outset, and include details.
2. Explain the importance of the problem and why the recipient should be involved in the solution.
3. State your hopes for the solution to the problem.
4. If you have had positive experiences with the person or organization in the past, mention that; it will help your cause.

2. Letters of apology

In the business world, you may receive letters from customers who are complaining about the service you offer or the product you provide. In a letter of apology (Figure 25.1), your goal is to fix or make up for the problem, reassure

---

Writing Responsibly — **Letters to the Editor**

When private citizens write a letter to the editor of a newspaper or magazine, they often feel strongly about something—a previous article in the publication, a political candidate, or a local problem. If you write such a letter, keep your emotions in check. Make your point, get your facts straight, assume a courteous tone, and avoid personal attacks against the publication or writer. Most publications now accept such letters via e-mail; read your submission over carefully and adjust the tone before hitting send.

to AUDIENCE

Professional Model Business Letter: Apology

October 10, 2012   REBECCA'S RESTAURANT
                      550 N. Wabash, Chicago, IL 60610 • 312-268-8539 • www.rebeccasrest.com

Ms. Lauren Grayson
6243 North Sheridan Road   *Inside address*
Chicago, IL 60610

Dear Ms. Grayson: *Salutation*

Gives reason for letter and offers apology
I am responding to your letter of September 28 about the difficulties you had in trying to purchase a gift certificate for your friends, the Websters. First let me say that I apologize and can assure you that the employee you spoke to on the phone apologizes as well.

Explains company policy
We do offer our guests the option of purchasing gift certificates via fax. The only things we require are faxed copies of identification and a credit card, and a filled-out gift certificate form—all of which you supplied. It is also our policy to keep guest information confidential at all times. In this instance, however, it is clear that we failed to execute our procedures.

Explains action taken and repeats apology
I have spoken to the employee involved and explained the importance of our system and guest satisfaction. I am enclosing a $75 gift certificate as a token of my apology.

Furthermore, I have sent a $75 gift certificate to the Websters, in the hope that they also accept our apologies and understand how important our guests are to us here at Rebecca's.

Closes cordially
Please feel free to contact me personally if you ever need anything in the future. I will do my best to help you in any way I can.

Sincerely,   *Closing*

Christopher Juarez   *Signature*

Christopher Juarez
General Manager

Enc.   *Enclosure indicated*

FIGURE 25.1 Sample letter of apology (full block style)

the customer that he or she is important, and restore the reputation of your company or organization.

Follow these steps in writing a letter of apology:

1. State the problem in the first paragraph, and apologize for it.

2. Explain your company's policy (if appropriate), and admit that correct procedures were not followed.
3. Tell the customer what you have done to correct the problem within your company, and what you are doing to make things right with the customer.
4. Repeat your apology, and offer further assistance if needed.

3. Letters of rejection

When you must turn down a request, a bid on a project, or a job application, your task is not only to communicate the bad news but also to maintain goodwill with the person to whom you are writing. An effective letter of rejection will do the following:

1. Begin with a positive statement, thanking the recipient for taking the time to apply for the job, submit the proposal, or do whatever the person has done.
2. Give the reason(s) for the rejection in a clear yet kind way.
3. Conclude the letter with an expression of goodwill that is particular to the recipient.

25c Writing Business Memos

On any given workday, you may write a memo to convey information to the advertising department, to raise a question with your supervisor, or to explain a new procedure to coworkers. You may write thousands of memos during your lifetime; they are the typical communication tool people use within a company or organization. Printed memos may be distributed, but they are now most frequently sent via e-mail (Figure 25.2). A few tips to help you write an effective memo follow.

> **Professional Model**
> Business memo (e-mail), 482

> **More about**
> Writing and answering e-mail, 172–76, 483

1. Use a standard memo format.

Insert the information in the sections of your e-mail's header *To, From, Date,* and *Subject.* (If you are sending a printed memo, type these headings at the top of the page or use the memo template that comes with your word processing program.) All memos should include a subject line that accurately summarizes the content of the message. If recipients are being copied, list them in the *Cc* line. Attachments to e-mailed memos usually appear in the header; for printed memos with attachments, add *Enc.* at the end of the message.

Professional Model: Business Memo

Recipients
To: Carter, Jane; Santos, Maria
From: Ng, Yuah

Specific subject line
Subject: Awards for Resident Advisers
Attachment: RA of the Year--Nomination Form.doc (20 KB)

Main point stated in 1st paragraph
Our resident advisers are on the front line of student affairs, dealing day to day with conflicts among students, difficulties new students face in adjusting to college life, and the enforcement of college policies. So this year, in conjunction with the Student Housing Office, and the Office of Student Affairs, we are recognizing the contribution resident advisers make by conferring a Resident Adviser of the Year award.

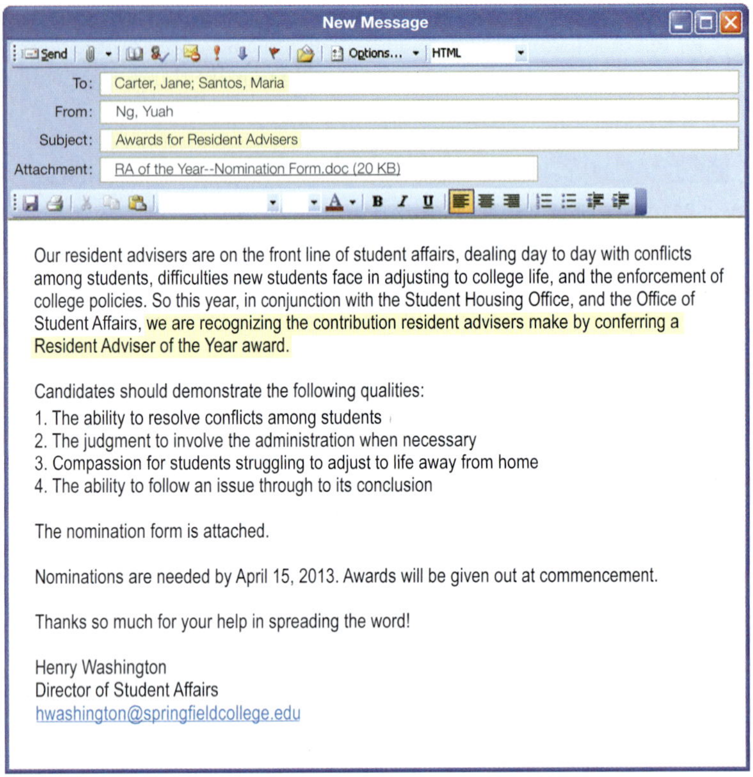

Candidates should demonstrate the following qualities:
1. The ability to resolve conflicts among students
2. The judgment to involve the administration when necessary
3. Compassion for students struggling to adjust to life away from home
4. The ability to follow an issue through to its conclusion

The nomination form is attached.

Nominations are needed by April 15, 2013. Awards will be given out at commencement.

Thanks so much for your help in spreading the word!

Henry Washington
Director of Student Affairs
hwashington@springfieldcollege.edu

FIGURE 25.2
Sample memo (e-mailed)

2. Get right to the point.

Use a tone appropriate for your reader, but be clear, specific, and concise. In your first paragraph, name the issue the memo is addressing and explain briefly why you are writing. In subsequent paragraphs or in a list, add any necessary details. A numbered or bulleted list is particularly effective in memos because it helps readers "see" your points or questions clearly. Conclude on a positive note, and thank the recipient if appropriate.

25d Writing Job Application Letters

A letter of application (Figure 25.3) is essentially a sales letter: Your goal is to sell yourself to a prospective employer and to get an interview. To do so, your

Quick Reference: E-mail Etiquette

Following e-mail etiquette (or *netiquette*) can make you more effective in social as well as professional settings. Here are fifteen tips for writing e-mail:

1. **Use accurate subject lines, and focus on a single topic.** Doing so will help your recipients manage their e-mail, and it will help you find your message later.
2. **Get right to the point, and keep messages brief.** Consideration for your reader's time is key.
3. **Maintain an appropriate tone.** Remain cordial and avoid *flaming* (or launching a personal attack).
4. **Include salutations (or greetings) and complimentary closings only in the most formal contexts.** Most e-mail messages do not require a formal salutation or closing.
5. **Follow the rules of capitalization.** Avoid writing all but the most informal messages in all lowercase (or all capital) letters. (Words in all capital letters are the equivalent of shouting.)
6. **Ask permission before sharing an e-mail message with someone to whom it was not addressed.** Sending along a message without asking permission may be unfair to the original sender.
7. **Reply promptly when your action is needed.** You may not always be able to answer swiftly, but do acknowledge receipt of the message, and let the sender know when to expect a full reply.
8. **Avoid hitting "reply all" unless every recipient will be interested in the reply.** With the quantity of e-mail circulating today, most recipients will appreciate *not* being included if the message is not directed toward them.
9. **Avoid "spamming" friends and colleagues.** Messages promising bad luck if you do not send the message on to five (or more) friends are commonplace on the Internet, but you can choose *not* to comply.
10. **Copy portions of previous messages, or reference the e-mail string for clarity.** If readers will need information from an earlier message, either copy and paste a portion of the message or refer the reader to a specific message.
11. **Never represent someone else's words as your own.** Acknowledge your use of any words or ideas you have borrowed from others. Usually, you need not provide a formal citation, but you should include the writer's name and any information needed to locate the source.
12. **Include your contact information with every message.** Make sure recipients know how to contact you in ways besides e-mail: Provide a telephone number and mailing address with each message.
13. **Edit your messages.** Even readers of e-mail deserve a text that is clear and correct.
14. **Pause before sending!** While the temptation to shoot off an angry message is sometimes great, avoid it. Treat the e-mail recipient with courtesy, even when you are annoyed.
15. **Archive your messages.** If you are likely to need to refer to a message you have sent or received, either print it out or save an electronic copy.

> **More about**
> Conciseness, 496–504 (ch. 26)
> Flaming, 182
> Tone, 15–16, 136, 543, 548–50
> Capitalization, 807–13 (ch. 54)

letter should be enthusiastic yet formal. Before you begin to write, learn something about the company or organization. You can then reveal a bit of your knowledge in your letter, which will show the recipient that you are serious about the job. Like other types of business correspondence, letters of application should follow some common guidelines concerning format and content:

> **Writing Responsibly** — **Personal E-mails and IM at Work**
>
> When you send e-mail on computers that are the property of a business or organization, the correspondence is considered the property of the organization and is subject to search should there be a suspicion of abuse. Therefore, write responsibly at work, and assume that your e-mail (or instant messages) may be viewed by others.
>
> to SELF

- Use one of the two standard letter formats: block format (Figure 25.1) or modified block format (Figure 25.3), and limit the letter's length to a single page.
- Address the letter to a specific person, even if you have to phone the company to determine who that is.
- Start by mentioning the specific job you are applying for and how you learned about it.
- In the next paragraph or two, explain why you are applying for this job, and list your specific qualifications.
- Point out the items in your résumé that are a good "fit" for this job, but do not just repeat the résumé.

Conducting Global Business in the United States Here are a few tips that may help you get a job and be successful at it:

- *Take advantage of your language skills.* Because many corporations operate globally and have clients from diverse backgrounds, be sure to mention—on your résumé and in a job interview—any languages besides English in which you are fluent.
- *Do not include personal information (such as age, religion, marital status) or a photograph on your résumé.* It is not the custom in the United States to include personal information or a photograph with a job application, and US employers are legally barred from assessing job qualifications on the basis of these factors.
- *Be direct and concise in your business writing.* Although your culture of origin or your other writing experiences may suggest a more indirect approach, follow the advice in this chapter if you are writing to a US organization.

Student Model **Job Application**

7716 W. Birchwood Street
Chicago, IL 60648

July 1, 2012

Modified block style: Return address and date align right of center

Mr. Aaron Gieseke
Recruitment, Human Resources
Museum of Science and Industry
57th Street and Lake Shore Drive
Chicago, IL 60637

Addresses specific person formally

Dear Mr. Gieseke:

I am applying for the entry-level position of assistant to the curator, which you advertised in the June 30 issue of the *Chicago Tribune*. Since childhood, I have been delighted by the museum's extraordinary exhibits, from Colleen Moore's Fairy Castle to the walk-through heart and chick hatchery. I would welcome the opportunity to put my skills and knowledge to work at your renowned institution.

Mentions specific job and shows familiarity with museum

Two years ago, I was fortunate to take several in-depth courses in museum curatorship at James Cook University. With European curators as teachers, I came to understand the many facets of running a museum, including preserving artifacts and tapping sources of funding. I also learned about the myriad jobs that go on behind the scenes and decided that museum life was where I wanted to be in my professional life.

Highlights educational ties to job

This decision was reinforced many times over while I was an intern at the Smithsonian last summer. I especially enjoyed working with researchers on new interactive exhibits and using my French language skills with international visitors. Inasmuch as the Museum of Science and Industry was the first to initiate interactive exhibits and welcomes thousands of overseas travelers each year, I believe my qualifications are ideal for the job.

Links work experience to job and shows knowledge of museum

My résumé is enclosed. I would be delighted to meet with you for an interview at any time. You may phone me at (312) 555–5683 or e-mail me at sonjaja1996@yahoo.com. I look forward to hearing from you.

Asks for interview and gives contact information

Sincerely,

Sonja Jacques

Sonja Jacques

Modified block style: Closing and signature align with return address

Enc.

FIGURE 25.3 **Sample job application letter (modified block style)**

- Conclude by asking for an interview and providing information about how you may be reached.
- Edit and proofread your letter carefully: A job application letter must be well written and contain no errors.

Throughout the letter, you need to walk a fine line: Do not be too modest about your accomplishments, but do not exaggerate your qualifications, either.

25e Writing Résumés

A *résumé* is a brief document that summarizes your work and educational experience for a prospective employer. Like a job application letter, it is a tool for selling yourself and obtaining an interview. Thus, in drafting a résumé, keep your audience and purpose in mind: Who will read this résumé? What will they want to know? Especially for those new to the workforce, focus on the skills you have acquired from your work experience. For example, you might explain that you "maintained good customer relations" and "presented a positive corporate image" in your job at a fast-food restaurant. If you are changing careers—from computer programming to advertising, for example—revise your résumé accordingly.

> Sample résumés:
> Traditional, 487
> Scannable, 489

Tell the truth on your résumé, but cast the information in a positive light. Also think about what you have done that is appropriate for this particular job. You may have nearly forgotten the tutoring you did at your campus literacy center when you were a first-year student, but that experience is relevant if you are applying for a teaching position.

Quick Reference: Designing a Print Résumé

- Leave plenty of white space; avoid a crowded look to make your résumé more readable.
- Use a slightly different design for your name and contact information to make your résumé more attractive and attention getting (Figure 25.4).
- Use a table format for other sections, aligning items on the left and setting off headings in boldface or capitals. You may want to use the résumé template that comes with your word processing software or add other design elements. However, be careful not to overdesign the document—keep it simple and easy to read.
- Single-space all sections, and put an extra line of space between them.
- Proofread your résumé until you are sure the document has no grammatical or typographical errors.
- Use a standard font, such as Times New Roman, and print your résumé on 8½ × 11–inch white or off-white paper. Use black ink only.

Student Model Traditional Résumé

Name and contact information set off from rest of résumé

Sonja Jacques
7716 W. Birchwood Street
Chicago, IL 60648
(312) 555–5683
sonjaja1996@yahoo.com

OBJECTIVE:	To obtain an assistant to curator position at a museum
EDUCATION:	**B.S., University of Illinois, Chicago Circle, June 2012.** History major; International studies minor GPA: 3.8 (on a 4-point scale) **Summer studies in Museum Curatorship, James Cook University, North Queensland, Australia, 2010.** Courses in artifact preservation, program management, museum funding.
EMPLOYMENT:	**Workstudy employee, UIC University Library, fall 2010–spring 2012.** Trained workstudy employees in library policies; shelved returned books. **Intern, Smithsonian Institution, Washington, DC, summer 2011.** Conducted museum tours for school groups; catalogued textual archives; assisted researchers. **Sales clerk, Moheiser's, Park Ridge, IL, summer 2008–spring 2010.** Organized inventory; waited on customers; learned apparel business.
SPECIAL SKILLS AND HONORS:	Fluent in French. Tutored 7th graders in French, Ebinger School, Chicago, IL, 2010–2011. Experience with Microsoft Word, PageMaker, and Internet research. President, Phi Kappa Phi Honor Society, UIC chapter, 2011. Dean's list, 2011–2012.
REFERENCES:	Available on request.

Education first, as typical for recent graduate

FIGURE 25.4
Sample printed résumé

1. Traditional print résumés

A résumé (Figure 25.4) arranges information in standard categories and a familiar sequence to make it easy for prospective employers to glean your qualifications quickly. This is not the place to demonstrate your flair for creative writing or flamboyant design. (The Quick Reference box on page 486 includes some basic guidelines for designing and formatting a print résumé.) Here are some tips to help you keep the content of your résumé on track:

> **More about**
> Document design,
> 162–70 (ch. 9)

- Arrange each section in reverse chronological order, with most recent job or degree first. If there are major gaps in your work history, or if you have changed careers, you may want to organize your résumé according to the skills that are particularly relevant to the job you are applying for. Keep in mind, however, that most employers prefer to read résumés in reverse chronological order.

> **More about**
> Active versus passive voice, 535–37
> Parallelism, 518–26 (ch. 28)

- Use active verbs and parallel construction throughout. For example, if you use *managed* for the first verb, you might use *organized* and *researched* thereafter.

- Limit your résumé to one page unless your work experience is extensive. Most recent college graduates should write a one-page résumé.

Most résumés include the following sections:

Contact information List your full name, mailing address, telephone number, and e-mail address at the top of the résumé. If you have separate home and school addresses, give them both, but make it clear to the recipient (perhaps in your cover letter) how and when you can be contacted at each location.

> **More about**
> Portfolios, 99–103

Career objective Indicate the specific position you are applying for or your career objective. Instead of *position in publishing,* say *entry-level editorial position in children's publishing.*

Education List the degrees you hold (college and above), the institutions that granted them, the date you received them (or anticipate receiving them), and your major and minor. Mention any honors such as being on the dean's list, and include your grade-point average if it is high (say, 3.5 or above on a 4-point scale). Include certificates, such as teaching certification.

Employment history Give the names and addresses of employers, titles of jobs, primary duties, and dates of employment.

Skills, awards, or memberships List computer skills (such as proficiency in PageMaker, Excel, or Dreamweaver) and other skills that are relevant to the job, such as fluency in a foreign language. Include awards and memberships that are pertinent. For example, if you were applying for a job at a community organization, you would want to state that you served as a volunteer and on the board of directors of Big Brothers Big Sisters.

References Provide names, mailing addresses, phone numbers, and e-mail addresses of three to six people who have agreed to serve as your references, or at

Genre Matters • Writing Résumés **25e** 489

Student Model Scannable Résumé

Sonja Jacques
7716 W. Birchwood Street
Chicago, IL 60648
(312) 555–5683
sonjaja1996@yahoo.com

Keywords for employer's database search

KEYWORDS: curator, curatorship, assistant, French, museum, archives, artifact, research, researchers

OBJECTIVE
Assistant to curator at museum

Headings set in all capitals, flush left, with no boldface, italics, or other design features

EDUCATION
B.S. University of Illinois, Chicago Circle, June 2012.
History major; International studies minor
GPA: 3.8 (on a 4-point scale)

Summer studies in Museum Curatorship, James Cook University, North Queensland, Australia, 2010.
Courses in artifact preservation, program management, museum funding.

Nouns used instead of verbs (trainer not trained) throughout

EMPLOYMENT
Workstudy employee, UIC University Library, fall 2010–spring 2012.
Trainer of workstudy employees in library policies; shelver of returned books.

Intern, Smithsonian Institution, Washington, DC, summer 2011.
Conductor of museum tours for school groups; cataloguer of textual archives; assistant to researchers.

Sales clerk, Moheiser's, Park Ridge, IL, summer 2008–spring 2010.
Inventory organization; customer service; experience with apparel business.

SPECIAL SKILLS AND HONORS
Fluent in French
Tutor of 7th graders in French, Ebinger School, Chicago, IL, 2010–2011
Experience with Microsoft Word, PageMaker, and Internet research
President, Phi Kappa Phi Honor Society, UIC chapter, 2011
Dean's list, 2011–2012

REFERENCES
Available on request

FIGURE 25.5
Sample scannable résumé

the bottom of your résumé add *References available on request.* In either case, be sure to obtain permission to list someone as a reference in advance.

2. Scannable or electronic résumés

Employers may request a scannable or electronic résumé (Figure 25.5)—one that is sent within the text of an e-mail message or as an attachment—so they can scan it to include in a database. To meet this requirement, a traditional print résumé needs to be revised and redesigned:

- Position all copy flush with the left margin. Use only capitals to set off headings. Eliminate italics, boldface, and all other design or format features.
- Wherever possible, change your skills from verbs (*supervised*) to concise nouns (*supervisor of*). If you have the job description, try to use the keywords it mentions. (Employers frequently use keywords to screen out inappropriate applications.)
- Below your contact information, list keywords from your résumé, such as titles of positions you have held (*assistant*) or skills you possess (*French*).
- When your scannable résumé is complete, e-mail it to yourself first, to make sure it is error-free and that the layout is readable.

NOTE Conventions for electronic or scannable résumés change over time and may vary from company to company. Check with your prospective employer to make sure your résumé fits the company's requirements.

Make It **Your Own**

Find an appealing job ad in a local paper, or find a posting in your school's job center. Then draft a résumé for the position following the recommendations in the section above.

Work **Together**

In groups of three or four, review each other's résumés. How could you rephrase the career objectives to tailor them more specifically to the job description? How might you revise the résumé to make it more appealing to the target audience?

Student Models
Research projects: "The Power of Wardrobe," Heather DeGroot, 381–88
"Nature Versus Nurture," Robyn Worthington, 461–68

25f Writing Reports and Proposals

As a student, you may have written reports about research you have conducted. You may have written proposals as well, perhaps suggesting to your college administration that campus parking be expanded. In this case, you would have done some research on parking problems to back up your suggestions. When you write as an employee or as a volunteer, reports and proposals have these same attributes: They provide information for a specific purpose, they usually involve research and analysis, and they may suggest some kind of change. Proposals, in particular, offer solutions for problems and seek funding for the project.

Reports and proposals may vary greatly in length, from a single page to more than a hundred pages. Long reports and proposals usually follow specific formats (which are dictated by the organization you are writing for), they include a table of contents, and they are divided into sections (with subheadings) such as the following:

- **Abstract, executive summary, or overview.** A one-paragraph summary of the entire report or proposal that highlights its purpose, major findings, and conclusions or recommended actions

- **Introduction or statement of the problem.** A discussion of the topic or problem that explains succinctly what is at issue and why it is important

- **Research methods and results.** A clear description of how you gathered information and what you discovered from your research (if appropriate, use graphs or tables to bolster your written explanation)

- **Conclusion or proposed solution.** A discussion of the relevance of your report or of the specific solution you are proposing (for a proposal, be sure to help readers see that your solution is preferable to other possible solutions and that it is feasible in terms of financing, staffing, or other potential roadblocks)

> **More about**
> Choosing the appropriate information graphic, 74–78
> Revising information graphics, 78–81
> Persuasive arguments, 134–37
> Tone, 15–16, 136, 543, 548–550

(The cover and first page of the executive summary of a report on school crime and safety appear in Figure 25.6 on page 492.)

As you draft a report or proposal, maintain an objective tone, and include only relevant and reliable information. Keep your purpose and audience in mind. It is not unusual for reports and proposals to be read by many different people (such as managers, sales representatives, and accountants). When this is the case, think about their various concerns and the questions they will want answered. For example, if you are proposing that the sales staff

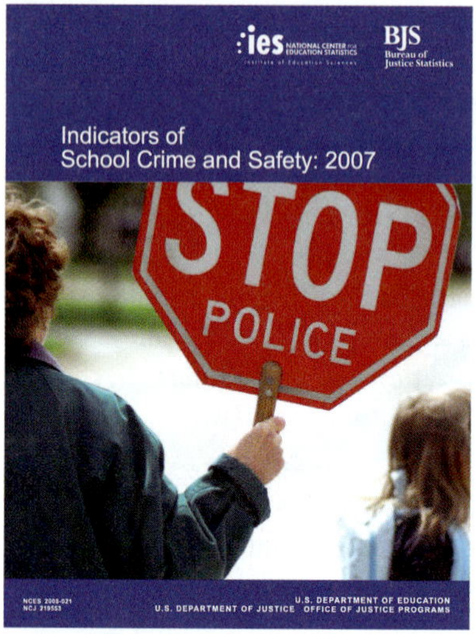

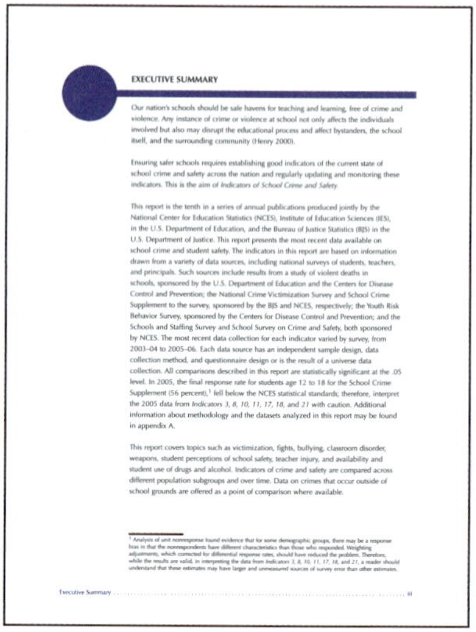

EXECUTIVE SUMMARY

Our nation's schools should be safe havens for teaching and learning, free of crime and violence. Any instance of crime or violence at school not only affects the individuals involved but also may disrupt the educational process and affect bystanders, the school itself, and the surrounding community (Henry 2000).

Ensuring safer schools requires establishing good indicators of the current state of school crime and safety across the nation and regularly updating and monitoring these indicators. This is the aim of *Indicators of School Crime and Safety.*

This report is the tenth in a series of annual publications produced jointly by the National Center for Education Statistics (NCES), Institute of Education Sciences (IES), in the U.S. Department of Education, and the Bureau of Justice Statistics (BJS) in the U.S. Department of Justice. This report presents the most recent data available on school crime and student safety. The indicators in this report are based on information drawn from a variety of data sources, including national surveys of students, teachers, and principals. Such sources include results from a study of violent deaths in schools, sponsored by the U.S. Department of Education and the Centers for Disease Control and Prevention; the National Crime Victimization Survey and School Crime Supplement to the survey, sponsored by the BJS and NCES, respectively; the Youth Risk Behavior Survey, sponsored by the Centers for Disease Control and Prevention; and the Schools and Staffing Survey and School Survey on Crime and Safety, both sponsored by NCES. The most recent data collection for each indicator varied by survey, from 2003–04 to 2005–06. Each data source has an independent sample design, data collection method, and questionnaire design or is the result of a universe data collection. All comparisons described in this report are statistically significant at the .05 level. In 2005, the final response rate for students age 12 to 18 for the School Crime Supplement (56 percent),[1] fell below the NCES statistical standards; therefore, interpret the 2005 data from *Indicators 3, 8, 10, 11, 17, 18,* and *21* with caution. Additional information about methodology and the datasets analyzed in this report may be found in appendix A.

This report covers topics such as victimization, fights, bullying, classroom disorder, weapons, student perceptions of school safety, teacher injury, and availability and student use of drugs and alcohol. Indicators of crime and safety are compared across different population subgroups and over time. Data on crimes that occur outside of school grounds are offered as a point of comparison where available.

[1] Analysis of unit nonresponse found evidence that for some demographic groups, there may be a response bias in that the nonrespondents have different characteristics than those who responded. Weighting adjustments, which corrected for differential response rates, should have reduced the problem. Therefore, while the results are valid, in interpreting the data from *Indicators 3, 8, 10, 11, 17, 18,* and *21*, a reader should understand that these estimates may have larger and unmeasured sources of survey error than other estimates.

Executive Summary iii

FIGURE 25.6 Sample report The full report appears online at nces.ed.gov/pubs2008/2008021.pdf

have larger, more expensive cars, how will you justify the extra cost to the financial experts?

25g Writing Press Releases

Press, or *media, releases,* like the one shown in Figure 25.7, are brief articles that announce events to newspapers, magazines, and online media outlets. If you work in the advertising or marketing department of an organization, part of your job might be writing press releases. Similarly, you could write them as a volunteer for a local charity or sporting club. Whatever organization they are written for, press releases follow a standard format because reporters and editors need to read them quickly and decide whether or not to use the information they contain. Here are some guidelines to follow when drafting a press release:

- Use your organization's letterhead, if possible, and include all pertinent contact information (address, phone number, e-mail address, website URL, and so on).
- At the top of the first page, type *For Immediate Release* and the date.

Professional Model Press Release

march of dimes
march for babies

March of Dimes Foundation

Karin Roseland
State Director

North Dakota Chapter
1330 Page Dr. #102
Fargo, ND 58103
Telephone 701-235-5530
Fax: 701-235-8725
EMAIL: kroseland@marchofdimes.com

marchforbabies.com

FOR IMMEDIATE RELEASE JAN. 16, 2008

For more information contact:
(Karin Roseland 701-235-5530)

— Uses letterhead
— "For immediate release" and date at top of first page

Family Teams Key to March for Babies
Premier March of Dimes Fundraising Event

— Article title in bold

(Fargo ND), January 17, 2008—1st Fargo/Moorhead March for Babies will take place on April 26, 2008 at 8:00 a.m. at West Fargo Veterans Memorial Arena. Formerly known as WalkAmerica, March for Babies is the March of Dimes' largest fundraising event that benefits all babies – those born healthy as well as those who need help to survive and thrive. The event has been renamed to make a clear connection to what the March of Dimes is all about—the health of babies.

— Most important information in first paragraph

Family Teams are made up of friends and family members who want to honor their own children or children they know – babies born prematurely or with a birth defect; babies who didn't survive; or healthy, full-term babies. Family Teams help remind everyone of the urgency of the mission of the March of Dimes. More than 12,000 Family Teams participated nationwide in 2007, raising nearly $11.5 million.

"We love to walk each year as a Family Team," said Jenny Smith, team captain. "Our first years, we participated because our neighbor's daughter was born premature. Now we walk to celebrate our own children – each born full-term and healthy. We know how fortunate we are."

"We hope many new Family Teams will be inspired to join us this year with the common goal of helping the March of Dimes improve baby health by preventing premature birth, birth defects and infant mortality," says Stacy Jacobs, Family Team committee member.

"It's easy to join or start a family team," added Jacobs. "Just visit marchforbabies.org or call toll-free 1-800-525-9255 to sign up or to donate to help babies be born healthy."

In 2008, national March for Babies sponsors are CIGNA, Continental Airlines, Famous Footwear, Farmers, FedEx, Grain Foods Foundation, Liberty Tax Services, nesting.com, and Kmart, the March of Dimes' number one corporate partner which has raised more than $63 million for babies. Additional national sponsorship is provided by Discovery Health, Mead Johnson Nutritionals, Outdoor services and Ther-Rx.

"In this community, we are proud also to be sponsored by U.S. Bank, BCBS, Loaf & Jug, and many other partners," Jacob said.

\#   \#   \#

About March of Dimes
The March of Dimes is the leading nonprofit organization for pregnancy and baby health. With chapters nationwide and its premier event, March for Babies, the March of Dimes works to improve the health of babies. For the latest resources and information, visit marchofdimes.com

FIGURE 25.7 Sample press release (Printed with the permission of Karin Roseland, North Dakota March of Dimes)

- Include an article title in bold or capital letters.
- To enable editors to cut your release for length easily, put the most important information up front and less important details toward the end.
- Use an objective tone, and make sure the content is factual and newsworthy.

Make It Your Own

Draft a press release announcing a student activity on campus (real or imagined). Make sure to include the most important information in the first paragraph and to provide information that is newsworthy.

Work Together

Exchange press releases with a classmate, and take turns role-playing the position of editor of a local newspaper. Would you publish your partner's press release? Why or why not?

Part Seven

Style Matters

Writing Engagingly

26 Writing Concisely 496
27 Using Coordination and Subordination 505
28 Using Parallelism 518
29 Engaging Readers with Variety and Emphasis 527
30 Choosing Appropriate Language 540
31 Choosing Effective Words 548
32 Using the Dictionary and Spelling Correctly 558

26 Writing Concisely

IN THIS CHAPTER

a. Eliminating wordiness, 497
b. Eliminating repetition, 499
c. Avoiding indirect constructions, 500
d. Consolidating, 502

Young children just learning to play soccer tend to swarm around the ball, each one duplicating the effort of the others, so that they move the ball toward the goal uncertainly. In practiced teams like those shown here, however, players work together efficiently to control the ball. Every player counts; none wastefully duplicates the work of another.

Wordy writing is like young children's soccer: The point gets made haltingly if at all. Sentences crowded with unnecessary words compel readers to separate what matters from what does not. *Concise* writing, in contrast, is like the play of a practiced team: Each point is made forcefully and without duplication of effort. Every word counts. Consider an example:

WORDY	The fact is that there is only one thing that should make us experience the emotion of fear and that is to all intents and purposes the emotion of fear itself.
CONCISE	The only thing we have to fear is fear itself.

—Franklin Delano Roosevelt, first inaugural address

> **More about**
> Sentence length and variety, 528–31

Writing Responsibly: Conciseness versus the Too-Short Paper

Effective writing should be concise but not necessarily brief. Concise writing provides readers with all the information they need without distractions, but it does not skimp on essential detail. It may take a long sentence to express a complex thought. Do not shortchange your readers—or your ideas—by omitting necessary detail.

to AUDIENCE

The first sentence is crowded with wordy expressions (*the fact is*), redundancies (*the emotion of fear*), and roundabout constructions (*there is only one thing*). The second, concise and direct, helped rally Americans to confront the Great Depression.

> **Quick Reference** — **Strategies for Writing Concisely**
> - Cut wordy expressions. (497)
> - Cut ineffective or unnecessary repetition. (499)
> - Revise roundabout constructions. (500)
> - Consolidate phrases, clauses, and sentences. (502)

Most of us write inadvertently wordy first drafts. As you revise, look for opportunities to tighten your prose. The Quick Reference box above offers some strategies.

26a Eliminating Wordy Expressions

First-draft writing sometimes contains common but wordy expressions that pad and clutter sentences. As you revise, prune these away.

Conciseness What one culture considers wordy, another may consider elegant. Not only culture but also context affects what readers expect: In literary contexts and even in some personal writing, US readers sometimes appreciate rich, expansive sentences. In academic contexts, however, US readers usually prefer writing that is concise and to the point.

1. Empty phrases

Some wordy expressions, like *to all intents and purposes, in fact, the fact is,* and *in the process of,* carry no information, and you can delete them:

▸ The passengers were ~~in the process of~~ boarding the plane when ~~in fact~~ the flight was canceled.

Similarly, intensifiers—modifiers like *absolutely, actually, definitely, really,* and *totally*—may add little meaning to the words they modify.

▸ The tourists were ~~absolutely~~ thrilled. None of them had ~~actually~~ seen a polar bear before.

Phrases built around words like *aspect, character, kind, manner,* and *type* are also often mere filler.

▸ They ~~are the kind of people who~~ have always ~~behaved in a generous manner.~~ *been generous.*

2. Roundabout expressions

Some wordy expressions say in many words what is better said with one.

Wordy Expression	Concise Alternative
at the present time	*now* (or delete entirely)
at that point in time	*then* (or delete entirely)
until such time as	until
at all times	always
at no time	never
most of the time	usually
in this day and age	today
due to the fact that	because
in spite of the fact that	although, even though
has the ability to	can
in the event that	if
in the neighborhood of	around

▶ ~~Due to the fact that~~ ^Because^ the housing market is ~~weak at this point in time~~ ^weak,^ many homeowners are waiting to sell until ~~such time as~~ conditions improve.

3. Redundant expressions

Some wordy expressions are **redundant,** stringing together two or more words that convey the same meaning.

Wordy Expression	Concise Alternative
blue in color	blue
in close proximity	close
each and every	*each* (or *every*)
end result	result
few/many in number	few/many
final outcome	outcome
past history	history
plans for the future/ future plans	plans
repeat again	repeat
round in shape	round
sum total	total

> **Tech** **Style Checkers and Wordiness**
>
> Although they might occasionally flag an inappropriate roundabout construction, computer style checkers are generally unreliable judges of wordiness. Rely on readers—yourself, your instructor, writing center tutors, your friends—to help you determine what is and is not acceptable.

▸ The candidate's mistakes during the campaign were ~~few in number~~ *few,* but they cost her the election, and she plans ~~for the future~~ never to repeat them ~~again~~.

26b Eliminating Ineffective or Unnecessary Repetition

Ineffective or unnecessary repetition can dull your prose and tire your readers.

1. Repetition and redundancy

As you revise your writing, look for words repeated unnecessarily, whether exactly or in varied form.

DRAFT   The author's informative overview provides particularly revealing information about the Johnson administration.

REVISION   The author's informative overview is particularly revealing about the Johnson administration.

Redundancy, another form of unnecessary repetition, is not restricted to the kind of stock phrases listed in the previous section; it happens whenever one expression duplicates the meaning of another.

▸ The portrait is ~~a likeness~~ of Gertrude Stein.

   A portrait *is* a likeness of a particular person.

2. Elliptical constructions

Sometimes grammatically necessary words can be omitted from a sentence when the context makes their meaning and function clear, and you can take advantage of such ***elliptical constructions*** to tighten your prose.

▸ On Saturday afternoons I went to the double feature, and on Sunday *mornings,* ~~mornings I went~~ to church.

> **EXERCISE 26.1 Eliminating wordy expressions and unnecessary repetition**
>
> Edit the following sentences to eliminate wordy expressions and unnecessary repetition.
>
> **EXAMPLE**
>
> The ~~beginning of the~~ Harry Potter books ~~starts when Harry discovers the fact~~ that he has magical abilities. *(begin with Harry's discovery)*
>
> 1. When the seventh and final book of J. K. Rowling's popular series of books about Harry Potter, called *Harry Potter and the Deathly Hallows,* was released in July 2007, people everywhere all over the world lined up outside bookstores to buy a copy due to the fact that the series is so popular and this was the last book in the series.
>
> 2. Those people who read carefully and know about such things can find references in the Harry Potter series to other writers who wrote before Rowling, such as the writers Dante and George Orwell.
>
> 3. In spite of the fact that Rowling's work has the ability to impress many people and is popular, the critic Harold Bloom complained that Rowling's style is very repetitive and also complained that she used too many clichés that she did not need to use in order to tell her story.
>
> 4. Others have complained about contradictions in the books that are small but really annoying to readers, such as the fact that in spite of all of the amazing spells everyone can make, no one makes a spell to get rid of Eloise's acne.

26c Avoiding Indirect Constructions

Certain sentence patterns tend toward wordiness and indirection. These include *expletive constructions,* sentences in the *passive voice,* and sentences built around weak verbs.

> *More about*
> Expletive constructions, 705–06

1. Sentences that begin with *There are . . . , It is . . .*)

Expletive constructions are sentences that begin with expressions like *there are, there is,* or *it is.* (Do not confuse *expletive* in this sense with its other sense of

Style Matters • Avoiding Indirect Constructions · 26c · 501

swear word or *curse*.) Revising to eliminate expletives will often make a sentence more direct and concise.

DRAFT	There are several measures that institutions can take to curb plagiarism.
REVISION	Institutions can take several measures to curb plagiarism.

2. Passive voice

In an active-voice sentence, the subject performs the action of the verb. In a passive-voice sentence, the subject receives the action.

> **More about**
> Passive versus active voice, 535–37, 652–55

	subj. verb
ACTIVE	Jared photographed the bear.
	subj. verb
PASSIVE	The bear was photographed by Jared.

Rewriting to use the active voice usually makes sentences more concise and direct.

DRAFT	A motion was proposed by the committee chair that the vote be delayed until the cost of the program could be accurately determined by the finance subcommittee.
REVISION	The committee chair proposed to delay the vote until the finance subcommittee could accurately determine the program's cost.

3. Sentences built around nouns derived from verbs

If the sentence is built around a weak verb such as *is, are, were,* or *was* (all forms of the verb *to be*), sometimes replacing the verb can produce a more concise and vivid result.

	noun verb
DRAFT	The destruction of the town by the tornado was complete.
	verb
REVISION	The tornado destroyed the town.

> **EXERCISE 26.2 Eliminating indirect constructions**
>
> Edit the following sentences to eliminate roundabout constructions.
>
> **EXAMPLE**
>
> ~~It is sleep deprivation that~~ *Sleep deprivation* is a serious problem for many college students.
>
> 1. In college, it is students who must plan their schedules and extracurricular activities carefully so they get enough sleep.
> 2. There are several sleep-related consequences that college students face if they do not manage their time.
> 3. Schoolwork is more difficult for students who are sleep deprived.
> 4. The reduction in the ability to concentrate as a result of inadequate sleep is serious.
> 5. Illness is also more frequent for sleep-deprived college students due to the fact that lack of sleep depletes the immune system.

26d Consolidating Phrases, Clauses, and Sentences

> **clause** A word group with a subject and a predicate
>
> **phrase** A group of related words that lacks a subject, predicate, or both

You can often make your writing more concise by reducing *clauses* to *phrases* and clauses or phrases to single words.

DRAFT Scientists cite glaciers, which have been retreating, and the polar ice caps, which have been shrinking, as evidence of global climate change.

REVISION Scientists cite retreating glaciers and shrinking polar ice caps as evidence of global climate change.

Sometimes you can also combine two or more sentences into one more concise, effective sentence.

DRAFT Scientists note that glaciers have been retreating and the polar ice caps have been shrinking. Most of them now agree that these phenomena are evidence of global climate change.

REVISION Most scientists now agree that retreating glaciers and the shrinking polar ice caps are evidence of global climate change.

EXERCISE 26.3 Combining sentences for conciseness

Reduce clauses to phrases and phrases to words as appropriate to combine each of the following passages into a single concise sentence.

EXAMPLE

Scientists in the United States have been analyzing the results of studies that connect obesity and sleep deprivation. Scientists in the United Kingdom have also been analyzing data about sleep and obesity.

Scientists in the United States and the United Kingdom have been studying the connection between obesity and sleep deprivation.

1. Some scientists conclude from their data that lack of sleep can be the cause of weight gain. Other scientists conclude from the same data that obesity and related health problems are more likely to cause lack of sleep.

2. Scientists in the United Kingdom and scientists in the United States worked together on one study, and they found as a result of their research that there is a relationship between sleep and hormones that control appetite. In that study they compared two groups of people. In one group were people who sleep for less than five hours a night. In the other group were people who sleep for more than eight hours a night.

3. The study found that people who sleep for less than five hours a night have 15 percent more of the hormone ghrelin, which increases appetite. The study found that people who sleep for less than five hours a night also have 15 percent less of the hormone leptin, which suppresses appetite.

4. Another study was reported by Swiss scientists. They studied 496 people between twenty-seven and forty years of age. The study lasted for thirteen years. The study found that twenty-seven-year-olds who slept for only a "short duration" were much more likely to be obese than forty-year-olds who got the same amount of sleep. This study found that the connection between sleep and obesity started to diminish after age thirty-four.

EXERCISE 26.4 Editing for conciseness

Use the strategies described in this chapter to make the following passage concise and direct.

> It is a fact that citizen, or amateur, scientists have the ability to contribute to the work of professional scientists. They can be of use in many different scientific fields of endeavor. For example, in the area of biology, citizen scientists can report the observations that they make. They have the ability to report observations about bird migration, seasonal change, and other factors that they can view in the vicinity of their own backyards. The widespread, detailed data provided by amateurs can help scientists bring their studies to completion.
>
> In the area of astronomy, discoveries that are very significant have been made by amateurs. These include the very first sightings of many comets. They also include important observations of variable stars. Variable stars are stars that change in brightness over time. There are organizations and even awards for amateur astronomers. This shows how important their work is.

Make It **Your Own**

Reread a piece of your writing, ideally a recent or current project, and look for sentences that could be made more concise. If you find any, make a note of the problem and how you could fix it, then add this to your list of areas to consider as you revise your prose.

Work **Together**

Working with two or three classmates, read a piece of each other's writing and identify where and how your classmates' sentences could be made more concise. Compare your results with those of the others in the group. What did each of you see that others did not? Write a few sentences reflecting on how this collaborative activity might help you revise your own work in the future.

27 Using Coordination and Subordination

IN THIS CHAPTER

a. Coordinating terms, phrases, and clauses, 506
b. Coordinating effectively, 507
c. Subordinating information, 510
d. Combining coordination and subordination, 515

Alexander Calder, *Untitled*, 1976

Look up as you enter the East Wing of the National Gallery of Art in Washington, DC, and a dramatic sight confronts you. Hanging from the skylight over the building's large atrium is a giant sculpture by Alexander Calder—a 920-pound, 76-foot-long mobile made of multicolored metal rods and plates—that despite its size and weight sweeps gracefully overhead. Calder achieved this elegant effect by carefully coordinating elements of equal weight, balancing heavy elements with a series of lighter subordinate elements that descend in a branching cascade from the cable that secures the mobile to the ceiling. The subordinated and coordinated elements combine to convey Calder's visual message.

Writers can similarly use coordination and subordination to craft sentences that best convey their intended meaning. ***Coordination*** establishes the equal weight or importance of two or more sentence elements.

equal weight
▶ We entered the museum, and a dramatic sight confronted us.

equal weight
▶ The mobile is made of rods and plates.

> **Tech** **Style Checkers and Coordination and Subordination**
>
> Using coordination and subordination requires you to figure out the logical relationships among the ideas you want to express and to decide on their relative importance, so that you can make these relationships clear to your audience. A computer style checker cannot do that for you.

505

Subordination establishes the supporting or modifying role of one or more sentence elements.

▶ Heavy elements balance lighter elements that descend in a branching cascade from the cable that secures the mobile to the ceiling.

27a Coordinating Terms, Phrases, and Clauses

> **phrase** A group of related words that lacks a subject, a predicate, or both
> **clause** A word group with a subject and predicate. An ***independent clause*** can stand alone as a sentence; a ***subordinate clause*** cannot.

Coordination can link or contrast two or more equally important terms, ***phrases,*** or ***clauses.***

1. Terms and phrases

To coordinate terms and phrases requires either a coordinating conjunction (such as *and, but, for, nor, or, so,* or *yet*) or a correlative conjunction (such as *both . . . and, either . . . or,* or *neither . . . nor*). Usually no punctuation separates two coordinated words or phrases.

> **More about**
> Coordinating and correlative conjunctions, 583–84

▶ Both Steven Spielberg and George Romero attended the New York Film Academy.

▶ London's Theatre Royal in Drury Lane has staged performances by the Shakespearean actor Edmund Kean and by the Monty Python comedy troupe.

Commas usually separate more than two terms or phrases in a coordinated series.

▶ From John Webster's point of view in 1612, the greatest playwright might have been George Chapman, William Shakespeare, or Ben Jonson.

2. Independent clauses

> **More about**
> Punctuating coordinated independent clauses, 611–19

To coordinate two independent clauses, use a comma and a coordinating conjunction, a semicolon, or a semicolon and a conjunctive adverb such as *for example, however, in addition,* or *therefore.*

- Today we consider Shakespeare to be the greatest English playwright, but his contemporaries regarded him as just one among many.
- Adele's debut CD was a huge success; it sold millions of copies.
- The play received glowing reviews and won a Tony award; however, it closed after only a short run.

27b Coordinating Effectively

Coordinating elements in a sentence gives them equal importance or weight. How you coordinate those elements shows your readers the relationship among them.

1. Conjunctions and their meaning

Conjunctions differ in meaning, and some can have more than one meaning depending on context (see the Quick Reference box on the next page).

A conjunction whose meaning does not match the relationship between coordinated elements might confuse readers and obscure the writer's point. In the following sentence, for example, changing *and* to *but* reveals what the writer intended to emphasize: the contrast between Einstein's youth and his accomplishments.

- Einstein was still young, ~~and~~ *but* he had revolutionized physics.

2. Independent clauses joined with a semicolon

Use a semicolon to join two independent clauses that have a logical connection to each other. The second clause can contrast with the first, provide an example of it, or give a reason for it.

> **More about**
> Semicolons, 766–72

CONTRAST	During the polar winter, the sun never rises; during the polar summer, it never sets.
EXAMPLE	The movie was a financial success; it set a record for opening-day box office receipts.
EXPLANATION	She wanted to be sure to have the assignment done for tomorrow; Spanish is her favorite class.

Quick Reference: Conjunctions and Their Meaning

Meaning	Conjunctions	Examples
addition	and, both ... and	*Both* advances in ship design *and* the introduction of the magnetic compass helped make possible the European voyages of discovery.
sequence	and	The lawyer turned *and* faced the jury.
cause and effect	so, for, (sometimes) and	The housing market has softened, *so* sellers have had to lower their prices.
choice	or, whether ... or, either ... or, nor, neither ... nor	Tournament games can be played on neutral courts *or* home courts. *Neither* ESPN *nor* any other network wants to show empty arenas.
contrast	but, yet	The police raided the house, *but* the suspect had fled. The poll indicates support for the law *yet* doubt about its chance for passage.
	not just ... but, not only ... but also	*Not just* the NCAA *but* the teams and fans should have a voice in the decision. [In addition to contrasting the coordinated elements, these conjunctions emphasize one over the other, suggesting that the first is commonplace and expected, the second new and noteworthy.]

When you join clauses with a semicolon and a conjunctive adverb, the conjunctive adverb specifies the relationship.

▶ During the polar winter the sun never rises; *in contrast,* during the polar summer, it never sets.

3. Inappropriate coordination

Coordination is inappropriate when it combines elements that are not of equivalent importance or weight. The following sentence, for example, puts an incidental fact—Einstein's year of birth—on an equal footing with a statement about his early accomplishments. The revision subordinates the minor information in a modifying phrase.

INAPPROPRIATE COORDINATION	Albert Einstein was born in 1879, and by 1905 he had published four important scientific papers.
REVISED	Albert Einstein, born in 1879, had published four important scientific papers by 1905.

4. Excessive coordination

In everyday speech, people often coordinate long strings of sentences with *and* and other conjunctions. What is acceptable in speech, however, quickly becomes tedious, even confusing, in writing. As you edit, look for such ***excessive coordination.***

EXCESSIVE COORDINATION	Steven Spielberg graduated from Saratoga High School, in Saratoga, California, in 1965, and he applied to the University of Southern California's film school three times, but he was rejected each time, so he finally decided to attend California State University at Long Beach, and while he was at Cal State he started an unpaid internship at Universal Studios, and an executive was impressed by his talent, so in 1969 he was allowed to direct a television episode there, and by 1975 he was directing films like *Jaws,* and that was his first big hit as a movie director, so perhaps in the end he was lucky to have been rejected by USC.
REVISED	Steven Spielberg, who graduated in 1965 from Saratoga High School in Saratoga, California, applied to the University of Southern California's film school three times and was rejected each time. Finally, he decided to attend California State University at Long Beach. While he was at Cal State, he started an unpaid internship at Universal Studios. An executive there was impressed by his talent, so in 1969 he was allowed to direct a television episode there. By 1975, he was directing films like *Jaws,* his first big hit as a movie director. Perhaps, in the end, he was lucky to have been rejected by USC.

EXERCISE 27.1 Eliminating inappropriate and excessive coordination

Edit the following sentences to eliminate excessive or inappropriate coordination.

EXAMPLE

Your parents probably encouraged you to start the day with a good ~~breakfast, and~~ *breakfast, so* now a five-year study suggests they were ~~right, but the~~ *right. The* study found that the more likely adolescents are to eat breakfast, the less likely they are to be overweight.

1. The study was conducted in the public schools of the Minneapolis–St. Paul area, and researchers found that there was a direct relationship between eating breakfast and body mass index (BMI), yet the more often an adolescent had breakfast, the lower was his or her BMI.

2. The adolescents studied were an average of fifteen years old at the start of the study, and those who ate breakfast consumed more carbohydrates and fiber, received fewer calories from fat, so got more exercise.

3. The relationship between breakfast eating and BMI was consistent throughout the study's entire five years, but the researchers controlled for age, sex, race, socioeconomic status, smoking, and concerns about diet and weight.

4. The study only observed an association between breakfast-eating habits and body mass, yet it did not prove a causal relationship, and nevertheless, one of the authors said that the research provided some useful guidance for healthy eating.

5. He noted that eating a healthy breakfast would encourage healthy eating for the rest of the day, yet it might help to lessen the urge for fast food or vending-machine food, and parents could also contribute, he added, by setting a good example and having a good breakfast themselves.

27c Identifying Important Ideas and Supporting Information with Subordination

Unlike coordination, which links equal ideas, subordination indicates which part of the sentence contains your important ideas, and which parts contain supporting examples, explanations, and details. Putting information in a sub-

Style Matters • Identifying Important Ideas and Supporting Information with Subordination

ordinate structure de-emphasizes it, showing that it is supporting material rather than major claims.

▶ The evidence is conclusive; my client is innocent.
  (main idea / main idea)

Coordination gives each idea equal weight.

▶ As the evidence proves conclusively, my client is innocent.
  (subordinated idea / main idea)

The emphasis is on the client.

▶ The evidence proves conclusively that my client is innocent.
  (main idea / subordinated idea)

The emphasis is on the evidence.

Subordination can also clarify the logical relationship among a series of ideas. The revised version of the following passage clarifies the chronological relationship among the facts listed in the draft, and it emphasizes the most significant fact—that comic books did not become widely popular until 1938.

DRAFT The first comic books appeared in the early 1920s. Nearly four decades earlier, comic strips had begun appearing in the major newspapers. Comic books did not gain widespread popularity until June 1938. Writer Jerry Siegel and artist Joe Shuster debuted their character Superman in June 1938.

REVISED Although comic books first appeared in the 1920s, which was nearly four decades after comic strips had begun to appear in the major newspapers, they did not gain widespread popularity until June 1938, when writer Jerry Siegel and artist Joe Shuster debuted their character Superman.

1. Subordinating techniques

To subordinate information within a sentence, put it in a subordinate clause, reduce it to a modifying phrase or word, or include it in an appositive.

- **Subordinate clause.** Subordinate clauses begin with a ***subordinating*** word, usually either a subordinating conjunction (such as *after, although, because, before, that,* or *when*) or a relative pronoun (such as *that, what, which, who,* or *whose*).

  ▶ Hatshepsut was one of only a few women to rule ancient Egypt.
    (insert: , whose reign was from 1473 to 1458 BCE,)
    ~~Her reign was from 1473 to 1458 BCE.~~

> **More about**
> Subordinating conjunctions and relative pronouns, 594–96, 602–03

> **Quick Reference** — **Subordination and Punctuation**
>
> In most cases, a comma follows a subordinate structure that begins an independent clause.
>
> > After the 1965 Newport festival, fans complained about Dylan's switch from acoustic to electric guitar.
>
> A subordinate structure that interrupts or ends an independent clause may or may not be set off with punctuation, depending on whether the information in it is ***essential*** (restrictive) or ***nonessential*** (nonrestrictive). A structure is essential if it specifically identifies the word or words it modifies. No punctuation sets off interrupting or concluding restrictive structures.
>
> > Athletes who win Olympic gold medals often earn money by endorsing products.
>
> A structure is nonessential if the meaning or identity of the word or words it modifies is clear without it. A comma or other punctuation usually sets off interrupting or concluding nonessential structures. (See pp. 757–59.)
>
> > Michael Phelps, who won eight gold medals in 2008, is a published author.

- **Modifying phrase or word.**

    Enticed by months of clever advance marketing, millions
    ▶ ~~Millions~~ of people bought the new multimedia smartphone within days of its release. ~~They had been enticed by months of clever advance marketing.~~

> **appositive** A noun or noun phrase that renames a preceding noun or noun phrase

- **Appositive.**

    , a giant mobile made of multicolored metal rods and plates,
    ▶ The sculpture sweeps gracefully overhead. ~~It is a giant mobile made of multicolored metal rods and plates.~~

2. Choosing a subordinating term

Understanding the meaning of subordinating terms is essential to using subordination effectively (see the Quick Reference box on the next page).

Use a subordinating term whose meaning matches the relationship you intend to convey between a subordinate element and the element it modifies. The following sentence uses a term referring to cause in a context that calls for a term referring to purpose. Revising requires either changing the term or rewording the clause.

DRAFT   He ran for mayor because he could bring the town's budget under control.

Quick Reference: Subordinating Terms and Their Meaning

Meaning	Conjunctions	Examples
time	after, as, before, since, until, when, whenever, while	Comics grew in popularity *after* Superman appeared in 1938.
place	where, wherever	Home is *where* the hearth is.
cause or effect	as, because, since, so that	*Because* of the water main break, traffic came to a standstill.
condition	even if, if, provided that, since, unless	*If* you finish the job today, you can take a vacation day tomorrow.
purpose	in order that, so that, that	She finished the job quickly *so that* she could have a day off.
identification	that, when, where, which, who	Adichie is the author *who* won the Orange Broadband Prize for fiction in 2007.
contrast or comparison	as, although, as if, even though, though, whereas	*Although* Einstein was still a young man, he had revolutionized physics.

REVISED   He ran for mayor so that he could bring the town's budget under control.

or

He ran for mayor because he wanted to bring the town's budget under control.

Be particularly careful with the subordinating conjunctions *as* and *since*, which can refer ambiguously to both cause and time.

DRAFT   As she was applying the last coat of varnish, Lisa declared the restoration complete.

REVISED   While she was applying the last coat of varnish, Lisa declared the restoration complete.

or

Because she was applying the last coat of varnish, Lisa declared the restoration complete.

3. Avoiding illogical subordination

State key ideas in an independent clause, and put illustrations, examples, explanations, and details in subordinate structures. Illogically subordinating a main idea to a supporting idea can confuse readers. The following sentence subordinates the idea of Einstein's accomplishments to the idea of his youth, illogically implying that he was young in spite of his accomplishments rather than accomplished in spite of his youth.

ILLOGICAL SUBORDINATION	Einstein was still young, although he had revolutionized physics.
REVISED	Although he was still young, Einstein had revolutionized physics.

4. Avoiding excessive subordination

Excessive subordination—stringing together too many subordinate structures—can make a sentence hard to read. The string of subordinate structures in the following sentence leaves readers unsure by the end where they began. The revision into two sentences clarifies the information the writer wants to convey.

EXCESSIVE SUBORDINATION	San Francisco, although generally an ideal habitat for peregrine falcons, is not entirely so, as became clear recently when rescuers had to remove falcon eggs from a nest on the Bay Bridge, despite the parents' protests, because once hatched, the fledglings would probably have drowned while learning to fly.
REVISED	San Francisco, although generally an ideal habitat for peregrine falcons, is not entirely so. Rescuers had to remove falcon eggs from a nest on the Bay Bridge recently, despite the parents' protests, because once hatched, the fledglings would probably have drowned while learning to fly.

EXERCISE 27.2 Eliminating excessive or illogical subordination

Edit the following passage to eliminate excessive or illogical subordination.

> An increasing number of high school seniors, although possessing excellent grades and good prospects for gaining admittance into the colleges of their choice, are opting for another alternative called a "gap year," which involves spending the year after graduating from high school doing something other than going to college. One recent graduate said she worked so hard in high school that she felt as if she had been continually running a marathon, without enough time for her three college-level physics courses, her clarinet practice, her band competitions, and her volunteer work, all of which often left her exhausted at the end of the day. She was accepted at several colleges, although she spent her gap year teaching English in Japan. This woman, who felt so pressured by her high school schedule that she chose to postpone college, has plenty of company, which includes a young man working on a farm in Costa Rica, a man who cares for injured sled dogs in Canada, a woman who builds guitars in England, and a woman who studies ballet in New York City, all activities that, according to the man in Costa Rica, "give you a break from being a student so you can reclaim the person inside." Even if many young people feel that their gap year gives them a refreshing, stimulating, and maturing change, they are delaying their start at college.

27d Using Coordination and Subordination Together

Used together, coordination and subordination can add grace and variety to your writing and help readers identify the points you want to emphasize. In this passage from a paper on Shakespeare's views on war in his play *Henry V*, Jonathan Adler, a student at Syracuse University, holds readers' interest and guides them to his concluding point by using both coordination and subordination in sentences of varied length.

> **More about**
> Variety and emphasis, 527–37

> Instead of glorifying war, Shakespeare shows us in *Henry V* that war is costly and that it has consequences. For his own security, however, Shakespeare had to disguise these views about war; speaking out against the government during his time was a risky thing to do. This need for disguise is where his dark comedy or satire comes in. In comedy and satire he can hide his anti-war sentiments while at the same time expressing them and mocking the entire process of going to war.
>
> —Jonathan Adler, Syracuse University

Coordination and Subordination Mastery of subordination is considered a sign of sophistication in American academic writing, but this is not true of all languages or cultures. If academic style in your native language or your style in other contexts favor coordination over subordination, you may need to make a conscious effort to use more subordinated structures in your writing. If your style favors subordination over coordination, you may have a tendency to oversubordinate your sentences in academic English. Your goal should be to strike a balance between both coordination and subordination.

EXERCISE 27.3 Combining sentences with coordination and subordination

Use coordination and subordination to combine sentences in the following passages in the way that seems most effective to you. Try to vary the coordination and subordination techniques you use.

1. Every holiday season, some people complain about the need to exchange gifts. Many are annoyed by the crowds, the expense, the materialism, and the overall stress of finding and buying suitable presents.

2. There are people who even refuse to take part in gift giving during the holidays. Some psychologists say that these people may be passing up an important opportunity to bond with their family and friends.

3. People's gift lists indicate who is important and unimportant in their lives, researchers note. A partner can use gift giving to show interest, strengthen a relationship, or even signal that the connection should end.

4. A recent study examined gift giving by pet owners. Researchers heard from owners why they gave their pets gifts. Owners said they wanted to make the pets happy. They also wanted to improve their pets' care and make them feel more comfortable.

5. Especially noteworthy is that the pets cannot return the gifts they receive. The act of giving itself makes the pet owners feel good. Simply knowing they are taking care of their pets gives them pleasure.

➤ EXERCISE 27.4 Using coordination and subordination correctly

Edit the following passage to correct any errors in the use of coordination and subordination.

> It is a task almost everyone does twice a day for just about their entire lives, yet not many people do it well, for tooth brushing is supposed to take more time than nearly anyone wants to spend on it, and we usually do not do it properly. The American Dental Association is the country's foremost authority on dental hygiene, and it tells us to brush each tooth to the gum line. Although most people are too impatient to brush as long as they should, the entire process ought to take two minutes. While people have been using a form of the standard toothbrush, with bristles attached to a six-inch-long handle, for more than 5,000 years, the task has always been the same, which is to remove the leftover bits of food from our last meal, but we brush for too short a time, and we also commonly brush too hard, no matter what our dentists tell us, even though brushing too hard can cause serious harm to teeth and gums, and this damage can be expensive to repair. People's ineptitude at brushing has inspired an entire industry of toothbrush devices that are elaborate technological wonders that do the brushing for us provided that we reposition the electric toothbrushes when they beep, and we passively wait for them to do their job. Most tooth-brushing devices are made by well-known companies, and they all claim that their products are superior at cleaning teeth. Nevertheless, there are few well-controlled studies showing one brush to be better than any other. Whereas most dental experts agree that using a standard toothbrush thoroughly and gently will remove plaque from teeth as well as an electronic gadget will, an expensive tooth-cleaning machine does have one advantage, which is that people are more likely to use it than the ordinary toothbrush they get from their dentist for free.

⌐ Make It **Your Own**

Reread a piece of your writing, ideally a recent or current project, and identify coordinate and subordinate structures. Look for any that need to be revised. If you find any, make a note in the margins of the paper identifying which section of this chapter explains the revision and add this to your list of areas to consider as you revise your prose.

28 Using Parallelism

IN THIS CHAPTER

a. Using paired and series items, 520

b. Maintaining parallelism, 522

c. Including function words, 522

d. Maintaining parallelism in lists and outlines, 523

e. Using parallelism for emphasis, 525

Andy Warhol, *Marilyn Diptych*, 1962

This silkscreen painting by Andy Warhol, called *Marilyn Diptych* (1962), has two matching, or parallel, parts. Each part consists of twenty-five images of Marilyn Monroe, but the black-and-white panel on the right contrasts dramatically with the gaudily colored panel on the left. The images embedded within each panel are also parallel: All are copies of the same original, all are the same size, and all are equally spaced in a grid. Within this structure, however, the images differ. Those in the left panel vary subtly in color; those in the right panel vary in clarity and definition, with some smeared almost beyond recognition and others faded almost to invisibility. The overall effect suggests, to some viewers, life and death, the transience of fame, and the way image obliterates individuality.

Warhol uses visual parallelism to convey his message. Similarly, writers use grammatical ***parallelism***—the expression of equally important ideas in similar grammatical form—to increase the clarity of their writing and to emphasize important points. Abraham Lincoln, for example, deployed parallelism to powerful effect as he urged his fellow citizens to persevere in the Civil War in this closing passage from the Gettysburg Address:

> It is for us the living, rather, to be dedicated here to the unfinished work which they who fought here have thus far so nobly advanced.
>
> It is rather for us to be here dedicated to the great task remaining before us—
>
> > that from these honored dead we take increased devotion to that cause for which they gave the last full measure of devotion—
> >
> > that we here highly resolve
> >
> > > that these dead shall not have died in vain—
> > >
> > > that this nation, under God, shall have a new birth of freedom—
> > >
> > > and that government
> > >
> > > > of the people,
> > > > by the people,
> > > > for the people,
> > >
> > > shall not perish from the earth.

— Parallel sentences
— Parallel clauses
— Parallel clauses
— Parallel phrases

EXERCISE 28.1 Identifying parallelism

Identify and describe the parallel structures in the following passages.

1. It was the best of times, it was the worst of times, it was the age of wisdom, it was the age of foolishness, it was the epoch of belief, it was the epoch of incredulity, it was the season of Light, it was the season of Darkness, it was the spring of hope, it was the winter of despair, we had everything before us, we had nothing before us, we were all going direct to heaven, we were all going direct the other way—in short, the period was so far like the present period, that some of its noisiest authorities insisted on its being received, for good or for evil, in the superlative degree of comparison only.   —Charles Dickens, *A Tale of Two Cities*

2. Those who see quickly, will resolve quickly and act quickly.
   —Jane Austen, *Mansfield Park*

3. We shall not flag or fail. We shall go on to the end. We shall fight in France, we shall fight on the seas and oceans, we shall fight with

growing confidence and growing strength in the air, we shall defend our island, whatever the cost may be, we shall fight on the beaches, we shall fight on the landing grounds, we shall fight in the fields and in the streets, we shall fight in the hills. We shall never surrender.

—Winston Churchill

4. We shall pay any price, bear any burden, meet any hardships, support any friend, oppose any foe to assure the survival and the success of liberty.

—John F. Kennedy

28a Using Parallelism for Paired Items and Items in a Series

For clarity and to avoid awkwardness, express paired ideas and items in a series in parallel form. Join subordinate clauses with similarly structured clauses, join phrases with similarly structured phrases, and join individual terms with other terms of the same form.

1. Items paired with a conjunction such as *and* or *but*

> **More about**
> Coordinating conjunctions, 583–84

Coordinating conjunctions include *and, but, for, nor, or, so,* and *yet.*

▶ Girls learn at a young age to be passive and ~~that they should be~~ deferential.

The original uses *and* to pair an infinitive phrase (*to be passive*) with a subordinate clause (*that they should be deferential*); the revision uses *and* to join a pair of adjectives (*passive* and *deferential*).

▶ The course always covers the twentieth century through World War II but sometimes ~~touching~~ *also touches* on the beginning of the Cold War ~~is possible also~~.

In the revision, the verbs *covers* and *touches on* are in parallel form.

Deceptive Parallelism Parallel structure is found in most languages, so the concept will probably not be unfamiliar to you. Use caution, however, to ensure that items that seem parallel are all grammatically equivalent. For example, in "He spoke only positively and friendly about his previous professor," *positively* and *friendly* appear parallel, but *positively* is an adverb whereas *friendly* is an adjective. To be parallel, the sentence requires restating along these lines: "He had only positive and friendly things to say about his previous professor."

2. Items paired with correlative conjunctions

Conjunctions such as *both . . . and, either . . . or, neither . . . nor,* and *not only . . . but also* are **correlative conjunctions.** They come in pairs, and they link ideas of equal importance. Readers expect items linked by a correlative conjunction to be parallel. To be parallel, however, the items linked by the correlative conjunctions must have the same grammatical form.

> **More about**
> Correlative conjunctions, 583–84

FAULTY PARALLELISM   The defense attorney not only convinced the jury that her client had no motive for committing the crime, but also was nowhere near the scene of the crime when it occurred.

This suggests that the defense attorney, not her client, was nowhere near the crime scene.

STILL FAULTY   The defense attorney convinced the jury not only that her client had no motive for committing the crime, but also was nowhere near the scene of the crime when it occurred.

A clause beginning with *that* follows *not only,* so a clause beginning with *that* should follow *but also.*

REVISED   The defense attorney convinced the jury not only that her client had no motive for committing the crime, but also that he was nowhere near the scene of the crime when it occurred.

3. Items in a series

Like paired items, three or more equivalent items in a series should be in parallel form.

FAULTY PARALLELISM   The detectives secured the crime scene, examined it for clues, and the witnesses were then called in for questioning.

REVISED   The detectives secured the crime scene, examined it for clues, and then called in the witnesses for questioning.

Tech   **Parallelism and Computer Style Checkers**

A computer's style checker cannot identify ideas that merit parallel treatment in an otherwise grammatical sentence.

More about
Clear comparisons, 674–77
Including function words, 700–01

28b Maintaining Parallelism in Comparisons

When you compare two items with *than* or *as,* the items should be in the same grammatical form.

▸ Getting into debt is unfortunately much easier than ~~to get~~ *getting* out of it.

28c Including Function Words to Maintain Parallelism

Words such as articles (*a, an, the*), conjunctions, and prepositions indicate the relationships among other words in a sentence. They should be included or repeated as needed in linked items for clarity and grammar as well as for parallelism.

▸ The trail leads over high mountain passes and *through* dense forests.

Trails lead *over* passes but *through* forests.

▸ EXERCISE 28.2 Correcting parallelism errors

Correct any errors in parallelism in the following sentences.

EXAMPLE

This spot offers a good view not only of herons but ~~you can~~ also ~~see~~ *of* egrets.

1. Many types of wading birds, some rare, are attracted to this island to rest during migration, to feed, and they nest here as well.

2. Perhaps surprisingly, this habitat is located not in a national park or wildlife refuge but it is found in the middle of New York harbor.

3. However, until ten or fifteen years ago, the area was inhospitable to wildlife because it was missing one crucial factor: not food or shelter but the presence of clean water.

4. Starting with the Clean Water Act of 1972 and accelerating within the last fifteen years with state legislation, regional planning, and as more federal funds were appropriated, the water in the harbor has become hospitable to wildlife.

5. Today, more than 2,000 pairs of shorebirds, including not only several species of herons, snowy egrets, but also great egrets, and glossy ibis nest on the different islands.

Writing Responsibly
Using Parallelism to Clarify Relationships among Ideas

An important component of the writing process is figuring out the *relationships* among your ideas and making those relationships clear to your readers. As you revise, ask yourself questions like these: What is the cause and what is the effect? What items are truly a part of the group and what items are not? Which ideas are important and which ideas provide supporting information?

Using parallelism can help you emphasize for your reader that certain ideas are of equal importance. (Coordination and subordination, discussed in the previous chapter, can also help you emphasize that ideas or information are of equal or unequal importance.)

Experimenting with some of the techniques you are learning in this chapter, and in other chapters in this part, can lead to new insights about your topic.

to AUDIENCE

28d Maintaining Parallelism for Items in Lists and Outlines

Each item in a list or an outline should be in the same grammatical form as the others.

1. Items in a list

Whenever you have a list of three or more items, those items should be in the same grammatical form. The following list is difficult to read in its draft form because the first and third items begin with independent clauses, whereas the other three begin with a noun followed by a bit of commentary. The revision puts them all in the noun followed by commentary form.

DRAFT LIST

Among the top ten most healthful foods, these are my favorites:

1. <u>Avocados are delicious unadorned</u>. I also enjoy them sliced in half with the hole filled with a mixture of olive oil and lime juice.

2. <u>I like nuts because they are so portable</u>.

3. <u>Berries</u>. All of them are delicious, except blackberries.

4. <u>Yogurt</u>. I avoid the kind with fruit on the bottom.

5. <u>Garlic</u>. I like it, but it doesn't like me.

REVISED

Among the top ten most healthful foods, these are my favorites:

1. <u>Avocados</u>. They are delicious unadorned. I also enjoy them sliced in half with the hole filled with a mixture of olive oil and lime juice.

2. <u>Nuts</u>. I like them because they are so portable.

3. <u>Berries</u>. All of them are delicious, except blackberries.

4. <u>Yogurt</u>. I avoid the kind with fruit on the bottom.

5. <u>Garlic</u>. I like it, but it doesn't like me.

2. Items in outlines

Maintain parallelism in outlines and headings by keeping all items at the same level in the same form. In the original version of the following outline, three of the top-level headings—I, II, and IV—are noun phrases whereas III is a question. Likewise, under heading I, the first subheading begins with a noun whereas the second and third are **gerund** phrases, and under heading IV, the last item is an independent clause. Revising the outline so that the headings are parallel makes it easier to understand.

> **gerund** The *-ing* form of a verb used as a noun

DRAFT OUTLINE	REVISED OUTLINE
I. Types of literary fraud	I. Types of literary fraud
A. Plagiarism	A. Plagiarism
B. Forging documents	B. Forgery
C. Misrepresenting the facts	C. Misrepresentation
II. Examples of literary fraud	II. Examples of literary fraud
A. Kaavya Viswanathan	A. Kaavya Viswanathan
B. The Donation of Constantine	B. The Donation of Constantine
C. James Frey	C. James Frey
III. Why do people commit literary fraud?	III. Motives for literary fraud
A. Financial gain	A. Financial gain
B. Personal glory	B. Personal glory
C. Insecurity	C. Insecurity
D. Weak writing skills	D. Weak writing skills
E. Busy schedule	E. Busy schedule
IV. Problems with literary fraud	IV. Problems with literary fraud
A. Copyright infringement	A. Copyright infringement
B. Breach of faith	B. Breach of faith
C. Readers take actions based on erroneous assumptions	C. Reader actions based on erroneous assumptions

➤ EXERCISE 28.3 Parallelism in lists

Correct the parallelism errors in the following list.

Favorite Leisure Activities

1. Reading, especially contemporary novels
2. I really enjoy going to the movies with my friends.
3. To hike in the woods and to camp out
4. On the weekends, I enjoy online role-playing game marathons
5. Listening to classic rock and folk music

28e Using Parallelism to Create Emphasis

Placing ideas in parallel form highlights their differences and similarities.

▸ All the images are copies of the same original, ~~the~~ same size, and ~~they have equal space between them~~ within a grid of rows and columns.

all are (inserted before "same size")
all are equally spaced (replacing the struck-through text)

> *More about*
> Parallelism and emphasis, 534–35

As the passage from Lincoln's Gettysburg address at the beginning of this chapter illustrates, parallelism can be a forceful tool for emphasizing important ideas. Martin Luther King, Jr., provides another example in his famous "I have a dream" speech. Notice how King's parallelisms generate an almost musical cadence that drives us toward the speech's conclusion.

> When we let freedom ring, when we let it ring from every village and every hamlet, from every state and every city, we will be able to speed up that day when all of God's children, black men and white men, Jews and Gentiles, Protestants and Catholics, will be able to join hands and sing in the words of the old Negro spiritual, "Free at last! Free at last! Thank God Almighty, we are free at last!"
>
> —Martin Luther King, Jr., from speech delivered August 28, 1963, Washington, DC

➤ EXERCISE 28.4 Parallelism and emphasis

Use parallelism to combine and emphasize the ideas in the following groups of sentences.

EXAMPLE

The ancestor of the modern horse evolved in North America about 4 million years ~~ago. It~~ *ago,* spread to Eurasia over the Bering land ~~bridge. Horses~~ *bridge, and then* became extinct in North America at the end of the last Ice Age about 12,000 years ago.

1. Scientists have long debated where and when the horse was domesticated. They have also debated where and when dogs and the pig were domesticated. The time and place of the domestication of other animals, such as cattle, sheep, and goats, is much clearer.

2. Dogs were domesticated before horses. Cattle were domesticated before horses. Goats were domesticated before horses. Pigs were domesticated before horses. Sheep were domesticated before horses.

3. Scientists now believe that horses were domesticated about 6,000 years ago in Central Asia. This conclusion is based on DNA evidence. It is also based on evidence obtained from archaeological remains. It is also based on studies of contemporary nomadic peoples whose lifestyles may resemble those of the people who first domesticated the horse.

4. All the evidence about horse domestication points to a complicated process. This process went on over a long time. This process occurred at many different places. This process was further complicated by climate changes during the last Ice Age, which altered the wild horses' habitat and forced them to migrate north.

Make It **Your Own**

Reread three pieces of your recent writing and identify examples of parallelism. Look for faulty parallelism, and if you find any, make a note in the margins of the paper identifying which section of this chapter explains the revision. Add this to your list of areas to consider as you revise your prose.

29 Engaging Readers with Variety and Emphasis

IN THIS CHAPTER

a. Varying sentence length, structure, 528
b. Varying sentence openings, 529
c. Creating emphasis with rhythm, 531
d. Creating emphasis with punctuation, 533
e. Using questions, commands, exclamations, 534
f. Using strategic repetition, 534
g. Choosing emphatic verbs, 535
h. Choosing active or passive voice, 535
i. **Writing Responsibly** Blending Voices in Your Text, 538

In this painting, *At the Opera*, artist Mary Cassatt captures our interest with a variety of visual elements, among them the large figure of the woman in the foreground; the more sketchily rendered figures in the background; the curving form of the balconies; the bright points of red and white; and the contrasting large, dark areas. Cassatt also structures the painting to emphasize certain elements over others and to direct our attention to a story unfolding within the scene. Our eyes go first to the woman in the foreground; then we follow her gaze through her opera glasses and let the curve of the balcony railing draw our attention to the upper left, where a male figure also is looking through opera glasses—not toward the stage, however, but at the woman in the foreground.

Writers also use variety and emphasis to capture and hold their readers' attention and to direct those readers to the subtleties of the story being told. Speakers use intonation, tone of voice, and timing to avoid monotony and emphasize or de-emphasize particular words or phrases. Writers use variety and emphasis to help readers "hear" the words of the text in their mind's ear.

Quick Reference — Achieving Variety and Emphasis

- Vary sentence length and structure. (528)
- Vary sentence openings. (529)
- Use rhythm strategically. (531)
- Choose appropriate punctuation. (533)
- Introduce questions, commands, and exclamations when appropriate. (534)
- Use strategic repetition. (534)
- Choose emphatic verbs and favor the active voice. (535)

527

> **simple sentence** One independent clause and no subordinate clauses
> **compound sentence** Two or more independent clauses and no subordinate clauses
> **complex sentence** One independent clause with at least one subordinate clause
> **compound-complex sentence** Two or more independent clauses with one or more subordinate clauses

29a Varying Sentence Length and Structure

Confronting readers with page after page of sentences of uniform length—long, short, or in between—can tire them and make it hard for them to pick out important details. To hold readers' attention and direct it to the points you want to emphasize, vary the length of your sentences and include a mix of sentence structures: *simple, compound, complex,* and *compound-complex.*

Short sentences deliver information concisely and dramatically. They are most emphatic, however, when they are mixed with longer sentences. In the following passage, too many short sentences in a row create a choppy effect, leaving the reader with the impression that each point is equally important. The revision combines most of the short sentences into longer sentences that clarify the relationship among the ideas the writer wants to convey. The writer's main point is now dramatically isolated in the one short sentence that remains.

DRAFT
: The whole planet is at risk. We need to put a stop to the wild spread of this disease. The key is education. First, we should educate the victims. Then we should let them educate the world. They can help us win this war against AIDS. They can help other people understand that everyone is vulnerable.

REVISION
: With the whole planet at risk, we need to put a stop to the wild spread of this disease. The key is education. First, we should educate the victims; then we should let them educate the world. They can help us win this war against AIDS by helping other people understand that everyone is vulnerable.

EXERCISE 29.1 Editing for varied sentence length and structure

Revise the paragraph to create a more coherent result with a mix of sentence lengths and types.

> In Central America and Mexico 3,000 years ago, people played a ballgame. It was called *Tlatchtil* in Náhuatl, which was their language. It used solid rubber balls; they weighed about 6 lbs. They kept the ball in motion by hitting it with their hips. It was played in elaborate stone ballcourts with rings on the sides. The team that got the ball through the ring won. There is some evidence of ballgames ending in sacrifice of players to the gods. We don't know whether the winners or the losers died. Other evidence suggests the game was played to settle conflicts and avoid war.

29b Varying Sentence Openings

In the default structure of an English sentence, the subject comes first, then the verb, and then the direct object if there is one. Reflecting this structure, most sentences start with the subject. However, a long string of subject-first sentences can make your text monotonous. Use modifying clauses and phrases to vary your sentence openings and to emphasize important information.

Adverbs and adverbial phrases and clauses Where you place an ***adverb***, and the phrases and clauses that function as adverbs, affects the rhythm of a sentence and the information it emphasizes.

> **adverb** A word that modifies a verb, adjective, other adverb, or entire phrase or clause and that specifies how, where, when, and to what extent or degree

ADVERBIAL SUBORDINATE CLAUSE

Stocks can be a risky investment because they can lose value.

Because they can lose value, stocks can be a risky investment.

Stocks, because they can lose value, can be a risky investment.

ADVERBIAL PREPOSITIONAL PHRASES

We eat pancakes for breakfast on Sundays.

On Sundays, we eat pancakes for breakfast.

For breakfast, we eat pancakes on Sundays.

> **More about**
> Sentence structure, 585–99

NOTE Moving an adverb can sometimes alter the meaning of a sentence. Consider these two examples:

- The test was surprisingly hard.
- Surprisingly, the test was hard.

In the first, *surprisingly* modifies *hard,* suggesting that the writer found the test harder than expected; in the second, *surprisingly* modifies the whole clause that follows it, suggesting that the writer expected the test to be easy.

Adjectival phrases The placement of ***adjectives*** and most adjectival phrases and clauses is less flexible than the placement of adverbs. However, participles and ***participial phrases,*** which act as adjectives, can often come at the beginning of a sentence as well as after the terms they modify.

> **adjective** A word that modifies a noun or pronoun with descriptive or limiting information
> **participial phrase** A phrase in which the present or past participle acts as an adjective

- New York City's subway system, flooded by torrential rains, shut down at the height of the morning rush hour.
- Flooded by torrential rains, New York City's subway system shut down at the height of the morning rush hour.

Subject complement An adjective, pronoun, or noun phrase that follows a linking verb and describes or refers to the subject of the sentence

An adjective phrase that functions as a *subject complement* can also sometimes be repositioned at the beginning of a sentence.

▶ The Mariana Trench is almost seven miles deep, making it the lowest place on the surface of the earth.

▶ Almost seven miles deep, the Mariana Trench is the lowest place on the surface of the earth.

More about
Placement of adjectives, 669–77

Appositives and absolute phrases An *appositive* is a noun or noun phrase that renames another noun or noun phrase. Because they designate the same thing, the appositive and the original term can switch positions.

▶ The governor, New York's highest official, ordered an investigation into the subway system's failure.

▶ New York's highest official, the governor, ordered an investigation into the subway system's failure.

An *absolute phrase*, consisting of a noun or pronoun with a participle, modifies an entire independent clause. It can often fall either before or after the clause it modifies.

▶ The task finally completed, the workers headed for the parking lot.

▶ The workers headed for the parking lot, the task finally completed.

More about
Transitional expressions, 54–55

Transitional expressions A *transitional expression* relates the information in one sentence to material that precedes or follows. Its placement affects the emphasis that falls on other parts of the sentence. The second passage below, for example, calls more attention to Superman's distinctiveness than the first does.

▶ Most comic book characters from the 1930s quickly fell into obscurity. However, Superman was not one of them.

▶ Most comic book characters from the 1930s quickly fell into obscurity. Superman, however, was not one of them.

EXERCISE 29.2 Varying sentence openings

Revise the following sentences to begin with something other than the subject.

EXAMPLE

Soaring in search of food, ravens
~~Ravens~~ patrol the misty blue sky high above the valley, ~~soaring in search of food.~~

1. The Canaan Valley, one of the highest valleys east of the Mississippi, was designated a National Natural Landmark in 1974.
2. This ecosystem, with its many species of plants and animals, is an example of northern forest.
3. It seems out of place, located here in West Virginia.
4. The valley is more than 3,000 feet deep and enjoys cool summers and snowy winters.
5. The valley is likely to remain wild and natural for many years to come because it is protected by federal and state governments.

29c Creating Emphasis with Rhythm

Sentences, like music, have rhythm, and within that rhythm, some beats get more stress than others. Readers readily notice the beginning of a sentence, where they usually find the subject, and they notice the end, where everything wraps up. Take advantage of readers' habits by slotting important or striking information into those positions. In the following example, the writer changed the subject of the sentence from *ready availability* to the more significant *free news* and moved *financial ruin* to the end, dramatically underscoring the seriousness of the challenge newspapers face.

DRAFT   The ready availability of free news on the Internet threatens financial ruin for traditional newspapers.

REVISED   Free news, readily available on the Internet, threatens traditional newspapers with financial ruin.

A common way to organize information in longer sentences is with a cumulative or loose structure. A *cumulative sentence* begins with the subject and verb of an independent clause and accumulates additional information in subsequent modifying phrases and clauses.

> That's the news from Lake Wobegon, where all the women are strong, all the men are good-looking, and all the children are above average.
> —Garrison Keillor, tag line from the radio show *A Prairie Home Companion*

A *periodic sentence,* in contrast, reserves the independent clause for the end, preceded by modifying details. The effect is to build suspense that highlights key information when it finally arrives.

> Through the center of town, up the strip, past the housing developments and shopping malls, street lights giving way to the thin streaming illumination of

the headlights, trees crowding the asphalt in a black unbroken wall: **that was the way to Greasy Lake.**

—T. Coraghessan Boyle, "Greasy Lake"

An interrupted periodic sentence begins with the subject of the independent clause but leaves the conclusion of the clause to the end, separating the two parts with modifying details. In the following example, the subject of the sentence is highlighted in yellow, and the predicate is highlighted in blue.

The archaeologist Howard Carter, peering through the small opening to the main chamber of Tutankhamen's tomb at treasures hidden from view for more than three millennia, when asked what he saw, *replied "wonderful things."*

An *inversion* is a sentence in which, contrary to normal English word order, the verb precedes the subject. Inverted sentences call attention to themselves. Used sparingly, they can help you emphasize a point or create a sense of dramatic tension.

▶ Into the middle of town *rode* (verb) *the stranger* (subj.).

Developing an Ear for Sentence Variety Many of the sentence structures that add variety to written English are uncommon in conversation and as a result may not come naturally to you even if you are fluent in conversational English. To develop an ear for sentence variety in your academic writing, try going through this chapter and imitating some of the structures it describes with examples of your own. Ask an instructor or another skilled writer of English to check your work to see if you have produced effective sentences.

EXERCISE 29.3 Cumulative and periodic sentences

Combine the sentences in each of the following passages into a single cumulative sentence. Then combine them again, this time into a periodic sentence.

CUMULATIVE SENTENCE

Mosses generally live in shady areas. ~~These areas~~ *, which* are more likely to be damp. ~~This reduces~~ *and therefore reduce* the risk of the moss drying out.

PERIODIC SENTENCE

Because mosses need to avoid drying out and shady areas tend to be damp, mosses generally live in shady areas. ~~Mosses generally live in shady areas. These areas are more likely to be damp. This reduces the risk of the moss drying out.~~

1. Moss is often killed by gardeners. It can inhibit the growth of small plants. It absorbs water through its leaves, preventing the water and fertilizer from reaching the roots of plants around it.

2. Moss is important in Japanese temple gardens. Some believe it to be calming. It is also used in bonsai gardening. The moss is believed to add a sense of age.

3. Water run-off from roofs fills sewers and is a problem in many cities. Modern sustainable buildings often have green roofs. Moss is a common plant for green roofs. It is light in weight. It does not have deep roots. It absorbs water.

29d Creating Emphasis with Punctuation

One way to draw your readers' attention to significant material is to place it at the end of a sentence after a colon or dash.

> **More about**
> Colons, 800–02
> Dashes, 796–98

- ▸ According to photographer William Klein, the advertising campaign for fashion designer John Galliano wasn't just influenced by Klein's visual techniques—it stole them.

- ▸ The judge had two words for Galliano's use of Klein's signature visual style: copyright infringement.

You can also draw attention to nonessential phrases or clauses within an independent clause when you set them off with dashes instead of commas.

> **More about**
> Essential and nonessential modifiers, 757–59

- ▸ The judge had two words—copyright infringement—for Galliano's use of Klein's signature visual style.

The punctuation between two independent clauses can affect the way readers perceive the relationship between them. A dash (as we have just seen) or a period creates a more emphatic separation than a semicolon or a comma and coordinating conjunction.

> **More about**
> Periods, 792–93
> Semicolons, 766–72
> Commas, 748–65

- ▸ The jury convicted the defendants. The judge sentenced them to life.
- ▸ The jury convicted the defendants; the judge sentenced them to life.
- ▸ The jury convicted the defendants, and the judge sentenced them to life.

29e Using Questions, Commands, and Exclamations

> **More about**
> Sentence categories, 597–99

Most sentences are *declarative:* They make a statement—declare something—about their subjects. Other types of sentences include questions, commands, and exclamations. When used sparingly, these can add variety to prose and draw attention to important ideas. Overused, they sound gimmicky or childish.

Most questions in academic writing are **rhetorical;** they are meant to call attention to an issue, not to elicit an answer.

> [F]or all our focus on happiness it is by no means clear that we are happier as a result. Might we not even say that our contemporary concern is something of an inauspicious sign, belying a deep anxiety and doubt about the object of our pursuit? Does the fact that we worry so much about being happy suggest that we are not?
> —Darrin M. McMahon, "The Pursuit of Happiness in Perspective"

> **More about**
> Person, 438–39

Commands are a type of second-person sentence: The subject of a command, even when unstated, is always *you.* The second person is best reserved for addressing the reader directly, and commands, in particular, are useful for describing a process or conveying advice.

> When in doubt tell the truth.
> —Mark Twain, *Following the Equator*

Exclamations are emphatic statements or expressions of strong emotion. Interjections are exclamatory words that stand alone within a sentence. Both are usually punctuated with exclamation marks, and both are rare in academic writing.

> The one fact that I would cry from every housetop is this: the Good Life is waiting for us—here and now!
> —B. F. Skinner, *Walden II*

29f Using Strategic Repetition

Redundancy and other forms of unnecessary repetition clutter writing and distract readers. Repetition is sometimes necessary, however, for clarity and to maintain parallelism.

Writers can also use repetition strategically for emphasis, calling attention to important ideas, as the writer Flannery O'Connor does with her repetition of the word *grotesque* in the following passage.

I doubt if the texture of Southern life is any more grotesque than that of the rest of the nation, but it does seem evident that the Southern writer is particularly adept at recognizing the grotesque; and to recognize the grotesque, you have to have some notion of what is not grotesque and why.
—Flannery O'Connor, talk delivered at Notre Dame University

Repetition for emphasis works especially well within parallel structures, as in this sentence from a paper by Syracuse University student Jessica Toro.

> Some children are never told that they are adopted, never given the opportunity to search for their biological parents.

Toro could have used *or* instead of the second *never*, but the repetition dramatically underscores her concern about the consequences of a particular policy toward adopted children.

> **More about**
> Parallelism, 518–26

29g Creating Emphasis with Emphatic Verbs

Verbs that describe an action directly are often more emphatic than verbs like *be*, *have*, or *cause* that combine with nouns or adjectives to describe an action indirectly.

▶ Many economists ~~have a belief~~ *believe* that higher gasoline taxes would ~~be beneficial to~~ *benefit* the economy in the long run. The increased costs would ~~have a stimulating effect on~~ *stimulate* research into alternate energy sources and eventually ~~cause a reduction in~~ *reduce* both carbon emissions and our dependence on oil.

29h Choosing the Active or Passive Voice

In an active-voice sentence, the subject performs the action of the verb; in a passive-voice sentence, the subject receives the action of the verb. Active-voice sentences are usually more emphatic, direct, and concise than their passive-voice counterparts.

> **More about**
> Voice in verbs, 637, 652–55
> Passive voice and wordiness, 500–02

ACTIVE VOICE: EMPHATIC
Rising oil prices stimulate research into alternate energy sources.

PASSIVE VOICE: UNEMPHATIC
Research into alternate energy sources is stimulated by rising oil prices.

However, if you want to emphasize the recipient of an action over the performer, or agent, of the action, the passive voice can be an appropriate choice. In this famous sentence from his address to the nation on December 8, 1941, for example, President Franklin Delano Roosevelt used the passive voice to focus on the United States as the victim of the attack on Pearl Harbor.

> Yesterday, December 7th, 1941—a date which will live in infamy—the United States of America was suddenly and deliberately attacked by naval and air forces of the Empire of Japan.

Because it can allow the agent to remain unidentified, the passive voice can also be an appropriate choice when the identity of the agent is unknown or unimportant.

> According to the coroner, the victim had been murdered between 3 and 4 in the morning.
>
> The identity of the murderer is unknown.

> *Harry Potter and the Philosopher's Stone,* the first book in the Harry Potter series, was published in 1997.
>
> The focus is on the date of publication, not the specific identity of the publisher.

Similarly, in science writing, the passive voice allows the description of procedures without constant reference to the individuals who carried them out.

> The effects of human activities on seagrasses were studied at Sandy Neck and Centerville beaches from 31 March 2011 to 30 March 2013.

Writing Responsibly

Voice and Responsibility

Because the passive voice allows the agent of an action to remain unnamed, it lends itself to misuse by people evading responsibility for their own or others' mistakes and misdeeds. Consider, for example, the classic dodge of the cornered politician or bureaucrat: "Mistakes were made."

Be on the lookout for this evasive use of the passive voice in your own writing and the writing of others. It is a usage that comes all too readily to hand when we need to convey unflattering or damaging information about ourselves or those we represent.

to TOPIC

EXERCISE 29.4 Emphatic verbs, active verbs

Revise each of the following sentences, replacing indirect expressions with emphatic verbs and, when appropriate, changing verbs from passive to active voice.

EXAMPLE

Many people ~~have a belief that Plymouth Colony was founded by advocates of~~ *believe that the founders of Plymouth Colony advocated* religious freedom.

1. The Pilgrims, as they came to be called, experienced persecution in England and made a decision to move to Holland.
2. In Holland, however, many members of the congregation found it a struggle to find employment and experienced economic suffering.
3. In addition, parents found the influence of Dutch language and culture on their children a source of worry and a threat to the group's survival.
4. Therefore, in 1619, a decision was made by the Pilgrims' leaders to move the entire group to the New World.
5. Although the Pilgrims wanted freedom to worship as they pleased, it was not assumed by them that religious freedom was desirable for all.
6. Rather, they were of the opinion that there was one proper way to worship and that proper way was the one observed by them.

Make It Your Own

Reread three pieces of your recent writing and edit them for variety and emphasis using the strategies covered in this chapter. If you find many sentences needing revision, add this to your list of areas to consider as you revise your prose.

Work Together

Working in a small group, review three examples of different types of writing—such as an advertisement, informational text, and a short story—and analyze the authors' use of the strategies covered in this chapter. What did each of you see that others did not? Write a few sentences reflecting on how this collaborative activity might help you revise your own work in the future.

Writing Responsibly
Blending Voices in Your Text

Make It Your Own! Good researched writing is more than collecting the ideas of others; it is instead an exploration of how the sources have helped researchers develop their own ideas. You will produce better work if, as you draft your project, you let your readers see *your* thinking.

Whenever you write from sources, you are blending the voices of your sources with one another and with your own. Although *voice* sometimes refers to the difference between passive and active voice, it also refers to who is talking in the text—the writer or the source.

Your audience wants to know whose voice it is "hearing." When you quote, it knows you are importing the voice of the source. When you **paraphrase** (rewrite the information in fresh language), your audience hears you talking. But when you **patchwrite** (copy from sources and make minor changes to its language, but not actually paraphrase), you lead your audience to the mistaken belief that it is hearing you when in fact it is neither your voice nor the source's, but rather an inappropriate mixture of the two. To blend voices successfully, you need to avoid patchwriting and show the beginning and end of your use of sources.

Most readers consider it plagiarism when a writer patchwrites. Regardless of whether he or she classifies it as plagiarism, no reader considers patchwriting good writing. The following passage from a source discussing the history of child psychology, followed by a student's first-draft writing from that source, illustrates the issue:

Passage from source

> In the 1910s and later, as child psychology became an academic discipline, teachers increasingly looked to educational researchers rather than librarians as the central experts in children's reading.

Patchwriting

> From the 1910s on, child psychology became a discipline, and teachers more and more thought that educational researchers rather than librarians were the main experts in children's reading (248).

The patchwriting follows the original sentence, deleting a few words and substituting some others, but still dependent on the language and arrangement of the source sentence. Not knowing that this is a blend of two voices—the writer's and the source's—the reader is misled to think this is the student's voice.

Paraphrase

> Child psychology emerged as an academic discipline in the early twentieth century, prompting teachers to look to researchers for expertise about children's reading. Librarians were no longer the primary authority on the topic (248).

Style Matters • Blending Voices in Your Text

The paraphrase appropriately uses keywords from the original, such as *discipline* and *child psychology*, but it otherwise uses fresh language and fresh sentence arrangement to restate the source.

Ground your own writing in paraphrase and summary, include some quotation, and avoid patchwriting altogether. This will allow your voice, rather than those of your sources, to dominate your text. This strategy requires your conscious effort and practice. Writing true paraphrase is an advanced skill that many college writers do not practice (see chart), but those who master this skill write the most successful research projects.

To let your readers know when you are paraphrasing or summarizing, use a signal phrase at the beginning of the source use and a parenthetical citation at the end. If your use of sources is lengthy, you can also occasionally mention the source or the author as you write, just to remind your readers that they are reading your summary or paraphrase of a source:

Students' Use of Sources
DATA FROM **The Citation Project**

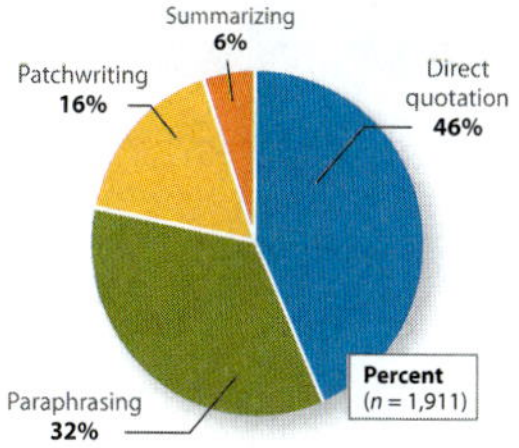

- Summarizing 6%
- Patchwriting 16%
- Direct quotation 46%
- Paraphrasing 32%

Percent (*n* = 1,911)

Researchers found that while most college research writers use quoting and patchwriting, the best projects were by those who use summary and paraphrase.

Marking where the source use begins and ends

Signal phrase at beginning of source use	McDowell explains that the academic discipline of child psychology, which emerged in the early twentieth century, looked to researchers for expertise about children's reading. Librarians were no longer the leading authorities on the topic. Both librarians and child psychologists were interested in children's reading patterns, but for different reasons. The librarians, McDowell says, wanted to understand what sorts of texts would interest children so they could get them into the library. Child psychologists, in contrast, wanted to understand the children themselves. Both groups collected information about children's reading, but they did it in different ways. The librarians observed children's reading and reported on their observations, while the child psychologists conducted scientific research (248–49).

- Paraphrase of a sentence from the source
- Summary of two pages in the source
- Parenthetical citation at end of source use

Signal phrase within the source use

Source: McDowell, Kathleen. "Toward a History of Children as Readers, 1890–1930." *Book History* 12 (2009): 240–65. Print.

Self Assessment

Review your work with each source, revising as necessary, to be sure you:

☐ Use paraphrase and summary. Did you avoid overreliance on quotations?
▶ *Summarizing, 256–58; paraphrasing, 252–56; patchwriting, 247*

☐ Paraphrase while avoiding patchwriting. Did you restate source material in fresh language and fresh sentences? ▶ *Taking notes and avoiding plagiarism, 250–51*

☐ Use signal phrases and parenthetical citations. Did you let your audience know where your paraphrase and summary begins and ends? ▶ *Voice, 278–80*

30 Choosing Appropriate Language

IN THIS CHAPTER

a. Using language in context, 540

b. Avoiding biased, hurtful language, 544

"We have only jobs here, Mr. Sanderson, not 'gigs.'"

During a job interview, both the applicant and the interviewer need to dress appropriately, behave appropriately, and use language appropriately. Neither would be likely to show up in a bathing suit, jump up and down on a couch, use language that might offend the other, or, like the applicant in this cartoon, refer to the position casually as a "gig." Such issues of appropriateness apply to your writing as well. In every document you write, use language that is appropriate to the context and avoids bias.

30a Using Language in Context

We all adjust our language to suit our audience and purpose. No form of the language is intrinsically better or more correct than another, but certain forms have become standard for addressing a broad audience in an academic setting or in the workplace. In this context, using appropriate language usually means the following:

- Avoiding nonstandard dialects
- Avoiding regionalisms, colloquialisms, and slang

540

- Avoiding overly technical terminology (jargon and neologisms)
- Adopting a straightforward tone, one that is neither overly informal nor pompously inflated

1. Nonstandard dialects

A ***dialect*** is a variant of a language with its own distinctive pronunciation, vocabulary, and grammar. A linguist once quipped that the only difference between the standard form of a language and its other dialects is that the standard form has an army and a navy. The standard form, in other words, became standard because it is the dialect of the elite and powerful.

Nonstandard dialects of English are not "bad" English, as many mistakenly believe. If you speak a dialect like Appalachian English or African American Vernacular English and you are addressing an audience of peers from your community, then your home dialect *is* appropriate. If you are addressing a broader audience or writing in an academic or workplace context, however, the dialect known as Standard American English, or Edited English, is usually the appropriate choice.

> **More about**
> The grammar of Standard American English, 574–99

2. Regionalisms, colloquialisms, and slang

Regionalisms are expressions that are characteristic of particular areas. Saying the car "needs washed" is acceptable in Pittsburgh but not in Boston. The expression "I might could do it" might be acceptable in Pikeville, Kentucky, but not in Des Moines, Iowa. Regionalisms can be appropriate in conversation or informal writing but are usually out of place in formal academic writing.

▸ Many scientists believe that we might ~~could~~ *be able to* slow global warming if we can reduce carbon emissions.

Colloquialisms are informal expressions common in speech but usually out of place in formal writing.

▸ An R rating designates a movie that is not appropriate for ~~kids~~ *children* under 17 who are not accompanied by ~~a grown up.~~ *an adult.*

Used judiciously, however, the occasional colloquialism can add verve to your writing.

▸ The musicians were only kids, none of them more than ten years old, but they played like seasoned professionals.

> ## Writing Responsibly
> **Avoiding Online Shortcuts**
>
> Users of text messaging, instant messaging, and social networking sites have developed a host of acronyms and abbreviations—like *BTW* for "by the way" and *IMO* for "in my opinion"—that save typing time and space on the tiny screens of mobile phones. With the possible exception of informal e-mail, these expressions are almost never appropriate in other contexts, particularly not in academic or business writing. The same applies to emoticons like :-) and :-(and to other shortcuts such as writing entirely in lowercase without punctuation, as in *i saw her this am.*
>
> to SELF

Slang is the extremely informal, inventive, often colorful (and sometimes off-color) vocabulary of a particular group. In general, slang is inappropriate in formal writing, but as with colloquial language, when used sparingly and judiciously, it can enliven a sentence and help emphasize an important point.

3. Neologisms and jargon

The world changes. Technology advances, new cultural trends emerge, and new research alters our understanding of ourselves and gives rise to new fields of study. As these changes occur, people necessarily invent new words and expressions—*neologisms.* Some neologisms gain wide currency and establish themselves as acceptable vocabulary for formal writing. Other neologisms, however, soon disappear or never move from informal to formal usage. When you consider using a neologism, ask yourself whether a more familiar synonym might serve as well. If the neologism is necessary but you are not sure your audience will be familiar with it, define it.

▶ Some instructors use wikis*, websites that allow a group of users to create and edit content collectively,* as tools for teaching collaborative writing.

The term *jargon* refers to the specialized vocabulary of a particular profession or discipline. Doctors speak of *adenomas* and *electroencephalograms.* Automobile mechanics speak of *camber angles* and *ring-and-pinion gears.* Lawyers speak of *effluxions of time* and *words of procreation.* English professors speak of *discursive historicity* and *terministic screens.* For an audience of specialists, this kind of insider vocabulary can efficiently communicate concepts that might otherwise take several sentences, even paragraphs, to explain. If you are addressing other specialists, jargon may be appropriate. If you are addressing a general audience, however, it is usually inappropriate. In most cases, avoid it. When a specialized term is needed, define it.

▶ The tenants lost the apartment ~~due to the effluxion of time on their lease~~. *when their lease expired.*

4. Appropriate formality

When you speak or write to close friends and intimates from your own age group, your language will probably—and appropriately—be relaxed and informal, sprinkled with dialect, slang, and colloquial expressions. Writing for most college courses or in the workplace, however, requires a formal tone and clear, straightforward language free of slang and colloquialisms. Clear and straightforward, however, should not mean simpleminded or condescending. Use challenging vocabulary if it aptly expresses your meaning, but do not try to impress your readers by inflating your writing with fancy words mined from a thesaurus.

> **More about**
> Using a thesaurus, 560

INAPPROPRIATELY INFORMAL	Tarantino is always ripping scenes from earlier flicks to use in his own.
POMPOUS	It is a characteristic stylistic mannerism of the auteur Quentin Tarantino to allusively amalgamate scenic quotations from the repertory of his cinematic forebears in his own oeuvre.
APPROPRIATE	In his movies, the director Quentin Tarantino routinely alludes to scenes from earlier movies.

➔ EXERCISE 30.1 Editing for language in context

Edit the following passage to establish appropriate formality for a college paper and to eliminate inappropriate regionalisms, colloquialisms, slang, and jargon.

> There are many reasons why folks are now trying essentially to effect a truncation of their consumption of meat. Some believe that having less meat will make them healthier. Some are desirous of losing weight by cutting their intake of fat. Some are doing it merely to be copycats. Regardless of the motivation, nutrition experts say that reducing meat

Writing Responsibly: Euphemisms and Doublespeak

We use **euphemisms** in place of words that might be offensive or emotionally painful. We speak to mourners about a relative who has *passed away*, and we excuse ourselves saying we have to go *to the bathroom* without referring to specific bodily functions.

The polite or respectful use of euphemisms, however, can easily shade into a more evasive reluctance to address harsh realities. Why use *correctional institution*, for example, when what you mean is *prison* or *jail*? Why use *ill-advised* when what you mean is *foolish* or *rash*?

Euphemisms that are deliberately deceptive, used to obscure bad news or sanitize an ugly truth, are called **doublespeak**. A company that announces that it is *downsizing*, not that it is about to lay off half of its workforce, is using doublespeak. *Terrorists* who call themselves *freedom fighters* are using doublespeak.

When reading, ask yourself: Does this word obscure or downplay the truth? When writing, think carefully about your motives: Are you using a euphemism (or doublespeak) to avoid hurting someone's feelings, or to evade responsibility for an uncomfortable truth?

to AUDIENCE

---

consumption is not rocket science and can be effectuated by following some simple steps.

To begin with, chill out about getting enough protein. Plants supply protein too, and some, such as spinach and lentils, proffer greater quantities of protein per calorie than a cheeseburger does. Per capita, Americans currently scarf up about a half pound of meat per day. The biggest bump in the road can be cooking more meat than you need, so start buying less meat than you usually do. When you have less meat on hand, you'll eat less of it. Have a go at planning meals with meat on the side of the plate instead of smack dab in the middle. Ramp up the amount of vegetables you buy, and dig up recipes for yummy vegetable dishes. Promulgate some rules for yourself; for example, you may want to have meatless breakfasts and lunches, and then eat whatever you like for dinners. Buckle down on this, and you'll soon find that meat plays a smaller role in your meals.

30b Avoiding Biased or Hurtful Language

> **More about**
> Stereotyping,
> 138–40, 156

Biased or ***hurtful language*** unfairly or offensively characterizes a particular group and, by extension, its individual members. It can be as blatant as a hatefully uttered racial, ethnic, or sexual slur, but it can also be subtle and unintentional, as in thoughtless stereotyping or an inappropriately applied label.

A ***stereotype*** is a simplified, uncritical, and often negative generalization about an entire group of people: *Blondes are ditzy; athletes are weak students; lawyers are unscrupulous; politicians are dishonest.* Even when they seem positive, stereotypes lump people together in ways that offensively ignore their individuality. In an article in the *New York Times,* for example, Chinese American writer Vivian S. Toy remembers among her "painful experiences of being different" that a college adviser once recommended that she switch her major to biology "since Chinese are better suited for the sciences."

We label people whenever we call attention to a particular characteristic about them. ***Labeling*** is appropriate when it is relevant.

▸ Barack Obama is the first African American president.

Labeling is inappropriate, and usually offensive, when it is irrelevant.

▸ President Obama, an African American, is an articulate debater.

To appreciate how irrelevant the label "African American" is in that last sentence, consider the following:

▸ Senator John McCain, who is of Scots-Irish and English descent, is an articulate debater.

1. Gender bias

English has no pronouns that designate an individual person without also designating that person's gender (*she, he, her, him, hers, his, herself, himself*). This lack creates problems when a writer uses the singular to refer generically to a whole class of people or to people in general.

▸ The sensible student is careful what [*he? she?*] posts about [*himself? herself?*] on social networking sites like Facebook and Twitter.

Until about the 1970s, the conventional solution to this problem was to use the masculine pronoun as the generic pronoun. In other words, depending on context, *he* referred either to a particular male human or to "he or she," a generic human of either gender. On the other hand, *she* always meant "female," never "she or he." Similarly, the terms *man* and *mankind* could refer generically to humanity as a whole, but *woman* and *womankind* only to women. Since the 1970s, writers have been replacing this usage—together with other vocabulary that reinforces gender stereotypes—with gender-neutral alternatives.

***Avoid generic* he** One way to avoid the generic *he*—and often the most graceful way—is to switch from singular to plural.

> ▶ ~~The sensible student is~~ *Sensible students are* careful what ~~he posts~~ *they post* about ~~himself~~ *themselves* on social networking sites like Facebook and Twitter.

Another alternative is to use *he or she* (or *she or he*).

> ▶ The sensible student is careful what he or she posts on social networking sites.

Be sparing with this option, however; used many times in quick succession, it becomes awkward.

> **AWKWARD** The sensible student is careful what <u>he or she</u> posts about <u>himself or herself</u> on the social networking sites <u>he or she</u> frequents.

> **More about**
> Pronoun-antecedent agreement, 630–35

NOTE The use of *they* as a generic pronoun for singular antecedents is common in speech, and some people consider it an acceptable alternative to generic *he* in writing as well. Most readers consider this usage ungrammatical, however, so it is best to avoid it.

> ▶ ~~The sensible student is~~ *Sensible students are* careful what they post about themselves.

***Avoid generic* man** Replace terms like *man, men,* and *mankind* used to represent all human beings with gender-neutral equivalents such as *humanity, humankind,* or *humans.*

> ▶ ~~Man is the only animal~~ *Humans are the only animals* to have ventured into space.

Replace occupational names that have the term *man* in them with gender-neutral alternatives.

> ▶ ~~Congressmen~~ *Members of Congress* have excellent health insurance.

Avoid gender stereotypes and inappropriate gender labeling Some occupations with gender-neutral names are stereotypically associated with either men or women. Avoid perpetuating those stereotypes with inappropriate gender labeling.

▶ Nursing is an ancient, honorable profession. ~~Women~~ ^People^ who choose it can expect a rewarding career.

▶ ~~Women~~ ^Job seekers^ with children may want to apply to companies that offer flexible hours to working ~~mothers.~~ ^parents.^

▶ ~~Ladies~~ ^Women^ and men will be evaluated according to the same criteria.

2. Racial, ethnic, and other labels

Racial and ethnic labels are appropriate only when race or ethnicity is relevant to the topic under discussion. The same is true for references to disabilities, sexual orientation, or other personal characteristics. When you do use labels, avoid terms that may give offense; instead, call people what they want to be called. The term *African American* is now widely accepted as a designation for Americans of African descent. People from Asia are *Asians,* not *Orientals* (a term many find disparaging). *Native American* and *American Indian* (or just *Indian*), on the other hand, are generally acceptable to the people they designate. Best in all cases is to be as specific as context permits. If what you mean is *Vietnamese,* or *Japanese,* or *Inuit,* or *Lakota,* or *Catalan,* or *Sicilian,* then use those terms, not the more general *Asian,* or *Native American,* or *European.*

31 Choosing Effective Words

IN THIS CHAPTER

a. Finding the right word, 548

b. Choosing compelling words and figures, 550

c. Mastering idioms, 554

d. Avoiding clichés, 555

Describing the image in this ad as a woman in a bathing suit dancing to the music from her iPod is literally accurate, but it omits the important emotional associations—"sexy," "carefree," "ecstatic"—that make the ad so effective. This image says "Buy an iPod, and you can be like her" (or, perhaps, "attractive to someone like her"). Like images, words have both literal meaning and emotional associations. ***Diction,*** or the choice of words to best convey an idea, requires attention to both.

> **More about**
> Commonly confused words, 565, G14–G19

31a Diction: Finding the Right Word

The literal meaning of a word, its dictionary definition, is its ***denotation.*** When you use a word, be sure its denotation matches your intended meaning. Be particularly careful, for example, not to misuse words that are similar in pronunciation or spelling.

> ▶ The name of the *Harry Potter* character Minerva McGonagall ~~eludes~~ *alludes* to Minerva, the Roman goddess of wisdom.
>
> To *elude* is to evade or escape; to *allude* is to make an indirect reference.

Tech — Word Choice and Grammar and Style Checkers

The grammar and style checkers in most word processing programs offer only marginal help with effective word choice. They often cannot distinguish an incorrectly used word from a correctly used one—*affect* from *effect*, for example—nor can they differentiate the emotional associations of words whose literal meaning is similar.

▸ The psychology of perception includes the study of optical ~~allusions~~ *illusions*.

   An *allusion* is an indirect reference; an *illusion* is a mistaken perception.

Be careful, too, with words that differ in meaning even though they are otherwise closely related.

▸ Many people owe their lives to the ~~heroics~~ *heroism* of volunteer firefighters.

   Heroics are melodramatic, excessive acts; *heroism* is courageous, potentially self-sacrificing behavior.

EXERCISE 31.1 Denotation

Consult a dictionary, style guide, the Quick Reference box on p. 565, or the Glossary of Usage at the end of this book as needed to find and correct any misused words in the following sentences.

EXAMPLE

The reporter tried but failed to ~~illicit~~ *elicit* a comment about climate change from the candidate.

1. Most scientists now except human activity as a cause of global warming.
2. Melting glaciers and rising sea levels are often sited as affects of global warming.
3. People in coastal areas may have trouble adopting to rising sea levels.
4. Another eminent result of global warming may be the breakup of ice shelves in Antarctica.
5. The strength of any one hurricane, however, cannot feasibly be attributed to global warming.

The secondary meanings of a word—the psychological or emotional associations it evokes—are its **connotations.** The word *walk,* for example, has many synonyms, including *amble, saunter, stride,* and *march.* Each of these, however, has distinctive connotations, as their effect in the following sentence suggests:

The candidate { ambled / sauntered / walked / strode / marched } to the podium to address her supporters.

The verb *walk* in this context is emotionally neutral, but the others all have connotations that suggest something about the candidate's state of mind. *Amble* suggests a relaxed aimlessness, whereas *saunter* suggests a jaunty self-confidence. *Stride* and *march* both suggest purposefulness, but *march,* with its military associations, also carries a hint of aggressiveness.

A word's connotations can also vary from reader to reader. To some people, for example, the word *wilderness* evokes a place of great danger; to others, a place of excitement; and to still others, a treasure to be preserved.

> **EXERCISE 31.2 Word choice and tone**
> Using a blog search engine such as Technorati or Google Blog Search, find two blogs on the same general topic (the environment or politics, for example). What is the tone of each? How do the writers' word choices create that tone? Discuss the denotation and connotations of five words in each blog that help set its tone. Explain which of the two blogs you find more appealing, and why.

31b Choosing Compelling Words and Figures

Some words are general, some specific, and others fall between:

← more general		more specific →
consume	eat	devour
fruit	apple	Granny Smith
mountain	California peak	Mt. Whitney

In addition, some words are concrete, designating things or qualities that can be seen, heard, felt, smelled, or touched; and others are abstract, designating concepts like *justice, capitalism,* or *democracy.*

Writing Responsibly: Word Choice and Credibility

The denotation and connotation of the words you choose can powerfully influence the tone of your writing, the effect you have on your readers, and what your readers conclude about you. Highly charged vocabulary, as in the following examples, might lead readers to question the writer's reliability:

> Hippie tree huggers are threatening the jobs of thousands of hardworking loggers.

> Conscientious activists are trying to protect endangered forests from rapacious, tree-murdering logging companies.

In academic writing, you will enhance your credibility if you describe conflicting positions in even-toned language:

> Environmentalists discuss their conflict with the logging industry in terms of the threat industry practices pose to a critical resource; the logging companies, contending that they are responsible forest stewards, describe the conflict in terms of their contribution to local economies.

Once you have looked at the issue fairly, nothing prevents you from then supporting one of these positions and challenging the other.

to AUDIENCE

1. Compelling words

Bring your writing to life by combining general and abstract language with the specific and concrete. Use general and abstract language to frame broad issues, and specific, concrete language to capture readers' attention and help them see things through your eyes. Using general language without specifics leaves readers to fill in the blanks on their own, and using specific language without the general and abstract leaves readers wondering what the point is.

The first of the two following descriptions of the Badwater ultramarathon lacks specific language that can tell us how long the race is, why it is challenging, or exactly where it takes place. The second fills in those details with concrete words—like "hottest spot in America," "stinking water hole," "135 miles," "Death Valley," "piney oasis," "8,300 feet up the side of Mt. Whitney," and "asphalt and road gravel." With these specifics, the writer David Ferrell evokes the challenges of the race without recourse to the abstract word *challenging*.

GENERAL AND ABSTRACT	Badwater is a long, physically challenging race over a partially paved course that begins in a geological depression and ends partway up a mountain.
CONCRETE AND SPECIFIC	Badwater is a madman's march, a footrace through the summer heat of the hottest spot in America. It extends 135 miles from a stinking water hole on the floor of Death Valley to a piney oasis 8,300 feet up the side of Mt. Whitney. The

course is nothing but asphalt and road gravel. Feet and knees and shins ache like they are being whacked with tire irons. Faces turn into shrink-wrap.

—David Ferrell, "Far Beyond a Mere Marathon"

Quick Reference: Figures of Speech

Figure and Definition	Examples
simile: An explicit comparison between two unlike things, usually expressed with *like* or *as*	Feet and knees and shins ache like they are being whacked with tire irons. —*David Ferrell*
	Only final exams, like the last lap of a long race, lay between the members of the senior class and their diplomas.
metaphor: An implied comparison between unlike things stated without *like, as,* or other comparative expressions	Faces turn into shrink-wrap. —*David Ferrell*
	After crossing the finish line of their last exams, seniors looked forward to that moment on the victory stand when the president of the college would bestow a diploma on them.
analogy: An extended simile or metaphor, often comparing something familiar to something unfamiliar. Well-constructed analogies can be particularly effective for explaining difficult concepts.	What that means [that the universe is expanding] is that we're not at the center of the universe, after all; instead, we're like a single raisin in a vast lump of dough that is rising in an oven where all the other raisins are moving away from each other, faster and faster as the oven gets hotter and hotter. —*David Perlman, "At 12 Billion Years Old, Universe Still Growing Fast"*
personification: The attribution of human qualities to nonhuman creatures, objects, ideas, or phenomena	The plague that rampaged through Europe in the fourteenth century selected its victims indiscriminately, murdering rich and poor in equal proportion.
hyperbole: Deliberate exaggeration for emphasis	That little restaurant on Main Street makes the best pizza on the planet.
understatement: The deliberate use of less forceful language than a subject warrants	The report of my death was an exaggeration. —*Mark Twain, clearly alive and well, responding to an obituary about him in a London paper*
irony: The use of language to suggest the opposite of its literal meaning or to express an incongruity between what is expected and what occurs	I come to bury Caesar, not to praise him. —*Mark Antony, in Shakespeare's play* Julius Caesar, *in a speech that praises the murdered leader effusively*

2. Figures of speech

In the example above, notice how Ferrell, in addition to providing concrete specifics, also uses striking comparisons and juxtapositions to paint a vivid picture of the rigors of the race and to suggest the mind-set required to compete in it. He calls the race "a madman's march," for example, and conjures up a beating with a tire iron and an image of a shrink-wrapped face to convey the physical punishment contestants endure. These are examples of ***figurative language,*** or ***figures of speech,*** the imaginative use of language to convey meaning in ways that reach beyond the literal meaning of the words involved.

Among the most common figures of speech are similes and metaphors. A ***simile*** is an explicit comparison between two unlike things, usually expressed with *like* or *as*: "Feet and knees and shins ache like they are being whacked with tire irons." A ***metaphor*** is an implied comparison between two unlike things stated without *like, as,* or other comparative expressions: "Faces turn into shrink-wrap." (A list of common figures of speech appears in the Quick Reference box on p. 552.)

> **EXERCISE 31.3 Compelling words and figures**
>
> Use your imagination—and additional sentences, if need be—to flesh out the following sentences with concrete, specific words and figurative language where appropriate. If you use figures of speech, make a note identifying each and explaining how it is used.
>
> **EXAMPLE**
>
> The party last night was fun because we played games and I met some people I like.
>
> *Last night's party at Jan's house was hopping until about 3 a.m., but I didn't notice the time rushing by because we played an absorbing role-playing game in which each of us tried to capture all of the others without being captured. I also met Brad, who shares my interest in composing music, and Mia, with whom I talked about anime for an hour.*
>
> *(Comment: "Time rushing by" is a metaphor that is used to emphasize how quickly the evening passed.)*
>
> 1. Alexandra's apartment is rather small and plain.
> 2. Next year, I will study abroad at the place I've always dreamed of visiting.
> 3. This meal was delicious and surprisingly healthful.
> 4. The movie was not for squeamish people.
> 5. I know the exact features I want in a car.

3. Inappropriate figures of speech and mixed metaphors

Used judiciously, figures of speech can spice up your writing. Used in the wrong context or piled inconsistently one on the other in *mixed metaphors,* they can be jarring, even silly. The original simile in the following example incongruously invokes the image of a pole vaulter, an athlete who goes mostly up and down, to describe a speeding train, which travels mostly horizontally. The revision, comparing the train to a race horse, is more apt.

▶ The new high-speed train, like a champion ~~pole vaulter,~~ *thoroughbred,* made it from Boston to Washington in record time.

Mixed metaphors—which combine multiple, conflicting images for the same concept—confuse readers.

| MIXED METAPHOR | Confronted with the tsunami of data available on the Internet, researchers, like travelers caught in a blinding desert sandstorm, may have trouble finding the nuggets of valuable information buried in a mountain of otherwise worthless ore. |

The sentence above, seeking to emphasize the challenges of online research, invokes tsunamis, sandstorms, mountains, and mining.

| REVISED | As they mine the mountain of data available on the Internet, researchers may have trouble identifying the nuggets of valuable information buried with the otherwise worthless ore they dig up. |

The revision elaborates a single metaphor that compares finding useful information online to mining for precious minerals.

31c Mastering Idioms

Idioms are expressions whose meaning does not depend on the meanings of the words that compose them. Each idiom is a unified package of meaning with its own denotations and connotations. The following sentence, for example, would make no sense if you tried to interpret it based on the literal meaning of the words *call, on,* and *carpet:*

▶ The directors called the CEO on the carpet for the company's poor sales in 2012.

Of course, the expression *call on the carpet* has nothing to do with calls or carpets. It is an idiom that, understood as a whole, means *to reprimand* or *scold*.

Most dictionaries list idiomatic uses of particular words. The entry for *call* in the *Merriam-Webster Online Dictionary,* for example, provides definitions for the idioms *call for, call forth, call into question, call it a day,* and *call it quits,* among others. For more detailed information on the history and meaning of particular idioms, consult a specialized dictionary such as the *American Heritage Dictionary of Idioms.*

> **More about**
> Specialized dictionaries, 558–60

Idioms, Prepositions, and Phrasal Verbs Because idioms can be understood only as a whole, you have to learn them as a whole, just as you would any unfamiliar word. Pay particular attention to the way prepositions combine with other words in idiomatic ways. A ***phrasal verb,*** for example, is a combination of a verb with one or more prepositions that has a different meaning than the verb alone.

> Raisa *saw* the flat tire on her car. [She looked at it.]

> Raisa *saw to* the flat tire on her car. [She had it repaired.]

> **More about**
> Prepositions, 739–46
> Phrasal verbs, 722–24

31d Avoiding Clichés

A ***cliché*** is a figure of speech, idiom, or other expression that has grown stale from overuse (see the Quick Reference box on the next page for some examples). Clichés come quickly to mind because they encapsulate common wit and wisdom in widely recognized phrases. For the same reason, they provide an easy substitute for fresh thought and expression. They may help you frame a subject in the early drafts of a paper, but they can also make your writing sound trite and unimaginative. You should edit them out as you refine your ideas. As the following example indicates, writing that is loaded with clichés is often also loaded with mixed metaphors.

CLICHÉ LADEN	As the campaign pulled into the home stretch and the cold hard fact of the increasingly nip-and-tuck polls sank in, the candidates threw their promises to stay on their best behavior to the wind and wallowed in the mire of down-and-dirty attack ads.
REVISED	As Election Day neared and the polls showed the race tightening, the candidates abandoned their promises of civility and released a barrage of unscrupulous attack ads.

Quick Reference — **Dodging Deadly Clichés**

When you encounter clichés like these in your writing, delete them or replace them with fresher images of your own.

best thing since sliced bread	hit the nail on the head	smart as a whip
beyond a shadow of a doubt	a hundred and one percent	straight and narrow
cold, hard fact	in the prime of life	think outside the box
cool as a cucumber	just desserts	throw [something] to the wind
down and dirty	nip and tuck	tried and true
down the home stretch	no way, shape, or form	wallow in the mire
easier said than done	on their best behavior	without a moment's hesitation
face the music	one foot out the door	zero tolerance
faster than greased lightning	plain as the nose on your face	
green with envy	slow as molasses	

What Is the Difference between an Idiom and a Cliché? The only thing that separates an idiom from a cliché is the frequency with which it is used. If you are a native English speaker, be alert to idioms that appear often in popular sources and in conversation, and try to avoid those in academic and professional writing. If you are not a native English speaker, you may not recognize an idiom as a cliché if you have not encountered it often in your reading. If you have questions about clichés and idioms, ask your instructor or consult a dictionary of idioms, such as *McGraw-Hill's Dictionary of American Idioms and Phrasal Verbs* or the *Longman American Idioms Dictionary*.

→ **EXERCISE 31.4 Avoiding clichés and mixed metaphors**

Edit the following sentences to eliminate clichés and mixed metaphors.

EXAMPLE

Mayor Wyndham has been reelected regularly because people feel that she is ~~tried and true~~ *reliable* and does not do anything unexpected.

1. Her new proposal hit the town council like a ton of bricks.
2. She wanted to have the county reroute the main road to the capital smack dab through town, forcing traffic to run a gauntlet through our commercial center.

3. Store owners, who have recently seen their sales sink like a stone, thought the plan hit the nail on the head and were happy as clams.

4. However, most townspeople flooded the mayor's office with an avalanche of angry calls and e-mails opposing the proposal.

5. Opponents insisted that in no way, shape, or form would they take to a proposal that threatened the peace and quiet that had attracted them to the town in the first place.

Make It Your Own

Review one of your recent writing projects and identify any passages that include misused words, words with an inappropriate connotation, or words that are overly general or abstract. If you find many areas needing revision, add this to your list of areas to consider as you revise your prose.

32 Using the Dictionary and Spelling Correctly

IN THIS CHAPTER

a. Choosing a dictionary, 558
b. Using a dictionary, 560
c. Avoiding common spelling problems, 562
d. Remembering spelling rules, 564
e. Forming plurals, 569
f. Improving your day-to-day spelling, 571

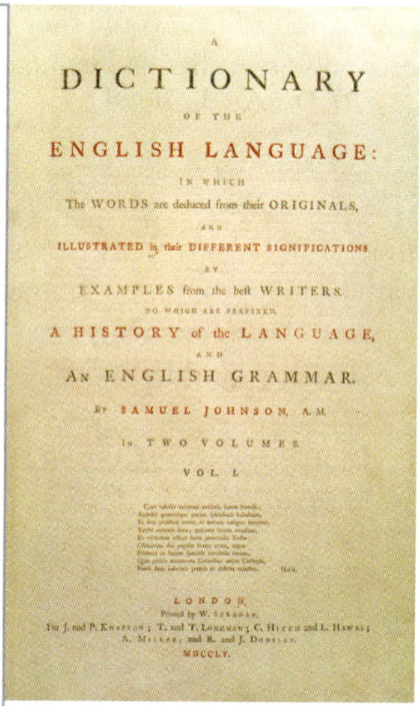

Samuel Johnson's *Dictionary of the English Language* (1755), although not the first ever published, established many of the conventions still found in dictionaries today. Johnson identified a core vocabulary of some 43,500 words; labeled each word's part of speech; briefly traced its origins; provided a concise, elegant (and sometimes humorous) definition of the word in all its senses; and accompanied each definition with an illustrative quotation. Johnson hoped to define and fix a standard of proper spelling and usage, but his dictionary, like those that have followed it, also reflects the state of the language in the time and place in which it was created.

32a Choosing a Dictionary

Dictionaries today come in a variety of forms, both printed and electronic, large and small, general purpose and specialized.

Abridged dictionaries Sometimes referred to as "desk dictionaries," these handy volumes contain information on approximately 200,000 words. Examples include the *American Heritage College Dictionary*, *Merriam-Webster's Collegiate Dictionary*, the *Random House Webster's College Dictionary*, and *Webster's New World College Dictionary*. The *American Heritage College Dictionary* is available online at *Yahoo! Education*. *Merriam-Webster's Collegiate Dictionary* is available online as the *Merriam-Webster Online Dictionary*. Most word processing programs also include a built-in dictionary with many features of an abridged dictionary.

Unabridged dictionaries Unabridged dictionaries contain detailed entries for most words in the English language, some half a million words in total. The most comprehensive unabridged dictionary is the twenty-volume *Oxford English Dictionary* (known as the *OED*). Others include *Random House Webster's Unabridged Dictionary* and *Webster's Third New International Dictionary, Unabridged.*

Both the *OED* and *Webster's Third New International* are available online for a fee. You should be able to find an unabridged dictionary in the reference section of any library, however, and many libraries provide access to online versions.

Dictionaries for Second-Language Learners In addition to translation dictionaries and standard abridged and unabridged dictionaries, you may also want to consult an all-English dictionary tailored for the second-language learner, such as *Heinle's Newbury House Dictionary of American English,* the *Longman Dictionary of American English,* or the *Oxford Dictionary of American English.* To understand American slang and idioms, consult a dictionary such as *McGraw-Hill's Dictionary of American Slang and Colloquial Expressions.* Since slang and idioms change rapidly, you should also consult native-speaking peers.

Specialized dictionaries Specialized dictionaries focus on a particular aspect of English vocabulary.

- Dictionaries of usage provide guidance about the use of particular words or phrases. Examples include the *American Heritage Book of English Usage* (available online at Bartleby.com) and *Right, Wrong, and Risky: A Dictionary of Today's American English Usage.* The *New Fowler's Modern English Usage* provides guidance on British as well as American usage.

- Subject-specific dictionaries explain the specialized terminology of particular fields and professions. Examples include the *Dictionary of Anthropology, Black's Law Dictionary,* and *A Dictionary of Business and Management.* For links to subject-specific dictionaries and glossaries available online, try Glossarist and YourDictionary.com.

> **More about**
> Subject-specific dictionaries, 206–10

Writing Responsibly: Choose Accurate Synonyms

When you consult a thesaurus, be sure you check both the meanings (*denotations*) and the associations (*connotations*) of the words you find there. A carelessly chosen synonym can distort the information you intend to convey. Suppose, for example, that you wanted to replace *intimidate* in the sentence "The professor's brilliance intimidated her students." Looking in a thesaurus, you might find both *overawe* and *bludgeon* listed as synonyms. *Overawe* is an appropriate substitute, probably more precisely reflecting the effect of the professor on her students than *intimidate*. *Bludgeon*, in contrast, inaccurately conjures visions of a bloody crime scene.

to TOPIC

> **More about**
> Denotation and connotation, 15–16, 548–50

- Thesauruses and synonym dictionaries provide lists of words that are equivalent to or that overlap in meaning with one another (**synonyms**), as well as words that have contrasting meanings (**antonyms**). They can help you find just the right word for a particular context or an alternative to a word you have been overusing. Examples include *Merriam-Webster's Dictionary of Synonyms* and the *New American Roget's College Thesaurus*. Note also that most word processing programs have a built-in thesaurus.

EXERCISE 32.1 Using a thesaurus

Look up one of the following words in a thesaurus. Choose three synonyms for that word and write a separate sentence for the original word and for each synonym that accurately reflects both its meaning and connotation.

make	problem	funny
talent	strange	fight

32b Using a Dictionary

Figure 32.1 shows the entry for the word *respect* in the *Merriam-Webster Online Dictionary*, the online counterpart to the eleventh edition of *Merriam-Webster's Collegiate Dictionary*. Although most online and printed abridged dictionaries present the same kinds of information, each has its own format and system of abbreviations.

> **More about**
> Hyphenation, 830–35

Spelling, word division, and pronunciation Entries begin with the word correctly spelled followed by acceptable variant spellings, if any. Dots show the division of the word into syllables, indicating where to put a hyphen if you must break the word between lines of text. Next, the pronunciation of the word is

Style Matters • Using a Dictionary **32b** 561

FIGURE 32.1 The entry for *respect* in the *Merriam-Webster Online Dictionary*

Annotations on the figure:
- First entry (as noun)
- Pronunciation with audio link
- Definitions and links to related online entries
- Idioms with links to related online entries
- Usage examples
- Etymology and date of earliest use
- Synonyms and antonyms

given. The print version has a key to pronunciation symbols; the online version has a link to this key, but it also gives the pronunciation in an audio link.

Grammatical functions and forms Labels indicate the part of speech and other grammatical aspects of a word. Most dictionaries specify the forms of irregular

> **More about**
> Regular and irregular verbs, 638–39
> Regular and irregular plurals, 569–71

verbs (*draw, drew, drawn*) but not of regular verbs like *respect,* and they provide irregular plurals (*woman, women*) but not regular plurals (*dogs*). The entry shown in Figure 32.1 includes a definition of the plural form *respects* because it has a usage that does not apply to the singular form.

> **More about**
> Idiomatic expressions, 554–55

Definitions and examples If a word has more than one definition, each is numbered, and any additional distinctions within a definition are labeled with a letter. Several definitions in the entry for *respect* as a noun include examples of the word used in context. At the end of the entry are the definitions of several idiomatic expressions that include *respect.*

> **More about**
> Usage in "A Glossary of Usage," G14–G19

Synonyms and usage Most dictionaries list synonyms for the entry word; in online dictionaries, clicking on a synonym will take you to the full entry for that word. Usage labels offer guidance on how to use a word appropriately.

> **EXERCISE 32.2 Using a dictionary**
> Look up the following words in a dictionary. Write down any alternate spellings, mark its division into syllables, and underline the stressed syllable.
>
> permanent   develop   approximate
> addition   opportunity   component

32c Avoiding Common Spelling Problems

For most people, spelling does not come easily. Even voracious readers and expert writers need to review common spelling problems, such as spelling from pronunciation, confusing homonyms, and confusing different forms of the same word.

Using a Bilingual Dictionary as an Aid to English Spelling If your first language has, like Spanish, a more phonetic spelling system than English has, a bilingual or translation dictionary can help you find the spelling of English words. For example, if you think *physician* begins with the letter *f,* you will have a hard time finding the correct spelling in an English dictionary, but if you look up *médico* in a Spanish-English dictionary, you will immediately find the proper spelling.

1. The unreliability of pronunciation

The word *Wednesday* is pronounced without the first *d* and the second *e* ("Wensday"). The letters *ow* in *sow* are pronounced as in *cow* when *sow* is used as a noun meaning "female pig." When *sow* is used as a verb meaning "to plant seeds," however, the letters *ow* are pronounced like the *ew* in *sew*. As these examples indicate, you cannot rely on the way a word sounds to guide you to its correct spelling.

2. Homonyms and other problematic words

Many spelling errors result from confusion over homonyms and near-homonyms like those in the Quick Reference box on page 565.

- ***Homonyms*** are groups of words that sound exactly alike but have different spellings and meanings, such as *to/too/two* and *cite/sight/site*.
- ***Near-homonyms*** are groups of words such as *personal/personnel* and *conscience/conscious* that are close but not the same in pronunciation. Near-homonyms also include groups such as *breath/breathe* and *advice/advise* that are different forms of the same word.

There is no easy formula for mastering these words. If any of them give you trouble, try to memorize their spellings and meanings, and always check for them as you proofread your writing.

> **More about**
> Confusing words and phrases in "A Glossary of Usage," G14–G19

Use American Rather Than British Spelling Multilingual writers who began their study of English outside the United States may be accustomed to British spelling, which is often different from American, as the following list shows. Some writers striving for formality mistakenly believe that British spellings are preferable. If you are writing for a US audience, be sure to follow American style. When in doubt, consult an American dictionary, which will give the preferred American spelling before any alternates.

American	British
airplane	aeroplane
labor/mold	labour/mould
theater	theatre
check	cheque
counseled	counselled
defense	defence
plagiarize	plagiarise
program	programme

EXERCISE 32.3 Using homonyms and near-homonyms

In each of the following sentences, underline the correct word from among the choices in parentheses.

EXAMPLE

In a popular cooking show, contestants (our, <u>are</u>) asked to (device, <u>devise</u>) each (<u>course</u>, coarse) of a meal in less (then, <u>than</u>) thirty minutes.

1. Each contestant must use the ingredients in a basket (to, too, two) produce a (grate, great) dish with his or her own (personnel, personal) (flair, flare).

2. (It's, Its) often the (forth, fourth) ingredient that (presents, presence) problems in the (dessert, desert) course.

3. The judges (compliment, complement) each chef's ability to (elicit, illicit) the full flavor of each ingredient, explain where the meal is (week, weak), and offer (advise, advice) about (where, were) each chef can improve.

4. They (our, are) very (fair, fare) and follow (their, they're, there) (conscience, conscious), but at the end of each round (its, it's) not always clear (which, witch) chef will be "chopped."

32d Remembering Spelling Rules

Mastering a few key rules—and noting their exceptions—can improve the accuracy of your spelling.

Writing Responsibly — Spelling Errors

A misspelled word is not an important issue when you are texting friends, but in other situations it may signal that you are careless about details. If you misspell *accountant* in a job-application letter to a financial firm, for example, the recipient may wonder how accurate you are about numbers. If you misspell a name, people may interpret it as a sign of indifference or disrespect.

to SELF

Quick Reference: Some Homonyms and Near-Homonyms

accept (to take willingly)
except (to exclude)

advice (counsel)
advise (to offer counsel)

affect (to influence; feeling)
effect (to cause; a result)

all ready (fully prepared)
already (by this time)

allude (to mention indirectly)
elude (to avoid)

allusion (an indirect reference)
illusion (a deceptive or false perception)

altar (a raised structure for religious ritual)
alter (to change)

are (form of *be*)
our (relating to us)

ascent (upward advance)
assent (to concur)

bare (unclothed; to make known)
bear (an animal; to support)

board (a piece of wood; to get on a vehicle)
bored (uninterested)

brake (stopping mechanism)
break (to wreck; a pause)

capital (seat of government)
capitol (building for the legislature)

cite (to acknowledge a source)
sight (something to see)
site (a place)

complement (to complete)
compliment (an admiring remark)

conscience (moral awareness)
conscious (awake, mindful)

council (a governing or advisory group)
counsel (advice; to advise)

descent (downward movement)
dissent (disagreement)

desert (desolate area; to abandon)
dessert (a meal's last course)

device (a contrivance)
devise (to contrive)

discreet (prudent, unpretentious)
discrete (distinct)

elicit (to bring out)
illicit (illegal)

eminent (highly regarded)
imminent (about to happen)
immanent (inherent)

fair (attractive; impartial)
fare (a price for transportation)

forth (forward)
fourth (following *third*)

gorilla (a great ape)
guerrilla (a fighter in unconventional warfare)

grate (to grind or irritate)
great (large or superior)

hear (to perceive sound)
here (at this place)

hole (an opening)
whole (complete)

incidence (rate of occurrence)
incidents (occurrences)

its (possessive of *it*)
it's (*it is* or *it has*)

lead (a metal; to go ahead of)
led (past tense of *lead*)

meat (edible animal flesh)
meet (to encounter)

passed (past tense of *pass*)
past (before the present)

patience (calm persistence)
patients (people under medical care)

peace (tranquility)
piece (a part)

personal (private; individual)
personnel (employees)

plain (not complicated)
plane (aircraft; carpenter's tool)

presence (being in attendance)
presents (gifts)

principal (most significant; chief)
principle (rule or tenet)

rain (precipitation)
reign (monarch's period of rule)
rein (strap used to control an animal; to restrain)

raise (to lift)
raze (to demolish)

respectfully (with respect)
respectively (in the order given)

right (correct; opposite of *left*)
rite (ceremony or ritual)
wright (one who fashions a thing)
write (to form words on a surface)

road (street)
rode (past tense of *ride*)

stationary (immobile)
stationery (writing paper)

than (compared to)
then (at that time; therefore)

their (possessive of *they*)
there (in that place)
they're (*they are*)

to (toward)
too (also)
two (number after *one*)

waist (midriff; narrow part)
waste (garbage; to squander)

weak (not strong)
week (seven days)

wear (to have on)
where (in what direction or place)
were (past tense of *be*)

weather (condition of the atmosphere)
whether (word that introduces choices or alternatives)

which (what one)
witch (sorcerer)

who's (*who is* or *who has*)
whose (possessive of *who*)

your (possessive of *you*)
you're (*you are*)

1. The *ie/ei* rule

The traditional rule—"*i* before *e* except after *c* or when sounded like *ay* as in *neighbor* and *weigh*"—will help you spell words like *believe, receive,* and *sleigh* correctly.

I BEFORE E	diesel, piece, pier, retrieve, shield, siege
E BEFORE I AFTER C	ceiling, conceit, conceive, deceit, perceive, receipt
EI SOUNDS LIKE AY	beige, deign, eighteen, reindeer, sleigh, veil

Some exceptions: *feisty, forfeit, heifer, height, heir, neither, protein, sovereign, seize, their, weird.*

> **EXERCISE 32.4** Spelling *ie* and *ei* words
>
> Correct any misspellings in the following sentences.
>
> **EXAMPLE**
>
> When Angie ~~recieved~~ *received* the ~~reciept~~ *receipt* for her rental deposit, she knew she had reached a milestone in her life.
>
> 1. It was her first apartment, and the cielings were eighteen feet high!
> 2. With that hieght, she could retreive her tall sculpture from her parents' backyard and install it in her apartment.
> 3. Of course, creating such an oversized sculpture had been a conciet, but she had always beleived that art should have no boundaries.
> 4. Now that fiesty conviction in the form of a huge peice of biege metal would take palpable shape in the very first home of her own.

2. Prefixes

Prefixes attach to the beginning of a root word to modify its meaning. Prefixes have no effect on the spelling of the rest of the word, even if the last letter of the prefix and the first letter of the root word are the same. For example, *re-* combines with *wind* to form *rewind, dis-* combines with *inherit* to form *disinherit,* and *mis-* combines with *statement* to form *misstatement.* In some cases, however, a hyphen separates a prefix from the rest of the word, as in *anti-inflammatory.*

> **More about**
> Prefixes and hyphenation, 831–32

3. Suffixes

> **More about**
> Suffixes and hyphenation, 831–32

Suffixes attach to the end of a root word to change its meaning and grammatical form. The suffix *-ly*, for example, changes the adjective *sweet* to the adverb *sweetly*. Unlike prefixes, suffixes often affect the spelling of the preceding root.

Words that end with a silent e In most instances, drop the silent *e* if the suffix starts with a vowel:

    observe → observant   response → responsible   revoke → revoked

Retain the silent *e* if the suffix starts with a consonant:

    hope → hopeful   love → lovely   polite → politeness

Some exceptions: *advantageous, argument, duly, enforceable, judgment, serviceable.*

Words that end with y For most words that end with a consonant and *y*, change the *y* to an *i* when you add a suffix:

    apology → apologize   deny → denies

    heavy → heavier   merry → merriment

Retain the *y* if the suffix is *-ing*, if a vowel precedes the *y*, or if the word ending in *y* is a proper name:

    spy → spying   play → playful   McCoy → McCoys

Suffixes -cede, -ceed, and -sede To avoid confusing these three suffixes, remember these facts:

1. *Supersede* is the only English word that ends in *-sede*.
2. *Exceed, proceed,* and *succeed* are the only words that end in *-ceed*.
3. All other similar words use the suffix *-cede: accede, concede, precede, secede.*

Suffixes -ally versus -ly and -efy versus -ify When a word ends in *ic*, use the suffix *-ally*. In all other instances, use *-ly*:

    basic → basically   magic → magically

    brisk → briskly   confident → confidently

Only four words use the suffix *-efy: liquefy, putrefy, rarefy, stupefy.* All other such words use the suffix *-ify: beautify, certify, justify, purify.*

Words that end with a consonant Do not double a final consonant if the suffix begins with a consonant (*commitment, fearless, kinship, poorly*). For suffixes that begin with a vowel, follow these guidelines:

- **One-syllable root words.** Double the final consonant if only one vowel precedes it:

  bi<u>t</u> → bi<u>tt</u>en   cha<u>t</u> → cha<u>tt</u>y   ski<u>p</u> → ski<u>pp</u>ing

  For other one-syllable words, do not double the consonant:

  char<u>t</u> → char<u>t</u>ed   droo<u>p</u> → droo<u>p</u>ing   spea<u>k</u> → spea<u>k</u>er

- **Multisyllable words.** Double the final consonant if only one vowel precedes the final consonant and if the final syllable of the root is accented in the new word containing the suffix:

  ad**mit** → ad**mitt**ance   con**cur** → con**curr**ent

  con**trol** → con**troll**ed

For multisyllable words that do not meet these criteria, do not double the final consonant:

devi<u>l</u> → devi<u>l</u>ish   paralle<u>l</u> → paralle<u>l</u>ism

erup<u>t</u> → erup<u>t</u>ed   proclai<u>m</u> → proclai<u>m</u>ing

In *devilish* and *parallelism,* the accent is on the first syllable of the root word; the final *t* in *erupt* is preceded by a consonant; and the final *m* in *proclaim* is preceded by two vowels.

→ EXERCISE 32.5 Adding suffixes

Correct any misspelled words in the following list, and circle those that are spelled correctly.

changable	truely	begining	tragicly
deploing	argueable	replys	runing
supercede	regreted	optimally	angryly
principally	soly	sponsored	

> **Tech** **Use Spelling Checkers Cautiously**
>
> Most of today's word processing programs correct some misspelled words while you type, identify other words that may be misspelled, and let you run a manual spelling check whenever you wish. Although these features are helpful, you cannot depend on them alone to guarantee error-free spelling.
>
> - Spelling checkers do not differentiate homonyms and commonly confused words, such as *descent, dissent* or *too, two*. If you type a correctly spelled word that happens not to be correct for the context, a spelling checker will not mark it wrong.
> - If you misspell a word, a spelling checker may suggest replacing it with the wrong word. For example, if you type *retify* for *rectify*, the checker's first recommendation might be *ratify*, which is clearly the wrong word.
> - A spelling checker will not catch the misspelling of most proper names unless you enter them in its dictionary.
> - A spelling checker will not alert you to most errors in capitalization.
>
> Spelling checkers, then, are a useful tool but not a replacement for a dictionary and careful proofreading. Check the spelling checker.

> **More about**
> Capitalization, 807–13

32e Forming Plurals

Most English nouns form the plural by adding the suffix *-s* or *-es*. Some nouns, however, like *child* (plural *children*) and *man* (plural *men*), have irregular forms, and some compound nouns form the plural on a word that is not the last one in the compound.

1. Regular plurals

- To form the plural of most English nouns, add an *-s*.

    letter → letters   shoe → shoes   Erickson → the Ericksons

- To form the plural of nouns that end with *s*, *sh*, *ch*, *x*, or *z*, add *-es*.

    miss → misses   dish → dishes   latch → latches

    box → boxes   fez → fezzes   Davis → the Davises

- To form the plural of some nouns that end with *f* or *fe*, change the *f* to a *v* and add *-s* or *-es*.

    loaf → loaves   scarf → scarves   thief → thieves

    knife → knives   wife → wives

However, words that end in *ff* or *ffe* and some words that end in *f* or *fe* form the plural just with the addition of an *-s*.

bluff → bluffs   giraffe → giraffes

chief → chiefs   safe → safes

- To form the plural of nouns that end with *o*, add *-s* if the *o* is preceded by a vowel or if the word is a proper noun.

duo → duos   ratio → ratios   video → videos

Add *-es* if the *o* is preceded by a consonant.

echo → echoes   potato → potatoes   veto → vetoes

Some exceptions: *autos, ponchos, sopranos, tacos*

- To form the plural of words that end with *y*, add *-s* if the *y* is preceded by a vowel or if the word is a proper noun.

decoy → decoys   essay → essays   Hagarty → the Hagartys

Change the *y* to *i* and add *-es* if the *y* is preceded by a consonant.

berry → berries   enemy → enemies   family → families

2. Irregular plurals

The only way to learn irregular plurals is to memorize them. Many nouns have irregular plurals that have survived from earlier forms of English.

woman → women   child → children   deer → deer

foot → feet   ox → oxen   sheep → sheep

mouse → mice

Other nouns with irregular plurals were borrowed into English from languages such as Greek, Latin, and French and retain the plural form of the original language.

analysis → analyses   criterion → criteria   phenomenon → phenomena

alumna → alumnae   medium → media   tableau → tableaux

alumnus → alumni   nucleus → nuclei

For many such words, a regularized plural form is acceptable as an alternative to the irregular form: *index, indices/indexes; fungus, fungi/funguses.*

3. Plurals of compound nouns

To form the plural of compound nouns composed of separate or hyphenated words, add *-s* or *-es* to the main noun in the compound.

    brigadier general*s*   chief*s* of staff   runner*s*-up

If there is no main noun, add *-s* or *-es* at the end: *singer-songwriters*

For compounds that are spelled as one word, add *-s* or *-es* at the end.

    keyboard*s*   spaceship*s*   touchdown*s*

An exception: *passersby*

▶ EXERCISE 32.6 Forming plurals

Write the plural form of each of the following singular nouns.

buzz	rally	half	ploy
mother-in-law	domino	study	tooth
handcuff	moose	studio	goose
spoof	person	tomato	

32f Improving Your Day-to-Day Spelling

Writers who have mastered all the rules in this chapter may still misspell some words sometimes. Here are a few tips for further reducing misspellings in your work:

- If you tend to misspell the same word or types of words repeatedly, keep track of them in a vocabulary log and check for them specifically when you proofread.
- Use a dictionary often, and keep one handy next to your computer.
- Remember that pronunciation may lead you astray in your spelling. Although you may say "goverment," do not forget that *govern* is the root word, so the word is spelled *government,* with an *n*.
- Use a spelling checker with caution (see the Tech box on p. 569), and proofread carefully.

Make It **Your Own**

With the spelling checker on, type this sentence into a blank word processing document:

> Fore score and seven yours ago, are fathers brought fourth on this continence anew nation, conceived in liberty and dedicated to the preposition that awl men our created equal.

Now compare the sentence to the first sentence of Abraham Lincoln's Gettysburg Address <loc.gov/exhibits/gadd/images/Gettysburg-2.jpg>. How many errors did the spelling checker catch? Introduce two or more similar errors into other famous passages (or into passages from a textbook or a newspaper or magazine article), and see how dependably the spelling checker catches them. For famous quotations, consult a printed collection like *Bartlett's Familiar Quotations,* the *Yale Book of Quotations,* or the *Oxford Dictionary of Quotations.* Or consult an online source like The Quotations Page <quotationspage.com> or the quotations sections of The Other Pages <theotherpages.org/quote.html>.

Work **Together**

With a classmate, exchange printouts (double-spaced) of the sentences with the errors you introduced in the Make It Your Own exercise above. Correct the sentences by hand; then check your work against the original sources.

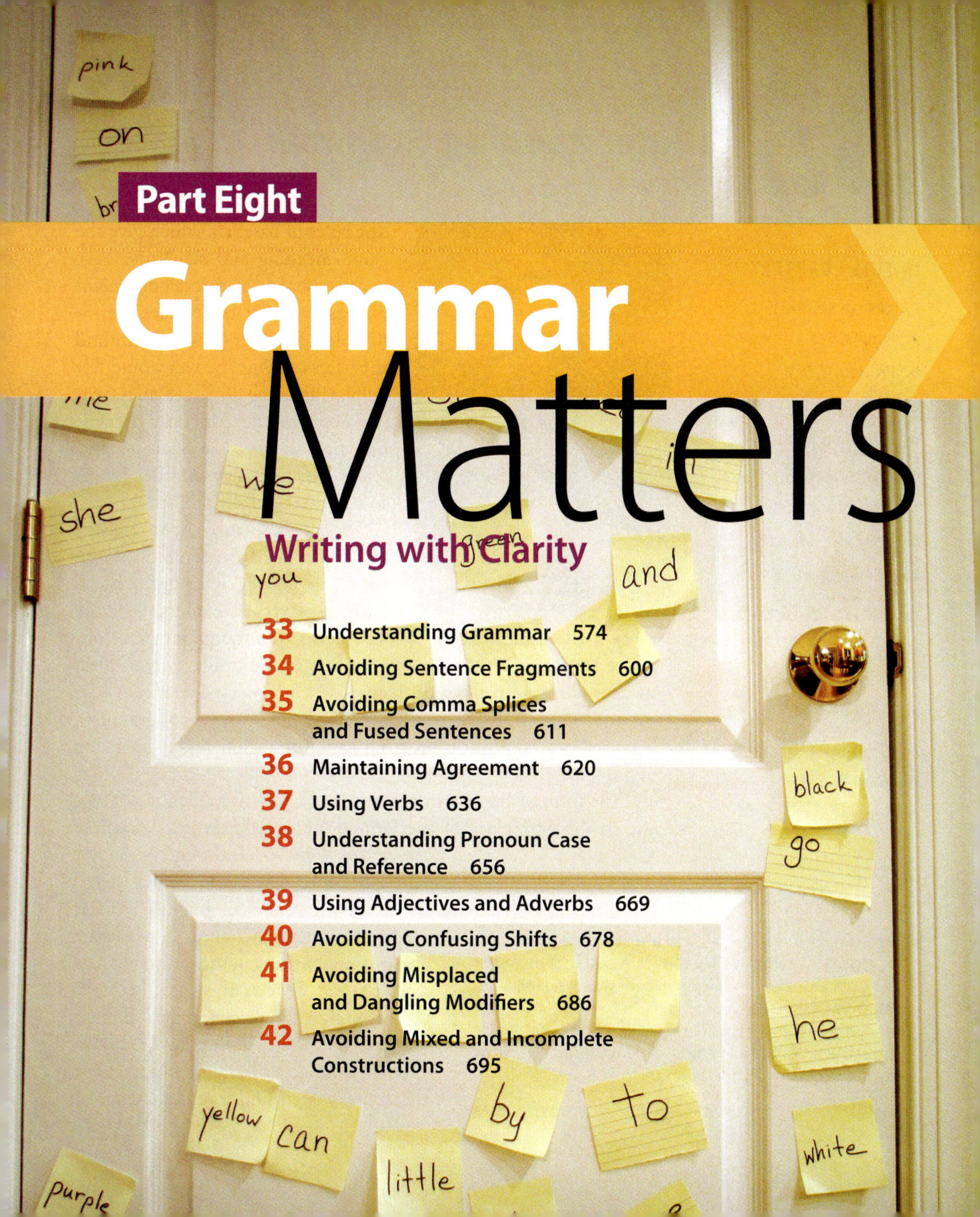

Part Eight

Grammar Matters

Writing with Clarity

33 Understanding Grammar 574
34 Avoiding Sentence Fragments 600
35 Avoiding Comma Splices and Fused Sentences 611
36 Maintaining Agreement 620
37 Using Verbs 636
38 Understanding Pronoun Case and Reference 656
39 Using Adjectives and Adverbs 669
40 Avoiding Confusing Shifts 678
41 Avoiding Misplaced and Dangling Modifiers 686
42 Avoiding Mixed and Incomplete Constructions 695

33 Understanding Grammar

IN THIS CHAPTER

PARTS OF SPEECH
a. Nouns, 575
b. Pronouns, 577
c. Verbs, 577
d. Adjectives, 580
e. Adverbs, 581
f. Prepositions, 582
g. Conjunctions, 583
h. Interjections, 584

SENTENCE STRUCTURE
i. Subjects, 585
j. Predicates, 587
k. Sentence patterns, 588
l. Phrases, 591
m. Clauses, 594
n. Sentence types, 597

Writing Responsibly
Why Grammar Matters

Writers have a responsibility to use language their readers regard as grammatically correct. A shared standard of grammar eases communication, and when you follow it, you show respect for your readers. In contrast, when you use language your readers regard as grammatically incorrect, you distract and confuse them, raising questions about the quality of your writing.

to AUDIENCE

The rules of baseball, which give the game meaning and structure, have become second nature to proficient players. Most of these rules are inflexible: A player who ran around the bases carrying the ball would not be playing baseball. Some rules vary, however: In the American League but not in the National League, teams can designate another player to bat instead of the pitcher.

Languages, too, have rules—*grammars*—that structure words so they can convey meaning. Just as baseball players have internalized the rules of the game, so have we all internalized the grammar of our native language. Most rules of grammar are inflexible. Any English speaker, for example, would recognize a statement like *throw Maria ball the base first to* as ungrammatical. Some aspects of grammar, however, can vary over time, from region to region, and from group to group.

The form of English that is accepted today in academic settings and in the workplace in the United States is known as **Standard American English.** Although it is not better or more correct than other varieties, Standard American English is what readers expect to encounter in academic and business writing in the United States. This chapter reviews the rules of Standard American English grammar, and the chapters that follow it in part 8 focus on particular aspects of grammar and usage that many writers find troublesome.

PARTS OF SPEECH

The term *parts of speech* refers to the functions words play in a sentence. English has eight parts of speech:

- nouns
- pronouns
- verbs
- adjectives
- adverbs
- prepositions
- conjunctions
- interjections

The same word can have more than one function, depending on the context in which it appears.

▶ Many students work to help pay for college. [*Work* is a verb.]
▶ Mastering calculus requires hard work. [*Work* is a noun.]

33a Nouns

Nouns name ideas (*justice*), things (*chair*), qualities (*neatness*), actions (*judgment*), people (*Albert Einstein*), and places (*Tokyo*). They fall into a variety of overlapping categories:

- ***Proper nouns*** name specific places, people, or things and are usually capitalized: *Nairobi, Hudson Bay, Hillary Rodham Clinton*, the *Taj Mahal*. All other nouns are **common nouns**, which name members of a class or group: *turtle, sophomore, skyscraper*.

- ***Collective nouns*** name a collection that can function as a single unit: *committee, administration, family*.

- ***Concrete nouns*** name things that can be seen, touched, heard, smelled, or tasted: *planet, liquid, symphony, skunk, pepper*. ***Abstract nouns*** name qualities or ideas that cannot be perceived by the senses: *mercy, fear*.

- ***Countable*** (or ***count***) ***nouns*** name things or ideas that can be counted. They can be either ***singular*** or ***plural***: *cat/cats, assignment/assignments, idea/ideas*.

- ***Uncountable*** (or ***noncount***) ***nouns*** name ideas or things that cannot be counted and do not have a plural form: *homework, knowledge, pollution*.

> **More about**
> Count and noncount nouns, 713–14, 718–20

Countable and Noncountable Nouns In many languages the classification of nouns as count or noncount affects the way they combine with articles (*a, an, the*) and other determiners (*my, your, some, many, this, these*). Awareness of the effect of this aspect of nouns on sentence grammar will help you avoid errors.

> **More about**
> Noun plurals,
> 569–71

Most nouns form the plural with the addition of a final *-s* or *-es*: *book/books, beach/beaches, country/countries*. A few have irregular plurals:

Quick Reference: The Parts of Speech

Parts of Speech	Functions	Examples
Nouns	name ideas, things, qualities, actions, people, and places	**Sarah** usually drives her blue **car** to **work**, but, alas, it needs expensive **repairs.**
Pronouns	rename or take the place of nouns or noun phrases	Sarah usually drives **her** blue car to work, but, alas, **it** needs expensive repairs.
Verbs	express action, occurrence, or state of being	Sarah usually **drives** her blue car to work, but, alas, it **needs** expensive repairs.
Adjectives	modify nouns or pronouns with descriptive or limiting information, answering questions such as *What kind? Which one?* or *How many?*	Sarah usually drives her **blue** car to work, but, alas, it needs **expensive** repairs.
Adverbs	modify verbs, adjectives, and other adverbs as well as entire phrases and clauses, answering such questions as *How? Where? When?* and *To what extent or degree?*	Sarah **usually** drives her blue car to work, but, alas, it needs expensive repairs.
Prepositions	relate nouns or pronouns to other words in a sentence in terms of time, space, cause, and other attributes	Sarah usually drives her blue car **to** work, but, alas, it needs expensive repairs.
Conjunctions	join words, phrases, and clauses to other words, phrases, or clauses and specify the way the joined elements relate to each other	Sarah usually drives her blue car to work, **but**, alas, it needs expensive repairs.
Interjections	express strong feeling but otherwise serve no grammatical function	Sarah usually drives her blue car to work, but, **alas**, it needs expensive repairs.

woman/women, life/lives, mouse/mice. For some nouns, the singular and the plural forms are the same: *deer/deer, fish/fish.*

Nouns indicate possession with a final *s* sound, marked in writing with an apostrophe: *Rosa's idea, the students' plan.*

> **More about**
> Apostrophes and possession, 773–77

33b Pronouns

Pronouns rename or take the place of nouns or ***noun phrases.*** The noun that a pronoun replaces is called its ***antecedent.*** The Quick Reference box on page 578 summarizes the types of pronouns and their functions.

> **noun phrase** A noun and its modifiers

> **More about**
> Pronouns, 630–35, 656–68

> **EXERCISE 33.1 Identifying nouns and pronouns**

Circle the nouns and underline the pronouns in the following sentences.

EXAMPLE

On his way to pick up his aunt at the airport, Bradley found himself stuck in traffic.

1. Making the situation even worse, the driver behind him kept honking his horn.
2. Bradley felt his car shake a bit and realized that the driver behind him had bumped his rear fender slightly while pulling out to change lanes.
3. The other driver was out of sight by the time Bradley reminded himself to get the car's license number.
4. He arrived at the airport a few minutes late, saw that his car's fender was unharmed, scanned the monitor for information about incoming flights, and learned that many, including his aunt's, were an hour behind schedule.

33c Verbs

Verbs express action (*The quarterback throws a pass*), occurrence (*The play happened in the second half*), or state of being (*The fans are happy*). Verbs also carry information about time (tense), as well as person, number, voice, and mood.

> **More about**
> Verb forms, 636–44

Two kinds of verbs combine to make up a ***verb phrase: main verbs*** and ***helping*** (or ***auxiliary***) ***verbs.*** Main verbs carry the principal meaning of a verb phrase. Almost all verb constructions other than the present and past tense, however, require a combination of one or more helping verbs with a form of

Quick Reference: Pronouns and Their Functions

Type and Function	Forms	Examples
Personal pronouns take the place of specific nouns or noun phrases.	**Singular:** *I, me, you, he, him, she, her, it* **Plural:** *we, us, you, they, them*	Yue bought the tickets for Adam, and she gave them to him before the concert.
Possessive pronouns are personal pronouns that indicate possession.	**Singular:** *my, mine, your, yours, his, her, hers, its* **Plural:** *our, ours, your, yours, their, theirs*	Adam gave one of the tickets to his roommate.
Reflexive pronouns refer back to the subject of a sentence.	**Singular:** *myself, yourself, himself, herself, itself, oneself* **Plural:** *ourselves, yourselves, themselves*	Laetitia reminded herself to return the books to the library.
Intensive pronouns rename and emphasize their antecedents.	Same as reflexive pronouns	Dr. Collins herself performed the operation.
Demonstrative pronouns rename and point to nouns or noun phrases. They can function as adjectives as well as nouns.	**Singular:** *this, that* **Plural:** *these, those*	Yameng visited the Forbidden City. That was his favorite place in China. That place was his favorite.
Relative pronouns introduce subordinate clauses that describe the pronoun's antecedent.	*who, whom, whoever, whomever, what, whose, whatever, whichever, that, which*	I. M. Pei is the architect who designed the East Wing of the National Gallery.
Interrogative pronouns introduce questions.	*who, whoever, whom, whomever, what, whatever, which, whichever, whose*	Who designed the East Wing of the National Gallery?
Indefinite pronouns do not refer to specific people or things.	**Singular:** *anybody, anyone, anything, each, either, everybody, everyone, everything, much, neither, nobody, no one, nothing, one, somebody, someone, something* **Singular or plural:** *all, any, more, most, some* **Plural:** *both, few, many, several*	Everybody talks about the weather, but nobody does anything about it. —Attributed to Mark Twain
Reciprocal pronouns refer to the individual parts of a plural antecedent.	*each other, one another*	The candidates debated one another many times before the primary.

the main verb. Some helping verbs (forms of *be*, *have*, and *do*) also function as main verbs. Others, called ***modal verbs*** (*can, could, may, might, must, shall, should, will, would,* and *ought to*), function only as helping verbs.

Modal Auxiliaries Modal auxiliaries can pose special problems for multilingual students because other languages use very different grammatical strategies to express intention, possibility, or expectation. For more on their meaning and use, see pages 728–30.

Helping verbs always precede the main verb in a verb phrase.

|— verb phrase —|
▶ The player **hit** a long home run. [main verb]

▶ The home run **may have broken** a distance record. [helping verbs / main verb]

▶ The children **have been playing** for two hours. [helping verbs / main verb]

NOTE Do not confuse ***verbals*** with complete verbs. Verbals are verb forms functioning as nouns, adjectives, or adverbs, not as verbs within a predicate.

> **More about**
> Verbals, 592, 601

- ▶ The potters *fired* the vessels in their kiln. [*Fired* is a verb.]
- ▶ The *fired* clay is rock hard. [*Fired* is a verbal, in this case an adjective modifying *clay*.]

EXERCISE 33.2 Identifying verb phrases

Underline the verb phrases in the following sentences, and circle the main verb in each. Note that some sentences may have more than one verb phrase.

1. Rennie has been to the zoo more often this year than ever before.
2. Her twin nieces began walking recently, and since then their favorite activity has been going to the zoo with Aunt Rennie.
3. This spring the twins were excited about the newly arrived pandas.
4. By the time Rennie and the twins finally got to the zoo, the pandas had become accustomed to visitors and chewed calmly on some bamboo.

33d Adjectives

> **More about**
> Adjectives, 669–77

Adjectives modify nouns or pronouns with descriptive or limiting information. They answer questions such as *What kind? Which one?* or *How many?*

	adj. noun
WHAT KIND?	a warm day
WHICH ONE?	the next speaker
HOW MANY?	twelve roses

Adjectives most commonly fall before nouns in a noun phrase and after *linking verbs* as **subject complements.**

> **linking verb** A verb that conveys a state of being linking a subject to its complement
> **subject complement** An adjective, pronoun, or noun phrase that follows a linking verb and describes or refers to the sentence subject

▸ The *young* musicians played a *rousing* concert.
     adj. noun   adj.   noun

▸ They were *enthusiastic.*
  pro- link. adj.
  noun verb

> **More about**
> Comparative adjectives, 674–75

Many adjectives change form to express comparison: *young, younger, youngest; enthusiastic, more/less enthusiastic, most/least enthusiastic.*

Possessive, demonstrative, and indefinite pronouns that function as adjectives—as well as the articles *a, an,* and *the*—are known as **determiners** because they specify or quantify the nouns they modify. Determiners always precede other adjectives in a noun phrase. Some, like *all* and *both,* also precede any other determiners.

▸ The *new* gym is in *that* building with *all those solar* panels on the roof.
  det. adj. noun   det. noun   dets. adj. noun
  det. noun

The Ordering of Adjectives The ordering of adjectives in noun phrases and the use of articles and other determiners in English can be challenging for multilingual writers. English sentences tend to place adjectives before nouns, while adjective placement in other languages varies, and some languages do not use articles at all. For more on these topics, see pages 733 and 714–21.

33e Adverbs

Adverbs modify verbs, adjectives, and other adverbs, as well as entire phrases and clauses. They answer such questions as *How? Where? When?* and *To what extent or degree?*

> **More about**
> Adverbs, 669–77

HOW? Embarrassingly, my cell phone rang loudly.
(adverb / verb / adv.)

The adverb *loudly* modifies the verb *rang*. The adverb *embarrassingly* modifies the whole sentence.

WHEN? Dinner is finally ready.
(adv. / adj.)

The adverb *finally* modifies the adjective *ready*.

WHERE?
EXTENT? Stop right there!
(verb / adv. / adv.)

The adverb *right* modifies the adverb *there,* which modifies the verb *stop*.

Like adjectives, many adverbs change form to express comparison: *far, farther, farthest; frequently, more/less frequently, most/least frequently.*

> **More about**
> Comparative adverbs, 674–75

A **conjunctive adverb** is a transitional expression that can link one independent clause to another. The conjunctive adverb modifies the second clause and specifies its relationship to the first. A period or semicolon, not a comma, should separate independent clauses linked with a conjunctive adverb.

▶ Writers have several options for joining independent clauses; a comma alone, however, is not one of them.

Quick Reference: Common Conjunctive Adverbs

accordingly	however	otherwise
also	indeed	similarly
anyway	instead	specifically
as a result	likewise	still
besides	meanwhile	subsequently
certainly	moreover	suddenly
finally	nevertheless	then
for example	next	therefore
furthermore	nonetheless	thus
hence	now	

> **More about**
> Adjective and adverb phrases, 592, 689–90
> Adjective and adverb clauses, 595–96

NOTE In addition to individual words, whole phrases and clauses can function as adjectives and adverbs within sentences.

EXERCISE 33.3 Identifying adjectives and adverbs

Underline the adjectives and circle the adverbs in the following sentences.

1. Grace had always liked to have a tidy bedroom.
2. She decided to ask Maritza gently if they could have a little chat about neatness.
3. The two were good friends as well as roommates, so they agreeably worked out a compromise.
4. They split their small room into equal halves, and each cleaned her half as thoroughly as she wished.

33f Prepositions

Prepositions relate nouns or pronouns to other words in a sentence in terms of time, space, cause, and other attributes.

▸ The lecture begins at noon in the auditorium.

As the Quick Reference box on the next page indicates, prepositions can consist of more than one word.

EXERCISE 33.4 Identifying prepositions

Underline the prepositions in each of the following sentences.

1. Many people drink coffee despite worrying about the health risks.
2. Over the last twenty years, research has shown that coffee is safe in moderation, and it may even offer some health benefits.
3. According to some studies, regular coffee drinkers have a lower incidence of type 2 diabetes than people who do not drink coffee.
4. However, because the main ingredient in coffee is caffeine, a mildly addictive stimulant, excessive use is not recommended.

Quick Reference: Common One-Word and Multiword Prepositions

about	at	far from	near	past
above	because of	for	near to	since
according to	before	from	next to	through
across	behind	in	of	to
after	below	in addition to	off	toward
against	beneath	in case of	on	under
ahead of	beside	in front of	on account of	underneath
along	between	in place of	on behalf of	until
among	by	in spite of	on top of	up
around	by means of	inside	onto	upon
as far as	close to	inside of	out of	with
as to	down	instead of	outside	within
as well as	during	into	outside of	without
aside from	except	like	over	

33g Conjunctions

Conjunctions join words, phrases, and clauses to other words, phrases, or clauses and specify the way the joined elements relate to each other.

- *Coordinating conjunctions* (*and, but, or, for, nor, yet,* and *so*) join grammatically equivalent elements, giving them each equal significance.

    ▶ Ingenious **and** energetic entrepreneurs can generate effective **but** inexpensive publicity. [The conjunction *and* pairs two adjectives; the conjunction *but* contrasts two adjectives.]

- *Correlative conjunctions* are pairs of terms that, like coordinating conjunctions, join grammatically equivalent elements. Common correlative conjunctions include *either . . . or, neither . . . nor, both . . . and, not only . . . but also,* and *whether . . . or.*

    > **More about**
    > Independent and subordinate clauses, 594–97

    ▶ Fred Thompson has been **both** an actor **and** a presidential candidate.

- *Subordinating conjunctions* link subordinate clauses to the independent clauses they modify.

    ▶ The party could not begin **until** the guest of honor had arrived.

> **Quick Reference** — **Common Subordinating Conjunctions**
>
> | | | | |
> |---|---|---|---|
> | after | before | since | when |
> | although | even if | so that | where |
> | as | even though | though | while |
> | as if | if | unless | |
> | because | once | until | |

EXERCISE 33.5 Identifying conjunctions

Underline the conjunctions in the following sentences, and label the type of conjunction (coordinating, correlative, or subordinating) each is.

1. Photography was Randall's hobby, so he volunteered to take photos at the community service club's fundraising car wash.

2. He said he would send the story and photos not only to the local newspaper but also to the school's TV station.

3. After the car wash, Randall had to decide whether to download the photos to his computer or ask to use his friend Amita's computer, which was faster and had more memory than his.

4. Although he decided to ask Amita, he ended up using his own computer anyway because hers needed repairs.

5. In the end, once he had followed up his photo story submission with phone calls, both the newspaper and TV station decided to run the story.

33h Interjections

Interjections are words like *alas, bah, oh, ouch,* and *ugh* that express strong feeling—of regret, contempt, surprise, pain, or disgust, for example—but otherwise serve no grammatical function.

▶ Ugh! That's the worst coffee I ever tasted.

▶ "Bah," said Scrooge.

—Charles Dickens, *A Christmas Carol* (1843)

SENTENCE STRUCTURE

All sentences have two basic parts: a subject and a predicate. The **subject** is the thing the sentence is about. The **predicate** states something about the subject.

|—— subject ——||—————— predicate ——————|
▸ Digital technology transformed the music industry.

Sentences fall into one of four functional categories:

- *Declarative sentences* (the most common type) make a statement.
  ▸ Digital technology transformed the music industry.
- *Imperative sentences* give a command.
  ▸ Join the digital bandwagon to survive in today's competitive media marketplace.
- *Interrogative sentences* ask a question.
  ▸ Will digital technology make printed books obsolete?
- *Exclamatory sentences* express strong or sudden emotion.
  ▸ How I hate updating software on my computer!

33i Subjects

The *simple subject* of a sentence is a noun or pronoun. The *complete subject* consists of the simple subject plus any modifying words or phrases.

|— complete subject —|
       simple
       subject
▸ *Two robotic* <u>vehicles</u> have been exploring Mars since January 2004.

A *compound subject* contains two or more simple subjects joined by a conjunction.

|————————— compound subject —————————|
                    ss   conj   ss
▸ *The six-wheeled, solar-powered* <u>Spirit</u> *and the identical* <u>Opportunity</u> landed within three weeks of each other.

In imperative sentences (commands), the subject, *you,* is unstated.

▸ [<u>You</u>] Learn about space exploration at www.nasa.gov.

> **Quick Reference** — **Finding the Subject**
>
> The complete subject of a sentence is the answer to the question "Who or what did the action or was in the state defined by the verb?"
>
> |—complete subject—| verb
> ▶ Two robotic vehicles landed safely on Mars in January 2004.
>
> What landed on Mars in January 2004? Two robotic vehicles did. The subject is *two robotic vehicles*.
>
> |————complete subject————| verb
> ▶ The scientists and engineers who designed the rovers cheered.
>
> Who cheered? The scientists and engineers who designed the rovers did. The subject is *the scientists and engineers who designed the rovers*.
>
> The subject usually precedes the verb, but it is not always the first element in a sentence. In the following sentence, for example, the phrase *in July 2007* modifies the rest of the sentence but is not part of the subject.
>
> |—subject—| verb
> ▶ In July 2007, Martian dust storms restricted the activity of the rovers.

In interrogative sentences (questions), the subject falls between a helping verb and the main verb or, if the main verb is a form of *be,* after the verb.

helping   main
verb |—subject—| verb
▶ Did   the rovers   find evidence of water on Mars?

verb |———subject———|
▶ Were *Spirit* and *Opportunity* more durable than expected?

Writers occasionally invert normal word order and place the subject after the verb for emphasis.

verb |———subject———|
▶ Out of the swirling dust emerged the hardy Mars rover.

The subject also follows the verb in sentences that begin with *there* followed by a form of *be.* In these **expletive constructions,** the word *there* functions as a placeholder for the delayed subject.

v |—subject—|
▶ There are two vehicles roaming the surface of Mars.

> **More about**
> Word order and emphasis, 531–32

English Word Order In English, word order is less flexible than in many other languages, and the position of a word often affects its grammatical function and meaning. English sentences tend to place subjects before verbs and verbs before their objects. English readers expect this order, so using other word orders can cause confusion.

More about English word order, 704–12

33j Predicates

The ***simple predicate*** of a sentence is the main verb and any helping verbs. The ***complete predicate*** is the simple predicate together with any objects, complements, and modifiers.

complete predicate
simple pred.

▸ Polynesian mariners *settled the Hawaiian Islands.*

complete predicate
simple pred.

▸ The first settlers *may have arrived as early as the fourth century CE.*

A ***compound predicate*** is a complete predicate with two or more simple predicates joined by a conjunction.

complete predicate
simple pred. / sp

▸ Polynesian mariners *navigated thousands of miles of open ocean and settled the islands of the South Pacific.*

EXERCISE 33.6 Identifying subjects and predicates

For each of the following sentences, underline and label the simple subject and simple predicate; then circle and label the complete subject and complete predicate.

1. Carlynn had never gone on a camping trip before.
2. Everyone else was diligently working to set up the campsite.
3. Carlynn's cousin Marilupe handed Carlynn a hatchet and told her to find some dead wood for the campfire.

4. Later, an exhausted Carlynn and a still energetic Sara stacked the wood and assembled some large rocks in a circle.

5. Then Marilupe amazed Carlynn as well as everyone else by demonstrating how to start a fire without matches.

33k Verb Types and Sentence Patterns

There are three kinds of verb, *intransitive, linking,* and *transitive,* and they combine with other elements in the predicate in five basic sentence patterns.

1. Subject → intransitive verb

Intransitive verbs require no object and can stand alone as the only element in a predicate. They are often modified, however, by adverbs and adverbial phrases and clauses.

▶ The volcano *erupted*.
       |—subj.—| verb (intrans.)

▶ The volcano *erupted* suddenly in a powerful blast of ash and steam.
       |—subj.—| verb (intrans.) |———— adverbial modifiers ————|

Quick Reference — Five Sentence Patterns

1. subject → intransitive verb
       s   iv
   ▶ The lights dimmed.

2. subject → linking verb → subject complement
       s   lv   sc
   ▶ The audience fell silent.

3. subject → transitive verb → direct object
       s   tv   do
   ▶ The orchestra played the overture.

4. subject → transitive verb → indirect object → direct object
       s   tv   io   do
   ▶ The show gave the audience a thrill.

5. subject → transitive verb → direct object → object complement
       s   tv   do   oc
   ▶ The applause made the actors happy.

2. Subject → linking verb → subject complement

A ***subject complement*** is an adjective, pronoun, or noun phrase that describes or refers to the subject of a sentence. A ***linking verb*** connects the subject to its complement. Linking verbs express states of being rather than actions. The verb *be*, when used as a main verb, is always a linking verb. Other verbs that can function as linking verbs include *appear, become, fall, feel, grow, look, make, prove, remain, seem, smell, sound,* and *taste*.

▸ |—subj.—| |link. vb.| |—subj. comp.—|
  The Oscar   is   a coveted award.

▸ The patient felt   better.

3. Subject → transitive verb → direct object

Transitive verbs have two *voices:* active and passive. ***Transitive verbs*** in the ***active voice*** require a ***direct object***—a pronoun or noun phrase that receives the action of the verb.

> **More about**
> Voice in verbs, 652–55
> Voice and style choices, 535–37

▸ |————subject————| |active trans. vb.| |—do—|
  The undersea volcano   created   a new island.

The ***passive voice*** reverses the role of the subject, making it the recipient of the action of the verb. An active-voice sentence can usually be transformed into a passive-voice sentence of the same meaning. The subject of the passive-voice version is the direct object of the active-voice version.

▸ |—subject—| |passive trans. verb|
  A new island   *was created*   by the undersea volcano.

In the passive voice, the agent of the action can be left unstated.

▸ A new island *was created*.

NOTE Many verbs can be either transitive or intransitive.

	|—do—|
TRANSITIVE	My sister *won* the Scrabble game.
INTRANSITIVE	My sister always *wins*.

When in doubt about the usage of a verb, check a dictionary.

4. Subject → transitive verb → indirect object → direct object

Some transitive verbs can take an *indirect object* as well as a direct object. The indirect object, which precedes the direct object, identifies the beneficiary of the action of the verb.

▶ Juan [s] lent [tv] Ileana [io] his notes. [do]

▶ The donor bought the library a new computer center.

Often, the indirect object can also be stated as a prepositional phrase that begins with *to* or *for* and follows the direct object.

▶ Juan lent his notes *to Ileana*.

▶ The donor bought a new computer center *for the library*.

Verbs that can take an indirect object include *ask, bring, buy, call, find, get, give, hand, leave, lend, offer, pass, pay, promise, read, send, show, teach, tell, throw,* and *write*.

> **More about**
> Indirect objects, 707–09

Indirect Objects The use of indirect objects is highly idiomatic in English. The verbs that take them are similar to others that do not. Likewise, in some situations an indirect object before the direct object is interchangeable with a prepositional phrase after it, but in others only one or the other is acceptable. Learning how to use indirect objects effectively, then, requires exposure to a broad variety of English-language situations and texts.

5. Subject → transitive verb → direct object → object complement

An *object complement* is an adjective or noun phrase that follows the direct object and describes the condition of the object or a change that the subject has caused it to undergo.

▶ The fans [s] considered [tv] the umpire's call [do] mistaken. [oc]

▶ The manager named David Ortiz designated hitter.

EXERCISE 33.7 Identifying objects and complements

In the following sentences, underline the objects and complements. Then write DO above each direct object, IO above each indirect object, SC above each subject complement, and OC above each object complement.

1. Before he died, my grandfather wrote my mother a long letter.
2. It is actually a family history in letter form.
3. In it, my grandfather describes his own parents' arduous journey from their homeland to their new home in America.
4. The story makes me grateful for their courage.

33l Phrases

A *phrase* is a group of related words that lacks a subject, a predicate, or both. Phrases function in various ways within sentences, but cannot function as sentences by themselves. A phrase by itself is a *fragment,* not a sentence.

> **fragment** An incomplete sentence punctuated as if it were complete

1. Noun phrases

A *noun phrase* consists of a noun together with any modifiers. Noun phrases function as subjects, objects, and complements within sentences.

▶ *Sam's mouth-watering apple pie* emerged piping hot from the oven. [noun phrase/subject]

▶ The guests devoured *Sam's mouth-watering apple pie.* [noun phrase/direct object]

▶ The high point of the meal was *Sam's mouth-watering apple pie.* [noun phrase/subj. comp.]

An *appositive phrase* is a noun or noun phrase that renames a noun or noun phrase and is grammatically equivalent to it.

▶ The high point of the meal, *Sam's mouth-watering apple pie,* emerged piping hot from the oven. [appositive]

2. Verb phrases

A ***verb phrase*** consists of a main verb and all its helping verbs. Verb phrases function as the simple predicates of sentences and clauses.

▶ By Election Day, the candidates *will have been campaigning* for almost two years. [verb phrase: *will have been campaigning*]

3. Prepositional phrases

A ***prepositional phrase*** is a preposition followed by the ***object of the preposition:*** a pronoun or noun and its modifiers. Prepositional phrases function as adjectives and adverbs.

▶ The train arrives in an hour. [The prepositional phrase *in an hour* functions as an adverb modifying the verb *arrives*.]

▶ She recommended the book about Einstein. [The prepositional phrase *about Einstein* functions as an adjective modifying the noun *book*.]

> **EXERCISE 33.8 Identifying prepositional phrases**
>
> In the following sentences, underline each prepositional phrase, write above it the type (adjective or adverb), and circle the words it modifies.
>
> 1. Roger said he was a little nervous before he stepped into the canoe.
> 2. Miguel told Roger to sit in the front of the canoe.
> 3. Miguel, who had been on many canoe trips before, expertly steered from the canoe's back seat.
> 4. The trip down the river was enjoyable for both Roger and Miguel.

4. Verbal phrases

Verbals are verb forms that function as nouns, adjectives, or adverbs. Although they may have objects and complements, verbals lack the information about tense, person, and number required of a complete verb.

A ***verbal phrase*** consists of a verbal and any modifiers, objects, or complements. There are three kinds of verbal phrases: gerund phrases, infinitive phrases, and participial phrases.

Gerunds A ***gerund*** is the present participle (or *-ing* form) of a verb used as a noun; and like nouns, gerunds and gerund phrases can function as subjects, objects, and complements.

▶ <u>*Increasing automobile fuel efficiency*</u> will reduce carbon emissions. *(gerund phrase/subject)*

▶ The mayor recommends <u>*improving the city's mass transit system.*</u> *(gerund phrase/dir. obj.)*

Infinitives An ***infinitive*** is the *to* form of the verb (*to decide, to eat, to study*). Infinitives and infinitive phrases can function as adjectives and adverbs as well as nouns.

▶ The goal of the law is <u>*to increase* fuel efficiency.</u> *(noun phrase/subj. comp.)*

▶ Congress passed a law <u>*to increase* fuel efficiency.</u> *(adjective phrase)*

▶ <u>*To reduce* traffic congestion,</u> the city improved its mass transit system. *(adverb phrase)*

Infinitive versus Gerund after the Verb Some verbs can be followed by a gerund but not an infinitive, others by an infinitive but not a gerund, and still others by either a gerund or an infinitive. Lists of verbs and what can follow them do exist, but learning specific examples is a matter of experience with a broad variety of English-language situations and texts.

> **More about**
> Infinitive versus gerund after verbs, 725–26

Participial phrases In a ***participial phrase*** the present participle or past participle of a verb acts as an adjective. The present participle ends in *-ing.* The past participle of regular verbs ends in *-ed,* but some verbs have irregular past participles.

▶ <u>*Surveying* the disheveled apartment,</u> Grace wondered whether it would be possible to room with Maritza.

▶ <u>*Deeply concerned,*</u> she asked, "How long have you lived alone?"

> **More about**
> Irregular past participles, 638–42

> **EXERCISE 33.9 Identifying verbal phrases**
>
> In the following sentences, underline each verbal phrase. Then write above it the type (gerund, infinitive, or participial).
>
> 1. Seeking economic opportunity or freedom from political or religious repression, millions of immigrants came to the United States between the end of the Civil War and the early 1920s.
> 2. Many of the newcomers intended to return to their homelands.
> 3. Most immigrants during this period came from southern and eastern Europe, replacing the Irish and German immigrants who had predominated before the Civil War.
> 4. Leaving home and settling in a new environment must have been difficult.
> 5. Not always welcomed in their new communities, immigrants often settled together in ethnic enclaves.

5. Absolute phrases

Absolute phrases modify entire sentences rather than particular words within sentences. They usually consist of a pronoun or noun phrase followed by a participle. Set off by commas, they can often fall flexibly before, after, or within the rest of the sentence.

▶ *All our quarrels forgotten,* we sat before the fire and talked quietly.

When the participle in an absolute phrase is a form of *be,* it is often omitted as understood.

▶ *Her interview [having been] successful,* she was offered the job on the spot.

33m Independent and Subordinate Clauses

A *clause* is a word group with a subject and a predicate. An ***independent*** (or ***main***) *clause* can stand alone as a sentence.

|—— independent clause ——|
▶ Sam's pie won first prize.

A *subordinate* (or *dependent*) clause is a clause within a clause.

▶ Sam baked the pie that won first prize.

That is, a subordinate clause functions inside an independent clause (or another subordinate clause) as a noun, adjective, or adverb but cannot stand alone as a sentence. A subordinate clause by itself is a *fragment*. A subordinating word—either a ***subordinating conjunction*** (see the Quick Reference box on p. 584) or a ***relative pronoun*** (see the Quick Reference box on p. 578)—usually signals the beginning of a subordinate clause.

> **More about**
> Subordinate clause fragments, 607–08
> Punctuating subordinate clauses, 512, 751–53, 757–59

1. Adjective clauses

Like adjectives, ***adjective clauses*** (also called ***relative clauses***) modify nouns or pronouns. They usually begin with a relative pronoun that immediately follows the word the clause modifies and refers back to it.

▶ Sam baked the pie that won first prize.

▶ The donor who paid for the library's new computer center is a recent graduate.

In both of these examples, the relative pronoun is the subject of the subordinate clause, and the clause follows normal word order, with the subject before the verb. When the relative pronoun is the direct object, however, it still comes at the beginning of the clause, reversing normal word order.

▶ The candidate whom we supported lost the election.

> **More about**
> Who versus whom, 663–64

Adjective clauses can also begin with the subordinating conjunctions *when* and *where*.

▶ Tupelo, Mississippi, is the town where Elvis Presley was born.

It is sometimes acceptable to omit the relative pronoun that introduces an adjective clause when the meaning of the clause is clear without it.

▶ The candidate [*whom*] *we supported* lost the election.

> **More about**
> The meaning of subordinating conjunctions, 513

2. Adverb clauses

Adverb clauses usually begin with a subordinating conjunction, which specifies the relation of the clause to the term it modifies. Like adverbs, adverb clauses can modify verbs, adjectives, and adverbs as well as whole phrases and clauses.

- The baby boom **began** *as World War II ended.*
  The adverb clause modifies the verb *began.*

- The economy grew **faster** *than many Americans thought it would.*
  The adverb clause modifies the adverb *faster.*

- The 1950s were an affluent decade, *although the general prosperity did not extend to all.*
  The adverb clause modifies the preceding independent clause.

3. Noun clauses

Noun clauses do not modify other parts of a sentence but instead replace noun phrases as subjects, objects, or complements within an independent clause. Noun clauses can begin with a relative pronoun as well as with certain subordinating conjunctions, including *how, if, when, whenever, where, wherever, whether,* and *why.*

- *Whoever crosses the finish line first* [subject] wins the race.

- Home is *where the heart is.* [subject comp.]

- The evidence proves *that the defendant is not guilty.* [direct object]

> **EXERCISE 33.10 Identifying subordinate clauses**

In the following passage, underline the subordinate clauses. Then write above each clause its function (noun, adverbial, or adjectival).

> Spring break is a time when most students want just to take it easy and have fun. Martin usually did just that, although he sometimes thought he should spend the time more productively. However, he never could figure out how he could turn this desire to be useful into reality. Then he saw a story in the school newspaper about the community service club's spring break project, which was to help build a home for someone in need. He decided that this was his opportunity to do something different. That he had to pay for the trip himself required Martin to spend many hours working to raise the funds. He washed cars, shoveled snow, babysat, walked dogs, and did other errands for his neighbors over the winter until he had the $600 that he needed. The bus took Martin and the other participants to the home site, which was four hundred miles from the school. The days at the construction site started earlier than the students usually liked to get up, but they all found it exciting to learn how to build a house. The construction had progressed substantially by the end of the spring break week. Martin and his fellow student home builders returned feeling as though they had used their week off doing something useful.

33n Sentence Types

Sentences fall into four types depending on the combination of independent and subordinate clauses they contain. Including a mix of types in your writing and choosing the appropriate type for the information you intend to convey can help you hold your readers' attention and emphasize important points.

> **More about**
> Sentence variety, 527–31

1. Simple sentences

A *simple sentence* has only one independent clause and no subordinate clauses.

|———————— independent clause ————————|
▶ Lance Armstrong won the Tour de France seven times.

A simple sentence need not be short or even uncomplicated. A sentence with a compound subject, a compound predicate, or both is still a simple sentence as long as it has a single complete subject, a single complete predicate, and no subordinate clauses.

▶ Lance Armstrong and Miguel Indurain have each won the Tour de France and dominated professional cycling. *[independent clause]*

2. Compound sentences

A *compound sentence* has two or more independent clauses but no subordinate clauses. A comma and a coordinating conjunction, a semicolon, or a semicolon and a conjunctive adverb usually join the clauses in a compound sentence.

> **More about**
> Avoiding comma splices and fused sentences, 611–19 (ch. 35)

▶ Lance Armstrong won the Tour de France seven times, and in 2002, *Sports Illustrated* named him Sportsman of the Year. *[independent clause / independent clause]*

▶ Armstrong's seven wins were in consecutive years; two other cyclists had previously won in five consecutive years. *[independent clause / independent clause]*

3. Complex sentences

A *complex sentence* consists of a single independent clause with at least one subordinate clause.

▶ After he won his seventh Tour in 2005, Armstrong retired from racing. *[subordinate clause / independent clause]*

▶ The Tour de France, which is the world's longest cycling race, covers nearly 2,000 miles in 22 days. *[independent clause / subordinate clause]*

4. Compound-complex sentences

A *compound-complex sentence* has two or more independent clauses with one or more subordinate clauses.

▶ The Tour has long been plagued by allegations of doping among contestants, but the 2007 race, which saw three riders disqualified for doping-related offenses, was particularly scandal ridden.

(independent clause: The Tour has long been plagued by allegations of doping among contestants; independent clause: but the 2007 race ... was particularly scandal ridden; subordinate clause: which saw three riders disqualified for doping-related offenses)

EXERCISE 33.11 Identifying sentence types

Next to each of the following sentences, write the type of sentence it is: simple, compound, complex, or compound-complex.

1. Lindsay practices her breathing exercises every day with her husband, Larry, who coaches her enthusiastically.
2. Lindsay and Larry attend weekly childbirth classes, meet other expectant parents, learn about the stages of labor, and practice massage and relaxation techniques.
3. One couple, although friendly to Lindsay and Larry, often interrupt the instructor, so Larry is sometimes annoyed by them.
4. Lindsay and Larry will be first-time parents, but they are learning important information by attending the classes.
5. As they learn more, Lindsay and Larry gain confidence as prospective parents; however, the childbirth video made them nervous at first.

Make It Your Own

Write down five sentences from a reading assignment or from a newspaper article. Identify the independent and dependent clauses in each sentence, and label each sentence as simple, compound, complex, or compound-complex.

Work Together

Exchange your sentences and your analysis of them with those of another student, and check each other's work. Consult your professor if you disagree about any sentences.

34 Avoiding Sentence Fragments

IN THIS CHAPTER

a. Recognizing fragments, 600
b. Correcting fragments, 604
c. Using intentional fragments, 609

An open drawbridge is not a complete bridge; it is two bridge fragments, neither of which, by itself, will get travelers all the way across a river. Similarly, a sentence *fragment* is not a complete sentence. It may begin with a capital letter and end with a period (or a question mark or an exclamation point), but it lacks all the elements of a complete sentence. It takes readers only partway through the writer's thought, leaving them searching for the missing pieces. Although writers may use them intentionally in certain contexts, fragments are almost always out of place in academic and business writing.

34a Recognizing Fragments

A sentence must have at least one ***independent clause,*** which is a group of related words that has a ***complete verb*** and a ***subject*** but does not start with a subordinating term such as *although, because, who,* or *that.* A word group punctuated like a sentence that does not satisfy these conditions is a fragment, not a sentence.

1. No verb

A ***complete verb*** consists of a main verb together with any helping verbs needed to express tense, mood, and voice. If a word group lacks

> **subject** A noun or pronoun that names the topic of a sentence
> **complete verb** A main verb together with any helping verbs needed to indicate tense, voice, and mood

> **More about**
> Verbs, 636–55 (ch. 37)

> **Quick Reference** — **Identifying Fragments**
>
> To determine whether a word group is a fragment or a sentence, ask yourself these questions:
>
> 1. **Does it have a complete verb?** If the answer is no, it is a fragment.
> 2. **Does it have a subject?** If the answer is no, it is a fragment.
> 3. **Does it begin with a subordinating word but otherwise stand alone?** If the answer is yes, it is a fragment.

a complete verb, it is a *phrase,* and if that phrase is punctuated as a sentence, it is a phrase fragment.

FRAGMENT (NO VERB)	Her beautiful new sports car.
SENTENCE	Her beautiful new sports *car was smashed* beyond repair. (subj. / complete verb)

Verbals are words that look like verbs—they are derived from verbs—but they lack the information about tense required of a complete verb. Instead, they function as nouns, adjectives, or adverbs. Verbals can include past participles (the *-ed* form in most verbs), present participles (the *-ing* form), and infinitives (the *to* form). Verbal phrases, by themselves, are fragments, not sentences.

> **More about**
> Verbals, 579, 592–94, 725–26

FRAGMENT	An *inspired* teacher *making* a difference in her students' lives. (verbal / verbal)
SENTENCE	An *inspired* teacher, *she is making* a difference in her students' lives. (verbal / subj. / verb)

2. No subject

The subject of a sentence is the answer to the question "Who or what did the action defined by the verb?" If a word group lacks a subject, it is a phrase. If the phrase is punctuated like a sentence, it is a phrase fragment.

FRAGMENT	*Serves* no purpose. (verb)
SENTENCE	*The breadmaker* in my cupboard *serves* no purpose. (subject / verb)

> **More about**
> Imperatives, 650

Imperatives (*commands*) look like they do not have a subject. Actually their subject is understood to be *you,* and they are sentences, *not* fragments.

	verb
IMPERATIVE SENTENCE	Come here right now!

Including a Stated Subject Unlike in most other languages, all sentences in formal English except commands always require an explicitly stated subject. See chapter 43, "Understanding English Word Order and Sentence Structure."

3. Begins with a subordinating term

> **More about**
> Subordinate clauses, 594–97

A subordinate clause and an independent clause both have a subject and verb, but a subordinate clause begins with a subordinating term, either a subordinating conjunction or a relative pronoun (see the Quick Reference box on the next page). The subordinating term links the subordinate clause to another clause, where it functions as a noun, adjective, or adverb. A subordinate clause cannot stand alone as a sentence, and if it is punctuated like a sentence, it is a subordinate clause fragment.

	subordinator
FRAGMENT	When the drawbridge closes.

	subordinator
SENTENCE	We will cross the river when the drawbridge closes.

	subordinator
FRAGMENT	Which made driving hazardous.

	subordinator
SENTENCE	The storm left a foot of snow, which made driving hazardous.

Be careful to distinguish between relative pronouns used to introduce a subordinate clause and the same words used as interrogative pronouns to introduce questions. Questions beginning this way are complete sentences.

	relative pronoun
FRAGMENT	Who will be attending.

	interrogative pronoun
SENTENCE	Who will be attending?

Grammar Matters • Recognizing Fragments

Quick Reference: Subordinating Terms

Subordinating Conjunctions

after	before	since	unless	whereas
although	even if	so that	until	while
as	even though	than	when	why
as if	if	that	whenever	
because	once	though	where	

Relative Pronouns

that	who	whom	whose	which
what	whoever	whomever	whatever	whichever

EXERCISE 34.1 Identifying fragments

Identify each of the following word groups as a sentence or a fragment; then further label each fragment as a phrase fragment or a subordinate clause fragment.

> **More about**
> Different types of pronouns, 578

EXAMPLE

Which have women heads of state. *[fragment, subordinate clause]*

1. In 2006, Michelle Bachelet became the first female president of Chile.
2. Who would have predicted such a turn of events just a few years earlier?
3. Not many observers at the time.
4. Because Chile was for many years a bastion of gender conservatism.
5. Electing Bachelet changed all that.
6. The voters went to the polls.
7. With an open mind.
8. The people of Chile were excited.
9. Waving flags and banners, honking horns, blowing whistles, and chanting slogans.
10. Which is a promising sign for the future.

34b Correcting Fragments

Once you have identified a fragment, you have two options for correcting it:

1. Connect the fragment to a related independent clause.

   ▶ The first mission to Pluto was launched in 2006~~. Will arrive~~ *and will arrive* in 2015.

   ▶ He made 5,000 songs available over the university's server~~. Which~~ *, which* prompted the record companies to threaten legal action.

2. Convert the fragment into an independent clause.

   ▶ The first mission to Pluto was launched in 2006. ~~Will~~ *It will* arrive in 2015.

   ▶ He made 5,000 songs available over the university's server. ~~Which prompted~~ *In response,* the record companies ~~to threaten~~ *threatened* legal action.

These options apply to both phrase fragments and subordinate clause fragments. Either option can fix a fragment; deciding on the best one is a stylistic choice that depends on the context in which the fragment occurs.

Writing Responsibly: Sentence Fragments and Context

Although writers sometimes use them deliberately in certain contexts (see 34c), for a variety of reasons you should avoid sentence fragments in your academic or business writing. One is that fragments can create ambiguities, as in the following example:

▶ Our small town has seen many changes. Some long-time stores went out of business. Because the new mall opened. There are now more options for family entertainment.

Did the new mall put stores out of business, provide new entertainment options, or both? To clarify this ambiguity, the writer would need to attach the fragment to the preceding sentence or the following sentence, or rewrite these sentences in some other way.

Another reason to avoid fragments is that readers may interpret them as carelessness or a lack of competence, which would undermine your efforts to present yourself authoritatively.

to TOPIC

> **Tech** **Grammar Checkers and Sentence Fragments**
>
> The grammar checkers in word processing programs may miss some fragments and, in some cases, may incorrectly flag imperatives as fragments. Although your grammar checker can help you, you will still need to edit your prose carefully for fragments.

1. Phrase fragments

Phrase fragments lack a subject, a complete verb, or both. As you edit your writing, watch for fragments based on certain kinds of phrases in particular. These include prepositional phrases, verbal phrases, appositive phrases, the separate parts of compound predicates, and items in lists and examples.

Prepositional phrases A *prepositional phrase* consists of a preposition (such as *as, at, for, from, in addition to, to,* or *until*) followed by a pronoun or noun and its modifiers. You can usually correct a prepositional phrase fragment by attaching it to an adjacent sentence.

> **More about**
> Prepositions and prepositional phrases, 582–83, 592, 739–46

▶ The Kenyon College women won the NCAA Division III title ~~again. For~~ *for* the seventeenth consecutive year.

Verbal phrases Although verbals are derived from verbs, verbal phrases can function as adjectives, adverbs, or nouns within a sentence but not as sentences on their own. In the following example, *stranding* is a verbal.

▶ The car had run out of ~~gas. Stranding~~ *gas, stranding* us in the middle of nowhere.

Appositive phrases An *appositive phrase* is a noun or *noun phrase* that renames a preceding noun or noun phrase and is grammatically equivalent to it. Appositives become fragments when they are separated by a period from the phrases they rename.

> **More about**
> Appositives, 591
>
> **noun phrase** A noun together with any modifiers

▶ The diners eagerly awaited the culmination of the ~~meal. Sam's~~ *meal, Sam's* mouth-watering apple pie.

Compound predicates A *compound predicate* consists of two or more complete verbs, together with their objects and modifiers, that are joined by a

> **More about**
> Compound predicates, 587

coordinating conjunction (such as *or, and,* or *but*) and that share the same subject. A fragment results when the last part of a compound predicate is punctuated as a separate sentence.

▶ By the end of May, the band members hated each other. ~~But~~ *but* still had six weeks left to tour.

> **More about**
> Punctuation for lists, 797, 801

Lists and examples Lists become fragments when they are separated from the sentence to which they belong. To correct list fragments, link them to the sentence by rephrasing the passage or replacing the period with a colon or a dash.

FRAGMENT	Three authors are most commonly associated with the Beat movement. Allen Ginsberg, Jack Kerouac, and William Burroughs.
REVISED	Three authors are most commonly associated with the Beat movement: Allen Ginsberg, Jack Kerouac, and William Burroughs.
	or
	The three authors most commonly associated with the Beat movement are Allen Ginsberg, Jack Kerouac, and William Burroughs.

Examples or explanations that begin with transitional words such as *for example, in contrast,* and *in addition* can be sentences; they are fragments, however, if they are punctuated like a sentence but lack a subject or a complete verb, or otherwise consist of only a subordinate clause. In the following example, the writer corrected a phrase fragment by rephrasing and attaching it to the preceding sentence.

▶ People today have access to many sources of news and ~~opinion. For~~ *opinion, including, for* example, the Internet and cable television as well as broadcast television and print newspapers and magazines.

The writer of the next example corrected a subordinate clause fragment by deleting the subordinating word *that,* which turns the fragment into a sentence.

▶ Certain facts underscore the rapid growth of the Internet. For ~~example that~~ *example,* web browsers did not become widely available until the mid-1990s.

> **EXERCISE 34.2 Correcting sentence fragments**

Correct each sentence fragment below and write at the end what kind of fragment it is (prepositional phrase, verbal phrase, appositive phrase, compound predicate, list or example).

EXAMPLE

The most unforgettable character I know is my ~~grandfather. Jacob~~ Black.
                                                         ^ grandfather, Jacob

[appositive phrase]

1. Even though he was only five feet four inches tall, he was a championship boxer. During high school.

2. Boxing was what many young men pursued. Back in the 1940s.

3. Later, he joined the army. Becoming a first sergeant in the quartermaster corps.

4. He was responsible for setting up army camps in Korea. Also for supervising supplies, cooking, and recreation.

5. He must have been a pretty tough guy in those days. Not the warm and loving grandpa I knew later on.

2. Subordinate clause fragments

A subordinate clause has a subject and a verb but begins with a subordinating word or phrase—a subordinating conjunction or a relative pronoun—and cannot stand alone as a sentence. When you correct a subordinate clause fragment, be sure to consider the relationships among the ideas you are expressing before deciding whether to transform the subordinate clause into an independent clause or to connect it to a related independent clause. Subordinating conjunctions, for example, specify the relationship between the information in a subordinate clause and the clause it modifies. If that relationship is important, you will probably want to correct the fragment by connecting it to the independent clause to which it relates.

> ▸ Twitter continues to gain popularity as a source of information~~. Because~~ it can publish late-breaking news as soon as it occurs.
>   ^ because

> **More about**
> Subordination and subordinating conjunctions, 510–17

The correction retains the subordinating conjunction *because* and with it important information about the cause-and-effect relationship between the two parts of the sentence. That information would have been obscured if the writer had simply deleted the subordinating conjunction to change the fragment into a separate sentence: *They can publish late-breaking news as soon as it occurs.*

In other cases, revising a subordinate clause fragment into a separate sentence by deleting the subordinating word can produce a clearer, less awkward result than would attaching it to another sentence.

▶ Horses and camels have something in common. ~~That the~~ ^The ancestors of both originated in the western hemisphere and migrated to the eastern hemisphere.

> **More about**
> Punctuating subordinate clauses and other subordinate structures, 512, 757–59

A subordinate clause that begins with a subordinating conjunction is usually set off by a comma if it comes at the beginning of a sentence but not if it comes at the end. The punctuation of a subordinate clause that begins with a relative pronoun depends on whether the clause is ***essential*** (it specifically identifies the word or words it modifies) or ***nonessential*** (the identity of the word or words it modifies is clear without it).

▶ EXERCISE 34.3 Correcting subordinate clause fragments

Correct each fragment below and write at the end whether the fragment begins with a subordinating conjunction or a relative pronoun.

EXAMPLE

Northern Florida is dotted with natural ~~springs. That~~ ^*springs that* are direct outlets of a huge aquifer, or groundwater source. *[relative pronoun]*

1. The springs discharge millions of gallons of cool, clean, fresh water each day. Because the aquifer is very close to the surface.
2. The area contains many rivers, lakes, and ponds. That are fed from the springs.
3. Although the area still seems rural and remote. The water attracts many vacationers.
4. For many years people came to visit area tourist attractions. That included "mermaid" shows and glass-bottom boat rides.
5. Today, however, the region has gained a reputation for ecotourism. Because it abounds with state parks, water trails, and campgrounds.

34c Using Intentional Fragments Effectively and Judiciously

Writers sometimes use fragments not in error but intentionally for emphasis or to reflect how people actually speak. Exclamations and the answers to questions often fall into this category.

- Another loss! Ouch!
- What caused this disaster? The collapse of our running game.

Intentional fragments are also common in advertising copy, and many writers use them for effect when the context makes their full meaning clear.

- All science. No fiction.
  —Toyota advertisement
- Man is the only animal that blushes. Or needs to.
  —Mark Twain, *Following the Equator*

Consider your writing situation, your context and genre, and especially your audience before deciding to use a sentence fragment deliberately. If your purpose is careful reporting or analysis, you should probably avoid the intentional sentence fragment because it can create ambiguity (see the Writing Responsibly box on p. 604). In academic or business writing, where clarity of expression is highly prized, fragments are frowned upon and can undermine your authority. On the other hand, if your purpose is expressive or you are writing in an informal context or genre (for example, in a blog or for a fanzine), the occasional intentional fragment can be highly effective.

EXERCISE 34.4 Correcting sentence fragments

Identify and correct any sentence fragments in the following paragraph.

> On January 2, miners of the morning shift reported for work. As usual beginning the descent to the coal seam deep underground. Not all had descended into the mine when the explosion happened. There were two crews. One still aboveground. The explosion occurred at 6:31 a.m. Causing a power outage throughout the mine. Which filled with smoke. And deadly carbon monoxide. A mine rescue team was called. But not until 8:04 a.m. Because it took the mine supervisors that long to ascertain what had happened. Meanwhile, the trapped miners had only a limited supply of oxygen. Distraught families gathered aboveground waiting

for news. At last a shout rang out. "Alive!" A collective sigh of relief and thanksgiving was audible. As family members waited to see their loved ones once again.

Make It **Your Own**

Reread three texts you have written recently or a draft you are working on and look for sentence fragments. If you find any, make a note of what kind they are and correct them; then add this to your list of areas to consider as you revise your prose.

Work **Together**

Exchange texts and analyze your classmate's writing for sentence fragments. Underline any you find and make a note of what kind they are. Compare your results with those of the others in the group. What did each of you see that others did not? Were some types of fragments easier to find than others? If so, make a note of any you had difficulty finding and add them to your revision checklist.

35 Avoiding Comma Splices and Fused Sentences

IN THIS CHAPTER

a. Correctly joining independent clauses, 611

b. Identifying comma splices and fused sentences, 612

c. Recognizing when comma splices and fused sentences occur, 613

d. Correcting comma splices and fused sentences, 615

> **More about**
> Clauses, 594–96

If not properly joined with a coupling mechanism like the one in this picture, railway cars would either pull apart when the lead car accelerated or crash into each other when the lead car braked. Like railway cars, two independent clauses joined in a compound sentence need a proper coupling mechanism. If the clauses are incorrectly joined with a comma alone in a *comma splice,* they may seem to readers to pull apart confusingly. If the clauses crash into one another with no separating punctuation in a *fused* (or *run-on*) *sentence,* readers will not know where one ends and the other begins.

35a Correctly Joining Independent Clauses

An *independent clause* can stand on its own as a sentence. Related independent clauses can follow one another as separate sentences, each ending in a period.

▶ Richard Harris played Dumbledore in the first two Harry Potter movies. Michael Gambon played the role after Harris's death in 2002.

> **More about**
> Coordination, 505–10

Alternatively, you can join (or *coordinate*) independent clauses in a compound sentence with a variety of coupling mechanisms that let readers know one clause is ending and another beginning. Of these, two are the most common:

- A comma and a coordinating conjunction (*and, but, or, nor, for, so, yet*)
  - ▸ Richard Harris played Dumbledore in the first two Harry Potter movies, but Michael Gambon played the role after Harris's death in 2002.
- A semicolon
  - ▸ Richard Harris played Dumbledore in the first two Harry Potter movies; Michael Gambon played the role after Harris's death in 2002.

You can also use a colon or a dash between independent clauses when the first clause introduces the second or the second elaborates on the first. (The colon is usually more appropriate in formal writing.)

▸ Two actors have played Dumbledore: Michael Gambon succeeded Richard Harris in the role after Harris's death in 2002.

35b Identifying Incorrectly Joined Independent Clauses: Comma Splices and Fused Sentences

When a writer improperly joins two independent clauses with a comma alone, the result is a *comma splice*.

COMMA SPLICE |—independent clause—| |—independent clause—| Ronald Reagan was originally an actor, he turned to politics in the 1960s.

When a writer runs two independent clauses together with no punctuation between them, the result is a *fused sentence* (also called a *run-on sentence*).

Writing Responsibly **Clarifying Boundaries**

Comma splices and fused sentences obscure the boundaries between linked ideas. If you leave them uncorrected in your writing, you burden readers with a task that should be yours: to identify where one idea ends and another begins and to specify how those ideas relate to each other.

to AUDIENCE

Grammar Matters • Recognizing When Comma Splices and Fused Sentences Tend to Occur   cs/fs **35c**

Quick Reference: Identifying Comma Splices and Fused Sentences

When two independent clauses are joined by	The result is
A comma and coordinating conjunction	**Not** a comma splice or fused sentence
A semicolon	**Not** a comma splice or fused sentence
A colon or dash	**Not** a comma splice or fused sentence
A comma alone	A **comma splice—revise**
No punctuation at all	A **fused sentence—revise**

FUSED SENTENCE

|———————— independent clause ————————| |—
Politics and acting have something in common they
|———————— independent clause ————————|
both require an affinity for public performance.

35c Recognizing When Comma Splices and Fused Sentences Tend to Occur

To avoid comma splices and fused sentences in your own work, pay attention to situations in which they are particularly likely to occur:

1. When the second clause begins with a conjunctive adverb (such as *for example, however,* or *therefore*) or other transitional expression

    COMMA SPLICE   In the first two Harry Potter movies, Richard Harris played Dumbledore, however, after Harris's death in 2002, Michael Gambon played the role.

    REVISED   In the first two Harry Potter movies, Richard Harris played Dumbledore; however, after Harris's death in 2002, Michael Gambon played the role.

2. When the grammatical subject of the second clause is a pronoun whose antecedent is the subject of the first clause

Tech: Comma Splices, Fused Sentences, and Grammar Checkers

Grammar checkers in word processing programs do not reliably identify comma splices or fused sentences. They catch some, but they miss many more.

COMMA SPLICE	Ronald Reagan was originally an actor, he turned to politics in the 1960s.
REVISED	Ronald Reagan was originally an actor, **but** he turned to politics in the 1960s.

3. When the first clause introduces the second or the second explains or elaborates on the first

FUSED SENTENCE	Politics and acting have something in common they both require a willingness to perform in public.
REVISED	Politics and acting have something in common: They both require a willingness to perform in public.

4. When one clause is positive and the other negative

COMMA SPLICE	We were not upset that the exam was postponed, we were relieved.
REVISED	We were not upset that the exam was postponed; we were relieved.

> **EXERCISE 35.1 Identifying comma splices and fused sentences**
>
> In each of the following sentences, underline the independent clauses. Then write CS after each comma splice, write FS after each fused sentence, and circle the numbers of sentences that are correct as is.

Writing Responsibly — Is a Comma Splice Ever Acceptable?

Comma splices often show up in compound sentences composed of two short, snappy independent clauses in parallel form, particularly when one is negative and the other positive or when both are commands. This usage is common, for example, in advertising:

> Buy one, get one free.

It can crop up, too, in the work of experienced writers, who may use it deliberately because they feel a period, semicolon, or comma and coordinating conjunction would be too disruptive a separation in sentences like these:

> You're not a man, you're a machine.
>
> —George Bernard Shaw, *Arms and the Man*

> Go ahead, make my day.
>
> —Joseph C. Stinson, screenplay to *Sudden Impact*

However, this usage looks like an error and will confuse readers, and thus it is best avoided in academic writing.

to AUDIENCE

EXAMPLE

<u>This is our dog her name is Dusty</u>. *[FS]*

1. Dusty is a mutt, she is not a purebred dog.
2. Some people think she is a German shepherd others just ask what kind of dog she is.
3. I always say she is just a dog.
4. Dogs like Dusty are called a variety of names, mongrel is probably the most common.
5. Mutt and mixed-breed are other common names that are used for these dogs.
6. Mixed-breed dogs have fewer genetic disorders than do purebred dogs the inbreeding of purebreds has created genetic problems.
7. For example, German shepherds often have hip problems, collies often have eye diseases.
8. One type of mixed-breed is the crossbreed, a deliberate cross between two purebred strains.
9. As for Dusty, she certainly looks like a German shepherd she also looks like a Norwegian elkhound.
10. To me, she is the world's greatest dog, I love her very much.

35d Correcting Comma Splices and Fused Sentences

The Quick Reference box on page 616 lists five strategies for correcting comma splices and fused sentences. The strategy you choose should depend on the logical relationship between the clauses and the meaning you intend to convey.

1. Separate sentences

Correcting a comma splice or fused sentence by dividing the independent clauses into separate sentences makes sense when one or both of the clauses are long or when the two clauses do not have a close logical relationship.

▶ My friends and I began our long-anticipated trip to Peru in early July ~~we~~ . We arrived in Lima on Saturday morning and flew to Cuzco that same day.

Quick Reference — **Ways to Correct Comma Splices and Fused Sentences**

1. Use a period to divide the clauses into separate sentences. (615)
2. Join the clauses correctly with a comma and coordinating conjunction. (616)
3. Join the clauses correctly with a semicolon. (616)
4. Join the clauses, if appropriate, with a colon or dash. (617)
5. Change one independent clause into a subordinate clause or modifying phrase. (617)

Use a period also when the second clause is a new sentence that continues a quotation that begins in the first clause.

▶ "We must not be enemies," Abraham Lincoln implored the South in his first inaugural address_. "Though passion may have strained, it must not break our bonds of affection."

2. Coordinating conjunction

> *More about*
> The meaning of coordinating conjunctions, 507–08

When you join independent clauses with a comma and a coordinating conjunction (*and, but, or, nor, for, so,* or *yet*), choose the conjunction that best fits the logical relationship between the clauses.

▶ We needed to adjust to the altitude before we began hiking in the Andes_{, so} we spent three days sightseeing in Cuzco.

3. Semicolon

> *More about*
> Coordinating with a semicolon, 507–08, 767–68

Join two independent clauses with a semicolon when they have a clear logical relationship, either of contrast, example, or explanation.

▶ Most languages spoken in Europe belong to the Indo-European language family_; a few, such as Basque, Finnish, and Hungarian, do not.

Using a semicolon in combination with a conjunctive adverb or other transitional expression can clarify the relationship between the clauses.

▶ Most languages spoken in Europe belong to the Indo-European language family_{; however,} Basque, Finnish, and Hungarian are exceptions.

4. Colon or dash

You can use a colon or, less commonly, a dash to join independent clauses when the first clause introduces the second or the second explains or elaborates on the first. This usage can create a more emphatic separation between the clauses than would a semicolon.

> **More about**
> Punctuating for emphasis, 533
> Colons, 800–02
> Dashes, 796–98

- The message is clear, smoking kills. [colon inserted]

- Don't get kicked out of school, learn to study effectively. [dash inserted]

5. Subordinate clause and modifying phrase

You can correct a comma splice or fused sentence by turning one of the independent clauses into a subordinate clause or by reducing the information in it to a modifying phrase. Note, however, that putting information in subordinate clauses and phrases usually de-emphasizes it in relation to the information in the independent clause it modifies.

> **More about**
> Subordination and emphasis, 510–11

COMMA SPLICE Spanish, like French and Italian, is a Romance language, it derives from Latin, the language of the Romans.

REVISED: SUBORDINATE CLAUSE Spanish, like French and Italian, is a Romance language |———— subordinate clause ————| because it derives from Latin, the language of the Romans.

REVISED: MODIFYING PHRASE |———— modifying phrase ————| Spanish, a Romance language like French and Italian, derives from Latin, the language of the Romans.

➔ EXERCISE 35.2 Correcting comma splices and fused sentences

Choose one of the methods described above to correct each comma splice or fused sentence. Circle the numbers of any sentences that are correct as is.

EXAMPLE

Disaster films are almost as old as film itself the first was made in 1901. [semicolon inserted]

1. Obviously, disasters are natural subjects for films they are dramatic and visually interesting.

2. Early disaster movies focused on natural events such as fires, floods, and earthquakes, later ones showed human-made tragedies.

3. The first modern disaster movies were made in the 1950s, they focused on airplane crashes.

4. The golden age of disaster movies was probably the 1970s, the most popular of all was *Airport,* released in 1970.

5. It was followed by numerous sequels as well as by other hugely successful examples of the genre, such as *The Towering Inferno.*

6. Since that time, the summer blockbuster has remained everyone's idea of a good time it usually includes enough romance and drama, as well as special effects, to please everyone.

7. The genre even spawned its own subgenre, the disaster spoof, represented by the hits *Airplane* and *Airplane II.*

8. With the increasing sophistication of computerized special effects in the 1990s disaster films enjoyed a huge revival they had flagged in popularity in the 1980s.

9. However, 9/11 may have changed all that how much fun is it to see a film like *The Towering Inferno* today?

10. Other disaster films that refer to real events, such as *The Day After Tomorrow,* which focused on the effects of global warming, have been successful only time will tell whether the genre will survive.

EXERCISE 35.3 Correcting comma splices and fused sentences

Revise the following passage to correct any comma splices or fused sentences.

Opera is an art form that combines music, lyrics, and dialog, so is musical comedy, however. Then what is the difference between them? Perhaps it is their origins opera arose in the seventeenth century primarily in Italy as an attempt to revive classical Greek drama. Musical comedy arose in the United States in the twentieth century out of vaudeville and other plotless musical shows such as burlesque and reviews. Regardless, there is a great deal of overlap between the two forms today although the famous composer and lyricist Stephen Sondheim says that if something is performed in an opera house, it is an opera, but if it is performed in a theater, it is a musical comedy, today many works are performed in both places.

Make It **Your Own**

Choose a text you have recently written or are writing. On one page of that text, underline each independent clause and check each sentence to be sure it does not include fused sentences or comma splices; if it does, revise the sentences accordingly and add this to your revision checklist.

Work **Together**

Exhange your revised pages with a classmate and double-check each other's work. Where do you have differences of opinion? Review this chapter to resolve any differences.

36 Maintaining Agreement

IN THIS CHAPTER

SUBJECT-VERB AGREEMENT

a. How subjects and verbs agree, 620
b. Intervening words, 622
c. Compounds, 623
d. Indefinite pronouns, 625
e. Collective nouns, 625
f. Numbers, 626
g. Singular nouns that end in -s, 627
h. Titles, words as words, and gerund phrases, 627
i. *Who, which,* or *that,* 628
j. Subject after verb, 629
k. Linking verbs, 629

PRONOUN-ANTECEDENT AGREEMENT

l. Indefinite words, 631
m. Collective nouns, 634
n. Compounds, 634

In many languages, the grammatical form of some words in a sentence must match the form of other words. When the forms match, the reader can easily understand the sentence; when they do not, the effect can be like trying to force a square peg into a round hole, leaving the reader distracted or confused. In English, subjects and verbs require this kind of matchup, or *agreement,* as do pronouns and the words to which they refer.

SUBJECT-VERB AGREEMENT

A verb and its subject have to agree, or match each other, in person and number. ***Person*** refers to the form of a word that indicates whether it corresponds to the speaker or writer (*I, we*), the person addressed (*you*), or the people or things spoken or written about (*he, she, it, they, Alice, milkshakes*). ***Number*** refers to the form of a word that indicates whether it is singular, referring to one thing (*a student*), or plural, referring to more than one (*two students*).

36a Understanding How Subjects and Verbs Agree

With just a few exceptions, it is only in the present tense that verbs change form to indicate person and number. Even in the present

> **Tech** **Grammar Checkers and Subject-Verb Agreement**
>
> Grammar checkers in word processing programs can alert you to many subject-verb agreement problems, but they can also miss errors and can flag some constructions as errors that are not. Make your own informed judgment about any changes the computer might recommend.

620

tense, they have only two forms. One form, which ends in *-s*, is for third-person singular subjects; the other is for all other subjects.

	Singular		Plural	
	subject	**verb**	**subject**	**verb**
First Person	I	vote	we	vote
Second Person	you	vote	you	vote
Third Person	he, she, it, the student	vote**s**	they, the students	vote

> **More about**
> The forms of regular and irregular verbs, 636–44

Most nouns form the plural with the addition of an *-s* (*dog, dogs*) or *-es* (*coach, coaches*).

In other words, an *-s* on a noun makes the noun plural; an *-s* on a present-tense verb makes the verb singular:

> **More about**
> Regular and irregular plural nouns, 569–71

	Noun	**Verb**
Singular	The dog	bark**s**
Plural	The dog**s**	bark

NOTE Nouns with irregular plurals include *woman* (plural *women*), *foot* (plural *feet*), *child* (plural *children*), and *phenomenon* (plural *phenomena*).

> **verb phrase** A *main verb* together with any *auxiliary*, or *helping*, *verbs*. The main verb carries the principal meaning of the phrase; the auxiliaries provide information about tense, voice, and mood.

1. Agreement with *be* and with helping verbs

Unlike any other English verb, *be* has three present-tense forms (*am, are, is*) and two past-tense forms (*was, were*). In **verb phrases** that begin with a form of *be, have,* or *do* as a helping verb, the subject agrees with the helping verb.

	⊢— subject —⊣	⊢— verb phrase —⊣
SINGULAR	The *price* of oil	*has* been fluctuating.
PLURAL	Commodity *prices*	*have* been fluctuating.
SINGULAR	The *price*	*was* fluctuating.
PLURAL	*Prices*	*were* fluctuating.

> **More about**
> Forms of *be, have,* and *do,* 639–41

The modal auxiliaries—*can, could, may, might, must, shall, should, will, would,* and *ought to*—have only a single form; they do not take an *-s* ending for third-person singular subjects.

> **More about**
> Modal auxiliaries, 628–31

	⊢subject⊣	⊢verb phrase⊣
SINGULAR	The *price*	*can* change.
PLURAL	*Prices*	*can* change.

Writing Responsibly | Dialect Variation in Subject-Verb Agreement

The rules of subject-verb agreement are not the same in all dialects of English. In various communities in the English-speaking world, you might hear people say things like *"The cats is hungry," "We was at the store," "That coat needs washed,"* or *"She be walking to school."* In the contexts in which they occur, these variations are not mistakes; they reflect rules, but those rules are different from those of Standard American English. Still, the subject-verb agreement rules of Standard American English are what most readers in the United States expect to encounter.

to AUDIENCE

2. Subject-verb agreement pitfalls

> **More about**
> Identifying sentence subjects, 585–87

The basic rules of subject-verb agreement may be clear, but writers (and speakers) nonetheless often trip over them. As the Quick Reference box on the next page indicates, these errors usually involve problems identifying the subject of a sentence and determining whether it is singular or plural.

36b Ignoring Words That Intervene between the Subject and the Verb

In English, the subject of a sentence is usually near the verb. As a result, writers sometimes mistakenly treat words that fall between the subject and the verb as if they were the subject. The writer of the following sentence mistook the singular noun phrase *Order of the Phoenix* for the true subject, the plural noun *members*. The revision corrects the agreement error.

FAULTY The members of the Order of the Phoenix is dedicated to thwarting Voldemort.

REVISED The members of the Order of the Phoenix are dedicated to thwarting Voldemort.

NOTE When a singular subject is followed by a phrase that begins with *as well as, in addition to, together with,* or some similar expression, the verb is singular, not plural.

▶ Harry Potter, together with the other members of the Order of the Phoenix, ~~are~~ *is* determined to thwart Voldemort.

Grammar Matters • Distinguishing Plural from Singular Compound Subjects   agr   **36c**   623

> **Quick Reference** — Avoiding Subject-Verb Agreement Pitfalls
>
> 1. Ignore words that intervene between the subject and the verb. (622)
> 2. Distinguish plural from singular compound subjects. (623)
> 3. Distinguish singular from plural indefinite pronouns. (625)
> 4. Understand collective noun subjects. (625)
> 5. Find agreement when the subject is a measurement, a number, or the word *number*. (626)
> 6. Recognize that some nouns that end in *-s* are singular. (627)
> 7. Treat titles, words as words, and gerund phrases as singular. (627)
> 8. Match the number of a relative pronoun subject (*who, which, that*) to its antecedent. (628)
> 9. Match the verb to the subject when the subject follows the verb. (629)
> 10. Match a linking verb with its subject, not its subject complement. (629)

36c Distinguishing Plural from Singular Compound Subjects

A *compound subject* consists of two or more subjects joined by a *conjunction* (*Jack and Jill, one or another*).

> **conjunction** Part of speech that joins words, phrases, or clauses to other words, phrases, or clauses and specifies the way the joined elements relate to each other

1. Compounds joined by *and* or *both . . . and*

Most compound subjects joined by *and* or *both . . . and* are plural.

▸ Twitter *and* Facebook *are* two popular social networking websites.

▸ *Both* Twitter *and* Facebook *allow* users to post links to photos and videos.

A compound subject joined by *and* is singular, however, if the items in the compound refer to the same person or thing.

▸ The winner *and* next president *is* the candidate with the most electoral votes.

A compound subject joined by *and* is also singular if it begins with *each* or *every*.

▸ *Each* paper *and* exam *contributes* to your final grade.

However, if it is followed by *each*, a compound joined by *and* is plural.

▸ The research paper *and* the final exam *each contribute* 25 percent toward your final grade.

2. Compounds joined by *or, nor, either . . . or, neither . . . nor*

When a compound subject is joined by *or, nor, either . . . or,* or *neither . . . nor,* the verb agrees with the part of the compound that is closest to the verb.

▶ *Neither* the coach *nor* the players <u>were</u> worried by the other team's early lead.

> The second part of the compound is plural, so the verb is plural.

Applying this rule can produce an awkward result when the first item in a compound is plural and the second is singular. Reversing the order often resolves the problem.

AWKWARD   *Neither* the players *nor* the coach <u>is</u> happy about last night's loss.

REVISED   *Neither* the coach *nor* the players <u>are</u> happy about last night's loss.

Sometimes the result is so awkward that the only solution is to reword the sentence. This happens particularly when the subject includes the pronouns *I, we,* or *you* and the verb is a form of *be.*

AWKWARD   *Neither* Carla *nor* I <u>am leaving</u> until the job is finished.

REVISED   Carla *and* I <u>are not leaving</u> until the job is finished.

or

Neither Carla *nor* I <u>will leave</u> until the job is finished.

➔ EXERCISE 36.1 Making subjects and verbs agree

Underline the subject in each of the following sentences, and then circle the verb that agrees with it.

EXAMPLE

Mr. Jefferson's <u>computer</u>, as well as its programs, (is)/ are) out of date.

1. The members of the panel (agrees/agree) that he needs a new computer.
2. Many students today (has/have) their own very fast computers.
3. Both Ms. Lopez and Mr. Handler (is/are) installing new software on their computers.
4. Mr. Jefferson's old computer (prevents/prevent) him from using that software.
5. His new computer and software (is/are) scheduled to arrive next week.

36d Distinguishing Singular and Plural Indefinite Pronouns

Indefinite pronouns (see the Quick Reference box below) refer to unknown or unspecified people, quantities, or things. Most indefinite pronouns always take a singular verb:

▶ *Everybody talks* about the weather, but *nobody does* anything about it.
—Attributed to Mark Twain

Some indefinite pronouns (*both, few, many, others, several*) always take a plural verb:

▶ *Many* of us *make* New Year's resolutions, but *few* of us *keep* them.

Some indefinite pronouns (*all, any, more, most, some*) are either singular or plural, depending on context:

▶ *Some* of these questions *are* hard.

▶ *Some* of this test *is* hard.

In the first sentence, *some* takes a plural verb because it refers to the plural noun *questions;* in the second sentence, *some* takes a singular verb because it refers to the singular noun *test*.

36e Understanding Collective Noun Subjects

A **collective noun** designates a collection, or group, of individuals: *audience, chorus, committee, faculty, family, government.* In US English, a collective noun is singular when it refers to the group acting as a whole.

> **Quick Reference** — **Common Indefinite Pronouns**
>
> **Always singular:** *another, anybody, anyone, anything, each, either, everybody, everyone, everything, much, neither, nobody, no one, nothing, one, somebody, someone, something*
>
> **Always plural:** *both, few, many, others, several*
>
> **Variable:** *all, any, more, most, some*

> The *faculty is* revising the general education requirements.
>
> The group acts as a whole.

A collective noun is plural when it refers to the members of the group acting individually.

> The *faculty are* unable to agree on the new requirements.
>
> The individual members of the group disagree among themselves.

If this usage sounds odd to you, however, you can reword the sentence with a clearly plural subject.

> The *members* of the faculty *are* unable to agree on the new requirements.

36f Finding Agreement When the Subject Is a Measurement, a Number, or the Word *Number*

Numbers, fractions, and units of measure take a singular verb when they refer to an undifferentiated mass or quantity.

> Almost *400,000,000 gallons* of gasoline *is* consumed every day in the United States.

> *One-fourth* of the world's oil *is* consumed in the United States.

> *Seven thousand dollars is* too high a price for that car.

Numbers, fractions, and units of measure take a plural verb when they refer to a collection of individual people or things.

> Recently, *more than 600,000 immigrants* annually *have become* naturalized citizens of the United States.

- *About a third* of the citizens naturalized in 2007 <u>were</u> from Asia.

- *More than 7 billion pennies* <u>were</u> minted in 2007.

The word *number* is plural when it appears with *a* but singular when it appears with *the*.

- *A number* of voters <u>are</u> in favor of the transportation bond.

- *The number* of voters in favor of the transportation bond <u>is</u> low.

36g Recognizing Nouns That Are Singular Even Though They End in -s

Some nouns that end in *-s* are singular. Examples include diseases like *diabetes* and *measles*.

- *Measles* <u>is</u> a contagious disease.

Words like *economics, mathematics,* and *physics* are singular when they refer to an entire field of study or body of knowledge.

- *Economics* <u>is</u> a popular major at many schools.

They are plural, however, when they refer to a set of individual traits related to the field of study.

- *The economics* of the music industry <u>are</u> changing rapidly.

36h Treating Titles, Words as Words, and Gerund Phrases as Singular

The titles of books, articles, movies, and other works; the names of companies and institutions; the names of countries; and words treated as words are all singular even if they are plural in form.

- *Harry Potter and the Order of the Phoenix is* the fifth of J. K. Rowling's seven Harry Potter books.

- *The Centers for Disease Control and Prevention helps* protect the nation's health.

- *The United States is* one of the world's largest food exporters.

- *Fungi is* one of two acceptable plural forms of the word *fungus; funguses is* the other.

> **gerund** The present participle (*-ing* form) of a verb used as a noun

Gerunds and gerund phrases are also always singular.

- *Conducting excavations is* just one part of an archaeologist's job.

36i Matching a Relative Pronoun (*Who, Which,* or *That*) to Its Antecedent When the Pronoun Is the Subject of a Subordinate Clause

> **More about**
> Pronouns and their antecedents, 630–35, 664–68

A relative pronoun (*who, which,* or *that*) that functions as the subject of a subordinate clause is singular if its **antecedent** (the word it refers to) is singular, but it is plural if its antecedent is plural.

- People *who live* in glass houses should not throw stones.

- The cactus is a plant *that thrives* in a hot, dry environment.

Be careful with antecedent phrases that include the expressions *one of* or *only one of*. *One of* usually signals a plural antecedent; *only one of* signals a singular antecedent.

- Bill Clinton is *one of several presidents* of the United States *who were elected* to two terms.

  Several presidents were elected to two terms, and one of them was Clinton. The pronoun *who* refers to the plural noun *presidents*.

Grammar Matters • Matching a Linking Verb with Its Subject, Not Its Subject Complement **agr 36k** 629

▶ Franklin D. Roosevelt is *the only one* of those presidents *who was elected* to more than two terms.

Only one president, Roosevelt, was elected to more than two terms. The pronoun *who* refers to that particular one and is singular.

36j Finding Agreement When the Subject Follows the Verb

If you reverse normal order and put the subject after the verb for emphasis or dramatic effect, be sure the verb agrees with the actual subject, not a different word that precedes the verb.

> **More about**
> Inverted word order, 532

▶ Onto the tennis court *stride* the defending champion and her challenger.

The subject is the plural compound *the defending champion and her challenger,* not the singular term *tennis court.*

The subject also follows the verb in sentences that begin with *there* followed by a form of *be* (*there is, there are, there was, there were*).

▶ ~~There's~~ *There are* more people registered to vote than actually vote on Election Day.

The subject, *people,* is plural, so the verb should be plural.

36k Matching a Linking Verb with Its Subject, Not Its Subject Complement

A **linking verb** (such as *was* or *were*) connects the subject of a sentence to a **subject complement,** which describes or refers to the subject. When either the subject or the subject complement is singular but the other is plural, make sure the verb agrees with the subject.

> **More about**
> Linking verbs and subject complements, 589

▶ One influential voting bloc in the election ~~were~~ *was* young voters.

The subject is the singular noun *bloc,* not the plural noun *voters.*

EXERCISE 36.2 Making subjects and verbs agree

Underline the subject in each of the following sentences and circle the verb. If the verb agrees with the subject, do nothing else. If the subject and verb do not agree, write the correct form of the verb at the end of the sentence.

EXAMPLE

sounds
The traffic sound very loud.

1. The number of vehicles using Reynolds Road have nearly doubled in a year.
2. Mr. Ojiba is the only one of the Town Council members who agrees with the proposal to install traffic-slowing speed bumps in the road.
3. A significant number of residents is opposed to installing traffic lights.
4. There was no other solution proposed to the Council.
5. The road provides a much more direct route into the city.
6. Everyone want there to be a solution to this problem.

PRONOUN-ANTECEDENT AGREEMENT

Pronouns rename or take the place of nouns, noun phrases, or other pronouns. The word or phrase that a pronoun replaces is its ***antecedent.*** Pronouns and their antecedents must agree in person (first, second, or third), number (singular or plural), and gender (neuter, feminine, or masculine). The antecedent usually appears before the pronoun but sometimes follows it. The two pronouns in the following example have the same antecedent—*Emma*—which follows the first pronoun and precedes the second.

▶ In *her* haste, *Emma* shut down the computer without saving *her* work.

A Possessive Pronoun Agrees with Its Antecedent, Not the Word It Modifies
In English, a possessive pronoun (such as *his, hers,* or *its*) agrees with its antecedent, not the word it modifies. In the following example, *father* is the antecedent, so the pronoun should be masculine.

▶ The father beamed joyfully at ~~her~~ *his* newborn daughter.

Grammar Matters • Matching Pronouns with Indefinite Pronoun and Generic Noun Antecedents   agr   **36l**   **631**

> **Tech** **Grammar Checkers and Pronoun-Antecedent Agreement**
>
> Grammar checkers in word processing programs cannot identify pronoun-antecedent agreement errors.

As with subject-verb agreement, the basic rule of pronoun-antecedent agreement—match the pronoun to its antecedent in person, number, and gender—is uncomplicated. However, writers often find themselves uncertain how to apply the rule in certain situations, as the Quick Reference box below summarizes.

36l Matching Pronouns with Indefinite Pronoun and Generic Noun Antecedents

Antecedents that are singular but have a plural sense are among the most common sources of pronoun-antecedent confusion. These include the following:

> **More about**
> Singular and plural indefinite pronouns, 625

- **Indefinite pronouns** such as *each, everybody,* and *everyone* that are singular even though they refer to groups.
- **Generic nouns**—that is, singular nouns used to designate a whole class of people or things rather than a specific individual. In this sentence, for example—*The aspiring doctor faces years of rigorous training*—the expression *aspiring doctor* generically designates all would-be doctors.

1. Singular indefinite pronoun or generic noun antecedents

A pronoun with a singular indefinite pronoun or generic noun antecedent should be singular. Do not let the plural sense of the antecedent distract you.

▸ The dog is a domesticated animal, unlike ~~their~~ *its* cousins the wolf and coyote.

The antecedent is the singular generic noun *dog,* so the pronoun should be singular too.

> **Quick Reference** **Avoiding Pronoun-Antecedent Agreement Pitfalls**
>
> 1. Match pronouns with indefinite pronoun and generic noun antecedents. (631)
> 2. Match pronouns with collective noun antecedents. (634)
> 3. Match pronouns with compound antecedents. (634)

More about
Avoiding gender bias, 545–47

This rule creates a problem, however, when the indefinite antecedent refers to both women and men. Correct agreement requires a singular pronoun, but using *he* as a substitute for either *man* or *woman* results in gender bias.

GRAMMATICALLY CORRECT BUT GENDER-BIASED AGREEMENT

In past downturns *the affluent consumer* continued to spend, but now even *he* is cutting back.

Writers often try to avoid this conflict with a gender-neutral plural pronoun such as *they*, resulting in faulty pronoun-antecedent agreement.

UNBIASED BUT GRAMMATICALLY INCORRECT AGREEMENT

In past downturns, *the affluent consumer* continued to spend, but now even *they* are cutting back.

This usage is common in everyday speech, but it is inappropriate for formal writing (although, as the Writing Responsibly box on the next page suggests, some language experts now think differently).

You can avoid both gender bias and faulty agreement by rephrasing according to one of these strategies:

1. Make both the antecedent and the pronoun plural.

   ▶ In past downturns, ~~the affluent consumer~~ *affluent consumers* continued to spend, but now even ~~he is~~ *they are* cutting back.

2. Rephrase the sentence without the pronoun.

   ▶ ~~In past downturns, the~~ *Even the* affluent consumer continued to spend *, who* ~~but now even he~~ is cutting back. *in past downturns, now*

Quick Reference

Three Strategies for Avoiding Gender Bias with Indefinite Antecedents

1. Make both the antecedent and the pronoun plural.
2. Rephrase the sentence without the pronoun.
3. Use *he or she, she or he,* or the appropriate variant (for example, *him or her* or *her or him*), but sparingly.

Writing Responsibly: Using a Plural Pronoun with a Singular Antecedent

The use of a plural pronoun with singular indefinite antecedents is common in everyday speech, and many language experts now maintain that it should be acceptable in formal writing, too. It is a usage, after all, that some of the finest writers in the English language have seen fit to employ:

> God send everyone their heart's desire!
> —Shakespeare, *Much Ado About Nothing*, 3.4

> Everybody who comes to Southampton finds it either their duty or pleasure to call upon us....
> —Jane Austen, from a letter

Nonetheless, many readers still find the usage grating, so it is best to avoid it when you are writing for a general audience in an academic or business context.

to AUDIENCE

3. Use *he or she* or the appropriate variant (for example, *him or her* or *her or him*), but sparingly.

   ▶ In past downturns, the affluent consumer continued to spend, but even ^(she or) he is now cutting back.

CAUTION Avoid overusing the phrases *he or she* and *his or her*. They can make your text sound stuffy and strained.

2. Plural or variable indefinite pronoun antecedents

Although most indefinite pronouns are singular, some (*both, few, many, others, several*) are always plural.

   ▶ *Both* of the candidates released *their* income tax returns.

Others (*all, any, more, most, some*) are singular or plural depending on the context.

   ▶ When the teacher surprised the *students* with a pop quiz, she discovered that *most* had not been doing *their* homework.

   ▶ Although some of the river's *water* is diverted for irrigation, *most* still makes *its* way to the sea.

36m Matching Pronouns with Collective Noun Antecedents

Collective nouns (for example, *audience, chorus, committee, faculty, family, government*) are singular when they refer to a group acting as a whole.

▸ *My family* traces *its* roots to West Africa.

Collective nouns are plural when they refer to the members of a group acting individually.

▸ *The billionaire's family* fought over *their* inheritance.

36n Matching Pronouns with Compound Antecedents

Compound antecedents joined by *and* are usually plural and take a plural pronoun.

▸ *Clinton and Obama* were the leading candidates for *their* party's nomination.

Pronouns with compound antecedents joined by *or, nor, either . . . or,* or *neither . . . nor* agree with the nearest antecedent. To avoid awkwardness when one of the antecedents is plural and the other singular, put the plural antecedent second.

▸ *Neither the coach nor the players* worried that *their* team might lose.

When the antecedents differ in gender or person, however, the results of the "nearest antecedent" rule can be so awkward that the only solution is to reword the sentence:

AWKWARD	It was clear after the New Hampshire primary that either Barack Obama or Hillary Clinton would find herself the Democratic Party's nominee for president.
REVISED	It was clear after the New Hampshire primary that either Barack Obama or Hillary Clinton would be the Democratic Party's nominee for president.

EXERCISE 36.3 Editing for pronoun-antecedent agreement

Edit the following sentences to correct errors in pronoun-antecedent agreement and avoid gender bias.

EXAMPLE

Zoe and her parents felt as though something was missing from ~~her~~ *their* family.

1. Nearly every home in their neighborhood had their own dog, cat, or other type of pet.
2. That is why the Conyer family was slowly walking through the animal shelter, looking over every animal as Zoe, Robert, and their parents passed his cage.
3. Some of the dogs they passed barked frantically, but others just lay idly in his or her cages.
4. Then Robert pointed to a puppy enthusiastically pawing at their cage and whining to attract the family's attention.
5. That's when they found Molly, a cheerful, agreeable, and gentle dog who immediately immersed itself in the life of the Conyer family.

Make It **Your Own**

Reread several papers that you have recently written and note where you handled agreement issues well. If you see areas in need of revision, edit them and add this issue to your revision checklist.

37 Using Verbs

IN THIS CHAPTER

VERB FORMS

a. Basic verb forms, 636
b. Regular and irregular verbs, 638
c. Complete verbs, 639
d. *-s* or *-es*, *-d* or *-ed* endings, 642
e. *rise/raise, sit/set, lie/lay*, 643

TENSE

f. Verb tenses, 644
g. Uses of the present tense, 647
h. Tense sequence, 648

MOOD

i. Verb moods, 650
j. The subjunctive, 650

VOICE

k. Verb voice, 652
l. Active versus passive, 653

Verbs are the driving force in a sentence. They specify the action (*Sylvia won the race*), occurrence (*She became a runner in high school*), or state of being (*She was tired after the meet*) that affects the subject. Verbs also provide information about time (**tense**), the identity of the subject (**person** and **number**), whether the subject is acting or being acted on (**voice**), and the attitude or manner of the writer or speaker (**mood**) (see the Quick Reference box on the next page).

VERB FORMS

37a Understanding the Basic Forms of Verbs

With the exception of the verb *be*, all verbs have five forms: base, *-s* form, past tense, past participle, and present participle.

	Base Form	*-s* Form	Past Tense	Past Participle	Present Participle
Regular Verb	campaign	campaigns	campaigned	campaigned	campaigning
Irregular Verb	choose	chooses	chose	chosen	choosing

636

> **Quick Reference** — **What Information Do Verbs Reveal?**
>
> Verbs provide information about tense, person and number, voice, and mood.
> - **Tense.** When does the action occur? In the **present** (*laugh/laughs*), **past** (*laughed*), or **future** (*will laugh*)?
> - **Person.** Does the verb form tell you that the subject is speaking (*I laugh*), spoken to (*You should laugh*), or spoken about (*He laughs*)?
> - **Number.** Are the subject and its accompanying verb **singular** (*He laughs*) or **plural** (*They laugh*)?
> - **Mood.** Is the verb **indicative**, stating or questioning something about the subject (*He laughs*)? Is it **imperative**, giving a command (*Douse the coach!*)? Is it **subjunctive**, expressing a possibility (*If the coach were doused again, she might lose patience with her players*)?
> - **Voice.** Is the verb **active**, with the subject performing the action (*He laughs*), or **passive**, with the subject being acted upon (*The coach is doused with water by her players*)?

- The *base form* is what you find when you look up a verb in the dictionary. Use it with a plural noun or the pronouns *I, we, you,* or *they* to express a present or habitual action, occurrence, or state of being.

  ▸ Presidential candidates *campaign* every four years.

  ▸ I usually *choose* candidates based on their policies.

- The *-s form* is the base form plus *-s* or *-es.* Use it with a singular noun or a singular pronoun (*he, she, it*) to express present or habitual action, occurrence, or state of being.

  > **More about**
  > Verb tenses, 644–52
  > Voice, 652–55

  ▸ My favorite senator always *campaigns* in our town.

  ▸ She *chooses* positive messages instead of negative ones.

- The past-tense form of regular verbs such as *campaign* is the base form plus *-d* or *-ed;* the past-tense forms of irregular verbs such as *choose* vary. Use the past tense with singular or plural subjects to express past action, occurrence, or state of being.

  ▸ The mayor *campaigned* downtown yesterday.

  ▸ Some people *chose* to protest his appearance.

- The past participle is the same as the past tense in most verbs but varies in some irregular verbs. Use the past participle in combination with forms of *have* to form the perfect tenses and with forms of *be* to form the passive voice.

  ▸ The candidate *has campaigned* nonstop.

  ▸ Our town *was chosen* by the candidate for his last campaign stop.

- The present participle of all verbs, regular and irregular, is formed by adding *-ing* to the base form. Use the present participle with forms of *be* to form the progressive tenses.

    ▶ Senator Brown *is campaigning* here today.

    ▶ They *have been choosing* a running mate.

NOTE Past and present participles sometimes function as **verbals**, not verbs. Past participles, for example, can sometimes be modifiers (*an educated public*), and present participles can be modifiers (*her opening statement*) or nouns (*campaigning is exhausting*).

> **More about**
> Verb forms as modifiers, 592–94

> **verbal** A verb form that functions as a noun, adjective, or adverb

37b Using Regular and Irregular Verb Forms Correctly

The vast majority of English verbs are **regular**, meaning that their past-tense and past-participle forms end in *-d* or *-ed*:

Base	Past Tense	Past Participle
climb	climb**ed**	climb**ed**
analyze	analyze**d**	analyze**d**
copy	cop**ied**	cop**ied**

However, about two hundred English verbs are **irregular**, with past-tense and past-participle forms that do not follow one set pattern:

Base	Past Tense	Past Participle
build	built	built
eat	ate	eaten
see	saw	seen

The forms of irregular verbs can easily be confused.

▶ My wool shirt ~~shrunk~~ *shrank* when I washed it in hot water.

Tech Grammar Checkers and Verb Problems

Grammar checkers in word processing programs will spot some errors that involve irregular or missing verbs, verb endings, and the subjunctive mood, but they will miss other errors and may suggest incorrect solutions. You must look for verb errors yourself and carefully evaluate any suggestions from a grammar checker.

If you are unsure whether a verb is regular or irregular or what form you should use in a particular situation, consult a dictionary or the Quick Reference box on page 640. In the dictionary, you will find any irregular forms listed in the entry for the base form of a verb.

EXERCISE 37.1 Choosing the correct irregular verb

In the following sentences, fill in the blank with the correct form of the word in parentheses.

EXAMPLE

The *Titanic* __sank__ (sink) after it __struck__ (strike) an iceberg.

1. Today, ships with special hulls _____ (cut) through new ice to _____ (take) tourists to _____ (see) Antarctica.
2. One photographer on an arctic cruise _____ (say) she _____ (take) a photograph of Gentoo penguins that _____ (have) bright orange beaks.
3. She _____ (write) in her journal that she _____ (see) their big tails _____ (swing) from side-to-side as they walked.
4. When a naturalist _____ (tell) them these birds may _____ (become) extinct because the temperature has _____ (rise), reducing the _____ (freeze) area where they live, she _____ (feel) very sad.

37c Combining Main Verbs with Helping Verbs to Form Complete Verbs

Almost all verb constructions other than the present and past tenses require the combination of a ***main verb*** with one or more ***helping verbs*** (or ***auxiliary verbs***) in a ***verb phrase***. The most common helping verbs are *be, have,* and *do,* all three of which can also function as main verbs (*they <u>are</u> hungry; she <u>had</u> lunch; they <u>did</u> the dishes*). *Be,* unlike any other English verb, has eight forms.

FORMS OF *BE*

Base		be
Present Tense	I	am
	we, you, they	are
	he, she, it	is
Past Tense	I, he, she, it	was
	we, you, they	were
Past Participle		been
Present Participle		being

Quick Reference: Common Irregular Verbs

Base Form	Past Tense	Past Participle	Base Form	Past Tense	Past Participle
arise	arose	arisen	leave	left	left
be	was/were	been	lend	lent	lent
bear	bore	borne, born	let	let	let
beat	beat	beaten	lie (recline)†	lay	lain
become	became	become	lose	lost	lost
begin	began	begun	make	made	made
bid	bid	bid	mean	meant	meant
bite	bit	bitten, bit	pay	paid	paid
blow	blew	blown	prove	proved	proved, proven
break	broke	broken	quit	quit	quit
bring	brought	brought	read	read	read
build	built	built	ride	rode	ridden
burst	burst	burst	ring	rang	rung
buy	bought	bought	rise	rose	risen
catch	caught	caught	run	ran	run
choose	chose	chosen	say	said	said
come	came	come	see	saw	seen
cost	cost	cost	send	sent	sent
cut	cut	cut	set	set	set
dig	dug	dug	shake	shook	shaken
dive	dived, dove	dived	shoot	shot	shot
do	did	done	shrink	shrank	shrunk
draw	drew	drawn	sing	sang	sung
drink	drank	drunk	sink	sank	sunk
drive	drove	driven	sit	sat	sat
eat	ate	eaten	sleep	slept	slept
fall	fell	fallen	slid	slid	slid
feel	felt	felt	speak	spoke	spoken
fight	fought	fought	spend	spent	spent
find	found	found	spread	spread	spread
flee	fled	fled	spring	sprang, sprung	sprung
fly	flew	flown	stand	stood	stood
forget	forgot	forgotten, forgot	steal	stole	stolen
freeze	froze	frozen	strike	struck	struck, stricken
get	got	gotten, got	swim	swam	swum
give	gave	given	swing	swung	swung
go	went	gone	take	took	taken
grow	grew	grown	teach	taught	taught
hang (suspend)*	hung	hung	tear	tore	torn
have	had	had	tell	told	told
hear	heard	heard	think	thought	thought
hold	held	held	throw	threw	thrown
hide	hid	hidden	wake	woke, waked	waked, woken
hit	hit	hit	wear	wore	worn
keep	kept	kept	win	won	won
know	knew	known	wind	wound	wound
lay	laid	laid	write	wrote	written
lead	led	led			

*Hang is regular—hang, hanged, hanged—when used to mean "kill by hanging."
†Lie is regular—lie, lied, lied—when used to mean "to be untruthful."

FORMS OF *HAVE* AND *DO*

Present Tense (Base and -s Form)	I, you, we, they he, she, it	have has	do does
Past Tense		had	did
Past Participle		had	done
Present Participle		having	doing

The ***modal verbs**—can, could, may, might, must, shall, should, will, would,* and *ought to*—function only as helping verbs. Modals indicate ability, intention, permission, possibility, desire, and suggestion. They do not change form to indicate number or tense.

Modal Verbs English modal verbs have a range of meanings and unusual grammatical characteristics that you may find challenging. For example, they do not change form to indicate number or tense:

> More about
> Modals, 728–30

▸ In a close election, one vote ~~cans~~ *can* make a difference.

The main verb carries the principal meaning of the verb phrase; the helping verbs, if any, carry information about tense and voice. A **complete verb** is a verb phrase with all the elements needed to determine tense, voice, and mood. Main verbs can stand alone as complete verbs only in their present-tense and past-tense forms.

▸ The candidates [*main verb:* campaigned] until Election Day.

Main verbs in other forms (past or present participles) require helping verbs.

▸ The candidates [*helping verbs:* have been] [*main verb:* campaigning] for almost two years.

Sometimes in informal speech you can drop needed helping verbs, and some dialects allow certain constructions as complete verbs that Standard English does not allow. Helping verbs can sometimes be contracted (*they've voted already, we'll register tomorrow*) but in formal writing should never be omitted entirely.

▸ The candidates *have* been campaigning for almost two years.

CAUTION Do not use *of* for *have* in a verb phrase with a modal. When you use informal contractions like *could've* or *might've* in speech, remember that they mean *could have* and *might have*.

37d Including -s or -es, -d or -ed Endings When Required

> **More about**
> Subject-verb agreement, 620–30

Sometimes when speaking informally, you can omit the verb endings *-s*, *-es*, *-d*, or *-ed* or blend the sound of an ending inaudibly with the initial sound of the following word. Some dialects do not always require these endings. In formal writing, include them, or not, as standard usage requires.

▶ My dad ~~say~~ *says* I am ~~suppose~~ *supposed* to mow the lawn. I also ~~needs~~ *need* to trim the hedges. Before he ~~move~~ *moved* to Phoenix, my brother ~~use~~ *used* to do the mowing.

> **More about**
> Phrasal verbs, 722–24

Phrasal Verbs Phrasal verbs, such as *ask out* and *give in*, combine a verb with one or more prepositions or adverbs known as particles. The verb and particle combination of a phrasal verb has a distinct meaning, one that is different from the stand-alone words that form it. Because phrasal verbs are idiomatic, native English speakers are usually comfortable using them spontaneously. But that does not mean they can explain why one "gets on" a plane but "gets in" a boat.

EXERCISE 37.2 Correcting verb endings

In the following sentences, correct any verbs that have the wrong or missing verb endings *-s*, *-es*, *-d*, or *-ed*.

EXAMPLE
In our first year of college, many of us ~~mix~~ *mixed* studying with partying, but not one of us ~~do~~ *does* that now.

1. Tonight, Eyal and Aaron wants to see the movie, but Franco and I are determine to get our papers finish before we goes out.
2. I use to do my work at the last minute, so I never revise my papers.
3. Last semester I declare my major, so now I am concern about my grades.

4. My roommate say she go to the Writing Center, and they have always helps her.
5. I schedule an appointment for next week, before we go to the party.

37e Distinguishing *Rise* from *Raise*, *Sit* from *Set*, *Lie* from *Lay*

The forms of *rise* and *raise, sit* and *set,* and *lie* and *lay* are easily confused. One verb in each pair (*rise, sit,* and *lie*) is **intransitive,** meaning that it does not take a direct object. The other verb in each pair (*raise, set,* and *lay*) is **transitive,** meaning that it does take a direct object (underlined in the following examples).

> **More about**
> Transitive and intransitive verbs, 588–91

- *Rise* means "to move or stand up." *Raise* means "to cause something (the direct object) to rise."
    ▶ The plane *rises* into the air. The pilot *raises* the landing gear.
- *Sit* means "to be seated." *Set* means "to place or put something (the direct object) on a surface."
    ▶ The passengers in coach *sit* in cramped seats. The attendants *set* drinks on their trays.
- *Lie* means "to recline." *Lay* means "to place or put something (the direct object) on a surface."
    ▶ The passengers in first class *lie* in fully reclining seats. During the landing, the pilot *lays* the plane gently on the runway.

Quick Reference: Distinguishing *Rise* from *Raise*, *Sit* from *Set*, and *Lie* from *Lay*

Base Form	-s Form	Past Tense	Past Participle	Present Participle
rise (to get up)	rises	rose	risen	rising
raise (to lift)	raises	raised	raised	raising
sit (to be seated)	sits	sat	sat	sitting
set (to place)	sets	set	set	setting
lie (to recline)	lies	lay	lain	lying
lay (to place)	lays	laid	laid	laying

A further difficulty with *lie* and *lay* is their confusing overlap of forms: The past tense of *lie* is *lay,* whereas the past tense of *lay* is *laid.* Changing the previous example to the past tense illustrates the issue.

▶ The passengers in first class ~~laid~~ *lay* in fully reclining seats. During the landing, the pilot ~~lay~~ *laid* the plane gently on the runway.

➤ EXERCISE 37.3 Using *rise/raise, sit/set,* and *lie/lay* correctly

In the following paragraph, correct any errors involving *rise/raise, sit/set,* and *lie/lay.*

> Senna began her daily exercise routine as soon as she raised from bed. She seldom laid in bed long after her alarm went off. She usually set the alarm to go off at 4:30 a.m. Most of her neighbors were still laying in their beds when she was rising barbells over her head. Each time she rose a weight, she held it up for several seconds, then gently sat it down. She would also set on the floor and later lay down flat for some stretching exercises. After these warm-ups, Senna went out for a run and watched the sun raise over the lake. As she ran, she tried not to rise her knees too high, and she never let her arms lay idly at her side. Home again from her run, she would sometimes lay down again for a few minutes before beginning her workday.

TENSE

37f Understanding Which Verb Tense to Use

Verb *tenses* provide information about the time in which an action or event occurs—past, present, or future—about whether or not the action is ongoing or completed, and about the time of one action relative to another.

1. Simple tenses

Use the *simple present tense* for current or habitual actions or events and to state general truths. Accompanied by a reference to a future event, the simple present can also indicate a future occurrence (also see *section 37h*).

CURRENT ACTION	Hernando *opens* the door to his classroom.
HABITUAL ACTION	He *enjoys* teaching second-graders.

| GENERAL TRUTH | Earth *is* the third planet from the sun. |
| FUTURE OCCURRENCE | Winter *ends* in two weeks. |

Use the *simple past tense* for completed actions or occurrences.

▶ The bell *rang*. Hernando *asked* his students to be quiet.

Use the *simple future tense* for actions that have not yet occurred.

▶ He *will give* them a spelling test this afternoon.

2. Perfect tenses

The perfect tenses generally indicate the completion of an action before a particular time. Use the *present perfect tense* for an action that started in the past but is now completed or for an action that started in the past but is ongoing.

| COMPLETED ACTION | I *have read* all the Harry Potter books. |
| ONGOING ACTION | I *have read* books all my life. |

Use the *past perfect tense* for actions completed by a specific time in the past or before another past action.

▶ Because the students *had studied* hard for their test, they knew most of the spelling words.

The studying—*had studied* (past perfect)—came before the knowing—*knew* (simple past).

Use the *future perfect tense* for an action that will be completed by a definite time in the future.

▶ By the time the semester ends, Hernando's students *will have improved* their spelling grades.

3. Progressive tenses

The progressive tenses indicate ongoing action. Use the *present progressive tense* for an action that is ongoing in the present.

▶ Matilda *is learning* Spanish.

Use the *past progressive tense* for an action that was ongoing in the past.

▶ Last night, Yue *was practicing* for her recital.

> **Reference** — **An Overview of Verb Tenses and Their Forms**
>
> **Simple Tenses**
>
> | Tense | Form | Example |
> |---|---|---|
> | Simple present | base or *-s* form | I *learn* something new every day. |
> | Simple past | past tense form | I *learned* Spanish many years ago. |
> | Simple future | *will* + base form | I *will learn* to ski next winter. |
>
> **Perfect Tenses**
>
> | Tense | Form | Example |
> |---|---|---|
> | Present perfect | *has/have* + past participle | I *have learned* to water ski already. |
> | Past perfect | *had* + past participle | I *had learned* to water ski by the time I was nine. |
> | Future perfect | *will have* + past participle | I *will have learned* how to skydive by September. |
>
> **Progressive Tenses**
>
> | Tense | Form | Example |
> |---|---|---|
> | Present progressive | *am/is/are* + present participle | I *am learning* about Japanese food. |
> | Past progressive | *was/were* + present participle | I *was learning* to make sushi yesterday. |
> | Future progressive | *will be* + present participle | I *will be learning* new skills next week. |
> | Present perfect progressive | *have/has been* + present participle | I *have been cooking* seriously since I was a teenager. |
> | Past perfect progressive | *had been* + present participle | I *had been preparing* simple dishes even before then. |
> | Future perfect progressive | *will have been* + present participle | I *will have been enjoying* this hobby for two decades by the end of the year. |

Use the *future progressive tense* for an ongoing action that will occur in the future.

▶ Elena *will be working* as a publishing company intern next summer.

Use the *present perfect progressive tense* for an ongoing action that began in the past.

▶ Hernando *has been working* on his master's degree in education since 2008.

Use the *past perfect progressive tense* for an ongoing past action that is now completed.

▶ Until this semester, he *had been taking* education courses at night.

Use the *future perfect progressive tense* for an ongoing action that will be finished at a definite time in the future.

▶ By the end of August, Hernando *will have been studying* education for more than six years.

Do Not Use the Progressive Tenses with All Verbs Certain verbs, typically those that convey a mental process or a state of being, are not used in the progressive tenses. Examples include *appreciate, belong, contain, envy, fear, know, like, need, owe, own, remember, resemble, seem,* and *want*.

▶ She ~~is seeming~~ [seems] angry with her boyfriend. He ~~was owing~~ [owed] her an apology.

37g Following Conventions for the Use of the Present Tense

The present tense is conventionally used for describing works of art, for describing events in literary works, and for stating scientific facts.

▶ In his 2007 novel *Bridge of Sighs,* Richard Russo ~~told~~ [tells] an engrossing story about the Lynch family, who ~~lived~~ [live] in a small town in upstate New York.

▶ Watson and Crick discovered that DNA ~~had~~ [has] a double helix structure.

Although the discovery was in the past, it remains true.

In general, use the present tense to introduce a quotation, paraphrase, or summary.

▶ As Harriet Lerner ~~noted,~~ [notes,] "Anger is neither legitimate nor illegitimate, meaningful nor pointless. Anger simply is."

> **More about**
> APA documentation style, 347–88

EXCEPTION The APA documentation style calls for the use of the past tense or the past perfect tense for reporting findings or introducing cited material.

▸ Chodoff (2002) ~~claims~~ *claimed* that in their efforts to put a diagnostic label on "all varieties and vagaries of human feelings," psychiatrists ~~risk~~ *risked* medicalizing "the human condition itself."

37h Using Tense Sequence to Clarify Time Relationships

> **More about**
> Inappropriate shifts in tense, 678–79

When a sentence contains two separate actions, readers need a clear idea of the time relationship between them, which writers communicate by their choice of tenses, or ***sequence of tenses.*** Change verb tenses when there is reason to do so, but do not shift tenses unnecessarily.

In a sentence with two past actions, for example, use the simple past tense for both verbs if the actions occurred simultaneously.

▸ When he *arrived* at the station, the train *departed*.

He arrived and the train departed at the same time.

If the actions happened at different times, use the past perfect tense for the action that occurred first.

▸ By the time he *arrived* at the station, the train *had departed*.

The train departed before he arrived.

1. Infinitives and tense sequence

An ***infinitive*** consists of *to* followed by the base form of the verb (*to listen, to go*). Use this form, the *present infinitive,* for an action that occurs after or simultaneously with the action of the main verb.

▸ Ivan is known to be a good student.

The knowing and the being happen together.

▸ Everyone expects Ivan to ace the exam.

The expectation is about Ivan's future performance on the exam.

Use the *perfect infinitive*—*to have* and the past participle (*to have listened, to have gone*)—for an action that happened before the action of the main verb.

- Ivan is said *to have studied* all weekend.
  The studying took place before the talk about it.

2. Participles and tense sequence

Use the present participle (*listening, going*) to express action that happens simultaneously with the action of the main verb, regardless of the tense of the main verb.

- *Handing* her son Robbie a cup of coffee, Mona offered him some brownies.

Use the past participle (*listened, gone*) or the present perfect participle (*having listened, having gone*) to express action that happens before the action of the main verb.

- *Discouraged* by her daughter's aloofness, Mona asked her son to help.
  Mona was discouraged before she asked.

- *Having mediated* their disagreements for years, Robbie refused to intervene.
  Robbie mediated before he refused.

EXERCISE 37.4 Editing for verb tense and verb tense sequence

In the following paragraph, correct any errors in verb tense and revise sentences if necessary to achieve appropriate verb tense sequence.

EXAMPLE

Having worked ~~Working~~ on many knitted items in the past, I realized I ~~will~~ *would* like to earn a living as a knitter.

By the end of this year, I have been knitting for over fifteen years. I was a knitter for as long as I can remember. My mother told me that, when I was about five, she has begun teaching me how to knit. All through my childhood I had always knitted whenever I had sat down to watch television. Once, when my dad had driven us from Memphis to Denver for a vacation, I knitted practically the entire way. By the time we will have arrived in Denver, I knitted most of a sweater for my brother. While I was in high school, I was starting a knitting club. At first, there were only two or three people in the club, but gradually we had recruited several new members, and it was getting to be a lot of fun. Recently, I begun knitting scarves, hats, mittens, and other items to sell on a crafts website. I believe that sometime in the future I will have been making a good living from my knitting.

MOOD

37i Understanding Verb Mood

The *mood* of a verb indicates whether a speaker or writer views what is said as a fact, a command, or a possibility. Most English sentences are in the *indicative mood,* which states facts or opinions and asks questions.

- Our research papers *are* due tomorrow morning.
- *Did* you *say* the deadline had changed?

The *imperative mood* issues commands, gives instructions, or makes requests. The subject of an imperative sentence (*you*) is usually left unstated.

- *Hand in* your papers by Friday afternoon.
- *Turn* left at the third stoplight.
- Please *pass* the salt.

The *subjunctive mood* expresses possibility (or impossibility), as in hypothetical situations, conditions known to be untrue, wishes, suggestions, and requirements.

- If I *were* finished, I could go to bed.
- The doctor suggests that he *get* more exercise.

37j Using the Subjunctive Mood Correctly

The subjunctive has three tenses: present, past, and past perfect. The present subjunctive is always the base form of the verb, regardless of the person or number of the subject: *Ramon asks that his teacher give* (not *gives*) *him an*

Writing Responsibly — Using the Subjunctive in Formal Writing

Because the subjunctive has been fading from everyday usage, the indicative may seem more acceptable to you. Most readers, however, still expect to find the subjunctive used in formal writing.

▶ I wish that I ~~was~~ *were* finished.

to AUDIENCE

---

extension. The past subjunctive of *be* is *were*: *I wish I were* (not *was*) *finished*. For all other verbs, the past subjunctive is identical to the past tense. Similarly, the past perfect subjunctive is identical to the past perfect indicative.

The subjunctive has been fading from everyday usage, and as a result, the indicative (*I wish I was finished*) may seem an acceptable alternative to you. Most readers, however, expect to find the subjunctive used appropriately (*I wish I were finished*) in formal writing.

Clauses with verbs in the subjunctive are always subordinate clauses. They include **conditional clauses** that begin with *if, as if,* or *as though* and describe a condition known to be untrue. Conditional clauses put forward a set of circumstances and modify a main clause that states what follows from those circumstances.

▶ If I *were* taller, I would try out for basketball.

▶ The candidate acts as though he *were* already the winner.

If the main clause includes a modal auxiliary such as *would, could,* or *should,* do not use a similar construction instead of the subjunctive in the *if* clause.

▶ If I ~~would have been~~ *were* taller, I would try out for basketball.

Verbs in the main clause that express a wish, request, recommendation, or demand also trigger the subjunctive in the subordinate clause.

▶ The hikers wished their campground ~~was~~ *were* not so far away.

▶ Citizens are demanding that the government ~~fixes~~ *fix* the economy.

- ▶ Senators have requested that the president ~~is~~ *be* more responsive to the middle class.
- ▶ Alicia's adviser recommended that she ~~takes~~ *take* calculus.

→ EXERCISE 37.5 Using the subjunctive mood correctly

In each of the following sentences, circle the correct verb form.

EXAMPLE

If Cally (was / **were**) a morning person, she would be more alert for her 8:00 a.m. classes.

1. The professor requests that students (be/are) in their chairs at the beginning of class.
2. He reacts to tardiness as if it (was/were) a personal insult.
3. One student's adviser recommended that she (get/gets) more sleep and breakfast.
4. If this class (were/was) part of her major, she would be more inclined to do so.
5. She just wishes the semester (were/was) over.

VOICE

37k Understanding Voice

The term *voice* refers to the role of the subject in a sentence. Only transitive verbs—verbs that take a direct object—can be in the passive voice. In the ***active voice,*** the subject is the actor and the direct object is acted upon.

ACTIVE

David hit the ball out of the park.

David is the subject, and *the ball* is the direct object.

In the ***passive voice,*** the subject is acted upon. To change an active-voice sentence into the passive voice, make the direct object the subject, combine the appropriate form of *be* with the past participle of the main verb, and identify the actor in a phrase beginning with *by*.

PASSIVE

The ball was hit out of the park by David.

The passive voice also permits you to leave the actor unidentified.

PASSIVE (AGENT UNIDENTIFIED)

The ball was hit out of the park.

To change the passive voice to active, make the subject into the direct object and the actor into the subject, and change the verb from the passive form to its active form.

▸ David's ~~baseball career was enhanced by his~~ generosity off the field. *enhanced his baseball career.*

If the passive-voice sentence leaves the actor unidentified, you will need to supply one.

▸ ~~The~~ *Americans elected the* country's first African American president ~~was elected~~ in 2008.

37l Choosing between the Active and Passive Voice

The active voice is usually preferable to the passive voice because it is the livelier and more direct of the two. The passive voice, in contrast, can deaden prose and obscure a writer's point.

> **More about**
> Style and voice, 535–37

In certain situations, however, the passive voice can be the appropriate choice:

- When the recipient of an action is more important than the actor or the identity of the actor is unimportant

    ▸ Hillary Clinton's appointment as secretary of state *was confirmed* by the Senate today.

    The writer wants to focus on Hillary Clinton, the receiver of the action.

    ▸ Hillary Clinton was confirmed as secretary of state on January 21, 2009.

    The focus is on the date of Clinton's confirmation, not the identity of the confirming body.

- In reports of scientific procedures
  ▶ Five hundred patients *were treated* with Cytoxan over a six-month period.

  The purpose of a scientific report is to describe what happened, not to focus on the scientists who conducted the research.

- When the actor is unknown or cannot be identified
  ▶ Our home *was burglarized* while we were on vacation.

EXERCISE 37.6 Changing passive voice to active

Revise each of the following sentences, changing the passive voice to the active voice.

EXAMPLE

Passive: The stage directions for the play were adapted by the director.

Active: *The director adapted the stage directions for the play.*

1. The costumes and props had been designed in order to increase the play's grandeur.
2. Taylor's performance was made more compelling than it otherwise would have been by the brilliant staging of the scene.
3. Because the play's scenes were rehearsed by the actors every day, excitement about the play spread across the campus.
4. Folding chairs were brought by the maintenance crew so the unexpected attendees on opening night could sit.

EXERCISE 37.7 Revising verbs

In the following paragraph, correct any verb errors.

My trip back to Chicago from San Francisco start out just fine. It was a beautiful afternoon, the plane boarding went fairly quickly, and the flight left right on schedule. I lied back in my seat for a nice nap when the pilot announced that there was some rough weather ahead, but it should not have affected our flight's arrival time. I heard this type of announcement once before on what turned out to be a horrible flight, so I should of start worrying right then. I was thinking that if I were to check the weather that morning, my flight might have been changed and I might have avoided this. We soon heard that the storm got so serious that all airports in the Chicago area will have been shut down and we will be landing in Topeka, Kansas, instead. It was evening by the time we had gotten our luggage at Topeka's airport, where we learned that all hotels had already been booked. I end up renting a car and I drive all night. It was rainy and windy when I arrive in Chicago, but most of the storm passed by then.

Make It **Your Own**

Write a paragraph about a true or fictional event that did not go according to plan. Write what you or the protaganist expected to happen, why things went wrong, how it turned out, and, finally, what might have been done differently.

Work **Together**

Exchange your paragraph with a classmate and circle each other's verbs. If you see any that need to be revised, underline them and in the margin write the pages in this chapter that discuss the issue. When you have both finished, review the recommended revisions and write a brief reflection about how they might make your paragraph easier to understand. If you found this difficult, add verbs to your revision checklist.

38 Understanding Pronoun Case and Reference

IN THIS CHAPTER

PRONOUN CASE

a. In subject complements, 658
b. In compounds, 658
c. In appositives, 660
d. For *we* and *us* before nouns, 660
e. With infinitives, 661
f. With *-ing* words, 661
g. In comparisons, 662
h. *Who* and *whom*, 663

CLEAR PRONOUN REFERENCE

i. Ambiguous reference, 665
j. Broad reference, 665
k. Implied reference, 666
l. *You*, 666
m. Indefinite *they* and *it*, 666
n. Reference to people with *who* and *whom*, 667

> **More about**
> Subjects and objects, 585–91

When you play an online multiplayer game like World of Warcraft or Halo, you may be interacting with dozens of other players who could be located almost anywhere in the world. Neither you nor they are physically present in the game. Instead, you all have virtual stand-ins—avatars—to represent you. Your avatar acts on your orders and may even change form—from human to animal or student to soldier, for example—depending on the way in which you want it to function in a particular environment.

Like avatars, pronouns are stand-ins. They represent other words—their ***antecedents***—from one place to another in speech or writing. Also like avatars, they sometimes change form depending on the role you want them to play within a sentence.

PRONOUN CASE

Nouns, and the pronouns that represent them, can play various roles within a sentence. They can be subjects:

	subject	
NOUN	**The Steelers**	lost.
PRONOUN	**They**	lost.

656

They can be objects (including direct objects, indirect objects, and objects of prepositions):

	subject		direct object
NOUN	The Bears	beat	**the Steelers.**
PRONOUN	We	beat	**them.**

They can indicate possession:

	possessive			possessive	
NOUN	**Chicago's**	team	beat	**Pittsburgh's**	team.
PRONOUN	**Our**	team	beat	**their**	team.

> **More about**
> Indicating possession with apostrophes, 773–77

The term *case* refers to the different forms a noun or pronoun takes—*subjective, objective,* or *possessive*—depending on which of these roles it serves. Nouns do not change much—they have the same form as subjects that they do as objects, and they indicate possession with an *s* sound that is marked in writing with an apostrophe (*Chicago's team*). In contrast, most **personal pronouns** and some **relative** and **interrogative pronouns** are shape shifters—they have distinct forms for many of their roles:

personal pronouns Pronouns that take the place of nouns or noun phrases
relative pronouns Pronouns that introduce subordinate clauses that describe the pronoun's antecedent
interrogative pronouns Pronouns that introduce questions

		Subjective Case	Objective Case	Possessive Case
Personal Pronouns				
Singular	1st person	I	me	my, mine
	2nd person	you	you	your, yours
	3rd person	he	him	his
		she	her	her, hers
		it	it	its
Plural	1st person	we	us	our, ours
	2nd person	you	you	your, yours
	3rd person	they	them	their, theirs
Case-Variant Relative and Interrogative Pronouns		who	whom	whose
		whoever	whomever	

Some case errors are easy to detect because they sound wrong to native speakers of English.

▶ Hermione is one of Harry's best friends, and ~~her~~ *she* often gives ~~he~~ *him* sound advice.

In many situations, however, the ear is an unreliable guide to proper case usage.

case Grammar Matters • Understanding Pronoun Case and Reference

38a Using the Subjective Case for Subject Complements

A pronoun that functions as a ***subject complement*** following a form of *be* used as a main verb should be in the subjective case, not the objective case.

> **subject complement** An adjective, pronoun, or noun phrase that follows a linking verb and describes or refers to the sentence subject

▶ Asked who spilled the milk, my sister confessed that the guilty one was ~~her.~~ *she.*

If this usage sounds overly formal, try reversing the subject and subject complement.

▶ Asked who spilled the milk, my sister confessed that the guilty one ~~was her.~~ *she was* one.

38b *She and I* or *Her and Me?* Keeping Track of Case in Compounds

Pronouns that are part of compound subjects or subject complements should be in the subjective case.

▶ My friends and ~~me~~ *I* chat online while we play computer games. [compound subject]

Pronouns that are part of compound objects should be in the objective case.

▶ My parents call my brothers and ~~I~~ *me* every weekend. [compound dir. obj.]

Pronouns that are part of compound possessives should be in the possessive case.

▶ My father often gets ~~me~~ *my* and my brother's names confused. [compound possessive]

Grammar Matters • *She and I* or *Her and Me*? Keeping Track of Case in Compounds

Quick Reference: Editing for Case in Compounds

To determine the correct case of a pronoun in a compound, isolate the pronoun from the rest of the compound; then read the result aloud to yourself. If the pronoun sounds wrong, replace it with the one that sounds right.

Faulty	[My friends and] me chat online while we play computer games.
Revised	My friends and I chat online while we play computer games.

Me chat online is clearly wrong. Replacing the objective pronoun *me* with the subjective pronoun *I* corrects the problem.

Faulty	My parents call [my siblings and] I every weekend.
Revised	My parents call my siblings and me every weekend.

My parents call I is clearly wrong. Replacing the subjective pronoun *I* with the objective pronoun *me* corrects the problem.

Faulty	My father often gets me [and my brother's] names confused.
Revised	My father often gets my and my brother's names confused.

My father gets me names confused is clearly wrong. Replacing the objective pronoun *me* with the possessive pronoun *my* corrects the problem.

EXERCISE 38.1 Pronoun case in subject complements and compounds

Circle the correct pronoun from each pair in parentheses.

EXAMPLE

When we were about twelve, Sofia and (**I**/ me) were intensely interested in rocketry.

1. Actually it was (she/her) who first joined the rocketry club, and then she got me involved.
2. We got so good at building and launching model rockets that other kids would call (she or I/her or me) whenever they had problems.
3. As we got older and our interests changed, (she and I/her and me) gradually lost our fascination with rocketry.
4. Now that I'm in college, one of (me/my) and my roommate's favorite pastimes has become rocketry.

appositive phrase
A noun or noun phrase that renames a preceding noun or noun phrase and is grammatically equivalent to it

38c Keeping Track of Pronoun Case in Appositives

The case of a pronoun in an *appositive phrase* should reflect the function of the phrase the appositive renames. If the original phrase is a subject or subject complement, as in the first of the following examples, the pronoun should be in the subjective case; if it is an object, as in the second example, the pronoun should be in the objective case.

▶ The two most talented actors in our school, Valentino and ~~her,~~ *she*, always get the best roles in school productions.

▶ The director always wants the best artists, ~~she~~ *her* and ~~I~~ *me*, to work on the scenery.

38d Deciding between *We* and *Us* before Nouns

In expressions that combine *we* or *us* with a noun, use *we* with nouns that function as subjects or subject complements and *us* with nouns that function as objects. To decide which is which, say the sentence to yourself with the pronoun alone.

▶ ~~Us~~ *We* gamers live vicariously in the game world through our avatars.

Us live vicariously is clearly wrong. The subjective pronoun *we* should replace the objective pronoun *us*.

▶ Our avatars act vicariously in the game world on behalf of ~~we~~ *us* gamers.

Avatars act on behalf of we is clearly wrong. The objective pronoun *us* should replace the subjective pronoun *we*.

→ **EXERCISE 38.2** Pronoun case in appositives and before nouns

Circle the correct pronoun or pronouns from each pair in parentheses.

EXAMPLE

As spring break approached, it became clear that both of us, (Owen and I / Owen and me), had no ride home.

1. As a result, (we/us) non–car owners started asking all of our friends how they got home in this situation.
2. Everyone took pity on the two stranded guys, (Owen and I/Owen and me), but nobody was able to offer us a ride.
3. Eventually, someone told (we/us) that (we/us) simply had to take the bus from our small college town to the train station in the state capital.
4. This way, the two seemingly abandoned non–car owners, (Owen and I/Owen and me), became informed and even empowered commuters.

38e Using the Objective Case Both before and after an Infinitive

Both the subject and object of an ***infinitive*** should be in the objective case.

> **infinitive** The *to* form of a verb (*to decide, to eat, to study*)

▶ I asked *her* to recommend *me* for the job.

Both *her,* the subject of the infinitive *to recommend,* and *me,* its direct object, are in the objective case.

38f Deciding on Pronoun Case with the *-ing* Form of a Verb

In most cases, use the possessive form of a noun or pronoun with a ***gerund*** (the present participle, or *-ing* form of a verb used as a noun).

> **More about**
> Gerunds, 593

▶ Professor Nolan, I appreciate ~~you~~ *your* taking time to advise me on my résumé.

Use the objective form of a noun or pronoun, however, when the *-ing* word functions as a modifier rather than a noun.

PRONOUN IS THE MODIFIER   Margo is a Tiger Woods fan. She admires *his* playing.

PRONOUN IS MODIFIED   Margo saw *him* playing at the US Open.

38g Clarifying Pronoun Case in Comparisons with *Than* or *As*

In comparisons with *than* or *as,* the choice of pronoun case can sometimes result in two otherwise identical sentences with significantly different meanings.

- Amy likes her new car more than I.
- Amy likes her new car more than me.

In the first sentence, the subjective case (*I*) signals a comparison between Amy's and the writer's fondness for Amy's car (she thinks better of it than the writer does). In the second sentence, the objective case (*me*) signals a comparison between Amy's fondness for her car and her fondness for the writer (she thinks better of her car than of the writer). To avoid confusing readers in situations like this, identify which pronoun your meaning requires by supplying any words needed to make the comparisons explicit.

- Amy likes her new car more than I *do.*
- Amy likes her new car more than *she likes* me.

EXERCISE 38.3 Pronoun case with infinitives, gerunds, and comparisons

Circle the correct pronoun from each pair in parentheses.

EXAMPLE
My uncle has put an enormous amount of time into (him /(his)) gardening.

1. When he was very young, his mother taught (he/him) to help (she/her) in their backyard garden.
2. Now that he has his own backyard, it turns out that he loves gardening even more than (she/her).
3. While I certainly like to watch (him/his) gardening, I don't enjoy doing it myself.
4. Even before I could walk and talk, it was obvious that I didn't like gardening as much as (he/him).
5. I must admit, though, that I allowed (he/him) to show (I/me) how to care for a few of his fruit trees.

38h Using *Who*, *Whom*, *Whoever*, and *Whomever*

The pronouns *who*, *whom*, *whoever*, and *whomever* have two jobs. As **relative pronouns** they introduce **subordinate clauses**. As **interrogative pronouns** they introduce questions.

> **subordinate clause**
> A word group with a subject and predicate that cannot stand alone as a sentence but instead functions within a sentence as a noun, adjective, or adverb

- Use *who* or *whoever* for the subject of a subordinate clause or question.

  |—— subordinate clause ——|
  subj.
  ▸ Tiger Woods, *who* began playing as a toddler, has long dominated golf.

  |—————— question ——————|
  subj.
  ▸ *Who* began playing golf as a toddler?

- Use *whom* or *whomever* for the object of a subordinate clause or question. Notice, however, that contrary to normal word order, in which direct objects follow verbs, *whom* and *whomever* usually come at the beginning of a clause or question.

  |—— subordinate clause ——|
  dir. obj.
  ▸ Woods, *whom* many golf fans admire, was sidelined by a knee injury in 2008.

  |—————— question ——————|
  dir. obj.
  ▸ *Whom* do many golf fans admire?

- The case of a relative pronoun is determined by its role in a clause, not the role of the clause in the sentence. The relative pronoun in the following example is the subject of its clause and so should be in the subjective case—*whoever*—even though the clause as a whole is the object of the preposition *to*.

Writing Responsibly / Case and Tone

Many people now ignore the distinction between *who* and *whom*, using only *who*. In academic and business writing, however, many readers will assume that you do not understand correct usage if you use *who* when *whom* is called for. So, even if *whom* and *whomever* sound inappropriately formal, even old-fashioned, to your ear, consider what your reader's expectations are and adjust your usage accordingly.

to AUDIENCE

▶ In professional golf, the winner's prize goes to ~~whomever~~ *whoever* completes the course in the fewest strokes.

- Match the pronoun to its verb, not to the verb of an intervening clause. In the following example, the pronoun should be the subjective case *who* because it is the subject of *was,* not the object of *know.*

▶ Thomas Edison, ~~whom~~ *who* many people know was the inventor of the lightbulb, was also the inventor of the phonograph.

EXERCISE 38.4 Distinguishing *who, whom, whoever, whomever*

Circle the correct pronoun from each pair in parentheses.

EXAMPLE

Ayrton, (*who* / whom) grew up in southern California, was visiting New York City for the first time.

1. It was the middle of winter, and taxis seemed to stop for (whoever/whomever) stood furthest into the street, but not for him.
2. (Whoever/Whomever) would have guessed that when Ayrton slipped on some ice and fell on his back, everybody on the street would surround him and reach down to help him up?
3. These were not the uncaring people (who/whom) he had assumed New Yorkers were.
4. He was soon back on his feet thanks to a tough-looking old man (who/whom) Ayrton invited to join him for a coffee.

CLEAR PRONOUN REFERENCE

Pronoun reference involves the clarity of the relationship between a pronoun and its antecedent. With clear pronoun reference, readers can easily identify the antecedent of a pronoun.

▶ Mario talked to his sister Roberta about her career plans.

The pronoun *his* clearly refers to Mario; the pronoun *her* clearly refers to Mario's sister.

Pronoun reference is unclear when readers cannot be certain what a pronoun's antecedent is.

▶ Mario talked to Paul about his career plans.

  Did Mario and Paul talk about Mario's career plans or Paul's? Without more information, readers will be uncertain.

38i Avoiding Ambiguous Reference

The reference of a pronoun is ambiguous when it has two or more equally plausible antecedents.

▶ Mario talked to Paul about his career plans.

One way to resolve ambiguous reference is to replace the pronoun with the appropriate noun.

▶ Mario talked to Paul about Paul's career plans.

To avoid repeating the noun, rephrase the sentence in a way that eliminates the ambiguity.

▶ Paul talked about his career plans with Mario.

  The position of the pronoun *his* associates the plans clearly and unambiguously with Paul, not Mario.

38j Avoiding Confusingly Broad Reference with *It, This, That,* and *Which*

When pronouns such as *it, this, that,* and *which* refer broadly to an entire clause, sentence, or series of sentences, readers may be uncertain about what specific information the pronouns cover.

▶ Who owns Antarctica? Several countries—including Argentina, Australia, Chile, France, New Zealand, Norway, the United Kingdom, and the United States—all claim or reserve the right to claim all or part of the continent. ~~This makes it~~ *These competing claims make the question of ownership* difficult to answer.

  The revision specifies what information the writer meant by *this* and *it*.

38k Avoiding Implied Reference

A pronoun should have a clearly identifiable antecedent, not an unstated, or implied, antecedent. In the following example, the only word that could serve grammatically as the antecedent to *they* is *stories,* but stories are not places. The writer's intended antecedent is implied in the adjective *small-town,* as the revision makes clear.

DRAFT	From her stories of her small-town childhood, they seem like great places to grow up.
REVISED	Her stories of her childhood make small towns seem like great places to grow up.

Similarly, in the next example, the antecedent to *he*—*Einstein*—is implied, confusingly, in the possessive form *Einstein's.*

▶ According to Einstein's theory of relativity, ~~he showed that~~ mass and energy are interchangeable.

38l Reserving *You* for Directly Addressing the Reader

In formal writing, reserve the pronoun *you* (and the implied *you* of commands) to address the reader directly, as in "you, the reader." Do not use *you* as a substitute for indefinite words such as *anybody, everybody,* or *people.*

▶ Before computers and the Internet, ~~you~~ *people* got ~~your~~ *their* news mostly from newspapers, radio, and television.

38m Avoiding the Indefinite Use of *They* and *It*

In formal writing, the pronouns *they* and *it* need specific antecedents. Avoid using these pronouns to refer to unspecified people or things.

▶ At Hogwarts School of Witchcraft and Wizardry, ~~they~~ *students* use owls, not e-mail, for sending messages.

Grammar Matters • Designating People with *Who, Whom,* and *Whose,* Not *That* and *Which*   ref   **38n**   **667**

▶ ~~In the~~ **The** beginning of the chapter~~, it~~ compares pronouns to computer-game avatars.

38n Designating People with *Who, Whom,* and *Whose,* Not *That* and *Which*

When you are speaking, you are as likely to use *that* as you are to use *who* or *whom* to refer to people. In formal writing, however, you should usually use only *who* and *whom* to refer to people.

▶ According to his website, the people ~~that~~ **who** most inspire Tiger Woods are his parents and Nelson Mandela.

Use *that* and *which* for animals and things.

▶ The stray cats ~~who~~ **that** live in the alley sometimes howl at night.

For pets and other named animals, however, *who* or *whom* is often more appropriate than *that* or *which*.

▶ Our cat Juniper, ~~which~~ **who** is now twelve years old, is still healthy and spry.

The possessive pronoun *whose* is also best reserved for people but can apply to animals and things when avoiding it requires the awkward use of the phrase *of which*.

▶ The polar bear is an animal ~~the~~ **whose** habitat ~~of which~~ is threatened by global warming.

EXERCISE 38.5 Editing for pronoun reference

Edit the following passage to eliminate problems with pronoun reference.

> Everyone who knew Colin identified him as someone that loved music. When you wanted to know about a band's background, you would ask Colin, who had made a life's work of studying the histories of musicians and composers. When Sydnee Sandford, a popular host on his college's

radio station, interviewed Colin about the 1960s rock musicians that she was featuring on her show, he became instantly famous on campus. That is what started it. A week later, the radio station manager told Colin that they would like to know if he wanted his own radio program. It appealed to him, but he also understood that he was a person that was quite shy and uncomfortable with public speaking. Based on his past experiences at speaking before audiences, they caused him to avoid giving her an answer. Sensing his obvious discomfort, she pointed out that she herself was also shy and had long been terrified of public speaking. She said that her answer was that you would discuss on your show and interview others about what interested you the most. Colin remembered how easy it was to talk on her show because he enjoyed the topic.

Colin's show aired at 3 to 4 a.m., and the only person the taste of which in music he used as a guide was himself. Soon he attracted a huge listenership on campus.

Make It Your Own

Write a true or fictional paragraph about giving someone a birthday present. Consider writing about deciding what to give, how you found the present, and how the recipient reacted. Use at least six different pronouns, with at least one from each of the three pronoun cases: subjective, objective, and possessive.

Work Together

Exchange your paragraph with a classmate and circle each other's pronouns. If you see any that need to be revised, underline them, and in the margin write the pages in this chapter that discuss the issue. When you have both finished, review the recommended revisions and write a brief reflection about how they might make your paragraph easier to understand. If you found this difficult, add pronouns to your revision checklist.

39 Using Adjectives and Adverbs

IN THIS CHAPTER

a. Differentiating adjectives and adverbs, 669

b. Using adjectives as subject complements, 670

c. Choosing *bad* or *badly*, *good* or *well* 671

d. Using negatives correctly, 673

e. Avoiding nouns as adjectives, 673

f. Using comparative forms, 674

> **More about**
> The characteristics of English adjectives, 732–34

The clothing, jewelry, and hairstyles we choose—our modifiers—send a message to others about how we want them to perceive us. A flamboyant dress, a tattoo, eye-catching jewelry, and flowing hair send one impression; a tailored business suit sends another. Similarly, we send readers a message about how we want our words to be understood by our choice of adjectives and adverbs to modify them.

39a Differentiating Adjectives and Adverbs

Adjectives modify (or describe) nouns and pronouns, answering questions such as *What kind? Which one?* or *How many? Adverbs* modify verbs, adjectives, other adverbs, and entire phrases, clauses, and sentences; they answer questions such as *How? Where?* or *When?*

Although many adverbs end in the suffix *-ly*, many do not (*later, often, quite, seldom*), and dozens of adjectives do (*elderly, lowly, scholarly*). The only reliable way to distinguish an adjective from an adverb is not from its form but from its function (see the Quick Reference box on p. 670).

English Adjectives Do Not Have Plural Forms In English, adjectives do not change form to agree with the words they modify.

Relaxing in a rocking chair, I watched ~~olds~~ old movies on TV.

669

> **Quick Reference** — **The Functions of Adjectives and Adverbs**
>
> **Adjectives modify:**
> Nouns — *sunny* day
> Pronouns — someone *responsible*
>
> **Adverbs modify:**
> Verbs — spoke *forcefully*
> Adjectives — *painfully* loud
> Adverbs — *very* cautiously
> Phrases — *finally* over the finish line
> Clauses and sentences — *Eventually*, the story ended.

39b Using Adjectives, Not Adverbs, as Subject Complements after Linking Verbs

Linking verbs express a state of being rather than an action or occurrence. They link the subject to a **subject complement,** which describes or refers to the subject. In other words, the subject complement modifies the subject, not the verb; it can be an adjective or a noun, but not an adverb.

The verb *be,* when used as a main verb, is always a linking verb.

▸ The *food* is *delicious*.

   The adjective *delicious* modifies the subject, *food*.

> **More about**
> Linking verbs and subject complements, 589

Other verbs, such as *appear, become, feel, look, prove, sound,* and *taste,* may function as linking verbs in one context and action verbs in another. A word following one of these verbs should be an adjective if it modifies the subject and an adverb if it modifies the verb.

▸ *Maria* looked *anxious* to the dentist.

   Looked is a linking verb and the adjective *anxious* is a subject complement that describes Maria's state of mind as the dentist perceived it.

▸ Maria *looked anxiously* at the dentist.

   Looked is an action verb modified by the adverb *anxiously,* which describes the manner in which Maria performed the action of looking.

39c Choosing *Bad* or *Badly, Good* or *Well*

In casual speech, we commonly mingle adjectives and adverbs. In writing, however, use adjectives to modify nouns and pronouns and use adverbs to modify verbs, adjectives, or other adverbs. Do not confuse *bad* with *badly, good* with *well*, or *real* with *really*. Use the adjective form of these pairs for subject complements. Include *-ly* endings when needed, and use an adjective, not an adverb, to modify a direct object.

> **Tech** **Grammar Checkers and Adjective-Adverb Problems**
>
> Grammar checkers in word processing programs catch some adjective and adverb errors but miss many others. A grammar checker, for example, missed errors such as *The Patriots played bad, the boat rocked gentle,* and *Tomás looked well in his tuxedo.*

- *Bad* is an adjective; *badly* is an adverb.

    ▶ The Patriots played ~~bad~~ *badly* in the fourth quarter.

    Badly modifies the action verb *played*.

    ▶ The quarterback feels ~~badly~~ *bad* about the loss.

    Feels is a linking verb; *bad* modifies *quarterback*.

- The word *good* is an adjective, and *well* is its adverb counterpart. *Well* is an adjective, however, when it is used to mean "healthy."

    ▶ Leah did ~~good~~ *well* on her final exams.

    The adverb *well* modifies the verb *did*.

    ▶ Tomás looks ~~well~~ *good* in his tuxedo.

    Looks is a linking verb; the adjective *good* modifies *Tomás*.

    ▶ After a late-night graduation party, Leah is not feeling ~~good~~ *well*.

    Well is used as an adjective because it refers to health.

- Do not confuse the adjective *real* with the adverb *really*.

    ▶ The actors are ~~real~~ *really* enthusiastic about tonight's performance.

NOTE Intensifiers like *really* often add little or no meaning to a sentence and can usually be dropped in the interest of conciseness.

> **More about**
> Conciseness,
> 496–504 (ch. 26)

- Do not confuse adverbs that end in -*ly* with their adjective counterparts that do not.

  ▸ You should play ~~gentle~~ *gently* with small children.

  The adverb *gently* modifies the verb *play*.

- Never use an adverb to modify a direct object. When a modifier follows a direct object, ask yourself, "What word is being modified?" If the answer is "the verb," then the modifier should be an adverb, but if the answer is "the direct object," then the modifier is an **object complement** and should be an adjective or noun.

  ▸ The divorce left Kayla *cautious* about future relationships.
  The adjective *cautious* modifies the direct object *Kayla*.

  ▸ She *conducted* herself *cautiously* with potential new friends.
  The adverb *cautiously* modifies the verb *conducted*, not the direct object *herself*.

> **More about**
> Direct objects and object modifiers, 588–91, 707–09

object complement An adjective or noun phrase that follows the direct object and describes the condition of the object or a change the subject has caused it to undergo

➤ EXERCISE 39.1 Correcting common adjective-adverb problems

Revise the following sentences to correct any adjective or adverb errors.

EXAMPLE

Most people are ~~real~~ *really* surprised to learn that Bennett and Raul are roommates and even ~~well~~ *good* friends.

1. Raul takes unusual good care of his clothes and dresses fashionable.
2. Bennett feels indifferently about clothes and dresses real sloppy.
3. Of course, Raul always keeps his side of their room awful messily.
4. Bennett, on the other hand, puts absolute everything careful in its proper place.
5. Despite these stark differences, the two of them get along real good.

39d Using Negatives Correctly

In a sentence with a *double negative,* two negative modifiers describe the same word. Because one negative cancels the other, the message becomes positive. In Standard American English, double negatives can be acceptable, but only to emphasize a positive meaning. The sentence *It is not unlikely that the attorney will be disbarred,* for example, means that the attorney's disbarment is likely. Although some dialects allow the use of double (and more) negatives to emphasize a negative meaning, and many people use them that way in casual speech, you should avoid them in formal writing. Remember that the negative word *not* is part of contractions such as *couldn't* and *shouldn't* and that words like *barely, hardly,* and *scarcely* have a negative meaning.

▶ Students ~~shouldn't~~ *should* never park in a faculty-only lot.

▶ The children ~~can't~~ *can* hardly wait to open their presents.

39e Avoiding Long Strings of Nouns Used as Adjectives

One noun can often function as an adjective to modify another: *government worker, traffic violation, college course.* Multiple nouns strung together this way, however, can be cumbersome and confusing.

CONFUSING The *teacher education policy report* will be available tomorrow.

REVISED The *policy report on teacher education* will be available tomorrow.

Order of Adjectives in a Series When more than one adjective modifies a noun, the adjectives usually need to follow a specific order:

▶ a ~~European~~ *European* stunning racehorse

Charts like the one on page 733 may help you learn what that order is, but to follow that order reliably, you will need consistent exposure to a broad range of English-language situations and texts. For guidance on ordering multiple adjectives, see page 733.

39f Using Comparative and Superlative Adjectives and Adverbs

Most adjectives and adverbs have three forms for indicating the relative degree of the quality or manner they specify: positive, comparative, and superlative. The *positive form* is the base form—the form you find when you look the word up in the dictionary.

> **POSITIVE** Daryl is *tall*.

The *comparative form* indicates a relatively greater or lesser degree of a quality.

> **COMPARATIVE** Daryl is *taller* than Ivan.

The *superlative form* indicates the greatest or least degree of a quality.

> **SUPERLATIVE** Daryl is the *tallest* player on the team.

Regular adjectives and adverbs form the comparative and superlative with either the suffixes *-er* and *-est* or the addition of the words *more* and *most* or *less* and *least*. A few adjectives and adverbs have irregular comparative and superlative forms (see the Quick Reference box on the next page). If you are not sure whether to use *-er/-est* or *more/most* for a particular adjective or adverb, look it up in a dictionary. If the entry shows *-er* and *-est* forms, use them. If no such forms are listed, use *more* or *most*.

1. Comparative or superlative

Use the comparative form to compare two things, the superlative to compare three or more.

▶ Between Jon Stewart and Stephen Colbert, I think Colbert is the ~~funniest~~ *funnier*.

▶ Of all comedians ever, I think Buster Keaton was the ~~funnier~~ *funniest*.

2. Redundant comparisons

Do not combine the comparative words *more/most* with adjectives or adverbs that are already in comparative form with an *-er* or *-est* ending.

▶ Trains in Europe and Japan are ~~more~~ faster than trains in the United States.

Quick Reference: Forming Comparatives and Superlatives

Regular Forms

	Positive	Comparative	Superlative
Adjectives	bold	bolder/less bold	boldest/least bold
	helpful	more/less helpful	most/least helpful
Adverbs	far	farther	farthest
	realistically	more/less realistically	most/least realistically

Irregular Forms

	Positive	Comparative	Superlative
Adjectives	bad	worse	worst
	good	better	best
	little	less (quantity)/littler (size)	least (quantity)/littlest (size)
	many	more	most
	much	more	most
	some	more	most
Adverbs	badly	worse	worst
	well	better	best

3. Complete comparisons

Make sure your comparisons are logical and that readers have all the information they need to understand what is being compared to what.

> **More about**
> Complete comparisons, 701–02

▶ The nurses' test scores were higher. *than those of the pre-med students.*

The original makes us ask, "Higher than what?" The addition clarifies the comparison.

4. Absolute terms

Expressions like *more unique* or *most perfect* are common in everyday speech, but if you think about them, they make no sense. *Unique, perfect,* and other words such as *equal, essential, final, full, impossible, infinite,* and *unanimous* are absolutes, and absolutes are beyond compare. If something is unique, it is by definition one of a kind. If something is perfect, it cannot be improved upon. In formal writing, then, avoid using absolute terms comparatively.

▶ Last night's performance of the play was the ~~most perfect~~ *best* yet.

EXERCISE 39.2 Revising errors with comparatives and superlatives

In the following sentences, correct any errors with the comparative or superlative forms of adjectives and adverbs.

EXAMPLE

Cameron is more ~~frugaller~~ *frugal* than even I am and may be the most ~~frugallest~~ *frugal* person I know.

1. Cameron's apartment is the most coldest of anyone's.
2. He must have the lower fuel bill in our area although his house is probably not more energy efficient.
3. Cameron feels that it is most essential for him to spend the smaller amount of money he can on anything.
4. According to him, people are more unhappy when they spend more.
5. I don't know whether I feel most admiration or disgust for Cameron's frugality, but I admit I have learned from him more useful pointers on saving money.

EXERCISE 39.3 Revising for problems with adjectives and adverbs

In the following paragraphs, correct any errors in adjective or adverb usage.

It was her last year of college, and Gillian was finding life to be extreme exhilarating and real overwhelming at the same time. She had worked hardest in the previously three years to complete her required courses so that this year she could be more selective about the courses she took. That is why, although she was a chemistry major, she was taking several courses that scarcely had nothing to do with chemistry. She was furthering her study of Russian and was doing a lot of translating between Russian and English, which was terrible stressful at times. Her opera course was a purely delight, and she also loved studying European history from 1500 to 1789, although that required an immense amount of reading.

She was also enjoying her extracurricular activities, but she couldn't barely fit them all into her demanding schedule. Playing flute in the wind ensemble was fun, especially since she was the more accomplished musician in the group. However, playing in the band for the musical was bad taxing because the score was highly intricate.

Make It **Your Own**

Write a paragraph describing what you would have in your dream house if you were fabulously rich. Use at least six adjectives and six adverbs in your descriptions of your house's features, making at least two of the adjectives or adverbs comparative or superlative.

Work **Together**

Exchange your paragraph with a classmate and circle each other's adjectives and adverbs. If you see any that need to be revised, underline them and in the margin write the pages in this chapter that discuss the issue. When you have both finished, review the recommended revisions and write a brief reflection about what effect they would have on your paragraph. If you found this difficult, add adjectives and adverbs to your revision checklist.

40 Avoiding Confusing Shifts

IN THIS CHAPTER

a. Avoiding shifts in tense, 678

b. Avoiding shifts in mood and voice, 679

c. Avoiding shifts in person and number, 681

d. Avoiding shifts in direct and indirect discourse, 683

> **More about**
> Verb tenses, 644–50

When NASCAR drivers round the curves or head into the straightaway, they need to shift gears, but an expert driver shifts only when doing so will provide a clear advantage. Similarly, good writers try not to jar their readers with unnecessary shifts in style or grammar.

40a Avoiding Awkward Shifts in Tense

Verb tenses place events in a sentence in time. Sentences with more than one verb may require a shift in tense from one to another if the verbs refer to events that occur at different times.

▶ Yesterday *was* snowy, and today *is* cloudy and cold, but according to the weather report, the weekend *will be* warm and sunny.

The sentence contrasts past, present, and future weather conditions.

Shifts from one tense to another not grounded in a corresponding shift in time, however, are confusing. Avoid such inappropriate shifts, particularly when you are telling a story or describing a sequence of events.

▶ The guide waited until we had all reached the top of the pass; then she ~~leads~~ *led* the way down to the river and ~~makes~~ *made* sure sure everybody ~~is~~ *was* safe in camp.

Convention dictates the use of the present tense for writing about literary events and characters as well as about films, plays, and other similar works.

▶ In Madame Defarge, the principal villain of *A Tale of Two Cities,* Charles Dickens ~~depicted~~ *depicts* the cruel ironies of the French Revolution.

40b Avoiding Awkward Shifts in Mood and Voice

Two other characteristics of verbs are mood and voice; as with tense, shifts in mood and voice should help make clear what the writer intends to convey.

1. Shifts in mood

English verbs have three moods: indicative, imperative, and subjunctive. Most sentences are consistently in the indicative mood, which is used to state or question facts and beliefs. You may, however, inadvertently shift inappropriately between the imperative mood—used for commands, directions, and entreaties—and the indicative mood when explaining a process or giving directions.

> **Tech** **Catching Confusing Shifts**
>
> The grammar and style checkers in word processing programs are unreliable at differentiating appropriate and confusing shifts. One style checker, for example, had no objection to this absurd statement: "Yesterday it will rain; tomorrow it snowed two feet." On the other hand, the same style checker flags every occurrence of the passive voice, regardless of whether it is appropriate to the passage in which it appears.

▶ Dig a narrow hole about six inches deep, place the tulip bulb firmly at the bottom of the hole, and then ~~you can~~ fill the hole with dirt.

The subjunctive mood is used in certain situations to express a wish or demand or to make a statement contrary to fact. Although many of us often replace it with the indicative in everyday speech, readers expect to encounter it in formal writing.

> **More about**
> Mood, 650–52

▶ If the presidential primary ~~was~~ *were* held earlier in the year, our state's voters would have a greater voice in the outcome of the race.

2. Shifts in voice

Avoid shifting needlessly between the active voice, in which the subject performs the action of the verb (*I wrote the paper*) and the passive voice, in which the subject receives the action (*The paper was written by me*). As originally

> **More about**
> Voice, 535–37, 652–55

shift Grammar Matters • Avoiding Confusing Shifts

written, the following passage started out in the active voice (*British consumed, Italians favored*) but then shifted to the passive voice for no reason:

> ▸ During the eighteenth century, the British consumed most of their carbohydrates in the form of processed sugar. The Italians favored pasta, whereas sourdough bread ~~was preferred by the French.~~ *the French preferred*

➔ EXERCISE 40.1 Correcting verb shifts in tense, mood, and voice

Correct the following sentences to make the verbs consistent in tense, mood, and voice. Check for shifts both within and between sentences. If a sentence needs no revision, circle its number.

EXAMPLE

After she mowed the lawn and pulled some weeds, Kris ~~relaxes~~ *relaxed* on the porch watching the hummingbirds until supper ~~is~~ *was* ready.

1. As most birdwatchers know, hummingbirds can do many things that other birds could not do.
2. With their wings being beaten an astonishing fifty times a second or more, hummingbirds sometimes fly as fast as sixty miles per hour.
3. Because hummingbirds expend so much energy, they needed to eat often, usually every twenty minutes.
4. With the highest metabolic rate of any animal, they burn energy faster than tigers, elephants, and all other birds.
5. Hummingbirds' most amazing feature, though, is their ability to fly in any direction—including upside down—something no other bird was capable of doing.
6. When birdwatchers study hummingbirds up close, the uniqueness of the species can be fully appreciated.
7. In addition, get a good view of the birds' long bills and stunning iridescent feathers.
8. Given hummingbirds' constant need for food, which they obtain from nectar and flowers, one would expect to have found them only in warm climates.

9. However, if birdwatchers are able to travel around the country, they would discover some species in chilly locales, such as the Rocky Mountains and Alaska.
10. Many hummingbirds migrate to warmer areas during winter months, but they returned to cooler areas in the spring and summer.

40c Avoiding Awkward Shifts in Person and Number

Person refers to the identity of the subject of a sentence and the point of view of the writer. In the first person (*I, we*), the writer and subject are the same. In the second person (*you*), the reader and subject are the same. In the third person (*he, she, it, they, Marie Curie, electrons*), the subject is the writer's topic of discussion, what the writer is informing the reader about. ***Number*** refers to the quantity (singular or plural) of a noun or pronoun.

> **More about**
> Person and number, 620–22

1. Shifts in person

Many situations require a shift in person. You might be telling a story in the first person, for example, but you will almost certainly have to relate some parts of it in the third person.

▶ We approached the spooky old house with trepidation. The front door creaked open. We stepped inside.

Arbitrary shifts in person, in contrast, are distracting to readers. The writer of the following passage, for example, began in the first person but shifted jarringly to the second person. The revision establishes a consistent first-person point of view.

▶ When I get together with my friends in the tech club, we usually discuss the latest electronic devices. ~~You~~ *We* tend to forget, though, that a garden spade and a ballpoint pen are also technological tools and that thousands of nonelectronic items become part of ~~your~~ *our* technological world every year.

Most academic writing is in the third person. The second person, including commands, is best reserved for addressing readers directly, telling them how to do something or giving them advice. (You have probably noticed that this handbook often addresses you, the reader, in just this way.) Be consistent, however, and avoid shifting arbitrarily between second and third person.

▶ To train your dog properly, ~~people~~ *you* need plenty of time, patience, and dog biscuits. You should start with simple commands like "sit" and "stay."

2. Shifts in number

> **More about**
> Avoiding gender bias, 545–47, 631–33

Most inappropriate shifts in number are errors in agreement between a pronoun and its antecedent and are often the result of a writer's desire to avoid gender bias. These kinds of errors arise most commonly when the antecedent is a singular generic noun (*person, doctor*) or indefinite pronoun (*anyone, everyone*).

FAULTY	When a <u>person</u> witnesses a crime, <u>they</u> should report it to the police.

The antecedent of the plural pronoun *they* is the singular generic noun *person*.

Several options are available for revising such shifts. One is to use the plural throughout. Another is to replace the plural pronoun with *he or she* (although this expression becomes tedious when overused). A third is to rephrase the sentence to avoid the problem entirely.

REVISED: PLURAL THROUGHOUT	When people witness a crime, they should report it to the police.
REVISED: HE OR SHE	When a person witnesses a crime, he or she should report it to the police.
REVISED: REPHRASED	Anybody who witnesses a crime should report it to the police.

Look, too, for illogical shifts in number between two related nouns. As originally written, for example, the following sentence suggests that the passengers shared a single computer.

▶ All passengers had to open their ~~computer~~ *computers* for a security inspection.

EXERCISE 40.2 Correcting shifts in person and number

Correct the following sentences so that they are consistent in person and number.

EXAMPLE

Although ~~a historian~~ *historians* may understand past migrations, they do not have all the answers to current urban expansions.

1. During the nineteenth century, miners, merchants, and entrepreneurs flocked to the thriving river town of Galena, Illinois, to seek your fortune.
2. Galena was indeed "the west" in those days because you could not yet find any major cities west of the Mississippi River.
3. A Galenian can boast that their city, once the lead-mining capital of the world, was also home to Ulysses S. Grant and nine Civil War generals.
4. A Galenian is also likely to be proud of their town's renowned collection of original nineteenth-century architecture.
5. The mines are long closed, and the river resembles a meandering stream, but Galena remains a historic treasure where a visitor can step into yesterday, escape their busy life, and you can relax.

40d Avoiding Awkward Shifts in Direct and Indirect Quotations and Questions

Direct quotations reproduce someone's exact words and must always be enclosed in quotation marks: *My roommate announced, "The party will start at 8 p.m."* ***Indirect quotations*** report what someone has said but not in that person's exact words: *My roommate announced that the party would start at 8 p.m.*

Abrupt shifts between direct and indirect quotations, like the one in the following example, are awkward and confusing. Both of the revised versions are clearer and easier to follow than the original. In this instance, however, direct quotation is the best choice because Berra's own words express his humor most effectively.

> **More about**
> Punctuating direct and indirect quotations, 780–82, 785–89
> Quoting sources, 259–62, 312–33
> Direct sources, 790–91

AWKWARD SHIFT	Yogi Berra says that you should go to other people's funerals or "otherwise, they won't come to yours."
REVISED: DIRECT QUOTATION	As Yogi Berra says, "You should always go to other people's funerals. Otherwise, they won't come to yours."
REVISED: INDIRECT QUOTATION	Yogi Berra says that you should go to other people's funerals because, otherwise, they won't come to yours.

> **More about**
> Punctuating direct and indirect questions, 793–94

Abrupt shifts between direct and indirect questions are likewise confusing. A ***direct question*** is stated in question (interrogative) form and ends with a question mark: *When does the library open?* An ***indirect question*** reports a question in declarative form and ends with a period: *I wonder when the library opens.*

AWKWARD SHIFT	The author asks how much longer can the world depend on fossil fuels and whether alternative sources of energy will be ready in time.
REVISED: DIRECT QUESTION	The author asks two questions: How much longer can the world depend on fossil fuels, and will alternative sources of energy be ready in time?
REVISED: INDIRECT QUESTION	The author asks how much longer the world can depend on fossil fuels and whether alternative sources of energy will be ready in time.

> **EXERCISE 40.3 Revising confusing shifts**
>
> Revise the following passage to eliminate confusing shifts.
>
> In a blind taste test described in the *New York Times,* a cross section of the country's population sampled thousands of products in several locations, and store brands were given high marks by the testers. When the testers tried both national and store brands for such products as cereal, cream, pizza, and chicken nuggets, the researchers determine that the store brands were preferred over national brands by testers. While the testers did favor some national-brand products, such as chicken nuggets, cheese pizza, chocolate ice cream, and potatoes au gratin, the testers overwhelmingly prefer store-brand raisin bran. Store-brand frozen broccoli and chocolate chip cookies were also winners.

Grammar Matters • Avoiding Awkward Shifts in Direct and Indirect Quotations and Questions

Although store brands have achieved a near equality with national brands in the minds of many consumers, shoppers are still careful in their choices. A shopper might ask, why shouldn't I buy a store brand if it tastes as good as a name brand? But if you find the store brand isn't good enough, you wouldn't buy it even if it was a lot cheaper.

Make It Your Own

Write a five- or six-sentence paragraph describing your favorite vacation, real or imaginary. Include in your paragraph as many types of awkward shifts in tense, mood, voice, person, and number as you can. You may include shifts both within and between sentences. Label this paragraph "Version A." Then rewrite your paragraph, eliminating the awkward shifts. Label this "Version B."

Work Together

Exchange Version A with a classmate and edit each other's paragraph to eliminate the unnecessary shifts. Compare your corrections with your classmate's Version B. Discuss and resolve any differences. If you found this difficult, add it to your revision checklist.

41 Avoiding Misplaced and Dangling Modifiers

IN THIS CHAPTER

MISPLACED MODIFIERS

a. Avoiding confusing or ambiguous placement, 687

b. Avoiding disrupting placement, 689

DANGLING MODIFIERS

c. Identifying dangling modifiers, 692

d. Correcting dangling modifiers, 693

Since 1886 the Statue of Liberty has dominated New York harbor, holding aloft a torch in the hand of her outstretched right arm. In 1876, however, while work on the rest of the statue continued in France, the arm and torch stood incongruously at the Philadelphia Centennial Exhibition, displayed there, and later in New York's Madison Square Park, to help raise funds for the construction of the statue's pedestal. This photograph of the display may strike you as strange because this huge piece of sculpture does not belong in a park; it is supposed to be attached appropriately to the rest of the statue. Similarly, when you misplace modifiers in your sentences, you may inadvertently confuse or surprise your readers.

MISPLACED MODIFIERS

A modifying word, phrase, or clause is misplaced if readers have to puzzle out what it modifies or if they stumble over it while trying to get from one part of a sentence to the next. Look for such ***misplaced modifiers*** as you revise your drafts.

> **Tech** Misplaced Modifiers and Grammar and Style Checkers
>
> The grammar and style checkers in word processing programs usually cannot tell what a modifier is supposed to modify, so they rarely flag those that are misplaced confusingly far from their intended targets or that seem ambiguously to modify more than one term. They do flag most split infinitives and some other disruptive modifiers.

41a Avoiding Confusing or Ambiguous Placement

Place modifiers so that they clearly refer to the words you intend them to modify and only those words.

1. Modifiers confusingly separated from the words they modify

We tend to associate modifiers with the words closest to them. A modifier positioned far from its intended target might appear to modify some other part of the sentence instead—and might confuse or amuse your readers.

▶ The couple moved to a bigger apartment *because they needed more space* after their first child was born ~~because they needed more space~~.

The couple's need for space did not cause the birth of their child.

▶ For more than four years, the two rovers *that landed in January 2004* have been exploring the surface of Mars ~~that landed in January 2004~~.

The rovers landed, not the surface of Mars.

EXERCISE 41.1 Correcting confusingly placed modifiers

Revise the following sentences so that all modifiers are clearly and logically positioned.

EXAMPLE

Mr. Doyle walked down Main Street to Town Hall, the building that housed all the town's administrative offices, with determination.

Mr. Doyle walked with determination down Main Street to Town Hall, the building that housed all the town's administrative offices.

1. Because it was a quiet, peaceful, and relaxing town, he knew that a lot of people had chosen to move there, and he knew that like him they didn't like the changes.

2. So he had decided to go to Town Hall and formally protest the installation of a traffic light on Reynolds Road in the main intersection of town, dressed in his finest suit.

3. He went straight to the main desk, walking through the large, ornate doors of the building.

4. He was there to protest the proposed traffic light, he told the receptionist, which was a direct threat to the town's long-standing harmony and tranquility.

5. The receptionist said that after holding several public meetings on the issue, he was very sorry but the Town Council had already voted for the traffic light.

2. Squinting modifiers

A *squinting modifier* confuses readers by appearing to modify both what precedes it and what follows it.

DRAFT   People who study hard usually will get the best grades.

Do people who make a practice of studying hard get the best grades, or do the best grades usually (but not always) go to people who study hard? The following revisions show that the sentence can be clarified in two different ways:

REVISION   People who usually study hard will get the best grades.

REVISION   People who study hard will usually get the best grades.

3. Ambiguous limiting modifiers

Limiting modifiers include qualifying words such as *almost, even, exactly, hardly, just, merely, only, scarcely,* and *simply*. Always place these words in front of the words you intend to modify. Do not place them in front of a verb unless they modify the verb. Otherwise, you risk ambiguity.

In the following example, the ambiguous placement of the limiter *just* leaves the reader with a variety of possible interpretations. If *just* is understood to modify *offers,* the sentence makes the unlikely suggestion that the only class the math department offers is Calculus III at night on Thursdays. The revisions provide three equally likely alternative readings.

AMBIGUOUS   The math department just offers Calculus III at night on Thursdays.

REVISED	At night on Thursdays, the math department offers just Calculus III. [That is the only math course you can take on Thursday nights.]
REVISED	On Thursdays, the math department offers Calculus III just at night. [That is the only time you can take the class on Thursdays.]
REVISED	The math department offers Calculus III at night just on Thursdays. [That is the only day you can take the class at night.]

41b Avoiding Disruptive Placement

A modifier is disruptive when it awkwardly breaks the flow among grammatically connected parts of a sentence.

1. Separation of subject from verb or verb from object

Long adverbial phrases and clauses tend to be disruptive when they fall between subjects and verbs (as in the first example below), within verb phrases (as in the second example), or between verbs and their objects (as in the third example).

▶ *The Sopranos*, ~~well after its last episode aired in June 2007,~~ continued to elicit admiring commentary and analysis ∧ *well after its last episode aired in June 2007.*

▶ *If it maintains a large following,* ∧ ~~The~~ show might, ~~if it maintains a large following,~~ appear in reruns for years to come.

▶ The show often jarringly contrasts, ~~leaving the viewer torn between empathy and revulsion,~~ the mundane events of Tony's family life with the callous brutality of the mobster's world ∧ *, leaving the viewer torn between empathy and revulsion.*

An adjective phrase or clause that modifies the subject of a sentence is not usually disruptive when it falls between subject and verb. On the contrary, it would likely be misplaced in any other location.

▶ The two Mars rovers, *which both landed in January 2004,* were designed to last only 90 days.

2. Split infinitives

An infinitive consists of *to* and the base form of a verb (*to share, to jump, to remember*). An infinitive splits when a modifier is inserted between the *to* and the verb. Grammarians have traditionally considered infinitives to be indivisible units and split infinitives to be improper. Although many authorities now consider them acceptable, split infinitives can be awkward and often should be revised, particularly in formal writing.

▶ Grant's strategy was *to* ~~relentlessly~~ attack Lee's army *relentlessly* despite the heavy losses the Union army suffered as a result.

Sometimes, however, a modifier is less awkward when splitting an infinitive than in any other spot in a sentence. If the adverb *relentlessly* were placed anywhere else in the following sentence, for example, it would not clearly and unambiguously modify only the word *attack*. Placed before the infinitive or at the end of the sentence, it could be understood to modify *urged;* placed after the infinitive, it could be understood to modify *retreating*.

▶ Lincoln urged his generals to *relentlessly* attack retreating enemy forces.

Writing Responsibly: Misplaced Modifiers in the Real World

Misplaced modifiers can sometimes cause real distress. A confusing instruction like the one below from the website of the Federal Emergency Management Agency (FEMA) might bewilder a homeowner struggling to recover from a natural disaster.

> You will need your social security number, current and pre-disaster address, phone numbers, type of insurance coverage, total household annual income, and a routing and account number from your bank *if you want to have disaster assistance funds transferred directly into your bank account.* [Emphasis added.]

As written, this suggests that an applicant for relief needs all of the listed items in order to have disaster assistance deposited directly into a bank account. Here is what the writer probably meant to say:

> You will need your social security number, current and pre-disaster address, phone numbers, type of insurance coverage, total household annual income, and, *if you want to have disaster assistance funds transferred directly into your bank account,* a routing and account number from your bank.

to TOPIC

EXERCISE 41.2 Correcting disruptive modifiers

In the following sentences, move any disruptive modifiers, and revise any awkward split infinitives.

EXAMPLE

Amber's laptop, ~~ever since she'd owned it,~~ had worked flawlessly. *ever since she'd bought it.*

1. Over the last week, however, she had been, mainly with the keyboard, having problems with it.
2. Often, when she hit the *r* key, she would see an *x* on her screen, and hitting, even when tapping gently and carefully, the *o* key gave her a *b* on the screen.
3. The technical support specialist with whom she spoke finally, after talking Amber through several troubleshooting routines, instructed her to mail the computer to a repair facility.
4. She worried that the repair process, leaving her to indefinitely rely on her library's computers, would take a long time.
5. When the repaired computer, two weeks later, arrived in the mail, Amber discovered that the repair staff had considerably replaced not only the laptop's keyboard, but its motherboard as well, and the computer worked better than ever.

DANGLING MODIFIERS

Consider the following sentence:

▶ While paddling the canoe toward shore, our poodle swam alongside.

Who or what is paddling the canoe? Surely not the poodle, yet that is what the sentence seems, absurdly, to suggest. The problem here is that the phrase *while paddling the canoe toward shore* does not actually modify the subject, *poodle,* or anything else in the sentence. It dangles, unattached, leaving it to the reader to infer the existence of some unnamed human paddler. Correcting this ***dangling modifier*** requires either making the paddler the subject of the sentence (as in the first revision below) or identifying the paddler in the modifier (as in the second revision).

> While paddling the canoe toward shore, our poodle ~~swam~~ *swimming* alongside. [*I saw* inserted before "swimming"]

> While ~~paddling~~ *I paddled* the canoe toward shore, our poodle swam alongside.

41c Identifying Dangling Modifiers

Dangling modifiers have the following characteristics:

- They are most often phrases that include a **verbal** (a gerund, infinitive, or participle) that has an implied but unstated actor.
- They occur most often at the beginnings of sentences.
- They appear to modify the subject of the sentence, so readers expect the implied actor and the subject to be the same.
- They dangle because the implied actor and the actual subject of the sentence are different.

verbal Verb form that functions as a noun, adjective, or adverb

> **More about**
> Phrases and clauses, 591–97

DANGLING INFINITIVE PHRASE

To learn about new products, the company's sales meeting occurs annually in August. [Meetings do not learn.]

DANGLING PARTICIPIAL PHRASE

Hoping to boost morale, an attractive resort hotel is usually selected for the meeting. [Resorts cannot hope.]

DANGLING PREPOSITIONAL PHRASE WITH GERUND OBJECT

After traveling all day, the hotel's hot tub looked inviting to the arriving sales reps. [The sales reps traveled, not the hot tub.]

41d Correcting Dangling Modifiers

Simply moving a dangling modifier will not correct it.

DANGLING To learn more about new products, the company's sales meeting occurs annually in August.

STILL DANGLING The company's sales meeting occurs annually in August to learn more about new products.

To correct a dangling modifier, first determine the identity of the modifier's unstated actor. You then have two options:

1. Rephrase to make the implied actor the subject of the sentence
2. Rephrase to include the implied actor in the modifier

Use the approach that works best given the purpose of the sentence in your draft.

MAKING THE IMPLIED ACTOR THE SUBJECT

To learn about new products, the company's sales meeting ~~occurs annually~~ *sales reps attend annual* in August.

Hoping to boost morale, an attractive resort hotel ~~is usually selected~~ *management usually selects* for the meeting.

In both these cases, the implied actor—*sales reps* in the first, *management* in the second—was missing entirely from the original sentence.

INCLUDING THE IMPLIED ACTOR IN THE MODIFIER

As the sales reps arrived after ~~After~~ traveling all day, the hotel's hot tub looked inviting to ~~the arriving sales reps.~~ *them.*

In this case, the implied actor, *sales reps,* appeared in the original sentence but needed to be repositioned.

EXERCISE 41.3 Correcting dangling modifiers

Revise the following sentences to eliminate dangling modifiers.

EXAMPLE

As soon as Derek stepped aboard,
~~On stepping aboard,~~ the boat began to roll back and forth.

1. To avoid seasickness in the bobbing boat, focusing on the distant shoreline was a great help.
2. Having little hope of actually catching anything, expectations for success were low.
3. Having dropped his line into the water, a tug indicated that he had a bite.
4. Reeling in the fish, everyone cheered because the first-timer had made the first catch.
5. Catching a few more fish and not getting seasick, the trip was clearly a success.

Make It Your Own

Reread several papers that you have recently written and note where you handled modifiers well. Circle any confusingly placed, ambiguous, disruptive, or dangling modifiers and edit them using the information in this chapter. If you found several, add this issue to your revision checklist.

42 Avoiding Mixed and Incomplete Constructions

IN THIS CHAPTER

MIXED CONSTRUCTIONS

a. Correcting mixed constructions, 695
b. Correcting mismatched subjects, predicates, 697

INCOMPLETE CONSTRUCTIONS

c. Using essential words, 700
d. Avoiding incomplete comparisons, 701

M. C. Escher, *Waterfall,* 1961

This disorienting image by artist M. C. Escher shows an impossible building, a mixed construction with a water channel that appears to flow horizontally but somehow ends up two stories higher than it begins, with the water cascading back to its source. As you edit your writing, look for sentences that similarly start in one direction but turn disorientingly in another, leaving readers unsure where you have taken them. Look, too, for sentences that omit words readers need to grasp fully your intended meaning.

MIXED CONSTRUCTIONS

When a sentence begins one way and then takes an unexpected turn—in grammar or logic—the result is a ***mixed construction.*** To find and correct mixed constructions in your drafts, keep your eye on the way your sentences begin, and make sure every predicate has a grammatically and logically appropriate subject.

42a Recognizing and Correcting Grammatically Mixed Constructions

Grammatically mixed constructions can occur when a writer treats an introductory phrase or clause that cannot function as the subject of a sentence as if it were the subject. The following example starts with a long prepositional phrase (underlined) that the writer mistakenly uses as the subject of the sentence. A prepositional phrase, although it can modify the subject or other parts of a sentence, cannot be the subject. The result is a ***sentence fragment,*** not a sentence.

> **sentence fragment**
> An incomplete sentence punctuated as if it were complete.

> **MIXED** As a justification by American leaders for dropping atomic bombs on Hiroshima and Nagasaki maintained that doing so persuaded the Japanese to surrender without the need for an invasion that might have cost hundreds of thousands of casualties.

Fixing a sentence like this requires identifying a grammatical subject and isolating it from the introductory phrase. Here is one possible revision (with the subject underlined):

> **REVISED** As a justification for dropping atomic bombs on Hiroshima and Nagasaki, <u>American leaders</u> maintained that doing so persuaded the Japanese to surrender without the need for an invasion that might have cost hundreds of thousands of casualties.

Here is a more concise alternative that eliminates the introductory phrase altogether:

> **REVISED** <u>American leaders</u> maintained that dropping atomic bombs on Hiroshima and Nagasaki persuaded the Japanese to surrender without the need for an invasion that might have cost hundreds of thousands of casualties.

> **More about**
> Clauses, 594–97
> Relating ideas with subordination, 510–17

In the next example, the writer follows a subordinate clause (*Because the bombings had devastating effects*) with the verb *provoked*, which has no subject. The editing changes the first part of the sentence into a noun phrase subject for *provoked*.

▶ ~~Because the bombings had devastating effects~~ *The devastating effects of the bombings* provoked intense debate over the morality of the military decision.

Mixed constructions also occur when a writer treats a modifying phrase or clause as if it were the predicate of a sentence. Look for this kind of mixed construction, especially in sentences that begin with the phrase *the fact that*. The following example begins with a subject, *the fact,* followed by a long adjective *that* clause that modifies the subject but cannot at the same time be the predicate of the sentence.

> **subject complement**
> An adjective, pronoun, noun, or noun phrase that follows a linking verb and refers to the subject of the sentence

> **MIXED** The fact that Hiroshima and Nagasaki, which were devastated by the bomb, are once again thriving cities.

One way to revise this sentence is to add the verb *is,* making the *that* clause into a ***subject complement.***

> **REVISED** The fact is that Hiroshima and Nagasaki, which were devastated by the bomb, are once again thriving cities.

Better yet is simply to eliminate the phrase *the fact that,* a wordy expression that adds no information to the sentence.

> **More about**
> Eliminating wordy expressions, 497–99

REVISED   Hiroshima and Nagasaki, which were devastated by the bomb, are once again thriving cities.

When you are drafting a paper, you may find yourself not only mixing constructions but also confusingly mixing up several ideas in the effort to get your thoughts down. Clarifying snarls like these may require you to pull the ideas apart and sort them into separate sentences.

MIXED   While the first atomic bomb had been successfully tested by scientists of the Manhattan Project on July 16, 1945, at Alamogordo, New Mexico, then less than one month later an American plane, after years of intensive research, dropped the bomb that destroyed Hiroshima on August 6.

REVISED   After years of intensive research, scientists of the Manhattan Project successfully tested the first atomic bomb on July 16, 1945, at Alamogordo, New Mexico. On August 6, less than one month later, an American plane dropped the bomb that destroyed Hiroshima.

42b Recognizing and Correcting Mismatched Subjects and Predicates

The error of ***faulty predication*** occurs when a subject and predicate are mismatched—when they do not fit together logically. For example, the original subject of the following sentence, *recommendation,* does not work with the verb *insisted.* Recommendations cannot insist; doctors can.

> **linking verb** A verb that connects a subject to a subject complement

▶ The ~~doctor's recommendation~~ *doctor* insisted that Joe be hospitalized immediately.

Many instances of faulty predication involve a mismatch between the subject and subject complement in sentences in which the verb is a form of *be* or other **linking verb.**

MISMATCHED   Only students who are absent because of illness or a family emergency will be grounds for a makeup exam.

REVISED   Only students who are absent because of illness or a family emergency will be permitted to take a makeup exam.

Two forms of expression involving the verb *be* that have become commonplace in everyday speech are examples of faulty predication and should be avoided in formal writing. These are the use of *is where* or *is when* in definitions and the use of *the reason is . . . because* in explanations.

1. Is where, is when

Definitions with the expressions *is when* and *is where* usually result in logical mismatches because the terms defined involve neither a place (*where*) nor a time (*when*).

▶ A tornado is ~~where~~ *a violent storm in which* high winds swirl around in a funnel-shaped cloud.

A tornado is a storm, not a place.

▶ A friend is ~~when~~ *who* someone cares about you and has fun with you.

A friend is a person, not a time.

The expressions result in grammatical mismatches, too, because *where* and *when* introduce adverb clauses, which cannot function as subject complements.

2. The reason . . . is because

Explanations using the expression *the reason . . . is because* are similarly mismatched both logically (*the reason* and *because* are redundant) and grammatically (*because* introduces an adverb clause, which cannot function as a subject complement). The following example shows two simple ways to fix this kind of faulty predication—by changing the subject of the sentence or by substituting *that* for *because*.

▶ ~~The reason~~ I wrote this paper ~~is~~ because my instructor required it.

▶ The reason I wrote this paper is ~~because~~ *that* my instructor required it.

> **More about**
> Including a stated subject and eliminating redundant subject and object pronouns, 704–07

Obligatory Words and Unacceptable Repetitions in English Unlike some languages, formal written English requires a stated subject in all sentences except commands.

▶ *It rained* ~~Rained~~ all day yesterday.

On the other hand, formal written English does not permit the use of a pronoun to emphasize an already stated subject or direct object.

▶ Maria~~, she~~ forgot to take her umbrella.

EXERCISE 42.1 Correcting mixed constructions

Revise the following sentences to eliminate mixed constructions. Some sentences may be revised in more than one way.

EXAMPLE

While discouraging human athletes from using chemicals to improve performance ~~ignores~~ ⟨, we ignore⟩ the reality that animals use any chemicals they can to gain an advantage.

1. Because a hedgehog needs to avoid predators gnaws on the skin of poisonous toads.
2. The reason the hedgehog does this is because it gets the toad's toxin and then spread it over its body, making itself immune to enemies.
3. As male cardinals and house finches eat as many berries as they can in the fall unconcerned with the low nutritional value of the food.
4. Eating the berries is where the birds obtain carotenoids, the red and orange pigments that make their feathers so colorful in the spring.
5. The fact that the male *Cosmosoma myrodora* moth, which also collects steroid toxins to help attract the opposite sex.
6. The male moth's drive to lap up toxin from the leaves of certain vines stores a supply of the toxin in pouches on his abdomen.
7. When the male moth's abdominal pouches get large and heavy attracting female moths.
8. During their mating is when the male's pouches burst and spread the steroid toxins all over the female.
9. The fact is that this is how the female *Cosmosoma myrodora* moth becomes inedible to spiders.
10. By denying human athletes the use of steroids is unfair when animals use the chemicals to such great advantage?

INCOMPLETE CONSTRUCTIONS

As you draft sentences, you may unintentionally leave out grammatically or logically essential words. Sometimes these omissions result in sentence fragments. Often, however, they create seemingly minor but nonetheless distracting grammatical or idiomatic bumps. As you proofread and edit your drafts, be especially alert for such missing words in compound and other constructions and in comparisons.

More about
Writing concisely,
496–504 (ch. 26)

42c Adding Essential Words to Compound and Other Constructions

In compound constructions, the omission of *nonessential* repetitions can often help tighten prose.

- Abigail needed a new dress to wear to the graduation party and [to] the wedding reception. First she shopped at Macy's and then [she shopped] at Kohl's.

elliptical construction A construction in which otherwise grammatically necessary words can be omitted because their meaning is understood from the surrounding context

Such *elliptical constructions* work, however, only when the stated words in one part of a compound match the omitted words in other parts. When grammar or idiom requires different words—different verb forms, different prepositions, or different articles, for example—those words should be included.

- The candidate claimed that she always had and always would ^{supported}^ support universal health care coverage.

    The word *supported* is needed because *had support* would be ungrammatical.

- On the campaign trail and ⁱⁿ^ debates, her opponent for the nomination insisted that his plan was better than hers.

    In this situation, the word *debates* requires the preposition *in*, not *on*.

- A yearning for change, ^{an}^ unsettled economy, and ^{the}^ character of the candidates themselves combined to sustain high voter turnout during the primary season.

    The word *unsettled* requires a different form of the indefinite article (*a, an*) than *yearning,* and in this situation the word *character* requires the definite article (*the*) rather than the indefinite article.

Occasionally, you may need to repeat a modifier for clarity.

- The candidates asked their loyal backers and ^{their}^ opponents to support the winner, whoever that might be.

    The repeated *their* makes clear that the adjective *loyal* applies only to *backers* and not to *opponents.*

Although you can often omit the word *that* without obscuring the meaning of a subordinate clause, sometimes you need to include it to avoid confusion.

▶ I know *that* Sheila, who is a sympathetic person, will not be terribly upset about the stains on the silk shirt ~~that~~ I borrowed from her.

In the original, without the first *that*, *Sheila* could be understood as the object of *know* rather than the subject of the long subordinate clause that follows. On the other hand, the *that* at the end of the sentence can be eliminated because no such ambiguity affects the subject (*I*) of the clause it introduces.

42d Avoiding Incomplete or Ambiguous Comparisons

Comparisons show how two items are alike or different. For comparisons to be clear, the items they juxtapose must be logically equivalent. The original version of the following sentence confusingly compares a group of people, children, to a process, growing up. The editing makes the two sides of the comparison equivalent.

> **More about**
> Comparisons, 674–75

▶ Children who grow up on farms are more active than ~~growing up in~~ *those who grow up in* big cities.

To be complete, comparisons must fully specify what is being compared to what.

▶ The Log Cabin Restaurant is better *than Joe's Diner*.

Be careful how you use the terms *any* and *any other* when you compare one item to others that belong to the same category.

▶ Mount Everest is higher than any *other* mountain in the world.

Mount Everest is a mountain in the world, so without the modifier *other*, the sentence suggests that Mount Everest is higher than itself.

▶ Aconcagua, the highest mountain in South America, is higher than any ~~other~~ mountain in North America.

The sentence compares a mountain in South America to mountains in North America, not to other mountains in South America.

Be sure, also, to include any information you need to avoid ambiguity in your comparisons. In its draft form, the following comparison has two possible interpretations, as the revisions make clear.

inc Grammar Matters • Avoiding Mixed and Incomplete Constructions

DRAFT	Yvette is more concerned about me than my brother.
REVISED	Yvette is more concerned about me than <u>she is about</u> my brother.
REVISED	Yvette is more concerned about me than my brother <u>is</u>.

When you use the word *as* in a comparison, be sure to use it twice.

▶ Stephen King's horror stories are scary as Edgar Allan Poe's.
                                                         as

▶ EXERCISE 42.2 Correcting incomplete constructions

Revise the following sentences to eliminate incomplete constructions. Some sentences may be revised in more than one way.

EXAMPLE

Traveling by airplane was once more convenient than *traveling by* train.

1. Yuko understood, from what she heard on the news, air travel had become more difficult in recent years.
2. The airline Yuko chose for her trip to Los Angeles had a more reliable on-time record than any air carrier.
3. She thought she had been careful about her flight planning as she possibly could have been.
4. Unfortunately, she could not have planned for a sudden severe storm during her flight, resulting disruptions in the country's air travel system, and unexpected landing of her flight at Albuquerque, New Mexico, at midnight.
5. She learned that the plane would need repairs and the airline unable to continue the flight to Los Angeles for days.
6. Yuko knew Helen, who sat next to her on the plane, was willing to rent a car and drive the rest of the way to Los Angeles.
7. After an all-night drive, an exhausted Yuko concluded that, whenever available, train travel would be better.

Make It **Your Own**

Reread several papers that you have recently written and note where you handled sentence constructions well. If you see examples of mixed or incomplete constructions, or ambiguous comparisons, edit them and add this issue to your revision checklist.

Part Nine

Language Matters
Issues for Multilingual Writers

43 Understanding English Word Order and Sentence Structure   704
44 Using Nouns and Noun Determiners   713
45 Managing English Verbs   722
46 Managing Adjectives and Adverbs   732
47 Using Prepositions   739

43 Understanding English Word Order and Sentence Structure

by Ted E. Johnston and M. E. Sokolik

IN THIS CHAPTER

a. Observing normal word order, 704

b. Including a stated subject, 704

c. Managing *there* and *it* constructions, 705

d. Eliminating redundant pronouns, 706

e. Direct objects, indirect objects, and object complements, 707

f. Observing word-order patterns, 709

g. Observing inverted word order, 710

> **More about**
> Sentence types, 585
> Word order in questions, 709–10

```
                    Sentence
                   /        \
              Subject      Predicate
                           /        \
              Noun       Verb       Noun
               ↓           ↓          ↓
            The dog     chased     the cat.
            The cat     chased     the dog.
```

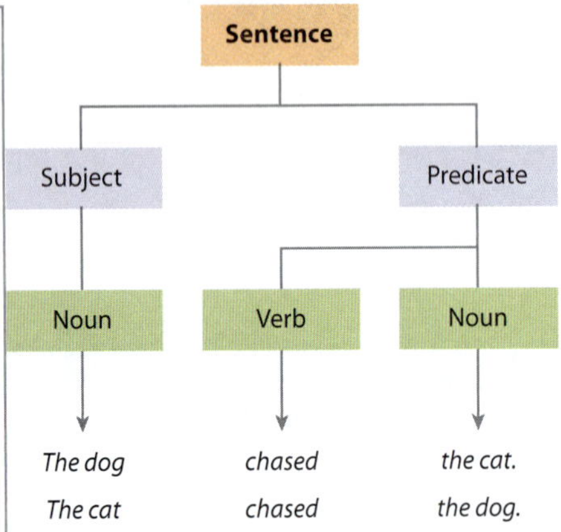

English is a word-order language, which means that the position of a word in a sentence often determines its grammatical function. As a result, *The dog chased the cat* means something different from *The cat chased the dog*. This chapter describes and explains word order and related aspects of English sentence structure.

43a Observing Normal Word Order

In declarative sentences (as opposed to questions or commands), normal word order is subject-verb-object (or S-V-O). That is, the subject comes first, then the verb, and then the direct object, if there is one, or any other words that make up the predicate.

FAULTY WORD ORDER	Chased the cat the dog. (V ? ?)
NORMAL WORD ORDER	The dog chased the cat. (S V O)

43b Including a Stated Subject

> **clause** A word group with a subject and a predicate. An ***independent clause*** can stand alone as a sentence; a ***subordinate clause*** cannot.

Except for commands, English sentences and *clauses* require a subject to be stated, even if the identity of the subject is clear from a previous sentence or clause. In the following example, the pronoun *he,* referring to the subject of the first sentence, can serve as the subject of both clauses of the second sentence.

▸ Nico has a hard life for a ten-year-old. ^(He is)Is just a boy, but ^(he)is expected to work like a man.

Similarly, a subordinate clause requires a stated subject even if its subject is a pronoun or another noun phrase that obviously refers to the same entity as the subject of the clause that precedes it.

▸ Lucy asked for directions because ^(she)was lost. *(sub. clause)*

In commands, the subject is unstated but is understood to be "you."

▸ [you] Leave now!

43c Managing *There* and *It* Constructions

Expletives are words that are empty of content; that is, they do not refer to anything. In English, the words *there* and *it* are often used as expletives.

In *there* constructions, *there* precedes a form of *to be*. *There,* however, is not the subject. The subject follows the verb, and the verb is either singular or plural, depending on the subject. The expletive *it,* on the other hand, is always the singular subject of its clause. *It* constructions are often used to indicate an environmental condition or some aspect of time. The verb in expletive *it* constructions is often a form of *be,* but other verbs can be used, especially those related to process (for example, *start, continue, end*). The expletives *there* and *it* cannot be omitted from such clauses, even though they do not refer to anything.

▸ ^(There are)~~Are~~ not enough reasons to support your argument.

▸ Waiter, I am not pleased that ^(there)is a fly in my soup.

▸ When ^(it)was almost 3:00 p.m., ^(it)started hailing really hard.

In a similar construction, the pronoun *it* is not empty, but refers to content that follows the verb. In the following sentence, for example, *it* refers to *to drive during a snowstorm*. In either case, empty or meaningful, *it* is the subject and cannot be omitted.

▶ ~~Is~~ *It is* dangerous to drive during a snowstorm.

43d Eliminating Redundant Subject and Object Pronouns

Although English requires a stated subject in all clauses except commands, the use of a pronoun to reemphasize an already stated subject is not acceptable in writing, even though such constructions often occur in informal speech.

▶ Rosalinda, ~~she~~ left early for the airport. *[subj. / redundant subject]*

Similarly, when *which* or *that* begins a clause and serves as the clause's subject or direct object, do not also add *it* to serve as the subject or direct object. In the following sentences, for example, both *which* and *it* refer redundantly to the movie *Pan's Labyrinth*; to correct the sentences requires eliminating one or the other pronoun.

▶ Last night I saw *Pan's Labyrinth*, which ~~it~~ impressed me very much. *[subj. / redundant subject]*

or

▶ Last night I saw *Pan's Labyrinth*, ~~which~~ it impressed me very much.

▶ I liked *Pan's Labyrinth*, which many of my friends liked ~~it~~ too. *[dir. obj. / redundant object]*

or

▶ I liked *Pan's Labyrinth*, ~~which~~ many of my friends liked it too.

Language Matters • Direct Objects, Indirect Objects, and Object Complements

EXERCISE 43.1 Using normal word order and including a subject

In the following sentences, correct word-order errors involving subjects or omissions of *it* or *there*.

EXAMPLE
It was
~~Was~~ obvious the students hadn't studied for the test.

1. Without a doubt, is nothing more breathtaking than seeing a double rainbow after a storm.
2. I am excited by this letter, which I received it late yesterday.
3. Was still too early to plant the tomatoes, so died all of them.
4. We read that are several new dance clubs opening this weekend.
5. We left the office because was after five o'clock.
6. Don't you think is a little silly to argue about who is the better cook?
7. My aunt and uncle, they are both working in California as computer programmers.
8. Is completely impossible to dislike that professor!
9. This is an uplifting story because has such an optimistic ending.
10. I read a controversial article that it claims North and South America were settled much earlier than previously thought.

43e Structuring Sentences with Direct Objects, Indirect Objects, and Object Complements

Direct objects, indirect objects, and object complements can follow a transitive verb.

1. Direct and indirect objects

A ***direct object*** receives or carries the action of a transitive verb. Certain transitive verbs—such as *ask, find, give, order, send, show, teach, tell,* and *write*—can also take an ***indirect object***, which names the recipient of the direct object. The indirect object falls between the verb and the direct object.

> **More about**
> Direct and indirect objects, 588–90

      s   v   io   do
▸ She sent Michiko a book on Scandinavian cuisine.

Alternatively, the recipient of the direct object can be identified in a phrase beginning with a preposition, usually *to,* that follows the direct object.

▶ She sent a book on Scandinavian cuisine to Michiko.
     s v   do   alternative phrase

When the direct object is a personal pronoun, the verb must be followed by a prepositional phrase, not an indirect object.

▶ She sent ~~Michiko~~ it. *to Michiko.*

Several common verbs do not take indirect objects even though the actions they refer to are similar to those of verbs that do. These verbs include *answer, carry, change, close, complete, deliver, describe, explain, keep, mention, open, propose, put, recommend, repair* (or *fix* when it means *repair*), and *say.* With these verbs, the function of the indirect object can be performed only by a prepositional phrase beginning with *to* (or sometimes *for*) that follows the direct object.

▶ The doctor explained ~~my father~~ the dangers of secondhand smoke. *to my father.*

▶ The professor opened ~~us~~ the door to understanding. *for us.*

2. Object complements

An **object complement** follows a direct object and describes a condition of the object or a change in the object that the subject has caused the object to undergo.

▶ Some workers here make my job impossible.
                            do   obj. comp.

Placing an object complement before the direct object will either make a sentence ungrammatical or change its meaning. The following sentence, as originally written, was ungrammatical.

▶ The players have just elected ~~their team captain~~ Paul. *their team captain.*

The following sentences, in contrast, are both grammatical but have different meanings.

▶ We need to keep all the <u>happy</u> workers.

▶ We need to keep all the workers <u>happy</u>.

The first sentence, with the adjective *happy* before the direct object, recommends retaining the workers who are already happy, but not necessarily those who are not. The second, with *happy* in the object complement position after the direct object, recommends taking action to make sure that not one of the workers feels unhappy.

EXERCISE 43.2 Using objects and object complements

Correct any errors related to indirect objects or object complements in the following sentences. Next to sentences with an error, write IO if the problem is related to indirect objects and OC if it is related to object complements. Mark any correct sentences OK.

EXAMPLE

We want the ~~closed~~ door, please.   *closed,*   OC

1. We painted the yellow walls because yellow is a cheerful color.
2. She sent me a very informative letter.
3. I consider his inappropriate remarks and refuse to respond to them.
4. The owner described me the house in great detail.
5. The president appointed me his new assistant.
6. Frank has a build very muscular.
7. I had an extra blanket, so I gave a homeless man it.
8. We ordered the carpet baby blue, not the beige one.
9. The last treatment did to the patient more harm than good.
10. The teacher explained the students the assignment one more time.

43f Observing Word-Order Patterns in Questions

In questions, unlike declarative statements, a verb nearly always precedes the subject.

- To form a question with one-word forms of the verb *be,* simply invert subject and verb.

  s   v   v   s
  The grapes are ripe.   Are the grapes ripe?

- In all other cases, a question requires a helping verb as well as a main verb. The subject goes after the first helping verb in a verb phrase and before the rest of the verb phrase.

   s   hv   mv   hv s mv
  They have left for New York.   Have they left for New York?

     s   hv mv   hv   s   mv
  The children can go with us.   Can the children go with us?

     s   hv hv mv   hv   s   hv   mv
  The painters should have finished.   Should the painters have finished?

- To form a question with one-word verbs other than forms of *be,* use the appropriate form of *do* as the helper.

    s   v   hv   s   mv
  The prisoner escaped.   Did the prisoner escape?

- Questions that begin with question words like *what, who,* and *why* normally follow the same word order as other questions.

     hv   s   mv
  What is the engineer saying about the project?

- If the question word is the subject, however, the question follows subject-before-verb word order.

   s   v   do
  Who is saying these things about the project?

43g Observing Inverted Word Order When Certain Conjunctions or Adverbs Begin a Clause

When they appear at the beginning of a sentence or clause, certain adverbs, adverb phrases, correlative conjunctions (such as *neither . . . nor* and *not only . . . but also*), and the conjunction *nor* by itself require inverted word order similar to that used in questions.

▶ *Neither* ~~the parents~~ have called the principal, *nor* ~~they~~ have informed the school board. [the parents] [they]

▶ The twins don't bowl, *nor* they play tennis. [do]

The adverbs *rarely, seldom, no sooner, no longer,* and similar negating or limiting expressions also require inverted word order when they start a sentence or clause. Such sentences have a formal tone.

▶ *Seldom* ~~the dancers~~ have had the opportunity to perform in public. [the dancers]

Moving the adverb to the interior of the sentence cancels the inversion.

> **More about**
> Adverbs, 669–77, 734–38

▶ The dancers have *seldom* had the opportunity to perform in public.

Usually, this less formal, noninverted version of such sentences is preferable to the inverted version.

➔ EXERCISE 43.3 Working with word-order inversions

In the following sentences, correct any word-order errors related to inversions. Mark any correct sentences OK.

EXAMPLE
Neither we want to go the party, nor we want to help pay for it. [do] [do]

1. Neither he takes classes at the university, nor he works.
2. Jossette has been working on her research project?
3. When Chen bought his new computer?
4. We rarely went to dinner with friends.
5. Rarely it rains in the desert.
6. Goes she often to parties?
7. Couldn't Fatima have done something sooner about the error?
8. Why smoking should be banned in bars?
9. Not only she works hard, but she also studies hard.
10. Mark neither reads French nor speaks it.

Make It **Your Own**

In an issue of a newsmagazine such as *Time,* the *Economist, U.S. News and World Report,* or the *Week,* find two examples each of sentences with indirect objects, object complements, and inversions involving "not only," "neither/nor," or some other initial adverb or adverbial phrase. Copy the sentences and underline the components in each sentence identifying the feature. Write two examples of your own for each type of sentence patterned on the examples you found.

Work **Together**

In small groups, check the examples group members found and wrote on their own in the Make It Your Own activity above. Does everyone agree with the results? Why or why not? Ask your instructor if you are uncertain about any of the examples.

44 Using Nouns and Noun Determiners
by Ted E. Johnston and M. E. Sokolik

IN THIS CHAPTER

a. Understanding different types of nouns, 713
b. Using nouns with articles and other determiners, 714

"What can I say? I was an English major."

English nouns rarely appear by themselves. Most of the time they are paired with words such as *a, an, the, my, that, each, one, ten, several, more, less,* and *fewer.* These words are known as **determiners** because they help us figure out—or determine—how a noun works and what it means when we encounter it in a sentence. As this cartoon suggests, learning to use nouns and determiners appropriately can sometimes challenge native speakers as much as it does multilingual students.

44a Understanding Different Types of Nouns

To use a noun properly, you need to know whether it is a *proper noun* or a *common noun,* and, if it is a common noun, whether it is *count* or *noncount.* A **common noun** identifies a general category and is usually not capitalized: *woman, era, bridge, corporation, mountain, war.* A **proper noun** identifies someone or something specific and is usually capitalized: *Hillary Clinton, Middle Ages, Golden Gate Bridge, Burger King, Himalayas, World War II.*

Count nouns name discrete, countable things. **Noncount nouns** (also called **noncountable** or **mass** nouns) usually name entities made of a continuous substance or of small, indistinguishable particles, or they refer to a general quality. A *drop,* a *grain,* and a *suggestion,* for example, are count nouns, but *water, sand,* and *advice* are noncount nouns.

> **More about**
> Types of nouns, 575–77

> **More about**
> Forming noun plurals, 569–71

- Count nouns can be singular (*drop*) or plural (*drops*). Most noncount nouns are singular, even those that end in *-s,* and

713

thus should be matched with singular verbs. Noncount nouns cannot be preceded by a number or any other term that would imply countability (such as *a, an, several, another,* or *many*), nor can they be made plural if they are singular.

▶ Aerobics ~~help~~ *helps* me to relax.

Here are some examples of contrasting count and noncount nouns:

Count	Noncount
car/cars	traffic
dollar/dollars	money
noodle/noodles	spaghetti
pebble/pebbles	gravel
spoon/spoons	silverware

- Many nouns can be noncount in one context and count in another.
  ▶ While speaking of *love* [noncount], my grandmother recalled the three *loves* [count] of her life.

  In the opening phrase, *love* is an abstraction. In the main clause, *loves* refers to the people the grandmother has loved.

- All languages have count and noncount nouns, but a noun that is count in one language may be noncount in another.

44b Using Nouns with Articles (*a, an, the*) and Other Determiners

The ***articles** a, an,* and *the* are the most common determiners. Other determiners include possessives (*my, your, Ivan's*), numbers (*one, five, a hundred*), and other words that quantify (*some, many, a few*) or specify (*this, those*).

1. Articles with common nouns

The main function of the ***indefinite articles,** a* and *an,* is to introduce nouns that are new to the reader. The ***definite article,** the,* usually precedes nouns that have already been introduced or whose identity is known or clear from the context. Noncount nouns and plural count nouns also sometimes appear with no article (or the ***zero article***).

Language Matters • Using Nouns with Articles (*a, an, the*) and Other Determiners

Quick Reference: Some Common Noncount Nouns

Although there is no hard-and-fast way to distinguish noncount from count nouns, most noncount nouns do fall into a few general categories.

Abstractions and Emotions	advice, courage, happiness, hate, jealousy, information, knowledge, love, luck, maturity, patriotism, warmth
Mass Substances	air, blood, dirt, gasoline, glue, sand, shampoo, water
Food Items	beef, bread, corn, flour, gravy, pork, rice, salt, sugar
Collections of Related Items	cash, clothing, equipment, furniture, graffiti, information, jewelry, luggage, mail, traffic
Games and Other Activities	aerobics, baseball, checkers, homework, news, Pilates, poker, pool, soccer, tennis, volleyball
Weather-Related Phenomena	cold, drizzle, frost, hail, heat, humidity, lightning, rain, sleet, snow, sunshine, thunder
Diseases	arthritis, chicken pox, diabetes, influenza, measles
Fields of Study	botany, chemistry, mathematics, physics, sociology

- Use *a* before a consonant sound (*a cat*) and *an* before a vowel sound (*an elephant*). Do not be misled by written vowels that are pronounced as consonants (*a European tour*) or written consonants that are pronounced as vowels (*an hour early*). Be especially careful with words that begin with *h* (*a hot stove, an honorary degree*) and *u* (*a uniform, an upheaval*).

- Use *a* or *an* only with singular count nouns. A singular count noun *must* be preceded by an article or some other determiner even if other modifiers come between the determiner and the noun.

   ▶ A friend of mine bought an antique car on eBay.

- Never use *a* or *an* with a noncount noun.

   ▶ A good advice is hard to find.
       Good

- Use *a* or *an* when you first introduce a singular count noun if the specific identity of the noun is not yet known to the reader or is not otherwise clear from the context. Use *the* for subsequent references to the same noun.

- ▸ A friend of mine bought <u>an</u> antique car on eBay. She restored <u>the</u> car and sold it for <u>a</u> tidy profit. <u>The</u> profit came in handy when she took <u>a</u> vacation.

  The is appropriate for *car* in the second sentence because it refers to the same car introduced in the first sentence. The word *profit* in the second sentence takes *a* because it is making its first appearance there. The third sentence continues the process.

- Use *the* with both count and noncount nouns whose specific identity has been previously established or is clear from the context.

  - ▸ We admired <u>the</u> antique car that my friend bought on eBay.

    The modifying clause *that my friend bought on eBay* identifies a specific car.

  - ▸ She sold it for <u>a</u> tidy profit and used <u>the</u> money for <u>a</u> vacation.

    The context clearly identifies the money with the profit.

  - ▸ My friend is traveling around <u>the</u> world for three months.

    The noun *world* logically refers to the planet we live on—not, say, Mars or Venus.

  - ▸ Vicky is <u>the</u> fastest runner on her team.

    The superlative *fastest* refers specifically to one person.

> **More about**
> Superlatives, 674–75

- No article is used to introduce noncount nouns or plural count nouns used generically—that is, to make generalizations.

  - ▸ Good advice is hard to find.
  - ▸ Good teachers can change lives.

- Both the definite and indefinite articles can introduce singular nouns used generically. Sometimes either is appropriate:

  - ▸ <u>The</u> good teacher can change lives.
  - ▸ <u>A</u> good teacher can change lives.

  Sometimes the generic meaning is clear with only one or the other:

  - ▸ Thomas Alva Edison invented ~~a~~ *the* lightbulb.

2. Articles with proper nouns

Proper nouns in English almost never occur with the indefinite article (*a, an*), and most occur with no article:

▶ Ruby grew up in Lima, Peru, but now lives in Wichita, Kansas.

There are many exceptions, however:

- Certain place names always occur with *the: the* Bronx, *the* Philippines, *the* Northeast, *the* Pacific Ocean.
- The names of ships (including airships) conventionally occur with *the: the* Queen Mary, *the* Challenger.
- Many product names can be used with *a* or *the* or sometimes both: *the* Cheerios, *an/the* iPhone, *a/the* Toyota.
- Many multiword proper nouns occur with *the: the* United States, *the* Brooklyn Bridge, *the* Department of State, *the* War of 1812. Others do not, however. The city of Chicago, for example, is home to both *the Wrigley Building* (with article) and *Wrigley Field* (no article).
- Most plural proper nouns occur with *the: the* Bartons, *the* Chicago Cubs.

EXERCISE 44.1 Using articles correctly

Insert *a, an, the,* or no article as appropriate in the blanks in the following paragraph.

I feel ___¹ anger whenever I see ___² poor child suffering from ___³ hunger. In ___⁴ United States, we believe that ___⁵ children need ___⁶ good breakfast every morning to do well in ___⁷ school, so schools provide ___⁸ breakfast for them. I realize that ___⁹ economic situation is often worse in ___¹⁰ other countries than here, but even here, there is more hunger than ___¹¹ people realize. ___¹² hungriest children are found in ___¹³ rural areas of our country. ___¹⁴ boy I once knew told me that many nights he went to bed hungry after working in ___¹⁵ fields. ___¹⁶ boy later moved to ___¹⁷ nearby city and his family was able to get ___¹⁸ assistance from ___¹⁹ various charitable organizations.

art Language Matters • Using Nouns and Noun Determiners

> **More about**
> Order of adjectives, 732–33

3. Nouns and other determiners

As with articles, the use of other determiners with nouns depends on the kind of noun in question, particularly whether it is singular or plural, count or noncount. In all cases, determiners precede any other adjectives that modify a noun.

Possessive nouns or pronouns Use possessive nouns (*Julio's*) and possessive pronouns (*my, our, your, his, her, its, their, whose*) with any count or noncount noun.

sing. count	plural count	noncount
Ann's book	*Ann's* books	*Ann's* information
her book	*her* books	*her* information

This, that, these, those The demonstrative pronouns *this, that, these,* and *those* specify, or single out, particular instances of a noun. Use *this* and *that* only with noncount nouns and singular count nouns. Use *these* and *those* only with plural count nouns.

sing. count	plural count	noncount
this book	—	*this* information
that book	—	*that* information
—	*these* books	—
—	*those* books	—

Quantifying words or phrases Use numbers only with count nouns: *one shirt, two shirts.* See the Quick Reference box on the next page for a list of other quantifying words and how they work with different kinds of nouns in most contexts.

Few *versus* a few *and* little *versus* a little The determiners *few* and *a few* (for count nouns) and *little* and *a little* (for noncount nouns) all indicate a small quantity, but they have significant differences in meaning. *Few* means a negligible amount, whereas *a few* means a small but significant number. Likewise, *little* means *almost none,* whereas *a little* means *some.*

▸ Rhoda has *few* good friends.
   She is almost friendless.

▸ Rhoda has *a few* good friends.
   She has significant companionship.

Language Matters • Using Nouns with Articles (*a, an, the*) and Other Determiners

Quick Reference: Matching Nouns with Quantifying Words and Phrases

Quantifying Word or Phrase	Singular Count Nouns	Plural Count Nouns	Noncount Nouns	Examples
any, no	✓	✓	✓	You can read any book on the list. Have you read any books this summer? Do you have any information about the reading list?
another, each, every, either, neither	✓	no	no	I read another book last week.
the other	✓	✓	✓	The other book is a murder mystery. I haven't finished the other books on the reading list. The other information is the most reliable.
a couple of, a number of, both, few, a few, fewer, fewest, many, several	no	✓	no	The professor assigned fewer books last term.
a lot of, lots of, all, enough, more, most, other, some	no	✓	✓	Some books are inspiring. Some information is unreliable.
little, a little, much, a great deal of, less, least	no	no	✓	I need a little information about the course requirements.

▶ Pete provided *little* help before the party.
  He didn't do his share.

▶ Pete gave me *a little* help after everyone left.
  He made himself useful.

Indicating extent or amount with noncount nouns Because a noncount noun is always singular, do not make it plural or add a determiner that implies a plural form. For example, do not use a determiner such as *a large number of, many,* or *several* immediately before a noncount noun. Instead, use a determiner such as *a great deal of, less, little, much,* or *some*—or revise the sentence another way.

44b art Language Matters • Using Nouns and Noun Determiners

▸ The city is doing ~~researches~~ *some* on the proposal.

The modifier *some* is appropriate for the noncount noun *research* because it does not imply plurality.

▸ Gina bought two ~~breads~~ *loaves of* at the store.

In the edited version, *two* modifies the count noun *loaves*.

▸ We do not have many ~~violences~~ *incidents of violence* in our neighborhood.

▸ A ~~large number~~ *great deal* of information is available on your topic.

A large number of, which suggests plurality, cannot be used with *information,* a noncount noun.

▸ EXERCISE 44.2 Editing for noun and determiner usage

Correct any errors resulting from the improper use of nouns and determiners in the following passage.

> A great deal of students showed up at the class party this past weekend. Everyone seemed to have fairly good time despite few major problems that I am now being blamed for. However, whenever we plan this kinds of events in future, we need much more people to help. So little people actually helped that I essentially had to do all work on my own. Therefore, I refuse to take a blame for all things that went wrong. Everyone should be aware that other person (who will remain nameless) who had agreed to help me organize event didn't do his share of job. He was supposed to coordinate the individuals who had volunteered to set up and decorate hall and then to remind others who had indicated that they would provide necessary items not to forget to do so. Because he didn't call anyone, that tasks never got done, but I did best I could by myself. Not surprisingly, biggest problem we had was that there were not enough supplies. For example, we had less sodas than we needed, so some guests had to drink lot of water because it was so hot that evening. Another examples was that we didn't have as many ice as we needed, and there weren't enough plastic glasses or napkins. I had to send someone out to buy much of this items using my own moneys.

Language Matters • Using Nouns with Articles (*a, an, the*) and Other Determiners

Make It Your Own

Write five sentences with plural references using noncount nouns from five of the categories in the Quick Reference box on page 715. For example, you might write, "The recipe calls for *five cups of flour.*" Next, referring to the Quick Reference box on page 719, write three sentences with count nouns and three with noncount nouns using different quantifiers. For example, you might write, "I read *a couple of* science fiction *novels* over spring break."

Work Together

In small groups, exchange your work on the exercise above. Discuss your differences, and consult your instructor if you need help arriving at a consensus.

45 Managing English Verbs
by Ted E. Johnston and M. E. Sokolik

IN THIS CHAPTER

a. Using phrasal verbs, 722
b. Using gerunds and infinitives, 725
c. Using participles as adjectives, 727
d. Using helping verbs, 728

Verbs can express an action or occurrence (*The dog jumps for the Frisbee*) or indicate a state of being (*The dog is frisky*). In many languages, verbs can have several forms. For example, they may change to indicate the identity of a subject or object or the time frame in which an event happens. English verbs, in contrast, have only a few forms, but these combine with other words to accomplish the same functions.

45a Using Phrasal Verbs

> **More about**
> Verbs and verb phrases, 592, 621, 636–55

Phrasal verbs—sometimes called *multiword verbs*—consist of a verb and one or two **particles**. The particle takes the form of a preposition or adverb, and it combines with the verb to create a new verb with a new meaning. For example, the verb *throw* means to project something through the air. The phrasal verb *throw out* consists of the verb *throw* and the particle *out*; it means to dispose of something.

▸ Segundo threw out his old notebook.
      phrasal vb. — *particle*

▸ Segundo threw his old notebook on his bed.
      verb

The meaning of a verb-and-particle combination differs from the meaning of the same words in a verb-and-preposition combination. The phrasal verb *look up*, for example, means to consult or find something in a reference work, which is different from the meaning of *look* followed by a phrase that happens to begin with the preposition *up*.

	phrasal vb.
PHRASAL VERB	Svetlana looked up the word in the dictionary.
	verb prep.
VERB WITH PREPOSITIONS	Svetlana looked up the steep trail and began to hike.

A transitive phrasal verb is ***separable*** if its direct object can fall either between the verb and the particle (separating them) or after the particle.

▸ She looked up the address online.

▸ She looked the address up online.

Quick Reference: Some Common Phrasal Verbs and Their Meanings

SEPARABLE

ask out	invite for a date
calm down	make calm, become calm
give up	surrender
hand in	submit
hand out	distribute
look up	find something in a reference work
put back	return to original position
put down	criticize meanly; suppress
take back	return; retract
take off	remove
take on	assume responsibility for
take up	begin a hobby or activity
throw out	dispose of

INSEPARABLE

add up to	total
barge in on	interrupt unannounced
call on	visit, or ask for a response directly
come across	find accidentally
drop in	visit unannounced
get out of	evade an obligation, exit
give in	surrender
grow up	mature
hint at	suggest
look down on	disdain
look up to	admire
put up with	tolerate
run into	encounter; collide
stand in for	substitute for
turn up	show up, arrive

vb Language Matters • Managing English Verbs

If the direct object of a separable phrasal verb is a pronoun, it must come between the verb and the particle.

I decided to hand ~~in it~~. *it in.*

A phrasal verb is ***inseparable*** if no words can fall between the verb and the particle.

FAULTY	I came an old photo across in the drawer.
REVISED	I came across an old photo in the drawer.

The meaning of a phrasal verb changes when the particle changes (see the Quick Reference box on page 723). The phrasal verb *take on,* for example, means "to assume responsibility for."

▸ She took on the editing of the newsletter.

The phrasal verb *take back,* in contrast, means "to return" or "to retract."

▸ She took all her overdue books back to the library.

EXERCISE 45.1 Using phrasal verbs correctly

Put a check by the sentences that use verbs and phrasal verbs incorrectly, and then revise those sentences so they are correct.

EXAMPLE

After the accident, the EMT calmed down ~~him~~. *him* ✓

1. I hear that Lisa is sick. Who is going to stand in for her?
2. I cannot find my glasses. Have you come them across?
3. The instructor handed the assignment out yesterday.
4. Is there any way for us to get this assignment out of?
5. If you do not understand a word, look up it.
6. That jacket looks too warm. Why don't you take off it?
7. Will you take these back to the store?
8. I ran an old friend into at the movie theater.

45b Using Gerunds and Infinitives after Verbs and Prepositions

A ***gerund*** is the *-ing* form of a verb used as a noun (*listening, eating*). An ***infinitive*** is the base form of a verb preceded by *to* (*to listen, to eat*).

1. Gerunds and infinitives after verbs

- Only gerunds can follow some verbs, and only infinitives can follow others.

    ▶ The committee recommended ~~to submit~~ *submitting* the proposal for a vote.

    ▶ Rosa Parks refused ~~sitting~~ *to sit* in the back of the bus.

- Some verbs can be followed by either gerunds or infinitives. For some of these verbs, the choice of gerund or infinitive has little effect on meaning, but for a few the difference is significant.

SAME MEANING	The economy *continued* to grow.
	The economy *continued* growing.
DIFFERENT MEANINGS	Juan *remembered* to e-mail his paper to his professor. [He didn't forget to do it.]
	Juan *remembered* e-mailing his paper to his professor. [He recalled having done it already.]

- Some verbs that can be followed by an infinitive can also be followed by an infinitive after an intervening noun or pronoun.

    ▶ Yue *wanted* to study the violin.

    ▶ Yue's parents *wanted* her to study the violin.

    Certain verbs, however, take an infinitive only after an object noun or pronoun.

    ▶ The candidate *urged* citizens to vote on Election Day.

A few verbs (for example, *feel, have, hear, let, look at,* and *see*) require an ***unmarked infinitive***—the base verb alone, without *to*—after an intervening noun or pronoun.

▶ Paolo let his children ~~to go~~ *go* to the movies.

▶ Jen heard a dog ~~to bark~~ *bark* late at night.

2. Gerunds after prepositions

Only a gerund, not an infinitive, can be the object of a preposition.

▶ The article is about ~~to travel~~ *traveling* in South America.

Quick Reference: Gerund or Infinitive after Selected Verbs

Some verbs that can be directly followed by a gerund but not an infinitive

admit	discuss	imagine	practice	risk
avoid	enjoy	mind	quit	suggest
consider	escape	miss	recall	tolerate
deny	finish	postpone	resist	understand

Some verbs that can be directly followed by an infinitive but not a gerund

agree	claim	hope	offer	refuse
appear	decide	manage	plan	wait
ask	expect	mean	pretend	want
beg	have	need	promise	wish

Some verbs that can be directly followed by a gerund or an infinitive with little effect on meaning

begin	hate	love	start
continue	like	prefer	

Some verbs for which choice of gerund or infinitive affects meaning

forget	remember	stop	try

Some verbs that take an infinitive only after an intervening noun or pronoun

advise	command	force	persuade	tell
allow	convince	instruct	remind	urge
cause	encourage	order	require	warn

45c Using Participles as Adjectives

Both the present participle and the past participle of a verb can function as adjectives, but they convey different meanings, especially if the base verb refers to an emotion or state of mind such as anger or boredom. The ***present participle*** (or *-ing* form) usually describes the cause or agent of a state of affairs. The ***past participle*** (the *-ed* form in regular verbs) usually describes the result of the state of affairs.

> **More about**
> Regular and irregular verb forms, 636–40, 640

State of Affairs	Cause	Result
Physics class bored me today. (verb)	The class was boring. (adj.)	I was bored. (adj.)
Dr. Sung's lecture interested me. (verb)	The lecture was interesting. (adj.)	I was interested. (adj.)

EXERCISE 45.2 Using gerunds, infinitives, and participial adjectives

Use the verbs in parentheses to correctly complete each sentence. The first one is done as an example. Some may have more than one correct solution.

1. That movie was really *boring* (bore). I fell asleep after twenty minutes.
2. Juan was _____ (astonish) to see a rare bird in his backyard.
3. Martine advised Hugo _____ (see) the museum exhibit. Our father begged us not _____ (drive) there in the icy weather.
4. We had to postpone _____ (give) our parents an anniversary party because my mother had to work Saturday.
5. We enjoy _____ (cook) for our friends.
6. The customer inquired about _____ (purchase) a new microwave oven.
7. Nikolai admitted _____ (borrow) his roommate's computer without _____ (ask).
8. Mike continued _____ (watch) TV during dinner.
9. The sergeant commanded the advancing troops _____ (march) up the hill.

> **More about**
> Verb forms, 636–44
> Subject-verb agreement, 620–30

45d Using Helping Verbs for Verb Formation

Most English verb constructions, other than the present and past tenses, consist of a main verb with one or more helping (auxiliary) verbs. The main verb carries the principal meaning, and the helping verbs carry information about time, mood, and voice. There are two kinds of helping verb: simple and modal.

- The simple helping verbs—*have, do,* and *be*—also function as main verbs, and like other main verbs, they change form to indicate person and tense.

- The modal helping verbs—including *can, could, may, might, must, ought to, shall, should, will,* and *would*—carry information about attributes of the main verb such as ability, intention, permission, possibility, desire, and suggestion (see the Quick Reference box on the next page). Unlike the simple auxiliaries, the modal auxiliaries do not change form to indicate number or tense.

  ▶ All the contestants at the Olympics can swim fast, but Michael Phelps ~~cans~~ *can* swim faster than any of the others.

  ▶ William should work all day today, and he ~~shoulded work~~ *should have worked* yesterday too.

NOTE When you hear such contractions as *should've* or *could've* in speech (or similar contractions with other modals), remember that the contracted word is *have* (*should have, could have*), not *of*.

- In a verb phrase, auxiliaries almost always precede the main verb, and modals precede any other auxiliaries.

  ▶ In June, Chen *will* [modal] *have been* [simple auxiliaries] *living* [main verb] in Seattle for ten years.

- When forming verbs, include needed auxiliaries.

  ▶ Demetrio *is* taking six courses this semester.

  ▶ My grandparents *have* been visiting Scotland every year.

Quick Reference: Modals and Meaning

Modals	Meaning	Examples
can, could	Used to indicate ability, possibility, and willingness and to request or grant permission	Sam can paint wonderful watercolors. [ability] You can leave class early today. [grant permission] Could we meet at the library? [request permission] I'm so hungry I could eat a horse. [possibility] I could work your shift if you need me to. [willingness]
may, might	Used to request and grant permission and to offer suggestions. For requests, *might* has a more hesitant and polite connotation than *may,* but they are otherwise usually interchangeable.	May I see the comments you wrote? [request permission] Might I borrow your car this afternoon? [more polite request for permission] It may/might rain this afternoon. [possibility] You may/might want to bring an umbrella. [suggestion]
must	Expresses necessity, prohibition (in the negative), and logical probability	Passengers must pass through airport security before boarding. [necessity] Passengers must not leave their seats while the seatbelt sign is illuminated. [prohibition] We must be on our final approach. [logical probability]
shall, should, ought to	*Should* and *ought to* express advisability and expectation, usually interchangeably. *Shall* expresses intention as well as advisability, but in American English it usually appears only in questions.	Shall/Should we eat in or go out for dinner tonight? [advisability] We should/ought to eat out less to save money. [advisability] The pizza should/ought to arrive in 20 minutes or so. [expectation]
will, would	*Will* expresses intention, willingness, and expectation. *Would* expresses intention, willingness, typical or repeated action, and logical assumption, and it is also used for polite requests.	I will finish the laundry if you want. [willingness] I will apply to graduate school next year. [intention] The bus will arrive soon. [expectation] Would you mind opening the window? [request] Amalia decided she would apply to graduate school. [intention] When preparing dinner, he would always clean up as he cooked. [repeated action] That alarm you're hearing would be the monthly test of the emergency system. [logical probability]

45d vb Language Matters • Managing English Verbs

- In general, never follow a modal with another modal, and always follow a modal with the base form of a simple auxiliary or main verb.

▶ Tomás should ~~can~~ *be able to* finish his calculus homework before the movie starts.

▶ Yuki must ~~to~~ take three more courses to graduate.

EXERCISE 45.3 Using modal auxiliaries

The following e-mail message has six errors in the use of modals and auxiliaries. Edit the message to correct these errors. The first error has been found for you.

Hi Mario,

I hope everything is going well. I *am* writing to ask you a favor. We want to organize an auction for the baseball team. If you might could contribute a little time, that would to be great! We need someone who cans contact potential donors, assign starting bids for items, and mail out publicity. We think we might raise as much as $10,000 for team uniforms if we can get enough volunteers. I really hope you will to help us out. Do you think you come on Saturday for a short meeting?

Thanks in advance!

Bill

Make It **Your Own**

Review a recent piece of writing you completed for one of your classes. Print a new copy and circle all the verbs, gerunds, infinitives, and participial adjectives. Note any that you find confusing or that were marked by your instructor as incorrectly used. Make notes about their correct use by consulting this book, your instructor, or your college writing center.

Work **Together**

The use of modals affects how polite (or impolite) a piece of writing is considered to be. Working with a partner, consider the following pairs of sentences. Decide which in each pair is more polite, and discuss why. Does it depend on your audience? Be prepared to discuss your conclusions with your class.

1. a. Can you open the window?
   b. Would you mind opening the window?
2. a. Might I have a bite of your cake? It looks delicious.
   b. Could I have a bite of your cake?
3. a. Can I get a letter of recommendation from you?
   b. May I ask you to write me a letter of recommendation?

46 Managing Adjectives and Adverbs
by Ted E. Johnston and M. E. Sokolik

IN THIS CHAPTER

a. Placing adjectives in the proper order, 732

b. Choosing the correct prepositions, 733

c. Placing adverbs correctly, 734

d. Dealing with confusing adverbs, 736

> **More about**
> Articles and other determiners, 714–21
> Cumulative versus coordinate adjectives, 755–56

linking verbs *Be* and other verbs that express a state of being rather than an action and connect a subject to its subject complement

Just as a coat of paint can change our perception of the surface it covers, adjectives and adverbs color our understanding of the words they modify. ***Adjectives*** modify nouns and pronouns. ***Adverbs*** modify verbs, adjectives, other adverbs, and entire phrases, clauses, and sentences. This chapter will help you use adjectives and adverbs correctly and place them appropriately in your sentences.

46a Placing Adjectives in the Proper Order

- Most English adjectives have only one form, regardless of whether the noun they modify is singular or plural.

  ▶ Serena wants a white dress, but many of these white dresses are not to her liking.

- English adjectives usually come before a noun (*Serena has a white dress*) or after a **linking verb** (*Serena's dress is white*).

- When multiple adjectives cumulatively modify the same noun, the kind of information they convey determines their proper order (see the Quick Reference box on the next page).

NOTE More than three adjectives in a sequence can be awkward. Instead, vary your sentences to distribute the adjectives without confusing your readers.

Language Matters • Choosing the Correct Prepositions with Adjectives

Quick Reference: Putting Cumulative Adjectives in Standard Order

Article or Other Determiner	Overall Evaluation or Opinion	Size	Shape or Other Intrinsic Aspect	Age	Color	Essence: Nationality, Material, or Purpose	Noun
two		big			red	rubber	balls
an	exciting			new		mystery	novel
my		tiny	helpless	newborn			kitten
those	funny			old	black-and-white		sitcoms
the	delicious		round			French	pastry

46b Choosing the Correct Prepositions with Adjectives

On a particular day, you might be excited *by* a lecture, mad *at* a friend, or happy *about* the election in Pakistan. As these phrases reveal, you need to be careful when combining adjectives and prepositions. When in doubt, consult a dictionary to make sure you are using the proper idiom. The editing in the following paragraph gives additional examples of correct idiomatic usage:

Ally is delighted ~~in~~ *With* her midterm grades. She had been nervous ~~of~~ *about* flunking biochemistry. Ally is grateful ~~at~~ *to* her instructors. When she struggled, they were not disappointed ~~at~~ *in* her, and they were proud ~~about~~ *of* her when she succeeded. She is dedicated ~~with~~ *to* completing her nursing degree.

> **More about**
> Prepositions, 739–46

EXERCISE 46.1 Using adjectives correctly

Correct problems with adjective order or prepositions used after adjectives in the following sentences. (The Quick Reference box above will help you with some of these.) If a sentence has no problems, circle its number.

EXAMPLE

The ~~new~~ ridiculous *new* parking regulations are hurting students financially.

1. In our old cozy kitchen, we had a blue round table.
2. The professor gave a historical lengthy overview World War II.
3. The mayor is devoted for eliminating gang violence in our city.
4. There used to be a beige big leather sofa in the waiting room.
5. The lawyer's final pathetic defense of his client was embarrassing.
6. Everyone should be alarmed with global warming.
7. My economical new hybrid car helps me cope with the price of gas.
8. The witness said he saw a green old van leave the scene of the crime.
9. That gray-haired wise doctor still maintains a practice private.
10. The residents are worried from the possibility of another hurricane.

46c Placing Adverbs Correctly

- An adverb cannot be located between a verb and its object.

  ▶ Susan plays ~~beautifully~~ the piano*beautifully*.

  In this sentence, *beautifully* fits correctly only at the end, after *piano*, the direct object.

- Many adverbs, primarily those related to time (such as *often* and *frequently*), may be placed either before the subject or verb or after the direct object.

  ▶ *Recently*, Susan learned ~~recently~~ a new concerto.

  ▶ Susan *recently* learned ~~recently~~ a new concerto.

  ▶ Susan learned ~~recently~~ a new concerto *recently*.

- When a main verb has no helping verbs, the adverb should precede it. When the main verb has helping verbs, the adverb should usually be placed between the first helper and the main verb.

  ▶ Carla *carelessly wasted* gas by leaving the motor running.

> Carla ~~carelessly~~ *has been wasting* gas by leaving the motor running.
>   ^ *carelessly*

Some adverbs (but not all) can be placed between the second helper and the main verb.

> Carla ~~carelessly~~ has been *wasting* gas by leaving the motor running.
>   ^ *carelessly*

- In most instances, place an adverb first if it modifies the entire sentence.

  > <u>Surprisingly</u>, she has decided to change her major to psychology.

- When certain negative adverbs or adverb phrases begin a sentence, they require a change in the standard subject-verb order. Included in this group are *not only, at no time, never, rarely,* and *seldom.*

  > Seldom I ~~have~~ been so proud of my brother.
  >   ^ *have*

> **More about**
> Inverted word order when certain negative adverbs start a sentence, 710–12

EXERCISE 46.2 Putting adverbs in the right place

Correct any adverb placement problems in the following sentences. Circle the number of any sentences that are already correct.

EXAMPLE

The doctor gave me ~~unintentionally~~ the wrong information.
                  unintentionally
                  ^

1. The children played fast and furiously the game and then fell instantly asleep.
2. Sam is doing well in math now that he is doing diligently the homework.
3. Seldom does the manager promote new employees so quickly.
4. We should consider always the suggestions of our employees rather than implementing suddenly changes.
5. Not only Tom works on Saturday, but also on Sunday.
6. Little Ralph has sadly never learned to read.
7. The judge soon should make his decision.
8. Do you really think that Ivan treats Martha unfairly?

46d Dealing with Confusing Adverbs

Certain English adverbs seem similar but actually have significantly different connotations and functions. Often-confused words include *too* with *so, too* with *either, not* with *no, hard* with *hardly,* and *such* with *so.*

1. *Too* and *so*

To give an adjective a negative or more negative meaning, use *too* in most instances. To intensify any adjective, use *so* or *very* or a similar adverb.

▶ The professor realized her first test had been ~~so~~ *too* difficult and was surprised to find us still ~~too~~ *so* excited about the class.

2. *Too* and *either*

When following up a statement about one subject's action with a statement about another subject's doing likewise, use *either* after a verb that is grammatically negative (as with *not* or *never* or *won't* or *hasn't*), and use *too* after a verb that is grammatically positive. Remember that unless verbs such as *avoided* or *refused* are used with a negative adverb (such as *not*), they are grammatically positive, even though by themselves they have negative meanings.

▶ Floyd <u>didn't join</u> the fraternity, and I <u>didn't, either</u>.
   Neither one joined.

▶ Floyd <u>joined</u> the fraternity, and I <u>did, too</u>.
   Both joined.

▶ Floyd <u>refused to join</u>, and I <u>did, too</u>.
   Neither one joined.

▶ Floyd <u>didn't refuse to join</u>, and I <u>didn't, either</u>.
   Both were willing to join.

3. *Not* and *no*

Because *no* is an adjective, it can only modify a noun. The adverb *not,* however, can modify an adjective, a verb, or another adverb. The expression *not a* (*an*) can replace the adjective *no* in front of a noun.

> ▸ Keith is ~~no~~ *not* friendly. Because he will ~~no~~ *not* talk to me, he is ~~not~~ *no (or not a)* friend of mine.

4. *Hard* and *hardly*

The word *hard* can be either an adjective or an adverb. As an adverb, it means *intensely* or *with great effort*. The adverb *hardly* means *just a little* or *almost not at all*.

> ▸ Juan got an *A* after he studied <u>hard</u> for the exam. Laura got a *D* because she <u>hardly</u> looked at her notes.

5. *Such* and *so*

Such a (an), *such*, or *so* can emphasize a type or a quality. Use *such a (an)* before an adjective that precedes a concrete noun: *She is <u>such a</u> wise person.* Use *such* by itself directly in front of an abstract noun: *<u>Such</u> wisdom is rare.* To intensify any freestanding adjective, as in the case of a subject complement, use *so*: *She is <u>so</u> wise.*

➔ EXERCISE 46.3 Correcting easily confused adverbs

Correct any adverb errors in the following sentences, and circle the number of those sentences that have no errors.

EXAMPLE

Jack didn't go to the party, and I didn't, ~~too.~~ *either.*

1. We worked hardly on this project, and all we got was a *C*.
2. We don't feel guilty about this decision, and you shouldn't, too.
3. The waiters here are so slow; we may never get our food.
4. Mark is not millionaire, but he is so generous person.
5. I really admire that she helps her elderly parents too much.
6. We have come so far to give up now.

ad Language Matters • Managing Adjectives and Adverbs

Make It Your Own

Review a text that you were assigned to read in one of your classes, and find examples of cumulative adjectives used before a noun. Look for strings of two, three, or more adjectives not separated from one another by commas, being sure to include any noun determiners. Use the Quick Reference box on page 733 to account for the order in which the adjectives appear. Do any examples violate the usual order?

Work Together

Join with several other students and compare the examples of cumulative adjectives you analyzed in the exercise above. Consult your instructor if your group disagrees about the analysis of any of the examples.

47 Using Prepositions
by Ted E. Johnston and M. E. Sokolik

IN THIS CHAPTER

a. Recognizing prepositions, 739
b. The functions of prepositions, 740
c. Using prepositions correctly, 744
d. Necessary and unnecessary prepositions, 745

Prepositions are words that specify a relationship between other words or phrases. They usually combine with nouns, pronouns, or noun phrases to form *prepositional phrases*. In the sentence "I found my socks under the washing machine," for example, *under the washing machine* is a prepositional phrase introduced by the preposition *under*.

To help you learn to use prepositions correctly, this chapter explains how to identify prepositions (*section 47a*), how to determine the function they serve (*47b*), and how to use them correctly (*47c* and *d*).

47a Recognizing Prepositions

Although there are fewer than one hundred single-word prepositions in use in English, many additional multiword prepositions function in similar ways. The Quick Reference box on the next page lists some of the most common of both.

➤ EXERCISE 47.1 Recognizing prepositions

Identify the prepositional phrases in the following sentences. Underline the prepositional phrase, and circle each preposition.

EXAMPLE
A small air carrier might assume responsibility (for) the freight (from) the customer.

1. The Dehkhoda Institute, which is devoted to the teaching of Farsi, was founded in 1945.

Quick Reference: Common Single-Word and Multiword Prepositions

Single-Word Prepositions

about	beneath	like	to
above	beside	near	toward
across	between	of	under
after	by	off	underneath
against	down	on	until
along	during	onto	up
among	except	out	upon
around	for	outside	with
at	from	over	within
before	in	past	without
behind	inside	since	
below	into	through	

Multiword Prepositions

according to	by means of	in front of	on account of
ahead of	close to	in place of	on behalf of
as far as	due to	in spite of	on top of
as to	far from	inside of	out of
as well as	in accordance with	instead of	outside of
aside from	in addition to	near to	
because of	in case of	next to	

2. The black-backed jackal is an African canine with a foxlike appearance.
3. The first cricket test match was played in 1877 between Australia and England.
4. In November, snow fell on the coast, which is rare so early in the season.
5. The citywide depression lasted for two centuries, through famine and war, until the 1990s.

47b The Functions of Prepositions

Every preposition has multiple possible functions depending on the context in which it occurs. As a result, it is often easier to understand prepositions in terms of their function than to try to memorize what each one means.

Language Matters • The Functions of Prepositions   prep   **47b**

The most basic use for a preposition is to indicate *location*. Other important functions are to indicate *time*, to indicate *condition* or *degree*, to specify *cause* or *reason*, and to designate *possession*, *attribute*, or *origin*.

> **Quick Reference**
>
> **Identifying Functions of Prepositions**
>
> Common functions of prepositions include the following:
>
> 1. To indicate *location* (741)
> 2. To indicate *time* (741)
> 3. To indicate *condition* or *degree* (742)
> 4. To specify *cause* or *reason* (742)
> 5. To designate *possession, attribute,* or *origin* (743)

1. Location

The most basic prepositions for indicating the location of things are *at, on,* and *in.*

- *At* specifies a general point of orientation.
  - ▸ Meet me at the station.
- *On* specifies contact between two things.
  - ▸ The book is on the table.
  - ▸ The clipboard hangs on the wall.
- *In* specifies that one thing is contained within another.
  - ▸ The solution is in the beaker.
  - ▸ Liz is in San Francisco.

NOTE Many locations operate like *surfaces* or *containers.* Generally, use *in* for locations that seem like containers and *on* for locations that seem like surfaces.

CONTAINER	He sat in his car. [**Not:** *He sat on his car,* which would mean he was on top of it.]
SURFACE	He sat on the bus. [Buses, trains, and airplanes are usually considered surfaces because people can walk around on them.]
CONTAINER	We walked in the hallway.
SURFACE	We walked on the sidewalk.

2. Time

The most common prepositions for relating things to a moment in or period of time are *at, in, on,* and *by.*

- *At* designates a particular point in time.
  - ▸ Let's meet at 4:00.
  - ▸ The party ended at midnight.
- *In* can designate either a future time or a particular period.
  - ▸ I'll leave in 10 minutes.
  - ▸ We'll finish the job in April.

- *On* designates a particular day or date.
- *By* indicates *no later than*.

▶ His birthday is on Friday.
▶ Her birthday is on the twelfth.
▶ Turn in your essay by 3:00 p.m.
▶ They decided to leave by 5:00 a.m. to avoid rush hour.

3. Condition / Degree

Prepositions of condition or degree indicate the state of the object. Some common prepositions in this category are *of, on, in, about,* and *around.*

- *In* or *on* can specify a condition. These uses are often idiomatic.

▶ The house is on fire.
▶ She is on vacation.
▶ Charlie is not in trouble.
▶ Darlene left her desk in perfect order.

- *Of* is used in phrases indicating fractions or portions.

▶ Three of the books are required for the course.
▶ One of those coats is mine.

- *Around* or *about* can indicate approximation.

▶ That book costs around twenty dollars.
▶ I walked about ten miles.

4. Cause / Reason

Prepositions showing cause include *from, of, for,* and *because of.*

- *From* indicates cause or explains a condition.

▶ We were wet from the rain.
▶ We were tired from walking all day.

- *For* often indicates a cause and answers the question *Why?*

▶ Oregon is famous for its forests.
▶ He got an award for selling more cars than anyone else.

- *Of* and *because of* both show a reason.

▶ The patient died of pneumonia.
▶ I sneezed because of my cold.

5. Possession / Attribute / Origin

The most common prepositions showing possession, attribute, or origin are *of*, *from*, and *with*.

- Possession is typically shown with *of*.
  - ▶ That song is one of Wilco's.
  - ▶ The composer of the song is Jay Bennett.

- An attribute can be indicated by *with*.
  - ▶ He was a man with real talent.
  - ▶ He is the one with the red beard.

- *From* can show origin.
  - ▶ Bennet was from Illinois.
  - ▶ The CD came from a website.

NOTE Indicating possession with *of* instead of *'s* or *s'* is often awkward.

AWKWARD	the bike of Bob
PREFERRED	Bob's bike

→ EXERCISE 47.2 Determining the function of a preposition

Write in the function of the underlined preposition in the space to the right of each sentence. Choose from *Location, Time, Condition/Degree, Cause/Reason,* or *Possession/Attribute/Origin*.

EXAMPLE
She bought the car <u>with</u> greater fuel efficiency. *attribute*

1. The construction will be completed <u>in</u> 2012. _____
2. In 1946, Margolin moved <u>to</u> Lebanon. _____
3. Bellatrix is described as a tall woman <u>with</u> pale skin. _____
4. Let's meet <u>at</u> the library to study tonight. _____
5. We were dying <u>of</u> thirst. _____
6. He's having a birthday party <u>in</u> July. _____
7. Hearing loss is estimated to begin <u>at</u> age 30. _____
8. There are no students <u>from</u> Japan here. _____

47c Using Prepositions Correctly

Certain verbs or nouns will suggest the use of particular prepositions. It may help to memorize these phrases:

- *give* something *to* someone
- *take* something *from* someone
- *sell* something *to* someone
- *buy* something *from* someone
- *lend* something *to* someone
- *borrow* something *from* someone
- *get married* or *engaged to* someone
- *fill* something *with* something
- *shout to* someone (in greeting)
- *shout at* someone (in anger)

In addition, some prepositions serve a particular grammatical function. For example, in passive constructions, the preposition *by* identifies who or what did something.

- The car was repaired *by* Pat.

Similarly, indirect objects, when placed after rather than before a direct object, are usually preceded by *to:*

- Theo gave the present *to* his father.

> **More about**
> Passive voice, 535–37, 652–55
> Direct and indirect objects, 589–91, 707–09

EXERCISE 47.3 Using prepositions correctly

Insert the correct preposition into the blanks below. In some cases, more than one preposition may be acceptable.

EXAMPLE
He came *from* a small village *in* the middle *of* the country.

1. Our sense ___ identity—___ who we are and what we have done—is tied ___ our memories.
2. *The Big Knife* is a 1955 film directed and produced ___ Robert Aldrich and based ___ the play ___ Clifford Odets.

3. Ronald and Reginald Kray were identical twin brothers and the foremost organized crime leaders ___ London ___ the 1950s and 1960s.
4. The original manuscripts ___ Oscar Wilde today are found ___ many collections, but ___ far the largest collection is found ___ the William Andrews Clark Memorial Library ___ UCLA.
5. Tortell is a Catalan pastry stuffed ___ marzipan, which ___ some special occasions is topped ___ glazed fruit. It is traditionally eaten ___ January 6.

47d Necessary and Unnecessary Prepositions

Unfortunately, there is no rule of grammar to tell when a preposition is needed. Consider these examples:

- I like to listen ^*to* music.
- She was looking ^*at* the book.

Similarly, there is no rule to tell when one is not needed:

- ~~In one~~ *One* block from the school, there is a coffee shop.
- We were discussing ~~about~~ climate change in class.

To make things more complicated, sometimes a phrase is acceptable with or without a preposition.

- I've lived here for six years.
- I've lived here six years.

One strategy for mastering these usages, some of them idiomatic, is to notice in your reading when you encounter unfamiliar constructions involving prepositions. Some students keep a grammar log or other notebook to help them remember these constructions.

EXERCISE 47.4 Distinguishing between necessary and unnecessary prepositions

Correct the following passage for preposition usage. Cross out any prepositions that are not needed, insert any that are missing, and leave unchanged any that are correctly used. There are thirteen preposition errors in the passage, not including the one in the example.

EXAMPLE

Flip the Frog is an animated cartoon character created *by* an American cartoonist, Ub Iwerks, who also helped ~~with~~ to create another famous character—Mickey Mouse.

Flip starred a series cartoons distributed by MGM from 1930 to 1933. Apart Flip, the series had many other characters, including Flip's dog and a mule named of Orace.

Flip's first appearance was in a cartoon called by *Night*. Iwerks animated this short feature while working his friend Walt Disney in 1930. After a number disagreements between them, Iwerks left Disney and went on to accept an offer to open a cartoon studio his own a salary of $300 a week. Disney at the time couldn't match with this offer. The first cartoon series Iwerks was expected to create featured on a character called Tony the Frog, but Iwerks didn't like the name and had it changed Flip.

Make It **Your Own**

In a paper you have recently written or are now writing, look for preposition errors. How many do you find? What functions of these prepositions do you recognize (location, time, etc.)? How would you fix the errors?

Work **Together**

For a paper you have recently written or are now writing, exchange texts with a classmate and analyze your classmate's writing for prepositional errors. How many do you find? How would you correct them? (If your partner is a native speaker of English, you may find very few errors. If this is the case, note any preposition usages that are unfamiliar to you and discuss their meaning with your partner.) Be prepared to discuss what you gained from this exercise.

Part Ten

Detail Matters

Punctuation and Mechanics

- **48** Using Commas   748
- **49** Using Semicolons   766
- **50** Using Apostrophes   773
- **51** Using Quotation Marks   780
- **52** Using End Punctuation   792
- **53** Using Other Punctuation Marks   796
- **54** Capitalizing   807
- **55** Italics and Underlining   814
- **56** Using Abbreviations   820
- **57** Using Numbers   826
- **58** Using Hyphens   830

48 Using Commas

IN THIS CHAPTER

a. In compound sentences, 750

b. After introductory elements, 751

c. With conjunctive adverbs and transitional phrases, 753

d. With interjections and similar elements, 753

e. To separate items in a series, 754

f. To separate coordinate adjectives, 756

g. To set off nonessential elements, 757

h. With quotations, 759

i. With numbers, names and titles, place names and addresses, and dates, 760

j. To avoid ambiguity, 762

k. Not between subjects and verbs, verbs and objects, 763

Commas function as dividers within—but not between—sentences: Think of each sentence as a room. If the periods are walls between these rooms, then the commas are screens used to make subdivisions within them. As a screen might set off a dressing area from a larger bedroom, so a comma sets off information within the main sentence. As a screen might divide a work space into offices, so commas mark divisions between independent clauses. Problems with commas can be caused not only by omitting them but also by inserting them where they are *not* needed: Imagine having a screen in your kitchen between your stove and refrigerator.

The rules for comma placement are fairly straightforward. A list of the rules writers use most often appears in the Quick Reference box on the next page.

Writing Responsibly | Commas and Clarity

Like Alice in Wonderland, most of us aim to say what we mean and mean what we say. But sometimes in writing an incorrect use of commas can have us saying something we do not mean (or meaning something we do not say). Consider this example, with and without commas:

This sentence . . .	*means* . . .
Writing to my mother is a terrible chore.	I find writing to my mother a real pain!
Writing, to my mother, is a terrible chore.	My mother finds writing a real pain!

You have a responsibility to your reader to look carefully at your use of commas when editing a document; ask yourself, "Do I mean what I say and say what I mean?" If the answer is no, correct your use of commas.

to AUDIENCE

Detail Matters • Using Commas **48** **749**

Quick Reference — Common Comma Do's and Don'ts

Do use a comma . . .

. . . to separate independent clauses joined by a coordinating conjunction. (750)

                      coord.
   independent clause   conj.   independent clause

▶ Hip-hop music was born in the 1970s, **but** it continues to flourish.

. . . to set off introductory elements from an independent clause. (751)

   subordinate clause   independent clause

▶ **Although it was born in New York City**, rap has become popular around the world.

. . . to separate three or more items in a series. (754)

▶ Some early hip-hop artists include **Afrika Bambaataa**①, **Grandmaster Flash**②, **Run DMC**③, and **LL Cool J**④.

. . . to separate coordinate (but not cumulative) adjectives. (756)

                      coordinate adjectives

▶ Hip-hop soon grew to have a **huge**, **enthusiastic** audience outside the New York club scene.

. . . to set off nonessential elements. (757)

                 nonessential clause

▶ Afrika Bambaataa, **who adopted the name of a Zulu chieftain**, formed Zulu Nation to attract kids toward hip-hop and away from gangs.

Do *not* use a comma . . .

. . . following a coordinating or subordinating conjunction. (750, 751)

▶ Run DMC is popular enough to be featured on the game Guitar Hero,
   sub. conj.
although, the songs the group plays are by the band Aerosmith.

. . . to separate paired elements. (750)

▶ Even scholars are writing about **hip-hop music, and culture.**

. . . to separate independent clauses not joined by a coordinating conjunction. (750)

▶ LL Cool J's 1985 *Radio* was perhaps the first mainstream rap hit, it went platinum within five months.

. . . preceding the first item or following the last item in a series. (754)

▶ Hip-hop has also merged with musical styles such as, **hip house**①, **nu soul**②, **reggaetón**③, and **merenrap**④, to create exciting sounds.

. . . between a subject and its verb or a verb and its object or complement. (763)

   subj   verb   direct obj.

▶ LL Cool J, has had, **eight platinum records** in a row since then.

48a Using Commas in Compound Sentences

Quick Reference

The Seven Coordinating Conjunctions

| and | but | or | nor |
| for | so | yet | |

In a *compound sentence* a comma and *coordinating conjunction* work together: The comma marks the break between the two **independent clauses,** and the coordinating conjunction joins them into a single sentence. When a coordinating conjunction combines two independent clauses, place a comma *before* it (not *after* it):

▶ My heart is in San Francisco, but my body is in New York.
   (independent clause) (coord. conj.) (independent clause)

compound sentence
Two or more independent clauses linked by a comma and a coordinating conjunction or a semicolon

NOTE Unless readers will be confused, the comma can be omitted when the two independent clauses are very short:

▶ I sing in Italian but I speak only English.

independent clause
A word group that includes a subject and a predicate that can stand alone as a sentence

Do not use a comma before the conjunction if both parts cannot stand on their own as sentences:

▶ My accountant left the country, and took my bank balance with him.
   (independent clause) (verb phrase)

More about
Comma splices, 611–19 (ch. 35)
Semicolons, 766–72 (ch. 49)

Paired items should not be separated by a comma:

▶ Both my purse, and my bank account are empty.
   (pairs)

When the clauses are long and punctuated with commas already, readers might find the sentence clearer if you replace the comma before the coordinating conjunction with a semicolon:

▶ Comic books are gradually becoming more respectable as works of serious fiction, with graphic novels such as *Maus* and *Watchmen* earning tremendous critical acclaim; yet many people, including my girlfriend, refuse to take them seriously.

NOTE Without a coordinating conjunction, a comma between two independent clauses creates a **comma splice.**

EXERCISE 48.1 Correcting commas in compound sentences

Correct the sentences below by adding or deleting commas. (Some may already be correct!)

EXAMPLE

The dollar has dropped against the euro**,** so tourists have flocked to

the United States to shop.

1. The US dollar continues to be weak against both the euro, and the pound.
2. The yen remains strong against the US dollar but it fell against the Australian dollar as markets opened this morning.
3. The yen, and the yuan are strengthening.
4. The currencies of Latin America continue to be weak relative to the euro, but they are holding their own against the US dollar.
5. Japanese, and American travelers who visit Europe this summer will feel the pinch, but Australian, and Chinese visitors should find Europe a bargain.

48b Using a Comma after Introductory Elements

A word, phrase, or subordinate clause introducing an independent clause is usually followed by a comma. There are two exceptions:

- In an inverted sentence, where an introductory word group immediately precedes the verb

  ▶ <u>Into the deep, dark jungle</u> *introductory word group* <u>marched</u> *verb* Dr. Livingston.

- Following an introductory word group that acts as the subject of the sentence

  ▶ <u>Exploring deep, dark jungles</u> *subject* <u>is</u> *verb* what he does.

When the introductory element is very brief, some writers omit the comma. If readers might be confused, even for a moment, include it:

  ▶ Before eating**,** the missionaries said grace.

Detail Matters • Using Commas

> **subordinate clause** A word group that lacks a subject or predicate or that begins with a subordinating word or phrase; a word group that cannot stand alone as a sentence

1. Insert a comma after introductory clauses.

When a *subordinate,* or dependent, clause introduces an independent clause, place a comma between the two.

▸ *subordinate clause*
  Although Boythorn prided himself on his gruff demeanor, he doted on his pet bird.

▸ *subordinate clause*
  Because his theories addressed the Great Depression, John Maynard Keynes became the most influential economist of the 1930s.

> **phrase** A group of related words that lacks a subject, predicate, or both; it cannot stand alone as a sentence, but it can function *in* a sentence as a noun, a verb, or a modifier

2. Insert a comma after introductory phrases.

Insert a comma following an introductory *phrase* to signal the start of the main clause:

▸ *participial phrase*
  Lacking Mozart's natural abilities, Salieri formed an obsessive hatred for his rival.

▸ *prepositional phrase*
  In an unguarded moment, the politician muttered an unprintable phrase into the live microphone.

▸ *absolute phrase*
  A vegetarian for many years, he suddenly craved bacon.

> **More about**
> Participial phrases, 593
> Prepositional phrases, 592
> Absolute phrases, 594

➔ EXERCISE 48.2 Inserting commas after introductory elements

Supply a comma as needed after introductory elements in the sentences below. (You will not need to add a comma in every sentence.)

EXAMPLE

With infection rates continuing to rise, developing nations in southern Africa and around the world face shrinking populations.

1. With the advent of the AIDS epidemic around 1990 the rate of population growth in southern Africa has decreased substantially.

2. According to the US Census Bureau population growth rates in Zimbabwe and South Africa are expected to drop 75 percent or more by 2010.

3. In fact life expectancies in Zimbabwe have already fallen by twenty-six years.
4. In the next decade, the population of southern Africa is expected to be smaller by 71 million people than it would have been without the AIDS epidemic.
5. Developing countries like Haiti and Cambodia sadly are also experiencing AIDS-related drops in population growth rates.

48c Using Commas to Set Off Conjunctive Adverbs and Most Transitional Phrases

Transitional expressions and *conjunctive adverbs* are usually set off by commas.

> ▶ The basking shark, in fact, consumes only zooplankton and small fish. It may end up as dinner for an orca or tiger shark, however.

When the transitional expression or conjunctive adverb is used to link independent clauses, place a semicolon before it.

> ▶ The whale shark is the largest fish in today's oceans; nevertheless, it presents no threat to humans.

transitional expressions Words and phrases that show the relationship between sentences

conjunctive adverb A transitional expression that can link one independent clause to another; it modifies the second clause and specifies its relationship to the first

48d Inserting Commas to Set Off Interjections, Contrasting Information, Expressions of Direct Address, Parenthetical and Conversational Expressions, and Tag Questions

> ▶ Wow, that wind farm is gorgeous!
> ▶ Some people, sadly, think the industrial look of a wind farm is ugly.
> ▶ The current energy situation requires us to revise, not cling to, traditional notions of beauty.

- Professor Kinney, [direct address] how much do you know about offshore wind farming?

- The first US offshore wind farm, it turns out, [parenthetical] is on Nantucket Sound.

- No, [conversational expression] it isn't a single-handed solution to our energy problems.

- Wind farms will make a big contribution, won't they? [tag]

48e Using Commas to Separate Items in a Series

Place a comma between items in a series of three or more.

- Our new house will feature solar panels, a hilltop windmill, and rainwater conversion.

Some writers omit the comma before the coordinating conjunction (*and* in this example) in a series, but readers may find the final comma helpful in distinguishing paired and unpaired elements. The managing editor of the *Chicago Manual of Style* likes to quote this hypothetical dedication, which highlights the potential problems that can be caused by omitting the serial comma:

- I dedicate this book to my parents, Mother Teresa and the Pope.

To Use or Not to Use the Serial Comma English-speaking nations may share a common language, but their rules when using it sometimes differ. British writers have more or less dispensed with the serial comma (except to avoid confusion), while Americans (except for journalists) continue to use it. When writing for a US audience, use the serial comma.

> **More about**
> Using semicolons in a series, 769

When the items in the series are long or contain internal commas, substituting semicolons for commas can make the sentence easier to read:

- Phillis Wheatley was born in Senegal in 1753, was sold into slavery to a Boston, Massachusetts, family, studied Greek, Latin, and English, and became the first published African American writer.

Detail Matters • Using Commas to Separate Coordinate, Not Cumulative, Adjectives **48f**

EXERCISE 48.3 Inserting commas in conjunctive adverbs, transitional phrases, interrupting words and phrases, and items in a series

Supply commas as needed in the sentences below. (You will not need to add a comma in every sentence.)

EXAMPLE

My goodness, did I have a horrible cold last week!

1. I originally thought my sneezing was due to an allergy; however my doctor pointed out the difference between symptoms from an allergy and a cold.
2. A telltale sign for example is how quickly the symptoms develop.
3. Allergy symptoms start immediately, but cold symptoms, on the other hand, take a day or longer to develop and gradually worsen.
4. Allergies nearly always cause itchiness in the eyes nose and throat, while a cold usually does not.
5. My obvious cold symptoms according to my doctor were fever aches and chest congestion.

48f Using Commas to Separate Coordinate, Not Cumulative, Adjectives

Coordinate adjectives each modify the noun or pronoun they precede and are of equal weight; ***cumulative adjectives,*** on the other hand, modify not only the noun or pronoun they precede but also the next adjective in the series. Hence, the order of coordinate adjectives does not matter, but the order of cumulative adjectives does.

Consider the example below:

▶ The girl struggled to hide her brooding, moody nature from the [coordinate adjectives] sympathetic, insightful child psychologist she visited weekly. [coordinate adjectives] [cumulative adjectives]

> **More about**
> Adjective order,
> 732–33

While you could reverse *brooding* and *moody* or *insightful* and *sympathetic,* you could not reverse *insightful* and *child:* A *child insightful psychologist* does not make sense.

Quick Reference: Testing for Coordinate and Cumulative Adjectives

To determine whether two or more adjectives should be separated by a comma, try these two tests:

1. **Place the word *and* between the two adjectives.** If the phrase still makes sense, then the adjectives are coordinate, and you should put a comma between them:

   Yes: sexy and exciting boyfriend
   No: enormous and shoulder bag

2. **Reverse the order.** If the meaning remains the same no matter what order they appear in, then the adjectives are coordinate, and you should insert a comma between them:

   Yes: sexy, exciting boyfriend = exciting, sexy boyfriend
   No: enormous shoulder bag ≠ shoulder enormous bag

EXERCISE 48.4 Using commas with coordinate and cumulative adjectives

Add commas as needed in the sentences below.

EXAMPLE

How likely is it that a curious, adventurous sixth grader will take up smoking?

1. As part of a revealing new study, researchers interviewed 1,195 sixth graders and then spoke to them several times over the next four years.
2. The study suggested that two characteristics indicate a heightened identifiable risk level for becoming a smoker.
3. The clearest key indication for future smoking is that it is easy to get cigarettes.
4. The other demonstrated major characteristic is that young people tend to become smokers if they have friends who smoke.
5. Furthermore, combining these two characteristics is a strong indicative risk factor.

48g Using Commas to Set Off Nonessential Appositives, Phrases, and Clauses

Words, phrases, or clauses that add information to a sentence but do not identify the person, place, or thing being described are **nonessential** (or *nonrestrictive*) **elements** and are set off by commas from the rest of the sentence. Elements that identify the person, place, or thing being described are **essential** (or *restrictive*) and are *not* set off by commas. Consider the following sentence:

> More about
> Essential and nonessential elements, 609

▸ My coworker *Philip*, whom I had never seen without a tie, arrived at the office this morning wearing a toga. [essential: Philip; nonessential: whom I had never seen without a tie]

Philip picks out one coworker from among the rest, so that element is essential. The nonessential clause—*whom I had never seen without a tie*—provides important information about Philip, but it does not identify him from among the writer's colleagues, so it is nonessential.

Compare the sentence above to this sentence:

▸ My coworker, *Philip*, showed up at work this morning wearing a toga. [nonessential: Philip]

In this sentence, *Philip* is set off by commas, suggesting that the writer has only one colleague, so identifying him by name is not essential.

1. Use commas with nonessential appositives.

An ***appositive*** renames a preceding noun phrase. When it identifies, or specifies, the noun phrase, it is essential and is not set off by commas:

> **appositive** A noun or noun phrase that renames the noun, pronoun, or noun phrase that precedes it

▸ The Roman emperor *Claudius* suffered from an ailment that caused him to limp and to stammer uncontrollably. [noun phrase: The Roman emperor; essential appositive: Claudius]

In this case, *Claudius* distinguishes this Roman emperor from all the other Roman emperors, so it is essential and should not be set off by commas.

When the appositive adds information but does not identify, it is nonessential and is set off by commas.

▸ The fourth Roman Emperor, *Claudius*, suffered from an ailment that caused him to limp and to stammer uncontrollably. [noun phrase: The fourth Roman Emperor; nonessential appositive: Claudius]

Because there was only one *fourth Roman emperor*, the name *Claudius* is nonessential.

2. Use commas with nonessential phrases.

A phrase that acts as an adjective, modifying a noun, pronoun, or noun phrase, can also be essential or nonessential: If it identifies what it is describing, then it is essential and should *not* be set off by commas; if it does not identify, then it is nonessential and *should* be set off by commas.

- The girl, asked by her father to behave, said, "I am being haive." *(noun / nonessential phrase)*
- The girl asked by her father to behave is my niece. *(noun / essential phrase)*

3. Use commas with nonessential clauses.

A subordinate (or dependent) clause can also act as an adjective, modifying a noun, pronoun, or noun phrase. When it identifies the noun, pronoun, or noun phrase, it is essential and is *not* set off by commas; when it does not, it is nonessential and *is* set off by commas.

Adverb clauses The placement of an adverb clause indicates whether it is essential or nonessential: If it appears at the beginning of the sentence, it is generally nonessential and set off by a comma; if it appears in the middle of the sentence, it is generally essential and is not set off by commas:

- Because he found the politics required to win an Academy Award demeaning, George C. Scott refused to accept an Oscar for his performance in the movie *Patton*. *(nonessential adv. clause / noun)*
- George C. Scott refused to accept an Academy Award for his performance in the movie *Patton* because he found the politics required to win an Oscar demeaning. *(noun / essential adv. clause)*

That *clauses* versus which *clauses* Subordinate clauses beginning with the word *that* are always essential and thus never set off by commas.

- Produce that has been genetically modified differs from its non–GM counterpart by a human-made alteration to its DNA. *(essential clause)*

The word *which,* on the other hand, is used today to introduce both essential and nonessential clauses:

▶ Genetically modified produce, *which is sold in grocery stores throughout the United States,* is still looked on with suspicion by many consumers.   [nonessential clause]

NOTE Some writers (and instructors), especially in the United States, believe *which* should be used exclusively with nonessential clauses.

➔ EXERCISE 48.5 Using commas with appositives, phrases, and clauses

Correct the errors in the following sentences by inserting or deleting commas as necessary.

EXAMPLE

Lyme disease, a bacterial infection, was named for the town in Connecticut where it was first identified.

1. The malady, Lyme disease, is transmitted by deer ticks.
2. A person can become infected by deer ticks, that wait among tall grass for someone or something to latch onto.
3. When someone gets Lyme disease he or she will sometimes develop a reddish rash that looks like a spreading bull's-eye.
4. Lyme disease is difficult to diagnose because many people, who have it, do not remember getting bitten by a tick.
5. There is a good protective measure completely covering the arms and legs whenever walking in tall grass that can help a person avoid deer ticks and the Lyme disease that they carry.

48h Using Commas with Quotations

In most cases, separate a ***direct quotation*** from a ***signal phrase*** with a comma:

▶ After learning that he had been appointed poet laureate, *Charles Simic exclaimed,* "I'm almost afraid to get out of bed—too much good luck in one week."   [signal phrase]

---

direct quotation The exact words someone has used; direct quotations must be placed in quotation marks to avoid plagiarism

signal phrase A noun or pronoun plus an appropriate verb identifying the writer from whom you are borrowing words or ideas

Exceptions

- When the quotation begins the sentence and ends with a question mark or exclamation point, no comma should be added.
    - ▶ "When shall we three meet again, in thunder, lightning, and in rain?" asks the first witch in Shakespeare's *Macbeth*.
- When the quotation is integrated into your own sentence, omit the comma:
    - ▶ Friar Lawrence warns Romeo that "these violent delights have violent ends."
- When the signal phrase is incorporated into a complete sentence that makes sense without the quotation, use a colon before the quotation:
    - ▶ Hamlet exits the graveyard scene with a veiled threat: "The cat will mew, and dog will have his day."

Indirect quotations should *not* be set off by commas.

▶ New poet laureate Charles Simic confessed that having so much good luck worried him.

> **indirect quotation**
> A quotation that has been paraphrased (put into the writer's own words), instead of taken word-for-word from the source

48i Using Commas with Numbers, Names and Titles, Place Names and Addresses, and Dates

Numbers, names and titles, place names and addresses, and dates are each punctuated according to specialized conventions, some of which vary from one community or discipline to another.

> **More about**
> Numbers, 826–29 (ch. 57)

1. In numbers

The following conventions are standard in most American English usage:

- In four-digit numbers, using a comma to mark divisions of hundreds is optional, except with years, when no comma should be included:
    - ▶ The company paid $9347 for those supplies in 2012.
    - ▶ The company paid $9,347 for those supplies in 2012.
- In five-digit numbers, a comma is used to mark divisions of hundreds.
    - ▶ Workers have filed 93,471 unemployment claims since January.

2. Between personal names and titles

Use a comma to separate a personal name from a title that follows it:

- Send the request to Janet Woodcock, director of the Center for Drug Evaluation and Research.

Use no comma when a title precedes the name or when the "title" consists of roman numerals:

- Send the request to **Doctor** Janet Woodcock.
- My son will be named Albert Farnsworth **IV**.

The titles Jr. and Sr. may appear with or without commas:

- Ken Griffey, Jr., appears in the *Simpsons* episode "Homer at the Bat."
- Ken Griffey Jr. appears in the *Simpsons* episode "Homer at the Bat."

3. In place names and addresses

Use a comma to separate names of cities from states, provinces, regions, or countries:

- Boston, Massachusetts, was the birthplace of Benjamin Franklin. Famous as an American patriot, Franklin also lived for several years in London, England, and Paris, France. He died at age eighty-four in Philadelphia, Pennsylvania.

Do *not* place a comma between the name of a state and the zip code:

- The Franklin Institute, founded to honor Benjamin Franklin, is located at 222 North 20th Street, Philadelphia, Pennsylvania 19103.

4. In dates

Use commas to set off dates in which the day follows the month and when dates include the time of day or the day of the week:

- I will never forget that my son was born at 5:17 a.m., Tuesday, March 17, 2009.

No comma is needed in dates when only the month and year are used or when the day *precedes* the month:

- My niece was born in February 2000.
- Her exact birth date is 13 February 2000.

EXERCISE 48.6 Using commas with numbers, names, places, and dates

In the following sentences, add commas as necessary to mark numbers, names and titles, place names and addresses, and dates. (Not all sentences will need correction.)

EXAMPLE

The board of directors met on Tuesday, June 5, 2012, at 3:00 p.m. in the institute's new offices in Swansea, Massachusetts.

1. Yvonne Gesinghaus, MD, disagrees with the board's decision.
2. According to Dr. Gesinghaus "We should spend the $10500 on research, not on a party in San Antonio Texas."
3. Nevertheless, she requests that we send an invitation to William Green Sr. 217 Adamson Parkway Seattle WA 90107.
4. His invitation must go out by 7 October 2014.
5. The next meeting of the board of directors has been rescheduled to Monday January 10 2013.
6. The finance officer told Dr. Gesinghaus that, the meeting on Monday will start promptly at 5 p.m.
7. Also, please change your records to reflect her new job title: Yvonne Gesinghaus Director of Research and Development.
8. The foundation she now works for is located in a suburb of Fall River Massachusetts.
9. The new director's annual salary will be $165000.
10. The increase will take effect in January 2014.

48j Using Commas to Avoid Ambiguity

A comma can separate ideas that might otherwise be misinterpreted, and it can mark places where words have been deleted.

Detail Matters • Avoiding Commas between Subjects and Verbs, Verbs and Objects

1. To separate ideas

When two ideas could be misread as a single unit, add a comma to separate the two:

▶ My friends who can afford toˏ take taxis frequently.

2. To replace omitted words and avoid repetition

Replace a repeated word with a comma after its first use:

▶ I vacationed in the Adirondacks, my brother ~~vacationed~~ in British Columbia.

48k Avoiding Commas between Subjects and Verbs, Verbs and Objects

A single comma should not separate a subject from its verb or a verb from its object unless another rule calls for it:

▶ The Senate finance committee, is the focus of much attention.
  (subject) (verb)

▶ The committee must explain, its decision to a nervous public.
  (verb) (object)

➔ EXERCISE 48.7 Using commas to resolve ambiguity

Correct the following sentences by inserting or deleting commas as necessary. (Not all sentences will need correction.)

EXAMPLE

The members who want toˏ contribute their time to painting the club's meeting hall.

1. Fiona is painting a wall, and Helen the baseboards.
2. Those who can stay and keep painting through the second shift.
3. Although most members never help, those who do devote a great deal of their spare time to it.

4. Jason worked ten hours this week, Alika eight, and Jesse fifteen.
5. The members who do enjoy a sense of satisfaction that they have made a difference.

EXERCISE 48.8 Avoiding unnecessary commas

Delete any unnecessary commas from the following sentences.

EXAMPLE

Current treatments for multiple myeloma include,/ chemotherapy, radiation, and stem-cell transplantation, but,/ other treatments are under development.

1. In April 2007, researchers at the Mayo Clinic, discovered that a by-product of wood mold, chaetocin, kills multiple, myeloma, cells more effectively than current treatments, such as thalidomide, or stem-cell transplantation.
2. The doctor, who led the study told reporters, that the team had found chaetocin to cause myeloma cell, death in mice and, that it had also provided new avenues for research.
3. This cancer of the bone marrow cells, is currently incurable, but this new research on chaetocin holds, promise for a cure.
4. Chaetocin kills myeloma cells in mice by, accumulating in the cancer cells, slowing the growth of myeloma cells, and causing biological changes in cancer cells that led to, their death.
5. Dr. Bible, who led the team of researchers, noted that treatments are still several years off, but expects that his team's discovery will help patients in the future.

EXERCISE 48.9 Using commas correctly

Add or delete commas as needed in the paragraph below.

EXAMPLE

Americans‸instead of losing their spirit of creativity‸ seem to be getting more inventive,/ than ever.

The United States Patent Office, is so overwhelmed that it now has a backlog of 700000 applications and its average review time is now thirty-one months. In an attempt to deal with the flood of applications the office has proposed new rules. The new rules would make inventors provide more information than they now do; in addition the agency would also allow expanded public review of applications. What's more and this may be of greater concern to inventors the office is now approving a smaller percentage of applications. In 2007 it approved approximately 50 percent of applications which is down from 72 percent in 2000. To improve the chances of approval inventors, need to be sure that their inventions are both new, and useful. The description of an invention whether it is simple, or highly complex should also be understandable, and written clearly. Today American inventiveness is not only thriving but it is also more competitive than ever before.

Make It Your Own

Review your use of commas in a recent writing project of two or more pages. Add commas where needed and cross through unnecessary ones. Then analyze the impact these changes would have on your reader. (Refer to the sections in this chapter as needed.)

Work Together

Exchange your work on Exercise 48.9 with a partner. Check your classmate's use of commas. Did he or she make any errors? If so, refer to sections in this chapter to help you explain the effect these errors had on you as a reader. (Be specific.)

49 Using Semicolons

IN THIS CHAPTER

a. Linking independent clauses, 767

b. Before a conjunctive adverb or transitional phrase, 768

c. Marking a series with internal commas, 769

d. Repairing a comma splice, 769

e. Avoiding overuse, 770

'I think Lassie is trying to tell us something, ma.'

Although there are other uses of the semicolon, its main function is to link two independent clauses into a single sentence. The comma and a coordinating conjunction also play this role, so what makes the semicolon useful? It is the signal the semicolon sends to the reader; it tells the reader that the clause that follows will specify consequences, restate meaning, or introduce a contrast.

A list of the most important rules for using semicolons appears in the Quick Reference box on the next page.

Writing Responsibly | Sending a Signal with Semicolons

Writers who do not understand the role of the semicolon may use it to connect independent clauses randomly, and this can lead readers to see a connection between ideas that the writer did not intend or cannot defend. Consider this sentence: *Angelina is working in New York; Brad has a headache.* The semicolon here suggests that there is a logical relationship between the two clauses, that one is the cause or effect of the other, when, in fact, the two may reflect mere coincidence. Avoid conveying more than you meant; use the semicolon with care.

to TOPIC

Detail Matters • Using a Semicolon to Link Independent Clauses   **;**   **49a**

Quick Reference — Common Semicolon Do's and Don'ts

***Do* use a semicolon . . .**

. . . to link two closely related independent clauses when the second clause specifies the consequence of the first, restates its meaning, or introduces a contrast. (767)

▶ In 1911, Italian nationalist Vincenzo Peruggia stole the *Mona Lisa* from the Louvre in France; he believed fervently that da Vinci's painting should be displayed in Italy.

. . . when a conjunctive adverb or transitional phrase links them. (768)

▶ Peruggia was arrested while trying to sell the painting to a Florence art gallery; however, his mission was not entirely in vain.

. . . to distinguish items in a series with internal commas. (769)

▶ Before arresting Peruggia, authorities questioned Guillaume Apollinaire, a French poet; Pablo Picasso, a Spanish painter and founder of cubism; and various Louvre employees.

. . . to repair a comma splice. (769)

▶ Before the *Mona Lisa* was restored to Paris, it was exhibited in museums across Italy; as a result, Peruggia was hailed as a national hero and served only a brief prison term.

***Do not* use a semicolon . . .**

. . . to link an independent clause to anything except another, related independent clause. (768)

▶ During his trial, Peruggia leapt to his feet*[independent clause]*, *[phrase]* raging at the prosecutor, the judge, and even his own lawyer.

▶ Peruggia claimed he was motivated only by patriotism*[independent clause]*, *[subordinate clause]* even though he had demanded a "reward" of half a million lire.

. . . to introduce a list. (769)

▶ Despite an outcry, the *Mona Lisa* was returned to France after visiting the following Italian cities*[:]* *[list]* Naples, Rome, Florence, Venice, and Milan.

49a Using a Semicolon to Link Independent Clauses

When two ***independent clauses*** are closely related and balanced, a semicolon emphasizes their relationship.

▶ Adjusting to life in a new country does not come easily; I learned that firsthand.
  [independent clause 1]   *[independent clause 2]*

> **independent (or main) clause** A word group that contains a subject and a main verb and that does not begin with a subordinating conjunction, relative pronoun, or relative adverb

Detail Matters • Using Semicolons

> **More about**
> Parallelism, 518–26 (ch. 28)
> Commas, 748–65 (ch. 48)
> End punctuation, 792–95 (ch. 52)
> Dashes, 796–98
> Colons, 800–02
> Coordinating conjunctions (list), 750

A semicolon replaces a comma and coordinating conjunction:

- Summer traffic to Jones Beach can be slow*;* *so* you might want to take the train instead. *[coord. conj.]*

- Summer traffic to Jones Beach can be slow*;* you might want to take the train instead.

A semicolon is often used when the second clause emphasizes the consequences of the first, restates the first, or offers a contrast with the first:

- My mother's taste is always changing*;* just when I think I know what she likes, she proves me wrong. *[emphasizes consequences]*

- When the French arrived, this area was very different from what it has become*;* Detroit was once a deep forest. *[restates]*

- People think of Franklin Delano Roosevelt as the architect of the New Deal*;* he actually designed buildings, too. *[contrasts]*

Do not use a semicolon to link a phrase or a subordinate clause to an independent clause:

- The new Harry Potter film proved successful*~~;~~*, grossing $22 million in the first night. *[phrase]*

49b Using a Semicolon before a Conjunctive Adverb or Transitional Phrase Linking Two Independent Clauses

> **More about**
> Conjunctive adverbs (list), 581
> Transitional words and phrases (list), 55

When a conjunctive adverb (such as *therefore, however,* and *furthermore*) or a transitional phrase such as *on the other hand* or *for example* comes between two independent clauses, precede it with a semicolon (and follow it with a comma).

- *Shakespeare in Love* introduced the playwright to a new generation of moviegoers*;* *moreover,* it was an entertaining film. *[semi. + conj. adv. + comma]*

When the conjunctive adverb or transitional phrase is placed within one of the independent clauses rather than between them, retain the semicolon between the clauses and insert a comma before and after the conjunctive adverb or transitional phrase:

▶ Film is a popular form of entertainment*;* it can be*,* in addition*,* a means of exploring literature's classic themes in contemporary contexts.

49c Using a Semicolon to Mark a Series with Internal Commas

Ordinarily, commas are used to mark items in a series:

▶ You can create an off-grid home by building with straw bales, using solar power, and generating additional energy with windmills on the property.

However, when the items are especially long or complex or when an item in the series has internal punctuation, use semicolons. Do not use a semicolon to introduce a list.

▶ The architectural firm of Hanover, Harvey, and Witkins recommends creating an off-grid home by building with straw bales; packing them tightly, which makes them flame-resistant; utilizing solar power; and generating additional energy through windmills on the property.

▶ I used the following in my "green" home: straw bales, solar panels, and water-conserving fixtures.

49d Repairing a Comma Splice

One way to repair a ***comma splice*** is to replace the comma between the two independent clauses with a semicolon.

▶ Reporters without Borders fights restrictions placed on journalists; the group also raises awareness about this increasingly important issue.

> **comma splice** Two independent clauses joined by a comma alone

Sometimes a comma splice occurs because a comma is placed before a conjunctive adverb or transitional phrase that links two independent clauses. To correct it, replace the comma with a semicolon:

▶ Most people don't think of babies as prospective employees, however, in Hollywood infants can become working actors at fifteen days old.

49e Avoiding Overuse

> **More about**
> Sentence variety, 527–31

complex sentence
One or more subordinate clauses linked to an independent clause

Use semicolons sparingly to avoid suggesting that everything in the passage is of equal importance. Overusing semicolons can also be a sign that you need to vary your sentence structures. You can turn some independent clauses into phrases or create **complex sentences** by turning some of your independent clauses into subordinate clauses.

DRAFT

According to the *Los Angeles Times*, the earliest known gunshot victim in the Americas died in 1536; archaeological exploration in Peru has uncovered a pierced skull. The Inca warrior was shot by Spanish conquistadors. Historical records verify that a battle took place at the location in which the skull was found; the battle is now known as the "siege of Lima." As many as 72 victims' remains have been found; most were not shot; most were bludgeoned to death.

> Combines independent clauses 2 and 3; clause 3 becomes a subordinate clause introduced by the relative pronoun *who*.

> Combines independent clauses 4 and 5; clause 5 becomes a phrase.

REVISION

According to the *Los Angeles Times*, the earliest known gunshot victim in the Americas died in 1536. Archaeological exploration in Peru has uncovered the pierced skull of an Inca warrior who was shot by Spanish conquistadors. Historical records verify that the skull was found at the site of a battle now known as the "siege of Lima." As many as 72 victims' remains have been found. **Most were not shot but were instead** [phrase] **bludgeoned to death.**

> Combines independent clauses 7 and 8; clause 8 becomes a phrase.

EXERCISE 49.1 Correcting the use of semicolons

Add or delete semicolons or replace them with a different punctuation mark to correct or improve the sentences below. (Some sentences may be correct.)

EXAMPLE

About 10 percent of Americans are dyslexic, they have a learning disability that causes them to have difficulty with written language, particularly reading and spelling.

1. Very few corporate managers are dyslexic; and this is understandable, since corporate management requires strong reading and writing skills.
2. Their disability does seem to exclude dyslexics from participating in this major business sector, however, according to a recent study, dyslexics are well represented as entrepreneurs or small-business owners.
3. About 35 percent of the entrepreneurs surveyed identified themselves as dyslexic apparently, it is common for dyslexics to develop important strengths precisely because of their weakness.
4. The study concluded that dyslexics were more likely than nondyslexics to be willing to delegate authority, to be especially adept at key business skills, such as oral communication and problem solving, and to be owners of two or more businesses.
5. Researchers noted that dyslexics' willingness to delegate authority gives them a specific advantage over nondyslexic entrepreneurs; the ability to focus on what they do best.

EXERCISE 49.2 Using semicolons correctly

Add or delete semicolons or replace them with a different punctuation mark to correct or improve the paragraph below.

EXAMPLE

Many elderly people worry that they may lose certain mental abilities, such as memory*;* recently, researchers have uncovered some potentially useful methods of maintaining mental sharpness.

In general, the idea is for the aging to get plenty of mental and physical stimulation just as physical exercise strengthens muscles, mental exercise strengthens the brain. The brain needs novelty; new challenges; and continued stresses to maintain or increase its strength, this type of stimulation creates new nerve cells and connections between them. It is common for some cells of an elderly person's brain to deteriorate, however; the newly developed brain tissue may compensate for the lost brain cells. So those who knit should try ever more complicated patterns, those who like listening to opera should try to learn the libretto, and those who like crossword puzzles should try new kinds of puzzles; such as Sudoku and double crostics. Also important for keeping mentally sharp is to pursue stimulating activities with other people, these can include taking classes; playing bridge; or participating in a reading group.

Make It **Your Own**

Review your use of semicolons in a recent writing project of two or more pages. Add semicolons where needed and cross through unnecessary ones. Then analyze the impact these changes would have on your reader. (Refer to the sections in this chapter as needed.)

Work **Together**

Exchange Exercise 49.2 with a partner. Check your classmate's use of semicolons. Did he or she make any errors? If so, refer to sections in this chapter to help you explain the effect these errors had on you as a reader. (Be specific.)

50 Using Apostrophes

IN THIS CHAPTER

a. Using apostrophes to indicate possession, 773

b. Using apostrophes in contractions, abbreviated years, 777

c. Moving away from using apostrophes with plurals of abbreviations, dates, numbers, and words or letters as words, 777

Apostrophes, like pins, replace something that is missing: Pins replace stitches; apostrophes replace letters in contractions (*can't, ma'am*). Apostrophes also make nouns and indefinite pronouns possessive (*Edward's* or *somebody's horse*). Centuries ago, English speakers indicated possession with a pronoun (*Edward his horse*), so, in fact, today's possessive form (*Edward's horse*) is also an age-old contraction. A list of the most important rules for using apostrophes appears in the Quick Reference box on the next page.

50a Using an Apostrophe to Indicate Possession

In English, you can indicate possession (ownership) in nouns and indefinite pronouns by using the preposition *of*:

▶ Many admired the commitment of the **students**. But the involvement of everybody is needed to make real progress.

Writing Responsibly | Contractions in Formal Writing

Contractions and other abbreviations provide useful shortcuts in speech and informal writing, and they are finding their way into more formal academic and business writing. They are still not fully accepted, however. To determine whether contractions will be acceptable to your readers or will undermine your authoritative tone, check with your instructor, look for contractions in academic journals in your field, or consult reports or business letters written by other company employees. If you are in any doubt, spell the words out.

to SELF

773

Quick Reference: Common Apostrophe Do's and Don'ts

***Do* use an apostrophe . . .**

. . . to indicate possession (with singular and plural nouns and indefinite pronouns) (773)

- The book's cover promised "a thrilling read," but we were skeptical.
- Everyone's taste is different.
- Most books' covers are beautifully designed.
- She borrowed Socrates' book, not Jess's.

. . . to form a contraction or abbreviate a year (777)

- Didn't you forget your anniversary last year?
- You only got married in '08!

Do *not* use an apostrophe . . .

. . . with possessive pronouns, especially *its* (775)

- Now that they've played their CD, I want to play our~~'~~s.
- Sadly, it~~'~~s sales are lagging.

. . . with plurals (775)

- I've got load~~'~~s of song~~'~~s in my brain just itching to get out.

. . . with dates, letters, and numbers (777)

- The members of her club were born in the 1950~~'~~s.

. . . with verbs ending in *-s* (776)

- My mom still hope~~'~~s to sell downloads to members of her book club.

You can also do so by adding an apostrophe, with or without an *-s:*

- Many admired the **students**' [noun] commitment. But **everybody's** [indef. pron.] involvement is needed to make real progress.

1. With singular nouns and indefinite pronouns (but not personal pronouns)

Singular **nouns** and **indefinite pronouns** add an apostrophe and an *-s* to indicate possession:

- The factory's smokestacks belched thick, black smoke.
- No one's health was unaffected.

---

noun A word that names ideas, things, qualities, actions, people, and places

indefinite pronouns Pronouns that do not refer to specific people or things, such as *all, anybody, either, everybody, few, many, either, no one, someone*

> **Tech** **Apostrophes and Spelling or Grammar Checkers**
>
> Be wary of apostrophe-related "errors" identified by your word processor's spelling or grammar checker. These programs may mistake *its* for *it's* (or vice versa).
>
> Pay attention to the program's suggestions, but always double-check them for accuracy.

Even for most singular nouns that already end in *-s*, add an *-'s*:

▶ Dolores's asthma was particularly aggravated.

Add an apostrophe alone to a singular noun or pronoun only when adding an *-'s* would make the word difficult to pronounce:

▶ Socrates' pneumonia became so serious he had to be hospitalized.

Personal pronouns are *never* made possessive by adding an apostrophe. Be sure to use the possessive form, *not* a contraction.

▶ We regret that ~~you're~~ *your* new power plant will have to close, but ~~they're~~ *their* health is more important.

> **personal pronouns** Pronouns that replace specific nouns or noun phrases, such as *I, me, he, him, she, her, it, we, us, you, they, them*

Be especially careful with *its*:

- *It's* (*it is*) is a contraction like *don't* (*do not*) and *can't* (*cannot*).
- *Its* is a **possessive pronoun** like *his* and *hers*.

If you tend to confuse *it's* and *its*, remember that the contraction *always* takes an apostrophe, but the personal pronoun *never* does:

▶ Buca Di Becco serves Italian cuisine at *its* (possessive) best, so *it's* (contraction) a good idea to call ahead for reservations.

> **possessive pronouns** Pronouns that indicate ownership, such as *my, his, yours, mine*, and *theirs*

2. With plural nouns

To make plural nouns possessive, first form the plural and then the possessive. When the plural form ends in *-s*, just add an apostrophe; when it does not end in *-s*, add an apostrophe and *-s*.

Singular	Plural	Possessive
lady	ladies	ladies'
person	people	people's

- By midnight, the ladies' maids were exhausted.
- I'm often amazed by people's consideration for the well-being of others.

This rule applies to family names that end in *-s,* too: Make the name plural and then possessive.

- The ~~William's~~ *Williamses'* parties always ended at dawn.

NOTE Just because a word ends with an *-s* does not mean that it needs an apostrophe. Delete apostrophes from plural nouns and singular verbs:

- Your dog~~'~~s bark wildly, but my cat remain~~'~~s placid. *(noun (plu.) / verb (sing.))*

3. To indicate joint or individual ownership or possession

First, decide whether the apostrophe indicates *joint* or *individual ownership.* When the nouns share possession, make only the last noun possessive:

- Giorgione and Titian's painting *Portrait of a Venetian Gentleman* (c. 1510) is on view at the National Gallery of Art in Washington, DC.

  Giorgione and Titian painted the portrait collaboratively.

When the nouns each possess the same object, quality, or event, make each noun possessive:

- Giorgione's and Titian's paintings of Venus are important milestones in the art of the High Renaissance.

  Each produced paintings of Venus that are important milestones.

4. With compound nouns

While number (singular or plural) is usually attached to the core noun in a compound noun, the possessive is attached to the last noun:

- Jeremiah is driving his sisters-in-law crazy. *(core (plural))*

  Jeremiah has more than one sister-in-law, and he is driving them all crazy. Attach number to the core noun, *sister.*

- Jeremiah is driving his sister-in-law's [last] car.

  Jeremiah is using the car belonging to his sister-in-law; attach possession to the last noun, *law*.

- Jeremiah has his sisters-in-law's [core (plural)] [last] unwavering support.

  Jeremiah has more than one sister-in-law, and he has their unwavering support; attach the plural to the core noun (*sisters*) and possession to the last noun (*law's*).

50b Using Apostrophes in Contractions and Abbreviated Years

An apostrophe can stand in place of missing letters or numbers in a contraction or in an abbreviated year.

- I am — I'm
- He is, she is — He's, she's
- It is/has — It's
- They are — They're
- You are — You're

- Cannot — Can't
- Could not — Couldn't
  Would not — Wouldn't
- Let us — Let's
- Who is — Who's
- 2012 — '12

50c Moving Away from Using Apostrophes to Form Plurals of Abbreviations, Dates, Numbers, and Words or Letters Used as Words

Only a few years ago, *-'s* was a common way of creating the plural for abbreviations, dates, and words or characters used as words. These practices are now in flux, but using apostrophes for this purpose seems to be falling out of fashion. Unless the style guide you use instructs otherwise, do not use apostrophes to form these plurals.

- My brother has stayed in more YMCA's than anyone else I know.
- He spent the 1990's traveling around the United States playing music.
- Now he minds the *p*'s and *q*'s of students in composition classes.
- His students give him 5's on his evaluations.

50c · Detail Matters • Using Apostrophes

NOTE The Modern Language Association (MLA) still recommends the use of an apostrophe with the plurals of letters:

> Now he minds the *p*'s and *q*'s of students in composition classes.

Use an apostrophe to form a plural letter if its absence might cause confusion.

CONFUSING	You've dotted your *t*s and crossed your *i*s. *(may be misread as* is*)*
CLEAR	You've dotted your *t*'s and crossed your *i*'s.

→ EXERCISE 50.1 Correcting apostrophes

Supply or delete apostrophes as appropriate. (Some sentences may be correct.)

EXAMPLE

The sopranos voice crack's whenever she thinks about PhD's in musicology assessing her performance.

1. It was one of her biggest crowd's since the 1990's.
2. Many of the audience member's were fans who gave the performance 10's.
3. The auditorium resounded with they're *bravo*'s and *more*'s.
4. Personally, I think singer's who can't hit the high notes should issue IOU's with each performance.
5. This singer's high *C*'s are always flat, and she deserve's *F*'s for how she manage's the tempo of her concerts.
6. My two sisters and brothers-in-laws applause was among the most enthusiastic of the entire audience.
7. At our' dinner after the concert, my sister's were in agreement over their appreciation of the soprano, and Suzie's and Amber's praise for the soprano was fervent and wholehearted.
8. I didn't want to hurt Suzies and Ambers feelings, so I kept my criticisms about the soprano to myself' during dinner.
9. On the way to our's car I tugged my husband Marks arms and I told him how shocked I was at my sisters's not noticing the soprano's lack of professionalism.

10. Mark smiled and said, "Your wise to let you're sisters' savor the performance, but I think you should be honest but tactful at next weeks concert when we sit in the Jones' special box at the opera house."

EXERCISE 50.2 Using apostrophes correctly

In the following paragraph, add or delete apostrophes as necessary.

One of Adam Smiths contributions to modern economic's is the distinction between use value and exchange value. Writing in the 1700's, Smith defined *use value* as the ability to satisfy peoples wants. In Smiths analysis, *exchange value* is the amount of good's or service's that people are willing to pay for something. His economics can help us understand our's. Smiths pointing out the difference between use value and exchange value can help contemporary economist's understand that value doesnt just derive from price. Jeremy Reiss essay clearly reflects this understanding.

Make It Your Own

Review your use of apostrophes in a recent writing project of two or more pages. Add apostrophes where needed and cross through unnecessary ones. Then analyze the impact these changes would have on your reader. (Refer to the sections in this chapter as needed.)

Work Together

Exchange Exercise 50.2 with a partner. Check your classmate's use of apostrophes. Did he or she make any errors? If so, refer to sections in this chapter to help you explain the effect these errors had on you as a reader. (Be specific.)

51 Using Quotation Marks

IN THIS CHAPTER

a. Setting off direct quotations, 780

b. Indicating titles of short works, 783

c. Indicating words used in a special sense, 784

d. Misusing, 784

e. Punctuating quotations, 785

f. Altering quotations: ellipses and brackets, 786

g. Introducing and identifying quotations, 787

h. Writing Responsibly
Acknowledging indirect sources, 790

Indicating who said what is an important use of quotation marks. When we fail to indicate that words were spoken or written by others—whether accidentally or on purpose—we open ourselves up to charges of plagiarism. Misusing quotation marks can also confuse or annoy your readers. (Think how much better the couple in the cartoon would get along if the man would learn to use quotation marks correctly!) Learning when to use—and when *not* to use—quotation marks is an important part of a writer's responsibilities. A list of the most important rules for using quotation marks appears in the Quick Reference box on the next page.

51a Setting Off Direct Quotations

Double quotation marks (" ") indicate the beginning and end of direct quotations (someone's exact words, whether written or spoken):

▶ Of grappling with the unknown, Albert Einstein wrote this: "The most beautiful thing we can experience is the mysterious. It is the source of all true art and all science."

Single quotation marks (' ') indicate quotations within quotations:

▶ Barbara Jordan, the first black woman to represent a southern state in Congress, felt that when the Constitution was written she "was not included in that 'We, the people.'"

Detail Matters • Setting Off Direct Quotations " " **51a** **781**

Quick Reference: Common Quotation Mark Do's and Don'ts

***Do* use quotation marks . . .**

. . . to set off direct quotations. 780

▶ Eisenhower once said that any person "who wants to be president is either an egomaniac or crazy."

. . . to indicate irony (use sparingly). 784

▶ After an unsuccessful stint as president of Columbia University, Eisenhower let himself be "persuaded" to run for the US presidency.

. . . to refer to words as words. 784

▶ "Popular" is an adjective often attached to Eisenhower's presidency.

(Italics are also widely used for this purpose.)

***Do not* use quotation marks . . .**

. . . to set off indirect quotations (paraphrases). 782

▶ Eisenhower once said that "lunatics or narcissists are the only people who would desire the presidency."

. . . for emphasis. 784

▶ Eisenhower was a five-star general and "Supreme" Commander of Allied forces in Europe during World War II.

. . . with slang or clichés. 785

▶ "Snafus" occur regularly in the army, but Eisenhower generally avoided them through careful planning.

In formal contexts, consider recasting to avoid slang. Clichés are rarely appropriate; rewrite to avoid them.

Quotation Marks in American English Use of quotation marks varies from place to place and culture to culture. In contemporary American English, double quotation marks signal a quotation, and single quotation marks signal a quotation within a quotation:

▶ John complained, "For the third time this month, Mary said, 'I need a few bucks to tide me over till payday.' And it's only June 15!"

British usage is the opposite:

▶ John complained, 'For the third time this month, Mary said, "I need a few bucks to tide me over till payday." And it's only June 15!'

Writing Responsibly: Using Quotations Fairly

You have a responsibility to your reader and other writers to supply quotation marks whenever you borrow language from a source. Omitting quotation marks when needed can undermine your reputation as a writer to be trusted.

to OTHER WRITERS

More about
Plagiarism, 246–63
Patchwriting, 252–56

> **Tech** **Smart Quotes versus Straight Quotes**
>
> Word processing programs usually default to *smart*, or curly, quotation marks ("/"). Smart quotes may look more professional than straight quotes ("/"), but they often turn to gibberish when they are pasted into an online document or uploaded to a web page. If you plan to e-mail or post content that includes quotation marks, change your program's preferences to straight quotation marks. Use the Help function to locate this option.

>**More about**
>Paraphrasing, 252–56

Indirect quotations, which paraphrase someone's words, do *not* use quotation marks:

- Albert Einstein said that ~~"~~the unknown inspires scientists as well as artists.~~"~~

- Barbara Jordan felt that ~~"~~she was excluded by the founding fathers when they drafted the US Constitution.~~"~~

1. In dialog

When quoting dialog, start a new paragraph each time the speaker changes, and put all spoken words in quotation marks:

- "Have you brought women here before?" He smiled and kept chewing, so I said, "Do you always use the same tricks?"
  —"What tricks?" He looked at me like he didn't understand.
  —Leslie Marmon Silko, "Yellow Woman"

If one speaker continues for more than a paragraph, use quotation marks at the beginning of each paragraph, but omit closing quotation marks until the end of the speech.

2. With long quotations

> Generally, introduce block quotations with a complete sentence plus a colon.

> In block quotations, use double quotation marks for quotations within a quotation.

For lengthy quotations, omit quotation marks, and indent quotations in a block from the left margin:

- Lucio Guerrero examines how local Goths feel about their lifestyle's mass-market appeal:

   > For some, that suburbanization of Goth may be what saves the subculture. "If someone who identifies as Goth doesn't have easy access

to the fashion or accouterments that they feel drawn to, but they do have access to a store like Hot Topic, then it's a positive thing," said Scary Lady Sarah, a local DJ and supporter of Chicago's Goth community.

—Lucio Guerrero, "Like a GOTH," *Chicago Sun-Times*

> **More about**
> Formatting block quotations, 292, 334 (MLA style), 377 (APA style)

3. With quotations from poetry

When quoting one to three lines of poetry, use quotation marks and run the lines into your text. Indicate the end of each line by inserting a slash, with a space on each side:

▶ Furthermore, lines 21–22 ("In the pay of a man / From town") and 25–26 ("And here we must draw / Our line") have a marching cadence, a rhythm that reinforces the battlefield symbolism.

When quoting four or more lines, omit quotation marks, set the poetry as a block, and retain the original line breaks:

▶ Gary Snyder's "Front Lines" begins powerfully:

> The edge of the cancer
> Swells against the hill—we feel
> A foul breeze—
> And it sinks back down. (lines 1–4)

51b Indicating Titles of Short Works

Most American style guides suggest placing titles of short works in quotation marks and titles of long works in italics:

- Lahiri's short story "Year's End" appeared in the collection *Unaccustomed Earth*.
- "Front Lines," a poem by Gary Snyder, is from his book *No Nature*.
- Ben Brantley's review of *Romeo and Juliet*, "Rash and Unadvis'd Seeks Same," ran in the *New York Times*.
- *Grey's Anatomy* is my guilty pleasure; "I Am a Tree" is my favorite episode.

> **More about**
> Italicizing titles of longer works, 814–15

- The podcast "Of Two Minds, One Consciousness" from the *Scientific American* website uses results from split-brain studies to explore thought.
- "Bleeding Love," from Leona Lewis's album *Spirit,* reached the top of the Billboard charts.

In APA, CSE, and the *Chicago Manual of Style* parenthetical style, omit quotation marks from the titles of short works in bibliographic entries.

> **More about**
> Citing and documenting sources 288–346 (MLA style, ch. 18), 347–88 (APA style, ch. 19), 389–415 (*Chicago* style, ch. 20), 416–30 (CSE style, ch. 21)

51c Indicating Words Used in a Special Sense

Quotation marks can call attention to words used in a special sense. When talking *about* a word, enclose it in quotation marks to avoid confusion:

▶ Many people confuse "lay" and "lie."

Italics can also be used for this purpose.

To signal that you are using a word ironically or sarcastically, place it in quotation marks:

▶ I didn't know that the Indian "problem" on the plains began in the 1860s....

—James Welch, *Killing Custer*

Use quotation marks sparingly for indicating irony. Overuse can annoy readers. Your words should usually be able to convey irony on their own.

Set a term to be defined in italics and the definition in quotation marks:

▶ Many writers don't realize that *e.g.* stands for "for example" in Latin.

51d Misusing Quotation Marks

It is important to use quotation marks where needed; it is also important to omit them where they are not needed.

> **More about**
> Using italics for emphasis, 816

1. *Not* for emphasis

▶ Paul Potts's debut album was "amazing," selling 130,000 copies in its first week alone.

Let your words and the rhythms of your sentences create emphasis. On the rare occasion when something more is needed, use *italics,* not quotation marks.

2. *Not* with slang

If slang is acceptable in the context, use it without the apology that quotation marks represent; if it is not (as in business or academic writing), choose a more appropriate word or phrase:

▶ Daniel Radcliffe ~~"beat out"~~ *bested* hundreds of competitors to win the role of Harry Potter.

3. *Not* with clichés

Clichés are rarely appropriate; instead of attempting to justify them with quotation marks, revise the sentence to avoid them altogether:

▶ I left the party before ~~the "sun was over the yardarm."~~ *drinks were served.*

51e Punctuating Quotations

Whether punctuation appears before or after the closing quotation mark depends on the punctuation mark.

> **More about**
> Periods, 792–93
> Commas, 748–65 (ch. 48)
> Question marks, 793–94
> Exclamation points, 794–95
> Dashes, 796–98

1. With periods and commas

In American English, commas and periods go *inside* the closing quotation mark, except when a citation follows the quotation:

▶ "Sacred cows," said the sixties radical Abbie Hoffman, "make the tastiest hamburger."

▶ According to sixties radical Abbie Hoffman, "sacred cows make the tastiest hamburger" (qtd. in Albert 43).

> **More about**
> Citing indirect sources, 790–91; 300–01 (MLA), 356 (APA)

Commas and Periods with Quotation Marks In Britain as well as in many other countries that use the roman alphabet, commas and periods follow the closing quotation mark. Since American punctuation rules require that commas and periods come before the closing quotation mark, be sure to adjust your usage to meet US readers' expectations.

2. With question marks, exclamation points, and dashes

Question marks, exclamation points, and dashes go *inside* the closing quotation mark when they are part of the quotation:

> In *The Graduate* (1967), a family friend offers Benjamin career advice: "I just want to say one word to you... plastics!"

They go *outside* the closing quotation mark when they are not:

> Why does Robert Duvall's character in *Apocalypse Now* (1979) say "I love the smell of napalm in the morning"? He explains that "it smells like victory"!

3. With colons and semicolons

Colons and semicolons go outside the closing quotation mark:

> "Love means never having to say you're sorry"; so wrote Erich Segal in *Love Story*.

> "Lions and tigers and bears": These are the only problems Dorothy doesn't encounter on her yellow-brick road to self-knowledge.

51f Altering Quotations with Ellipses and Square Brackets

Student Model
"My View from the Sidelines," 446–51

To fit a quotation into your own sentence, you may alter the wording (but not the meaning) by adding, changing, or deleting words. You have a responsibility, though, to alert your readers to your changes: Enclose additions or changes in brackets, and replace deleted words with ellipses:

Original: "Sometimes driven behind the origin is the rhythm, and the rhythm, as it comes out, causes the rest of the poem to follow. Rhythm is, in a very real sense, primary."

> Snyder explains in the video that "[s]ometimes driven behind the origin is the rhythm.... Rhythm is, in a very real sense, primary" (*Gary Snyder*).
>
> —Rita McMahan, "My View from the Sidelines"

changed letter in brackets
deletion marked by ellipses

More about
Altering quotations fairly, 786, 800, 803

Remember, too, it is unethical to distort the meaning of the original text by altering a quotation or taking a quotation out of context.

NOTE In MLA style, if you must change a capital to a lowercase letter (or vice versa), place brackets around the letter to alert readers to the change.

51g Introducing and Identifying Quotations

Use a colon to introduce a quotation if the clause preceding the quotation could stand on its own as a sentence and could make sense without the quotation:

> Darwin's own words clarify the issue: "It is not the strongest of the species that survive . . . but the ones most responsive to change."

> **More about**
> Clauses, 594–97

Use a comma with signal phrases such as "Darwin said" or "she wrote":

> *signal phrase*
> Charles Darwin said, "It is not the strongest of the species that survive . . . but the ones most responsive to change."

> **More about**
> Using signal phrases, 276–78, 288–90, 347–49

Use no punctuation if the quotation is needed to complete the sentence (as when the word *that* precedes it), and do not capitalize the first word in the quotation:

> Darwin asserts that "[i]t is not the strongest of species that survive . . . but the ones most responsive to change."

If a signal phrase interrupts the quotation, insert a comma before the closing quotation mark and after the signal phrase:

> *signal phrase*
> "It is not the strongest of species that survive," Darwin asserts, ". . . but the ones most responsive to change."

EXERCISE 51.1 Correcting problems with quotation marks and other punctuation

Edit the sentences below as needed to correct problems with quotation marks and other punctuation.

EXAMPLE

Ashley said that "~~Our~~ our library research would go a lot faster if we did it ~~together"~~ together," and I said ~~why not.~~ , "Why not?"

1. On our way to the library, I said You're right. Some sources just aren't available online.
2. In fact, didn't Professor Fass say "Only one-third of your sources may be online?" asked Ashley.

3. "Yes," I said, but that depends on what the word online means; "I pointed to a copy of the *New York Times* that I found lying on a table."

4. Opening it to an article titled Resisting the Rush to a World of No Cash, I said that "I found this in the library, but why can't I get it online and simply pretend that I got it from the periodicals room"?

5. Ashley smiled and said What you call "pretending" is what some might call cheating.

6. In any case, she added, "I don't think I could find this copy of Michael Chabon's short story, The Little Knife, online, and she pointed out that at the library she could also thumb through the magazine in which it originally appeared for more information."

7. "I actually knew you were right," I said, because I needed to go to the library to do this: I was looking through the "Oxford English Dictionary" for the derivation of the word turncoat.

8. Then I noted that "in my paper on Vidkun Quisling, I'd like to go beyond the standard definition of turncoat: One who traitorously switches allegiance".

9. Ashley asked Can you work into your paper the quote from the *Godfather* trilogy, "Keep your friends close, but your enemies closer?"

10. As I searched the library's catalog, I said that "I'd try, but I thought I'd find so much useful material in the library that I might not be able to fit it in."

→ EXERCISE 51.2 Correcting errors with quotation marks

Edit the passage below to correct problems with quotation marks and other punctuation.

EXAMPLE

Ross said that "he came across this quote attributed to Albert Einstein"/: Only two things are infinite, the universe and the stupidity of people, and I'm not so sure about the universe.

These, said Ross, are from the collection of references I found during research but did not use. He showed us a copy of a book by Abbie Hoffman titled, "*Steal This Book*," noting that 'it is hard to find even in libraries because many people followed the title's advice.' Then he said, I was researching what people sell when I opened a copy of the newspaper "*The Rock Ridge Record*" to the want ads in the back". He pointed to a want ad that offered the following. Used tombstone: Perfect for someone named Hancock Arnold Henry Field. One only. Then Ross continued, 'Here is one of several quotes I've collected by Woody Allen': "Why does man kill? He kills for food. And not only food: frequently there must be a beverage." Ross added that "Woody Allen also wrote one of his favorite short stories," which was titled, Notes from the Overfed: After reading Dostoevsky and the new "*Weight Watchers*" magazine on the same plane trip. "Finally", said Ross, "for an English essay, I found this play on the word "strip" by Groucho Marx: If you want to see a comic strip, you should see me in the shower."

Make It **Your Own**

Review your use of quotation marks in a recent writing project of two or more pages. Add quotation marks where needed and cross through unnecessary ones. Then analyze the impact these changes would have on your reader. (Refer to the sections in this chapter as needed.)

Work **Together**

Exchange Exercise 51.2 with a partner. Check your classmate's use of quotation marks. Did he or she make any errors? If so, refer to sections in this chapter to help you explain the effect these errors had on you as a reader. (Be specific.)

51h " " Detail Matters • Using Quotation Marks

Writing *Responsibly*
Acknowledging Indirect Sources

Make It Your Own! Confusing direct and indirect sources is a common problem. Fortunately, the procedures for correctly representing indirect sources in your research papers are not hard to learn, and following them will subtly enhance your writing.

When you cite sources, you do not just inform your audience about where you obtained your information; you also have a responsibility to let your audience know who is speaking in the source. If your source quotes or uses ideas from another writer, that other writer is for you an indirect source[1]: You are not reading that other writer yourself but are reading what he or she said. If you want to use that material from the indirect source, you should acknowledge the indirect source as well as the source that was talking about it. This is a sophisticated technique that takes practice to master; researchers with the Citation Project discovered that citing indirect sources accurately was a challenge for first-year college writers, separating them from experienced writers.

The following example, from a paper exploring the Graduate Equivalency Diploma (GED) alternative to traditional high schools, shows how the problem occurs:

Student's first draft

> **[Paraphrase of passage in source]** Nontraditional high school students in the GED Options Pathway program shouldn't be labeled "GED kids"; they should be judged on their individual accomplishments. **[Quotation from source]** "This is supposed to be the land of the free and equal opportunity and all that stuff" (Peterson). **[In-text citation]**

Peterson, who is cited in the sample above, is the writer of the newspaper story in which the quotation appears. However, Peterson does not speak the sentence in quotation marks. That sentence is being spoken by another source, whom Peterson is quoting in the following passage:

Passage from source

> The program does use the Graduate Equivalency Degree, or GED, as a tool. The students all have to pass the test's five sections, but when they complete the program they earn a regular high school diploma. This is an important point for Robbins, and she stresses that her students will get to graduate with their classes.
>
> "In fact, I'm trying to get everybody to quit calling them those GED kids," she said.
>
> **[Quoted passage]** "Number one, they've labeled them. That irritates me. This is supposed to be land of the free and equal opportunity and all that stuff. Don't label my kids. Let them prove what they can do. Let the test scores speak."

[1] The terms *indirect source* and *indirect quotation* are often used interchangeably.

Detail Matters • Acknowledging Indirect Sources   **51h**   **791**

When you are drawing on material from a source that is quoting, paraphrasing, or summarizing another, your citations should accurately indicate who is speaking and should also indicate where you found the material. This can be accomplished in a parenthetical citation, a signal phrase, or a combination of the two:

Parenthetical citation: Name the speaker, write "qtd. in" (quoted in), then name the source's author

Paraphrase of passage in source	Students in the GED Options Pathway program should not be labeled "GED kids"; they should be judged on their individual accomplishments. "This is supposed to be the land of the free and equal opportunity and all that stuff" (Robbins, qtd. in Peterson).	Parenthetical citation identifies speaker and source
Quotation from source		

Signal phrase: Name both the speaker and the source in your text

Signal phrase identifies source and speaker	Journalist Erica Peterson reports teacher Anastasia Robbins's beliefs: Students in the GED Options Pathway program should not be labeled "GED kids"; they should be judged on their individual accomplishments. "This is supposed to be the land of the free and equal opportunity and all that stuff," says Robbins.	Paraphrase of passage in source / Quotation

Combination of signal phrase and parenthetical citation:

Signal phrase identifies the speaker	Teacher Anastasia Robbins believes that students in the GED Options Pathway program should not be labeled "GED kids"; they should be judged on their individual accomplishments. "This is supposed to be the land of the free and equal opportunity and all that stuff" (qtd. in Peterson).	Paraphrase of passage in source / Quotation
Parenthetical citation identifies the source		

Source: Peterson, Erica. "W.Va. Program Gives High-Risk Students an Option." *wvgazette.com*. West Virginia Gazette, 24 Apr. 2011. Web. 4 May 2012.

Providing the name of the person being quoted (regardless of whether it is a person who was interviewed or another author) is all you need for acknowledging your indirect source; that name should not be in the list of works cited at the end of your paper, since you did not read the original article or interview that person. The source you were reading, though, should be both cited in your paper and included in your list of works cited.

Self Assessment

Review your work to be sure that whenever you work from an indirect source, you:

☐ Cite the direct source. Did you name the source in which you found the material and include only the direct source in your list of works cited?
   ▸ *Direct versus indirect sources, 683–84*

☐ Use parenthetical citation, signal phrases, or a combination of both to acknowledge the name of the speaker in the indirect source and the author of the source in which you found the material. Did you make clear who is speaking? ▸ *Signal phrases, 276–77*

52 Using End Punctuation

Periods, Question Marks, and Exclamation Points

IN THIS CHAPTER

a. Using periods, 792

b. Using question marks, 793

c. Using exclamation points, 794

Imagine that each of the people in these photographs has just uttered the words "you're here." Just by looking at their faces, can you guess who was perplexed, thrilled, or neutral? In face-to-face encounters, sight and sound play a huge role in how we interpret tone and meaning, but in a written text, we depend on words and punctuation—especially the punctuation ending the sentence—to signal mood. Think of the question mark as a raised eyebrow, the exclamation point as wide eyes and an open mouth, and the period as the neutral expression we usually wear.

52a Using Periods to End Statements and Mild Commands

Periods mark the end of most sentences, including statements (or *declarative sentences*), *indirect* (or reported) *questions,* and mild commands:

STATEMENT	Our library has survived a flood and two fires.
MILD COMMAND/ INSTRUCTION	Please urge the council to situate the new library building on higher ground.
INDIRECT QUESTION	She wondered whether the water had ever risen so fast before.

Periods are also used with some, but not all, abbreviations.

> **More about**
> Using periods with abbreviations, 820

52b Using Question Marks to End Direct (Not Indirect) Questions

Most writers do not need a handbook to tell them to use a question mark to end a *direct question:*

- When did Uzbekistan declare its independence?
- Did you know that the median age in Uzbekistan is only 23.2 years?

Use a period, not a question mark, to punctuate *indirect* questions, that is, questions that are reported, not asked directly:

- Dr. Wilson asked why the median age in Uzbekistan is so low.

Use a period, not a question mark, in requests phrased as questions to soften the tone:

- Would you please find out the life expectancy in Uzbekistan.

Writing Responsibly — Question Marks and Exclamation Points

In an e-mail to a friend, you might use a series of question marks or exclamation points to convey surprise or lend emphasis:

- Isn't it about time Joey got rid of the goatee???!

But such techniques are not appropriate in more formal contexts, such as an e-mail to an instructor:

- I look forward to studying Indiana government with you next term.!!!!

Your responsibility to yourself as an authoritative writer is to use restraint, for overusing exclamation points or other punctuation may undermine your credibility with readers.

to SELF

Detail Matters • Using End Puctuation

A question mark in parentheses can also suggest doubt about a date, number, or word.

▶ Life expectancy at birth in Uzbekistan is 67 (?).

You may also punctuate a series of questions with question marks, even when they are part of the same sentence:

> Note that capital letters are optional if each question is not a complete sentence.

▶ Do you know what Uzbekistan's primary crop is? what language the majority speaks? what countries surround this landlocked nation?

52c Using Exclamation Points with Strong Commands or to Express Excitement or Surprise

When giving an emphatic command or expressing sudden excitement or surprise, use an exclamation point to end the sentence:

▶ Don't go there!

▶ "Mom is coming!"

The same sentence, when ended with a period, conveys much less urgency:

▶ Don't go there.

▶ "Mom is coming."

Tech — Using Exclamation Points in E-mail Messages

Because warmth can be difficult to convey in e-mail, writers often use an exclamation point to soften the tone. Compare:

▶ We look forward to seeing you next week.

▶ We look forward to seeing you next week!

EXERCISE 52.1 Using end punctuation

Write six sentences modeled on the examples above that use periods, question marks, and exclamation points appropriately. The context for this exercise is academic.

EXERCISE 52.2 Editing end punctuation

Insert end punctuation—periods, question marks, and exclamation points—as needed. If multiple end punctuation is appropriate, explain why you chose the punctuation mark you did.

EXAMPLE

"Could you repeat the question?" That's the most common response law professor David Cole gets when he calls on disengaged students during class at Georgetown University.

The laptop—the favorite in-class tool for college and university students across the country—is coming unplugged When used responsibly—for taking notes or quickly accessing research—a laptop provides valuable educational support But when used irresponsibly—for watching YouTube, surfing the Web, emailing, IM-ing, playing games, checking sports scores, and shopping for shoes instead of engaging in class—laptops become the scourge of professors, some of whom are now banning them, especially in law schools
. . . Herzog banned all laptops from his classes for a day, and was so "stunned by how much better the class was," that he has vowed to make the embargo permanent in the fall

—Kathy McManus, "Class Action: Laptops Not Allowed,"
Responsibility Project

Make It **Your Own**

Review your use of end punctuation in a recent writing project of two or more pages. Add end punctuation where needed and cross through unnecessary ones. Then analyze the impact these changes would have on your reader. (Refer to the sections in this chapter as needed.)

Work **Together**

Exchange Exercise 52.2 with a classmate. Check your partner's use of end punctuation. Did he or she make any errors? If so, refer to sections in this chapter to help you explain the effect these errors had on you as a reader. (Be specific.)

53 Using Other Punctuation
Dashes, Parentheses, Brackets, Colons, Ellipses, and Slashes

IN THIS CHAPTER
a. Using dashes, 796
b. Using parentheses, 798
c. Using brackets, 800
d. Using colons, 800
e. Using ellipses, 803
f. Using slashes, 805

Writers thinking about punctuation typically focus on the comma, the semicolon, the period, and maybe the quotation mark—the star players of the punctuation team. But dashes, parentheses, brackets, colons, ellipses, and slashes also play key roles. Think of these other marks as the special teams of punctuation: While you may call on them in only a limited number of situations, when needed, there is no better punctuation mark for the job. The Quick Reference box on the next page summarizes how these punctuation marks are used.

53a Using Dashes

Dashes can be used singly, when the information to be set off falls at the end of the sentence, or in pairs, when it falls in the middle. They are used to lend emphasis and to mark examples, explanations, and appositives:

▶ In almost every era of Western culture, women's clothing has been decidedly restrictive and uncomfortable—*and the garments of the mid–nineteenth century are a prime example.* [example]

▶ To be fashionable, women had to wear clothing that hampered their mobility—*cumbersome petticoats and long dresses dragged in puddles and snagged on stairways, turning even a short walk into a navigational challenge.* [explanation]

796

Quick Reference: What These Punctuation Marks Do

Dashes lend emphasis and set off examples, explanations, appositives, contrasts, definitions, series items, interruptions, and shifts.

Parentheses set off information of lesser importance.

Brackets set off a writer's insertions in a quoted passage or replace parentheses within parentheses.

Colons link introductory independent clauses to examples, explanations, appositives; they introduce lists (when the introductory clause does *not* include the words *including, like,* or *such as*); and they introduce quotations (when the introductory clause can stand on its own and make sense without the quotation).

Ellipses indicate an omission or a delay for dramatic effect.

Slashes divide lines of poetry, fractions, and URLs. In formal writing, slashes are not used to separate alternatives (*and/or, he/she*) or parts of dates (*10/23/09*).

▶ In the 1870s another torture device—*the bustle* [appositive]—was introduced.

Dashes also emphasize contrasts, definitions, and items in a list:

▶ The bustle, which emphasized a woman's backside, was considered erotic in its day—*but from a modern perspective, it is quite modest.* [contrast]

▶ For both daytime and evening wear, women were strapped into corsets—*close-fitting undergarments that laced tightly around the torso.* [definition]

▶ The trappings of mid-nineteenth-century dress—*six petticoats, a long hem, a bulky bustle, and a tight corset* [list]—guaranteed women's discomfort.

Dashes can also be used to indicate a break in thought, speech, or tone:

▶ Women's dress today ranges from the prim to the promiscuous—*anything goes!* [break (tone)]

Tech — Typing a Dash

Keyboards do not have a single key for dashes, but you can usually create them with a special series of keystrokes or from the Insert menu. If you cannot find your word processor's combination for typing a dash, type two hyphens (--) instead.

More about
Apostrophes, 773–79 (ch. 50)

CAUTION If you use dashes more than once or twice over several pages, consider replacing one or more with commas: As with antibiotics, overuse of dashes undermines their effectiveness.

53b Using Parentheses

Use parentheses to set off supplementary information (such as examples, dates, abbreviations, or citations) to avoid distracting readers from the main point. Parentheses also enclose letters or numbers delineating items in a list.

▶ The English word for a trifling flaw or offense (*peccadillo*) [example] comes from the Spanish word for a small sin, but many other borrowings from Spanish (*barbecue, chocolate, hammock, potato, tomato*) [examples] actually originated in languages of the peoples whom the Spanish conquered in the Caribbean, Mexico, and South America.

▶ In 1991, the Spanish government founded the Instituto Cervantes (IC) [abbrev.], named for Miguel de Cervantes (1547–1616) [dates], the author of *Don Quixote* (1605, 1615) [dates].

> Unless a complete sentence is enclosed, punctuation goes outside closing parenthesis.

Writing Responsibly: Dashes, Parentheses, or Commas?

Responsible writers remain alert to the tone their punctuation conveys. Compare these three versions of the same sentence and consider the effect the punctuation has on you as a reader:

- Echinacea is reputed—despite many scientists' skepticism—to prevent and relieve colds.
- Echinacea is reputed (despite many scientists' skepticism) to prevent and relieve colds.
- Echinacea is reputed, despite many scientists' skepticism, to prevent and relieve colds.

The dashes lend emphasis—sometimes even a touch of drama—to the material they enclose, while the parentheses downplay that material. The comma is the most neutral mark. Select the punctuation mark best suited to the effect you want your words to have on your readers.

to AUDIENCE

▶ The goals of the IC are (1) to promote the study of Spanish worldwide, (2) to improve the methods of teaching Spanish as a second language, and (3) to advance understanding of Spanish and Latin American cultures.

▶ The proverb "Make hay while the sun shines" first appeared in *Don Quixote* (vol. 1, ch. 11).

EXERCISE 53.1 Choosing between dashes and parentheses

Edit the sentences below to add dashes or parentheses as needed. If either is possible, explain why you chose one over the other.

EXAMPLE

Getting old does not necessarily mean getting frail — spending decades in pain, being stooped over, and having to use a walker — for many people are now in good mental and physical health well into their nineties.

I used dashes here to emphasize the description of "getting frail."

1. People over 85 constitute the fastest-growing segment of our population, and by 2050 researchers project that a substantial number of Americans 800,000 will be over 100 years old.

2. Many studies predicting the length of people's lives indicate that about 35 percent of the factors are determined by genes that we cannot control which leaves about 65 percent that we may be able to influence.

3. One particular long-term study it tracked elderly men for 25 years pointed out that the men who lived to at least age 90 were primarily the ones who did not smoke; prevented diabetes, obesity, and high blood pressure; and exercised regularly.

4. A key indicator for many of the "young-elderly" 70-year-olds is eating healthily limiting calories, saturated fat, and sugar as well as getting high-quality protein and whole grains with plenty of fiber.

5. In addition, several long-term studies have shown that exercise for both women and men is the strongest predictor of healthy longevity.

Detail Matters • Using Other Punctuation

> **More about**
> Altering quotations with ellipses and brackets, 786

53c Using Brackets

Square brackets have two primary uses—to indicate additions or changes to a quotation and to replace parentheses within parentheses:

> *Capital replaced to fit quotation into writer's sentence.*

- Ramo and Burke explain that "[i]n 1456, when the first Bible rolled off [Gutenberg's] press, there were fewer than 30,000 books in Europe."

> *Gutenberg's replaces his in source for clarity.*

> *Freshwater added to explain an antiquated meaning of "sweet."*

- Only four years after Gutenberg printed his first book, the Spanish explorer Vincente Yanez Pinzón reached the mouth of the Amazon, which he called Río Santa María de la Mar Dulce ("River St. Mary of the Sweet [Freshwater] Sea").

Square brackets are also used to enclose the Latin word *sic*, which means *thus* or *so*. It is inserted into a quotation following an error to make clear that it was the original writer, not the person using the quotation, who made the mistake:

> *Writer uses [sic] to point out subject-verb agreement error (are should be is).*

- The most compelling review noted that "each of these blockbusters are [sic] flawed in a different, and interesting, way."

NOTE The Modern Language Association (MLA) and the Council of Science Editors (CSE) do not recommend underlining or italicizing *sic*; the *Chicago Manual of Style* and the American Psychological Association (APA), on the other hand, do recommend setting this Latin word in italics.

53d Using Colons

> **More about**
> Independent clauses, 594–96, 611–13

A colon is usually used after an independent (or main) clause to introduce and call attention to what follows. Colons are also used to separate titles from subtitles and in other conventional ways.

Writing Responsibly — Using [sic]

Use *[sic]* cautiously: Calling attention to an error simply to point out another writer's mistake can make you look impolite or even condescending and might undermine your reputation (or ethos) as a respectful writer. When you come across a simple typographical error in a passage you want to quote (the writer typed *teh* instead of *the*, for example), either paraphrase or simply correct the error.

to SELF

1. To introduce an example, explanation, appositive, or list

Use a colon following an independent (or main) clause to introduce an example, an explanation, an appositive, or a list:

- Cervantes was unlucky**:** *examples* At the battle of Lepanto, he lost the use of his left hand, and on the return journey, he was captured by Algerian pirates.

- Writing *Don Quixote* gave its impoverished author something more than just satisfaction**:** *appositive* the opportunity to make some money.

- A number of important writers died on April 23**:** Rupert Brooke, *list* William Wordsworth, Miguel de Cervantes, and William Shakespeare.

A dash can substitute for a colon in these cases, but a colon is more appropriate in formal writing.

Colons are also used to introduce a list that is preceded by the phrases *as follows* or *the following*:

- The following writers all died on April 23**:** *list* William Wordsworth, Miguel de Cervantes, and William Shakespeare.

Do not introduce a list with a colon when the introductory clause concludes with *like*, *such as*, or *including*:

- A number of important writers all died on April 23, including ~~:~~ William Wordsworth, Miguel de Cervantes, and William Shakespeare.

> **More about**
> Using commas in quotations, 759–60

2. To introduce a quotation

Use a colon to introduce a quotation only when it is preceded by an independent clause that would make sense without it, but not when the quotation is introduced by a signal phrase such as *she said* or *Hughes asks*.

COLON *ind. clause makes sense without quotation* In 1918, William Strunk, Jr., gave writers a piece of timeless advice**:** "Omit needless words."

COMMA *signal phrase needs quotation to make sense* In 1918, William Strunk, Jr., said**,** "Omit needless words."

3. Other conventional uses

- Between title and subtitle and between publication date and page numbers (for periodicals) and location and publisher (for books) in bibliographic citations for some documentation styles

    Langford, David. "Hogwarts Proctology Class**:** Probing the End of Harry Potter." *New York Review of Science Fiction* 20.2 (2007)**:** 1, 8–11. Print.

    Satrapi, Marjane. *Persepolis 2***:** *The Story of a Return*. New York**:** Pantheon, 2004. Print.

- Following the salutation and following *cc* in formal business correspondence

    ▸ Dear Professor Howard:

    ▸ cc: KM

- Between chapter and verse in scripture; between hours, minutes, and seconds; in ratios:

    ▸ Song of Solomon 3:1–11

    ▸ 4:30 p.m.

    ▸ Women outnumber men in college 2:1.

4. Common mistakes with colons

- Do not insert a colon between a verb and its complement or object.

    ▸ Young readers awaited ~~:~~ the next volume in Stephenie Meyer's vampire love saga.

- Do not insert a colon between a preposition and its object.

    ▸ *Vogue* announced a return to ~~:~~ hippie-style clothing.

More about
MLA style, 288–346 (ch. 18)
APA style, 347–88 (ch. 19)
Chicago style, 389–415 (ch. 20)
CSE style, 416–30 (ch. 21)

More about
Business letter formats, 476–81

> **EXERCISE 53.2** Using colons in a sentence
>
> Write two sentences using colons, one to introduce an example or explanation and the other to introduce an appositive, list, or quotation. (See the section above for examples.)

53e Using Ellipses

Ellipses are sets of three periods, or *ellipsis points,* with a space between each. They are most often used to replace words removed from quotations, but they are also sometimes used to create a dramatic pause or to suggest that the writer is unable or unwilling to say something.

1. To indicate deletions from quotations

Although it is not acceptable to alter the meaning of a quotation, writers can and do omit words from quotations as needed to delete irrelevant information or to make a quotation fit into their own sentence. The ellipses alert readers that a change has been made:

> ▸ *Don Quixote* begins like a fable: "In a village of La Mancha**,** . . . there lived not long since one of those gentlemen that keep a lance**,** . . . a lean hack**,** . . . and an old greyhound for coursing**.** . . ."
>   *(comma + ellipses)* *(comma + ellipses)* *(comma + ellipses)* *(period + ellipses)*

> Use four dots—a period plus the ellipses—if a deletion occurs at the end of the sentence.

With a parenthetical citation, insert the ellipses before the closing quotation marks and the period after the citation.

> ▸ "They will have it his surname was Quixada . . ." (1).
>   *(ellipses + close quote)* *(citation + period)*

When only a few words are quoted or when the quotation begins with a lowercase letter, it is obvious that words have been omitted from the quotation, so no ellipses are needed:

> ▸ That *Don Quixote* keeps "a lean hack" suggests that he is no romantic hero, but instead minor, rather poor, country gentry.

NOTE If you are quoting a complete sentence, no ellipses are needed to indicate that the sentence comes from within a longer passage.

> **More about**
> Altering quotations, 284–86, 786, 800

Writing Responsibly — Altering Quotations

Exercise care when changing quotations: Never make a change that might distort the original or that might mislead readers, and always use ellipses and brackets to indicate an alteration.

to OTHER WRITERS

2. To indicate the omission of a line (or lines) of poetry

Use not a single ellipsis mark (three dots) but a whole line of dots to replace one or more missing lines of poetry:

▶ One of the most famous lines in Robert Frost's poem "Mending Wall" is "Good fences make good neighbors," but the speaker's meaning is lost when this line is taken out of context:

> There where it is we do not need the wall:
> . . . .
> My apple trees will never get across
> And eat the cones under his pines, I tell him.
> He only says, "Good fences make good neighbors." (lines 23–27)

3. To indicate a dramatic pause or interruption in dialog

An ellipsis can indicate an incomplete thought, a dramatic pause, or an interruption in speech:

▶ The disgruntled writer muttered, "The only word to describe my editor is . . . unprintable."

> **EXERCISE 53.3** Using brackets and ellipses with quotations
>
> Write a paragraph in which you quote a passage from another text, marking deletions with ellipses and enclosing additions in brackets. Your paragraph must include at least one addition and two deletions. Be sure to identify the quoted passage by using a signal phrase and parenthetical page number.

> **More about**
> Signal phrases,
> 276–84, 288–93,
> 347–49

53f Using Slashes

The slash (or *virgule*) is used to mark the ends of lines in poetry when the poetry is run into a sentence:

▶ *Don Quixote* opens with some "commendatory verses" that warn the writer "Whoso indites frivolities, / Will but by simpletons be sought" (lines 62–63).

Slashes are also used in fractions and URLs:

▶ 1/2   1/3   3/4

▶ www.unh.edu/writing/cwc/handouts/

In informal contexts, the slash is sometimes used to indicate that either term is applicable:

▶ I've got so many courses this semester that I decided to take Spanish pass/fail.

In more formal contexts (such as academic or business writing), replace the slash with the word *or,* or rewrite the sentence:

DRAFT	An effective writer revises his/her work.
BETTER	An effective writer revises his or her work.
BEST	Effective writers revise their work.

Slashes are also used in dates, but only in informal or technical contexts or in tables where space is at a premium.

TECHNICAL OR INFORMAL	6/26/13
FORMAL	June 26, 2013 or 26 June 2013

EXERCISE 53.4 Editing dashes, parentheses, brackets, colons, ellipses, and slashes

In the following paragraph, add or delete dashes, parentheses, brackets, colons, ellipses, and slashes as necessary.

The Welsh poet Dylan Thomas 1914–1954 wrote many memorable poems but is perhaps most famous for one "Do not go gentle into that good night." Thomas's poem attempts to arouse his dying father a robust and vigorous man throughout most of his life to avoid leaving life weakly. The poem states its plea in its first two lines "Do not go gentle into that good night, Old age should burn and rave at close of day." The poem's second stanza begins: "Though wise men at their end know dark is right," pointing out that people often are aware "at the end know" of the finality of death. However, the stanza ends with "Do not go gentle into that good night." Stanzas 2 through 5 of the poem where Thomas shows it's only fitting to fight death to the very end explain that wise men, good men, wild men, and grave men do not leave life softly. The poem's last two lines demonstrate (as well as plead) "Do not go gentle into that good night. Rage, rage against the dying of the light." Perhaps the most moving line [in the poem] is also in the last stanza "Curse, bless, me now with your fierce tears, I pray." Here, Thomas's words they become increasingly stirring when one repeats them aloud express how his father's "fierce tears" would be both a misfortune and a mercy.

Make It **Your Own**

Review your use of dashes, parentheses, brackets, colons, ellipses, and slashes in a recent writing project of two or more pages. Add punctuation marks where needed and cross through unnecessary ones. Then analyze the impact these changes would have on your reader. (Refer to the sections in this chapter as needed.)

Work **Together**

Exchange Exercise 53.4 with a classmate. Check your partner's use of punctuation. Did he or she make any errors? If so, refer to sections in this chapter to help you explain the effect these errors had on you as a reader. (Be specific.)

54 Capitalizing

IN THIS CHAPTER

a. First word of a sentence, 807

b. Proper nouns and proper adjectives, 809

c. Titles and subtitles, 810

d. Pronoun *I* and interjection *O*, 811

e. Abbreviations and acronyms, 812

> **More about**
> Nouns, 575–77
> Adjectives, 580, 669–77
> Titles and subtitles, 783–84, 810–11, 814–15
> Pronouns, 577–78

Like a spire soaring over surrounding rooftops, a capital letter beckons the reader, calling attention to the word it adorns. But just as architecture varies from place to place, so the rules of capitalization vary from language to language.

In English, capital letters are used to call the reader's attention in a variety of contexts. The Quick Reference box on page 808 outlines the most important rules of capitalization in English. For cases not covered here, or when you are not sure, consult a dictionary. Your readers will think better of you if you avoid overcapitalizing.

Capitalization English capitalization can be confusing to people for whom English is a foreign language. In Spanish, French, and German, the first-person singular pronoun is lowercase (*yo, je, ich*), but in English it is capitalized (*I*), although the other personal pronouns are not. In Spanish and French, the names of months and days of the week are lowercased, but not in English. In German, all nouns are capitalized, but in English only proper nouns are. Languages such as Arabic and Korean have no capital letters at all. Proofread your work carefully to adhere to the conventions of capitalization in the language in which you are writing, referring to this chapter and a good college dictionary as needed.

54a Capitalizing the First Word of a Sentence

Capitalize the first letter of the first word of every sentence:

807

cap Detail Matters • Capitalizing

> **Quick Reference** **Common Capitalization Do's and Don'ts**
>
> **Do capitalize . . .**
> **. . . the first word of a sentence. (807)**
> ▶ The day broke gray and dull.—Somerset Maugham, *Of Human Bondage*
>
> **. . . proper nouns and proper adjectives. (809)**
> ▶ Aunt Julia, Beijing, Dad (used as a name), Band-Aid, Shakespearean, Texan
>
> **. . . the first, last, and important words in titles and subtitles. (810)**
> ▶ *Harry Potter and the Order of the Phoenix*
>
> **. . . the first-person pronoun *I*. (811)**
> ▶ I think; therefore, I am. —René Descartes
>
> **. . . abbreviations and acronyms. (812)**
> ▶ Eng. Dept., UCLA, NYPD
>
> **Do *not* capitalize . . .**
> **. . . common nouns. (809)**
> ▶ dog, cat, aunt, city, my dad, bandage
>
> **. . . compass directions. (810)**
> ▶ north, south, northwest, southeast
>
> **. . . seasons or academic years and terms. (810)**
> ▶ spring, freshman, intersession

▶ (In response to Franklin Roosevelt's long tenure, the US Congress passed an amendment limiting a president to two terms.)

This rule applies even to sentences in parentheses, unless they are incorporated into another sentence:

> **More about**
> Parentheses, 798–99

▶ His vice president, Harry S. Truman, decided not to run for reelection, although the amendment did not apply to him. (The sitting president was exempted.)

▶ Although the amendment did not apply to him (the sitting president was exempted), Truman decided not to run for reelection.

Capitalize the first word of a sentence you are quoting, even when it is incorporated into your own sentence:

- In response to a question about the amendment, President Eisenhower said, "By and large, the United States ought to be able to choose for its president anybody that it wants, regardless of the number of terms he has served."

Do not capitalize the first word when you are quoting only a phrase:

- President Eisenhower's "faith in the long-term common sense of the American people" made him feel the amendment was unnecessary.

When interrupting a quoted sentence, do not capitalize the first word of the second part:

- "By and large," Eisenhower said, "the United States ought to be able to choose for its president anybody that it wants, regardless of the number of terms he has served."

NOTE In MLA style, if you must change a capital to a lowercase letter (or vice versa) to incorporate a quotation into your sentence, place brackets around the letter to alert readers to the change.

> **More about**
> Brackets, 800
> Altering quotations, 786, 800, 803–04

If a colon links two *independent clauses,* capitalizing the first word following the colon is optional, but be consistent:

- Before Franklin Roosevelt, no US president had held office for more than two terms: That precedent was broken with Roosevelt's third inauguration.

or

- Before Franklin Roosevelt, no US president had held office for more than two terms: that precedent was broken with Roosevelt's third inauguration.

> **independent (or main) clause** A word group that contains a subject and a main verb and that does not begin with a subordinating conjunction, relative pronoun, or relative adverb

54b Capitalizing Proper Nouns and Proper Adjectives

Capitalize the first letter of ***proper nouns*** (the names of specific people, places, and things) and the adjectives derived from them. Do not capitalize common nouns (names for general groups of people, places, and things). The Quick Reference guide on page 810 provides examples of words in each group.

Quick Reference: Capitalize Proper Nouns and Proper Adjectives, but Not Common Nouns

Proper Nouns and Proper Adjectives	Common Nouns
ACADEMIC DEPARTMENTS AND DISCIPLINES	
Political Science Department, Linguistics 101	political science, linguistics
PEOPLE	
Senator Robert C. Byrd, Mom (used as a name), Dickensian	the senator, my mother, novelistic
PLACES, COMPASS DIRECTIONS	
Yosemite National Park, Neptune, the Northwest	the park, that planet, northwest, midwestern
TIME PERIODS AND HOLIDAYS	
Tuesday, June, Memorial Day	a weekday, this summer, spring break
HISTORICAL EVENTS, PERIODS, AND DOCUMENTS	
Korean War, Roaring Twenties, the Emancipation Proclamation	the war, the twenties, the proclamation
ORGANIZATIONS, OFFICES, COMPANIES	
National Wildlife Federation, General Accounting Office, National Broadcasting Corporation	a conservation group, the legislative branch, the network, the corporation
TRADE NAMES	
Coke, Kleenex, Xerox	a soda, a tissue, a photocopy
NATIONS, ETHNIC GROUPS, RACES, AND LANGUAGES	
Pakistan, Pakistani, African American, Caucasian, Swahili	her country, his nationality, their language
RELIGIONS, RELIGIOUS DOCUMENTS, AND RELIGIOUS TERMS	
Buddhism, Jewish, Vedas, Bible, Allah, God	your religion, a religious group, a sacred text, biblical, the deity
TRANSPORTATION	
Greyhound, Amtrak, U.S.S. *Constitution*	a bus, the train, this battleship

54c Capitalizing Titles and Subtitles

In general, capitalize the first and last words of titles and subtitles, as well as any other important words: nouns (*Pride, Persuasion*), verbs (*Is, Ran*), pronouns (*It, Their*), adjectives (*Green, Starry*), and adverbs (*Slow, Extremely*). Do not capitalize prepositions (*in, at, to, by*), coordinating conjunctions (*and, but, for, nor, or, so, yet*), *to* in infinitive verbs, or articles (*a, an, the*) unless they begin or end the title or subtitle.

Extremely Loud and Incredibly Close: A Novel

"In the Basement of the Ivory Tower" (article)

Pokémon XD: Gale of Darkness (game)

"I Kissed a Girl" (song)

The Dark Knight (movie)

Flying Popcorn (software)

NOTE Style guides may recommend different capitalization for titles and subtitles in reference lists and bibliographies. Check the style guide you are using and follow the rules described there.

> **More about**
> MLA style, 288–346 (ch. 18)
> APA style, 347–88 (ch. 19)
> *Chicago* style, 389–415 (ch. 20)
> CSE style, 416–30 (ch. 21)

54d Capitalizing the First-Person Pronoun *I* and the Interjection *O*

In all formal contexts, capitalize the first-person singular pronoun *I*:

- I wish I could meet myself in twenty years.

Although rarely used in contemporary prose, the interjection *O* should always be capitalized:

- Awake, O north wind, and come, O south wind! —Song of Solomon 4.16

However, the word *oh* should be capitalized only when it begins a sentence:

- "Oh literature, oh the glorious art, how it preys upon the marrow in our bones." —D. H. Lawrence

Writing Responsibly — Capitalizing in E-mail and IM

In general, the rules of capitalization are the same online as they are in print. But while in print a writer may sometimes type a word in all capital letters for emphasis, in e-mail or other online contexts, words typed in all capital letters are interpreted as shouting. When formatting is available, use italics (or boldface type) for emphasis in online writing; when such formatting is unavailable, place an asterisk before and after the word you want to emphasize. Also, although omitting capital letters in e-mail and instant messages may be acceptable in informal contexts, to maintain a professional tone you should follow the rules of capitalization when texting or e-mailing in business or academic settings.

to SELF

54e Capitalizing Abbreviations and Acronyms

> **More about**
> Abbreviations,
> 820–25 (ch. 56)

Abbreviations of proper nouns should be capitalized, and acronyms should be typed in all capital letters:

ABBREVIATIONS	U. of Mich., Anthro. Dept.
ACRONYMS	RADAR, NASA, OPEC

> **acronym** Word formed from the first letter of each major word in a name

EXERCISE 54.1 Correcting capitalization

The following sentences have been typed entirely in lowercase letters. Supply correct capitalization.

EXAMPLE

~~when~~ *When* ~~i~~ *I* moved into my first apartment this ~~september~~ *September*, ~~i~~ *I* quickly realized that ~~i~~ *I* had to watch my pennies at ~~stop~~ *Stop* and ~~shop~~ *Shop*.

1. when i went shopping with my friend jason, he called me a dumb shopper.
2. my cart was filled with products with names like kellogg's, maxwell house, and tide, but his cart had mostly store brands.
3. i told him that my mom would ask me, "why do you always have to have levi's? aren't the sears jeans just as good?" now that it was my own money, i understood.
4. on monday, I saw jason in the english class we have together, and as we opened up our books to a short story titled "king of the bingo game," i whispered to him, "thanks to you i saved fifteen dollars at the supermarket yesterday."
5. as we walked out of tyler hall and headed west to our history class, he said, "you'll have more money to spend on fashion if you spend less on detergent and ketchup."

Make It **Your Own**

Review your use of abbreviations and acronyms in a recent writing project of two or more pages. Add abbreviations and acronyms where needed and cross through unnecessary ones. Then analyze the impact these changes would have on your reader. (Refer to the sections in this chapter as needed.)

Work **Together**

The rules of capitalization have not always been in place for writers of English. In groups of two or three, revise the passage below to follow today's rules of capitalization in English. Refer to this chapter or to a good dictionary to settle any disputes.

> I do here in the Name of all the Learned and Polite Persons of the Nation, complain to your Lordship, as First Minister, that our Language is extremely imperfect; that its daily Improvements are by no means in proportion to its daily Corruptions; and the Pretenders to polish and refine it, have chiefly multiplied Abuses and Absurdities; and, that in many Instances, it offends against every Part of Grammar.
>
> —Jonathan Swift, *Proposal for Correcting, Improving, and Ascertaining the English Tongue* (1712)

55 Italics and Underlining

IN THIS CHAPTER

a. Titles of longer works, 814
b. Emphasis, 816
c. Names of vehicles, 816
d. Words, letters, and numbers used as words, 816
e. Unfamiliar non-English words, 817
f. Hyperlinks, 817

Before the computer, writers typed on typewriters and used underlining to emphasize words; set off the titles of longer works; distinguish words, letters, and numbers used as words; set off unfamiliar non-English words; and call out the names of ships, airplanes, spacecraft, and other vehicles. Now writers type on computers and use italics for these purposes. The Quick Reference box on the next page outlines the most important rules for using italics and underlining.

> *More about*
> Using quotation marks with titles of shorter works, 783–84

55a Italicizing Titles of Longer Works

Use italics (or underlining) for titles of longer works, such as books, periodicals (magazines, journals, and newspapers), films, CDs, television series, and websites; use quotation marks for shorter works, such as stories, articles, songs, television episodes, and web pages:

▶ Annie Proulx's collection *Close Range: Wyoming Stories* includes the story "Brokeback Mountain," which originally appeared in the *New Yorker* magazine. Kenneth Turan, critic for the *Los Angeles Times,* called the 2005 film *Brokeback Mountain* "groundbreaking," and Roger Ebert of the *Chicago Sun-Times* gave it two thumbs up. The *Brokeback Mountain* soundtrack on CD includes songs like "He Was a Friend of Mine" by Willie Nelson and "The Devil's Right Hand" by Steve Earle.

Detail Matters • Italicizing Titles of Longer Works ital **55a** **815**

> **Quick Reference** — **Common Italics Do's and Don'ts**
>
> ***Do* use italics . . .**
>
> **. . . with titles of longer works. (814)**
>
> ▶ We will be discussing the novel *Wuthering Heights* for the next two weeks. By the way, the novel's main character has nothing to do with the comic strip *Heathcliff.*
>
> **. . . for emphasis. (816)**
>
> ▶ I ask you *not* to read beyond the first chapter until we have discussed it in class.
>
> (Use italics for emphasis sparingly in academic prose.)
>
> **. . . with words, letters, and numbers used as words. (816)**
>
> ▶ You will notice that several of the characters' names begin with the letter *h;* this can be confusing.
>
> **Do *not* use italics . . .**
>
> **. . . with titles of short works. (814)**
>
>   "Girl"
> ▶ Jamaica Kincaid's story ~~*Girl*~~ is only one page long.
>
> **. . . with historical documents and religious works. (815)**
>
>   Declaration of Independence   Bible
> ▶ The ~~*Declaration of Independence*~~ and the ~~*Bible*~~ take pride of place on my grandmother's bookshelf.
>
> **. . . with links to websites and web pages (underline if a hyperlink). (818)**
>
> ▶ If you do not want to buy the book that was discussed in Salon.com, you can download it from Project Gutenberg <u><www.gutenberg.org/etext/768></u>.

In addition, stand-alone items like court cases and works of art (paintings and sculptures) are italicized:

- *Bowers v. Hardwick*
- *Mona Lisa*
- *The Bronco Buster*

In contrast, the titles of major historical documents and religious works are not italicized:

- Magna Carta, Mayflower Compact, Kyoto Protocol
- Bible, Qur'an, Vedas

> ## Writing Responsibly
> **Using Italics for Emphasis**
>
> When using italics for emphasis, consider your reader. Sometimes italics can help convey the writer's feelings, but will readers be interested? In a personal context, the use of italics in the sentence below might be acceptable:
>
> ▶ Should *I* call *him*, or should I wait for *him* to call *me*?
>
> But such emphasis on the writer's emotions is usually inappropriate in a business or academic context.
>
> *to AUDIENCE*

55b Italicizing for Emphasis

Italics are sometimes used for emphasis:

▶ Rowling wants readers to *identify* with Harry, not merely to *sympathize* with him.

In the sentence above, the italics heighten attention to the contrast. To be effective, use italics sparingly for emphasis. Using italics haphazardly or overusing them can annoy or even confuse readers:

▶ He wanted *readers* to know *his* characters, not *merely* to observe them.

55c Italicizing Names of Vehicles

The names of individual trains, ships, aircraft, and spacecraft are all italicized:

Titanic, Spirit of St. Louis, Challenger

However, vehicles referred to by company, brand, or model names are not:

Corvette, Boeing 747

55d Italicizing Words, Letters, or Numbers Used as Words

When referring to words, letters, or numbers used as words, set them off from the rest of the sentence with italics:

▶ My chemistry teacher used the word *interesting* to describe the results I got on my last lab. He told me to be more careful next time, to dot all my *i*'s and cross all my *t*'s.

55e Italicizing Unfamiliar Non-English Words and Latin Genus and Species

> **More about**
> Plurals of letters, 777–78

English is an opportunistic language; when encountering new things or ideas, English speakers often adopt words already used in other languages. The word *raccoon,* for example, comes from Algonquian and the word *sushi* from Japanese. Once they are fully absorbed, they are typed with no special formatting. Until then, borrowings should be italicized:

▶ The review provides a good example of *diegesis* in that it describes the film without making a judgment about it.

To determine whether a non-English word warrants italics, check your dictionary: Words familiar enough to be found in a college dictionary should not be set in italics.

Latin genus and species names are also set in italics:

▶ *Acer saccharum* are the Latin genus and species for the sugar maple.

55f Underlining Hyperlinks

In recent years, underlining has taken on a new, specialized meaning: It is used (along with color) to indicate hyperlinks in both printed and online documents (Figure 55.1). Because many documents today will ultimately appear online, writers are increasingly reserving underlining for hyperlinks and using italics for all the other purposes outlined in this chapter.

> **EXERCISE 55.1 Correcting underlining and italics**
>
> Cross through any words or phrases that should not be italicized or underlined, and circle any words or phrases that should be.
>
> **EXAMPLE**
>
> The 1960s television show (Hogan's Heroes) depicted ~~Nazism~~ as a joke, and the show (F Troop) falsified the relationship between ~~Native Americans~~ and the military.
>
> 1. In a review of the book "Hot, Flat, and Crowded," by Thomas Friedman, David Victor reminds readers that the Soviet Union's 1957 launch of the spacecraft Sputnik galvanized the United States's space program and calls Friedman's book "a plea for a new Sputnik moment."

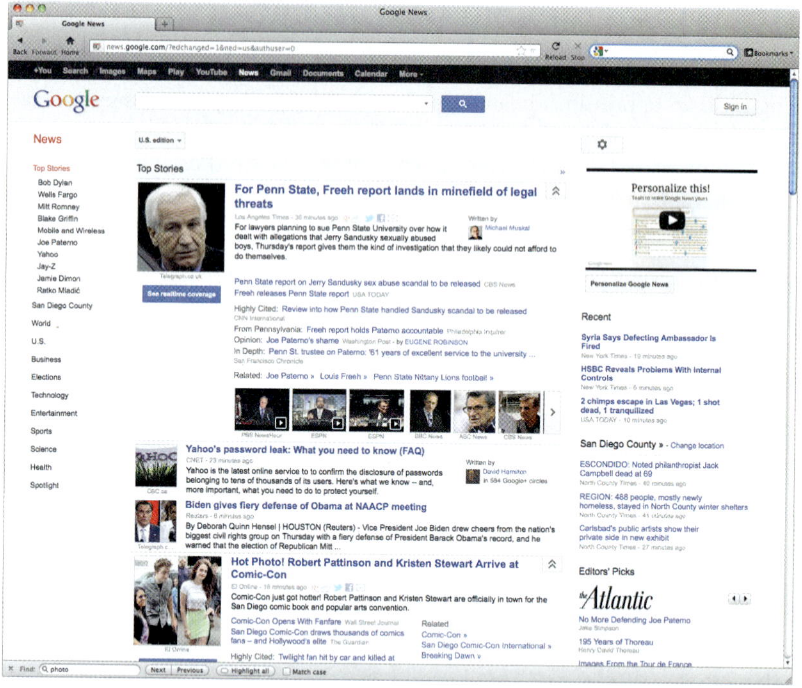

FIGURE 55.1 Hyperlinks The hyperlinks on many web pages (including the Google News page shown here) are set in bright-blue type to set them off from the surrounding text; they are often underlined as well or show underlining when a cursor rolls over the link.

2. The film The Matrix makes references to Plato's *Cave Allegory* from the book "The Republic" and is indebted to Buddhist philosophy in that it considers the world *maya*, or illusion, a concept expressed in the Buddhist religious works the *Tripitaka*.

3. Thomas Jefferson's motto while writing the Declaration of Independence might have been "novus ordo seclorum," a new order of the ages, for with that document a new nation was born.

4. In 1992, Vice President Dan Quayle mistakenly told a sixth grader that the student had spelled the word potato incorrectly and that the word should not end with an o but with an additional e.

5. Articles on these and other topics appear in Wikipedia, www.wikipedia.org, but remember that Wikipedia is often more *comprehensive* than *reliable*.

EXERCISE 55.2 Adding italics and underlining

Underline any words in the passage below that should be set in italics or underlined, and add quotation marks where needed.

A study reported in the journal Archives of General Psychiatry this month linked the father's age with the likelihood that his children will develop bipolar disorder. The study, called Advancing Paternal Age and Bipolar Disorder by Emma M. Frans et al., looked for a link between paternal, not maternal, age, although a slight correlation with maternal age was also found. The suspected cause is a type of random mutation among sperm cells called de novo mutations. An article called Advancing Paternal Age and Autism, published two years ago, also found a link between the likelihood of having an autistic child and paternal age. Both articles can be found at the Archives of General Psychiatry website: http://archpsyc.ama-assn.org/.

Make It Your Own

Review your use of italics and underlining in a recent writing project of two or more pages. Add italics and underlining where needed and cross through unnecessary ones. Then analyze the impact these changes would have on your reader. (Refer to the sections in this chapter as needed.)

Work Together

Exchange Exercise 55.2 with a partner. Check your classmate's use of italics and underlining. Did your partner make any errors? If so, explain the effect these errors had on you as a reader. (Be specific.)

56 Using Abbreviations

IN THIS CHAPTER

a. Abbreviating titles, 822
b. Using familiar abbreviations, 822
c. Abbreviating years, hours, numbers, dollars, 823
d. Avoiding certain abbreviations, 823
e. Replacing Latin abbreviations, 824

>*More about*
MLA style, 288–346 (ch. 18)
APA style, 347–88 (ch. 19)
Chicago style, 389–415 (ch. 20)
CSE style, 416–30 (ch. 21)

When you see this familiar symbol, you know at a glance that the object it adorns was made from recycled materials. When they are familiar to the audience, icons like this one communicate information briefly and quickly. Abbreviations accomplish a similar goal in writing: They convey information rapidly, but they work only when readers know what they stand for.

While used frequently in business, scientific, and technical contexts, abbreviations are used sparingly in writing in the humanities and for a general audience, except in tables (where space is at a premium) and in bibliographic citations.

When you do abbreviate, use a period with a person's initials and with most abbreviations that end in lowercase letters:

▸ J. K. Rowling   Martin Luther King, Jr.   St. John

▸ St.   Blvd.   Ave.

Use a period after each letter with abbreviations of more than one word:

▸ i.e.   e.g.   a.m.   p.m.

Most abbreviations made up of all capital letters no longer use periods:

▸ BS   MA   DVD   UN

The Quick Reference box on the next page outlines the most important rules for using abbreviations.

Quick Reference — Common Abbreviation Do's and Don'ts

Do use abbreviations . . .

. . . of titles before or after names. (822)
- Dr. Martin Luther King, Jr. *or* Martin Luther King, Jr., PhD

. . . when they are familiar to readers. (822)
- The role of the CIA has changed dramatically since 2001.

. . . with specific numerals and dates. (823)
- My class on ancient Rome meets at 8:30 a.m. to study the period from 509 BCE to 476 CE. The book for that class costs $87.50.

. . . in names of businesses when they are part of the official name. (824)
- Warner Bros. Entertainment Inc.   Spindletop Oil & Gas Co.

Do *not* use abbreviations . . .

. . . of titles not used with a proper name. (823)
- My ~~dr.~~ is married to a ~~col.~~ in the Marines.
  (*doctor*) (*colonel*)

. . . of popular online terms in formal prose. (823)
- ~~TMI~~ with very little focus makes this work a data parade without a point.
  (*Too much information*)

. . . of names, words, courses, parts of books, states and countries, days and months, holidays, and units of measurement in formal prose. (823)
- My ~~bros.~~ ~~Wm.~~ and ~~Jos.~~, even though they are both now over six ~~ft.~~ tall, still love waking up early in the ~~a.m.~~ on ~~Xmas~~.
  (*brothers William Joseph* ... *feet* ... *morning Christmas*)

. . . of Latin terms. (824)
(Replace with English equivalents in prose.)
- Leafy green vegetables, ~~e.g.~~, arugula, kale, and spinach, can reduce the risk of heart disease.
  (*for example*)

56a Abbreviating Titles before and after Names

- Mr. Tony Carter
- Ms. Aoife Shaughnessy
- Dr. Jonnelle Price
- Rev. Jane Genung

Christopher Aviles, PhD
Namazi Hamid, DDS
Robert Min, MD
Frederick C. Copelston, SJ

In most cases, avoid abbreviating titles when they are not used with a proper name:

- I'm hoping my English ~~prof.~~ *professor* will write me a letter of recommendation.

Academic degrees are an exception:

- My auto mechanic comes from a highly educated family: His father has an MS, his mother has an MLS, and his sister has a PhD.

Never use a title both before and after a name: Change *Dr. Hazel L. Cunningham, PhD* to either *Dr. Hazel L. Cunningham* or *Hazel L. Cunningham, PhD*.

56b Using Familiar Abbreviations: Acronyms and Initialisms

Acronyms and *initialisms* are abbreviations made of all capital letters formed from the first letters of a series of words. Acronyms are pronounced as words (*AIDS, CARE, NASA, NATO, OPEC*), while initialisms are pronounced as a series of letters (*DNA, HBO, JFK, USA*). Familiar acronyms and initialisms are acceptable in any context:

- Myanmar democracy advocate Aung San Suu Kyi met with a number of UN dignitaries during her trip to New York last month.

However, if the abbreviation is likely to be unfamiliar to readers, spell out the term on first use and follow it with the abbreviation in parentheses. Subsequently, just use the abbreviation:

- The International Olympic Committee (IOC) failed to take action following the arrest of two elderly Chinese women who had applied for permission to protest in the designated protest areas during the Beijing Olympics. A spokesperson claimed that the IOC has no control over the protest areas.

Detail Matters • Avoiding Abbreviations of Names, Words, and More **abbr 56d** 823

Writing Responsibly: Using Online Abbreviations Appropriately

A new breed of initialism has emerged in online discourse. Here are some examples:

BFN (bye for now)	OIC (oh, I see!)
IDK (I don't know)	OTOH (on the other hand)
IMO (in my opinion)	ROTFL (rolling on the floor laughing)
LOL (laughing out loud)	TMI (too much information!)

The irreverence of some of these initialisms corresponds with the freewheeling characteristics of online discourse. Use them in text messages or on informal networking sites, but avoid them in college and professional writing, including e-mails. While they might establish your online savvy, they might also annoy readers in more formal contexts, undermining your ethos (or credibility).

> **More about**
> Ethos, 143–44

to SELF

56c Using Abbreviations with Specific Years (BC, BCE, AD, CE), Hours (a.m., p.m.), Numbers (no.), Dollars ($)

▶ The emperor Augustus ruled Rome from 27 **BCE** until his death in 14 **CE**.

▶ The Roman historian Titus Livius (known as Livy) lived from 59 **BC** until **AD** 17.

▶ I didn't get home until 11:45 p.m., because the no. 27 bus was so late.

▶ I owe my sister $27.32, and she won't let me forget it.

> AD precedes the number; BC, BCE, and CE follow the number.

NOTE The abbreviations BCE (for *before the common era*) and CE (for *common era*) are now generally preferred over BC (*before Christ*) and AD (*anno domini*, "the year of the Lord" in Latin).

56d Avoiding Abbreviations of Names, Words, Courses, Parts of Books, States and Countries, Days and Months, Holidays, and Units of Measurement in Prose

▶ In ~~Fr.~~, people receive gifts not on ~~Xmas~~ but on ~~Jan.~~ 6.
    France,   *Christmas*   *January*

▶ On ~~Mon.~~ mornings, ~~Psych.~~ 121 meets in a tiny classroom: It is only
  Monday   *Psychology*

ten ~~ft.~~ wide.
    feet

▶ My ~~Eng.~~ teacher, ~~Eliz.~~ Santos, recommends that we always read the
     English   *Elizabeth*

~~intro.~~ first.
introduction

An exception is the names of businesses, when the abbreviation is part of the official name:

▶   Dun & Bradstreet, Inc., was ~~inc.~~ in New York ~~&~~ is still located there.
                                 incorporated   *and*

56e Replacing Latin Abbreviations with English Equivalents in Formal Prose

Latin abbreviations, like those below, are generally avoided in formal writing (except in bibliographies).

▶ e.g.   for example   ▶ cf.   compare
▶ i.e.   in other words   ▶ et al. and others
▶ etc.   and so forth   ▶ N.B.   note especially

NOTE Both *etc.* and *and so forth* are best avoided in formal prose. Instead, include all the items or precede a partial list with *such as* or *for example*. Follow *e.g.* and *i.e.* with a comma if you use them in tables or parenthetical material. Common Latin abbreviations are not italicized or underlined.

EXERCISE 56.1 Correcting abbreviations

Correct the use of abbreviations in the following sentences, which were written for an academic reader in the humanities.

EXAMPLE

This ~~spr.~~ I am taking ~~Astro.~~ 121, the ~~Hist.~~ of ~~Astro.~~
     spring   *Astronomy*   *History* *Astronomy*

Detail Matters • Replacing Latin Abbreviations with English Equivalents in Formal Prose   **abbr**   **56e**   **825**

1. My prof. (Dr. Wm. Irvine, PhD.) assigned a fascinating book on Ptolemy (83–168 A.D.), a Gr. astron. and astrol. who lived in Egypt.
2. Ptol. wrote his great treatise on astron., the *Almagest,* in 147 A.D.
3. In addition to the *Almagest,* Ptol. wrote other works, e.g., *Tetrabiblios, Harmonics,* and *Optics,* that are important in their fields.
4. The National Aeronautics and Space Administration has a good website, and one of its pages mentions Ptol.'s model for predicting eclipses, but it says he developed it in about BC 150, which I think is a mistake.
5. The final for this class is scheduled for Jan. 5, after Xmas, so I'm hoping Santa will bring me a copy of the *Almagest,* trans. by GJ Toomer.
6. I would buy a copy of it for myself but, OMG, it costs over 67.50 dollars.
7. To understand Ptol. more fully, I read ch. 2 from Seilik's book, which explains Ptol.'s geocentric model of the universe.
8. Cf. that with Evans's discussion in ch. 1 of *The Hist. and Pract. of Ancient Astro.*
9. I would major in astro. except that all the classes are held in a bldg. on a noisy blvd.
10. Instead, I will major in accounting, get a job with Deloitte & Touche or Kraft Bros., and study astro. on the side.

Make It **Your Own**

Rewrite a recent text message to avoid abbreviations. Then write a paragraph explaining how this change affects the tone of the message. (If you do not have such a text message, write one using at least two of the abbreviations in the Writing Responsibly box on p. 823.)

Work **Together**

In groups of two or three, craft a text message using as many abbreviations and initialisms as you can. Then trade messages with another group and translate.

57 Using Numbers

IN THIS CHAPTER

a. Spelling numbers of one or two words, 827

b. Using numbers for dates, times, other quantitative information, and parts of literary works, 827

Are we "number one" or "#1"? It depends on the context. At a football game, while dressed in your team's colors, you would probably use the numeral: The context is informal and, besides, the word *one* might not fit as well on the giant hand! But just as you would not attend an interview with your face painted orange and white, in many formal contexts spelling out the number is more appropriate.

Rules for deciding whether to use numerals or to spell out numbers vary widely according to context. In business and the news, single-digit numbers are usually spelled out, while numerals are used for numbers over ten. In the humanities, numbers that can be written in one or two words are usually spelled out, while numerals are used for larger numbers. In the sciences, numerals are customarily used for all numbers. The best practice is to choose a style that will make sense to your audience, and then be consistent in its use. The rules below are appropriate to an academic audience in the humanities.

> ### Writing Responsibly   Ethos and Convention
>
> Using numbers and symbols in conventional ways does not normally affect meaning. Yet conventional usage is important, especially in formal contexts like school or the workplace, because it lends support to your ethos, or credibility. As a marker of appropriateness, it can subtly affect the way your audience perceives you and how seriously they take what you have to say.
>
> to SELF

>**More about**
>Appropriate language, 540–47 (ch. 30)
>Ethos, 143–44

57a Spelling Out Numbers When They Can Be Expressed in One or Two Words

Spell out numbers under a hundred and round numbers—numbers that can be expressed in one or two words:

▸ Satchel Paige pitched sixty-four scoreless innings and won twenty-one games in a row.

If your text uses a combination of numbers—some that can be expressed in one or two words and others that cannot—use numerals throughout for consistency's sake:

▸ Satchel Paige pitched an estimated ~~two thousand~~ *2,000* baseball games during his career. At his first game, 78,383 fans were in attendance, and at his first game as a starter, 72,434 spectators looked on.

Avoid beginning a sentence with numerals. Instead, spell out the number or revise your sentence:

▸ ~~78,000~~ *Seventy-eight thousand* people attended Satchel Paige's first game as a pitcher.

▸ Satchel Paige's first game as a pitcher drew 78,000 fans.

Numbers over a million are often best expressed as a combination of words and numerals:

▸ Over 10 million fans attended Negro League baseball games in 1930.

57b Following Conventions for Dates, Times, Addresses, Specific Amounts of Money and Other Quantitative Information, and Divisions of Literary Works

- **Dates:** May 4, 2013   the fourth of May   429 BCE   1066 CE   AD 1066

- **Times, years:** 4:15 p.m.   seven o'clock   1990s   the nineties   1999–2009   from 1999 to 2009

- **Phone numbers, addresses:** (800) 624-5789
  26 Peachtree Lane   221 W. 34th Street
  Atlanta, GA 30303   New York, NY 10001

- **Exact sums of money:** $10.95 $579.89 $24 million
- **Decimals and fractions:** half   ½   three-quarters   ¾   4⅞   3.95

NOTE MLA style generally recommends using the percent symbol (%) with numerals. The *Chicago Manual* recommends using the word *percent* with numerals in writing for the humanities and the symbol % with numerals in writing for the sciences.

- **Scores, statistics, and percentages:** 5 to 4   42–28   13.3 percent (or 13.3%)   3 out of 10
- **Measurements:** 55 mph   90–100 rpm   135 pounds   5 feet   9 liters   41°F
- **Divisions of books, plays, poems:** part 3   book 7   chapter 15   page 419 or p. 419   act 1   scene 3   lines 4–19

Punctuating Numbers in American English Conventions for punctuating numbers differ across cultures. In many European countries, for instance, commas separate whole numbers from decimal fractions, where periods mark divisions of thousands. In the United States, the convention is reversed:

▶ 2,541   94.7

EXERCISE 57.1 Correcting numbers: Spelling out numbers or using numerals

Revise the following sentences according to the rules for using numerals or spelling out numbers discussed above.

EXAMPLE

At about ~~six thirty~~ *6:30* a.m., the planet Venus is visible low on the horizon; ~~30~~ *thirty* minutes before that, you can also see Jupiter.

1. 1965 saw the first probe reach Mars; it took 22 close-up pictures of the planet and 2 pictures of its moons.
2. The *Mars Pathfinder* was launched on December four, nineteen ninety-six and landed seven months later, on July four, nineteen ninety-seven.

3. *Pathfinder* collected over 16,000 images and conducted 20 tests of the soil.

4. In all, *Pathfinder* collected over two billion bits of data.

5. Mars has a mountain that is seventy-eight thousand feet tall and a canyon that is six to seven times as deep as the Grand Canyon.

6. A Martian day is forty-five minutes longer than an Earth day.

7. Mars is about fifty percent smaller in diameter than Earth: Its diameter is about 4,200 miles, whereas Earth's is about eight thousand miles.

8. Venus, the 6th largest planet, is roughly the size of Earth, at about seven thousand seven hundred miles in diameter.

9. The 2nd closest planet to the sun, its surface can heat up to 900 degrees F.

10. I love to study the night sky, but living at 253 6th Avenue, New York, NY, I can see it only when I travel.

Make It Your Own

Review your use of numerals in a recent writing project of two or more pages. Add numerals where needed and cross through unnecessary ones. Then analyze the impact these changes would have on your reader. (Refer to the sections in this chapter as needed.)

Work Together

Read the student paper in chapter 19 (pp. 381–88). In groups of two or three, discuss whether Heather DeGroot has followed the rules for using numbers laid out in this chapter. What effect does context have on following the rules? What effect would changing her treatment of numbers have on her intended audience?

58 Using Hyphens

IN THIS CHAPTER

a. Forming compounds, 830
b. Breaking words at ends of lines, 833

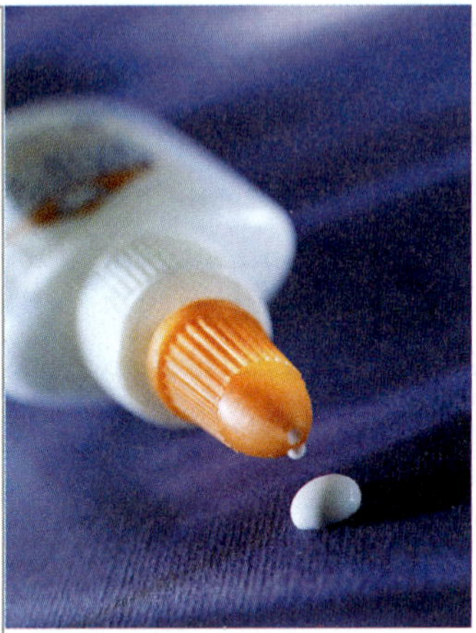

Just as glue can hold pieces of paper, plastic, wood, and glass together, hyphens can bind pieces of a word into a single whole. They join parts of a compound adjective or number, link some prefixes and suffixes to the root word, connect numbers in a fraction, and link word parts that split at the end of a line.

Keep in mind, though, that while some words, like *cross-purposes* or *cross-examination,* use a hyphen, not all compounds need that glue: Some are so closely bound by usage that they have become a single unit (*crosscurrent*), while others are linked merely by placement (*cross hairs*). Consult a dictionary to determine how the parts of a compound should be connected, and if a compound word is not in the dictionary, follow the rules below.

> **More about**
> Using a dictionary, 560–62

58a Using Hyphens to Form Compounds

1. Hyphenate compound adjectives before the noun but not after.

Hyphenate compound modifiers when they precede the noun but not when they follow it:

> ▸ The well-intentioned efforts [noun] by the International Olympic Committee (IOC) to allow peaceful protests were thwarted by the Chinese government.

Writing Responsibly
Hyphenating with Readers in Mind

Correct hyphenation can make reading easier for your audience, but over-hyphenating may drive readers crazy. When editing your paper, check a dictionary to make sure not only that all compounds are hyphenated correctly but also that you have not added hyphens where they are not needed. Keep a particularly close eye on phrasal (or multiword) verbs and subject complements, which do not need hyphens:

- *phrasal verb*
  The police knocked on our door after Fred turned up the volume on the stereo.
- *subject complement*
  Sometimes Fred seems like a thirteen year old.

to AUDIENCE

> **More about**
> Phrasal verbs, 722–24
> Subject complements, 589

- *noun*
  The efforts of the IOC to allow peaceful protests were well-intentioned but ill-conceived.

When an adverb ending in *-ly* is part of a compound adjective, no hyphen is necessary:

- In China, politically-sensitive websites are blocked by the government.

When two or more parallel compound adjectives share the same base word, avoid repetition by putting a space after the first hyphen and stating the base word only once:

Class- and race-based analyses of *To Kill a Mockingbird* show that Harper Lee was not completely able to rise above her social background.

2. Use a hyphen to link certain prefixes and suffixes to the root word.

In general, hyphens are not needed to attach prefixes and suffixes to the root word:

*de*compress   *pre*test   *re*define   *sub*category

But the prefixes *all-*, *ex-*, and *self-* and the suffix *-elect* are always attached to the root word with a hyphen:

- *all*-star   *ex*-boyfriend   *self*-absorbed   president-*elect*

When *all, elect, self,* and even *ex* (a word in Latin, meaning *from*) are freestanding words, they do not need a hyphen:

- *all* the participants in the game
- her sense of *self*
- to *elect* the candidates
- an *ex* officio member

In most cases, to avoid double or triple letter combinations, add a hyphen:

- *anti*-inflationary   *multi*-institutional   *re*-education   ball-*like*
- Exceptions: override   cooperate

If the prefix will be attached to a numeral or to a root that begins with a capital letter, insert a hyphen:

- post-1914   pre-1945   anti-Semite   un-American

Finally, if the prefix-plus-root combination could be misread as another word, add a hyphen to avoid confusion:

- He finally recovered from a bout of the flu.
- We re-covered the sofa with a floral fabric.

3. Use a hyphen in compound numbers under one hundred, between scores (in sports), and between numbers (to replace *from . . . to*).

Numbers over twenty and under one hundred are hyphenated when written out:

- Workaholics would work twenty-four hours a day, seven days a week, fifty-two weeks a year if their bodies would cooperate.

In sports scores, use a hyphen between numbers instead of *to*.

- The Vikings lost to the Bengals 23-17.

A hyphen can replace the words *from* and *to* with dates:

- The years from 1919 to 1938 offered a brief respite between the two world wars.

or

- The years 1919-1938 offered a brief respite between the two world wars.

But do not combine methods:

- from 1919~~-~~1938 [to] or ~~from~~ 1919-1938

58b Using Hyphens to Break Words at the Ends of Lines

Word processing programs generally "wrap" text (that is, they move a too-long word at the end of a line to the beginning of the next line). Still, you may occasionally need to break words manually. If you do, follow these rules:

- Break words between syllables. (Check your dictionary for syllable breaks, such as those shown in Figure 58.1.)

    - CIA operatives in the Middle East have found it impossible to ~~infiltr-~~ [infil-] ~~trate~~ [ate] al Qaeda.

> re•spon•si•bil•i•ty (ri spon'sə bil'i tē), *n., pl.* **-ties.** 1. the state, fact, or quality of being responsible. 2. an instance of being responsible: *The responsibility for this mess is yours!* 3. a particular burden of obligation upon one who is responsible: *the responsibilities of authority.* 4. a person or thing for which one is responsible. [1780–90]
>
> (dots between syllables)

FIGURE 58.1 Syllable breaks in the dictionary Dictionaries indicate syllabification by placing dots between syllables.

- Break compound words between parts or after hyphens.

    - Washington DC's long-standing handgun ban was ~~overturn-~~ [over-] ~~turned~~ [ed] in 2008 by the Supreme Court.

- Do not break one-syllable words or contractions.

    - To determine surface area, multiply the ~~wid-~~ [width] ~~th~~ of a room by its length.

- Break words so that at least two letters remain at the end of a line and at least three letters move down to the beginning of the next line.

    - Increases in the cost of gas and food have ~~reduc-~~ [re-] ~~duced~~ discretionary spending.

Tech — Breaking URLs and E-mail Addresses

Most word processing programs offer automatic hyphenation of words. However, you must break URLs or e-mail addresses manually. If you are following MLA or CSE style guidelines, break URLs only after a slash. If you are following *Chicago Manual* guidelines, break a URL or e-mail address before a period or other punctuation, or after the @ symbol, a single or double slash, or a colon. Do *not* insert a hyphen.

EXERCISE 58.1 Adding and deleting hyphens

Add and delete hyphens as needed in the following sentences. (You may consult a dictionary.)

EXAMPLE

The Deadhead phenomenon began in the mid-1960s, when the Grateful Dead became active in the Haight-Ashbury music scene.

1. In 1971, a long time friend of the Grateful Dead took on a self assigned project to put together a mailing list to keep fans informed of upcoming shows.
2. Clearly, there were more than just fifty or seventy five people on this list, because city to city caravans of tie dye wearing Deadheads soon sprang up.
3. Their long distance travel was motivated by changes night to night in the songs the musicians played.
4. Shows sold out for the long lived and well loved band, and a true blue community of Deadheads was created.
5. Although the band is now defunct, well and long proven loyalty is still highly-visible in thruway rest stops, where large groups of slack jawed fans, exhausted from concerts by Grateful Dead spinoff bands like RatDog and Phil Lesh and Friends, still congregate.

EXERCISE 58.2 Correcting hyphens

Using a dictionary, correct the passage below, adding and deleting hyphens or revising as needed:

Attention Deficit Hyperactivity Disorder (ADHD) was first described in a children's book called "The Story of Fidgety Philip" (1845), written for the author's three year old son. Today, the National Institute of Mental Health estimates that from 3-5 percent of children have ADHD. But diagnosis is difficult because loss of self control and attention is common. To be diagnosed, children must have difficulties in two or more of the following areas: school-, social-, community-, home-, or playground-behavior. Other causes of inattention or hyperactivity include middle-ear infections that cause hearing loss, seizure disorders, and learning disabilities. Baby-sitters and class-room teachers frequently notice problems and recommend testing, but well-qualified and highly-experienced clinicians are best able to diagnose the disorder and recommend treatment.

Make It **Your Own**

Review your use of hyphens in a recent writing project of two or more pages. Add hyphens where needed and cross through unnecessary ones. Then analyze the impact these changes would have on your reader. (Refer to the sections in this chapter as needed.)

Work **Together**

Exchange Exercise 58.2 with a classmate. Check your partner's use of hyphens. Did he or she make any errors? If so, explain the effect these errors had on you as a reader. (Be specific.)

Glossary of Key Terms

A

absolute phrase (530, 594) A phrase consisting of a noun or pronoun followed by a participle (the *-ing* or *-ed* form of a verb) that modifies an entire clause or sentence: *Our spirits rising, we began our vacation.*

abstract (109, 215, 428) Overview of a text, including a summary of its main claims and most important supporting points.

abstract noun (575) See *noun*.

acronym (315, 812, 822) An abbreviation formed from the first letters of a series of words and pronounced as a word (*AIDS, NASA*). Compare *initialism*.

active voice (501, 589, 625) See *voice*.

adjective (529, 580, 669, 732) A word that modifies a noun or pronoun with descriptive or limiting information, answering questions such as *what kind, which one,* or *how many: a happy camper, the tall building.*

adjective clause (595) A subordinate clause, usually beginning with a relative pronoun (such as *who, whom, which,* or *that*), that modifies a noun or pronoun: *Sam baked the pie that won first prize.* Adjective clauses can also begin with the subordinating conjunctions *when* and *where*.

adverb (529, 581–82, 669, 732) A word that modifies a verb, adjective, other adverb, or entire phrase or clause, answering questions such as *how? where? when?* and *to what extent or degree? The door opened abruptly.*

adverb clause (595, 758) A subordinate clause, usually introduced by a subordinating conjunction such as *although, because,* or *until,* that functions as an adverb within a sentence: *I walk to work because I need the exercise.*

agreement (620–65) The matching of form between one word and another. Verbs must agree with, or match, their subjects in person and number (subject-verb agreement), and pronouns must agree in person, number, and gender with their antecedents (pronoun-antecedent agreement). See also *antecedent, gender, number, person*.

alignment (162) Arrangement in a straight line (vertical, horizontal, or diagonal) of elements on a page or screen to create connections among parts and ideas.

alternating pattern of organization (60) A method of organizing a comparison-contrast paragraph or essay by discussing each common or divergent trait of both items before moving on to the next trait. See also *block pattern of organization.*

analogy (552) An extended comparison of something familiar with something unfamiliar. (See also *figurative language, simile, metaphor.*) An analogy becomes a false analogy (150) when the items being compared have no significant shared traits.

analysis (62, 119–22, 193) The process of dividing an entity, concept, or text into its component parts to study its meaning and function. Analysis is central to critical reading and is a common strategy for developing paragraphs and essays in academic writing. Also called *classification, division.*

annotated bibliography (203–05) A bibliography that includes not only retrieval information for each source but also information about the source, such as its content, its relevance to the writer's project, or the writer's evaluation of it.

annotation (114, 117) The process of taking notes on a text, including writing down definitions, identifying key concepts, highlighting unfamiliar vocabulary and words that reveal tone, and making connections or noting personal responses.

antecedent (577, 630, 656) The noun or noun phrase to which a pronoun refers. In the sentence *The pitcher caught the ball and threw it to first base,* the noun *ball* is the antecedent to the pronoun *it*.

antonyms (560) Words with opposite meanings—for example, *good* and *bad*. Compare *synonyms.*

APA style (347–89) The citation and documentation style of the American Psychological Association, used frequently in the social sciences.

appeals (142–44) Efforts to engage the reader. Emotional appeals (**pathos**) engage the reader's feelings; intellectual appeals (**logos**) engage the reader's rational faculties; ethical appeals (**ethos**) engage the reader's sense of fairness and respect for good character.

appositive (530, 591, 605, 660) A noun or noun phrase that renames a preceding noun or noun phrase and is grammatically equivalent to it: *Miguel, my roommate, avoids early morning classes.*

arguable claim (134–60) A claim on which reasonable people might hold differing opinions and that can be supported by evidence.

argument (11, 134) An attempt to persuade others to accept your opinion by providing logical supporting evidence. See also *persuasive argument, purpose.*

article (714–21) The words *a, an,* and *the. A* and *an* are **indefinite articles**; *the* is a **definite article**. The **zero article** refers to nouns that appear with no article.

asynchronous media (182) Communication media such as e-mail and discussion lists that allow users to

G1

participate at their own convenience. Compare *synchronous media;* see also *discussion list.*

audience (9–16, 84, 163, 183) The intended readers for a written text or listeners for a presentation.

authority (126, 157) An expert on a topic. An authority becomes a false authority when the person from whom the writer draws evidence is not truly an expert on the topic.

B

bar graph (74, 75) An information graphic that compares data in two or more categories using bars of different heights or lengths.

belief (138–39) A conviction based on values.

biased or hurtful language (115, 544) Language that unfairly or offensively characterizes a group and, by extension, the individual members of that group.

bibliographic notes (332) Notes that add information or point readers to other sources on the topic.

bibliography (210–14) A list of works cited in a text, with full retrieval information (usually including author, title, publisher, date of publication, and type of publication) for each entry. Bibliographies are usually constructed following a style sheet such as MLA or APA. In *Chicago* style, the word bibliography is used for the end-of-project source list; in APA, it is called a reference list; and in MLA, it is called list of works cited.

block pattern of organization (60) A method of organizing a paragraph or text by discussing all the significant traits of one item (such as a source, event, or theory) before moving on to discuss all the traits of another item. See also *alternating method.*

block quotations (292) Exact quotations of longer than four lines (MLA style) or forty words (APA style) in which quotation marks are omitted and the quotation is indented as a block from the left margin of the text.

block-style letter (477) A format for business letters in which all text is flush with the left margin and a line space is inserted before paragraphs. In **modified block style,** all text begins flush left except for the return address, date, closing, and signature.

blog (or **weblog**) (177, 321) An online journal that chronicles thoughts, opinions, and information often on a single topic. See also *asynchronous media.*

body (33–34, 185) The portion of a text or presentation that develops and supports the thesis.

Boolean operator (218–20) The terms *and, not,* and *or* used in databases and search engines for refining keyword searches.

brainstorming or listing (22) A technique for generating ideas by listing all the ideas that come to you during a fixed amount of time; brainstorming can also take place in groups.

C

case (656–65) The form of a noun or pronoun that corresponds to its grammatical role in a sentence. Many pronouns have three cases: **subjective** (for example, *I, we, he, she, they, who*), **objective** (for example, *me, us, him, her, them, whom*), and **possessive** (for example, *mine, ours, his, hers, theirs, whose*). Nouns change form only to indicate possession.

cause and effect (62) A method of paragraph or essay development that explains why something happened or what its consequences were or will be.

Chicago **style** (201) The citation and documentation style recommended in the *Chicago Manual of Style,* used frequently in the humanities.

chronological organization (35) A pattern of organization in which events are discussed in the order in which they occurred; chronological organization is used when telling a story (narrative) or explaining a process (process analysis).

citation (274, 288, 347) The acknowledgment of sources in the body of a research project, usually tagged to a bibliography, works-cited list, or reference list. See also *in-text citation, parenthetical citation, signal phrase.*

citation-name system (417–18) In CSE style, a system of acknowledgment for research projects that provides a superscript number in the text and a list of references, numbered in alphabetical order (usually by author's surname) at the end of the project.

citation-sequence system (417–18) In CSE style, a system of acknowledgment for research projects that provides a superscript number in the text and a list of references, numbered in order of appearance, at the end of the project.

claim (31, 32, 134, 138, 139) An assertion that is supported by evidence. A *claim of fact* asserts a verifiable piece of information; it can be a central claim in an informative text but not in an argumentative text. A *claim of causation* asserts the causes or effects of a problem; a *claim of policy* asserts how best to resolve a problem or what is the best course of action to take; a *claim of judgment or value* asserts that one's personal beliefs or convictions should be embraced. Claims of causation, policy, and value are all appropriate central claims in argumentative texts.

classical model (154) A model for organizing an argument composed of five parts: introduction, background, evidence, counterclaims and counterevidence, and conclusion. Compare *Rogerian* and *Toulmin models.*

classification See *analysis.*

clause (502–04, 511–14, 594–97, 704) A word group with a subject and a predicate. An **independent clause** can stand on its own as a sentence. A **subordinate** (or **dependent**) **clause** functions within a sentence as a noun, adjective, or adverb but cannot stand as a sentence on its own. See also *sentence.*

cliché (555–57) A figure of speech, idiom, or other expression that has grown stale from overuse. See also *figurative language, idiom.*

click trail (178) The sequence of links followed while navigating pages on a website.

climactic organization (35–36) A pattern of organization that orders supporting paragraphs from least to most engaging or compelling.

clustering or mapping (22–23) An idea-generating technique for organizing, developing, or discovering connections among ideas by writing a topic in the center of the page, adding related topics and subtopics around the central topic, and connecting them to show relationships.

coauthorship (45) Two or more writers working together to research, brainstorm, compose, revise, or edit a text.

coherence, coherent (37, 46, 52–59) The quality of a text in which sentences and paragraphs are organized logically and clearly so that readers can move from idea to idea without having to puzzle out the relationships among parts.

collaborative learning (26–28, 45) A process by which classmates or colleagues enhance understanding by studying together and reviewing one another's writing.

collective noun (625) See *noun*.

colloquialism (541) An informal expression common in speech but usually out of place in formal writing.

comma splice (611–19, 750, 769) The incorrect joining of two independent clauses with a comma alone—without a coordinating conjunction.

common knowledge (249) General information that is available from a number of different sources and that is considered factual and incontestable. Common knowledge does not require documentation.

common noun (713) See *noun*.

commonplace book (20–21) A written record (quotations, summaries, paraphrases) of the ideas of others and your own reactions to those ideas, preserved in a notebook or online document.

comparative form (674–77) See *comparison of adjectives and adverbs*.

comparison and contrast (60–61) A pattern of paragraph or essay development in which the writer points out the similarities and differences among items. See also *alternating method, block method*.

comparison of adjectives and adverbs (674–76) The form of an adjective or adverb that indicates the relative degree of the quality or manner it specifies. The **positive form** is the base form of the adjective (for example, *brave*) or adverb (for example, *bravely*). The **comparative form** indicates a relatively greater or lesser degree (*braver, more bravely*). The **superlative form** indicates the greatest or least degree (*bravest, most bravely*).

complement (588–91) See *subject complement, object complement*.

complete predicate (587) See *predicate*.

complete subject (585) See *subject*.

complete verb (600–01) A main verb together with any helping verbs needed to express tense, mood, and voice.

complex sentence (528, 598, 770) See *sentence*.

compound-complex sentence (528, 598) See *sentence*.

compound predicate (605–06) See *predicate*.

compound sentence (528, 597, 750) See *sentence*.

compound subject (550, 623) See *subject*.

conciseness (496) The statement of something in the fewest and most effective words needed for clarity and full understanding.

conclusion (33–34, 109, 185) The closing paragraph or section in a text. An effective conclusion provides readers with a sense of closure.

concrete noun (575) See *noun*.

conditional clause (651–52) A subordinate clause that begins with *if* and describes a set of circumstances (*conditions*) and that modifies an independent clause that describes what follows from those circumstances.

conjunction (583, 623) A word that joins a word, phrase, or clause to other words, phrases, or clauses and specifies the way the joined elements relate to one another. **Coordinating conjunctions** (*and, but, or, for, nor, yet,* and *so*) join grammatically equivalent elements, giving them each equal significance: *Jack and Jill went up the hill.* **Correlative conjunctions** are pairs of terms (such as *either . . . or, neither . . . nor,* and *both . . . and*) that join grammatically equivalent elements: *Both Jack and Jill fell down.* **Subordinating conjunctions** link subordinate clauses to the clauses they modify. *After Jack and Jill went up the hill, they both fell down.*

conjunctive adverb (581, 753) A transitional expression (such as *for example, however,* and *therefore*) that can relate one independent clause to a preceding independent clause.

connected (46) See *transition*.

connotation (15, 87, 550) The emotional resonance of a word. Compare *denotation*.

content notes (332) Footnotes or endnotes that clarify or justify a point in your text or that acknowledge the contributions of others in the preparation of your project.

context (9, 16–17, 164, 183) The social, rhetorical, and historical setting in which a text is produced or read. The context in which Lincoln's Gettysburg Address was produced is different from the context in which it may be read today, but both are important for fully understanding the text.

contrast (162) In design, differences that call attention to and highlight one element among others.

coordinate adjectives (75) Two or more adjectives that separately and equally modify the noun they precede. Coordinate adjectives should be separated by a comma: *an innovative, exciting vocal group*.

coordinating conjunction (750) See *conjunction*.

coordination (505–10) The joining of elements of equal weight or importance in a sentence. See also *subordination*.

correlative conjunction (521) See *conjunction*.

counterevidence (135, 145–47) Evidence that undermines or contradicts your claim.

count noun (or **countable noun**) (713) See *noun*.

critical reading and thinking (108–33) A careful, systematic approach to a text or idea, going below the surface to uncover meaning and draw conclusions. Critical reading and thinking begins with reading actively; it requires analysis, interpretation, synthesis, and critique.

critique (125–31, 433, 440) An evaluation based on evidence accumulated through careful reading, analysis, interpretation, and synthesis. It may be positive, negative, or a bit of both.

CSE style (201) The citation and documentation style recommended in *Scientific Style and Format: The CSE Manual for Authors, Editors, and Publishers*, used frequently in the sciences.

cumulative adjectives (755) Two or more adjectives that modify not only the noun or pronoun they precede but also the next adjective in the series. Cumulative adjectives should not be separated by commas: *A great American rock band.*

cumulative sentence (531) A sentence that begins with the subject and verb of an independent clause and accumulates additional information in subsequent modifying phrases and clauses: *The mountaineers set off, anticipating the view from the peak but wary of the dangers they faced to get there.*

D

dangling modifier (691–94) A word, phrase, or clause that erroneously does not actually modify the subject or anything else in a sentence, leaving it to the reader to infer the intended meaning. In the sentence *As your parent, you should put on a sweater when it is cold*, the phrase *as your parent* dangles; it appears illogically to modify the subject, *you*, but actually refers to the speaker, as in *As your parent, I recommend that you put on a sweater when it is cold.*

database (217–20, 315) A collection of data, now usually available in digital form. In research, databases provide citations to articles in academic journals, magazines, and newspapers.

declarative sentence (534) See *sentence*.

deductive reasoning (135–37) A form of reasoning that moves from a general principle to a specific case to draw a conclusion; if the premises are true, the conclusion must be true. Compare *inductive reasoning*; see also *syllogism*.

definite article (714) See *article*.

definition (62–63, 115, 301) An explanation of the meaning of a word or concept made by including it in a larger class and then providing the characteristics that distinguish it from other members of that class: In the definition *People are reasoning animals*, *people* is the term to be defined, *animals* is the larger class to which people belong, and *reasoning* is the trait that distinguishes people from other animals. Also, a pattern of paragraph or essay development in which the writer explains the special meaning of a term by explaining what the term includes and excludes.

degree (674–76) See *comparison of adjectives and adverbs*.

demonstrative pronouns (577) The pronouns *this, that, these,* and *those* used as nouns or adjectives to rename and point to nouns or noun phrases: *These are interesting times we live in.*

denotation (87, 548) The literal meaning of a word; its dictionary definition. Compare *connotation*.

dependent clause (594) A subordinate clause. See *clause*.

description (59) A pattern of paragraph or essay development that draws on specific, concrete details to depict a scene or object in terms of the senses: seeing, hearing, smelling, touching, tasting.

determiner (580, 713) An article (*a, an,* or *the*) or a possessive, demonstrative, or indefinite pronoun that functions as an adjective to specify or quantify the noun it modifies: *a cat, some cats, that cat, her cat.*

development (40–42, 59–63, 270–72) The depth at which a topic or idea is explored.

dialect (541) A language variety with its own distinctive pronunciation, vocabulary, and grammar.

diction (548) The choice of words that will best convey an idea.

direct object (589, 707) See *object*.

direct question (684) A sentence that asks a question and ends with a question mark. Compare *indirect question*.

direct quotation (683, 759) A copy of the exact words that someone has written or spoken, enclosed in quotation marks or, for longer quotations, indented as a block. Compare *indirect quotation*.

direct source (683, 790–91) A text that you are yourself reading (as contrasted to a source *quoted in* a text you are reading).

discussion (379, 429) In APA and CSE style, the last section of a research project; the Discussion section provides the writer's opinion of the implications of the research.

discussion list (181–82) An electronic mailing list that enables a group of people to participate in e-mail conversations on a specific topic. See also *asynchronous media*.

division (62, 119–22, 193) See *analysis*.

documentation (288, 347) Information in a bibliography, reference list, or list of works cited that allows readers to locate a source cited in the text. See also *citation*.

document design (162–69) The arranging and formatting of text elements on a page or screen using proximity (nearness), alignment, repetition, and contrast to indicate their relative importance and their relation to each other.

DOI (200, 399, 423) Digital object identifier, a permanent identifier assigned to electronic publications.

domain (237–39) The ending of the main portion of a URL; the most common domains are *.com* (commercial), *.edu* (educational), *.gov* (governmental), and *.net* (network).

double-entry reading journal (117–19) An online or printed journal with one column for passages from sources (quotations, summaries, or

Glossary of Key Terms G5

paraphrases) and another column for the writer's response to the passage.

doublespeak (544) Euphemisms that are deliberately deceptive, used to obscure bad news or sanitize an ugly truth.

drafting (38–42, 270–72) The stage of the writing process in which the writer puts ideas on paper in complete sentences and paragraphs.

E

editing (88–90) The stage of the writing process in which the writer fine-tunes the draft by correcting words and sentences and revises them to enhance clarity and power.

ellipses (803–04) A set of three periods, or *ellipsis points*, with a space between each. Ellipses are used to replace words deleted from quotations; they are also sometimes used to create a dramatic pause or to suggest that the writer is unable or unwilling to say something.

elliptical construction (499, 700) A construction in which grammatically necessary words can be omitted as understood because their meaning and function are otherwise clear from the context: *The movie [that] we saw last night is excellent.*

endnote (390) A note that appears in a list at the end of the project.

entertaining text (10) See *purpose.*

essential (or **restrictive**) **element** (608, 758) A word, phrase, or clause that provides essential information about the word or words it modifies. Essential elements are not set off by commas: *The train that she is on has been delayed.* See also *nonessential element.*

et al. (294, 353) Abbreviation of the Latin phrase *et alia,* "and others."

ethos (143) See *appeals.*

euphemism (544) An inoffensive word or expression used in place of one that might be offensive or emotionally painful.

evaluation (230–45) In research, assessment of sources to determine their relevance and reliability.

evidence (84) The facts, examples, statistics, expert opinions, and other information writers use to support their claims.

excessive coordination (509–10) The joining of tediously long strings of independent clauses with *and* and other conjunctions.

excessive subordination (509, 514) The stringing together of too many subordinate structures.

exclamatory sentence (585) See *sentence.*

exemplification (60) A pattern of paragraph or essay development that explains by example or illustration.

expletive construction (500, 586, 705) A kind of inverted construction in which *there* or *it* precedes a form of the verb *to be* and the subject follows the verb: *There are seven days in a week.*

explicate (440) To read a text closely, analyzing it line by line or even word by word; explications of a text are common in literary analysis.

exploratory argument (134) An argument in which the author considers a wide range of evidence before arriving at the most plausible position; in exploratory arguments, the thesis is often offered at the conclusion of the text. See also *argument, persuasive argument, purpose.*

expository report (138) See *informative report.*

expressive text (10) See *purpose.*

F

fact (138) A piece of information that can be verified.

fallacy (115, 156) A mistake in reasoning.

familiar to unfamiliar (35) A method of organization that begins with material that is known by the audience and moves toward material that the audience will not know.

faulty predication (697–99) A logical or grammatical mismatch between subject and predicate.

field research (226–29) The gathering of research data in person rather than from sources. Field research includes interviews, observational studies, and surveys. See also *primary source.*

figurative language or figures of speech (553–54) The imaginative use of language to convey meaning in ways that reach beyond the literal meaning of the words involved. See *analogy, hyperbole, irony, metaphor, personification, simile, understatement.*

flaming (182) Writing a scathing, often ad hominem, response to someone with whom the writer disagrees, usually in e-mail or on Internet forums.

focused freewriting (22) See *freewriting.*

font (165–66) Typeface; fonts may be serif (such as Times Roman) or sans serif (such as Arial), may be set in boldface, italics, or underlining, and may be in a larger or smaller size (the most common sizes are 10 point and 12 point).

footer (332) Material (most often a page number, sometimes accompanied by title or author's name) appearing at the bottom of every page of a text.

footnote (390) A note that appears at the bottom of the page.

formal outline (36–37) See *outline.*

formalist approach (433) An approach to literature and art that focuses on the work itself rather than on the author's life or other theoretical approaches.

format (95–99) The look of a document created by choice of font and color and use of white space, lists, headings, and visuals. See also *layout.*

fragment (591, 600) An incomplete sentence punctuated as if it were complete, beginning with a capital letter and ending with a period, question mark, or exclamation point.

freewriting (21–22) An idea-generating technique that requires writing nonstop for a fixed period of time (often ten to fifteen minutes); in *focused freewriting,* the writer writes nonstop about a specific topic or idea.

function word (522) A word that indicates the relationship among other words in a sentence. Examples include **articles, conjunctions,** and **prepositions.**

funnel introduction (63–65) An essay introduction that begins with broad statements and narrows in focus to conclude with the thesis statement. See also *introduction*.

fused sentence or run-on sentence (611–19) A sentence in which one independent clause improperly follows another with no punctuation or joining words between them.

future perfect progressive tense (647) See *tense*.

future perfect tense (645) See *tense*.

future progressive tense (646) See *tense*.

future tense (645–47) See *tense*.

G

gender (630) The classification of nouns and pronouns as feminine (*woman, mother, she*), masculine (*man, father, he*), or neuter (*table, book, it, they*).

gender bias (545) Stereotyping people according to their gender.

general to specific (35) A method of organization that begins with a general statement (the **thesis statement** or **topic sentence**) and proceeds to provide specific supporting evidence.

generalization (156) A broad statement. If not supported by specific details, a generalization becomes a hasty generalization (jumping to conclusions) or a sweeping generalization (application of a claim to all cases when it applies only to a few).

generic noun (631) A noun used to designate a whole class of people or things rather than a specific individual or individuals: *the average child*.

genre (9, 16–18, 164, 183) A category or type of writing; in literature, genres include poetry, fiction, and drama; in college writing, genres may include analytical essays, case studies, or observational reports.

gerund (524, 592, 628, 661, 725) The present participle of a verb (the *-ing* form) used as a noun: <u>Walking</u> *is good exercise*.

grammar (574) The rules of a language that structure words so they can convey meaning.

grounds (142) In an argument, the evidence that supports the claim. See *Toulmin model*.

H

header (332–33) Material (most often a page number, sometimes accompanied by title or author's name) appearing at the top of every page of a text.

heading (168–69) A brief caption describing or labeling a section of text.

helping verb or auxiliary verb (577, 579, 639–42) A verb that combines with a main verb to provide information about tense, voice, mood, and manner. Helping verbs include forms of *be, have,* and *do* and the modal verbs *can, could, may, might, must, shall, should, will, would,* and *ought to*.

home page (100, 176, 178) On a website, the page designed to introduce visitors to the site.

homonyms (561, 565) Words that sound exactly alike but have different spellings and meanings: *their, there, they're*.

HTML (180, 215, 399) Hypertext Markup Language, a coding system used to format texts for the web.

hyperbole (552) Deliberate exaggeration for emphasis: *That restaurant makes the best pizza in the universe.* See *figurative language*.

hyperlink (178) A navigation tool that allows users to jump from place to place on a web page or from web page to web page; hyperlinks (or links) appear as highlighted words or images on a web page.

hypertext (177) An online text that provides links to other online files, texts, images, audio files, and video files, allowing readers to jump to other related sites rather than reading *linearly*.

hypothesis (195–96, 228) A proposed answer to a research question that is subject to testing and modification during the research process.

I

idea journal (20–21) An online or printed record of your thoughts that you can draw on to develop or explore a topic.

idiom (554) A customary expression whose meaning cannot be determined from the literal meaning of the words that compose it: *They struggled to make ends meet.*

imperative (602, 650) See *mood, sentence*.

indefinite article (714–21) See *article*.

indefinite pronoun (625, 631, 774) A pronoun such as *anybody, anyone, somebody, some,* or *several* that does not refer to a specific person or thing.

independent clause (594, 598, 611, 750, 767, 809) See *clause*.

indicative (650) See *mood*.

indirect object (590, 707) See *object*.

indirect question (684) A sentence that reports a question and ends with a period: *My teacher asked us if we texted each other even when we're in the same room.* Compare *direct question*.

indirect quotation (683, 760) A sentence that uses paraphrase or summary to report what someone has said rather than quoting word-for-word. Indirect quotations need to be cited but should not be marked with quotation marks or block indenting. Compare *direct quotation*.

indirect source (300–01, 356, 407, 790–91) If you read a text that quotes or uses ideas from another source, that other source is for you an "indirect source": You are not reading that other source yourself but are reading about its ideas. If you want to use that material from the indirect source, you should acknowledge the indirect source as well as the source that was talking about it.

inductive reasoning (135) A form of reasoning that draws conclusions based on specific examples or facts. Compare *deductive reasoning*.

infinitive (593, 648, 661, 725–26) A verbal formed by combining *to* with the base form of the verb (*to decide, to eat, to study*). Infinitives can function as adjectives and adverbs as well as nouns. See *verbal*.

informal (scratch) outline (35) See *outline*.

information graphics (74–77) Graphics that convey and depict relationships among data; information graphics include tables, bar graphs, line graphs, and pie charts.

informational note (376–77, 382) In APA style, a note that occurs on the first page of a text to identify the author, provide contact information, and acknowledge support and conflicts of interest; student projects usually omit informational, or author, notes.

informative (or **expository**) **report** (10, 31, 138) A text in which the main purpose is to explain a concept or report information. See also *purpose*.

initialism (822) Abbreviation formed from the first letters of a series of words and pronounced as letters (*DNA, HBO*). Compare *acronym*.

inseparable (725) A transitive phrasal verb whose direct object can fall only after the particle, not before it.

intensive pronoun (578) A pronoun that renames and emphasizes its antecedent: *Dr. Collins herself performed the operation.*

interjection (584) Words like *alas* and *ugh* that express strong feeling but otherwise serve no grammatical function.

interpret, interpretation (119–23, 433) Explain the meaning or significance of a text, artwork, or event.

interpretive analysis (440–42) An in-depth interpretation of the meaning or significance of literary texts, cultural works, political events, and so on.

interrogative pronoun (657, 663) A pronoun such as *who, whom, whose, what,* or *which* used to introduce a question: *What did she say?*

interrogative sentence (585) See *sentence*.

interesting (46) Paragraphs and essays that make the audience want to continue reading.

in-text citation (275, 288, 347, 416) A citation that appears in the body of the research project. See also *parenthetical citation, signal phrase*.

intransitive verb (588, 643–44) A verb that does not require a direct object: *The child smiled.*

introduction (34, 63, 109, 185, 428) The opening paragraph or section of a text. An effective introduction should identify your topic and your stance toward the topic, establish your purpose, and engage your readers. See also *funnel introduction*.

invention techniques (20–25) Prewriting strategies that help you generate and explore ideas. See *brainstorming, freewriting*.

inversion (532) An inversion is a sentence in which, contrary to normal English word order, the verb precedes the subject, usually to emphasize the point being made.

inverted-funnel conclusion (65) A conclusion that begins with a restatement of the thesis (in different words) and broadens out to discuss implications, next steps, or possible solutions. See also *conclusion*.

irony (552) The use of language to suggest the opposite of its literal meaning or to express an incongruity between what is expected and what occurs. See *figurative language*.

irregular verb (638–39) A verb that does not form the past tense or past participle by adding -*ed* to the base form.

J

jargon (542) The specialized vocabulary of a particular profession or discipline; inappropriately technical language.

journal (117–19) A place to record observations and ideas in writing. Also, a periodical that publishes scholarly articles. See also *periodical*.

journalists' questions (plus two) (23–24) Questions that ask *who, what, where, when, why,* and *how* to help you explore a topic. In college writing, also ask yourself about the significance of your topic (*Is it important?*) and its consequences (*What are its effects?*).

K

keyword (210–11) (a) A term entered into an Internet search engine, online database, or library catalog to find sources of information. (b) A word or phrase in a text that highlights or is essential to the message of the text.

L

labeling (545) Applying a word or phrase to describe an entire group, such as *autistic, Cub Scout,* or *Asian American.* When the label does not apply to all group members, or when it unfairly characterizes the group, it contributes to **stereotyping**.

layout (165) The visual arrangement of text and images using proximity (nearness), alignment, repetition, and contrast. See also *format*.

level of diction (15) The choice of words to convey a tone (formal or informal) appropriate to the audience. See *tone, connotation*.

linear text (177) A document, such as a novel or magazine article, that is arranged so that readers begin at page 1 and read through to the end. Compare *hypertext*.

line graphs (75, 77) A type of information graphic that uses lines and points on a graph to show changes over time.

link (178, 201, 239) See *hyperlink*.

linking verb (580, 589, 629, 670, 697) A verb that expresses a state of being rather than an action and connects the subject to its subject complement. The verb *be,* when used as a main verb, is always a linking verb. *They are excited.* See also *subject complement*.

logical fallacy (156–60) See *fallacy*.

logical organization (35) The arrangement of a sentence, paragraph, or entire text in a way that will seem sensible to readers, that will not confuse or puzzle them.

logos (142, 143) See *appeals*.

lurk (238) Read online discussions without contributing.

M

main verb (577, 639–42) The part of a verb phrase that carries its principal meaning. See *verb phrase*.

mechanics (807–35) Conventions controlling capitalization, italics, abbreviation, numbers, and hyphenation.

menu (101, 177) A list of the main sections of a website.

metaphor (552, 553) An implied comparison between unlike things stated without *like*, *as*, or other comparative expressions: *Her mind buzzed with original ideas.* See *figurative language*, *simile*.

metasearch engine (211–12) Internet search engines that return the top search results from several search engines at once, with duplicate entries deleted.

methods (228, 379, 428) In APA and CSE style, the section of a research project that explains the research methods and describes any research participants (such as people interviewed) or data collected.

misplaced modifier (686–91) An ambiguously, confusingly, or disruptively placed modifying word, phrase, or clause.

mixed construction (695–99) A sentence with parts that do not fit together grammatically or logically.

mixed metaphor (554) A combination of multiple conflicting figures of speech for the same concept. See *figurative language*.

MLA style (274–86) The citation and documentation style of the Modern Language Association, used frequently in literature and languages.

modal verb (579, 641) See *helping verb*.

modified block-style letter (477) See *block-style letter*.

modifier (529–31) A word, phrase, or clause that functions as an adjective or adverb to qualify or describe another word, phrase, or clause.

mood (637, 650–51) The form of a verb that indicates how the writer or speaker views what is written or said. The **indicative mood** states facts or opinions and asks questions: *I finished my paper.* The **imperative mood** issues commands, gives instructions, or makes requests: *Hand in your papers by Friday.* The **subjunctive mood** expresses possibility, as in hypothetical situations or wishes: *If I were finished, I could go to bed.*

N

name-year system (417–18) In CSE style, a system of acknowledgment for research projects that includes the last name of the author and the year of publication in parentheses in the text; is accompanied by an alphabetical list of references at the end of the project.

narration (59) A pattern of paragraph or essay development that tells a story, usually in chronological (time) order. See also *chronological organization*.

near-homonyms (563, 565) Words that are close but not the same in pronunciation (*moral*, *morale*) or are different forms of the same word (*breath*, *breathe*).

neologism (542) A newly coined word or expression.

netiquette (483) A word composed of parts of the words *Internet* and *etiquette* that refers to conventions of politeness in online contexts.

noncount noun (or **uncountable** or **mass noun**) (713) See *noun*.

nonessential (or **nonrestrictive**) **element** (608, 700, 757) A modifying word, phrase, or clause that adds information to the element it modifies but does not identify it. Commas should set off nonessential elements from the rest of the sentence. *My grandfather, who recently retired, worked for the same company for forty-five years.*

noun (575–77) A word that names an idea (*justice*), thing (*chair*), quality (*neatness*), action (*judgment*), person (*Albert Einstein*), or place (*Tokyo*). **Proper nouns** name specific places, people, or things and are usually capitalized: *Nairobi*, *Hillary Rodham Clinton*. **Common nouns** name members of a class or group: *turtle*, *skyscraper*. **Collective nouns** name a collection that can function as a single unit: *committee*, *family*. **Concrete nouns** name things that can be seen, touched, heard, smelled, or tasted: *planet*, *symphony*, *skunk*. **Abstract nouns** name qualities or ideas that cannot be perceived by the senses: *mercy*, *fear*. **Count** (or **countable**) **nouns** name countable things and can be either singular or plural: *cat/cats*, *idea/ideas*. **Noncount** (or **uncountable** or **mass**) **nouns** name ideas or things that cannot be counted and do not have a plural form: *knowledge*, *pollution*.

noun clause (596) A subordinate clause that functions as a noun. See *clause*.

noun phrase (577, 591, 605) A noun and its modifiers.

number (620, 637, 681) The form of a word that indicates whether it is singular, referring to one thing (*a student*), or plural, referring to more than one (*two students*).

O

object (589–91, 707–09) A noun or pronoun (or a noun phrase or noun clause) that receives or benefits from the action of a transitive verb or that follows a preposition. A **direct object** receives the action of the verb: *My friend wrote a letter.* An **indirect object** benefits from the action of the verb: *My friend wrote me a letter.* The **object of a preposition** usually follows a preposition to form a prepositional phrase. *She sent the letter by mail.*

object complement (590, 708) An adjective or noun phrase that follows the direct object and describes the condition of the object or a change that the subject has caused it to undergo: *The candidate declared his opponent incompetent.*

objective case (656–64) See *case*.

objectivity (138–41, 233) A text is objective when it makes reasonable claims supported by logical evidence; recognizes alternative perspectives; and treats those alternatives respectfully.

object of a preposition (592) See *object*.

opinion (138) The most plausible answer for now, based on an evaluation of the available facts. Opinions are subject to revision in light of new evidence and are often the basis of argumentation.

organization (84, 173) Arranging the parts of a sentence, paragraph, or essay so that readers can most readily understand and appreciate it.

outline (35) A method of classifying information into main points, supporting points, and specific details. An **informal** (or **scratch**) **outline** arranges ideas in order of presentation; a **formal outline** uses roman and arabic numerals, upper- and lowercase letters, and indentions to classify information into main points, supporting points, and specific details; a **sentence outline** writes out main points, supporting points, and specific details in complete sentences; a **topic outline** uses words and phrases to indicate the ideas to be discussed.

P

paragraph (47–52) A group of sentences that focus on a single topic or example, often organized around a *topic sentence.*

parallelism (518–26) In writing, the expression of equivalent ideas in equivalent grammatical structures. In an outline, the use of the same pattern or form for headings at each level.

paraphrase (110, 249, 252–56) The statement of the ideas of others in one's own words and sentence structures.

parenthetical citation (275, 289, 291, 349) A citation to a source that appears in parentheses in the body of a research paper. Compare *signal phrase;* see also *in-text citation.*

participial phrase (529, 593) A phrase in which the present or past participle of a verb acts as an adjective: *the writing assignment, the written word.*

participles (593–94, 636–38) Forms of a verb that combine with helping verbs to form certain tenses and that, as verbals, can function as adjectives. The **present participle** is the *-ing* form of the verb. The **past participle** is the *-ed* form in regular verbs (the same as the past tense) but takes various forms in irregular verbs. See *participial phrase, tense, verbal.*

particle (722–24) A preposition or adverb that combines with a verb to create a new verb with a meaning that differs from the verb's meaning on its own—for example, *throw away* versus *throw.*

parts of speech (575–84) The categories in which words can be classified according to the role they play in a sentence. English has eight parts of speech: *noun, pronoun, verb, adjective, adverb, preposition, conjunction,* and *interjection.*

passive voice (500–01, 652) See *voice.*

past participle (727) See *participle.*

past perfect progressive tense (647) See *tense.*

past perfect tense (645) See *tense.*

past progressive tense (644–50) See *tense.*

past tense (644–50) See *tense.*

patchwriting (100, 247) A faulty paraphrase that relies too heavily on the language or sentence structure of the source text. Patchwritten texts may replace some terms from the source passage with synonyms, add or delete a few words, or alter the sentence structure slightly, but they do not put the passage fully into fresh words and sentences. At some colleges and universities, *patchwriting* is considered plagiarism.

pathos (144) See *appeals.*

patterns of development (59–63) See *analysis, cause and effect, comparison and contrast, definition, description, exemplification, narration,* and *process analysis.*

PDF (Portable Document Format) (180, 215, 399) A file format developed by Adobe that allows documents to be opened in different systems without altering their formatting.

peer revising (90–92) A revising strategy in which the writer solicits feedback on a text from classmates, colleagues, or friends. See also *revising.*

perfect progressive tense (644–50) See *tense.*

perfect tenses (644–50) See *tense.*

periodical (215) A publication, such as a magazine, newspaper, or scholarly journal, that is issued at regular intervals—daily, weekly, monthly, quarterly. See also *journal.*

periodic sentence (531–33) A sentence that reserves the independent clause for the end, building suspense that highlights key information when it finally arrives.

person (620, 637, 681) The form of a word that indicates whether it corresponds to the speaker or writer (*I, we*), the person addressed (*you*), or the people or things spoken or written about (*he, she, it, they, Marta, milkshakes*).

persona (7, 87) The personality of the writer as reflected in tone and style.

personal pronoun (657, 775) The pronouns *I, me, you, he, him, she, her, it, we, us, they, them,* which take the place of specific nouns or noun phrases.

personal statement (101) In a portfolio, the writer's description of the contents and explanation for the choice and arrangement of selections. See also *portfolio.*

personification (552) The attribution of human qualities to nonhuman creatures, objects, ideas, or phenomena: *The tornado swallowed the house.* See *figurative language.*

persuasive argument (11, 32, 134) An argument that advocates for a claim. The writer's purpose is to convince readers to agree with or at least to respect a position on a debatable issue. See also *argument, exploratory argument, purpose.*

phrasal verb (642, 722–24) A verb combined with one or two particles that together create a new verb with a meaning different from that of the original verb alone. See *particle.*

phrase (502–04, 591–94, 601, 752) A group of related words that lacks a subject, predicate, or both. A phrase cannot stand alone as a sentence, but it can function *in* a sentence as a noun, a verb, or a modifier.

pie chart (74–75)   An information graphic that depicts the relationship of the parts to the whole; its sections must add up to 100 percent.

plagiarism (199, 247–56)   Presenting a work or a portion of a work of any kind—a paper, a photograph, a speech, a web page—by someone else as if it were one's own.

plain text (165)   A computer text format that does not allow for styling such as boldface and italics.

plural (620–22)   Referring to more than one thing. See *number*.

point of view (435)   The perspective of the narrator in a work of literature.

portfolio (99–101)   A printed or online collection of a writer's work. A portfolio may contain the writer's best work, a range of types of writing (a proposal, a report, a set of instructions), or a collection of texts from a single project (prewriting, outline, first draft, revised draft). A portfolio usually also includes a table of contents and a personal statement. See also *personal statement*.

positive form (674–77)   See *comparison of adjectives and adverbs*.

possessive case (656–64)   See *case*.

possessive pronoun (775)   The pronouns *my, mine, your, yours, his, hers, its, our, ours, your, yours, their,* and *theirs*, which indicate possession.

predicate (587–88)   The part of a sentence or clause that states (*predicates*) something about the subject. The **simple predicate** consists of a main verb together with any helping verbs: *Marta is writing her parents a long e-mail.* The **complete predicate** consists of the simple predicate together with any objects, complements, and modifiers: *Marta is writing her parents a long e-mail.* A **compound predicate** is a complete predicate with two or more simple predicates joined with a conjunction: *Marta wrote the e-mail but decided not to send it.*

prefix (566)   A group of letters that attaches to the beginning of a root word to modify its meaning: *act, react*.

prejudice (138, 140)   Ascribing qualities to an individual based on generalities about a group, generalities that are often inaccurate. See also *stereotype*.

premise (135–37)   A claim or assumption on which the conclusion of an argument is based. See *syllogism*.

preposition (582, 739–46)   A word or term that relates nouns or pronouns to other words in a sentence in terms of time, space, cause, and other attributes.

prepositional phrase (592, 605)   A preposition followed by its object—a noun or pronoun and its modifiers. Prepositional phrases function as adjectives and adverbs: *the cat with gray fur*.

present participle (727)   See *participle*.

present perfect progressive tense (645–47)   See *tense*.

present perfect tense (645)   See *tense*.

present progressive tense (644–47)   See *tense*.

present tense (644–47)   See *tense*.

press, or media, releases (482–94)   Brief articles that announce events to newspapers, magazines, and online media outlets.

previewing (109)   Scanning the title, subtitle, abstract, introduction, conclusion, sidebars, key terms, headings, subheadings, figures, and illustrations of a text to get a sense of its content, organization, and emphases before reading it in full.

primary source (226–29, 259–62, 456)   Firsthand information, such as an eyewitness account, a research report, a recorded interview, or a work of literature or art. See also *field research*.

process analysis (59)   A pattern of paragraph or essay development that explains a process step by step.

progressive tenses (644–47)   See *tense*.

pronoun (56, 577, 630)   A word that renames or takes the place of a noun or noun phrase.

pronoun reference (644–68)   The relationship between a pronoun and its antecedent (the word it replaces). Pronoun reference is clear when readers can tell effortlessly what a pronoun's antecedent is.

proofreading (93–94)   Reading a text to identify and correct spelling and typographical mistakes as well as punctuation and mechanical errors.

proper noun (713–809)   See *noun*.

proximity (162)   In design, the arrangement of content to show relationships. Material that is related should be placed close together; material that is unrelated should be placed at a distance.

purpose (9, 10–12, 164, 183)   Your main reason for writing: to express your feelings or impressions or to entertain, inform, or persuade your audience.

Q

quantifier (718, 719)   An adjective such as *some, many, much, less,* or *few* that indicates the amount of a noun.

quotation (248–49, 259–62)   A restatement of what someone else has said or written, either in a *direct quotation* (word for word) or an *indirect quotation* (a report of what was said or written). See *direct quotation, indirect quotation*.

R

reading journal (117–19)   An online or printed record of a reader's reactions to, analysis of, or critique of a text.

reciprocal pronoun (577–78)   A pronoun that refers to the individual parts of a plural antecedent: *The candidates debated one another*.

redundancy (498–99)   Unnecessary repetition: *It was a cloudy, overcast day*.

reference list (358, 378, 416, 428–29)   In APA and CSE style, a section at the end of a writing project in which the writer provides full bibliographic information for all sources cited in the text.

reference work (206–29)   Sources, such as dictionaries, encyclopedias, bibliographies, almanacs, and atlases, that provide overview and background information on a word or topic. Specialized reference works

Glossary of Key Terms

may be appropriate sources for college projects, but general reference works are not.

reflection (114–19) The process of thinking about, annotating, and writing about a text in a reading journal; reflection is a necessary step for coming fully to terms with the text. See also *annotation, reading journal.*

reflexive pronoun (577–78) A pronoun that refers back to the subject of a sentence: *She helped herself to the buffet.*

regionalism (541) Nonstandard usage characteristic of people in a particular locality.

regular verbs (638–39) Verbs whose past-tense and past-participle forms end in *-d* or *-ed.*

relative clause (595) An adjective clause introduced by a relative pronoun such as *who, whom,* or *that.* See *adjective clause.*

relative pronouns (594, 657, 663) Pronouns such as *who, whom, whose, that,* and *which* used to introduce a subordinate clause that describes the pronoun's antecedent: *The apartment that I rented is small.*

relevance (46, 48, 230–31) The extent to which supporting evidence not only addresses the general topic of a text but also contributes to the reader's understanding of or belief in the text's main idea (the *thesis*). A relevant source offers information that will enrich understanding, provide background information or evidence to support claims, or suggest alternative perspectives.

reliability (230–36) The extent to which a source is accurate and trustworthy.

research hypothesis (195–96) A tentative assertion of what the writer expects the research to prove.

research log (198–200) A journal in which a researcher records research questions and hypotheses; a working thesis; information gathered from sources; interpretation, analysis, synthesis, and critique of sources; and ideas for next steps.

research questions (195–96) Questions about a topic that research might answer.

response (115, 432–36) Your own reactions to and insights about a text. Response occurs while a reader reads, and it often changes and develops as a result of re-reading and studying the text.

restrictive element (757–759) See *essential element.*

résumé (486–90) A brief summary of an applicant's qualifications and experience.

revising (82–103, 174) The stage of the writing process in which the writer assesses global issues such as whether the text fulfills its purpose, addresses its intended audience, is fully developed, and is organized clearly and logically; also the stage in which the writer assesses local issues such as word choice, sentence variety and emphasis, and wordiness. See also *conciseness, peer revising.*

rhetorical appeal (142) See *appeal.*

rhetorical citation (281) Identifying the source of information, words, or ideas while providing information about the source or your evaluation of it.

rhetorical question (534) A question that is meant to call attention to an issue, not to elicit an answer.

Rogerian model (154–55) A model for organizing an exploratory argument that discusses evidence and counterevidence before drawing a conclusion. Compare *classical* and *Toulmin models.*

roundabout expression (498) A wordy expression that should be more concise.

S

scholarly sources (232–36) Peer-reviewed journal articles and books by experts, often published by university presses.

scratch (informal) outline (35) See *outline.*

search engine (207–20) Computer software that retrieves information from the internet, online databases, and library catalogs.

secondary sources (259–62) Sources that describe, evaluate, or interpret primary sources or other secondary sources. A textbook is a secondary source.

sentence (527–39) A word group with a subject and predicate that does not begin with a subordinating expression. A **declarative sentence** makes a statement: *The phone rang.* An **imperative sentence** gives a command: *Answer the phone.* An **interrogative sentence** asks a question: *Did the phone ring?* An **exclamatory sentence** expresses strong or sudden emotion: *How I hate annoying ring tones!* A **simple sentence** has only one independent clause and no subordinate clauses: *The phone rang.* A **compound sentence** has two or more independent clauses but no subordinate clauses: *The phone rang, and I answered it.* A **complex sentence** consists of a single independent clause with at least one subordinate clause: *My cell phone rang while I was in the elevator.* A **compound-complex sentence** has two or more independent clauses with one or more subordinate clauses: *My cell phone rang, but I didn't answer it because I was in a crowded elevator.*

sentence fragment (695) A word group punctuated like a sentence but lacking one or more of the essential parts of a sentence: an independent clause, a complete verb, and a subject.

sentence outline (36) See *outline.*

separable (723) A transitive phrasal verb is *separable* if its direct object can fall either between the verb and the particle (separating them) or after the particle.

sequence of tenses (648–50) The choice of tenses that best reflect the time relationship among the events described in the clauses of a sentence.

server (177) A computer that links other computers into a network.

setting (435) In works of literature, where and when the action occurs.

signal phrase (276, 289, 291, 348–49, 417, 759) A phrase that identifies, discusses, or describes the author or source being cited: *"How do I know* what I think," E. M. Forster asked, "until I see what I say?"

simile (552–53) An explicit comparison between two unlike things, usually expressed with *like* or *as*: *run like the wind* (see also *figurative language, metaphor*).

simple future tense (645) See *tense*.

simple past tense (645) See *tense*.

simple predicate (587) See *predicate*.

simple present tense (644, 645) See *tense*.

simple sentence (528, 597) See *sentence*.

simple subject (585) See *subject*.

simple tenses (644–45) See *tense*.

singular (620–21) Referring to one thing.

site map (178) A list of a website's contents.

slang (542) The informal, inventive, often colorful (and off color) vocabulary of a particular group. Slang is usually inappropriate in formal writing.

slash (804–05) Punctuation used to mark the ends of lines in poetry when the poetry is run into a sentence.

spam (483) Unsolicited advertising sent to e-mail or social software accounts such as Twitter.

spatial organization (35) An organizational strategy that structures a description visually, from left to right, from inside to outside, from top to bottom, and so on.

sponsors (288) Corporations, agencies, and organizations that are responsible for creating and making available a website's content.

squinting modifier (688) A modifier that appears confusingly to modify both what precedes it and what follows it.

Standard American English (574) The dialect of English that prevails in academic and business settings in the United States.

stereotype (545) A simplified, uncritical, and often negative generalization about an entire group of people. See also *prejudice*.

styles of documentation (288, 347, 389, 416) A set of specifications for citing and documenting sources. Most of the well-known style sheets, such as MLA, APA, *Chicago*, and CSE, are sponsored and updated by professional organizations or publishers.

subject (585–87, 600) The part of a sentence that identifies what the predicate is making a statement about. The **simple subject** is a noun or pronoun: *The cat hissed at the dog*. The **complete subject** is the simple subject with any modifying words or phrases: *The excitable gray cat chased the dog*. A **compound subject** is a complete subject with two or more simple subjects joined with a conjunction: *The cat and the dog usually get along*.

subject complement (530, 580, 589, 629, 658, 670, 696) An adjective, pronoun, or noun phrase that follows a linking verb and describes or refers to the sentence subject: *This food is delicious*.

subject directory (25, 212–14) A collection of websites organized into groups by topic and arranged hierarchically from most general to most specific.

subjective case (656–64) See *case*.

subjunctive mood (650–52) See *mood*.

subordinate clause, or **dependent clause** (511–14, 594, 663, 752) See *clause*.

subordinating conjunction (594) See *conjunction*.

subordination (506, 510–15) The incorporation of secondary or modifying elements into a sentence or clause: *Although he got a late start, he arrived on time*.

suffix (567–68) A group of letters that attaches to the end of a root word to change its meaning and grammatical form: *act, action*.

summary (110–11, 249, 256–59) A passage restating the main idea and major supporting points of a source text in the reader's own words and sentence structures. A summary should be at least 50 percent shorter than the text it restates.

superlative form (674–77) See *comparison of adjectives and adverbs*.

superstition (138) A belief with no basis in fact: *A wish made on a falling star will come true*.

s.v. (396) Abbreviation of the Latin phrase *sub verbo*, "under the word."

symbolism (435) The use of a character, event, or object to represent something more than its literal meaning.

synchronous media (182) Communication media such as instant messaging and online chat in which participants discuss topics in real time. Compare *asynchronous media*.

synonyms (56) Words with similar meanings—for example, *wrong* and *incorrect*. Compare *antonyms*.

synthesis (112, 123–25) The process of making connections among ideas in a text, ideas in other texts, and the writer's own ideas and experiences. Synthesis is an important component in critical thinking and reading and is central to much successful college writing.

T

table (74) An information graphic that organizes data into rows and columns.

tense (637, 644) The form of a verb that indicates the time in which an action or event occurs, when it occurred relative to other events, and whether it is ongoing or completed. The three **simple tenses** are the simple present (*I practice*), the simple past (*I practiced*), and the simple future (*I will practice*). The **perfect tenses** generally indicate the completion of an action before a particular time. They include the present perfect (*I have practiced*), the past perfect (*I had practiced*), and the future perfect (*I will have practiced*). The **progressive tenses** indicate ongoing action. They include the present progressive (*I am practicing*), the past progressive (*I was practicing*), the future progressive (*I will be practicing*), the present perfect progressive (*I have been practicing*), the past perfect progressive (*I had been practicing*), and the future perfect progressive (*I will have been practicing*).

tense sequence (648–50) See *sequence of tenses.*
theme (432) The main point of a work of literature.
thesis statement (29–33, 83–84, 196) A brief statement (one or two sentences) of a text's main idea.
title page (100) A cover sheet for a printed portfolio, with identifying information, including the work's title, author's name, course number, and date of submission.
tone (9, 15–16, 115) The attitude of the writer toward the audience, the topic, and the writer her- or himself as conveyed through word choice, style, and content.
topic (9, 20, 25, 31, 163) The subject of a text.
topic outline (36) See *outline.*
topic sentence (47–52) A sentence (sometimes two) that states a paragraph's main idea.
Toulmin model (155) A model for organizing an argument based on *claims* (or assertions), *grounds* (or evidence), and *warrants* (or assumptions linking claims to grounds). Compare *classical* and *Rogerian models.*
transitional expressions (54, 530, 753) Words and phrases, such as *in addition, however,* and *since,* that show the relationship between sentences or paragraphs.
transitive verb (589–91, 643–44) A verb that takes a direct object.
tree diagram (33) A way to depict the relationships among topics and subtopics visually by placing the main idea at the top of the page and letting topics and subtopics branch off below it.

U

understatement (552) The deliberate use of less forceful language than a subject warrants. *An A average is pretty good.* See *figurative language.*
unfamiliar to familiar (35) An organization pattern that presents surprising ideas, examples, or information first, before moving on to familiar ground.
unified, unity (37, 47) A quality of a text in which all the examples and evidence support the paragraph's topic sentence and in which each of the supporting paragraphs supports the text's thesis statement.
unmarked infinitive (725) The base verb alone, without *to.*
URL (236–38) Universal resource locator, a website's Internet address.

V

verb (577–79, 636–55) A word that expresses action (*The quarterback throws a pass*), occurrence (*The play happened in the second half*), or state of being (*The fans are happy*). Verbs also carry information about time (tense), as well as person, number, voice, and mood.
verbal (579, 592, 601, 638, 692) A verb form that functions as a noun, adjective, or adverb. Verbals may have objects and complements, but they lack the information about tense required of a complete verb.
verb phrase (591, 592, 621–22, 639) A main verb with any helping (or auxiliary) verbs.
verbal phrase (577, 605) A verbal and any modifiers, objects, or complements.
vested interest (233) A participant or stakeholder who might personally benefit from the results of a decision, event, or process has a vested (not objective) interest in that decision, event, or process and thus might influence it not for the welfare of others but for personal gain.
voice (500–01, 637, 652–53) In grammar, the form of a transitive verb that indicates whether the subject is acting or acted upon. In the **active voice**, the subject performs the action of the verb: *The dog chased the cat.* In the **passive voice**, the subject receives the action of the verb: *The cat was chased by the dog.* Also, in writing, the sense of the writer's personality as conveyed through the writer's word, style, and content choices. See also *persona, tone.*

W

warrant (147) An unstated assumption that underlies an argument's main claim. See *Toulmin model.*
web browser (180) The software program that interprets HTML code, making it possible for users to view websites and web pages.
weblog (or **blog**) (177, 321) See *blog.*
web pages (176) Files on a website in addition to the home page; web pages may include text, audio, video, still images, and database files.
website (176) A collection of files located at a single address (URL) on the World Wide Web.
well developed (46) Paragraphs or essays that supply the information readers need to be persuaded of the writer's point.
white space (166) The portion of a page or screen with no text, graphics, or images.
wiki (177) A website designed for collaborative writing and editing.
working bibliography (200–05) A list of sources a researcher compiles before and during the research process.
working thesis (441) The first version of a thesis that a writer can imagine for the text he or she is writing. Typically the working thesis goes through several revisions as the writer drafts and revises the text.
works-cited list (288, 305, 332) In MLA style, a section at the end of a research project in which the writer provides full bibliographic information for all sources cited in the text.
writing process (9–106) The process a writer engages in to produce a writing project. The writing process includes analyzing the assignment, planning the project, generating ideas, drafting, revising, editing, designing, proofreading, and publishing.
writing situation (9–17) The characteristics of a text, including its purpose, audience, context, and genre, as well as its length, due date, and format.

Z

zero article (714) See *article.*

Glossary of Usage

This usage glossary includes words that writers often confuse (*infer, imply*) or misuse (*disinterested, uninterested*) and expressions that are nonstandard and sometimes even pretentious. As a responsible writer, strive to avoid words and expressions that will confuse or distract your readers or that will undermine their confidence in you. Of course, not all words and expressions that cause writers problems are listed here; if a word or expression with which you have trouble is *not* included here, check the index, review chapters 30 and 31 ("Choosing Appropriate Language" and "Choosing Effective Words"), review the list of homonyms and near homonyms on p. 565, consult the usage notes in a dictionary, or consult another usage guide, such as *Fowler's Modern English Usage*, *The New York Times Manual of Style and Usage*, *100 Words Almost Everyone Confuses and Misuses*, or *The American Heritage Book of English Usage*.

A

a, an *A* and *an* are indefinite articles. Use *a* before a word that begins with a consonant sound: *a car, a hill, a one-way street*. Use *an* before a word that begins with a vowel sound: *an appointment, an hour, an X-ray*.

accept, except *Accept* is a verb meaning "agree to receive": *I accept the nomination*. *Except* is a preposition that means "but": *Everyone voted for me except Paul*.

adapt, adopt *Adapt* means "to adjust": *Instead of migrating, the park's ducks adapt to the changing climate*. *Adopt* means "to take as one's own": *I adopted a cat from the shelter*.

adverse, averse *Adverse* means "unfavorable" or "hostile"; *averse* means "opposed": *She was averse to buying a ticket to a play that had received such adverse criticism*.

advice, advise The noun *advice* means "guidance"; the verb *advise* means "to suggest": *I advised her to get some sleep. She took my advice and went to bed early*.

affect, effect As a verb, *affect* means "to influence" or "to cause a change": *Study habits affect one's grades*. As a noun, *affect* means "feeling or emotion": *The defendant responded without affect to the guilty verdict*. As a noun, *effect* means "result": *The decreased financial aid budget is an effect of the recession*. As a verb, *effect* means "to bring about or accomplish": *Submitting the petition effected a change in the school's policy*.

aggravate, irritate *Aggravate* means "to intensify" or "worsen": *Dancing until dawn aggravated Giorgio's bad back*. *Irritate* means "to annoy": *He was irritated that his chiropractor could not see him until Tuesday*. Colloquially, *aggravate* is often used to mean *annoy*, but this colloquial usage is inappropriate in formal contexts.

agree to, agree with *Agree to* means "to consent to": *Chris agreed to host the party*. *Agree with* means "be in accord with": *Anne agreed with Chris that a party was just what everyone needed*.

ain't *Ain't* is a nonstandard contraction for *am not, are not,* or *is not* and should not be used in formal writing.

all ready, already *All ready* means "completely prepared"; *already* means "previously": *They were all ready to catch the bus, but it had already left*.

all right, alright *All right* is the standard spelling; *alright* is nonstandard.

all together, altogether *All together* means "as a group": *When Noah's family gathered for his graduation, it was the first time they had been all together in years*. *Altogether* means "completely": *Noah was altogether overwhelmed by the attention*.

allude, elude, refer to *Allude* means "to refer to indirectly"; *elude* means "to avoid" or "to escape": *He eluded further questioning by alluding to his troubled past*. Do not use *allude* to mean "refer directly"; use *refer to* instead: *The speaker referred to [not alluded to] slide six of her PowerPoint presentation*.

allusion, illusion An *allusion* is an indirect reference: *I almost missed the author's allusion to Macbeth*. An *illusion* is a false appearance or belief: *The many literary quotations he drops into his speeches give the illusion that he is well read*.

almost, most *Almost* means "nearly"; *most* means "the majority of": *My roommate will tell me almost [not most] anything, but I talk to my sister about most of my own problems*.

a lot, alot *Alot* is nonstandard; always spell *a lot* as two words.

among, amongst *Amongst* is a British alternative to *among;* in American English, *among* is preferred.

among, between Use *among* with three or more nouns or with words that stand for a group composed of three or more members; use *between* with two or more nouns: *I'm double majoring because I could not decide between biology and English. Italian, art history, and calculus are among my other favorites*.

amoral, immoral *Amoral* means "neither moral nor immoral" or "indifferent to moral standards"; *immoral* means "violating moral standards": *While secularists believe that nature is amoral, religionists often view natural disasters as punishments for immoral behavior*.

amount, number Use *amount* with items that cannot be counted (noncount or mass nouns); use *number* with items that can be counted

G14

Glossary of Usage

(count nouns): *The dining hall prepares the right amount of food based on the number of people who eat there.*

an See *a, an.*

and/or *And/or* is shorthand for "one or the other or both." It is acceptable in technical and business writing, but it should be avoided in most academic writing.

ante-, anti- The prefix *ante-* means "before," as in *antebellum*, or "before the war"; the prefix *anti-* means "against," as in *antibiotic* ("against bacteria").

anxious, eager *Anxious* means "uneasy": *Dan was anxious about writing his first twenty-page paper. Eager* indicates strong interest or enthusiasm: *He was eager to finish his first draft before spring break.*

anybody, any body; anyone, any one *Anybody* and *anyone* are singular indefinite pronouns: *Does anybody [or anyone] have an extra pen? Any body and any one are a noun and pronoun (respectively) modified by the adjective any: She was not fired for making any one mistake but, rather, for making many mistakes over a number of years.*

anymore, any more *Anymore* means "from now on": *She does not write letters anymore*. *Any more* means "additional": *I do not need any more stamps*. Both are used only in negative contexts, for example, with *not* or other negative terms such as *hardly* or *scarcely*.

anyplace *Anyplace* is an informal way of saying *anywhere*. *Anywhere* is preferable in formal writing.

anyways, anywheres *Anyways* and *anywheres* are nonstandard; use *anyway* and *anywhere* instead.

as *As* should not be used in place of *because, since,* or *when* if ambiguity will result: *As people were lining up to use the elliptical machine, the management posted a waiting list.* Does this sentence mean that management posted the sign *while* people were lining up, or does it mean that the management posted the sign *because* there was such demand for the machine?

as, as if, like Use *as,* or *as if,* not *like,* as a conjunction in formal writing: *The president spoke as if* [not *like*] *he were possessed by the spirit of Abraham Lincoln. Like* is acceptable, however, as a preposition that introduces a comparison: *The president spoke like a true leader.*

at *At* is not necessary to complete *where* questions: *Where is Waldo?* not *Where is Waldo at?*

averse, adverse See *adverse, averse.*

awful, awfully In formal writing, use *awful* and *awfully* to suggest the emotion of fear or wonder, not as a synonym for *bad* or to mean *very*. *The high priest gave forth an awful cry before casting the captive from the top of the pyramid toward the crowd below.*

awhile, a while *Awhile* is an adverb: *They talked awhile before going to dinner. A while* is an article and a noun, and should always follow a preposition: *Rest for a while between eating and exercising.*

B

bad, badly In formal writing, use the adjective *bad* to modify nouns and pronouns and after linking verbs (as a subject complement): *Because I had a bad day, my husband feels bad.* Use the adverb *badly* to modify verbs, adjectives, and adverbs: *Todd's day went badly from start to finish.*

being as, being that *Being as* and *being that* are nonstandard substitutes for *because*: *Because* [not *being as*] *Marcus did well as a teaching assistant, he was asked to teach a class of his own the next year.* Avoid them.

beside, besides *Beside* is a preposition that means "next to" or "alongside of": *You will always find my glasses beside the bed. Besides* is an adverb meaning "furthermore" or a preposition meaning "in addition to": *Besides, it will soon be finals. Besides chemistry, I have exams in art history and statistics.*

between, among See *among, between.*

bring, take Use *bring* when something is coming toward the speaker and *take* when it is moving away: *When the waiter brought our entrees, he took our bread.*

burst, bursted; bust, busted *Burst* is a verb meaning to break apart violently; the past tense of *burst* is also *burst*, not *bursted*. *Bust* is slang for *to burst* or *to break* and should be avoided in formal writing: *The boiler burst* [not *bursted* or *busted*] *in a deadly explosion.*

C

can, may Use *can* when discussing ability: *I know she can quit smoking.* Use *may* when discussing permission: *The server told her that she may not smoke anywhere in the restaurant.*

capital, capitol *Capital,* a noun, can mean "funds," or it can mean "the city that is the seat of government": *The student council did not have enough capital to travel to Harrisburg, Pennsylvania's capital.* The word *capitol* means "the building where lawmakers meet": *The state's capitol is adorned with a golden dome.* When capitalized, *Capitol* refers to the building in Washington, DC, where the US Congress meets.

censor, censure *Censor* means both "to delete objectionable material" (a verb) and "one who deletes objectionable material" (a noun): *The bedroom scenes, but not the battle scenes, were heavily censored.* Clearly, the censors object more to sex than to violence. *Censure* means both "to reprimand officially" (verb) and "an official reprimand" (noun): *The ethics committee censured the governor for lying under oath. Members of his party were relieved that a censure was all he suffered.*

cite, sight, site *Cite,* a verb, means "to quote" or "mention": *Cite your sources according to MLA format. Sight,* a noun, means "view" or "scene": *The sight of a field of daffodils makes me think of Wordsworth. Site,* a noun, means "location" or "place" (even online): *That site has the best recipes on the Internet.*

climactic, climatic *Climactic* is an adjective derived from the noun *climax* and means "culminating" or "most intense"; *climatic* is an adjective derived from the noun *climate: The climactic moment of a thunderstorm occurs when the center of the storm is overhead. Tornados are violent climatic phenomena associated with thunderstorms.*

complement, compliment *Complement* is a noun meaning "that which completes or perfects something else"; it can also be used as a verb meaning "the process of completing or making perfect." *Compliment* means either "a flattering comment" or "the act of giving a compliment": *My husband complements me and makes me whole; still, it annoys me that he rarely compliments me on my appearance.*

conscience, conscious *Conscience* is a noun meaning "sense of right and wrong": *Skipping class weighed heavily on Sunil's conscience. Conscious* is an adjective that means "aware" or "awake": *Maria made a conscious decision to skip class.*

continual(ly), continuous(ly) *Continual* means "repeated frequently": *The continual request for contributions undermined her resolve to be more charitable. Continuous* means "uninterrupted": *The continuous stream of bad news forced her to shut off the television.*

could care less *Could care less* is an illogical, and nonstandard, substitute for *could not care less: If one could care less, then one must care, at least a little, and yet this is not the intended meaning.*

could of, must of, should of, would of These are misspellings of *could have, must have, should have,* and *would have.*

criteria, criterion *Criteria* is the plural form of the noun *criterion,* Latin for "standard": *His criteria for grading may be vague, but I know I fulfilled at least one criterion by submitting my paper on time.*

D

data, media, phenomena *Data, media,* and *phenomena* are plural nouns (*datum, medium,* and *phenomenon* are their singular forms): *The data suggest that the economy will rebound by the time you graduate. The news media raise the alarm about public corruption, but it is the voters who must take action. The Aurora Borealis is one of many amazing natural phenomena.* (*Data* is increasingly used as a singular noun, but continuing to use it as a plural is never wrong.)

differ from, differ with *Differ from* means "to lack similarity": *Renaissance art differs greatly from art of the Middle Ages. Differ with* means to disagree: *Martin Luther's forty-nine articles spelled out the ways in which he differed with the Catholic Church.*

discreet, discrete *Discreet,* an adjective, means "tactful" or "judicious": *Please be discreet—don't announce that you saw Ada crying in the bathroom. Discrete* means "distinct" or "separate": *The study revealed two discrete groups, those who can keep a secret and those who cannot.*

disinterested, uninterested *Disinterested* means "impartial": *A judge who cannot be disinterested should recuse him- or herself from the case. Uninterested* means "indifferent": *The book seems well-written, but I am uninterested in the topic.*

don't, doesn't *Don't* is a contraction of *do not;* it is used with *I, you, we, they,* and plural nouns: *I don't want to drive, but the trains don't run very often. Doesn't* is a contraction of *does not;* it is used with *he, she, it,* and singular nouns: *It doesn't matter whether you're a little late; Fred doesn't mind waiting.*

E

each and every *Each and every* is a wordy substitute for *each* or *every;* use one or the other but not both.

eager, anxious See *anxious, eager.*

effect, affect See *affect, effect.*

e.g., i.e. *E.g.* is an abbreviation of a Latin phrase meaning "for example" or "for instance"; *i.e.* is an abbreviation of a Latin phrase meaning "that is." In formal writing, use the English equivalents rather than the Latin abbreviations; the Latin abbreviations are acceptable in tables, footnotes, and other places where space is at a premium.

elicit, illicit *Elicit,* a verb, means "to draw out": *Every week, American Idol contestants try to elicit enough support to avoid elimination.* Illicit, an adjective, means "illegal" or "impermissible": *In 2003, American Idol contestant Frenchie Davis was disqualified for posing in illicit photos.*

elude, allude, refer to See *allude, elude, refer to.*

emigrate from, immigrate to *Emigrate from* means "to leave one's country and settle in another": *Jake's grandmother emigrated from Poland in 1919. Immigrate to* means "to move to and settle in a new country": *Jake's grandmother immigrated to the United States in 1919.*

eminent, imminent, immanent *Eminent* means "renowned": *The university hosts lectures by many eminent scientists. Imminent* means "about to happen" or "looming": *In the last year of the Bush administration, many felt that a recession was imminent. Immanent* means "inherent" or "pervasive throughout the world": *Many religions teach that God's presence is immanent.*

enthused *Enthused* is a colloquial adjective meaning "enthusiastic." In formal writing, use *enthusiastic: Because of the team's excellent record, Eric was enthusiastic* [not *enthused*] *about joining.*

etc. *Etc.* is an abbreviation of the Latin phrase *et cetera,* meaning "and others." Because *et* means "and," adding the word *and* before *etc.* is redundant. In a series, include a comma before *etc.: A great deal of online media are used in classes today: blogs, wikis, Blackboard, Facebook, etc.* In most formal writing, concluding with a final example or *and so on* (the English equivalent of *etc.*) is preferable.

everybody, everyone; every body, every one *Everybody* and *everyone* are interchangeable singular indefinite pronouns: *Everybody* [or *everyone*] *who went to the concert got a free T-shirt. Every body* and *every one* are

Glossary of Usage

a noun and a pronoun (respectively) modified by the adjective *every*: *Coroners must treat every body they examine with respect.*

except, accept See *accept, except.*

expect, suppose *Expect* means "to anticipate": *I expect to be home when she arrives. Suppose* means "to presume": *I suppose she should have a key just in case.*

explicit, implicit *Explicit*, an adjective, means "overt" or "stated outright": *The rules are explicit: "No running." Implicit* is an adjective that means "implied": *Implicit in the rules is a prohibition against skipping.*

F

farther, further Use *farther* with distances: *I'd like to drive a hundred miles farther before we pull over for dinner.* Use *further* to mean "more" or "in addition": *I have nothing further to add.*

fewer, less Use *fewer* with items that can be counted (count nouns). Use *less* with items that cannot be counted (noncount or mass nouns): *This semester, I am taking three fewer classes than I took in the fall, but because I have a job now, I have less time to study.*

first, firstly *Firstly* is used in Britain, but it sounds overly formal in the United States. *First* (and *second* and *third*) is the standard form in the United States.

flaunt, flout *Flaunt* means "to parade" or "show off"; *Ivan flaunted his muscular torso on the quad. Flout* means "to disobey" or "ignore": *He flouted school policy by parading about without his shirt on.*

further, farther See *farther, further.*

G

get Many colloquial expressions with *get* should not be used in formal writing. Avoid expressions such as *get with the program, get your act together, get lost,* and so on.

good, well *Good* is an adjective; *well* is an adverb: *Playing well in the tournament made Lee feel good.* In references

to health, however, *well* is an adjective: *She had a cold, but now she is well and back at work.*

H

hanged, hung Use the past-tense verb *hanged* only to describe a person executed by hanging. Use the past-tense verb *hung* to describe anything else (pictures, clothing) that can be suspended.

hardly Use *can hardly* instead of *can't hardly*, a double negative: *I can hardly keep my eyes open.*

he, she; he/she; s/he Historically, the pronoun *he* was used generically to mean *he or she*; in informal contexts, writers avoid bias by writing *he/she* or *s/he.* In formal writing, however, revise your sentence to avoid a gendered pronoun: *Sensible students are careful what they post on social networking sites* [not *The sensible student is careful what he posts about himself on social networking sites*].

hisself *Hisself* is a nonstandard substitute for *himself.* Avoid it.

I

i.e., e.g. See *e.g., i.e.*

if, whether Use *whether* not *if* when alternatives are offered: *If I must go out, I insist that we go to a decent restaurant. I do not care whether we eat Chinese food or Italian, but I refuse to eat at Joe's.*

illicit, elicit See *elicit, illicit.*

illusion, allusion See *allusion, illusion.*

immigrate to, emigrate from See *emigrate from, immigrate to.*

imminent, eminent, immanent See *eminent, imminent, immanent.*

immoral, amoral See *amoral, immoral.*

implicit, explicit See *explicit, implicit.*

imply, infer *Imply* means "to suggest indirectly": *The circles under Phillip's eyes implied that he had not slept much. Infer* means "to conclude": *From the way he devoured his dinner, I inferred that Raymond was famished.*

incredible, incredulous *Incredible* means "unbelievable": *Debbie told an incredible story about meeting the Dalai Lama. Incredulous* means

"unbelieving": *I am incredulous of everything that the tabloids print.*

infer, imply See *imply, infer.*

in regards to *In regards* to is nonstandard. Use *in regard to, as regards,* or *regarding* instead.

irregardless *Irregardless* is nonstandard; use *regardless* instead.

irritate, aggravate See *aggravate, irritate.*

is when, is where Avoid these phrases in definitions: *An oligarchy is a system of government in which the many are ruled by a few,* or *Oligarchy is government of the many by the few* [not *An oligarchy is when the many are ruled by a few*].

it's, its *It's* is a contraction of "it is" or "it has," and *its* is a possessive pronoun: *It's been a long time since the ailing pigeon flapped its wings in flight.* One trick for distinguishing the two is to recall that contractions such as *it's* are often avoided in formal writing, while possessive pronouns like *its* are perfectly acceptable.

K

kind, kinds *Kind* is a singular noun: *This kind of weather is bad for asthmatics. Kinds* (a plural noun) is used only to denote more than one kind: *Many kinds of pollen can adversely affect breathing.*

kind of, sort of *Kind of* and *sort of* are colloquial; in formal writing, use "somewhat" or "a little" instead: *Julia was somewhat* [not *kind of*] *pleased to be going back to school.* Use *kind of* and *sort of* in formal writing only to mean "type of": *E.E. Cummings's poetry creates a new kind of grammar.*

L

lay, lie *Lay* means "to place"; it requires a direct object. Its main forms are *lay, laid,* and *laid*: *She laid her paper on the professor's desk. Lie* means "to recline"; it does not take a direct object. Its main forms are *lie, lay,* and *lain*: *She fell asleep as soon as she lay down.*

leave, let *Leave* means "to go away"; *let* means "to allow." *If I leave early, will you let me know what happens?*

less, fewer See *fewer, less.*

like, as, as if See *as, as if, like.*

loose, lose The adjective *loose* means "baggy" or "not securely attached": *I have to be careful with my glasses because one of the screws is loose.* The verb *lose* means "to misplace": *I am afraid I will lose the screw and have to attach the earpiece with duct tape.*

lots, lots of *Lots* and *lots of* are colloquial and should be avoided in academic writing; use terms like *much, many,* and *very* instead.

M

may, can See *can, may.*

maybe, may be The adverb *maybe* means "possibly" or "perhaps": The verb phrase *may be* means "have the possibility to be": *Maybe I'll apply for an internship next semester, but if I wait too long all of the positions may be filled.*

may of, might of *May of* and *might of* are misspellings of *may have* and *might have.*

media See *data, media, phenomena.*

moral, morale *Moral* means "ethical lesson": *Aesop's fables each have a moral, such as "don't judge others by their appearance." Morale* means "attitude" or "spirits": *April's warm weather significantly raised student morale.*

most, almost See *almost, most.*

must of See *could of, must of, should of, would of.*

myself, himself, herself, etc. Use pronouns that end with *-self* to refer to or intensify other words: *Obama himself made an appearance.* Do not use them when you are unsure whether to use a pronoun in the nominative case (*I, she, he, we, they*) or the objective case (*me, her, him, us, them*): *This conversation is between him and me* [not *himself and myself*].

N

nohow, nowheres *Nohow* and *nowheres* are nonstandard forms of *anyway, in any way, in any place, in no place,* and *nowhere.* Avoid them.

number, amount See *amount, number.*

O

off of Omit *of: Sarah took the pin off* [not *off of*] *her coat.*

OK, O.K., okay These are all acceptable spellings, but the term is inappropriate in formal writing. Choose a more specific word instead: *Food served in the dining hall is mediocre* [not *okay*].

P

phenomena See *data, media, phenomena.*

plus Avoid using *plus* as a substitute for the coordinating conjunction *and* or the transition *moreover.*

precede, proceed *Precede* means "come before"; *proceed* means "continue": *Despite warnings from those who preceded me, I proceeded to take six classes in one semester.*

principal, principle *Principal,* a noun, refers to the leader of an organization. *Principal,* used as an adjective, means "main." *Principle,* used as a noun, means "belief" or "standard": *The school principal's principal concern is the well-being of her students. She runs the school on the principle that fairness is essential.*

proceed, precede See *precede, proceed.*

R

raise, rise The verb *raise* means "lift up" or "move up" and takes a direct object: *Joseph raised the blinds.* The verb *rise* means "to go upward" and does not take a direct object: *We could see the steam rise as the solution started to boil.*

real, really Do not use *real* or *really* as a synonym for *very: Spring break went very* [not *real* or *really*] *fast.*

reason is because, reason why To avoid redundancy and faulty predication, choose either *the reason is that* or *because: The reason Chris fell is that he is uncoordinated. It is not because his shoe was untied.*

refer to, allude, elude See *allude, elude, refer to.*

relation, relationship Use *relation* to refer to a connection between things: *There is a relation between the amount one sleeps and one's overall health.* Use *relationship* to refer to a connection between people: *Tony has always had a close relationship with his grandfather.*

respectfully, respectively *Respectfully* means "with respect": *Ben treats his parents respectfully. Respectively* means "in the given order": *My mother and father are 54 and 56, respectively.*

rise, raise See *raise, rise.*

S

set, sit The verb *set* means "to place" or "to establish," and it takes a direct object. *The professor set the book on the desk.* The verb *sit* means "to assume a sitting position," and it does not take a direct object: *You can sit in the waiting room until the doctor is ready.*

shall, will In the past, *shall* was used as a helping verb with *I* and *we,* and *will* was used with *he, she, it,* and *they: I shall go on dancing,* and *they will go home.* Now *will* is generally used with all persons: *I will go on singing, and they will all cover their ears. Shall* is used mainly with polite questions (*Shall we invite your mother?*) and in rules and regulations (*No person shall enter these premises after dusk.*).

should of See *could of, must of, should of, would of.*

since *Since* can mean "because" or "from that time," so use it only when there is no chance that readers will infer the wrong meaning. In the sentence that follows, either meaning makes sense: *Since I moved to the country, I have had no trouble sleeping.* Revise to make your meaning clear: *Since January, when I moved to the country . . .* or *Because I moved to the country, . . .*

sit, set See *set, sit.*

site, sight, cite See *cite, sight, site.*

somebody, someone *Somebody* and *someone* are interchangeable singular indefinite pronouns: *Someone* [or *somebody*] *is at the door.*

sometime, sometimes *Sometime* is an adverb meaning "at an indefinite

Glossary of Usage **G19**

time"; *sometimes* is an adverb meaning "on occasion," "now and then": *Sometimes I wish my future would come sometime soon.*

somewheres *Somewheres* is nonstandard; use *somewhere* instead.

stationary, stationery *Stationary* means "not moving"; *stationery* means "writing paper." (Thinking of the *e* in "stationery" as standing for *envelope* may help.)

supposed to, used to *Supposed to* means *should; used to* means "did regularly in the past." In speech, the final *-d* is often dropped, but in writing, it is required: *I was supposed [not suppose] to practice piano daily; instead, I used [not use] to play hockey.*

sure and, sure to; try and, try to *Sure to* and *try to* are standard; *sure and* and *try and* are not.

T

take, bring See *bring, take.*

than, then *Than* is a conjunction used in comparisons; *then* is an adverb of time. *If Betsy is already taller than I, then I will be impressed.*

that, which In formal writing, *that* is generally used with essential (or restrictive) clauses and *which* with nonessential (nonrestrictive) clauses: *The project that I am working on now is due on Monday, which is why I really have to finish it this weekend.*

that, who In formal writing, use *who* or *whom,* not *that,* to refer to people: *I. M. Pei is the architect who [not that] designed this building.*

their, there, they're *Their* is a possessive pronoun, *there* is an adverb of place, and *they're* is a contraction of "they are": *They're always leaving their dishes in the sink. Why must they leave them there instead of putting them in the dishwasher?*

theirself, theirselves, themself *Theirself, theirselves,* and *themself* are nonstandard. Use *themselves* instead.

them In colloquial speech, the pronoun *them* is sometimes used in place of the demonstrative adjective *those;* avoid this nonstandard usage: *Those [not them] are the books I need for class.*

then, than See *than, then.*

this here, these here, that there, them there *This here, these here, that there,* and *them there* are nonstandard for *this, these, that,* and *them.*

to, too, two *To* is a preposition, *too* is an adverb, and *two* is a number: *To send two dozen roses to your girlfriend for Valentine's Day is too expensive.*

try and, try to See *sure and, sure to; try and, try to.*

U

uninterested, disinterested See *disinterested, uninterested.*

unique *Unique* means "the one and only thing of its kind," so it is illogical to modify it with words like *somewhat* or *very* that suggest degrees: *Your approach to the issue is unique [not somewhat unique].*

usage, use The noun *usage,* which means a "customary manner, approach," should not be used in place of the noun *use: The use [not usage] of cell phones in this restaurant will not be tolerated.*

use, utilize The verb *utilize,* which means "to use purposefully," should not be used in place of *use: Students must use [not utilize] parking lots D, E, and F, not those parking lots reserved for faculty and staff.*

W

wait for, wait on Although *wait on* is sometimes used colloquially as a substitute for "wait for," it is nonstandard. Use *wait on* to mean "serve" and *wait for* to mean "await": *I am waiting for [not waiting on] my mother, who is always late.*

ways *Ways* is sometimes used colloquially as a substitute for "distance." Avoid this usage in formal writing: *We still have quite a distance [not ways] to go before we get to a rest area.*

weather, whether *Weather,* a noun, means "the state of the atmosphere"; *whether,* a conjunction, indicates a choice between alternatives: *It does not matter whether you prefer rain or snow; the weather will be what it will be.*

well, good See *good, well.*

whether, if See *if, whether.*

which, that See *that, which.*

who, that See *that, who.*

who, whom Use *who* for the subject of clauses; use *whom* for the object of clauses: *Who will be coming to the party? Whom did you ask to bring the cake?*

who's, whose *Who's* is a contraction of "who is" or "who has"; *whose* is a possessive pronoun: *Who's at the door? Whose coat is this?*

will, shall See *shall, will.*

would of See *could of, must of, should of, would of.*

Y

you *You* (the second-person singular pronoun) should be used only to refer to the reader, not to refer to people in an indefinite sense (to replace *one*): *In medieval society, subjects [not you] had to swear an oath of allegiance to the king.*

your, you're *Your* is a possessive pronoun; *you're* is a contraction of "you are": *You're as stubborn as your brother.*

Credits

Text Credits

PART 1: Fig. 1.1 University of Arizona Library website, *Facsimiles of Illuminated Manuscripts: The Kennicott Bible* <http://www.library.arizona.edu/exhibits/illuman/15_01.html>. University of Arizona Libraries, Special Collections. Used by permission. **p. 8** Jeff Gurney, "Plagiarism Cheats Students," *The Globe* (Salt Lake Community College), 23 Nov. 2005. Copyright © 2005. Reprinted by permission of the author. **p. 12** Jo Goodwin Parker, From "What Is Poverty?" from George Henderson, *America's Other Children: Public Schools Outside Suburbia* (University of Oklahoma Press, 1971). Copyright © 1971 by University of Oklahoma Press, Norman. Reprinted by permission of the publisher. All rights reserved. **p. 41** Michael Specter, "The Long Ride," *The New Yorker.* Copyright © 2002 by Michael Specter for The New Yorker. Originally published in *The New Yorker.* **p. 47** Brent Staples, "How Hip-Hop Music Lost Its Way and Betrayed Its Fans," *The New York Times,* online edition, May 12, 2005. © 2005 The New York Times. All rights reserved. Used by permission and protected by the Copyright Laws of the United States. The printing, copying, redistribution, or retransmission of the Material without express written permission is prohibited. **pp. 50–51** Jeff Reid, "The DNA-ing of America," *Utne Reader,* Sept.–Oct. 1995, pp. 26–27. Reprinted from Utne Reader, www.utne.com. Copyright © 1995 Ogden Publications, Inc. Used by permission. **p. 53** Arthur Lubow, from "The Murakami Method," *The New York Times,* April 3, 2005. © 2005 The New York Times. All rights reserved. Used by permission and protected by the Copyright Laws of the United States. The printing, copying, redistribution, or retransmission of the Material without express written permission is prohibited.

p. 53 Daniel Etherington, "Nasty Cartoons from Japan." www.bbc.co.uk, November 14, 2002. Copyright © bbc.co.uk/news. **pp. 54–55** Peter Canby, "The Cat Came Back," *Harper's Magazine,* March 2005. Copyright © 2005 by Peter Canby for *Harper's Magazine.* Reprinted by permission of International Creative Management, Inc. **pp. 55–56** Castle Freeman, "Surviving Deer Season: A Lesson in Ambiguity," *Atlantic Monthly,* December 1995. Reprinted by permission of the author. **p. 57** Tad Friend, "The Harriet-the-Spy Club," *The New Yorker,* July 31, 2000. Reprinted by permission of International Creative Management, Inc. Copyright © 2000 by Tad Friend for *The New Yorker.* **p. 59** Virginia Morell, "OK, There It Is—Our Mystery Mollusk," from "Monterey Menagerie," *National Geographic,* June 2004. Copyright © 2004 by Virginia Morell. Reprinted by permission of the author. **p. 60** Barbara Ehrenreich, "What I've Learned from Men: Lessons for a Full-Grown Feminist," published in *Ms. Magazine,* 1985. Copyright 1985. Reprinted by permission. **p. 61** Copyright © 1988 by Richard Selzer. Originally appeared in *The New York Times,* (August 21, 1988). Reprinted by permission of Georges Borchardt, Inc., on behalf of the author. **p. 62** Stephen King, "Why We Crave Horror Movies," first published in *Playboy* magazine, January 1981. © Stephen King. All rights reserved. Reprinted With Permission. **pp. 69–71** Al Gore, *An Inconvenient Truth: The Planetary Emergency of Global Warming and What We Can Do About It.* (Rodale Books, 2006). Copyright © 2006 by Al Gore. Permission granted by Rodale, Inc., Emmaus PA 18098.

PART 2: Ex. 7.1 Wray Herbert, "Why Uncertainty May Be Bad for Your Health," *Newsweek,* Web Exclusive, Sept. 19, 2006, accessed March 15, 2007.

<http://www.medecus.com/index.php?q=no-sugarcoat-doc> updated: 9:15 a.m. ET Sept 19, 2006. Reprinted by permission of the author. **pp. 116–17** Brent Staples, "How Hip-Hop Music Lost Its Way and Betrayed Its Fans," *The New York Times,* online edition, May 12, 2005. © 2005 The New York Times. All rights reserved. Used by permission and protected by the Copyright Laws of the United States. The printing, copying, redistribution, or retransmission of the Material without express written permission is prohibited. **Ex. 7.7** "USA Snapshots: What type of transportation should the government pay more attention to?" by Anne R. Carey and Sam Ward. Source: National Association of Realtors and Transportation. <http://www.usatoday.com/news/snapshot.htm> *USA TODAY,* May 12, 2009. Reprinted with permission.

PART 3: Fig. 9.1 From Boston Public Library <www.johnadamslibrary.org/>. Courtesy of the John Adams Library at the Boston Public Library. **Fig. 10.4** Massachusetts Bay Transportation Authority (MBTA) 2007 Webby-award-winning site. Reproduced by permission of the Massachusetts Bay Transportation Authority.

PART 4: Fig. 13.1 Copyright © 2009 Google. **Fig. 13.2** Copyright © 2009 Google. **Fig. 13.3** Reproduced by permission of EBSCO Host Copyright Agent. **Fig. 13.4** Copyright © 2005 Regents of the University of Minnesota. All rights reserved. **Fig. 13.5** SUMMIT Catalog Libraries of Syracuse University and SUNY Environmental Sciences and Forestry, http://summit.syr.edu . Copyright © 2009 Syracuse University Library. Reproduced by permission. **Fig. 13.6** SUMMIT Catalog Libraries of Syracuse University and SUNY Environmental

C1

Sciences and Forestry, http://summit.syr.edu . Copyright © 2009 Syracuse University Library. Reproduced by permission. **Ex. 15.1** Yugi Noguchi, "On Capitol Hill, Playing WikiPolitics; Partisanship Tests Web Site's Policies." *The Washington Post*, 4 Feb 2006: A1. © 2006 The Washington Post. All rights reserved. Used by permission and protected by the Copyright Laws of the United States. The printing, copying, redistribution, or retransmission of the Material without express written permission is prohibited. **Ex. 15.3** Katharine Q. Seelye, "A Fabled Bureau Exits Eastern Kentucky's Coal Country," *The New York Times*, 30 Jan 2006: C1. Copyright © 2006 The New York Times. All rights reserved. Used by permission and protected by the Copyright laws of the United States. The printing, copying, and redistribution, or retransmission of the Material without express written permission is prohibited. **Ex. 15.3** Charlene Ryan, "Gender Differences in Children's Experience of Musical Performance Anxiety." *The Psychology of Music*, 32.1 (2004): 89–103. Copyright © 2004, Society for Education, Music, and Psychology Research. Reprinted by permission of SAGE.

PART 5: p. 333, Microsoft toolbars showing margins & indentation. Created with Microsoft Office Word® software. **p. 337,** Adrian Tomine, 8-panel cartoon "Optic Nerve #6," p. 22, from Drawn and Quarterly, February 1999. © 1999 by Adrian Tomine. Reproduced by permission.

PART 6: Fig. 22.1 Gary Snyder, "Front Lines," from Turtle Island, copyright © 1974 by Gary Snyder. Reprinted by permission of New Directions Publishing Corp. **pp. 452–54,** Ben Brantley, "Rash and Unadvis'd in Verona Seeks Same" (review of "Romeo and Juliet"), *The New York Times*, 25 June 2007, pp. E1, E7. <http://theater2.nytimes.com/2007/06/25/theater/reviews/25bran.html?scp=1&sq=%22Romeo%20and%20Juliet%22%202007&st=cse>. © 2007 The New York Times. All rights reserved. Used by permission and protected by the Copyright laws of the United States. The printing, copying, and redistribution, or retransmission of the Material without express written permission is prohibited. **p. 25.2** Sample Microsoft Outlook screen shot of an emailed memo. Created with Microsoft Outlook software. **p. 25.7** Sample Press Release, "Family Teams Key to March for Babies," March of Dimes, North Dakota Chapter, January 1, 2008. Reprinted with the permission of Karin Roseland, State Director, March of Dimes North Dakota Chapter.

PART 7: p. 519 Winston Churchill, speech to House of Commons, 4 June 1940. Copyright © Winston S. Churchill. Reproduced with permission of Curtis Brown Ltd., London, on behalf of The Estate of Winston Churchill. **p. 525** Martin Luther King Jr., speech, Washington, DC, August 26, 1963. Copyright 1963 Dr. Martin Luther King Jr.; copyright renewed 1991 Coretta Scott King. Reprinted by arrangement with The Heirs to the Estate of Martin Luther King Jr., c/o Writers House as agent for the proprietor, New York, NY. **p. 534** Darrin M. McMahon, "The Pursuit of Happiness in Perspective," April 8, 2007, *Cato Unbound*, <www.cato-unbound.org/2007/04/08/darrin-m-mcmahon/the-pursuit-of-happiness-in-perspective>. All Rights Reserved, ©2008 Cato Institute. **p. 535** Flannery O'Connor, talk delivered at Notre Dame University, 1957, published in *Mystery and Manners: Occasional Prose* by Flannery O'Connor. Selected and edited by Sally Fitzgerald and Robert Fitzgerald. New York: Farrar, Straus and Giroux, 1969. Reprinted by permission of Farrar, Straus & Giroux and the Harold Matson Company, Inc. © 1957 by Flannery O'Connor. © Renewed 1985 by Regina Cline O'Connor. Reprinted by permission of the Mary Flannery O'Connor Charitable Trust via Harold Matson, Inc. **p. 561** Dictionary definition of "Respect" from *Merriam-Webster's Collegiate Dictionary* online, © 2012. Reprinted with permission by Merriam-Webster. **p. 764** By Gerard Whyman, reproduced by permission from www.CartoonStock.com. **p. 780** Copyright © 2003 Mark Stivers, www.markstivers.com. Reproduced by permission. **pp. 781–82** Lucio Guerrero, "Like a GOTH," courtesy of *The Chicago Sun-Times*. **p. 55.1** Search engine, copyright © 2012 by Google.

Photo Credits

PART 1: Opener: Jeff J. Mitchell/Getty Images; **p. 2:** Stockbyte/PunchStock RF; **p. 3:** Bill Aron/PhotoEdit; **p. 9:** image100/Alamy RF; **p. 29:** © Car Culture/Corbis; **p. 46:** Frank Lloyd Wright, Stained-glass window, 1912. Glass, zinc, 86¼ x 28 x 2 in. (219.1 x 71.1 x 5.1 cm). Purchase, Edgar J. Kaufmann Foundation and Edward C. Moore Jr. Gifts, 1967 (67.231.1). The Metropolitan Museum of Art/Art Resource, NY. © 2012 Frank Lloyd Wright Foundation, Scottsdale, AZ/Artists Rights Society (ARS), New York; **p. 47:** Kiki Smith, *Untitled*, 1993. Paper and papier-maché, life-size. © Kiki Smith, courtesy The Pace Gallery; **p. 54:** Richard Stonehouse/Camera Press/Redux; **p. 60:** Library of Congress, Rare Book and Special Collections; **p. 73:** WDCN/University College London/Photo Researchers, Inc.; **p. 74:** "Worry" by Nation Magazine from the November 13, 2000 issue of *The Nation*. Reprinted with permission from The Nation.; **p. 78:** Charles Gatewood/The Image Works; **p. 81:** Courtesy of the Ad Council; **p. 82:** Scala/Art Resource, NY; **p. 86:** Erich Lessing/Art Resource, NY.

PART 2: Opener: © The McGraw-Hill Companies, Inc.; **p. 108:** Guiseppe Dall'Arche/Grand Tour/Corbis; **p. 109 (top):** L. Clark/Corbis RF; **p. 109 (bottom):** S. Solum/PhotoLink/Getty Images RF; **p. 119:** Boris Roessler/dpa/Corbis; **p. 122:** Courtesy of the Ad Council; **p. 129:** Kiki Smith, *Untitled*, 1993. Paper and papier-maché, life-size. © Kiki Smith, courtesy The Pace Gallery; **p. 134:** Tony Freeman/PhotoEdit; **p. 135:** Courtesy of the Ad Council; **p. 138:** Concept & Photography: Erik Adigard/M-A-D; **p. 143:** Courtesy of NASA; **p. 145 (top):** Digital Vision/Getty RF; **p. 145 (bottom):** PA Wire/PA Photos/AP Images; **p. 156:** Courtesy of The Advertising Archives; **p. 158:** Illustration by Oleg Volk, olegvolk.net.

Credits

PART 3: Opener: Olaf Kowalzik/Getty Images; **p. 162:** Werner Forman/Art Resource, NY; **p. 167 (left):** Digital Image © The Museum of Modern Art/Licensed by SCALA / Art Resource, NY; **p. 167 (right):** Courtesy the Los Angeles Times; **p. 171:** © 2012 Jenny Holzer Studio, member Artists Rights Society (ARS), New York; **p. 183:** Everett Collection, Inc.

PART 4: Opener: Don Farrall/Getty Images RF; **p. 192:** © Jan Cartwright, collage, *Self-Portrait,* 2001; **p. 202:** The screen shots and the contents are published with permission of ProQuest LLC. Further reproduction is prohibited without permission.; **p. 203:** Courtesy of WebMD, www.webmd.com.; **p. 204:** Courtesy of © 2000–2012 ITHAKA/JSTOR. All Rights Reserved.; **p. 205:** Project MUSE, The Johns Hopkins University Press; **p. 206:** © Images.com/Corbis; **p. 230:** © Marty Bucella. Reproduced by permission from www.CartoonStock.com; **p. 232: (left):** Book jacket art reprinted from SOUTH BEACH DIET by Arthur Agaston. Permission granted by Rodale, Inc. Emmaus, PA 18098; **p. 232: (right):** Susan Bordo, *Unbearable Weight: Feminism, Western Culture, and the Body.* © 2004 by the Regents of the University of California. Published by the University of California Press. © 2012 Estate of Pablo Picasso/Artists Rights Society (ARS), New York; **p. 234:** © The McGraw-Hill Companies, Inc./Mark Dierker, photographer; **p. 237:** The Library of Congress; **p. 240:** Franklin D. Roosevelt Presidential Library and Museum; **p. 242 (left):** Writing Tutorial Services, Courtesy of Center for Innovative Teaching and Learning. © The Trustees of Indiana University; **p. 242 (right):** © Plagiarism.org; **p. 246 (top):** Getty Images for Meet the Press; **p. 246 (center):** Adrian Dennis/AFP/Getty Images; **p. 246 (bottom):** Courtesy of Harold Garner, Southwestern Medical Center; **p. 264:** STScI /NASA; **p. 271:** Jacket Cover from *Jimmy Corrigan: The Smartest Kid on Earth* by Chris Ware, © 2000, 2003 by Mr. Chris Ware. Used by permission of Pantheon Books, a division of Random House, Inc.; **p. 274:** © The McGraw-Hill Companies, Inc./Mark Dierker, photographer.

PART 5: Opener: Image Source/Getty Images RF; **p. 336:** Courtesy of Lydia Nichols; **p. 340 (left):** Jack Kirby and Steve Ditko, *Amazing Fantasy* #15. SPIDERMAN TM & © 2010 Marvel Characters, Inc. Used with permission. p. 340 (right): © Robert Crumb, 2013. Used by permission, Agence Littéraire Lora Fountain & Associates, Paris, France; **p. 341:** Adrian Tomine, *Optic Nerve,* #6, p. 22. (Montreal: *Drawn and Quarterly,* Feb. 1999); **p. 343:** Jacket Cover from *Jimmy Corrigan: The Smartest Kid on Earth* by Chris Ware, © 2000, 2003 by Mr. Chris Ware. Used by permission of Pantheon Books, a division of Random House, Inc.; **p. 388:** Photographs courtesy of Jane Carter; **p. 410:** David Rumsey Map Collection: carto@luna-img.com.

PART 6: Opener: Matthew Salacuse/Getty Images; **p. 432:** Stephen Webster/Photonica/Getty Images; **p. 452:** Sara Krulwich/The New York Times/Redux; **p. 455:** Alexander Joe/AFP/Getty Images; **p. 469:** Corbis Premium/Alamy Images RF; **p. 474 (left):** Warner Bros/The Kobal Collection/Art Resource, NY; **p. 474 (right):** Polygram/Working Title/The Kobal Collection/Art Resource, NY; **p. 476:** Steve Coleman/Digital Vision/Getty Images RF; **p. 491:** Printed with the permission of Karin Roseland, North Dakota March of Dimes; **p. 493:** U.S. Department of Education. Institute of Education Sciences, National Center for Education Statistics.

PART 7: Opener: Walter B. McKenzie/Getty Images; **p. 496:** AFP/Getty Images; **p. 505:** © Alexander Calder, *Untitled,* 1976. Aluminum and steel, overall: size 910.3 x 2315.5 cm (358 3/8 x 911 5/8 in.) gross weight: 920 lb. Gift of the Collectors Committee, 1977.76.1. © The National Gallery of Art, Washington DC. Photo © Randy Duchaine/Alamy; **p. 518:** © 2012 The Andy Warhol Foundation for the Visual Arts/ARS, NY. Tate Gallery, London, Great Britain/Art Resource, NY; **p. 527:** Mary Cassatt, *At the Opera,* 1880. © Burstein Collection/Corbis; **p. 540:** *The New Yorker,* July 8, 1996. © The New Yorker Collection, 1996. Mick Stevens from cartoonbank.com. All Rights Reserved.; **p. 548:** © The McGraw-Hill Companies, Inc./Lars A. Niki, photographer; **p. 558:** Private Collection/The Bridgeman Art Library International.

PART 8: Opener: John Lee/Aurora/Getty Images; **p. 574:** Jamie Squire/Getty Images; **p. 600:** Chad Baker/The Image Bank/Getty Images RF; **p. 611:** Martin Diebel/fstop/Getty Images RF; **p. 620:** Chad Baker/Stone/Getty Images; **p. 636:** Comstock/Getty Images RF; **p. 656:** Waltraud Grubitzsch/EPA/Newscom; **p. 669:** Jumpstart Studios/Getty Images; **p. 678:** Transtock/Jupiterimages/Getty Images; **p. 686:** Library of Congress, Prints & Photographs Division; **p. 695:** M.C. Escher, *Waterfall,* 1961. © 2013 The M.C. Escher Company-Holland. All rights reserved. www.mcescher.com.

PART 9: Opener: Image Source/Getty Images RF; **p. 713:** *The New Yorker,* July 28, 2008. © J. C. Duffy/The New Yorker Collection/cartoonbank.com; **p. 722:** Howard Berman/The Image Bank/Getty Images; **p. 732:** Andrew Paterson/Photographer's Choice/Getty Images; **p. 739:** Courtesy of School of the Photographic Arts: Ottawa. Ric Frazier/Masterfile.

PART 10: Opener: Tetra images/Getty Images RF; **p. 748:** Courtesy of Cherry Tree Design, Bozeman, MT; **p. 766:** © Gerard Whyman. Reproduced by permission from www.CartoonStock.com; **p. 773:** Nick Pope/Dorling Kindersley/Getty Images; p. 780: © 2003 Mark Stivers. 11/19/03. www.markstivers.com. Reproduced by permission.; **p. 792 (top left):** BananaStock/PictureQuest RF; **p. 792 (right):** RedChopsticks/Getty Images RF; **p. 792 (left bottom):** Rachel Watson/Getty Images RF; **p. 796:** G. Newman Lowrance/Getty Images;

p. 807: De Agostini Picture Library/Getty Images; **p. 814:** Index Stock/Getty Images RF; **p. 826:** Brand X/Superstock RF; **p. 830:** © The McGraw-Hill Companies, Inc.

Documentation Foldout:

Book (Printed) MLA Style
Woolf, Virginia. *The Three Guineas.* Copyright 1938 by Harcourt Inc. Copyright renewed 1966 by Leonard Woolf. Reprinted by permission of Houghton Mifflin Harcourt Publishing Co.

Journal Article (Printed) MLA Style
Table of Contents, *English Journal,* vol. 101, no. 5, May 2012. First page of "Juxtaposing Immigrant and Adolescent Girl Experiences: Literature for All Readers," by Mary Amanda Stewart," *English Journal,* v01. 101, No. 5, May 2012. Copyright © Mary Amanda Stewart and The National Council of Teachers of English. Reprinted by permission.

Journal Article from an Online Database MLA Style
EBSCO Host Academic Search Premier page showing listing and abstract of "Teaching History with Comic Books: A Case Study of Violence, War, and the Graphic Novel by Alicia C. Decker. *History Teacher,* vol. 45, Issue 2, February 2012, 169–188. Reproduced by permission of EBSCO Host Copyright Agent.

Short Work on a Website MLA Style
Screenshot of the journal article, "E-books and the Personal Library," by Joseph Esposito, *The Scholarly Kitchen,* August 20, 2012. Copyright © Joseph Esposito. Reprinted by permission.

Book (Printed) APA Style
Title and copyright page, *Theories of Personality.* Jess Feist, Gregory J. Feist, Tomi-Ann Roberts, Eighth Edition. Copyright © 2013 by Jess Feist, Gregory J. Feist, and Tomi-Ann Roberts. Reprinted by permission of The McGraw-Hill Companies.

Journal Article (Printed) APA Style
Table of contents, *American Educator,* vol. 36, No. 1, Spring, 2012. First page of "Cognitive Scientist: Why Does Family Wealth Affect Learning," by Daniel T. Willingham, *American Educator,* vol. 36, No. 1, Spring, 2012. Copyright © American Educator and Daniel T. Willingham. Reprinted by permission.

Journal Article from an Online Database APA Style
EBSCO Host Academic Search Premier page showing listing and abstract of "Scientific cousins: The Relationship between Charles Darwin and Francis Galton' by Raymond E. Fancher. *American Psychologist,* 64(2), 84–92. Reproduced by permission of EBSCO Host Copyright Agent.

Short Work on a Website APA Style
Screenshot of "Memory Enhanced by Simple Break after Reading," from the Psyblog Website by Jeremy Dean. Copyright © 2012 Jeremy Dean. Reprinted by permission.

Index

A

a, an, 580, 713–16, G14. *See also* Articles
(*a, an, the*)
Abbreviations, 820–24
    acronyms, 354, 808, 812, 822
    apostrophes in plurals of, 777
    to avoid, 823–24
    of business names, 821
    capitalizing, 808, 812, 820
    common do's and don'ts, 821
    in government documents, 329
    of group authors, 295, 353–54
    initialisms, 822, 823
    Latin, 821, 824
    online, 542, 823
    parentheses around, 798
    periods in, 820
    in personal names, 822
    of specific years, hours, numbers, and dollars, 823
    of titles before and after names, 821–22
    of titles in citations, 295, 301–02
    unfamiliar, 822
about, 742
Abridged dictionaries, 558–59
absolutely, 497
Absolute phrases, 530, 594, 675
Abstract nouns, 575
Abstracts
    in APA papers, 365, 369–70, 379, 382
    in business reports and proposals, 491
    in critical reading, 109, 231
    in database searching, 215, 220
    in dissertations, 365
    in previewing, 231
    in research or laboratory reports, 460
Abstract words, 88, 186, 551–52, 575
Academic context, 16
Academic degrees, 822
Academic honesty/integrity. *See* Plagiarism
Academic Info, 213
Academic Onefile, 215
Academic Search Premier, 215, 217

Academic writing. *See also* Literature and humanities, writing in; Sciences and social sciences, writing in
    analysis of assignments, 17–19
    audience, 12–16
    collaborative, 26–28
    critical framework for, 121
    discipline-specific vocabulary in, 457–58, 542–43
    essay exams, 469–75
    evidence in, 40–42
    format of, 95–99
    genre and context for, 16–17
    idea generation in, 20–25
    in literature and humanities, 432–54
    organization of, 33–40
    paragraph development in, 59–63
    portfolios in, 99–103
    purpose of writing, 10–11, 17
    responsibilities to readers, 4
    sample papers, 43–44, 95–99, 127–30, 147–53, 336–46, 381–88, 408–15, 429–30, 442–46, 448–51, 461–68
    style guide selection, 95, 200, 437, 457
    subjunctive in, 651
    thesis statement in, 29–32. *See also* Thesis/thesis statement
    tone in, 15–16
    topic selection in, 20–26. *See also* Topic
Academic years and terms, 808
Academy of American Poets, 225
accede, 567
accept, except, 565, G14
Accessibility of website, 165, 181
Accuracy
    in science writing, 456
    in source representation, 791
    in synonyms, 560
    in visuals, 78–80
Acknowledgments, 379
Acknowledging sources. *See also* Citations; Documentation styles
    common knowledge and, 249–50
    reasons for, 288, 347, 389, 416
    responsibilities for, 5–7

Acronyms
    as abbreviations, 822
    brackets around, 354
    capitalizing, 808, 812
    definition of, 822
    in online communication, 172, 542
    pronunciation of, 822
Action verbs, 670
Active listening, 190
Active reading. *See* Critical reading and thinking
Active voice
    concise writing and, 501
    definition of, 652
    emphasis from, 535–36
    in the humanities, 439
    passive voice *vs.,* 652–54
    reasons for using, 536, 653–54
    in résumés, 488
    shifting voice, 652–53, 679–80
    transitive verbs and, 589
actually, 497
AD, BC, CE, BCE, 823
adapt, adopt, G14
Addresses
    for business correspondence, 477–78
    commas in, 761
    e-mail, 834
    numbers in, 827
add up to, 723
Ad hominem fallacy, 7, 159
Adjective(s), 669–75
    absolute, 675
    adverbs *vs.,* 669–70
    bad and *good,* 671–72
    commas separating, 749, 755, 756
    comparative form, 580, 581, 674–75
    compound, 830–31
    coordinate, 755, 756
    cumulative, 755, 756
    definition of, 529, 580
    functions of, 576, 669–70
    grammar checkers and, 671
    -ly endings on, 672
    nouns used as, 673
    as object complements, 672
    ordering of, 580, 673, 732–33, 756

I1

Index

Adjective(s) (*continued*)
  overuse of, 732
  participles and participial phrases as, 529, 593, 638, 727
  placement of, 529, 580
  plurals not used for, 669
  positive form, 674
  prepositions with, 592, 733
  pronouns as, 580
  proper, 809–10
  as subject complements after linking verbs, 670, 671
  superlative form, 580, 674–75
Adjective clauses, 595
Adjective phrases, 529–30
admit, 726
adopt, adapt, G14
Adverb(s), 669–75
  adjectives *vs.*, 669–70
  badly and *well*, 671–72, G15
  beginning a sentence, 710–11
  clauses, 576, 596, 758
  comparative form, 581, 674–75
  in compound adjectives, 831
  conjunctive. *See* Conjunctive adverbs
  definition of, 529
  functions of, 581, 669–70
  grammar checkers and, 671
  hard and *hardly*, 737
  hyphens and, 831
  negative, 735
  not and *no*, 736–37
  not used with direct objects, 671
  as particles, 722
  phrases, 529
  placement of, 529, 734–35
  positive form, 674
  prepositional phrases as, 592
  sentence variety and, 529
  such and *so*, 737
  superlative form, 674–75
  too and *either*, 736
  too and *so*, 736
  word order and, 711, 734–35
Adverb clauses
  commas setting off nonessential, 758
  functions of, 576, 596
  placement of, 529
adverse, averse, G14
Advertisements
  comma splices in, 614
  critique of, 121–22
  documenting: APA style for, 374; MLA style for, 328
  as visual arguments, 134

advice, advise, 563, 565, G14
advise, 726
affect, effect, 565, G14
African Americans, 547
after, 511, 513, 603
Afterwords, citing, 311, 363, 396
aggravate, irritate, G14
a great deal of, 719
agree, 726
Agreement. *See* Pronoun-antecedent agreement; Subject-verb agreement
agree to, agree with, G14
ain't, G14
Alignment, in design, 162
all
  count and noncount nouns with, 719
  placement of, 580
  pronoun-antecedent agreement, 633
  subject-verb agreement, 625
all-, 831–32
Alliteration, 447
allow, 726
all ready, already, 565, G14
all right, alright, G14
all together, altogether, G14
allude, elude, refer to, 565, G14
Allusion, 435
allusion, illusion, 565, G14
-ally and *-ly* suffixes, 567
Almanac of American Politics, 209
Almanacs, 209
almost, 688
almost, most, G14
a lot, alot, G14
already, 55
already, all ready, 565, G14
alright, all right, G14
altar, alter, 565
Alternating method, in comparison-contrast, 60–61
"Alternative Energy: Does It Really Offer an Alternative?" (Smith), 43–44, 96–99
Alternative viewpoints, 145–46
although
  in sentence fragments, 600
  in subordination, 511, 513, 603
altogether, all together, G14
always, avoiding statements with, 135
am, 639
a.m., 823
Ambiguity
  as and, 513
  comma use to avoid, 748, 762–63

in comparisons, 701–02
in limiting modifiers, 688
in pronoun reference, 665
in sentence fragments, 604
American Heritage Book of English Usage, 559
American Heritage College Dictionary, 558
American Heritage Dictionary of Idioms, 555
American Indians, 547
American National Biography, 209
American Psychological Association style guidelines. *See* APA style
American Rhetoric, 225
among, amongst, G14
among, between, G14
amoral, immoral, G14
amount, number, G14
Amounts, subject-verb agreement in, 626–27
Ampersand, 352
an, a, 580, 713–16, G14. *See also* Articles (*a, an, the*)
Analogous colors, 168
Analogy
  definition, 552
  false, 156–57
Analysis
  of assignments, 17–19, 192–93, 270–72
  of drama, 451–54
  of essay exam questions, 471–72
  of fiction, 440–46
  of genres, 9, 17–18, 435
  interpretive, 440–46
  as method of development, 193
  in note making, 262–63
  in paragraph development, 62
  of poetry, 446–51
  prior to writing, 120–22, 433
  process analysis, 59–60
  in research projects, 192–93, 270–72
  in revising, 82–83
  of thesis statement, 31–33
  of writing situation, 9–17
analyze, 18, 192, 472
and
  in compound subjects, 585, 623
  in coordinating independent clauses, 583, 616, 750
  in parallel structures, 520
  pronoun-antecedent agreement, 634
  in sequences, 508
  subject-verb agreement, 623
AND, as Boolean operator, 219

and/or, G15
and others, 294, 824. *See also* et al.
and so forth, 824
Anecdotes, 35, 64
Annotated bibliographies, 203–04
Annotation
  of images, 115
  note making *vs.*, 251
  on notes, 470
  of online texts, 114
  in reading critically, 114–17
  in summaries, 256
  of working bibliographies, 203–04
  in writing about literature, 432–33, 434
Anonymous (unsigned) sources
  APA style for: in-text citations, 354; reference list entries, 359
  Chicago style for, 393–94
  MLA style for: in-text citations, 295; entry in works-cited list, 308
another
  count and noncount nouns with, 719
  subject-verb agreement, 625
answer, 708
ante-, anti-, G15
Antecedents of pronouns. *See also* Pronoun-antecedent agreement
  agreement of, 630–34
  clarity of pronoun reference to, 664–67
  collective nouns as, 634
  compound, 634
  definition of, 577, 630
  generic noun as, 631–33, 682
  indefinite pronouns as, 631–33
  singular *vs.* plural, 628–29
Anthologies, documenting
  APA style for, 363
  Chicago style for, 395
  MLA style for, 297, 309–10
anti-, ante-, G15
Antonyms, 560
Anxiety, in presentations, 187
anxious, eager, G15
any
  in comparisons, 701
  count and noncount nouns with, 719
  pronoun-antecedent agreement, 633
  subject-verb agreement, 625
anybody, 625, G15
anymore, any more, G15
anyone
  pronoun-antecedent agreement, 682
  subject-verb agreement, 625

anyone, any one, G15
any other, 701
anyplace, G15
anything, 625
anyways, anywheres, G15
APA style, 347–88. *See also* In-text citations, APA-style; Reference list, APA-style
  abstracts in, 379, 382
  author notes in, 382
  directory to models: in-text citations, 350; reference list entries, 360–61
  disciplines using, 201, 457
  formatting a paper in, 377–81
  in-text citations models, 347–57
  notes in, 376–77
  parenthetical notes: described, 349; directory to, 350; models, 348–57
  printing, paper, and binding, 380, 381
  reasons for citing sources, 347
  reference lists: directory to, 360–61; model entries, 358–76
  sample paper in, 381–88
  [sic] in, 800
Apology, letters of, 479–81
Apostrophes, 773–78
  common do's and don'ts, 774
  in compound nouns, 776–77
  in contractions and abbreviated years, 774, 777
  grammar checkers and, 775
  misuse of, 774
  plurals and, 774, 775–76, 777–78
  possession indicated by, 657, 773–77
Appeals
  analyzing, 120
  bandwagon appeal fallacy, 157
  to credibility (ethos), 143
  to emotions (pathos), 144–45
  to intellect (logos), 142–43
  wise use of, 144
appear
  infinitive after, 726
  as linking verb, 589, 670
Appendixes, in research reports, 460–61
Appositives/appositive phrases
  colons and, 801
  commas and, 757
  dashes and, 796–97
  definition of, 512, 530, 591, 660, 757
  as fragments, 605
  placement of, 530

pronoun case in, 660
to subordinate information, 511, 512
appreciate, 647
Appropriate language, 541, 543
Architectural renderings, 77
Archive.org, 225
are, 501, 639
are, our, 565
Arguable claim, 73
argue, 18, 192
Argumentative writing. *See* Persuasive argument
Arguments, 134–60
  appeals in, 120, 142–45, 157
  assumptions in, 147
  audience for, 142–44
  circular, 157
  claims in, 134, 138–41
  classical model, 154
  counterevidence in, 84, 135, 145–47, 190, 267
  evidence in. *See* Evidence
  exploratory, 120, 134–35, 137, 147–53
  logical fallacies in, 156–59
  logical reasoning in, 135–37, 154
  oral, 144
  organization models, 154–55
  persuasive, 134–35
  purpose of, 11
  revising, 159
  Rogerian model, 154–55
  sample paper, 147–53
  thesis-driven, 120, 134–35, 137, 147–53
  tone in, 136
  topic selection in, 140
  Toulmin model, 155
  visuals as, 134
around, 742
Articles *(a, an, the)*
  a or *an* usage, 713–16, G14
  in alphabetizing titles, 308, 359
  capitalizing, in titles and subtitles, 810–11
  with common nouns, 714–16
  definite and indefinite, 714–16
  definition of, 714
  as determiners, 580
  with proper nouns, 717
  the usage, 713, 715–16
  zero, 714
Articles in periodicals (online and printed)
  copying from databases, 220

Articles in periodicals (online and printed) (*continued*)
  databases of: general, 215–17; specialized, 437
  documentation: APA style for, 366–70; *Chicago* style for, 397–402; CSE style for, 422–26; MLA style for, 315–19
  documenting articles from online databases, 306–07, 315–18, 366–68, 392, 399–400, 401, 423, 424
  documenting online articles, 315–16, 366–69, 399–400, 401
  documenting printed articles, 315–18, 328–31, 366–70, 374–76, 397–98, 400–02, 406, 422–23, 424, 425, 428
  finding, 215–20
  finding bibliographic information for, 315–19, 366–67, 398–400, 422–24
  format for online. *See* Online articles, documenting
  magazine, 316–17, 367–68, 400, 424–25
  microform, 318–19
  newspaper, 317–18, 368–69, 400–02, 425–26
  in PDFs, 215, 218, 315
  quotation marks around titles of, 783–84
  URLs of, 316, 367, 400, 425
Arts and Humanities Citation Index, 437
Art works, documenting
  APA style for, 374
  Chicago style for, 405
  MLA style for, 327
as
  ambiguity of, 513
  in comparisons, 522, 662, 702
  to indicate time, 512
  pronoun case with, 662
  in similes, 553
  in subordination, 513, 603
as, as if, like, G15
as, because, since, G15
ascent, assent, 565
as cited in, 356
as follows, 801
Asians, Orientals, 547
as if
  subjunctive with, 651
  in subordination, 513, 603

as if, as, like, G15
ask
  indirect object with, 590, 707
  infinitive after, 726
Ask.com, 213
ask out, 642, 723
aspect, 497
assent, ascent, 565
assess, 18, 192
Assignment(s)
  analyzing, 17–19
  assignment calculators, 194
  due dates for, 18
  in literature and humanities, 440
  for research projects, 192–93
  scheduling, 18, 19
  in sciences and social sciences, 459
Assignment calculators, 194
Assistive Technology Resource Center, 181
Assonance, 447
Assumptions, in arguments, 147, 155
Asterisks
  in e-mails, 174, 811
  in wildcat searches, 219
as though, 651
as well as, 622
Asynchronous media, 182. *See also* Blogs and blog postings; Discussion list postings; E-mails
at
  to indicate location, 741
  to indicate time, 741
  in *where* questions, G15
at all times, 498
Atlases. *See* Maps
at no time, 498
Attachments, e-mails, 174
at that point in time, 498
At the Opera (Cassatt), 527
at the present time, 498
Audience
  academic, 12–16
  analyzing, 9, 12–17
  appealing to, 142–44
  for business reports and proposals, 491
  design and, 163
  for e-mails, 172
  general *vs.* specialist, 13
  information provided to, 13
  instructor as, 14–15, 17
  language and, 13
  for multimedia presentations, 184
  for portfolios, 100

  for research projects, 193
  responsibilities to, 4
  revising for, 84
  tone and, 15–16
  for websites, 176
audience, 625
Audio aids, in presentations, 187
Audiobooks, documenting
  APA style for, 373
  MLA style for, 325
Audio sources, documenting
  APA style for, 372–74
  Chicago style for, 404–05
  MLA style for, 322–28
Author(s)
  anonymous, 295, 308, 354, 359, 393–94
  in anthologies, 297, 309, 363, 395
  APA style: in-text citations, 350–55; reference list, 358–62
  of audio and visual sources, 322–23
  avatars, 322
  Chicago style, 391–95
  CSE style, 418–22
  editors and, 309–10, 394, 395
  expertise of, 233
  group or corporate, 295, 309, 353–54, 362, 394, 420–21
  MLA style: in-text citations, 293–96; Works-cited list, 305–09
  multiple. *See* Multiple authors
  pseudonyms of, 309
  with the same surname, 296, 355, 362
  single. *See* Single authors
  two or more sources by the same, 290, 296, 309, 354–55, 360–62, 394
  with two or more works published in the same year, 355, 360–61
  use of name in writing about literature, 439
  vested interests of, 233
Author-date system, 389. *See also* APA style; CSE style
Authority. *See* Credibility
Author notes, 382, 459
Auxiliary verbs. *See* Helping (auxiliary) verbs
Avatars, 322, 656. *See also* Persona
averse, adverse, G14
avoid, 726
avoided, 736
awful, awfully, G15
awhile, a while, G15
Awkward shifts. *See* Shifts

B

Background information, 13, 14, 64, 115, 210
Backup of data files, 199
bad, badly, 671–72, G15
Bandwagon appeal fallacy, 157
bare, bear, 565
barely, 673
barge in on, 723
Bar graphs, 74–76, 80
Bartleby.com, 306, 559
Base form, of verbs, 636, 637, 640
Bcc (blind carbon copy), 173
BCE, CE, BC, AD, 823
be
    in expletive constructions, 705–06
    faulty predication and, 697–98
    forms of, 639
    as helping verb, 621, 639, 728
    as linking verb, 589, 670
    omitted from absolute phrases, 594
    questions beginning with, 710
    subject-verb agreement with, 621
bear, bare, 565
because
    in sentence fragments, 600
    as subordinating term, 511, 513, 603
because, as, since, G15
because of, 742
become, 589, 670
been, 639
before, as subordinating term, 511, 513, 603
beg, 726
Begging the question fallacy, 157
begin, 726
being, 639
being as, being that, G15
Beliefs, claims of value and, 139
belong, 647
beside, besides, G15
between, among, G14
Bhagavad-Gita, citation of, 299
Bias
    in field research, 228
    gender, 545–47, 632
    in interviews, 227
    keeping an open mind, 234
    in language, 87, 544–47
    in observations and surveys, 228
Biased language, 87, 544–47
Bible, citation of. *See also* Sacred texts
    in APA style, 356, 365
    in *Chicago* style, 397
    in MLA style, 299–300, 313–14

Bibliographic notes, 250, 331–32, 407–08
Bibliographies. *See also* Reference list, APA-style; Reference list, CSE-style; Works cited list, *Chicago*-style; Works cited list, MLA-style
    annotated, 203–04
    list of works consulted, 305
    notes for, 250, 331–32, 407–08
    as sources, 210
    working, 200–05
Bilingual dictionaries, 562
Bing search engine, 213
Biographical criticism, 436
Biographical reference works, 209
Black's Law Dictionary, 559
Blackwell Dictionary of Political Science, 207
Blind carbon copy (Bcc), 173
Block method, in comparison-contrast, 60–61
Block quotations
    APA style for, 377
    MLA style for, 334
    placement of in-text citation in, 292
    punctuation of, 782–83
Block-style business letters, 477–78
Blogs and blog postings
    documenting: APA style for, 371–72; *Chicago* style for, 404; CSE style for, 427; MLA style for, 321
    evaluating, 236–39
    language shortcuts in, 542, 823
    locating, 214, 215
    sarcasm in, 136
    vlogs, 372–73
Blog search engines, 214
blue in color, 498
board, bored, 565
Body
    of business letter, 478
    of multimedia presentations, 185
    paragraph development in, 59–63
    planning, 34
    revising globally, 82–83
Boldface type, 165, 811
Bookending borrowed material, 253, 291
Bookmarking, 251
Book Review Digest, 437
Books
    avoiding abbreviating parts of, 823–24
    commonplace, 20
    divisions of, using numerals with, 828

    documenting: APA style for, 358–65; *Chicago* style for, 390–97; CSE citation-sequence style for, 417–18; CSE documentation style for, 418–22; CSE name-year style for, 418–20; MLA style for, 305–15
    e-books, 307–08, 392–93
    editions other than the first, 311, 363, 395
    introductions, prefaces, forewords, or afterwords by a different author, 311, 363, 396
    popular *vs.* scholarly, 197, 231, 232–33
    reprinted or republished, 313, 355–56, 364
    series of, 313, 397
    titles of, 173, 359, 815
Book series, documenting
    Chicago style for, 397
    MLA style for, 313
Boolean operators, 218, 219
bored, board, 565
borrow from, 744
both
    count and noncount nouns with, 719
    placement of, 580
    pronoun-antecedent agreement, 633
    subject-verb agreement, 625
both...and
    as correlative conjunctions, 521, 583
    indicating addition, 506, 508
    subject-verb agreement and, 623
Brackets
    for acronyms in in-text citations, 354
    in quotations, 786, 800
    to replace parentheses within parentheses, 800
    with *sic,* 800
Brainstorming, 22, 470
brake, break, 565
Brantley, Ben, 452–54
Breadcrumb (click) trails, 178, 179
break, brake, 565
breath, breathe, 563
bring, 590
bring, take, G15
British English
    commas and periods with quotation marks, 785
    serial commas in, 754
    single and double quotations marks in, 781
    spelling, 563

Broadening, of topic, 25–26
Brochures, documenting
  APA style for, 375
  MLA style for, 314
Browsers, 79, 180, 181
burst, bursted; bust, busted, G15
Business and public writing
  e-mail etiquette, 483
  job application letters, 482–86
  letters of complaint, apology, and rejection, 479–81
  memos, 481–82
  press releases, 314, 492–94
  reports and proposals, 490–92
  résumés, 486–90
  standard letter format, 477–79, 802
Business letters. *See also* Business and public writing
  colons in, 802
  envelopes and addresses for, 477–78
  format for, 477–78
  guidelines for, 477
  on plain paper, 478–79
  sample, 478–79
  standard elements in, 478–79
Business names
  abbreviations in, 824
  capitalizing, 810
  as singular, 627–28
bust, busted; burst, bursted, G15
but
  in contrast, 508
  in coordination, 506, 583, 750
  in correcting comma splices and fused sentences, 616
  in parallelism, 520
buy, 590
buy from, 744
by, 741–42, 744

C

Cached results, 370
Calder, Alexander, 505
Calendars, 18–19
call, 590
call for, 555
call forth, 555
call into question, 555
call it a day, 555
call it quits, 555
Call numbers, searching by, 223
call on the carpet, 723
calm down, 723
can
  meanings of, 729
  as modal verb, 579, 641, 728, 729
  subject-verb agreement, 621
can, could, 729
can, may, G15
capital, capitol, 565, G15
Capitalization, 807–12
  of abbreviations and acronyms, 812, 820
  altering with brackets, 786, 800
  common do's and don'ts, 808
  in e-mails, 483
  of first-person pronouns, 808
  of first word of a sentence, 807–09
  of independent clauses linked by colons, 809
  of interjection *O,* 811
  omitting, 811
  prefixes before, 832
  of proper nouns and adjectives *vs.* common nouns, 808, 809–10
  of questions that are incomplete sentences, 794
  of quoted sentences, 808–09
  spelling checkers and, 569
  in titles and subtitles, 381, 808, 810–11
Captions of figures, 279–80, 304, 335–36, 407
Caricatures, 74
carry, 708
Cartoons, MLA style for, 327–28
Case. *See* Pronoun case
Cassatt, Mary, 527
Causation, claim of, 140
cause, 726
Cause, prepositions indicating, 742
Cause and effect
  conjunctions and, 508
  for in, 742
  in paragraph development, 62
  prepositions and, 742
  subordinating terms and, 607–08
  transitional expressions indicating, 55
Cc line, in communications, 172, 478, 481, 802
CD-ROMS
  APA style for, 373
  Chicago style for, 404
  MLA style for, 312, 322
CE, AD, with dates, 823
-cede, -ceed, -sede suffixes, 567
censor, censure, G15
Cézanne, Paul, 86
cf., 824
-ch, plurals of words that end in, 569
change, 708
character, 497
Characters, literary, 435, 679
Charts. *See also* Visuals
  MLA style for, 303–04, 328
  pie, 74–76
Chat, online. *See* Instant messaging
Chicago Manual of Style, 16th ed., 389, 437. *See also Chicago* style
Chicago Manual online, 389
Chicago style, 389–415. *See also* Works cited list, *Chicago*-style
  abbreviated *vs.* complete notes, 390
  audio and visual sources in, 404–05
  author-date system, 389
  basic bibliographic entry format in, 390, 391–92
  bibliographic models, 392–407
  bibliography page format in, 408, 415
  books in, 390–97
  directory to models, 391
  disciplines using, 201, 389
  endnotes in, 413–14
  formatting a paper in, 407–08
  government publications in, 406
  indirect sources in, 407
  interviews in, 406
  note and bibliography system, 390
  other electronic sources in, 402–04
  percent symbols in, 828
  periodicals in, 397–402
  personal communications in, 406
  reasons for citing sources, 389
  sample paper in, 408–15
  [sic] in, 800
  tables and figures in, 407
child, children, 621
Choice, expressions of, 508
chorus, 625
Chronological organization, 35
Chronology, transitional expressions of, 55
CIA Factbook, 209
Circular reasoning, 157
Citation indexes, 235
Citation management software, 201, 217
Citation-name system. *See* Citation-sequence and citation-name systems, CSE
Citation Project, 104, 132, 244, 790
Citations, 274–86. *See also* APA style; *Chicago* style; CSE style; MLA style
  APA in-text citations, 347–57
  author's voice *vs.,* 278–80

common knowledge and, 249–50
CSE in-text citations, 416–18
in first draft, 270–72
identifying type of source, 282
integrating into text, 275–76, 284–85, 289
MLA in-text citations, 288–305
in paraphrases, 249, 253, 275–76
reasons for, 288, 347, 389, 416
source boundaries in, 276–80, 348–49
source summaries with, 282–83
in summaries, 249, 275–76
Citation-sequence and citation-name systems, CSE
for books with group or corporate authors, 421
for books with one author, 419–20
for books with two or more authors, 420
for discussion lists or blog postings, 427
for dissertations, 422
for edited books, 421
for edited book selections or conference proceedings, 421–22
for e-mails, 428
information in, 417–18
for magazine articles, 424–25
for newspaper articles, 425–26
numbering, 429
for scholarly journal articles, 423–24
for technical reports or government documents, 428
for web pages and websites, 427
cite, site, sight, 563, G15
claim, 726
Claim-based arguments, 134, 138–41
Claims
absolute, 135
analysis of, 120–21
of causation, 140
of fact, 31–32, 138, 139
of judgment, 32, 134, 139–40
linked to grounds by warrants, 147
of policy, 139–40
signal verbs indicating, 277
supporting with appeals to readers, 142–45
supporting with reasons and evidence, 40–42
of value, 32, 139
visual, 75, 138, 156
Class discussions, contributing to, 184
Classical model of arguments, 154

Classics, 356, 365, 436
Classification. *See* Analysis
Clauses
adjective, 595
adverb, 520, 576, 596, 758
capitalization of, 809
colons and, 612, 613
commas and, 512, 758–59
conditional, 651
consolidating, 502
coordinating independent, 506–07, 750
dashes and, 533, 612, 613
definition of, 506, 594, 704
dependent. *See* Subordinate clauses
independent. *See* Independent clauses
noun, 596
as sentence fragments, 595, 602–03, 607–08
stated subject in, 704–05
subordinate. *See* Subordinate clauses
Clichés
avoiding, 555–56
not used in conclusions, 67
quotation marks not used for, 781, 785
Click (breadcrumb) trails, 178, 179
climactic, climatic, G15–G16
Climactic organization, 35
close, 708
Close reading, 18, 440. *See also* Critical reading and thinking
Closing paragraphs. *See* Conclusions
Closings
in e-mails, 174
in letters, 478
Clustering, 22–23, 33
Coauthored projects, 45. *See also* Collaboration
"Code of Best Practices in Fair Use for Media Literacy Education," 6
Code shifting, between media, 3
Coherence
in outlines, 37–38
in paragraphs, 46, 52–58
revising for, 86
Collaboration, 26–28, 45
Collective nouns
definition of, 575, 625
as pronoun antecedents, 634
as subjects, 625–26
subject-verb agreement, 625–26
Colloquialisms, 541
Colons, 800–02
appositives and, 801

in bibliographic citations, 802
in business letters, 802
coordinating conjunctions and, 612
in correcting fragments, 606, 617
emphasis and, 533
in formal business correspondence, 802
introducing examples, explanations, appositives, or lists, 801
joining independent clauses, 612, 613
not between preposition and object, 802
not between verb and object, 802
quotations and, 760, 786, 787, 801
in ratios, 802
in scripture, 802
before subtitles, 800, 802
in time notations, 802
Colors, in document design, 167–68
Color-vision impairment, 168
Color wheel, 168
The Columbia Dictionary of Modern Literary and Cultural Criticism, 437
.com sites, reliability and, 236–37
come across, 723
Comic books, 327–28
command, 726
Commands
for describing processes, 534
end punctuation of, 792–93, 794
imperative mood in, 650
subject in, 602
unstated subjects in, 534, 585, 602, 705
Commas, 748–63. *See also* Commas, common misuses; Comma splices
absolute phrases and, 752
with appositives, 757
British use of, 754, 785
clarity and, 748
common do's and don'ts, 749
in compound sentences, 598, 750
with conjunctive adverbs and transitional phrases, 753
with contrasting information, 753
in coordinate adjectives, 755, 756
coordinating conjunctions and, 598, 612, 750
in dates, 761–62
in expression of direct address, 753–54
in interjections, 753
after introductory elements, 749, 751–52

Commas (*continued*)
  in names and titles, 761
  as neutral marks, 798
  nonessential elements and, 608, 757–59
  in numbers, 760
  in parenthetical and conversational expressions, 753–54
  in place names and addresses, 761
  with quotations, 759–60, 785, 787
  to replace omitted words, 763
  to separate ideas, 763
  to separate independent clauses, 612, 613
  to separate items in a series, 506, 749, 754
  with signal phrases, 759–60, 787
  subordinate structures and, 512
  with tag questions, 753–54
Commas, common misuses
  common do's and don'ts, 749
  after coordinating conjunctions, 749
  before coordinating conjunctions, 754
  between cumulative adjectives, 756
  with indirect quotations, 760
  before or after a series, 749
  between paired elements, 749, 750
  to set off essential elements, 757
  to set off *that* and *which* clauses, 758–59
  between subjects and verbs, verbs and objects, 749, 763
  after subordinating conjunctions, 749
Comma splices, 611–18
  in advertising, 614
  boundaries obscured by, 612
  causes of, 613–14
  correcting, 615–17
  definition of, 611, 769
  identifying, 612–13
  semicolons and, 616, 767, 769–70
committee, 625
Common knowledge, 249–50
Commonly confused words. *See* Homonyms
Common nouns. *See also* Noun(s)
  articles with, 714–16
  count *vs.* noncount, 713–14, 715
  definition of, 575, 713
  not capitalized, 808
Commonplace books, 20
Company names
  abbreviations in, 824
  capitalizing, 810
  as singular, 627–28

Comparative adjectives and adverbs, 580, 581, 674–75
compare, 192, 472
Comparison and contrast. *See also* Comparisons; Contrast
  block *vs.* alternating method, 60–61
  paragraph development through, 60–61
  transitional expressions in, 55
Comparisons
  of adjectives and adverbs, 674–75
  as in, 662
  incomplete or ambiguous, 701–02
  parallelism in, 522
  redundant, 674
  than in, 662
  transitional expressions in, 55
Compass directions, 808, 810
Compelling words, 550–53
Complaint letters, 479
complement, compliment, 565, G16
Complementary colors, 168
Complements
  object, 590, 672, 708–09
  subject. *See* Subject complements
complete, 708
Complete predicates, 587
Complete subjects, 585
Complete verbs, 600–01, 639–42
Complex sentences, 528, 598, 770
Composition. *See* Drafting
Compound adjectives, 830–31
Compound antecedents, 634
Compound-complex sentences, 528, 598–99
Compound nouns, 571, 776–77
Compound numbers, hyphenation of, 832
Compound objects, pronoun case in, 658
Compound possessives, 658
Compound predicates, 587, 605–06
Compound sentences
  commas in, 598, 750
  comma splices in, 614
  conjunctive adverbs and, 598
  coordinating conjunctions and, 598, 750
  definition of, 528, 598, 750
  elliptical constructions in, 700–01
  semicolon overuse and, 750
  in sentence variety, 528
Compound subjects
  agreement of pronouns with, 634
  definition of, 585
  pronoun case in, 658, 659
  subject-verb agreement with, 623–24

Compound words
  hyphens in, 776–77, 833
  plurals of, 571
  possessives of, 658, 659, 776–77
Comprehension, in reading, 108–14
Compressed music files, 326
Computerized databases. *See* Databases
Computerized library catalogs. *See* Library catalogs
Computerized sources. *See* Electronic sources; Online sources
Computers. *See also* Internet; Websites and web pages
  assignment calculators, 194
  backing up, 199
  calendars, 18–19
  citation management software, 201, 217
  electronic calendars, 18
  in essay exams, 473
  grammar checkers. *See* Grammar checkers
  peer revising on, 90–92
  spelling checkers, 93, 569, 775
  style checkers. *See* Style checkers
Computer software. *See also specific software*
  citation management, 201, 217
  documenting: APA style for, 372; MLA style for, 322
  presentation, 187, 188
concede, 567
Concentration, 108
Concessions
  in arguments, 146
  signal verbs indicating, 277
Concise Columbia Electronic Encyclopedia, 208
Conciseness, 496–504
  brevity *vs.*, 496
  in business memos, 481–82
  in business writing, 486
  elliptical constructions and, 499, 700–01
  empty phrases and, 497
  expletive constructions and, 500–01
  nouns derived from verbs and, 501
  passive voice and, 501. *See also* Passive voice
  repetition and redundancy and, 498–99
  roundabout expressions and, 498
  strategies to increase, 88–89, 502
  style checkers and, 499
  wordy expressions and, 497–99

Conclusions
　in business reports and proposals, 491
　five don'ts for, 67
　inverted-funnel, 65
　in multimedia presentations, 185
　planning, 34
　previewing, 231
　in research or laboratory reports, 460
　revising, 84
　thesis restatement, 65–66
　transitional expressions in, 55
　writing, 65–68
Concrete vs. abstract words
　choosing between, 551–52
　definitions of, 575
　in multimedia presentations, 186
　in revising, 88
Conditional clauses, subjunctive verbs in, 651
Conference presentations, APA style for, 373
Conference proceedings, documenting
　APA style for, 376
　CSE style for, 421–22
　MLA style for, 314
Confidentiality, in e-mails, 173
Confusing shifts. *See* Shifts
congressional documents, MLA style for, 329
Conjunctions
　addition and, 508
　in compound subjects, 585, 623–24
　coordinating. *See* Coordinating conjunctions
　correlative, 506, 521, 583, 710–11
　definition of, 623
　functions of, 576, 583
　inverted word order and, 710–11
　meaning of, 507, 508
　in parallelism, 520, 521
　subordinating, 511, 583–84, 595–96, 602–03
Conjunctive adverbs
　commas and, 753
　comma splices and, 613, 616
　in compound sentences, 598
　in coordinating independent clauses, 508
　definition of, 581, 753
　list of, 581
　semicolons and, 598, 767, 768–69
Connecting paragraphs, 69–72
Connotation
　credibility and, 551
　emotional associations, 87
　in poetry, 447
　of synonyms, 550, 560
　tone and, 15, 87
Conrad, Abrams, 409–15
conscience, conscious, 565, G16
Consequences, discussing, 768
consider
　in assignments, 18
　gerund after, 726
Consistency. *See* Pronoun-antecedent agreement; Subject-verb agreement
Consonance, 447
Consonants, suffixes for words that end with, 568
contain, 647
Content notes
　APA style for, 376–77
　Chicago style for, 390–407
　creating, 332
　MLA style for, 331–32
Context
　analyzing, 9
　audience and, 16–17
　design and, 164
　in e-mails, 172
　in multimedia presentations, 184
　sentence fragments and, 604
　in websites, 176
continual(ly), continuous(ly), G16
continue, 726
Contractions
　apostrophes in, 774, 777
　double negatives in, 673
　at the ends of lines, 833
　in formal writing, 773
　with *have* not *of,* 642, 728
　in helping verbs, 641–42
Contrast. *See also* Comparison and contrast; Comparisons
　commas and, 753
　conjunctions indicating, 508
　in design, 162
　paragraph development and, 60–61
　semicolons and, 768
　subordinating terms and, 513
　transitional expressions and, 54, 55
in contrast, 55, 606
contrast, in essay exams, 472
Controlling idea. *See* Thesis/thesis statement
Convention, credibility and, 826
Conversational expressions, commas after, 753–54
convince, 726

Coordinate adjectives, 755, 756
Coordinate sentences. *See* Compound sentences
Coordinating conjunctions
　colons with, 612
　commas and, 598, 612, 750
　in compound predicates, 606
　in compound sentences, 598, 750
　in correcting comma splices and fused sentences, 616
　dashes with, 612
　function of, 506, 583
　list of, 750
　meanings of, 507, 508
　in parallelism, 520
　semicolons and, 612, 768
　in titles and subtitles, 810
Coordination. *See also* Coordinating conjunctions
　definition of, 505
　excessive, 509
　inappropriate, 508–09
　of independent clauses, 506–07
　in parallelism, 520
　punctuation in, 506, 612, 749–50, 754–56, 768
　style checkers and, 505
　subordination used with, 515
　of terms and phrases, 506
Copyright clearance
　for academic work, 6–7
　for borrowed images, 78
　for web material, 178
Corporate authors. *See* Group or corporate authors
Correlative conjunctions
　examples of, 506, 583
　function of, 583
　in parallelism, 521
　word order and, 710–11
could
　for ability, possibility, and willingness, 728, 729
　in *if* clauses, 651
　meanings of, 729
　as modal verb, 579, 641, 728, 729
　subject-verb agreement with, 621
could, can, 729
could care less, G16
could of, must of, should of, would of, G16
could've, could have, 728
council, counsel, 565
Council of Science Editors style. *See* CSE style

Index

Counterevidence
  alternative viewpoints as, 145–47
  inductive reasoning and, 135
  in multimedia presentations, 190
  in revising, 84
  in the Rogerian model, 155
  thesis statement revision from, 266
Count (countable) nouns
  articles with, 714–16
  definition, 575
  determiners with, 718–20
  examples of, 713–14
  importance of, on grammar, 576
Country names, 810
a couple of, 719
Courses, avoiding abbreviations of, 823–24
Court cases
  documenting, MLA style, 304
  italics for, 815
Cover letters, in job applications, 482–86
CQ Press Electronic Library, 224
Creative Commons License, 178
Credibility
  citations and, 5, 272, 275
  convention and, 826
  ethos, 143, 826
  evaluating, 120, 126, 262
  exclamation points and, 793
  fair use of quotations and, 260
  introductions and, 65
  online abbreviations and, 823
  plagiarism and, 246
  typographical errors and, 477
  of visuals, 239–41
  of websites, 181
  of Wikipedia, 208, 238
  word choice and, 551
Credo, 208
criteria, criterion, G16
Critical approaches, 436
Critical reading and thinking
  alternative viewpoints, 145–46
  analyzing, 120–22
  annotating, 114–17
  assumptions and, 147, 155
  comprehension in, 108–14
  critiquing, 125–31
  drawing inferences, 124
  engaging, 108
  enjoying, 111–12
  evaluation of sources, 230–45
  interpreting, 122–23
  journal keeping, 117–19, 470
  logical fallacies and, 156–59

logical reasoning and, 135–37
note taking, 251–63
paraphrasing, 110, 132
preparing to write, 119–31
previewing, 109–10
rate of reading, 109
reflecting, 114–19
sample critiques, 121–22, 127–30
steps in developing, 121
study guides and, 433
summarizing, 110–11, 132–33, 432
synthesizing, 123–24
visuals and, 126
for writing about literature, 432–35
Critical response, 123, 127–30
Critical thinking. *See* Critical reading and thinking
Critical understanding, 121
criticism, 125
Critiques
  definition of, 120, 125
  of drama, 451–54
  of literature, 433, 440–46. *See also* Literature and humanities, writing in
  of poetry, 446–51
  preparing to write, 120–27
  sample critique, 121–22, 127–30
  of sources, 125–27
  understanding *criticism,* 125
CSE style, 416–30. *See also* Citation-sequence and citation-name systems, CSE; Reference list, CSE-style
  books in, 418–22
  citation-name system in, 417–18
  citation-sequence system in, 417–18
  directory to models, 419
  disciplines using, 201, 457
  formatting papers in, 428–29
  in-text citations, 416–18
  name-year system in, 417
  parenthetical notes in, 416–18
  periodicals in, 422–26
  reasons for citing sources, 416
  reference list in, 418–28
  sample reference section, 429–30
  sections of paper in, 428–29
  [sic] in, 800
  superscript numbers in, 417
Cultural knowledge, 250
Cumulative adjectives, 755, 756
Cumulative sentences, 531
Cyberstalking, 178

D

-d, -ed endings, 637. *See also* Verb(s)
DAI (Dissertation Abstracts International), 365
Dangling modifiers, 691–93
Dashes, 796–98
  avoiding, in e-mails, 174
  avoiding overuse of, 798
  in correcting fragments, 606, 617
  creating emphasis with, 533, 796, 797, 798
  functions of, 796–97
  to indicate a break in thought, 797
  to join independent clauses, 533, 612, 613
  parentheses and commas *vs.,* 798
  quotation marks and, 786
  to set off information in a sentence, 796
  typing, 797
data, media, phenomena, G16
Databases
  abstracts on, 215, 220
  Boolean searches of, 218, 219
  copying articles from, 220
  documenting: APA style for, 366–68; *Chicago* style for, 392, 399–400, 401; CSE style for, 423, 424; MLA style for, 306–07, 315–16, 317, 318
  hidden benefits of library, 217
  HTML *vs.* PDF in, 315
  locating documentation information on, 201–03
  searching, 217–20
  secondary sources found in, 437
  selecting, 215–17
  specialized, 437
  in topic selection, 195
Data sets, 375
Dates
  abbreviations in, 823
  of access, 307, 312
  apostrophes in, 773, 777
  assignment due dates, 18
  in business letters, 478
  citations with missing, 314
  commas in, 761–62
  as common knowledge, 249
  formats for, 827
  hyphens in, 832–33
  in parentheses, 798
  question marks in parentheses after, 794
  slashes in, 805

Days of the week, 823
Debates, documenting, MLA style for, 327
decide, 726
Decimals, 828
Declarative sentences
  definition of, 534, 585
  periods at end of, 793
  sentence variety and, 534
  word order in, 704
Deconstructionist approach to criticism, 436
Deductive order of paragraphs, 53
Deductive reasoning, 120, 135–37, 154
define, 472
Definite article *(the)*, 713, 714–16. *See also* Articles *(a, an, the)*
definitely, 497
Definition, as pattern of development, 62–63
Definitions
  dashes and, 797
  in dictionary entries, 562
  extended, 62
  in paragraph development, 62–63
Degree. *See* Comparative adjectives and adverbs
Degrees, academic, abbreviating, 822
DeGroot, Heather, 381–88
Deliberate (intentional) fragments, 604, 609
deliver, 708
Delivering a presentation, methods, 186, 189
Demands, verbs in, 651–52
Demonstrative pronouns, 578
Denotation, 87, 548–49, 551, 560
deny, 726
Dependent clauses. *See* Subordinate clauses
descent, dissent, 565
describe
  in assignments, 18, 192
  indirect objects not taken by, 708
Description, as pattern of development, 59
desert, dessert, 565
Design principles, 162–63. *See also* Document design; Electronic document design
Desk dictionaries, 558–59
dessert, desert, 565
Determiners. *See also* Articles
  articles as, 580
  definition of, 713

few, a few, 718–19
less, fewer, G17
little, a little, 718–19
nouns with, 580
possessive nouns or pronouns as, 580, 718
preceding adjectives, 718
pronouns as, 580
quantifying words or phrases as, 718–20
this, that, these, and *those,* 718
word order of, 733
Development
  analysis, interpretation, and synthesis in, 193
  patterns of, 59–63
  in research projects, 193
device, devise, 565
Diagrams, 75
Dialects
  appropriate use of, 541
  definition of, 541
  double negatives in, 673
  helping verbs in, 641
  omission of verb endings in, 642
  subject-verb agreement in, 622
Dialog
  ellipses in, 804
  quotation marks in, 782
Diaries, MLA style for, 330–01
Diction. *See also* Word(s)
  connotation and, 87, 550
  definition of, 548
  denotation in, 548–49
  grammar and style checkers and, 549
  level of, 15–17
  tone and, 15
Dictionaries
  abridged, 558–59
  bilingual, 562
  discipline-specific, 207, 208, 457
  documentation of: *Chicago* style for, 396; MLA style for, 301–02, 311–12
  information in, 560–62, 733, 833
  online, 558–59
  sample entry, 561
  subject-specific, 559
  thesauruses, 560
  unabridged, 207, 559
  of usage, 559
  using, 560–62
Dictionary of Anthropology, 559
Dictionary of Business and Management, 559

Dictionary of the English Language (1755), 558
differ from, differ with, G16
Digital literacy, 3
Digital media, documenting
  CD-ROMS, 312, 322, 404
  CDs, 373
  DVD-ROMS, 312
  DVDs, 323, 404
Digital object identifiers. *See* DOI
Digital portfolios, 100–01
Digital sources. *See* Online sources
Direct address, commas after, 753–54
Direct discourse. *See* Quotation(s)
Directions, compass, 808
Direct objects
  in adjective clauses, 595
  adverbs not used to modify, 672
  of phrasal verbs, 723–24
  pronouns as, 724
  sentence structure and, 707–08
  of transitive verbs, 589
Directors, 452
Direct questions, 684, 793–94
Direct quotations, 683–84, 759–60, 780–83. *See also* Quotation(s)
Disabilities
  biased language and, 547
  website accessibility and, 165, 181
Disciplines
  capitalizing, 810
  databases for, 216
  dictionaries for, 207, 208, 457
  noncount nouns for, 715
  plagiarism and, 248
  style guide selection, 95, 200, 437, 457
  tone and, 15
  visuals and, 169
discreet, discrete, 565, G16
discuss
  in assignments, 18, 192
  gerund after, 726
Discussion list postings
  documenting: APA style for, 371; *Chicago* style for, 404; CSE style for, 427; MLA style for, 321
  evaluating, 238–39
  locating, 214, 215
Discussion section, reports in the sciences and social sciences, 460
Diseases, noncount nouns for, 715
disinterested, uninterested, G16
Disruptive modifiers, 689–90
dissent, descent, 565

Dissertation Abstracts International
(DAI), 365
Dissertations, documenting
APA style for, 365
Chicago style for, 397
CSE style for, 422
MLA style for, 314–15
Distortion, in visuals, 80, 81
Division, as pattern of development, 62
do
forms of, 641
as helping verb, 621, 639, 710, 728
in questions, 710
Documentation styles. *See also specific documentation style*
APA, 347–88
Chicago, 389–415
CSE, 416–30
MLA, 288–346
Document design, 163–70. *See also* Electronic document design; Format; Web design
abstracts, 365, 369–70
for academic texts, 95–99, 164–70
design principles, 162–63
in e-mails, 173–74
figure captions, 279–80, 304, 335–36, 407
figures: APA-style, 379–80; *Chicago*-style, 407; MLA-style, 334–36, 379–80
fonts, 95, 165–66
headers, 333
headings in, 95, 168–69
indentations, 95, 332, 333, 377–78
layout in, 165
for letters, 477–78
for lists, 166–67
margins, 95, 332, 335, 377–78
in MLA style, 332–36
overall impression in, 164–65
page numbers, 278, 316, 357, 378
portfolios, 100–01
reference lists: APA-style, 378, 380–81; CSE-style, 428–30
résumés, 486
spacing, 332, 377, 477
table numbers, 95, 334–35, 379–80, 407
visuals in, 169–70
white space in, 166
works-cited lists: *Chicago*-style, 408, 415; MLA-style, 346
for writing in the sciences and social sciences, 459–61

writing situation and, 163–64
doesn't, don't, G16
DOI (digital object identifiers)
APA style for, 358, 359, 366–67
checking, 370
Chicago style for, 399–400
in working bibliography, 200
Domains, 236. *See also* URLs
don't, doesn't, G16
Double (redundant) comparisons, 674
Double-entry reading journals, 118
Double negatives, 673
Double quotation marks. *See* Quotation marks
Double spacing, 332
Doublespeak, 544
Double (redundant) superlatives, 674–75
Drafting, 38–44. *See also* Organizing a project
acknowledging sources in first draft, 272
analysis, interpretation, and synthesis in, 265, 270–72
of body paragraphs, 41, 46–59
in collaborative projects, 45
of conclusions, 65–67
deciding whether to use visuals, 73–74
of essays in literature, 440–42
of essays in science, 457–59
evidence and counterevidence in, 40–41, 265, 267. *See also* Counterevidence; Evidence
explaining and supporting ideas, 40–41
figure captions in, 279–80, 304, 335–36, 407
integrating quotations in, 275–76, 284–85
of introductions, 63–65
organizing ideas in, 33–37, 265
outlining in, 35–37
preparing for, 38–40
prewriting in, 33
protecting your work, 42
sample paper, 42–44
signal phrases in, 276, 277, 279. *See also* Signal phrases
summaries, paraphrases, and quotations in, 272
summary of steps in, 265
supporting claims in, 270–72
thesis statements in, 264–66. *See also* Thesis/thesis statement

visuals as evidence in, 74–77, 270
writer's block and, 38, 39–40
writing methods in, 270
Drama
documenting, in MLA style, 297–98, 310
numbers in divisions of plays, 828
writing about, 451–54
Drawings. *See* Visuals
Dropbox, 174
drop in, 723
Due dates, 334
due to the fact that, 498
DVDs, documenting
Chicago style for, 404
MLA style for, 312, 323

E

each
count and noncount nouns with, 719
as determiner, 713
pronoun-antecedent agreement, 631
subject-verb agreement, 623, 625
each and every, 498, G16
eager, anxious, G15
e-books, documenting
APA style for, 358–59
Chicago style for, 392–93
MLA style for, 307–08
Economist website, 209
ed., eds., 309–10, 394, 395
Edited books, documenting
APA style for, 363
Chicago style for, 394, 395
CSE style for, 421
MLA style for, 309
Editing. *See* Revising
Editing checklists, 89
Edition numbers, 311
Editorials
connecting paragraphs in, 69–71
documenting: *Chicago* style for, 401–02; MLA style for, 319
Editors, in documentation
APA style for, 363
Chicago style for, 394, 395
MLA style for, 309–10
.edu sites, reliability and, 236–37
Education FullText, 216
effect, affect, 565, G14
-efy and *-ify* suffixes, 567
e.g., 824
e.g., i.e., 824, G16
ei/ie spelling rule, 566

either
    count and noncount nouns with, 719
    subject-verb agreement, 625
either, too, 736
either . . . or
    in coordination, 506, 508, 583
    parallelism with, 521
    pronoun-antecedent agreement, 634
    subject-verb agreement, 624
Either-or fallacy, 158
-elect, 831–32
Electronic document(s). *See also* Electronic document design; *specific electronic documents*
    backing up, 199
    designing, 165–70
    documenting: APA style for, 358–59, 370–72; *Chicago* style for, 392–93, 396, 397–407; CSE style for, 420, 423–28; MLA style for, 320–22, 328–31, 358–59, 370–72
    research logs, 198–99, 250
    résumés, 489–90
Electronic document design. *See also* Websites and web pages
    breadcrumb (click) trails, 178, 179
    color in, 167–68
    design principles in, 162–63, 180
    e-mails, 173–74, 811
    fonts in, 165–66
    genre, 176
    headings in, 168–69
    home page, 100, 176–78
    layout in, 165
    links in, 101, 178, 815, 817, 818
    lists in, 166–67
    navigation tools for, 177–78, 179
    overall impression in, 164–65
    visuals in, 169–70, 180, 188
    website content in, 179–80
    website structure, 177
    white space in, 166
Electronic résumés, 489–90
Electronic sources, documenting. *See also* Online sources
    APA style for, 370–72
    Chicago style for, 402–04
    CSE style for, 418–28
    MLA style for, 302–03, 305–31
elicit, illicit, 565, G16
Ellipses
    in APA style, 359
    in dialog, 804
    omitted lines of poetry and, 804
    in quotations, 260, 786, 803
Ellipsis points. *See* Ellipses
Elliptical construction, 499, 700–01
elude, allude, refer to, 565, G14
e mails
    addresses, line breaks in, 834
    answering, 172, 175–76, 483
    archiving, 174, 175, 483
    attachments to, 174
    capitalization in, 483, 811
    confidentiality in, 173, 175
    contact information in, 174, 483
    design conventions, 173–74
    documenting: APA style for, 357, 376; *Chicago* style for, 406; CSE style for, 428; MLA style for, 300, 303
    emoticons in, 172, 542
    etiquette for, 483
    exclamation points in, 794
    online abbreviations in, 542, 823
    paragraph format in, 174
    personal, at work, 484
    quotation marks in, 782
    revising, 174, 483
    spam in, 483
    tone in, 172, 173, 483
    writing, 172–74
Em dashes. *See* Dashes
emigrate from, immigrate to, G16
eminent, imminent, immanent, 565, G16
Emoticons, 172, 542
Emotional appeals, 144–45
Emotional associations. *See* Connotation
Emphasis
    active or passive voice in, 535–36
    asterisks for, 811
    colons for, 617
    dashes for, 617, 796, 797, 798
    in e-mails, 174, 811
    emphatic verbs, 535
    inverted word order for, 586
    italics in, 785, 815, 816
    multiple question marks and exclamation points, 793
    paragraph ordering and, 53
    parallelism and, 525
    punctuation and, 533
    quotation marks and, 781, 784–85
    quotations used for, 260
    repetition for, 56, 535
    rhythm and, 531–32
    transitional expressions and, 55
Empirical research, 455

Empty phrases, 497
encourage, 726
Encyclopedia of Life, 238–39
Encyclopedias
    appropriate use of, 207–08
    discipline-specific, 208, 457
    documenting: APA style for, 364; *Chicago* style for, 396; MLA style for, 301–02, 311–12
    Wikipedia, 208, 238
EndNote, 201
Endnotes
    APA style for, 376–77
    Chicago style for, 413–14. *See also Chicago* style
    definition, 390
    MLA style for, 331–32, 345
End punctuation, 377, 792–94. *See also* Exclamation points; Period; Question marks
end result, 498
engaged to, 744
English as a second language (ESL), 703–46
    a, an, 713, 715–16
    adjectives, 580, 669, 673, 732–33
    adverbs, 710–11, 734–35
    a great deal of, 719–20
    agreement, pronoun-antecedent, 630
    American *vs.* British English, 563, 754, 781, 785
    arguments, exploratory *vs.* persuasive, 137
    articles, 713–16, 717
    ask out, 723
    audience, understanding one's, 14
    to be, 705–06, 710
    bilingual dictionaries, 562
    borrow from, 744
    British *vs.* American English, 563, 754, 781, 785
    business, conducting in the US, 484
    buy from, 744
    can, could, 729
    capitalization, 807
    class discussions, contributing to, 184
    clichés, 556
    code-switching, by bilingual speakers, 3
    common nouns, 713, 714–16
    conciseness, 497
    conjunctions, word order and, 710–11
    connotation, 15
    continue, 705, 726

English as a second language (ESL) (*continued*)
  contractions, 728
  coordination and subordination, 516
  could, can, 729
  count nouns, 576, 713–16, 718–20
  declarative sentences, 704
  demonstrative pronouns, 718
  determiners, 718–20
  dictionaries, 559
  direct objects, 707–08
  either and *too,* 736
  e-mails, task-oriented, 173
  end, 705
  engaged to, 744
  ethos and logos, in the US, 143
  expletives, 705–06
  explicit subjects, 602
  few, a few, 718–19
  fill with, 744
  gerunds, 593, 725–26
  gestures, 189
  give in, 723
  give to, 744
  a great deal of, 719–20
  h-, articles for words beginning with, 715
  hard and *hardly,* 737
  helping verbs, 728–30
  idea generation, 20
  idioms, 555, 556
  in, 741, 742
  indirect objects, 590, 707–08
  infinitives, 593, 725–26
  introductory paragraphs, 63
  it, 705
  job applications, 74, 484
  lend to, 744
  less, fewer, 713
  little, a little, 718–19
  look up, 723
  main idea, stating the, 29
  married to, 744
  may, might, 729
  modal verbs, 579, 641, 728–30
  much, 719–20
  must, 729
  noncount nouns, 713–16, 718–20
  not and *no,* 736–37
  note making in English, 252
  nouns, 714–20
  numbers, 828
  object complements, 708–09
  obligatory words, 698
  on, 741–42

ought to, should, shall, 729
parallelism, deceptive, 520
participles, as adjectives, 727
peer revising, 90
personal experiences, writing about, 10
phrasal verbs, 555, 642, 722–24
plagiarism, 6, 247
praise for the reader, avoiding, 63
prepositions, 555, 733, 739–45
present participle, 727
progressive tenses, 647
pronouns, 630, 706, 719–20
proofreading, 94
proper nouns, 713, 717
punctuation, 512, 781, 785, 828
quantifying words or phrases, 718–20
questions, word order in, 709–10
quotation marks, 781, 785
reading for comprehension, 109
repetitions, 698
sell to, 744
sentence structure, 704–06, 710–11
sentence variety, developing an ear for, 532
serial comma, 754
shall, should, ought to, 729
should've, should have, 728
shout at, shout to, 744
so and *such,* 737
so and *too,* 736
some, 719–20
sources, conversations with, 275
spelling, 563
start, 705
study groups, 470
subjects, stated, 602, 698, 704–05
subordination and coordination, 516
such and *so,* 737
take back, 723, 724
take from, 744
take on, 723, 724
take up, 723
that, 706, 713, 718
the, 713, 715–16
there and *it* constructions, 705
these, 718
thesis statements, 29
this, 718
those, 718
throw, throw out, 723
to be, 705–06, 710
too and *either,* 736
too and *so,* 736

transitive verbs, 707–08, 723
verbs, 722–30
which, 706
will, would, 729
word order, 587, 704–11, 732–33, 734–35
Writing Responsibly around the World, 6
English language
  British, 563, 754, 781, 785
  dialects, 541, 622, 641, 642, 673
  idioms, 554–55, 556
  regionalisms, 541
  slang, 542, 781, 785
  Standard American, 574
enjoy, 726
enough, 719
enthused, G16
Envelopes, for business letters, 477
envy, 647
equal, 675
-er, in comparisons, 674
Errami, Mounir, 246–47
escape, 726
ESL. *See* English as a second language
Essay exams, 469–75
  analyzing questions on, 471–72
  common verbs in, 472
  computer use in, 473
  parameters of the exam, 470–71
  practice questions, 470
  previewing the exam, 471–72
  reading and developing a strategy, 471
  reviewing notes for, 469–70
  sample answers, 474–75
  study groups for, 470
  writing effective answers in, 472–73
essential, 675
Essential elements, 512, 608, 757
-est, in comparisons, 674
et al.
  APA style for, 353
  avoiding, in formal writing, 824
  English equivalent of, 294
  MLA style for, 294–95, 308
etc., 824, G16
Ethical appeals, 143
Ethical issues. *See also* Bias; Plagiarism
  biased language, 87, 544–47
  blind copies in e-mails, 173
  in interviews, 227
  keeping an open mind, 234
  in observations and surveys, 228
Ethnic group names, 810

Ethnic labels and bias, 547
Ethos, 143, 826
Euphemisms, 544
evaluate, 18, 192, 472
Evaluation. *See* Credibility; Sources, evaluating
even, 688
even if, 513, 603
even though, 513, 603
every, 623, 719
everybody, 625, 631
everybody, everyone; every body, every one, G16–G17
everyone
    pronoun-antecedent agreement, 631, 682
    subject-verb agreement, 625
everyone, everybody; every one, every body, G16–G17
everything, 625
Evidence
    analyzing, 120–21
    counterevidence and, 84, 135, 145–47, 190, 267
    made-up, 41
    ordering paragraphs by, 53
    qualitative *vs.* quantitative, 456–57
    revising, 84
    types of, 40–41
    visuals as, 74–78, 270
    in writing about literature and humanities, 441–42
    in writing about sciences and social sciences, 456–57
ex-, 831–32
exactly, 688
Examinations. *See* Essay exams
Examples
    colons to introduce, 801
    dashes to set off, 796, 797
    in dictionary entries, 562
    as fragments, 606
    paragraph development through, 60
    in parentheses, 798
    supporting ideas by, 41
    transitional expressions and, 55
exceed, 567
except, accept, 565, G14
Exclamation points
    in e-mails, 794
    in exclamations, 534, 609
    quotation marks and, 786
    series of, 793
    strong commands and excitement and, 793, 794

Exclamations, 534, 609
Exclamatory sentences, 585
Executive summaries, 491
Exemplification, 60
expect, 726
expect, suppose, G17
Experimental research, 455
Expertise, source reliability and, 233
explain, 18, 472, 708
Explanations, colons before, 801
Expletive constructions, 500–01, 586, 705–06
Expletives, 705
Explicating a text, 440, 446, 448–51
explicit, implicit, G17
Exploitative images, 78
"Exploration and Empire: James Cook and the Pacific Northwest" (Conrad), 409–15
Exploratory arguments, 120, 134–35, 137, 147–53
Exploring topics. *See* Idea generation
Expository reports. *See* Informative reports
Expressive writing, 10
Eye contact, in presentations, 189

F

-f, -fe, -ff, -ffe, plurals of words that end in, 569–70
Facebook, 229
the fact is, 497
Facts
    claims of, 31–32, 138, 139
    as common knowledge, 249
    as evidence, 40–41
    in letters to the editor, 479
Fact sheets, 375
the fact that, 696–97
faculty, 625
fair, fare, 565
Fair use, in copyright law, 6–7
fall, 589
Fallacies, logical, 156–59
False analogy fallacy, 156–57
False authority fallacy, 156, 157
False cause fallacy, 158
False dilemma fallacy, 158
Familiar-to-unfamiliar order, 35
family, 625
FAQs (frequently asked questions), 210
far, farther, farthest, 581
fare, fair, 565
Farmhouse in Normandy (Cézanne), 86
farther, further, G17

Faulty predication, 697–98
Favorites list, 251
fear, 647
Federated searching, 220
feel
    as linking verb, 589, 670
    unmarked infinitives after, 725
feet, foot, 621
Feminist criticism, 436
few
    count and noncount nouns with, 719
    pronoun-antecedent agreement, 633
    subject-verb agreement, 625
few, a few, 718–19
a few, 719
fewer, 713, 719
fewer, less, G17
fewest, 719
few in number, 498
Fiction, writing about, 440–46. *See also* Literature and humanities, writing in
Field research, 226–29, G17
fig./Fig., 334, 335
Figurative language (figures of speech), 447, 552–56
Figure, 379–80
Figure captions, 279–80, 304, 335–36, 407
Figures
    APA style for, 379–80
    captions for, 279–80, 304, 335–36, 407
    Chicago style for, 407
    MLA style for, 303–04, 334–35
    in research or laboratory reports, 460
Figures of speech, 447, 552–56
fill with, 744
Films
    documenting: APA style for, 372; *Chicago* style for, 404; MLA style for, 300, 323
    movie stills, 75, 77
    primary sources in writing about, 436
final, 675
final outcome, 498
find, 590, 707
finish, 726
first, firstly, G17
First draft, 42–44, 270–72. *See also* Drafting
First person
    in academic writing, 15
    capitalization of *I*, 808, 811
    in writing in the humanities, 438–39

"Five-paragraph theme," 34
fix, 708
Flaming, 182, 483
flaunt, flout, G17
Flickr, 214
Focused freewriting, 22
the following, 801
Fonts (typeface)
  APA style for, 378
  font size, 165, 174, 332
  MLA style for, 332
  selecting, 95, 165–66, 174
foot, feet, 621
Footers, 379
Footnotes. *See also* Endnotes
  APA style for, 376–77
  Chicago style for, 390–407. *See also* *Chicago* style
  in critical reading, 115
  definition, 390
  MLA style for, 331–32
  superscript numbers for, 376–77, 417
for
  in coordination, 506, 508, 583, 750
  in correcting comma splices, 616
  to indicate cause, 742
  in indirect-object phrase, 590
  in parallel constructions, 520
force, 726
Foreign languages. *See* English as a second language
Forewords, documenting
  APA style, 363
  Chicago style, 396
  MLA style, 311
for example
  in comma splices and fused sentences, 613
  in coordination, 506
  semicolons and, 768
  in transitions, 606
forget, 726
Formal diction, 15. *See also* Diction
Formalist approach to literature, 433
Formality, appropriate, 543
Formal outlines, 36–37. *See also* Outlines
Format
  of academic texts, 95–99
  of APA-style papers, 377–81
  of block quotations, 782–83
  of block-style letters, 477–79
  of *Chicago*-style papers, 407–08
  of CSE-style papers, 428–29
  of dates, 827
  of fractions, 828

of letters, 477–79
of MLA-style papers, 332–36
PDF, 215, 218, 315
plain text, 173–74
of portfolios, 100–01
of scientific reports, 459–61
of URLs, 804
Formatting academic texts
  in APA style, 377–81
  in *Chicago* style, 407–08
  in CSE style, 428–29
  first page, 96
  in MLA style, 332–36
  sample paper, 96–99
forth, fourth, 565
Forums, online. *See* Discussion list postings
Fractions
  formats for, 828
  slashes in, 804
  subject-verb agreement and, 626–27
Fragments. *See* Sentence fragments
Freewriting, 21–22
frequently, 734
frequently, more/less frequently, most/least frequently, 581
Frequently asked questions (FAQs), 210
friendly, 520
from, 742, 743
from . . . to, 832–33
full, 675
Full block-style business letters, 477–78, 480
"Full text"/"full text PDF," 215, 218
Function words, parallelism and, 522
fungus, fungi, funguses, 570
Funnel introductions, 63
further, farther, G17
furthermore, 768
Fused (run-on) sentences, 611–18
  boundaries obscured by, 612
  causes of, 613–14
  correcting, 615–17
  identifying, 612–13
Future perfect progressive tense, 646, 647
Future perfect tense, 645, 646
Future progressive tense, 646
Future tenses, 645–47

G

Garner, Harold, 246–47
Gender agreement, 630, 632
Gender bias, avoiding, 545–47, 632
Generalizations, 67, 716
General-to-specific organization, 53

General *vs.* abstract words, 551
Generic nouns
  articles with, 716
  in pronoun-antecedent agreement, 631–33, 682
Genre(s)
  analyzing before writing, 9, 17–18, 435
  design and, 164
  of literature, 17
  of multimedia presentations, 184
  of websites, 176
Genus and species names, italicizing, 817
Geographic names
  articles with, 717
  capitalization of, 810
  as singular, 627–28
Gerund(s). *See also* Gerund phrases
  definition of, 524, 593, 628, 725
  functions of, 593
  after prepositions, 726
  pronoun case with, 661
  subject-verb agreement, 627–28
  after verbs, 593, 725–26
Gerund phrases
  functions of, 593
  parallelism of, 524
  pronoun case with, 627–28
  subject-verb agreement, 627–28
Gestures, in presentations, 189
get, 590, G17
get out of, 723
Gigablast, 213
give, 590, 707
give in, 642, 723
give to, 744
give up, 723
Glossarist, 559
Glossary
  of key terms, G1–G13
  of usage, G14–G19
Goals of writing. *See* Purpose of writing
good, well, 671–72, G17
Goodwin, Doris Kearns, 246
Google
  blog searching, 214, 215
  keyword searching in, 210–11, 236
  news alerts from, 214
  number of links to sites, 210
  Web searching, 210–11, 212
Google Blog Search, 215
Google Docs, 174, 229, 390
Google Groups, 215
Google Scholar, 216, 235

Gore, Al, 69–71, 183
gorilla, guerrilla, 565
.gov sites, reliability and, 237–38
government, 625
Government publications
 abbreviations in, 329
 documenting: APA style for, 374–75; *Chicago* style for, 406; CSE style for, 428; MLA style for, 295, 304, 328–29
 finding, 224
Grammar, 561, 574. *See also specific grammatical elements*
Grammar checkers
 adjective-adverb problems and, 671
 apostrophes and, 775
 comma splices and fused sentences and, 613
 confusing shifts and, 679
 misplaced modifiers and, 686
 pronoun-antecedent agreement and, 631
 sentence fragments and, 605
 subject-verb agreement and, 620
 verb problems and, 638
Grammatical shifts. *See* Shifts
Graphic novels, documenting, in MLA style, 328
Graphics. *See* Visuals
Graphs, 74–77. *See also* Visuals
grate, great, 565
a great deal of, 719–20
Grounds, 142. *See also* Evidence
Group or corporate authors, in documenting
 APA style for, 353–54, 362
 Chicago style for, 394
 CSE style for, 420–21
 MLA style for, 295, 309
grow up, 723
guerrilla, gorilla, 565
Guilt by association fallacy, 159
Gurney, Jeff, 8

H

Hackman, Tom, 147–53
hand, 590
hand in, 723
hand out, 723
hanged, hung, 640, G17
Hanging indent
 in APA reference list, 378, 380
 in *Chicago* works-cited list, 408
 in MLA works-cited list, 332
hard, hardly, 737

hardly
 as limiting modifier, 688
 negative meaning of, 673
hardly, can hardly, G17
has the ability to, 498
Hasty generalization fallacy, 156
hate, 726
have
 forms of, 641
 as a helping verb, 621, 639, 728
 infinitive after, 726
 in perfect tenses, 637
 unmarked infinitives after, 725
he or she, 546
he (generic), 545–46
he, she; he/she; s/he, G17
Headers
 in academic texts, 96
 in APA style, 378, 379
 in e-mails, 173, 481
 in MLA style, 332, 333, 337
Headings
 in critical reading, 109, 231
 in document design, 168–69
 heading levels, 95
 parallelism in, 524
hear, 725
hear, here, 565
Heinle's Newbury House Dictionary of American English, 559
Helping (auxiliary) verbs
 in complete verbs, 639–42
 contraction and omission of, 641–42
 in dialects and informal speech, 641
 functions of, 577, 579
 kinds of, 728–30
 modal verbs, 579, 641, 728–30
 placement of, 579, 586, 734–35
 in questions, 710
 simple, 728
 subject-verb agreement and, 621
he or she, 633, 682
her or him, 633
herself, himself, myself, etc., G18
Highlighting, 251, 469–70
him or her, 633
himself, herself, myself, etc., G18
hint at, 723
his or her, 633
hisself, G17
Historical Abstracts, 437
Historical documents, not italicized, 815
Historical events, capitalization of, 810
hole, whole, 565

Holiday names
 abbreviating, 824
 capitalizing, 810
"Holy Underground Comics, Batman! Moving Away from the Mainstream" (Nichols), 337–46
Home pages. *See also* Websites and web pages
 constructing, 176–78
 MLA style for, 320–21
 planning, 176
 in portfolios, 100
Homonyms
 definition of, 563
 list of, 563, 565
 near-homonyms, 563, 565
 spelling checkers and, 93
hope, 726
how, 596
however
 in comma splices and fused sentences, 613
 in coordination, 506
 semicolons and, 768
 as transitional expression, 530
"How Hip-Hop Music Lost Its Way and Betrayed Its Fans" (Staples), 116–17
HTML (HyperText Markup Language)
 Chicago style for files in, 399
 in creating websites, 179–80
 in databases, 215, 399
 definition of, 399
 PDF *vs.,* 218, 315, 399
 in source copies, 201
HTML editors, 180
Hub-and-spoke structure, 177
Hulu, 225
Humanities, writing in. *See* Literature and humanities, writing in
humanity, humankind, humans, 546
hung, hanged, G17
Hurtful (biased) language, 87, 544–47
Hyperbole, 552
Hyperlinks. *See* Links
HyperText Markup Language. *See* HTML
Hypertextual organization, 177
Hyphens, 830–34
 in APA style, 377
 automatic hyphenation, 834
 to avoid confusion, 832
 before capital letters, 832
 in compound adjectives, 830–31
 in compound nouns, 776–77
 in compound numbers, 832

Hyphens (*continued*)
    between dates, 832–33
    at the ends of lines, 560–61, 833–34
    overuse of, 831
    plurals and, 571
    after prefixes and suffixes, 566, 831–32
    in sports scores, 832
    in URLs and e-mail addresses, 834
Hypotheses
    drafting, 195–96, 265–66
    in field research, 228
    from research questions, 195–96, 265–66

I

I
    in academic writing, 15
    capitalization of, 808, 811
    in writing in the humanities, 438–39
Ibid., 413
-ic, suffixes with words that end in, 567
Icons, 181
Idea generation, 20–25
    brainstorming, 22
    clustering, 22–23
    discussing topics with others, 24–25
    freewriting, 21–22
    idea journals and commonplace books, 20
    Internet, library, and classroom tools for, 25
    journalists' questions, 23–24
    in thesis drafting, 30
Idea journals, 20
Ideas. *See also* Idea generation
    citing, 249
    explaining and supporting, 40–41
    organizing, 33–37, 265, 266–69
    support for. *See* Evidence
    transitional expressions and, 55
Identification, conjunctions used for, 333–34
Idioms, 554–55, 556, 642
i.e., 824
i.e., e.g., 824, G16
ie/ei spelling rule, 566
if
    in noun clauses, 596
    in subjunctive clauses, 651
    as subordinating conjunction, 513, 603
if, whether, G17
-ify and *-efy* suffixes, 567

Ignoring the question (red herring) fallacy, 158
illicit, elicit, 565, G16
illusion, allusion, 565, G14
illustrate, 472
Illustrations. *See* Visuals
IM. *See* Instant messaging
Imagery, in poetry, 447
Images. *See also* Visuals
    annotating, 115
    as evidence, 77–78
    manipulated, 41, 236, 240, 248
    manipulative, 78, 81
    writing about, 126
imagine, 726
immigrate to, emigrate from, G16
imminent, eminent, immanent, 565, G16
immoral, amoral, G14
Imperative mood, 650, 679
Imperative sentences, 585, 602
implicit, explicit, G17
imply, infer, G17
impossible, 675
Imprints, MLA style for documenting, 311
in, indicating location or time, 741, 742
in addition, in addition to, 506, 606, 622
incidence, incidents, 565
in close proximity, 498
including, 801
Incomplete sentences, 699–702. *See also* Sentence fragments
in contrast, 508, 606
"An Inconvenient Truth" (Gore), 69–71
incredible, incredulous, G17
indeed, 55
Indefinite articles (*a, an*), 580, 713–16, G14
Indefinite pronouns
    definition of, 774
    forms of, 578
    possessive, 774–75
    pronoun-antecedent agreement, 631, 633
    subject-verb agreement and, 625
Indentation
    in academic texts, 95
    in APA format, 377–78
    in *Chicago* format, 408
    in MLA format, 332, 333
Independent clauses
    capitalization of, 807–09
    colons after, 800
    comma splices of, 612–14
    commas to separate, 749
    coordinating, 506–07, 750

in correcting fragments, 604–08, 612–14
    definition of, 506, 594, 704, 750, 767, 809
    linking, 611–13
    punctuation between two, 507–08, 533, 612, 613, 767–68
index, indexes, indices, 570
Indexes
    citation, 235
    searching, 215–20
Indians, 547
Indicative mood, 650, 679
indices, indexes, 570
Indirect objects, 590, 707–08
Indirect questions, 684, 792–93
Indirect quotations
    acknowledging, 790–91
    in awkward shifts, 683–84
    punctuation and, 760, 782
Indirect sources, documenting
    APA style for, 356
    Chicago style for, 407
    MLA style for, 300–01
Inductive order of paragraphs, 53
Inductive reasoning, 120, 135
in fact, 497
infer, imply, G17
Inferences, drawing, 124
infinite, 675
Infinitive(s)
    dangling, 692
    definition of, 593, 725
    in fragments, 601
    gerunds *vs.,* 593
    objective case pronouns and, 661
    split, 686, 690
    unmarked, 725–26
    verb tenses used with, 648–49
Infinitive phrases, 520, 592, 593, 692
Info.com, 213
Infomine, 213
Informal diction. *See* Diction
Informal outlines, 35–36. *See also* Outlines
Informational notes
    APA style for, 376–77
    MLA style for, 331–32
Information graphics, 74–77, 239–41. *See also* Visuals
Information literacy, 3
Informative reports
    approach in, 18
    claims of fact in, 138
    purpose of, 10–11

Index **I19**

research assignments and, 192
thesis statements in, 31–32
Infospace, 213
-ing words, 593. *See also* Gerund(s)
Initialisms, 822, 823. *See also* Acronyms
Initials, periods with, 820
in order that, 513
Inquiry-based (exploratory) arguments, 120, 134–35, 137, 147–53. *See also* Arguments
in regards to, G17
Inseparable phrasal verbs, 723–24
Inside address, in business letters, 478
Insider terminology (jargon), 542–43
in spite of the fact that, 498
Instant messaging (IM)
  acronyms in, 172, 823
  capitalizing in, 811
  language shortcuts in, 542, 823
  MLA style for, 330
  personal, at work, 484
  writing precautions in, 181–82
instead, 54
instruct, 726
Instructors
  as audience, 14–15
  interviewing, 226
  revising with, 92
  vocabulary used by, 458
Intellectual property. *See* Copyright clearance
Intensifiers, 671
Intensive pronouns, 578
Intentional fragments, 604, 609. *See also* Sentence fragments
Interactive media
  blog postings. *See* Blogs and blog postings
  discussion lists, 214, 215, 238–39
  e-mails. *See* E-mails
  flaming in, 182, 483
  instant messaging. *See* Instant messaging
  searching, 214–15
  social networking sites, 229, 542
  synchronous *vs.* asynchronous media, 182
  wikis, 238–39
  writing in, 181–82
Interjections
  capitalization of *O,* 811
  commas after, 753
  definition of, 584
  examples of, 584
  functions of, 576, 584

Internet. *See also* Online sources; Websites and web pages
  collaborating on, 45
  documenting information from, 249
  downloads from, 324
  electronic portfolios on, 100–01
  evaluating sources on, 236–39
  flaming on, 182, 483
  idea generation and, 25
  peer revising on, 90–92
  plagiarism and, 236
  social bookmarking sites on, 251
  subject directories on, 25, 212
  website and web page creation on, 176–81
Interpretation
  of literature, 433
  of sources, 121
  of texts, 122–23
  thesis example, 123
Interpretive analysis, 440–46
Interrogative pronouns
  case in, 657
  definition of, 657
  examples of, 578
  relative pronouns *vs.*, 602
  who, whom, whoever, and *whomever,* 663–64
Interrogative sentences, 585, 586
Interrupted periodic sentences, 532
Interviews
  conducting, 226–27
  documenting: APA style for, 357, 376; *Chicago* style for, 406; MLA style for, 303, 330
  job, 482, 484
In-text citations. *See also* In-text citations, APA-style; In-text citations, MLA-style
  APA style for, 347–57
  CSE style for, 416–18
  general principles of, 290
  MLA style for, 288–305
In-text citations, APA-style, 347–57
  authors with two or more works published in the same year, 355
  directory of models, 350
  general principles of, 348
  group or corporate authors, 353–54
  indirect sources, 356
  multiple authors, 352–53
  one author, 350–52
  parenthetical citations, 349–50, 351, 352

personal communications, interviews, or e-mails, 357
placement of, 348–50
reprinted or republished works, 355–56
sacred texts, 356
signal phrases in, 276, 277, 348–49, 351
two authors, 352
two or more authors with the same surname, 355
two or more sources by the same author, 354–55
two or more sources in one citation, 354
unnamed or anonymous authors, 354
websites or other electronic sources, 357
In-text citations, CSE-style, 416–18
In-text citations, MLA-style, 288–305
  anthology selections, 297
  block quotations, 292
  dictionary or encyclopedia entries, 301–02
  directory of models, 294
  of entire source, 290, 296–97
  general principles of, 290
  government documents, 295, 304
  group or corporate authors, 295
  indirect sources, 300–01
  legal sources, 304
  literary sources, 297–99
  more than three authors, 294–95
  motion picture, television or radio broadcast, 300
  multiple sources in one citation, 305
  multiple sources in one sentence, 304–05
  multivolume sources, 297
  one author, 293
  parenthetical note format, 290
  personal communications, 303
  placement of, 290–92
  reasons for, 288
  sacred texts, 299–300
  signal phrases in, 289, 291, 293
  tables, charts, or figures, 303–04
  two authors with the same surname, 290, 296
  two or more sources by the same author, 290, 296
  two or three authors, 293
  unnamed or anonymous authors, 295
  of unpaginated sources, 290, 291, 302
  web pages, 290, 291

In-text citations, MLA-style (*continued*)
  websites or other electronic sources, 302–03
in the event that, 498
in the neighborhood of, 498
in the process of, 497
in this day and age, 498
Intransitive verbs, 588, 643–44
Introduction(s)
  APA style for, 363
  avoiding praise for the reader in, 63
  in business reports and proposals, 491
  Chicago format for, 396
  funnel, 63
  length of, 64, 84
  MLA style for, 311
  for multimedia presentations, 184
  planning, 34
  in research or laboratory reports, 460
  revising, 83–84
  seven don'ts for, 65
  writing, 63–65
Introductory elements, commas after, 749, 751–52
Invention. *See* Idea generation
Inverted-funnel conclusions, 65
Inverted word order
  conjunctions or adverbs beginning clauses and, 710–11
  for emphasis, 532, 586
  subject-verb agreement in, 629
Irony
  definition of, 552
  in literature, 435
  quotations marks indicating, 781, 784
irregardless, G17
Irregular verbs, 561, 638–39, 640
Irrelevant argument, 157–58
irritate, aggravate, G14
is, 501, 639
Issue numbers, 203, 204, 205, 398
is where, is when, 698, G17
it
  as confusingly broad reference, 665
  as expletive, 705
  indefinite use of, 666–67
  as stated subject, 698
Italics
  common do's and don'ts, 815
  in court cases, 304, 815
  in document design, 165
  in e-mails, 811
  for emphasis, 785, 815, 816
  in genus and species names, 817

not used for links, 101, 178, 239, 815, 817
  sacred text titles and, 815
  in talking about a word, 816
  in titles of longer works, 372, 380, 814
  in titles within titles, 364–65
  in unfamiliar non-English words, 817
  in vehicle names, 816
  in words, letters, or numbers used as words, 784, 815, 816
  in works of art, 815
it is . . . , sentences beginning with, 500–01
it's, its, 565, 774, 775, G17

J

Jargon, 542–43
Job applications
  cover letter format, 484
  photographs in, 74, 484
  portfolios in, 99–103
  references in, 488–89
  résumés in, 486–90
  sample, 485
  writing in, 482–84
Job interviews, 482, 484
Joint ownership, apostrophes and, 776
Journalists' questions, 23–24
Journal or diary entries, MLA documentation for, 330–31
Journals. *See* Periodicals
Journals, keeping
  double-entry reading, 117–19
  essay exams and, 470
  idea generation and, 20
Judgment, claims of, 32, 139–40
Jumping on the bandwagon fallacy, 157
Jumping to conclusions, 156
just, 688

K

Keefe, Alicia, 429–30
keep, 708
Keynote, 187
Key terms
  glossary of, G1–G13
  in paraphrases, 252–53
  in reading critically, 109
  in résumés, 490
Keyword searches, 210–11, 218–19, 221–22
kind, 497
kind, kinds, G17
kind of, sort of, G17

know, 647
Knowledge, common, 249–50
Ky, Rachana, 102–03

L

Labeling people, 545. *See also* Biased language
Laboratory notebooks, 459
Laboratory reports
  format, 459–61
  sample, 462–68
Language. *See also* Word(s)
  abstract *vs.* concrete, 88, 186, 551–52, 575
  active *vs.* passive voice, 536, 652–54. *See also* Voice
  appropriate formality in, 541, 543
  audience and, 13
  biased or hurtful, 87, 544–47
  British *vs.* American English, 563, 754, 781, 785
  capitalization of names of, 810
  colloquialisms, 541
  dialects, 541, 622, 641, 642, 673
  diction, 15–17, 87, 548–50
  doublespeak, 544
  euphemisms, 544
  figurative, 447, 552–56
  first and third person, 15, 438–39, 458, 808
  formal, 87
  idioms, 554–55, 556, 642
  jargon, 542–43
  in literature, 435
  neologisms, 542
  online shortcuts, 542
  in presentations, 186
  regionalisms, 541
  in sciences and social sciences, 457–59
  slang, 542, 781, 785
  Standard American English, 574
a large number of, 719–20
Latin abbreviations, 821, 824
lay, lie, 640, 643–44, G17–G18
Layouts, 165
lead, led, 565
least
  count and noncount nouns with, 719
  as superlative, 674
leave, 590
leave, let, G17
Lectures, documenting
  APA style for, 373–74
  MLA style for, 327

Legal cases, documenting
  APA style for, 376
  MLA style for, 304, 329
lend, 590
lend to, 744
less
  in comparisons, 674
  count and noncount nouns with, 719–20
  as determiner, 713
less, fewer, 713, G17
let, 725
let, leave, G17
Letters. *See also* Letters to the editor
  of apology, 479–81
  business, 477–79
  of complaint, 479
  documenting: APA style for, 357, 376; *Chicago* style for, 406; MLA style for, 303, 329–30
  to the editor, 479
  envelopes for, 477
  formats in, 477–78
  job application, 482–86
  letterhead, 492
  of rejection, 481
Letters to the editor
  documenting: APA style for, 369; *Chicago* style for, 402; MLA style for, 319
  writing, 479
Letters used as words, apostrophes and, 774, 777–78
Level of diction, 15–17. *See also* Diction
LexisNexis Academic, 216
LexisNexis Congressional, 224
Library catalogs
  browsing, 223
  idea generation and, 195
  media in, 225
  reliability of sources in, 235–36
  searching, 207–08, 220–23
  subject headings in, 222–23
Library databases. *See* Databases
Library of Congress, 225
Library stacks, 223
Library websites, 25, 221
lie, lay, 640, 643–44, G17–G18
like
  colons not used after, 801
  gerund or infinitive after, 726
  not used in progressive tense, 647
  in similes, 553
like, as, as if, G15
Limiting modifiers, 688–89

Line graphs, 75–77
Line length, 447
Lines, of poetry, 298–99
Linking verbs
  adjectives after, 670, 732
  definition of, 580, 697, 732
  faulty predication and, 697–98
  sentence pattern with, 589
  subject-verb agreement, 629
  verbs that function as, 589
Links (hyperlinks)
  in document design, 101, 178, 815, 817, 818
  evaluating reliability by, 239
  italicizing, 101, 178, 239, 815, 817
  in portfolios, 101
  underlining, 818
  in websites, 101, 178, 210, 239, 815
list, 472
List(s)
  colons before, 801
  dashes in, 797
  in document design, 166–67
  as fragments, 606
  parallelism in, 167, 523
  parentheses around numbers in, 798–99
Listening, active, 190
Listing (brainstorming), 22, 470
List of works cited. *See* Reference list, APA-style; Reference list, CSE-style; Works cited list, *Chicago*-style; Works cited list, MLA-style
List of works consulted, 305
Literacies, types of, 2–3
Literary analyses. *See* Literature and humanities, writing in
Literary Criticism Index, 437
Literary sources, MLA style for, 297–99
Literature, elements of, 435
Literature and humanities, writing in, 432–54
  abbreviations in, 820
  active voice in, 439
  analysis of the text, 433
  assignment types, 440
  author's name in, 439
  critical framework in, 433, 435, 436
  drama, 451–54
  elements of literature in, 435
  evidence in, 441–42
  fiction, interpretive analysis of, 440–46
  first and third person in, 438–39

formalist approach in, 433
genres in, 17
language of literature in, 437–40
numbers in, 826–28
past and present tense in, 438, 647, 679
percent in, 828
poetry, 446–51
primary sources for, 435–36
reading actively and reflectively, 432–33
sample paper, 442–46
secondary sources for, 437
shifts in person in, 681–82
style guide selection, 200, 437
thesis statements, 440–41
title in, 440, 443, 452
verb tenses in, 438
vocabulary, specific, 437, 542–43
Literature reviews, in the sciences, 459
little, 719–20
little, a little, 718–19
Live performances, documenting, MLA style for, 326
Location, prepositions for, 741
Logical fallacies, 156–59
Logical organization, 35, 53
Logical reasoning, 135–37
Logos, appeals to, 142–43
Longman Dictionary of American English, 559
look, 589, 670
look at, 725
look down on, 723
look up, 723
look up to, 723
loose, lose, G18
a lot of, 719
lots, lots of, G18
lots of, 719
love, 726
Lurking, 238
-ly and *-ally* suffixes, 567, 672, 831
Lycos (search engine), 213

M

Made-up evidence, 41. *See also* Evidence
Magazine articles, documenting. *See also* Periodicals
  APA style for, 367–68
  Chicago style for, 400
  CSE style for, 424–25
  MLA style for, 316–17
Main clauses. *See* Independent clauses

Main idea, statement of, 29, 51. *See also* Topic sentences
Main verbs, 577, 639, 641
make, 589
man, mankind (generic, sexist use), 545, 546
manage, 726
Manipulative images, 81
manner, 497
Manuscript, formatting. *See* Document design
-man words, gender bias and, 545–46, 632
many
    count and noncount nouns with, 719–20
    pronoun-antecedent agreement, 633
    subject-verb agreement, 625
many in number, 498
Mapping, 22–23
Maps
    MLA style for, 328, 374
    as visual evidence, 75, 77
Al-Marashi, Ibrahim, 246
Margins
    in APA style, 377–78
    in MLA style, 332, 335
Marilyn Diptych (Warhol), 518
married to, 744
Marxist criticism, 436
Mass (noncount) nouns, 715
may
    meanings of, 729
    as modal verb, 579, 641, 728, 729
    subject-verb agreement with, 621
may, can, G15
may, might, 729
maybe, may be, G18
may of, might of, G18
McGraw-Hill's Dictionary of American Slang and Colloquial Expressions, 559
McMahan, Rita, 448–51
mean, 726
Meanings
    of coordinating conjunctions, 507, 508
    modals and, 729
    of phrasal verbs, 722–24
Measurement units. *See* Units of measure
meat, meet, 565
media, data, phenomena, G16
Media releases, 314, 492–94
Media sources, documenting
    APA style for, 373

Chicago style for, 404, 405
    MLA style for, 300, 324–25
Memoranda (memos)
    business, 481–82
    documenting, in MLA style, 330
men (generic), 545, 546
mention, 708
Menus, in websites, 101, 177
merely, 688
Merriam-Webster Online Dictionary, 555
Merriam-Webster's Collegiate Dictionary, 558
Merriam-Webster's Dictionary of Synonyms, 560
Metaphors, 552, 553
Metasearch engines, 211–12, 213
Methods section, 460, 491
Microform articles, documenting, MLA style for, 318–19
Microsoft Academic Search, 235
Microsoft Word
    footnote/endnote numbering in, 390
    header creation in, 332, 333
might
    meanings of, 729
    as modal verb, 579, 641, 728, 729
    subject-verb agreement with, 621
might, may, 729
might of, may of, G18
mind, 726
Misplaced modifiers, 686–90
    ambiguous limiting modifiers, 688–89
    dangling modifiers, 691–93
    importance of avoiding, 690
    separation from modified words, 687
    separation of subject from verb, 689–90
    separation of verb from object, 689–90
    split infinitives, 686, 690
    squinting modifiers, 688
miss, 726
MIT Open Courseware, 225
Mixed constructions, 695–98
    faulty predication, 697–98
    grammatically mixed, 695–97
Mixed metaphors, 554
MLA Handbook for Writers of Research Papers (7th ed.), 288, 437. *See also* MLA style
MLA International Bibliography, 437
MLA style, 288–346. *See also* In-text citations, MLA-style; Works cited list, MLA-style

apostrophes in plurals of letters, 778
for audio and visual sources, 323–28
for books, 305–15
brackets for changed capitals in quotations, 786
changing capitalization in quotations, 285, 809
citations in figures and tables, 304, 335
content and bibliographic notes in, 331–32
disciplines using, 200
format of paper in, 332–36
indentation, 332, 333
in-text citations in, 288–305
for miscellaneous sources, 307–31
for notes, 331–32
parenthetical notes in, 289, 291, 293
percent symbols in, 828
for periodicals, 315–19
portfolios in, 335
printing and binding a paper in, 335
reasons for citing sources in, 288
sample paper in, 336–46
[sic] in, 800
URLs and e-mail addresses, 834
Works cited list in, 305–31
Modal auxiliaries, 579, 641, 728–30. *See also* Helping (auxiliary) verbs
Modern Language Association style guidelines. *See* MLA style
Modified block-style business letters, 477–78
Modifiers. *See also* Adjective(s); Adverb(s); Misplaced modifiers
    absolute phrases as, 530, 594, 675
    appositives as, 530
    dangling, 691–93
    disruptive, 689–90
    grammar checkers and, 686
    limiting, 688–89
    misplaced, 686–90
    repeated in elliptical construction, 700
    squinting, 688
    in subordination, 511, 512
Money, 823, 828
Months, 823
Mood, in verbs
    awkward shifts in, 679
    imperative, 650, 679
    indicative, 650, 679
    information from, 650
    subjunctive, 650, 679
moral, morale, G18

Index

more
  in comparatives and superlatives, 674
  count and noncount nouns with, 719
  as determiner, 713
  pronoun-antecedent agreement, 633
  as quantifier, 719
  subject-verb agreement, 625
more unique, 675
most
  in comparatives and superlatives, 674
  count and noncount nouns with, 719
  pronoun-antecedent agreement, 633
  as quantifier, 719
  subject-verb agreement, 625
most, almost, G14
most of the time, 498
most perfect, 675
Motives for writing. *See* Purpose of writing
Movies. *See* Films
Movie stills, 75, 77
MP3/MP4 files, MLA style for, 326
much
  count and noncount nouns with, 719–20
  subject-verb agreement, 625
Multilingual writers. *See* English as a second language (ESL)
Multimedia presentations, 183–90
  delivery of, 189
  gestures in, 189
  listening actively in, 190
  organizing, 185
  preparing and rehearsing, 186–89
  presentation anxiety in, 187
  presentation software in, 187, 188
  purpose, audience, context, and genre in, 183–84
  speaking responsibly, 189–90
  topic and thesis selection in, 184
  visuals in, 187
Multimedia resources. *See also* Visuals
  borrowing *vs.* creating, 78
  documenting. *See* Audio sources, documenting; Visual sources
  illustrations, 144, 249
  locating, 225
Multiple authors. *See also* Group or corporate authors
  ampersand in, 352
  documenting: APA style for, 352–53, 362; *Chicago* style for, 393; CSE style for, 420; MLA style for, 293–95, 305, 308, 359
  et al. in, 294–95, 308, 353, 824

Multivolume works, documenting
  APA style for, 364
  Chicago style for, 396
  MLA style for, 297, 312–13
Music, 405
Musical compositions, 326
Musicals and other audio recordings, 325–26, 373
must
  meanings of, 729
  as modal verb, 579, 641, 728, 729
  subject-verb agreement with, 621
must of, could of, should of, would of, G16
my, 713
myself, himself, herself, etc., G18
"My View from the Sidelines: Gary Snyder's 'Front Lines'" (McMahan), 448–51

N

n. pag., 316
Names
  abbreviations of, 822
  commas with, 761
  of companies, 627–28, 810, 824
  of countries, 810
  of genus and species, 817
  geographic, 627–28, 717, 810
  of holidays, 810, 824
  of occupations, 546
  of organizations, 627–28, 810
  personal, 761, 810, 820
  of places, 627–28, 717, 761, 810
  of races, 810
  of religions, 810
  subject-verb agreement and, 627–28
  title abbreviations in, 295, 301–02
  of vehicles, 816
Name-year system, CSE. *See also* In-text citations, APA-style; In-text citations, MLA-style
  books with group or corporate authors, 420
  books with one author, 418–20
  books with two or more authors, 420
  discussion lists or blog postings, 427
  dissertations, 422
  edited books, 421
  edited book selections or conference proceedings, 421
  e-mails, 428
  information in, 417
  magazine articles, 424–25
  newspaper articles, 425–26
  order of entries in, 429

  scholarly journal articles, 422–24
  technical reports or government documents, 428
  websites and web pages, 426–27
Narration, 59–60
Narrowing topic, 25, 32, 195
National Aeronautics and Space Administration (NASA), 225
National Park Service, 225
Native Americans, 547
Natural sciences. *See* Sciences and social sciences, writing in
"Nature Versus Nurture: Does Birth Order Shape Personality?" (Worthington), 462–68
Navigation tools, 177–78, 179
N.B., 824
Near-homonyms, 563, 565
Necessity, modals expressing, 729
need
  infinitive after, 726
  not used in progressive tense, 647
Negatives
  double, 673
  placement of, 735
  too and *either* and, 736
neither
  count and noncount nouns with, 719
  subject-verb agreement, 625
neither . . . nor
  in coordination, 506, 508, 583
  indicating choice, 508
  inverted word order and, 710–11
  parallelism with, 521
  pronoun-antecedent agreement and, 634
  subject-verb agreement, 624
Neologisms, 542
.net sites, reliability and, 237
Netiquette, 483
NetTutor, 92
never, 135
The New American Roget's College Thesaurus, 560
The New Encyclopedia Britannica, 208
The New Fowler's Modern English Usage, 559
New historicist approach to criticism, 436
News alerts, 214
Newspaper articles, documenting
  APA style for, 368–69
  Chicago style for, 400–02
  CSE style for, 425–26
  MLA style for, 317–18
Nichols, Lydia, 337–46

no, not, 736–37
nobody
    count and noncount nouns with, 719
    subject-verb agreement, 625
nohow, nowheres, G18
no longer, 711
Noncount (noncountable) nouns
    articles with, 714–16
    definition, 575
    determiners with, 718–20
    examples of, 713–14, 715
    importance of, on grammar, 576
Non-English words, italicizing, 817
Nonessential elements
    commas and, 608, 749, 757–59
    dashes and, 533
    omission of, 700–01
    subordination of, 512, 608
Non sequitur fallacy, 157–58
Nonsexist language. *See* Gender bias, avoiding
no one, 625
nor
    choice indicated by, 508
    in coordination, 506, 508, 583, 750
    in correcting comma splices and fused sentences, 616
    inverted word order and, 710–11
    in parallelism, 520
    pronoun-antecedent agreement and, 634
no sooner, 711
NOT, as Boolean operator, 219
not, no, 736–37
Note(s). *See also* Endnotes; Footnotes
    APA style for, 376–77
    bibliographic, 250, 331–32, 407–08
    Chicago format for, 407–08, 413–14. *See also Chicago* style
    complete *vs.* abbreviated, 390
    content, 250
    for figures and tables, 279–80, 304, 335–36, 407
    MLA style for, 331–32
    organizing, 250–51, 267
    for speaking, 186
    superscript numbers for, 376–77, 417
Note making, 251–63
    analyzing, interpreting, synthesizing, and critiquing sources, 262–63
    annotating *vs.,* 251
    for essay exams, 469–70
    highlighting *vs.,* 251
    by non-native writers of English, 252
    paraphrasing in, 110, 134, 252–55

    plagiarism and, 21, 250–55
    quotations in, 260–61
    research notes, 251
    source and page number in notes, 250
    summarizing in, 256–58
    types of notes, 250–51
    in writing about literature, 432–33, 434
Notepad, 180
nothing, 625
not just . . . but, 508
not only . . . but also
    in contrast, 508
    as correlative conjunctions, 521, 583
    inverted word order with, 710–11
Noun(s), 713–20
    a, an, the with, 580, 714–17
    abstract *vs.* concrete, 88, 186, 551–52, 575
    as adjectives, 673
    appositives. *See* Appositives/appositive phrases
    collective, 575, 625–26
    common *vs.* proper, 575, 713
    compound, 571
    count *vs.* noncount, 575, 576, 713–16, 718–20
    definition of, 774
    determiners and, 580
    as direct objects, 589
    functions of, 576
    generic, 631–33, 682, 716
    gerund phrases as, 524, 593, 627–28
    gerunds, 524, 593, 627–28, 725, 726
    as object complements, 672
    plurals of, 576–77, 621
    possessive, 577, 718, 774–77
    present participles as, 638
    quantifying words or phrases with, 718–20
    singular, that end in *s,* 627
Noun clauses, 596
Noun phrases, 591, 605
Novels, documenting, MLA style for, 297–98, 310. *See also* Literature and humanities, writing in
nowheres, nohow, G18
n.p., 314
Number
    definition of, 620, 681
    shifts in, 682
number, amount, G14
number, no., 823
a number of, 719

Numbers
    apostrophes in, 777
    at the beginning of a sentence, 827
    commas in, 760, 828
    hyphens in, 832–33
    italicizing, 815, 816
    numerals *vs.* spelled-out, 827
    periods in, 828
    prefixes in, 832
    shifts in, 682
    specific formats in, 827–28
    subject-verb agreement in, 626–27
    superscript, 376–77, 417

O

-o, plurals of words that end in, 570
O (interjection), 811
Object(s)
    complements, 590, 672, 708–09
    compound, 658
    direct, 589, 595, 672, 707–08
    indirect, 590, 707–08
    of prepositions, 592, 708
  object complements
    adjectives or nouns as, 672
    definition of, 590, 672
    sentence structure and, 590, 708–09
Objective case, in pronouns, 657, 658, 660, 661
Objectivity
    in sources, 233
    in writing, 83
Object of a preposition, 592
Obligatory words, 698
Observational studies, 228
Occupation names, avoiding gender-specific, 546
OED *(Oxford English Dictionary),* 207, 559
of
    with fractions or portions, 742
    to indicate cause or condition, 742
    to indicate possession, attribute, or origin, 743, 773
    not used with a modal, 642
    to show a reason, 742
off, of, G18
offer, 590, 726
often, 734
oh, 811
OK, O.K., okay, G18
on, 741–42
once, 603
one, 625, 713
one of, 628–29

Online articles, documenting. *See also* Online sources
   in APA style, 366–69
   in *Chicago* style, 399–401
   in MLA style, 315–16
Online assignment calendars, 194
Online books. *See* e-books
Online chat. *See* Instant messaging
Online communication. *See also* Blogs and blog postings; e-mails; Instant messaging
   discussion list postings, 214, 215, 238–39
   open *vs.* moderated forums, 238–39
   social networking, 229, 542
   synchronous *vs.* asynchronous media, 182
Online databases. *See* Databases
Online dictionaries, 558–59
Online forums. *See* Discussion list postings
Online journals, documenting
   APA style for, 366–70
   Chicago style for, 397–402
   CSE style for, 422–26
   MLA style for, 315–19
Online magazines, documenting
   APA style for, 367–68
   Chicago style for, 400
   CSE style for, 424–25
   MLA style for, 316–17
Online media. *See* Interactive media
Online newspapers, documenting
   APA style for, 368–69
   Chicago style for, 400–01
   CSE style for, 425–26
   MLA style for, 317–18
Online postings. *See* Blogs and blog postings; Discussion list postings
Online sources. *See also* Online sources, evaluating; Online sources, finding; *specific online sources*
   almanacs and yearbooks, 209
   annotating, 203–04
   databases. *See* Databases
   dictionaries and encyclopedias, 558–59
   discussion list postings, 238–39. *See also* Discussion list postings
   evaluating, 230–34, 236–39
   government publications. *See* Government publications
   HTML *vs.* PDF in, 218, 315
   instant messaging. *See* Instant messaging
   multimedia, 225
   open *vs.* moderated forums, 238–39
   periodicals. *See* Periodicals
   plagiarism in, 236
   social networking sites, 229, 542
   synchronous *vs.* asynchronous media, 182
   websites and web pages. *See* Websites and web pages
   in working bibliographies, 200–05
Online sources, finding. *See also* Databases
   advanced search options, 211, 212
   almanacs and yearbooks, 209
   bibliographies, 210
   biographical reference works, 209
   Boolean searches, 218, 219
   copying database articles, 220
   on databases, 217–20
   dictionaries and encyclopedias, 207–08
   Google Scholar, 216
   government publications, 224
   interactive media, 214–15
   keyword searches, 210–11
   library catalogs, 207–08, 220–23
   metasearch engines in, 211–12, 213
   multimedia, 225
   RSS feeds and news alerts, 214
   search engines, 210
   subject directories, 25, 212
   subject headings, 222–23
   Wikipedia, 208, 238
Online surveys, 229
Online video clips, 324
only, 688
only one of, 628–29
on the other hand, 768
open, 708
Open Directory Project, 213
Opinion, claims of, 139–40
Opposing arguments. *See* Counterevidence
or
   choice indicated by, 508
   in coordination, 506, 508, 583, 750
   in correcting comma splices and fused sentences, 616
   in parallelism, 520
   pronouns matched with compound antecedents, 634
   slashes instead of, 805
OR, as Boolean operator, 219
Oral arguments, 144
Oral presentations. *See* Multimedia presentations
order
   indirect object with, 707
   infinitive after, 726
.org sites, reliability and, 237–38
Organizational path, 202, 204
Organizational strategies, 35
Organizing a project, 29–40. *See also* Drafting
   arguments, 154–55
   checking for unity and coherence, 37–38
   choosing an organizational strategy, 35
   crafting a thesis, 29–33, 265
   multimedia presentations, 185
   organizing ideas, 33–37, 265, 266–69
   outlining, 35–37
   planning shape of essay, 33–34
   preparing to draft, 38–40
   résumés, 487–89
   websites, 177
Orientals, Asians, 547
Origin, prepositions indicating, 743
Orphaned phrases. *See* Sentence fragments
other, 719
the other, 719
others
   pronoun-antecedent agreement, 633
   subject-verb agreement, 625
ought to
   meanings of, 729
   as modal verb, 579, 641, 728, 729
   subject-verb agreement with, 621
ought to, shall, should, 729
our, are, 565
Outlines
   for essay exam answers, 473
   in organizing ideas, 267–69, 470
   outlining techniques, 35–37
   parallelism in, 524
   in revising, 83
   scratch, 35–36, 267
   sentence, 36–37, 267
   for speaking, 186
   topic, 36–37, 267–69
Overgeneralization, 140, 156
owe, 647
own, 647
Oxford Dictionary of American English, 559

The Oxford Encyclopedia of British Literature, 437
Oxford English Dictionary (OED), 207, 559

P

Page, definition of, 2–3
Page numbers
  APA style for, 357, 378
  in electronic documents, 278, 316, 357
  in MLA style, 316
Pamphlets, documenting
  APA style for, 375
  MLA style for, 314
Paper clips on papers, 334, 380, 408, 429
Paragraphs
  coherence in, 46, 52–58
  concluding, 65–68
  connecting, 69–72
  in e-mails, 174
  introductory, 63–65
  main idea implied in, 51
  numbered, 302–03, 357
  organization of, 53–54, 84, 86
  patterns of development in, 59–63
  pronouns and synonyms in, 56–57
  relevance in, 46, 47, 48
  repetition in, 55–57
  topic sentences in, 47, 48, 49–51
  transitions within and between, 54–55
  unity in, 46, 47–52
Parallelism, 518–26
  comparisons and, 522
  coordinating conjunctions and, 520
  correlative conjunctions and, 521
  deceptive, 520
  definition of, 518
  emphasis from, 525
  example of, 518–19
  formal outlines and, 524
  function words and, 522
  in headings, 168–69
  items in a list, 523
  items in a series, 521
  items in outlines, 524
  phrases and, 519, 520, 524
  in repetition, 535
  in résumés, 488
  in speaking, 186
  subordinate clauses and, 520
Paraphrases
  in critical reading, 110, 132
  definition of, 252

documenting, in APA style, 350–51, 370–71
length of, 252
by non-native writers of English, 252
in note making, 252
parenthetical citation for, 249, 253, 275–76
patchwriting in, 110, 134, 252–55
source boundaries in, 277–78
of unpaginated source material, 278
used to support claims, 132–33
verb tense in introducing, 547–48
writer's voice in, 538–39
Parentheses, 798–99
  around dates, 798
  around numbers in a list, 798–99
  around question marks, 794
  in Boolean searches, 219
  capitalization of sentences in, 808
  commas and dashes *vs.,* 798
  downplaying material in, 798
  within parentheses, 800
  punctuation and, 798
  for supplementary information, 798
Parenthetical expressions, commas after, 753–54
Parenthetical notes
  APA style, 348–57. *See also* In-text citations, APA-style
  CSE style, 416–18
  MLA style, 289, 291, 293. *See also* In-text citations, MLA-style
Participial phrases
  as dangling modifiers, 692
  definition of, 529, 593
  placement of, 529
Participles. *See also* Past participles; Present participles
  as adjectives, 727
  infinitives and, 649
  participial phrases, 529, 593
  placement of, 529
  tense sequence and, 649
Particles, 722–24
Parts of speech, 575–84. *See also specific parts of speech*
pass, 590
passed, past, 565
Passive voice
  active voice *vs.,* 652–54
  concise writing and, 501
  definition of, 652
  emphasis and, 535–36
  past participles in, 637
  reasons for using, 653–54

responsibility and, 536
  in science and social science writing, 458, 536, 654
  shifting voice, 652–53, 679–80
  transitive verbs in, 589, 652
past history, 498
Past participles
  as adjectives, 638, 727
  forms of, 637
  with infinitives, 649
  of irregular verbs, 636, 640–41
  in participial phrases, 593
  tense sequences and, 649
  as verbals, 601, 638
Past perfect progressive tense, 646, 647
Past perfect subjunctive, 651
Past perfect tense, 645, 646, 648
Past progressive tense, 645, 646
Past subjunctive mood, 651
Past tenses
  of irregular verbs, 636, 640–41
  in literature and humanities writing, 438
  of regular verbs, 636, 637
  in science and social science writing, 458–59, 648
  simple, 645
  in verb phrases, 639
Patchwriting. *See also* Plagiarism
  definition of, 247
  examples of, 253–54, 538
  in paraphrasing, 110, 132, 252–55
  in summarizing, 256–57
Pathos, appeals to, 144–45
patience, patients, 565
Patterns of development, 59–63. *See also* Paragraphs
  analysis, 62
  cause and effect, 62
  comparison-contrast, 60–61
  for connecting paragraphs, 69
  definition, 62–63
  description, 59
  exemplification, 60
  narration, 59–60
pay, 590
PDF (Portable Document Format)
  APA style for files in, 366
  Chicago style for files in, 399
  database articles in, 215
  definition of, 180
  HTML *vs.,* 218, 315
  MLA style for files in, 303
  in posting documents online, 180
  for source copies, 201

peace, piece, 565
Peer review, 90–92, 232
Penguin Dictionary of Literary Terms and Literary Theory, 437
Pen names, 309
Percents, 828
perfect, 675
Perfect infinitive, 649
Perfect progressive tenses, 646, 647
Perfect tenses, 645–47, 649
Performances
  documenting: *Chicago* style for, 405; MLA style for, 326
  writing about, 451–54
Period(s)
  in abbreviations, 820
  in correcting comma splices, 616
  in questions, to soften tone, 793
  quotation marks and, 785
  in sentences and mild commands, 792–93
  spaces after, 377
Periodicals. *See also* Online articles
  abstracts from, 215, 220
  in critical reading
  documenting: APA style for, 366–70; *Chicago* style for, 397–402; CSE style for, 422–26; MLA style for, 315–19
  finding articles in, 215–20
  issue numbers, 203, 204, 205, 398
  scholarly *vs.* popular, 231, 234
Periodic sentences, 531–32
Permission for borrowed images. *See* Copyright clearance
Perry Castañeda Library Map Collection, 225
Person
  definition of, 620, 681
  first, 15, 438–39, 808
  plurals and, 621
  second, 534, 666, G19
  shifts in, 681–82
  third, 438–39, 458, 681–82
  use of, 681–82
Persona, 7, 87
personal, personnel, 563
Personal attacks, 159
Personal beliefs, 130
Personal communications, documenting
  APA style for, 357, 376
  Chicago style for, 406
  MLA style for, 303
Personal context, 17

Personal correspondence, documenting, MLA style for, 330
Personal experiences, writing about, 10
Personal names
  abbreviations in, 820
  capitalization in, 810
  commas and, 761
Personal pronouns, 578, 657, 775
Personal statements, in portfolios, 101–03, 335
Personification, 552
personnel, personal, 563
Perspective, gaining, 82–83
persuade, 726
Persuasive argument. *See also* Arguments
  approach in, 18
  deductive logic in, 120, 135–37
  editorials as, 11
  in research assignments, 192
  thesis statements in, 32–33
phenomena, data, media, G16
phenomenon, phenomena, 621
Philosopher's Index, 437
Phone numbers, 827
Photographs. *See also* Visuals
  in emotional appeals, 144–45
  as evidence, 74–75, 77
  finding, 225
  in job applications, 74, 484
Phrasal verbs
  as idioms, 555, 642
  list of, 723
  particles in, 722–24
  separable *vs.* inseparable, 723–24
Phrases
  absolute, 530, 594
  as adjectives, 529–30, 582
  as adverbs, 529, 582
  appositive. *See* Appositives/appositive phrases
  commas to set off nonessential, 608, 758
  in concise writing, 502
  coordinating, 506
  definition of, 506, 591, 752
  as disruptive, 689–90
  empty, 497
  as fragments, 591, 601, 605–06, 695–96
  gerund, 524, 593, 627–28
  infinitive, 520, 592, 593, 692
  introductory, 749, 751–52
  noun, 591, 605
  in parallelism, 519, 520, 524
  participial, 529, 592, 593, 692

  prepositional. *See* Prepositional phrases
  quantifying, 718, 719
  signal. *See* Signal phrases
  transitional, 54–55, 530
  verb, 577, 579, 592, 621, 639–42, 728–30
piece, peace, 565
Pie charts, 74–76
Pinterest, 214
Place names
  articles with, 717
  capitalization of, 810
  commas with, 761
  as singular, 627–28
Plagiarism, 246–63
  acknowledging sources, to avoid, 6
  college policy on, 6
  common knowledge and, 249–50
  culture and, 247
  definition of, 247, 248
  electronic research logs and, 199
  examples of, 253–55
  note taking and, 21, 250–51
  in online sources, 236
  patchwriting, 132, 247, 252–57, 538
  prevalence of, 246–47
  quoting and, 259–61, 790–91
  source materials requiring citation, 248–49
  student essay on, 8, 148–53
  summarizing and, 256–58
  unintentional, 199, 247
  valuing research, 248
  of visuals, videos, and sound files, 249
"Plagiarism Cheats Students" (Gurney), 8
plain, plane, 565
Plain form (unmarked) infinitives, 725–26
Plain text, 173–74
plan, 726
plane, plain, 565
Planning a project, 9–28. *See also* Organizing a project
  analyzing an assignment, 17–19
  analyzing the writing situation, 9–17
  collaborative projects, 26–28
  determining purpose of writing, 10–12
  generating ideas, 20–25
  identifying and addressing one's audience, 12–15
  narrowing or broadening the topic, 25–26

Planning a project (*continued*)
  setting the assignment calendar, 18, 19
  setting tone and genre, 15–17
plans for the future, 498
Plays
  documenting, in MLA style, 297–98, 310
  numbers in divisions of plays, 828
  writing about, 451–54
Plot, 435
Plurals
  apostrophes and, 774, 775–78
  articles and, 714
  awkward shifts and, 682
  of compound nouns, 571
  of count nouns, 713–14
  in dictionary entries, 561
  indefinite pronouns and, 625
  irregular, 570, 576–77, 621
  possession in plural nouns, 577, 774
  of pronouns, 578
  of proper nouns, 570
  quantifying words with, 719
  regular, 569, 576, 621
  of verbs, 621, 637
plus, G18
p.m., 823
Podcasts, documenting
  APA style for, 373
  Chicago style for, 405
  MLA style for, 325
Poetry. *See also* Literature and humanities, writing in
  divisions of, 828
  documenting, MLA style for, 297–99
  elements of, 447
  ellipses in, 804
  explication sample, 446, 448–51
  lines of, 298–99
  quotations from, 783
  slashes to mark ends of lines in, 783, 804
  writing about, 446–51
Point of view, 435
Policy, claims of, 139–40
Portfolios
  contents of, 99–101
  electronic, 100–01
  format of, 100–01
  in MLA-style papers, 336
  personal statements in, 101–03
  sample, 101–03
  submission of, 101

Positive form of adjectives and adverbs, 674
Possession, prepositions indicating, 743
Possessive case
  apostrophes in, 657, 773–77
  compound, 658, 659, 776–77
  determiners in, 580, 718
  with gerunds, 661
  of to indicate possession, 743
  its in, 775
  nouns and, 577, 718
  prepositions and, 743
  pronoun-antecedent agreement, 630
  pronoun forms in, 578, 657–58
Possibility
  modals expressing, 728, 729
  verb mood and, 650
Postal abbreviations, 478
Postcolonial criticism, 436
Poster sessions, documenting, APA style for, 373–74
Post hoc, ergo propter hoc fallacy, 158
Postings. *See* Blogs and blog postings; Discussion list postings
postpone, 726
"The Power of Wardrobe: Male Stereotype Influences" (DeGroot), 382–88
PowerPoint, 187. *See also* Multimedia presentations
practice, 726
precede, 567
precede, proceed, G18
Predicates
  complete, 587
  compound, 587, 605–06
  faulty predication, 697–98
  in mixed construction, 696–97
  simple, 587
Prefaces, citing, 311, 363, 396
prefer, 726
Prefixes, 566, 831–32
Prejudices, 140. *See also* Bias
Premises, in deduction, 135–36
Preparing to write, 29–40. *See also* Critical reading and thinking
Preposition(s), 739–45. *See also* Prepositional phrases
  adjectives with, 733
  for cause or reason, 742
  for condition or degree, 742
  definition of, 582, 739
  functions of, 576, 740–43
  gerunds after, 726

lists of common, 583, 740
multiword, 740
necessary and unnecessary, 745
objects of, 592
  as particles, 722–24
  in phrasal verbs, 555
  recognizing, 739–40
  specified for certain verbs or nouns, 744
  in titles and subtitles, 810
Prepositional phrases
  as adjectives and adverbs, 529, 592
  as dangling modifiers, 692
  definition of, 592
  direct object recipients in, 708
  as fragments, 605, 695–96
  functions of, 592
  as indirect objects, 590
  list of, 583, 740
  time and, 741–42
presence, presents, 565
Presentation anxiety, 187
Presentations. *See* Multimedia presentations
Presentation software, 187, 188
Present infinitive tense, 648
Present participles
  as adjectives, 638, 727
  forms of, 636, 638, 641
  as nouns, 638
  tense sequences and, 649
  as verbals, 601, 638
Present perfect participles, 649
Present perfect progressive tense, 646
Present perfect tense, 645, 646
Present progressive tense, 645, 646
Present subjunctive mood, 650–51
Present tenses, 620–21, 644–49
Press releases, 314, 492–94
pretend, 726
Previewing, in reading critically, 109–10, 230–31
Prewriting, 33, 123
Primary sources, 435–36, 456, G18
principal, principle, 565, G18
Print sources. *See specific sources*
Privacy, e-mails and, 175
Probability, modals expressing, 729
Problem-solution organization, 54, 70
proceed, 567
proceed, precede, G18
Process analysis, 59–60
Professional titles, 478
Progressive tenses, 638, 645–47
promise, 590, 726

Pronoun(s). *See also* Pronoun-antecedent agreement; Pronoun case
 as adjectives, 580
 for coherence, 56–57
 in comma splices, 613–14
 definition, 630
 demonstrative, 578
 as determiners, 580, 718
 as direct objects, 724
 functions of, 576, 577, 578
 gender bias and, 545–46, 632
 implied references for, 666
 indefinite, 578, 625, 631, 633, 774–75
 intensive, 578
 interrogative, 578, 602, 657, 663–64
 objective case, 657, 658, 660, 661
 in paragraphs, 56–57
 personal, 578, 657, 775
 possessive case in. *See* Possessive case
 pronoun reference, 664–67
 reciprocal, 578
 redundant subject and object pronouns, 706
 reflexive, 578
 relative. *See* Relative pronouns
 as subject complements, 658
 subjective case, 656–57, 658, 664
 subject-verb agreement, 624
 they and *it* as indefinite, 666–67
 this, that, these, and *those* as determiners, 718
 types of, 578
 who, whom, whoever, and *whomever* as, 663–64
 you, to address reader directly, 666, G19
Pronoun-antecedent agreement, 630–34
 collective noun antecedents and, 634
 compound antecedents and, 634
 gender bias and, 545–46, 632
 generic noun antecedents, 631–33, 682
 grammar checkers and, 631
 indefinite pronouns and, 631–33
 "nearest antecedent" rule in, 634
 plural or variable indefinite pronouns and, 633
 plural pronouns with singular antecedents, 633
 possessive pronouns and, 630
 in subordinate clauses, 628–29
Pronoun case, 656–64
 in appositives, 660
 in comparisons with *than* or *as,* 662

 in compounds, 658, 659
 forms of, 656–57
 with infinitives, 661
 with the *-ing* form of a verb, 661
 interrogative, 657
 objective, 657, 658
 personal pronouns, 657
 possessive, 578, 580, 657, 658, 659, 661, 718
 subjective, 656–57, 658, 664
 tone and, 663
 we or *us* before a noun, 660
 with *who, whom, whoever,* and *whomever,* 663–64
Pronoun reference, 664–67
Pronunciation
 in dictionaries, 561
 spelling and, 562–63
Proofreading, 93–94, 181
Proper adjectives, 809–10
Proper nouns
 articles with, 717
 capitalizing, 808, 809–10
 function of, 575, 713
Proposals, 490–92
propose, 708
ProQuest Central, 215, 217
prove, 589, 670
provided that, 513
Proximity, in design, 162
Pseudonyms, 309
Psychology, style guide for, 200
PsycINFO, 195, 216, 217
Publication Manual of the American Psychological Association (6th ed.), 347, 377. *See also* APA style
Public context, 16–17
Punctuation. *See also specific punctuation marks*
 in compound sentences, 598, 750
 conjunctive adverbs and, 581
 in coordination, 506, 749, 754–56
 emphasis and, 533
 end, 377, 792–94
 of nonessential subordinate clauses, 512, 533, 608, 700–01, 749, 757–59
 in proofreading, 94
 in quotations, 260, 759–60, 785–87, 801, 803
 in subordination, 512, 749, 752, 758–579
 in URLs and DOIs, 359, 804
Purpose of writing
 in assignments, 10–11, 17

 in business letters, 477
 definition of, G18
 design and, 164
 in e-mails, 172
 to entertain, 10
 to express, 10
 to inform, 10–11
 in multimedia presentations, 183–84
 to persuade or argue, 11
 in research projects, 192, 265
 source evaluation and, 233
 statement of, 265, 477
 tone and, 15–16
 in websites, 176
put, 708
put back, 723
put down, 723
put up with, 723

Q

Qualifiers, in arguments, 139
Qualitative data, 456
Quantifiers, 718–20
Quantitative data, 456–57
Queer approach to criticism, 436
Question(s). *See also* Question marks
 answers to, 609
 direct, 684, 793–94
 incomplete sentences as, 794
 indirect, 684, 792–93
 in introductions, 64
 periods used to soften tone, 793
 relative pronouns beginning, 602–03
 research, 195–96, 266
 rhetorical, 534
 series of, 794
 shifts between direct and indirect, 684
 tag, 753–54
 in titles, 87
 verb mood in, 650
 word order in, 586, 709–10
Question marks
 in direct questions, 793–94
 multiple, 793
 in parentheses, 794
 quotation marks and, 786
 in a series of questions, 794
 in wildcard searches, 219
Questionnaires (surveys), 228–29
quit, 726
Quotation(s). *See also* Quotation marks
 APA style for, 351–52
 block or long, 292, 334, 782–83
 bookending, 253, 291

Quotation(s) (*continued*)
brackets in, 786, 800
capitalizing first words in, 808–09
capital letters changed to lowercase in, 786
circumstances for use of, 259–60
citing, 248–49, 351–52
claims supported by, 132–33
colons and, 760, 786, 787, 801
commas between signal phrases and, 759–60, 787
contexts for, 133, 245
copying into notes, 260–61
direct, 683–84, 759–60, 780–83
ellipses in, 260, 786, 803
indirect, 683–84, 790–91
integrating into text, 275–76, 284–85, 289. *See also* Signal phrases
interrupted by signal phrases, 787, 801, 809
overusing in notes, 260
overusing in research papers, 272
from poetry, 783
from primary *vs.* secondary sources, 260
within quotations, 780–81, 782–83
shifts between direct and indirect, 683–84
source's authority established with, 260
using fairly, 260
verb tense in introducing, 547–48
Quotation marks, 780–87
in American *vs.* British usage, 785
common do's and don'ts, 781
in definitions, 784
in dialog, 782
in direct quotations, 780–83
double changed to single, 780–81
in irony, 781, 784
in keyword searches, 211, 219
not for emphasis, 781, 784–85
not in long quotations, 782–83
not in parenthetical style, 784
not with clichés, 781, 785
not with indirect quotations, 781, 782
not with slang, 781, 785
punctuation in quotations and, 785
in quotations from poetry, 783
single, 780–81
smart *vs.* straight, 782
source boundaries and, 276–80

in specialized terms in paraphrases, 253
in titles of short works, 783–84
in titles within titles, 313
for words used as words, 781, 784
Qur'an, documenting
APA style for, 356, 365
MLA style for, 299, 313–14

R

Races, names of, 810
Racial labels, 547
Radio broadcasts, documenting
APA style for, 373
MLA style for, 300, 324–25
rain, reign, rein, 565
raise, raze, 565
raise, rise, 643, G18
Random House Webster's Unabridged Dictionary, 558, 559
rarely, 711
"Rash and Unadvis'd in Verona Seeks Same" (Brantley), 452–54
Ratios, colons in, 802
raze, raise, 565
read, 590
Reader response approach to criticism, 436
Readers, responsibilities to, 56. *See also* Audience
Reading. *See also* Critical reading and thinking
actively and reflectively, 432–33
aloud, 83, 88
for comprehension, 108–14
of essay exams, 471
proofreading, 93–94
with study guides, 433
Reading journals, 117–19, 470
real, really, 671–72, G18
really, 497, 671
Reason, prepositions indicating, 742
Reasoning, logical, 135–37
reason is because, reason why, 698, G18
Reasons for writing. *See* Purpose of writing
recall, 726
Recipients, in e-mails, 172, 175
Reciprocal pronouns, 578
recommend, 708
Recordings, 373
Red herring fallacy, 158
Redundant comparisons, 674
Redundant expressions, 498–99, 674

Reference list, APA-style, 358–76
abstracts, 365, 369–70
anthology selections, 363
art works, 374
audio and visual sources, 372–74
authors with two or more works published in the same year, 360–61
blogs and blog postings, 371–73
book editions other than the first, 363
books with author and editor or translator, 362–63
books with authors of the same surname and first initial, 362
books with group or corporate authors, 362
books with multiple authors, 359, 362
books with one author, 358, 361
books with two authors, 359
books with unnamed or anonymous authors, 359
computer software, 372
conference proceedings, 376
directory of models, 360–61
discussion list postings, 371
dissertations, 365
DOIs and URLs in, 358, 359, 366–67, 370
edited books or anthologies, 363
electronic sources, 358–59, 370–72
fact sheets, brochures, and pamphlets, 375
format of, 378, 380–81
government publications, 374–75
lectures, speeches, or conference presentations, 373–74
legal sources, 376
letters to the editor, 369
magazine articles, 367–68
motion pictures, 372
multiple sources with an author and various coauthors, 362
multivolume works, 364
musical or other audio recordings, 373
newspaper articles, 368–69
personal communications, 376
presentation slides, 372
reference work entries, 364
reports, nongovernmental, 375
republished books, 364
reviews, 369
sacred or classical sources, 365
in sample paper, 387
scholarly journal articles, 366–67
television or radio broadcasts, 373

two or more books by the same author, 360–62
vlogs, 372–73
websites and web pages, 370–71
wiki articles, 371
Reference list, *Chicago*-style. *See* Works cited list, *Chicago* style
Reference list, CSE-style, 418–28
   books with group of corporate author, 420–21
   books with one author, 418–20
   books with two or more authors, 420
   directory to models, 419
   discussion lists or blog postings, 427
   dissertations, 422
   edited books, 421
   edited book selections or conference proceedings, 421–22
   e-mails, 428
   format of, 428–30
   magazine articles, 424–25
   newspaper articles, 425–26
   sample reference list, 429–30
   scholarly journal articles, 422–24
   technical reports or government documents, 428
   URLs and e-mail addresses, 834
   web pages, 427
   websites, 426–27
Reference list, MLA-style. *See* Works cited list, MLA-style
References, in job applications, 488–89
Reference Universe, 208
Reference works
   almanacs and yearbooks, 209
   bibliographies, 210
   biographical, 209
   citation indexes, 235
   databases, 195, 201–03, 215–20, 437
   dictionaries, 207–08, 457, 558–62, 733
   documenting: APA style for, 364; *Chicago* style for, 396; MLA style for, 311–12
   encyclopedias, 207–08, 457
   idea generation and, 25
   library catalogs as, 195, 207–08, 220–23, 225, 235–36
   locating, 206–10
   subject-specific, 207, 208
   uses of, 206
refer to, allude, elude, G14
Reflecting, 114–19
"Reflecting on Brent Staples's Editorial 'How Hip-Hop Music Lost Its Way and Betrayed Its Fans'" (Wratten), 128–30
Reflexive pronouns, 578
refuse, 726
refused, 736
RefWorks, 201, 217
Regionalisms, 541
Regular verbs, 636–38
Rehearsing presentations, 187, 189
reign, rain, rein, 565
Rejection, letters of, 481
relation, relationship, G18
Relative (adjective) clauses, 595
Relative pronouns
   in adjective clauses, 595
   case in, 657, 663–64
   definition of, 657
   forms of, 578
   interrogative pronouns *vs.,* 602, 663
   list of, 603
   in noun clauses, 596
   omitting, 595
   in questions, 602–03
   subject-verb agreement and, 578, 628–29
   in subordinate clauses, 511, 595
   who, whom, whoever, and *whomever* as, 663–64
Relevance
   of paragraphs, 46, 47, 48
   of sources, 230–31, 240–41
Reliability. *See* Credibility
Religion names, 810
Religious works. *See* Sacred texts
remain, 589
remember, 647, 726
remind, 726
repair, 708
repeat again, 498
Repetition
   in design, 162, 165
   emphasis and, 535
   in paragraphs, 55–57
   in poetry, 447
   in speaking, 186
   strategic, 534–35
   unacceptable, 698
   unnecessary, 499
   using commas to replace omitted words, 763
reply all, 175, 483
Reports. *See also* Sciences and social sciences, writing in
   business, 490–92
   laboratory, 459–68
   sample paper, 461–68
   standard format for, 459–61
   thesis statements in, 10–11, 18, 31–32, 138, 192
   writing, 457–59
Republished or reprinted works, 313, 355–56, 364
Requests, 651–52
require, 726
Research, field, 226–29, G17
Research hypothesis, 195–96, 265–66
Research logs, 198–99, 250
Research notebooks, 251, 459
Research papers
   analysis, interpretation, and synthesis in, 270–72
   assignment analysis, 192–93
   factors in planning, 194
   field research, 226–29
   finding sources for. *See* Sources, finding
   format for, 459–61
   informative *vs.* persuasive, 192–93
   note making for, 459
   organizing ideas, 266–69
   plagiarism, avoiding, 199, 272
   purpose and audience for, 192–93
   questions and hypotheses in, 195–96, 265–66
   research logs in, 198–99, 250
   revising, 273
   sample paper, 461–68
   schedule in, 18, 194
   source selection strategies in, 197–98
   thesis statement in, 264–66
   topic selection in, 195
   working bibliographies in, 200–05
Research questions, 195–96, 265–66
Research topics, 195. *See also* Topic
resemble, 647
resist, 726
respectfully, respectively, 565, G18
Response, critical, 123, 127–30
Restrictive (essential) elements, 512, 608, 757
Results section, 460
Résumés
   designing, 486
   sample, 487, 489
   scannable or electronic, 489–90
   traditional print, 487–89
Return address, 478

Reviews
  documenting: APA style for, 369; *Chicago* style for, 402; MLA style for, 319
  of drama, 451–54
Revising, 82–93
  arguments, 159
  audience and, 84
  the big picture in, 85
  for coherence and unity, 84, 86, 473
  e-mails, 174
  evidence and counterevidence, 84
  globally and locally, 82–83
  with instructors or tutors, 92
  peer, 90–92
  perspective gained in, 82–83
  proofreading in, 93–94
  sentences, 88–89
  support for ideas in, 84, 85
  thesis statements, 31–33, 83–84
  titles, 86–87
  visuals, 78–81
  websites, 181
  words, 87–88
Rhetorical appeals, 142
Rhetorical questions, 534
Rhyme, 447
Rhythm, 447, 531–32
right, rite, wright, write, 565
Right, Wrong, and Risky: A Dictionary of Today's American English Usage, 559
rise, raise, 643, G18
risk, 726
rite, right, wright, write, 565
road, rode, 565
Rogerian model of arguments, 154–55
Rogers, Carl, 154–55
Roundabout constructions, 499
Roundabout expressions, 498–99
round in shape, 498
RSS feeds, 214
run into, 723
Run-on sentences. *See* Fused (run-on) sentences

S

-s, -es
  as plural noun ending, 569
  subject-verb agreement and, 627
  as verb ending, 636, 637, 774
Sacred texts
  capitalization of, 810
  chapter and verse notations, 802
  documenting: APA style for, 356, 365; *Chicago* style for, 397; MLA style for, 299–300, 313–14
  not italicized, 815
Salutations
  in business letters, 478
  in e-mails, 172–73, 483
Sample papers
  in APA style, 381–88
  argument, 147–53
  business memo, 482
  in *Chicago* style, 408–15
  claims and evidence analysis, 121
  connecting paragraphs, 69–71
  critique, 127–30
  in CSE style, 429–30
  drama review, 451–54
  essay exam answers, 474–75
  fiction, interpretive analysis of, 442–46
  final draft, 95–99
  first draft, 42–44
  job application, 485
  letter of apology, 480
  in MLA style, 336–46
  outlines, 268–69
  personal statement for portfolio, 101–03
  poetry explication, 446, 448–51
  press release, 493
  prewriting, 123
  report, 492
  research report, 461–68
  résumé, print, 487
  résumé, scannable, 489–90
  in sciences and social sciences, 461–68
  scratch outline, 36
  summaries, 111, 257–58
  summary notes with writer's assessment, 263
  textual analysis, 434
  thesis statement, 265–66
Sarcasm, 784
say, 708
Scannable résumés, 489–90
scarcely, 673, 688
Scheduling
  assignment calculators, 194
  assignments, 18, 19
  in collaborative projects, 28
  first draft, 39
  research projects, 194
Scholarly journals, documenting
  APA style for, 366–67
  Chicago style for, 398–99
  CSE style for, 422–24
  MLA style for, 310, 315–16
Science Direct, 216
Sciences and social sciences, writing in
  approaches to, 11, 455–56
  discipline-specific vocabulary in, 457–58, 542–43
  passive voice in, 458, 536, 654
  past and present tense in, 458–59, 647
  qualitative and quantitative data in, 456–57
  reference list in, 460, 467
  sample report, 461–68
  standard format for, 459–61
  style guide selection in, 201, 416, 457
  third person in, 458
  types of, 459
Scientific Style and Format: The CSE Manual for Authors, Editors, and Publishers (7th ed.), 416. *See also* CSE style
Scopus, 235
Scores, in sports, 828
Scratch outlines, 35–36, 267. *See also* Outlines
screen, screens, 302
Screenshots, 75, 77
Search.com (metasearch engine), 213
Search engines
  blog, 214, 215
  database, 217–20
  examples of, 213
  federated searching on, 220
  metasearch, 211–12, 213
  using, 210
secede, 567
Secondary sources, 437
Second-language learners. *See* English as a second language
Second person
  addressing the reader, 666, G19
  in commands, 534
see, 725
seem, 589, 647
seldom, 711
self-, 831–32
sell to, 744
Semicolons, 766–71
  in compound sentences, 598
  conjunctive adverbs and, 581, 768–69
  coordinating conjunctions and, 612, 768

Index

do's and don'ts, 767
in in-text citations, 305, 354
linking independent clauses with, 507–08, 612, 613, 750, 753, 767–68
between long items in a series, 754, 767, 769
not before lists, 767, 769
overuse of, 770–71
quotation marks and, 786
in repairing comma splices, 616, 767, 769–70
sending a signal with, 766
in series, 754, 767, 769
stressing equal importance with, 770
in transitional expressions, 768–69
send, 590, 707
Sentence(s)
capitalization of first word in, 807–09
commands, 534
common problems in, 88–89
complete, 600–03
complex, 528, 598, 770
compound. *See* Compound sentences
compound-complex, 528, 598–99
cumulative, 531
declarative, 534, 585, 704, 793
exclamations, 534
exclamatory, 585
imperative, 585, 602
interrogative, 585
interrupted periodic, 532
inverted word order in, 532, 586, 629, 710–11
length of, 528
periodic, 531–32
questions. *See* Question(s)
revising, 88–89
simple, 528, 597–98
stated subject requirement in, 698, 704–05
topic, 47, 48, 49–51
variety and emphasis in, 527–39
Sentence fragments, 600–10
ambiguities from, 604
context and, 604
correcting, 604–08
definition of, 591, 695
grammar checkers and, 605
imperatives *vs.,* 602
intentional, 604, 609
lists and examples as, 606
mixed construction and, 695–96
with no subject, 601–02

with no verb, 600–01
phrases as, 591, 601, 605–06, 695–96
prepositional phrases as subjects in, 605, 695–96
recognizing, 600–03
subordinate clauses as, 595, 602–03, 607–08
verbals as, 601, 605
Sentence outlines, 36–37, 267. *See also* Outlines
Sentence structure, 585–99. *See also* Word order
certain conjunctions or adverbs beginning a clause, 710–11
direct and indirect objects in, 591
elliptical constructions, 499, 700–01
faulty predication, 697–98
grammatically mixed, 695–97
incomplete constructions, 699–702
inverted word order in, 532, 586, 629, 710–11
normal word order in, 704
object complements in, 590
in paraphrasing, 253
in questions, 586
redundant subject and object pronouns in, 706
sentence patterns, 588–90
stated subject, 698, 704–05
subject and predicate in, 585–88
there and *it* constructions, 586
variety in, 428, 528–32
verb types and, 588–90
Sentence variety, 428, 528–32
Separable phrasal verbs, 723–24
Sequence of tenses, 648–49
Sequences, conjunctions and, 508
Sequiera, Shona, 443–46
Serial commas, 506, 749, 754
Series
of books, 313, 397
commas separating items in, 506, 749, 754
dashes setting off, 797
parallelism and, 521
semicolons in, 754, 767, 769
Servers, 174, 176
set, sit, 643, G18
Setting, 435
several
count and noncount nouns with, 719–20
as determiner, 713
pronoun-antecedent agreement, 633
subject-verb agreement, 625

Sexist language. *See* Gender bias, avoiding
Sexual orientation, 547
-sh, plurals of words that end in, 569
shall
meanings of, 729
as modal verb, 579, 641, 728, 729
subject-verb agreement with, 621
shall, should, ought to, 729
shall, will, G18
she, he; he/she; s/he, G17
she or he, 546, 633, 682
Shifts, 678–84
in number, 682
in person, 681–82
in questions, 683–84
in quotations, 683–84
in verb mood, 679
in verb tense, 678–79
in voice, 679–80
should
advisability and expectation and, 729
with *if* clauses, 651
meanings of, 729
as modal verb, 579, 641, 728, 729
subject-verb agreement with, 621
subjunctive used with, 651
should, shall, ought to, 729
should of, would of, could of, must of, G16
should've, should have, 728
shout at, 744
shout to, 744
show, 590, 707
sic, 800
sight, cite, site, 563, G15
Signal phrases
APA style for, 348–49, 351
authority of source and, 276–77
in bookending, 253, 291
commas with, 759–60, 787
definition of, 759
format of, 289
interrupting quotations, 787, 801, 809
introducing quotations, 787, 801
MLA style for, 289, 291, 293
in presentations, 190
in research papers, 244–45
signal verb list, 277
source boundaries and, 279, 348–49
in summaries, 257
for writer's voice, 281–83, 293, 539
Signal verbs, 277
Signatures, in letters, 478
Signposts, in presentations, 190
Silent *-e,* words that end in, 567

Similes, 552, 553
Simple future tense, 645, 646
Simple past tense, 645, 646
Simple predicates, 587
Simple present tense, 644–45, 646
Simple sentences, 528, 597–98
Simple subjects, 585
Simple tenses, 644–45, 646
simply, 688
since
    meanings of, 513, G18
    as subordinating conjunction, 513, 603
since, because, as, G15
Single authors, documenting
    APA style for, 350–52, 358, 361
    Chicago style for, 391–93
    CSE style for, 418–20
    MLA style for, 293, 305–08
Single quotation marks, 780–81
sit, set, 643, G18
site, sight, cite, 563, G15
Site maps, 178
Slang, 542, 781, 785
Slashes
    functions of, 804–05
    in poetry quotations, 783, 804
Slippery slope fallacy, 159
Smarthinking, 92
Smart quotation marks, 782
smell, 589
Smith, Betsy, 43–44, 96–99
Snyder, Gary, 434
so
    in coordination, 506, 508, 583, 750
    in correcting comma splices, 616
    in parallelism, 520
so, such, 737
so, too, 736
Social networking sites, 229, 542
Social sciences, writing in. *See* Sciences and social sciences, writing in
Software. *See* Computer software
some
    count and noncount nouns with, 719–20
    pronoun-antecedent agreement, 633
    as quantifying word, 719
    subject-verb agreement, 625
somebody, 625
somebody, someone, G18
someone, 625
something, 625
sometime, sometimes, G18
somewheres, G19

sort of, kind of, G17
so that, 513, 603
sound, 589, 670
Sound recording. *See* Audio sources
Source(s). *See also* Citations; Sources, evaluating; Sources, finding
    accurate and fair representation of, 791
    acknowledging, 272
    analyzing, interpreting, synthesizing, and critiquing, 119–33
    bookending borrowed material, 253, 291
    citation management software, 201, 217
    common knowledge, 249–50
    complex, 244–45
    copying, 201, 220
    establishing authority of, in papers, 276–77
    evaluation of, 230–45
    in field research, 226–29
    multimedia, 78, 225
    online. *See* Online sources
    popular *vs.* scholarly, 197, 231, 232–33, 234
    in presentations, 190
    primary *vs.* secondary, 435–37
    printed, 197
    relevance of, 230–31, 240–41
    selection strategies, 197–98
    summarizing, 110–11, 132–33, 432
    unpacking, 244–45
    working bibliographies, 200–05
    for writing about literature, 435–36, 437
    for writing in the sciences and social sciences, 197–98
Sources, evaluating, 230–45. *See also* Credibility
    critiquing, 125–27
    interactive media, 214
    online texts, 236–39
    popular *vs.* scholarly sources, 232–33, 234
    for relevance, 230–31
    for reliability, 232–36, 239
    visual sources, 239–41
Sources, finding, 206–29. *See also* Online sources, finding
    abstracts, 215, 220
    blogs and blog postings, 214, 215
    databases and indexes, 215–20
    government publications, 224
    interactive media and, 214–15

    library catalogs and, 207–08, 220–23
    multimedia sources, 225
    reference works, 206–10
    on the Web, 210–13
Spacing
    in APA style, 377
    in business letters, 477
    in MLA style, 332
Spam/spamming, 483
SparkNotes, 433
Spatial organization, 35
Spatial relationships, transitional expressions for, 55
Speaking, 186, 189–90. *See also* Multimedia presentations
Specialized databases, 437
Specialized dictionaries, 207
Special pleading fallacy, 157
Specific words, 551–52
Speeches, 144, 327, 373–74. *See also* Multimedia presentations
Spelling
    American *vs.* British, 563
    bilingual dictionaries and, 562
    dictionaries and, 560–61
    of homonyms and near-homonyms, 563, 565
    ie/ei rule, 566
    impact of errors in, 564
    improving, 571
    plurals, 569–71
    prefixes, 566
    pronunciation and, 562–63
    proofreading, 93–94
    spelling checkers, 93, 569, 775
    suffixes, 567–68
Spelling checkers, 93, 569, 775
Split infinitives, 686, 690
Sponsors, of websites, 238
Sports scores, 832
Square brackets. *See* Brackets
Squinting modifiers, 688
Stacking the deck fallacy, 157
Stage fright, 187
Standard American English, 574
Standard word order, 704
stand in for, 723
Stanzas, 447
Staples, Brent, 115–17
Staples on papers, 334, 380, 408, 429
start, 726
Statement of purpose. *See* Thesis/thesis statement
stationary, stationery, 565, G19
Statistics, 35, 41, 828

Stereotypes, 545, 546–47
stop, 726
Strategic repetition, 534–35
Student example papers. *See* Sample papers
Study groups, 470
Study guides, 433
Style. *See* Appropriate language; Biased language; Conciseness; Coordination; Dictionaries; Emphasis; Parallelism; Subordination; Variety; Words; Wordy expressions
Style checkers
confusing shifts and, 679
coordination and subordination and, 505
misplaced modifiers, 686
parallelism and, 521
word choice and, 549
wordiness and, 499
Style guide selection, 95, 200, 437, 457
Styles of documentation. *See also specific documentation style*
APA, 347–88
Chicago, 389–415
CSE, 416–30
MLA, 288–346
Subject(s)
complements. *See* Subject complements
complete, 585
compound, 585, 623–24
dangling modifiers and, 692
definition, 600
in expletive constructions, 586
explicit, 602
finding the, 586
fragments and, 601–02
in imperatives, 602
in interrogative sentences, 586
question words as, 710
redundant subject and object pronouns, 706
shifting voice to maintain, 652–53
simple, 585
there as, 586
unstated, 534, 585, 602, 705
word order and, 586–87
Subject complements
adjective phrases as, 530
adjectives as, 580, 670, 671
compound, 658
definition of, 530, 580, 658, 696
mixed constructions with, 696–97
placement of, 530

pronouns as, 658
sentence pattern with, 588, 589
subject-verb agreement and, 629
Subject directories, 25, 212
Subject headings, 222–23
Subjective case, in pronouns, 656–57, 658, 664
Subject-verb agreement, 620–29
with *be,* 621
collective nouns and, 625–26
compound subjects and, 623–24
dialects and, 622
faulty predication and, 697–98
grammar checkers and, 620
helping verbs and, 621
indefinite pronouns and, 625
intervening words and, 622
linking verbs and, 629
measurement or number subjects and, 626–27
person and number definitions, 626–27
pitfalls in, 623
relative pronouns and, 628–29
singular nouns ending in *-s,* 627
subject following the verb and, 629
with *there,* 629
titles, names, and words treated as words, 627–28
Subject-verb-object (S-V-O) order, 704
Subject-verb order. *See* Word order
Subjunctive mood, 650–52, 679
Subordinate clauses
adverbial, 529
commas and, 752, 758–59
comma splices and, 617
definition of, 506, 595, 663, 704, 752
as fragments, 595, 602–03, 607–08
functions of, 510–11
fused sentences and, 617
introducing an independent clause, 752
in mixed construction, 696
parallelism and, 520
punctuation and, 512, 768
relative pronouns in, 595
semicolons and, 768
in sentence structure, 506
stated subject required in, 704–05
as subjects, 696
subjunctive in, 651
subordinating conjunctions in, 595
techniques of, 511–12
types of, 511–12

whom or *whomever* as object of, 663
who or *whoever* as subject of, 663
Subordinating conjunctions
in adjective clauses, 595
in adverb clauses, 596
functions of, 583
list of, 584, 603
in noun clauses, 596
in sentence fragments, 602
in subordinate clauses, 511, 595
Subordination. *See also* Subordinate clauses; Subordinating conjunctions
coordination used with, 515
in correcting comma splices, 617
definition of, 506
essential *vs.* nonessential information and, 512, 608
excessive, 514
functions of, 510–11
illogical, 514
punctuation and, 512, 749, 752, 758–579
style checkers and, 505
techniques of, 511–12
term selection in, 512–13
Subtitles
capitalization of, 808, 810–11
colons before, 800, 802
succeed, 567
such, so, 737
such as, 801, 824
Suffixes, 567–68, 831–32
suggest, 726
Summaries
in assignments, 17
in critical reading, 110–11, 132–33, 432
executive, 491
introducing, 257
length of, 256, 258
source boundaries in, 277–78
student models, 111, 257–58, 263
to support claims, 133, 151
thesis example, 66–67
verb tense in introducing, 547–48
writer's voice in, 538–39
writing, 256–58, 432
summarize, 472
sum total, 498
Superlative adjectives and adverbs, 674–75
Superscript numbers, 376–77, 417
supersede, 567
Superstitions, 138

Index

Support. *See* Evidence
suppose, expect, G17
supposed to, used to, G19
sure and, sure to, G19
Surveys, 228–29
S-V-O (subject-verb-object) order, 704
Sweeping generalization fallacy, 156
Syllables, in dictionary entries, 560–61, 833
Symbolism, 435
Synchronous media, 182
Synonym dictionaries, 560
Synonyms
    accurate, 560
    for coherence, 56–57
    in dictionary entries, 562
    in paragraphs, 56–57
    in paraphrasing, 252–53
    in thesauruses, 560
Synthesis
    in critical reading, 123–24
    of literature texts, 433
    in viewing visuals, 126

T

Table of contents, 101
Tables
    APA style for, 379–80
    Chicago style for, 407
    MLA style for, 303–04, 327, 334–35
    in research or laboratory reports, 460
    as visual evidence, 74, 75, 78–79
Tag questions, commas after, 753–54
take, bring, G15
take back, 723, 724
take from, 744
take off, 723
take on, 723, 724
take up, 723
Talmud, documenting
    in APA style, 356, 365
    in MLA style, 299
taste, 589, 670
teach, 590, 707
Technology. *See* Computers
Technorati, 215
Television broadcasts, documenting
    APA style for, 373
    MLA style for, 300, 324–25
tell
    indirect object with, 590, 707
    infinitive after, 726
Tenses. *See* Verb tenses
Tense sequences, 648–49
Test-taking. *See* Essay exams

Textbooks, as sources, 457
TextEdit, 180
Text-messaging, 17, 172, 542, 823
Textual analysis, 433, 434
than
    in comparisons, 522, 662
    pronoun case and, 662
    as subordinating conjunction, 603
than, then, 565, G19
Thank-you notes, 227
that
    antecedents of, 628
    confusingly broad use of, 665
    count and noncount nouns with, 718
    as determiner, 713
    identification indicated by, 513
    omitted from elliptical constructions, 700–01
    in parallel clauses, 521
    people not designated by, 667
    preceding quotations, 787
    purpose indicated by, 513
    redundant object pronouns with, 706
    as relative pronoun, 603
    in sentence fragments, 600, 606
    subject-verb agreement and, 628
    subordinate clauses beginning with, 511
    as subordinating conjunction, 513, 603
that, which, G19
that, who, G19
that clauses, commas not used with, 758–59
that there, them there, these here, this here, G19
the, 713, 715–16. *See also* Articles (*a, an, the*)
their, there, they're, 565, G19
theirself, theirselves, themself, G19
them, those, G19
Theme, in literature, 432, 435
them there, that there, these here, this here, G19
then, 55
then, than, 565, G19
there, as expletive, 586, 705
there, their, they're, 565, G19
there are, 500–01, 629
therefore
    in comma splices, 613
    in coordination, 506
    semicolons and, 768
there is, 629
there was, 629

there were, 629
Thesauruses, 560
these, 718
these here, this here, that there, them there, G19
Theses. *See* Dissertations
Thesis-driven arguments. *See* Exploratory arguments
Thesis/thesis statement, 29–32
    arguable theses, 139
    counterevidence and, 266
    devising, 265, 472–73
    drafting, 29–31, 265, 441
    in essay exam answers, 473
    for multimedia presentations, 184
    placement of, 53, 63
    from research questions and hypotheses, 196, 264–66
    revising, 31–33, 85, 265
    samples, 265–66, 474–75
    in summaries, 256
    in writing about literature, 440–41
they, 546, 666–67
they're, their, there, 565, G19
Third person, 438–39, 458, 681–82
this, 665, 718
this here, these here, that there, them there, G19
those, 718
those, them, G19
though, 513, 603
throw, 590
throw out, 723
Time, formats for, 827
Time management
    in assignments, 18, 19, 194
    in collaborative projects, 28
    in drafting, 39
Time relationships
    adverbs and, 734
    colons and, 802
    prepositions and, 741–42
    sequence of tenses and, 648–49
    transitional expressions indicating, 55
Time sequences, 648–49
Title(s)
    abbreviating, 295, 301–02
    capitalizing, 381, 808, 810–11
    composing, 86–87
    in e-mails, 173
    of home pages, 178
    italics in, 372, 380, 814
    of journals, 315, 423
    of long works, 372, 380, 783–84, 814
    in MLA style, 334

of people, 478, 761, 810, 821–22
quotation marks around, 783–84, 814
revising, 86–87
of sacred texts, 299–300
of short works, 783–84, 814
subject-verb agreement, 627–28
subtitles, 800, 802, 808, 810–11
of tables, 407
within titles, 313, 364–65, 440
Title page
in academic texts, 96
in APA format, 378–79, 382
in *Chicago* format, 409
in MLA format, 334, 337
in portfolios, 100
in research or laboratory reports, 334, 459
to
direct objects and, 708
indirect objects and, 590, 744
in infinitives, 593, 686, 690
in titles and subtitles, 810
to, too, two, 563, G19
to all intents and purposes, 497
to be. See be
to do. See do
together with, 622
to have. See have
tolerate, 726
Tone
audience and purpose and, 15–16
in business letters, 477
in e-mails, 172, 173, 483
in memos, 482
pronoun case and, 663
in visuals, 74
well-tempered, 136
too, either, 736
too, so, 736
too, to, two, 563, G19
Topic. *See also* Idea generation
assignment and, 17
broadening, 25–26
choosing an engaging, 140
design and, 163
fresh, 140
for multimedia presentations, 184
narrowing, 25, 32, 195
in research assignments, 196
responsibilities to, 4–5
Topic outlines, 36–37, 267–69. *See also* Outlines
Topic sentences, 47, 48, 49–51
totally, 497

Toulmin, Stephen, 155
Toulmin model of arguments, 155
Trade names, 810
"Transcending Stereotypes in Hurston's *Their Eyes Were Watching God*" (Sequiera), 443–46
Transition(s). *See* Signal phrases
Transitional expressions
commas and, 753
comma splices and fused sentences and, 613, 616
definition of, 753
examples of, 55
within and between paragraphs, 54–55
placement of, 530
semicolons and, 767, 768–69
Transitional paragraphs, 54–55
Transitive verbs
active voice and, 589
direct objects with, 589, 707
examples of, 643–44
indirect objects with, 590
passive voice and, 589, 652
phrasal, 723–24
Translation dictionaries, 559
Translators, documenting
APA style for, 362–63
Chicago style for, 395
MLA style for, 309–10
Tree diagrams, 33–34
try, 726
try and, try to, G19
turn up, 723
Twitter, 214, 229
two, to, too, 563, G19
type, 497
Typefaces. *See* Fonts

U

Unabridged dictionaries, 207, 559
unanimous, 675
Uncountable (noncount) nouns, 575, 713–16, 718–20
Underlining, 165, 173, 814–18
understand, 726
Understatement, 552
Unfamiliar-to-familiar order, 35
unify, unity, G19
Unintentional plagiarism, 199, 247
uninterested, disinterested, G16
unique, 675, G19
Units of measure, 626–27, 824
Unity
in outlines, 37–38

in paragraphs, 46, 47–52
revising for, 84, 86, 473
unity, unify, G19
unless, 513, 603
Unmarked infinitives, 725–26
Unnamed authors, documenting
APA style for, 354, 359
Chicago style for, 393–94
MLA style for, 295, 308
Unpublished dissertations, documenting
APA style for, 365
Chicago style for, 397
MLA style for, 315
until, 513, 603
until such time as, 498
urge, 726
URLs
APA style and, 358–59
checking, 370
Chicago style and, 392, 399
digital object identifiers and, 359
in e-mails, 174
line breaks in, 392, 834
locating, 237
for magazine articles, 316, 367, 400, 425
for personal websites, 238
slashes in, 804
source evaluation by, 236–37
us
before a noun, 660
as personal pronoun, 578, 775, G9
Usage
in dictionary entries, 562
glossary of, G14–G19
usage, use, G19
use, utilize, G19
used to, supposed to, G19

V

Valid arguments, 157
Validity. *See* Credibility
Value, claims of, 32, 139
Variety, 528–32, 534
Vehicle names, 816
Verb(s), 636–54, 722–30. *See also* Subject-verb agreement; Verbals; Verb tenses
as adjectives, 727
basic forms of, 636–38
complete, 600–01, 639–42
in dictionary entries, 561
emphatic, 535
on essay exams, 471
functions of, 576, 577, 636

Index **137**

Verb(s) (*continued*)
gerunds and infinitives after, 593, 725–26
grammar checkers and, 638
helping. *See* Helping (auxiliary) verbs
imperative mood, 650
indicative mood, 650, 679
indirect objects taken by, 590, 707–08
information revealed in, 637
-*ing* form, pronoun case with, 661
intransitive, 588, 643–44
in inverted sentences, 532, 586, 629
irregular, 561, 636–39, 640
lie, lay, 643–44
linking. *See* Linking verbs
main, 577, 639, 641
modal, 579, 641, 728–30
mood. *See* Mood, in verbs
nouns derived from, 593
phrasal, 555, 722–24
regular, 636–38
rise, raise, 643
sentence fragments and, 600–01
sentence patterns and, 588–90
signal, 277
sit, set, 643
-*s* or -*es* and -*d* or -*ed* endings on, 636, 637, 642, 774
transitive, 589–90, 643–44, 652, 707
verbal phrases, 592–93, 601, 605, 629
verbals, 579, 592, 638, 692
verb phrases, 577, 579, 592, 621, 639–43, 728–30
Verbal phrases
as fragments, 601, 605
functions of, 592
helping verbs in. *See* Helping (auxiliary) verbs
subject-verb agreement and, 629
types of, 592–93
Verbals
complete verbs *vs.*, 579
dangling modifiers and, 692
definition of, 592, 638, 692
examples of, 638
past and present participles as, 638
Verb mood. *See* Mood, in verbs
Verb phrases
definition of, 592
forming, 639–42
functions of, 577, 579
subject-verb agreement with, 621
types of verbs in, 728–30

Verb-subject agreement. *See* Subject-verb agreement
Verb tenses, 644–50
awkward shifts in, 678–79
choosing, 644–47
definition of, 644
future tenses, 645–47
infinitives and, 648–49
in literature and humanities writing, 438, 647
past, 438, 636–37, 639–41, 645, 648
past perfect subjunctive, 651
past subjunctive, 651
perfect, 645, 646, 647
perfect infinitive, 649
perfect progressive, 646, 647
present, 620–21, 644–49
present infinitive, 648
present subjunctive, 650–51
progressive, 645–47
in science writing, 458–59, 647
sequences, 648–49
in signal phrases, 276
simple, 644–45, 646
subjunctive, 650–52, 679
Verse form, 447
Video blogs (vlogs), 372–73
Video games, 322
Videos, in websites, 180
Video sources
documenting: APA style for, 372; *Chicago* style for, 404; MLA style for, 323–24
finding, 225
Virgules. *See* Slashes
Visual claims, 75, 138, 156
Visual fallacies, 156
Visual impairments, 165, 181
Visual literacy, 3
Visuals. *See also* Visual sources
accuracy in, 78–80
annotating, 115
as arguments, 134, 138, 156
captions for, 169–70, 279–80, 304, 335–36, 407
clarity of, 78
copyright clearance for, 78
critiques of, 126
decision to include, 73–74
distortion of, 80, 81
document design and, 169–70
document size and, 79
in emotional appeals, 144
evaluating, 239–41
as evidence, 74–78

exploitative, 78
false dilemmas in, 158
finding, 225
high- *vs.* low-resolution, 180
information graphics, 74–77
in intellectual appeals, 142–43
manipulative, 81
maps, 75, 77
in multimedia presentations, 187, 188
original *vs.* borrowed, 78
personal statements as, 335
photographs in job applications, 74, 484
placement of, 169–70
previewing, 231
reading critically, 110
revising, 78–81
text references to, 169
in websites, 180, 249
Visual sources
documenting: APA style for, 372–74; *Chicago* style for, 404–05; MLA style for, 322–28, 334–35
evaluating, 239–41
Vlogs, 372–73
Vocabulary, specialized, 437, 542–43
Vocabulary logs, 571
Voice. *See also* Active voice; Passive voice; Tone
emphasis and, 535
in-text citations and, 278–80
persona, 7, 87
responsibility and, 536
shifts in, 679–80
writer's, 281–83, 293, 538–39
in writing for sciences and social studies, 458, 536
Volume numbers, 203, 204, 205
Volumes. *See* Multivolume works

W

waist, waste, 565
wait, 726
wait for, wait on, G19
want, 647, 726
Warhol, Andy, 518
warn, 726
Warrants, 147
was, 501, 639
waste, waist, 565
ways, G19
we
before a noun, 660
as personal pronoun, 660, 775, G9
weak, week, 565

Weak claims, 138
wear, where, were, 565
weather, whether, 565, G19
Web. *See* Websites and web pages
Web browsers, 79, 180, 181
Web design, 163–70. *See also* Electronic document design
 breadcrumb (click) trails, 178, 179
 color in, 167–68
 content in, 179–80
 design principles in, 162–63, 180
 fonts in, 165–66
 headings in, 168–69
 home page, 176–78
 layout in, 165
 links in, 101, 178, 815, 817, 818
 lists in, 166–67
 maintaining, 181
 navigation tools in, 177–78, 179
 overall impression in, 164–65
 revising, 181
 site structure, 177
 visuals in, 169–70, 180, 188
 web pages in, 176
 white space in, 166
 writing situation in, 176, 179–80
Web forums, 238–39
Weblogs. *See* Blogs and blog postings
Web of Knowledge, 235
Websites and web pages. *See also* Internet; Web design
 accessibility of, 165, 181
 bookmarking, 251
 college library, 25, 221
 conciseness in, 89
 content creation in, 179–80
 copyright protection of, 178
 creating, 176–81
 designing, 163–70
 documenting: APA style for, 357, 370–71; *Chicago* style for, 403; CSE style for, 426–27; MLA style for, 290–91, 302–03, 320–21
 editing and revising, 181
 evaluating, 236–40
 FAQs on, 210
 finding source titles and publishers, 201–03
 home pages, 100, 176–78
 links to, 101, 178, 239, 815
 locating, as sources, 210–13
 maintaining, 181
 metasearch engines and, 211–12, 213
 online surveys in, 229
 personal, 238
 plagiarism and, 236
 planning, 176–79
 searching, 210–13
 site structure, 177
 sponsors of, 238
 subject directories in, 25, 212
 URL extensions, 236–37
 visuals in, 180
 writing situation and, 176
Webster's New World College Dictionary, 558
Webster's Third New International Dictionary, Unabridged, 559
well, good, 671–72, G17
Well-tempered tone, 136
were, 501, 639
were, where, wear, 565
what
 as relative pronoun, 603
 in subordinate clauses, 512
 word order in questions with, 710
whatever, 603
when
 in adjective clauses, 595
 in adverb clauses, 698
 to indicate time, 513
 in noun clauses, 596
 in sentence fragments, 602–03
 to show identification, 513
 in subordinate clauses, 512, 513, 603
whenever
 in noun clauses, 596
 as subordinating conjunction, 513, 603
where
 in adjective clauses, 595
 in adverb clauses, 698
 to indicate place, 513
 in noun clauses, 596
 to show identification, 513
 as subordinating conjunction, 513, 603
where, wear, were, 565
whereas, 513, 603
wherever, 513, 596
whether, 596
whether, if, G17
whether, weather, 565, G19
whether . . . or, 508, 583
which
 antecedents of, 628–29
 commas and, 758–59
 confusingly broad use of, 665
 identification shown by, 513
 people not designated by, 667
 redundant object pronouns with, 706
 as relative pronoun, 603
 in sentence fragments, 602
 subject-verb agreement, 628
 in subordinate clauses, 512, 513
which, that, G19
which, witch, 565
whichever, 603
while, 513, 603
White space, 166
who
 antecedents of, 628–29
 designating people with, 667
 identification shown by, 513
 as interrogative pronoun, 663
 as relative pronoun, 603, 663–64
 in sentence fragments, 602
 subject-verb agreement, 628
 in subordinate clauses, 512, 513
 word order in questions with, 710
who, that, G19
who, whom, 663–64, G19
whoever, 603, 663–64
Whois.net, 238
whole, hole, 565
whom
 designating people with, 667
 as interrogative pronoun, 663
 as relative pronoun, 603, 663–64
whom, who, G19
whomever, 603, 663–64
who's, whose, 565, G19
whose
 designating people with, 667
 as relative pronoun, 603
 in subordinate clauses, 512
why
 in noun clauses, 596
 as subordinating conjunction, 603
 word order in questions with, 710
"Why Students Cheat: The Complexities and Oversimplifications of Plagiarism" (Hackman), 148–53
Wikipedia, 208, 238
Wikis
 documenting: APA style for, 371; *Chicago* style for, 403; MLA style for, 321, 371
 evaluating, 238–39
Wildcard characters, 219
will
 meanings of, 729
 as modal verb, 579, 641, 728, 729
 subject-verb agreement with, 621

will, shall, G18
will, would, 729
Windows SkyDrive, 174
wish, 726
Wishes, verbs in, 650, 651–52
witch, which, 565
with, 743
woman, women, 621
womankind, 545
Word. *See* Microsoft Word
Word(s). *See also* Spelling
　abbreviating, 823–24
　abstract *vs.* concrete, 88, 186, 551–52, 575
　breaking at the ends of lines, 833–34
　choosing, 87–88
　clichés, 67, 555–56
　compelling, 550–53
　compound, 571, 658, 659, 776–77, 833
　connotation of, 87, 550
　credibility and, 551
　denotation, 87, 548–49
　division of, 560–61
　empty, 497
　figures of speech, 447, 552–56
　formality of, 87
　general *vs.* specific, 551–52
　grammar and style checkers and, 549
　homonyms and near-homonyms, 93, 563, 565
　idioms, 554–55, 556
　mixed metaphors, 554
　non-English, 817
　numbers spelled-out, 827
　referred to as words, 627–28, 777–78, 781, 784, 816
　revising and, 87–88
Word division, in dictionaries, 560–61
Wordiness, 88–89. *See also* Conciseness
Word order. *See also* Misplaced modifiers
　in adjective clauses, 595
　adjectives in, 580, 673, 732–33, 756
　adverbs in, 711, 734–35
　conjunctions or adverbs beginning a clause, 710–11
　inverted, 532, 586, 629, 710–11
　of multiple adjectives, 673
　in questions, 586, 709–10
　subject-verb-object, 704
　variety in, 529–30
　in verb phrases, 728, 730
　with *whom* or *whomever,* 663
Words, used as words
　apostrophes in plurals of, 777–78

italicizing, 816
quotation marks for, 781, 784
subject-verb agreement, 627–28
Wordy expressions, eliminating, 497–99
Working bibliographies, 200–05
Working (preliminary) thesis, 29–31, 265, 441
Workplace writing. *See* Business and public writing
Works cited list, APA-style. *See* Reference list, APA-style
Works cited list, *Chicago*-style
　anthology or edited book selections, 395
　basic bibliographic entry format, 390, 391–92
　book editions other than the first, 395
　books in a series, 397
　books with authors and editors or translators, 395
　books with editors (no author), 394
　books with group or corporate authors, 394
　books with more than three authors, 393
　books with one author, 391–93
　books with two or three authors, 393
　books with unnamed (anonymous) author, 393–94
　CD-ROMs, 404
　discussion list or blog postings, 404
　dissertations or theses, 397
　format of, 408, 415
　government publications, 406
　indirect sources, 407
　interviews, 406
　introductions, prefaces, forewords, or afterwords, 396
　letters to the editor, 402
　magazine articles, 400
　motion pictures, 404
　multivolume works, 396
　music or other audio recordings, 405
　newspaper articles, 400–02
　performances, 405
　personal communications, 406
　podcasts, 405
　reference book entries, 396
　reviews, 402
　sacred texts, 397
　scholarly journal articles, 398–400
　titles of short works in, 784
　web pages or wiki articles, 403
　websites, 403

works by the same author, 394
works of art, 405
Works cited list, CSE-style. *See* Reference list, CSE-style
Works cited list, MLA-style, 305–31
　advertisements, 328
　art works, 327
　audio and visual sources, 322–28
　avatars different from actual name, 322
　basic entry for printed books, 305–06
　blogs and blog postings, 321
　book editions other than the first, 311
　books from imprint of larger publishing company, 311
　books in series, 313
　books with author and editor or translator, 309–10
　books with author using pen name, 309
　books with group or corporate authors, 309
　books with more than three authors, 308
　books with one author, 305–08
　books with two or three authors, 308
　books with unnamed or anonymous authors, 308
　comics or cartoons, 327–28
　computer software, 322
　conference proceedings, 314
　diary or journal entries, 330–31
　directory, 306–07
　discussion list postings, 321
　dissertations, 314–15
　DVD extras, 324
　edited books or anthologies, 309–10
　editorials, 319
　format of, 346
　government publications, 328–29
　home page (academic), 320–21
　instant messages, 330
　Internet downloads, 324
　interviews, 330
　in-text citations and, 289–90, 295, 300
　introductions, prefaces, forewords, or afterwords, 311
　lectures, speeches, or debates, 327
　legal sources, 329
　letters, 329–30
　letters to the editor, 319
　live performances, 326
　magazine articles, 316–17

maps or charts, 328
memoranda, 330
microform articles, 318–19
missing publication information, 314
motion pictures, 323–24
multivolume works, 312–13
musical compositions, 326
musicals or other audio recordings, 325–26
newspaper articles, 317–18
pamphlets, brochures, or press releases, 314
periodicals, 315–19
personal correspondence, 330
podcasts, 325
reference work entries, 311–12
republished books, 313
reviews, 319
sacred texts, 313–14
scholarly journal articles, 315–16
sources published in more than one medium, 322
student model of, 346
television or radio broadcasts, 324–25
titles within titles, 313
two or more works by the same author, 309
video games, 322
videos, 323–24
web pages, 320
websites, 320
wiki articles, 321
Works of art, 327, 647, 815
World Almanac and Book of Facts, 209
World Wide Web. *See* Websites and web pages
Worthington, Robyn, 462–68
would
 with *if* clauses, 651
 intention or willingness indicated by, 729
 meanings of, 729
 as modal verb, 579, 641, 728, 729
 subject-verb agreement with, 621
would, will, 729
would of, could of, should of, must of, G16
Wratten, Alea, 124, 128–30
wright, write, rite, right, 565
write, 590, 707
Writer's block, 38, 39–40
Writers-in-progress, 7
Writer's voice, 281–83, 293, 539
Writing. *See* Academic writing; Drafting; Literature and humanities, writing in; Sciences and social sciences, writing in
Writing situation, 9–12. *See also* Audience; Context; Genre(s); Purpose of writing; Tone
WYSIWYG, 180

X

-x, plurals of words that end in, 569

Y

-y
 plurals of words that end in, 570
 suffixes for words that end with, 567
Yahoo!, 210, 213
Yahoo! Education, 558
Yahoo! Groups, 215
Yearbook of Immigration Statistics, 209
Yearbooks, 209
Years, 777, 823, 827. *See also* Dates
yet
 in coordination, 506, 508, 583, 750
 in correcting comma splices, 616
 in parallelism, 520
Yippy (metasearch engine), 213
you
 to address reader directly, 666, G19
 unstated, 534, 585, 602, 705
your, you're, 565, G19
YourDictionary.com, 559
YouSendIt, 174
YouTube, 214, 225, 324

Z

-z, plurals of words that end in, 569
Zero article, 714
Zip codes, 761
Zotero, 201

ESL Index

A

a, an, 715–16
Adjectives
  agreement and unchanging form of, 669, 732
  determiners as, 580, 733
  nouns used as, 673
  ordering a cumulative series of, 580, 732–33
  past participle as, 727
  placement of, 580, 732
  present participle as, 727
Adverbs
  hard and *hardly,* 737
  not and *no,* 736–37
  placement of, 734–35
  such and *so,* 737
  too and *either,* 736
  word order and, 710–11
Agreement and adjectives, 669
Agreement, pronoun-antecedent, 630
Arguments, exploratory *vs.* persuasive, 137
Articles *(a, an, the)*
  common nouns and, 714–16
  count and noncount nouns and, 714–16
  as determiners, 713, 714
  indefinite *(a, an)* and definite *(the),* 714–16
  proper nouns and, 717
  zero, 714
Attribute, prepositions of, 743
Audience, understanding one's, 14
Auxiliary verbs. *See* Helping (auxiliary) verbs

B

Bilingual dictionaries, 562
British *vs.* American English, 563, 754, 781, 785
Business, conducting in the US, 484

C

can, could, meaning of, as modals, 729
Capitalization, 807

Cause, prepositions of, 742
Class discussions, contributing to, 184
Clichés and idioms, 556
Code-switching, by bilingual speakers, 3
Common nouns, 713, 714–16
Comprehension, reading for, 109
Conciseness, 497
Condition, prepositions of, 742
Conjunctions, word order and, 710–11
Connotation, recognizing language differences in, 15
could, can, meaning of, as modals, 729
Count nouns, 576
  articles with, 714–16, 717
  other determiners with, 718–20

D

Declarative sentences, 704
Definite article *(the),* 713, 715–16
Degree, prepositions of, 742
Demonstrative pronouns with nouns, 718
Determiners, 713, 714, 718–20
Dictionaries
  bilingual, as spelling aids, 562
  for second-language learners, 559
Direct objects and word order, 707–08

E

-ed verb form (past participle) as adjective, 727
e-mails, cultural differences, 173
Ethos and logos, in the US, 143
Expletives, 705–06
Explicit subjects, requirements for, 602

F

few, a few, 718–19

G

Gerunds, after verbs and prepositions, 593, 725–26
Gestures during presentations, US audiences and, 189

H

h-, a vs. *an* for words beginning with, 715

hard and *hardly,* 737
Helping (auxiliary) verbs, 579
  modal, 728–30
  simple *(have, do,* and *be),* 728

I

Idea generation, 20
Idioms
  clichés and, 555–56
  prepositions and phrasal verbs and, 555
Indefinite articles *(a, an),* 714–16
Indirect objects
  prepositions and, 744
  verbs that take, 590, 708
  word order and, 707–08
Infinitives
  after verbs and prepositions, 593, 725–26
  unmarked, 725–26
-ing verb form (present participle) as adjective, 727
Inseparable phrasal verbs, 642, 722–24
Introductions, not praising the reader in, 63
Inverted word order, 710–11
it, as expletive, 705

J

Job applications, photographs and, 74, 484

L

less, fewer, 713
little, a little, 718–19
Locations, prepositions of, 741
Logos and ethos, in the US, 143

M

Main idea, stating the, 29
may, might, meaning of, as modals, 729
Modal helping (auxiliary) verbs, 579, 728–30
  meanings of, 641, 728–30
must, meaning of, as modal, 729

ESL1

ESL2 ESL Index

N

Noncount nouns
- articles with, 714–16
- definition of, 713–14
- examples of, 715
- other determiners with, 718–20

not and *no*, 736–37
Note making, in English, 252
Nouns, 714–20
- articles with, 714–17
- common, 714–16
- count and noncount, 576, 714–20
- other determiners with, 718–20
- proper and common, 714–17
- quantifying words with, 718–20

Numbers
- with count nouns, 713
- punctuating, 828

O

Object complements, word order and, 708–09
Objects
- direct, 707–08
- indirect, 590, 707–08
- redundant pronouns with, 706

Obligatory words, 698
Origin, prepositions of, 743
ought to, should, shall, meaning of, as modals, 729

P

Parallelism, deceptive, 520
Participles, as adjectives, 727
Past participles, 727
Peer revising, with native speakers, 90
Personal experiences, writing about, 10
Photographs in job applications, 74, 484
Phrasal verbs
- idioms and, 555
- list of common, 723
- separable *vs.* inseparable, 642, 722–24

Plagiarism, cultural differences and, 6, 247
Possession, prepositions of, 743
Praising the reader, avoiding, 63
Prepositional phrases, 708
Prepositions, 739–45
- adjectives with, 733
- of cause and reason, 742
- of condition and degree, 742
- definition of, 739
- examples of, 740
- functions of, 740–43, 744
- gerunds after, 726
- idioms and, 555
- infinitives after, 726
- of location, 741
- necessary and unnecessary, 745
- in phrasal verbs, 722–23
- of possession, attribute, origin, 743
- recognizing, 739–40
- of time, 741–42

Present participle, 727
Progressive tenses, 647
Pronouns
- antecedent agreement with, 630–34
- demonstrative, as determiners, 718
- possessive, as determiners, 718
- redundant, 706

Proofreading, 94
Proper nouns, 713, 717
Punctuation
- commas, 754, 785
- of numbers, 828
- periods, 785
- quotation marks, 781, 785
- subordination and, 512

Q

Quantifying words or phrases, 718–20
Questions, word order in, 709–10
Quotation marks
- in American English, 781
- with periods and commas, 785

R

Reading for comprehension, 109
Reason, prepositions of, 742
Redundant pronouns, 706
Repetitions, unacceptable, 698

S

sell to, 744
Sentences. *See also* Sentence structure
- commands, 705
- declarative, 704–05
- questions, 709–10

Sentence structure
- direct and indirect objects in, 707–08
- object complements in, 708–09
- stated subjects in, 704–05
- *there* and *it* constructions in, 705–06
- variety in, 532

Separable phrasal verbs, 642, 722–24
Serial comma, 754
shall, should, ought to, meaning of, as modals, 729
should've, should have, 728
Sources, conversations with, 275
Spelling
- American *vs.* British, 563
- bilingual dictionaries as aids to, 562

Study groups, 470
Subjects
- explicit (stated), 602, 698, 704–05
- redundant pronouns in, 706
- in *there* and *it* constructions, 705–06

Subordination, punctuation and, 512, 516
such and *so*, 737

T

that, as noun determiner, 718
that or *which* clauses, redundant pronouns with, 706
the, 715–16
there and *it* constructions, 705–06
these, as noun determiner, 718
Thesis statements, 29
this, as noun determiner, 718
those, as noun determiner, 718
Time, prepositions of, 741–42
too and *either*, 736
too and *so*, 736
Transitive verbs, objects with, 707–08, 723

U

Unmarked infinitives, 725–26

V

Verbs, 722–30
- gerunds and infinitives after, 725–26
- *have, do, be*, as helping verbs, 728
- helping (auxiliary), 728–30
- modal helping, 579, 728–30
- phrasal, 722–24
- progressive tenses, 647
- transitive, objects with, 707–08, 723

W

which or *that* clauses, redundant pronouns with, 706
will, would, meaning of, as modals, 729

Word order
    adjectives and, 732–33
    adverbs and, 734–35
    of direct and indirect objects, 707–08
    inflexibility of, 587
    inverted, 710–11
    normal S-V-O, 704
    of object complements, 708–09
    in questions, 709–10
    in *there* and *it* constructions, 705–06

would, will, meaning of, as modals, 729
Writing Responsibly around the World, 6

Z

Zero article, 714

Notes

Notes

Notes

Notes

Notes

Quick Reference *A Menu of Resources*

Model Papers

Student Models
Newspaper Article: Plagiarism Cheats Students 8
Freewrite 21
Brainstorm 22, 26
Journalists' Questions 24
Informal (or Scratch) Outline 36
Topic Outline and Sentence Outline 36
First Draft 42
Final Draft 95
Personal Statement 101
Summary 111
Double-Entry Reading Journal 118
Claims and Evidence Analysis 121
Advertisement Critique 121
Prewrite 123
Critical Response Essay 127
Exploratory Argument 147
Summary 257
Reading Note 261
Summary Note with Writer's Assessment 263
Thesis Statement 265
Outline 268
Research Project: MLA Style 336

Research Project: APA Style 381
Research Project: *Chicago* Style 408
Research Project: CSE-Style Reference List 429
Textual Analysis 434
Writing about Fiction: Interpretive Analysis 442
Writing about Poetry: Explication 448
Research Report 461
Effective Essay Exam: Response 474
Job Application 485
Traditional Résumé 487
Business Letter: Scannable Résumé 489

Professional Models
Editorial: "An Inconvenient Truth" by Al Gore 69
Essay: "Why Uncertainty May Be Bad for Your Health" by Wray Herbert 112
Editorial: "How Hip-Hop Music Lost Its Way and Betrayed Its Fans" by Brent Staples 116
Writing about Drama: Review of a Play 451
Business Letter: Apology 480
Business Memo 482
Press Release 493

Self-Assessment Checklists

Ensuring Your Group is Effective 27
Revising a Thesis 31
Checking Your Draft 85
Proofreading 94
Reviewing Your Work with Each Source 105, 133, 245, 539, 791
Annotating an Image 115

Preparing to Write about a Visual 126
Revising Your Argument 159
Ten Steps to Using Presentation Software Effectively 188
Summarizing 257
Analyzing, Interpreting, Synthesizing, and Critiquing a Source 262
As You Revise Projects 286

Quick Reference *A Menu of Resources*

ESL Notes

Writing Responsibly around the World 6
Writing about Personal Experiences 10
Getting Help in Understanding Your Audience 14
Recognizing Differences in Connotation 15
Generating Ideas in English or Your First Language 20
Stating the Main Idea 29
Avoid Praising the Reader in Your Introduction 63
Photographs in Job Applications 74
Peer Review with Multilingual Students 90
Proofreading When English Is Not
    Your First Language 94
Reading for Comprehension 109
Exploratory versus Persuasive Approaches
    to Argument 137
Logos and Ethos in the United States 143
Task-Oriented E-mails Get Right to the Point 173
Contributing to Class Discussion 184
Adjusting Your Gestures to Appeal
    to a Multicultural Audience 189
Plagiarism and Culture 247
Making Notes in English 252
Having a Conversation with Sources 275
Study Groups 470
Conducting Global Business in the United States 484
Conciseness 497
Coordination and Subordination 516
Deceptive Parallelism 520
Developing an Ear for Sentence Variety 532
Idioms, Prepositions, and Phrasal Verbs 555
What Is the Difference between an Idiom
    and a Cliché? 556
Dictionaries for Second-Language Learners 559
Using a Bilingual Dictionary as an Aid
    to English Spelling 562
Use American Rather Than British Spelling 563
Countable and Noncountable Nouns 576
Modal Auxiliaries 579
The Ordering of Adjectives 580
English Word Order 587
Indirect Objects 590
Infinitive versus Gerund after the Verb 593
Including a Stated Subject 602
A Possessive Pronoun Agrees with Its Antecedent,
    Not the Word It Modifies 630
Modal Verbs 641
Phrasal Verbs 642
Do Not Use the Progressive Tenses with All Verbs 647
English Adjectives Do Not Have Plural Forms 669
Order of Adjectives in a Series 673
Obligatory Words and Unacceptable Repetitions
    in English 698
To Use or Not to Use the Serial Comma 754
Quotation Marks in American English 781
Commas and Periods with Quotation Marks 785
Capitalization 807
Punctuating Numbers in American English 828

Tech Tips

Protecting Your Work 42
Consider the Size of Your Document 79
Annotating Online Texts 114
Use a Lower Resolution to Avoid
 Memory-Hogging Image Files 180
Using an Assignment Calculator 194
Back Up Your Electronic Research Log 199
Citation Management Software 201
Using Google Scholar 216
Hidden Benefits of Library Databases 217
HTML versus PDF 218
Online Surveys 229
Identifying Personal Websites 238
Bookmarking and Listing Favorites 251
Page References and Web Pages 291
Creating a Header 332, 379
Indention 333, 378
Citing Electronic Sources: Digital Object Identifiers
 (DOIs) and URLs 359
Checking URLs and DOIs 370
Creating Footnotes and Endnotes 390
Guidelines for Formatting URLs 392
Creating Superscript Numbers 417
Style Checkers and Wordiness 499
Style Checkers and Coordination
 and Subordination 505
Parallelism and Computer Style Checkers 521
Word Choice and Grammar and Style Checkers 549
Use Spelling Checkers Cautiously 569
Grammar Checkers and Sentence Fragments 605
Comma Splices, Fused Sentences,
 and Grammar Checkers 613
Grammar Checkers and Subject-Verb Agreement 620
Grammar Checkers and
 Pronoun-Antecedent Agreement 631
Grammar Checkers and Verb Problems 638
Grammar Checkers and Adjective-Adverb Problems 671
Catching Confusing Shifts 679
Misplaced Modifiers and Grammar
 and Style Checkers 686
Apostrophes and Spelling or Grammar Checkers 775
Smart Quotes versus Straight Quotes 782
Using Exclamation Points in E-mail Messages 794
Typing a Dash 797
Breaking URLs and E-mail Addresses 834

Quick Reference *A Menu of Resources*

Quick Reference Guidance

Your College's Plagiarism Policy 6
Analyzing the Purpose of an Assignment 18
Overcoming Writer's Block 40
Sample Transitional Expressions 55
Seven Don'ts for Introductions 65
Five Don'ts for Conclusions 67
Matching Visual Evidence to Claims 75
Seven Ways to Gain Objectivity about Your Work 83
Formatting Academic Texts 95
Steps in Developing Critical Understanding 121
Devising an Arguable Thesis 139
Including Visuals (Images and Graphics) 169
Consider Your Writing Situation when Composing E-Mail 172
Creating a Website? Consider Your Writing Situation 176
Overcoming Presentation Anxiety 187
Factors in Planning a Research Project 194
Dictionaries and Encyclopedias 208
Almanacs and Yearbooks 209
Biographical Reference Resources 209
Search Engines and Subject Directories 213
Blog and Discussion List Search Engines 215
Conducting a Boolean Search 219
Accessing Government Information Online 224
Multimedia Resources 225
Judging Reliability 231
Scholarly versus Popular Periodicals 234
Drafting the Research Paper 265
Writing the First Draft 270
Signal Verbs 277
General Principles of In-Text Citations 290, 348
Examples of MLA-Style In-Text Citations 294
Examples of MLA-Style Works-Cited Entries 306
Examples of APA-Style In-Text Citations 350
Examples of APA-Style Reference List Entries 360
Examples of *Chicago*-Style Note and Bibliography Entries 39
Examples of CSE-Style Reference List Entries 419
Elements of Literature 435
Critical Approaches to Literature 436
Writing about Poetry 447
Writing about Drama 452
Common Verbs on Essay Exams 472
What an Effective Answer Does— and Does Not Do 473
E-mail Etiquette 483
Designing a Print Resume 486
Strategies for Writing Concisely 497
Conjunctions and Their Meaning 508

Subordination and Punctuation 512
Subordinating Terms and Their Meaning 513
Achieving Variety and Emphasis 527
Figures of Speech 552
Dodging Deadly Clichés 556
Some Homonyms and Near-Homonyms 565
The Parts of Speech 576
Pronouns and Their Functions 578
Common Conjunctive Adverbs 581
Common One-Word and Multiword Prepositions 583
Common Subordinating Conjunctions 584
Finding the Subject 586
Five Sentence Patterns 588
Identifying Fragments 601
Subordinating Terms 603
Identifying Comma Splices and Fused Sentences 613
Ways to Correct Comma Splices and Fused Sentences 616
Avoiding Subject-Verb Agreement Pitfalls 623
Common Indefinite Pronouns 625
Avoiding Pronoun-Antecedent Agreement Pitfalls 631
Three Strategies for Avoiding Gender Bias with Indefinite Antecedents 632
What Information Do Verbs Reveal? 637
Common Irregular Verbs 640
Distinguishing *Rise* from *Raise*, *Sit* from *Set*, and *Lie* from *Lay* 643

An Overview of Verb Tenses and Their Forms 646
Editing for Case in Compounds 659
The Functions of Adjectives and Adverbs 670
Forming Comparatives and Superlatives 675
Some Common Noncount Nouns 715
Matching Nouns with Quantifying Words and Phrases 719
Some Common Phrasal Verbs and Their Meanings 723
Gerund or Infinitive after Selected Verbs 726
Modals and Meaning 729
Putting Cumulative Adjectives in Standard Order 733
Common Single-Word and Multiword Prepositions 740
Identifying Functions of Prepositions 741
Common Comma Do's and Don'ts 749
The Seven Coordinating Conjunctions 750
Testing for Coordinate and Cumulative Adjectives 756
Common Semicolon Do's and Don'ts 767
Common Apostrophe Do's and Don'ts 774
Common Quotation Mark Do's and Don'ts 781
What These Punctuation Marks Do 797
Common Capitalization Do's and Don'ts 808
Capitalize Proper Nouns and Proper Adjectives, but Not Common Nouns 810
Common Italics Do's and Don'ts 815
Common Abbreviation Do's and Don'ts 821

Quick Reference *A Menu of Resources*

Writing Responsibly Notes

Your Responsibilities as a Writer 5
Taking Yourself Seriously as a Writer 7
Seeing and Showing the Whole Picture 13
Note Taking and Plagiarism 21
Made-up Evidence 41
Guiding the Reader 56
Exploitative Images 78
The Big Picture 85
Making an Essay Long Enough without Wordiness 89
Beware the Spelling Checker! 93
Explaining Your Choice of Sources 104
Engaging with What You Read 108
Drawing Inferences 124
Understanding *Criticism* 125
Understanding and Representing the Entire Source 132
The Well-Tempered Tone 136
Choosing an Engaging Topic 140
Establishing Yourself as a Responsible Writer 144
Preparing Oral Arguments 144
Visual Claims and Visual Fallacies 156
Selecting Fonts with Readers in Mind 165
Establishing a Consistent Font 166
Designing for Those with Impaired Color Vision 168
Maintaining Confidentiality in E-Mail 173
Making Considerate Attachments 174
Understanding E-mail and Privacy 175
Checking Accessibility 181
Flaming 182
Listening Actively 190
Using Printed Sources 197
Avoiding Accidental Plagiarism 199
Using Wikipedia 208
Going beyond Reference Sources 210
Really Reading *Real* Sources 216
Conducting Interviews Fairly 227
Avoiding Manipulation and Bias in Observations 228
Reporting Results Fairly 229
Keeping an Open, Inquiring Mind 234
Online Plagiarism 236
Choosing and Unpacking Complex Sources 244
Using Illustrations and Avoiding Plagiarism 249

Highlighting versus Making Notes 251
Using Quotations Fairly 260
Acknowledging Counterevidence 267
Citing and Documenting Sources 288, 347, 389, 416
Using Signal Phrases to Show Relationships with Sources 293
Of Deadlines and Paperclips 334, 380, 408, 429
Reading with Study Guides 433
Presenting Data Accurately 456
Using Your Computer during an Essay Exam 473
Letters to the Editor 479
Personal E-mails and IM at Work 484
Conciseness versus the Too-Short Paper 496
Using Parallelism to Clarify Related Ideas 523
Voice and Responsibility 536
Blending Voices in Your Text 538
Avoiding Online Shortcuts 542
Euphemisms and Doublespeak 544
Word Choice and Credibility 551
Choose Accurate Synonyms 560
Spelling Errors 564
Why Grammar Matters 574
Sentence Fragments and Context 604
Clarifying Boundaries 612
Is a Comma Splice Ever Acceptable? 614
Dialect Variation in Subject-Verb Agreement 622
Using a Plural Pronoun with a Singular Antecedent 633
Using the Subjunctive in Formal Writing 651
Case and Tone 663
Misplaced Modifiers in the Real World 690
Commas and Clarity 748
Sending a Signal with Semicolons 766
Contractions in Formal Writing 773
Using Quotations Fairly 781
Acknowledging Indirect Quotations 790
Question Marks and Exclamation Points 793
Dashes, Parentheses, or Commas? 798
Using *[sic]* 800
Altering Quotations 803
Capitalizing in E-mail and IM 811
Using Italics for Emphasis 816
Using Online Abbreviations Appropriately 823
Ethos and Convention 826
Hyphenating with Readers in Mind 831